## If you're wondering why you should buy this new edition of Comparative Politics Today, here are 8 good reasons!

**1.** Chapters 1–7 present the latest political events, data, and political theory to help you learn the **latest methods and insights** in the field of comparative politics.

**2.** Chapter 8, "Politics in Britain," covers the transition from Tony Blair to Gordon Brown as prime minister and examines the political and economic challenges faced by the **new Labour government**.

**3.** Chapter 9, "Politics in France," brings you up to date on the policy departures of President Nicolas Sarkozy and **France's changing role in Europe** and its relations with the European Union.

**4.** Chapter 10, "Politics in Germany," discusses the **Grand Coalition** under the leadership of Germany's first woman chancellor, Angela Merkel, including the political context leading up to the 2009 Bundestag elections.

**5.** Chapter 11, "Politics in Japan," reviews the rapid changes in political leadership from **Abe to Fukuda to Aso.** The chapter considers the implications of these leadership changes for Japan's domestic policies and international position.

**6.** Chapter 12, "Politics in Russia," includes new material on the **2008 presidential election of Dmitry Medvedev** and Vladimir's Putin's transition to become Russia's premier, including a description of the slide into an increasingly authoritarian regime.

**7.** Chapter 14, "Mexico," analyzes the reforms of President Felipe Calderón and **Mexico's evolving relationship with the United States**.

**8.** Chapter 19, "Politics in the United States," describes the **historic election of President Barack Obama** in November 2008. The chapter also discusses the challenges of the current financial and economic crisis facing the Obama administration.

PEARSON

# CONTRIBUTORS

OLADIMEJI ABORISADE
Obafemi Awolowa University, Nigeria

GABRIEL A. ALMOND
Stanford University

HOUCHANG E. CHEHABI
Boston University

WAYNE A. CORNELIUS
University of California, San Diego

RUSSELL J. DALTON
University of California, Irvine

FRANCES HAGOPIAN
University of Notre Dame

ARANG KESHAVARZIAN
New York University

THAD KOUSSER
University of California, San Diego

A. CARL LEVAN
American University

MELANIE MANION
University of Wisconsin

SUBRATA K. MITRA
Universität Heidelberg, Germany

ROBERT J. MUNDT
Late, University of North Carolina at Charlotte

G. BINGHAM POWELL, JR.
University of Rochester

AUSTIN RANNEY
Late, University of California, Berkeley

THOMAS F. REMINGTON
Emory University

RICHARD ROSE
University of Aberdeen, Scotland

FRANCES ROSENBLUTH
Yale University

MARTIN A. SCHAIN
New York University

KAARE STRØM
University of California, San Diego

MICHAEL F. THIES
University of California, Los Angeles

JEFFREY A. WELDON
Instituto Technologico Autónomo de Mexíco
(ITAM)

*Acquisitions Editor:* Vikram Mukhija
*Associate Editor:* Donna Garnier
*Editorial Assistant:* Toni Magyar
*Senior Media Editor:* Regina Vertiz
*Marketing Manager:* Lindsey Prudhomme
*Production Manager:* Eric Jorgensen
*Project Coordination, Text Design, and Electronic Page Makeup:* GGS Higher Education Resources, A Division
   of PreMedia Global, Inc.
*Cover Design Manager:* Wendy Ann Fredericks
*Cover Photo:* VEER Geoff Graham/Photonica/Getty Images
*Photo Researcher:* Jody Potter
*Senior Manufacturing Buyer:* Dennis J. Para
*Printer and Binder:* Edwards Brothers, Inc.
*Cover Printer:* Lehigh-Phoenix Color

**Library of Congress Cataloging-in-Publication Data**

Comparative politics today : a world view / Gabriel A. Almond ... [et al]. —9th ed., update.
      p. cm.
   Includes bibliographical references and index.
   ISBN-13: 978-0-205-58596-0
   ISBN-10: 0-205-58596-5
 1. Comparative government—Textbooks.   I. Almond, Gabriel A. (Gabriel Abraham), 1911–2002
   JF51.C62 2010
   320.3—dc22

                                                         2009019111

2 3 4 5 6 7 8 9 10—EDW—12 11 10

**Longman**
is an imprint of

www.pearsonhighered.com

ISBN-13: 978-0-205-58596-0
ISBN-10:    0-205-58596-5

UPDATED NINTH EDITION

# COMPARATIVE POLITICS TODAY

## A WORLD VIEW

Gabriel A. Almond
Late, Stanford University

G. Bingham Powell, Jr.
University of Rochester

Russell J. Dalton
University of California, Irvine

Kaare Strøm
University of California, San Diego

**Longman**

New York    San Francisco    Boston
London    Toronto    Sydney    Tokyo    Singapore    Madrid
Mexico City    Munich    Paris    Cape Town    Hong Kong    Montreal

The editors and coauthors of the ninth edition update of
*Comparative Politics Today* dedicate this book to the
memory of Austin Ranney— a colleague, a friend,
a leader in the study of American politics,
and for many years, a contributor to this book.
He passed away on July 24, 2006, at the age of 85.

# BRIEF CONTENTS

# DETAILED CONTENTS

## CHAPTER 10

# Politics in Germany   252
### Russell J. Dalton

## CHAPTER 11

# Politics in Japan   304
### Frances Rosenbluth and Michael F. Thies

## CHAPTER 12

# Politics in Russia   354
### Thomas F. Remington

## CHAPTER 13

# Politics in China   400
### Melanie Manion

# A GUIDE TO COMPARING NATIONS

This analytic index provides a guide to where specific themes are addressed in each chapter.

| Topics | Chapters 1–7 | Britain | France | Germany | Japan | Russia |
|---|---|---|---|---|---|---|
| **History** | — | 160–63 | 202–03 | 255–60 | 308–11 | 358–62 |
| **Social Conditions** | 10–23 | 156–60 | 203–05 | 260–63 | — | 389–91 |
| **Executive** | 103–07, 113–20 | 168–73 | 205–06 | 263–67 | 312 | 362–69 |
| **Parliament** | 103–07, 110–13 | 171–73 | 206–07 | 264–65 | 311–12 | 364–66 |
| **Judiciary** | 107–09 | 164–65 | 208 | 267 | 314–15 | 391–92 |
| **Provincial Government** | 107 | 156–58 | 241–43 | 263 | 312–14 | 370–73 |
| **Political Culture** | 43–52 | 173–76 | 208–12 | 267–72 | 332–35 | 370–72 |
| **Political Socialization** | 52–57 | 176–79 | 212–16 | 272–74 | 335–38 | 372–74 |
| **Participation/Recruitment** | 60–64 | 179–82 | 216–18, 230–35 | 274–76 | 327–28 | 374–77 |
| **Interest Groups** | 64–76, 80–81 | 182–85 | 218–22 | 277–80 | 328–30 | 377–81 |
| **Parties and Elections** | 81–98 | 185–90 | 223–30 | 280–89 | 315–27 | 381–86 |
| **Policy Process** | 31–38 | 190–97 | 235–41 | 289–93 | 338–43 | 364–66 |
| **Outputs and Outcomes** | 38–39, 127–45, 147–49 | 154–56, 196–97 | 201–02, 243–47 | 254–55, 297–00 | 306–07, 343–45, 347–49 | 356–58, 391–94, 394 |
| **International Relations** | 145–47 | 155–56 | 246–47 | 299–300 | 307, 344–47 | 394–95 |

| China | Mexico | Brazil | Iran | India | Nigeria | United States |
|---|---|---|---|---|---|---|
| 404–08 | 455–60 | 503–06 | 559–64 | 606–10 | 656–60 | 709 |
| 408–09 | 460–63 | 506–10 | 591–95 | 610–15 | 660–64 | 710–11 |
| 412–13, 416–17 | 473–77 | 511 | 564–66 | 616–20, 620–22 | 676–77, 681–83 | 714–15 |
| 410–12, 413–14 | 467–69, 470–73, 475–77 | 511–513 | 566–67 | — | 681–83 | 714–15 |
| 413 | 494 | 513–14 | 567 | 622 | 683–84 | 715 |
| — | 469–70 | 511 | 574–77 | 623–25 | 679–81 | 713–14 |
| 422–23 | 463–64 | 515–21 | 577–82 | 635–37 | 666–72 | 716–18 |
| 420–22 | 464–65 | 521–22 | 571, 74 | 637–38 | 672–76 | 718–19 |
| 418, 423–28 | 465–67, 477–78 | 522–27, 527–31 | 577–82 | 638–40 | 676–78, 687 | 719–23 |
| 428–30 | 479–80 | 531–39 | 568–74 | 629–35 | 687–93 | 727–35 |
| 413–18 | 449–55, 480–88 | 539–42 | | 629–35 | 687–93 | 727–35 |
| 428–36 | 471–73 | 501–03 | 567–68, 586–90 | 621–22 | — | 735–38 |
| 402–03, 436–42 | 455, 488–495 | 542–49 | 558–59, 590–95 | 604–06, 641–45 | 655–56, 694–700 | 707–09, 738–42 |
| 442 | 460–61 | 549–51 | 595–96 | 604–05, 646 | 664–65, 700–01 | 711–12, 707–08 |

We are used to thinking about reading written texts critically—for example, reading a textbook carefully for information, sometimes highlighting or underlining as we go along—but we do not always think about "reading" visuals in this way. We should, for images and informational graphics can tell us a lot if we read and consider them carefully. Especially in the so-called information age, in which we are exposed to a constant stream of images on television and the Internet, it is important for you to be able to analyze and understand their meanings. This brief guide provides information about the types of visuals you will encounter in *Comparative Politics Today: A World View* and offers some questions to help you analyze everything from tables to charts and graphs to news photographs.

## TABLES

Tables are the least "visual" of the visuals we explore. They consist of textual information and/or numerical data arranged in columns and rows. Tables are frequently used when exact information is required and when orderly arrangement is necessary to locate and, in many cases, to compare the information. For example, Table 1.4 makes data on the income distribution of many nations organized and easy to compare. Here are a few questions to guide your analysis:

- What is the purpose of this table? What information does it show? There is usually a title that offers a sense of the table's purpose.

| Income Distribution for Selected Nations | | | | TABLE 1.4 |
|---|---|---|---|---|
| **Country** | **Year** | **Wealthiest 10%** | **Poorest 40%** | **Wealthy/Poor Gap** |
| Germany | 2000 | 22.1 | 22.2 | −0.1 |
| Russia | 2002 | 23.8 | 20.9 | 2.9 |
| Japan | 1993 | 21.7 | 24.8 | 3.1 |
| France | 1995 | 25.1 | 19.8 | 5.3 |
| India | 1999 | 28.5 | 21.2 | 7.3 |
| Britain | 1999 | 28.5 | 17.5 | 11.0 |
| United States | 2000 | 29.9 | 16.2 | 13.7 |
| Iran | 1998 | 33.7 | 19.5 | 14.2 |
| China | 2001 | 33.1 | 13.7 | 19.4 |
| Nigeria | 1996 | 35.4 | 12.6 | 22.8 |
| Mexico | 2000 | 43.1 | 10.3 | 32.8 |
| Brazil | 2001 | 46.9 | 8.3 | 38.6 |

Source: World Bank, *World Development Indicators 2005*, table 2–7 (www.worldbank.org); distribution of income or consumption.

- What information is provided in the column headings (the table's top row)? How are the rows labeled? Are there any clarifying notes at the bottom of the table?
- Is a time period indicated, such as July to December 2005? Or, are the data as of a specific date, such as January 1, 2006? Are the data shown at multiple intervals over a fixed period or at one particular point in time?
- If the table shows numerical data, what do these data represent? In what units? Dollars spent on social service programs? Percentage of voters who support the British Labour Party? Projected population increases?

- What is the source of the information presented in the table? Is it government information? Private polling information? A newspaper? A corporation? The United Nations? An individual? Is the source trustworthy? Current? Does the source have a vested interest in the data expressed in the table?

## CHARTS AND GRAPHS

Charts and graphs depict numerical data in visual forms. The most common kinds of graphs plot data in two dimensions along horizontal and vertical axes. Examples that you will encounter throughout this

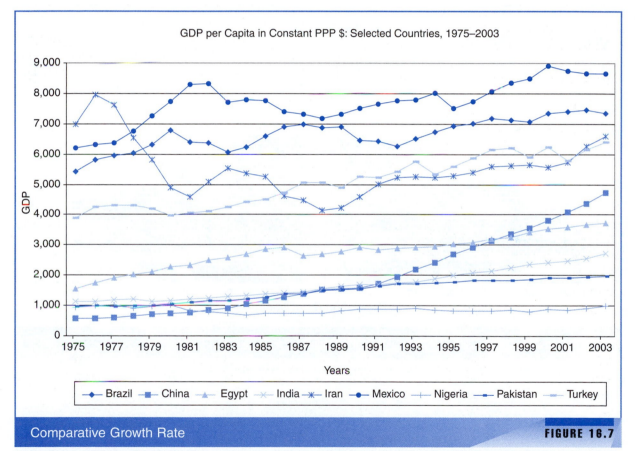

GDP per Capita in Constant PPP $: Selected Countries, 1975–2003

Legend: Brazil, China, Egypt, India, Iran, Mexico, Nigeria, Pakistan, Turkey

**Comparative Growth Rate**

**FIGURE 16.7**

Source: Based on data from Massoud Karshenas and Hassan Hakimian, "Oil, Economic Diversification and the Democratic Process in Iran," *Iranian Studies* 38, no. 1 (March 2005), 67–90.

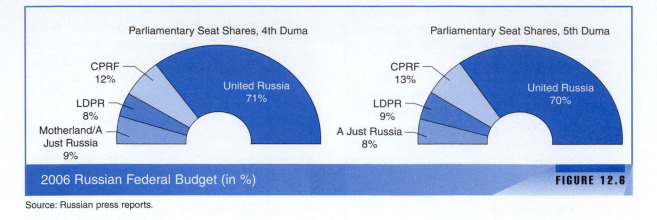

2006 Russian Federal Budget (in %)

FIGURE 12.6

Source: Russian press reports.

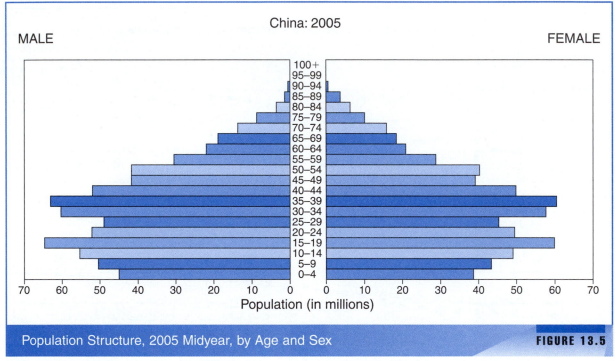

Population Structure, 2005 Midyear, by Age and Sex

FIGURE 13.5

Source: U.S. Census Bureau, International Data Base at http://www.census.gov/ipc/www/idbpyr.html.

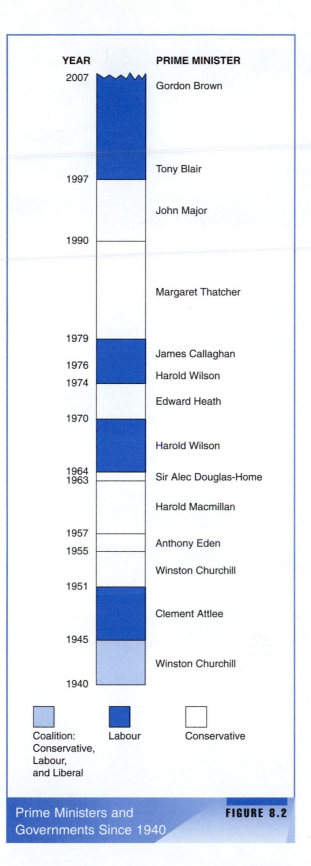

| YEAR | PRIME MINISTER |
|---|---|
| 2007 | Gordon Brown |
| | Tony Blair |
| 1997 | |
| | John Major |
| 1990 | |
| | Margaret Thatcher |
| 1979 | |
| 1976 | James Callaghan |
| 1974 | Harold Wilson |
| | Edward Heath |
| 1970 | |
| | Harold Wilson |
| 1964 | |
| 1963 | Sir Alec Douglas-Home |
| | Harold Macmillan |
| 1957 | |
| 1955 | Anthony Eden |
| | Winston Churchill |
| 1951 | |
| | Clement Attlee |
| 1945 | |
| | Winston Churchill |
| 1940 | |

Coalition: Conservative, Labour, and Liberal    Labour    Conservative

**Prime Ministers and Governments Since 1940**

**FIGURE 8.2**

book are line graphs, pie charts, bar graphs, and time-lines. These kinds of visuals emphasize data relationships: at a particular point in time, at regular intervals over a fixed period of time, or, sometimes, as parts of a whole. Line graphs show a progression, usually over time (as in Figure 16.7, Comparative Growth Rate). Pie charts (such as Figure 12.6, 2006 Russian Federal Budget) demonstrate how a whole (total government spending) is divided into its parts (different types of government programs). Bar graphs compare values across categories, showing how proportions are related to each other (as in Figure 13.5, showing the male and female populations in China by age bracket). Bar graphs can present data either horizontally or vertically. Timelines show events and changes over a defined period of time (such as the list of prime ministers of Britain in Figure 8.2). You will also encounter charts that map out processes and hierarchies throughout this book (as in the structure of the government of Nigeria shown in Figure 18.4).

Many of the same questions you ask about tables are important when analyzing graphs and charts also (see above). Here are more questions to help you:

- In the case of line and bar graphs, how are the axes labeled? Are symbols or colors used to represent different groups or units?
- Are the data shown at multiple intervals over a fixed period or at one particular point in time?
- If there are two or more sets of figures, what are the relationships among them?
- Is there distortion in the visual representation of the information? Are the intervals equal? Does the area shown distort the actual amount or the proportion? Distortion can lead you to draw an inaccurate conclusion on first sight, so it's important to look for it.

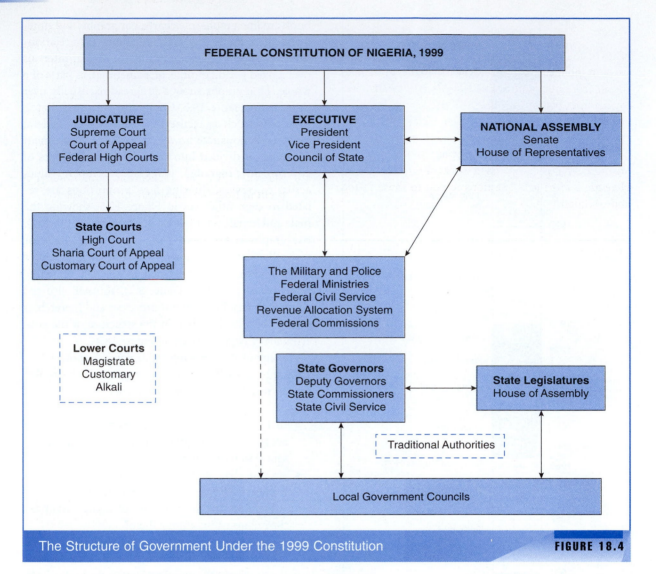

**FEDERAL CONSTITUTION OF NIGERIA, 1999**

**JUDICATURE**
Supreme Court
Court of Appeal
Federal High Courts

**EXECUTIVE**
President
Vice President
Council of State

**NATIONAL ASSEMBLY**
Senate
House of Representatives

**State Courts**
High Court
Sharia Court of Appeal
Customary Court of Appeal

The Military and Police
Federal Ministries
Federal Civil Service
Revenue Allocation System
Federal Commissions

**Lower Courts**
Magistrate
Customary
Alkali

**State Governors**
Deputy Governors
State Commissioners
State Civil Service

**State Legislatures**
House of Assembly

Traditional Authorities

Local Government Councils

The Structure of Government Under the 1999 Constitution

**FIGURE 18.4**

## MAPS

Maps of countries, regions, and the world are very often used in political analysis to illustrate demographic, social, economic, and political issues and trends. See, for example, Figure 14.7, Levels of Social Well-Being by State, in 2000 (page xix). Though tables and graphs might sometimes give more precise information, maps help us to understand in a geographic context data that are more difficult to express in words or numbers alone. Here are a few more questions to add to those in the above sections:

- What does the map key/legend show? What are the factors that the map is analyzing? Are symbols or colors used to differentiate sections of the map? Maps can express information on political boundaries, natural resources, ethnic groups, and many other topics, so it is important to know what exactly is being shown.
- What is the region being shown? How detailed is the map?
- Maps usually depict a specific point in time. What point in time is being shown on the map?

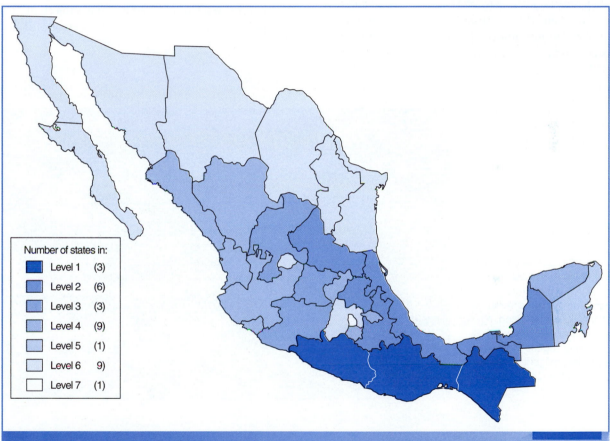

Number of states in:

| | | |
|---|---|---|
| Level 1 | (3) |
| Level 2 | (6) |
| Level 3 | (3) |
| Level 4 | (9) |
| Level 5 | (1) |
| Level 6 | 9) |
| Level 7 | (1) |

Levels of Social Well-Being by State, in 2000    **FIGURE 14.7**

Level 1: Chiapas, Guerrero, Oaxaca
Level 2: Campeche, Hidalgo, Puebla, San Luis Potosí, Tabasco, Veracruz
Level 3: Guanajuato, Michoacán, Zacatecas
Level 4: Colima, Durango, Jalisco, Morelos, Nayarit, Querétaro, Sinaloa, Tlaxcala, Yucatán
Level 5: Quintana Roo
Level 6: Aguascalientes, Baja California, Baja California Sur, Coahuila, Chihuahua, México, Nuevo León, Sonora, Tamaulipas.
Level 7: Distrito Federal

Note: Level of social well-being is measured by characteristics of dwellings (have electricity, refrigerator, television, concrete vs. dirt floors, sewerage connection, private bathroom; number of rooms; use something other than firewood or coal for cooking) and population characteristics (percentage economically active; literate; 6–19-year-olds who attend school; receive health care; live in urban area; average number of children born to women over age 12).

Source: Instituto Nacional de Estadística, Geografía e Informática, www.inegi.gob.mx.

## NEWS PHOTOGRAPHS

Photos can have a dramatic—and often immediate—impact on politics and government. Think about some photos that have political significance. For example, do you remember the photos from the September 11, 2001, terrorist attacks? Visual images usually evoke a stronger emotional response than do written descriptions. For this reason, individuals and organizations have learned to use photographs to document events, to make arguments, to offer evidence, and even in some cases to manipulate the viewer into having a particular response. The photo of a student protester confronting tanks in Tiananmen Square (page xx) captured the attention of the world and drew attention to the violent response of the Chinese government to the protesters. Here are a few questions to guide your analysis:

- When was the photograph taken? (If there is no date given for the photograph in its credit line or caption, you may be able to approximate the date according to the people or events depicted in the photo.)
- What is the subject of the photograph?
- Why was the photo taken?
- Is it spontaneous or posed? Did the subject know he or she was being photographed?
- Who was responsible for the photo (an individual, an agency, or an organization)? Can you discern the photographer's attitude toward the subject?
- Is there a caption? If so, what information does it provide? Does it identify the subject of the photo? Does it provide an interpretation of the subject?

In 1989, ordinary Chinese participated in the largest spontaneous protest movement the communists had ever faced. A lone protester shows defiance of regime violence in his intransigent confrontation with a Chinese tank.

AP Images

With great pleasure we introduce this ninth and substantially revised edition of *Comparative Politics Today: A World View,* which for the past three decades has been among the most influential textbooks in comparative politics. As the world grows more interdependent and as students are exposed to more cultures and communities, an appreciation of comparative politics is becoming ever more essential. As a text, *Comparative Politics Today* is ideally suited for courses that combine a broad and comprehensive thematic overview with rich and high-quality country studies written by expert scholars in their respective fields.

This edition of *Comparative Politics Today* continues to embody the system, process, and policy framework that Gabriel Almond introduced as a method to describe and explain politics in different political systems. Earlier editions of this book in the 1970s pioneered the teaching of systematic comparison of the political cultures, structures, processes, and policy performances of the world's political systems. Later editions described how enormous changes—such as democratization, the break-up of the Soviet empire, and intensified threats from ethnic conflict—have shaped politics in many nations. Throughout, these editions reflect Almond's creativity and the applicability of his framework to the changing concerns of students of political science.

## FEATURES

This edition begins by explaining why governments exist, what functions they serve, and how they create problems as well as solutions. Chapter 1 also introduces the three great challenges facing most states in the world today: building a common identity and sense of community; fostering economic and social development; and securing democracy, human rights, and civil liberties. Chapter 2 sketches the concepts needed to compare politics in very different societies: political systems and their environments, structures and functions, policy performance and its consequences. Jointly, these two chapters spell out the unique framework that this book employs.

Chapters 3 through 7 elaborate on important political structures, functions, and processes. They discuss the causes and consequences of political cultures, interest groups, parties and other aggregation structures, and constitutions, key policymaking structures, and types of public policies and their consequences. These chapters give comprehensive and unusually rich accounts of political processes in different political systems and provide a set of theoretical foci and empirical benchmarks for the country chapters that follow.

The continuing and unprecedented spread of democracy is not only a development to be celebrated, but also a reason that the issues of democratic representation, as discussed in Chapters 4 through 6, are becoming increasingly relevant to an ever larger share of the world's population. Growing prosperity in many parts of the world means that the issues of development and public policy (Chapters 1 and 7) are changing. While the global incidence and intensity of war has happily declined in recent years, conflicts still devastate or threaten communities in areas such as Iraq, Afghanistan, Lebanon, South Asia, Sudan, and other parts of Africa. And the world faces enormous challenges, new as well as old, in such areas as climate change, migration, economic globalization, epidemic disease, international terrorism, and nuclear proliferation. All of these developments make it more important than ever to understand how political decisions are made, and what their consequences might be, in the very different political systems that make up our political world.

The rest of this book presents systematic analyses of politics in twelve selected countries. In each case, distinguished specialists begin by discussing the current policy challenges facing citizens of that country and provide a historical perspective on its development. Each chapter then uses the system, process, and policy framework to highlight the distinctive features of that country's politics. The systematic application of a consistent framework facilitates comparison among countries. These rich country studies cover all the major regions of the world, including five developed democratic countries (Britain, France, Germany, Japan, and the United States), six developing countries at various levels of democratization (Brazil, China, India, Iran, Mexico, and Nigeria), and Russia, with its fascinating blend of development and poverty, and of democracy and authoritarianism. This book thus includes most of the world's large and influential countries and illustrates a wide range of political possibilities, problems, and limitations.

## NEW TO THIS UPDATED EDITION

This updated version of *comparative Politics Today* represents another learning opportunity for instructors and students in comparative politics. With the world seemingly changing at an ever faster pace, education must link students to ongoing events. The chapters on four European nations that are co-published in *European Politics Today* have been fully revised. We have also reviewed and updated every chapter to include the most recent developments in each country. And we have continued our effort to make the book more compact and reader-friendly, so that the overall length has been reduced.

Notable updates to the country chapters include:

- Britain—Covers the transition from Tony Blair to Gordon Brown as prime minister. The fully revised chapter examines the political and economic challenges faced by the new prime minister and the Labour government.
- France—Reports on the policy departures of President Nicolas Sarkozy and France's changing role in Europe and its relations with the European Union.
- Germany—Discusses the political experiences of the Grand Coalition government of the CDU/CSU

and SPD under the leadership of Germany's first woman chancellor, Angela Merkel. It also describes the political context leading up to the 2009 Bundestag elections.

- Russia—Adds new material on the 2008 presidential election of President Dmitry Medvedev, and Vladimir's Putin's transition to become Russia's premier. The chapter also describes the slide into an increasingly authoritarian regime.
- United States—Describes the historic election of President Barack Obama in November 2008. The chapter also discusses the challenges of the current financial and economic crisis facing the Obama administration.
- Japan—Reviews the rapid changes in the country's political leadership from Abe to Fukuda to Aso. The chapter considers the implications of these leadership changes for Japan's domestic policies and international position.
- Mexico—Analyzes the reforms of President Felipe Calderón and Mexico's evolving relationship with the United States.

With these and many other updates, we hope and believe that *Comparative Politics Today: A World View* will serve students and instructors across the world better than ever.

## ACKNOWLEDGMENTS

We are pleased to acknowledge the contributions of some of the many people who helped us prepare this ninth edition of *Comparative Politics Today*. But first we want to note that our new chapter on Iran has replaced the chapter on Egypt that appeared in previous editions. This was a painful decision, and we are sincerely grateful to Ann Mosely Lesch for her excellent contributions to many previous editions of this book.

We would like to thank the following individuals for their careful review and analysis of the book: Jim Peterson, Valdosta State; Michael Brittingham, University of Louisville; and Jon Jonassen, Brigham Young University-Hawaii. We are also grateful to Farhat Popal for research assistance and to Sonal R. Desai for assistance in developing the index.

Our coauthors wish to acknowledge their gratitude to a number of individuals who have contributed to their respective chapters. Melanie Manion wishes to thank Russell Dalton for his helpful comments and Michel Oksenberg and Nina Halpern for their comments on an earlier version of the China chapter. Wayne Cornelius and Jeffery Weldon thank Claudia Y. Carmona and Luis Estrada for research assistance on the Mexico chapter. Arang Keshavarzian thanks Adrian Dumitru, Nicola Gaye, and Katayon Kholdi-Haghighi for their research assistance. Subrata Mitra wishes to thank Karsten Frey and Alexander Fischer for research assistance on the chapter on India. Oladimeji Aborisade and A. Carl LeVan thank Claire Christian of American University for research assistance. In addition, Aborisade thanks Robert LaGamma, Curtis Huff, Arlene Jacquerre, and Charlotte Peterson for bringing together himself and Robert Mundt under the auspices of the U.S. Information Agency. He also thanks John A. Ayoade, Cecil Brown, Roger Brown, Charles Coe, Alex Gboyega, Jim Mean, Aladosu Oyelakin, Gary Rassel, Jim Svara, and Deil Wright for their help on earlier versions of the Nigeria chapter. Thad Kousser would like to thank Mike Binder and Nancy Ranney.

Our thanks also go to the team at Longman and GGS Higher Education Resources: Eric Stano, Vikram Mukhija, Toni Magyar, Donna Garnier, Regina Vertiz, Eric Jorgensen, Dennis Para, Wendy Fredericks, Lindsey Prudhomme, and Suganya Karuppasamy.

G. BINGHAM POWELL, JR.
RUSSELL J. DALTON
KAARE STRØM

# ISSUES IN COMPARATIVE POLITICS

## WHAT IS POLITICS?

Some people love politics. They relish the excitement of political events, such as a presidential election, as they would an exciting athletic contest (the World Series of baseball or the World Cup of soccer, perhaps). Others are fascinated with politics because they care about the issues and their consequences for people in their own communities and around the world. Still others hate politics, either because it sets groups and individuals against each other, or because it involves abuse of power, deceit, manipulation, and violence. Finally, some people are indifferent to politics because it has little to do with the things that matter most to them. All of these reactions involve kernels of truth about politics. Indeed, most of us react to politics with a mixture of these sentiments. Politics has many faces and can be a force for good as well as evil. The core of politics, however, is about human beings making important decisions for themselves and for others.

This book is about the comparative study of politics. In order to make political comparisons, we need to understand what politics is as well as what it means to study politics comparatively. Comparative politics thus involves two separate elements:

- It is a subject of study—comparing the nature of politics and the political process across different political systems.
- It is a method of study—involving how and why we make such comparisons.

We address the first point in this chapter; Chapter 2 discusses the second.

Politics deals with human decisions, and political science is the study of such decisions. Yet, not all decisions are political, and many of the social sciences study decisions that are of little interest to political scientists. For example, consider when you go with a friend to an event, such as a concert or a soccer match. You can spend your money on the tickets (to get the best seats possible) or on food and drink, or you can save your money for the future. Economists study the sorts of spending decisions people make, and perhaps how they reach them. Psychologists, on the other hand, might study why you went to the event with this friend and not another, or who suggested going in the first place.

Political scientists seldom examine such personal experiences, unless they have political consequences. Instead, we examine the political process and its impact on the citizens. Political decisions constantly touch our lives in many ways, our careers, and our families. Our jobs are structured by government regulations, our homes are built to conform to government housing codes, our public schools are funded and managed by the government, and even when we go to a concert or sporting event, we travel on roads maintained by the government and monitored by the police. We might not think of politics as omnipresent in our lives, but it affects us in many important ways. Therefore, it is important to study how political decisions are made and what their consequences are.

Political decisions are *public* and *authoritative*. There is no such thing as political solitaire, playing politics by yourself. Political decisions take place within some community that we call a *political system*, which we describe below. Yet, not all social decisions are public. Most of what happens within families, among friends, or in social groups belongs to the *private sphere*. Actions within this sphere do not bind anyone outside that group. In most societies, your choice of concert partners and food are private decisions.

The *public sphere* deals with collective decisions that extend beyond the individual, typically involving government action. In totalitarian societies, like Hitler's Third Reich and some communist nations, the public sphere is very large and the private sphere is very limited. The state tries to dominate the life of its people, even intruding into family life. On the other hand, in some less developed nations the private domain may almost crowd out the public one. People in many African nations, for instance, may be unaware of what happens in the capital city and untouched by the decisions made there. Western democracies have a more balanced mix of private and public spheres. However, the boundaries between the two spheres get redrawn all the time. A few decades ago, the sex lives of U.S. presidents or members of the British royal family were considered private matters, not to be discussed in public. These norms are changing in Britain and the United States, but the traditional standards remain in other countries. Similarly, at one time in British history certain religious beliefs were considered treasonous. Today, religious beliefs are considered private matters in most modern democracies, but not in many other parts of the world. Even though politics may be influenced by what happens in the private domain, it deals directly with only those decisions that are public.

Politics is also *authoritative*. Authority means that formal power rests in individuals or groups whose decisions are expected to be carried out and respected. Thus, political decisions are binding for members of that political system. Governments may use force to ensure compliance, although authority is not always backed up by force. For instance, a religious authority, such as the Pope, has few coercive powers. He can persuade, but rarely compel, the Catholic Church's followers. In contrast, tax authorities, such as the U.S. Internal Revenue Service, can both exhort and compel people to follow their rules.

Thus, politics refers to activities associated with the control of public decisions among a given people and in a given territory, where this control may be backed up by authoritative means. Politics involves the crafting of these authoritative decisions—who gets to make them and for what purposes.

We live in one of the most exciting times to study politics. The end of the Cold War created a new international order, although its shape is still uncertain. The democratic transitions in Eastern Europe and many developing nations have transformed the world, although it is unclear whether these new democracies will endure and what forms they might take. In Western nations, new challenges and choices have arisen that divide their citizens. Some of these problems—such as confronting global warming and achieving international peace—are transnational. Part of their solutions, we hope, lies in the political choices that people make about their collective future. Our goal in this book is to give you a sense of how governments and politics function to address these challenges.

## GOVERNMENTS AND THE STATE OF NATURE

**Governments** are organizations of individuals who have the power to make binding decisions on behalf of a particular community. Governments thus have authoritative and coercive powers. Governments do many things. They can wage war or encourage peace; cultivate or restrict international trade; open their borders to the exchange of ideas and art or close them; tax their populations heavily or lightly and through different means; allocate resources for education, health, and welfare or leave such matters to others. People who are affected by such decisions may well agree with them and indeed welcome them, but there is also often heated disagreement about the proper role of government decisions.

Debates over the nature and appropriate role of government are far from new. They reflect a classic polemic in political philosophy. For centuries, philosophers have debated whether governments are a force for good or evil. In the seventeenth and eighteenth centuries—the time of the English, French, and American revolutions—much of this debate was couched in arguments concerning the **state of nature.**

Philosophers thought about the state of nature as the condition of humankind if no government existed. In some cases, they thought that such a situation existed before the first governments were formed. These philosophers used their ideas about the state of nature to identify an ideal social contract (agreement) on which to build a political system. Even today, many philosophers find it useful to make such a mental experiment to consider the consequences of having governments.

These debates have shaped our images of government, even to the present. The contrast between Thomas Hobbes' and Jean-Jacques Rousseau's ideas about the state of nature is most striking. Hobbes was the ultimate pessimist. He thought of the state of nature as mercilessly inhospitable, a situation of eternal conflict of all against all, and a source of barbarism and continuous fear. He pessimistically argued that "[i]n such condition, there is no place for Industry; because the fruit thereof is uncertain: and consequently no Culture of the Earth; no Navigation, nor use of the commodities that may be imported by Sea; no commodious Building, . . . no Arts; no Letters; no Society; and which is worst of all, continuall feare, and danger of violent death; And the life of man, solitary, poor, nasty, brutish, and short."[1]

Rousseau, in contrast, was more optimistic. For him, the state of nature represented humanity before its fall from grace, without all the corruptions that governments have introduced. "Man is born free," Rousseau observed in *The Social Contract*, "and yet everywhere he is in chains." Rousseau saw governments as the source of power and inequality, and these conditions in turn as the causes of human alienation and corruption. "The extreme inequality in our way of life," he argued, "excess of idleness in some, excess of labor in others; . . . late nights, excesses of all kinds, immoderate ecstasies of all the passions; fatigues and exhaustion of mind, numberless sorrows and afflictions . . . that most of our ills are our own work; that we would have avoided almost all of them by preserving the simple, uniform, and solitary way of life prescribed to us by nature."[2]

John Locke's ideas have been particularly important for the development of Western democracies. He took a position between those of Hobbes and Rousseau. Compared with Hobbes, Locke thought of human beings as more businesslike and less war prone. Yet, like Hobbes he proposed a social contract to replace the state of nature with a system of government. While Hobbes thought the main task for government is to quell disorder and protect against

violence and war, Locke saw the state's main role as protecting property and commerce and promoting economic growth. He believed government would do this by establishing and enforcing property rights and rules of economic exchange. Whereas Hobbes thought government needed to be a Leviathan—a benevolent dictator to whom the citizens would yield all their power—Locke favored a limited government.[3]

Although these debates began centuries ago, they still underlie current discussions on the appropriate role of government. To some, government is the solution to many human needs and problems—a theme that former U.S. President Bill Clinton often advocated. To others, the government is often part of the problem—a theme that former U.S. President Ronald Reagan articulately argued. To some, government exists to create the social order that protects its citizens; to others, the government's rules limit our freedoms. This tension is part of the political discourse in many contemporary nations, including the United States. We explore these contrasting views and different examples of government structures in this book.

## WHY GOVERNMENTS?

A recent libertarian science fiction book begins with the scenario of a group of travelers landing at an airport after a long overseas flight. As they disembark from the plane, they notice there are no police checking passports, no customs officers scanning baggage, and no officials applying immigration rules.[4] They had landed in a society without government, and the puzzle was what having no government would mean for the citizenry. The answer is a lot (see Box 1.1). As philosophers have pointed out, there are many reasons why people create governments and prefer to live under such a social order. We shall discuss some of these, beginning with activities that help generate a stable community in the first place and then those that help this community prosper.

### Community- and Nation-Building

One of the first purposes of governments is to create and maintain a community in which people can feel safe and comfortable. While humans may be social beings, it is not always easy to build a community in which large numbers of people can communicate, feel

## U.S. Government's Top Ten List

**BOX 1.1**

Paul Light surveyed 450 historians and political scientists to assess the U.S. government's greatest achievements in the past half century. Their top ten list is as follows:

- Help rebuild Europe after World War II
- Expand the right to vote for minorities
- Promote equal access to public accommodations

- Reduce disease
- Reduce workplace discrimination
- Ensure safe food and drinking water
- Strengthen the nation's highway system
- Increase older Americans' access to health care
- Reduce the federal deficit
- Promote financial security in retirement

Source: Paul Light, *Government's Greatest Achievements of the Past Half-Century* (Washington, DC: Brookings Institution, 2000) (www.brookings.edu/comm/reformwatch/rw02.pdf).

at home, and interact constructively. Governments can help generate such communities in many different ways, for example, by teaching a common language, instilling common norms and values, creating common myths and symbols, and supporting a national identity. However, sometimes such actions create controversy because they threaten the values of minority groups.

Nation-building activities help instill common world views, values, and expectations. Using a concept discussed more in Chapter 3, governments can help create a national **political culture.** The political culture defines the public's expectations toward the political process and its role within the process. The more the political culture is shared, the easier it is to live in peaceful coexistence and engage in activities for mutual gain, such as commerce.

## Security and Order

Government activities partially reflect Hobbes' belief that only strong governments can make society safe for their inhabitants. Providing security and law and order is among the most essential tasks that governments perform. Externally, security means protecting against attacks from other political systems. Armies, navies, and air forces typically perform this function. Internally, security means protecting against theft, aggression, and violence from members of one's own society. In most societies providing this protection is the function of the police.

Providing security and order is a critical role of modern governments. While governments worldwide have privatized many of the services they once performed—for example, those involving post offices, railroads, and telecommunications, few, if any, governments have privatized their police or defense forces. This shows how security is one of the most essential roles of government. The international terrorist attacks in New York City and Washington, D.C., on September 11, 2001, and subsequent attacks in London, Madrid, and other cities underscore the importance of security.

## Protecting Rights

John Locke considered property rights to be particularly critical to the development of prosperous communities. Without effective protection of property rights, people will not invest their goods or energies in productive processes. Also, unless property rights exist and contracts can be negotiated and enforced, people will not trust their neighbors enough to engage in trade and commerce. Anything beyond a subsistence economy requires effective property rights and contracts. Therefore, Locke believed that the primary role of government is to establish and protect such rights. Similarly, contemporary authors argue that social order is a prerequisite for development and democratization.[5]

Effective property rights allocate ownership and provide security against trespass and violations. Such rights must also make the buying and selling of property relatively inexpensive and painless. Finally, people must have faith that their property rights can be defended. Thus, many analysts argue that one of the most restrictive limitations on development in the Third World is the government's inability (or unwillingness) to guarantee such rights. Peasant families who have lived for generations on a plot of land cannot claim ownership, which erodes their incentive and opportunity to invest in the future.

Although Locke was most concerned with economic property rights, governments also protect many other social and political rights. Among them are freedoms of speech and association and protection against various forms of discrimination and harassment. Indeed, the protection of these rights and liberties is one of the prime goals of government—with other factors such as nation-building, security, and property rights providing a means toward this goal. Governments also play a key role in protecting the rights of religious, racial, and other social groups. Human development stresses the expansion of these rights and liberties, and governments play a key role in this process.

## Promoting Economic Efficiency and Growth

Economists have long debated the government's potential role in promoting economic development. Neoclassical economics shows that markets are efficient when property rights are defined and protected, when competition is rigorous, and when information is freely available. When these conditions do not hold, markets may fail and the performance of the economy may suffer.[6] At least in some circumstances, governments can lessen the results of market failure.

Governments may be especially important in providing **public goods,** such as clean air, a national defense, or disease prevention. Public goods have two things in common. One is that if one person enjoys them, they cannot be withheld from anyone else. The second is that one person's enjoyment or consumption of the goods does not detract from anyone else's. Consider clean air. For most practical purposes, it is impossible to provide one person with clean air without also giving it to his or her neighbors. Moreover, my enjoyment of clean air does not mean that my neighbors have any less of it. Analysts therefore argue that people in a market economy will not pay enough for public goods. They claim that only government can provide such public goods. Otherwise, people will not voluntarily pay for public goods because they can benefit from the goods that others provide, or they will not act until they are assured others will also contribute.

Governments can also benefit society by controlling the **externalities** that occur when an activity produces costs that are not borne by the producer or the user. For instance, many forms of environmental pollution occur when those who produce or consume goods do not pay all of the environmental costs. Polluting factories, waste dumps, prisons, and major highways can impose large costs on those who live near them. NIMBY ("not in my backyard") groups are an example of citizens complaining about these costs. Governments can help protect people from such unfair externalities or ensure that burdens are fairly shared.

Governments also can promote fair competition in economic markets. For example, governments can assure that all businesses follow minimum standards of worker protection and product liability. In other cases, the government may control potentially monopolistic parts of the economy to ensure that suppliers do not take advantage of their market power. This happened in the nineteenth century with railroad monopolies, and now in the twenty-first century with technology monopolies, such as Microsoft, or telecommunications companies. In these cases the government acts as the policeman to ensure that the economically powerful do not exploit their power. Sometimes, the government itself may become the monopolist. There are some markets in which very large start-up costs or prohibitive costs of coordination mean that there should be only one producer. The government may then set itself up as that monopolist, or it may decide to tightly control a private monopolist. Telecommunications have commonly been a government monopoly, as have mail services and strategic defense industries.

## Social Justice

Governments can also play a role in dividing the fruits of economic growth in equitable ways. Many people argue that governments are needed to promote social justice by redistributing wealth and other resources among citizens. In many countries the distribution of income or property is highly uneven. Moreover, in many societies income and wealth inequalities worsen over time. Brazil, for example, has one of the most severe income inequalities in the world, an inequality that grew in every decade from the 1930s to the 1990s.

Under such circumstances, social justice may require a "new deal," especially if inequalities deprive many individuals of education, adequate health care, or other basic needs. Government can intervene to redistribute resources from the better-off to the poor. Some theorists argue that such transfers should attempt to equalize the conditions of all citizens. Others prefer governments to redistribute enough to equalize opportunities, and then let individuals be responsible for their own fortunes.

Many private individuals, organizations, and foundations attempt to help the poor, but they generally lack the capacity to effect large-scale redistribution. Governments do, at least under some circumstances. Many tax and welfare policies effectively redistribute income, although the degree of redistribution is often hotly disputed. Yet most individuals agree that governments should provide their citizens with the opportunities to reach certain minimum standards of living and a social safety net.

## Protecting the Weak

We commonly rely on the government to protect individuals and groups that are not able to speak for themselves. Groups such as the poor or the homeless or future generations cannot effectively protect their own interests. Governments, however, can protect the interests of the unborn and prevent them from getting saddled with economic debts or environmental degradation. In recent decades, governments have become much more involved in protecting groups that are politically weak or disenfranchised, such as children, the old, and the infirm or disabled, as well as nonhumans—from whales and birds to trees and other parts of our natural environment.

## WHEN DOES GOVERNMENT BECOME THE PROBLEM?

There are many reasons that governments may become involved in human affairs, but such intervention is not always welcomed. When and how government intervention is necessary and desirable are among the most disputed issues in modern politics. During the twentieth century, the role of governments expanded enormously in most nations. At the same time, criticisms of many government policies have persisted and sometimes intensified. Such skepticism is directed at virtually all government activities, especially the economic role of government.

## Destruction of Community

Whereas some see governments as a way to build community, others argue that governments destroy natural communities. Government, they hold, implies power and inequality among human beings. And power corrupts. In Lord Acton's famous words, "Power corrupts, and absolute power corrupts absolutely."

While those who have power are corrupted, those without it are degraded and alienated. According to Rousseau, only human beings unfettered by government can form bonds that allow them to develop their full human potential. By imposing an order based on coercion, hierarchy, and the threat of force, governments destroy natural communities. The stronger government becomes, the more it creates inequalities of power that have negative consequences. Such arguments stimulated Western criticism of communism as limiting the potential and freedom of its citizens.

Others argue that strong governments create a "client society," in which people learn to be subservient to authorities and to rely on governments to meet their needs. In such societies, governments patronize and pacify their citizens, as seen in many developing nations today.

## Violations of Basic Rights

Just as governments can help establish many essential rights, they can also use their powers to violate these rights in the most serious manner. The twentieth century witnessed enormous progress in the extension of political, economic, and social rights in societies worldwide. At the same time, however, some governments violated basic **human rights** on an unprecedented scale. The millions of lives lost to political persecution is the most serious example of this. Such horrors happened not only in Nazi extermination camps and during Stalin's Great Terror in the Soviet Union, but also on a huge scale in China, Cambodia, and Rwanda, and on a smaller scale in Iraq, Argentina, the Sudan, and Afghanistan.

These extreme abuses of government power illustrate a dilemma that troubled James Madison and other Founders of the American Revolution: the tension between creating a government strong enough to govern effectively but not so strong that it could destroy the rights of its citizens. They understood the irony that to protect individuals from each other, societies can create a government that has even more power to coerce the individual.

## Economic Inefficiency

Governments can help economies flourish, but they also can distort and restrict a state's economic potential. President Robert Mugabe, for instance, has destroyed the economy of a once developing Zimbabwe, and similar examples exist in many struggling economies. Economic problems might arise even if government officials do not actively abuse their power. Government regulation of the economy may distort the terms of trade and lower people's incentives to produce. Further inefficiencies may arise when governments actually own or manage important economic enterprises. This is particularly likely if the government holds a monopoly on an important good, since monopolies generally cause goods to be undersupplied and overpriced. Moreover, government industries may be especially prone to inefficiency and complacency because management and workers often have better job protection than those in the private sector. Therefore, they may worry less about the economic performance of the firm. Such experiences stimulate calls to restrict the economic role of governments in both developing and advanced industrial economies.

## Government for Private Gain

Society also may suffer if government officials make decisions to benefit themselves personally, or select policies to get themselves reelected regardless of whether those policies would be the best for the society. These actions are like a game in which one person's gain is another person's loss. A politician or political group may use the government to unfairly reap benefits at the public's expense—what is called "rent seeking." *Rents* are benefits created through government intervention in the economy—for example, tax revenue or profits created because the government has restricted competition. Rent seeking refers to efforts by individuals, groups, firms, or organizations to reap such benefits. The idea is really quite simple. For instance, a local mayor plans an economic development project that will benefit his friends who own land in the area or who will supply contracts for the project. Rent seeking can impose large net costs on society because policies are chosen for the private benefits that they produce rather than for their social efficiency and because groups may expend large amounts of resources to control the spoils of government. Rent seeking may turn into outright corruption when influence is traded for money or other advantage (see Box 1.2).

Political exploitation is a particularly serious problem in poor societies. Holding political office is often an effective way to enrich oneself when other political actors are too weak to constrain the abuse of government officials. Besides, many developing societies do not have strong norms against using government for private gain. On the contrary, people often expect those in government to use their power to benefit themselves, their families, and their neighbors. Even in many advanced democratic societies public officeholders are expected to appoint their supporters

---

### The Case of Mobutu Sese Seko

**BOX 1.2**

What happens if politicians use their power in their own self-interest or to benefit individuals or groups that support them? President Mobutu Sese Seko (1930–1997) of Zaire offers a tragic example of the costs that rent-seeking politicians can impose on their societies. After seizing power in a 1965 coup, Mobutu ruled the large African state of Congo (which he renamed Zaire) for more than thirty years. During his long rule, President Mobutu used government funds, including aid from Western states such as the United States, to amass a huge personal fortune, which he invested abroad. In addition to large sums of money, he is reported to have owned about thirty luxury residences abroad, including a number of palatial estates on the French Riviera. Meanwhile, living standards in Zaire, a poor country despite significant natural resources, plummeted, and the country was racked with epidemic disease and civil war. Mobutu died of natural causes shortly after his ouster.

to ambassadorships and other public posts, constrained in part by civil service rules designed to reward merit over patronage. The temptations of officeholding are great. Despite formal rules, press scrutiny, and citizen concerns, few governments anywhere finish their terms of office untainted by some corruption scandal.

## Vested Interests and Inertia

Government-created private gains are difficult to change or abolish once they have been established. Some people enjoy the benefits of government jobs, contracts, or other favors that they otherwise might not have had. The larger the government and the more attractive the benefits it provides, the more likely it is that such vested interests will resist change (unless change means even larger benefits). Therefore, any government will foster a group of people with a vested interest in maintaining or enlarging the government itself. Such groups may become a powerful force in favor of the status quo.

Vested interests make it difficult to change government policies or make them more efficient. Once established, agencies and policies can live on far beyond their usefulness. For example, when the Spanish Armada threatened to invade England in 1588, the government posted a military observation post at Land's End in southwest England. This observation post remained in place for four centuries! In the United States, the Rural Electrification Administration was created in 1935 to bring electricity to rural America; it persisted for almost sixty years until it was finally merged into the Rural Utilities Service in 1994.

Vested interests are particularly likely in political systems that contain a lot of safeguards against rapid political change. While the checks and balances in political systems such as in the United States are designed to safeguard individual rights, they may also protect the privileges of vested interests. Yet, even political systems that contain far fewer such checks may exhibit an excess of political inertia. Britain is an excellent example. Until recently, the House of Lords represented the social groups that dominated British society before the Industrial Revolution more than 200 years ago (noblemen, bishops, and judges). Only in the last few years has Britain begun reforming the House of Lords to eliminate features that reflect Britain's feudal and preindustrial past.

This debate and struggle over the proper role of government are an ongoing part of politics. In the past twenty-five years or so, there has been a clear trend away from extensive government regulation of many economic sectors. Since the 1970s especially, many societies have moved to privatize many economic sectors and to deregulate others. Government regulation has become less extensive in some areas, but it has grown in others—for example, through enacting laws to protect the environment or the rights of children. The overall size of governments in advanced industrial countries has not changed very much. In the former communist countries and in some developing countries, however, the government's size has shrunk quite dramatically. Yet, countries vary widely in the size of their governments, and they are likely to continue to do so.

## POLITICAL SYSTEMS AND STATES

We began by discussing governments, but governments are only one part of a larger political system. Since the term **political system** is a main organizing concept of this book, it deserves a full explanation. A system necessarily has two properties: (1) it has a set of interdependent parts, and (2) it has boundaries between the system and its environment.

Political systems are a particular type of social system that is involved in the making of authoritative public decisions. Central elements of a political system are the institutions of government—such as parliaments, bureaucracies, and courts—that formulate and implement the collective goals of a society or of groups within it.

Political systems also include important parts of the society in which governments operate. For example, political organizations, such as political parties or interest groups, are part of the political system. Such organizations do not have coercive authority, except insofar as they control the government. Likewise, the mass media only indirectly affect elections, legislation, and law enforcement. A whole host of institutions—beginning with the family and including communities, churches, schools, corporations, foundations, and think tanks—influence political attitudes and public policy. The term *political system* refers to the whole collection of related, interacting institutions and agencies.

The political systems that we compare in this book are all independent states. They represent some of the important countries in the contemporary world. At the same time, they reflect the diversity of political systems that exist today. A **state** is a particular type of political system. It has **sovereignty**—an independent legal authority over a population in a particular territory, based on the recognized right to self-determination. Sovereignty rests with those who have the ultimate right to make political decisions.

External sovereignty means the right to make binding agreements (treaties) with other states. For instance, France's external sovereignty means that it can enter into treaties with other states. The city of Bordeaux, however, does not have this right (nor do other subnational units of government in France). Internal sovereignty means the right to determine matters having to do with one's own citizens. For example, the French government has internal sovereignty so that it can impose taxes on French citizens.

Yet, states mold and are molded by a domestic environment and an international environment. The system receives inputs from these environments and shapes them through its outputs. The boundaries of political systems are defined in terms of persons, territory, and property. Most people have citizenship rights in only one country. Similarly, territory is divided between states. A given piece of land is supposed to belong to only one country. Of course, disputes over citizenship, territory, and property are by no means uncommon and are among the most frequent causes of international conflict.

Every state faces some constraints on its external and internal sovereignty. For example, with the increasing integration of France into the **European Union (EU),** the French government has given up parts of its sovereignty to the EU, and this loss of sovereignty is a major topic of political debate. In the United States, we confuse things a bit by calling the fifty constituent units "states," even though they enjoy much less sovereignty than France. The states of the United States share the power and authority of the "state" with the federal government in Washington, D.C.

We often think of the world as a patchwork of states with sizable and contiguous territories and a common identity shared by their citizens. A nation is a group of people, often living in a common territory, who have such a common identity. We call the cases in which national identification and sovereign political authority largely coincide **nation-states.** We have come to think of nation-states as the natural way to organize political systems, and often as an ideal. The national right to self-determination—the idea that every nation has a right to form its own state if it wants to do so—was enshrined in the Treaty of Versailles signed at the end of World War I.

Nation-states are often a desirable way to organize a political system. However, the national right to self-determination is a relatively modern invention. Until the end of the Middle Ages, Europe consisted of many very small political systems and a few very large ones, whose territorial possessions were not always very stable or contiguous. Nor did states always consist of people with the same national identity. Gradually, a set of European nation-states evolved, and the 1648 Treaty of Westphalia established that principle for the political organization of Europe. The nation-state thus emerged as the dominant political system during the eighteenth and nineteenth centuries in Europe.

Since then, Europe has transformed itself into distinct nation-states. This did not happen accidentally—indeed, the governments of the emerging nation-states had a lot to do with it. They sought to instill a common national identity among the peoples they controlled. They did so, often heavy-handedly, by promoting a common language, a common educational system, and often a common religion. While this process of *nation-building* was often harsh, it produced a Europe in which the inhabitants of most states have a strong sense of community.

Many societies in the developing world today face similar challenges. Especially in Africa, the former colonial powers (particularly Britain and France) left the newly independent states with very weak national identities. In many parts of Africa, large-scale national communities simply did not exist at the time of colonization. Even where they did exist, they were rarely reflected in the boundaries that the colonial powers drew between their possessions. After independence, many new states have therefore faced huge nation-building tasks.

There are additional challenges to contemporary nation-states. After World War II, power in Western states began to shift downward from the state to local governments, and upward to supranational organizations, such as the EU. Most of the industrialized countries of Western Europe have gradually created a common market economy. Originally consisting of six countries—France, Germany, Italy, Belgium, the Netherlands, and Luxembourg—the EU has expanded to twenty-seven members with the addition of two members in 2006.

The **United Nations (UN),** formed at the end of World War II in 1945, has also acquired new responsibilities since the collapse of the Soviet Union in the 1990s. As of early 2006, UN forces were peacekeepers in fifteen countries. These operations—involving more than 100,000 peacekeepers—separate combatants in domestic and international conflicts, settle disputes, and form effective governing institutions. The UN has increased authority over world security, constraining, supporting, and sometimes replacing the unilateral actions of individual states. While the sovereignty of states may be diminishing, they are still the most important political systems. That, of course, is the main reason that they are the subject of our study.

## THE DIVERSITY OF STATES

Just about the entire surface of the world today is covered by independent states. There were 192 UN "member-states" in 2009.[7] A few countries are not members of the UN (Taiwan, Switzerland, and the Vatican), and some independence movements would create even more states. When the United States declared its independence in 1776, most independent states were European (see Figure 1.1). Much of the rest of the world existed as colonies to one of the European empires. In the nineteenth and early twentieth centuries, the number of states increased, principally in Latin America, where the Spanish and Portuguese empires broke up into twenty independent states. In Europe, newly independent countries emerged in the Balkans, Scandinavia, and the Low Countries.

Between the two world wars, national proliferation extended to North Africa and the Middle East; and Europe continued to fragment as the Russian and Austro-Hungarian empires broke up. Since World War II, the development of new states has taken off. By 2009, 125 new countries had joined the sixty-eight states that existed in 1945. The largest group of new states is in Sub-Saharan Africa. More than twenty new countries formed in the 1990s—mostly the successor states of the Soviet Union, Yugoslavia, and Czechoslovakia.

All these countries—new as well as old—share certain characteristics. They have legal authority over their territories and people; most have armies, air forces, and

The United Nations is the most inclusive organization of states. As of 2009, the United Nations had 192 member states, represented by the flags flying outside its headquarters in New York City.

Joseph Sohm–ChromoSohm, Inc./Corbis

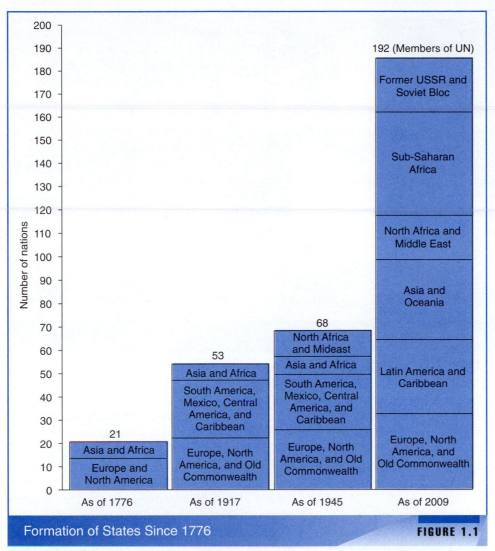

Formation of States Since 1776    **FIGURE 1.1**

Source: For Contemporary Members, Information Office, United Nations. Data to 1945 from Charles Taylor and Michael Hudson, *World Handbook of Political and Social Indicators* (New Haven, CT: Yale University Press, 1972), 26 ff.

in some cases navies; they collect taxes and spend money; they regulate their economies, maintain public order, and pursue their general welfare. Countries send and receive ambassadors; most belong to several international organizations. They also vary, often profoundly, in physical size, histories, institutions, cultures, religions, economies, and social structures—factors that shape their politics.

## Big and Small States

Nations come in all sizes. The smallest legally independent political entity in both geographic extent and population is Vatican City, the headquarters of the Catholic Church, with less than half a square kilometer of turf and fewer than a thousand residents.

The contrasts between geographic size and population size can be graphically seen in the following two maps. Map 1.1 is the familiar global map in which countries are displayed according to their size. Russia, with its landmass extending over eleven contiguous time zones, is the world's largest state with more than 17 million square kilometers. The United States falls about midpoint in this range, with just more than 9 million square kilometers. Many of the established democracies in Europe are relatively small (Britain has 242,000 square kilometers and Germany 349,000).

Map 1.2 is more provocative because is displays nations by their population size. Instantly we see China and India balloon in size because of their large populations. China alone accounts for almost a quarter of the world's population (with 1.3 billion people), and India is not far behind (with 1.1 billion). The European democracies we compare—Britain, France, and Germany—look smaller in these comparisons because their populations range from about 60 million to 80 million. Even more dramatically, Australia shrinks from a continent in the first map to a small dot in the population map because of its small population size (20 million). The United States in this global perspective seems relatively small in population terms

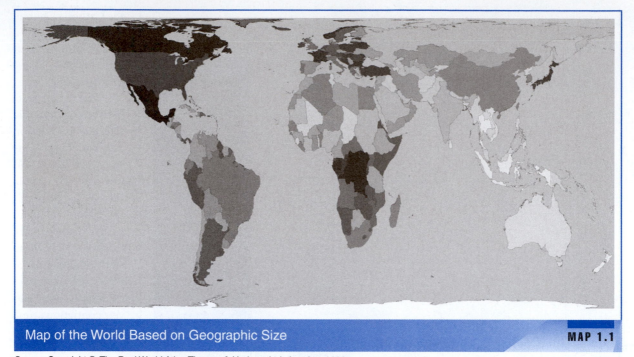

Map of the World Based on Geographic Size                                                              MAP 1.1

Source: Copyright © *The Real World Atlas,* Thames & Hudson, Ltd., London, 2008.

(298 million), even though it has roughly the same area as China and is geographically larger than India. And even though Russia has almost twice as much land as any other country, it has a modest population size (142 million) that is barely half as large as the United States, and Russia is shrinking.

The political implications of these striking contrasts in population size and geographic area are not always obvious. Big countries are not always the most important and do not always prevail over the small ones: Cuba has challenged the United States for almost forty years; Israel stands off the Arab world; and tiny Vatican City has great power and influence. Nor do area and population size determine a country's political system. Both little Luxembourg and large India are democracies. Authoritarian regimes are found in small, medium, and large countries. These enormous contrasts in size show only that the states now making up the world differ greatly in their physical and human resources.

A state's geographic location can also have important strategic implications. In the sixteenth through nineteenth centuries, European states typically required a large land army to protect themselves from the threats of their neighbors. These nations had difficulties developing free political institutions, since they needed a strong government to extract resources on a large scale and keep the population under control. Britain was protected by the English Channel and could defend itself through its navy, a smaller army, lower taxation, and less centralization of power—which aided political liberalization. Most peoples of Asia, Africa, and Latin America were colonized by the more powerful Western nations. Those that had the richest natural resources and the most benign climates tended to attract the largest numbers of settlers.

Whether they are old or new, large or small, most of the world's states face a number of common challenges. The first is building community. Most states do not have a homogeneous population, and instilling a sense of shared identity can be a serious challenge. Second, the ability to foster economic and social development is a challenge that is shared even by the wealthiest states. Finally, most states face significant challenges in advancing democracy and civil liberties. These challenges should be familiar from our discussion of the purposes and dangers of governments. In the remainder of this chapter, we discuss these challenges successively.

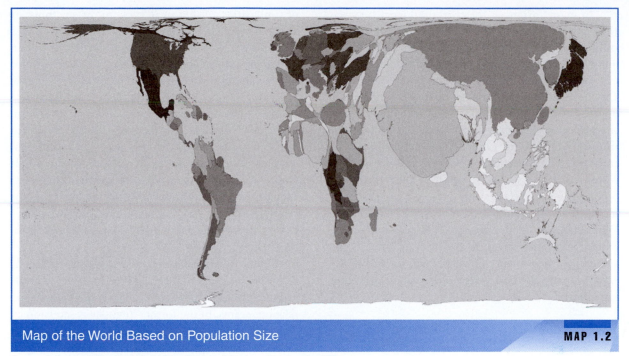

Map of the World Based on Population Size    MAP 1.2

Source: Copyright © *The Real World Atlas,* Thames & Hudson, Ltd., London, 2008.

## BUILDING COMMUNITY

One of the most important challenges facing political systems worldwide is to build a common identity and a sense of community among the citizens. The absence of a common identity can have severe political consequences. Conflicts over national, ethnic, or religious identities are among the most explosive causes of political turmoil, as we have witnessed in Northern Ireland, the former Yugoslavia, Rwanda, and elsewhere. But while building community is a pervasive challenge, some countries are in a much better situation than others. Japan, for example, has an ethnically homogeneous population, a common language, and a long national political history. A large majority of the Japanese share in the religions of Buddhism and Shintoism, and the country is separated by miles of ocean from its most important neighbors. Nigeria, in contrast, is an accidental and artificial creation of British colonial rule and has no common precolonial history. The population is sharply divided between Muslims and Christians; the Christians are divided equally into Catholics and Protestants. There are some 250 different ethnic groups, speaking a variety of local languages, in addition to English. Obviously, the challenges of building community are much greater in Nigeria than they are in Japan. Although few countries face problems as complicated as those of the Nigerians, the community-building challenge is one of the most serious issues facing many states today.

### States and Nations

The word *nation* is sometimes used to mean almost the same as the word *state*, as in the name the United Nations. Strictly speaking, however, we wish to use the term **nation** to refer to a group of people with a common identity. When we speak of a "nation," we thus refer to the self-identification of a people. That common identity may be built upon a common language, history, race, or culture, or simply upon the fact that this group has occupied the same territory. Nations may or may not have their own state or independent government. In some cases—such as Japan, France, or Sweden—there is a close correspondence between the memberships of the state and the nation. Most people who identify themselves as Japanese do in fact live in the state of Japan, and most people who live in Japan identify themselves as Japanese.

In many instances, the correspondence between the nation and the state is not so neat. Nor is it obvious that it should be. In some cases, states are *multinational*—consisting of a multitude of different nations. The Soviet Union, Yugoslavia, and Czechoslovakia were multinational states that broke apart. In other cases, some nations are much larger than the corresponding states, such as Germany for most of its history or China. Some nations have split into two or more states for political reasons, such as Korea today and Germany between 1949 and 1990. Some groups with claims to be nations have no state at all, such as the Kurds, the Basques, and the Tamils. When states and nations do not coincide, it can cause explosive political conflict, as discussed later. At the same time, the presence of several nations within the same state can also be a source of diversity and cultural enrichment.

## Nationality and Ethnicity

There is a fine line between nations and *ethnic groups,* which may have common physical traits, languages, cultures, or history. Like nationality, **ethnicity** need not have any objective basis in genetics, culture, or history. The German sociologist Max Weber defined ethnic groups as "those human groups that entertain a subjective belief in their common descent because of similarities of physical type or of customs or both, or because of memories of colonization and migration.... [I]t does not matter whether or not an objective blood relationship exists."[8] Similarly, groups that are physically quite similar, but differ by language, religion, customs, marriage patterns, and historical memories (for example, the Serbs, Croats, and Muslim Bosnians) may believe they are descended from different ancestors and hence are physically different as well. Over centuries, originally homogeneous populations may intermix with other populations, even though the culture may continue. This is true, for example, of the Jewish population of Israel, which has come together after more than two millennia of global dispersion.

Ethnic differences can be a source of political conflict.[9] Since the end of the Cold War, many states of the former Soviet bloc have come apart at their ethnic and religious seams. In the former Yugoslavia, secession by a number of provinces triggered several wars. The most brutal of these was in Bosnia-Herzegovina, where a Muslim regime faced rebellion and murderous "ethnic cleansing" by the large Serbian minority. Intervention by the UN, the North Atlantic Treaty Organization (NATO), and the United States contained Serbian aggression and led to an uneasy settlement, but considerable tension remains. Similar tensions and violent aggression occurred in Kosovo as well.

With the Chinese government encouraging economic growth and foreign investment, the Shanghai skyline is now a mix of highrises and construction cranes.

Wolf Kern/VISUM/The Image Works

In many developing countries, boundaries established by former colonial powers cut across ethnic lines. In 1947 the British withdrew from India and divided the subcontinent into a northern Muslim area—Pakistan—and a southern Hindu area—India. The most immediate consequence was a terrible civil conflict and "ethno-religious" cleansing. There still are almost 100 million Muslims in India. Similarly, thirty years ago the Ibo "tribe" of Nigeria fought an unsuccessful separatist war with the rest of Nigeria, resulting in the deaths of millions of people. The Tutsi and Hutu peoples of the small African state of Rwanda engaged in a civil war of extermination in the 1990s, with hundreds of thousands of people slaughtered, and millions fleeing the country in fear of their lives.

The migration of labor, forced or voluntary, across state boundaries is another source of ethnic differentiation. The American descendants of Africans forcefully enslaved between the seventeenth and the nineteenth centuries are witnesses of the largest coercive labor migration in world history. In contrast, voluntary migration takes the form of Indians, Bangladeshi, Egyptians, and Palestinians seeking better lives in the oil sheikhdoms around the Persian Gulf; Mexican and Caribbean migrant workers moving to the United States; and Turkish and North African migrants relocating to Europe. Some migration is politically motivated, triggered by civil war and repression. Two scholars refer to the contemporary world as living through an "Age of Migration,"[10] comparable in scale to that of the late nineteenth and early twentieth centuries.

Table 1.1 provides examples of politically significant "ethnicity," broadly defined, in our selected twelve countries. Five sets of traits are included, beginning with physical differences, then language, norms against intermarriage, religion, and negative historical memories. The table illustrates the importance of each distinction to ethnic identity. The most important bases of distinction lie in intermarriage, religion, and historical memories. Language differences are of great importance in four cases and of some importance in six; and finally, and perhaps surprisingly, physical differences are of great importance in only two cases. Recent migration has made such previously homogeneous states as France, Japan, and Germany more multiethnic. Other countries, such as the United States and Canada, have long been multiethnic and have become even more so. Indeed, globalization and migration seem destined to increase the diversity of many societies worldwide.

| | Physical Differences | Language | Norms Against Intermarriage | Religion | Negative Historical Memories |
|---|---|---|---|---|---|
| **Examples of Ethnicity: Its Bases and Their Salience*** | | | | | **TABLE 1.1** |
| Brazil: Blacks | XX | O | XX | X | X |
| Britain: South Asians | X | O | X | XX | X |
| China: Tibetans | X | XX | XX | XX | XX |
| France: Algerians | X | X | XX | XX | XX |
| Germany: Turks | X | XX | XX | XX | O |
| India: Muslims | O | X | XX | XX | XX |
| Iran: Kurds | X | XX | XX | XX | XX |
| Japan: Buraku-min | O | O | XX | O | XX |
| Mexico: Mayan | X | X | XX | X | XX |
| Nigeria: Ibo | O | X | XX | XX | XX |
| Russia: Chechens | X | XX | XX | XX | XX |
| United States: | | | | | |
|    African-Americans | XX | X | XX | O | XX |
|    Hispanics: | X | X | X | O | X |

*Salience is estimated at the following levels: O = none or almost none; X = some; XX = much importance in affecting differences.

## Language

Language can be a source of social division that may overlap with ethnicity. There are approximately 5,000 different languages in use in the world today, and a much smaller number of language families. Most of these languages are spoken by relatively small tribal groups in North and South America, Asia, Africa, or Oceania. Only 200 languages have a million or more speakers, and only eight may be classified as world languages.

English is the most truly international language. There are approximately 380 million people who speak English at home, and 1.8 billion who live in countries where it is one of the official languages. Other international languages include Spanish (more than 300 million home speakers), Arabic (200 million), Russian (165 million), Portuguese (165 million), French (100 million), and German (100 million). The language with the largest number of speakers, though in several varieties, is Chinese (1.2 billion). The major languages with the greatest international spread are those of the former colonial powers—Great Britain, France, Spain, and Portugal.[11]

Linguistic divisions can create particularly thorny political problems. Political systems can choose to ignore racial, ethnic, or religious differences among their citizens, but they cannot avoid committing themselves to one or several languages. Linguistic conflicts typically show up in controversies over educational policies, or over language use in the government. Occasionally, language regulation is more intrusive, as in Quebec, where English-only street signs are prohibited and large corporations are required to conduct their business in French.

## Religious Differences and Fundamentalism

States also vary in their religious characteristics. In some—such as Israel, the Irish Republic, and Pakistan—religion is a basis of national identity for a majority of the population. Iran is a theocratic regime, in which religious authorities govern and religious law is part of the country's legal code. In other societies, such as Poland under communism, religion can be a rallying point for political movements. In many Latin American countries, the clergy have embraced a liberation theology that fosters advocacy of the poor and criticism of government brutality.

Table 1.2 indicates that Christianity is the largest and most widely spread religion, which is divided into three major groups—Roman Catholics, Protestants (of many denominations), and Orthodox (e.g., Greek and Russian). The Catholics are dominant in Europe and Latin America; there is a more equal distribution of Catholics and Protestants elsewhere. While the traditional Protestant denominations have declined in North America in the last decades, three forms of Protestantism—Fundamentalist, Pentecostal, and Evangelical—have increased.

The Muslims are the second largest religious group and the most rapidly growing religion. Muslims are primarily concentrated in Asia and Africa, as well as substantial numbers in Europe and North America, and are becoming revitalized in the Asian successor

| Adherents of All Religions by Six Continents (mid-2004, in millions) | | | | | | | | TABLE 1.2 |
|---|---|---|---|---|---|---|---|---|
| Religion | Africa | Asia | Europe | Latin America | North America | Oceania | Total | Percentage |
| Christians | 401.7 | 341.3 | 553.6 | 510.1 | 273.9 | 26.1 | 2,106.2 | 33.0 |
| Muslims | 350.4 | 892.4 | 33.2 | 1.7 | 5.1 | .4 | 1,283.4 | 20.1 |
| Nonreligious and Atheists | 6.4 | 724.2 | 130.6 | 18.6 | 33.1 | 4.2 | 917.7 | 14.4 |
| Hindus | 2.6 | 844.5 | 1.4 | .8 | 1.4 | .4 | 851.2 | 13.3 |
| Buddhists | .1 | 369.3 | 1.6 | .7 | 3.0 | .4 | 375.4 | 5.9 |
| Jews | .2 | 5.3 | 1.9 | 1.2 | 6.1 | .1 | 14.9 | .2 |
| Other | 107.7 | 693.5 | 3.2 | 17.6 | 6.3 | 1.0 | 828.8 | 13.1 |
| Total | 869.1 | 3,870.5 | 725.5 | 550.7 | 328.9 | 32.6 | 6,377.6 | 100% |

Source: Adherents as defined in *Encyclopedia Britannica 2006.*

states of the Soviet Union. Muslims have been particularly successful in missionary activities in Sub-Saharan Africa.

Religion can be a source of intense antagonism, since beliefs may take the form of deep personal convictions that are difficult to compromise. Religious groups often battle over such issues as the rules of marriage and divorce, childrearing, sexual morality, abortion, euthanasia, the emancipation of women, and the regulation of religious observances. Religious communities often take a special interest in educational policies in order to transmit their ideas of nature and humankind, right and wrong. On such issues, religious groups may clash with one another as well as with more secular groups. Although religious groups can coexist peacefully, and are often the source of exemplary acts of compassion and reconciliation, they may also commit acts of violence, cruelty, and terrorism.[12]

Even societies in which most people supposedly belong to the same community of faith may be split by conflicts between "fundamentalists" and those who are more moderate in their beliefs. **Religious fundamentalism** has recently emerged in some form in all major faiths in reaction to social modernization. Fundamentalists have frequently been technologically adaptive, even while militantly rejecting some elements of modernity (see Box 1.3).

Judaism, Christianity, and Islam are all "religions of the book," although not exactly the same book. The Jews believe only in the Old Testament; the Christians add on the New Testament; and the Muslims add the Koran to these two. While each religion disagrees over the interpretation of these texts, Jewish, Christian, and Muslim, fundamentalists all believe in the truth of their respective sacred books and attack some of their own clergy for lukewarm defense of these sacred texts. There are also Hindu and Buddhist fundamentalists. The rise of fundamentalism has affected the entire world.

The extremist wings of fundamentalist movements employ violence in many forms: from threats and property destruction to assassination and destructive suicide, as young people turn themselves into bombs. The terrorism of these acts lies in their enormity. They stagger the imagination and are intended to weaken the will. From this point of view, the September 11, 2001, attacks on the World Trade Center and the Pentagon were acts of mega-terrorism, involving not only suicide pilot-hijackers but also aircraft filled with volatile fuel and innocent passengers converted into immense projectiles. (See Box 19.1 in Chapter 19.) These attacks were followed by terrorist assaults in Bali, Madrid, London, Riyadh, and other cities. Dealing with international terrorism by religious fundamentalists is now a challenge that faces many nations worldwide.

## FOSTERING ECONOMIC DEVELOPMENT

Two major forces are transforming political systems and nations, and the lives of their citizens; they provide major sources of comparison across the nations in this book. The first is the process of economic development, and the second is political democratization.

---

### The Origins of "Fundamentalism"

BOX 1.3

Fundamentalism got its name in the decades before World War I when some Protestant clergymen in the United States banded together to defend the "fundamentals" of religious belief against the secularizing influences of a modernizing society. This was a reaction to new biblical scholarship at the time that questioned the divine inspiration and authorship of the Bible, and to the expansion of science and Darwinist theories of evolution. These church leaders were also distressed by the apparent erosion of morality and tradition in the United States. In 1920, a journalist and Baptist layman named Curtis Lee Laws appropriated the term "fundamentalist" as a designation for those who were ready "to do battle royal for the Fundamentals." The fundamentalists affirmed the inerrancy (the absolute truth) of the Bible and formed enclaves to protect themselves from error and sin. Religious fundamentalism has recently emerged in some form in all major faiths in reaction to social modernization.

A political system cannot generally satisfy its citizens unless it can foster social and economic development. Thus, as significant as nation-building may be, the level of economic and social development and the rate of economic growth are exceptionally important. Economic development implies that citizens can enjoy new resources and opportunities. Many people are primarily concerned that government can improve their living conditions through economic growth, providing jobs and raising income standards. However, development can also create social strains and damage nature. For better or worse, the social changes that result from economic development transform the politics of developing countries. The success of governments—both democratic and autocratic—is often measured in these terms.

For many affluent advanced industrial societies, contemporary living standards provide for basic social needs (and much more) for most of the public. Indeed, the current political challenges in these nations often focus on problems resulting from the economic successes of the past, such as protecting environmental quality or managing the consequences of growth. New challenges to social welfare policies are emerging from the medical and social security costs of aging populations. For most of the world, however, substantial basic economic needs still exist, and governments focus on improving the socioeconomic conditions of the nation.

Over the past two decades, globalization, democratization, and marketization have begun to transform living conditions in many nations. The United Nations Development Program (UNDP) combines measures of economic well-being, life expectancy, and educational achievement into what it calls the Human Development Index (HDI).[13] The HDI shows dramatic improvements in life conditions in many regions of the world over the past three decades (Figure 1.2). East Asia and South Asia have made substantial improvements since 1975. For instance, in 1975 South Korea and Taiwan had

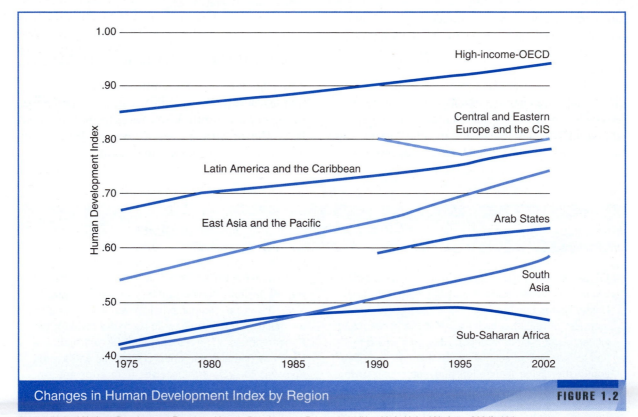

**Changes in Human Development Index by Region**

**FIGURE 1.2**

Source: United Nations Development Program, *Human Development Report 2004* (New York: United Nations, 2004), 134.

a standard of living close to many poor African nations, and they are now affluent societies. Even more striking is the change in the two largest nations in the world. China improved from an HDI of .52 in 1975 (the same as Botswana or Swaziland) to .75 in 2003 (similar to the Philippines or Ecuador); India improved from an HDI of .41 to .60. These statistics represent improved living conditions for billions of people. At the same time, other regions of the world are not sharing in these advances. Living conditions have changed only marginally in Sub-Saharan Africa over this period—the poorest of the poor nations have not improved. In addition, many of the postcommunist nations of Central and Eastern Europe have suffered economically following the transition from communism to capitalism and democracy. The HDI for Russia, for instance, has stagnated since 1990.

The process of economic development typically follows a similar course. One element is a transformation of the structure of the labor force. The five advanced industrial countries in our comparisons all have agricultural employment as less than 10 percent of the labor force. The three poorest countries—China, India, and Nigeria—have more than two-thirds of their labor forces employed in agriculture. The middle-income countries—Mexico and Brazil—have about a third to a

fifth of their labor forces in agriculture. In addition, economic development is typically linked to urbanization, as peasants leave their farms and move to the cities. In nations undergoing rapid economic development, such as China, urban migration creates new opportunities for the workers but also new economic and social policy challenges for the governments.

The UNDP's Human Development Index provides a means to compare the differences in current life conditions across the twelve comparison nations in this chapter (Table 1.3). Perhaps the most striking feature of this table is the wide gap in living standards that still exists across nations worldwide. For instance, the **gross national product (GNP)** per capita, which is a measure of national economic development, is nearly thirty times higher in the Western advanced industrial democracies than in Nigeria.[14] Similarly, there are notable gaps in life expectancy and educational opportunities between the affluent Northern societies and the developing nations in Africa and Asia. In highly industrialized countries, education is virtually universal and practically everyone over age 15 can read and write. In India and Nigeria, less than two-thirds of the adult population has this minimal level of education. Moreover, the countries with the fewest literate citizens also have the fewest radios and television sets—even

| Human Development Indicators | | | | | | TABLE 1.3 |
|---|---|---|---|---|---|---|
| Nation | Life Expectancy | Percent Enrolled in School | GNP/capita (ppp) | 2003 HDI | 1975 HDI | 2003 World Rank |
| United States | 77.4 | 93 | 37,562 | .944 | .867 | 10 |
| Japan | 82.0 | 84 | 27,967 | .943 | .857 | 11 |
| United Kingdom | 78.4 | — | 27.147 | .939 | .845 | 15 |
| France | 79.5 | 92 | 27,677 | .938 | .853 | 16 |
| Germany | 78.7 | 89 | 27,756 | .930 | — | 20 |
| Mexico | 75.1 | 75 | 9,168 | .814 | .689 | 53 |
| Russia | 65.3 | 90 | 9,230 | .795 | — | 62 |
| Brazil | 70.5 | 91 | 7,790 | .792 | .645 | 63 |
| China | 71.6 | 69 | 5,003 | .755 | .525 | 85 |
| Iran | 70.4 | 69 | 6,995 | .736 | .566 | 99 |
| India | 63.3 | 60 | 2,892 | .602 | .412 | 127 |
| Nigeria | 43.4 | 64 | 1,050 | .453 | .318 | 158 |

Source: United Nations Development Program, *World Development Report 2005* (New York: United Nations, 2005) (www.undp.org).

though these devices do not require literacy. Economic development is also associated with better nutrition and medical care. In the economically advanced countries, fewer children die in infancy, and the average citizen has a life expectancy at birth of over seventy-five years. Improvements in living conditions have substantially increased life expectancy in many low-income nations, such as Mexico and China. However, the average life expectancy of an Indian is sixty-three years; and the Nigerian little more than forty years. Material productivity, education, exposure to communications media, and longer and healthier lives are closely interconnected.

In order to become more productive, a country needs the resources to develop a skilled and healthy labor force and to build the infrastructure that material welfare requires. Preindustrial nations face most urgently the issues of economic development: how to improve the immediate welfare of their citizens yet also build and invest for the future. Typically, these are newer nations that also face the challenges of building community and effective political institutions. Political leaders and celebrities, such as Bono and Angelina Jolie, have mobilized public awareness that these differences in living conditions are a global concern—for those living in the developing world, the affluent nations and their citizens, and international organizations such as the United Nations and the World Bank.

## Problems of Economic Development

The HDI or GNP per capita measure the overall wealth, income, and opportunity in a nation, but these factors are not evenly distributed within nations. The unequal distribution of resources and opportunities is among the most serious causes of political conflict. A large GNP may conceal significant differences in the distribution of resources and opportunities. A high rate of national growth may benefit only particular regions or social groups, leaving large parts of the population unrewarded or even less well off than before. The "inner cities" of the United States, the older parts of such Indian cities as Delhi and Calcutta, the peripheral ramshackle settlements around the cities of Latin America, many rural areas in China, and the arid northeast of Brazil all suffer from poverty and hopelessness. At the same time, other parts of the countries experience growth and improved welfare. Moreover, there is some evidence that rapid economic development tends to increase such inequalities.

A country's politics may be sharply affected by internal divisions of income, wealth, and other resources. Table 1.4 displays income distributions for our twelve comparison countries. Generally speaking, economic development improves the equality of income, at least past a certain stage of economic growth. Wealthy nations like Japan, Germany, and

Poverty in Third World cities is illustrated by this scene of a back street in Calcutta, in India, where the poor make their beds in the street. Similar scenes, though on a lesser scale, are to be encountered in modern American cities where homeless people sleep on the sidewalks and in doorways.

Jehangir Gazdar/Woodfin Camp & Associates

| Income Distribution for Selected Nations | | | | TABLE 1.4 |
|---|---|---|---|---|
| Country | Year | Wealthiest 10% | Poorest 40% | Wealthy/Poor Gap |
| Germany | 2000 | 22.1 | 22.2 | −0.1 |
| Russia | 2002 | 23.8 | 20.9 | 2.9 |
| Japan | 1993 | 21.7 | 24.8 | 3.1 |
| France | 1995 | 25.1 | 19.8 | 5.3 |
| India | 1999 | 28.5 | 21.2 | 7.3 |
| Britain | 1999 | 28.5 | 17.5 | 11.0 |
| United States | 2000 | 29.9 | 16.2 | 13.7 |
| Iran | 1998 | 33.7 | 19.5 | 14.2 |
| China | 2001 | 33.1 | 13.7 | 19.4 |
| Nigeria | 1996 | 35.4 | 12.6 | 22.8 |
| Mexico | 2000 | 43.1 | 10.3 | 32.8 |
| Brazil | 2001 | 46.9 | 8.3 | 38.6 |

Source: World Bank, *World Development Indicators 2005*, table 2-7 (www.worldbank.org); distribution of income or consumption.

France have relatively more egalitarian income distributions than middle- or low-income countries. Still, the wealthiest 10 percent in Japan receive about the same total income as the poorest 40 percent receive. This is a large gap in life conditions between rich and poor, but the gap is even wider in less affluent nations. In Mexico, a middle-income country, the ratio is closer to 10 to 1; and in Brazil it is more than 20 to 1. The table also suggests that a nation's political characteristics make a difference. India has consciously worked to narrow inequality, which places it higher in the table, while inequality in the United States is as great as several poor nations, such as China.

Although industrialization and high productivity may eventually encourage a more equal distribution of income, the first stages of industrialization may actually increase **income inequality.** As economies modernize they create a dual economy—a rural sector and an urban industrial and commercial sector, both with inequalities of their own. These inequalities increase as education and communication spread more rapidly in the modern sector, which may contribute to the political instability of developing countries. Moreover, there is no guarantee that inequality will diminish in later stages of development. In Brazil, for instance, income inequality has increased for decades, even as the economy has developed. In the United States, income inequality increased substantially from the 1970s to the mid-1990s because of changes in economic structure, the increase in single-parent families,

and a lowering of income taxes. In Russia and other postcommunist societies, the development of new capitalist markets was accompanied by new income inequalities. Inequality is an issue that many nations face.

Several studies have proposed various policy solutions to mitigate the hardships economic inequality causes in developing societies.[15] Taiwan and South Korea are models showing how early land reforms equalized opportunity at the outset of the developmental process. Investment in primary and secondary education, in agricultural inputs and rural infrastructure (principally roads and water), and in labor-intensive industries produced remarkable results for several decades. A comparative advantage in cheap and skilled labor enabled Taiwan and South Korea to compete effectively in international markets. Thus, some growth policies mitigate inequalities, but it can be very difficult to put them into practice, especially where substantial inequalities already exist.

Another correlate of development is population growth. The book *The Population Explosion* drew attention to the social burden that may follow from the population growth that typically accompanies economic development.[16] As health care improves, living standards increase, and life expectancies lengthen, population sizes grow. This is a positive development because it represents improved living conditions for these people, but rapid population growth also can pose policy challenges for many developing nations.

| | In 1990 | | Projected to 2015 | |
| --- | --- | --- | --- | --- |
| **Economic Development Level** | **Number** | **Percentage** | **Number** | **Percentage** |
| Low-income economies | 1,777 | 33.9 | 2,794 | 39.4 |
| Middle-income economies | 2,588 | 49.3 | 3,299 | 46.5 |
| High-income economies | 887 | 16.8 | 1,007 | 14.1 |
| Total | 5,252 | 100 | 7,100 | 100 |

**TABLE 1.5**

Population by Economic Development Level in 1990 and Projected to 2015 (in millions)

Source: World Bank, *World Development Report Indicators 2005*, table 2-1 (www.worldbank.org), population dynamics.

Table 1.5 puts this issue in sharp relief. The table divides the world population into three strata: low-income economies, middle-income economies, and high-income economies. In 1990 the low-income countries had a population total of almost 2 billion, or about a third of the total world population. In contrast, the high-income nations had about a sixth of the world's population.

Some projections estimate that world population in 2015 will increase to 7 billion and that the poorer countries will see a more rapid rate of growth. In 2005, Hania Zlotnik of the UN population division estimated that "out of every 100 persons added to the [world's] population in the coming decade, 97 will live in developing countries."[17] Rapid economic growth in the developing world can create significant burdens for these nations.

These prospects have produced a development literature that mixes both light and heat. Economist Amartya Sen warns of a "danger that in the confrontation between apocalyptic pessimism on one hand, and a dismissive smugness, on the other, a genuine understanding of the nature of the population problem may be lost."[18] He points out that the first impact of "modernization" on population is to increase it rapidly, as new sanitation measures and modern pharmaceuticals reduce the death rate. As an economy develops, however, changing conditions tend to reduce fertility. With improved education (particularly of women), health, and welfare, the advantages of lower fertility become clear, and population growth declines.

Fertility decreased in Europe and North America as they underwent industrialization. Today, in many European nations the native populations are decreasing because fertility rates are below levels necessary to sustain a constant population size. This pattern appears to be occurring in the developing world. Thus annual population growth in the world has declined from 2.2 percent to 1.7 percent in the last two decades. The rate of population growth in India, for example, rose to 2.2 percent in the 1970s and has since declined. Latin America peaked at a higher rate and then came down sharply. The major problem area is Sub-Saharan Africa, with an average growth rate of more than 2.7 percent each year during the 1990s.[19] The fertility rate in Africa has recently dropped dramatically because of the tragically rising death rate from the AIDS epidemic.

While population growth rates appear to be slowing, governments are addressing this issue in different ways. China adopted a coercive policy of limiting families to a single child, which in urban areas produced dramatic results at great costs. India followed a collaborative approach involving governmental intervention and market and education to affect family choices.[20] Kerala in southern India is a dramatic example of what can be accomplished by the collaborative approach, where expanding education (particularly among women) and otherwise improving living conditions has reduced fertility more than in China.

Economic growth can have other social costs. For instance, advanced industrial societies are dealing with the environmental costs of their industrial development. Despoiled forests, depleted soils and fisheries, polluted air and water, nuclear waste, endangered species, and a threatened ozone layer now burden their legislative dockets. With increasing industrialization and urbanization in the developing world, many of these environmental problems could worsen. Thus, economic development can impose serious environmental costs as well as benefits. At the same time, some environmental problems are even more acute in less developed countries, where rapid increases in population and urbanization create shortages of clean air, clean water, and adequate sanitation.[21] Thus,

The world's increasing energy use is causing serious environmental challenges. The burning of fossil fuels—such as coal, oil, and gas—pollutes our air, water, and atmosphere, whereas nuclear power plants, such as this one in Northern Bohemia, pose the risk of nuclear radiation.

Sean Sprague/Panos Pictures

economic development generally improves the living conditions of the public, but in the process it produces new policy problems that governments must address.

## FOSTERING DEMOCRACY, HUMAN RIGHTS, AND CIVIL LIBERTIES

The second major force transforming contemporary political systems is the process of democratization, which includes the enhancement of human rights and the expansion of freedom. Democracy is the form of government to which most contemporary countries, more or less sincerely and successfully, aspire. A **democracy,** briefly defined, is a political system in which citizens enjoy a number of basic civil and political rights, and in which their most important political leaders are elected in free and fair elections and are accountable under a rule of law. Democracy literally means "government by the people."

In small political systems, such as local communities, it may be possible for "the people" to share directly in debating, deciding, and implementing public policy. In large political systems, such as contemporary states, democracy must be achieved largely through indirect participation in policymaking. Elections, competitive political parties, free mass media, and representative-

assemblies make some degree of democracy, some degree of "government by the people," possible. This indirect, or representative, democracy is not complete or ideal. But the more citizens are involved and the more influential their choices, the more democratic the system.

The most important general distinction in classifying political systems is between democratic systems and authoritarian systems. *Authoritarian* states lack one or several of the defining features of democracy. In democracies, competitive elections give citizens the chance to shape the policymaking process through their selection of key policymakers. In authoritarian systems the policymakers are chosen by military councils, hereditary families, dominant political parties, and the like. Citizens are either ignored or pressed into symbolic assent to the government's choices.

Authoritarian states can take several forms. (See Chapter 6.) In **oligarchies,** literally "rule by the few," important political rights are withheld from the majority of the population. South Africa until the abolition of apartheid in the early 1990s is a good example. Other authoritarian states, such as Egypt, are controlled by an individual dictator and his party or military supporters. **Totalitarian systems**—such as Nazi Germany, or the Soviet Union under Stalin, or North Korea today—are systems in which the government constricts the rights and privacy of its citizens in a particularly severe and intrusive manner.

As societies become more complex, richer, and more technologically advanced, the probability of citizen involvement and democratization increases. In the first half of the twentieth century most Western states were transformed from authoritarian regimes or oligarchies to democracies. After World War II, a second democratic wave—which lasted from 1943 until the early 1960s—saw both newly independent states (such as India and Nigeria) and defeated authoritarian powers (such as Germany and Japan) set up the formal institutions of democracy.[22]

Another round of democratic transitions began in 1974, involving Southern Europe, East Asia, Latin America, and a number of African states. The most dramatic changes came in Central and Eastern Europe, where in a few short years the Soviet empire collapsed, the nations of Eastern Europe rapidly converted to democracy, and many of these nations have now joined the European Union. The people power revolution in the Philippines, the end of the apartheid regime in South Africa, and the public protests for democratization in Indonesia were equally dramatic. Samuel P. Huntington speaks of this latest move toward democracy as a "Third Wave" of worldwide **democratization**.[23]

As a result of these three democratization waves, democracy has become a common goal of the global community (see Figure 1.3). As late as 1978, only a third of the world's independent countries had competitive party and electoral systems. Communist and other single-party governments and other authoritarian regimes dominated the landscape. By 2004, almost two-thirds of states had a system of electoral democracy, and human rights and liberties were similarly spreading to more of the world's population.[24] This democratization trend is continuing in the new millennium, with prospects for further progress in many nations.

This democratization process results from a combination of factors. Economic development transforms societies in ways that typically encourage democratization by creating autonomous political groups that demand political influence, by expanding the political skills of the citizenry, and by creating economic complexity that encourages systems of self-governance. Social modernization transforms the political values and political culture of the public, which increases demands for a more participatory system (see Chapter 3). New democracies are also much more likely to endure when founded in economically developed societies.[25]

Democracy is not an all-or-nothing proposition, however. No democracy is perfect, and we can speak of shades or gradations of democracy. Democracy typically does not come about overnight. It often takes time to establish democratic institutions and to have citizens recognize them and comply with the rules of the democratic process.

It can be especially difficult to consolidate democracy in less economically developed societies. Not all of the newly democratizing countries are succeeding beyond the first few years. In some, democratic processes fail to produce stable institutions and effective public policies and give way to some form of authoritarianism. In Nigeria, a democratic-leaning regime installed in 1979 was overthrown by a military coup in 1983, and a partial movement toward redemocratization was again aborted by the military in 1993 before being reestablished in 1999. Nigeria is by no

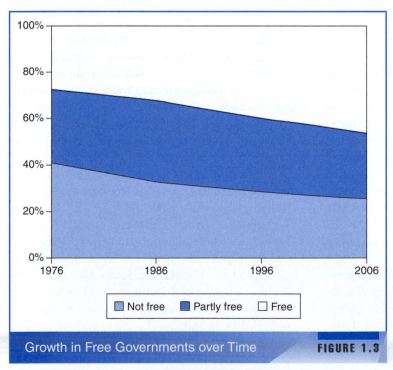

**Growth in Free Governments over Time**     **FIGURE 1.3**

Source: Freedom House, *Freedom in the World 2006* (www.freedomhouse.org).

## Women and Political Development

BOX 1.4

If a poor nation could do one thing to stimulate its development, what should it do? Opening the fiftieth session of the United Nations Commission on the Status of Women in 2006, UN Deputy-Secretary General Louise Fréchette said the international community finally comprehends that empowering women and girls around the globe is the most effective tool for a country's development. She stated that studies have repeatedly shown that by giving women equal education and work opportunities and access to a society's decision-making processes, a country can boost its economic productivity, reduce infant and maternal mortality rates and improve the general population's nutrition and health. These results are achieved because women's education and participation in the labor force increase family output, increase the likelihood that children will be better educated and benefit from health care, improve nutrition in the family, and better the quality of life for women and their families.

Source: UN News Center, February 27, 2006.

means unique. Transition can move in either direction, toward or away from democracy. The recent wave of democratization is supported by the more favorable environments of more modernized societies and because there are now more democracies in the world to support new democracies. However, democracy is difficult to sustain when severe economic or political problems face a nation, or where the public remains uncertain about democracy.

Even when states democratize, there is no guarantee that they will grant human rights and civil liberties to all their people. In some countries, majority rule turns into a "tyranny of the majority" against ethnic or religious minorities. Therefore, democracies have to balance between respecting the will of the majority and protecting the rights of the minority. Even when political rulers sincerely try to promote human rights and civil liberties (which is by no means always the case), they do not always agree on the nature of those rights.

A good example of the spread of rights and liberties—and cultural differences in the definition of rights—involves gender issues. Governments in Western industrial societies favor gender policies that guarantee equality for women in society, the workplace, and politics. The United Nations and other international organizations have become advocates of women's rights. But gender norms often vary across cultural zones. The UN's statistics indicate that many developing nations hesitate to grant equal rights to women, restricting their education and involvement in the economy and politics.[26] Restrictions on women's rights are even starker in many Arab states. Ironically, other research indicates that improving the status of women is one of the most productive ways to develop a nation politically and economically (see Box 1.4). In short, expanding human rights is an ongoing process in the world today, and there is much room for further progress.

## LOOKING FORWARD

The last several decades have been a period of tremendous social, economic, and political change in the world. Economic development, improved living standards, the spread of human rights, and democratization improved the life chances and life conditions of billions of individuals. In most of the world, the average child born today can look forward to a longer, better, and freer life than his or her parents—especially if she is a girl.

At the same time, continuing social, economic, and political problems remain. Progress in one area can create new opportunities, but also new problems in another. Economic development, for example, can sometimes stimulate ethnic strife and destabilize political institutions. Economic development can also disrupt social life. And the process of development has been uneven across and within nations. Many basic human needs still remain in too short supply.[27]

Even in the affluent democracies, as one set of policy issues is addressed, new issues come to the fore. Western democracies struggle to address issues of environmental quality, changing lifestyles, and the challenges of globalization and multiculturalism. A more affluent and information-driven citizenry can also limit the effectiveness of political parties, interest groups, parliaments, and political executives. Success in meeting these old and new challenges can improve the living conditions for the world's populations, decrease international conflict, and come closer to meeting the ideals of humankind.

Governments and politics have played a large role in promoting the successes and failures of the past. Just as we can point to governments whose actions improved life for their citizens, there are other governments that took regressive actions. Governments and their activities are central to our political futures. Our goal in this book is to examine the ways in which citizens, policymakers, and governments address the policy challenges that face them today.

## REVIEW QUESTIONS

- What is politics?
- What are the contrasting images of the "state of nature" of humankind?
- What are the potential positive and negative outcomes of government activity?
- What are the main challenges that countries face in building a political community?
- What are the causes and consequences of economic development?
- What are the causes and consequences of democratization?

## KEY TERMS

democracy
democratization
ethnicity
European Union (EU)
externalities
governments

gross national product (GNP)
human rights
income inequality
nation
nation-states

oligarchies
political culture
political system
public goods
religious fundamentalism
sovereignty

state
state of nature
totalitarian systems
United Nations (UN)

## SUGGESTED READINGS

Chenery, Hollis et al. *Redistribution With Growth.* New York: Oxford University Press, 1981.

Cornelius, Wayne et al., eds. *Controlling Immigration: A Global Perspective.* Stanford, CA: Stanford University Press, 1995.

Dalton, Russell, and Doh Chull Shin, eds. *Citizens, Democracy, and Markets Around the Pacific Rim.* Oxford: Oxford University Press, 2006.

Diamond, Larry, ed. *Developing Democracy: Towards Consolidation.* Baltimore: Johns Hopkins University Press, 1999.

Ehrlich, Paul, and Anne Ehrlich. *The Population Explosion.* New York: Simon & Schuster, 1990.

Horowitz, Donald. *Ethnic Groups in Conflict.* Berkeley: University of California Press, 1985.

Huntington, Samuel. *The Third Wave: Democratization in the Late Twentieth Century.* Norman: University of Oklahoma Press, 1991.

———. *The Clash of Civilizations and the Remaking of World Order.* New York: Simon & Schuster, 1996.

Lijphart, Arend. *Patterns of Democracy.* New Haven, CT: Yale University Press, 1999.

Linz, Juan, and Alfred Stepan, eds. *Problems of Democratic Transitions and Consolidation.* Baltimore: Johns Hopkins University Press, 1996.

Marty, Martin, and Scott Appleby. *Fundamentalism Observed.* Chicago: University of Chicago Press, 1991.

Putnam, Robert. *Making Democracy Work: Civic Traditions in Modern Italy.* Princeton, NJ: Princeton University Press, 1993.

Przeworski, Adam et al. *Democracy and Development: Political Institutions and Well-being in the World 1950–1990.* New York: Cambridge University Press, 2000.

Sachs, Jeffrey. *The End of Poverty: Economic Possibilities for Our Time.* New York: Penguin, 2005.

United Nations. *World Development Report.* New York: Oxford University Press, annual editions.

Weiner, Myron. *The Global Migration Crisis: Challenge to States and to Human Rights.* New York: HarperCollins, 1995.

Zakaria, Fareed. *The Future of Freedom: Illiberal Democracy at Home and Abroad.* New York: Norton, 2003.

# ENDNOTES

1. Thomas Hobbes, *Leviathan,* ed. C. B. Macpherson (New York: Penguin, 1968), 186.

2. J. J. Rousseau, *Second Discourse on Inequality, The First and Second Discourses* (New York: St. Martin's Press, 1964), pp. 109–10.

3. Two other philosophical groups are especially outspoken critics of government: libertarians and anarchists. Adherents of **libertarianism** are individualists who see society as composed of individual human beings with fundamental rights that must be protected. The main problem with government, libertarians argue, is that the more tasks it takes on, the more prone it is to violate such basic rights. Adherents of **anarchism** claim that governments produce undesirable effects; they see societies not as collections of individuals but as communities of people who in their natural condition are equal. Governments and power corrupt such communities and lead to oppression and alienation.

4. Martin Greenberg and Mark Tier, *Visions of Liberty* (New York: Baen Publishers, 2004).

5. See, for example, Fareed Zakaria, *The Future of Freedom: Illiberal Democracy at Home and Abroad* (New York: Norton, 2003).

6. See, for example, Douglas North, *Institutions, Institutional Change, and Economic Performance* (Cambridge: Cambridge University Press, 1990); Mancur Olson, "The New Institutional Economics: The Collective Choice Approach to Economic Development," in C. Clague, ed., *Institutions and Economic Development.* (Baltimore: Johns Hopkins University Press, 1997; S. Knack and P. Keefer, "Institutions and Economic Performance," *Economics and Politics* 7 (1995) 207–29.

7. The Vatican and Switzerland are not members of the UN but maintain permanent observer missions at the UN headquarters. Taiwan was expelled from the UN in 1971 to accommodate mainland China (the People's Republic).

8. Max Weber, *Economy and Society,* ed. Guenther Roth and Claus Wittich (Berkeley: University of California Press, 1978), 389.

9. Even before the end of the Cold War, ethnic autonomy movements in parts of old countries—such as the United Kingdom (the Scots and Welsh) and Canada (the Quebecois)—sought to break free or achieve greater autonomy.

10. Stephen Castles and Mark J. Miller, *The Age of Migration: International Population Movements in the Modern World* (New York: Guilford, 1994).

11. Erik V. Gunnemark, *Countries, Peoples, and Their Languages: The Geolinguistic Handbook* (Gothenburg: Lanstryckeriet, 1991).

12. A book dealing with this theme is R. Scott Appleby, *The Ambivalence of the Sacred* (Lanham, MD: Rowman & Littlefield, 2000).

13. United Nations Development Program, *Human Development Report 2005* (New York: United Nations). See also www.undp.org for additional data and interactive presentations.

14. The per capita *gross national product (GNP)* is the total economic output per person. Rather than the traditional measures computed according to the exchange rates of the national currencies, the *purchasing power parity (PPP)* index takes into account differences in price levels from one country to another. Most analyses assume that the GNP/ppp statistics are more comparable measures of living conditions. The income gap increases, however, if one uses the traditional exchange rate measure of GNP.

15. For example, see Hollis Chenery et al., *Redistribution with Growth* (New York: Oxford University Press, 1981).

16. Paul Ehrlich and Anne Ehrlich, *The Population Explosion* (New York: Simon & Schuster, 1990).

17. Hania Zlotnik, "Statement to the Thirty-Eighth Session of the Commission on Population and Development," April 4, 2005 (www.un.org/esa/population/cpd/Statement_HZ_open. pdf).

18. Amartya Sen, "Population: Delusion and Reality," *New York Review of Books,* 22 Sept. 1994, pp. 62ff.

19. World Bank, *World Development Report, 1998–1999* (New York: Oxford University Press, 1999).

20. Sen, "Population: Delusion and Reality."

21. Regina Axelrod, David Downie, and Norman Vig, eds., *The Global Environment: Institutions, Law, and Policy* (Washington, DC: CQ Press, 2004); Yale Center for Environmental Law and Policy and Center for International Earth Science Information Network, *2005 Environmental Sustainability Index: Benchmarking National Environmental Stewardship* (New Haven, CT: Yale University, 2005) (http://www.yale.edu/esi/).

22. While many countries became formally democratic in these years, most of them quickly lapsed into authoritarianism. Many of these would-be democracies failed in their first decade; another "reverse wave" in the 1960s and early 1970s swept away some older democracies (Chile, Greece, and Uruguay, for example) as well.

23. Samuel Huntington, *The Third Wave* (Norman: University of Oklahoma Press, 1991).

24. Freedom House, *Freedom in the World 2004* (Washington, DC: Freedom House, 2005) (www. freedomhouse.org).

25. Seymour Martin Lipset, "Some Social Requisites of Democracy," *American Political Science Review 53* (September 1959), 69–105 Larry Diamond, "Economic Development and Democracy Reconsidered," in G. Marks and L. Diamond, eds., *Reexamining Democracy* (Newbury Park, CA: Sage, 1992); Tatu Vanhanen, *Prospects of Democracy* (New York: Routledge, 1997); Adam Przeworski et al., *Democracy and Development: Political Institutions and Well-being in the World 1950–1990* (New York: Cambridge University Press, 2000).

26. See United Nations Development Program, *Human Development Report 2005* (New York: United Nations) (http://hdr.undp.org/reports/global/2005/), tables 25–30, and associated discussion.

27. Many of these issues are addressed by the United Nations' Millennium Development Goals. Visit the UN website (http://www.un.org/millenniumgoals/) or see United Nations, *Millennium Development Goals Report 2005* (New York: United Nations) (http://unstats.un.org/unsd/mi/pdf/MDGBook.pdf).

# COMPARING POLITICAL SYSTEMS

## WHY WE COMPARE

The great French interpreter of American democracy, Alexis de Tocqueville, while traveling in America in the 1830s, wrote to a friend explaining how his own ideas about French institutions and culture entered into his writing of *Democracy in America*. Tocqueville wrote: "Although I very rarely spoke of France in my book, I did not write one page of it without having her, so to speak, before my eyes."[1]

On a more general note about the comparative method, he offered this comment: "Without comparisons to make, the mind does not know how to proceed."[2] Tocqueville was telling us that comparison is fundamental to all human thought. We add that it is the methodological core of the humanistic and scientific methods. It is the only way we can fully understand our own political system. Comparing our experience with that of other countries deepens our understanding of our own institutions. Examining politics in other societies permits us to see a wider range of political alternatives. It illuminates the virtues and shortcomings of our own political life. By taking us beyond our familiar arrangements and assumptions, comparative analysis helps expand our awareness of the possibilities of politics.

Comparison is also at the methodological core of the scientific study of politics. Comparative analysis helps us develop explanations and test theories of the ways in which political processes work and in which political change occurs. The goals of the comparative methods used by political scientists are similar to those used in more exact sciences. But political scientists cannot normally design experiments, a major path to knowledge in many of the natural sciences. We cannot control and manipulate political arrangements and observe the consequences. We are especially limited when dealing with large-scale events that drastically affect many people. For example, researchers cannot and would not want to start a social revolution to see its effects.

We can, however, use the comparative method to describe and explain the different combinations of political events and institutions found in different societies. More than two thousand years ago, Aristotle in his *Politics* contrasted the economies and social structures of Greek city-states in an effort to determine how the social and economic environments affected political institutions and policies (see Box 2.1). More contemporary political scientists also try to explain differences between the processes and performance of political systems. They compare two-party democracies with multiparty democracies, parliamentary with presidential regimes, democracies in poor countries with those in rich countries, elections in new party systems with those in established democracies. These and many other comparisons have greatly enriched our understanding of politics.

## HOW WE COMPARE

We study politics in several different ways: we describe it; we seek to explain it; sometimes we try to predict it. These are all parts of the scientific process. Each of them may use the comparative method.

## Aristotle's Library

BOX 2.1

There is historical evidence that Aristotle had accumulated a library of more than 150 studies of the political systems of the Mediterranean world of 400–300 B.C. Many of these had probably been researched and written by his disciples.

While only the Athenian constitution survives of this library of Aristotelian polities, it is evident from the references to such studies that do survive that Aristotle was concerned with sampling the variety of political systems then in existence, including the "barbarian" (Third World?) countries, such as Libya, Etruria, and Rome: "[T]he references in ancient authorities give us the names of some 70 or more of the states described in the compilation of 'polities.' They range from Sinope, on the Black Sea, to Cyrene in North Africa; they extend from Marseilles in the Western Mediterranean to Crete, Rhodes, and Cyprus in the East. Aristotle thus included colonial constitutions as well as those of metropolitan states. His descriptions embraced states on the Aegean, Ionian, and Tyrrhenian Seas, and the three continents of Europe, Asia, and Africa."

Source: Ernest Barker, ed., *The Politics of Aristotle* (London: Oxford University Press, 1977), 386.

The first stage in the study of politics is description. If we cannot describe a political process or event, we cannot really hope to understand or explain it. Much less can we predict what might happen next or in similar situations. In order to describe politics, we need a set of concepts that are clearly defined and well understood. We speak of this as a conceptual framework. The easier this set of concepts is to understand, and the more generally it can be applied, the more helpful it is to the study of politics. Conceptual frameworks are not generally right or wrong, but they may be more or less useful to the task at hand.

## POLITICAL SYSTEMS: ENVIRONMENT AND INTERDEPENDENCE

*Comparative Politics Today* suggests that we compare political systems with a structural-functional systems framework. To do so, we need to discuss three general concepts that we use throughout this book: (1) system, (2) structure, and (3) function. **System,** as we defined it in Chapter 1, suggests an object having interdependent parts, acting within a setting or an **environment.** The **political system** is a set of institutions and agencies concerned with formulating and implementing the collective goals of a society or of groups within it. **Governments** are the **policymaking** parts of political systems. The decisions of governments are normally backed up by legitimate coercion, and obedience may be compelled. (We discuss legitimacy at greater length in Chapter 3.)

Figure 2.1 tells us that a political system exists in both an international environment and a domestic environment. It is molded by these environments and it tries to mold them. The system receives **inputs** from these environments. Its policymakers attempt to shape them through its outputs. In the figure, which is quite schematic and simple, we use the United States as the central actor. We include other countries as our environmental examples—Russia, China, Britain, Germany, Japan, Mexico, and Iran.

Exchanges among countries may vary in many ways. For example, they may be "dense" or "sparse"; U.S.–Canadian relations exemplify the dense end of the continuum, while U.S.–Nepalese relations would be at the sparse end.

Relationships among political systems may be of many different kinds. The United States has substantial trade relations with some countries and relatively little trade with others. Some countries have an excess of imports over exports, whereas others have an excess of exports over imports. Military exchanges and support with such countries as the NATO nations, Japan, South Korea, Israel, and Saudi Arabia have been of significant importance to the United States.

The interdependence of countries—the volume and value of imports and exports, transfers of capital, international communication, the extent of foreign

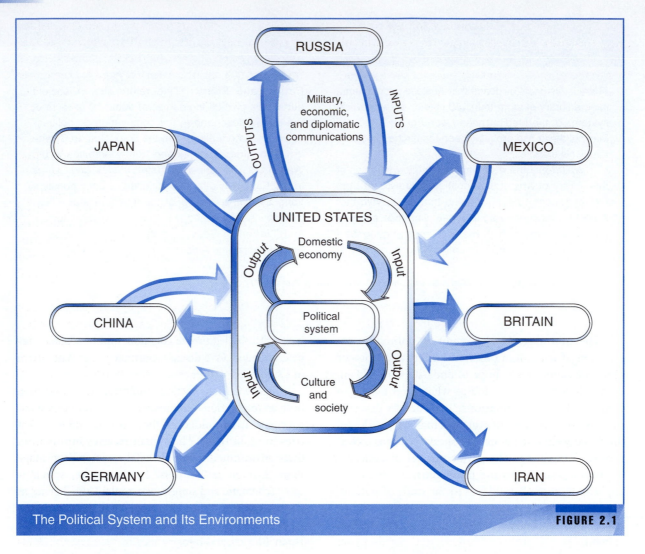

RUSSIA

Military, economic, and diplomatic communications

OUTPUTS     INPUTS

JAPAN     MEXICO

UNITED STATES

Output     Domestic economy     Input

Political system

Input     Culture and society     Output

CHINA     BRITAIN

GERMANY     IRAN

**The Political System and Its Environments**     **FIGURE 2.1**

travel and immigration—has increased enormously in the last decades. This increase is often called **globalization.** We might represent this process as a thickening of the input and output arrows between the United States and other countries in Figure 2.1. Fluctuations in this flow of international transactions and traffic attributable to depression, inflation, protective tariffs, international terrorism, war, and the like may wreak havoc with the economies of the countries affected.

The interaction of a political system with its domestic environment—the economic and social systems and the political culture of its citizens—is also depicted in Figure 2.1. We can illustrate this interaction in the U.S. case by the rise of the "high-tech information-based economy."

The composition of the U.S. labor force, and consequently its citizenry, has changed dramatically in the last century. Agriculture has declined to under 2 percent of the gainfully employed. Employment in heavy extractive and manufacturing industries has decreased substantially. Newer, high-technology occupations, the professions, and the service occupations have increased sharply as proportions of the labor force. The last half-century has also witnessed significant improvements in the educational level of the U.S. population. Many more young people complete high school and go on to college. Moreover, people move more easily from one region to another. These and other changes in the U.S. social structure have altered the challenges facing the U.S. system and the resources available to meet these challenges.

These changes in the economy and the citizenry are associated with changes in American **political culture.** (Political culture—the attitudes, beliefs, and values of the people in a country—is discussed at more length in Chapter 3.) People want different things from politics. For example, an educated and culturally sophisticated society is more concerned with quality of life, the beauty and healthfulness of the environment, and similar issues.

At the same time, the globalization of the economy leads to demands from firms and workers in some industries for protection of their jobs. Natural disasters, such as the hurricane that devastated New Orleans in 2005, spur calls for the national government to lead reconstruction. Local issues are seen as the responsibility of the entire country. People live longer. An aging population demands that governments do more to help with medical benefits. In input-output terms, socioeconomic changes transform the political demands of the electorate and the kinds of policies that it supports.

Thus a new pattern of society results in different policy outputs, different kinds and levels of taxation, changes in regulatory patterns, and changes in welfare expenditures. The advantage of the system-environment approach is that it directs our attention to the **interdependence** of what happens between and within countries. It provides us with a vocabulary to describe, compare, and explain these interacting events.

If we are to make sound judgments in politics, we need to be able to place political systems in their domestic and international environments. We need to recognize how these environments both set limits on and provide opportunities for political choices. This approach keeps us from reaching quick and biased political judgments. If a country is poor in natural resources and lacks the capabilities necessary to exploit what it has, we cannot fault it for having a low industrial output or poor educational and social services. Each country chapter in the second half of this book begins by discussing the current policy challenges facing the country and its social and economic environment.

## POLITICAL SYSTEMS: STRUCTURES AND FUNCTIONS

Governments do many things—from establishing and operating school systems, to maintaining public order, to fighting wars. In order to carry on these disparate activities, governments have specialized agencies, or **structures,** such as parliaments, bureaucracies, administrative agencies, and courts. These structures perform **functions,** which in turn enable the government to formulate, implement, and enforce its policies. The policies reflect the goals; the agencies provide the means to achieve them.

Figure 2.2 locates six types of political structures—political parties, interest groups, legislatures, executives, bureaucracies, and courts—within the political system. These are formal organizations engaged in political activities. They exist in most contemporary political systems. This list is not exhaustive. Some structures, such as ruling military councils or governing royal families, are found in only a few countries. Some, such as Iran's Council of Guardians, are unique to their political system.

We might think that if we understand how such structures work in one political system, we can apply this insight to any other system. Unfortunately, that is not always the case. The sixfold classification will not carry us very far in comparing political systems with each other. The problem is that similar structures may have very different functions across political systems. For example, Britain and China have all six types of political structures. However, these institutions are organized differently in the two countries. More importantly, they function in dramatically different ways. They do different things in the political processes of their countries.

The political executive in Britain consists of the prime minister, the ministers assigned to the Cabinet, and the larger ministry, which consists of all the heads of departments and agencies. All these officials are usually selected from Parliament. There is a similar structure in China, called the State Council, headed by a premier and consisting of the various ministers and ministerial commissions. But while the British prime minister and Cabinet have substantial policymaking power, the State Council in China is closely supervised by the general secretary of the Communist Party, the Politburo, and the Central Committee of the party.

Both Britain and China have legislative bodies—the House of Commons in Britain and the National People's Congress in China. Their members make speeches to each other and vote on prospective public policies. But while the House of Commons is a key institution in the policymaking process, the Chinese Congress meets for only brief periods, ratifying decisions made mainly by the Communist Party authorities.

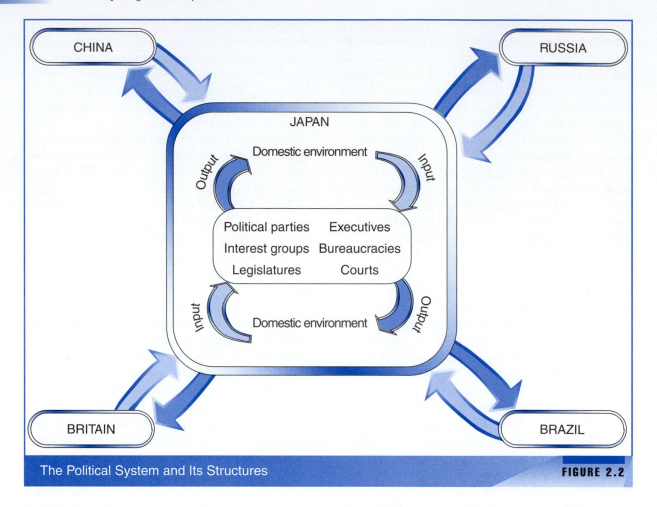

**The Political System and Its Structures**

**FIGURE 2.2**

Usually the Chinese delegates do not even consider alternative policies.

There are even larger differences between political parties in the two countries. Britain has a competitive party system. The majority in the House of Commons and the Cabinet are constantly confronted by an opposition party or parties, competing for public support. They look forward to the next election when they may unseat the incumbent majority, as happened in 1997, when the Labour Party replaced the Conservatives in government. In China the Communist Party controls the whole political process. There are no other political parties. The principal decisions are taken in the Politburo and to some extent in the Central Committee of the Communist Party. The governmental agencies implement the policies, which are initiated or approved by the top Communist Party leaders.

Thus, an institution-by-institution comparison of British and Chinese politics that did not spell out their interdependence and the functions that they perform would not bring us far toward understanding the important differences in the politics of these two countries. Each country study in this book includes a figure that shows how some of the major structures select and control each other. Another figure illustrates how they fit into the policymaking process.

Figure 2.3 shows the functions of the political process that we can use to compare all political systems. The center of Figure 2.3 under the heading **"process functions"** lists the distinctive activities necessary for policy to be made and implemented in any kind of political system.

- **Interest articulation** involves individuals and groups expressing their needs and demands.
- **Interest aggregation** combines different demands into policy proposals backed by significant political resources.

This meeting of the National Assembly of the People's Republic of China in the Great Hall of the People in Beijing illustrates the importance of structural functionalism. While this is called the "National People's Congress" and the delegates are raising their hands in a vote, the vote is purely formal, since there is no real choice between alternatives.

Mark Avery/AP Images

- **Policymaking** decides which policy proposals are to become authoritative rules.
- **Policy implementation** carries out and enforces public policies; **policy adjudication** settles disputes about their application.

(We discuss each concept in greater detail in Chapters 4, 5, and 6.) We call these process functions because they play a direct and necessary role in the process of making policy.

Before policy can be decided, some individuals and groups in the government or the society must decide what they want and hope to get from politics. The political process begins as these interests are expressed or articulated. The many arrows on the left of the figure show these initial expressions.

To be effective, however, these demands must be combined (aggregated) into policy alternatives—such as higher or lower taxes or more or fewer social security benefits—for which substantial political support can be mobilized. Thus the arrows on the left are consolidated as the process moves from interest articulation to interest aggregation.

Governments then consider alternative policies. Whoever controls the government backs one of them and authoritative policymaking takes place. The policy must be enforced and implemented, and if it is challenged, there must be some process of adjudication.

Each policy may affect several different aspects of a society, as reflected in the three arrows for the implementation phase.

These process functions are performed by such political structures as parties, legislatures, political executives, bureaucracies, and courts. The **structural-functional approach** stresses two points. One is that *in different countries, the same structure may perform different functions.* A second is that while a particular institution, such as a legislature, may have a special relationship to a particular function, such as policymaking, *institutions often do not have a monopoly on any one function.* Presidents and governors may share in the policymaking function (veto powers), as do the higher courts (judicial review of statutes for their constitutionality).

The three functions listed at the top of the figure—socialization, recruitment, and communication—are not directly involved in making and implementing public policy but are of fundamental importance to the political system. We refer to these three functions as **system functions.** They determine whether or not the system will be maintained or changed. For example, will policymaking continue to be dominated by a military council or be replaced by competitive parties and a legislature? Will a sense of national community persist, or will it be eroded by new experiences?

The arrows leading from these three functions to all parts of the political process suggest their crucial

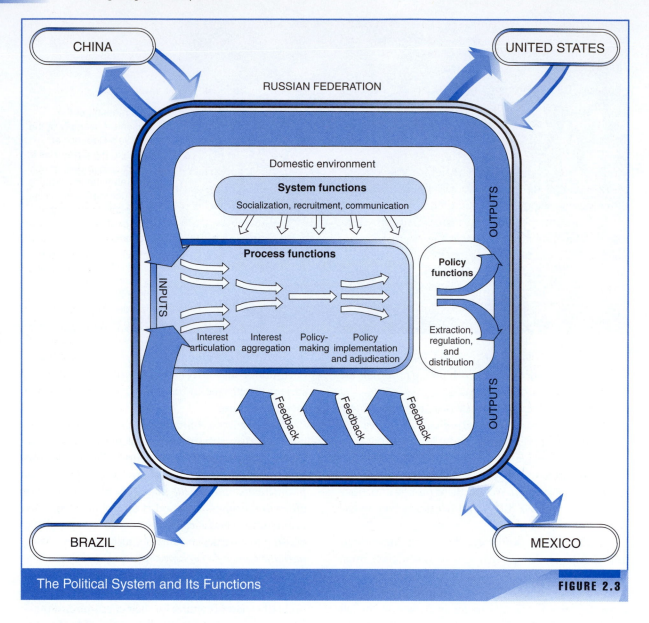

**The Political System and Its Functions**    **FIGURE 2.3**

role in underpinning and permeating the political process.

- **Political socialization** involves families, schools, communications media, churches, and all the various political structures that develop, reinforce, and transform the political culture, the attitudes of political significance in the society. (See Chapter 3.)
- **Political recruitment** refers to the selection of people for political activity and government offices. In a democracy, competitive elections play a major role in political recruitment. In authoritarian systems,

recruitment may be dominated by a single party, as in China, or unelected religious leaders, as in Iran.

- **Political communication** refers to the flow of information through the society and through the various structures that make up the political system. Gaining control over information is a key goal of most authoritarian rulers, as shown in the elaborate efforts of Chinese leaders to control content on the Internet.

Understanding the performance of the system functions is essential to understanding how political systems respond to the great contemporary challenges of building community, fostering economic development, and securing democracy that we discussed in Chapter 1.

On the right side of Figure 2.3 we see the consequences of the policy process. The **outputs** are the implementations of the political process. These are the substantive impacts on the society, the economy, and the culture. They include various forms of **extraction** of resources in the form of taxes and the like, **regulation** of behavior, and **distribution** of benefits and services to various groups in the population. The **outcomes** of all these political activities reflect the way the policies interact with the domestic and international environments. Sometimes these outcomes are the desired results of public policies. But sometimes the complexities of policy and society result in unintended consequences. Among these may be new demands for legislation or for administrative action, or increases or decreases in the amount of support given to the political system and incumbent officeholders. We shall return to the policy level, after providing an example of a structural-functional comparison.

The functional concepts shown in Figure 2.3 describe the activities carried on in any society regardless of how its political system is organized or what kinds of policies it produces. Using these functional categories, we can determine how institutions in different countries combine in making and implementing different kinds of public policy. Each country study in this book discusses the ways the different political functions are performed.

## AN ILLUSTRATIVE COMPARISON: REGIME CHANGE IN RUSSIA

Figures 2.4 and 2.5[3] offer a simplified graphic comparison of structures and functions in Russia before and after the breakdown of communist rule in the Soviet Union. They illustrate the use of the comparative method to assess the way a political regime changed significantly in a short period of time. The point here is to illustrate how we can use the tools of political analysis, rather than provide the details of the Russian case (which are discussed in depth in Chapter 12).

The figures depict the changes in the functioning of the major structures of the political system brought about by the collapse of communism. These include two revolutionary changes. One is the end of the single-party political system dominated by the Communist Party of the Soviet Union, which held together the vast, multinational Soviet state. The other is the dissolution of the Soviet Union itself into its fifteen member republics. As a result of these two remarkable events, Russia, the republic that was the core republic of the old union, became an independent noncommunist state.

In June 1991, Boris Yeltsin, a bitter rival to the Soviet president, Mikhail Gorbachev, was elected president of Russia. Six months later, the Soviet Union collapsed and Gorbachev gave up his office. In December 1993, Russian voters were called on to ratify a new constitution, which provided for a powerful executive presidency and at the same time elected a new parliament dominated by a diverse range of political parties.

In the new Russia, democratic tendencies competed with pressures for authoritarian rule. Overall, the new system was a mixture of pluralism with vestiges of the old, bureaucratically run, state socialist order. New political parties were represented in Parliament and tried to develop national political bases of support for the next elections. A reborn Communist Party—called the Communist Party of the Russian Federation—regularly denounced Yeltsin and called for the restoration of a strong state and more social protection. Parliament had become a meaningful site for policy debate and decisionmaking. The mass media were no longer tightly controlled by the Communist Party. New organized interest groups, such as business associations and labor unions, were actively involved in policymaking. The bureaucracy remained a powerful central player in the political process, however, with substantial continued control over the economy.

These and subsequent changes are reflected in the differences between the two figures. In 1985 (the year that the reform leader Mikhail Gorbachev came to power), the Soviet Union was a communist regime. Its Communist Party ruled the country. The top leader of the country was the general secretary of the Communist Party. Although the country had the formal trappings of democracy, power actually flowed downward from the decisionmakers at the top to government and society.

Figure 2.4 therefore shows how the basic functions of the political system were performed in 1985. The Communist Party was the dominant political institution of the country, overseeing schools and media, the arts and public organizations, the economy and

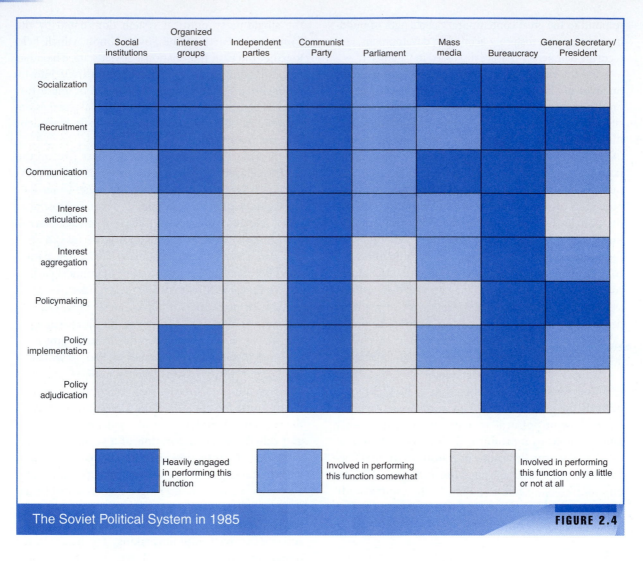

| | Social institutions | Organized interest groups | Independent parties | Communist Party | Parliament | Mass media | Bureaucracy | General Secretary/ President |
|---|---|---|---|---|---|---|---|---|
| Socialization | | | | | | | | |
| Recruitment | | | | | | | | |
| Communication | | | | | | | | |
| Interest articulation | | | | | | | | |
| Interest aggregation | | | | | | | | |
| Policymaking | | | | | | | | |
| Policy implementation | | | | | | | | |
| Policy adjudication | | | | | | | | |

Heavily engaged in performing this function

Involved in performing this function somewhat

Involved in performing this function only a little or not at all

**The Soviet Political System in 1985**

**FIGURE 2.4**

the courts. For this reason, all the cells of the chart in the column marked "Communist Party" are shaded dark, as are the cells under the column marked "Bureaucracy." Although social institutions—such as the family, workplace, arts, and hobby groups— exercised some influence over such system-level functions as socialization, recruitment, and communication, it was the Communist Party and state bureaucracy that dominated process-level functions. Under their tutelage, the mass media in 1985 were a key agent of communist political socialization and communication. Parliament was a compliant instrument for ratifying decisions made by the party and bureaucracy. No other parties could exist beside the Communist Party. The only organized interest groups were those authorized by

the party. The party's general secretary was the most powerful official in the country, since there was no state presidency.

By 2000 the political system had undergone fundamental changes, as shown in Figure 2.5. Many more structures played a role in the political process, as is immediately evident by the larger number of cells that are heavily shaded. In particular, Parliament, independent political parties, and regional governments all acquired important new powers in policymaking. The freedom enjoyed by ordinary citizens to articulate their interests and to organize to advance them had expanded enormously. The Communist Party, no longer an official or monopolistic party, had declined substantially in power and

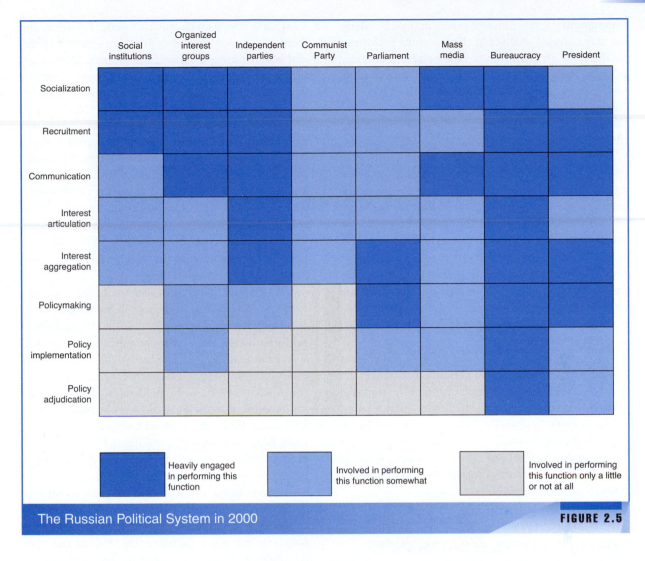

The Russian Political System in 2000

FIGURE 2.5

was playing by the rules of the parliamentary game. The lighter shading for the Communist Party in Figure 2.5 shows its diminished influence. The state bureaucracy remained an important element in the political system, although adapting itself to the new trend of movement toward a market economy by adopting quasi-commercial forms.

The presidency, now occupied by Vladimir Putin, has been a dominating policymaking institution in the new Russia, as shown in Figure 2.5. The Parliament, although fairly representative of the diversity of opinion in the country, was frustrated in its policymaking and oversight roles by the inertia of the vast state bureaucracy, by its inability to compel compliance with its laws, by its weak links with the electorate, and by the president's power to make policy by decree. Nevertheless, it played a much greater role than before in aggregating interests and making policy, as shown when comparing Figures 2.4 and 2.5.

An updating of Figure 2.5 would show the eclipse of parties, Parliament, and the mass media by the President and the Bureaucracy after 2000. This movement in a more authoritarian direction, although not back to communism, would be shown by fewer dark-shaded columns in the middle of the figure. These further developments are discussed in detail in Chapter 12.

The brief comparisons presented here illustrate the use of the structural-functional approach. This approach enables us to examine how the same functions are performed in different countries, or in the same country at two different points in time. Similarly, we may examine changes in the functions performed by the same structures over time or across different political systems. In a country undergoing as rapid and dramatic a transition as Russia in the 1990s, this framework helps us to analyze changes in the distribution of power among the major institutions making up the political system.

Neither the analysis of structures nor that of functions is complete without the other. A structural analysis tells us the number of political parties, or the organization of the legislature. It describes how the executive branch, the courts, the bureaucracy, the mass media, interest groups, and other structures of a political system are set up and by what rules or standards they operate. A functional analysis tells us how these institutions and organizations interact to produce and implement policies. This kind of analysis is especially essential when we are comparing very different kinds of political systems.

The country chapters of this book do not present formal structural-functional sketches like Figures 2.4 and 2.5. But at the core of each chapter is a set of discussions of these functions and the structures that perform them. We can see these in the section headings of the country studies and in the analytic guide at the beginning of this book. These tools make it possible to compare the workings of the very different political systems in this book.

## THE POLICY LEVEL: PERFORMANCE, OUTCOME, AND EVALUATION

The important question is what these differences in structure and function do for the interests, needs, and aspirations of people. We call this the **policy level** of the political system.

Looking again at Figure 2.3, we see reflections of the relationships between the international environment, the domestic society, and the political system. At the left of Figure 2.3 are arrows signifying inputs of demands and supports from the society and the international system. Inputs also come from the independent initiatives of political leaders and bureaucrats. The structures performing the political process functions convert these inputs into the policies of the government. These policies extract resources, distribute benefits, and regulate behavior. They are designed

to achieve broad goals, such as welfare, justice, and freedom—or control and domination—as well as special benefits for groups and individuals. At the right are arrows signifying outputs and outcomes, the end products of the political process, the things a government does for and to its people.

We call the outputs of a political system—its extractions, distributions, regulations, and symbolic acts—its policy performance. We have to distinguish among these efforts, the things a government does, and the actual outcome of these efforts. Governments may spend equal amounts on education and health, or defense, but with different consequences. Government efficiency or corruption plays a role in the effectiveness of politics. But so do the underlying cultural, economic, and technological levels.

Americans spend more per capita on education than any other people in the world. But their children perform less well in some subjects, such as mathematics, than do children in some other countries that spend substantially less. The United States spent enormous sums and many lives on the war in Vietnam in the 1960s and 1970s, as did the Soviet Union on its war in Afghanistan in the 1980s. Yet, both countries were held at bay by small countries resolved to resist at all costs. Because of these costly failures, they were weakened internally. The outcome of public policy is never wholly in the hands of the people and their leaders. Conditions in the internal environment, conditions and events in the larger external world, and simple chance may frustrate the most thoughtfully crafted programs and plans. Each country study in this book concludes with a discussion of the country's performance, describing both policies and their outcomes.

Finally, we must step even further back to consider the whole situation of political system, process, and policy and the environment in order to evaluate what political systems are doing. Evaluation is complex because people value different things and put different emphases on what they value. We will refer to the different things people may value as political "goods." In Chapter 7, we discuss goods associated with the system level, such as the stability or adaptability of political institutions. We also discuss goods associated with the process level, such as citizen participation in politics. Finally, we consider goods associated with the policy level, such as welfare, security, and liberty. To evaluate what a political system is doing, we assess performance and outcomes in each of

The wall dividing California from Mexico illustrates the input-output model of comparative politics. The two men are trying to escape from the poverty of the Mexican economy. The wall is part of the output of the American political system, intended to frustrate illegal immigrants. The two figures illustrate the point that outputs do not necessarily produce the intended outcomes.

Les Stone/Corbis

these areas. We must also be aware of how outcomes affect individuals and subgroups in the society, of specific changes that may often be overlooked in presenting averages.

A particularly important problem of evaluation concerns building for the future as well as living today. The people of poor countries wish to survive and alleviate the suffering of today but also to improve their children's lot for tomorrow. The people of all countries, but especially rich ones, must deal with the costs to their children of polluted and depleted natural resources as the result of the thoughtless environmental policies of the past.

## HOW WE EXPLAIN

Once we are able to describe politics with the help of the conceptual framework that we choose, the next task is to explain it. What we mean by explaining political phenomena is seeking to identify relationships among them. For example, we might be interested in the relationship between democracy and international peace (see Box 2.2). Are democratic states more peaceful than others? If so, are they peaceful because they are democratic, are they democratic because they are peaceful, or are they perhaps both peaceful and democratic because they are more prosperous than other states?

These questions show that we often want explanations to go beyond associating one thing with another. Ideally, we want to put many political relationships in causal terms, so that we can say that one political feature is the cause of another, and the latter is the effect of the former.

Theories are statements about causal relationships between general classes of events—for example, about what causes democracy, war, or welfare policies. Scientific theories are always tentative; they are always subject to modification or falsification as our knowledge improves. And theories need to be testable. A good theory is one that holds up after continued trials and experiments. Yet, it can be further confirmed or modified as we test the theory again and again. A well-tested theory allows us to explain confidently what happens in specific cases or groups of cases: these two countries have a peaceful relationship because they are democracies (see Box 2.2).

Researchers in political science distinguish between studies based on large numbers (large "$n$") and small numbers (small "$n$"). In large "$n$" studies, it is often possible and helpful to use statistical analysis. Such studies are usually referred to as *statistical studies;* small "$n$" studies are usually called *case studies.* Large "$n$" studies have a sufficient number and variety of cases to enable the researcher to examine the relation among the variables. Variables are the features on which our cases differ—for

## Statistical Methods

**BOX 2.2**

A popular contemporary research program known as *democratic peace research* illustrates the pros and cons of statistical and case study research. It has been of primary interest to international relations scholars, who took the diplomatic history of the Cold War period and asked whether democratic countries are more peaceful in their foreign policy than authoritarian and nondemocratic ones. Many scholars in the democratic peace research group took the statistical route. They counted each year of interaction between two states as one case. With roughly half a century of diplomatic history involving a state system of 100 countries or more, they had a very large number of cases, even after eliminating the many irrelevant cases of countries that never, or rarely, had any relations with one another. Political scientists Andrew Bennett and Alexander George drew these conclusions after surveying the statistical research:

> Statistical methods achieved important advances on the issue of whether a nonspurious interdemocratic

peace exists. A fairly strong though not unanimous consensus emerged that: (1) democracies are not less war-prone in general; (2) they have very rarely if ever fought one another; (3) this pattern of an interdemocratic peace applies to both war and conflicts short of war; (4) states in transition to democracy are more war prone than established democracies; and (5) these correlations were not spuriously brought about by the most obvious alternative explanations.

Yet, although much was learned from the statistical studies, they were not as successful at answering "why" questions. Case studies make clinical depth possible, revealing causal interconnections in individual cases. Careful repetition of these causal tracings from case to case strengthens confidence in these relationships. Thus Bennett and George concluded that the best research strategy uses statistical and case study methods together, with each method having its own strengths.

Source: Andrew Bennett and Alexander George, "An Alliance of Statistical and Case Study Methods: Research on the Interdemocratic Peace," APSA-CP: *Newsletter of the APSA Organized Section in Comparative Politics* 9 (1998) no. 1: 6.

example, "form of government: democracy or dictatorship." Statistical analysis enables us to consider possible alternative causes at the same time, accepting some and rejecting others. Small "*n*" studies permit investigators to go deeply into a case, identify the particularities of it, get the clinical details, and examine each link in the causal process. Most researchers recognize that these methods are complementary (see Box 2.2).

Large "*n*" statistical studies allow us to be more certain and precise in our explanations. On the other hand, we need the depth that case studies provide. They encourage us to formulate insightful hypotheses for statistical testing in the first place. They allow us to trace the nature of the cause-and-effect relations (sometimes called "causal mechanisms") better than large "*n*" studies. In this manner, political scientists may come to know not only whether democracies are more peaceful than dictatorships, but more precisely why democratic leaders behave in the way that they do.

We can also generate and test hypotheses about the causes and consequences of political change by comparing countries at different historical periods. Tocqueville's study of the French Revolution contributed to a general theory of revolution by comparing pre- and postrevolutionary France.[4] Theda Skocpol based her theories of the causes of revolution on a comparison of the "old regimes" of France, Russia, and China with their revolutionary and postrevolutionary regimes.[5]

An example may suggest how you might go about theorizing in comparative politics, going beyond "just mastering the facts." It is well known that rich countries are more likely to be democracies than are poor countries; democracy and economic development are strongly associated. But there are many possible reasons for this association. Some have suggested that this relationship comes about because democracy encourages education and economic development. Others have argued that as countries develop economically, their new middle classes or better organized working class are more likely to demand democratization. Yet others have seen that both democracy and economic development are commonly found in some regions of the world, such as Western Europe, while both tend to be scarce in the Middle East and Africa. This fact suggests that certain cultures may encourage or discourage both of them.

We want to understand the causal nature of this association, for reasons of both science and policy. Fostering economic development and securing democracy are two of the significant political challenges that we discussed in Chapter 1. It is vitally important that we understand how they relate to each other.

A work of Adam Przeworski and his associates examined the full experience of democracies, nondemocracies, and transitions between them in all parts of the world between 1950 and 1990.[6] Their statistical analysis led them to conclude that the explanation for the association did not lie in regional effects or superior economic growth in democracy. Moreover, countries at any level of development seemed able to introduce democracy, although economically developed countries are somewhat more likely to do so. They argue that the key to the relationship lies rather

in the consistently greater fragility of democracies in societies at lower levels of economic development. Democracy can easily be introduced in poor societies with less educated populations. But in these social conditions it is often replaced by some kind of dictatorship. In rich countries, on the other hand, democracy tends to survive once it has been introduced. These democratic failures in poor countries produce a strong association between development and democracy. We still need to understand just why democracy is more precarious in less developed societies. But we are making progress in understanding the causal element in the relationship. We are better able to explain the relationship between development and democracy, as well as the failures of democratization in specific countries.

Comparative analysis is a powerful and versatile tool. It enhances our ability to describe and understand political processes and political change in any country by offering concepts and reference points from a broader perspective. The comparative approach also stimulates us to form general theories of political relationships. It encourages and enables us to test our political theories by confronting them with the experience of many institutions and settings.

## REVIEW QUESTIONS

- How do the main elements in the environment of a political system affect the way it performs?

- Why can't we compare political systems by just describing the different structures we find in them?

- What are the functions performed in all political systems as policies are made?

- What is the difference between outputs and outcomes of policy?

- How do we use theories to explain political events?

## KEY TERMS

| | | | |
|---|---|---|---|
| distribution | interdependence | policy level | process functions |
| environment | interest aggregation | policymaking | regulation |
| extraction | interest articulation | political culture | structural-functional |
| functions | outcomes | political communication |     approach |
| globalization | outputs | political recruitment | structures |
| governments | policy adjudication | political socialization | system |
| inputs | policy implementation | political system | system functions |

## SUGGESTED READINGS

Collier, David. "The Comparative Method," in Ada W. Finifter, ed., *Political Science: The State of the Discipline II.* Washington, DC: American Political Science Association, 1993.

Dogan, Mattei, and Dominique Pelassy. *How to Compare Nations: Strategies in Comparative Politics.* Chatham, NJ: Chatham House, 1990.

Goodin, Robert E., and Hans-Dieter Klingemann. Chapters 2 and 3, and Part 4 of *A New Handbook of Political Science.* New York: Oxford University Press, 1996.

King, Gary, Robert O. Keohane, and Sidney Verba. *Scientific Inference in Qualitative Research.* New York: Cambridge University Press, 1993.

Lichbach, Mark, and Alan Zuckerman. *Comparing Nations: Rationality, Culture, and Structure.* New York: Cambridge University Press, 1997.

Przeworski, Adam, and Henry Teune. *The Logic of Comparative Social Inquiry.* New York: Wiley, 1970.

## ENDNOTES

1. Alexis de Tocqueville to Louis de Kergolay, 18 October 1847, in *Alexis de Tocqueville: Selected Letters on Politics and Society*, ed. Roger Boesche (Berkeley: University of California Press, 1985), 191.

2. Alexis de Tocqueville to Ernest de Chabrol, 7 October 1831, ibid, 59.

3. Figures 2.4 and 2.5 and the text of this section were contributed by Thomas Remington.

4. Alexis de Tocqueville, *The Old Regime and the French Revolution,* trans. Stuart Gilbert (New York: Doubleday, 1955).

5. Theda Skocpol, *States and Social Revolutions* (New York: Cambridge University Press, 1979).

6. Adam Przeworski et al., *Democracy and Development* (Cambridge: Cambridge University Press, 2000).

# POLITICAL CULTURE AND POLITICAL SOCIALIZATION

Do you remember the first time you traveled to a foreign country? You probably were surprised by how many of the normal things in your life were different there. The food was different, people wore different clothes, houses were constructed and furnished differently, and the pattern of social relations differed (for instance, whether they talked to strangers or stood in queues). You were observing how social norms shape what people eat, how they dress, how they live, and maybe even on which side of the road they drive.

Similarly, each nation has its own political norms that influence how people think about and react to politics. Americans' strong feelings of patriotism, the Japanese deference to political elites, and the French proclivity for protest all illustrate how cultural norms shape politics. The way political institutions function at least partially reflects the public's attitudes, norms, and expectations. Thus, the English use their constitutional arrangements to sustain their liberty, while the same institutions were once used as a means of repression in South Africa and Northern Ireland. When a new regime forms, a supportive public can help develop the new system, while the absence of public support may weaken the new system. To understand the political tendencies in a nation, we must begin with public attitudes toward politics and their role within the political system—what we call a nation's political culture.

Chapter 1 stated that one main goal of any government, and a special challenge for a new government, is to create and maintain a political community. In part, this involves developing common structures and systems (such as a single economy), common political institutions, and common political processes. At the level of the public, this involves developing common world views, values, and expectations among the public that together comprise the nation's political culture. So studying political culture partially explains how a political community is created and sustained.

In this chapter we map the important parts of political culture. We then discuss political socialization: how individuals form their political attitudes and thus, collectively, how citizens form their political culture. We conclude by describing the major trends in political culture in world politics today.

## MAPPING THE THREE LEVELS OF POLITICAL CULTURE

A nation's **political culture** includes its citizens' orientations at three levels: the political system, the political and policymaking process, and policy outputs and outcomes (Table 3.1). The *system* level involves how people view the values and organizations that comprise the political system. Do citizens identify with the nation and accept the general system of government? The *process* level includes expectations of how politics should function, and individuals' relationship to the political process. The *policy* level deals with the public's policy expectations for the government. What should be the policy goals of government and how are they to be achieved?

| The Aspects of Political Culture | **TABLE 3.1** |
|---|---|

| Aspects of Political Culture | Examples |
|---|---|
| System | Pride in nation |
| | National identity |
| | Legitimacy of government |
| Process | Role of citizens |
| | Perceptions of political rights |
| Policy | Role of government |
| | Government policy priorities |

## The System Level

Orientations toward the political system are important because they tap basic commitments to the polity and the nation. It is difficult for any political system to endure if it lacks the support of its citizens.

Feelings of national pride are considered an affective, emotional tie to a political system. National pride seems strongest in nations with a long history that has emphasized feelings of patriotism—the United States is a prime example (see Figure 3.1). Such a common sense of identity and national history often binds a people together in times of political strain. The figure indicates that high levels of pride exist in nations with very different political and economic systems, such as the United States and Poland. In contrast, national pride is low in Japan and Germany, two nations that have avoided nationalist sentiments in reaction to the World War II regimes and their excesses. In other cases, ethnicity, language, or history divide the public, which may strain national identities and ultimately lead to conflict and division.

Feelings of popular **legitimacy** are another foundation for a successful political system. When people believe that they ought to obey the laws, legitimacy is high. If they see no reason to obey or if they comply only from fear, legitimacy is low. Because it is much easier for government to function when citizens believe in the legitimacy of the system, virtually all governments, even the most brutal and coercive, try to encourage people to believe that they should obey the laws. A political system and a government with high legitimacy are typically more effective in carrying out policies and are more likely to overcome hardships and reversals.

Citizens may grant legitimacy to a government for different reasons. In a traditional society, legitimacy may depend on the ruler's inheriting the throne or on the ruler's commitment to religious customs. In a modern democracy, the legitimacy of the authorities depends on their selection by voters in competitive elections and on the government following constitutional procedures. In other political cultures, the leaders may base their claim to legitimacy on their special wisdom or ideology, which they claim will transform people's lives for the better, even though the government does not respond to specific public demands or follow prescribed procedures.[1] Theocratic regimes, such as Iran, base their legitimacy on adherence to religious principles. Thus, legitimacy also presumes an agreement on the broad form of government that defines the political system and thus the standards of legitimacy: monarchical rule, a tribal system, a communist order, or a democratic system.

Whether legitimacy is based on tradition, ideology, elections, or religion, feelings of legitimacy reflect a basic understanding between citizens and political authorities. Citizens obey the laws and in return the government meets the obligations set by the terms of its legitimacy. As long as the government meets its obligations, the public is supposed to be supportive and act appropriately. If legitimacy is violated—the line of succession is broken, the constitution is subverted, or the ruling ideology is ignored—the government may expect resistance and perhaps rebellion.

In systems with low legitimacy, people often resort to violence or extra-governmental actions to solve political disagreements. Legitimacy is lacking where the public disputes the boundaries of the political system (as in Northern Ireland or Kashmir), rejects the current arrangements for recruiting leaders and making policies (as when Ukranians took to the streets in 2004–05 demanding new democratic elections), or loses confidence that the leaders are fulfilling their part of the political bargain (as when the Thai opposition forced the prime minister from office in 2006).

The Soviet Union disintegrated in the early 1990s because all three legitimacy problems appeared. After the communist ideology failed as a legitimizing force, there was no basis for a national political community in the absence of common language or ethnicity. Similarly, the loss of confidence in the Communist Party as a political organization led many people to

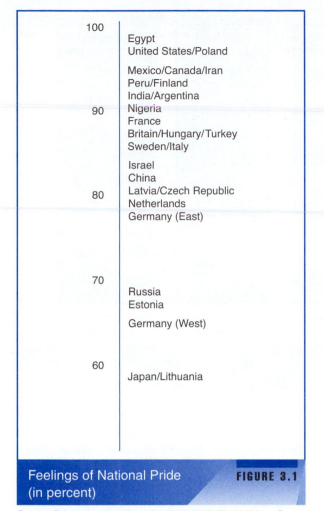

| | |
|---|---|
| 100 | Egypt |
| | United States/Poland |
| | |
| | Mexico/Canada/Iran |
| | Peru/Finland |
| | India/Argentina |
| 90 | Nigeria |
| | France |
| | Britain/Hungary/Turkey |
| | Sweden/Italy |
| | |
| | Israel |
| | China |
| 80 | Latvia/Czech Republic |
| | Netherlands |
| | Germany (East) |
| | |
| | |
| 70 | Russia |
| | Estonia |
| | Germany (West) |
| | |
| 60 | Japan/Lithuania |

**Feelings of National Pride (in percent)**    **FIGURE 3.1**

Source: Selected nations from the 2000–2002 *World Values Survey* and the 1999 *European Values Survey*. Figure entries are the percent "proud" and "very proud"; missing data are excluded from the calculation of percentages.

call for institutional reform. Finally, shortages of food and consumer goods caused people to lose faith in the government's short-term economic and political policies. Soviet President Mikhail Gorbachev failed in his efforts to deal with all three problems at the same time.

## The Process Level

The second level of the political culture involves what the public expects of the political process. Whether you are English or Nigerian, what do you think about the institutions of your political system and what is expected of you as a citizen?

Broadly speaking, three different patterns describe the citizen's role in the political process:[2]

- **Participants** are, or have the potential to be, involved in the political process. They are informed about politics and make demands on the polity, granting their support to political leaders based on performance.
- **Subjects** passively obey government officials and the law, but they do not vote or actively involve themselves in politics.
- **Parochials** are hardly aware of government and politics. They may be illiterates, rural people living in remote areas, or simply people who ignore politics and its impact on their lives.

As shown in Figure 3.2, in a hypothetical modern industrial democracy a majority are participants, a third are simply subjects, and a small group are parochials. This distribution provides enough political activists to ensure competition among political parties and sizable voter turnout, as well as critical audiences for debate on public issues by parties, candidates, and pressure groups. At the same time, not all citizens feel the need to be active in or concerned about the political system.

The second column in Figure 3.2 shows the pattern we expect in an industrialized authoritarian society, such as the former communist nations of Eastern Europe. A small minority of citizens are involved in a one-party system, which penetrates and oversees the society, as well as decides government policies. Most other citizens are mobilized as subjects by political institutions: political parties, the bureaucracy, and government-controlled mass media. People are encouraged and even forced to cast a symbolic vote of support in elections and to pay taxes, obey regulations, and follow the dictates of government. Because of the effectiveness of modern social organization and the efforts of the authoritarian power structure, few people are unaware of the government and its influence on their lives. If such a society suddenly attempts to democratize its politics, many people must learn to become democrats and participants.

The third column shows an authoritarian society that is partly traditional and partly modern, such as in Iran or China. In spite of an authoritarian political system, some participants—students and intellectuals, for example—oppose the system and try to change it

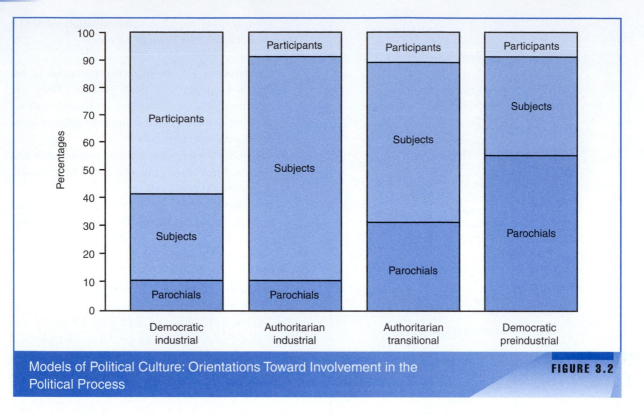

Models of Political Culture: Orientations Toward Involvement in the Political Process

FIGURE 3.2

by persuasion or acts of protest. Favored groups, like business people and landowners, discuss public issues and engage in lobbying. Most people in such systems are passive subjects, aware of government and complying with the law but not otherwise involved in public affairs. The parochials—poor and illiterate urban dwellers, peasants, or farm laborers—have limited contact with the political system.

The fourth column shows the democratic preindustrial system, perhaps India or Nigeria, which has a predominantly rural, illiterate population. In such a country, the few political participants are chiefly educated professionals, business people, and landowners. A much larger number of employees, workers, and farmers are directly affected by government taxation and other official policies. The largest group of people are illiterate peasants, whose knowledge of and involvement with national politics are minimal. Such a society faces a significant challenge to create a more aware public that can participate meaningfully and shape government policies through democratic means.

Attitudes toward the citizen's role are also shaped by the political form of the regime. In the early 1900s, many different political systems existed worldwide.

Fascism was on the rise in Europe, communism was establishing itself in the Soviet Union, colonial administrations governed large parts of the world, and monarchical or authoritarian governments ruled other nations. All of these systems encouraged a restrictive role for the citizens. Western Europe and North America were the democracies in this sea of conflicting currents.

Today, many of these nondemocratic forms of governance are no longer widely accepted. Communism still has strongholds in China and Cuba, but it has lost its image as a progressive force for global change. Some nations still accept autocratic or religiously based systems of government. However, the global wave of democratization since the early 1990s has raised democratic principles to a position of prominence (see Figure 1.3 in Chapter 1). Democratic norms emphasize the importance of a participatory system, majority rule and minority rights, and the values of political tolerance. Most of the people in the world today seem to favor democratic principles even if they differ in how those principles should be applied.[3]

The distribution of these citizen types and political norms is affected by the process of social and

## Becoming Modern

Alex Inkeles and David Smith report how one Nigerian worker replied to a question about how his new job in a factory made him feel. "Sometimes like 9 feet tall with arms a yard wide. Here in the factory I alone with my machine can twist any way I want a piece of steel that all the men in my home village together could not begin to bend at all." Such experiences—and the parallel changes in educational levels and access to information—can create a more modern political culture.

Source: Alex Inkeles and David Smith, *Becoming Modern* (Cambridge: Harvard University Press, 1974), 158.

economic **modernization** that we introduced in Chapter 1. Industrialization, urbanization, and improved living standards transform the social base of a nation. Exposure to modernity through work, education, and the media shapes an individual's personal experiences and sends messages about norms in other societies. It encourages citizen participation, a sense of individual equality, the desire for improved living standards and increased life expectancy, and government legitimacy based on policy performance. It also frequently disrupts familiar ways of life, traditional bases of legitimacy, and political arrangements that depend on citizens remaining parochials or subjects. In addition, the secularizing influences of science can alter economic and social systems, which then reshape the political culture. This modernization trend has powerful effects as it penetrates societies (or parts of societies). Alex Inkeles and David Smith's classic study of modernization emphasized how factory experience can create an awareness of the possibilities of organization, change, and control over nature that empowers the individual (see Box 3.1).

This modernization process is spread unevenly across the globe. The advanced industrial societies have the largest proportion of citizens who are participants and cognitively engaged in politics. The recent economic growth in East Asia is similarly transforming the political culture and political behavior in these nations.[4] In contrast, modernization has proceeded more slowly and uncertainly in Africa and Arab nations. Some political leaders in these nations even reject the principles of modernization as incongruent with their national values. However, there is persuasive evidence that where social and economic modernization occurs, it transforms the political culture to emphasize self-expression, participatory values, and autonomy.[5]

### The Policy Level

What is the appropriate role of government? If you ask political theorists, you get a wide range of answers—from the minimal state to the all-encompassing polity (see Chapter 1). And if you travel to other nations, you quickly realize that there is wide variation in how people answer this question.

The policy activities of a country are influenced by public images of what constitutes the good society and the government's role in achieving these goals. Should government manage the economy, or should private property rights and market forces guide economic activity? Should the state intervene in addressing social and moral issues, or should it follow a minimalist strategy? The ongoing debates over "big government" versus "small government" in democratic states, and between socialist and market-based economies, reflect these different images of the scope of government.

We can illustrate differences in policy expectations with an opinion survey question that asks whether the government is responsible to provide for everyone (see Figure 3.3). The range in opinions is considerable; about three-quarters of respondents in Nigeria and Sweden believe this is a government responsibility compared with only a quarter of the French or West Germans. In general, people in developing nations and in the formerly communist nations of Eastern Europe are more supportive of a large government role—reflecting both their social condition and their past political ideologies. In some Western nations, such as Sweden and Finland, traditions include a large role for the government. In general, however, support for government action generally decreases as national affluence increases.[6]

Cubans wave flags at a
pro-government rally
organized by the Castro
government.

AP Images

Policy expectations also involve specific issue demands.[7] Indeed, each country study in this book begins with a discussion of the policy challenges facing the nation and the public's issue concerns. This sets the agenda of politics that responsive governments should address.

Some policy goals, such as economic well-being, are valued by nearly everyone. Concern about other policy goals may vary widely across nations because of the nation's circumstances and because of cultural traditions. People in developing countries are more likely to focus on the government's provision of basic services to ensure public welfare. Advanced industrial societies have the resources to provide for basic needs. In these nations, people are often more concerned with quality-of-life goals, such as preservation of nature and even government support for the arts.[8] One basic measure of a government's performance is its ability to meet the policy expectations of its citizens.

Another set of expectations involves the functioning of government. Some cultures put more weight on the policy outputs of government, such as providing welfare and security. Other cultures also emphasize how the process functions, which involves values such as the rule of law and procedural justice. Among

Germans, for example, the rule of law is given great importance; in many developing nations political relations are personally based, and there is less willingness to rely on legalistic frameworks.

## Consensual or Conflictual Political Cultures

Although political culture is a common characteristic of a nation, values and beliefs can also vary within it. Political cultures may be consensual or conflictual on issues of public policy and, more fundamentally, on views of legitimate governmental and political arrangements. In some societies, citizens generally agree on the norms of political decisionmaking and their policy expectations. In other societies—because of differences in histories, conditions, or identities—the citizens are sharply divided, often on both the legitimacy of the regime and solutions to major problems.[9]

When a country is deeply divided in its political values and these differences persist over time, distinctive **political subcultures** may develop. The citizens in these subcultures may have sharply different points of view on some critical political matters, such as the boundaries of the nation, the nature of the regime, or the correct ideology. They may affiliate with different political parties

| | |
|---|---|
| 80 | |
| | Nigeria |
| | Sweden/Tanzania |
| 70 | India |
| | Turkey/Argentina |
| | Egypt |
| | Finland |
| | Latvia |
| 60 | Iran |
| | Estonia |
| | Mexico |
| | Germany (East) |
| 50 | Peru |
| | Italy/Russia |
| | China |
| | Poland/Lithuania |
| 40 | |
| | Canada/Czech Republic |
| | Netherlands |
| | United States/Japan |
| 30 | Britain |
| | France/Germany (West) |

**The Government Should
Ensure Everyone Is Provided
For (percent agreeing)**

**FIGURE 3.3**

Source: Selected nations from the 2000–2002 *World Values Survey* and 1999 *European Values Survey*; missing data are excluded from the calculation of percentages.

and interest groups, read different newspapers, and even have separate social clubs and sporting groups. Thus, they are exposed to different information about politics. For instance, such subcultural differences characterize the publics in India, Nigeria, and Russia today.

In some instances, historical or social factors generate different cultural trajectories. For instance, *ethnic, religious,* or *linguistic* identities in many parts of the world shape citizen values.[10] Moreover, as such groups increase their political skills and self-confidence, they may express their identities and demand equal treatment. In fact, the processes of globalization might actually heighten these cultural contrasts.[11] The migration of peoples into new areas—made possible by easier transportation and encouraged by wars, political conflicts, and the desire for economic betterment—can seem to threaten the way of life of the host society. The exposure to values from other cultures also may intensify one's own self-image, which may increase cultural tensions. Although such exposure may eventually lead to greater tolerance, that outcome is not guaranteed.

## WHY CULTURE MATTERS

Political culture does not explain everything about politics. Even people with similar values and skills might behave differently from each other when they face different situations. Nor is political culture unchangeable. However, cultural norms typically change slowly and reflect stable values. Thus, political culture is important first because it encapsulates the history, traditions, and values of a society. To understand how most people in a nation think and act politically, we can begin by understanding their political culture. Political culture can create the common political community that is one goal of government.

In addition, the distribution of cultural patterns is typically related to the type of political process that citizens expect and support. This is the principle of *congruence theory*. For instance, support for a democratic system is typically higher in societies that have a more participatory political culture. Authoritarian states are more likely to endure when the public is characterized by subjects and parochials—where individuals lack the skills or motivations to participate and the state discourages their participation. These cultural norms represent the "rules of the game" for the political system, and the system works better when citizens accept these rules. Where political structures and political cultures are mutually reinforcing, a more stable political system is likely to emerge.

We can illustrate the logic of congruence theory in terms of the relationship between political culture and the democratic development of a nation (Figure 3.4). The horizontal axis of the figure displays the public's adherence to self-expressive values, reflecting the participatory norms we discussed earlier. The vertical axis represents the democratic development of the nation based on a variety of expert evaluations. You can see that as participatory values increase, so too does the democratic development of the nation. The nations

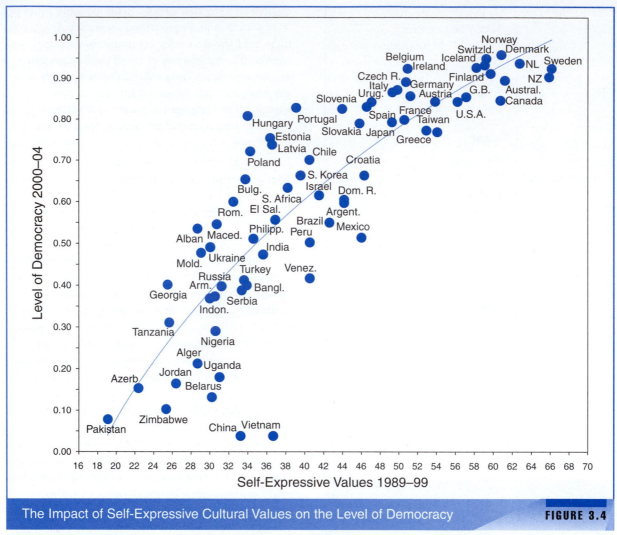

**The Impact of Self-Expressive Cultural Values on the Level of Democracy**    **FIGURE 3.4**

Source: The self-expressive values measure is from the *World Values Survey*; higher scores represent more citizen emphasis on self-expression. The level of democracy measure is a composite of the ranking of democracy by the Freedom House and other national rankings. Higher scores indicate a higher level of democratic development. For additional discussion of these measures see Ronald Inglehart and Christian Welzel, *Modernization, Cultural Change and Democracy: The Human Development Sequence* (New York: Cambridge University Press, 2005).

in this book that are included in these analyses show a clear differentiation between the established Western democracies, relatively new democracies (such as Russia and other East European nations), and nondemocracies (such as China and several Middle East nations). Structure and culture do overlap in these nations.[12]

Do democracies create a participatory democratic public or does such a political culture lead to a democratic political system? It works both ways. For example, immediately after World War II, Germans were less supportive of democracy, but political institutions and political experiences transformed their culture over the next generation.[13] At the same time, democracy

endured in Britain during the strains of the Great Depression and World War II, at least in part because the British public supported the democratic process. The important conclusion is that there is normally a relationship between political culture and political structures.

Beyond shaping the structure of the political system, a nation's political culture also influences the style of politics and the content of policymaking. We have stressed how the policy elements of a political culture can influence the content of policy. In addition, research suggests that cultural factors, such as social trust and engagement, influence the efficiency and effectiveness of government.[14]

Finally, while the political culture may help build a national community, it may also provide a basis of division. For instance, where political subcultures coincide with ethnic, linguistic, or religious differences—as in Northern Ireland, Bosnia, and Lebanon—the divisions can be enduring and threatening. The fragmentation of the Soviet empire, the breakup of Yugoslavia, and the impulses toward autonomy and secession among ethnically distinct regions (such as in Scotland or separatist movements in Africa) all reflect the lasting power of language, culture, and historical memory to create and sustain the sense of ethnic and national identity among parts of contemporary states. In broader international terms, Samuel Huntington has divided the world into different civilizations defined by their religious and cultural traditions.[15] He then predicted that these cultural differences will be a major source of international conflict in this century. While culture may have the power to divide, it is counterbalanced by its potential to build a common political community.

## POLITICAL SOCIALIZATION

Political cultures are sustained or changed as people acquire their attitudes and values. *Political socialization* refers to the way in which political values are formed and the political culture is transmitted from one generation to the next. Most children acquire their basic political values and behavior patterns by

adolescence.[16] Some of these attitudes will evolve and change throughout their lives, while other attitudes may remain part of their political self throughout life.

At any specific time, a person's political beliefs are a combination of various feelings and attitudes. At the deepest level, there are general identifications, such as nationalism, ethnic or class self-images, religious and ideological commitments, and a fundamental sense of rights and duties in the society. At the middle level, people develop attitudes toward politics and governmental institutions. Finally, there are more immediate views of current events, policies, issues, and personalities. All these attitudes can change, but those in the first level usually were acquired earliest, have been most frequently reinforced, and tend to be the most durable.

Three points about political socialization deserve mention. First, the socialization process can occur in different ways. Direct socialization involves an actor explicitly communicating information, values, or feelings toward politics. Examples of direct socialization include civics courses in the schools, public education programs of the government, and the political information campaigns of interest groups. Communist political systems also heavily use direct indoctrination programs (see Box 3.2). Indirect political socialization occurs when political views are inadvertently molded by our experiences. For example, children normally learn important political values by observing the behavior of their parents, teachers, and friends. Or, people may learn by observing the political and social

---

### Socializing Values                                                                              **BOX 3.2**

Communist East Germany had a special ceremony for eighth graders to mark their passage to adulthood. The heart of the ceremony was the endorsement of the following four pledges:

- As young citizens of our German Democratic Republic, are you prepared to work and fight loyally for the great and honorable goals of socialism, and to honor the revolutionary inheritance of the people?
- As sons and daughters of the worker-and-peasant state, are you prepared to pursue higher education, to cultivate your mind, to become a master of

your trade, to learn permanently, and to use your knowledge to pursue our great humanist ideals?
- As honorable members of the socialist community, are you ready to cooperate as comrades, to respect and support each other, and to always merge the pursuit of your personal happiness with the happiness of all the people?
- As true patriots, are you ready to deepen the friendship with the Soviet Union, to strengthen our brotherhood with socialist countries, to struggle in the spirit of proletarian internationalism, to protect peace and to defend socialism against every imperialist aggression?

context that surrounds them, watching what governments do and how other citizens react.

Second, socialization is a lifelong process. Early family influences can create an individual's initial values, but subsequent life experiences—becoming involved in new social groups, moving from one part of the country to another, shifting up or down the social ladder, becoming a parent, finding or losing a job—may change one's political perspectives. More dramatic experiences—such as relocating to a new country or suffering through an economic depression or a war—can alter even basic political attitudes. Such events seem to have their greatest impact on young people, but people at any age are affected to some degree.

Third, patterns of socialization can unify or divide. Governments design public education systems, for instance, to create a single national political culture. Some events, such as international conflict or the death of a popular public figure, can affect nearly the entire nation similarly. In contrast, subcultures in a society can have their own distinctive patterns of socialization. Social groups that provide their members with their own newspapers, their own neighborhood groups, and perhaps their own schools can create distinctive subcultural attitudes. Divisive patterns of socialization can lead to a political gap among members of a nation.

## AGENTS OF POLITICAL SOCIALIZATION

Individuals in all societies are affected by **agents of political socialization:** individuals, organizations, and institutions that influence political attitudes. Some, like civics courses in schools, are direct and deliberate sources of political learning. Others, like playgroups and work groups, affect political socialization indirectly.

### The Family

The direct and indirect influences of the family—the first socialization source that an individual encounters—are normally powerful and lasting. The family has distinctive influences on attitudes toward authority. Participation in family decisionmaking can increase a child's sense of political competence, providing skills for political interaction and encouraging active participation in the political system as an adult. Similarly, unquestioning obedience to parental decisions may lead

a child toward a role as a political subject. The family also shapes future political attitudes by defining a social position for the child: establishing ethnic, linguistic, class, and religious ties; affirming cultural values; and influencing job aspirations.

The nature of the family is changing in many societies. Family sizes are generally decreasing, which changes the pattern of family life. In addition, there has been a marked rise of single-parent families, especially in the advanced industrial democracies. The impact of these structural changes on family socialization patterns is still unclear.

In addition, gender roles are changing in many industrial nations, although they persist in many less-developed nations.[17] The rise of the women's movement and self-help groups has encouraged women to become politically active and change social cues about how women should relate to politics. The lessening of gender differences in self-images, in parental roles, and in relations to the economy and the political system is significantly affecting patterns of political recruitment, political participation, and public policy. A more open family, equality of parenting, and the early exposure of children to childcare and preschool group experiences have modified the impact of the family in the socialization process. Especially in the developing world, the changing role of women may have profound influences in modernizing the society.[18]

### Schools

Schools educate children about politics and their role in the process, providing them with information on political institutions and relationships. Schools can also help shape attitudes about the political system, the rules of the political game, the appropriate role of the citizen, and expectations about the government. Schools typically reinforce attachments to the political system and reinforce common symbols, such as the flag and pledge of allegiance, that encourage emotional attachments to the system. When a new nation comes into being, or a revolutionary regime comes to power in an old nation, it usually turns immediately to the schools as a means to supplant "outdated" values and symbols with new ones more congruent with the new ideology.

In some nations, educational systems do not provide unifying political socialization but send starkly different messages to different groups. For instance, some Muslim nations segregate girls and boys within the school system. Even if educational experiences are intended to be equal, segregation creates different experiences and expectations. Moreover, the content of education often differs between boys and girls. Perhaps the worst example occurred under the Taliban in Afghanistan, where for several years young girls were prohibited from attending school. Such treatment of young girls severely limits their life chances, and ensures they will have restricted roles in society and the economy—which was the intent of the Taliban system. The new Afghanistan government reversed this policy, and now young girls are being included in the education system, and their future life prospects are improving as a result.

Education also affects the political skills and resources of the public. Educated people are more aware of the impact of government on their lives and pay more attention to politics.[19] The better educated have mental skills that improve their ability to manage the world of politics. They also have more information about political processes and participate in a wider range of political activities.

## Religious Institutions

The religions of the world are carriers of cultural and moral values, which often have political implications. The great religious leaders have seen themselves as teachers, and their followers have usually attempted to shape the socialization of children through schooling, preaching, and religious services. In most nations, there are formal ties between the dominant religion and the government. In these instances, religious values and public policy often overlap. Catholic nations, for instance, are less likely to have liberal abortion policies, just as Islamic governments enforce strict moral codes.

Religious institutions of many kinds offer valuable moral and ethical guidance that individuals often need to make choices in complex societies. Religious affiliations are often important sources of partisan preferences and can guide people in making other political choices. Thus, even though church attendance is decreasing in many nations, the political relevance of religion continues.

Where churches teach values that may be at odds with the controlling political system, the struggle over socialization can be intense. These tensions can take a wide variety of forms: the clash between secular and religious roles in the French educational system, the efforts of American fundamentalists to introduce prayer in the schools, or the conflict between Islamic fundamentalists and secular governments in Algeria and Egypt. In such cases, religious groups may oppose the policies of the state, or even the state itself.

The emergence of religious fundamentalism in recent decades has influenced the society and politics of countries as diverse as the United States, India, Israel, Lebanon, Iran, Pakistan, Algeria, and Nigeria. Such **fundamentalism** is often a defensive reaction against the spread of scientific views of nature and human behavior, and the libertarian values and attitudes that accompany these views.[20] The influence of fundamentalism has been most visible in the Middle East and in Muslim countries, but it is important in Christian countries as well. Both Protestant and Catholic versions of fundamentalism exist in the United States, Europe, and Latin America. Versions of fundamentalism also exist, combined with ethnic and nationalist tendencies, in the Confucian, Buddhist, and Hindu countries of Asia. Broadly speaking, fundamentalism seeks to raise conservative social, moral, and religious issues to the top of the contemporary policy agenda.

## Peer Groups

Peer groups also shape political attitudes. They include childhood playgroups, friendship cliques, school and college fraternities, small work groups, and other groups in which members share relatively equal status and close ties. They can be as varied as a group of Russian mothers who meet regularly at the park, to a street gang in Brazil, to a group of Wall Street executives who are members of a health club.

A peer group socializes its members by motivating or pressuring them to conform to the attitudes or behavior accepted by the group. Individuals often adopt the views of their peers because they like or respect them or because they want to be like them. Similarly, an individual may become interested in politics or attend a political demonstration because close friends do so. One example of peer networks is the international youth culture symbolized by rock music, T-shirts, and blue jeans (and more liberal political values). Some observers claim that it played a major role in the failure of communist officials to mold Soviet and

Eastern European youth to the "socialist personality" that was the Marxist-Leninist ideal. Likewise, the "skinheads" groups that have sprouted up among lower class youth in many Western countries have adopted political views that are based on peer interactions.

## Social Class

Most societies have significant social divisions based on class or occupation. Individuals live in different social worlds defined by their class position. For instance, industrialization in Britain created a working class that was concentrated in particular neighborhoods. This working class developed its own forms of speech, dress, recreation, and entertainment, as well as its own social organizations (such as social clubs, trade unions, and political parties). Similarly, the life experience of the rural peasantry in many less developed nations is radically different from that of urban dwellers. Often, these social divisions are politically relevant: identifying yourself as a member of the working class or the peasantry leads to distinct political views about what issues are important and which political groups best represent your interest.

## Interest Groups

Interest groups, economic groups, and similar organizations also shape political attitudes. In most industrial countries, the rise of trade unions transformed the political culture and politics, created new political parties, and ushered in new social benefit programs. Today, unions are active participants in the political process and try to persuade their members on political matters. Other professional associations—such as groups of peasants and farmers, manufacturers, wholesalers and retailers, medical societies, and lawyers—also regularly influence political attitudes in modern and modernizing societies. These groups ensure the loyalty of their members by defending their economic and professional interests. They can also provide valuable political cues to nonmembers, who might identify with a group's interests or political ideology. For instance, when a group that you like (or dislike) publicly supports a policy, it gives you information on the likely content of the policy.

The groups that define a civil society are also potential agents of socialization. These groups might include ethnic organizations, fraternal associations, civic associations (such as parent-teacher associations), and policy groups (such as taxpayers' associations, women's groups, and environmental groups). Such groups provide valuable political cues to their members and try to reinforce distinct social and political orientations. They also provide settings to learn about how making political choices in small groups can be extended to politics. For instance, Vietnam has an active network of social groups that socialize individuals into the norms of the communist regime, while civil society groups in the United States are treated as

The international press cover an emergency summit of the Organization of the Islamic Conference (OIC) called to discuss the Iraqi crisis in March 2003.

AP Images

democracy-building organizations.[21] In addition, these groups—using the media and other sources—send out large quantities of information on political, social, and economic issues to the public and elites.

## Political Parties

Political parties normally play an important role in political socialization. In democratic systems, political parties attempt to mold issue preferences, arouse the apathetic, and find new issues to mobilize support. Party representatives provide the public with a steady flow of information on the political issues of the day. Party organizations regularly contact voters by mail or phone, and in many nations party activists visit voters at home. In addition, every few years there is an election in which parties present their accomplishments and discuss the nation's political future. Elections can serve as national civics lessons, and the political parties are the teachers.

In competitive democratic party systems, partisan socialization can be also a divisive force. In their efforts to gain support, party leaders may appeal to class, language, religion, and ethnic divisions and make citizens more aware of these differences. The Labour and Conservative parties in Britain, for example, use traditional symbols of class to attract supporters. Similarly, the Congress Party in India tries to develop a national program and appeal, but other parties emphasize the ethnic and religious divisions. Leaders of preindustrial nations often oppose competitive parties because they fear such divisiveness. Although this is sometimes a sincere concern, it is also self-serving to government leaders, and is increasingly difficult to justify against contemporary demands for multiparty systems.

Authoritarian governments often use a single party to inculcate common attitudes of national unity, support for the government, and ideological agreement. The combination of a single party and controlled mass media is potent: the media present a single point of view, and the party activities reinforce that perspective by directly involving the citizen. In a closed environment, single-party governments can be potent agents of socialization.

## Mass Media

The mass media—newspapers, radio, television, magazines—are important in socializing attitudes and values in nations around the globe. The mass media are typically the prime source of information on the politics of the day. There is virtually no place so remote that people lack the means to be informed about events elsewhere: in affluent nations the public is wired to the Internet, satellite dishes sprout from houses in Iran, inexpensive transistor radios are omnipresent even in Third World villages far removed from urban centers.

There is one thing most people in the world share in common: we sit before our televisions to learn about the world.[22] Television can have a powerful cognitive and emotional impact on large public audiences by enlisting the senses of both sight and sound. Watching events on television—such as the broadcasts of government affairs or the war in Iraq—gives a reality to the news. Seeing the world directly can shape political attitudes. Today, the Internet provides another powerful source of news for those with access to it.

Access to information thus becomes an important political commodity in the contemporary world. Western democracies put a premium on freedom of the media, even if they frequently complain about what the media reports. In many European nations, the government still manages television and radio stations because it views the media as a public service. Autocratic governments typically seek to control the media and what they can report, as well as the public's access to information (see Box 3.3). Similarly, the communist regimes of Eastern Europe had tried to limit access to news reports from the West because they feared it would undermine their regimes, and the movements for democracy in the region were partially created by the image of the way of life in the West. In the contemporary world of Internet and satellite broadcasting, it is becoming increasingly difficult for governments to control the spread of information.

## Direct Contact with the Government

In modern societies, the wide scope of governmental activities brings citizens into frequent contact with various bureaucratic agencies. One survey of Americans found that about a third had had contact with a government official (federal, state, or local) in the preceding year.[23] Citizens contacted a wide range of government offices, from federal officials, to state and local governments, to school boards and the police. In addition, the government touches our lives in a myriad of other ways, from running the public schools to providing retirement

## The Great Firewall of China

**BOX 3.3**

The People's Republic of China currently has the largest number of Internet users of any nation in the world, except the United States, and this fact has government officials worried. Chinese "netizens" find themselves surfing in the shadow of the world's most sophisticated censorship machine. There is now an estimated 30,000-strong Internet police force, which—with the aid of Western-provided technology—is dedicated to monitoring websites and e-mails. On a technical level, the five gateways that connect China to the global Internet filter traffic coming into and going out of the country. Keyword blocking technology—much of it provided by U.S. companies such as Microsoft and Google—prevents access to offending sites. Even the country's 110,000 Internet cafes are now highly regulated and state-licensed, and all are equipped with standard surveillance systems.

Source: Richard Taylor, "The Great Firewall of China," *BBC News*, January 6, 2006.

checks to providing social services. The degree of government intervention in daily life, and hence the necessity for contacts with government, varies greatly across nations as a function of their political system and the role of government in the society.

These personal experiences are powerful agents of socialization, strengthening or undercutting the images presented by other agents. Does the government send retirement checks on time? Do city officials respond to citizen complaints? Are the schools teaching children? Do unemployment offices help people find jobs? Are the highways well maintained? These are very direct sources of information on how well the government functions. No matter how positive the view of the political system that people have learned as children, citizens who face a different reality in everyday life are likely to change their early-learned views. Indeed, the contradictions between ideology and reality proved to be one of the weaknesses of the communist systems in Eastern Europe.

In summary, the country chapters in this book all examine the patterns of political socialization for several reasons. The sources of political socialization often determine the content of what is learned about politics. If people learn about new events from their friends at church, they may hear different information than people who rely on their workplace or the television for information. The role of these different socialization agents and the content of their political messages also vary systematically across nations. In addition, the ability of a nation to recreate its political culture in succeeding generations is an important factor in perpetuating the political system. Finally, cultures change when new elements are added to the process of political learning.

Thus, socialization provides the feedback mechanism that enables a political culture to endure or change.

## TRENDS SHAPING CONTEMPORARY POLITICAL CULTURES

A political culture exists uniquely in its own time and place. Citizens' attitudes and beliefs are shaped by personal experiences and by the agents of political socialization. Yet, in any historical period there may be trends that change the culture in many nations. The major social trends of our time reflect both general societal developments and specific historic events.

For the past two decades, a major new development is the trend toward democracy in Eastern Europe, East Asia, and other parts of the developing world. This **democratization** trend reflects long-term responses to modernity as well as immediate reactions to current events. Modernization gradually eroded the legitimacy of nondemocratic ideologies, while the development of citizens' skills and political resources made their claim to equal participation in policymaking (at least indirectly) more plausible. Thus, many studies of political culture in Eastern Europe and the former Soviet Union uncovered surprising support for democratic norms and processes among the citizenry as the new democratic system formed.[24]

Ironically, as democracy has begun taking root in Eastern Europe, citizens in many Western democracies are increasingly skeptical about politicians and political institutions. In 1964, three-quarters of Americans said they trusted the government; today only a third of the public say as much—and the malaise is spreading to

Western Europe and Japan.[25] At the same time, public support for democratic norms and values has strengthened over time in most Western democracies. Thus, these publics are critical of politicians and political parties when they fall short of these democratic ideals. Although this cynicism is a strain on democratic politicians, it presses democracy to continue to improve and adapt, which is ultimately democracy's greatest strength.

Another recent major trend affecting political cultures is a shift toward **marketization**—that is, an increased public acceptance of free markets and private profit incentives, rather than a government-managed economy. One example of this movement appeared in the United States and many Western European nations beginning in the 1980s, where economies had experienced serious problems of inefficiency and economic stagnation. Margaret Thatcher in Britain and Ronald Reagan in the United States rode to power on waves of public support for reducing the scale of government. Public opinion surveys show that people in these nations felt that government had grown too large (see again Figure 3.3).

Just as Western Europeans began to question the government's role in the economy, the political changes in Eastern Europe and the Soviet Union transformed the discussion. The command economies of Eastern Europe were almost exclusively controlled by state corporations and government agencies. The government set both wages and prices and directed the economy. The collapse of these systems raised new questions about public support for marketization. Public opinion surveys generally find that Eastern Europeans support a capitalist market system and the public policies that would support such an economic system.[26]

**Globalization** is another trend affecting political cultures of many nations. Increasing international trade and international interactions tend to diffuse the values of the overall international system. Thus, as developing nations become more engaged in the global economy and global international system, the development of certain norms—such as human rights, gender equality, and democratic values—increases.[27] People in developing nations also learn about the broader opportunities existing in other nations, which can spur cultural change as well as economic change. Thus, although globalization has been a deeply divisive political issue for the past decade in many nations, the Pew Global Values Survey found broad support for globalization among citizens worldwide—especially in developing nations where it is seen as improving living standards and life chances.[28]

Clearly, political culture is not a static phenomenon, so our understanding of political culture must be dynamic. It must encompass how the agents of political socialization communicate and interpret historic events and traditional values. It must juxtapose these factors with the exposure of citizens and leaders to new experiences and new ideas. But it is important to understand the political culture of a nation, because these cultural factors influence how citizens act, how the political process functions, and what policy goals the government pursues.

## REVIEW QUESTIONS

- What are the three key elements of a political culture?
- Why does political culture matter?
- Why is the process of political socialization important?
- What are the main agents of political socialization?
- What are the major trends in cultural change in the contemporary world?

## KEY TERMS

| | | | |
|---|---|---|---|
| agents of political socialization | globalization | parochials | political socialization |
| democratization | legitimacy | participants | political subcultures |
| fundamentalism | marketization | political culture | subjects |
| | modernization | | |

## SUGGESTED READINGS

Almond, Gabriel A., and Sidney Verba. *The Civic Culture.* Princeton, NJ: Princeton University Press, 1963.

———, eds. *The Civic Culture Revisited.* Boston: Little Brown, 1980.

Barnes, Samuel, and Janos Simon, eds. *The Postcommunist Citizen.* Budapest: Erasmus Foundation, 1998.

Bratton, Michael, Robert Mattes, and E. Gyimah-Boadi. *Public Opinion, Democracy, and Market Reform in Africa.* Cambridge: Cambridge University Press, 2004.

Cleary, Matthew, and Susan C. Stokes. *Democracy and the Culture of Skepticism: Political Trust in Argentina and Mexico.* New York: Russell Sage, 2006.

Dalton, Russell. *Democratic Challenges, Democratic Choices: The Erosion of Political Support in Advanced Industrial Democracies.* Oxford: Oxford University Press, 2004.

Harrison, Lawrence, and Samuel P. Huntington, eds. *Culture Matters: How Values Shape Human Progress.* New York: Basic Books, 2000.

Horowitz, Donald. *Ethnic Groups in Conflict.* Berkeley: University of California Press, 2000.

Huntington, Samuel. *The Clash of Civilizations and the Remaking of World Order.* New York: Simon & Schuster, 1996.

Inglehart, Ronald, and Pippa Norris. *Sacred and Secular: Religion and Politics Worldwide.* Cambridge: Cambridge University Press, 2004.

Inglehart, Ronald, and Christian Welzel. *Modernization, Cultural Change, and Democracy: The Human Development Sequence.* New York: Cambridge University Press, 2005.

Inkeles, Alex, and David H. Smith. *Becoming Modern.* Cambridge: Harvard University Press, 1974.

Jennings, M. Kent. "Political Socialization," in Russell Dalton and Hans-Dieter Klingemann, eds. *Oxford Handbook of Political Behavior.* Oxford: Oxford University Press, 2007.

Jennings, M. Kent, and Richard Niemi. *Generations and Politics: A Panel Study of Young Adults and Their Parents.* Princeton, NJ: Princeton University Press, 1981.

Klingemann, Hans Dieter, Dieter Fuchs, and Jan Zielonka, eds. *Democracy and Political Culture in Eastern Europe.* London: Routledge, 2006.

Norris, Pippa, ed. *Critical Citizens: Global Support for Democratic Government.* Oxford: Oxford University Press, 1999.

Norris, Pippa, and Ronald Inglehart. *Rising Tide: Gender Equality and Cultural Change Around the World.* New York: Cambridge University Press, 2003.

Pharr, Susan, and Robert Putnam. *Disaffected Democracies: What's Troubling the Trilateral Democracies?* Princeton, NJ: Princeton University Press, 2000.

Putnam, Robert. *The Beliefs of Politicians.* New Haven, CT: Yale University Press, 1973.

———. *Making Democracy Work: Civic Traditions in Modern Italy.* Princeton, NJ: Princeton University Press, 1993.

Pye, Lucian W., and Sidney Verba, eds. *Political Culture and Political Development.* Princeton, NJ: Princeton University Press, 1965.

Rochon, Thomas. *Culture Moves: Ideas, Activism, and Changing Values.* Princeton, NJ: Princeton University Press, 1998.

Rose, Richard, Christian Haerpfer, and William Mishler. *Testing the Churchill Hypothesis: Democracy and Its Alternatives in Postcommunist Societies.* Cambridge, UK: Polity/Baltimore: Johns Hopkins University Press, 2000.

## ENDNOTES

1. This concept of legitimacy and its bases in different societies draws on the work of Max Weber. See, for example, Max Weber, *Basic Concepts in Sociology*, trans. H. P. Secher (New York: Citadel Press, 1964), chs. 5–7.

2. These terms were developed in Gabriel A. Almond and Sidney Verba, *The Civic Culture: Political Attitudes and Democracy in Five Nations* (Princeton, NJ: Princeton University Press, 1963).

3. Ronald Inglehart and Christian Welzel, *Modernization, Cultural Change, and Democracy: The Human Development Sequence* (New York: Cambridge University Press, 2005); Pippa Norris, ed., *Critical Citizens: Global Support for Democratic Government* (Oxford: Oxford University Press, 1999).

4. Russell Dalton and Doh Chull Shin, eds., *Citizens, Democracy, and Markets Around the Pacific Rim* (Oxford: Oxford University Press, 2006).

5. Inglehart and Welzel, *Modernization, Cultural Change, and Democracy.*

6. Ronald Inglehart, *Modernization and Postmodernization* (Princeton, NJ: Princeton University Press, 1997), chs. 6–7.

7. Ole Borre and Elinor Scarbrough, eds., *The Scope of Government* (Oxford: Oxford University Press, 1995).

8. Ronald Inglehart, *Culture Shift in Advanced Industrial Societies* (Princeton, NJ: Princeton University Press, 1990).

9. Even within established Western democracies, there are internal differences in the appropriate role of government, the role of the citizen, and the perceived goals of government. See Max Kaase and Ken Newton, *Beliefs in Government* (Oxford: Oxford University Press, 1995).

10. W. Kymlicka and N. Wayne, eds., *Citizenship in Divided Societies* (Oxford: Oxford University Press, 2000); Donald Horowitz, *Ethnic Groups in Conflict* (Berkeley: University of California Press, 2000).

11. Amy Chua, *World on Fire: How Exporting Free Market Democracy Breeds Ethnic Hatred and Global Instability* (New York: Doubleday, 2003).

12. See also Inglehart and Welzel, *Modernization, Cultural Change, and Democracy*.

13. Kendall Baker, Russell Dalton, and Kai Hildebrandt, *Germany Transformed* (Cambridge: Harvard University Press, 1981).

14. Robert Putnam, *Making Democracy Work: Civic Traditions in Modern Italy* (Princeton, NJ: Princeton University Press, 1993); Robert Putnam, *Bowling Alone* (New York: Simon & Schuster, 2000).

15. Samuel P. Huntington, *The Clash of Civilizations and the Remaking of World Order* (New York: Simon & Schuster, 1996); see also Fareed Zakaria, *The Future of Freedom* (New York: Norton, 2003).

16. See Almond and Verba, *Civic Culture*, ch. 12; M. Kent Jennings, Klaus R. Allerbeck, and Leopold Rosenmayr, "Generations and Families," in Samuel H. Barnes, Max Kaase, et al., *Political Action* (Beverly Hills, CA: Sage, 1979), chs. 15–16.

17. Pippa Norris and Ronald Inglehart, *Rising Tide: Gender Equality and Cultural Change Around the World* (New York: Cambridge University Press, 2003).

18. Martha Nussbaum and Jonathan Glover, eds., *Women, Culture, and Development* (New York: Oxford University Press, 1995).

19. For example, see Sidney Verba, Norman H. Nie, and Jae-on Kim, *Participation and Political Equality* (New York: Cambridge University Press, 1978); Barnes, Kaase, et al., *Political Action*, ch. 4.

20. See Martin Marty and Scott Appleby, *Fundamentalism Observed* (Chicago: University of Chicago Press, 1991).

21. Robert Putnam, ed., *Democracies in Flux* (Oxford: Oxford University Press, 2002).

22. The Pew Global Attitudes Project found that over two-thirds of the public in most nations cited television as their main source of political information. Only in poor African nations did this statistic fall below 50 percent, and in these nations the radio provided an alternative. Pew Global Attitudes Project, *What the World Thinks in 2002* (Washington, DC: Pew Global Attitudes Project, 2002) (http://pewglobal.org/).

23. Sidney Verba et al., *The American Participation Study 1990* (Ann Arbor: Interuniversity Consortium for Political and Social Research, University of Michigan).

24. Arthur Miller, William Reisinger, and Vicki Hesli, eds., *Public Opinion and Regime Change* (Boulder, CO: Westview Press, 1993); William Mishler and Richard Rose, "Trajectories of Fear and Hope: Support for Democracy in Post-communist Europe," *Comparative Political Studies* 28 (1995): 553–81. Compare to Robert Rohrschneider, "Institutional Learning Versus Value Diffusion," *Journal of Politics* 58 (1996): 442–66.

25. Norris, *Critical Citizens*; Russell Dalton, *Democratic Challenges, Democratic Choices*.

26. See William Zimmerman, *The Russian People and Foreign Policy: Russian Elite and Mass Perspectives* (Princeton: Princeton University Press, 2002), ch. 2; Raymond Duch, "Tolerating Economic Reform," *American Political Science Review* 87 (1993): 590–608. Russian support for marketization noticeably lags behind that of most Eastern Europeans.

27. Wayne Sandholtz and Mark Gray, "International Integration and National Corruption," *International Organization* 57 (Autumn 2003): 761–800; Mark Gray, Miki Kittilson, and Wayne Sandholtz, "Women and Globalization: A Study of 180 Countries, 1975–2000," *International Organization* 60 (Spring 2006): 293–333.

28. Pew Global Attitudes Project, *Views of a Changing World, June 2003* (Washington, DC: Pew Global Attitudes Project, 2003): 71–81 (http://pewglobal.org/reports/display.php?ReportID=185).

# INTEREST ARTICULATION

Every political system has some way for people and social groups to express their needs and demands to the government. This process, known as **interest articulation,** can take many forms. For example, a person might contact a city council member, or in a more traditional system she might meet with the village head or tribal chieftain. Or, a group of people might work together on a common concern. In large, established political systems, formal interest groups are a primary means of promoting political interests.

As societies have become internally more complex and the scope of government activity has widened, the quantity and variety of methods to articulate public interests have grown proportionately. People work together to address local and national needs, ranging from providing clean water in a village to passing national clean water standards. Social movements involve the public in issues as diverse as protecting the rights of indigenous people in the Amazon to debating nuclear power. Formal, institutionalized interest groups develop to represent labor, farmers, businesses, and other social interests. Interest groups, in large numbers, work in capitals like London, Washington, D.C., and Tokyo. Some of these headquarter buildings are as imposing as those housing major governmental agencies. Today, Internet chatrooms and blogging provide another forum for expression. In countries with powerful local governments, interest groups are active at the provincial or local level as well.

This chapter considers the multiple ways that people can express their interests in contemporary political systems. First we discuss the means of interest articulation that are available to individual citizens. Then we describe how formal interest groups and associations provide another means of interest articulation. For example, in most countries that allow them, labor unions, manufacturers' associations, farm groups, and associations of doctors, lawyers, engineers, and teachers represent these interests. In the end, most political systems rely on many different forms of interest articulation to determine what the public and social groups want from their government.

## CITIZEN ACTION

One aspect of interest articulation involves what you might do as an individual citizen. Suppose an unjust or unfair law was being passed by the government—what could you do to express your dissatisfaction and try to stop the legislation? Or suppose you see a need that the government is not addressing—what could you do to encourage government action? These are the questions that often face us as citizens—what choices do we have for making our interests and needs known to policymakers?

Individual citizens can use various methods to make requests and demands for policies (Table 4.1).[1] Each of these forms of citizen action has different characteristics, as described in the table. The most common form of citizen participation is voting in an election. When elections are free and meaningful, they enable people to express their interests and to make a collective choice about the government's past progress

| | | TABLE 4.1 |
|---|---|---|
| **Forms of Citizen Interest Articulation** | | |
| **Form** | **Scope of Interests** | **Degree of Pressure on Elites** |
| Voting, participation in elections | Broad, collective decision on government leaders and their programs | Modest pressure, but not policy focused |
| Informal group | Collective action focused on a common interest | High pressure |
| Direct contact on personal matter | Normally deals with specific, personal problem | Low pressure |
| Direct contact on policy issue | Action on a government policy | Modest pressure |
| Protest activity | Highly expressive support for specific interests | High pressure |
| Political consumerism | Focused on specific issues, activities | High pressure |

and the future policies for the nation. Although elections select political elites, they often are a blunt policy tool because they involve many different issues, and between elections officeholders may stray from the voters' preferences.

People can also work with others in their community to address common needs, as when parents work to better the local schools or residents express their worries about how the community is developing. These activities are typically very policy focused and exert direct pressure on decisionmakers. Such group activity exists in both democratic and authoritarian systems, although nondemocracies may limit the methods of expression to ones that do not openly confront authorities.

Some interest articulation involves direct contact with government, such as writing a letter to an elected official or to a government bureaucracy (see Box 4.1, page 63). Some direct contact involves personal issues, such as when a veteran writes to his legislator for help in getting benefits approved, or when a homeowner asks the local party precinct leader to get her driveway snow-plowed regularly. These forms of personal contact are universal across political systems, including the authoritarian ones. Other direct contact involves broader political issues facing the government, such as campaigns to support or block new legislation. Direct contact on policy issues occurs primarily in democratic systems, where citizen input is broadly encouraged. However, even in autocratic nations the public often finds ways to petition the government on policy matters.[2]

The expression of interests also may involve **protests** or other forms of contentious action. The spontaneous gathering of outraged ghetto dwellers,

the public protests that overthrew the communist governments of Eastern Europe, and the environmental protests of Greenpeace are all examples of how protest articulates policy interests. Protests and other direct actions tend to be high-pressure activities that can both mobilize the public and directly pressure elites; these activities can also be very focused in their policy content.

Recent participation studies found that political consumerism—buying or boycotting a product for political reasons—is another active form of participation, at least in Western democracies.[3] Such participation allows individuals to protest the activities of a firm that pollutes or has unfair labor practices. Several boycotts of American and Western products have been organized in Arab nations to protest Western policies toward the region. Such efforts are very focused. If they become politically visible, they can have broader policy effects as well.

In summary, people can take many routes to express their interests, and each of these routes has particular characteristics associated with it.

## HOW CITIZENS PARTICIPATE

The amount of citizen political participation varies widely according to the type of activity and the type of political system. Table 4.2 shows examples of the types of citizen participation in several of the nations examined in this book.

The most frequent forms of political participation revolve around elections: turning out to vote, trying to convince others how to vote, or working with political

| | **TABLE 4.2** |
|---|---|
| **Citizen Participation Across Nations (percentage)** | |

| Type of Participation | United States | Britain | France | Germany | Japan | Russia | Mexico | Brazil | China | Iran | Nigeria |
|---|---|---|---|---|---|---|---|---|---|---|---|
| Voter turnout in most recent national elections | 54% | 61% | 60% | 78% | 68% | 56% | 59% | 78% | — | 60% | 49% |
| Discussed politics with others | 74 | 46 | 65 | 84 | 64 | 75 | 58 | 58 | 70 | 69 | 74 |
| Participated in political party activity | 18 | 3 | 2 | 3 | 4 | 1 | 5 | — | 10 | — | — |
| Participated in citizen interest group | 36 | 7 | 6 | 7 | 9 | 2 | 11 | — | 3 | — | — |
| Signed a petition | 81 | 81 | 68 | 52 | 63 | 12 | 19 | 47 | — | — | 7 |
| Participated in lawful protest demonstration | 21 | 13 | 39 | 28 | 13 | 24 | 4 | 25 | — | — | 17 |

Sources: Election turnout data is percent of registered public for most recent national legislative election from the International Institute for Elections and Democracy, downloaded from www. idea.org; 2000–2002 *World Values Survey* and the 1999 *European Values Survey* for other statistics. Some of the participation questions were not asked in each survey, and these missing items are noted by a dash in the table.

parties. Because elections are the most common form of public involvement in the political process, they are important forms of interest articulation. During elections, citizens speak their minds on current issues by engaging in conversations, attending meetings, contributing to campaigns, and even expressing their opinions to pollsters. Ultimately, individuals decide their preferences in their ballot choices. At the same time, however, elections perform many other functions: aggregating political interests, recruiting political elites, and even socializing political values and preferences through the campaign process (see Chapter 2).

Among the democracies, the United States stands out for its rather low levels of national voting participation: both West Europeans (with their long democratic experience) and Russians (who are new to democratic elections) vote more frequently than Americans. However, as the table shows, Americans' low level of election turnout does not simply reflect apathy. Americans are much more likely than the British to try to discuss politics with others, and Americans are much more likely to work for a party or candidate than either the British or Germans.

Public efforts to express political interests and influence public policy extend beyond elections. Grassroots politics—people working together to address a common problem—is a very direct method for articulating political interests and attempting to

influence policy. Alexis de Tocqueville considered such grassroots community action as the foundation of democracy in America. Today, such activities are often identified with middle-class participation in affluent societies—such as parent-teacher association groups, community associations, and public interest groups—but group activity occurs in almost any nation.[4] Indian villagers working together to build a communal latrine or to develop rural electricity and indigenous people protecting their land rights are other examples of community action.

Table 4.2 indicates that group action is frequent in the advanced industrial democracies. Nearly a third of Americans are members of a citizen interest group, and significant numbers are active in Europe as well.[5] Such activity is high in Mexico, perhaps because this survey overlaps with the politicization of Vicente Fox's election in 2000. However, surveys from the developing world suggest that these activities are regularly used, albeit less frequently than in more developed nations.

Perhaps the most expressive and visible form of citizen action involves participation in protests, demonstrations, or other direct actions (see Box 4.2). For instance, many environmentalists believe that direct actions—hanging an environmental banner from a polluting smokestack, staging a mass demonstration outside of parliament, or boycotting

## The *Shangfang* System

BOX 4.1

In 1949, the communist government in China created the *Shangfang* system that allows individuals to formally petition the government to intervene on their behalf. This system was intended as a safety valve to allow disgruntled individuals to express their grievances, and as a method for the state to mobilize expression of support from the populace. The petitioners typically are concerned about personal problems or local issues, and this system allows them to bypass unresponsive local officials and petition Beijing.

Sometimes they even travel to the capital to present their petition in person. The use of Shangfang has ebbed and flowed over time, but it illustrates how even authoritarian governments seek input from their citizens. In 2004, the government's petition office received more than 10 million petitions, ranging from a complaint over an eviction notice to protests about the effects of the Three Gorges Dam. However, only a miniscule fraction of these petitions receive a government response.

Source: Kevin O'Brien. (See "Rightful Resistance," *World Politics* 49 (1996): 31–55.

polluters—effectively generate media attention and public interest in their cause. Political protests arise for quite different reasons. On the one hand, protest and direct action is often used by individuals and groups that feel they lack access to legitimate political channels. The mass demonstrations in Eastern Europe in the late 1980s and the public rallies and marches of black South Africans against apartheid illustrate protests as the last resort of the disadvantaged. On the other hand, peaceful protests are also increasingly used by the young and better-educated citizens in Western democracies. To many democratic citizens, protest is the continuation of "normal" politics by other means.

A majority in most nations have signed a petition, a form of political action that has become so common that it no longer can be described as unconventional (see again Table 4.2). Roughly a fifth of Americans and Germans have at some time participated in a legal demonstration. Many different sectors of society now use protests and direct action.[6] The French have more protest involvement than most other established democracies, with nearly two-fifths of the population reporting participation at some point. These numbers reflect both French traditions of popular protest and the difficulties citizens often find in getting the attention of government. The Russian patterns are also striking. In 1990, only 4 percent of Russians reported participating in a protest, reflecting the communist government's repression of such activities. A decade later, nearly a quarter of Russians said they had participated in a legal demonstration—they are learning to express their grievances in a more democratic setting.

The table also indicates that protest activities are less frequent in developing societies, such as Mexico and Nigeria.

Citizen participation thus reflects the way that people use the opportunities existing within a political system. In nations with active political parties and competitive elections, many people participate in the electoral process. In nations where such activities are limited, people may turn to group-based activity or protest in order to express their preferences, but it is more likely that they are politically inactive. As we noted in Chapter 3, a participatory political culture—of all forms—is a by-product of political modernization.

Cross-national research shows that better educated and higher social status individuals are more likely to use the various opportunities for participation. These individuals tend to develop attitudes that encourage participation, such as feelings of efficacy and a sense of civic duty.[7] They also possess the personal resources and skills that are useful in becoming politically active when duty calls or a need arises. Skill and confidence are especially important for demanding activities, such as organizing new groups or becoming a leader in an organization. This inequality in participation is less for easier activities, such as voting. The tendency for the better-off to be politically active is more evident in societies (such as the United States) with weak party organizations, weak working-class groups (such as labor unions), and less party attention to lower class interests. In nations with stronger working-class parties and labor unions, organizational networks encourage the participation of less affluent citizens.

Participation patterns are important for several reasons. For citizens to influence government policy, they first need to articulate their interests to the government. A wider choice of activities presumably increases the citizens' ability to express their interests and be heard. Moreover, the forms of action differ in their policy content and political pressure (see again Table 4.1). Finally, individuals differ in their level of political activities and the types of activities that they use. These differences in voice are likely reflected in policy outputs if the government responds to public pressures. In other words, those who are more active in articulating their interests are more likely to have their interests addressed by policymakers.

## INTEREST GROUPS

Interest articulation can also occur through the actions of social or political groups that represent a set of people. Some groups are poorly organized and unfocused, and often short-lived. Other groups have a permanent organizational base, often with professional staffs to provide expertise and representation. In addition, interest groups often participate in the political process, serving on government advisory bodies and testifying at parliamentary hearings. Interest groups vary in structure, style, financing, and support base, and these differences may influence a nation's politics, its economics, and its social life. We begin by defining four types of interest groups: anomic, nonassociational, institutional, and associational.

### Anomic Groups

**Anomic groups** are spontaneous groups that suddenly form when many individuals react to an event that stimulates frustration, disappointment, or other strong emotions. They are flash affairs, rising and subsiding suddenly. Without previous organization or planning, frustrated individuals may suddenly take to the streets to vent their anger as news of a government action touches deep emotions or as a rumor of new injustice sweeps the community. Their actions may lead to violence, although not necessarily. Particularly where organized groups are absent or where they have failed to get adequate political representation, smoldering discontent may be sparked by an incident or by the emergence of a leader. It may then suddenly explode in relatively unpredictable and uncontrollable ways.

Some political systems, including both developed and developing nations, report a rather high frequency of violent and spontaneous anomic behavior.[8] This behavior often involves spontaneous public demonstrations or acts of violence, rather than the planned and orchestrated protests of institutionalized political groups. Other countries are notable for the infrequency of such disturbances, which may reflect either the limited opportunities for action or the nation's political culture.

In France, for example, protests have become part of the tradition of politics (see again Table 4.2). In the late 1960s, the French government nearly collapsed as a result of protests that began when university students stimulated a mass protest against the government. In 2006, another wave of mass protests nearly brought the economy to a standstill and forced the government to withdraw unpopular labor regulations. In a typical year, Paris might experience protests by students, shopkeepers, farmers, homemakers, government employees, environmentalists, women's groups, and a host of other interest groups. Protest is almost a national political sport in France.

Anger over the assassination of a popular political leader or other catastrophic event can also stimulate a public outburst. For instance, one commonly sees relatively spontaneous public demonstrations when one nation makes a hostile action toward another nation. Wildcat strikes (spontaneous strike actions by local workers, not organized actions by national unions), long a feature of the British trade union scene, also occur frequently in such European countries as France, Italy, and Sweden.

Sometimes anomic groups are a subset of individuals drawn from a larger social grouping, such as a racial or an ethnic group. For instance, in 1992 there was rioting and looting by some residents in minority neighborhoods of Los Angeles following the acquittal of police officers accused of excessive violence in the beating of an African-American suspect. Similarly, in 1992, riots broke out in Algeria when some Muslim fundamentalists protested the government's invalidation of the recent election. We treat these as anomic group actions because there is no structure or planning to the event, and the people involved disperse after the protest ends.

We must be cautious, however, about calling something an anomic political behavior when it really

## Attacks on Globalization

BOX 4.2

In July 2001 tens of thousands of protestors arrived in Genoa to demonstrate at the G8 Summit Meeting. Hundreds of different groups came to protest at the meetings, and several of the more radical groups engaged in running battles with the police. Many of the most violent clashes involved what became known as the "Black Block." The Block was comprised of several loosely organized anarchist and radical groups, wearing trademark black clothing, black hoods, and gas masks. Confrontations with police often appeared choreographed in advance, coordinated by cell phones, and videotaped by sympathetic activists—and subsequently distributed on the Internet. Many other protest groups in Genoa were worried that the radical anarchist goals of the Block detracted attention from their policy concerns about the economic and social impacts of globalization. After two days of violent clashes, the summit ended. Damage ran into the tens of millions of dollars, 200 protestors were arrested, and one protestor was shot in a clash with police. In the end, the violence in the streets overshadowed both the elected politicians at the summit and the policy goals of the nonviolent groups in Genoa.

Source: BBC World News.

is the result of detailed planning by organized groups. For instance, the demonstrations against the World Trade Organization in Seattle in 1999 and Genoa in 2001 owed much to indignation but little to spontaneity (see Box 4.2).

### Nonassociational Groups

Like anomic groups, **nonassociational groups** rarely are well organized, and their activity is episodic. They differ from anomic groups because they are based on common interests and identities of ethnicity, region, religion, occupation, or perhaps kinship. Because of these economic or cultural ties, nonassociational groups have more continuity than anomic groups. Subgroups within a large nonassociational group (such as an ethnic minority or workers) may act as an anomic group, as in the 1992 Los Angeles riots, the 2005 Paris riots, and the Middle East protests against the Danish cartoons of Mohammed in 2006. Throughout the world, ethnicity and religion, like occupation, are powerful identities that can stimulate collective activity.

Two kinds of nonassociational groups are especially interesting. One is a large group that is not formally organized, although its members may perceive common interests. Many ethnic, regional, and occupational groups fit into this category. The members share a common interest or need, but there is no formal group to represent their interests.

It can be very difficult to organize such groups because although members share a common problem, none of them will undertake the effort to organize other members. This is commonly known as the **collective action problem.**[9] Moreover, if large collective benefits—for example, ending discriminatory legislation or cleaning up water pollution—are achieved, they will be shared even by those who did not work, the so-called free riders. This pattern of people waiting for the rewards without sharing the cost or risk of action affects other types of groups as well. For instance, students who might benefit from lower tuition fees are typically underrepresented because there is no organization to articulate their interests. Understanding the collective action problem helps us to see why some groups (including governments and revolutionary challengers) become organized and others do not, and under what circumstances the barriers to collective action are overcome.

A second type of nonassociational group is the small village, an economic or ethnic subgroup whose members know each other personally. A small, face-to-face group has some important advantages and may be highly effective in some political situations. If its members are well connected or its goals unpopular or illegal, the group may remain informal or even inconspicuous. Such groups may undertake various actions, such as engaging in work stoppages, circulating student petitions to demand better support and training, requesting that a bureaucrat continue a grain tariff to benefit landowners, or asking a tax collector for favored treatment to benefit relatives. As the last example suggests, personal interest articulation may

The British Society of Civil Servants, a well-organized and unusually effective associational interest group, assembles for an orderly meeting in a London hall to plan a 24-hour work stoppage.

Les Wilson/Photri

often have more legitimacy and perpetuate itself by invoking group or personal ties.

## Institutional Groups

**Institutional groups** are formal and have other political or social functions in addition to interest articulation. Political parties, business corporations, legislatures, armies, bureaucracies, and churches often have separate  political groups with special responsibility for representing a group's interests. Either as corporate bodies or as smaller groups within these bodies (legislative blocs, officer cliques, groups in the clergy, or ideological cliques in bureaucracies), such groups typically express the interests of their members. The influence of institutional interest groups is usually drawn from the strength of their primary organizational base—for instance, the size of their membership or their income. A group based on a governmental institution has direct access to policymakers.

In industrial democracies, bureaucratic and corporate interests use their resources and special information to affect policy. In the United States, for instance, the military industrial complex consists of the combination of the U.S. Department of Defense and defense industries that support military expenditures. Similarly, the farm lobby and the U.S. Department

of Agriculture often advocate agricultural policies. Political parties are among the most active institutional participants in the policy process of most democracies. And as in most societies, government bureaucracies do not simply react to pressures from the outside, they also can act as independent forces of interest representation.

Nonpolitical institutional groups can also participate in the political process. In Italy, for example, the Roman Catholic Church has exerted significant influence on the government. In electoral politics, the Church used to ask Catholics to vote against the Communists. Less overtly, the Church has members of the clergy call on officeholders to express opinions on matters of concern to the Church. In Islamic countries, fundamentalist clergy pursue a similar role, prescribing what morals public policy should follow, actively lobbying governmental officials, and sometimes participating in the governing process.

In authoritarian regimes, which prohibit or at least control explicit political groups, institutional groups can still play a large role. Educational officials, party officials, jurists, factory managers, officers in the military services, and government bodies representing other social units had significant roles in interest articulation in communist regimes.[10] In preindustrial societies, which usually have fewer associational groups and with limited popular support, military groups, corporations, party factions, and bureaucrats often play prominent political roles. Even where the military does not seize power directly, the possibility of such action often forces close government attention to military requests.

## Associational Groups

**Associational groups** are formed explicitly to represent the interests of a particular group, such as trade unions, chambers of commerce, manufacturers' associations, and ethnic associations. These organizations have procedures for formulating interests and demands, and they usually employ a full-time professional staff. Associational groups are often very active in representing the interests of their members in the policy process. For instance, in recurring debates about health care in the United States there is an enormous mobilization of pressure groups and lobbyists—from representatives of doctors and health insurance organizations to consumer groups and the like—seeking to influence legislation.

Associational interest groups—where they are allowed to flourish—affect the development of other types of groups. Their organizational base gives them an advantage over nonassociational groups, and their tactics and goals are often recognized as legitimate in society. Labor unions, for example, are often central political actors because they represent the mass of the working class; in the same way, business associations often speak for the corporate interests of the nation.

A special subset of associational groups consists of citizens who are united not by a common economic or individual self-interest but by a common belief in a political ideology or a policy goal.[11] The environmental movement, many women's groups, and other civic groups are examples of this kind of associational group. In some of these issue groups, the members may seldom interact directly and not even share common social characteristics (such as employment or ethnicity), but are bound together by their support of a political organization, such as Greenpeace or Amnesty International. On the organizational side, many of these new social groups have fluid and dynamic organizations, with frequent turnover in both leadership and membership. On the tactical side, they use a wide range of approaches, often discounting

the value of partisan campaigning and conventional lobbying in favor of unconventional protests and direct actions.

Civic associations represent another way for citizens to articulate their policy goals by supporting groups that advocate their preferred policy positions. Such groups have proliferated in most advanced industrial democracies in the past generation, and they are now spreading to the developing world.

In summary, a social interest can manifest itself in many different groups. We can illustrate this point with examples of different groups that might involve members of the working class:

*Anomic group:* a spontaneous group of working-class individuals living in the same neighborhood

*Nonassociational group:* the working class as a collective

*Institutional group:* the labor department within the government

*Associational group:* a labor union

Distinguishing among the types of groups is important for several reasons. The nature of a group typically reflects the resources it can mobilize to support its political efforts. Perhaps one of the most important resources is an institutional structure that will sustain political efforts until the government responds to the group's interests. The nature of a group also may signify the tactics it uses to gain political access (see Table 4.3, page 75). Finally, since the articulation of interest is the first step in policy influence, the nature of groups suggests what types of interests are more likely to get a hearing in the political system and which interests may be underrepresented.

## Civil Society

Political analysts have devoted increasing attention to whether an extensive network of interest groups and public participation in these groups creates a **civil society**—a society in which people are involved in social and political interactions free of state control or regulation. Community groups, voluntary associations, and even religious groups—as well as access to free communication and information through the mass media and the Internet—are important parts

Pakistanis in Karachi, Pakistan, protest publication in Europe of offensive cartoons depicting Muhammed.

Ilyas Dean/The Image Works

of a civil society.[12] Participation in associational and institutional groups can socialize individuals into the political skills and cooperative relations that are part of a well-functioning society. People learn how to organize, express their interests, and work with others to achieve common goals. They also learn the important lesson that the political process itself is as important as the immediate results. Thus, a system of active associational groups can lessen the development of anomic or nonassociational activity. Group activity can help citizens to develop and clarify their own preferences, provide important information about political events, and articulate the interests of citizens more clearly and precisely than parties and elections.[13] Thus, an active public involved in various interest groups provides a fertile ground for the development of democratic politics.

As political and economic conditions become interdependent across nations, there is also increasing attention directed toward the development of a global civil society. Individuals and groups in one nation are connected to groups with similar concerns in other nations, and jointly reinforce their individual efforts.

Environmental groups in the Western democracies, for example, assist environmental groups in developing nations with the expertise and organizational resources to address the issues facing their country. National groups meet at international conferences and policy forums, and the network of social relations, as well as Internet connections, extends across national borders.[14] This is another sign of how the international context of domestic politics is growing worldwide.

One problem facing the nations of Eastern Europe and other newly democratizing nations is building a rich associational group life in societies where the government had suppressed or controlled organized groups.[15] The Communist Party and the government bureaucracy dominated the nations of Eastern Europe for over forty years. The process of building new, independent associational groups to articulate the interests of different citizens is underway and will be important to the democratic process. Similarly, many less economically developed nations need to create a civil society of associational groups to involve citizens in the political process and represent their interests if democratization is to succeed.

# INTEREST GROUP SYSTEMS

The nature of the connection between interest groups and government policymaking institutions is another important feature of the political process. Different types of connections create different interest group systems. All modern societies have large numbers of interest groups, but their relationships with government can follow different models. Interest group systems are classified into three major groupings: pluralist, democratic corporatist, and controlled.[16]

**Pluralist interest group systems** have several features involving both how interests are organized and how they participate in the political process:

- Multiple groups may represent a single societal interest.
- Group membership is voluntary and limited.
- Groups often have a loose or decentralized organizational structure.
- There is a clear separation between interest groups and the government.

For instance, not only are there different groups for different social sectors (such as labor, business, and professional interests), but there may be many multiple labor unions or business associations within each sector. These groups compete among themselves for membership and influence, and all simultaneously press their demands on the government. The United States is the best-known example of a strongly pluralist interest group system; Canada and New Zealand are also cited as examples. Despite its greater labor union membership and somewhat greater coordination of economic associations, Britain tends to fall on the pluralist side in most analyses, as do France and Japan.

Democratic **neo-corporatist interest group systems** are characterized by a much more organized representation of interests:

- A single peak association normally represents each societal interest.
- Membership in the peak association is often compulsory and nearly universal.
- Peak associations are centrally organized and direct the actions of their members.
- Groups are often systematically involved in making and implementing policy.

For instance, in a neo-corporatist system there may be a single peak association that represents all the major industrial interests; a pluralist system may have several different business groups that act autonomously. Equally important, interest groups in these systems often regularly and legitimately work with the government agencies and/or political parties as partners in negotiating solutions to policy problems.

The best-studied democratic neo-corporatist arrangements involve economic problems. Democracies with business and labor peak associations that negotiate with each other and the government have had better records than more pluralist countries in sustaining employment, restraining inflation, and increasing social spending.[17] In addition, there is also evidence that neo-corporatist systems are more effective in implementing other public policies, such as environmental protection.[18]

In many advanced industrial societies, however, membership in labor unions has decreased and some bargaining patterns have become less centralized. Thus, some countries that have relied on neo-corporatist patterns have adapted this system to these new consequences and applied corporatism in new ways.[19] In contrast, several nations in Eastern Europe have attempted to develop more corporatist structures to develop interest group politics, but the system of autonomous interest groups remains underdeveloped. The experience with neo-corporatist models in developing nations is even more varied.[20]

Because different sectors of a society may vary in their organized interest groups and in their government relations, we must be cautious about generalizing too much about interest group systems. Figure 4.1, however, shows the striking differences in organization of the labor movements across many of the nations in this book. Britain, the United States, France, and Japan are examples of more pluralist systems. Less than half the British labor force is unionized, and these unions are not as highly coordinated as those in corporatist countries. The member unions in the British Trades Union Congress have strong traditions of individual autonomy and are themselves relatively decentralized. Moreover, the influence of the labor unions on government policymakers has waned over the past few decades. In the United States and France, the labor movement is somewhat fragmented. These countries also lack a tradition of "social partnership" between government, unions, and employer associations. In the area of labor policy, at

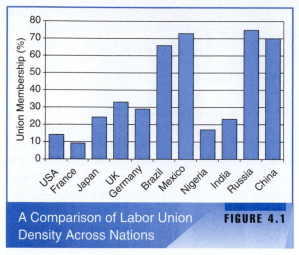

A Comparison of Labor Union Density Across Nations    **FIGURE 4.1**

Source: International Labor Organization, *World Labour Report 1997–1998*, The Statistical Annex, Table 1.2 (www.ilo.org). The figure plots union membership as a percentage of wage earners.

least, these are highly pluralist, not corporatist, interest group systems. However, corporatist-type arrangements among individual industries, trade associations, and governmental bureaucracies (without organized labor involvement) exist in Japan.

Germany is a closer fit to the neo-corporatist model (see Chapter 10). The most thoroughly corporatist interest group systems are in Austria, Finland, the Netherlands, Norway, and Sweden. These nations are characterized by a high level of union membership among the nonagricultural labor force, and a highly centralized and united labor movement. In addition, under the corporatist model interest groups such as labor unions often have special access to government. For instance, German labor unions have formal membership on many government commissions, special access to policy administration, and are very influential through informal channels of influence.

Mexico and Brazil are examples of another form of corporatist politics. Union membership in many Latin American nations is fairly high, and the trade unions and peasant associations are closely tied to political parties or religious interests. Usually, these groups mobilize support for the political parties or social institutions that dominate them, and are closely tied to the state when their party is in power. This system is changing in both Mexico and Brazil, as democratization encourages the unions to become more politically independent and influential (see Chapters 14 and 15).

Nigeria and India illustrate a pattern common in other developing democracies. Interest groups, such as unions, are often not well developed and have a limited mass membership. They are participants in the process, but without the mass membership or formal access that gives labor unions influence in established Western democracies of either the pluralist or corporatist model.

Finally, **controlled interest group systems** follow a different pattern:

- There is a single group for each social sector.
- Membership is often compulsory.
- Each group is normally hierarchically organized.
- Groups are controlled by the government or its agents in order to mobilize support for government policy.

The last point is the most important: Groups exist to facilitate government control of society. The best examples are the traditional communist systems in which the party penetrates all levels of society and controls all the permitted associational groups. For instance, Figure 4.1 shows that 70 percent of wage earners in China belong to a union.[21] Unions and other interest associations are subordinated to the Communist Party, and they are only rarely permitted to articulate the interests of their members. Russia also once followed this communist model, and the unions have large memberships as a result of this experience. Chapter 12 on Russia discusses how the unions are struggling to gain autonomy from the state and play an influential role in the postcommunist system. But they have made limited progress.

These nations limit interest articulation to leaders of institutional groups, who can use their positions in political institutions as a base for expressing their demands. Numerous institutional interest groups can also emerge in these societies, especially from parts of the party and bureaucracy, such as the military, as well as informal nonassociational groups.

## ACCESS TO THE INFLUENTIAL

To be effective, interest groups must be able to reach key policymakers through **channels of political access.** Otherwise, groups may express their members' interests yet fail to have an impact on policymakers.

Political systems vary in the ways they respond to political interests. Interest groups vary in the tactics they use to gain access. Group tactics are partially shaped by the opportunities offered by the structure of policymaking, as well as by their own values and preferences.

There is a significant distinction between legitimate and constitutional channels of access (such as the mass media, parties, and legislatures) and illegitimate, coercive access channels. These two channels reflect the types of resources that groups can use to influence elites as well as the group's perceptions of which tactics will be most successful. Groups with substantial resources—money, members, or status—typically have an easier time working through legitimate constitutional channels. Groups with limited resources or legitimacy may feel they must act through coercive channels because they are not accepted by the political system. In democracies, groups tend toward legitimate channels because the system expects and allows group activity. In contrast, nondemocratic systems typically limit legitimate access, which might stimulate illegitimate or coercive activities.

## Legitimate Access Channels

The legitimate channels of access can take many forms, and these are often seen in both democratic and nondemocratic systems. For instance, personal connections are an important means of reaching political elites in all societies—the use of family, school, local, or other social ties. An excellent example is the information network among the British elite based on old school ties originating at Eton, Harrow, or other "public" schools, or at Oxford and Cambridge universities. Similarly, in Japan many alumni of the University of Tokyo Law School hold top positions among the political and bureaucratic elites who interact because of these personal ties. Although personal connections are commonly used by nonassociational groups representing family or regional interests, they serve other groups as well. Face-to-face contact is one of the most effective means of shaping attitudes and conveying messages. Interests communicated by a friend or neighbor carry much more weight than a formal letter from a stranger. In modern nations, personal connections are usually cultivated with special care. In Washington, D.C., the business of advising interest groups and individuals on access to politicians

is an increasingly lucrative profession (and, increasingly a target of government regulation and potential corruption). These activities are often carried on by former officeholders who use their personal governmental contacts for their lobbyist clients.

The **mass media**—television, radio, newspapers, and magazines—are another important access channel in democratic societies. The mass media and the Internet can mobilize support for interest group efforts, leading to donations of time and money, and encouraging sympathizers to support the group. Many interest groups thus hire skillful public relations specialists, purchase direct advertising, and seek favorable attention in the media. Interest groups encourage media reports on their needs as well as coverage of their views on specific policies. When a cause receives national media attention, the message to policymakers carries added weight if politicians know that millions of voters are interested in the issue. Moreover, groups believe that in an open society, "objective" news coverage has more credibility than sponsored messages. However, multiple conflicting messages and a lack of specific focus can limit the effectiveness of the mass media for many smaller groups.

The potential power of the media could be seen when the communist governments in Eastern Europe loosened control over the media in the late 1980s. This action gave a huge boost to democracy movements. For instance, when asked what caused the democratic revolution in Poland in the 1990s, Lech Walesa pointed to a television and said "that did." Media reports on the failures in communist government policy and the contrasting lifestyles in the West undermined the legitimacy of the regimes. As democratic protests spread across Eastern Europe, stories of successful protests in other parts of the country, or in other countries, enhanced the confidence of demonstrators. Citizen protests encouraged by mass media reports helped convince the ruling groups that their support had vanished.

Political parties are another important access point. Democratic political parties often rely on interest groups for financial and voter support, and act as representatives of these interests within government. In a nation like Germany, the various components of the party organization, particularly parliamentary committees, are important channels for transmitting demands to the cabinet and the party in power. In some cases, other factors limit the role of parties as interest representatives. For instance, highly ideological

## Lobbying Behind the Scenes

British beer companies use a variety of means to support their industry. For example, the industry contributed funds to Labour MPs who recently voted for longer opening hours for British pubs. They also provide travel support for MPs who are favorable to the industry. A group of MPs who support the industry formed the All-Party Parliamentary Beer Group (APBG). The group's announced goal is "to promote the wholesomeness and enjoyment of beer and the unique role of the pub in UK society." The parliamentary group campaigned to have beer taxes reduced, conducted hearings on whether the government overregulates British pubs, and supported the extension of pub hours. The group hosts a series of functions at Westminster, giving industry chiefs the opportunity to meet MPs and showcase their products. The parliamentary group also selects a "beer drinker of the year," who receives an award at their annual dinner. The parliamentary group receives direct financial support from breweries, and the secretary for the group is paid by the alcohol industry.

Visit the APBG website: www.publications.parliament.uk/pa/cm/cmparty/memi140.htm.

parties with a hierarchical structure, such as most communist parties, are more likely to control affiliated interest groups than to communicate the interest groups' demands. Decentralized party organizations, like those in the United States, may be less helpful than individual legislators in providing access.

Legislatures are another common target of interest group activities (see Box 4.3). Standard lobbying tactics include making appearances before legislative committees and providing information to individual legislators. In the United States, political action committees raise campaign contributions for individual members of Congress and usually receive some political attention in exchange. In Britain and France, the strong party discipline in the legislature lessens the importance of individual members of Parliament (MPs) as access channels for interest groups. In contrast, in the United States the combination of loose party discipline and a decentralized legislative system makes the individual members of the Congress major targets of group efforts.

Government bureaucracies are also a major access point in most political systems. Contacts with the bureaucratic agencies may be particularly important where the bureaucracy has policymaking authority or where interests are narrow and directly involve few citizens. A bureaucrat sympathetic to a group may try to respond to its demands without leaving bureaucratic-channels, by exercising administrative discretion. A government official may also give public consideration to an issue or frame an issue in a way that receives a sympathetic hearing by policymakers. The bureaucracy may be an especially important access point in nondemocratic systems because other legitimate channels of citizen access do not exist.

Government officials may consider protest demonstrations, strikes, and other forms of dramatic and direct pressure on government as legitimate or illegitimate tactics, depending on the political system. Protests may be either spontaneous actions of an anomic group or a planned use of unconventional channels by an organized group. In democratic societies, demonstrations often mobilize popular support—or electoral support—or media attention for the group's cause. The mass demonstrations on immigration reform in 2006 are examples of efforts to shape and influence the U.S. public debate on legislation being considered by Congress. On a regular basis, the Mall in Washington, D.C., hosts other groups protesting other policy issues. In nondemocratic societies, such demonstrations are more hazardous and often represent more extreme dissatisfaction that cannot find voice through conventional channels of access.

Lawful protest can be a tactic of society's powerless, those who do not have access or resources to influence policymakers through conventional channels. As a political tactic, protest activity is especially attractive to young people and minority groups, who are not among the elite. Protests are also a favored tactic of groups whose ideological commitments focus on challenging the established social and political order. Yet, protests are increasingly used as a means of interest articulation by organized and accepted interests who feel that dramatic actions can heighten support for their cause. Protests can supplement other channels, especially in gaining the attention of the mass media in an age when television comes to every household. Thus we find doctors in New Delhi, farmers in Japan, and "gray panthers" (the elderly) in Germany using a tactic that once was limited to the poor and minorities.[22]

## Coercive Access Channels and Tactics

Most scholars see the level of collective violence as closely associated with the character of a society and the circumstances in the nation. In his studies of civil strife, Ted Robert Gurr argued that feelings of relative deprivation motivate people to act aggressively. Gurr defined relative deprivation as a "discrepancy between people's expectations about the goods and conditions of life to which they are entitled, on the one hand, and, on the other, their value capabilities—the degree to which they think they can attain these goods and conditions."[23]

Feelings of relative deprivation are a source of frustration, discontent, and anger. The more such discontent and anger persist, the greater the chance of collective violence. People also tend to turn to violence if they believe it is justified and if they believe it will lead to success. If they think that their government is illegitimate and that the cause of their discontent is justified, they will more readily turn to political violence. To this end, it is the responsibility of the government and its institutions to provide peaceful alternatives to violence as a means of change.

This general description of political violence should not overlook the differences among the types of violent political activities. A riot, for example, involves the spontaneous expression of collective anger and dissatisfaction by a group of citizens. Though riots have long been dismissed as aberrant and irrational action by social riffraff, modern studies have shown that rioters vary greatly in their motivation, behavior, and social background.[24] Most riots seem to follow some fairly clear-cut patterns, such as confining destruction or violence to particular areas or targets. Relative deprivation appears to be a major cause of riots, but the release of the frustrations is not as aimless as is often supposed.

Although the 2005 riots in Paris were triggered by the accidental deaths of two teenagers, most analysts see their deaths as only a proximate cause, a "spark" that ignited already volatile factors. Gangs of minority youth burned thousands of automobiles, damaged shops, and attacked police who attempted to quell the violence. The French president and then the Parliament declared a state of emergency in reaction to the violent protests, establishing a curfew and limiting civil liberties. Even though much of the mayhem seemed poorly related to effective political action, it was a cry for attention. Youth from immigrant families had high levels of unemployment and felt that social and economic discrimination was limiting their life chances. Even in a democracy, the government sometimes overlooks the needs of its own citizens and allows such frustrations to explode into violence.

While deprivation may help fuel the discontent, strikes and obstructions are typically carried out by well-organized associational or institutional groups. For instance, violent protests in Seattle and Genoa against the World Trade Organization and globalization involved highly organized activities among some of the more radical groups participating in the protests (see again Box 4.2).

Historically, labor unions used the general strike to pressure the government or employers on fundamental issues. The influence of strikes and obstructions has varied, however, depending on the legitimacy of the government and coercive pressure from other groups. A massive truckers' strike helped bring down the government in Chile in 1972–1973, but student-inspired boycotts in Korea in the 1980s had only a modest impact on the government. Most spectacularly, the strikes, obstructions, and demonstrations in Eastern Europe in 1989 and 1990, like the earlier people's power movement in the Philippines, had massive success against regimes that had lost legitimacy.

Finally, **political terror tactics**—including deliberate assassination, armed attacks on other groups or government officials, and mass bloodshed—are sometimes used by radical groups. The tragedies in Northern Ireland; the suicide bombings by Palestinians in Israel; and the attacks of Jihadist terrorists in New York City, Madrid, London, Bali, and other cities demonstrate the use of such tactics. The use of terrorism typically reflects the desire of some group to change the rules of the political game or to destroy a political system, rather than to gain political access.

The use of political terror is more often likely to produce negative consequences rather than construct

Protesters held a massive demonstration in front of Mexico's electoral court to demand a ballot-by-ballot recount of the disputed 2006 presidential election.

AP Images/Eduardo Verdugo

positive policy change. Massive deadly violence may destroy a democratic regime, leading to curtailment of civil rights or even military intervention when many people and leaders feel that any alternative is preferable to more violence. For example, democratically elected governments justified their suppression of democratic institutions in Peru in 1992 and India in 1975 (see Chapter 17) in response to the violent actions of terrorists. An authoritarian, repressive response often promises quick results against terrorists; however, small-group terrorism usually fails when confronted by united democratic leadership.[25] In a democratic society, violence often forfeits the sympathy that a group needs if its cause is to receive a responsive hearing. The current conflict between the West and jihadist terrorists has renewed the debate on how democratic governments should balance the need for security against the preservation of civil liberties.

## POLICY PERSPECTIVES ON INTEREST ARTICULATION

As we pointed out in Chapter 2, we need to examine the structures performing political functions from both process and policy perspectives. In order to understand the formation of policies, we need to know which groups articulate interests and their policy preferences. Many associational interest groups specialize in certain policy areas. The concerns of other interest groups, such as anomic or institutional groups, may be less easily discerned, but they are equally important for the policy process.

Table 4.3 provides examples of legitimate and coercive interest articulation for different types of interest groups. Each case provides an example of the differences in legitimate access channels, such as informal meetings by Mexican business leaders lobbying their government to Greenpeace testifying before European Parliament committees. Similarly, coercive acts range from spontaneous outbursts by anomic groups to Hamas using terror tactics on the West Bank. This framework also helps us to think about how a single interest group might pursue its goals through multiple channels, including protests, representation by institutional groups, and lobbying by associational groups. For instance, honeybee farmers in the United States have lobbied their representatives in Congress to maintain federal price supports, and they have also used their allies in the U.S. Department of Agriculture to support their position (will honeybee protests be next?). This table presents examples from many nations in order to suggest the varied possibilities that exist in each nation. If we were studying interest articulation patterns in one nation, we could build a table showing the structures, policies, and channels involved during a particular period.

## INTEREST GROUP DEVELOPMENT

One consequence of modernization is a widespread belief that the conditions of life can be altered through human action. Modernization normally involves education, urbanization, rapid growth in public communication, and improvement in the physical conditions of life. These changes are closely related to increases in political awareness, participation, and feelings of

**Process and Policy Perspectives on Interest Articulation**

TABLE 4.3

**Examples of Interest Articulation**

*Channel of Access*

| Types of Interest Groups | Legitimate Channel | Coercive Channel |
|---|---|---|
| Anomic groups | Russian workers strike to protest price increases | Iranians attack Danish embassy to protest cartoons depicting Mohammed |
| Nonassociational groups | Mexican business leaders discuss taxes with president | Minorities in France riot in 2005 over their social conditions |
| Institutional groups | U.S. Department of Agriculture advocates subsidies for honey production | Indonesian army supports democracy movement to overthrow Suharto regime (1997) |
| Associational groups | Greenpeace lobbies the European Parliament to ban genetically modified foods | Palestinian Hamas launches terror attacks on Israel |

political competence. Such participant attitudes encourage more diverse and citizen-based interest articulation.

At the same time, modernization produces an increasing diversity of life conditions and a specialization of labor as people work in many types of jobs—a process that leads to the formation of large numbers of special interests. The interdependence of modern life, the exposure provided by mass communications, and a larger policy role of government further multiply political interests. These interests are organized into different interest groups. Thus, the diversity of interest groups is another by-product of modernization.

Successful democratic development leads to the emergence of complex interest group systems that express the needs of groups and individuals in the society. Yet, this process is by no means automatic. The problems of organizing large groups for collective action are huge. Societies vary widely in the extent to which people engage in associational activity. One factor explaining participation is the level of trust shared among members of the society. Robert Putnam and his colleagues found that an active associational life in Northern Italian communities was associated with widespread trust in others. Furthermore, these qualities of the political culture were related to economic growth and a participant political life.[26] Ronald Inglehart has shown similar continuity in social trust across nations.[27] Alternatively, modernization may weaken traditional structures in some societies,

but then fail to develop effective associational groups in their place because of restrictive social attitudes. A nation's ability to achieve either stability or democracy will be hindered as a result.

In other cases, authoritarian parties and bureaucracies may control associational groups and choke off the channels of political access. Eastern Europe offers a situation in which forty years or more of authoritarian domination suppressed autonomous interest groups. Eventually, the processes of economic modernization pressured these authoritarian systems to allow more open organization and expression of political interests. In addition, social change led to an expansion of interest articulation activity and a need for associational groups to provide regular and organized expression for citizens' interests.

The recent development of organized interest groups in Eastern Europe should not, however, lead us to conclude that every conceivable group now has equal standing. Using the American experience as an example, the articulation of interests is frequently biased toward the goals of the better-off, who are also often better organized.[28] It is often pointed out that the American Association of Retired Persons (AARP) is an effective group that is not counterbalanced by a "Young Taxpayers Group," and that the traditional labor-management competition leaves consumers underrepresented.

We might test the breadth of citizen representation by evaluating systems in terms of their

An Italian environmentalist in front of Rome's U.S. Embassy protests the refusal of the United States to ratify the Kyoto Protocol on global warming.

AP Images/Dario Pignatelli

inclusiveness: what proportion of the population is represented to what degree in national-level politics? South Africa under apartheid illustrates the extreme case where the majority was prevented outright from forming associational groups. In the Third World, competing interests in the capital rarely involve the interests of rural peasants; sometimes peasant organizations are brutally suppressed, while urban middle- and upper-class groups can petition authorities. It seems to be no coincidence that the bias in group inclusion appears greatest where the gaps in income and education are widest. We previously suggested that, pushed to the extreme, those excluded from the process may engage in anomic activity or resort to

violence, a conclusion supported by statistical studies of inequality and violence.[29] Even in less extreme cases, the presence of different levels of political awareness means that every interest group system is somewhat biased. Democratization involves not only the provision of competitive elections but also the reduction of the bias in interest representation.

Another challenge faces the patterns of interest articulation and representation in advanced industrial democracies. There are claims that participation in associational groups is decreasing in the United States, and perhaps in other established democracies.[30] For instance, memberships in labor unions and formal church engagement have steadily trended downward in most Western democracies over the past several decades. Some scholars argue that this trend represents a growing social isolation in developed nations, as people forsake social and political involvement for the comfort of their favorite chair and their favorite television program. However, other researchers argue that we are witnessing a change in how citizens organize and express their interests, such as through public Interest groups, Internet networks, and blogging.[31] Even in nations such as India and China, millions of people are now using the Internet to learn about politics and how they can articulate their interests.

What can be said for certain is that democratic politics rests on a participatory public that uses individual and group methods to express and represent its interests. Thus, developing an active social and political life is an important standard for measuring the political development of a nation.

## REVIEW QUESTIONS

- How do the different forms of citizen action vary in their potential influence on policy makers?

- What are the main types of interest groups?

- How does a "civil society" differ from a noncivil society?

- What are the key differences among pluralist, neo-corporatist, and controlled interest group systems?

- What are the consequences when an interest group works through legitimate channels of influence rather than coercive channels?

- What factors increase the diversity of interest groups and their efforts to influence the political process?

## KEY TERMS

anomic groups

associational groups

channels of political access

civil society

collective action problem

controlled interest group
    systems

institutional groups

interest articulation

mass media

neo-corporatist interest
    group systems

nonassociational groups

pluralist interest group
    systems

political terror tactics

protests

## SUGGESTED READINGS

Dahl, Robert A. *Polyarchy: Participation and Opposition.* New Haven, CT: Yale University Press, 1971.

———. *Democracy and Its Critics.* New Haven, CT: Yale University Press, 1989.

Dalton, Russell J. *Citizen Politics: Public Opinion and Political Parties in Advanced Industrial Democracies,* 5th ed. Washington, DC: CQ Press, 2008.

Denardo, James. *Power in Numbers: The Political Strategy of Protest and Rebellion.* Princeton, NJ: Princeton University Press, 1985.

Hirschman, Albert. *Exit, Voice, and Loyalty.* Cambridge: Harvard University Press, 1970.

Howard, Marc Morjé. *The Weakness of Civil Society in Post-Communist Europe.* New York: Cambridge University Press, 2003.

Keck, Margaret, and Kathryn Sikkink. *Activists Beyond Borders: Advocacy Networks in International Politics.* Ithaca, NY: Cornell University Press, 1998.

Lichbach, Mark. *The Rebel's Dilemma.* Ann Arbor: University of Michigan Press, 1994.

Meyer, David, and Sidney Tarrow, eds. *The Social Movement Society: Contentious Politics for a New Century.* Lanham, MD: Rowman & Littlefield, 1998.

Norris, Pippa. *Democratic Phoenix: Reinventing Political Activism.* New York: Cambridge University Press, 2003.

Olson, Mancur. *The Logic of Collective Action.* Cambridge: Harvard University Press, 1965.

Putnam, Robert. *Bowling Alone: The Collapse and Revival of American Community.* New York: Simon & Schuster, 2000.

Putnam, Robert D., ed. *Democracies in Flux: The Evolution of Social Capital in Contemporary Society.* Oxford: Oxford University Press, 2002.

Richardson, Jeremy J., ed. *Pressure Groups.* New York: Oxford University Press, 1993.

Rootes, Christopher. *Environmental Movements: Local, National, and Global.* London: Frank Cass, 1999.

Shi, Tianjian. *Political Participation in Beijing.* Cambridge: Harvard University Press, 1997.

Tarrow, Sidney. *The New Transnational Activism.* New York: Cambridge University Press, 2005.

Thomas, Clive. *Political Parties and Interest Groups: Shaping Democratic Governance.* Boulder, CO: Lynn Rienner, 2001.

Van Deth, Jan et al. *Social Capital and European Democracy.* New York: Routledge, 1999.

Verba, Sidney, Norman H. Nie, and Jae-on Kim. *Participation and Political Equality.* Cambridge: Cambridge University Press, 1978.

Verba, Sidney, Kay Schlozman, and Henry Brady. *Voice and Equality.* Cambridge: Harvard University Press, 1996.

Wattenberg, Martin. *Where Have All the Voters Gone?* Cambridge: Harvard University Press, 2003.

Wiarda, Howard J. *Corporatism and Comparative Politics: The Other Great "ism."* Armonk, NY: Sharpe, 1997.

## ENDNOTES

1. This framework draws on Sidney Verba, Norman N. Nie, and Jae-on Kim, *Participation and Political Equality* (Cambridge: Cambridge University Press, 1978), ch. 2.

2. See, for example, the range of activities of Beijing residents described in Tianjin Shi, *Political Participation in Beijing* (Cambridge: Harvard University Press, 1997).

3. Dietlind Stolle, Marc Hooghe, and Michele Micheletti, "Politics in the Supermarket: Political Consumerism as a Form of Political Participation," *International Political Science Review* 26 (2005): 245–70.

4. Pippa Norris, *Democratic Phoenix: Reinventing Political Activism* (New York: Cambridge University Press, 2003), Verba, Nie, and Kim, *Participation and Political Equality.*

5. Citizen interest group activity includes membership in groups working on local community issues, environmental interests, humans rights issues, women's issues, and the peace movement.

6. Russell Dalton, *Citizen Politics,* 5th ed. (Washington, DC: CQ Press, 2008, 2002), ch. 4; Norris, *Democratic Phoenix,* ch. 10.

7. See Verba, Nie, and Kim, *Participation and Political Equality;* and Samuel Barnes, Mox Kaase, et al., *Political Action* (Beverly Hills: Sage Publications, 1979).

8. See the evidence in J. Craig Jenkins and Kurt Schock, "Political Process, International Dependence, and Mass Political Conflict: A Global Analysis of Protest and Rebellion, 1973–1978," *International Journal of Sociology* (2004) 33:41–63.

9. Studies of these problems were stimulated by the now classic work of Mancur Olson, *The Logic of Collective Action* (Cambridge: Harvard University Press, 1965). See also Mark Lichbach, *The Rebel's Dilemma* (Ann Arbor: University of Michigan Press, 1994); Mancur Olson, "Dictatorship, Democracy, and Development," *American Political Science Review* 87, no. 3 (Sept. 1993): 567–76; Todd Sandler, ed., *Collective Action: Theory and Applications* (Ann Arbor: University of Michigan Press, 1992).

10. See G. F. Skilling and F. Griffiths, eds., *Interest Groups in Soviet Politics* (Princeton, NJ: Princeton University Press, 1971); the essays by Frederick C. Barghoorn and Skilling in Robert A. Dahl, *Regimes and Oppositions* (New Haven, CT: Yale University Press, 1973); and Roman Kolkowicz, "Interest Groups in Soviet Politics," *Comparative Politics* 2, no. 3 (April 1970): 445–72.

11. Christopher Rootes, ed., *Environmental Movements: Local, National, and Global* (London: Frank Cass, 1999); Amrita Basu, ed., *The Challenges of Local Feminism: Women's Movements in Global Perspective* (Boulder, CO: Westview, 1995).

12. Jean Cohen and A. Arato, *Civil Society and Political Theory* (Cambridge: MIT Press, 1992); M. Walzer, ed., *Toward a Global Civil Society* (Oxford: Berghahn Books, 1995).

13. See Table 4.1; John Pierce et al., *Citizens, Political Communication, and Interest Groups: Environmental Organizations in Canada and the United States* (Westport, CT: Praeger, 1992).

14. Sidney Tarrow, *The New Transnational Activism* (New York: Cambridge University Press, 2005); Margaret Keck and Kathryn Sikkink, *Activists Beyond Borders: Advocacy Networks in International Politics* (Ithaca: Cornell University Press, 1998).

15. Marc Morjé Howard, *The Weakness of Civil Society in Post-Communist Europe* (New York: Cambridge University Press, 2003); Russell Dalton, "Civil Society and Democracy," in Russell Dalton and Doh Chull Shin, eds. *Citizens, Democracy, and Markets Around the Pacific Rim* (Oxford: Oxford University Press, 2006).

16. Philippe Schmitter, "Interest Intermediation and Regime Governability," in Suzanne Berger, ed., *Organizing Interests in Western Europe* (New York: Cambridge University Press, 1981), ch. 12; Arend Lijphart and Markus Crepaz, "Corporatism and Consensus Democracy in 18 Countries," *British Journal of Political Science* 21, no. 2 (April 1991): 235–46; Wyn Grant, ed., *The Political Economy of Corporatism* (New York: St. Martin's Press, 1985).

17. On the relative success of the corporatist systems in economic performance, see Miriam Golden, "The Dynamics of Trade Unionism and National Economic Performance," *American Political Science Review* 87, no. 2 (June 1993): 439–54; Arend Lijphart, Ronald Rogowski, and R. Kent Weaver, "Separation of Powers and Cleavage Management," in R. Kent Weaver and Bert A. Rockman, *Do Institutions Matter? Government Capabilities in the United States and Abroad* (Washington: Brookings Institution, 1993), 302–44.

18. Lyle Scruggs, "Institutions and Environmental Performance in Seventeen Western Democracies," *British Journal of Political Science* 29 (1999): 1–31.

19. Oscar Molina and Martin Rhodes, "Corporatism: The Past, Present and Future of a Concept," *Annual Review of Political Science* 2 (2002): 305–31.

20. Howard Wiarda, ed. *Authoritarianism and Corporatism in Latin America—Revisited* (Gainesville: University Press of Florida, 2004); Julius E. Nyang'Oro and Timothy M. Shaw, *Corporatism in Africa: Comparative Analysis and Practice* (Boulder, CO: Westview Press, 1990).

21. We should also note that most Chinese work and live in rural areas and are not wage earners. The figure is based on the share of the labor force that receives a regular salary, which in China means urban workers. But India has a comparable labor structure, and many fewer Indian wage earners are unionized.

22. Norris, *Democratic Phoenix.*

23. Ted Robert Gurr, "A Comparative Study of Civil Strife," in Hugh David Graham and Ted Robert Gurr, eds., *The History of Violence in America* (New York: Bantam Press, 1969), 462–63.

24. See Pippa Norris, Stefaan Walgrave, and Peter van Aelst, "Does Protest Signify Disaffection? Demonstrators in a Postindustrial Democracy," in Mariano Torcal and Jose Ramón Montero, eds., *Political Disaffection in Contemporary Democracies: Social Capital, Institutions and Politics* (London: Routledge, 2006): 279–307; Mark Baldassare, ed., *The Los Angeles Riots: Lessons for the Urban Future* (Boulder, CO: Westview, 1994).

25. On violence and democratic survival, see G. Bingham Powell, Jr., *Contemporary Democracies: Participation, Stability, and Violence* (Cambridge: Harvard University Press, 1982), ch. 8; see also the contributions to Juan J. Linz and Alfred Stepan, eds., *The Breakdown of Democratic Regimes* (Baltimore: Johns Hopkins University Press, 1978).

26. Robert D. Putnam, *Making Democracy Work: Civic Traditions in Modern Italy* (Princeton, NJ: Princeton University Press, 1993).

27. Ronald Inglehart, *Culture Shift in Advanced Industrial Societies* (Princeton, NJ: Princeton University Press, 1990), 34–36; see also Almond and Verba, *Civic Culture*, ch. 11.

28. Jeffrey M. Berry, *The Interest Group Society* (New York: Longman, 1997).

29. Many of these studies are reviewed by Mark I. Lichbach, "An Evaluation of 'Does Economic Inequality Breed Political Conflict' Studies," *World Politics* 41 (1989): 431–70. More recent references and analyses appear in T. Y. Wang et al., "Inequality and Political Violence Revisited," *American Political Science Review* 87, no. 4 (Dec. 1993): 979–93.

30. Robert Putnam, *Bowling Alone: The Collapse and Revival of American Community* (New York: Simon & Schuster, 2000); Robert Putnam, ed., *Democracies in Flux: The Evolution of Social Capital in Contemporary Society* (Oxford: Oxford University Press, 2002).

31. Cliff, Zukin et al., *A New Engagement? Political Participation, Civic Life, and the Changing American Citizen* (New York: Oxford University Press, 2006); Russell Dalton, *The Good Citizen* (Washington, DC: CQ Press, 2007), Ch. 4.

# INTEREST AGGREGATION AND POLITICAL PARTIES

**Interest aggregation** is the activity in which the political demands of individuals and groups are combined into policy programs. For example, in developing an economic policy program, politicians often have to balance farmers' desires for higher crop prices, consumers' preferences for lower prices and taxes, and environmentalists' concerns about water pollution and pesticides. Who prevails in such balancing acts depends in part on political institutions, which is the subject of Chapter 6. But interest aggregation depends also on political skills and resources, such as votes, campaign funds, political offices, media access, or even armed force.

How interests are aggregated is a key feature of the political process. The aggregation process determines which interests are heard, and what individuals and groups are allowed to participate. Interest aggregation can also help create a balanced government program out of competing policy goals. How stable and effective governments are also depend on their patterns of interest aggregation.

Interest aggregation can occur in many ways. An influential party leader or military dictator may have a considerable personal impact. Yet, large states usually develop more specialized organizations for aggregating interests. Political parties are just such organizations, and they play an important role in interest aggregation in democratic as well as in many nondemocratic systems. Each party (or its candidates) stands for a set of policies and tries to build a coalition of support for this program. In a democratic system, two or more parties compete to gain support for their alternative policy programs. In an authoritarian system, a single party or institution may try to mobilize citizens' support for its policies. In either type of system political parties may play a major role. In authoritarian systems the process is frequently covert and controlled, and the process is top-down rather than bottom-up. In other words, parties mobilize interests to support the government, rather than responding to demands by regular citizens or social interests.

It is important to remember that political parties may perform many different functions, and that different structures may aggregate interests. For instance, in addition to aggregating interests, parties frequently shape the political culture as they strive to build support for their ideologies, issue positions, and candidates. Parties recruit voters and select would-be officeholders. They articulate interests of their own and transmit the demands of others. Governing parties are also involved in making public policy and even in overseeing its implementation and adjudication. Yet, the distinctive and defining goal of a political party—its mobilization of support for policies and candidates—is especially related to interest aggregation. In this chapter we compare the role of parties in interest aggregation to those of other structures.

## PERSONAL INTEREST AGGREGATION

One way to bring political interests together in policymaking is through personal connections. Virtually all societies feature **patron-client networks**—structures in which a central officeholder, authority figure, or group provides benefits (patronage) to supporters in exchange for their loyalty. It was the defining principle of feudalism. The king and his lords, the lord and his knights, the knight and his serfs and tenants—all were bound by ties of personal dependence and loyalty. The American political machines of Boss Tweed of New York or Richard Daley, Sr., of Chicago were similarly bound together by patronage and loyalty. Personal networks are not confined to relationships cemented by patronage only. The president of the United States, for instance, usually has a circle of personal confidants, a "brain trust" or "kitchen cabinet," bound to their chief by ideological and policy propensities as well as by ties of friendship.

The patron-client network is so common in politics that it resembles the cell in biology or the atom in physics—the primitive structure out of which larger and more complicated political structures are composed. Students of politics in all countries report such networks. When interest aggregation is performed mainly within patron-client networks, it is difficult to mobilize political resources behind unified policies of social change or to respond to crises. This is because political decisions depend on ever-shifting agreements among many factional leaders (patrons). Patron-client politics thus typically means a static political system.

Contemporary research on patron-client relationships was pioneered in studies of Asian politics, where this structure runs through the political processes of countries such as the Philippines, Japan, and India.[1] But parallels exist in Europe, the Middle East, Latin America, and most regions of the world. Patron-client relationships affect recruitment to political office, interest aggregation, policymaking, and policy implementation. Yet as Table 5.1 shows, patron-client networks are a particularly important means of aggregating political interests in poorer countries.

## INSTITUTIONAL INTEREST AGGREGATION

In modern societies, as citizens become aware of larger collective interests and have the resources and skills to work for them, personal networks tend to be regulated, limited, and incorporated within broader organizations. Interest groups with powerful resources

Elections can stir strong feelings of joy or disappointment. Here, French protesters demonstrate against the election of President Nicolas Sarkozy in May 2007. The placard reads: "No to capitalism with a human face."

Jean Philippe Ksiazek/AFP/Getty Images

| | Extensiveness of Interest Aggregation by Actor | | | | |
|---|---|---|---|---|---|
| **Country** | **Patron-Client Networks** | **Associational Groups** | **Competitive Parties** | **Authoritarian Parties** | **Military Forces** |
| Brazil | Moderate | Moderate | Moderate | — | Moderate |
| Britain | Low | High | High | — | Low |
| China | Moderate | Low | — | High | High |
| France | Low | Moderate | High | — | Low |
| Germany | Low | High | High | — | Low |
| India | High | Moderate | Moderate | — | Low |
| Iran | High | Moderate | Low | — | Moderate |
| Japan | Moderate | High | High | — | Low |
| Mexico | Moderate | Moderate | Moderate | — | Low |
| Nigeria | High | Low | Moderate | — | Moderate |
| Russia | Moderate | Low | Moderate | — | Moderate |
| United States | Low | Moderate | High | — | Low |

**TABLE 5.1**

Structures Performing Interest Aggregation in Selected Contemporary Nations*

*Extensiveness of interest aggregation rated as low, moderate, or high. Rating refers to broad-level performance issue areas at different times. Blank implies that such actors do not exist.

can easily cross the subtle dividing line between interest articulation and aggregation. Associational groups (see Chapter 4) often support political contenders such as political parties. But they can occasionally wield sufficient resources to become contenders in their own right. For instance, the political power of the labor unions within the British Labour Party historically rested on the unions' ability to develop coherent policy positions and mobilize their members (who were formally represented in the party) to support those positions. As we discussed in Chapter 4, interest group systems of democratic corporatism empower both labor and business groups to get actively engaged in making economic policies. These arrangements include continuous political bargaining among organized labor, business interests, political parties, and government representatives. Such corporatist systems interconnect organizations that in other political systems play very different, often antagonistic, roles. Table 5.1 illustrates how associational groups tend to play a larger role in democratic politics that accept the independence of interest groups and their attempts to influence government policy.

**Institutional groups,** like bureaucratic agencies and military factions, can also be important interest aggregators. Indeed, the bureaucracy performs this function in most societies. Although established primarily to implement public policy, the bureaucracy may negotiate with interest groups to identify their preferences or to mobilize their support. Government agencies may even be "captured" by interest groups and used to support their demands. Bureaucrats often create client support networks to expand their organizations or to enhance their ability to solve problems in their areas of expertise. Military organizations, with their special control of physical force, can also be powerful interest aggregators. We shall have more to say about their role later in this chapter.

## COMPETITIVE PARTY SYSTEMS AND INTEREST AGGREGATION

In many contemporary political systems, parties are the primary structures of interest aggregation. Political parties are *groups or organizations that seek to place candidates in office under their label.* In any given society, there may be one party, two parties, or as many as ten or twenty. We refer to the number of parties, and the relationships among them, as properties of the **party system.** The most critical distinction runs between **competitive party systems,** which primarily try to build electoral support, and noncompetitive or **authoritarian party systems,** which seek to direct society. This distinction does not depend on the closeness of electoral victory, or on the number of parties. It depends instead on the ability of political parties to freely form and compete for citizen support, and on this competition for citizen support as the key to government control. Thus a party system can be competitive even if one party wins most of the votes in a certain area, or even dominates several consecutive national elections, as long as other parties can challenge its dominance at the polls.

The role of competitive parties in interest aggregation depends not only on the individual party but also on the structure of parties, electorates, electoral laws, and policymaking institutions. Typically, interest aggregation in a competitive party system takes place

at several stages: within the individual parties, as the party chooses candidates and adopts policy proposals; through electoral competition; and after the election through bargaining and coalition building with other parties in the legislature or executive.

Political parties have been around as long as there have been elections and representative assemblies, but modern democratic parties began developing in Europe and the Americas from about the mid-nineteenth century. They have since emerged in all societies that have adopted free and fair elections and democratic government. Parties differ in their purposes and organization. Some have elaborate policy platforms, whereas others are little more than vehicles for ambitious politicians to get elected (or even to enrich themselves). Some parties are highly structured mass organizations, whereas others are loose, *personalistic* groups dominated by their leaders (see Box 5.1).

The first parties were typically *internally created;* their founders were politicians who already held seats in the national assembly or other political

---

## Personalistic Parties

**BOX 5.1**

Political parties are typically formal organizations with officers, members, statutes, and official policy programs. Sometimes, however, parties can be much looser *personalistic* movements built around one political leader, or a small group of leaders. Personalistic parties are particularly common in new democracies. In Russia, for example, President Putin (2000–08) was able to form a party (United Russia) with a strong personal following. But even India and France have highly personalistic parties. In India, the Congress Party has been dominated by the families of its most important founders, Gandhi and Nehru. In France, most presidents have come out of the Gaullist movement, which has had many names but was dominated from the start by President Charles de Gaulle and later by some of his followers. Personalistic parties commonly do not have a very clear policy program. They are often susceptible to clientelistic politics and sometimes become vehicles for purely personal ambitions and rent seeking.

Shmuel Flatto-Sharon offers a blatant but extreme example. Flatto-Sharon is a French businessman of

Jewish background. In 1977 he fled to Israel because the French authorities wanted to prosecute him for embezzling $60 million. To avoid extradition, he decided to run for election to the Knesset (the Israeli national assembly), which would give him immunity from prosecution. He formed a party, which he ran as a one-man operation—it had no other candidates or officers. Flatto-Sharon refused to identify himself as left, right, or center. He appealed for Jewish solidarity, arguing that Israel should not allow him to be imprisoned in a gentile country (France). He also promised a free television set to all Israeli households (this was before television sets became inexpensive and commonplace). And he promised to pay anyone who voted for him. Remarkably, he won two parliamentary seats, even though as his party's only candidate he could not fill the second seat. In 1981, however, Flatto-Sharon lost his bid for reelection. He was convicted of bribery for his vote-buying scheme and sent to jail in Israel, but never extradited to France.

offices. These parties were often committed to broad constitutional principles (such as republican government, universal suffrage, or separation of church and state), but otherwise they often had only loose policy programs and little organization outside the legislature. They often had colorful names which said little about their policies, such as Whigs and Tories in Britain, Whites ("Blancos") and Reds ("Colorados") in several Latin American countries, Hats and Caps in Sweden, or for that matter Democrats and Republicans in the United States. Some of the descendents of these parties have kept their original names; others now call themselves Liberals (such as the previous Whigs) or Conservatives (such as the previous Tories).

During the late nineteenth century and early twentieth century, a series of other types of parties emerged, as the democratic countries industrialized and urbanized, and as larger and larger segments of the adult population gained the right to vote. The growth of the industrial working class led to the formation of socialist, social democratic, communist, and other workers' parties. Farming interests gained representation through agrarian parties, and other parties emerged to represent religious communities (such as Catholics or Hindus) or ethnic or linguistic minorities. In countries that were not independent, parties of national independence often became a dominant force. All of these parties were typically *externally created*—they organized outside parliament before they became a force inside that institution. They often had much stronger mass membership organizations than their older competitors, and they often also had (and continue to have) closer ties to specific interest groups. Thus, social democrats and communists tended to have strong ties to labor unions, agrarian parties to farmers' organizations, and many Christian Democratic parties (at least Catholic ones) to the Vatican and religious organizations.

Most of these parties still exist and continue to play a leading role. They have settled into stable *party families* of Social Democrats, Conservatives, Christian Democrats, Liberals, Nationalists, etc., which often maintain close contacts across national boundaries. The party systems of most countries show a great deal of stability, and many of the most important parties of the early twenty-first century were also the dominant parties a hundred years ago. Yet, two important new types of parties have emerged in the past thirty or forty years, particularly in advanced industrial countries. One is the "new left," or Green parties, that in many countries emerged in the 1960s or 1970s. These parties tend to champion international peace and disarmament, ecological and environmental protection, gender equality, a large welfare state, and minority rights. They are often more supportive of alternative life styles than traditional working-class parties of the left (such as Social Democrats). The other important type of new party is the "populist right." These parties tend to be critical of existing parties and political leaders, whom they see as elitist, corrupt, and out of touch. They favor strict law-and-order policies but criticize what they see as "politically correct" government interventionism. They dislike the distortions that the welfare state sometimes creates, such as policies that make it unattractive to work and easy to live off of welfare benefits (see Chapter 7). And they typically oppose large-scale immigration (see Box 5.2).

The party systems of most democratic countries reflect a mix of these various party families. But no two party systems are exactly alike, and not all party families are represented in all countries. The variations in party systems reflect differences in demographics, economic development, and political histories. They also depend on differences in electoral systems, as we shall discuss below.

## Elections

In democracies, political parties live and die by their performance in political elections. The act of voting, and giving support to a political candidate, party, or policy proposal, is one of the simplest and most frequently performed political acts. By aggregating these votes, the citizens can make a collective decision about their future leaders and public policies. Elections are one of the few devices through which diverse interests can be expressed equally and comprehensively.[2]

The simple act of voting can have profound implications. The voters' choice of parties and candidates helps aggregate political interests. Electoral outcomes determine who manages the affairs of government and makes public policy. And parties generally fulfill their electoral promises when they gain control of government.[3] When leftist governments come to power in Europe, they tend to expand the size and efforts of the government; whereas conservative parties generally slow the growth of government

BOX 5.2

## Parties Just for Fun

Some political parties seem to have no other purpose than to make fun of politics and politicians. One example is Britain's Official Monster Raving Loony Party (OMRLP), formed in 1983. Its founding leader was musician David Sutch, who called himself Screaming Lord Sutch. Sutch and the other founders were apparently inspired by the television series *Monty Python's Flying Circus*. The OMRLP has never won any seat in Parliament, but has captured a few seats in local British government. Sutch died in 1999 and was replaced as party leader by Alan "Howling Laud" Hope. In 2005, the party ran on a platform of abolishing the income tax, inviting the rest of Europe to adopt the British currency, retraining "stupid traffic cops" as clergy, and introducing a ninety-nine-pence coin to "save on change." These proposals may be political longshots, but one of the party's early goals, for British pubs to stay open all day, has actually been achieved.

In Denmark, comedian Jacob Haugaard has since 1979 several times contested parliamentary elections as a candidate for the Association of Deliberate Work Avoiders. In 1994, he won election to the Danish Parliament. His election platform included demands for disability pensions for people who lack a sense of humor, tailwinds on all Danish bike paths, more generous Christmas presents, more renaissance furniture at IKEA, and more whales in Danish waters. Haugaard also promised his voters free beer, and he used the public funds his party received from the Danish government to fulfill this campaign commitment (he bought beer and hot dogs for his supporters after the election).

programs and promote private enterprise. Republicans and Democrats in the United States also have been fairly responsible in keeping their promises. However, parties that want radical change or have not recently been in office often find it difficult to implement their programs when they eventually come to power. When, for example, the German Greens came to power in 1998 as part of a coalition government, they had to modify their promise to shut down Germany's nuclear power plants immediately. Instead they negotiated a phase-out over many years. But by and large, parties try hard to implement their programs, and citizens can therefore influence interest aggregation and policymaking through their role in selecting elites.

When they aggregate interests and make policy, party leaders are often caught between the demands of their party activists and the voters. Party activists often want policies that are more radical than those that most voters prefer. At any rate, activists will typically insist more vigorously that the party program should be implemented, whereas ordinary voters are often happier when governments try to compromise and listen to opinions outside their own parties. There is a broad and ongoing debate about the extent to which democracy requires political parties to be internally democratic. Advocates of participatory democracy strongly support

this idea, as do parties such as the European Greens. On the other hand, the famous Austrian economist Joseph A. Schumpeter argued that vigorous competition *between* parties is what matters for a healthy democracy and that democracy within parties is irrelevant or even harmful.[4] (See also Box 5.3.)

Elections often have other functions as well (see also Chapter 4). The communist nations of Eastern Europe and elsewhere utilized elections to legitimize their governments. They routinely reported turnout that exceeded 98 percent of the electorate. But the outcome was given in advance. Until 1990, voters in the Soviet Union were given only one candidate to vote for, and this person was always a nominee of the Communist Party. Voter participation was very high in these nations because the government pressured people to participate and express their symbolic support for the regime, not because the elections actually decided anything. Elections played a role in socializing and shaping citizens' attitudes, but had little to do with interest articulation or aggregation.[5]

In most democratic countries, voters can freely choose whether or not to vote. Some democratic countries, though, require citizens to vote and impose penalties on those who do not. Voting choices reflect a mix of motivations.[6] Many citizens try to judge the parties' policy promises. For others, elections are a

BOX 5.3

## The Iron Law of Oligarchy

Can political parties be the main vehicles of democratic representation if they do not govern themselves democratically? This has been a main concern among students of modern political parties. In 1911, the young German sociologist Robert Michels published a study of the German Socialist Party in which he formulated the "iron law of oligarchy," which states that all modern organizations tend towards oligarchy (rule by the few) rather than democracy. "Who says organization says oligarchy," Michels famously observed. He identified several forces that push organizations such as political parties towards oligarchy. One is the need for specialization and differentiation that exists in all large, modern organizations. A second cause of oligarchy lies in the fact that most ordinary members do not have the time or resources to hold their leaders accountable and that they often crave strong leadership. A third reason is that parties foster leaders who live "off" politics rather than "for" politics. They exploit their leadership positions to advance their own ambitions for wealth or power, often to the detriment of their followers. (In contemporary terms, we would refer to such self-interested pursuit of power as rent seeking.) Michels' study was particularly troubling because he found these tendencies even in a party, the German Socialist Party, with which he sympathized and which was considered particularly strongly committed to democratic ideals.

Source: Robert Michels, *Political Parties* (New York: Free Press, 1962).

simple referendum on government performance. They vote to throw the rascals out if times are bad, and to reelect them if times are good. In other cases, elections can be dominated by the charisma of a strong leader or the incompetence of a weak one. In each case, however, elections aggregate these diverse concerns to make a collective decision on the composition of government.

## Electoral Systems

The rules by which elections are conducted are among the most important structures that affect political parties. We refer to these rules as the **electoral system.** They determine who can vote, how people vote, and how the votes get counted. The rules that determine how voter choices are translated into election outcomes, how votes are converted into seats, are especially important. In the United States, Britain, and many countries influenced by Britain (such as India and Canada), the legislative election rules divide the country into many election districts. In each district, the candidate who has more votes than any other—a *plurality*—wins the election in the district. This simple, **single-member district plurality (SMDP) election rule** is often called "first past the post," a horse-racing term, because the winner need only finish ahead of the others but not win a majority of the votes. This system seems obvious and natural to Americans, but it is rarely used in continental Europe or in Latin America. Another version of single-member district elections is the **majority runoff** (or **double-ballot**) system used in France and in presidential elections in Russia. In this system, voting happens in two stages, normally separated by a couple of weeks. In the first round, it takes a majority of all votes (50 percent + 1) to win. The winning candidate, then, has to win not just more votes than any other candidate, but more votes than all other candidates combined. If there is no majority winner in the first round, then only a smaller number of candidates (in French and Russian presidential elections the top two) make it into the second round, in which whoever gets the largest number of votes is elected.

In contrast to the single-member district system, most democracies use some form of **proportional representation (PR)** in multimember districts. In these systems the country is divided into a few large districts, which may elect as many as twenty or thirty members apiece. These districts are often the states or provinces that make up the country. In the Netherlands and Israel, the entire country is a single electoral district with more than 100 members. The competing parties offer lists of candidates for the slots in each district. The number of representatives a party wins depends on the overall proportion of the votes it receives, though no system is perfectly proportional. A party receiving 4 percent of the vote would be awarded approximately 4 percent of the legislative seats. Sometimes parties must achieve a minimum threshold of votes, usually 3 to 5 percent nationally, to receive any seats at all. If so many parties compete that a lot of them fall below this threshold, many voters may be left unrepresented, as happened in Russia in 1995.

In order to compete effectively, parties must formulate appealing policy programs and nominate attractive candidates for office. They must anticipate the offerings of their competitors and the preferences of the voters. The procedure that parties use to develop policy positions varies greatly from country to country and from party to party. In the United States the national party conventions held at each presidential election formalize the party's policy positions, both by adopting a party platform and by selecting a slate of candidates. In other countries, parties have more regular congresses, and centralized party organizations issue party programs (also known as platforms or manifestos).[7] Whatever the system, a successful program must both spell out policy positions that are popular with the voters and aggregate interests within the party.

Parties must also offer candidates for office. In the United States, voters directly select these candidates through **primary elections.** But primaries are an unusually open form of candidate selection. In most other countries with **single-member district (SMD)** elections, party officials select the candidates, either locally or nationally. In proportional representation elections, the party draws up a list of candidates for each district. In **closed-list PR systems,** the elected representatives are then simply drawn from the top of this list, in declining order, and ordinary voters have no say about their candidates. In **open-list systems,** on the other hand, voters can give preference votes to individual candidates, and these votes are counted when it is decided which candidates will represent the party in that district. Besides adopting programs and selecting candidates, parties also attempt to publicize them and mobilize electoral support through rallies, media advertising, door-to-door campaigning, and other activities.

## Patterns of Electoral Competition

In democratic party systems, the electoral system is a major determinant of the patterns of electoral competition. Two famous political science theories help us

understand this connection: Duverger's Law and Downs' median voter result. **Duverger's Law,** which is named after the French political scientist Maurice Duverger, is one of the best-known theories in political science.[8] It states that there is a systematic relationship between electoral systems and party systems, so that plurality single-member district election systems tend to create two-party systems in the legislature, while proportional representation electoral systems generate multiparty systems. Duverger identified two mechanisms behind this regularity. He called them the mechanical effect and the psychological effect. The **mechanical effect** is to be found in the way that different electoral systems convert votes into seats. In single-member district systems, parties get no representation unless they finish first in at least one district. Therefore, smaller parties that run second, third, or fourth across many districts receive little or no representation. In the 2001 election in Britain, for example, the Liberal Democratic Party (Britain's third largest party) received 18 percent of the votes, but only 8 percent of the seats in Parliament. The **psychological effect** lies in the fact that both voters and candidates anticipate the mechanical effect. Therefore, voters do not throw their support behind "hopeless" parties and candidates. Instead, they may support their second-best (or even third-best) option in order to keep a party that they strongly dislike from winning. And knowing that the voters will not support them, minor party candidates are reluctant to run. Giving your support to a party or candidate that is not your first choice in order to avoid an even worse outcome is known as **strategic voting.** Duverger argues that strategic voting tends to work to the advantage of parties that are already large and to the disadvantage of small ones. In U.S. elections, it has been fairly common for third-party candidates to run well in the polls until close to the election date, when voters realize that these candidates are not going to win. Their support then often declines rapidly.

Anthony Downs examined the effects of the number of parties on their policy positions. He showed that in two-party systems in which the parties are competing along a left-right (or other) policy dimension and are interested only in winning elections, and where all voters choose the party closest to their policy preferences, the parties will moderate their policies so as to try to win the support of the median voter (the voter who is at the midpoint of the policy spectrum, with as many other voters to the right as to the left). Downs' contribution is known as the **median voter result.** According to this theory, two-party systems will exhibit a centrist pull or "convergence." In systems with only two parties, parties have to try to win a majority, so targeting the "center" of the electorate is critical. In PR systems with many political parties, however, no one group has much chance of winning a

majority, and parties can survive with much less support. Therefore, there is not the same centrist pull and parties may instead spread themselves out across the policy spectrum.[9]

Figure 5.1 offers a comparative "snapshot" of parties and voters in several democratic countries. It shows where party supporters in each country placed themselves on a left-right scale in public opinion surveys in

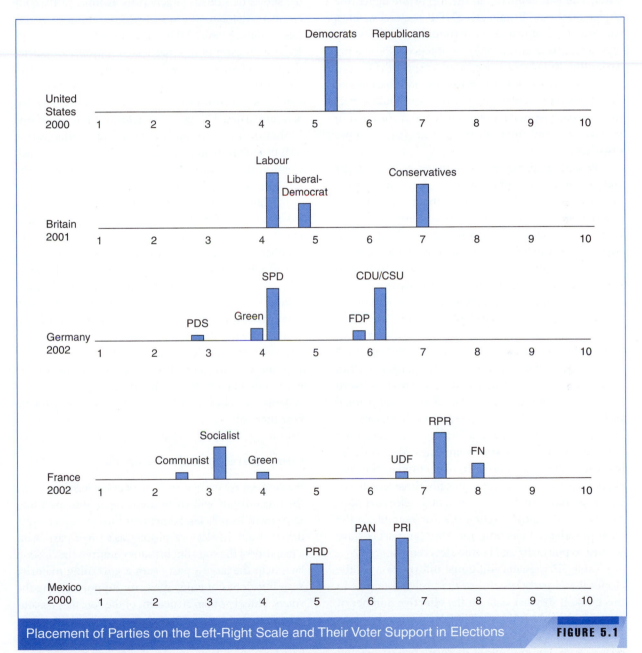

**Placement of Parties on the Left-Right Scale and Their Voter Support in Elections**    **FIGURE 5.1**

Source: Party positions from the self-placements of party voters. The height of the bar represents the percentage of the total vote won by that party in the legislative election identified on the left.

the early 2000s, with one identified as Left (or liberal in the United States) and 10 identified as Right (or conservative in the United States). Note that although the left-right placements reflect the relative positions of party supporters in their respective societies, the meaning of left, right, and center can be different in different societies. The height of the columns above the scale shows what percentage of the electorate voted for each party. The two countries at the top of the figure, the United States and Britain, use SMDP electoral systems, whereas France uses a majority runoff system, Mexico a mixed system, and Germany in practice a PR system. According to Duverger, we should expect the United States and Britain to have only two serious parties and the others more. Following Downs, we should expect the two-party systems to be centrist and clustered in policy space and the multiparty systems to be more dispersed.

By and large, Figure 5.1 supports both Duverger and Downs. In the countries at the top of the figure, especially in the United States, there are only two large parties. Moreover, the parties are fairly close to the center. Democrats are somewhat to the left and Republicans somewhat to the right, with a lot of overlap. The left-right "gap" between the average party supporters, although larger than it was twenty years ago, is still fairly small. In France, toward the bottom of the figure, many parties receive voter support. There is a very large distance between the left-most party (the Communists) and right-most party (the National Front), and even between the two largest parties (Socialists and RPR). Britain and Germany fall between these more extreme cases. As Duverger would predict, Britain looks more like the United States, but the parties are farther apart and the smaller Liberal Democratic Party falls between the two major ones. Mexico shows that even systems with proportional representation and more than two parties (though only three significant ones) can have convergent and centrist electoral politics. Yet, in the most recent years, for example in the 2006 presidential election, the Mexican parties have seemed to pull apart and become less centrist.

Table 5.2 presents additional information on the electoral and party systems of the twelve countries in this book. It displays data on the **effective number of parties** in each country. This measure takes into account both the overall number of parties and their relative sizes. For example, if there are two parties and they are exactly the same size, the effective number of parties is 2.0. If, however, one party has 80 percent of the votes and the other 20 percent, the effective number of parties is just below 1.5.[10] The effective number of parties can be calculated for either votes or seats, as we have done in Table 5.2. If Duverger's Law is correct, then the effective number of parties should be lower in countries that have SMDP electoral systems than in those that have other systems (particularly PR). Table 5.2 shows that this is largely true, as three of the four countries that have the lowest effective number of parties do indeed have SMDP elections. At the same time, India is an exception; it has a large number of parties despite an SMDP electoral system. But a closer look at India shows that even though the country has many parties overall, most electoral districts feature only two serious parties.[11] Thus, India helps us understand one limitation of Duverger's Law, which is that while SMDP systems tend to sustain only two parties in each election district, these two parties need not be the same throughout the country.

Table 5.2 also gives us a measure of the mechanical effect in Duverger's Law, the consequences of the counting rules themselves. By comparing the effective number of parties among the voters (vote shares) with the effective number of parties in the national assembly (seat shares), we can see how much the electoral system helps the large parties and disfavors the small ones. This bias exists in all countries and electoral systems, as the numbers in the column for seat shares are always consistently lower than those in the column for vote shares. Duverger's Law suggests that this difference should be greater in "first past the post" (SMDP) systems than elsewhere, but it is not clear that our data bear that out.

## Competitive Parties in Government

If a competitive party wins control of the legislature and the executive, it will (if unified) be able to pass and implement its policies. Sometimes this control emerges directly from the electoral process, as a single party wins a majority of the vote. But in many countries the election laws help the largest party gain a governing majority even if it does not enjoy majority support among the voters. Thus, less than 50 percent of the vote may be converted into more than 50 percent of the legislative seats. Such "artificial" or "manufactured" legislative majorities have been the rule in countries with "first past the post" (SMDP) electoral systems, such as Britain.[12]

| | | Effective Number of Parties— | Effective Number of Parties— | |
|---|---|---|---|---|
| Country | Electoral System | Vote Shares | Seat Shares | How Are Individual Candidates Selected? |
| Brazil | PR open list | 10.63 | 9.30 | Candidate preference vote |
| Britain | SMD plurality | 3.56 | 2.45 | Nominated by local constituency association |
| China | No contested elections | No contested elections | No contested elections | No contested elections |
| France | SMD majority run-off | 3.37 | 2.25 | Nominated by local constituency association |
| Germany | Mixed system: SMD plurality + PR closed list | 3.75* | 3.44* | National party + state party conventions |
| India | SMD plurality | 7.50 | 6.55 | Nominated by local constituency association |
| Iran | MMD majority run-off | No available data | 2.66 | Must be approved by Council of Guardians |
| Japan | Mixed system: SMD plurality + PR closed list | 3.72 | 2.26 | National party |
| Mexico | Mixed system: SMD plurality + PR closed list | 3.60 | 3.02 | Nominated by local constituency association + national party |
| Nigeria | SMD plurality | 2.62 | 2.34 | Nominated by local constituency association |
| Russia | PR closed list | 4.71 (under previous electoral system with SMD plurality + PR closed list) | 3.18 | National party |
| United States | SMD plurality | 2.17 | 2.00 | Primary elections |

**TABLE 5.2**

Elections—Lower House of National Legislature

Note: Data from the most recent national elections, as of October 1, 2006.

MMD = Multimember district

SMD = Single-member district

PR = Proportional representation

*Calculated using proportional representation results.

Sources: Arend Lijphart, *Patterns of Democracy* (New Haven: Yale University Press, 1999), www.Electionguide.org; www.Wikipedia.org.

For example, since 1974 either the Conservative Party or the Labour Party has consistently won a majority of seats in the British House of Commons, even though neither party has ever been supported by a majority of the voters in any of these elections. Margaret Thatcher's Conservative Party won a solid majority in the House of Commons in 1983 and 1987 with only about 42 percent of the vote. With almost exactly the same level of support, Tony Blair and the Labour Party won nearly two-thirds of the seats in 1997 and 2001. In 2005, Labour's share of the vote fell to about 35 percent, but the party still got a solid majority of the seats. In all these elections, the quarter of the electorate supporting the smaller British parties received only a handful of parliamentary seats.

In other countries, multiparty elections do not yield single-party majorities, but party coalitions formed before the election may still offer the voters a direct choice of future governments. Before the election, a group of parties may join forces, agree to coordinate their election campaigns, or agree to govern together if they jointly win a parliamentary majority. When such coalitions form, as they have in many (but not all) elections in France and Germany, it is almost like a two-party system. Voters can clearly identify the potential governments and reward or punish the incumbents if they so choose. They thus have the ability to choose the direction of government policy through their party choice.

When elections do not create a majority party, and there is no preelectoral coalition, the political parties and their leaders must negotiate a new government after the election. This is common in many multiparty parliamentary systems, such as the Netherlands and Italy.[13] In these nations interests are not aggregated through elections, because the election does not determine the government. Instead, the aggregation of interests occurs in government when a coalition is negotiated. (See also Chapter 6, and Figure 6.2.)

The aggregation of interests at the executive rather than electoral level can have both costs and benefits. On the one hand, when elite party coalitions determine government policy, voters may feel that the government is not accountable to them. And because interest aggregation occurs among political elites, different elite coalitions can form on different issues. This can be confusing to citizens (and even informed observers). It may be difficult for voters to assign clear responsibility for government policy, and it may seem unfair that the electoral losers sometimes get to

decide. This situation lessens the value of the vote as an instrument to shape future policy or to punish parties responsible for bad policy choices in the past.

On the other hand, there may be benefits for minority interests when all parties, not just the election winners, are represented in policymaking. All citizens hold minority opinions on some issues, and some are in the minority on many issues. If even minority representatives can influence policy between elections, they may feel that they have more political protection. Finally, even governments that win a majority of votes typically do not have majority support for all of their policy proposals. So there may be benefits for the nation as a whole when even the winners have to negotiate the different parts of their programs. Such bargaining may even increase the likelihood that policies reflect different majorities on different issues. The value of elections as instruments of representation may increase when interests are aggregated within a government coalition, though the value of elections as instruments of accountability may diminish.[14]

## Cooperation and Conflict in Competitive Party Systems

Competitive party systems can be classified by the number of parties as well as by the patterns of competition or cooperation among them. **Majoritarian**

Democratization means new political rights and, often, social change. Here, women line up to vote in Afghanistan's first democratic elections.

Caren Firouz/Reuters/Corbis

**two-party systems** are either dominated by just two parties, as in the United States, or they have two dominant parties and election laws that usually create legislative majorities for one of them, as in Britain. In **majority-coalition systems,** parties establish preelectoral coalitions so that voters know which parties will attempt to work together to form a government. Germany and France have in most elections been in this category. Purely **multiparty systems** have election laws and party systems that virtually ensure that no single party wins a legislative majority and no tradition of preelection coalitions. Interest aggregation then depends on a coalition of parties bargaining and coming to agreement after the election.

The degree of antagonism or polarization among the parties is another important party system characteristic. In a **consensual party system,** the parties commanding most of the legislative seats are not too far apart on policies and have a reasonable amount of trust in each other and in the political system. These are typically party systems like those shown toward the top of Figure 5.1. Bargaining may be intense and politics exciting, but it seldom threatens the system itself. In a **conflictual party system,** the legislature is dominated by parties that are far apart on issues or are antagonistic toward each other and the political system, such as the Russian party system in the 1990s.

Some party systems have both consensual and conflictual features. Arend Lijphart has used the term **consociational** (or **accommodative**) to describe party systems in which political leaders are able to bridge the intense differences between antagonistic voters through power-sharing, broad coalitions, and decentralization of sensitive decisions to the separate social groups.[15] A consociational system can enable a deeply divided nation to find a way to peaceful democratic development. In Austria and Lebanon after World War II, suspicious and hostile groups—the socialists and Catholics in Austria, and the Christians and Muslims in Lebanon—worked out a set of consociational understandings that made stable government possible. Austria's accommodation was based on a two-party system and Lebanon's on many small, personalistic religious parties. Austria's consociationalism was largely successful, but the Lebanese experiment was not. After 1975, the country fell victim to civil war.

South Africa also adopted consociational practices in its transition to democracy. Leaders of the major political parties of the white minority and two major segments of the black majority negotiated (with great difficulty) arrangements for a democratic transition. The "Interim Constitution" guaranteed a share in power and government—cabinet posts—to all parties winning over 5 percent of the vote. Later, this feature was abandoned.

As the contrasting examples of Austria and Lebanon suggest, consociational practices (and the ability even to agree to attempt them) offer deeply divided democracies hope but no guarantees of long-term success. One critical aspect of consociationalism is that many important decisions are taken by small groups of politicians behind closed doors. If these politicians are able to work together more constructively than their supporters, then consociationalism can be a happy solution. But if the politicians are intransigent or self-interested, it may not be the best option.

The number of parties does not always tell us much about the degree of antagonism. The United States and Britain are relatively consensual majoritarian party systems. They are not perfect two-party systems because minor parties exist in both countries, especially in Britain. Yet, one or the other of the two major British parties usually wins majority control and governs through disciplined party voting. In the United States, the degree of consensus changes from election to election because of the shifting programs of presidential candidates. Moreover, the looser cohesion of American parties and the frequency of divided government lead to postelection bargaining that is similar to consensual multiparty systems.

But not all majoritarian party systems are consensual. Austria between 1918 and 1934 is the best example of a conflictual majoritarian party system. Antagonism between the Socialist Party and the other parties was so intense that in the mid-1930s it produced a brief civil war. The Austrian experience also illustrates how party systems can change. After World War II, the leaders of the two major parties negotiated an elaborate coalition agreement of mutual power sharing—checks and balances—to contain the country's conflicts. After some twenty years of the consociational "Grand Coalition," party antagonism had greatly declined.

Consensual multiparty systems are found in Norway and Sweden, among other countries. France (1946–1958), Italy (1945–1992), and Weimar Germany (1919–1933), on the other hand, are historical examples of conflictual multiparty systems, with powerful communist parties on the left and conservative or fascist movements on the right. Cabinets had to form out of centrist movements, which were themselves divided on many issues. This resulted in instability, poor government performance, and loss of citizen confidence in democracy. These factors contributed to the collapse of the French Fourth Republic, to government instability and citizen alienation from politics in Italy, and to the overthrow of democracy in Weimar Germany.

New democracies, especially those divided by language or ethnicity, sometimes face similar challenges. Some of the emerging party systems in Central and Eastern Europe have fallen into the pattern of conflictual, multiparty competition. For instance, in the 1995 parliamentary elections in Russia, forty-three parties appeared on the ballot—ranging from unreformed communists on the left to nationalist parties on the right—and seven parties won representation in Parliament. But later elections greatly reduced the number of parties.

Thus, although the number of parties affects political stability, the degree of antagonism among parties is more important. Two-party systems are stable and effective, but they may be dangerous if society is too deeply divided. Multiparty systems consisting of relatively moderate parties can often offer stability and fairly effective performance, especially if the parties are willing to commit themselves to preelectoral coalitions. Pure multiparty systems without preelectoral coalitions are more prone to ineffectiveness, but some have worked well over long periods. Where social groups and parties are highly antagonistic, however, collapse and civil war are ever-present possibilities, regardless of the number of parties. When crises develop, the most critical factor is typically how committed party leaders are to working together to defend democracy. Sometimes party leaders in a multiparty, representational setting are more accustomed to such cooperation.[16]

## AUTHORITARIAN PARTY SYSTEMS

Authoritarian party systems can also aggregate interests. They deliberately attempt to develop policy proposals and to mobilize support for them, but they do so in a completely different way from competitive party systems. In authoritarian party systems, aggregation takes place within the party or in interactions with business groups, unions, landowners, and institutional groups in the bureaucracy or military. Although there may be sham elections, the citizens have no real opportunity to shape aggregation by choosing between party alternatives.

Authoritarian party systems can be distinguished according to the degree of top-down control within the party and the party's control over other groups in society. At one extreme is the **exclusive governing party,** which insists on almost total control over political resources. It recognizes no legitimate interest aggregation by groups within the party. Nor does it permit any free activity, much less opposition, from interest groups, citizens, or other government agencies. In its most extreme form, sometimes called totalitarianism, it penetrates the entire society and mobilizes support for policies developed at the top. Its policies are legitimated by a political ideology, such as communism or national socialism (Nazism), that claims to know the true interests of the citizens, regardless of what the citizens themselves believe.[17] At the other extreme is the **inclusive governing party,** which recognizes and accepts at least some other groups and organizations, but may repress those that it sees as serious challenges to its own control.

### Exclusive Governing Parties

In a purely totalitarian society, there is only one party with total top-down control of society, and no autonomous opposition parties or interest groups. Totalitarian single-party systems can be impressive vehicles of political mobilization. A clear ideology provides legitimacy and coherence, and the party penetrates and organizes society in the name of that ideology and in accordance with its policies. But totalitarianism is difficult to sustain. Although the ruling communist parties of the Soviet Union before 1985, of Eastern Europe before 1989, and of North Korea, Vietnam, and Cuba today resemble this model, few parties have long maintained such absolute control. China is an interesting mixed case. While the Chinese government has withdrawn from the direct administration of much of the economy, it still does not recognize the legitimacy of any opposition groups. The ruling party permits, within bounds, some interest articulation by individuals, but not mass mobilization against government policy.[18]

Not all exclusive governing parties are totalitarian, however. Many leaders committed to massive social change—for example, national independence from colonialism—have used the exclusive governing party as a tool for mass mobilization. Such exclusive governing parties may experience more internal dissent than is commonly recognized. Within the party, groups may unite around such interests as their region or industry, or behind leaders of different policy factions. Beneath the supposedly united front, power struggles may erupt in times of crisis. Succession crises are particularly likely to generate such power struggles, as at the death of Stalin in the Soviet Union and Mao Zedong in China. The Chinese Communist Party has several times had to rely on the army, even on coalitions of regional army commanders, to sustain its control.

It is difficult to build an exclusive governing party as an agent for social transformation. The seduction of power regularly leads to rent seeking or other abuses of power that are not checked by competitive democratic politics and that may distort the original party objectives. The exclusive governing parties in some African states also had limited capacity to control society. Furthermore, the loss of confidence in Marxist-Leninist ideology and in the Soviet model led all eight of the African regimes that had once invoked it to abandon that approach by the early 1990s.

As exclusive governing parties age, many enter a stage in which they maintain control but place less emphasis on mobilization. Some, such as North Korea, may degenerate into vehicles for personal rule and exploitation by the ruler's family and supporters.[19] Finally, as shown by the collapse of communism in the former Soviet Union and Eastern Europe, if and when the party leaders lose faith in the unifying ideology, it may be difficult to maintain party coherence.

## Inclusive Governing Parties

Among the preindustrial countries, especially those with notable ethnic and tribal divisions, the more successful authoritarian parties have been *inclusive*. These systems recognize the autonomy of social, cultural, and economic groups and try to incorporate them or bargain with them, rather than control and remake them. The more successful African one-party systems, such as Kenya and Tanzania, permitted aggregation around personalistic, factional, and ethnic groups within a decentralized party.

Inclusive party systems have sometimes been labeled *authoritarian corporatist systems*. Like the democratic corporatist systems (see Chapter 4), some of these systems encourage the formation of large organized interest groups that can bargain with each other and the state. Unlike the democratic corporatist systems, however, these authoritarian systems provide no political resources directly to the populace. Independent protest and political activity outside of official channels are suppressed. The party leaders permit only limited autonomous demands within the ranks of the party and by groups associated with it.

The inclusive authoritarian systems may permit substantial amounts of autonomous interest aggregation, which may take many forms. The party typically tries to gather various social groups under the general party umbrella and negotiate with outside groups and institutions. Some inclusive parties have attempted aggressive social change. Others have primarily been arenas for interest aggregation. Many inclusive party governments permit other parties to offer candidates in elections, as long as these opposition candidates have no real chance of winning. Indeed, one interesting feature of politics in the last thirty years or so, along with the increasing number of liberal democracies, has been the growth of **electoral authoritarianism.** This is where there is a facade of democracy providing "some space for political opposition, independent media, and social organizations that do not seriously criticize or challenge the regime."[20] The Mexican PRI was long a successful example of an inclusive governing party featuring electoral authoritarianism (see Box 5.4).

The fact that some inclusive authoritarian parties have been impressively durable does not necessarily mean that they are strong or successful. In many countries these parties coexist in uneasy and unstable coalitions with the armed forces and the civilian bureaucracy. In some countries the party has become window dressing for a military regime or personal tyranny. Seldom have these parties been able to solve the economic or ethnic problems that face their country.

These political systems were often created in a struggle against colonialism, and as colonialism becomes more distant, they may implode. As memories of the independence struggle fade and the leaders die off or retire, the ties of ideology and experience that hold these parties together weaken. These developments, in conjunction with the worldwide expansion of democracy, have led to a general loss of legitimacy for the single-party model. In some cases (as in Tanzania), they have adjusted by permitting

## Mexico's PRI

BOX 5.4

One of the oldest and the most inclusive authoritarian parties was the Partido Revolucionario Institucional (PRI) in Mexico. For more than fifty years the PRI dominated the political process and gave other parties no realistic chances of winning elections. The PRI attained this dominance after President Lázaro Cárdenas turned it into a "big-tent" coalition in the 1930s; it was also careful to control the counting of the ballots. It did not have to fear electoral competition, at least until the 1990s. The PRI incorporated many social groups, with separate sectors for labor, agrarian, and middle-class interests. The party dealt with its opponents in carefully designed ways. While some political dissidents were suppressed, others were deliberately enticed into the party. The party also gave informal recognition to political factions grouped behind such figures as former presidents. Various Mexican leaders mobilized their factions within the PRI and in other important groups not directly affiliated with it, such as big business interests. Bargaining

was particularly important every six years when the party had to choose a new presidential nominee, since the Mexican Constitution limits presidents to one term. This guaranteed some turnover of elites. In recent decades, however, rising discontent made it difficult to aggregate interests through a single party. The urban and rural poor who had not shared in Mexico's growth joined with reformers to demand a more fully democratic system. An armed uprising of peasant guerrillas in early 1994 shocked the political establishment and led to promises of genuine democratic competition. Legislative elections in 1997 were more open than earlier contests, and ended the seventy-year rule of the PRI, which then lost the presidency to the National Action Party (PAN) in 2000. After that election, the PRI has quickly diminished as a political force, even though it still controls many state and local governments. In 2006, its candidate ran a distant third in Mexico's presidential election. (See Chapter 14.)

real party competition. More frequently, they have resorted to electoral authoritarianism with varying degrees of manipulation to provide a veneer of domestic and international legitimacy. In more than a few cases, they have turned to naked coercion, with the military serving as final arbiter.

## THE MILITARY AND INTEREST AGGREGATION

After independence, most of the nations of the Third World adopted at least formally democratic governments. But in many countries these civil governments lacked effectiveness and authority, which often led to their breakdown and replacement by **military governments.** The military had instruments of force and organizational capacity, and in the absence of a strong constitutional tradition, it was an effective contender for power. Even under civilian rule, the military had substantial political influence and often constituted a significant power contender. In Brazil, for example, the military played a crucial role in interest aggregation even under the civilian government prior to the

coup of 1964. After that intervention, it was the dominant actor for the next twenty years. In many other countries, the military has long been a similarly important interest aggregator.

The military's virtual monopoly on coercive resources gives it great potential power. Thus, when aggregation fails in democratic or authoritarian party systems, the military may emerge by default as the only force able to maintain orderly government. If the legitimacy of the government is weak and the social order threatens to break down, a united military may be the only force that can sustain political cohesion. The military may also intervene for more self-interested reasons, such as protecting its autonomy or budgets from civilian interference. About two-fifths of the world's nations have confronted military coup attempts at some time, and in about a third of the nations these coups were at least partially successful in changing leaders or policy. Fewer than half of these coup attempts, however, focused on general political issues and public policy. Most coups seemed motivated by the professional interests of the military.

What happens after the military intervenes can vary. The soldiers may support the personal tyranny of

Rebel soldiers (on right), who staged an uprising against the Ivory Coast government and took over large areas of the country, meet with French troops monitoring a cease-fire in 2002.

Pascal Le Segretain/Getty Images

a civilian president or a dominant party. Or the armed forces may use their power to further institutional or ideological objectives. Military rulers may try to create military and/or bureaucratic versions of authoritarian corporatism, linking organized groups and the state bureaucracy with the military as final arbiter. They may undertake "defensive" modernization in alliance with business groups or even more radical modernization. In Latin America almost all the corporatist versions of authoritarian aggregation have had a strong military component and only rarely a dominant authoritarian party.

The major limitation of the military in interest aggregation is that its internal structures are not designed for interest aggregation. The military is primarily organized to have an efficient command structure. It is not set up to aggregate internal differences, to build compromise, to mobilize popular support, or even to communicate with social groups outside the command hierarchy. Nor do military regimes have the legitimacy in the international community that elections provide. Thus the military lacks many of the advantages held by party systems. These internal limitations may be less serious when the military is dealing with common grievances and putting pressure on—or seizing power from—unpopular authorities. The same limitations become a major problem, however, when a military government needs to stake out its own course

and mobilize support for it. For these reasons military governments frequently prove unstable and are often forced to share power with other institutions, or they simply voluntarily withdraw from politics.

## TRENDS IN INTEREST AGGREGATION

As we have previously noted, the democratic trend in the world has gained momentum since the end of the 1980s. Figure 5.2 classifies the world's regimes by their degree of freedom at four points: the end of the 1970s, the end of the 1980s, the late 1990s, and 2005–2006. The percentages should be viewed as estimates, often based on limited information. But the figure provides a rough idea of the importance of competitive interest aggregation across the world.

In 1978 fewer than one-third of the world's almost 200 independent countries were classified as free. These regimes, which tended to have competitive party systems as their predominant interest aggregation structures, were dominant in Western Europe and North America (including the Caribbean), not uncommon in Latin America and Asia, but rare in Africa and the Middle East. Nearly as many countries had some versions of a single-party regime, and about 40 percent were classified as not free. In slightly less than a quarter of all countries the military dominated

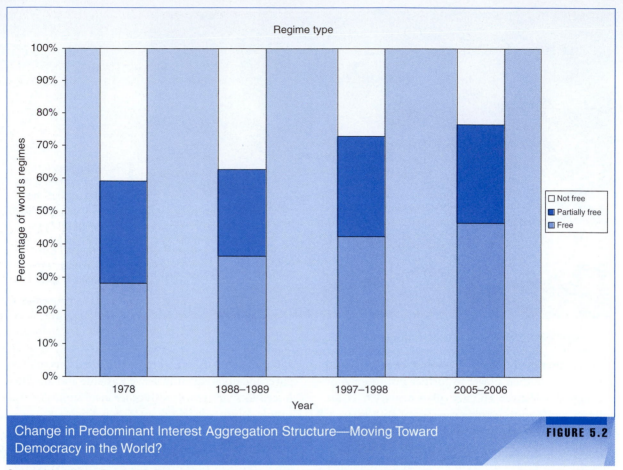

Change in Predominant Interest Aggregation Structure—Moving Toward Democracy in the World?

**FIGURE 5.2**

Source: Adapted from Raymond D. Gastil, *Freedom in the World 1979, 1988–1989, 1997–1998* (New York: Freedom House, 1979, 1989, 1998), and other data from www.freedomhouse.org.

interest aggregation, either formally (military governments) or in practice (military-dominated civilian governments). The military-dominated regimes accounted for about a third or more of the countries in Africa and Latin America. Single-party systems were the main form in Eastern Europe and relatively common in Africa and Asia and accounted for most of the remaining unfree countries.

A decade later, the trend was away from single-party governments. Across the world they declined from 30 to 24 percent of the world's nations, although still accounting for nearly 40 percent of African nations. As we already know, the decline of exclusive governing party regimes is even more striking. The proportion of military governments actually increased slightly, from 23 to 26 percent of the world's countries. There was a minor democratic trend toward competitive party and electoral systems, with

more than one-third of the world's governments now classified as free.

The trend toward democracy took off more dramatically beginning in 1989 in Eastern Europe, and with new pressures for democracy in the developing world. By the late 1990s, for the first time in world history there were more free than unfree states. The collapse of communism in Europe and elsewhere was in large part responsible, but the number of military dictatorships also declined. The declining acceptance of authoritarian governments, as well as the withdrawal of Soviet support, contributed to this trend, especially in Africa. Many African nations moved toward a more democratic and free system during the 1990s. Yet a few authoritarian party systems with exclusive governing parties are still around, such as China and Cuba. Most of the remaining unfree states are in the Middle East, Central Asia, and Africa. Many African nations still

## Trying to Make Democracy Work

BOX 5.5

Nigeria is in many ways typical of the rough road to democracy that many developing countries have traveled. The Nigerian military government, which had ousted an ineffective civilian government in 1983, responded to the democratization wave of the early 1990s by introducing careful and measured reforms. It initiated state-level elections in 1991 and federal legislative elections in 1992. Finally, after presidential elections scheduled for June 1993, the transition to civilian rule would be complete. But the military kept strict control of the electoral process and disqualified politicians who had held office under previous civilian regimes (because they were considered to be tainted by corruption). Voters were left with a choice of only two parties, both created by the government. Voting turnout was low because many voters became cynical about the process. These doubts were confirmed when the military annulled the presidential election, even before the results were announced, and installed an interim government instead. In November 1993, Defense Minister General Sani Abacha launched a military coup which overturned the interim government, banned all political activity, dissolved the legislature, dismissed the elected state governments, and thus ended Nigeria's cautious experiment with elections. In 1998, President Abacha suddenly died of a heart attack, and the reform process could begin anew. In spring 1999, the military government held a presidential election. The victor was a former army general, Olusegun Obasanjo, who went on to try to implement democratic reforms. He was reelected four years later. But continuing ethnic and religious violence, corruption, and abuses of power have made the Nigerian transition to democracy fragile. (See Chapter 18.)

feature some variety of the "electoral authoritarianism" discussed above, with severe constraints on civil freedom and electoral opposition. A few remain unabashed authoritarian systems (as in Zimbabwe) or are mired in deadly civil war (as in Sudan and Somalia).

Perhaps in deference to the decline in the legitimacy of authoritarianism, the military throughout the world is now more likely to dominate from behind the scenes than through direct rule. Latin America also has experienced the genuine replacement of military regimes by competitive party regimes in such important countries as Argentina, Brazil, Chile, and Uruguay. Although the era of confidence in the military as a solution to development seems to have passed, military domination remains likely when other types of government are unsuccessful.

Where there has been "backsliding" on the road to democracy, the military has often played a part. So we cannot assume that the democratizing trend will continue relentlessly. Multiparty regimes that seem unable to cope with economic and social problems often lose their legitimacy. Such is now the challenge facing parts of Eastern Europe, as well as much of the Third World. In many of these countries, competitive party systems exist, but citizens have very little trust in them and often consider them to be corrupt. And military coups continue to occur, as in Thailand and Fiji in the fall of 2006.

## SIGNIFICANCE OF INTEREST AGGREGATION

How interests are aggregated is an important determinant of what a country's government does for and to its citizens. Successful public policy depends on effective interest aggregation. One important function of interest aggregation is to narrow policy options, so that the desires and demands of citizens are converted into a few policy alternatives. Many possible policies are eliminated in the process. Those that remain typically have the backing of significant sectors of society. For instance, even though such policies have been adopted in other nations, there has never been a "serious" proposal that the United States government take over the country's steel industry, because no powerful group has ever favored it.

In democratic countries, competitive party systems narrow down and combine policy preferences. Through elections, voters throw their support behind some of these parties and thus shape party representation in the legislature. Even at the legislative stage, further consolidation and coalition building takes place. At some point, however, most policy options have been eliminated from consideration. Either no party backed them or the parties supporting them fared badly in the elections.

In noncompetitive party systems, military governments, and monarchies, aggregation works differently, but with the similar effect of narrowing policy options. On some issues, aggregation virtually determines policy, as when a military government or a faction of an authoritarian party can decide the government's program. In other cases the legislative assembly, military council, or party politburo may contain several factions that must negotiate over policy. The narrowing of policy choices also affects the influence and access of social interests.

But politics shapes its environment as well as reflecting it. Interest aggregation often alters the polarization that the political culture projects into policymaking. That is one reason why politics is so fascinating. Well-organized and well-led political parties might, at least for a while, be able to dominate politics and limit the strength of extremist groups in the legislature. Conversely, well-organized extremists might be able to appeal to the fears and prejudices of some groups and get their support at the polls, thus gaining more legislative strength in an otherwise consensual country.

Aggregation ultimately affects the government's adaptability and stability. Authoritarian interest aggregation tends to create political power structures that do not reflect popular opinion. In highly divided and conflict-ridden societies, rulers may portray such lack of representation as a virtue. Leaders of military coups often justify their overthrow of party governments by claiming to depolarize politics and rid the nation of conflict it cannot afford. Similarly, heads of authoritarian parties typically claim that their nation must concentrate all its energies and resources on common purposes and that party competition would be too polarizing.

In contrast, most proponents of democratic interest aggregation argue that the best hope for accommodating conflicting social and political interests lies in free and fair electoral competition, followed by negotiation among those groups that gain the voters' favor. Democracy thus leads policymakers to act as the people wish. In a polarized political culture, the division and uncertainty that interest aggregation implies may be seen as a high price to pay for citizen control. As the frequent instability in authoritarian governments indicates, however, it may be easier to do away with the appearance of polarization than with the reality. Competing demands may find their way to the surface anyway, and the citizens may end up without either freedom and participation or stability.

## REVIEW QUESTIONS

- What structures other than political parties aggregate interests?

- What is Duverger's Law? Which two effects does it imply?

- What is the median voter result, and why does it pertain only to two-party systems?

- What are the differences between totalitarian parties and other single-party systems?

- Why do many countries turn to military governments, and why are military governments often short-lived?

## KEY TERMS

accommodative party
    systems
authoritarian party systems
closed-list PR systems
competitive party systems
conflictual party system
consensual party system
consociationalism
double-ballot
Duverger's Law

effective number of
    parties
electoral authoritarianism
electoral system
exclusive governing party
inclusive governing party
institutional groups
interest aggregation
majoritarian two-party
    systems

majority-coalition systems
majority runoff
mechanical effect
median voter result
military governments
multiparty systems
open-list systems
party system
patron-client networks
plurality election rules

primary elections
proportional
    representation (PR)
psychological effect
single-member district
    (SMD)
single-member district
    plurality (SMDP)
    election rule
strategic voting

## SUGGESTED READINGS

Cox, Gary W. *Making Votes Count: Strategic Coordination in the World's Electoral Systems.* Cambridge: Cambridge University Press, 1997.

Dalton, Russell J., and Martin P. Wattenberg. *Parties Without Partisans: Political Change in Advanced Industrial Democracies.* New York: Oxford University Press, 2000.

Decalo, Samuel. *Coups and Army Rule in Africa,* 2nd ed. New Haven, CT: Yale University Press, 1990.

Downs, Anthony. *An Economic Theory of Democracy.* New York: Harper & Row, 1957.

Farrell, David. *Electoral Systems: A Comparative Introduction.* New York: St. Martin's Press, 2001.

Farrell, David, Ian Holliday, and Paul Webb, eds. *Political Parties in Democratic States.* Oxford: Oxford University Press, 2002.

Jackson, Robert H., and Carl G. Rosberg. *Personal Rule in Black Africa.* Berkeley: University of California Press, 1982.

Kitschelt, Herbert. *The Transformation of European Social Democracy.* New York: Cambridge University Press, 1994.

Laver, Michael, and Norman Schofield. *Multiparty Government.* New York: Oxford University Press, 1990.

Lijphart, Arend. *Electoral Systems and Party Systems.* New York: Oxford University Press, 1994.

———. *Patterns of Democracy.* New Haven, CT: Yale University Press, 1999.

Linz, Juan J. *Totalitarian and Authoritarian Regimes.* Baltimore: Johns Hopkins University Press, 2002.

Mainwaring, Scott. *Rethinking Party Systems in the Third Wave of Democratization.* Stanford, CA: Stanford University Press, 1999.

Michels, Robert. *Political Parties.* New York: Free Press, 1962.

Nordlinger, Eric A. *Soldiers in Politics: Military Coups and Governments.* Englewood Cliffs, NJ: Prentice-Hall, 1976.

Powell, G. Bingham, Jr. *Contemporary Democracies: Participation, Stability, and Violence.* Cambridge: Harvard University Press, 1982.

———. *Elections as Instruments of Democracy.* New Haven, CT: Yale University Press, 2000.

Riker, William H. *Liberalism Against Populism.* San Francisco: W. H. Freeman, 1982.

Strøm, Kaare, Wolfgang C. Müller, and Torbjörn Bergman, eds. *Cabinets and Coalition Bargaining: The Democratic Life Cycle in Western Europe.* Oxford: Oxford University Press, 2008.

## ENDNOTES

1. See, for example, Luis Roniger and Ayse Gunes-Ayata, eds., *Democracy, Clientelism, and Civil Society* (Boulder, CO: Lynne Rienner, 1994); S. Eisenstadt and L. Roniger, *Patrons, Clients, and Friends* (Cambridge: Cambridge University Press, 1984); Lucian W. Pye, *Asian Power and Politics* (Cambridge: Harvard University Press, 1985); and Martin Shefter, "Patronage and Its Opponents," in *Political Parties and the State* (Princeton, NJ: Princeton University Press, 1994).

2. Unfortunately, elections cannot solve all the problems of aggregating interests fairly. For example, giving each citizen one vote does not take into account the varying intensities with which different people may hold their opinions. Moreover, economists and political scientists have found that when there are three or more alternatives in any decision, there is no fair way to aggregate votes to select a single, best outcome ("Arrow's Paradox"). See Duncan Black, "On the Rationale of Group Decision Making," *Journal of Political Economy* 56 (1948): 23–34; and Kenneth Arrow, *Social Choice and Individual Values* (New Haven, CT: Yale University Press, 1951). For an accessible discussion of some political implications, see William H. Riker, *Liberalism Against Populism* (San Francisco: W. H. Freeman, 1982); and Kenneth A. Shepsle and Mark S. Bonchek, *Analyzing Politics: Rationality, Behavior, and Institutions* (New York: Norton, 1997), Part II.

3. Hans-Dieter Klingemann, Richard Hofferbert, and Ian Budge, eds., *Parties, Policy, and Democracy* (Boulder, CO: Westview, 1995); Michael, Gallagher, Michael Laver, and Peter Mair, *Representative Government in Western Europe,* 4th ed. (New York: McGraw-Hill, 2005); and Richard Rose, *Do Parties Make a Difference?* (Chatham, NJ: Chatham House, 1984), ch. 5.

4. Joseph A. Schumpeter, *Capitalism, Socialism, and Democracy* (New York: Harper, 1943).

5. However, in Communist China semicompetitive elections for village leadership positions since 1987 has in some areas brought the opinions of local leaders and ordinary citizens closer together. See Melanie Manion, "The Electoral Connection in the Chinese Countryside," *American Political Science Review* 90 (1996): 736–48.

6. See Russell J. Dalton, *Citizen Politics: Public Opinion and Political Parties in Advanced Industrial Democracies,* 5th ed. (Washington, DC: Congressional Quarterly Press, 2008).

7. Ian Budge, David Robertson, and Derek Hearl, eds., *Ideology, Strategy, and Party Change: Spatial Analyses of Post-War Election Programmes in 19 Democracies* (New York: Cambridge University Press, 1987); Richard Katz and Peter Mair, eds., *How Parties Organize: Change and Adaptation in Party Organizations in Western Democracies* (Thousand Oaks, CA: Sage 1994).

8. Maurice Duverger, *Political Parties: Their Organization and Activity in the Modern State,* [1954] trans. Barbara and Robert North (New York: Wiley, 1963). For a more contemporary contribution, see Gary W. Cox, *Making Votes Count* (Cambridge: Cambridge University Press, 1997).

9. Anthony Downs, *An Economic Theory of Democracy* (New York: Harper & Row, 1957).

10. The effective number of parties is calculated as follows: first calculate the proportion of seats (or votes) held by each party. Square each of these proportions and then add them all up. Finally, divide one by the sum of all the squared proportions. See Markku Laakso and Rein Taagepera, "'Effective' Number of Parties: A Measure with Application to West Europe," *Comparative Political Studies* 12 (1979): 3–27.

11. See Pradeep Chhibber and Kenneth Kollman, *The Formation of National Party Systems* (Princeton, NJ: Princeton University Press, 2004).

12. For analyses of the consequences of election laws, see Douglas Rae, *The Political Consequences of Election Laws* (New Haven, CT: Yale University Press, 1967); and Arend Lijphart, *Electoral Systems and Party Systems: A Study of Twenty-seven Democracies, 1945–1990* (Oxford: Oxford University Press, 1994).

13. On government coalitions, see especially Michael Laver and Norman Schofield, *Multiparty Government: The Politics of Coalition in Europe* (New York: Oxford University Press 1990); and Kaare Strøm, Wolfgang C. Müller, and Torbjörn Bergman, eds., *Cabinets and Coalition Bargaining: The Democratic Life Cycle in Western Europe* (New York: Oxford University Press, 2008).

14. On elections and the representation of votes and preferences, as well as the trade-off with accountability, see G. Bingham Powell, Jr., *Elections as Instruments of Democracy* (New Haven, CT: Yale University Press, 2000), chs. 5–10.

15. See Arend Lijphart, *Democracy in Plural Societies* (New Haven, CT: Yale University Press, 1977); and Arend Lijphart, *Patterns of Democracy* (New Haven, CT: Yale University Press, 1999).

16. See Lijphart, *Patterns of Democracy*; G. Bingham Powell, Jr., *Contemporary Democracies* (Cambridge: Harvard University Press, 1982), chs. 8 and 10; and Juan J. Linz and Alfred Stepan, eds., *The Breakdown of Democratic Regimes* (Baltimore: Johns Hopkins University Press, 1978).

17. Juan Linz, *Totalitarian and Authoritarian Regimes* (Boulder, CO: Lynne Rienner, 2000); Amos Perlmutter, *Modern Authoritarianism: A Comparative Institutional Analysis* (New Haven, CT: Yale University Press, 1981), especially 62–114.

18. See Melanie Manion, "Politics in China," Chapter 13 below; for the earlier period, see, for example, Franz Schurman, *Ideology and Organization in Communist China* (Berkeley: University of California Press, 1966).

19. Juan Linz calls these "sultanistic" regimes; see *Totalitarian and Authoritarian Regimes* (Boulder, CO: Lynne Rienner, 2000), 151–157; Houchang Chehabi and Juan Linz, ed. *Sultanistic Regimes* (Baltimore: Johns Hopkins University Press, 1998); and Robert H. Jackson and Carl G. Rosberg, *Personal Rule in Black Africa* (Berkeley: University of California Press, 1982).

20. Larry Diamond, "Thinking About Hybrid Regimes," *Journal of Democracy* 13 (2002): 26; and the articles by Andreas Schedler; Steven Levitsky and Lucan Way; and Nicolas van de Walle in the same issue.

# GOVERNMENT AND POLICYMAKING

**Policymaking** is the pivotal stage in the political process, the point at which bills become law or edicts are issued by the rulers. Later, policies are implemented and enforced. To understand public policy, we must know how decisions are made. Where is power effectively located in different political systems? What does it take to change public policy: a simple majority vote in the legislature or approval also by an independently elected executive? Or is it a decree issued by the military commanders or the party central committee? Or is it merely the whim of the personal dictator?

This chapter focuses on decision rules and on the policymaking role of government agencies, such as legislatures, chief executives, bureaucracies, and courts. Government agencies are at the core of policymaking. While parties, interest groups, and other actors may be very active in articulating and aggregating interests, government officials do most of the actual initiation and formulation of policy proposals. Interest group demands for tax relief or for the protection of endangered species cannot succeed unless they are transformed into policy by government officials according to some accepted decision rules. They cannot be effective until these policies are appropriately implemented by other officials.

Yet, government action does not flow in one direction only. The interaction between government and citizens is a two-way process. It includes an upward flow of influence and demands from the society, as well as a downward flow of decisions from the government. (See Figure 2.2 in Chapter 2.)

## CONSTITUTIONS AND DECISION RULES

A constitution establishes the basic rules of decision-making, rights, and the distribution of authority in a political system. We sometimes use the term "constitution" to refer to a specific document laying out such principles—for example, the one adopted by the Founders of the United States in 1787. But a constitution need not be embodied in a single document. In fact, it rarely is. We should therefore think of a constitution as a set of rules and principles, whether it is a specific written document, a set of customs or practices, or, as is usually the case, both. Even a military or party dictatorship typically sets procedures for having decrees proposed, considered, and adopted.

Written constitutions are particularly important in political systems based on the *rule of law*. This means that government should take no action that has not been authorized by law and that citizens can be punished only for actions that violate an existing law. Under the rule of law, the constitution is the supreme body of laws.

A constitution thus contains a set of **decision rules**—the basic rules governing how decisions are made. Policymaking is the conversion of social interests and demands into authoritative public decisions. Constitutions establish the rules by which this happens. They confer the power to propose policies on specific groups or institutions. They may give others the right to amend, reject, or approve such proposals, or to implement, police, or adjudicate them. They may specify how many resources are needed to make policies, as well as what these resources are.

Decision rules affect political activity because they determine what political resources are valuable in influencing decisions and how to acquire and use these resources. For example, in a federal and decentralized system such as the United States, a pressure group may have to approach both the legislative and the executive branches, and it may have to be active both at the state and the federal levels. If instead decisions are made by decree from the commander of the armed forces or the central committee of a single-party state, groups will need to influence these crucial policymakers.

Different decision rules have different attractions. More inclusive rules about policymaking—such as those that require the cooperation of several institutions or the support of over 50 percent of voters—can protect against hasty decisions. They can also prevent decisions that disadvantage large minorities (perhaps close to half) of the voters. At the same time, more inclusive rules can give a minority the power to block proposals favored by a majority. The more inclusive the voting rules are, as the percentage to approve approaches unanimity, the less likely it is that any decision can be made at all. Less inclusive decision rules make it easier to reach a policy, but many interests may be ignored.

Both the government as a whole and its institutions have decision rules. Decision rules may be simple or complex and apply to different circumstances. For example, the U.S. Congress has many different decision rules that apply under different circumstances, such as a simple majority in each house to pass a bill initially, but a two-thirds majority to override a presidential veto. The British House of Commons uses a much smaller set of rules (mainly simple majority rule). Decision rules may be more or less formal and precise. Most legislatures have formal and precise decision rules, whereas cabinets at the head of the executive branch often have informal and flexible rules.

Within any given branch of government or other political institution, numerous rules affect the policymaking process. In most modern assemblies the decision rules about voting are *egalitarian*, which is to say that each member has the same voting power. Simply speaking: one person, one vote. That is hardly ever true in government departments (ministries), however. Or in dictatorships. There, decisionmaking is *hierarchical*. Everybody is supposed to defer to his or her superior. In a pure hierarchy, only the vote of a person at the very top (for example, the minister) counts. Such a decision rule makes it easy to respond quickly in a policymaking emergency, but few interests or ideas may be taken into account.

Even when decisions are made through equal voting, the inclusiveness of the decision rules still shapes the outcomes. Many institutions operate through simple majority voting: in a choice between two options, whichever option gets the larger number of votes wins. Alternatively, more inclusive rules—such as "qualified" majorities of three-fifths, two-thirds, or even three-fourths—are sometimes required for particularly consequential decisions. For example, the U.S. Constitution requires two-thirds majorities in both houses of Congress in order to amend the Constitution or override a presidential veto. The most inclusive voting rule is unanimity, which means that any one member can block any decision.

It is important that decision rules in a democracy be transparent and stable. If they are not, citizens will not know what to expect from government. That may in turn cause them to be less trusting and less willing to invest or make other commitments. It may also lead to serious conflicts, and ultimately government may break down and issues be decided by force. The importance of having predictable decision rules was suggested by Thomas Jefferson in his introduction to the first Manual of the House of Representatives: "A bad set of rules is better than no rules at all."

## Making Constitutions

Making a constitution is a fundamental political act: it creates or transforms decision rules. Most current constitutions were formed as the result of some break, often violent, with the past—war, revolution, or rebellion against colonial rule. New decision rules were made to accommodate new internal or external powers. Thus, the defeated powers and the successor states of World Wars I and II all adopted new constitutions or had new constitutions imposed on them.

Britain is unusual in having not a formal written constitution but only a long accepted and highly developed set of customs and conventions, buttressed by important ordinary statutes. This reflects the British record of gradual, incremental, and (on the whole) peaceful political change. Nevertheless, the major changes in British decision rules—such as the shift of power from the Crown to Parliament in the seventeenth century, and the Reform Acts of 1832 and 1867, which established party and cabinet government and vastly extended the right to vote—followed on periods of civil war or unrest.

Perhaps the most significant exception to the association between disruptive upheavals and constitution creation is the peaceful development over the last fifty years of the constitution of the European Union, whose growing powers are altering the decision rules affecting about 460 million Europeans in twenty-seven countries. While there has been no violence associated with the formation and growth of the EU, its origins lie in the bitter lessons of World Wars I and II.

The decades since World War II have seen much constitutional experimentation. Not only the defeated powers, but many new states—such as India and Nigeria, which achieved independence with the breakup of colonial empires—introduced new political arrangements. Some of the new states in the developing areas, such as Nigeria, have subsequently changed their form of government several times. In the last two decades the worldwide trend toward democracy, the end of the Cold War, and the dissolution of the Soviet Union have produced a new round of constitutional design. The recent constitutional crafting in Eastern Europe, Russia, and the other Soviet successor states as well as in South Africa and elsewhere have reignited old debates about the virtues and faults of different constitutional arrangements, or about the very wisdom of constitutional engineering.[1]

## DEMOCRACY AND AUTHORITARIANISM

The most important distinction in policymaking is between democratic and authoritarian systems. **Democracy** means "government by the people." In small political systems, such as local communities, "the people" may share directly in debating, deciding, and implementing public policy. In large political systems, such as contemporary states, democracy must be achieved largely through indirect participation in policymaking. Policymaking power is delegated to officials chosen by the people.

Elections, competitive political parties, free mass media, and representative assemblies are political structures that make some degree of democracy, some "government by the people," possible in large political

systems. Competitive elections give citizens a chance to shape policy through their selection and rejection of key policymakers. Such indirect democracy is not complete or ideal. Moreover, the democratic opportunities in less economically developed societies are often meaningful to educated elites or to those living near the centers of government, but less relevant to the average citizen in the countryside. But the more citizens are involved and the more influential their choices, the more democratic the system.

In **authoritarian regimes,** in contrast, the policymakers are chosen by military councils, hereditary families, dominant political parties, and the like. Citizens are either ignored or pressed into symbolic assent to the government's choices.

The basic decision rules of political systems—both democratic and authoritarian—differ along three important dimensions:

1. the separation of powers among different branches of government;
2. the geographic distribution of authority between the central (national) government and lower levels, such as states, provinces, or municipalities; and
3. limitations on government authority.

We shall discuss these dimensions in order, beginning with the separation of authority between executive and legislative institutions.

## SEPARATION OF GOVERNMENT POWERS

The theory of **separation of powers** between different institutions of government has a long and venerable history going back at least to the work of Locke and Montesquieu.[2] Separation of powers, they argued, has the virtue of preventing the injustices that might result from an unchecked executive or legislature. Madison and Hamilton elaborated this theory in *The Federalist*,[3] which described and defended the institutional arrangements proposed by the U.S. Constitutional Convention of 1787.

Political theorists in the course of the nineteenth and first part of the twentieth centuries drew upon the two successful historical cases of representative democracy—Britain and the United States—to create the "classic" separation of powers theory. This theory argued that there are essentially two forms of

| | | TABLE 6.1 |
|---|---|---|
| **Distinguishing Features of Parliamentary and Presidential Democracies** | | |
| **Distinguishing Features[a]** | **Parliamentary Democracies** | **Presidential Democracies** |
| Title of chief executive | Prime minister (head of government) | President (head of state and government) |
| Selection of assembly | By citizens in competitive election | By citizens in competitive election |
| Selection of chief executive | By assembly after election or removal | By citizens in competitive election |
| Removal of chief executive before fixed term? | By assembly: (No) confidence vote | Fixed terms |
| Dismissal of assembly before fixed term? | Prime minister may call for early election[b] | Fixed terms |
| Authority to legislate | Assembly only | Assembly plus president (e.g., veto) |
| Party relations in assembly and executive | Same parties control both; cohesive party voting | Different party control possible; less cohesive party voting |

[a]These define the pure parliamentary and presidential types; as discussed in the text, many constitutional systems, especially in Eastern Europe, "mix" the features of the two types.

[b]Some constitutional systems that are parliamentary in all other ways do not allow for early legislative elections. All parliamentary democracies provide for legislative elections after some maximum time (from three to five years) since the last election.

representative democratic government: the presidential and the parliamentary.

The **democratic presidential regime** provides two separate agencies of government—the executive and the legislative—separately elected and authorized by the people. (See Table 6.1, column 3.) Each branch is elected for a fixed term; no one branch can by ordinary means unseat the other; and each has specific powers under the constitution. Ultimate power to authorize legislation and approve budgets in modern democracies resides with the legislature, whose relationships with the executive are then critical for concentration or dispersal of power. Different presidential regimes provide their presidents with a variety of different powers over government appointments and policymaking. For example, some presidents have the authority to veto legislation or to make policy by executive decree under some conditions.[4] In the United States, both the legislature and executive (Congress and the presidency) have large and significant roles in policymaking. In some other democratic presidential systems, such as Brazil, the president may have such a variety of constitutional powers (including the power to make laws through "emergency" decrees) that he or she can reduce the role of the legislature. But coordination between the separate institutions of executive and legislature must somehow be achieved to make policy.

The **parliamentary regimes,** in contrast, make the executive and legislative branches interdependent. (See Table 6.1, column 2.) First of all, only the legislative branch is directly elected. The prime minister and his or her cabinet (the collective leadership of the executive branch) emerge from the legislature. The cabinet is chaired by the prime minister, who is the head of government and selects the other cabinet members.[5] Typically, neither branch has a fixed term of office. The cabinet can be voted out of office at any time, and most often this is true of the legislature (the parliament) as well.

The critical feature that makes this possible is the **confidence relationship** between the prime minister and the parliamentary majority. In a parliamentary system, the prime minister and his or her cabinet must at all times enjoy the confidence of the parliamentary majority. Whenever the parliamentary majority for whatever reason votes a lack of confidence, the prime minister and all the other cabinet members have to resign. At the same time, the prime minister typically has the power to dissolve parliament and call new elections at any time. These two powers—the parliamentary majority's dismissal power and the prime minister's dissolution power—make the two branches mutually dependent. This structure induces agreement between them by forcing each branch to be acceptable to the other.

Prime ministers in parliamentary democracies lead precarious political lives. Unlike presidents in presidential systems, prime ministers can be voted out of office at any time, and for any reason, by a parliamentary majority. There are two ways in which this

## The Confidence Vote in Britain

BOX 6.1

British prime ministers can resort to the confidence motion in order to bring rebellious party members into line. Usually, the mere threat of a confidence motion is sufficient. But in 1993, Conservative Prime Minister John Major faced a parliamentary crisis over the ratification of the Maastricht Treaty, which expanded the powers of the European Union. Major had only a slim majority in the House of Commons. Many "Euroskeptics" in his own party were opposed to the Maastricht Treaty. About twenty of these Conservative dissidents voted with the Opposition and helped defeat the Maastricht Treaty in the House of Commons.

Immediately after this embarrassing defeat, however, Major introduced a confidence motion on his Maastricht policy. He announced that if he lost this vote, he would dissolve the House of Commons and hold new elections. Many of the Conservative dissidents feared that their party would do poorly in such an election and that they might personally lose their seats. Prime Minister Major's confidence motion passed by a vote of 339 to 299, and the House of Commons approved the Maastricht Treaty.

Thus, the confidence vote, which is generally available to prime ministers in parliamentary systems, helps explain why party discipline tends to be stronger in parliamentary than in presidential systems.

---

can happen. One is when parliament passes a motion expressing a lack of confidence in the prime minister—a no-confidence motion. The other possibility is when parliament defeats a motion expressing confidence in the prime minister—a confidence motion. No-confidence motions are typically introduced by the parliamentary opposition in the hope of bringing down the prime minister. Confidence motions, on the other hand, are normally introduced by prime ministers themselves.

Since one possible result of a confidence motion is being kicked out of office, it may seem like a form of Russian roulette. In reality, however, the confidence vote can be a powerful weapon in the hands of the prime minister. It is typically attached to a bill (a policy proposal) the prime minister favors, but the parliamentary majority does not. By attaching a confidence motion to the bill, the prime minister forces the members of parliament to choose between the bill and the fall of the cabinet. This can be a particularly painful choice for dissident members of the prime minister's own party. If they vote for the bill, they may bring down their own government, and perhaps immediately have to face the voters to boot (see Box 6.1). Thus, the possibility of a confidence motion actually helps explain why party discipline tends to be stronger in parliamentary than in presidential systems.

Thus parliamentary democracies do not experience the form of divided government that is common under presidentialism, when the party that controls the presidency does not control the legislature, or vice versa. Instead, the chief executive (prime minister and cabinet) becomes the agent of the parliamentary majority. In most parliamentary systems the cabinet consists largely of members of parliament. Conflicts between parliament and the executive are less likely to occur and decisionmaking tends to be more efficient than under presidentialism. Since the same party (or parties) controls both branches of government, the cabinet tends to dominate policymaking, and the legislature may be less influential than under a presidential constitution.

Not all democracies fit neatly into the presidential or parliamentary category. Some, such as France, are often characterized as mixed, or **"semipresidential."** In some of these mixed types, the president and the legislature are separately elected (as in presidential systems), but the president then has the power to dissolve the legislature (as in parliamentary systems). In such systems, the cabinet may be appointed by the president (as under presidentialism), but subject to dismissal by the legislature (as under parliamentarism). A variety of arrangements exist for such shared control. Their consequences are often sharply affected by which party or coalition controls the presidency and legislature. Many of the new constitutions of the emergent democracies of Eastern Europe and Asia are of this mixed type.

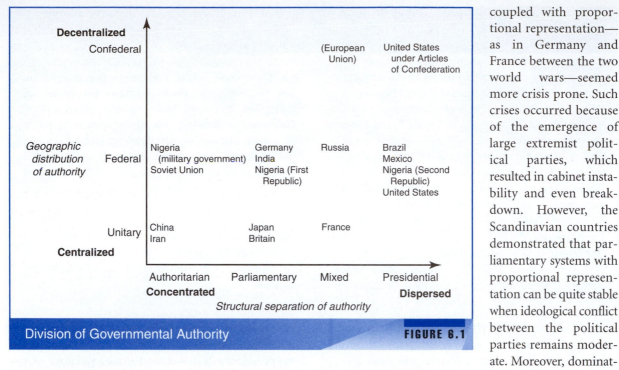

**Decentralized**
Confederal

**Geographic distribution of authority**    Federal

Unitary
**Centralized**

Authoritarian    Parliamentary    Mixed    Presidential
**Concentrated**    **Dispersed**
*Structural separation of authority*

| | Authoritarian | Parliamentary | Mixed | Presidential |
|---|---|---|---|---|
| Confederal | | | (European Union) | United States under Articles of Confederation |
| Federal | Nigeria (military government) Soviet Union | Germany India Nigeria (First Republic) | Russia | Brazil Mexico Nigeria (Second Republic) United States |
| Unitary | China Iran | Japan Britain | France | |

**Division of Governmental Authority**    **FIGURE 6.1**

Reading across Figure 6.1, we see political systems classified by the separation of policymaking powers between executive and legislative institutions, from concentrated to dispersed. The vertical dimension of the table shows geographic division of power, which is discussed in the next section. In authoritarian governments on the left of the figure, executive, legislative, and judicial power are typically concentrated. Two of the twelve countries discussed in this book—China and Iran—have authoritarian governments not chosen in competitive elections. Britain, Germany, Japan, and India are parliamentary systems in which executive and legislative powers are concentrated in cabinets responsible to the popularly elected lower houses of parliament. At the extreme right of Figure 6.1 are pure presidential systems, such as Brazil, Mexico, and the United States. Nigeria seems to be in transition to a presidential democracy. In between, we find mixed systems, such as France and Russia.

In the debate over the best system of representative democracy, many political theorists traditionally favored the British-style parliamentary system. This version of parliamentarism—coupling plurality voting rules that usually create clear single-party majorities in parliament with a cabinet and prime minister responsible to parliament—can result in fairly stable governments responsible to the public will. Parliamentarism

coupled with proportional representation—as in Germany and France between the two world wars—seemed more crisis prone. Such crises occurred because of the emergence of large extremist political parties, which resulted in cabinet instability and even breakdown. However, the Scandinavian countries demonstrated that parliamentary systems with proportional representation can be quite stable when ideological conflict between the political parties remains moderate. Moreover, dominating parliamentary majorities, as in Northern Ireland, can sometimes threaten minority groups and intensify conflict.[6] In comparison to both versions of parliamentary government, the U.S. presidential system has often been criticized for periodically producing divided government, which could result in stalemate or "grid lock."

The third wave of democratization reopened these parliamentary-presidential debates. Advocates of parliamentarism, particularly of the proportional variety, argue that it provides a consensual framework in which different economic, ethnic, and religious groups can find representation and negotiate their differences. Parliamentary systems also have the flexibility to change governments between elections if the people disapprove of actions of the executive. Since many of the current transitional democracies are deeply divided, a parliamentary, proportional representation system may be particularly suitable. Presidentialism, they argue, is more susceptible to social conflict and democratic breakdown. Under conditions of divided government, a confrontation between the two legitimately elected institutions representing the people can tear a political system apart. Or, a strong president can use executive powers to repress competition.

Other scholars point out that practical politics is producing presidential systems with significant executive power.[7] Even in the domain of the former British empire (such as in Nigeria) and in most of Eastern Europe and the Soviet successor states, the constitutions provide for powerful presidents. Latin America has been dominated by presidential regimes for more than a century. A 1993 referendum in Brazil reaffirmed its commitment to presidentialism. Presidentialism also offers the citizens a more direct choice of chief executive, and it puts more effective checks on the power of the majority in the legislature.

## GEOGRAPHIC DISTRIBUTION OF GOVERNMENT POWER

Another distinction between governmental structures is the geographic division of power: confederal systems at one extreme, unitary systems at the other extreme, and **federal systems** in the middle. (See the vertical dimension of Figure 6.1.) The United States under the Articles of Confederation was confederal. Ultimate power rested with the states. The central government had authority over foreign affairs and defense but depended on financial and other support from the states. Under the Constitution of 1787, the U.S. government changed from confederal to federal, which is to say that both central and state governments had separate spheres of authority and the means to implement their power. Today, the United States, Germany, Russia, India, Nigeria, Mexico, and Brazil are federal systems in which central and local units each have autonomy in particular spheres of public policy. These policy areas and powers are, however, divided among central and local units in varying ways. Britain, France, China, Japan, and Iran are unitary systems with power and authority concentrated in the central government. Regional and local units have only those powers specifically delegated to them by the central government, which may change or withdraw these powers at will.

Most of the world's states are unitary. In fact, only eighteen states are federal, or fewer than one in ten. Although the federal states are relatively few in number, they tend to be large and politically important. Thus, federal states account for more than one-third of the world's population and 41 percent of its land area. In general, the larger and the more diverse a state is, the more likely it is to be federal.

Federalism is commonly thought to have several advantages. In culturally divided societies, it may help protect ethnic, linguistic, or religious minorities, particularly if they are geographically concentrated. It may serve as a check on overly ambitious rulers and thus protect markets and citizen freedoms. Moreover, federalism may allow subunits (such as states) to experiment with different policy programs. Governments may thus learn from the experiences of others. In addition, citizens may be free to "vote with their feet" and choose the policy environment that best fits their preferences.

While federalism promotes choice and diversity, however, it does so at the expense of equality. Federalism allows local governments to pursue different policies. One implication is that citizens may get systematically different treatments and benefits from different local governments. Unitary governments may also be in a better position to redistribute resources from richer regions to poorer regions, if that is desirable.

In comparing confederal, federal, and unitary systems, we must distinguish between formal and actual distributions of power. In unitary systems, in spite of the formal concentration of authority at the center, regional and local units may acquire power that the central government rarely challenges. In federal systems, centralized party control may overcome apparent regional autonomy. Thus, the real differences between federal and unitary systems may be considerably less significant than their formal arrangements suggest.

Mexico is an example of the discrepancy between formal and actual federalism. Until recently the Partido Revolucionario Institucional (PRI) had centralized control in this formally federal system. Recent developments in Mexico, with oppositional parties winning ground in some states and the PRI power monopoly under challenge, have produced some "real" federalism to go along with the formalities.

## LIMITATIONS ON GOVERNMENT POWER

Unlike authoritarian regimes, democracies are characterized by some legal or customary limitation on the exercise of power. Systems in which the powers of various government units are defined and limited by a written constitution, statutes, and custom are called **constitutional regimes.** Civil rights—such as the right to a fair trial and freedom to speak, petition, publish, and assemble—are protected against government interference except under specified circumstances.

| Judicial Limitation of Governmental Authority | | TABLE 6.2 |
| --- | --- | --- |
| **Unlimited** | | **Limited** |
| **Nonindependent Courts** | **Independent Courts** | **Judicial Review** |
| China | Britain | United States |
| Iran | | India |
| Nigeria | | Germany |
| | | France |
| | | Brazil |
| | | Japan |
| | | Russia |

The courts are crucial to the limitations on governmental power. As illustrated in Table 6.2, governments may be divided into those, at one extreme, in which the power to coerce citizens is relatively unlimited by the courts, and those, at the other extreme, in which the courts not only protect the rights of citizens but also police other parts of the government to see that their powers are properly exercised. The United States, Germany, and India are systems in which high courts rule effectively on challenges that other parts of the government have exceeded the powers allocated by the constitution. This practice of **judicial review** is authorized to various degrees in about half of the world's democracies and seems to be growing in popularity. But judicial review is often weakened by lack of independence of the appointment or tenure of judges, as in Japan, or by their ineffectiveness in overcoming executive power, as in Russia.

Some other constitutional regimes have independent courts that protect persons against the improper implementation of laws and regulations, but cannot legally overrule the assembly or the political executive, as in Britain. The substantive rights of people in these systems are protected by statute, custom, self-restraint, and political pressure—which are also essential to the effectiveness of courts even where judicial review is authorized. In authoritarian systems, policymakers do not usually allow courts to constrain their use and abuse of power, even where brave judges attempt to rule against them.

Arend Lijphart characterizes only four of the thirty-six democratic systems he examines as having "strong" judicial review: Germany, India, the United States, and Canada after 1982.[8] The Supreme Court of India is most similar to the U.S. Supreme Court, having successfully overruled the prime minister and assembly by declaring over 100 national laws and ordinances to be unconstitutional.[9] The German Constitutional Court also has a substantial impact on national and state policymaking, both through its rulings and through government's anticipation of those rulings.

About a quarter of Lijphart's democracies had either strong or medium-strength judicial review. In both France and Germany, new legislation may be challenged in court by opposition members of parliament even before it takes effect, a process called "abstract" judicial review. Lijphart classified a little over half of his democracies as having "weak judicial review," with the powers of courts constrained by very limited constitutional authority (as in Sweden) or limited independence of government-appointed judges (as in Japan). In the remaining democracies, including Britain, courts enjoyed no power of judicial review of legislation, although, as suggested in Table 6.2, they may still protect individuals from government abuse not specifically authorized by law.

In many of the new democracies of Eastern Europe judicial review was proclaimed in the constitution, but proved harder to implement in practice. There have been striking successes in constraining governments in some countries, as in Bulgaria, but failures in others, such as Albania and Belarus. In Nigeria, the courts long retained a striking degree of judicial independence under a succession of otherwise undemocratic military regimes, but were shown little respect under the Abacha regime of the mid-1990s, which established special military tribunals to prosecute its perceived enemies.

China, in contrast, after explicit rejection of any limits on "mass justice" from the late 1950s to the 1970s, has gradually attempted to introduce a very limited "rule by law." This is seen by Chinese rulers as a way to encourage stability and economic growth and control corruption. However, the practice falls far short of the promise of limitation on governmental authority.

All written constitutions provide for amending procedures. Most framers of constitutions have recognized that basic decision rules must be adaptable, because of potential ambiguities, inefficiencies, changes in citizen values, or unforeseen circumstances. But if amendments are too easy to make, they may jeopardize important constitutional protections. Therefore, many constitutions provide that certain arrangements may not be amended (for example, the provision in the U.S. Constitution granting each state equal representation in the Senate).

Amending procedures vary widely, ranging from the complex to the simple. Perhaps the simplest case is that of the United Kingdom, where an ordinary parliamentary statute may alter the constitution. In some cases, constitutional amendments must be approved by a popular vote. The U.S. Constitution has the most difficult formal procedure.

One of the main points of Figure 6.1 and Tables 6.1 and 6.2 is that constitutions may concentrate or disperse government power along several dimensions.[10] There are necessary trade-offs involved in making such constitutional choices. Probably no one who favors democracy and individual liberties would argue for extreme centralization of power in an omnipotent dictator, as in Thomas Hobbes's *Leviathan* (see Chapter 1). However, constitutional democracies that concentrate power to a somewhat lesser degree, such as the British system, have some important advantages. Their governments tend to be effective and efficient, and by relying on majority rule, they tend to treat all citizens equally. No small group can hold up a decision favored by a solid majority. On the other hand, constitutions that disperse power, like more inclusive decision rules, have their own advantages. They are more likely to check potential abuses of power, such as the tyranny of a majority, and policies will tend to be more stable over time.

## CHECKING THE TOP POLICYMAKERS

One challenge of government is to control the excesses of top political leaders. In many authoritarian systems, there is no legal and institutionalized way to remove the top political leaders if they become unpopular or overstep whatever bounds they may face. Moreover, authoritarian leaders can usually change or simply ignore the constitution when it restricts their desires. Democracies have various procedures for keeping the leaders in check, but the procedures vary among the types of systems. In parliamentary systems, chief executives can be removed virtually at any time through a vote of no confidence if they lose the support of a parliamentary majority. In Germany, for example, Social Democratic Party Chancellor Helmut Schmidt was ousted by Helmut Kohl of the Christian Democratic Party in October 1982.

Democratic presidential systems fall somewhere in between. Unlike prime ministers under parliamentary constitutions, presidents have fixed terms of office. Most presidential systems provide for the removal of presidents before their term is up, but typically only if they are guilty of serious criminal or other wrongdoing. This procedure is called **impeachment.** Impeachment typically involves three components: (1) impeachable offenses are usually identified as presenting unusual danger to the public good or safety; (2) the penalty is removal from office (sometimes with separate criminal penalties); and (3) impeachment cases are decided by the legislature, but require more than ordinary majorities and may also involve the judiciary in some way. The positive value of impeachment is that it provides a way of legally mobilizing political power against a threat to the constitutional or legal order. At the same time, the danger is that it can be used for mere partisan or personal goals.

In the U.S. system, impeachment procedures can be used against the incumbents in top offices, even the president (as in the cases of Presidents Nixon and Clinton) or a Supreme Court justice, if their activities stray too far beyond legal bounds. No U.S. president has yet been convicted by the Senate and removed from office, although that fate has befallen other federal officials, such as judges.

Impeachment is associated with constitutions having powerful presidencies with fixed terms of office, such as those in the United States, Brazil, South Korea, and the Philippines. Impeachment rules have also been adopted in the constitutions of semipresidential regimes, such as Russia, and even in purely parliamentary regimes.

In the long run, the ultimate control of democratic order is periodic and competitive elections. This need to achieve and regularly renew their mandates is the fundamental device that leads politicians to respond to the needs and demands of citizens. It is deeply imperfect. It may be difficult to tell when elected officials are incompetent, deceitful, or just unlucky. The complexities of policymaking may baffle the attempt of even trained observers to assign responsibility for successes or failures. The multiplicity of political issues may leave citizens torn between their candidate choices. Or, none of the choices may seem very palatable. Yet, deeply

## Impeachment in Latin America

Brazil, Mexico, and many other Latin American nations with strong presidents have impeachment rules and traditions. These were often modeled on the U.S. Constitution. In Mexico, the president, the state governors, and federal judges are subject to impeachment. Brazil has an impeachment process similar to that of the United States, except that it takes a two-thirds vote in the lower house of the assembly to charge the president and other high civil officers with impeachable offenses. A two-thirds vote is also required in the Senate to convict. The clause was invoked in 1992 when Brazil's President Fernando Collor was impeached on charges of large-scale corruption. He resigned before trial in the Senate. Impeachment procedures also forced presidents from office in Venezuela in 1993 and Paraguay in 1999.

imperfect as it is, this remarkable recruitment structure gives every citizen some influence on the policymaking process. For this reason, we consider it the most significant democratic structure.

## ASSEMBLIES

Legislative **assemblies** have existed for thousands of years. Ancient Greece and Rome had them, as did many other ancient societies. Indeed, the Roman Senate has given its name to modern assemblies in the United States and many other countries.

Almost all contemporary political systems have assemblies, variously called senates, chambers, diets, houses, and the like. Assemblies are also known as "legislatures" (regardless of what role they actually play in legislating) or as "parliaments" (mainly in parliamentary systems). Their formal approval is usually required for major public policies. They are generally elected by popular vote, and hence are at least formally accountable to the citizenry. Today, more than 80 percent of the countries belonging to the United Nations have such governmental bodies. The almost universal adoption of legislative assemblies suggests that in the modern world a legitimate government must formally include a representative popular component.

## Assembly Structure

Assemblies vary in their size—from less than 100 to more than 1,000—and their organization. They may consist of one (in which case they are called unicameral) or two (bicameral) chambers. Most democracies, and some authoritarian systems, have bicameral (two-chamber) assemblies. Federal systems normally provide simultaneously for two forms of representation: often representation in one chamber is based on population and representation in the second chamber is based on geographic units. Even in unitary systems (such as France or Japan), **bicameralism** is common, but the purpose of the second chamber is to provide a check on policymaking rather than to represent subnational units. The bicameral U.S. Congress grew out of both federalism and the desire to separate the power of the federal government.

The U.S. system, in which the two chambers have roughly equal powers, is unusual. In most bicameral systems, one chamber is dominant, and the second (such as the Russian Council of the Federation or the French Senate) has more limited powers that are often designed to protect regional interests. While representatives in the dominant chamber are popularly elected, those in the second chamber are sometimes chosen by the regional governments (as in Germany) or in other indirect ways. The prime minister in most parliamentary systems is responsible only to the more popularly elected chamber, which therefore has a more important position in policymaking than the second chamber. (See the discussion of the vote of confidence procedure earlier in this chapter and in Box 6.1.) In such systems members of the prime minister's cabinet are usually chosen from the majority party or parties' leadership in this chamber.

Assemblies also differ in their internal organization in ways that have major consequences for policymaking. There are two kinds of internal legislative organization: party groups and formal assembly subunits (presiding officers, committees, and the like). There is often an inverse relationship between the strength of parties versus other subunits (such as committees). The stronger parties are, the weaker are committees, and vice versa. British members of Parliament vote strictly along party lines much more consistently than members of the U.S. Congress. As in most parliamentary systems, British members of Parliament rarely vote against the instructions of their party leaders. Because cabinets generally hold office only as long as they can command a parliamentary majority, deviating from the party line means risking the fall of the government and new elections.

In presidential systems, the president and the legislators are independently elected for fixed terms of office. Thus the fate of the governing party is less directly tied up with voting on legislative measures. In U.S. legislatures, party discipline operates principally on procedural questions, such as committee assignments or the selection of a presiding officer. On substantive policy issues, Democratic and Republican legislators are freer to decide whether or not to vote with their party leaders.

All assemblies have a committee structure, some organized arrangement that permits legislators to divide up their labor and to specialize in particular issue areas. Without such committees, it would be impossible to handle the large flow of legislative business. As we have seen, however, the importance of committees varies. In some legislatures—such as those in the United States, Japan, and Germany—committees are very influential. This is partially because they are highly specialized, have jurisdictions that match those of the executive departments, and have large staff resources. Strong committees tend to have a clear legislative division of labor that matches the executive branch, allowing for specialized oversight of executive activity. They are often arenas in which the opposition can be influential. British committees are much weaker than their opposite numbers in the United States, since they have small staffs, are dominated by the governing party, and get appointed for one bill at a time. Hence, they cannot accumulate expertise in a particular policy area. German and Japanese committees are stronger than those of Britain but weaker than their American counterparts.[11]

## Assembly Functions

Assembly members deliberate, debate, and vote on policies that come before them. Most important policies and rules must be considered and at least formally approved by these bodies before they have the force of law. Assemblies typically also control public spending decisions, so that control of the purse strings (budgeting) is one of their major functions. In addition, some assemblies have important appointment powers, and some (like the British House of Lords in criminal cases) may serve as a court of appeals. Although laws typically need assembly approval, in most countries legislation is actually formulated elsewhere, usually by the political executive and the upper levels of the bureaucracy.

When we compare the importance of assemblies as policymaking agencies, the U.S. Congress, which plays a very active role in the formulation and enactment of legislation, is at one extreme. The other extreme is represented by the National People's Congress of the People's Republic of China, which meets infrequently and does little more than listen to statements by party leaders and rubber-stamp decisions made elsewhere. Roughly midway between the two is the House of Commons in Britain. There, legislative proposals are sometimes initiated or modified by ordinary members of Parliament, but public policy is usually initiated and proposed by members of the Cabinet (who are, to be sure, chosen from the members of the parliamentary body). The typical assembly provides a deliberating forum, formally enacts legislation, and sometimes amends it.

Assemblies should not be viewed only as legislative bodies. All assemblies in democratic systems have an important relationship to legislation, but not necessarily a dominant role. Their political importance is based not just on this function, but also on the great variety of other political functions they perform. Assemblies can play a major role in elite recruitment, especially in parliamentary systems where prime ministers and cabinet members typically serve their apprenticeships in parliament. Legislative committee hearings and floor debates may be important sites for interest articulation and interest aggregation, especially if there is no cohesive majority party. Debates in assemblies can be a source of public information about politics and thus contribute to the socialization of citizens generally and elites in particular.

## Representation: Mirroring and Representational Biases

Contemporary legislative assemblies, especially in democratic systems, are valued particularly because they represent the citizens in the national policymaking process. It is not obvious, however, what the ideal linkage between citizens and government officials should be. Some argue that government officials should mirror the characteristics of the citizens as far as possible. This principle, also known as *descriptive representation*, is held to be particularly important with respect to potentially conflictual divisions (such as race, class, ethnicity, gender, language, and perhaps age).

However, descriptive representation is not the only concern in recruiting public officials. The limits of mirroring were inadvertently expressed by a U.S. senator. In defending a U.S. Supreme Court nominee who was accused of mediocrity, the senator lamely contended, "[E]ven if he were mediocre, there are a lot of mediocre judges and people and lawyers. They are entitled to a little representation, aren't they?"[12] Most people would probably not argue that government officials should mirror the general population in their abilities to do their jobs. Instead, we generally want political elites to be the best possible *agents* for their constituents. In this view, government officials should be selected for their ability to serve the interests of the citizens, whether or not they share the voters' background characteristics.

For politicians to be good agents, they need to have similar *preferences* to the citizens they represent *and* they need the appropriate *skills* to do their jobs. In democracies, political parties are the most important mechanism by which the preferences of citizens and leaders get aligned. As far as skills are concerned, education and experience are the most important factors. Political and governmental leadership—particularly in modern, technologically advanced societies—requires knowledge and skills that are hard to acquire except through education and training. Natural intelligence or experience may, to a limited degree, take the place of formal education.

Hence, it might be a good thing for government officials to be better informed, more intelligent, more experienced, and perhaps better educated than the people who they serve. Just as medical patients tend to look for the most capable physician rather than the one who is most like them, so, one could argue, citizens should look for the best qualified officeholder. In this view, selecting government officials, including representative policymakers, is like delegating to experts. It may be a hopeful sign that citizens in many modern democracies are increasingly willing to select leaders who do not share their background characteristics.

As in the case of so many other political choices, there is no obvious or perfect way to choose between mirroring and expert delegation. This is an old debate, and in many situations it is necessary to make a trade-off between the two. And different offices may require different considerations. Most people would, for example, probably put a higher emphasis on mirroring in their local assembly than in a regulatory agency overseeing nuclear technology.

The bad news is that political elites, even democratically elected members of legislative assemblies, hardly ever mirror the citizens they represent on any of the standard social characteristics. Even in democracies such as the United States, Britain, and France, political leaders tend to be of middle- or upper-class background or unusually well-educated and upwardly mobile individuals from the lower classes. There are exceptions. In some countries, trade unions or leftist political parties may serve as channels of political advancement for people with modest economic or educational backgrounds. These representatives acquire political skills and experience by holding offices in working-class organizations. Thus the Labour Party delegation in the British House of Commons and the Communist delegation in the French National Assembly have included substantial numbers of workers. And during the long domination of the executive by the Norwegian Labor Party (1935–1981), none of its prime ministers had even completed secondary school. But these are rare and vanishing examples. In most contemporary states, the number of working-class people in high office is small and declining.

Women have also been poorly represented in political leadership positions in most countries. History certainly offers examples of strong and influential female rulers, such as Queen Elizabeth I of England (who ruled from 1558 to 1603). Yet in most countries women did not have the right to vote until well into the twentieth century and have not held many political leadership positions.

That situation has changed significantly in the last twenty-five years. In 1980, women on average held fewer than 10 percent of the parliamentary seats in the advanced industrial democracies. By 1990, that figure was up to about 15 percent, and by 1997 women had surpassed 20 percent. Women have also held the chief executive office in a growing number of countries, particularly in Europe and Asia. (See Box 6.3.)

## Women as Chief Executives

**BOX 6.3**

From about 1970 on, women have gained chief executive office in a growing number of countries. Interestingly, many of them have been from Asian and Middle Eastern countries, where women's roles in public life traditionally have been limited. Sinmavo Bandaranaike of Sri Lanka (1960–1965 and 1970–1977), Indira Gandhi of India (1966–1977 and 1980–1984), and Golda Meir of Israel (1969–1974) were among the pioneers. In the 1980s and 1990s, women also came to power in the Philippines, Pakistan, Bangladesh, and again in Sri Lanka. In Burma, Nobel Peace Prize winner Aung San Suu Kyi won the elections of 1990 but the military prevented her from taking office.

Women have also made inroads in leadership positions in Europe and North America, though they are still few and far between in Africa and Latin America. The first female leader in a major European country was Prime Minister Margaret Thatcher of Britain (1979–1990). Her strong and decisive leadership made her one of Europe's most influential politicians in the 1980s. Women have come to power in other western countries as well. Ireland and Iceland have had female presidents. Canada, France, and Switzerland have had brief stints with female prime ministers. Angela Merkel is chancellor of Germany. In Norway, Gro Harlem Brundtland held the prime ministership for a total of about ten years between 1981 and 1996. Brundtland, a physician and environmentalist, later headed the World Health Organization.

The career paths of Asian women leaders have tended to differ from those in Europe. Many of the former have come from prominent political families, such as the Gandhi family in India and the Bhuttos in Pakistan. In several cases, they have been the widows or daughters of important political leaders. In Europe, women leaders are more likely to have made independent political careers, and they can rely on stronger women's interest groups.

---

Angela Merkel, for example, became chancellor of Germany in 2005.

But women's advancement has been uneven, and their representation remains low in the developing world. In many Northern European countries, such as Sweden, women by the late 1990s accounted for 30 to 40 percent of the legislators and a similar proportion of cabinet members. But in Russia, Mexico, Brazil, and Japan, women still accounted for fewer than one legislator in ten in the 1990s.[13]

Political elites also tend to be unrepresentative with respect to age. In many countries, legislators (much less chief executives) under age 40 are a rarity, whereas a large proportion of leading politicians are past normal retirement age. Japan is an extreme example. In 1990, there were about eight legislators over age 60 for every one member under age 40. In many countries, university graduates—and often lawyers and civil servants in particular—are vastly overrepresented, whereas ethnic, linguistic, and religious minorities are often underrepresented. Representational biases are thus numerous and pervasive. And while women's representation is increasing, class biases are getting worse.

## POLITICAL EXECUTIVES

In modern states, the executive branch is by far the largest, the most complex, and typically the most powerful branch of government. It is not easy to describe executives in simple ways, but it is sensible to start at the top. Governments typically have one or two **chief executives,** officials who sit at the very top of the often-colossal executive branch. Such executives have various names, titles, duties, and powers. They are called presidents, prime ministers, chancellors, secretaries general, or even leader (in Iran). There are even a few kings who still have genuine power. Titles may mislead us as to what functions these officials perform, but they tend to be the main formulators and executors of public policy.

### Structure of the Chief Executive

Democratic governments typically feature either a single chief executive (in presidential systems) or a split chief executive of two offices: a largely ceremonial head of state (who represents the nation on formal occasions) and a more powerful head of

| | | TABLE 6.3 |
|---|---|---|
| **Bases of Legislative Power of Chief Executives** | | |
| **Authoritarian** | **Democratic: Partisan Influence** | **Democratic: Constitutional Powers** |
| **Effective** | | |
| General Secretary, China | British Prime Minister | |
| | French Prime Minister | |
| | German Chancellor | |
| | Indian Prime Minister | |
| | Japanese Prime Minister | |
| | (Russian Prime Minister) | |
| **Ceremonial** | | |
| Chinese President | | British Queen or King |
| | | German President |
| | | Indian President |
| | | Japanese Emperor |
| **Ceremonial and Effective** | | |
| Iranian Leader | French President | Brazilian President |
| | | Mexican President |
| | | Nigerian President |
| | | Russian President |
| | | U.S. President |

government (who determines public policies). Table 6.3 distinguishes among executives according to the bases of their power to affect policymaking. In the left column we see the chief executives in authoritarian systems, whose power ultimately rests on coercion. The middle and right columns show the chief executives in democratic countries. The middle column shows executives whose power rests primarily on their partisan influence in the legislature, which is the case of the prime ministers in most parliamentary systems. The right column includes chief executives whose ability to influence legislation resides in powers directly granted them by the constitution, rather than partisan connection alone. Strong presidents may be able to veto legislation, for example, issue legal decrees, or introduce the budget. They usually have the power to appoint and dismiss members of the cabinet.

Reading down the table, we see the distinction between executives with effective power over policy, purely ceremonial roles, or both effective and ceremonial power. Political executives are effective only if they have genuine discretion in the enactment and implementation of laws and regulations, in budgetary matters, or in important government appointments. Where they do not have these powers, they are symbolic or ceremonial. In presidential systems, the ceremonial and effective roles are almost always held by the same person, the president, as we see in both authoritarian and democratic systems at the bottom of Table 6.3. In parliamentary democratic systems, and in some authoritarian systems, the two roles are separated between the "head of state," who is primarily a ceremonial official, and a "head of government," who makes and implements the decisions. The British, German, Indian, and Japanese prime ministers appear in column two at the top of the table, while their ceremonial counterparts appear at the center right.

These distinctions are not absolute. Some constitutions, such as the German, give substantial formal powers to their prime ministers. At the same time even largely ceremonial presidents can exert important influence if the parties are divided or by exercising special constitutional powers (or both, as has recently happened in India). Moreover, partisan influence in the legislature is useful even to the strongest democratic presidents. Still, it is usually easy to determine the primary sources of legislative power, even where the formal names may be misleading.

As noted earlier, a few countries, such as France and Russia, have both significant presidents and prime ministers. The balance of power between them depends on the constitutional powers of the president and on the partisan division in the legislature. In Russia, the constitutional powers of veto and decree of the president are very great, and expanded under recent authoritarian trends; until recently the prime minister has been mostly just another administrator, with little effective power. In France, however, the president's formal powers are much weaker; when the legislature is unified under opposition parties it has elected a prime minister who has effectively dominated policymaking, greatly reducing the president's political influence.

In China the chairman of the Communist Party is the most powerful political figure and the effective chief executive. The Chinese president is the head of state, which is a purely ceremonial role, without associated powers. However, in recent years the same individual (Jiang Zemin and now Hu Jintao) has held both offices, and also a key role as chairman of the party military commission. A third role was the premier, or head of government, which was a largely administrative position.

Monarchies are much more rare at the beginning of the twenty-first century than they were at the beginning of the twentieth. Some monarchs, such as the king of Saudi Arabia and some other Arab monarchs, still exercise real power. Most contemporary monarchs, however, have little or no actual political influence. Monarchs like the British queen or the Scandinavian kings are principally ceremonial and symbolic officers with very occasional political powers. They are living symbols of the state and nation and of their historical continuity. Britain's queen may bestow honors or peerages (appointments to the nobility) with a stroke of her scepter, but these are recommended by the prime minister. The Japanese monarchy has also traditionally been dignified and exalted and played an important role as a national symbol. In contrast, the Scandinavian and Low Country monarchies are more humdrum. Because members of these royal families occasionally use more humble means of transportation, these dynasties are sometimes called "bicycle monarchies." In republican democracies

Chief executives, including the new US President Barack Obama, and the German Chancellor Angela Merkl, attend an April 2009 NATO summit with their defense ministers, foreign ministers and NATO officials in Strasbourg, France.

Action Press-Pool/Getty Images

with parliamentary systems, presidents perform the functions that fall to kings and queens in parliamentary monarchies. Thus German presidents give speeches on important anniversaries and designate prime ministers after elections or when a government has resigned.

A system in which the ceremonial executive is separated from the effective executive has a number of advantages. The ceremonial executive symbolizes unity and continuity and can be above politics. The U.S. presidency, which combines both effective and ceremonial functions, runs the risk that the president will use his ceremonial and symbolic authority to enhance his political power or that his involvement in politics may make him a less effective symbolic or unifying figure.

Crown Princess Victoria, heir to the Swedish throne, illustrates why the Scandinavian and Low Country monarchies are commonly referred to as "bicycle monarchies."

Jonas Esktrmer/Scanpix Sweden/Sipa Press

## Recruitment of Chief Executives

Historically, finding generally acceptable ways to select the individuals to fill the top policymaking roles has been critical to political order and stability. A major accomplishment of stable democracies is regulating the potential conflict involved in leadership succession and confining it to the mobilization of votes instead of weapons. When we refer generally to "recruitment structures," we are thinking of how nations choose their top policymakers and executives. Table 6.4 shows the recruitment structures in the countries selected for this book.

The most familiar structures are the presidential and parliamentary forms of competitive party systems. In presidential systems, as in Brazil and the United States, parties select candidates for nomination, and the electorate chooses among them. Russia and France have directly elected presidents but also give an important role to the prime minister, who is appointed by the president but can be removed by the legislature.

Mexico appears similar to other presidential systems. But for half a century the Partido Revolucionario Institucional (PRI) had such control over the electoral process that the voters merely ratified the party's presidential nominee. That nomination itself was announced by the outgoing president after complex bargaining between party factions and other powerful groups. Mexico seemed to be moving to give the voters an honest role in choosing between alternative candidates, but until the remarkable July 2000 election many voters remained skeptical that a non-PRI president could really come to power. As the table shows, Mexico now seems a newly democratic presidential system, with parties nominating candidates and voters genuinely choosing among them, as in the very close election of 2006.

In both presidential and parliamentary democracies the tenure of the chief executive is limited, directly or indirectly. In the presidential system this is usually directly, through fixed terms of office for the chief executive. In the parliamentary system there is a maximum term for the parliament, which then indirectly also limits the life of the cabinet, since the prime minister is accountable to the new parliamentary majority and can be removed by it.

Table 6.4 also illustrates the role of noncompetitive parties and military organizations in China, the

| | **Recruitment of Chief Executive** | | **TABLE 6.4** |
|---|---|---|---|

| Country | Chief Executive Structure | Recruitment Structures | How Often Has This Type of Government Survived Succession?[b] |
|---|---|---|---|
| Brazil | President | Party and voters | Often |
| Britain | Prime minister | Party, House of Commons, voters | Very often |
| China | Party secretary[a] | Party and military | Often |
| France | President/Prime minister | Party, (Assembly) voters | Often |
| Germany | Chancellor | Party, Bundestag, voters | Often |
| India | Prime minister | Party, Lok Sabha, voters | Often (one interruption) |
| Iran | Leader, President | Religious elites, voters | Once |
| Japan | Prime minister | Party, Diet, voters | Often |
| Mexico | President | Party and voters | Twice |
| Nigeria | President | Military, party, voters | Once |
| Russia | President | Party, president, and voters | Twice |
| United States | President | Party and voters | Very often |

[a] "Party secretary" refers to that position or to a similar one as head of party in a communist regime.
[b] "Often" means that at least three successions have taken place under that type of government.

military in Nigeria, and nonelected religious elites in Iran. The important role played by political parties illustrates the great need to mobilize broad political support behind the selection of chief executives. The frequent appearance of parties also reflects, no doubt, the modern legitimacy of popular sovereignty: the promise that the rulers' actions will be in the interest of the ruled.

Authoritarian systems rarely have effective procedures for leadership succession. The more power is concentrated at the top, the riskier it is to transfer it from one person to the next. Very often, authoritarian leaders do not dare to relinquish their power, and leadership succession occurs only when they die or are overthrown. In communist regimes, the Communist Party selects the general secretary (or equivalent), who is the controlling executive force. Individual succession is not a simple matter. These systems do not limit the terms of incumbents, who are difficult to oust once they have consolidated their supporters into key party positions. Nonetheless, they always have to be aware of the possibility of a party coup of the type that ousted Nikita Khrushchev from the Soviet leadership in 1964. As a system, however, the Soviet leadership structure seemed quite stable until the dramatic 1991

coup attempt against Gorbachev. Although he was briefly restored to power, the events surrounding the coup stripped the Soviet presidency of power, and legitimacy passed to the presidencies and legislatures of the fifteen constituent republics. Russia managed its first democratic transition surprisingly smoothly, from Yeltsin to his chosen successor Vladimir Putin, who was elected as the new president in April 2000 and reelected in 2004. Putin arranged a less democratic transition in 2008.

The poorer nations show substantially less stability, and the regimes have usually had less experience at surviving succession crises.[14] Nigeria is typical. It experienced a succession of military coups and governments from 1966 until 1979, then introduced a competitive presidential system, which was overthrown by a military coup shortly after its second election in 1983. The military government again moved toward civilian rule in the early 1990s but then annulled the 1993 presidential election before the results were announced. The military rulers finally allowed a return to civilian rule in 1999.

Many African nations experience repeated coups. Military governments, stable or unstable, have also been common in Latin America and the

Middle East, although they are now more likely to dominate in coalition or from behind the scenes. (See Chapter 5.) The Chinese Communist Party has remained in power for fifty years but has suffered several periods of internal strife, and the army has been involved in recruitment at all levels. India's democracy, having persisted through assassinations and other crises, has been an exception to the rule among poorer nations. It has provided a number of democratic successions with a single interruption (authoritarian emergency rule that postponed elections for several years) in the 1970s.

## The Cabinet

In many political systems, the **cabinet** is the most important collective decisionmaking body. Its power can be particularly great in parliamentary systems, where its formation is closely linked to selection of the prime minister. It typically contains the leaders (often called "ministers" or "secretaries of state") of all the major departments (sometimes called "ministries") into which the executive branch is divided. The cabinet meets frequently, often several times per week. It is typically selected and led by the head of government: the president in presidential systems and the prime minister in parliamentary ones. In some parliamentary systems, the entire cabinet is collectively responsible to the legislature. The prime minister may be little more than "first among equals," especially under conditions of multiparty coalition governments. In other parliamentary systems, such as Germany, the constitution confers much more authority on the prime minister.[15]

How does the cabinet get selected? In presidential systems, selecting cabinet members is typically a presidential prerogative, though sometimes (as with the U.S. Senate), the legislature has to give its approval. The president can typically also dismiss cabinet members at will, whereas the legislature's ability to do so is most often severely limited.

In parliamentary systems, in contrast, the process is very different, since the prime minister and his or her cabinet need to maintain the confidence of the parliamentary majority. Therefore, cabinet formation depends on the result of parliamentary elections and on the composition of parliament. If a competitive party wins a parliamentary majority by itself, it will

Coalition partners emphasize their solidarity before the German Bundestag in February 2003: Chancellor Gerhard Schroeder of the Social Democratic Party (right) welcomes Foreign Minister Joschka Fischer of the Green Party. Their two parties had campaigned together in a preelection coalition in the 2002 parliamentary election and formed a majority coalition cabinet afterwards.

AP Images/Markus Schreiber

(if unified) be able to form a cabinet of its own members and can then pass and implement its policies. Sometimes the election directly determines who controls the majority. This will always be the case in pure two-party systems, where one party or the other will always have a parliamentary majority. It can also happen in multiparty systems, whenever one party gets more seats than all its competitors combined. But the more parties there are, the less likely it is that one of them will have a majority on its own. We call the outcome in which one party controls a parliamentary majority by itself a majority situation. Whenever majority situations occur in parliamentary systems, the majority party almost always forms a *majority single-party cabinet* by itself.

Far more often, no party wins a majority of votes. In most multiparty countries, the typical election result is that no party has a parliamentary majority by itself—a minority situation. Most commonly under such circumstances, several parties (two, three, or as many as six or seven) join forces and form a *coalition cabinet* in which they are all represented. Sometimes, parties anticipate this need to form coalitions before the election. They may then make a formal agreement with one another and inform the voters that they intend to govern together if they collectively get enough votes. The allied parties may thus encourage their voters to support the coalition partners' candidates where their own party's candidates seem weak and often take advantage of special provisions of voting laws. Many German and French governments have come to power in this fashion. In such cases, the voters can have a direct voice in the choice of the future cabinet, much as they do in two-party systems. Voters are thus given a major role in choosing the direction of government policy.

But parties often do not make such preelection commitments. Even when they do, they often fail to get the support they would need to control a parliamentary majority. If no party or preelection coalition wins control of the legislature through the election, then parties may bargain after the election, or between elections, to form a new cabinet. In the Netherlands, such bargaining took four months after the 2003 election. In Germany, about three weeks of bargaining was

necessary to form a "grand coalition" of the two largest parties after the 2005 parliamentary election.

Whether bargaining takes place before or after the elections, the parties in parliamentary systems typically have a lot of options concerning the composition of the cabinet. In minority situations, the result can be either a minority government or a majority coalition of several parties. In some cases, a single party decides that it can form a minority cabinet alone, often because the other parties disagree too much among themselves to offer any alternative. Figure 6.2 illustrates these various possibilities. In the minority case, the parties in the cabinet must continually bargain with other parties to get policies adopted and even to remain in office. In majority coalitions, bargaining will take place primarily among coalition partners represented in the cabinet. In both of these circumstances, the power of the prime minister may depend on the bargains he or she can strike with leaders of other parties.

These complications illustrate two of the problems of combining parliamentary government with electoral systems of proportional representation. Such systems tend to produce minority situations, which do not give the voters a very clear choice about who will control the executive branch. Instead, the parties may determine this behind closed doors after the election. Sometimes, the results are paradoxical, as when parties that have just lost votes in the elections are able to negotiate their way into a governing coalition. The second problem is that under minority situations, cabinets are sometimes

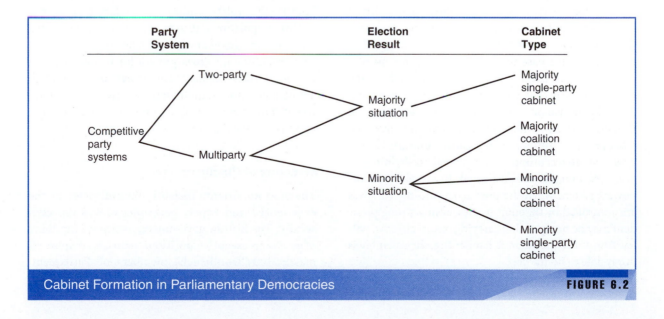

**Cabinet Formation in Parliamentary Democracies**    **FIGURE 6.2**

unstable. Italy, for example, has had on average more than one change of government per year since World War II. Yet, such problems need not always emerge. In Germany, for example, cabinets have been quite stable, and the voters have generally been given fairly clear options ahead of elections.

## Functions of the Chief Executive

Typically, the chief executive is the most important structure in policymaking. The executive normally initiates new policies. Depending on the division of powers with the legislature and the partisan balance, the executive also has a substantial part in their adoption. In presidential systems, the president very often has veto powers. Thus the chief executive not only has the first word in policymaking, he or she also typically has the last word. In parliamentary systems, on the other hand, the chief executive is less likely to be able to exercise a veto.

The political executive also oversees policy implementation and can hold subordinate officials accountable for their performance. The central decisions in a foreign policy crisis are generally made by the chief executive: the president (George W. Bush in the Iraq War) or the prime minister (Tony Blair in the Iraq War). Political initiatives and new programs typically originate in the executive. A bureaucracy without an effective executive tends to implement past policies, rather than to initiate new ones. Without politically motivated ministers, bureaucracies tend toward inertia.

The decision of a president, prime minister, cabinet, or central party committee to pursue a new foreign or domestic policy is usually accompanied by structural adaptations—the appointment of a vigorous minister, an increase in staff, the establishment of a special cabinet committee, and the like. Where the political executive is weak and divided, as in Fourth Republic France or contemporary Italy (at least until recently), this dynamic force is missing. Initiative then passes to the bureaucracy, legislative committees, and powerful interest groups—and general needs, interests, and problems may be neglected. In a separation-of-powers system when the presidency and the congress are controlled by different parties, even a strong president may be hampered in carrying out an effective policy. And if the president is hamstrung, the assembly is rarely able to fill the gap.

Chief executives also perform important system functions. Studies of childhood socialization show that the first political role perceived by children tends to be the chief political executive—the president, prime minister, and king or queen. In early childhood the tendency is to identify the top political executive as a parent figure. As the child matures, he or she begins to differentiate political from other roles, as well as to differentiate among various political roles (see Chapter 3). The conduct of the chief executive affects the trust and confidence that young people feel in the whole political system and they carry that with them into adulthood. The role of the chief executive in recruitment is obviously important, appointing the cabinet and other officials. The political executive also plays a central role in communication, in explaining and building support for new policies, or in improving performance in various sectors of the society and economy.

## THE BUREAUCRACY

Modern societies are dominated by large organizations, and the largest contemporary organizations are government **bureaucracies,** or their systems of public administration. These agencies, by which we mean all the members of the executive branch below the top executive (president/monarch, prime minister, and cabinet), are generally in charge of implementing government policy. The size of government bureaucracies increased over the course of the twentieth century. This is partly due to the efforts of governments to improve the health, productivity, welfare, and security of their populations. It may also be partly due to the tendency for government agencies, once they have been established, to seek growth for its own sake. In reaction to this tendency, and as part of the concern about government inefficiencies, there has been a recent movement to reduce government budgets and to downsize the bureaucracy (see Chapter 7).

## Structure of the Bureaucracy

The most important officials in bureaucracies are the experienced and expert personnel of the top **civil service.** The British "government," which we can think of as its top executive positions, consists of approximately 100 "frontbench" members of Parliament, some twenty of whom serve in the Cabinet, with the remainder named as ministers, junior ministers, and parliamentary secretaries. This relatively small group of political policymakers oversees some 3,000 permanent members of the **higher civil service,** largely recruited directly from the universities. They spend their lives as an elite corps, moving about from ministry to ministry, watching governments come and go, and becoming increasingly important as policymakers as they rise in rank. Below the higher civil service are a huge body of more than half a million permanent public employees, ordinary civil servants, organized into about twenty government departments and a number of other agencies. The total number of British civil servants rose from 100,000 in 1900 to more than 700,000 in 1979, but it then declined to under 500,000 under Conservative governments of the 1980s and 1990s.

The importance of the permanent higher civil service is not unique to Britain, though perhaps it has been most fully institutionalized there. In France, too, the higher civil service is filled with powerful generalists who can bring long tenure, experience, and technical knowledge to their particular tasks. In the United States, many top positions go to presidential appointees rather than to permanent civil servants. Despite this difference and a greater emphasis on technical specialization, there are permanent civil servants in the key positions just below the top appointees in such agencies as the Internal Revenue Service, the Federal Bureau of Investigation, the Central Intelligence Agency, the National Institutes of Health, and all the cabinet departments. These people tend to be specialists—such as military officers, diplomats, doctors, scientists, economists, and engineers—who exert great influence on policy formulation and execution in their specialties. Below these specialists and administrators are the vast numbers of ordinary government employees, postal workers, teachers, welfare case agents, and so forth, who see that governmental policies are put into practice. In 2004, the United States had 22 million public employees of all kinds, federal, state, and local, or about 17 percent of the total labor force. In many European countries, that proportion is even higher, approaching a third of the labor force in Norway, Denmark, and Sweden.

## The Functions of the Bureaucracy

Bureaucracies have great significance in most contemporary societies. One reason is that the bureaucracy is almost alone in implementing and enforcing laws and regulations. In so doing, they may have quite a bit of discretion. Most modern legislation is general and can be effectively enforced only if administrative officials work out its detail and implementation. Policy implementation and enforcement usually depend on bureaucrats' interpretations and on the spirit and effectiveness with which they put policies into practice. But the power of bureaucracies is not restricted to their implementation and enforcement of rules made by others. In Chapters 4 and 5 we discussed how bureaucratic agencies may articulate and aggregate interests. Departments like those for agriculture, labor, defense, welfare, and education may be among the most important voices of interest groups. Moreover, administrative agencies in modern political systems do a lot of adjudication. Tax authorities, for example, routinely determine whether citizens have faithfully reported their income and paid their taxes, and these authorities assess penalties accordingly. While citizens may in principle be able to appeal such rulings to the courts, relatively few actually do.

Finally, bureaucracies are involved in communication. Political elites, whether executives or legislators, base many of their decisions on the information they obtain from the public administration. Similarly, interest groups, political parties, the business elites, and the public depend on such information. Most major agencies in modern governments have spokespersons whose job it is to inform and influence the media. With the increasing media power in modern societies, top government executives are eager to present their versions of events. Increasingly, however, large parts of the journalistic professions refuse to recognize any limits on the publication of private as well as political information. Leaks of secret or confidential information and intelligence have become a veritable flood. Thus political executives and bureaucracies can no longer control information in the ways that they formerly did. In dealing with the media, top administrators now must have more complex strategies and professional assistance. The art of "spin control" has replaced their reliance on classification and "executive privilege."

## Bureaucracy and Performance

We commonly use the term "bureaucracy" to refer to all systems of public administration. Strictly speaking, however, bureaucracy refers to a particular way of organizing such agencies, a practice that gained favor in the latter part of the nineteenth century and the beginning of the twentieth century. According to the classical German sociologist Max Weber, bureaucracies have the following features:

1. Decisionmaking is based on fixed and official jurisdictions, rules, and regulations.
2. There are formal and specialized educational or training requirements for each position.
3. There is a hierarchical command structure: a firmly ordered system of super- and subordination, in which information flows upward and decisions downward.
4. Decisions are made on the basis of standard operating procedures, which include extensive written records.
5. Officials hold career positions, are appointed and promoted on the basis of merit, and have protection against political interference, notably in the form of permanent job tenure.[16]

No organization is perfectly bureaucratic in this sense, but professional armies come reasonably close, as do tax revenue departments.

These features of bureaucracies have a number of desirable effects. They promote competence, consistency, fair treatment, and freedom from political manipulation. Imagine what life could be like without bureaucracies. Before the advent of modern bureaucracy, public officials were often a sorry lot. Some of them inherited their jobs; others got them through family or political connections. Yet others bought their posts and used them either to enrich themselves or gain social status (or both). Many saw their jobs strictly as a sideline and devoted little time to their duties. No wonder, then, that public officials were often incompetent, uninterested in their jobs, corrupt, or all of the above. They often used their powers arbitrarily, to favor friends and neighbors, and to the disadvantage of others. Given the lack of rules and records, aggrieved citizens typically had few recourses.

But the negative connotations that the word "bureaucracy" has taken on suggest that such organizations have liabilities as well. Bureaucratic organizations can become stodgy, rule-bound, inflexible, and insensitive to the needs of their clients. In many cases, bureaucrats also have few incentives to be innovative and efficient, or even to work very hard. Although bureaucracies are supposed to be politically and ideologically neutral, in fact they tend to be influenced by the dominant ideologies of the time, to have conservative propensies, and to pursue institutional interests of their own.[17] Many citizens are exasperated with bureaucracy and its propensities for inefficiency and lack of responsiveness. This frustration is reflected in popular cynicism as well as in periodic attempts to reform government.

Mark Nadel and Francis Rourke suggest a variety of ways that government and societal agencies may influence and control bureaucracies, externally or internally.[18] The major external government control is the political executive. Although presidents, prime ministers, and ministers formally command subordinate officials and may have the power to remove them for nonperformance of duty, executives and bureaucracies actually depend on one another. Top executives typically try to persuade; rarely do they go to the extreme of dismissing or transferring civil servants. Centralized budgeting and administrative reorganization are other means of executive control. The threat to take away resources or authority may bring bureaucratic implementation into greater conformity with the aims of the political executive.

Modern authoritarian systems discovered that the bureaucracy was an essential tool of government control. Thus, recruitment of the bureaucracy was part of a larger pattern of control. Bureaucratic selection in the former Soviet Union, as in China today, was controlled through a device called *nomenklatura*. Under this procedure important positions were kept under the direct supervision of a party agency whose officials had the final word on recruitment. Moreover, the party offered a complicated set of inducements to control the behavior of the chosen officials. These inducements made it difficult for any but the topmost officials to have much freedom of action. Soviet leaders used normative incentives (such as appeals to party, ideology, and national idealism), financial incentives (such as better salaries, access to finer food and clothing, better housing, and freedom to travel), and coercive control (such as reporting by police, party, and bureaucrats). They used demotion or imprisonment, even execution, as penalties. To avoid a coup by police or military forces, the varied layers of command and inducement structures were interwoven, so that no layer could act independently.

In democracies, assemblies and courts also help control the bureaucracy. Legislative committee hearings or judicial investigations may bring bureaucratic performance into line with political desires. Sweden invented the institution of the **ombudsman** to prevent bureaucrats from doing injury or injustice to individuals.[19] This invention has been copied by other states. In the Scandinavian countries, Britain, Germany, and elsewhere ombudsmen now investigate citizen claims that they have suffered injury or damage as a result of government action. Ombudsmen typically have no power of their own, but report to the legislature for remedial action. Their cases rarely lead to criminal conviction, but often government officials change their policies as a result of embarrassing publicity. Thus, ombudsmen offer a more expeditious and less costly procedure than court action. Among the extragovernmental forces that constrain bureaucracies are public opinion and the mass media, as well as interest groups of various kinds.

All such controls on civil servants tend to be less effective outside the advanced industrial democracies. Authoritarian systems lack many of these controls, particularly external ones, such as elected political executives and legislators, independent courts, free mass media, and interest groups. Therefore, authoritarian regimes are particularly prone to bureaucratic inefficiency and inertia. Moreover, in many nonindustrial countries, mass media are neither independent nor influential, few citizens participate in politics, and lower level government employees are poorly trained and paid—all conditions that encourage bribery, extortion, and bureaucratic mismanagement.[20]

Successful democracy requires that public policies made by national assemblies and chief executives be implemented fairly and effectively; democracy depends on the rule of law. When ruling parties demand kickbacks of public money from construction firms seeking public works contracts, the democratic process is subverted by rent-seeking politicians. (See Chapter 1 and Box 1.2.) Similarly, when tax officials and border authorities are open to cash payments to overlook tax deficiencies and customs violations, democratic lawmaking is undermined. Citizens who must bribe teachers to get education for their children or health officials to get immunizations are deprived of the benefits of democratic public policies. Such practices are all too common in the poorer nations of the world.

Failure of the rule of law is difficult to study systematically, but some comparative insight into corruption in public bureaucracies is provided by the surveys of perceptions of corruption on the part of businesspeople, academics, and analysts in different countries. These have been combined into the Corruption Perceptions Index, which rates about one hundred countries each year on a scale from 0 ("highly corrupt") to 10 ("highly clean"). Figure 6.3 shows on the vertical dimension the ratings for 2005 (based on a three-year moving average) of the twelve countries studied in this book. As we see, all of the countries experience some levels of corruption. The world's top-rated country in 2005 was Iceland at 9.7. But Britain, Germany, the United States, France, and Japan (despite individually notorious cases in each) rated in the top half of the scale. Brazil, Mexico, China, Iran, and India are far more corrupt, with scores in the low range of the scale. Russia, plagued by many problems of its dual economic and political transitions, scores even worse. Nigeria, despite its recent efforts at democratic transition, is perceived as one of the world's most corrupt countries.

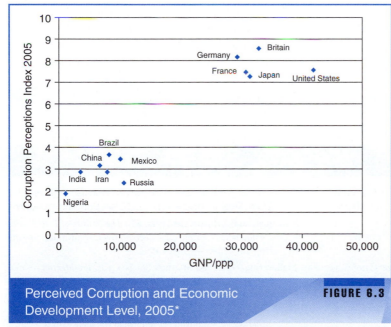

**Perceived Corruption and Economic Development Level, 2005***    **FIGURE 6.3**

*Economic development level from World Bank, downloaded from www.worldbank.org/data on July 6, 2006; Corruption Perception, Index from Transparency International, downloaded from www.transparency.org/cpi/index on July 6, 2006.

We can compare the perceived corruption scores with the purchasing power parity (ppp) measure of economic wealth and productivity on the horizontal dimension of Figure 6.3. This comparison shows that corruption and the failure of the rule of law are very strongly associated with poverty and underdevelopment, as well as with direct indicators of widespread misery (see also Table 1.3 in Chapter 1).[21] However, some individual countries do better or worse than we might expect. For example, Russia is somewhat more corrupt than we would expect from its middle-level income.

The ills of bureaucracy, including inefficiency and inertia, are pandemic. This is truly a dilemma because we are unlikely to invent any schemes for carrying out large-scale social tasks without the organization, division of labor, and professionalism that bureaucracy provides. Its pathologies can only be mitigated. The art of modern political leadership consists not only of defining and communicating appropriate goals and policies, but also of getting them implemented by a massive and complex bureaucracy—how and when to press and coerce it, reorganize it, reward it, teach it, or be taught by it.

## REVIEW QUESTIONS

- What are the advantages of more inclusive decision rules in making policies? What are the disadvantages?

- Why is the confidence relationship so important in parliamentary democracies?

- In what different ways can policymaking power be dispersed and limited by constitutional arrangements?

- What are the advantages and disadvantages of assembly representation that mirrors the characteristics of citizens?

- How are cabinets formed after national elections in parliamentary systems?

- Why are bureaucracies necessary but sometimes liabilities in policymaking?

## KEY TERMS

assemblies

authoritarian regimes

bicameralism

bureaucracies

cabinet

chief executives

civil service

confidence relationship

constitutional regimes

decision rules

democracy

democratic presidential regime

federal systems

higher civil service

impeachment

judicial review

ombudsman

parliamentary regimes

policymaking

semipresidential regime

separation of powers

## SUGGESTED READINGS

Aberbach, Joel, Robert D. Putnam, and Bert A. Rockman. *Bureaucrats and Politicians in Western Democracies.* Cambridge: Harvard University Press, 1981.

Döring, Herbert, ed. *Parliaments and Majority Rule in Western Europe.* New York: St. Martin's Press, 1995.

Huber, John D. *Rationalizing Parliament.* Cambridge: Cambridge University Press, 1996.

Laver, Michael, and Norman Schofield. *Multiparty Government: The Politics of Coalition in Europe.* Ann Arbor: University of Michigan Press, 1998.

Lijphart, Arend. *Democracy in Plural Societies.* New Haven, CT: Yale University Press, 1977.

———. *Patterns of Democracy: Government Forms and Performance in Thirty-Six Countries.* New Haven, CT: Yale University Press, 1999.

Linz, Juan, and Arturo Valenzuela, eds. *The Failure of Presidential Democracy: Comparative Perspectives.* Baltimore: Johns Hopkins University Press, 1994.

Mainwaring, Scott, and Matthew Shugart, eds. *Presidentialism and Democracy in Latin America.* New York: Cambridge University Press, 1997.

North, Douglass. *Institutions, Institutional Change, and Economic Performance.* Cambridge: Cambridge University Press, 1990.

Powell, G. Bingham. *Contemporary Democracies.* Cambridge: Harvard University Press, 1982.

Riker, William H. *Federalism: Origin, Operation, and Significance.* Boston: Little, Brown, 1964.

Sartori, Giovanni. *Comparative Constitutional Engineering.* New York: New York University Press, 1997.

Secondat, Charles de, Baron de Montesquieu. *The Spirit of the Laws.* London: Hafner, 1960.

Shugart, Matthew, and John Carey. *Presidents and Assemblies: Constitutional Design and Electoral Dynamics.* Cambridge: Cambridge University Press, 1992.

Stone-Sweet, Alec. *Governing with Judges: Constitutional Politics in Europe.* Oxford: Oxford University Press, 2002.

Strøm, Kaare. *Minority Government and Majority Rule.* Cambridge: Cambridge University Press, 1990.

Tsebelis, George. *Veto Players: How Political Institutions Work.* Princeton, NJ: Princeton University Press, 2002.

Weaver, Kent, and Bert Rockman, eds. *Do Institutions Matter? Government Capabilities in the United States and Abroad.* Washington, DC: Brookings Institution, 1993.

Weber, Max. "Bureaucracy." In H. H. Gerth and C. Wright Mills, eds. *From Max Weber.* New York: Oxford University Press, 1976, pp. 196–244.

Weingast, Barry R. "Political Foundations of Democracy and the Rule of Law." *American Political Science Review* 91, no. 2 (June 1997): 245–63.

## ENDNOTES

1. For a skeptical view of constitutional design, see James G. March and Johan P. Olsen, *Rediscovering Institutions: The Organizational Basis of Politics* (New York: Free Press, 1989), 171–72. For a more sanguine argument, see Giovanni Sartori, *Comparative Constitutional Engineering* (New York: New York University Press, 1995).

2. John Locke, *Two Treatises of Government*, ed. Peter Laslett (Cambridge: Cambridge University Press, 1960); and Charles de Secondat, Baron de Montesquieu, *The Spirit of the Laws* (London: Hafner, 1960).

3. *The Federalist: A Commentary on the Constitution of the United States* (Washington: National Home Library Foundation, 1937).

4. On presidential decree powers, see John M. Carey and Matthew S. Shugart, *Executive Decree Authority* (New York: Cambridge University Press, 1998); for more general discussions of presidential powers, see Matthew S. Shugart and John M. Carey, *Presidents and Assemblies: Constitutional Design and Electoral Dynamics* (Cambridge: Cambridge University Press, 1992); and Scott Mainwaring and Matthew S. Shugart, eds., *Presidentialism and Democracy in Latin America* (New York: Cambridge University Press, 1997).

5. It is important to avoid confusion between the formal titles of government officials and the source of their selection and bases of their powers—which determine the type of political system. For example, Germany is a parliamentary system, whose executive is headed by a prime minister, although his official title is chancellor; and as in many parliamentary systems the German head of state is a ceremonial president, chosen by the legislature, with little policymaking power. See also Table 6.3.

6. Arend Lijphart, *Democracy in Plural Societies* (New Haven, CT: Yale University Press, 1977); G. Bingham Powell, *Contemporary Democracies* (Cambridge: Harvard University Press, 1982); and Arend Lijphart, *Patterns of Democracy: Government Forms and Performance in Thirty-Six Countries* (New Haven, CT: Yale University Press, 1999).

7. Donald Horowitz, "Comparing Democratic Systems," in Larry Diamond and Mark F. Plattner, eds., *The Global Resurgence of Democracy* (Baltimore: Johns Hopkins University Press, 1993), 127 ff.

8. Arend Lijphart, *Patterns of Democracy*, 226.

9. George H. Gadbois, Jr., "The Institutionalization of the Supreme Court of India," in John R. Schmidhauser, ed., *Comparative Judicial Systems* (London: Butterworth Enterprises, 1987), 111–42.

10. A major trend in the division and limitation of policymaking powers in recent years has been the growth of independent central banks. Central banks, such as the Federal Reserve in the United States, have the critical task of regulating the supply of money and the interest rates, as well as many financial transactions for government and society. In most countries, such bank policy was long controlled by the chief executive as part of the government bureaucracy. But in the last 20 years, and especially since the early 1990s, many countries have given their central banks substantial independence and set for them the primary task of using monetary policy to maintain price stability and limit inflation. Their independence from the executive is encouraged by giving bank governors long terms of office free from the possibility of dismissal, as well as stipulated policy objectives and responsibilities. Such independence reassures investors, domestic and foreign, and seems to constrain inflation, but it limits the economic policy alternatives of the chief executive and cabinet.

11. For a survey of parliamentary committees in Europe, see Ingvar Mattson and Kaare Strøm, "Parliamentary Committees," in Herbert Doring, ed., *Parliaments and Majority Rule in Western Europe* (New York: St. Martin's Press, 1995), 249–307.

12. Senator Roman Houska quoted in *Time* magazine March 30, 1970.

13. See Pippa Norris, "Legislative Recruitment," in Lawrence LeDuc, Richard G. Niemi, and Pippa Norris, eds., *Comparing Democracies* (London: Sage, 1996), 184–215; and Richard E. Matland, "Women's Representation in National Legislatures: Developed and Developing Countries," *Legislative Studies Quarterly* 23, no. 1 (February 1998): 109–125.

14. Adam Przeworski, et al., *Democracy and Development* (New York: Cambridge University Press, 2000).

15. See the relevant chapters in Michael Laver and Kenneth A. Shepsle, *Cabinet Ministers and Parliamentary Government* (New York: Cambridge University Press, 1994).

16. See the discussion in Julien Freund, *The Sociology of Max Weber* (NY: Random House, 1969), 234–35.

17. See Joel Aberbach, Robert D. Putnam, and Bert A. Rockman, *Bureaucrats and Politicians in Western Democracies* (Cambridge: Harvard University Press, 1981).

18. Mark V. Nadel and Francis E. Rourke, "Bureaucracies," in Fred Greenstein and Nelson Polsby, eds., *Handbook of Political Science*, vol. 5 (Reading, MA: Addison-Wesley, 1975), 373–440.

19. See Frank Stacey, *The British Ombudsman* (Oxford: Clarendon Press, 1971); and Roy Gregory and Peter Hutchesson, *The Parliamentary Ombudsman: A Study in the Control of Administrative Action* (London: Allen & Unwin, 1975).

20. On the difficulties involved in reducing administrative corruption in developing countries, see Robert Klitgard, *Controlling Corruption* (Berkeley: University of California Press, 1989).

21. For a statistical analysis explaining scores on the Corruption Perceptions Index, see Daniel Triesman, "The Causes of Corruption: A Cross-National Study," *Journal of Public Economics* 76 (June 2000): 399–457, who suggests lower levels of economic development, shorter exposure to democracy, and federalism to be among the factors encouraging more perceived corruption.

# PUBLIC POLICY

Public policy consists of all the authoritative public decisions that governments make—the outputs of the political system. Policies or outputs are normally chosen for a purpose: they are meant to promote end results that we refer to as political outcomes. Different policies may be more or less efficient ways to reach the outcomes that policymakers want. But whether a particular outcome is good or bad ultimately depends on political goods and values. And whatever values and goals policymakers and citizens have will surely affect their evaluation of the political outcomes they actually reach. Since politicians and citizens often disagree over political goods and values, it is important to keep these goals in mind when we study public policy. In this chapter, we shall discuss these aspects of public policy in order, but we begin by considering what governments actually do.

## GOVERNMENT AND WHAT IT DOES

Governments do many things. Some things they do are timeless. In the days of the Roman Empire, for example, defense against external and internal enemies was a major government responsibility. It continues to be so in most societies today. In other ways, governments today do things that were unthinkable in the past. For example, contemporary governments regulate telecommunications and air traffic, policy areas that were unknown until the twentieth century.

Governments produce many goods and services, though exactly which ones vary a great deal from country to country. In most societies, governments provide law enforcement, roads, and postal services, and in many countries they do much more. In the former Soviet Union and other communist states, governments owned and operated most major industries and produced everything from military equipment to such consumer goods as clothing and shoes. In a capitalist society, such as the United States, most consumer goods are produced in the private sector. In much of Europe, the government produces more than in the United States, but far less than in the former Soviet Union. In some developing countries, the government produces very few goods or services.

The range of government involvement varies not just among countries, but also among different economic sectors within the same country. For example, one study showed that the U.S. government employed only 1 percent of the people engaged in mining and manufacturing, but 28 percent of those working for the utilities that supply gas, water, and electrical power; in France, the corresponding figures were 8 percent and 71 percent, respectively. Compared with socialist countries, governments in capitalist free-market societies tend to leave more production to private firms. Yet, there is no society in which the government produces no goods or services, and conversely no state in which all industries are run by the government. Even in the former Soviet Union, part of the agricultural sector was private, as were many simple consumer services, such as baby-sitting. Other ostensibly communist societies, such as China today, feature a lot of private enterprise, particularly in the consumer goods sector.

## Public Policies

The importance of governments goes far beyond their role as producers of goods and services. Indeed, this may not even be their most important role in most contemporary states. Governments also engage in various forms of public policy. In Chapter 1, we discussed three important challenges facing contemporary states: building community, fostering development, and securing democracy and human rights. Many **public policies** are wholly or in part directed at these challenges. Public policies are designed to strengthen national identity and community by reinforcing a common language or culture, or by promoting allegiance to a shared political heritage. A host of economic policies aims to promote economic and social development and to make its benefits broadly accessible. Finally, government policies establish or enhance democratic institutions that enable citizens to control political decisions. In the past century, most Western nations have been transformed from authoritarian, or oligarchic (systems ruled by the few), regimes to democracies. Government policy has increasingly been used to meet popular needs and demands. Even so, we cannot always assume that democratic governments do what is in the best interest of their citizens.

Public policies may be summarized and compared according to outputs—the actions that governments take to accomplish their purposes. We classify these actions or outputs under four headings:

1. **distribution**—of money, goods, and services—to citizens, residents, and clients of the state;
2. **extraction** of resources—money, goods, persons, and services—from the domestic and international environments;
3. **regulation** of human behavior—the use of compulsion and inducement to bring about desired behavior; and
4. **symbolic outputs**—political speeches, holidays, rites, public monuments and statues, and the like—used to exhort citizens to engage in desired forms of behavior, build community, or celebrate exemplary conduct (see Chapter 1).

Political systems have different policy profiles. Some governments produce a lot of goods and services but regulate little. Elsewhere, the government may be heavily engaged in extraction and distribution, but rely on the private sector to produce most goods and services. In the next sections, we shall discuss these four types of policies, beginning with distribution.

## DISTRIBUTION

The famous political scientist Harold D. Lasswell argued that the essence of government is deciding "who gets what, when, and how." Politics, he thought, is essentially about distribution. Whether or not we agree with Lasswell's point of view, there is no question that distributive policies are very important in contemporary societies. Whether or not they are democratic, all governments have to distribute resources in order to survive. Distributive policies include transfers of money, goods, services, honors, and opportunities to individuals and groups in the society. Such policies generally consume more government resources and employ more government officials than anything else that modern governments do.

### Distributive Policy Profiles

Health, education, and national defense are among the policy areas that consume the largest proportions of government spending worldwide. Figure 7.1 reports central governmental expenditures in these policy areas as a percentage of gross domestic product (GDP). Clearly, central government expenditures depend heavily on economic development. Developed countries generally allocate from one-half to two-thirds of their central government expenditures to education, health, and welfare. France, Germany, and Britain spend more than two-thirds of their budgets in these areas, compared with just under one-half in the United States, where a larger share of health care spending is in the private sector. Before 1989, the Soviet Union and the communist countries of Eastern Europe spent less on education, health, and welfare than the democracies of Western Europe. But as these Eastern European countries have introduced market economies, their expenditure patterns have become more similar to the West.

Since World War II especially, governments have greatly expanded their spending on education. Developing societies have made large efforts to provide at least primary education for all their citizens,

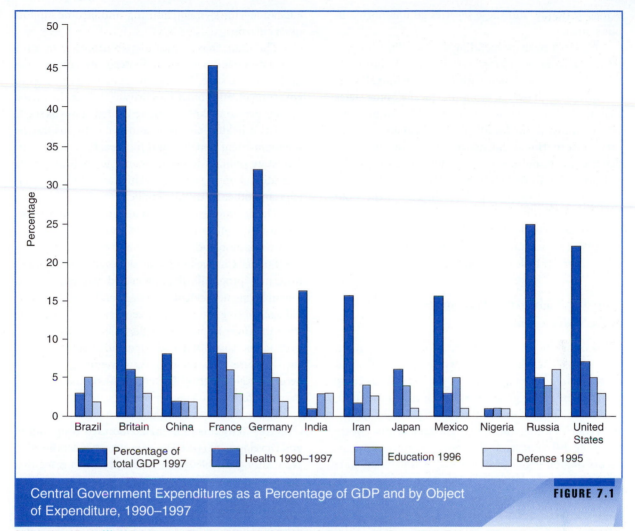

**Central Government Expenditures as a Percentage of GDP and by Object of Expenditure, 1990–1997**

**FIGURE 7.1**

Source: World Bank, *World Development Report: 1999–2000* (New York: Oxford University Press, 2000), Table 14, 256–57; Table 7, 242–43; Table 6, 240–41; Table 17, 262–63.

while most of the richer societies have also experienced a huge increase in secondary and university (tertiary) enrollments. A few decades ago, fewer than 5 percent of young adults in most European countries were able to get a college education. Today, those numbers have risen to 40 percent or more (see Table 7.4). Since most of these colleges and universities are public, government spending on secondary and higher education has risen substantially.

Public health is another major spending category. Some developing countries, such as India and Nigeria, typically spend less on health than on education. The government in Nigeria seems to have little impact on its people in these areas. India's efforts are only slightly better. Sadly, the countries that need them most have

the least to spend on education and health. Poor nations, with limited budgets and many pressing demands, cannot easily spare the resources for health and education. Also, social security expenditure in poor nations tends to be low, because shorter life expectancies and high birth rates mean that there are comparatively few older people. But part of the explanation of the low social expenditures in poor countries may also have to do with poor measures. Just as our GDP measures fail to include the subsistence economy and therefore underreport the wealth of the poorest countries (see Chapter 1), our measures of health expenditures may similarly underreport the efforts of the poorest states. In these societies the aged and the infirm typically receive some care through the extended family, and these services go unreported in our statistics.

National security spending shows a different pattern. Particularly among less-developed countries, spending varies as much with the international environment as with overall economic means. Some states that are locked in tense international confrontations (such as those in the Middle East) or that are trying to exert international influence make extraordinary defense efforts. Because of its worldwide security commitments, the United States is by far the heaviest military spender, although between the end of the Cold War and September 11, 2001, U.S. defense spending actually decreased. Japan, which spends as much as most Western countries on health and education, has spent relatively little on defense since World War II.

## From the Night Watchman State to the Welfare State

The importance of distributive policies has grown enormously over the past century or so, particularly in industrialized societies. Much of this growth has come about because the government performs more functions today than it did in the past. The **night watchman state** that was common in the nineteenth century was very different from the more expansive governments that emerged later. The night watchman state was a Lockean state (see Chapter 1), which primarily sought to regulate just enough to preserve law, order, a good business climate, and the basic security of its citizens.

With the twentieth century came the **police state,** the **regulatory state,** and the **welfare state.** The police state regulates much more intrusively and extracts resources more severely than the night watchman state. The most oppressive forms of the police state have been associated with the totalitarian ideologies (Nazism, fascism, and communism) that also left their mark on the past century. Fascist and communist governments typically call on their citizens to devote a lot of time to military or other community service and try to control their lives. But the twentieth century also produced more benign forms of big government. The regulatory state has evolved in all advanced industrial societies as they face the complexities of modern life. Finally, the welfare state, which is found particularly in prosperous and democratic societies, distributes resources extensively to provide for the health,

education, employment, housing, and income support of its citizens.

The main reason that distribution has become such a dominant concern in modern governments lies in the welfare state. The welfare state refers to a set of government, and sometimes private, policies involving old age pensions (known in the United States as social security); health, sickness, and accident insurance; unemployment benefits; and the like. Over time, welfare state policies have also come to include public education, housing subsidies, child and childcare benefits, and other distributive policies.

The first modern welfare state programs were introduced in Germany in the 1880s. In response to rapid industrialization and urbanization, the German government under Chancellor Bismarck began offering social insurance programs that protected workers against unemployment, accidents, sickness, and poverty during old age. During the twentieth century, and particularly from the Great Depression of the 1930s until the 1970s, most industrialized states adopted and greatly expanded such welfare state policies. As developing countries become wealthier, they also tend to spend more of their resources on welfare state services.

Figure 7.2 shows that the welfare state in advanced capitalist—**Organisation for Economic Co-operation and Development (OECD)**—countries has continued to grow during the 1980s and 1990s, albeit at a somewhat slower rate. As the figure shows, welfare state spending consists of two major categories: cash transfers to individuals and families, and direct government spending on services. Though both categories have grown, the transfer programs remain the largest. Among the individual programs that make up the welfare state, old-age pensions (social security) and health care loom particularly large. In many European countries with jobless rates of up to 10 or 15 percent, unemployment benefits are another major government outlay.

The welfare state is a mixture combining a social insurance scheme and a program of social redistribution. It is in part paternalistic (forcing people to put away money for their old age and potential illnesses) and in part Robin Hood (taking from the rich and giving to the poor). The balance between these two functions depends in part on which programs a particular country emphasizes and in part on how it finances them. Thus, not all welfare states are alike. Even among the advanced industrial countries, some welfare states are larger than others, and different

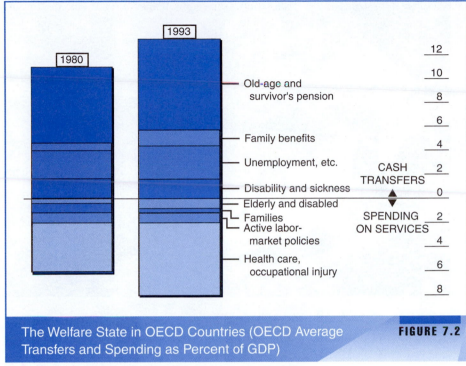

**The Welfare State in OECD Countries (OECD Average Transfers and Spending as Percent of GDP)**

**FIGURE 7.2**

Source: "Privatising Peace of Mind," *The Economist,* (October 24, 1998), 4.

political systems emphasize different benefits. All the wealthier nations try to assist the aged, the disabled, and the unemployed; but differences in expenditures reflect contrasts in priorities and historical experiences.

Because welfare benefits can be expensive and governments have limited funds, three principles govern most welfare state provisions. One is *need*: help and services are provided to those who need them the most. Social assistance is most commonly based on this idea. A second principle is *contribution*: benefits should go to those that have contributed to the program, for example, by paying taxes or insurance premiums. This is the basic idea behind social security in the United States, though other criteria also enter in. A third principle is *entitlement,* or *universalism*: everyone should have the benefit, regardless of specific circumstances. This is the principle that most countries apply to primary education or to immunization for young children.

The U.S. model stresses equality of opportunity through public education. Especially in higher education, the United States made a much greater and earlier effort than did most European nations. In contrast, on the European continent, social security and health

programs traditionally took precedence over education. Americans began spending on social security and welfare programs much later, and the U.S. government still does less in these areas than the governments of most other advanced democracies. And in many areas of welfare provision, U.S. programs are needs-based, whereas those in some European countries, such as Sweden, are entitlement-based (universalistic). For example, in the United States child benefits ("welfare") are given only to needy recipients for a limited period of time. In Scandinavia, on the other hand, all parents (billionaires as well as paupers) get the same payment from the government. In addition, they get generous parental leave at close to full pay. In sum, compared with Europeans, Americans have historically put more emphasis on equality of opportunity and less on welfare obligations. This may reflect the U.S. heritage as a nation of immigrants, many of whom arrived poor and have been expected to prosper by their own efforts.

Also, it is important to keep in mind that many welfare services in the United States are provided by private foundations, churches and other religious organizations, and individuals. In recent years, multi-billionaires, such as Warren Buffett and Bill and Melinda Gates, have made huge donations to charitable causes in the United States and abroad. And they are not alone. In 2005 Americans gave $260 billion to charitable organizations. More than three-fourths of these gifts came from living individuals, many of them people of very limited means. The nonprofit sector of the U.S. economy now accounts for 9 percent of the GDP, more than twice as much as in 1960. It employs close to 10 percent of the American workforce, more than the federal and state governments combined. This nonprofit sector exists in other

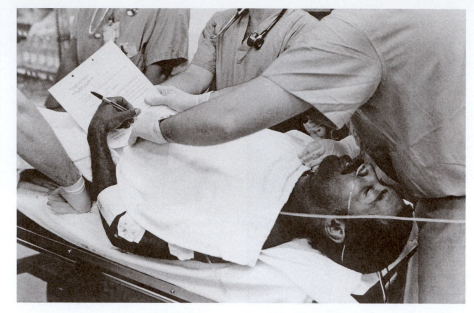

A seriously injured man is wheeled on a gurney into the emergency room of a Detroit, Michigan, hospital. He must sign the Medicaid form in order to activate his health benefits.

Leonard Freed/Magnum Photos, Inc.

developed states as well, but generally on a much smaller scale.

## Challenges to the Welfare State

Welfare states have many beneficial consequences. The Western European countries that pioneered these programs have virtually eradicated dire poverty, and they have created a much more "level playing field" for their citizens. Crime rates tend to be low in countries with extensive welfare states, and most of the programs are popular with ordinary citizens. Yet, the welfare state is also expensive. As government expenditures have grown to between one-third and one-half of GDP in most industrial democracies, they have caused serious concern about the ability of future generations to pay. One of the most serious problems is that at the same time that senior citizens are qualifying for greater pension benefits and health care costs are rising rapidly, the ranks of the elderly are swelling relative to those in the workforce. This is reflected in the dependency ratio, which is the proportion of those outside the workforce (because they are too young or too old) to those in the working-age population. Over the next decades, dependency ratios will increase in all advanced industrial societies, and particularly in such countries as Japan where the fertility rate is low and life expectancy high. Therefore, fewer working people

will have to pay higher taxes just to support existing health and welfare programs. In the United States, Medicare and Social Security may incur large deficits in the future. In other countries, social welfare programs are already costing more than their designated taxes are bringing in.

Another problem is that some welfare state policies give citizens few incentives to work. Norway and Sweden are among the leading countries in the world in life expectancy and public health statistics. Yet, workers in these countries are on sick leave about twice as often as those elsewhere in Europe, as the average Swedish worker misses about five or six weeks of work per year. In Norway, more than 10 percent of the working-age population is on disability pensions. This is partly because generous sick leave benefits let workers keep virtually their entire pay from the first day they miss work, and because it is fairly easy to qualify for disability benefits. But these policies are costly. In Sweden, sick pay and disability benefits account for more than 10 percent of the government's total spending.

These problems with the welfare state have stirred efforts to prevent further increases in spending obligations (entitlements) and to contain the costs of those already in effect. Thus the gradual expansion of welfare benefits that characterized most of the twentieth century can no longer be taken for granted.

# EXTRACTION

Since distribution means that governments spend, there must also be ways for governments to collect money and other resources. All political systems *extract* resources from their environments and inhabitants. When simple societies go to war, for example, individuals of specific age groups (most commonly young men) may be called on to fight. Anthropologists have estimated that in some hunter-gatherer societies, such obligations have been so onerous that about half of all males have died in warfare. (Thomas Hobbes would not have been surprised.) Such direct extraction of services is still found in modern states, in the form of compulsory military service, jury duty, or compulsory labor imposed on those convicted of crime.

The most common contemporary forms of resource extraction, however, are taxation and borrowing. *Taxation* is the extraction for governmental purposes of money or goods from members of a political system, for which they receive no immediate or direct benefit. Tax policies are designed to meet many different objectives, which sometimes conflict. On the one hand, governments often want to collect as much tax revenue as possible from their citizens in order to finance various services. On the other hand, they do not want to kill the goose that lays the golden egg. The more governments tax their citizens, the less these people are inclined to work, and if the tax burden becomes too onerous, they may try to evade taxes or even leave the country altogether. Another common trade-off in tax policies is between efficiency and equity. *Efficiency* means extracting the most tax revenue possible at the lowest cost to economic production. *Equity* means taxing in such a way that, as much as possible, no one is unfairly burdened, and particularly so that those who have the least are spared. In most societies, the tax system is designed to redistribute wealth in favor of the less well-off. Therefore, income taxes are generally progressive, which means that citizens with greater incomes are taxed at higher rates than those who earn less. Yet, there is a limit to how progressive income taxes can be. Highly progressive income taxes can reduce people's incentive to work and thus hurt capital formation. Therefore, they are often inefficient.

Personal and corporate income taxes and taxes on capital gains and wealth are called **direct taxes,** since they are directly levied on persons and corporations. Such taxes, as well as property taxes, tend to be progressive. But although corporate income taxes are meant to be progressive, corporations often avoid them through creative accounting or by moving their

Prison labor and community service are important forms of government extraction. This photo shows a female chain gang in the United States.

Jack Kurtz/The Image Works

operations to countries where taxes are lower. If personal income taxes become too high, similar things can happen. **Indirect taxes** include sales and value-added taxes, excise taxes, and customs duties. Their distributive effects depend on who purchases the relevant commodities and services. Since the poor spend more of their income on food and clothing than do those who are better off, sales (or value-added) taxes on such necessities are regressive (which means that the poor pay relatively more than the rich). But indirect taxes on luxury goods may be progressive, since the poor rarely purchase yachts, fine jewelry, or private planes. Payroll taxes, which are often used to finance pensions (for example, social security in the United States), tend to hit the middle class, since the wealthy often receive a larger share of their income from dividends, interest, or capital gains. Taxes on wages also penalize people in the labor force relative to retirees and homemakers and can therefore hurt employment or drive businesses into the "underground economy" in which they do not report their incomes.

Political systems that rely heavily on sales and payroll taxes are less likely to attain a progressive tax structure overall. On the other hand, such taxes are less "visible" than income taxes and seem to generate less resentment and tax avoidance. In many countries, particularly where the government does not have good financial records, indirect taxes are easier to collect. Finally, the more mobile a tax object is, the more difficult it is to tax. Financial investments tend to be highly mobile, which makes them difficult to tax. Land and buildings, on the other hand, are not very mobile, and many states tax them substantially.

Besides redistribution and efficiency, tax policies are often designed to promote such values as charity, energy conservation, or home ownership. For example, many countries stimulate home ownership by making mortgage interest payments tax deductible. The rationale is that home ownership promotes stable families who take an active interest in their neighborhoods. If such tax incentives are too generous, however, they can cause economic distortions. Families may put all their savings into housing, so that businesses are starved of capital. Moreover, mortgage deductions are primarily a middle-class benefit of little use to the truly poor, who rarely own their own homes.

Figure 7.3 shows the central government revenues as a percentage of **gross domestic product (GDP)**, the total value of goods and services produced by a country's residents in a year. For the average country, about a fifth of the GDP is extracted by the central government's taxes, but in some countries the proportion is much higher. Regional and local taxes add to the tax burden. In federal systems—such as Brazil, Germany, India, Russia, and the United States—these taxes can increase the total tax burden by a third or more.[1] Governments also derive revenues from nontax sources (the lighter columns in Figure 7.3), such as administrative fees and income from business enterprises that they run.

The tax profiles of different countries vary both in their overall tax burdens and in their reliance on different types of taxes. Sweden has the highest tax rates overall, as it extracts more than 50 percent of its GDP in taxes. France comes close to the 50-percent mark. Britain and Germany are among a number of advanced industrial societies that collect about 40 percent of GDP, while the United States and Russia extract about a third. Outside the European and North American areas, central government revenue rarely exceeds 20 percent of GDP. The central government revenue of India is under 15 percent, or about 20 percent more if we add state and local governments.

Countries also differ in how they collect their revenues. Some advanced industrial countries (including Germany and France) rely heavily on social security taxes imposed on both employers and employees. In both Germany and Britain, most of the revenue comes from social security and income taxes, but whereas Germany relies far more heavily on social security payments, Britain relies more on income taxes. The United States and Japan, which fall below average in total tax burden, depend to a large extent on direct income taxes rather than on sales and consumption taxes.[2] Poorer countries, such as Iran, India, and Mexico, receive most of their revenue from indirect taxes.

Although overall tax burdens continue to grow, income tax rates have decreased in Western countries since the early 1980s, as there has been a shift from direct income taxes to less visible indirect consumption taxes. Growing tax burdens led to taxpayer revolts and some scaling back of government extraction. From 1975 to 1990, British top marginal income tax rates declined by 43 percentage points, Swedish rates by 35 points, and Japanese rates by 25 points. During the same time period in the United States, federal rates

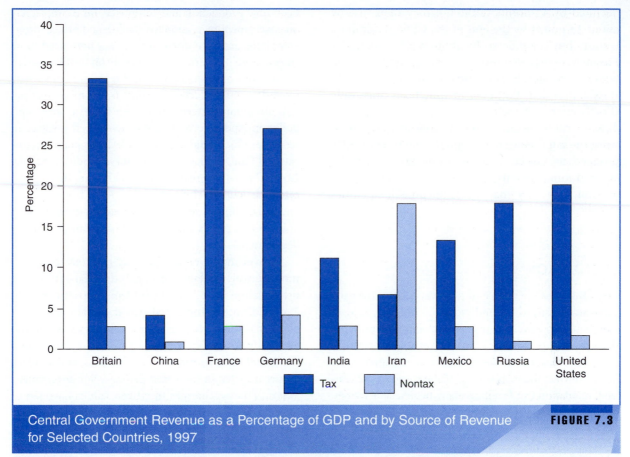

**Central Government Revenue as a Percentage of GDP and by Source of Revenue for Selected Countries, 1997**

FIGURE 7.3

Source: World Bank, *World Development Report, 1999–2000* (New York: Oxford University Press, 2000), Table 14, 256–57.

## Balancing the Books

BOX 7.1

In the long run, governments cannot spend more money than they raise. If governments fail to balance their books and instead run budget deficits, they have to borrow money, which creates debt that future generations of taxpayers have to pay off. Yet, even rich governments are notoriously bad at balancing their books, and many run budget deficits year after year. In 2004, nineteen of the twenty-eight (highly developed) Organisation for Economic Co-operation and Development (OECD) countries ran budget deficits, and the average deficit was equal to 3.5 percent of gross domestic product (GDP). The United States, which had run deficits most of the time since the Vietnam War,

briefly balanced its budget in the late 1990s, but then slid back into fiscal imbalance due to the stock market crash in 2000, the terrorist attacks of September 11, 2001, increased spending on homeland security, the invasion of Iraq, and tax cuts. As of 2006, however, the United States had reduced its deficit to 1.9 percent of GDP, well below European countries such as France, Germany, and Italy. When these countries in the 1990s decided to adopt a common currency, the Euro, they also committed themselves to keeping their respective national deficits smaller than 3 percent of GDP. In practice, however, they have often been unable to keep that promise.

declined by 42 points (although they then rose by about 13 points by the end of the Clinton administration, but came down by about 4.5 points under President George W. Bush). The average decline in top tax rates for all OECD countries was 18 percent.[3] In Russia, President Putin cut income taxes drastically shortly after he came to power. Tax rates have come down because of the spread of economic views that stress the importance of entrepreneurial incentives for productivity. Lower marginal income tax rates stimulate economic activity and lessen incentives for tax evasion, but they may cause income inequalities to grow.

## REGULATION

Regulation is the exercise of political control over the behavior of individuals and groups in the society. Most contemporary governments are not only welfare states, they are also regulatory states. Governments regulate for many reasons, as we discussed in Chapter 1. As social contract theorists such as Hobbes and Locke realized, regulation can facilitate many beneficial activities.

Economic production and commerce, for example, rely on government regulation to establish and protect property rights and to enforce contracts. There need to be rules to keep traffic moving smoothly on the freeways, in the air, and on the airwaves. Citizens and consumers often demand protections against fraud, manipulation, and obnoxious externalities, such as toxic waste and pollution. And governments are increasingly involved in setting product standards, particularly for pharmaceuticals and food, to make sure that these products are safe. Governments also regulate to shield their citizens, and often particularly children and women, from physical and other abuse, and to some extent they protect animals and plants against cruelty and environmental degradation.

Government regulation has proliferated enormously over the last century. Industrialization and urbanization have caused problems in traffic, health, and public order. Industrial growth has also generated concerns about industrial safety, labor exploitation, and pollution. Moreover, the growth of science and the belief that humanity can harness and control nature have led to increased demands for government action. Finally, changes in citizen values have led to

---

### Regulation and Development                                          BOX 7.2

In the advanced industrial countries of North America, Japan, and Western Europe, regulation has grown enormously along with their industrial and postindustrial economies. It is easy to think, therefore, that there is more regulation in wealthy countries than in poor ones. But this is not always true. In fact, low-income countries sometimes regulate more than rich ones. This is particularly true of regulations of business entry and competition. In many less developed countries, it is cumbersome and time-consuming, for example, to get the permits necessary to start a new business. Such regulations often mainly serve to create *rents* that government officials can exploit for their own benefit (see Chapter 1). They protect existing businesses by giving them monopolies or other protections. Many politicians expect the businesspeople who benefit from these regulations (often their family members, friends, or

business associates) to show their gratitude through kickbacks and other favors. Or business owners pay off politicians or civil servants to get around onerous regulations or to avoid long delays in handling their applications. Overregulation of this kind tends to hurt economic productivity and keep out foreign investment.

The Peruvian economist Hernando de Soto reports a sobering experience with abusive government regulation. As an experiment, he registered a small clothing factory in Lima, Peru, and decided in advance not to pay bribes. While he was waiting for his business to be registered, government officials asked him for bribes no fewer than ten times. Twice he broke his own rule and paid the bribe so that he would not be forced to give up his experiment. After ten months, his factory was finally registered. In New York, a similar procedure takes four hours.

Source: World Bank, *World Development Report 2005*, Chapter 5; William Easterly, *The Elusive Quest for Growth: The Economists' Adventures and Misadventures in the Tropics* (Cambridge: MIT Press, 2001), 233.

demands for new kinds of regulation. Thus, government regulation in the United States has extended to include gun control, protection of voting rights, prohibition of discrimination in employment, pollution abatement, and the like. At the same time, however, at least most Western societies have lessened their regulation of birth control, abortion, divorce, blasphemy, obscenity, and sexual conduct.

Governments regulate the lives of their citizens in many ways. Although we often associate regulation with legal means, there are other ways to regulate as well. Governments may control behavior by offering material or financial inducements or by persuasion or moral exhortation. For example, many governments try to reduce tobacco use by a combination of methods: bans on smoking, tobacco sales, or advertising; sales ("sin") taxes; and information campaigns to convince people of the hazards of smoking.

But even though there are many similarities in regulative policies across the world, states often differ substantially in their policy profiles. Patterns of regulation vary not only with industrialization and urbanization, for example, but also with cultural values. In the study of public policy, we describe and explain such differences among political systems by asking the following questions:

1. What aspects of human behavior and interaction are regulated and to what degree? Does the government regulate such domains as family relations, economic activity, religious activity, political activity, geographic mobility, professional and occupational qualifications, and protection of person and property? These questions have to do with the *domain* of government regulation.
2. What social groups are regulated, with what procedural limitations on enforcement, and what rights? Are these sanctions applied uniformly, or do they affect different individuals or groups differently? Are there rights of appeal? Such questions help us identify the *subjects* of regulation.
3. What sanctions are used to compel or induce citizens to comply? Does the government use exhortation and moral persuasion, financial rewards and penalties, licensing of some types of actions, physical confinement or punishment, or other forms of coercion? These questions help us map the *instruments*, or *mechanisms*, of regulation.

Although all modern states use sanctions, they vary in their goals and strategies. Yet, one aspect of regulation is particularly important politically: government control over political participation and communication. Recall from earlier chapters that democracy requires political competition. Governments in authoritarian systems often suppress political competition by prohibiting party organization, voluntary associations, and political communication. Government regulation in this area therefore has a crucial effect on democracy. Yet, governmental regulation is not always negative. Our civilization and amenities depend on regulation. Government regulation commonly promotes such values as the safety of persons and property, sanitation, prevention of environmental pollution, safe disposal of toxic wastes, maintenance of occupational safety, and equal access to housing and education.

Table 7.1 shows the political rights and civil liberties ratings for the countries included in this book,

| Political and Economic Rights and Liberties, 2004–2005 | | | **TABLE 7.1** |
|---|---|---|---|
| **Country** | **Political Rights** | **Civil Liberties** | **Economic Freedom** |
| Brazil | 2 | 3 | 5.9 |
| Britain | 1 | 1 | 8.1 |
| China | 7 | 6 | 5.7 |
| France | 1 | 1 | 7.3 |
| Germany | 1 | 1 | 7.6 |
| India | 2 | 3 | 6.7 |
| Iran | 6 | 6 | 6.1 |
| Japan | 1 | 2 | 7.5 |
| Mexico | 2 | 2 | 6.6 |
| Nigeria | 3 | 3 | 5.6 |
| Russia | 6 | 5 | 5.6 |
| United States | 1 | 1 | 8.2 |

Note: Expert ratings of political rights and civil liberties for each country on 1 (highest) to 7 (lowest) scale. Economic freedom scored on summary scale from 0 (low) to 10 (high).

Source: Freedom House website, www.freedomhouse.org (downloaded February 3, 2006); James Gwartney and Robert Lawson with William Easterly, *Economic Freedom of the World: 2006 Annual Report* (Vancouver: Fraser Institute, 2006), 13.

based on expert judgments. Political rights refers to citizen opportunities to participate in the choice of political leaders—voting rights, the right to run for office, and the like. Civil liberties refers to protections in such areas as freedom of speech, press, assembly, and religion, as well as to procedural rights, such as trial by a jury of peers and bans on arbitrary or cruel treatment. The rich democratic countries all have ratings of 1 or 2 for both political and civil rights. India, Brazil, and Mexico, which have improved significantly in recent years, follow next. At the other extreme, China, Iran, and most recently Russia substantially suppress both political rights and civil liberties. China in particular has tried to control the media comprehensively and sets few limits on government regulation vis-à-vis the individual. Nigeria is rated in the middle. These rankings, of course, vary over time. Rights and liberties in the United States have improved since the civil rights movement of the 1960s. Nigeria's military governments of the 1990s were repressive and frequently brutal, but things have improved there since power was turned over to an elected civilian president in 1999.

There is a strong correlation between political and civil rights. No country that scores high on participatory rights also scores very low on civil liberties, and no country low on participatory rights is high on civil liberties. This suggests a strong relationship between popular participation and the rule of law and equitable procedure. In a study of governmental repression in 153 countries during the 1980s, Steven C. Poe and C. Neal Tate found that positive civil and political rights records were best explained by democratic political institutions and conditions of peace and social order. Authoritarian states and those involved in internal or international war were the most frequent civil rights violators. A high level of economic development also helps explain a strong rights record.[4]

Table 7.1 also reports the level of economic freedom in each country. It is not always true that countries that are politically free also foster economic freedom, or vice versa. For example, China provides a lot less political freedom than Nigeria, but the level of economic freedom in the two countries is about the same. And even though Britain and France score the same on political rights and liberties, Britain has a higher level of economic freedom. On the whole, though, political and economic freedoms tend to go together.

## COMMUNITY-BUILDING AND SYMBOLIC OUTPUTS

A fourth type of output is symbolic policies. Much communication by political leaders takes the form of appeals to the courage, wisdom, and magnanimity embodied in the nation's past; or appeals to values and ideologies, such as equality, liberty, community, democracy, communism, liberalism, or religious tradition; or promises of future accomplishment and rewards. Political leaders appeal to such values for different reasons—for example, to win elections or to push their own pet projects. But at the same time many symbolic appeals and policies have the purpose of building community—for example, by boosting people's national identity, civic pride, or trust in government.

Symbolic outputs are also intended to enhance other aspects of performance: to make people pay their taxes more readily and honestly; comply with the law more faithfully; or accept sacrifice, danger, and hardship. Such appeals may be especially important in times of crisis. Some of the most magnificent examples are the speeches of Pericles in the Athenian Assembly during the Peloponnesian War, or those of Franklin D. Roosevelt in the depths of the Great Depression, or of Winston Churchill during Britain's darkest hours in World War II. But symbolic policies are important even in less extreme circumstances. Public buildings, plazas, monuments, holiday parades, and civic and patriotic indoctrination in schools all attempt to contribute to the population's sense of governmental legitimacy and its willingness to comply with public policy.

## OUTCOMES: DOMESTIC WELFARE

While we can describe different government policies, it is not always clear what their consequences will be. How do extractive, distributive, regulative, and symbolic policies affect the lives of citizens? Unexpected economic, international, or social events may frustrate the purpose of political leaders. Thus a tax rebate to stimulate the economy may be nullified by a rise in the price of oil. Increases in health expenditures may

| | **TABLE 7.2** |
|---|---|
| **Welfare Outcomes, 1990–2005** | |

| Country | Private Household Consumption Annual (%) Growth 1990–2003 | Population Below $2 per Day %, ca. 2000 | Access to Safe Water (%) 1990/2002 | Access to Sanitation (%) 1990/2002 |
|---|---|---|---|---|
| Brazil | 3.4 | 22.4 | 83/89 | 70/75 |
| Britain | 3.1 | ND | 100/100 | 100/100 |
| China | 8.5 | 46.7 | 70/77 | 23/44 |
| France | 1.6 | ND | 100/100 | 96/ND |
| Germany | 1.5 | ND | 100/100 | ND/ND |
| India | 4.9 | 80.6 | 68/86 | 12/30 |
| Iran | 3.5 | 7.3 | 91/93 | 83/84 |
| Japan | .4 | ND | 100/100 | 100/100 |
| Mexico | 2.8 | 26.3 | 80/91 | 66/77 |
| Nigeria | 3.7 | 90.8 | 49/60 | 39/38 |
| Russia | .9 | 7.5 | 94/96 | 87/87 |
| United States | 3.7 | ND | 100/100 | 100/100 |

Source: World Bank, *World Development Indicators 2005*, Tables 2.5, 2.15, 4.10 (downloaded February 3, 2006), from http://devdata.worldbank .org/wdipdfs/tab2_5.pdf, 2_15.pdf, from http://devdata.worldbank.org/wdi2005/Table4_10.htm; and previous editions.

have no effect because of unexpected epidemics or rising health costs, or health services may not reach those most in need. Sometimes policies have unintended and undesirable consequences, as when the introduction of benefits for troubled social groups lead others to simulate the same troubles to get the same favors. Consequently, to estimate the effectiveness of public policy, we have to examine actual welfare outcomes as well as governmental policies and their implementation.

Table 7.2 compares a number of welfare indicators. The first two columns report measures of economic well-being or its lack: growth in private consumption and the share of the population living on less than $2 per day. The severe problems of Nigeria and India are particularly notable: the vast majority of those populations live on less than $2 a day. The latter columns report the availability of critical public facilities: safe water and sanitation. While most of the people of the developed world have access to safe water, this is true for less than half of the population of many less-advantaged countries. In Nigeria, for example, only 49 percent of the population had access to safe water in 1990, though by 2002 this percentage had risen to 60. The good news

is that most of the poorer countries in our sample experienced solid progress over the past decade or so, although that progress may be more secure in China and India than in oil-dependent Nigeria.

In Chapter 1, we saw how income distribution tends to be most unequal in medium-income developing societies, such as Brazil, and more equal in advanced market societies as well as in low-income developing societies, such as India (see Table 1.4 in Chapter 1). In his studies of European economic history, Simon Kuznets showed that in the early stages of industrialization income distribution became more unequal, whereas in later stages of industrialization income distribution again came closer to equality.[5] This "Kuznets curve" reflects the fact that in the early stages of modernization, traditional farmers tend to be left behind as industry and commercial agriculture begin to grow. At higher levels of economic attainment, however, the number of poor farmers is reduced compared with the industrial and service sectors. In addition, when trade unions and democratic political parties emerge, they tend to make the income distribution more equal through taxation, wage policy, and welfare state policies.

## Government and the Rural Poor

BOX 7.3

Visitors from rich countries are often shocked and appalled at the poverty they see in the fast-growing cities of the developing world. Poverty in these teeming metropolises is often exacerbated by crime, violence, homelessness, and pollution. Yet, poverty is even more of a problem in the countryside than in the cities. The poorest countries in the world are overwhelmingly rural, and in most poor countries poverty rates in the country-side are much higher than in the cities. In Brazil, for example, only 15 percent of the urban population fell below the country's (modest) poverty line in 1998, whereas 51 percent of the rural population did so. There are many reasons that rural poverty is often so dire. In rural areas, there is often less investment in education and infrastructure. Farmers in poor countries often find it difficult to obtain title to their land or credit (see Box 7.4). And rural dwellers are more susceptible than city-dwellers to the vagaries of the climate.

But part of the problem of rural poverty can also result from government policy. In many African states, for example, the rulers tend to favor the urban popula-tion because they want the country to modernize and industrialize. Sometimes politicians also worry that a starving urban population might riot and bring down the government. For these reasons, governments tend to keep food prices artificially low, which hurts farmers. Governments also tend to prefer targeted government agricultural programs (often subsidies), which help particular groups of farmers (often wealthy ones). Such targeted programs help governments gain political sup-porters but are often wasteful. Even in democratic countries where the majority of voters are poor farmers, government policies often do little for them. Many vot-ers do not trust politicians who promise to deliver broad public goods (such as health care and education), but instead support candidates who promise targeted pri-vate goods (such as jobs and subsidies). Thus, even spending on schools becomes a way to create jobs rather than to educate children. In India, teachers' salaries account for 96 percent of recurrent expenditures in primary education. Even so, teacher absenteeism is rampant. When inspectors made unannounced visits to rural schools, about two-thirds of the teachers were absent.

Sources: Robert H. Bates, *Markets and States in Tropical Africa.* (Berkeley: University of California Press, 1981); Philip Keefer and Stuti Khemani, "Why Do the Poor Receive Poor Services?" *Economic and Political Weekly*, 28, February 2004, 935–43; World Bank, *World Development Report 2002*, 31–32.

Table 7.3 reports on health outcomes. During the 1990s, the average public health expenditure per capita for the economically developed countries was $2,505, compared with $182 for the developing countries. The average number of physicians per 1,000 people in the developed world was 2.8, compared with 1.3 in the developing world. But in Nigeria the number was only 0.2 in 1990 and 0.3 in 2004. The country has a high birth rate, but almost one out of ten infants fails to survive the first year of life, and more than one-third of Nigerian children under age 5 suffer from malnutri-tion. Nigerian citizens have a life expectancy at birth of just 45 years (compared with 75–80 years in advanced industrial countries).

Nigeria demonstrates the ills of poverty, but some poor countries cope more successfully than others. Consider the difference between China and India. With similar levels of GDP per capita, Chinese average life expectancy is 71 years and infant mortality is 30 per 1,000 live births, while those of India are 63 years and 63 per 1,000, respectively. China has three times as many physicians as India relative to its population. Almost half of India's children under age 5 are under-nourished, compared with a sixth of those in China. Fortunately, however, health conditions are improving in most of the poor countries, including India.

While the incidence of infant mortality and mal-nutrition is much lower in advanced economies, these problems are still serious among the poor in advanced industrial countries, such as the United States. The United States spends the largest proportion of its GDP on health care (approximately 15 percent) of any country. At the same time, however, the United States has a somewhat higher infant death rate than Japan and Western Europe due to more widespread poverty, drug abuse, and unequal access to health care. As Table 7.3 shows, Japan has an exceptional health record. It has the longest life expectancy and the

## Microcredit
**BOX 7.4**

One of the greatest obstacles to economic growth in many poor areas is the difficulty of obtaining credit. In advanced industrial countries, property owners (for example, farmers or home owners) typically have a recognized title to their property. If they want to invest to expand their business or start a new one, they can borrow against this collateral. People in poor countries rarely have this opportunity, and it is especially difficult for poor farmers and women to obtain loans. As a result, they often cannot get the funds they need to tide them over hard times or to take advantage of promising business opportunities.

Muhammad Yunus, a U.S.-educated professor of economics, had noticed these problems in his native country of Bangladesh. In 1974, he began extending small loans to poor people to help them out of these circumstances. His first loan amounted to $27 from his own pockets, which he lent to forty-two people, including a woman who made bamboo furniture, which she sold to support herself and her family. In 1976, Yunus founded Grameen Bank to make loans to poor Bangladeshis. The bank has since given out more than $5 billion in loans. To secure its loans, the bank sets up a system of "solidarity groups," which meet on a weekly basis and support each other's efforts. As of May 2006, Grameen Bank had almost 7 million borrowers, 97 percent of whom were women. Their repayment rate is 98 percent. In 2006, Muhammad Yunus and the Grameen Bank received the Nobel Peace Prize for these efforts to help poor people improve their lives.

## Health Outcomes, 1990–2004
**TABLE 7.3**

| Country | Total Health Expenditure as % of GDP, 2002 | Physicians per 1000 Citizens, 1990/2004 | Life Expectancy at Birth 2003 | Infant Mortality per 1,000 Live Births 2003 | Fertility Rate, 2003 |
|---|---|---|---|---|---|
| Brazil | 7.9 | 1.3/2.1 | 69 | 33 | 2.1 |
| Britain | 7.7 | 1.4/1.7 | 78 | 5 | 1.6 |
| China | 5.8 | 1.5/1.6 | 71 | 30 | 1.9 |
| France | 9.7 | 2.6/3.3 | 79 | 4 | 1.9 |
| Germany | 10.9 | 3.1/3.6 | 78 | 4 | 1.3 |
| India | 6.1 | 0.5/0.5 | 63 | 63 | 2.9 |
| Iran | 6.0 | 0.3/1.0 | 69 | 33 | 2.0 |
| Japan | 7.9 | 1.7/2.0 | 82 | 3 | 1.3 |
| Mexico | 6.1 | 1.1/1.7 | 74 | 23 | 2.2 |
| Nigeria | 4.7 | 0.2/0.3 | 45 | 98 | 5.6 |
| Russia | 6.2 | 4.1/4.2 | 66 | 16 | 1.3 |
| United States | 14.6 | 2.4/5.5 | 77 | 7 | 2.0 |

Source: World Bank, *World Development Indicators 2005*, Tables 2.14, 2.16, 2.17, 2.19 (downloaded February 7, 2006), from http://devdata.worldbank.org/wdi2005/Table2_14.htm, Table2_16.htm, Table2_17.htm, Table2_19.htm.

lowest infant mortality rate among all the study countries in this book. But its fertility rate of 1.3 means a declining population. (With no net migration, a fertility rate of approximately 2.1 results in a steady-state population.)

Table 7.4 tells us about access to education and information technologies, such as newspapers and personal computers. As we can see, many more people are reached by newspapers in rich and well-educated countries, such as Japan, than in the developing world. Yet even in poorer countries, communications have become much easier. Television has become widely available even in countries at middling development levels (e.g., Brazil and Mexico). Personal

| Education and Information | | | | | | **TABLE 7.4** |

| Country | Public Education Expenditure as Percent of Gov't Spending, 2002–03 | Gross Percentage of Relevant Age Group Enrolled, Tertiary, 2002–03 | Percentage 15 Years and Above Illiterate, Male/Female, 2002 | Female Share of Labor Force, 1998 | Newspapers per 1,000 Inhabitants, 2000 | Personal Computers per 1,000 Inhabitants, 2003 |
|---|---|---|---|---|---|---|
| Brazil | 12 | 18 | 14/13 | 35 | 46 | 75 |
| Britain | 11 | 64 | ND | 44 | 326 | 406 |
| China | ND | 13 | 5/13 | 45 | 59 | 28 |
| France | 11 | 54 | ND | 45 | 143 | 347 |
| Germany | 10 | 49 | ND | 42 | 291 | 485 |
| India | 13 | 11 | 32/55 | 32 | 60 | 7 |
| Iran | 18 | 21 | 16/30 | ND | 28 | 91 |
| Japan | 11 | 49 | ND | 41 | 566 | 382 |
| Mexico | 24 | 21 | 7/11 | 33 | 94 | 82 |
| Nigeria | ND | 8 | 26/41 | 36 | 25 | 7 |
| Russia | 12 | 70 | 0/1 | 49 | 105 | 89 |
| United States | 17 | 81 | ND | 46 | 215 | 659 |

Source: World Bank, *World Development Indicators 2005*, Tables 2.10, 2.11, 2.13; 5.10, 5.11 (downloaded February 7, 2006), from http://devdata .worldbank.org/wdi2005/Table2_10.htm,Table2_11.htm,Table2_13.htm, Table5_10.htm, Table5_11.htm: also World Bank, *World Development Indicators 2000* (for data on female labor force participation).

computers, however, are much rarer outside the advanced industrial economies. Compared with people in Brazil, people in the United States are three times more likely to own a television, but ten times more likely to own a personal computer. In the developed countries, most adults and many children have a cell phone, but in India and Nigeria there are about twenty-five people to a phone. Even so, the advent of cellular phones has made it much easier to connect the rural population in developing countries where there are often very few land lines.

Table 7.4 also provides a picture of educational attainment. The first column, showing public education expenditure as a percentage of GDP, gives a rough measure of the "priority" given to education. Remember, however, that private schools, which in some countries are very common, are not counted here. There are differences in educational requirements: Nigeria requires only children from ages 6 to 12 to attend school. And the differences in dollar expenditures per student are very large. The outcomes are predictable enough. At the high end in educational outcomes, France, Germany, Japan, and Britain have virtually all of their primary and secondary school-age

children in schools, and about half of the college-age population is in some form of advanced education. In the United States, college education is even more common. Nigeria has only 8 percent of the appropriate age cohort in tertiary education, by far the poorest record of these countries. India's figure is 11 percent.

The payoffs of development and education are clearly reflected in literacy rates: 30 to 40 percent of all adult Indians and Nigerians are unable to read or write. Yet China has less than 10 percent illiteracy. But because they are often based on the number of school years completed, not on actual reading ability, literacy figures are a crude measure of skill and competence and must be treated with caution. The high official literacy figures in the United States, for example, conflict with studies showing substantial functional illiteracy among American adults.

Women in developing countries often lag behind in literacy. For example, fewer than half of all adult females in India are reported to be literate. The discrepancy between male and female literacy rates tells us something of the status of women. Where women make up a smaller proportion of the labor force, female illiteracy also tends to be higher. Faced with

## Women and the Informal Economy

BOX 7.5

Parmila is an Indian widow in her thirties with two young children. Although she comes from a wealthy family, her husband's death forced her to take various part-time jobs. She collects wood from local forests, dries it, and then twice a week walks five miles to sell it at a local market. In the winter (November to January), she works on farms dehusking rice. She gets to keep some of the rice she produces. Outside of the rainy season, she also works as a laborer on a construction site, where her boss pays her about half of the Indian minimum wage. Parmila's total income is very low by Western standards, but it is enough to allow her to send her two children to school. Parmila does not ask for sympathy or for financial support from her relatives. "Even in times of acute crisis, I held my nerves and did not give in to circumstances," she says. "My God has always stood with me."

Women make up an increasing share of the world's workers. In most non-Islamic countries, they now make up 40 percent or more of the labor force. But in many parts of the world, most women work in the informal economy, where their work is often poorly paid. It commonly also escapes taxation and regulation. In India and in many African countries, for example, more than four out of five women who work outside of agriculture are in the informal economy. Many women choose such jobs voluntarily. They may do childcare for others or produce arts and crafts, often for local consumption. These jobs may be attractive because they can be performed at home while the women also take care of their own children or relatives. But many women also work in the informal sector because they face discrimination elsewhere. And some are enticed or forced into exhausting, dangerous, or degrading work in sweatshops or in the sex industry. While the informal economy can offer job flexibility, it can also be a place where there is little protection against abusive working conditions.

Source: William Easterly, *The Elusive Quest for Growth: The Economists' Adventures and Misadventures in the Tropics* (Cambridge: MIT Press, 2001), 45.

poverty, disease, and the absence of a social safety net, parents in poor countries traditionally want to have many children, to ensure that some survive and can support them in old age. But in large families mothers usually have few opportunities to educate themselves or hold jobs outside the home. Modernizing the status of women generally makes them better informed and more capable of making choices that lead to a more stable and healthy population. As women are educated and/or enter the labor force, they recognize the advantages of smaller families and become more aware of the importance of education and adequate health care.

Table 7.4 also reveals the sobering difficulties of trying to change societies, even in an area such as literacy, where modern technologies are available. It is hard for a poor country to spend a high percentage of its GDP on education, because it must then make sacrifices elsewhere. And the effects are limited if much of the country's productive effort has to go into feeding a rapidly growing population. No matter how large the educational effort may be, it does not translate into much per child, because the resource base is small and the population is growing rapidly. Moreover, since most older people are illiterate, the net effect on literacy is slow. And in many poorer countries, their best-educated young people often leave the country to take jobs in the big cities of the rich countries.

All of these data show how governmental and private efforts, in societies at different levels of economic development and of differing social structures and cultures, affect human life chances. Economic development affects economic prosperity; public health provisions, such as sanitation and the availability of potable water; and access to the outside world through telephone and television, roads, and other infrastructure. But although natural resources and socioeconomic structure constrain these outcomes, government and private efforts can make a big difference.

## OUTCOMES: DOMESTIC SECURITY

As Thomas Hobbes would have reminded us, maintaining domestic law and order and protecting persons and property are among the most basic government responsibilities. Without them the conduct of personal, economic, and civic life are impossible. It is therefore worrisome that until recently crime rates have been on the increase in many advanced industrial countries, as well as in the developing world. Thus in the United States the crime rate increased by almost 15 percent between 1982 and 1991. In France the 1990 incidence of crimes against persons and property was almost twice that of 1975. In Russia the crime rate doubled between 1985 and 1993, as the moral and legal order collapsed. The country now has a murder rate almost five times as high as the United States. Brazil and Mexico also have considerably higher murder rates than the United States, while those of such European countries as England, France, and Germany are a small fraction of the U.S. numbers. China has similarly low murder rates, whereas Japan is even lower.

High crime rates are primarily a problem of the larger urban areas where much of the population of modern countries resides. The causes of urban crime are complex. Rapidly increasing migration into the major cities, from the domestic countryside or from poorer foreign countries, increases diversity and often conflict. The pace of urbanization is particularly explosive in many developing countries, such as Brazil and Nigeria, where there are severe problems of poverty and infrastructure. The newly arrived city-dwellers often find themselves uprooted from their cultures, unwelcome, without a job, and living in squalor far apart from their families and traditional communities. Also, inequality of income and wealth, unemployment, and drug abuse lie behind this general decline in public order and safety. In some former communist countries, the situation is compounded by the fact that traditional authorities and law enforcement have collapsed.

Yet, crime rates have recently come down significantly in the United States and some other countries. The number of murders per 100,000 inhabitants in the United States peaked at 9.4 in 1994, and declined to 5.7 in 2003 (see Figure 7.4). There are several reasons that crime rates have recently come down in the United States and elsewhere. One is a strong economy, in which more young people have been able to find jobs. A second reason is stricter law enforcement. This is reflected in part in the number of police officers relative to total population, which ranges from one police officer for every 350 persons in the United States, to 820 in India, and 1,140 in Nigeria. In the United States, both federal and state governments have also sought to reduce crime by increasing the length of

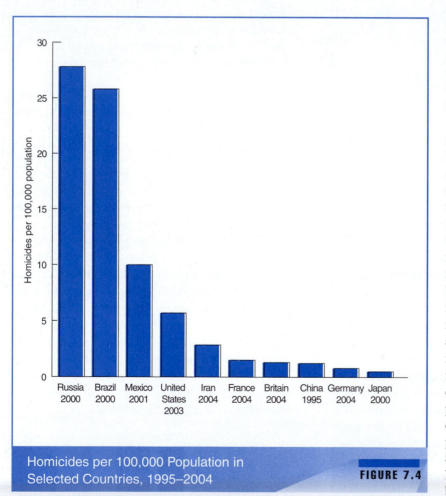

**Homicides per 100,000 Population in Selected Countries, 1995–2004**

**FIGURE 7.4**

Source: *United Nations Demographic Yearbook, 2002* (New York: United Nations, 2002) and "United Nations Surveys on Crime Trends and the Operations of Criminal Justice Systems," downloaded from http://www.unodc.org/unodc/en/crime_cicp_surveys.html.

imprisonment. By removing the criminally prone from the streets, these authorities have succeeded in cutting the crime rate, but at the cost of an exploding prison population. The United States now imprisons more people than any other country, including communist China. The total prison population in the United States in 2004 was around 2.2 million, including 1.3 million in state prisons and 700,000 in local jails awaiting sentencing or serving short sentences. The total U.S. prison population has for the past ten years been increasing at a rate of about 50,000 per year. Similarly, the French prison population almost doubled between 1983 and 1990.[6] A third cause of lower crime rates has been a decrease in the number of youth at the age at which most crimes are committed. Yet, as the 15- to 25-year-old male population in the United States is now on the rise, violent crime may increase once again.

## INTERNATIONAL OUTPUTS AND OUTCOMES

Most states engage in a great variety of international activities. Such economic, diplomatic, military, and informational activities may result in prosperity or depression, war or peace, secularization or the spread of particular beliefs.[7] The most costly outcome of the interaction among nations is warfare. Table 7.5 reports the numbers of deaths from international and internal collective violence for our twelve study countries for almost the entire twentieth century (1900–1995). The figures are mostly civilian and military deaths from interstate warfare, but they also include the slaughter of civilians in the efforts to implement communism in the Soviet Union, the holocaust of European Jews under the German Nazis (Hitler's National Socialist Party), many "ethnic cleansing" episodes in Europe and Africa, and civil wars in all parts of the world.

Over the long haul, the deadly costs of international warfare have gradually escalated. One authority estimates that more than 90 percent of the war deaths since 1700 occurred in the twentieth century. Civilian deaths caused by war increased even more rapidly than military ones. In the last decades of the twentieth century, more than three-quarters of the war deaths were civilian.[8]

Table 7.5 shows that the people of USSR/Russia, by a margin of more than two-to-one, were the most numerous victims of the tormented history of the twentieth century. The enormous Russian casualties during World War I destroyed the czarist regime. Its

**TABLE 7.5**

### Deaths from Collective Civilian-Military Violence, 1900–1995

| Country | Civilian Deaths | Military Deaths | Unspecified Deaths | Total Deaths |
|---|---|---|---|---|
| Brazil | — | 1,000 | 2,000 | 3,000 |
| Britain | 131,000 | 1,350,000 | — | 1,481,000 |
| China | 4,047,000 | 2,671,000 | 818,000 | 7,536,000 |
| France | 490,000 | 1,830,000 | — | 2,320,000 |
| Germany | 2,232,000 | 7,150,000 | — | 9,382,000 |
| India | 889,000 | 71,000 | 37,000 | 997,000 |
| Iran | 120,000 | 468,000 | 1,000 | 589,000 |
| Japan | 510,000 | 1,502,000 | — | 2,012,000 |
| Mexico | 125,000 | 125,000 | 10,000 | 260,000 |
| Nigeria | 1,005,000 | 1,000,000 | 6,000 | 2,011,000 |
| Soviet Union/Russia | 12,028,000 | 11,901,000 | 96,000 | 24,025,000 |
| United States | — | 524,000 | — | 524,000 |
| TOTALS | 21,577,000 | 28,593,000 | 970,000 | 51,140,000 |

Source: Adapted from Ruth Leger Sivard, "Wars and War Related Deaths, 1900–1995," *World Military and Social Expenditures 1996* (Washington, DC: World Priorities, 1996), 18–19. U.S. deaths add Korean and Vietnam war totals, from U.S. Department of State figures, to Sivard report of World War I and II deaths.

collapse was followed by the 1917 Bolshevik Revolution, the Civil War (1918–1921), and Stalin's Great Terror (particularly in the 1930s), each of which cost the lives of millions. Soviet suffering climaxed in World War II with a total of 17 million civilian and military dead. All told, the USSR/Russia suffered more than 24 million civilian and military deaths in the wars and political horrors of the twentieth century.

Germany suffered the second-largest number of deaths from twentieth-century collective violence. More than 3 million deaths, mostly military, occurred in World War I. In World War II, Germany suffered almost 5 million military and another 1.75 million civilian deaths. Other countries with huge losses include China (7 to 8 million) and Japan, whose more than 2 million deaths include half a million civilians, notably many residents of Hiroshima and Nagasaki. French and British sufferings were of roughly similar magnitude. Both countries took horrendous military casualties in the trench warfare of World War I. Since the Civil War, the United States has largely avoided the horrors of large-scale fighting on its own soil, but it still suffered over 120,000 deaths in World War I and close to half a million in World War II. While in the Korean and Vietnam wars, America suffered only moderate losses by these terrible standards, Korean and Vietnamese casualties were in the millions.

After World War II, the most devastating conflicts have occurred in the Third World. The partition of formerly British India into India, Pakistan, and Bangladesh has been associated with numerous deadly conflicts within and between the three countries. Some two million lives, mostly civilian, have been lost. In recent years, much of the world's media focus has been on conflicts in the Middle East, but conflicts in Africa have in fact been more frequent and devastating. Many African countries, newly independent from about 1960, but with borders arbitrarily drawn by colonial powers, have serious problems of national cohesion and have suffered from chronic civil war. Large-scale civil war in Nigeria (1967–1970) cost perhaps a million lives, and more sporadic conflict has continued to the present time. In 2002, for example, when the country hosted an international beauty contest, violent clashes erupted between Muslims and Christians that resulted in hundreds of deaths.

The end of the Cold War around 1990 witnessed a wave of instability and conflict in Eastern Europe and Central Asia. The breakup of the Soviet Union and Yugoslavia resulted in bloody border wars and secessional conflicts (for example, in Bosnia and Kosovo in the former Yugoslavia, and Chechnya in Russia). These conflicts brought another wave of ethnic slaughter, religious clashes, and struggles for power among different warlords. But since 1992, the number of wars and casualties has gradually and steadily declined. And although recent years have seen horrific acts of terrorism, its annual human toll has not changed much. Some students of international conflict see hope in what they call the "democratic peace," the fact that democratic countries hardly ever fight wars against one another. As more countries become democratic, will the world also become more peaceful?

The Uppsala Conflict Data Project reports 118 armed worldwide conflicts (defined as involving at least twenty-five battle deaths) from 1989 through 2004. In 2004, there were thirty ongoing conflicts, of which seven involved more than 1,000 deaths.[9] Each was a civil war occurring within state boundaries, although a few were internationalized in that foreign powers were also involved. In every year since the end of World War II in 1945, there have been more civil wars than interstate conflicts (wars between countries), and the civil wars have also caused more casualties than interstate wars. There are many reasons for the high incidence of civil war. Some are related to ethnic or religious conflicts. But others seem mainly due to struggles between warlords over lootable resources, such as diamonds, gold, or oil. External actors—such as the United Nations (UN), the United States, NATO, or strong regional powers—can sometimes help end civil wars, but in some cases (such as Angola) civil wars have been prolonged because foreign powers have been engaged on both sides of the conflict.

The UN in the post–Cold War world has intervened in some of these conflicts by providing peacekeeping missions when the parties to conflicts are ready to accept these mediations. More rarely the UN intervenes as a peacemaker, as in Bosnia and later in neighboring Kosovo in the 1990s, or when the peacekeeping mission in Sierra Leone (West Africa) was converted into a peacemaking effort. The UN's effectiveness in controlling domestic and international collective violence depends on consensus among the great powers. How tenuous this consensus can become is illustrated in the troubled efforts of the UN to disarm Iraq after the Gulf War of 1990–1991 and later to

United Nations weapons inspectors arrive at the Al-Rasheed missile propellant compound in Iraq in January 2003.

AP Images

prevent Saddam Hussein's government there from producing weapons of mass destruction, leading to the U.S.-led invasion of 2003.

The economic costs of national security can be high. Many countries face a massive national debt that often includes large deferred costs of borrowing for earlier wars and the maintenance of national defense. Many states, particularly in conflict-prone regions, feel that they need to spend significantly on national defense because of the "security dilemma"—they have to "take out insurance" against the possibility that their neighbors might be aggressive. While military expenditures in the world have declined since the collapse of the Soviet Union, the horrors of September 11, 2001, have led to a new costly mobilization of resources against international terrorism.

## POLITICAL GOODS AND VALUES

If we are to compare and evaluate public policy in different political systems, we need to consider the political goods that motivate different policies. That leads us back to the issues we discussed in Chapters 1 and 2, to the functions and purposes that governments serve. This book is organized around the concepts of system, process, and policy. We can think about values as "political goods" related to each of those levels of analysis.

At the system level, there is a long tradition in political analysis that emphasizes order, predictability,

and stability. Citizens are most free and most able to act purposefully when their environment is stable, transparent, and predictable. We call these conditions **system goods,** since they reflect the functioning and effectiveness of the whole political system. While people generally want some measure of change and new opportunities, most prefer stability to abrupt and unforeseeable change. Political instability—constitutional breakdowns, frequent leadership changes, riots, demonstrations, and the like—upsets most people's plans and can cost lives and cause material destruction. System goods have to do with the regularity and predictability with which political systems work, but also with their ability to adapt to environmental challenges.

Regularity and adaptability are typically somewhat in conflict. Sometimes order and stability are at the top of the agenda. In the United States, the administration of Warren Harding after World War I was such a period, called "a return to normalcy." There was a similar withdrawal from mobilization after World War II and the Korean War. On the other hand, the 1930s and the 1960s were periods of change and adaptation, in which the reach of governmental powers was extended. But the stress on change and adaptation can also be a call for reductions in the scope in government, as in the Thatcher administration in Britain or the Republican "Contract With America" of 1994–1995.

Another school of thought emphasizes goods associated with the political process—citizen participation and free political competition. Democracy is good and authoritarianism is bad, according to this school of thought, because of the way citizens are treated in the process, and not because democracy, for example, produces better economic results. Democratic procedures and various rights of due process, then, are **process goods.** Process goods include participation, compliance, and procedural justice. We value participation not merely as a means to responsive government, but for its own sake, since it enhances citizen competence and dignity. Compliance with authority can also be a good, as individuals respond to the impulse to serve others, which can be one of humanity's most gratifying experiences. U.S. President John F. Kennedy in his inaugural address called on such impulses to serve and sacrifice when he said, "Ask not what your country can do for you; ask what you can do for your country." Procedural justice (trial by jury, *habeas corpus,* no cruel and unusual punishment) is another crucial process value, without which citizens would have much greater reasons to fear their governments.

Procedural goods also include *effectiveness* and *efficiency.* A preference for effectiveness means that we prefer policies that actually lead to their desired purpose over policies that do not. Efficiency means that policies should attain their objectives at the lowest possible cost. If two alternative policies would lead to the same result but at very different costs, we would prefer the policy with the lower cost. In designing government agencies, most of us would prefer lean and inexpensive institutions to bloated agencies that produce no better results.

A third and final focus is on **policy goods,** such as economic welfare, quality of life, freedom, and personal security. We value a political system that improves welfare, decreases inequalities, enhances public safety, enables people to live lives they want for themselves, and cleans up its environment, whatever the political process that produces these results. Well-meaning people do not always agree which of these policy goods are most important. Yet, there are at least two important criteria that most of us would agree that government policy should meet. The first is *fairness.* The problem is that people often disagree over what is fair. In some situations, we believe that fairness requires all people to be treated equally (as when family members attempt to divide a tempting pie). In other situations, fairness demands that individuals be treated according to performance (as when grades are given in a college course). And in yet other situations, fairness means that people are treated according to their needs (for example, in cases of medical treatment). Thus fairness can imply *equal treatment* in some cases, *just desserts* (reward in proportion to merit or contribution) in others, and *treatment according to need* in yet others. Many distributive policies—for example, pension systems such as social security in the United States—rely on some combination of these criteria.

The debate over these various conceptions of fairness is never settled. In most cases, however, fairness would rule out practices that are *arbitrary* or *partial.* Few of us would find it fair if government officials threw dice to determine who would be imprisoned or be given pensions, or if they made such decisions solely on the basis of their personal prejudices or connections. We can think of fairness in this sense as reflected in the process good of *procedural justice.*

The second consideration is the promotion and preservation of *freedom.* As anarchists, libertarians, and other government skeptics would remind us, public policies should promote and protect freedom and basic human and political rights. If two policies are equally efficient and fair, then we would prefer the one that respects the rights and liberties of the citizens to the greater extent. But even in a democratic society, freedom is not always chosen over other political goods. The right to bear arms, protected in the Second Amendment to the U.S. Constitution, is a hotly contested issue, as many Americans would like to prevent those most likely to cause harm from carrying lethal weapons. Similarly, freedom of speech is a constitutional guarantee, but many people want to prohibit speech that is insulting, blasphemous, or offensive.

Liberty is sometimes viewed only as freedom from governmental regulation and harassment. Freedom is more than inhibition of government action, however, because even private individuals and organizations may violate the liberty and privacy of others. In such cases, liberty may be fostered by government intervention. Much legislation against racial segregation and discrimination generally has been impelled by this purpose. Liberty to act, organize, obtain information, and protest is an indispensable part of effective political participation. Nor is it irrelevant to social, political, and economic equality. Prior to the breakdown of communism in Eastern Europe and the Soviet Union,

| Political Goods | | TABLE 7.6 |
|---|---|---|
| **Levels of Political Goods** | **Classes of Goods** | **Content and Examples** |
| System level | System maintenance | The political system features regular, stable, and predictable decision-making processes. |
| | System adaptation | The political system is able to adapt to environmental change and challenges. |
| Process level | Participation in political inputs | The political system is open and responsive to many forms of political speech and action. |
| | Compliance and support | Citizens fulfill their obligations (e.g., military service and tax obligations) to the system and comply with public law and policy. |
| | Procedural justice | Legal and political procedures are orderly and fair (due process) and there is equality before the law. |
| | Effectiveness and efficiency | Political processes have their intended effects and are no more cumbersome, expensive, or intrusive than necessary. |
| Policy level | Welfare | Citizens have access to health care, learning, and material goods, which the government seeks to distribute broadly. |
| | Security | The government provides safety of person and property, public order, and national security. |
| | Fairness | Government policy is not discriminatory and recognizes individuals from different ethnic, linguistic, or religious groups; vulnerable or disadvantaged citizens are protected. |
| | Liberty | Citizens enjoy freedom from excessive regulation, protection of their privacy, and respect for their autonomy. |

it was a common view that the communist countries were trading liberty for equality. In contrast, capitalism was said to trade off equality for liberty. But one important thing that came to light after the collapse of communism was the extent of corruption and privilege in communist societies. While they had surely traded off liberty for a basic security of employment, it was not clear that the communists had otherwise gained much in the way of equality.

Table 7.6 draws on our three-level analysis of political systems to present a checklist of political goods or values. There is no simple way to say which value should prevail when they conflict. In fact, different preferences among such values as freedom, fairness, and efficiency set different cultures, parties, and political philosophies apart. One society or group of citizens may value fairness over liberty; another may make the opposite choice, as in Patrick Henry's famous exclamation, "Give me liberty or give me death!"

## TRADE-OFFS AND OPPORTUNITY COSTS

One of the hard facts about political goods is that we cannot always have them all simultaneously. A political system often has to **trade off** one value to obtain another. Spending funds on education is giving up the opportunity to spend them on welfare, or to leave them in the hands of those who earned them. **Opportunity costs** are what you lose in one area by committing your resources to a different good. They often arise when politicians have to decide how much to invest for the future rather than spend today (for example, when they determine future retirement benefits). Even more difficult are the trade-offs between security and liberty. Extreme liberty, as Hobbes would tell us, would give us a highly insecure world where the strong might bully the weak and where collective action would be difficult. Yet, without liberty, security may be little more than servitude or imprisonment.

The trade-offs between political goods are not the same under all circumstances. Sometimes increasing liberty will also increase security (for example, because riots against censorship will end). And under some conditions investment in education will be paid back many times in health and welfare, because trained citizens can better care for themselves and work more productively. These are positive trade-offs in which there may be no opportunity costs. But often you cannot "have your cake and eat it, too." One of the important tasks of social science is to discover the conditions under which positive and negative trade-offs occur.

Regrettably, political science has no way of converting units of liberty into units of safety or welfare. And we can never calculate the value of a political outcome gained at the cost of human life. Political decisionmakers often have to make such conversions, but as political scientists we can only point to value judgments that they are willing to make. The weight given to various goods differs across cultures and contexts. A religious faith or a political ideology may tell us how one value should be traded against another, and thus offer an orderly basis for choice. Such schemes may be invaluable for those pressed into action in the terrible circumstances of war, revolution, and famine. But when people do not share these underlying schemes and values, there may be serious conflicts. Sadly, there is no ideology, just as there is no political science, that can solve all these problems objectively.

## REVIEW QUESTIONS

- What explains the growth of the welfare state?
- What are the advantages and disadvantages of different types of taxes?
- Do some governments tend to promote political rights and others civil rights, or do civil and political rights tend to go together?
- How is the welfare outcome for women changing in developing countries today?
- What sorts of armed conflicts are most common in today's world, and what problems do they cause?

## KEY TERMS

direct taxes
distribution
extraction
gross domestic product (GDP)
indirect taxes

night watchman state
opportunity costs
Organisation for Economic Co-operation and Development (OECD)

outcomes
police state
policy goods
political goods and values
process goods
public policies

regulation
regulatory state
symbolic outputs
system goods
trade off
welfare state

## SUGGESTED READINGS

Bates, Robert H. *Markets and States in Tropical Africa*. Berkeley: University of California Press, 1981.

Bratton, Michael, and Nicholas van de Walle. *Democratic Experiments in Africa: Regime Transitions in Comparative Perspective*. New York: Cambridge University Press, 1997.

Castles, Francis G., ed. *The Comparative History of Public Policy*. Cambridge, UK: Polity Press, 1989.

Dahl, Robert. *Democracy and Its Critics*. New Haven, CT: Yale University Press, 1989.

Diamond, Larry, ed. *Democracy in Developing Countries*. Boulder, CO: Lynne Rienner, 1992.

Easterly, William. *The Elusive Quest for Growth: The Economists' Adventures and Misadventures in the Tropics*. Cambridge: MIT Press, 2001.

Flora, Peter, and Arnold Heidenheimer. *The Development of Welfare States in Europe and America*. New Brunswick, NJ: Transaction Books, 1981.

Gourevitch, Peter. *Politics in Hard Times*. Ithaca, NY: Cornell University Press, 1986.

Harbom, Lotta, and Peter Wallensteen. "Armed Conflict and Its International Dimensions, 1946–2004." *Journal of Peace Research* 42, no. 5, (2005): 623–35.

Jackson, Robert, and Carl Rosberg. *Personal Rule in Black Africa.* Berkeley: University of California Press, 1982.

Keefer, Philip, and Stuti Khemani. "Why Do the Poor Receive Poor Services?" *Economic and Political Weekly,* 28 February 2004, 935–43.

Lijphart, Arend. *Patterns of Democracy.* New Haven, CT: Yale University Press, 1999.

Lindblom, Charles E. *Politics and Markets.* New Haven, CT: Yale University Press, 1978.

Olson, Mancur. *The Rise and Decline of Nations.* New Haven, CT: Yale University Press, 1982.

———. *Power and Prosperity.* New York: Basic Books, 2000.

Putnam, Robert D. *Making Democracy Work.* Princeton, NJ: Princeton University Press, 1993.

Tsebelis, George. *Veto Players: An Introduction to Institutional Analysis.* Princeton, NJ: Princeton University Press, 2002.

Wilensky, Harold, *Rich Democracies: Political Economy, Public Policy, and Performance.* Berkeley: University of California Press, 2002.

Wilson, James G. *The Politics of Regulation in the United States.* New York: Basic Books, 1980.

## ENDNOTES

1. See World Bank, *Entering the 21st Century: World Development Report 1999–2000* (New York: Oxford University Press, 2000), Table A.1, 216–17.

2. Peter Flora and Arnold Heidenheimer, *The Development of Welfare States in Europe and America* (New Brunswick, NJ: Transaction Books, 1981); and Arnold Heidenheimer, Hugh Heclo, and Carolyn Teich Adams, *Comparative Public Policy,* 3rd ed. (New York: St. Martin's Press, 1990).

3. Heidenheimer, Heclo, and Adams. *Comparative Public Policy,* 211–19.

4. Steven C. Poe and C. Neal Tate, "Repression of Human Rights to Personal Integrity in the 1980s: A Global Analysis," *American Political Science Review* 88, no. 4 (December 1994): 853–72.

5. Simon Kuznets, "Economic Growth and Income Equality," *American Economic Review* 45 (1955): 1–28.

6. World Bank, *World Development Report: Infrastructure for Development* (New York: Oxford University Press, 1994), Overview, 1 ff.

7. Peter Gourevitch, in his book *Politics in Hard Times* (Ithaca, NY: Cornell University Press, 1986), analyzes the policy responses of five Western industrial nations—Britain, France, Germany, Sweden, and the United States—to the three world depressions of 1870–1890, 1930–1940, and 1975–1985. Gourevitch shows how these crises affected business, labor, and agriculture differently in each country; consequences for political structure and policy varied greatly. Thus the world depression of the 1930s resulted in a conservative reaction in Britain (the formation of a "National" government), a moderate left reaction in the United States (the "New Deal"), a polarization and paralysis of public policy in France ("Immobilisme"), a moderate social democratic reaction in Sweden, and a radical right and left polarization in Germany, leading to a breakdown of democracy and the emergence of National Socialism. While the causes of World War II were complex, the pacifism of Britain, the demoralization and defeatism in France, the isolationism of the United States, and the nihilism and aggression of Germany were all fed by the devastating worldwide economic depression of the 1930s.

8. Ruth Leger Sivard, *World Military and Social Indicators* (Washington, DC: World Priorities, 1993), 20.

9. See Lotta Harbom and Peter Wallensteen, "Armed Conflict and Its International Dimension, 1946–2004," *Journal of Peace Research,* 42, no. 5 (2005), 623–35.

N

ATLANTIC
OCEAN

NORTH
SEA

SCOTLAND

Wick

Inverness

Aberdeen

Glasgow

Edinburgh

Tyne

NORTHERN
IRELAND

Belfast

IRELAND

Irish Sea

NORTH

Leeds

NORTH
WEST

Liverpool

Manchester

Sheffield

Mersey

EAST
MIDLANDS

Norwich

Severn

ENGLAND

EAST
ANGLIA

WEST
MIDLANDS

Birmingham

WALES

SOUTH
EAST

Thames

Cardiff

London

SOUTH WEST

Portsmouth

Plymouth

English Channel

# POLITICS IN BRITAIN

*Richard Rose*

In a world of new democracies, Britain is different because it is an old democracy; its political system has been evolving for more than 850 years. In medieval times the King of England claimed to rule France and Ireland, as well as England. From the end of the fifteenth century onward, the claim to rule France was abandoned, and sovereignty was gained over Wales and Scotland. The government of the **United Kingdom** was created in 1801 by merging England, Scotland, Wales, and Ireland under the authority of Parliament in London.

Unlike new democracies in Eastern Europe, Latin America, and Asia, Britain did not become a democracy overnight. It became a democracy by evolution, rather than revolution. Democratization was a slow process. The rule of law was established in the seventeenth century, the accountability of the executive to Parliament was established by the eighteenth century, and national political parties organized in the nineteenth century.

Even though competitive elections had been held for more than a century, the right of every adult man and woman to vote was not recognized until the twentieth century.

The evolution of democracy in Britain is in contrast with a European history of countries switching between democratic and undemocratic forms of government. Whereas older British people have lived in the same political system all their lives, the oldest Germans have lived under four or five constitutions, two democratic and two or three undemocratic.[1]

At no point in history did representatives of the British people meet to decide what kind of government they would like to have, as happened in America and France at the end of the eighteenth century and in many democracies since. British politicians have been socialized to accept institutions and rules of the game as a legacy from distant predecessors. Ordinary citizens have been socialized to accept established institutions, too.

The influence of British government can be found in places as far-flung as Australia, Canada, India, and the United States. Just as Alexis de Tocqueville travelled to the United States in 1831 to seek the secrets of democracy, so we can examine Britain for secrets of stable representative government. Yet, the limitations of Britain as a model are shown by the failure of many attempts to transplant its institutions to countries gaining independence from the British Empire—and even more by the failure of its institutions to bring political stability to Northern Ireland.

## POLICY CHALLENGES FACING THE BRITISH GOVERNMENT

In Britain the term **government** is used in many senses. People may speak of the Queen's government to emphasize enduring and nonpartisan features, they may refer to a Labour or Conservative government or the government of the day to emphasize partisanship, or they may speak of Gordon Brown's government to stress its transitory personal feature. The departments headed by Cabinet ministers advised by senior civil servants are referred to collectively as **Whitehall,** after the London street on which many major government departments are located. **Downing Street,** where the prime minister works, is a short street off Whitehall. **Parliament**—that is, the popularly elected House of Commons and the nonelected House of Lords—is at one end of Whitehall. The term *Parliament* is often used as another way to refer to the House of Commons. Together, all of these institutions are often referred to as **Westminster,** after the district in London in which the principal offices of British government are located.

The constitutional doctrine that Parliament is sovereign was traditionally interpreted as holding that the government of the day can do whatever it wants, as long as it has the backing of a majority in the House of Commons. However, the claim to sovereignty of this island state stops at the water's edge. In a world in which many policy issues transcend national boundaries, the first challenge facing governors is to answer this question: Where does Britain belong? Prime ministers from Winston Churchill to Gordon Brown have claimed that Britain is a major world power because of its close ties with Commonwealth countries, the United States, and Europe.

The British Empire was transformed after World War II into the Commonwealth, a free association of 54 sovereign states with members on every continent. The independent status of its chief members is shown by the absence of the word *British* from their names. Commonwealth countries from Antigua and Australia to Zambia and Zimbabwe differ from each other in wealth, language, culture, and religion. They also differ in their commitment to democracy.

Every British prime minister claims a special relationship with the United States. The traditional view, dating back to the time of Winston Churchill and Franklin D. Roosevelt, was that "America provides the brawn and we provide the brains." However, the number of countries with which America has a special relationship keeps expanding, whereas British prime ministers have not built equally strong relationships with other countries. After the end of the Cold War, the emergence of the United States as a unique global force has made the relationship more attractive to Britain. However, the unilateralist policy of Washington under President George W. Bush reduced the influence that Britain and other countries may have hoped to have on American foreign policy.

When President Bush formed a "coalition of the willing" to attack Iraq, Prime Minister Tony Blair was more than willing, believing it desirable to do so to make the world a safer place. In response to doubts raised in the House of Commons, Blair argued that allying with the United States in Iraq would give Britain greater influence. However, both British Members of Parliament (MPs) and the public have had their doubts. In a June 2006 Populus poll of public opinion, two-thirds said Britain's relationship with the United States had become less important than its other international ties.

As countries such as Germany and France have regained economic and political significance, the British government has looked to Europe. In the jet age, the English Channel is no longer a barrier to travel to the European continent, and a tunnel under the English Channel provides a rail and road link to Paris that is shorter than that to the North of England or Scotland. Manufacturers such as Ford Motor Company link their plants in Britain with factories across Western Europe, just as Ford links factories across the United States.

Although the European Economic Community (EEC) was established in 1957, Britain did not join it until 1973. Since then the EEC has grown in membership and powers and has become the European Union (EU). The EU has the power to impose regulations affecting British business and limiting the government's economic policies. Government ministers spend an increasing amount of their time negotiating with other countries of the EU on matters ranging from political fundamentals to whether British beer should be served in metric units or by the traditional measure of a British pint.

Britain's governors accept the inevitability of globalization: In 2005 the prime minister, the deputy prime minister, the foreign secretary, and the ministers of Defence, Trade and Industry, and Environment each averaged more than one day a week traveling abroad. However, commitment to the EU remains limited. In small countries, which have always recognized the influence of bigger neighbors, exchanging nominal sovereignty to participate in the EU presents no problems. However, it is a shock to Britain's governors, who pride themselves on having a major role in three different international settings—the Commonwealth, Europe, and Washington, D.C.

When a public opinion poll asks whether Britain should act like a leading world power or a small neutral country like Sweden or Switzerland, 49 percent favor being a small power, as compared to 34 percent wanting the country to be a world power.[2] However, Britain's island status cannot insulate it from the rest of the world. It is not possible for Britain to become a small, rich country like Switzerland or Sweden. The effective choice today is between Britain being a big, rich country and Britain being a big, relatively less prosperous country.

A second set of challenges in the economic field makes the link between international and domestic policy very visible. For centuries Britain has depended on world trade, importing much food and many raw materials. To pay for these imports, it exports manufactured goods and "invisible" services of banks and other financial institutions in the city of London, and it does a big trade in tourism. The British pound sterling (£) is an international currency, but speeches by the prime minister and head of the Treasury do not determine its international value. This is decided in international markets in which currency speculators play a significant role. Since 1997 the value of the British pound in exchange for the dollar has ranged from $1.35 to $2.00.

Economic growth is important not only for British consumers, who borrow heavily, but also for the government, which usually runs a deficit to meet the bills for public spending. An aging population requires more health care and pensions, an educated population demands better education for their children, and a more prosperous society wants a better environment. However, the means of raising additional revenue without raising visible taxes are few. Moreover, any increase in deficit spending threatens inflation and a rise in interest rates by the independent Bank of England. The fiscal dividend of economic growth makes it much easier to meet these challenges.

Some challenges, such as fighting crime, cannot be resolved solely by spending money. Successive Conservative and Labour governments have spent more money on the police and built more prisons. However, their efforts have been accompanied by random crimes of street violence and stabbing, especially in London, and the use of guns in robberies and in shootings of police officers. Multiculturalism is another problem that cannot be met just by spending more money. The government seeks to promote a sense of "Britishness" among immigrants, giving lessons about the rights and obligations of citizens to immigrants wanting British passports. British-born offspring of immigrants automatically gain citizenship. Whether they choose to adopt British ways is greatly influenced by family and ethnic background and, in the case of a few Muslims, by jihadist activists.

Notwithstanding the power of the government of the day within Westminster, ministers are regularly confronted with challenges concerning the delivery of public services by local government, the National Health Service, and other institutions. Schools whose pupils have bad examination results embarrass the minister responsible for education, a social security official that loses computer disks with confidential details about millions of claims embarrasses the minister responsible for pensions, and the health minister is called to account when shortcomings of hospital cleaning staff lead to infections causing the death of patients These failings lead to calls for the government of the day to "do something," but it is not easy for a Cabinet minister in Whitehall to monitor the activities of more than a million health workers or millions of pupils. Whitehall has contracted with profit-making companies to deliver a variety of public services in a businesslike way. However, when these organizations make mistakes, the blame continues to fall on the government department that employed the faulty supplier.

With a general election due no later than Spring 2010, party leaders are concentrating on winning the next election. Gordon Brown, the leader of the **Labour Party,** faces a unique problem: As prime minister he must defend the record of a Labour government continuously in office since 1997. Labour's narrow margin of victory in 2005 makes its parliamentary majority vulnerable. After a "honeymoon" with the public after becoming prime minister in summer 2007, Brown has faced a legacy of taxing and spending problems and a worldwide economic and financial crisis. His hesitancy in making and explaining decisions, combined with a reserved personality, has led to an approval rating in the polls as low as that of his Labour predecessor, Tony Blair, at the end of Blair's prime ministership.

After losing three successive elections under three different leaders, the **Conservative Party,** the official Opposition, accepted the challenge to change by electing a youthful new leader, David Cameron. His strategy has much in common with that of Tony Blair in Opposition: to move the party from being promarket and antigovernment to occupying the political center by showing sympathy with measures to improve the environment, gay rights, and other liberal issues. Since Cameron has been an MP only since 2001, he cannot be identified with unpopular policies that led to his party's previous defeats. However, since neither he nor his principal associates have ever held office in government, inexperience raises questions about what a Cameron-led government would actually do if it were to win an election. As Opposition leader, Cameron has a problem in gaining public recognition. But since big majorities have come to disapprove of the Labour government's record under Blair and Brown, the Conservative Party has been ahead of Labour in the opinion polls because it offers a change from an unpopular government.

The **Liberal Democratic Party** is now the closest approximation to a "left" party that Britain has. It favors social and environmental policies and attacks government proposals that encroach on civil liberties. It is strongly in favor of the EU, where its leader, Nick Clegg, once worked as an official. It is also the only British party that opposed the Iraq War. Because of being third in seats in the House of Commons, the Liberal Democrats have no chance of forming a government on their own. But because the Conservative Party faces an uphill struggle to win an absolute majority in the House of Commons, it could hold the balance of power in the House of Commons after the next general election.

A change of government following the next general election would not change the problems facing government. A new government would then be challenged to realize its campaign promises. But this is easier said than done. As Tony Blair ruefully admitted five years after becoming prime minister, "In opposition, announcement is the reality. For the first period in government, there was a tendency to believe this is the case. It isn't. The announcement is only the intention."[3]

## THE ENVIRONMENT OF POLITICS: ONE CROWN, BUT FIVE NATIONS

The Queen of England is the best known monarch in the world, yet there is no such entity as an English state. In international law the state is the United Kingdom of Great Britain and Northern Ireland. Great Britain is divided into England, Scotland, and Wales. The most distinctive feature of **Wales** is that one-quarter of the population speaks an old Celtic language, Welsh, as well as English. **Scotland,** once an independent kingdom, has been an integral part of Britain since 1707. However, the Scots have separate legal, religious, and education institutions. The fourth part of the United Kingdom, **Northern Ireland,** consists of six counties of Ulster. The remainder of Ireland rebelled against the Crown in 1916 and established a separate Irish state in Dublin in 1921. The current boundaries of the United Kingdom, colloquially known as Britain, were fixed in 1921.

The United Kingdom is a unitary state because there is a single source of authority, the British Parliament. However, the institutions of government are not uniform throughout the United Kingdom. In the minds of its citizens, it is a multinational state, for people differ in how they describe themselves (Table 8.1). In England people often describe themselves as English or British without considering the different meanings of these terms. This does not happen elsewhere in the United Kingdom. In Scotland three-quarters see themselves as Scots. In Wales three-fifths identify themselves as Welsh. In Northern Ireland people divide three ways: almost half see themselves as British, one-quarter see themselves as Irish, and another one-quarter identify with Ulster (i.e., Northern Ireland).

Historically, Scotland and Wales have been governed by British Cabinet ministers accountable to Parliament. After decades of campaigning by nationalist parties seeking independence, in 1997 the Labour

| National Identities | England | Scotland | Wales | Northern Ireland |
| :--- | :--- | :--- | :--- | :--- |
| Identities vary within each nation | | | | **TABLE 8.1** |
| Self–identifying as: | | | | |
| British | 51% | 19% | 27% | 47% |
| English, Scots, Welsh, Irish | 38 | 75 | 60 | 27 |
| Other, don't know | 11 | 6 | 13 | 26* |

*Includes 21 percent identifying as Ulster.

Sources: England: British Social Attitudes Survey, 2004; Scotland: Scottish Social Attitudes Survey, 2004; Wales: Life and Times Survey, 2003; Northern Ireland: Life and Times Survey, 2004.

government endorsed **devolution**; an Act of Parliament gave responsibilities for policy to elected assemblies in Scotland and in Wales, and they came into being in 1999. The revenue of both assemblies comes from Westminster. It is assigned by a formula relating it to public expenditures on comparable policies in England.

The Scottish Parliament in Edinburgh has powers to legislate and to initiate a wide variety of social and environmental policies, including those delivered by Scottish local government. Elections to the 129-seat Parliament mix the traditional British **first-past-the-post electoral system** and proportional representation (PR), which are discussed in more detail later in the chapter. After the 1999 and 2003 elections, the Labour Party in Scotland formed a coalition government with the Liberal Party. In the May 2007 Scottish election, the unpopularity of the British Labour Party resulted in a one-seat margin for the Scottish National Party (SNP) over the Labour Party, 47 to 46. The remaining seats were divided among the Conservatives, 17; Liberal Democrats, 16; and others, 3.

Under the leadership of Alex Salmond as First Minister, the SNP established a minority government. Its first aim has been to demonstrate that the SNP was not just a protest party, but a party that was capable of governing as well as or better than parties that appeal for votes across the whole of Britain. Its second aim is to promote a referendum on independence for Scotland. The three Opposition parties have reacted by establishing a commission to recommend increases in powers devolved to Scotland, subject to approval by the British government in London. The chief dividing issue in Scotland today is what question or questions should be put to the Scottish people in a referendum that could take place in 2010 or 2011.

The 60-seat Welsh Assembly in Cardiff has power over a variety of local and regional services, and its activities are conducted in English and in Welsh. However, it does not have the power to enact legislation. It is elected by a mixed first-past-the-post and PR ballot. Labour has consistently been the biggest party at each election, but it has difficulty winning a majority of Assembly seats. After the May 2007 Assembly election, Labour held 26 seats, Plaid Cymru (the Welsh National Party) 14, Conservatives 12, Liberals 6, and others 2. Labour and Plaid Cymru together formed a coalition government. There is no effective political demand for independence.

Northern Ireland is the most un-English part of the United Kingdom. Formally, it is a secular polity, but differences between Protestants and Catholics about national identity dominate its politics. Protestants, who make up about three-fifths of the population, want to remain part of the United Kingdom. Until 1972 the Protestant majority governed through a home-rule Parliament at Stormont, a suburb of Belfast. Many of the Catholic minority did not support this regime, wanting to leave the United Kingdom and join the Republic of Ireland, which claims that Northern Ireland should be part of the Republic.

After Catholics launched protests against discrimination in 1968, demonstrations turned to violence in 1969. The illegal **Irish Republican Army (IRA)** was revived and in 1971 began a military campaign to remove Northern Ireland from the United Kingdom. Protestants organized illegal armed forces in response. More than 3,500 people have been killed in political violence since. After adjusting for population differences, this is equivalent to more than 140,000 political deaths in Britain or more than 700,000 such deaths in the United States.

Parliament has met in London by the River Thames for more than 700 years, and the clock tower of Big Ben is famous as a symbol of democracy in Canada and Australia as well as in Europe.

Steve Vidler/eStock Photo

In 1969 the British Army went into action in Northern Ireland to protect Catholics. In 1971 it helped intern hundreds of Catholics without trial in an unsuccessful attempt to break the IRA. In 1972 the British government abolished the Stormont Parliament, placing government in the hands of a Northern Ireland Office under a British Cabinet minister. In 1985 the British government took the unprecedented step of inviting the Dublin-based government of the Republic of Ireland to participate in institutions affecting the governance of Northern Ireland.

A stable settlement requires the support of paramilitary organizations, as well as political parties on both sides of the political divide. In 1994 the IRA announced a cessation of its military activity, and Sinn Fein, the political party of the Irish Republican movement, agreed to talks. Protestant paramilitary forces also announced a cessation of activities. On Good Friday of 1998, an agreement was reached that provided for an elected power-sharing executive and cross-border institutions involving both Dublin and Belfast. Contrary to the practice of government at Westminster, power-sharing means that whatever the outcome of a Northern Ireland election, government must be a coalition of parties representing both the pro–Britain Protestant majority and the pro–Irish Republic Catholic minority. The coalition

government initially formed along these lines collapsed in a dispute about whether the IRA had decommissioned its arsenal of weapons.

An election for the 108-seat Northern Ireland Assembly in 2007 gave the Democratic Unionist Party led by Dr. Ian Paisley 36 seats, the Republican Sinn Fein 27, the Ulster Unionist Party 18, the pro-Irish Social Democratic and Labour Party 16, the cross-religious Alliance Party 7, and others 4. After intensive negotiations in which London and Dublin offered incentives to Irish Republicans and put pressure on Ulster Unionists, a coalition government was formed with Dr. Ian Paisley, an outspoken Unionist and Protestant, as First Minister and Martin McGuinness, a Sinn Fein politician who had been active in the IRA, as Deputy First Minister, plus representatives of the Ulster Unionist Party and the Social Democratic and Labour Party.

While there is no agreement about national identity within Britain, there is no doubt about which nationality is the most numerous. England dominates the United Kingdom. It accounts for 84 percent of the United Kingdom population, as compared to 8 percent in Scotland, 5 percent in Wales, and 3 percent in Northern Ireland. Previous editions of this chapter have been called "Politics in England" because, as Tony

Blair once said, "Sovereignty rests with me, as an English MP, and that's the way it will stay."[4] However, changes in other parts of the United Kingdom have begun to affect politics in England. For example, in the 2005 British general election the Conservative Party won the most votes in England, but the Labour Party, thanks to its dominance in Scotland and Wales, won the most votes in the United Kingdom and a majority in the British Parliament. Demands by the Scottish National Party for independence have been met by English demands to reduce the share of British tax revenue that Westminster allocates to Scotland.

## A Multiracial Britain

Throughout the centuries England has received a relatively small but noteworthy number of immigrants from other parts of Europe. The Queen herself is descended from a titled family that came from Hanover, Germany, to assume the English throne in 1714. Until the outbreak of anti-German sentiment in World War I, the surname of the royal family was Saxe-Coburg-Gotha. By royal proclamation King George V changed the family name to Windsor in 1917.

The worldwide British Empire was multiracial, and so is the Commonwealth. Since the late 1950s, job seekers have been arriving in Britain from the West Indies, Pakistan, India, Africa, and other parts of the Commonwealth. Hundreds of thousands of people from Australia, Canada, the United States, and the member countries of the EU flow in and out of Britain as students or as workers. A strong British economy attracts temporary workers from Central and Eastern European countries in the EU. Public opinion has opposed unlimited immigration, and both Labour and Conservative governments have passed laws trying to limit the number of immigrants. However, these laws contain many exceptions.

Political disturbances around the world in the past two decades have increased the number of immigrants claiming asylum as political refugees from troubled areas in the Balkans, the Middle East, and Africa. Some have valid credentials as refugees, whereas others have arrived with false papers or make claims to asylum that courts have not upheld. In response to popular concern, the government has tried to make deportation of illegal immigrants easier. However, the government has admitted that hundreds of thousands of illegal immigrants now live in Britain.

The minority ethnic population of the United Kingdom has risen from 74,000 in 1951 to 4.6 million in the latest census, almost 8 percent of the total population. Official statistics define the minority population by the one characteristic that they have in common—they are not white. Because persons placed in this catchall category have neither culture nor religion in common, there is a further subdivision by race and ethnicity. West Indians speak English as their native language and have a Christian tradition, but this is often not the case for black Africans. Ethnic minorities from India, Pakistan, and Bangladesh are divided among Hindus, Muslims, and Sikhs, and most speak English as a second language. Chinese from Hong Kong have a distinctive culture. Altogether, almost half of the minority category comes from the Indian subcontinent, a quarter consists of black people from the Caribbean or Africa, one in seven is often of mixed British and minority origin, and the remainder come from many different countries.

With the passage of time, the ethnic minority population is becoming increasingly British-born and educated. This raises an important issue: What is the position of British-born offspring of immigrants? Whatever their country of origin, they differ in how they see themselves: 64 percent of Caribbean origin identify themselves as British, as do more than three-fifths of Pakistanis, Indians, and Bangladeshis and two-fifths of Chinese. However, some offspring of immigrants have rejected integration. A coordinated terrorist attack in London on July 7, 2005, that killed more than fifty people was organized by British-born offspring of Pakistani immigrants who had been converted to jihadism at British mosques. British-born jihadists have been able to receive training in Pakistan and neighboring Afghanistan.

In response to terrorist attacks, the government has shifted from promoting multiculturalism to stressing the integration of immigrant families into the British way of life. It has greatly increased police powers, justifying shoot-to-kill policies even when people wrongly suspected of being terrorists are the victims. Its program of cooperating with people it identifies as leaders of the Muslim community has faced difficulties. Those cooperating with the British government have found themselves in dispute with their coreligionists. Moreover, they have criticized police methods used in surveillance of the Muslim community and British military actions in Afghanistan and Iraq.

Many immigrants and their offspring are being integrated into electoral politics, since residential concentration makes their votes important in some parliamentary constituencies. Some candidates from different immigrant groups compete with each other. There are now hundreds of elected minority ethnic councillors in local government. The 15 ethnic MPs in the Commons today come from diverse backgrounds—India, Pakistan, the West Indies, Ghana, and Aden—and sit for the Labour, Liberal Democratic, and Conservative parties. A disproportionate number of minority ethnic people have voted Labour.

## THE LEGACY OF HISTORY

The legacy of the past limits current choices, and Britain has a very long past. Much of its legacy is positive, for many fundamental problems of governance were resolved centuries ago. The Crown was established as the central political authority in medieval times. The supremacy of the state over the church was settled in the sixteenth century when Henry VIII broke with the Roman Catholic Church to establish the Church of England. The power struggle between the English Crown and Parliament was resolved by a civil war in the seventeenth century in which Parliament triumphed and a weakened monarch was then restored. A Parliament chosen by an unrepresentative franchise was able to hold the Crown accountable in the eighteenth century.

The continuity of England's political institutions through the centuries is remarkable. Prince Charles, the heir to an ancient Crown, pilots jet airplanes, and a medieval-named chancellor of the Exchequer pilots the British economy through the deep waters of the international economy. Yet, symbols of continuity often mask great changes in English life. Parliament was once a supporter of royal authority. Today Parliament is primarily an electoral college deciding which party leader is in charge of government.

There is no agreement among political scientists about when England developed a modern system of government.[5] The most reasonable judgment is that modern government developed during the very long reign of Queen Victoria, from 1837 to 1901, when government institutions were created to cope with the problems of a society that was increasingly urban, literate, industrial, and critical of unreformed institutions. The creation of a modern system of government does not get rid of the problems of governing.

Developments since World War II can be divided into stages. The first stage, an all-party consensus on a mixed-economy Keynesian welfare state, built on the

The financial institutions of the City of London, such as the London Stock Exchange (pictured above), are a major source of earnings for the British economy when times are good and of losses where times are bad.

Anne Rippy/Getty Images

foundations of a wartime coalition government led by Winston Churchill. The Beveridge Report on social welfare, John Maynard Keynes's Full Employment White Paper, and the Butler Education Act of 1944 were initiatives named after Liberals and Conservatives. The 1945 British general election was won by a Labour government led by Clement Attlee. It combined social welfare policies, leading to the establishment of a comprehensive National Health Service, and socialist economic policies, under which many basic industries were taken into state ownership. Between 1951 and 1964, Conservative governments led by Winston Churchill, Sir Anthony Eden, and Harold Macmillan maintained a consensus about the mixed-economy welfare state. Keynesian techniques for promoting economic growth, full employment, and low inflation led to an era of consumer prosperity, and the availability of free university education was greatly expanded.

A flood of books on the theme "What's wrong with Britain?" proclaimed the need for faster economic growth and led to a second stage in which parties competed in innovation. The Labour Party under Harold Wilson won the 1964 election, campaigning with the vague activist slogan "Let's go with Labour." New names were given to government department offices, but behind their entrances many officials went through the same routines as before. The economy did not grow as predicted. In 1967 the government was forced to devalue the pound and seek a loan from the International Monetary Fund. Labour lost the 1970 election.

The major achievement of Edward Heath's 1970–1974 Conservative government was to make Britain a member of the EU. Doing so divided his own party and the Opposition. In trying to limit unprecedented inflation by controlling wages, Heath risked his authority in a confrontation with the left-wing-led National Union of Mineworkers, which struck for higher wages in what was then the state-owned coal industry. When Heath called the "Who Governs?" election in February 1974, no party won a majority of seats in the Commons. Labour formed a minority government, with Harold Wilson again as prime minister. A second election in October 1974 gave Labour a bare majority. Inflation, rising unemployment, and a contraction in the economy undermined Labour's program. James Callaghan succeeded Wilson as prime minister in 1976. Keynesian policies were abandoned in 1977 after Labour relied on a loan from the International Monetary Fund to stabilize the value of the pound in international markets.

When Margaret Thatcher won the 1979 election as leader of the Conservative Party, she became the first woman prime minister of a major European country (see Box 8.1). Thatcher's radical break with the economic policies of her predecessors introduced a third stage: She promoted free market policies and a reduction in the size of government. She regarded the economic failures of previous governments as arising from too much compromise. "The Old Testament prophets did not say 'Brothers, I want a consensus.' They said: 'This is my faith. This is what I passionately believe. If you believe it too, then come with me.'"[6]

Divisions among opponents enabled Thatcher to lead her party to three successive election victories, although never winning more than 43 percent of the total vote. Militant left-wing activists seized control of the Labour Party, and in 1981 four former Labour Cabinet ministers formed a centrist Social Democratic Party (SDP) in an alliance with the Liberal Party. The Labour Party's 1983 election manifesto was described as the longest suicide note in history. After Thatcher's third successive election victory in 1987, the SDP leadership merged with the Liberals to form the Liberal Democratic Party.

While proclaiming the virtues of the market and attacking big government, Thatcher did not court electoral defeat by imposing radical spending cuts on popular social programs. In consequence, public spending continued to grow in the Thatcher era. It was 40 percent of the gross domestic product in her last full year in office. While the Conservative majority in Parliament endorsed Thatcher's policies, it did not win the hearts and minds of the electorate. On the tenth anniversary of Thatcher's period as prime minister, an opinion poll asked whether people approved of "the Thatcher revolution." Less than one-third said they did.[7]

Within the Conservative Party, Thatcher's increasingly autocratic treatment of Cabinet colleagues created resentment, and during her third term of office, she became very unpopular in opinion polls. In autumn 1990 disgruntled Conservative MPs forced a ballot for the party leadership that caused her to resign. Conservative MPs elected a relatively unknown John Major as party leader. In 1992 Major won an unprecedented fourth consecutive term for the Conservative government. However, a few months afterward his economic policy,

## The Meaning of Thatcherism

BOX 8.1

Among modern British prime ministers, Margaret Thatcher has been unique in giving her name to a political ideology, Thatcherism.* Thatcher's central conviction was that the market offered a cure for the country's economic difficulties. She rejected the mixed-economy welfare state philosophy of her Conservative as well as her Labour predecessors. As Milton Friedman, the Nobel Prize–winning monetary economist, noted: "Mrs. Thatcher represents a different tradition. She represents a tradition of the nineteenth-century Liberal, of Manchester Liberalism, of free market free trade."[†]

In its economic policy, the Thatcher government experienced both successes and frustrations. The rate of economic growth increased and inflation dropped; however, unemployment rose. Industrial relations acts gave union members the right to elect their leaders and to vote on whether to hold a strike. State-owned industries and municipally owned council houses were sold to private owners. What were described as "businesslike" methods were introduced into managing everything from hospitals to museums.

As long as she was in control, Thatcher believed in strong government. In foreign policy she strongly promoted what she saw as Britain's national interest in dealings with the European Union and in alliance with President Ronald Reagan. The 1982 Argentine invasion of the Falkland Islands, a remote British colony in the South Atlantic, led to a brief and victorious war. Thatcher was also quick to assert her personal authority against colleagues in the Cabinet and against civil servants. The autonomy of local government was curbed, and a property tax on houses was replaced by a poll tax on each adult.

Following her departure from office, British Conservatives divided between those who sought to push market-oriented and anti–European Union measures further, the so-called Thatcherites, and those who believed the limits of cutbacks on the size of government had been reached.

*Cf. Margaret Thatcher, *The Downing Street Years* (New York: HarperCollins, 1993); Dennis Kavanagh, *The Reordering of British Politics* (Oxford, England: Oxford University Press, 1997).

[†]"Thatcher Praised by Her Guru," *The Guardian* (London), March 12, 1983.

---

based on a strong British pound, crashed under pressure from foreign speculators. A division opened up within the Conservative Party between hard-line Thatcherite opponents of Europe and those who supported Major's acceptance of EU initiatives. The Major government held onto office and maintained such Thatcherite policies as the **privatization** of the coal mines and railways.

A fourth stage opened after Tony Blair became Labour leader in 1994. Blair was elected leader because he did *not* talk or look like an ordinary Labour Party member. Instead of being from a poor background, he was educated at boarding school and studied law at Oxford. Instead of having grown up in the Labour movement, his parents were Conservatives. He joined the Labour Party due to the encouragement of a girlfriend, Cherie Booth, now his wife and a successful lawyer.

Blair first won office by proclaiming that he represented New Labour, a vague Third Way philosophy modeled on that of President Bill Clinton. It was invoked to show that he rejected socialist values and principles. In setting out Labour's manifesto, Blair proclaimed, "We are proud now to be the party of modern, dynamic business, proud now to be the party of law and order, proud now to be the party of the family, and proud now to be the party pledged not to increase income tax."[8] He pledged a pragmatic government that would do "what works" and appealed to the voters to "trust me" (see Box 8.2).

The first term of the Blair government (1997–2001) was devoted to demonstrating that Labour was fit for government. Blair and his chancellor of the Exchequer, Gordon Brown, endorsed Thatcher's efforts to limit public spending and payments to private-sector businesses to manage the delivery of major health, education, and other services. Five months after reelection in 2001, Blair responded to the September 11 attack by closely aligning himself with U.S. policies. Britain sent troops to Afghanistan and Iraq in 2003, but this policy lacked the full support of his party. It was endorsed in Parliament only with the support of Conservative MPs. In 2005 Labour again won a majority of seats in the

## The Accomplishments and Frustrations of Tony Blair

**BOX 8.2**

Tony Blair became the leader of the Labour Party with the goal of winning elections. To make the party electable, he abandoned traditional commitments to trade unions and to socialist policies. Blair's personality and actions appealed to middle-class voters, whose support Labour needed to win elections. Blair's efforts to create what he called a **New Labour Party** were rewarded with three straight Labour election victories in 1997, 2001, and 2005.

After becoming prime minister, Blair gave priority to running a perpetual election campaign through the media and used his rare appearances in the House of Commons to play to the television cameras there. The number of political appointees at 10 Downing Street increased substantially. Although they usually had no prior experience working in government, they were given unprecedented power to give orders to civil servants.

Blair promoted reforms in state-financed health and education services through competition intended to give citizens a measure of "consumer" choice in health and education. However, the methods chosen to do so angered many doctors, teachers, and public employees, who saw it as making their professional judgments subject to targets laid down by management consultants, continuing Thatcher's emphasis on making government businesslike, rather than a public service. Given that it takes years to deliver changes in social policies, many effects of Blair's measures may become evident only years after he has left office.

Major constitutional reforms included the devolution of executive responsibilities to elected assemblies in Scotland and Wales and to a power-sharing government in Northern Ireland. London was given a popularly elected mayor. Human rights laws were adopted. However, in the wake of terrorist attacks, the government drew protests from civil liberties groups because of the way it pursued terrorist suspects. Blair welcomed such criticism as proof of his toughness.

In international affairs Blair gave priority to close working relationships with Presidents Bill Clinton and George W. Bush. Following the September 11 attack on the United States, he committed British troops to Afghanistan and Iraq. Although Blair was successful in getting close to the White House, he failed in his declared goal of placing Britain at the heart of Europe—for example, by adopting the euro as Britain's currency. In his last full year in office, Blair was out of the country for 58 days on trips to more than two dozen different national capitals on six different continents.

Shortly after winning his first election victory, 75 percent approved of Blair as prime minister. Within a year of his second election victory, Blair's rating fell below 50 percent and never recovered. Blair's third election victory in 2005 was won with only 35.2 percent of the popular vote, a fall of 8.0 percent from his first victory. By June 2006, he reached a low: Only 23 percent approved of his performance as prime minister. A year later he resigned. Since then Blair has extended his public role as an envoy for peace between Israel and Palestine and has privately enriched himself through a part-time job advising Wall Street banker J.P. Morgan.

Tony Blair, *New Britain: My Vision of a Young Country* (London: Fourth Estate, 1996); Anthony Seldon, *Blair* (New York: Free Press, 2004); Anthony Seldon, Peter Snowdon, and Daniel Collings, *Blair Unbound* (New York: Simon and Schuster, 2007); Simon Jenkins, *Thatcher and Sons* (London: Allen Lane, 2006).

House of Commons, making Blair Britain's second-longest-serving prime minister in more than a century.

Since a prime minister does not have a fixed term of office, when Blair fell in the opinion polls, he came under pressure to fulfill his promise to retire rather than fight a fourth election. He did so in June 2007. The Labour Party unanimously elected Gordon Brown as its leader on the basis of his record as the government's chief economic minister, the chancellor of the Exchequer. During Brown's period as chancellor, the economy grew steadily, inflation was low, and unemployment fell, and Brown claimed that he had put an end to the recurring cycle of economic boom and bust. However, the turmoil in the world economy in 2008 showed this was not the case. After blaming the country's financial problems on world rather than domestic economic mistakes, Brown has initiated measures involving tens of billions of pounds in efforts to prevent the recession in the economy turning into a major depression.

## THE STRUCTURE OF GOVERNMENT

We must understand what government is as a precondition of evaluating what it does. Descriptions of a government often start with its constitution. However, Britain has never had a written constitution. In the words of constitutional lawyer J. A. G. Griffith, "The Constitution is what happens."[9]

The **unwritten constitution** is a jumble of acts of Parliament, court rulings, customs, and conventions that constitute the rules of the political game. The vagueness of the constitution makes it flexible, a point that political leaders such as Margaret Thatcher and Tony Blair have exploited to increase their own power. Comparing the written U.S. Constitution and the unwritten English constitution emphasizes how few are the constraints of an unwritten constitution (see Table 8.2). Whereas amendments to the U.S. Constitution must receive the endorsement of well over half the states and members of Congress, the unwritten constitution can be changed by a majority vote in Parliament or by the government of the day acting in an unprecedented manner.

The U.S. Constitution gives the Supreme Court the final power to decide what the government may or may not do. By contrast, in Britain the final authority is Parliament, where the government of the day commands a majority of votes. Courts do not have the power to declare an Act of Parliament unconstitutional; judges simply ask whether the executive acts within its authorized powers. Many statutes delegate broad discretion to a Cabinet minister or public authority. Even if the courts rule that the government has improperly exercised its authority, the effect of such a judgment can be annulled by a subsequent Act of Parliament retroactively authorizing the action.

The Bill of Rights in the U.S. Constitution allows anyone to turn to the courts for the protection of their personal rights. Instead of giving written guarantees to citizens, the rights of British people are meant to be secured by trustworthy governors. However, individuals who believed their personal rights infringed had no redress through the courts until the Blair government incorporated the European Convention of Human Rights into the country's laws.

In Britain the **Crown** is the abstraction that is used in place of the continental European idea of the state. It combines the dignified parts of the constitution, which sanctify authority by tradition and myth, with the efficient parts, which carry out the work of government. The Queen is only a ceremonial head of state. Some Britons argue that a monarchy is out of date, and the Labour government has sought to promote British values as an alternative focus of loyalty. The public reaction to the accidental death of Princess Diana was a media event, but not a political event like the assassination of President John Kennedy. Queen Elizabeth II does not influence the actions of what is described as Her Majesty's Government. While the Queen gives formal assent to laws passed by Parliament, she may not publicly state any opinion about legislation. The Queen is expected to respect the will of Parliament, as communicated to her by the leader of the majority party in Parliament, the prime minister.

### What the Prime Minister Says and Does

Leading a government with a complex structure (see Figure 8.1) is a political rather than a managerial task. Within the Cabinet the **prime minister** occupies a unique position, sometimes referred to as *primus inter pares* (first among equals). But as Winston Churchill

| Constitutional Comparison<br>Comparing an Unwritten and a Written Constitution | | TABLE 8.2 |
|---|---|---|
| | **Britain (unwritten)** | **United States (written)** |
| Origin | Medieval customs | 1787 Constitutional Convention |
| Form | Unwritten, indefinite | Written, precise |
| Final constitutional authority | Majority in Parliament | Supreme Court |
| Bill of individual rights | No | Yes |
| Amendment | Ordinary vote in Parliament; unprecedented action by government | More than majority vote in Congress, states |
| Policy relevance | Low | High |

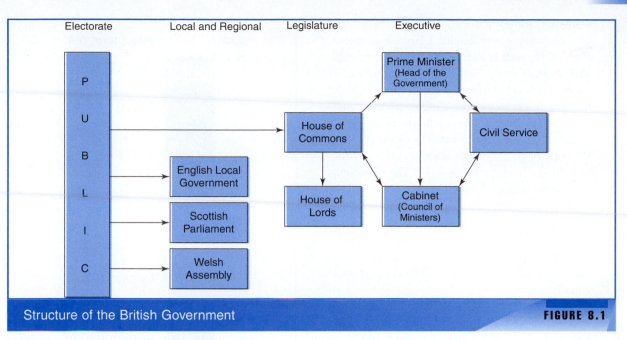

| Electorate | Local and Regional | Legislature | Executive |

**Structure of the British Government**    **FIGURE 8.1**

once wrote, "There can be no comparison between the positions of number one, and numbers two, three or four."[10] The preeminence of the prime minister is ambiguous. A politician at the apex of government is remote from what is happening on the ground. The more responsibilities attributed to the prime minister, the less time there is to devote to any one task. Like a president a prime minister is the prisoner of the law of first things first. Regardless of personality, a prime minister wears multiple hats as party leader, head of government, and spokesperson for the nation. Simultaneously, he or she is concerned with the following:

1. **Winning elections.** A prime minister may be self-interested, but he or she is not self-employed. To become prime minister, a politician must first be elected leader of his or her party. The only election that a prime minister must win is that of party leader. Seven prime ministers since 1945—Winston Churchill, Anthony Eden, Harold Macmillan, Alec Douglas-Home, James Callaghan, John Major, and Gordon Brown—initially entered Downing Street during the middle of a Parliament, rather than after a national election. In the 17 elections since 1945, the prime minister of the day has ten times led the governing party to victory and seven times to defeat.

2. **Campaigning through the media.** A prime minister does not need to attract publicity; it is thrust on him or her by the curiosity of television and newspaper reporters. During an election campaign, the prime minister gets four times as much coverage as any other member of his Cabinet team. Media eminence is a double-edged sword, for bad news puts the prime minister in an unfavorable light. The personality of a prime minister remains relatively constant, but during a term of office, his or her popularity can fluctuate by more than 45 percentage points in public opinion polls.[11]

3. **Dispensing patronage.** To remain prime minister, a politician must keep the confidence of a party. Potential critics can be silenced by appointing a quarter of MPs to posts as government ministers, who sit on front bench seats in the House of Commons. MPs not appointed to a post are backbenchers; many ingratiate themselves with the party leader in hopes of becoming a government minister. In dispensing patronage a prime minister can use any of four different criteria: (a) personal loyalty (rewarding friends), (b) cooption (silencing critics by giving them an office so that they are committed to support the government), (c) representativeness (for example, appointing a

woman or someone from Scotland or Wales), and (d) competence in managing a large department.

4. *Performing well in Parliament.* The prime minister appears in the House of Commons weekly for half an hour of questions from MPs, engaging in rapid-fire repartee with a highly partisan audience. Unprotected by a speechwriter's script, the prime minister must show that he or she is a good advocate of government policy or suffer a reduction in confidence. By being in the Commons and participating in votes there, the prime minister is able to judge the mood of the governing party. Whereas his predecessors would participate in at least a third of the votes in the Commons, Tony Blair turned his back on Parliament, in some years participating in as little as 6 percent of votes there.

5. *Making and balancing policies.* The overriding concern of a prime minister is foreign affairs because as head of the British government he or she deals with heads of other governments around the world. When there are conflicts between international and domestic policy priorities, the prime minister is the one person who can strike a balance between pressures from the world "out there" and pressures from the domestic electorate. The number of "intermestic" policies (that is, problems combining both an international and a domestic element) is increasing. The prime minister also makes policy by striking a balance between ministers who want to spend more money to increase their popularity and a Treasury minister who wants to cut taxes in order to boost his or her popularity.

While the formal powers of the office remain constant, individual prime ministers (see Figure 8.2) have differed in their electoral success, in how they view their job, and in their impact on government. Clement Attlee, Labour prime minister from 1945 to 1951, was a nonassertive spokesperson for the lowest common denominator of views within a Cabinet consisting of very experienced Labour politicians. When an aging Winston Churchill succeeded Attlee in 1951, he concentrated on foreign affairs and took little interest in domestic policy; the same was true of his successor, Anthony Eden. Harold Macmillan intervened strategically on a limited number of domestic and international issues, while giving ministers great scope

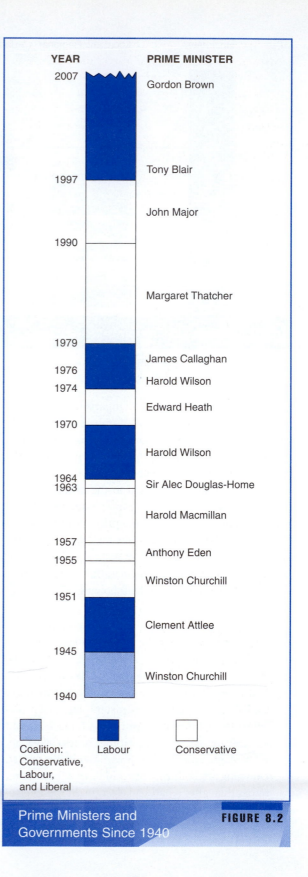

Prime Ministers and Governments Since 1940

**FIGURE 8.2**

on everyday matters. Alec Douglas-Home was weak because he lacked knowledge of economic affairs, the chief problem during his administration.

Both Harold Wilson and Edward Heath were initially committed to an activist definition of the prime minister's job. However, Wilson's major initiatives in economic policy were unsuccessful, and in 1974 the electorate rejected Heath's direction of the economy. Wilson won office again by promising to replace confrontation between management and unions with political conciliation. James Callaghan, who succeeded Wilson in 1976, also emphasized consensus, but economic crises continued.

Margaret Thatcher had strong views about many major policies; associates gave her the nickname TINA because of her motto: There Is No Alternative. Thatcher was prepared to push her views against the wishes of Cabinet colleagues and civil service advisors by any means necessary. In the end her "bossiness" caused a revolt of Cabinet colleagues that helped bring about her downfall. Her former colleagues welcomed John Major as a consensus replacement of a domineering Thatcher. However, his conciliatory manner was often interpreted as a sign of weakness. Sniping from ministers led Major to refer to his Cabinet colleagues as "bastards."

Tony Blair carried into the prime ministership the priority he gave in Opposition to campaigning through the media. Managing the flow of news to secure favorable media coverage was a top priority. Blair's communications director, Alastair Campbell, was given unprecedented powers to give orders to civil servants, and Cabinet ministers were supposed to support his media strategy on pain of losing favor with Downing Street. In the words of the former head of the civil service, the Blair government put "too much emphasis on selling" and "too little on careful deliberation." [12]

Gordon Brown came to the prime ministership with a reputation for success in managing the economy, which had enjoyed an unprecedented period of growth while he was in charge of the Treasury. He also used its power of the purse to influence Cabinet colleagues. Labour MPs unhappy with Tony Blair's endorsement of many policies of Margaret Thatcher hoped that Brown's left-wing views in youth would be reflected in policies promoting more egalitarian and socialist goals. After a brief honeymoon with public opinion Brown fell out of favor. By the end of the summer of 2008, his approval ratings in opinion polls were at a historic low, the Labour Party had lost two by-elections, and Labour MPs afraid of defeat at the next general election were publicly discussing the

During the Iraq War, Tony Blair was the foreign leader closest to President Bush.

AP Images

| | Britain (prime minister) | USA (president) |
|---|---|---|
| **Prime Minister and President** — Comparing the power of and processes for choosing a prime minister and a president | | **TABLE 8.3** |
| Media visibility | High | High |
| Route to top | Parliament | Governor, senator |
| Chosen by | Party vote | State primaries and caucuses |
| Elected by | Parliament | National election |
| Term of office | Flexible, insecure | Four years, secure |
| Constitution | Unitary | Federal |
| Domestic influence | High | So-so |
| International role | Semi-independent | Superpower |
| Checks | Informal | Congress, Supreme Court |

Source: Adapted from Richard Rose, *The Prime Minister in a Shrinking World* (Boston: Polity Press, 2001), p. 242.

desirability of another change of leadership, but the rules of the Labour Party make it difficult for dissatisfied members to mount an effective challenge to an incumbent.

Brown's quick response to the autumn 2008 financial crisis helped him regain some support, but continuing economic difficulties have continued to threaten his position.

Blair's innovations have led to charges that Britain now has a presidential system of government in which power is concentrated in the hands of one person. However, by comparison with a U.S. president, a British prime minister has less formal authority and less security of office (see Table 8.3). The president is directly elected for a fixed four-year term. A prime minister is chosen by his or her party for an indefinite term and is thus vulnerable to losing office if its confidence wanes. The president is the undoubted leader of the federal executive and can dismiss Cabinet appointees with little fear of the consequences; by contrast, senior colleagues of a prime minister are potential rivals for leadership and may be kept in the Cabinet to prevent them from challenging him or her.

However, with the support of the Cabinet and the majority of the governing party's MPs, a prime minister can be far more confident than a president that major legislative proposals will be enacted into law. Although the president is the chief of the executive branch of the federal government, the White House is without authority over Congress, state and local government, and the judiciary. By contrast, the prime minister is at the apex of a unitary government, with powers that are not limited by the courts or by a written constitution.[13]

## THE CABINET AND CABINET MINISTERS

The **Cabinet** consists of ministers appointed by the prime minister to head Whitehall departments. They must be members of either the House of Commons or the House of Lords. As ministers are leading figures in the majority party in Parliament, they contribute to what Walter Bagehot described as "the close union, the nearly complete fusion of the executive and legislative powers."[14]

Historically, the Cabinet was the forum in which the prime minister brought together leading members of the governing party, many with competing departmental interests and personal ambitions, to ensure agreement about major government policies. This was possible because the convention of Cabinet responsibility required that all Cabinet ministers give public support to, or at least refrain from public criticism of, what the government was doing, even if they opposed a policy in private. A minister unwilling to share responsibility was expected to resign from office.

The Cabinet is no longer a place for collective deliberation about policies. A half century ago there were usually two Cabinet meetings a week, and many took several hours to arrive at a political consensus. By the time of John Major, meetings were shorter and occurred less than once a week. Tony Blair further reduced the frequency of meetings and cut their average length to under an hour;

**BOX 8.3**

## Departmental Organization and Reorganization

British government departments are multipurpose organizations created as a result of the growth of government. Some departments focus on a clearly defined major function, while others combine multiple functions. The names and functions of departments are often reorganized to reflect changes in policy, political expediency, or fashion. For example, since 1964 responsibilities for trade, industry, and technology have been placed in departments labeled Trade and Technology, then Trade and Industry, then separate departments for Trade and for Industry, and again reunited as a single Trade and Industry department. Today the policies are divided between departments for Business, Enterprise, and Regulatory Reform and for Innovation, Universities, and Skills. Each time that the title on the front door of the department was changed, most officials and programs continued as before.

In March 2009 the government of Gordon Brown was organized as follows:

1. *External affairs:* foreign and commonwealth affairs; defense; international development.
2. *Economic affairs:* treasury; business, enterprise, and regulatory reform; transport; innovation, universities, and skills; energy and climate change.
3. *Legal and constitutional issues:* justice; home office; law officer's department; equalities office.
4. *Social services:* health; children, schools, and families; work and pensions; culture, media, and sport.
5. *Territorial:* environment, food, and rural affairs; communities and local government; Northern Ireland office; Scotland office; Wales office.
6. *Managing government business:* Cabinet office; leader of the House of Commons; chief whip in the House of Commons; leader of the House of Lords; chancellor of the Duchy of Lancaster; Privy Council office.

Source: www.parliament.uk.

he used them as a forum in which to exhort ministers to support Downing Street's media priorities. Gordon Brown has preferred to take charge of a wide range of issues, rather than trusting Cabinet colleagues.

Cabinet ministers remain important because the department that each heads is responsible for a major area of public policy and most decisions about what government does are taken within departments (see Box 8.3). Whitehall departments differ greatly from each other. For example, the Department of Business, Enterprise, and Regulatory Reform (DBER) has a larger staff than the Department of the Treasury. However, because of the importance of its responsibility for taxation and public expenditure, the Treasury has more senior civil servants. The DBER staff have a dispersed variety of concerns, including the competitiveness of industry, trade, employment, energy, and regulation. The Treasury staff concentrate on one big task, the management of the economy. The varied tasks of the DBER secretary make him or her much more vulnerable to adverse publicity if, for example, there is a financial scandal or

energy prices rise. The job of the chancellor of the Exchequer is more important politically, insofar as economic performance affects the governing party's electoral fate.

A Cabinet minister is both the head of a government department and a party politician. As a department head, he or she can initiate policies, select among alternatives brought forward from within the department, and try to avoid making an unpopular decision. A minister is responsible for actions taken by thousands of civil servants nominally acting on the minister's behalf and must answer for agencies to which Whitehall is increasingly contracting out responsibility for delivering public services. In addition, a minister is a department's ambassador to the world outside, including Downing Street, Parliament, the mass media, and interest or pressure groups. Not least, Cabinet ministers are individuals with ambitions to rise in politics. The typical minister is not an expert in a subject, but an expert in politics, and is willing to deal with any department that offers opportunities to further his or her political career.

The political reputation of Cabinet ministers depends on their success in promoting the interests of their department in Parliament, in the media, and in battles within Whitehall. Cabinet ministers are willing to go along silently with their colleagues' proposals in exchange for endorsement of their own measures. However, ministers often have to compete for scarce resources, making conflict inevitable between departments. Regardless of party, the ministers responsible for defense and education will press for increased spending, while the Treasury minister will oppose such moves. Cabinet ministers sometimes resolve their differences in Cabinet committees that include all ministers whose departments are most affected by an issue.

Tony Blair sought to exercise control over ministers through his personal staff. However, Blair did not have time during the week to go into the details of policy. Because he had never been a departmental minister, his public remarks sometimes showed naiveté about how the government actually worked—and the same was even more true of his staff. After years in office, Blair attacked the consequences of government by political advisors and spin doctors. In a leaked memo to Cabinet ministers, he criticized them for "too often" rushing out policies "in ignorance of the risks," thus making the government look bad.[15]

## The Civil Service

Although government could continue for months without new legislation, it would collapse overnight if hundreds of thousands of civil servants stopped administering laws and delivering public services that the government of the day had inherited from its predecessors. The largest number of civil servants are clerical staff with little discretion; they carry out the routine activities of a large bureaucracy. Only if these duties are executed satisfactorily can ministers have the time and opportunity to make new policies.

The most important group of civil servants is the smallest: the few hundred higher civil servants who advise ministers and oversee work of their departments. Top British civil servants deny they are politicians because of the partisan connotations of the term. However, their work is political because they are involved in formulating and advising on controversial policies. Thus, a publication aimed at recruiting bright graduates for the higher civil service declares: "You will be involved from the outset in matters of major policy or resource allocation and, under the guidance of experienced administrators, encouraged to put forward your own constructive ideas and to take responsible decisions."[16]

Top civil servants are not apolitical; they are bipartisan, being ready to work for whichever party wins an election. Their style is not that of the professional American athlete for whom winning is all-important. English civil servants have grown up playing cricket; its motto is that winning is less important than how one plays the game. However, ministers are more concerned with winning.

The relationship between ministers and higher civil servants is critical. A busy politician does not have time to go into details; he or she wants a brief that can catch a headline or squash criticism. Ministers expect higher civil servants to be responsive to their political views and to give advice consistent with their outlook and that of the governing party and Downing Street. Civil servants like working for a political heavyweight who can carry the department's cause to victory in interdepartmental battles. Civil servants prefer to work for a minister who has clear views on policy, but they dislike it when a minister grabs a headline by expressing views that will get the department into trouble later because they are impractical.

Both ministers and civil servants are concerned with political management in complementary ways. High-level civil servants are expected to be able to think like politicians, anticipating what their minister would want and objections that would be raised by Parliament, interest or pressure groups, and the media. Ministers are expected to be able to recognize the obstacles to achieving desirable goals that civil servants identify for them, However, this has caused activist prime ministers such as Margaret Thatcher and Tony Blair to regard much civil service advice as unhelpful to them in achieving their ambitions.

Ministers now have at hand political advisors to advise them on measures they can announce that will reflect credit on them in the media and in the governing party. This has caused civil servants to complain that ministers too often ignore advice that calls attention to the difficulties in achieving their intentions. In the words of a senior civil servant, "Just because ministers say to do something does not mean that we can ignore reality."[17] When ministerial decisions attract criticism, ministers may blame civil servants, rather than taking responsibility themselves. The head of the trade union of higher civil servants has argued, "There is a danger of descending into a search for scapegoats when problems emerge."[18]

The Thatcher government introduced a new phenomenon in Whitehall: a prime minister who believed civil servants were inferior to business people because they did not have to "earn" their living—that is, to make a profit. *Management* was made the buzzword in Whitehall, and departments were supposed to be run in a businesslike fashion, achieving value for money so that the government could profit politically by cutting taxes. Parts of government departments were "hived off" to form separate public agencies, with their own accounts and performance targets. The Blair government continued Thatcher's attempts to make the civil service more businesslike, in hopes of providing public services more cheaply.

During 11 years as head of the Treasury, Gordon Brown gathered around him a small team of political appointees and civil servants to further his efforts to manage the economy. As prime minister he has faced a different challenge: to concentrate attention on a few big decisions and to delegate tasks that he lacks the time to deal with. Cabinet ministers criticize Brown for trying to take charge of too many policies and then delaying decisions when all alternatives appear politically unpopular.

## The Role of Parliament

The principal division in Parliament is between the party with a majority of the seats in the House of Commons and the Opposition parties. The government expects to get its way because its members are the leading politicians in the majority party. MPs in the majority party almost invariably vote as the party leadership instructs because only by voting as a bloc can their party maintain control of government. If a bill or a motion is identified as a vote of confidence in the government, the government will fall if it is defeated.

The government's state of mind is summed up in the words of a Labour Cabinet minister who declared, "It's carrying democracy too far if you don't know the result of the vote before the meeting."[19] In the great majority of House of Commons votes, MPs vote along party lines. If a handful of MPs votes against the party whip or abstains, this is headlined as a rebellion. The Opposition cannot expect to alter major government decisions because it lacks a majority of votes in the

Commons. It accepts the frustrations going with its minority status for the life of a Parliament because it hopes to win a majority at the next election.

Whitehall departments draft bills presented to Parliament, and few amendments to legislation are carried without government approval. Laws are described as acts of Parliament, but it would be more accurate if they were stamped "Made in Whitehall." In addition, the government, rather than Parliament, sets the budget for government programs. The weakness of Parliament is in marked contrast to the U.S. Congress, where each house controls its own proceedings independent of the White House. A U.S. president may ask Congress to enact a bill, but cannot compel a favorable vote.

The chief functions of Parliament are political, rather than legislative. First of all, it weighs political reputations. MPs continually assess their colleagues as ministers or potential ministers and as allies or potential allies in internal party disputes about policy and personalities and promotion. A minister may win a formal vote of confidence, but lose status if his or her arguments are demolished in debate. They continually assess their leader as a person who will lead them to victory or defeat at the next election.

Second, backbench MPs can demand that the government do something about an issue and force a minister to explain and defend what he or she is responsible for. The party whip is expected to listen to the views of dissatisfied backbench MPs and to convey their concerns to ministers. In the corridors, dining rooms, and committees of the Commons, backbenchers can tell ministers what they think is wrong with government policy. If the government is unpopular and MPs feel threatened with losing their seats at the next election, they will be aggressive in demanding that something be done.

Publicizing issues is a third function of Parliament. MPs can use their position to call the media's attention to issues and to call the public's attention to themselves. Television cameras are now in Parliament, and a quick-witted MP can provide the media with sound bites.

Fourth, MPs can examine how Whitehall departments administer public policies. An MP may write to a minister about a department responsibility affecting a constituent or pressure group. MPs can request the parliamentary commissioner for administration (also known as the ombudsman, after the Scandinavian original) to investigate complaints about maladministration. Parliamentary committees scrutinize administration and policy, interviewing civil servants and ministers. However, as a committee moves from discussing details to discussing issues of government policy, it raises a question of confidence in the government, and this can divide a committee along party lines, with MPs in the governing party in the majority.

MPs are expected to promote the interests of their constituency and be helpful to individual constituents having trouble in dealing with a government department. However, the obligation to follow the party line when it comes to a vote limits the influence they can exert. Most MPs hold their seat by a comfortable majority conferred by partisan electors who identify with their party. When their party is in trouble nationally, constituency work and personal popularity cannot save MPs in seats held by a narrow margin from defeat.

A newly elected MP contemplating his or her role as one among 646 members of the House of Commons is faced with many choices. An MP may decide to be a party loyalist, voting as the leadership decides without participating in deliberations about policy. The MP who wishes more attention can make a mark by exhibiting brilliance in debates, by acting as an acknowledged representative of a pressure group, or by acting in a nonpartisan way—for example, helping look after unglamorous parliamentary services. An MP is expected to speak for constituency interests, but constituents accept that their MP will not vote against party policy if it is in conflict with local interests. The only role that an MP rarely undertakes is that of lawmaker—this job is undertaken in Whitehall departments.

Backbench MPs perennially demand changes to make their jobs more interesting and to give them more influence. However, the power to make major changes rests with the government, rather than the House of Commons. Whatever criticisms MPs made of Parliament while in Opposition, once in government they have an interest in existing arrangements that greatly limit the power of Parliament to influence or stop what ministers do.

The second chamber of the British Parliament, the House of Lords, is unique because it was initially composed of hereditary peers, now supplemented by lords appointed for life. However, in 1999 the Labour government abolished the right of all but 92 hereditary peers to sit in the House of Lords. Today a large majority of its members are life peers who have been

given a title later in life for achievement in one or another public sphere, government ministers who have been appointed without having a seat in the House of Commons, and prominent donors of money to a party. In Tony Blair's third term of office, the police investigated allegations that he had raised $50 million from rich backers hoping to be made into a lord and thereby being given a seat in the upper chamber of Parliament.

No party has a majority of seats in the House of Lords, and more than one-fifth of its members are cross-benchers who do not identify with any party. The government often introduces relatively noncontroversial legislation in the Lords. and it uses the Lords as a revising chamber to amend bills. Members of the Lords can raise party political issues or issues that cut across party lines, such as problems of the fishing industry or pornography. The Lords cannot veto legislation, but it can and does amend or delay the passage of some government bills.

Although all parties accept the need for some kind of second chamber to revise legislation, there is no agreement about what its composition or its powers should be. Current methods of appointment have raised concerns about the abuse of appointment powers. In 2007 a majority of MPs voted in favor of a completely elected House of Lords. However, the government has made no commitment to implement so large a reform. The last thing the government of the day wants is a reform that gives the upper chamber enough electoral legitimacy to challenge government legislation.

## Government as a Network

Policy making involves a network of prime minister, ministers, leading civil servants, and political advisors, all of whom share in what has been described as the "village life" of Whitehall. An English village is far smaller and more intimate than the city full of politicians inside the Washington, D.C., beltway.[20]

The growth of government has increased specialization so that policy makers see less and less of each other. For a given issue, a relatively small number of people are involved in the **core executive** group that makes a decision. However, members of the network are a floating population of people in Westminster; it is not the same for decisions about transport and agriculture or about health and defense.

The prime minister is the single most important person in government. Since there is no written constitution, a determined prime minister can challenge the status quo and turn government to fresh ends. But to say that the prime minister makes the most important decisions and leaves the less important ones to department ministers begs this question: What is an important decision? Decisions in which the prime minister is not involved are more numerous, require more money, and affect more lives than do most decisions taken at Downing Street. Scarcity of time is a major limitation on the influence of the prime minister. In the words of one Downing Street official, "It's like skating over an enormous globe of thin ice. You have to keep moving fast all the time."[21]

Within each department the permanent secretary, its highest-ranking civil servant, usually has much more knowledge of a department's problems than does a transitory Cabinet minister. Political advisors brought into a department to put the best spin on what their minister does know less about the department's work than its career civil servants. However, they have the political advantage of knowing the minister better.

## POLITICAL CULTURE AND LEGITIMACY

Political culture refers to values and beliefs about how the country ought to be governed. For example, there is a consensus that Britain ought to have a government accountable to a popularly elected Parliament. This view is held not only by the major parties, but also by parties that demand independence, such as the Scottish National Party.

The values of the political culture impose limitations on what government can do and what it must do. Regardless of party preference, the great majority of British people today believe that government ought to provide education, health services, and social security. Cultural norms about freedom of speech prevent censorship of criticism, and liberal laws on sexual relations and abortion allow for great freedom of choice in sexual matters.

Today many limits on the scope of public policy are practical, rather than normative. Public expenditure on popular policies, such as the health service, are limited by the extent to which the economy grows and the reluctance of Labour or Conservative governments to raise more money by increasing taxes. Trying

to introduce new legislation or reverse a major policy is difficult because of the need to take into account well-entrenched programs and interests.

There are three competing normative theories of how British government ought to operate. The **trusteeship theory of government** assumes that leaders ought to take the initiative in deciding what is collectively in the public interest. It is summed up in the epigram "The government's job is to govern." The trusteeship doctrine is always popular with the party in office because it justifies doing whatever the government wishes. The Opposition party rejects it because it is not in office.

The **collectivist theory** sees government as balancing the competing demands of collective groups in society. From this perspective, parties and pressure groups advocating group or class interests are more authoritative than individual voters.[22] Traditional Conservatives emphasized harmony between different classes in society, each with its own responsibilities and rewards. For socialists, group politics has been about class conflict. With changes in British society, party leaders have distanced themselves from close identification with representing collective interests, as they realize that votes are cast by individuals, rather than by business firms or trade unions.

The **individualist theory** postulates that political parties should represent people, rather than organized group interests. In the 1980s Margaret Thatcher was an outspoken advocate of economic individualism, regarding each person as responsible for his or her welfare. In an interview in 1987 she went so far as to declare, "There is no such thing as society." Liberal Democrats put emphasis on individual freedom from government enforcement of social norms, too. However, individuals are rarely offered a referendum allowing them to vote directly on what government does.

### The Legitimacy of Government

The legitimacy of government is shown by the British people simultaneously valuing their form of government with free elections to a representative Parliament, while making many specific criticisms about how it works.

Dissatisfaction with government encourages protest, but it is normally kept within lawful bounds. The World Values Survey finds that nearly every Briton says he or she might sign a petition and half might participate in a lawful demonstration. However, only one-sixth might participate in an illegal occupation of a building or factory. The readiness of groups in Northern Ireland to resort to armed action for political ends makes it the most "un-British" part of the United Kingdom.

The legitimacy accorded to British government is not the result of economic calculations about whether parliamentary democracy "pays" best. During the depression of the 1930s, Communist and Fascist parties received only derisory votes in Britain, while their support was great in Germany and Italy. Likewise, inflation and unemployment in the 1970s and 1980s did not stimulate extremist politics.

The symbols of a common past, such as the monarchy, are sometimes cited as major determinants of legitimacy. But surveys of public opinion show that the Queen has little political significance; her popularity derives from the fact that she is nonpolitical. The popularity of a monarch is a consequence, not a cause, of political legitimacy. In Northern Ireland, where the minority denies the legitimacy of British government, the Queen is a symbol of divisions between British Unionists and Irish Republicans, who reject the Crown. Habit and tradition appear to be the chief explanations for the persisting legitimacy of British government. A survey asking people why they support the government found that the most popular reason was "It's the best form of government we know."

Authority is not perfect or trouble free. Winston Churchill made this point when he told the House of Commons: "No one pretends that democracy is perfect or all wise. Indeed, it has been said that democracy is the worst form of government, except all those other forms that have been tried from time to time."[24] In the words of English writer E. M. Forster, people give "two cheers for democracy."

## Courts and Abuses of Power

The Constitutional Reform Act of 2005 authorized the creation of a Supreme Court as the highest judicial authority in the United Kingdom, with effect from autumn 2009. It ends the centuries-old practice of having a committee of the House of Lords operate as the highest court. The new Supreme Court consists of a president and 11 other justices appointed by the prime minister. Its chief function is to serve as the final court of appeal on points of law in cases initially heard by

courts in England, Wales, and Northern Ireland and in some cases by courts in Scotland, which maintains a separate system of courts, albeit the content of laws is usually much the same. Although the name of the new British Supreme Court is the same as that of the highest court in the United States, its powers are much more limited. It cannot declare an Act of Parliament unconstitutional, for Parliament remains the supreme authority in deciding what government can and cannot do.

In constitutional theory Parliament can hold ministers accountable for abuses of power by the government. In practice Parliament is an ineffective check on abuses of executive power because the executive consists of the leaders of the majority party in Parliament. When the government is under attack, the tendency of MPs in the governing party is to close ranks in its defense. The government can use this shield to protect itself from charges of abusing its power.

The decline of ministerial accountability to Parliament in recent decades has encouraged the courts to become more active in making rulings against the elected government of the day if ministers can be shown to have acted inconsistently with grants of power contained in acts of Parliament. Governments of both parties have responded by including clauses in acts that give ministers broad grants of discretionary power.

Britain's membership in the EU offers additional channels for judicial influence. The United Kingdom is now bound to act within laws and directives authorized by the EU. British judges can use EU standards when evaluating government actions, and plaintiffs can challenge British government actions at the European Court of Justice. The 1998 Human Rights Act of the Westminster Parliament allows citizens to ask British courts to enforce rights conferred by the European Convention on Human Rights.

Terrorist activities challenge conventional norms about individual rights and the collective interests of the state. At times British government forces dealt with the violence of the IRA and illegal armed Protestant groups by "bending" the law, implementing shoot-to-kill policies and fabricating evidence to produce convictions of terrorist suspects that the courts have subsequently overturned. As a response to jihadist terrorist bombings in London, the police are ready to use harsh measures against suspects, including shoot-to-kill responses when arresting suspects. The Labour government's proposals for reducing the rights of suspect terrorists have been condemned by

Opposition parties as creating a risk of a "siege" or "authoritarian" society.[24]

Tension is emerging between the principle that the elected government of the day should do what it thinks best and the judges' view that government should act in accord with the rule of law, whether an Act of Parliament or an obligation contained in a European treaty that the British government has endorsed. When judges make decisions that Labour government ministers do not like, the ministers have publicly attacked the decisions of the court. Judges reply by stating that they should not be attacked for enforcing the law. If the government does not like it, it should pass a new Act of Parliament or secure amendments to European treaties.

Both ministers and senior civil servants sometimes mislead Parliament and the public. A Conservative minister nominally responsible for open government told a Commons select committee in 1994 that "in exceptional cases it is necessary to say something that is untrue in the House of Commons." When accused in court of telling a lie about the British government's efforts to suppress an embarrassing memoir by an ex-intelligence officer, Robert Armstrong, then the head of the civil service and secretary to the Cabinet, described the government's statements as "a misleading impression, not a lie. It was being economical with the truth."

Whitehall practices of "cutting corners" or abusing powers have been protected from parliamentary scrutiny by legislation on **official secrecy**. This legislation treats information as a scarce commodity that should not be given out freely. Information about policy deliberations in departments is often deemed not in the "public" interest to disclose, for it can make government appear uncertain or divided. The Whitehall view is "The need to know still dominates the right to know."[25] Secrecy remains strong because it serves the interests of the most important people in government, Cabinet ministers and civil servants. A Freedom of Information Act has reduced, but not ended, the executive's power to keep secret the exchange of views within the Whitehall network. For example, in response to a request for information about its operation, a civil servant at the Histories, Openness, and Records Unit of the Cabinet Office wrote: "Releasing information which would allow analysis of policy decisions affecting the operation of the Act would of itself be detrimental to the Act's operation."[26]

Occasional abuses of executive power have created tensions for civil servants who believe that their job is not only to serve the elected government of the day, but also to maintain the integrity of government. This has led civil servants at times to leak official documents with the intention of preventing government from carrying out a policy that the leaker believes to be unethical or inadvisable (see Box 8.4).

## Conflicting Loyalties Among Civil Servants

**BOX 8.4**

The inability of Parliament to hold the government of the day accountable for palpable misdeeds disturbs senior civil servants who know what is going on and risk becoming accessories before the fact if they assist ministers in producing statements that mislead Parliament.

In one well-publicized case, a Ministry of Defence official, Clive Ponting, leaked to the House of Commons evidence that questioned the accuracy of government statements about the conduct of the Falklands War. He was indicted and tried for violating the Official Secrets Act. The judge asked the jury to think about the issue this way: "Can it then be in the interests of the state to go against the policy of the government of the day?" The jury concluded that it could be; Ponting was acquitted.

Most senior civil servants are unwilling to become whistle-blowers, challenging actions of ministers, and thereby jeopardizing their own careers. However, inquiries after major mistakes can show that these mistakes have occurred because ministers have refused to listen to cautions from civil servants or misrepresented their views. This was notably so in Tony Blair's justification of going to war in Iraq.

Graham Wilson and Anthony Barker, "Whitehall's Disobedient Servants? Senior Officials' Potential Resistance to Ministers in British Government Departments," *British Journal of Political Science* 27, no. 2 (1997): 223–246.

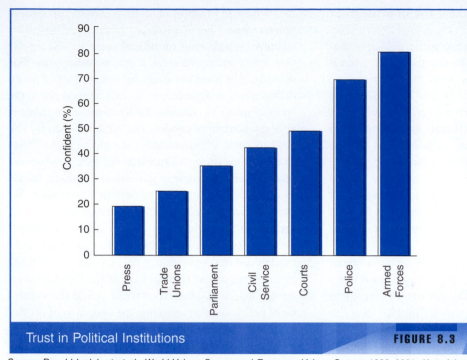

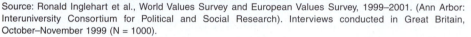

Trust in Political Institutions **FIGURE 8.3**

Source: Ronald Inglehart et al., World Values Survey and European Values Survey, 1999–2001. (Ann Arbor: Interuniversity Consortium for Political and Social Research). Interviews conducted in Great Britain, October–November 1999 (N = 1000).

British citizens have reacted to abuses of public office by becoming distrusting. Only a third of Britons report that they have a great deal or quite a lot of confidence in Parliament. The press and trade unions—institutions that theories of civil society describe as important in holding government accountable—are trusted by even fewer people. The most trusted public institutions today are those that maintain authority, led by the armed forces and the police (see Figure 8.3).

## POLITICAL SOCIALIZATION

Socialization influences the political division of labor between those who participate in politics and those who do not. The family's influence comes first chronologically; political attitudes learned within the family become intertwined with primary family loyalties. However, social change means that the views that parents transmit to their children may not be relevant by the time that their offspring have become 40 to 50 years old. In contemporary Britain whether one is a Christian or a Muslim is more relevant than whether one was brought up in the Church of England or the Methodist Church.

### Family and Gender

A child may not know what the Labour, Conservative, or Liberal Democratic Party stands for, but if it is the party of Mom and Dad, this can be enough to create a youthful identification with a party. However, the influence of family on voting is limited because 36 percent do not know how one or both of their parents usually voted or else their parents voted for different parties. Among those who report knowing which party both parents supported, just over half vote as their parents have. In the electorate as a whole, only 35 percent say that they know how both parents voted and that they vote for the same party.[27]

Children learn different social roles according to gender; yet, as adult citizens, men and women have the same legal right to vote and participate in politics. Bipartisan interest in appealing to women is illustrated by the 1976 Sex Discrimination Act, prohibiting discrimination in employment. It was enacted by a Labour government following a report by a Conservative government. For each general election, the votes of women are divided in much the same way as those of men.

Whether talking about economic, social, or international issues, politicians usually stress concerns common to both men and women. Men and women tend to have similar political attitudes. For example, more than half of women and half of men favor capital punishment, and a substantial minority in each group opposes it. Gender is less important than class, age, or education as an influence on party loyalties (see Table 8.4).

Gender differences do, however, lead to differences in political participation. Men are almost twice as likely as women to be local government councillors. Women

| Social Differences in Voting | | | | **TABLE 8.4** |

The Labour Party drew on a different electoral base than the Conservative Party in 2005

| | Labour | Conservative | Liberal Democratic | Other |
|---|---|---|---|---|
| *Gender* | | | | |
| Women | 39% | 34% | 22% | 5% |
| Men | 40 | 29 | 23 | 8 |
| Difference | −1 | 5 | −1 | −3 |
| *Age* | | | | |
| 18–29 | 44% | 20% | 30% | 6% |
| 30–59 | 40 | 30 | 23 | 7 |
| 60 plus | 36 | 41 | 18 | 5 |
| Difference | 8 | −21 | 12 | 2 |
| *Class* | | | | |
| Middle | 36% | 36% | 23% | 5% |
| Lower middle | 32 | 39 | 24 | 5 |
| Skilled manual | 48 | 27 | 18 | 7 |
| Unskilled manual | 52 | 18 | 20 | 10 |
| Difference | −16 | 18 | 3 | −5 |

Source: British Election Survey, 2005 (number of reported voters = 2,787).

are almost half the employees in the civil service, but are heavily concentrated in lower-level clerical jobs; women hold about 10 percent of the top appointments in the civil service. A record number of women candidates stood for the Commons in 2005, but male candidates still outnumbered women by a margin of four to one. A total of 128 women were elected to the House of Commons; it remains four-fifths male.

## Education

The majority of the population was once considered fit for only a minimum of education, but that minimum has steadily risen. In today's electorate the oldest voters left school at the age of 14 and the median voter by the age of 17. Less than 6 percent of young persons attend "public" schools—that is, fee-paying schools, which are actually private schools. Whereas half a century ago Britain had few universities, today there are more than one hundred universities and almost one-half of young persons are in postsecondary institutions, many of which lack the facilities of established research universities.

The stratification of English education used to imply that the more education a person had, the more likely that person was to vote for Conservatives. This is no longer the case. People with a university degree or its equivalent now divide their votes among the Conservative, Labour, and Liberal Democratic parties.

Education is strongly related to active participation in politics. The more education a person has, the greater the possibility of climbing the political ladder. University graduates make up more than two-thirds of the members of the House of Commons. The expansion of universities has broken the dominance of Oxford and Cambridge; barely one-quarter of MPs went to these two institutions. The concentration of graduates from many different British universities in top jobs is a sign of a meritocracy, in which officials qualified by education have replaced an aristocracy based on birth and family.

## Class

Historically, party competition has been interpreted in class terms; the Conservative Party has been described as a middle-class party and Labour as a working-class party. Class has appeared as relatively important in England because of the absence of major divisions of race, religion, or language, as are found in the United States, Canada, and Northern Ireland. The concept of **class** can refer to occupational status or serve as a shorthand term for the social status conferred by income and education. Occupation is the most commonly used indicator of class. Manual workers are usually described as the working class and nonmanual workers as the middle class.

Most Britons have a mixture of middle-class and working-class attributes. The mixed-class group has

Schools and street scenes in big cities show that Britain is now a multi-racial society.

J. C. Tordai/Panos Pictures

been increasing, as changes in the economy have led to a reduction in manual jobs and an increase in middle-class jobs. Many occupations such as computer technicians now have an indeterminate social status. When British citizens are asked whether they belong to a social class, 57 percent now reject placing themselves in either the middle or the working class.

The relationship between class and party has become limited. No party now wins as much as half the vote of middle-class electors. In the 2005 election, just over half of unskilled manual workers and just under half of skilled manual workers voted Labour (see Table 8.4). Due to the cross-class appeal of parties, less than half of the electorate conforms to the stereotypes of middle-class Conservative and working-class Labour voters.

Socioeconomic experiences other than occupation also influence voting. At each level of the class structure, people who belong to trade unions are more likely to vote Labour than Conservative. Housing creates neighborhoods with political relevance. People who live in municipally built council houses tend to vote Labour, while Conservatives do relatively well among home-owners, who are now a large majority of the electorate.

The focus of the mass media on what's happening today makes them an agency for resocializing people. The media's stress on what is new deemphasizes tradition. Today the upper class no longer commands deference, and celebrities owing their prominence to the media and achievements in sports, rock music, or the

like are better known than most MPs and even some Cabinet ministers. Moreover, the Internet provides people with alternative sources of information and opinion, and most Britons old enough to vote are able to find information there.

The British press is sharply divided. A few quality newspapers such as *The Times, The Guardian, The Daily Telegraph, The Independent,* and *The Financial Times* carry news and comment at an intellectual level higher than most American newspapers. Mass-circulation tabloids such as *The Sun,* Britain's best-selling newspaper, concentrate on trivia and trash. Most papers tend to lean toward one party. However, if the party that a paper normally supports becomes very unpopular, then the paper will criticize it or even lean toward whichever party has risen in popularity.

In the aggressive pursuit of news and audiences, journalists are prepared to grab attention by making the government of the day look bad, and television interviewers can gain celebrity by insulting MPs and ministers on air. A majority of MPs think that the media are to blame for popular cynicism about politicians and parties. However, a Populus poll in 2007 found that a majority of the electorate thinks that the conduct of politicians is just as much to blame for cynicism about politics as is the conduct of the media.

Television is the primary source of political news. Historically, radio and television were a monopoly of the British Broadcasting Corporation (BBC). Seeking to educate and to elevate, the BBC was also very respectful of all forms of authority, including government. The introduction of commercial television in the 1950s and commercial radio in the following decades has made all broadcasting channels populist in competing for audiences. There are now many television channels and a great variety of radio stations. The law forbids selling advertising to politicians, parties, or political causes.

Current affairs programs often seek audiences by exposing alleged failings of government, and television personalities make their names by the tough cross-examination of politicians of all parties. However, the government of the day controls the renewal of the broadcasting companies' licenses, and it sets the annual fee that every viewer must pay for noncommercial BBC programs, currently about $250 a year. Broadcasters try to avoid favoring one party because over a period of time control of government is likely to shift between parties and, with it, the power to make decisions that affect the companies' revenue and licenses.

Since political socialization is a lifetime learning process, the loyalties of voters are shaped by an accumulation of influences over many decades. Today there are still some members of the electorate who are old enough to have voted for or against Winston Churchill when he led the Conservative Party. However, the youngest electors had not been born until after Margaret Thatcher retired as leader of the Conservative Party. The median elector in the next British general election cast his or her first vote in the 1992 election.

## POLITICAL PARTICIPATION AND RECRUITMENT

### Participation

An election is the one opportunity people have to influence government directly. Every citizen aged 18 or over is eligible to vote. Local government officials register voters, and the list is revised annually, ensuring that nearly everyone eligible to vote is actually registered. Turnout at general elections averaged 77 percent in the 50 years since 1950. However, in 2001 it fell to 59 percent. In an attempt to boost turnout, the Labour government has experimented with encouraging people to vote by post, rather than in person. When postal ballots were mailed out in several North of England constituencies during the 2004 European Parliament election, three-fifths of those receiving a ballot did not bother to return it. In the 2005 general election, postal voting on demand led to serious allegations of fraud in several inner-city constituencies. Even then, turnout was only 61 percent.

Between elections there are additional opportunities to express political opinions (Figure 8.4). More than one-third have signed a petition on a public issue, and more than one-fifth say that politics has affected their shopping by causing them to boycott a product. The most

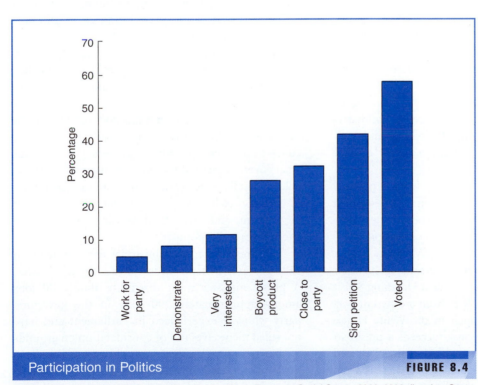

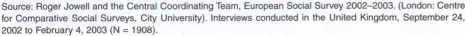

Participation in Politics — **FIGURE 8.4**

Source: Roger Jowell and the Central Coordinating Team, European Social Survey 2002–2003. (London: Centre for Comparative Social Surveys, City University). Interviews conducted in the United Kingdom, September 24, 2002 to February 4, 2003 (N = 1908).

politically involved—those who say they are very interested in politics, take part in a demonstration, or are active in a political party—make up no more than one-tenth of the electorate. However, a London-based protest by a few thousand people can get national media coverage, even though those participating make up only 0.01 percent of the electorate.

If political participation is defined as paying taxes and drawing benefits from public policies, then virtually every Briton is involved. Public programs provide benefits at each stage of the life cycle, from maternity allowances to mothers through education, employment and unemployment benefits, health care, and pensions in old age. The median British household receives two major benefits from public policies.

## Political Recruitment

The most important political roles in Britain are those of Cabinet minister, higher civil servant, partisan political advisor, and intermittent public person, which is analogous to a Washington insider. Each group has its own recruitment pattern. To become a Cabinet minister, an individual must first be elected to Parliament. Shortly after leaving university, ambitious politicians often become assistants to politicians and then "graduate" to becoming lobbyists, journalists, or MPs. Individuals enter the civil service shortly after leaving university by passing a highly competitive entrance examination; promotion is based on achievement and approval by seniors. Intermittent public persons gain access to ministers and civil servants because of the knowledge and position they have gained by making a career outside party politics.

In all political roles, starting early on a political career is usually a precondition of success because it takes time to build up the skills and contacts necessary to become a major political actor. Geography is a second major influence on recruitment. Ministers, higher civil servants, and other public persons spend their working lives in London. A change at Downing Street does not bring in policy makers from a different part of the country, as can happen in the White House when a president from Chicago succeeds a president from Texas. Since London is atypical of the cities and towns in which most British people live, there is a gap between the everyday lives of policy makers and those of the majority on whose behalf they act.

## MPs and Cabinet Ministers

For a person with ambitions to be a Cabinet minister, becoming an MP is the necessary first step. An ambitious person is not expected to begin in local politics and work his or her way gradually to the top at Westminster. Instead, at an early age an individual becomes a "cadet" recruit to a junior position such as a parliamentary assistant to an MP or a "gofer" for a Cabinet minister.

Nomination for a winnable or safe seat in the House of Commons is in the hands of local party committees. A candidate does not have to be resident in the constituency in which he or she is nominated. Hence, it is possible for a young person to go straight from university to a job in the House of Commons or party headquarters and then look around the country for a winnable seat for which to be nominated, a process that usually takes years. Once selected for a constituency in which his or her party has a large majority, the MP can then expect to be reelected routinely for a decade or more.

After entering the House of Commons, an MP seeks to be noticed. Some ways of doing so—for example, grabbing headlines by questioning the wisdom of the party leadership—make it difficult to gain promotion to the ministerial ranks. Other approaches assist promotion, such as successfully attacking Opposition leaders in debate or being well informed about a politically important topic. So, too, does showing loyalty to the party leader.

Experience in the Commons does not prepare an individual for the work of a minister. An MP's chief concerns are dealing with people and talking about what government ought to do. A minister must also be able to handle paperwork, relate political generalities to specific technical problems facing his or her department, and make hard decisions when all the alternatives are unpopular.

The restriction of ministerial appointments to MPs prevents a nationwide canvass for appointees. A prime minister must distribute about 100 jobs among approximately 200 MPs in the governing party who are experienced in Parliament and have not ruled themselves out of consideration on grounds of parliamentary inexperience, old age, political extremism, personal unreliability, or lack of interest in office. An MP has a better than even chance of a junior ministerial appointment if he or she serves three terms in Parliament. Exceptionally, Tony Blair gave a variety of ministerial posts to personal supporters whom he made life peers; they owed their posts to their patron, Blair, rather than to voters and to the Labour Party.

A minister learns on the job. Usually, an MP is first given a junior post as an under secretary and then promoted to minister of state before becoming a full member of the Cabinet. In the process an individual is likely to be shuffled from one department to another, having to learn new subject matter with each shift between departments. The average minister can expect to stay in a particular job for about two years and never knows when an accident of politics—a death or an unexpected resignation—will lead to a transfer to another department. The rate of ministerial turnover in Britain is one of the highest in Europe. The minister who gets a new job as the result of a reshuffle usually arrives at a department with no previous experience with its problems. Anthony Crosland, an able Labour minister, reckoned: "It takes you six months to get your head properly above water, a year to get the general drift of most of the field, and two years really to master the whole of a department."[28]

### Higher Civil Servants

Whereas MPs come and go from ministerial office with great frequency, civil servants can be in Whitehall for the whole of their working lives. Higher civil servants are recruited without specific professional qualifications or training. They are meant to be "the best and the brightest"—a requirement that has traditionally meant getting a prestigious degree in history, literature, or languages. The Fulton Committee on the Civil Service recommended that recruits have "relevant" specialist knowledge, but the committee members could not decide what kind of knowledge was relevant to the work of government.[29] The Civil Service Commission tests candidates for their ability to summarize lengthy prose papers, to resolve a problem by fitting specific facts to general regulations, to draw inferences from a simple table of social statistics, and to perform well in group discussions about problems of government.

Because bright civil service entrants lack specialized skills and need decades to reach the highest posts, socialization by senior civil servants is especially important. The process makes for continuity, since the head of the government's civil service usually started there as a young official under a head who had himself entered the civil service many decades before.

In the course of a career, civil servants become specialists in the difficult task of managing political ministers and government business. As the television series *Yes, Minister* shows, they are adept at saying "yes" to a Cabinet minister when they really mean "perhaps" and saying "up to a point" when they really mean "no." Increasingly, ministers have tended to discourage civil servants from pointing out obstacles in the way of what government wants to do; they look to "can do" advisors from outside the civil service.

### Political Advisors

Most advisors are participants in party politics, for their job is to mobilize political support for the government and for the Cabinet minister for whom they work. Because their background is in party politics and the media, such advisors bring to Whitehall skills that civil servants often lack and that their ministers value. But because they have no prior experience with the civil service, they are often unaware of its conventions and legal obligations. The methods used by political appointees to put a desirable spin on what the government is doing can backfire and cause public controversy. For example, when the September 11 disaster dominated the news, a Whitehall advisor emailed colleagues that this was a good time to put out news that revealed departmental mistakes, since the media would bury it beneath stories from the United States.

In addition, experts in a given subject area, such as environmental pollution or cloning, can act as political advisors. Even if inexperienced in the ways of Whitehall, they can contribute specialized knowledge that is often lacking in government departments, and they can be supporters of the governing party, too. For example, Margaret Thatcher brought in a free market economics professor, Alan Walters, to give her advice from a different perspective than that of the advice she received from what she regarded as a "socialist" civil service.

Most leaders of institutions such as universities, banks, churches, and trade unions do not think of themselves as politicians and have not stood for public office. They are principally concerned with their own organization. But when government actions impinge on their work, they become involved in politics. For example, university heads lobby Whitehall for more money for higher education, while simultaneously demanding freedom from ministerial directions that they describe as "political" interference. Because the actions of government are directly or indirectly relevant to almost all major institutions of society, in effect their leaders intermittently must participate in political debates on public policy.

## Selective Recruitment

Nothing could be more selective than an election that results in one person becoming prime minister of a country. Yet, nothing is more representative because an election is the one occasion when every adult can participate in politics with equal effect.

Traditionally, political leaders had high social status and wealth before gaining political office. Aristocrats, businesspeople, and trade union leaders can no longer expect to translate their high standing in other fields into an important political position. Today politics is a full-time occupation. As careers become more specialized, professional politicians become increasingly distant from other spheres of British life.

The greater the scope of activities defined as political, the greater the number of people actively involved in government. Government influence has forced company directors, television executives, and university heads to become involved in politics and public policy. Leadership in organizations outside Whitehall gives such individuals freedom to act independently of government, but the interdependence of public and private institutions, whether profit-making or nonprofit, is now so great that sooner or later they meet in discussions about the public interest.

## ORGANIZING GROUP INTERESTS

Civil society institutions have existed in Britain for more than a century. Their leaders regularly discuss their views of public policy with government officials in the expectation that this will put pressure on government to do what they argue is in their groups' interest, as well as the public interest.

The scope of group demands varies enormously from the narrow concerns of an association for single parents to the encompassing economic policies of organizations representing business or trade unions. Groups also differ in the nature of their interests: Some are concerned with material objectives, whereas others deal with single causes such as television violence or race relations.

The Confederation of British Industries is the chief representative organization of British business. As its name implies, its membership is large and varied. The Institute of Directors represents the highest-paid individuals at the top of large and small businesses. The largest British businesses usually have direct contacts with Whitehall and with ministers, whatever their party, because of the importance of these businesses' activities for the British economy and for its place in the international economy. For example, British Petroleum is one of the world's largest oil companies, and most of the oil it drills is found outside the United Kingdom. Government deems the success of such a company as important for national security, as well as for the national economy. The construction industry has access to government because home-building is important for the national economy, and Whitehall's tight control over land use influences where houses can be built.

The chief labor organization is the Trades Union Congress (TUC); its members are trade unions that represent many different types of workers, some white-collar and some blue-collar. Most member unions of the TUC are affiliated with the Labour Party, and some leading trade unionists have been Communists or Maoists. None has ever been a supporter of the Conservative Party.

Changes in employment patterns have eroded union membership; today only one-quarter of the labor force belongs to a trade union. Over the years the membership of trade unions has shifted from workers in such heavy industries as coal and railways to white-collar workers such as teachers and health service employees. Only one in six private-sector workers belongs to a trade union. By contrast, almost three-fifths of public-sector workers are union members. Elected representatives control their wages, and strikes or go-slow actions by teachers, hospital workers, or other public employees can cause political embarrassment to the government.

Britain has many voluntary and charitable associations, from clubs of football team supporters to the Automobile Association. It is also home to a number of internationally active nongovernmental organizations such as Oxfam, concerned with the problems of poor, developing countries, and Amnesty International, concerned with political prisoners. These nongovernmental organizations try to bring pressure not only on Westminster, but also on organizations such as the World Bank and on repressive governments around the world.

Unlike political parties, interest groups do not seek influence by contesting elections; they want to influence policies regardless of which party wins. Nonetheless, there are ties between interest groups and political parties. Trade unions have been institutionally part of the Labour Party since its foundation in 1900 and are the major source of party funds. The connection between business associations and the Conservatives is not formal, but the party's traditional commitment to private enterprise is congenial to business. Notwithstanding common interests, both trade unions and business groups demonstrate their autonomy by criticizing their party ally if it acts against the group's interest. Whichever party is in office, they seek to exercise influence.

Party politicians seek to distance themselves from interest groups. Conservatives know that they can win an election only by winning the votes of ordinary citizens, as well as prosperous businesspeople. Tony Blair sought to make the Labour government appear business friendly and reaped large cash donations from very wealthy businesspeople. However, this led union leaders to attack his government as unsympathetic, and a few small unions have left the Labour Party.

To lobby successfully, interest groups must be able to identify those officials most important in making public policy. They concentrate their efforts on Whitehall. When asked to rank the most influential offices and institutions, interest group officials named the prime minister first by a long distance; Cabinet ministers came second, the media third, and senior civil servants fourth (see Figure 8.5). Less than 1 percent thought MPs outside the ministerial ranks were of primary importance. However, interest groups do not expect to spend a lot of time at Downing Street. Most of their contacts are with officials within a government department concerned with issues of little public concern, but of immediate interest to the group.

## What Interest Groups Want

Most interest groups pursue four goals:

1. Sympathetic administration of established policies
2. Information about government policies and changes in policies

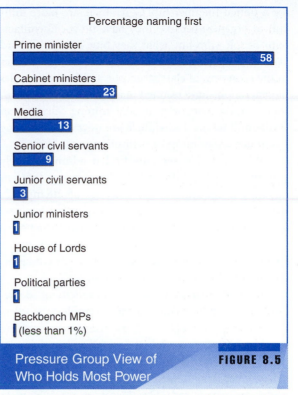

**Percentage naming first**

| | |
|---|---|
| Prime minister | 58 |
| Cabinet ministers | 23 |
| Media | 13 |
| Senior civil servants | 9 |
| Junior civil servants | 3 |
| Junior ministers | 1 |
| House of Lords | 1 |
| Political parties | 1 |
| Backbench MPs | (less than 1%) |

**Pressure Group View of Who Holds Most Power**          **FIGURE 8.5**

Source: Survey of officials of business, labor, and campaign groups, as reported in Rob Baggott, "The Measurement of Change in Pressure Group Politics," *Talking Politics* 5, 1 (1992): 19.

3. Influence on policy making
4. Symbolic status, such as being given the prefix "Royal" in their title

Whitehall departments are happy to consult with interest groups insofar as they can provide government officials with reciprocal benefits:

1. Cooperation in administering and implementing policies
2. Information about what is happening in their field
3. Evaluation of the consequences of policies under consideration
4. Support for government initiatives

As long as the needs of Whitehall and interest groups are complementary, they can bargain as professionals sharing common concerns. Both sides are ready to arrive at a negotiated agreement.

## Organizing for Political Action in Civil Society

The more committed members are to an interest group's goals, the more confidently leaders can speak for a united membership. Consumers are more difficult to organize because they have no social contacts with people who buy what they buy. Drivers of Ford cars are a category, rather than a social group. Changes in the economy, in class structure, and in the lifestyles of generations have resulted in a decline in the "dense" social capital networks of coal mining villages and textile mill towns. Individuals are now free to belong to a much wider range of institutions or to none.

Whitehall civil servants find it administratively convenient to deal with united interest groups that can implement agreements. But decades of attempts to plan the British economy demonstrate that business and union leaders cannot guarantee that their nominal followers will carry out bargains that leaders make. Group members who care about an issue can disagree, too, about what their leaders ought to do.

Individuals usually have a multiplicity of identities that are often in conflict—for example, as workers desiring higher wages and as consumers wanting lower prices. The spread of mass consumption and decline in trade union membership has altered the balance between these priorities. As a trade union leader has recognized, "Our members are consumers too."[30]

Even if a pressure or interest group is internally united, its demands may be counteracted by opposing demands from other groups. This is normally the case in economic policy, where interests are well defined, well organized, and competing. Ministers can play off producers against consumers or business against unions to increase their scope for choice and present their policies as "something for everybody" compromises.

The more a group's values are consistent with the cultural norms of society as a whole, the easier it is to equate its interest with the public interest. But in an open society such as Britain, the claims of one group to speak for the public interest can easily be challenged by competing groups. The centralization of authority in the British government means that interest groups must treat as given the political values and priorities of the governing party.

**Insider pressure groups** usually have values in harmony with every party. These groups are often noncontroversial, such as the Royal National Institute for the Blind. Insiders advance their case in quiet negotiations with Whitehall departments. Demands tend to be restricted to what is politically possible in the short term, given the values and commitments of the government of the day.[31]

**Outsider pressure groups** are unable to negotiate because their demands are inconsistent with the party in power. If their demands are inconsistent with the views of the Opposition as well, then outsider groups are completely marginalized. Outsider groups without any influence in Whitehall often campaign through the media. To television viewers their demonstrations appear as evidence of their importance; in fact, they are often signs of a lack of political influence. Green pressure groups face the dilemma of campaigning for fundamental change in hopes that eventually Whitehall departments will turn their way or of becoming insiders working within the system to improve the environment to some extent, but not as much as some ecologists would like.

## Keeping Interest Groups at a Distance

For a generation after World War II, ministers endorsed the corporatist philosophy of bringing together business, trade unions, and political representatives in tripartite institutions to discuss such controversial issues as inflation, unemployment, and the restructuring of declining industries. Corporatist bargaining assumed that there was a consensus on political priorities and goals and that each group's leaders could deliver the cooperation of those they claimed to represent. In practice, neither Labour nor Conservative governments were able to maintain a consensus. Nor were interest group leaders able to deliver their nominal followers. By 1979 unemployment and inflation were both zooming upward out of control because government could not manage the national economy and trade union and business association leaders were unable to get their nominal followers to stick to agreements that their leaders had made with government.

The Thatcher administration demonstrated that a government firmly committed to distinctive values can ignore group demands and lay down its own pattern of policy. It did so by dealing at arm's length with both trade unions and business groups. Instead of consulting with interest groups, it practiced state-distancing, keeping the government out of everyday marketplace activities such as wage bargaining, pricing, and investment.

A state-distancing strategy concentrates on policies that government can implement without the agreement of interest groups. It emphasizes the use of

Tony Blair, as Labour Prime Minister, and Gordon Brown, as Labour Chancellor of the Exchequer, were the two most powerful individuals in British government for a decade. However, they often did not see eye to eye.

Stephen Hird/Corbis

legislation to achieve goals, since no interest group can defy an Act of Parliament. Laws have reduced the capacity of trade unions to frustrate government policies through industrial action. The sale of state-owned industries has removed government from immediate responsibility for the operation of major industries, and Labour Chancellor Gordon Brown transferred to the Bank of England responsibility for monetary policy.

State-distancing places less reliance on negotiations with interest groups and more on the authority of government. Business and labor are free to carry on as they like—but only within the pattern imposed by government legislation and policy. Most unions and some business leaders do not like being "outside the loop" when government makes decisions. Education and health service interest groups like it even less because they depend on government appropriations to fund their activities and cannot effectively turn to the market as an alternative source of revenue.

## PARTY SYSTEM AND ELECTORAL CHOICE

British government is party government. A general election gives voters a choice of parties competing for the right to govern. Parties nominate parliamentary candidates and elect their leaders; one leader is the prime minister and the other leaders head Opposition parties.

## A Multiplicity of Choices

A general election must occur at least once every five years; within that period the prime minister is free to call an election at any time. The most recent general election was held in May 2005; the next election is therefore due no later than Spring 2010. Although every prime minister tries to pick a date when victory is likely, often this aim is frustrated by events. The winner nationally is the party that gains the most MPs. In 1951 and in February 1974, the party winning the most votes nationally did not win the most seats; the runner-up party in the popular vote formed the government.

An election offers a voter a very simple choice between parliamentary candidates competing to represent a constituency in the House of Commons. Within each constituency the winner is the candidate who is first past the post—that is, the candidate who has a plurality (the largest number) of votes, even if this is less than half the vote.

If only two parties contest a constituency, the candidate with the most votes will have an absolute majority. But since at least three candidates now contest almost all of the 646 constituencies, a candidate can often win with less than half the vote, thanks to its division among multiple competitors. For example, in a hard-fought contest among four parties in Inverness in 1992, the Liberal Democrats won the seat with only 26 percent of the constituency vote.

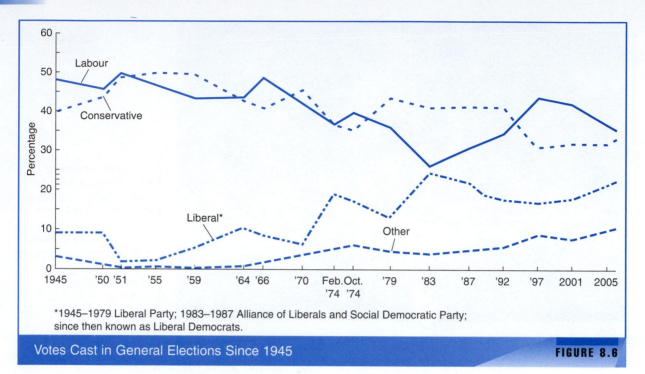

*1945–1979 Liberal Party; 1983–1987 Alliance of Liberals and Social Democratic Party; since then known as Liberal Democrats.

**Votes Cast in General Elections Since 1945**                    **FIGURE 8.6**

Between 1945 and 1970, Britain had a two-party system; the Conservative and Labour parties together took an average of 91 percent of the popular vote and in 1951 as much as 97 percent (see Figure 8.6). The Liberals had difficulty fielding candidates to contest a majority of constituencies and even more difficulty winning votes and seats. Support for the two largest parties was evenly balanced; Labour won four elections and the Conservatives won four.

In a two-party system, the failure of one party tends to benefit its opponent. However, when both the largest parties are discredited, this gives other parties an opportunity to gain support. A **multiparty system** emerged in the elections of 1974. The Liberals won nearly one-fifth of the vote, and nationalist parties did well in Scotland, Wales, and Northern Ireland. Together, the Conservative and Labour parties took only 75 percent of the vote. The Liberal Democratic and the nationalist parties have maintained their strength, as the results of the 2005 election show (see Table 8.5). The number of parties in the system today depends on the measure used.

1. The number of parties competing for votes varies from three to five in different parts of the United Kingdom. In England, three parties—the Labour, Conservative, and Liberal Democratic parties—compete for votes. In 2005 the United Kingdom Independence Party fought for a majority of seats, too, campaigning in opposition to the EU. In Scotland and Wales there are normally four parties, and the Scottish National and Plaid Cymru (Welsh Nationalist) parties elect MPs, too. In Northern Ireland at least five parties contest seats, two representing Unionist and Protestant voters, two Irish Republican and Catholic voters, and the weakest a cross-religious alliance of voters.

2. The two largest parties do not monopolize votes. Since 1974, the Conservative and Labour parties together have won an average of three-quarters of the vote and in the 2005 election together gained just 67.6 percent of the total vote. No party has won half the popular vote since 1935.

3. The two largest parties in the House of Commons often are not the two leading parties at the constituency level. During the 2005 election in more than one-quarter of constituencies, one or both of the two front-running parties were neither Labour nor Conservative.

4. More than half a dozen parties consistently win seats in the House of Commons. In 2005 so-called third parties won 93 seats in the Commons.

## The 2005 Election
### Party vote percentages by nation in 2005

TABLE 8.5

|  | England | Scotland | Wales | Northern Ireland | United Kingdom |
|---|---|---|---|---|---|
| Labour | 35.5 | 38.9 | 42.7 | 0 | 35.2 |
| Conservative | 35.7 | 15.8 | 21.4 | 0.1 | 32.4 |
| Liberal Democratic | 22.9 | 22.6 | 18.4 | 0 | 22.0 |
| Nationalists* | 0 | 17.7 | 12.6 | 93.3 | 4.6 |
| Others | 5.9 | 5.0 | 4.9 | 6.6 | 5.8 |

*Scottish National Party, Plaid Cymru (Wales), and in Northern Ireland the Democratic Union and Ulster Unionist parties and pro-Irish Republic Sinn Fein and the Social Democratic & Labour Party.

Source: *Colin Rallings and Michael Thrasher, ELECTION 2005: The Official Results. Plymouth LGC Elections Centre on behalf of the Electoral Commission, p. 178.* Official statistics.

5. Significant shifts in voting usually do not involve individuals moving between the Labour and Conservative parties, but in and out of the ranks of abstainers or between the Liberal Democrats and the two largest parties.

To win a substantial number of seats in the House of Commons, a party must either gain more than one-third of the popular vote nationally or concentrate its votes in a limited number of constituencies. For this reason the distribution of seats in the House of Commons is different from the distribution of the share of votes. In 2005 the Labour Party won more than 55 percent of the seats in the House of Commons with 35 percent of the popular vote (cf. Figures 8.6 and 8.7). The total vote for the Conservatives in England was actually higher than Labour's vote, but it won 92 fewer seats than Labour because more of its votes were where it finished second, whereas Labour candidates tended to come in either first or third.

Sitting in Opposition to the Labour government in the House of Commons are MPs whose parties have collectively won almost two-thirds of the popular vote. However, they have less than half the MPs because that vote is divided among more than eight different parties plus independents. Nationalist parties in Scotland, Wales, and Northern Ireland win seats because they concentrate their candidates in one part of the United Kingdom. Although the Liberal Democrats often win more than one-fifth of the popular vote, their support is spread relatively evenly across the country, making it far more likely that their candidates will finish second or third, rather than first.

The first-past-the-post electoral system manufactures a House of Commons majority for a party with two-fifths or less of the popular vote. Defenders of the British electoral system argue that proportionality is not a goal in itself. The first-past-the-post system is justified because it places responsibility for government

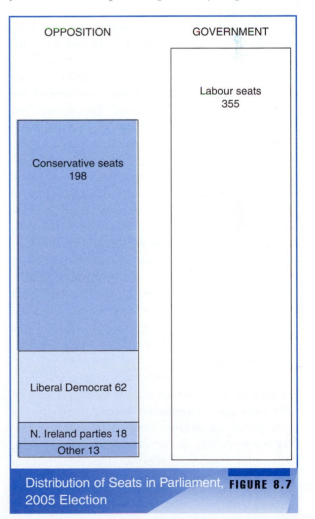

Distribution of Seats in Parliament, 2005 Election    **FIGURE 8.7**

in the hands of a single party. This justification is used in the United States, where the president can be described as representing all the people, whether he wins just over half or just under half the popular vote. In continental European countries, which use proportional representation, coalition or minority governments are the norm. When a coalition is necessary, a party finishing third in the popular vote can determine who governs by choosing the party that came in either second or first in the popular vote as its partner in creating a majority.

The strongest advocates of proportional representation are the Liberal Democrats. In a proportional representation system, the Liberal Democratic vote in 2005 would have given it 142 seats, more than twice what it actually received. A change is also supported by those who believe that a coalition government is a better government because it encourages a broad interparty consensus.

Successive British governments have altered the electoral system for contests that do not affect the composition of the Westminster Parliament.[32] All British Members of the European Parliament are elected by proportional representation, and it has been used in Northern Ireland for almost four decades. In the Scottish Parliament and the Welsh Assembly, there is a mixed electoral system: Some representatives are elected by first past the post and some by proportional representation. The mayor of Greater London is elected by the alternative vote, in which electors rank their candidates in order of preference and those with the fewest votes have their second preferences transferred to other candidates until one candidate has an absolute majority of preferences. The system for the Westminster Parliament remains unaltered because the decision about what kind of voting system to have is determined not by reasoning from abstract principles, but by the interests of the party that won power under the first-past-the-post system.

Political parties are often referred to as machines, but this description is very misleading, for parties cannot mechanically manufacture votes. Nor can they be commanded like an army. Parties are like universities; they are inherently decentralized, and people belong to them for a variety of reasons. Thus, party officials have to work hard to keep together three different parts of the party: those who vote for it, the minority active in its constituency associations, and the party in Parliament. If the party has a majority in Parliament,

there is a fourth group, the party in government. Whether the party leader is the prime minister or the leader of the Opposition, he or she must maintain the confidence of all parts of the party or risk ejection as leader (see Box 8.5).

The headquarters of each party provides more or less routine organizational and publicity services to constituency parties and to the party in Parliament. Each party has an annual conference to debate policy and to vote on some policy resolutions. Constituency parties are nationally significant because each selects its own parliamentary candidate. The decentralization of the selection process has allowed the choice of parliamentary candidates with a wide variety of political outlooks and abilities. Under Tony Blair the Labour Party introduced more central direction in choosing candidates. It was justified on the grounds of promoting more women MPs by restricting the selection of the candidate in a safe Labour constituency to a short list consisting exclusively of women.

The Liberal Democrats have a small central organization; they have sought to build up the party's strength by winning council seats in local government elections. In parliamentary elections it targets seats where the party is strong locally. This strategy has paid off; it has more than tripled its number of MPs, from 20 in 1992 to 62 in 2005, while its share of the vote increased by only 0.5 percent. The candidates for leadership are nominated by Liberal MPs, and the leadership is determined by vote of the party's membership.

## Party Images and Appeals

While the terminology of *left* and *right* is part of the language of elite politicians, it is rejected by the great majority of British voters. When asked to place themselves on a left-right scale, the median voter chooses the central position, and only a tenth place themselves on the far left or far right. Consequently, parties that veer toward either extreme risk losing votes.

When public opinion is examined across a variety of issues, such as inflation, protecting the environment, spending money on the health service, and trade union legislation, a majority of Conservative, Labour, and Liberal Democratic voters tend to agree. Big divisions in contemporary British politics often cut across party lines; for example, attitudes toward the EU divide both Labour and Conservative MPs, and so has the Iraq War. Any attempt to impute a coherent ideology to a political party is doomed to

## Electing and Ejecting a Party Leader

BOX 8.5

British voters decide which party has a majority in Parliament, while the majority party decides which of its MPs is its leader, and therefore prime minister. Opposition parties elect a leader in the hope that he or she will lead the party to election victory. The governing party wants its leader to win the next election, as well as the election thaDelivering Public Services on the Doorstept has given him or her office. If a party leader is unpopular and the party is trailing in opinion polls, MPs can try to eject their leader, even if he or she is prime minister.

A party leader is strongest when he or she is also prime minister. Constitutional principles and Cabinet patronage strengthen a prime minister's hand. Moreover, an open attack on a prime minister threatens electoral defeat as a result of conflict within the party. However, Margaret Thatcher lost the prime ministership by a vote of Conservative MPs in 1990. In 2006 Labour MPs were threatening to force a vote on Tony Blair's tenure if he did not leave office sooner rather than later. The following year Gordon Brown became unpopular and has faced demands to resign or be ejected after Labour began losing by-elections.

The Labour Party leadership is determined by an electoral college composed of three groups: Labour MPs, trade unions, and constituency party members. Each group has a very different number of members and method of deciding which candidate to back. In order to call a vote of confidence in a serving party leader, one-fifth of Labour MPs must sign a request for a vote on the leadership, and this must be endorsed by a party conference. This is difficult to achieve. If a vacancy results from the voluntary resignation of the leader or a resignation forced by Cabinet members calling for him or her to go, then there is an acting prime minister for several months while candidates compete for the party leadership.

Until 1965 the Conservative Party leader was not elected, but "emerged" as the result of consultation among senior MPs and members of the House of Lords. Since then the Conservatives have elected their leader in a two- or three-stage process. An election can be called if 15 percent of the party's MPs record their dissatisfaction in writing; their names are not supposed to be revealed. Alternatively, a leader can create a vacancy by resigning. Either way there is an initial ballot among Conservative MPs. The two MPs with the most votes are then voted on by the party membership at large, whose choice is decisive.

After Conservative Party members chose three leaders who were failures as vote-getters, it chose 39-year-old David Cameron in autumn 2005. They hoped that his youth would distance him from past Conservative defeats and his openness to change would appeal to middle-of-the-road voters needed for a Conservative election victory.

---

failure, for institutions cannot think and are not organized to debate philosophy.

Instead of campaigning by promoting an ideology or by appealing to collectivist economic interests, increasingly parties stress consensual goals, such as promoting prosperity and fighting crime. They compete in terms of which party or party leader can best be trusted to do what people want or on the basis of whether it is time for a change because one party has been in office for a long time. The titles of election manifestos are virtually interchangeable between the Conservative and Labour parties. In 2005 one party's manifesto was entitled "It's Time for Action," and the other urged "Britain Forward not Back."[33]

In office the governing party has the votes to enact any parliamentary legislation it wishes, regardless of protests by the Opposition. However, most of the legislation introduced by the government is meant to be so popular, and often noncontroversial, that the Opposition dare not vote against the bill's principle. For every government bill that the Opposition votes against on principle in the House of Commons, three are adopted with interparty agreement.[34]

Most policies of government are not set out in party manifestos; they are inherited from predecessors of the same or a different party. When the Thatcher administration entered office in 1979, it inherited hundreds of programs enacted by preceding governments, including some on the statute books since 1760.[35] It repealed some programs inherited from its predecessors—and it repealed some of its own programs that were quickly recognized as mistakes. When Margaret Thatcher left office, two-thirds of the programs for which the government was responsible had been adopted before she had taken office 11 years earlier.

Prior to the 1997 general election, the Labour Party pledged that in its first term it would be prudent with public money, maintaining public expenditures at the same level as the Conservative government. Tony Blair initiated major measures to reform the delivery of public services in his second term. By the time Gordon Brown entered office in 2007, the legacy left behind by Blair—and by his own taxing and spending policies in a decade in the Treasury—made it difficult to come up with fresh policies.

The freedom of action of the governing party is limited by constraints embedded in the obligations of office. Once in office ministers find that all the laws enacted by their predecessors must be enforced, even if the government of the day would not have enacted them. A newly elected government also inherits many commitments to foreign countries and to the EU. As a former Conservative minister said of his Labour successors, "They inherited our problems and our remedies."[36]

## CENTRALIZED AUTHORITY AND DECENTRALIZED DELIVERY OF GOVERNMENT POLICIES

In a unitary state, political authority is centralized. Decisions made by central government are binding on all public agencies through acts of Parliament and regulations prepared in Whitehall. In addition, Whitehall controls taxation and public expenditures to a degree unusual among other member states of the EU, where coalition government and federalism encourage decentralization.

For ordinary individuals the actions of government are tangible only when services are delivered locally at a school or a doctor's office or when rubbish is collected at their doorstep. However, Whitehall departments usually do not deliver policies themselves. Most public goods and services are delivered by agencies headquartered outside Whitehall. Moreover, five-sixths of public employees work for non-Whitehall agencies.[37] Thus, making and delivering public policies involves *intra*governmental politics.

### Whitehall

Running the *Whitehall obstacle race* is the first step in intragovernmental politics. Most new policies must take into account the effects of existing policies in a crowded policy "space." Before a bill can be put to Parliament, the Cabinet minister sponsoring it must determine with ministers in other departments how the new measure will affect existing programs and negotiate the terms of cooperation between departments to implement it. Such negotiations are time consuming. Often a department will begin work on a new initiative under one minister and complete it under another, or even under a different party in power.

*The Treasury controls public expenditures.* Before a bill can be put to Parliament, the Treasury must authorize the additional expenditure required because increased spending implies increased taxation. Ministers in charge of spending departments dislike constant Treasury reminders that there are strict limits on what they can spend. In the words of a veteran Treasury official, "the Treasury stands for reality."[38]

A minister anxious to gain attention by sponsoring a new policy must secure the approval of the prime minister's office before a bill can be put to Parliament. If the bill looks like it will produce favorable headlines and fit into Downing Street's overall strategy, it will be given a priority. Even if a measure is controversial, it can still go ahead as long as it will unite the governing party against attacks from Opposition parties and as long as public opinion will be on the government's side.

Once a bill becomes a law, there are many reasons why ministers do not want to be in charge of delivering services. Ministers may wish to avoid charges of political interference, allow for flexibility in the market, lend an aura of impartiality to quasi-judicial activities, allow qualified professionals to regulate technical matters, or remove controversial activities from Whitehall. The prime minister prefers to focus on the glamorous "high-level" politics of foreign affairs and economic management. However, since "low-level" services remain important to most voters' lives, ministers are under pressure to do something—or at least say something in response to media demands—when there is evidence of declining standards in schools, queues for hospital admission, or an increase of crime on the streets.

### Local Government

Within England, *local government* is subordinate to central government. Westminster has the power to write or rewrite the laws that determine what locally elected governments do and spend—and even to abolish local authorities and create new units of government with different boundaries. Changes in local government boundaries have reflected a vain search to find a balance between efficiency (assumed to correlate with fewer councils delivering services to more people spread over a wider geographical area) and responsiveness (assumed to require more councils with a smaller territory and fewer people).

Local council elections are fought on party lines. In the days of the two-party system, many cities were solidly Labour for a generation or more, while leafy suburbs and agricultural counties were overwhelmingly Conservative. The Liberal Democrats now win many seats in local elections and, when no party has a majority, introduce coalition government into town halls. However, being a councillor is usually a part-time job.

The Blair government introduced the direct election of the mayor of Greater London, citing New York and Chicago as positive examples. However, it has refused to give London the independence in taxing and spending that large U.S. cities enjoy.[39] Nevertheless, the office is a political platform that attracts media attention. London's first mayor, a left-wing independent, and its second, a Conservative eccentric, used their legitimacy as elected officials to challenge the views of government at Westminster.

Local government is usually divided into two tiers of county and district councils, each with responsibility for some local services. The proliferation of public-private initiatives and special-purpose agencies has reduced the services for which local government is exclusively responsible. Today there is a jumble of more or less local institutions delivering such public services as education, police protection, refuse collection, housing, and cemeteries (see Box 8.6). Collectively, local institutions account for about a fifth of total public expenditures.

Grants of money from the central government are the largest source of local government revenue. There is no local income tax, since the central government does not want to give local authorities the degree of fiscal independence that U.S. local governments have. The Thatcher government replaced the local property tax with a poll tax on every adult resident of a local authority, believing it would make voters more aware of the costs of local government and keep spending down. In practice, the tax produced a political backlash and was replaced by a community charge (tax) on housing, which the central government tends to control.[40] How to fund services that the local government delivers remains a contentious issue.

**Centralization** is justified in terms of **territorial justice**—that is, the same standards of public policy ought to apply everywhere in the country. For example, schools in inner cities and rural areas should have the same resources as schools in prosperous suburbs. This can be achieved only if tax revenues collected by the central government are redistributed from well-to-do to poorer parts of the country. In addition, ministers emphasize that they are accountable to a national electorate of tens of millions of people, whereas local councillors are accountable only to those who vote in their ward. Instead of small being beautiful, a big nationwide electorate is assumed to be better. The centralist bias of Westminster is illustrated by the statement of an activist law professor: "Local councillors are not necessarily political animals; we could manage without them."

*Devolution* to Scotland, Wales, and Northern Ireland is an extreme form of **decentralization.** Westminster delegates authority in different measures to elected assemblies. The Scottish government, accountable to a Parliament in Edinburgh, has the right to enact legislation on a broad range of social and public services of direct concern to individuals and communities, such as education, health, and roads. It is also responsible for determining spending priorities within the limits set by its block grant of money from the British Treasury. With the Scottish National Party in government, it has political incentives to challenge the authority of Westminster. The Welsh Assembly has administrative discretion, but no legislative or taxing powers. Northern Ireland is exceptional because the key service is police and security—and this is being kept under the control of British ministers until agreement is achieved under a power-sharing government that includes participants active in organizing its decades of civil war.

## Non-elected Institutions

*Executive agencies* are headed by nonelected officials responsible for delivering many major public services. The largest, the National Health Service (NHS), is not one organization, but a multiplicity of separate institutions with separate budgets, such as hospitals and doctors' offices. Access to the NHS is free of charge to every citizen. But health care is not costless. Public money is allocated to hospitals and to doctors and

## Delivering Public Services on the Doorstep

**BOX 8.6**

Government on the scale that the British people know it today could not exist if all its activities were concentrated in London, for five-sixths of the country's population lives elsewhere. As the demand for public services has increased, government has grown, chiefly through the multiplication of familiar institutions such as schools and hospitals. Devolution to Scotland and Wales has added to decentralization.

Education is an example of how different institutions relate. It is authorized by an Act of Parliament and principally financed by central government. Two Cabinet ministers divide responsibility: One is responsible for schools and another for universities. Both are Members of Parliament. However, the delivery of primary and secondary education is the responsibility of classroom teachers who are immediately accountable to the head of their school and not

to Parliament. Dissatisfaction with the management of schools by local government has led Whitehall to establish city academies, secondary schools independent of local government, but dependent on Whitehall for funding.

Increasingly, central government seeks to monitor the performance of schools in nationwide examinations and set targets that teachers and pupils are expected to achieve. But since the Whitehall department responsible for schools employs only 1 percent of the people working in education, success depends on actions taken by others. Conservative Minister of Education Lord Hailsham contrasted his position with that of a defense minister: As the latter, "You say to one person 'come' and he cometh and another 'go' and he goeth"; with the former, "You say to one man 'come' and he cometh not, and another 'go' and he stays where he is."

*See Richard Rose, Lord Hailsham is quoted in Maurice Kogan, The Politics of Education (Harmondsworth England: Penguin, 1971), P. 31. "The Growth of Government Organizations," in C. Campbell and B. G. Peters, eds., *Organizing Government, Governing Organizations* (Pittsburgh: University of Pittsburgh Press, 1988), 99–128.

dentists that must work to guidelines and targets established centrally. Because the central government picks up the bill, the Treasury, as the monopoly purchaser, regularly seeks to cut costs in providing increasingly expensive health care.

Public demand for more and better health care has increased with the aging of the population and the development of new forms of medical treatment. The government's rationing of the health care supply has led to lengthening queues, involving months of waiting before a person can see a medical specialist or have a hospital operation. British government has sought to deal with this problem through administrative changes intended to increase efficiency—that is, measures that will keep the total health care expenditure relatively constant by cutting the cost of individual services, while expanding the total number supplied. It has not adopted the practice common in most EU countries of asking patients to make a copayment to cover part of the cost of seeing a doctor or getting hospital treatment.

British government sponsors more than a thousand **quasi-autonomous nongovernmental organizations (quangos)**. All are created by an Act of Parliament or by an executive decision; their heads are

appointed by a Cabinet minister, and public money can be appropriated to finance their activities. Some quangos deliver services. When things go wrong, Parliament has difficulty assigning responsibility for decisions. Advisory committees draw on the expertise of individuals and organizations involved in programs for which Whitehall departments are nominally responsible. Ministry of Agriculture officials can turn to advisory committees for detailed information about farming practices; the department responsible for trade and industry can turn to business associations for information about a particular industry. Because they have no executive powers, advisory committees usually cost very little to run. Representatives of interest groups are glad to serve on such committees because this gives them privileged access to Whitehall and an opportunity to influence policies in which they are directly interested.

*Administrative tribunals* are quasi-judicial bodies that make expert judgments in such fields as medical negligence or handle small claims, such as disputes about whether the rent set for a rent-controlled flat is fair. Ministers may use tribunals to avoid involvement in politically controversial issues, such as decisions about deporting immigrants.

Tribunals normally work much more quickly and cheaply than do the courts. However, the quasi-judicial role of tribunals has created a demand for independent auditing of their procedures to ensure that they are fair to all sides. The task of supervising some seventy tribunals is in the hands of a quango, the Council on Tribunals.

## Turning to the Market

The 1945–1951 Labour government turned away from the market because its socialist leaders believed that government planning was better able to promote economic growth and full employment. It nationalized many basic industries, such as electricity, gas, coal, railways, and airlines. State ownership meant that industries did not have to run at a profit; some consistently made money, while others consistently lost money and required big subsidies. Government ownership politicized wage negotiations and investment decisions.

The Thatcher government promoted privatization by selling shares of nationalized industries on the stock market. Profit-making industries such as telephones, electricity, and gas were sold without difficulty. Selling council houses to tenants at prices well below their market value was popular with tenants. Industries that were losing money, such as British Airways, British Steel, and the coal mines, had to be reorganized, and unprofitable activities were shed to make them attractive to buyers. Industries needing large public subsidies to maintain public services, such as the railways, have continued to receive subsidies after privatization.

Privatization has been justified on grounds of economic efficiency (the market is better than civil servants at determining investment, production, and prices), political ideology (the power of government is reduced), service (private enterprise is more consumer oriented than are civil servants), and short-term financial gain (the sale of public assets can provide billions in revenue for government). Although the Labour Party initially opposed privatization, it quickly realized it would be electorally disastrous to take back privatized council houses and shares that people had bought at bargain prices.

Since many privatized industries affect the public interest, new regulatory agencies have been established to monitor telephones, gas, electricity, broadcasting, and water. Where there is a substantial element of monopoly in an industry, the government regulatory agency seeks to promote competition and often has the power to fix price increases at a lower rate than inflation. Even though it no longer owns an industry, government ministers cannot ignore things that go wrong. As an extreme example of government intervention, when several fatal accidents occurred on railway track maintained by a privatized transport company, the Blair government took it back into public ownership.

## From Trust to Contract

Historically, the British civil service has relied on trust in delivering policies. British civil servants are much less rule bound than are their German counterparts and less threatened with being dragged into court than are U.S. officials. Intragovernmental relations between Whitehall departments and representatives of local authorities were characterized by consensual understandings upheld by all sides on the basis of trust as well as law. However, the Thatcher government preferred to constrain local government through its use of law and its control of finance and to promote competition by establishing new agencies or contracting for public services with private-sector companies. Since 1997 the Labour government has continued this practice and has intensified the use of targets that agencies receiving public money should meet.

Trust has been replaced by contracts with agencies delivering such everyday services as automobile licenses and patents. In addition, the government has sought to keep capital expenditures from visibly increasing public debt through private finance initiatives. Banks and other profit-making companies loan money to build facilities that will be leased by government agencies or even operated by profit-making companies. The theory is that government can obtain the greatest value for its money by buying services from the private sector, ranging from operating staff canteens in government offices to providing prison services. However, the government's experience with cost overruns and failure to meet targets for information technology services costing hundreds of millions of pounds indicates that government officials often lack the skills to negotiate procurement contracts for large purchases involving expensive technology.

Government by contract faces political limits because departmental ministers must answer to Parliament when something goes wrong. The Prison

Service is a textbook example. It was established as an executive agency separate from Whitehall in 1993 to bring in private management to reduce unit costs in the face of a rising "demand" for prisons brought about by changes in crime rates and sentencing policies. However, when prisoners escaped and other problems erupted, the responsible Cabinet minister blamed the business executive brought in to head the Prison Service. The Prison Service head replied by attacking the minister's refusal to live up to the terms of the contract agreed to between them.

The proliferation of agencies, each with a distinctive and narrow responsibility for a limited number of policies, tends to fragment government. For example, parents may have to deal with half a dozen different agencies to secure all the public services to which they are entitled for their children. Tony Blair promoted "joined up" government, linking the provision of related services so that they could more easily be received by individual citizens. To many public agencies, this looked like a device to increase Downing Street's power. In fact, it had little effect and demonstrated the limits that result when a few dozen people at Downing Street determine what is done by millions of people delivering public services.

### The Contingency of Influence

The theory of British government is centralist: All roads lead to Downing Street, where the prime minister and the chancellor of the Exchequer have their homes and offices. The Foreign Office and the Treasury are only a few steps away. In practice, policy making occurs in many buildings, some within Whitehall and others far from London. Those involved can be divided horizontally between ministries and executive agencies and vertically between central government and local authorities and other nondepartmental public bodies that deliver particular services.

Influence is contingent: It varies with the problem at hand. Decisions about war and peace are made at Downing Street by the highest-ranking political and military officials. With respect to the decision to support the Iraq War, the prime minister's media advisor was also heavily involved. By contrast, the decisions as to whether a particular piece of land should be used for housing is normally made by local authorities far from London.

Most political decisions involve two or more government agencies and therefore require discussion and bargaining before decisions can be implemented. The making of policy is constrained by disputes within government much more than by differences between the governing party and its opponents. Many tentacles of the octopus of government work against each other, as public agencies often differ in their definition of the public interest. For example, the Treasury wants to keep taxes down, while the Ministry of Defence want more money for expensive equipment.

While the center of central government has been pressing harder on other public agencies, Whitehall itself has been losing influence because of its obligations in the EU. The Single Europe Act promotes British exports, but it also increases the potential for EU decisions to regulate the British economy. Whitehall has adopted a variety of strategies in its EU negotiations, including noncooperation and public dispute. Ironically, these are just the tactics that local government and executive agencies use when they disagree with Whitehall.

### WHY PUBLIC POLICY MATTERS

However a citizen votes, she or he does not need to look far to see the outputs of government. If there is a school-age child or a pensioner in the house, the benefits to the family are continuous and visible. If a person is ill, the care provided by doctors and hospitals is an important output of public policy; so, too, are police protection and tight controls on land use that maintain green belts and reduce suburban sprawl around cities.

To produce the benefits of public policy, government relies on three major resources: laws, money, and personnel. Most policies involve a combination of these resources, but they do not do so equally. Policies regulating individual behavior, such as marriage and divorce, are law intensive; measures that pay benefits to millions of people, such as social security, are money intensive; and public services, such as health care, are labor intensive.

Laws are the unique resource of government, for private enterprises cannot enact binding laws and contracts are effective only if they can be enforced by courts. The British executive centralizes the power to draft laws and regulations that can be approved without substantial amendment by Parliament. Moreover, many laws give ministers significant discretion in administration. For example, an employer may be required to provide "reasonable" toilet facilities, rather than having all features of lavatories specified down to the size and height of a toilet seat.

Public employees are needed to administer laws and deliver major services. The number of people officially counted as civil servants and public employees has been reduced by privatization. Nonetheless, more than a fifth of the entire British labor force depends on public spending for their jobs. The largest public employer is the National Health Service. The top civil servants who work in Whitehall are few in number.

To meet the costs of public policy, British government collects almost two-fifths of the gross national product in taxation. Income tax accounts for 29 percent of tax revenue; the top rate of taxation is 40 percent. Social security taxes are paid by deductions from wages and additional contributions of employers; these account for an additional 19 percent of revenue. Since there are no state or local income taxes, a well-to-do British person can pay taxes on income at a lower total rate than does an American subject to federal, state, and local taxation in New York City.

Taxes on consumption are important, too. There is a value-added tax of 17.5 percent on the sale of almost all goods and services. Gasoline, cigarettes, and alcohol are taxed very heavily, too. Taxes on consumption in total account for one-quarter of all tax revenue. Since profits fluctuate from year to year, the government prefers businesses to pay taxes on their gross revenues through a value-added tax and on their total wages bill through the employer's contribution to social security. Taxes on the profits of corporations provide under a tenth of tax revenue. Additional revenue comes from "stealth" taxes that ordinary citizens rarely notice and from taxes that do cause complaints, such as the council tax on houses. The government also raises money by taking a big cut from the National Lottery; more people play the lottery than vote in a general election.

Social security programs are the most costly government policies; they account for more than one-third of total public expenditures (Figure 8.8). They are also the most popular, transferring money from government to more than 10 million older people receiving pensions, plus millions of invalids, the unemployed, women on maternity leave, and poor people needing to supplement their limited incomes. Health and education are second and third, respectively, in their claims on the public purse. Together, these three social welfare programs

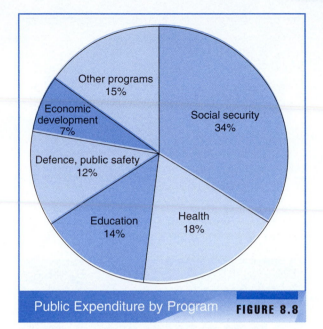

Public Expenditure by Program    **FIGURE 8.8**

Source: Office for National Statistics, 2004. *United Kingdom National Accounts. The Blue Book.* London: The Stationary Office, pages 276ff.

account for two-thirds of total public expenditures. A classic commitment of government—providing defense and maintaining public order and safety through the police, fire service, courts, and prisons—is fourth in spending importance.

Since there is no item in the public budget labeled as "waste," any government wanting to make a big cut in public spending must squeeze existing programs—and big savings can be made only by squeezing popular programs. But doing so would go against public opinion. When Margaret Thatcher entered office in 1979, the public divided into three almost equal groups: those wanting to spend more and tax more, those wanting to cut taxes even if it meant a reduction in public services, and a large middle group wanting to leave things as they were. Thatcher's campaign to cut taxes and public spending initially produced a reaction in favor of increasing public expenditure. By the time she left office, a majority favored increased spending even if it meant increased taxes. However, since a Labour government took office in 1997, the pendulum has swung back to an almost equal division between those who want to cut taxes and spending and those who want to increase both, with the median group wanting to keep both as they are (Figure 8.9).

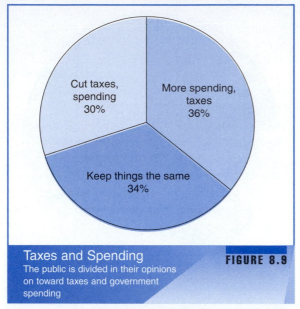

Cut taxes,
spending
30%

More spending,
taxes
36%

Keep things the same
34%

**Taxes and Spending**
The public is divided in their opinions
on toward taxes and government
spending

**FIGURE 8.9**

Source: Secondary analysis of British Social Attitudes Survey, 2006.
Number of respondents: 2,812.

## Policy Outcomes in Society

Public policies are meant to influence how people live, but only a totalitarian government would claim responsibility for everything that happens in society. In an open society such as Britain, social conditions reflect the interaction of public policies, the national and international economy, the not-for-profit institutions of civil society, and the choices that individuals and households make. Thus, the term *welfare state* is misleading to the extent that it implies that the state is the exclusive supplier of welfare. Total welfare in society is the sum of a "welfare mix," combining actions of government, the market, and the nonmonetized production of welfare in the household.[41]

Although commentators on British society often bemoan the country's decline relative to the much more populous United States and to continental European countries that have experienced dynamic economies, ordinary people do not compare their lives with those of people in other countries. The most important comparison is with their own past. Evaluating change across time shows great improvements in the living conditions of most people, as compared with their parents or grandparents. The longer the time span, the greater the improvement. Furthermore, in the production of such political "goods" as freedom from the state,

confidence in the honesty of public officials, and administrative flexibility, British government remains an international leader. The great majority of people are proud of the achievements of Britain and would not want to be citizens of any other country.

Defending the population against threats to security at home and abroad is a unique responsibility of government. In an interdependent world, British government participates in international alliances. Since World War II it has been a founding member of the North Atlantic Treaty Organization and has fought alongside the United States from the Korean War to the Iraq War. Maintaining order within the United Kingdom is a unique responsibility of Westminster. In Northern Ireland Whitehall has created a power-sharing government after very lengthy negotiations with Irish Republicans about giving up the use of arms.[42]

Since terrorist attacks by jihadists in London in 2005, the British government has pursued a multiplicity of measures in an attempt to identify, isolate, and, as appropriate, arrest and jail those planning violence. One strategy has been to encourage moderate Muslim groups to engage in the "self-policing" of their communities. Another has been to maintain surveillance on individuals and groups voicing fanatical opinions, including the endorsement of violence. A third has been to use extraordinary police powers to arrest and interrogate suspects.

Conservative as well as Labour governments accept responsibility for the economy. Most firms are profit-making, consumers can spend money as they like, and wages and prices are principally decided in the marketplace. Government influences the market through taxing and spending policies, interest rates, and policies on growth and unemployment. Increasingly, what happens to the British economy is also influenced by what happens elsewhere in the EU and on other continents, too, for British government cannot isolate the country from the global economy.

In each decade since World War II, the British economy has grown; compounding a small annual rate of growth over many decades results in a large rise in living standards. Per capita national income has more than tripled since 1945. Many consumer goods that were once thought of as luxuries—such as owning a car or a home or spending holidays abroad—are now mass-consumption goods. In addition, things unknown in 1945—such as color televisions, home computers, and mobile phones—are now commonplace. In the past decade the British economy has grown by one-third. Its growth rate has been higher than the average for the EU and for the G–7 nations.

Poverty can be found in Britain; the extent depends on the definition used. If poverty is defined in relative terms, such as having less than half the average wage, then about 10 percent of Britons are living in relative poverty. If poverty is defined as being trapped at a low income level for many years, then less than 4 percent are long-term poor.

Looking at all the major indicators of social well-being, the British people enjoy a higher standard of living today than they did a generation or two ago. Infant mortality has declined by more than four-fifths since 1951. Life expectancy for men and for women has risen by 12 years. A gender gap remains, as women on average live five years longer than men. The postwar expansion of schools has significantly raised the quantity of education available. Classes are smaller in size, and almost half of British youths go on to some form of further education, whether in universities or colleges, many of which did not exist in 1950. More than two-thirds of families now own their own home, and nine-tenths report satisfaction with their housing.

The outputs of public policy play a significant part in the everyday life of all Britons. Everyone makes major use of publicly financed health and education services. Children at school and patients seeing a doctor do not think of themselves as participating in politics. Yet, the services received are controlled and paid for by government. Social benefits such as free education, free health care, and the guarantee of an income in old age or during unemployment are so taken for granted today that most people see them as nonpolitical. People do not want a change in government after an election to result in radical changes in major social policies.

British people do not hold government responsible for what is most important in their lives; life satisfaction is evaluated very differently from public policy. When opinion polls annually ask what people think next year will be like for themselves and their family, nine-tenths of the time a majority say they expect the coming year to be all right for themselves, even when many expect economic difficulties for the country as a whole. When people are asked to evaluate their lives, they are most satisfied with their family, friends, home, and job and least satisfied with major political institutions of society.[43]

Satisfaction with the present goes along with acceptance of the principle of political change. However, even when a goal is agreed on, there are differences about the particular policy that can best achieve that goal. There are disagreements about the direction of change—for example, whether Westminster should take more responsibility for public services or devolve more responsibilities to regions and municipalities, and whether Britain should align itself more closely with the United States or with the EU. Politics in Britain is thus an ongoing debate about the direction, the means, and the tempo of adapting old institutions and inherited policies to the twenty-first century.

## REVIEW QUESTIONS

- How would you describe the unwritten constitution of Britain?
- What are the similarities and differences between being a president and being a prime minister?
- How many nations are there in the United Kingdom, and what are they?
- What are the continents and countries with which Britain has the closest links?
- How would you describe the different parties that have seats in the House of Commons?
- What policies claim the largest portion of public expenditures and why?
- What will be the main challenges facing the winning government after the next general election?

## KEY TERMS

Cabinet

centralization

class

collectivist theory of
 government

Conservative Party

core executive

Crown

decentralization

devolution

Downing Street

first-past-the-post
 electoral system

government

individualist theory

insider and outsider
 pressure groups

Irish Republican Army (IRA)

Labour Party

Liberal Democratic Party

multiparty system

New Labour Party

Northern Ireland

official secrecy

Parliament

prime minister

privatization

quasi-autonomous
 nongovernmental
 organization (quango)

Scotland

territorial justice

Thatcherism

trusteeship theory of
 government

United Kingdom

unwritten constitution

Wales

Westminster

Whitehall

## SUGGESTED READINGS

Bache, Ian, and Andrew Jordan, eds. *The Europeanization of British Politics*. Basingstoke, England: Palgrave Macmillan, 2006.

Butler, D. E., and Geraint Butler. *British Political Facts Since 1979*. Basingstoke, England: Palgrave Macmillan, 2006.

_____. *Twentieth Century British Political Facts, 1900–2000*. 8th ed. Basingstoke, England: Macmillan, 2000.

Flinders, Matthew. *The Politics of Accountability in the Modern State*. Aldershot, England: Ashgate, 2001.

Hazell, Robert, ed. *The English Question*. London: Constitution Unit, 2006.

Ingle, Stephen. *The British Party System*. 4th ed. London: Routledge, 2008.

Jordan, Grant, and William A. Maloney. *Democracy and Interest Groups*. Basingstoke, England: Palgrave Macmillan, 2007.

Kavanagh, Dennis, and David Butler. *The British General Election of 2005*. Basingstoke, England: Palgrave Macmillan, 2005.

McGarvey, Neil, and Paul Cairney. *Scottish Politics: An Introduction*. Basingstoke, England: Palgrave Macmillan, 2008.

Moran, Michael. *The British Regulatory State: High Modernism and Hyper-Innovation*. New York: Oxford University Press, 2003.

Norris, Pippa, and Joni Lovenduski. *Political Recruitment: Gender, Race, and Class in the British Parliament*. New York: Cambridge University Press, 1995.

Norris, Pippa, and Christopher Wlezien, eds. *Britain Votes 2005*. Oxford, England: Oxford University Press, 2005.

Oliver, Dawn. *Constitutional Reform in the United Kingdom*. New York: Oxford University Press, 2003.

Page, Edward C., and Bill Jenkins. *Policy Bureaucracy: Government with a Cast of Thousands*. Oxford, England: Oxford University Press, 2005.

Park, Alison, ed. *British Social Attitudes Survey: The 24th Report*. Thousand Oaks, CA: Sage, 2008.

Pattie, Charles, Patrick Seyd, and Paul Whitely. *Citizenship in Britain*. New York: Cambridge University Press, 2004.

Rallings, Colin, and Michael Thrasher. *British Electoral Facts, 1832–2006*. Aldershot, England: Ashgate, 2007.

Rose, Richard. *The Prime Minister in a Shrinking World*. Boston: Polity Press, 2001.

Rose, Richard, and Phillip L. Davies. *Inheritance in Public Policy: Change Without Choice in Britain*. New Haven, CT: Yale University Press, 1994.

Seldon, Anthony. *Blair*. New York: Free Press, 2004.

Seldon, Anthony, Peter Seldon, and Daniel Collings. *Blair Unbound*. New York: Simon and Schuster, 2007.

Smith, Martin J. *The Core Executive in Britain*. London: Macmillan, 1999.

*Social Trends*. London: Stationery Office, annual.

*Whitaker's Almanack*. London: J. Whitaker, annual.

Wilson, David, and Game, Chris. *Local Government in the United Kingdom*. 4th ed. Basingstoke, England: Palgrave Macmillan, 2007.

## INTERNET RESOURCES

Site of British government departments. **www.gov.uk.**

Site of the House of Commons and of the House of Lords. **www.parliament.uk.**

Prime Minister's site. **www.pm.gov.uk.**

Comprehensive coverage of United Kingdom and global news. **www.news.bbc.co.uk.**

Commentaries on current proposals to reform government, **www.ucl.ac.uk/constitution-unit.**

Reports results of its frequent public opinion polls. **www.ipsos-mori.com/polls.**

Official cite of the Political Studies Association, the professional body of British political scientists. **www.psa.ac.uk.**

## ENDNOTES

1. See Richard Rose, *What Is Europe? A Dynamic Perspective* (New York: Addison Wesley Longman, 1996), ch. 3.

2. *Gallup Political and Economic Index* (London) no. 390 (February 1993): 42.

3. Quoted in Krishna Guha, "Labour Escapes from Its Bloody Tower," *Financial Times,* August 24, 2002.

4. Quoted in John Kampfner and David Wighton, "Reeling in Scotland to Bring England in Step," *Financial Times,* April 5, 1997.

5. See Richard Rose, "England: A Traditionally Modern Political Culture," in *Political Culture and Political Development,* ed. Lucian W. Pye and Sidney Verba (Princeton, NJ: Princeton University Press, 1965), pp. 83–129.

6. Quoted in Richard Rose, *Do Parties Make a Difference?* 2nd ed. (Chatham, NJ: Chatham House, 1984), p. xv.

7. Andrew Dilnot and Paul Johnson, eds., *Election Briefing 1997* (Commentary 60) (London: Institute for Fiscal Studies, 1997), p. 2.

8. John Kampfner and David Wighton, "Blair Seals Labour's Switch to Low Tax Party," *Financial Times,* March 27, 1997.

9. Quoted in Peter Hennessy, "Raw Politics Decide Procedure in Whitehall," New Statesman (London), October 24, 1986, p. 10.

10. Winston Churchill, *Their Finest Hour* (London: Cassell, 1949), p. 14.

11. See Richard Rose, *The Prime Minister in a Shrinking World* (Boston: Polity Press, 2001), fig. 6.1.

12. Lord Butler of Brockwell, quoted in George Jones, "Blair Savaged on spain", *Daily Telegraph* (London) December 11, 2004.

13. For transatlantic comparisons of presidents and prime ministers, see Richard Rose, "Giving Direction to Government in Comparative Perspective," in *The Executive Branch,* ed. Joel Aberbach and Mark A. Peterson (New York: Oxford University Press, 2005), pp. 72-99.

14. Walter Bagehot, *The English Constitution* (London: World's Classics, 1955), p. 9.

15. David Leppard and Robert Winnett, "Blair Blames Ministers for Policy Gaffes," *Sunday Times* (London), April 18, 2004.

16. Careers in the Civil Service. London: First Division Association 1987, p.12.

17. Quoted by David Leppard, "ID Cards Doomed, Say Officials," *Sunday Times* (London), July 9, 2006. See also an interview with Sir Robin Butler, "How Not to Run a Country," *Spectator* (London), December 11, 2004.

18. Quoted in "Whitehall Remains Closed to Outsiders and Needs Radical Change, Report Says," *Times* (London), August 7, 2006.

19. Eric Varley, quoted in A. Michie and S. Hoggart, *The Pact* (London: Quartet Books, 1978), p. 13.

20. Hugh Heclo and Aaron Wildavsky, *The Private Government of Public Money* (London: Macmillan, 1974).

21. Bernard Ingham, press secretary to Margaret Thatcher, quoted in Richard Rose, "British Government: The Job at the Top," in *Presidents and Prime Ministers,* ed. R. Rose and E. Suleiman (Washington, DC: American Enterprise Institute, 1980), p. 43.

22. See Samuel H. Beer, *Modern British Politics,* 3rd ed. (London: Faber and Faber, 1982).

23. House of Commons, *Hansard* (London: Her Majesty's Stationery Office), November 11, 1947, col. 206.

24. The words of former Conservative Prime Minister John Major, "The Threat to Liberty Is Graver than Terrorism," *Times* (London), June 6, 2008.

25. Colin Bennett, "From the Dark to the Light: The Open Government Debate in Britain," *Journal of Public Policy* 5, no. 2 (1985): 209,

26. Quoted in Sean O'Neill, "Too Sensitive to Reveal, Minister," *Times* (London), October 3, 2005.

27. See Richard Rose and Ian McAllister, *The Loyalties of Voters* (Newbury Park, CA: Sage, 1990), ch. 3.

28. Quoted in Maurice Kogan, *The Politics of Education* (Harmondsworth, England: Penguin, 1971), p. 135.

29. See the Fulton Committee, *Report,* vol. 1, pp. 27ff., and Appendix E, especially p. 162.

30. Sir Ken Jackson, quoted in Krishna Guha, "Engineers and Electricians Turn Away from Moderate Traditions," *Financial Times,* July 19, 2002.

31. See W. A. Maloney, G. Jordan, and A. M. McLaughlin, "Interest Groups and Public Policy: The Insider/Outsider Model Revisited," *Journal of Public Policy* 14, no. 1 (1994): 17–38.

32. See Ministry of Justice, *Review of Voting Systems* (Cm. 7304) (London: Stationery Office, 2008).

33. The Conservative Party used the first title and the Labour Party the second.

34. For details, see Denis Van Mechelen and Richard Rose, *Patterns of Parliamentary Legislation* (Aldershot, England: Gower, 1986), tab. 8.2, and more generally, Rose, *Do Parties Make a Difference?*

35. Richard Rose and Phillip L. Davies, *Inheritance in Public Policy: Change Without Choice in Britain* (New Haven, CT: Yale University Press, 1994), p. 28.

36. Reginald Maudling, quoted in David Butler and Michael Pinto-Duschinsky, *The British General Election of 1970* (London: Macmillan, 1971), p. 62.

37. See *Better Government Services: Executive Agencies in the 21st Century* (London: Office of Public Service Reforms and the Treasury, 2002).

38. Sir Leo Pliatzky, quoted in Peter Hennessy, "The Guilt of the Treasury 1000," *New Statesman* (London), January 23, 1987.

39. See Paul Peterson, "The American Mayor: Elections and Institutions," *Parliamentary Affairs* 53, no. 4 (2000): 667–679.

40. David Butler, Andrew Adonis, and Tony Travers, *Failure in British Government: The Politics of the Poll Tax* (Oxford, England: Oxford University Press, 1994).

41. See Richard Rose, "The Dynamics of the Welfare Mix in Britain," in *The Welfare State East and West,* ed. Richard Rose and Rei Shiratori (New York: Oxford University Press, 1986), pp. 80–106.

42. Jonathan Powell, *Great Hatred, Little Room: Making Peace in Northern Ireland* (London: Bodley Head, 2008).

43. Richard Rose, *Ordinary People in Public Policy: A Behavioural Analysis* (Newbury Park, CA: Sage, 1989), pp. 175ff.

# POLITICS IN FRANCE

*Martin A. Schain*

## Country Bio

**Population**
63.8 million

**Territory**
211,208 square miles

**Year of Independence**
486

**Year of Current Constitution**
1958

**Head of State**
President Nicolas Sarkozy

**Head of Government**
Prime Minister François Fillon

**Languages**
French 100%, with rapidly declining regional dialects (Provença, Breton, Alsatian, Corsican, Catalan, Basque, Flemish)

**Religion**
Roman Catholic 89.5%, Muslim 7.5%, Protestant 2%, Jewish 1

FRANCE

Attracted by his dynamic image and promises of reform, a large majority of the French public elected Nicolas Sarkozy to the presidency of France in May 2007. A month later Sarkozy's party won a majority in the National Assembly, and he followed the election with a whirlwind of activities and initiatives. Two years later, however, as the economic crisis spread, Sarkozy's approval rating was as low as that of his predecessor, **Jacques Chirac,** and he was struggling to maintain the loyalty of his own majority.

The French electorate has been highly critical of those who have governed them under the **Fifth Republic.** In every legislative election between 1981 and 2007, they have favored the opposition. Nevertheless, French citizens now appear to have more confidence in the key institutions of the Republic than at any time in French history. Increasingly, however, they have little confidence in the politicians who are running them. The stability of the Republic has surprised many of the French, as well as the outside world. By combining two models of democratic government, the presidential and the parliamentary, the Fifth Republic has succeeded in a

constitutional experiment that now serves France well. For the first time since the French Revolution, there is no important political party or sector of public opinion that challenges the legitimacy of the regime.

## CURRENT POLICY CHALLENGES

At a time in U.S. history when the party system is highly polarized around fundamental socioeconomic issues and the government is immersed in a war that has divided the country, French politics—at least most of the time—seems almost tranquil by comparison. The French have lived with divided government (*cohabitation*) for most of the period since 1986 without its impeding government effectiveness or undermining institutional legitimacy. At the same time, the French electorate is clearly concerned about many of the same issues that concern Americans.

In 2008 French citizens were most worried about the economy, unemployment, crime, and urban violence. These problems are often considered problems of the "suburbs," since impoverished neighborhoods, frequently with large immigrant populations, are often found in the old working-class suburbs surrounding large cities. In the fall of 2005, suburban youth rioted for three weeks, burning thousands of automobiles and some public buildings. A few months later mostly middle-class students in high schools and universities closed down much of the education system. In 2009, as the economic crisis deepened, vast strike movements, which once again centered on the education system, spread throughout the country.

Unemployment rates in France have recently averaged about a third higher than U.S. rates. Anxiety about unemployment is related to deep concern about the consequences of being a member of the **European Union (EU).** This, in part, explains the rejection of the European constitutional treaty in 2005. Finally, voters are increasingly disturbed by their relatively new president.

We should emphasize that many of the issues at the heart of contemporary American politics are of little concern to the French. French citizens are not much concerned about the size of the state. Recent conservative governments have tried to reduce the level of public spending, but there is little support for massive cuts in the welfare state programs. Such welfare programs have always been more extensive in France than in the United States. In fact, surveys show that French voters are willing to sacrifice a great deal to maintain these programs, as well as state-subsidized social security and long vacations. Although unemployment rates in France are a third higher than those of the United States, its poverty rate is among the lowest in the advanced industrial democracies and less than half that of the United States.

On the other hand, unlike their American counterparts, French voters are deeply concerned about the environmental and health consequences of genetically modified organisms. Far more than Americans, French citizens are willing to pay for efforts to reduce pollution. Gas prices are more than double those in the United States, and state subsidies for a growing public transportation network are not challenged by public opinion.

Multiculturalism related to integrating a large and growing Muslim population (the largest in Europe) is another important policy challenge. In an effort to promote civic integration, the government passed legislation in 2004 prohibiting students in public schools from wearing conspicuous religious symbols, including Islamic head scarves worn by women. Since the riots of 2005 and 2006, the government has promised reforms to address the special needs of immigrants. These promises have resulted in few concrete proposals, but they have renewed public debates on public policy toward immigrants.

Finally, although there was widespread sympathy for the United States just after the September 11, 2001, attacks on the World Trade Center and the Pentagon, there was a perceptible rise in anti-American sentiment and distrust of American policy in the wake of these events. This distrust generated a major transatlantic crisis when France took the lead in resisting the American-led military action against Iraq in the spring of 2003. A broad consensus of public opinion and political parties supported French opposition to the war. These tensions have moderated since Sarkozy became president, but the U.S.-French relationship will experience further change with the new American administration that entered office in 2009.

Nicolas Sarkozy was swept into office in June 2007 and gained considerable acclaim by appointing both minority women and Socialists to his Cabinet. During his first year in office, however, the government passed relatively little legislation to deal with the problems on which he focused during the presidential campaign. An example of the challenges that he faced was the government's difficulty in passing what were widely considered to be uncontroversial constitutional reforms, even though the opposition Socialists generally agreed with Sarkozy's proposed reforms (although they wanted them to go further). The reforms finally passed by a single vote in July 2008. By the end of 2008, the president's program was constrained even further by the emerging economic crisis, and by massive strikes in reaction to presidential proposals to reorganize the education system. Indeed France was the only major industrial society in which the reaction to the declining economy has been growing social unrest.

## A HISTORICAL PERSPECTIVE

France is one of the oldest nation-states of Europe. The period of unstable revolutionary regimes that followed the storming of the Bastille in 1789 ended in the seizure of power by **Napoléon Bonaparte** a decade later. The French Revolution began with the establishment of a constitutional monarchy in 1791 (the First Republic), but the monarchy was overthrown the following year. Three more constitutions preceded Napoléon's seizure of power on the eighteenth day of the revolutionary month of Brumaire (November 10, 1799) and the establishment of the First Empire three years later. The other European powers formed an alliance and forced Napoléon's surrender, as well as the restoration of the Bourbon monarchy. Another revolution in 1830 drove the last Bourbon from the French throne and replaced him with Louis Philippe of the House of Orléans. He promised a more moderate rule bounded by a new constitution.

Growing dissatisfaction among the rising bourgeoisie and the urban population produced still another Paris revolution in 1848. With it came the proclamation of the Second Republic (1848–1852) and universal male suffrage. Conflict between its middle-class and lower-class components, however, kept the republican government ineffective. Out of the disorder rose another Napoléon, Louis Napoléon, nephew of the first emperor. He was crowned Napoléon III in 1852 and brought stability to France for more than a decade. However, his last years were marked by growing indecision and ill-conceived foreign ventures. His defeat and capture in the Franco-Prussian War (1870) began another turbulent period. France was occupied and forced into a humiliating armistice; radicals in Paris proclaimed the Paris Commune, which held out for two months in 1871, until crushed by the conservative government forces. In the commune's aftermath, the struggle between republicans and monarchists led to the establishment of a conservative Third Republic in 1871. The Third Republic was the longest regime in modern France, surviving World War I and lasting until France's defeat and occupation by Nazi Germany in 1940.

World War II deeply divided France. A defeated France was divided into a zone occupied by the Germans and a "free" Vichy zone in the southern half of France, where Marshall Pétain led a government sympathetic to the Germans. From July 1940 until August 1944, the government of France was a dictatorship. Slowly, a resistance movement emerged under the leadership of General **Charles de Gaulle**. It gained increased strength and support after the Allied invasion of North Africa and the German occupation of the Vichy zone at the end of 1942. When German forces were driven from occupied Paris in 1944, de Gaulle entered the city with the hope that sweeping reforms would give France the viable democracy it had long sought. After less than two years, he resigned as head of the Provisional Government, impatient with the country's return to traditional party politics.

In fact, the **Fourth Republic** (1946–1958) disappointed many hopes. Governments fell with disturbing regularity—twenty-four governments in twelve years. At the same time, because of the narrowness of government coalitions, the same parties and the same leaders tended to participate in most of these governments. Weak leadership had great difficulty coping with the tensions created first by the Cold War, then by the French war in Indochina, and finally by the anticolonialist uprising in Algeria.

When a threat of civil war arose over Algeria in 1958, a group of leaders invited de Gaulle to return to power and help the country establish stronger and more stable institutions. De Gaulle and his supporters formulated a new constitution for the Fifth Republic, which was enacted by a referendum in 1958. De Gaulle was the last prime minister of the Fourth Republic and then the first president of the newly established Fifth Republic.

## ECONOMY AND SOCIETY

Geographically, France is at once Atlantic, Continental, and Mediterranean; hence, it occupies a unique place in Europe. In 2008 a total of 63.8 million people, about one-fourth as many as the population of the United States, lived in an area one-fifteenth the size of the United States. More than 3.6 million foreigners (noncitizens) live in France, more than half of whom come from outside of Europe, mostly from North Africa and Africa. In addition, nearly 2 million French citizens are foreign-born. Thus, almost 10 percent of the French population is foreign-born, slightly less than the proportion of foreign-born in the United States.

Urbanization has come slowly to France, but it is now highly urbanized. In 1936 only sixteen French cities had a population of more than 100,000; they now number thirty-six. Compared with European countries with similar population (Britain and Germany), France has relatively few large cities; only Paris has more than a million people. Yet in 2002, 44 million people (three-quarters of the population) lived in urban areas, compared with half that number in 1936.

Almost one-quarter of the urban population—more than one-sixth of the entire nation and growing—lives in the metropolitan region of Paris. This concentration of people creates staggering problems. In a country with centuries-old traditions of administrative, economic, and cultural centralization, it has produced a dramatic gap in human and material resources between Paris and the rest of the country. The Paris region supports a per capita income almost 50 percent higher and unemployment substantially lower than the national average. The Paris region also has the highest concentration of foreigners in the country (twice the national percentage), and there are deep divisions between the wealthier and the poorer towns in the region.

Recent French economic development compares well with that of other advanced industrial countries. In per capita gross domestic product (GDP), France ranks among the wealthiest nations of the world, behind the Scandinavian countries, the United States, and Britain; it is ahead of Germany, Japan, and Italy and the average for the EU (see Chapter 1). During the period from 1996 to 2006, the French economy grew at about the EU average, but with an inflation rate at a little more than half the European average. Nevertheless, with estimates that the economy will contract by almost 3 percent by mid-2009, France now faces its greatest economic crisis since the Great Depression.[1]

Unemployment dipped after 1997 as the economy created new jobs, but it remains relatively high, compared with the averages of the EU and the United States. In 2008, with an unemployment rate of 7.8 percent, France was already experiencing some of the same problems as some of the poorer countries of Europe: long-term youth unemployment, homelessness, and a drain on social services. More than 40 percent of those unemployed in 2004 were the long-term unemployed (those without work for more than one year), a rate far higher than that of Britain, but less than those of Germany and Italy. Indeed, long-term unemployment rates have crept up, even though youth unemployment has declined significantly during the past fifteen years. All of these problems were projected to grow worse in 2009, as unemployment moved rapidly higher.

The labor force has changed drastically since the end of World War II, making France similar to other industrialized countries. During the 1990s the labor force grew by more than 1.6 million, continuing a growth trend that was greater than in most European countries. Most of these new workers were young people, and an increasing proportion consisted of women. For over a century, the proportion of employed women—mostly in agriculture, artisan shops, and factories—was higher in France than in most European countries. Today most women work in offices in the service sector of the economy. In 1954 women made up 35 percent of the labor force; today they make up 46 percent. The proportion of French women working (65 percent) is slightly lower than that of the United States, but one of the highest in Western Europe.

In 1938, 37 percent of French labor was employed in agriculture; this proportion was less than 3.5 percent in 2005. The percentage of the labor force employed in industry was down to about 24 percent, while employment in the service sector rose from 33 percent in 1938 to 71 percent today, slightly above the average for Western Europe.

By comparison with other advanced industrial countries, the agricultural sector of France remains important both economically and politically. France has more cultivated acreage than any other country in the EU. In spite of the sharp decline in the proportion of the population engaged in agriculture, agricultural production increased massively during the past quarter century.

Since 1945 there have been serious efforts to modernize agriculture, such as farm cooperatives, the consolidation of marginal farms, and improvements in technical education. Particularly after the development of the Common Agriculture Policy (CAP) in the European Community between 1962 and 1968, consolidation of farmland proceeded rapidly. By 1985 the average French farm was larger than that of any country in Europe except Britain, Denmark, and Luxembourg.

The EU has paid a large proportion of the bill for agricultural modernization, and subsidies have increased steadily. As a result, there are pressures (particularly from the British) to reduce CAP expenditures. With the enlargement of the EU in 2004 and the incorporation of more East European countries with large agricultural sectors, these pressures have increased. In addition to requiring the withdrawal of more land from production, major reforms in 1992, 1994, 1999, and 2003 at the European level have gradually moved subsidies away from price supports (that encourage greater production) and toward direct support of farm income. Nevertheless, total subsidies to French farmers through the CAP are greater than those provided to any other country.

French business is both highly dispersed and highly concentrated. Even after three decades of structural reorganization of business, about half of the 2.4 million industrial and commercial enterprises in France belong to individuals. In 1999, 54 percent of the salaried workers in the country worked in small enterprises with fewer than fifty workers. As in other advanced industrial societies, this proportion has been slowly increasing, primarily because of the movement of labor into the service sector.

From the perspective of production, some of the most advanced French industries are highly concentrated. The few firms at the top account for most of the employment and business sales. Even in some of the older sectors (such as automobile manufacture, ship construction, and rubber), half or more of the employment and sales are concentrated in the top four firms. The *Financial Times* reports that among the 500 largest industrial groups in the world in 2008, 31 were in France. France placed fifth in the number of firms on this list, behind the United States, Japan, the United Kingdom, and China, but ahead of all other European countries.

The organization of industry and commerce changed significantly during the 1990s. Privatization mandated by the EU has reduced the number of public enterprises by 24 percent and the number of those working in public enterprises by 31 percent. In 1997 among the top twenty enterprises in France, only four were public, compared with thirteen ten years before.

Despite a continuing process of privatization, relations between industry and the state remain close. In addition, more than 20 percent of the civilian labor force works in the civil service, which has grown about 10 percent during the past fifteen years.

## CONSTITUTION AND GOVERNMENT STRUCTURE

The **Constitution of 1958** is the sixteenth since the fall of the Bastille in 1789. Past republican regimes, known less for their achievements than for their instability, were invariably based on the principle that Parliament could overturn a government that lacked a parliamentary majority. Such an arrangement can work satisfactorily, as it does in most of Western Europe, when the country (and the parliament) embraces two—or a few—well-organized parties. The party or the coalition that gains a majority at the polls forms the government and can count on the support of its members in parliament until the next elections. At that time it is either kept in power or replaced by an equally disciplined party or coalition of parties.

### The Executive

De Gaulle's constitution for the Fifth Republic offered to remedy previous failings of French political parties and coalition politics. In preceding republics the president was little more than a figurehead. According to the new constitution, the **president of the Republic** is a visible head of state. He is to be placed "above the parties" to represent the unity of the national community. As guardian of the constitution, he is to be an arbiter who would rely on other powers—Parliament, the Cabinet, or the people—for the full weight of government action. He can appeal to the people in two ways. With the agreement of the government or Parliament, he can submit certain important legislation to the electorate as a referendum. In addition, after consulting with the prime minister and the parliamentary leaders, he can dissolve Parliament and call for new elections. In case of grave threat "to the institutions of the Republic," the president also has the option of invoking emergency powers.

Virtually all of the most powerful constitutional powers of the president—those that give the president formal power—have been used sparingly. Emergency powers were used only once by de Gaulle—in 1961 when the rebellion of the generals in Algiers clearly justified such use. De Gaulle dissolved Parliament twice (in 1962 and 1968), each time to strengthen the majority supporting presidential policies (see Figure 9.1).

Upon his election to the presidency in 1981, Socialist **François Mitterrand** dissolved the National Assembly. He did so again after his reelection seven years later in order have new parliamentary elections, expecting (correctly) that elections would provide him with a reliable majority. President Jacques Chirac dissolved the National Assembly in April 1997 in an attempt to extend the conservative majority into the next century and to gain political support for reduced public spending. The president lost his gamble.

| PRIME MINISTER | YEAR | PRESIDENT |
|---|---|---|
| Michel Debré | 1958 | Charles de Gaulle |
| Georges Pompidou | 1962 | |
| Maurice Couve de Murville | 1968 | |
| Jacques Chaban-Delmas | 1969 | Georges Pompidou |
| Pierre Messmer | 1972 | |
| Jacques Chirac | 1974 | Valéry Giscard d'Estaing |
| Raymond Barre | 1976 | |
| Pierre Mauroy | 1981 | François Mitterrand |
| Laurent Fabius | 1984 | |
| Jacques Chirac | 1986 | |
| Michel Rocard | 1988 | |
| Edith Cresson | 1991 | |
| Pierre Bérégovoy | 1992 | |
| Edouard Balladur | 1993 | |
| Alain Juppé | 1995 | Jacques Chirac |
| Lionel Jospin | 1997 | |
| Jean-Pierre Raffarin | 2002 | |
| Dominique di Villepin | 2005 | |
| François Fillon | 2007 | Nicolas Sarkozy |

**FIGURE 9.1**

French Presidents and Prime Ministers Since 1958

Direct popular elections to the office have greatly augmented the legitimacy and political authority of the president. Instead of the indirect election called for by the 1958 constitution, a constitutional amendment approved by referendum in 1962 provided for the popular election of the president for a renewable term of seven years. In September 2000 the presidential term was reduced to five years—again by constitutional amendment—to coincide with the normal five-year legislative term. France is one of six countries in Western Europe to select its president by direct popular vote.

De Gaulle outlined his view of the office when he said that power "emanates directly from the people, which implies that the Head of State, elected by the nation, is the source and holder of this power." Every president who has succeeded de Gaulle has maintained the general's basic interpretation of the office. But, as we shall see, there have been some changes in the way the presidency has functioned. The **prime minister** is appointed by the president and has responsibility for the day-to-day running of the government. In fact, the division of responsibility within the executive, between the president and the prime minister, has varied not only with the personalities of those who hold both offices, but also with the conditions under which they serve.

## The Legislature

The legislature is composed of two houses: the National Assembly and the Senate (see Figure 9.2). The **National Assembly** of 577 members is elected directly for five years by all citizens over age 18. The government may dissolve the legislature at any time, though not twice within one year. Experts have attributed the instability of previous regimes mostly to the constant meddling of Parliament with the activities of the executive. The 1958 constitution strove to end the subordination of government to Parliament. It imposed strict rules of behavior on each deputy and on Parliament as a body. These requirements, it was hoped, would ensure the needed equilibrium.

Under the 1958 rules, the government, rather than the legislature, controls proceedings in both houses and can require priority for bills it wishes to promote. The president, rather than the prime minister, generally chooses the Cabinet members, although this tends to be merely formal during periods of cohabitation. Parliament still enacts laws, but the domain of such laws is strictly defined. Many areas that in other democracies are regulated by laws debated

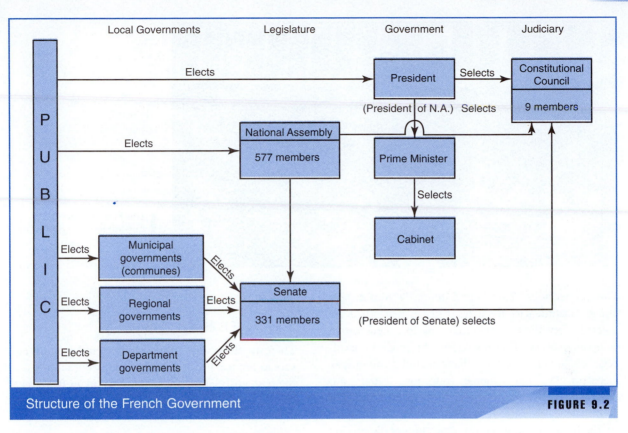

| Local Governments | Legislature | Government | Judiciary |
| --- | --- | --- | --- |

**Structure of the French Government**    **FIGURE 9.2**

and approved by Parliament are turned over to rule-making by the executive in France.

The nineteen standing committees of the National Assembly under the Fourth Republic were reduced to six in 1958. The sizes of the committees were enlarged to 73 to 145 members. This prevents interaction among highly specialized deputies who could become effective rivals of the ministers. Each deputy is restricted to one committee, and party groups are represented in each committee in proportion to their size in the National Assembly.

It is not surprising that the new constitution detailed the conditions under which the National Assembly could overthrow a government. More than one-half of the actual members of the house must formulate and pass an explicit motion of censure. Even after a motion of censure is passed, the government may resist the pressure to resign: The president can dissolve the National Assembly and call for new elections. During the first year after these elections, a new dissolution of the Assembly is prohibited by the constitution. The vote of censure is the only way Parliament can condemn the conduct of government, but

no government has been censured since 1962. Since that time every government has had a working (if not always friendly) majority in the National Assembly.

Thus, the government maintains considerable control over the legislative agenda, the content of legislation, and the conditions under which Parliament can debate legislative proposals. However, amendments to the constitution passed in July 2008 shifted the balance in important ways to the majority party. The National Assembly now has the right to fix its own agenda (half the time), and in the future it may be easier for Parliament to amend legislation. The number of parliamentary committees has been increased from six to eight. The bills considered by Parliament will be those reported out and amended by these committees, rather than those presented by the government (with a few exceptions).

The National Assembly shares legislative functions with the **Senate**. In all countries without a federal structure, the problem of how to organize a bicameral legislature is complex. How should the membership of the second chamber be defined if there are no territorial units to represent? The 331 members of the Senate

The French National Assembley, as seen from the Socialist seats.

Thomas Coex/AFP/Getty Images

(the "upper house") are elected indirectly from department constituencies for a term of six years (half are elected every three years—according to a new system adopted in 2003). They are selected by an electoral college of about 150,000, which includes municipal, departmental, and regional councilors. Rural constituencies are overrepresented. The Senate has the right to initiate legislation and must consider all bills adopted by the National Assembly. If the two houses disagree on pending legislation, the government can appoint a joint committee to resolve the differences. If the views of the two houses are not reconciled, the government may resubmit the bill (either in its original form or as amended by the Senate) to the National Assembly for a definitive vote (Article 45). Therefore, unlike the United States, the two houses are not equal in either power or influence (see again Figure 9.2).

### The Judiciary

Until the Fifth Republic, France had no judicial check on the constitutionality of the actions of its political authorities. The **Constitutional Council** was originally conceived primarily as a safeguard against any legislative erosion of the constraints that the constitution had placed on the prerogatives of Parliament.[2] Because of a constitutional amendment in 1974, however, the council now plays an important role in the legislative process. It is likely to play a more important judicial role as well because a constitutional amendment in 2008 gave the council appeal jurisdiction in cases in which the defendant claims that a law violates "rights and liberties" guaranteed by the constitution.

## POLITICAL CULTURE

### Themes of Political Culture

There are three ways that we understand political culture in France: history links present values to those of the past, abstraction and symbolism identify a way of thinking about politics, and distrust of government represents a dominant value that crosses class and generational lines.

*The Burden of History* Historical thinking can prove to be both a bond and—as the U.S. Civil War demonstrates—a hindrance to consensus. The French are so fascinated by their own history that feuds of the past are constantly superimposed on the conflicts of the present. This passionate use of historical memories—resulting in seemingly inflexible ambitions, warnings, and taboos—complicates political decisionmaking. In de Gaulle's words, France is "weighed down by history."

*Abstraction and Symbolism* In the Age of Enlightenment, the monarchy left the educated classes free to voice their views on many topics, provided the discussion remained general and abstract. The urge to discuss a wide range of problems, even trivial ones, in broad philosophical terms has hardly diminished. The exaltation of the abstract is reflected in the significance attributed to symbols and rituals. Rural communities that fought on opposite sides in the French Revolution still pay homage to different heroes two centuries later. They seem to have no real quarrel with each other, but inherited symbols and their political and religious habits have kept them apart.[3] This tradition helps explain why a nation united by almost universal admiration for a common historical experience holds to conflicting interpretations of its meaning.

*Distrust of Government and Politics* The French have long shared the widespread ambivalence of modern times that combines distrust of government with high expectations for it. The French citizens' simultaneous distrust of authority and craving for it feed on both individualism and a passion for equality. This attitude produces a self-reliant individual convinced that he is responsible to himself, and perhaps to his family, for what he was and might become. The outside world—the "they" who operate beyond the circle of the family, the family firm, and the village—creates obstacles in life. Most of the time, however, "they" are identified with the government.

Memories reaching back to the eighteenth century justify a state of mind that is potentially, if seldom overtly, insubordinate. A strong government is considered reactionary by nature, even if it pretends to be progressive. When citizens participate in public life, they hope to constrain government authority, rather than encouraging change, even when change is overdue. At times this individualism is tainted with anarchism. Yet, the French also accommodate themselves rather easily to bureaucratic rule. Since administrative rulings supposedly treat all situations with the same yardstick, they satisfy the sharp sense of equality possessed by a people who feels forever shortchanged by the government and by the privileges those in power bestow on others.

Although the Revolution of 1789 did not break with the past as completely as is commonly believed, it conditioned the general outlook on crisis and compromise and on continuity and change. Sudden change rather than gradual mutation, dramatic conflicts couched in the language of mutually exclusive, radical ideologies—these are the experiences that excite the French at historical moments when their minds are particularly malleable. In fact, what an outsider perceives as permanent instability is a fairly regular alternation between brief crises and prolonged periods of routine. The French are accustomed to thinking that no thorough change can ever occur except by a major upheaval (although this is not always true). Since the great Revolution, every French adult has experienced—

usually more than once—occasions of political excitement followed by disappointment. This process has sometimes led to moral exhaustion and widespread skepticism about any possibility of change.

Whether they originated within the country or were brought about by international conflict, most of France's political crises have produced a constitutional crisis. Each time, the triumphant forces have codified their norms and philosophy, usually in a comprehensive document. This explains why constitutions have never played the role of fundamental charters. Prior to the Fifth Republic, their norms were satisfactory to only one segment of the polity and hotly contested by others.

In the years immediately following 1958, the reaction to the constitution of the Fifth Republic resembled the reaction to previous French constitutions. Support for its institutions was generally limited to voters who supported the governments of the day. This began to change after 1962, with the popular election of the president. The election of Mitterrand to the presidency in 1981 and the peaceful transfer of power from a right to a left majority in the National Assembly laid to rest the 200-year-old constitutional debate among French elites. It proved to be the capstone of acceptance of the institutions of the Fifth Republic among the masses of French citizens.

Confidence in the Fifth Republic's constitutional institutions has been strong. And despite growing disillusionment with politicians, it has grown stronger. Moreover, there is little significant variation in trust in institutions among voters by their party identity.[4] French people invariably give the highest confidence ratings to institutions closest to them: to local officials, rather than to political parties or national representatives (see Figure 9.3). In recent years distrust of government officials has been high, but expectations of government remain high as well.

## Religious and Antireligious Traditions

France is at once a Catholic country—68 percent of the French population identified themselves as Catholic in 2002 (down from 87 percent in 1974)—and a country that the Church itself considers "dechristianized." Of those who describe themselves as Catholic, only 10 percent attend mass regularly (down from 21 percent in 1974), and 84 percent either never go to church or go only occasionally for ceremonies such as baptism or marriage.[5]

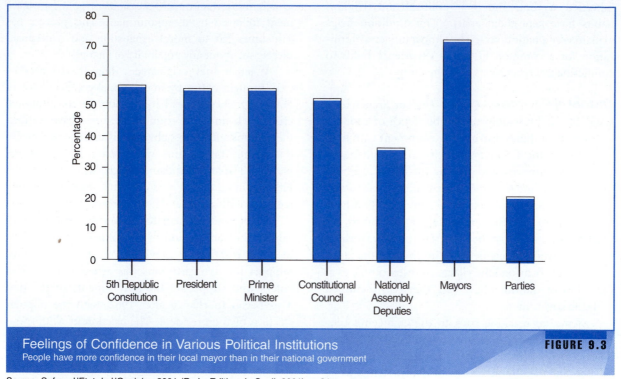

**Feelings of Confidence in Various Political Institutions**
People have more confidence in their local mayor than in their national government

**FIGURE 9.3**

Source: Sofres, L'Etat de L'Oopinion 2001 (Paris: Edition du Seuil, 2001), p. 81.

Until well into the twentieth century, the mutual hostility between the religious and the secular was one of the main features of the political culture. Since the Revolution, it has divided society and political life at all levels. Even now there are important differences between the political behavior of practicing Catholics and that of nonbelievers.

French Catholics historically viewed the Revolution of 1789 as the work of satanic men. Conversely, enemies of the Church became militant in their opposition to Catholic forms and symbols. This division continued through the nineteenth century. Differences between the political subcultures of Catholicism and anticlericalism deepened further with the creation of the Third Republic. After a few years, militant anticlericalism took firm control of the Republic. Parliament rescinded the centuries-old compact with the Vatican, expelled most Catholic orders, and severed all ties between church and state so that (in a phrase often used at the time) "the moral unity of the country could be reestablished." The Pope matched the militancy of the Republic's regime by excommunicating every deputy who voted for the separation laws in

1905. As in other European Catholic countries, the difference between the political right and left was largely determined by attitudes toward the Catholic Church.

The gap between Catholics and agnostics narrowed during the interwar period and after they found themselves working side by side in the resistance movement during World War II. Nevertheless, the depth of religious practice continues to be one of the best predictors of whether a voter will support an established party of the right.

Religious practice has been declining in France and many other industrialized countries since the 1950s. Less than 10 percent of the French population attends church regularly (once a week) today. Farmers are the most observant group, but their church attendance is only 23 percent. Blue-collar workers are the least observant: Now only 4 percent admit to attending church regularly.

In addition to secularization trends, important changes have occurred within the Catholic subculture. Today the vast majority of self-identified Catholics reject some of the most important teachings of the

Church, including its positions on abortion, premarital sex, and marriage of priests. Only 16 percent of identified Catholics perceive the role of the Church as important in political life, and Catholicism no longer functions as a well-integrated community with a common view of the world and common social values. In 2000 there were half the number of Catholic priests as in 1960 and a 75 percent decline of ordinations. Most private schools in France are nominally Catholic parochial schools, which the state subsidizes. The status of these schools (in a country in which state support for Catholic schools coexists with the separation of church and state) has never been fully settled. In 2008, 13 percent of primary schools and 31 percent of secondary schools were private.

French Jews (numbering about 600,000, or about 1 percent of the population) are sufficiently well integrated into French society that it is not possible to speak of a Jewish vote. One study demonstrates that, like other French voters, Jews tend to vote left or right, according to degree of religious practice. Anti-Semitic attitudes and behavior are not widespread in France. However, attacks against Jews and Jewish institutions—mostly by young Maghrebian men in mixed areas of large cities—increased dramatically in parallel with the emergence of the second intifada in the Middle East (2000–2002), but have since declined. These incidents were also related to emerging patterns of urban ethnic conflict in France.

Protestants (1.7 percent of the population and growing) have lived somewhat apart. There are heavy concentrations in Alsace, in Paris, and in some regions of central and southeastern France. About two-thirds of Protestants belong to the upper bourgeoisie. Protestants hold a large proportion of high public positions. Until recently, they usually voted more leftist than others in their socioeconomic position or in the same region. Although many Protestants are prominent in the Socialist Party, their electoral behavior, like their activities in cultural and economic associations, is determined by factors other than religion.

Islam is now France's second religion. There are 4 million to 4.5 million **Muslims** in France, two-thirds of whom are immigrants or their descendants from Muslim countries. The emergence of Islamic institutions in France is part of a larger phenomenon of integrating **new immigrants**. In the last decade, the affirmation of religious identification coincided with (and to some extent was a part of) the social and political mobilization of immigrants from Muslim countries.

There are now over a thousand mosques in France, as well as another thousand prayer rooms. In 2002 the government created the French Council of the Muslim Religion (CFCM) to represent Islam with public authorities (similar institutions exist for Jews and Catholics). A survey in 2005 notes that regular attendance of services at mosques is just above 20 percent—somewhat higher than average for the general population. More than 70 percent of those who identify as Muslims say that they attend services only occasionally.[6]

The growth of Muslim interests has challenged the traditional French view of the separation of church and state. Unlike Catholics and Jews, who maintain their own schools, or Protestants, who have supported the principle of secular state schools, some Muslim groups insist on the right both to attend state schools and to follow practices that education authorities consider contrary to the French tradition of secularism. Small numbers of Muslims have challenged dress codes, school curriculums, and school requirements and have more generally questioned stronger notions of *laïcité* (antireligious atheism).

In response to this challenge, the French Parliament passed legislation in 2004 that banned the wearing of "ostentatious" religious symbols in primary and secondary schools. Although the language is neutral about religion, the law is widely seen as an attempt to prevent the wearing of Islamic head scarves. The new law was widely debated, but it was also strongly supported by the French public. A sample of Muslim women surveyed two months before the law was passed also supported it.

Another response was the 2008 rejection by the administrative court (the Conseil d'Etat) of a citizenship application from a Moroccan woman who wore a burqua (a full-body covering), and was married to a man who was a French citizen. The court based the decision on what it termed practices "incompatible with essential values of the French community, notably with the principle of equality of the sexes."

Nevertheless, it is important to point out that surveys in 2006 indicated that French Muslims are better integrated than are those in other European countries (Britain and Germany, for example).[7] They have the strongest primary identity as French, rather than Muslim; the strongest commitment to "adopt national customs," rather than remaining distinct (78 percent);

and the most favorable view of their fellow citizens who are Christian and Jewish.

### Class and Status

Feelings about class differences shape a society's authority pattern and the style in which authority is exercised. The French, like the English, are conscious of living in a society divided into classes. But since equality is valued more highly in France than in England, deference toward the upper classes is far less developed, and resentful antagonism is widespread.

The number of citizens who are conscious of belonging to a social class is relatively high in France, particularly among workers. About two-thirds of workers in 2002 self-identified as working class.[8] There is some evidence that spontaneous class identity has been declining. However, a 1997 study showed an enduring and even a growing sense of class among white-collar workers and middle managers. In 2002 all social groups expressed a sentiment of belonging to a social class that was as high as or higher than that of workers.

Economic and social transformations have not eradicated subjective feelings about class differences and class antagonism. Indeed, periodic strike movements intensify class feelings and commitments to act. A survey in April 2006 revealed that half of those polled were prepared to participate in a demonstration to defend their ideas. In addition, as the number of immigrant workers among the least qualified workers has grown, traditional class differences are reinforced by a growing sense of racial and ethnic differences.

## POLITICAL SOCIALIZATION

French political attitudes have been shaped through experience with the political system, as well as through some key institutions and agents. Some agents, such as political associations, act to socialize political values quite directly, while others, such as the family and the media, act in a more indirect manner.

In an old country like France, agents of political socialization change slowly, even when regimes change rapidly. Socializing agents are carriers of a broader cultural tradition. Like any other teaching process, political socialization passes on from one generation to the next "a mixture of attitudes developed in a mixture of historical periods." But "traditions,

everyone agrees, do not form a constituted and fixed set of values, of knowledge and of representations; socialization never functions as a simple mechanism of identical reproduction [but rather as] an important instrument for the reorganization and the reinvention of tradition."[9]

### Family

For those French who view their neighbors and fellow citizens with distrust and the institutions around them with cynicism, the family is a safe haven. Concern for stability, steady income, property, and continuity were common to bourgeois and peasant families, though not to urban or agricultural workers. The training of children in bourgeois and peasant families was often marked by close supervision, incessant correction, and strict sanctions.

Particularly during the last forty years, the life of the French family, the role of its members, and its relationship to outsiders have undergone fundamental, and sometimes contradictory, changes. Very few people condemn the idea of couples living together without being married. In 2001, 44 percent of all births were outside of marriage (compared with 6 percent in 1968), a percentage only slightly lower than in the United States and higher than almost any other European country. The proportion of births outside of marriage is highest among women outside of the labor force and working-class women (with the notable exception of immigrant women). Very few of these children are in one-parent families, however. In virtually all cases, they are legally recognized by both parents before their first birthday. Nevertheless, 18 percent of young people below age 25 lived with only one of their natural parents in 2005, mostly due to divorce. The number of divorces was more than 40 percent of the number of marriages in 2000, and it has almost doubled since 1976, when new and more flexible divorce legislation came into effect.

Legislative changes have only gradually modified the legal restrictions on married women that existed in the Napoléonic legal codes. Not until 1970 did the law proclaim the absolute equality of the two parents in the exercise of parental authority and for the moral and material management of the family. Labor-saving devices for house and farm are described as the "secret agents of modernity" in the countryside.[10] Almost half of all women over age 15 are now employed, and

80 percent of French women between the ages of 25 and 49 are now working during their adult years.

The employment of more married women has affected the family's role as a vehicle of socialization. Working women differ from those who are not employed in regard to religious practice, political interest, electoral participation, party preference, and so on. In their attitudinal orientations, employed women are far closer to the men of the same milieu, class, or age group to which they belong than to women who are not employed.[11]

Although family structure, values, and behavior have changed, the family remains an important structure through which political values broadly conceived are transmitted from generation to generation. Several studies demonstrate a significant influence of parents over the religious socialization and the left-right political choices made by their children.[12]

There is perhaps no greater tribute to the continuing effectiveness of the French family than the results of a survey of French youth in 1994. With 25 percent of 18- to 24-year-olds unemployed, it was hardly surprising that 78 percent of young people had little confidence in the schools' ability to prepare them for the future. More surprising, more than 75 percent felt that their parents had confidence in them, that they were loved at home, and that their families had prepared them well for the future. In a survey taken in 1999, the family was ranked second only to school as a source of deep and durable friendship.

The effectiveness of the family in socializing general religious and ideological orientations does not mean that succeeding generations do not have formative experiences of their own or that there are no significant political differences by age. Therefore, political socialization is a product not only of the family experiences, but also of childhood experiences with peers, education, and the changing larger world. For instance, young people of Algerian origin, born in France, are somewhat more likely than their counterparts of French origin to practice their faith, but far less likely than their counterparts born in Algeria to practice their faith. Nevertheless, young people of Algerian origin were more likely to practice their religion in 2005 than they were in 1995.[13]

## Associations and Socialization

The French bias against authority might have encouraged social groups and associations if the egalitarian thrust and the competition among individuals did not work in the opposite direction. The French ambivalence about participation in group life is not merely negativistic apathy, but also reflects a lack of belief in the value of cooperation. On the one hand, this cultural ambivalence is reinforced by legal restrictions on associational life, as well as by a strong republican tradition hostile to groups serving as intermediaries between the people and the state. On the other hand, the state and local governments traditionally subsidize numerous associations (including trade unions). Some associations (not always the same ones that were subsidized) receive privileged access to decisionmaking power.

After World War II, *overall* membership in associations in France was comparable to that in other European countries, but lower than in the United States. However, group membership in France was concentrated in politicized associations that reinforced existing social divisions and was less common for independent social and fraternal groups. Membership in key professional organizations, especially trade unions, was much lower in France than in other European countries.

The number of associations has sharply increased over the past two decades, while the overall percentage of membership among the adult population has remained relatively constant. In a 2002 survey, 36 percent claimed to belong to one or more associations. This percentage has increased during the last thirty years, but has remained about the same for the last decade.

The pattern of association membership, however, has changed considerably. The traditional advocacy and political groups, politicized unions, and professional associations suffered sharp declines in absolute (and proportional) membership. Sports associations, self-help groups, and newly established ethnic associations now attract larger numbers of people. As more middle-class people have joined associations, working-class people have dropped out.[14]

To some extent these changes reflect shifting attitudes about political commitment in France. Although associational life remains strong, *militantisme* (voluntary work, with its implication of deep and abiding commitment) has clearly diminished. Older advocacy and professional associations that were built on this kind of commitment have declined. Newer groups are built on different and often more limited commitment.

New legislation has also produced changes. A 1981 law made it possible for immigrant groups to form their own organizations. This encouraged the emergence of thousands of ethnic associations. Decentralization legislation passed a few years later encouraged municipalities to support the creation of local associations, some to perform municipal services.

Even with these changing patterns, there remain uncertainties about the role of associations, old and new, in the socialization process. Some observers seem to confirm that membership in French organizations involves less actual participation than in American or British organizations and hence has less impact on social and political attitudes. Cultural distrust is manifest less in lower overall membership than in the inability of organizational leaders to relate to their members and to mobilize them for action.

## Education

One of the most important ways a community preserves and transmits its values is through education. Napoléon Bonaparte recognized the significance of education. Well into the second half of the twentieth century, the French educational system remained an imposing historical monument, in the unmistakable style of the First Empire. The edifice Napoléon erected combined education at all levels, from primary school to postgraduate professional training, into one centralized corporation: the imperial university. Its job was to teach the national doctrine through uniform programs at various levels.

As the strict military discipline of the Napoléonic model was loosened by succeeding regimes, each has discovered that the machinery created by Napoléon was a convenient and coherent instrument for transmitting the values—both changing and permanent—of French civilization. The centralized imperial university has therefore never been truly dismantled. The minister of education presides over a ministry that employs more than a million people and controls curriculums and teaching methods, the criteria for selection and advancement of pupils and teachers, and the content of examinations.

Making advancement at every step dependent on passing an examination is not peculiar to France (it is also found in Japan and other countries). What is distinctly French is an obsessive belief that everybody is equal before an examination. The idea that education is an effective weapon for emancipation and social

betterment has had popular as well as official recognition. The **baccalauréat**—the certificate of completion of the academic secondary school, the lycée—remains almost the sole means of access to higher education. Such a system suits and profits best those self-motivated middle-class children for whom it was designed.

Nevertheless, during the Fifth Republic, the structure of the French educational system has undergone significant change. The secondary schools, which trained only 700,000 students as late as 1945, now provide instruction for 5.5 million. Between 1958 and 2007, the number of students in higher education rose from 170,000 to 2.3 million. By 2006 the proportion of 20- to 24-year-olds in higher education (40 percent) was comparable to that in any other European country.[15]

The introduction of a comprehensive middle school with a common core curriculum in 1963 basically altered the system of early academic selection. Other reforms eliminated rigid ability tracking. However, the implementation of reforms, whether passed by governments of the right or the left, has often faced difficult opposition from middle-class parents and from teachers' unions of the left.[16] Although more than 80 percent of the students who sat for the examination passed the baccalauréat in 2006 (more than double the proportion of 1980), education reforms have altered only slightly the vast differences in the success of children from different social backgrounds.

Because of the principle of open admission, every holder of the baccalauréat can gain entrance to a university. There is, as in some American state universities, a rather ruthless elimination at the end of the first year (particularly for students in such fields as medicine) and sometimes later. Students of lower-class backgrounds typically fare worse than the others. In addition, the number of students from such backgrounds is disproportionately large in fields in which diplomas have the lowest value in the professional market and in which unemployment is greatest.

The most ambitious attempt to reform the university system came in the wake of the student rebellion of 1968, followed by other reforms in the 1970s and 1980s. They strove to encourage the autonomy of each university; the participation of teachers, students, and staff in the running of the university; and the collaboration among different disciplines. The government subsequently withdrew some of the reforms. Others failed to be implemented because of widespread resistance by those concerned. Administrative autonomy has remained fragmentary, as the ministry has held the financial purse strings, as well as the right to grant degrees. Today the widely lamented crisis of the university system has hardly been alleviated, although the size of the student population appears to have stabilized.

Since 2003 the most important symbolic change in French higher education has been the introduction of affirmative action programs for students in "priority education zones"—schools in poor areas, generally in or near larger cities. Some of the elite institutions of higher education (Sciences-Po in Paris, for example) have created links to some of these schools and have established special conditions of admission for their best students. Although these programs involve only a handful of students, these experiments are important because they represent the first affirmative effort to integrate potential leaders from immigrant communities into the French system (which we will discuss later).

An additional characteristic of the French system of higher education is the parallel system of **grandes écoles**, a sector of higher education that functions outside of the network of universities under rules that permit a high degree of selectivity. As university enrollment has multiplied, the more prestigious grandes écoles have only modestly increased the number of students admitted upon strict entrance examinations.[17] For more than a century, the grandes écoles have been the training ground of highly specialized elites. These schools prepare students for careers in engineering, business management, and the top ranks of the civil service. Their different recruitment of students and of teaching staffs, as well as their teaching methods, influences the outlook and even the temperament of many of their graduates. In contrast to university graduates, virtually all graduates of the grandes écoles find employment and often assume positions of great responsibility.

## Socialization and Communication

The political effectiveness of the mass media is often determined by the way in which people appraise the media's integrity and whether they believe that the media serve or disturb the functioning of the political system. In the past business firms, political parties, and governments (both French and foreign) often backed major newspapers. Today the press operates under the same conditions as it does in other Western democracies. Most newspapers and magazines are owned by business enterprises, many of them conglomerates that extend into fields other than periodical publications.

In spite of a growth in population, the number of daily newspapers and their circulation have declined since World War II. The decline in readership, a common phenomenon in most European democracies, is

Demonstration by medicl interns in Paris, in early 2003.

Pascal Le Segretain/Getty Images

due to competition from other media, such as television, radio, and the Internet.

Television has replaced all other media as a primary source of political information in France and other Western democracies.[18] It is increasingly the primary mediator between political forces and individual citizens, and it has an impact on the organization and substance of politics. First, a personality that plays well on television (not just a unique personality such as Charles de Gaulle) is now an essential ingredient of politics. As in other countries, image and spectacle are important elements of politics. Second, television helps set the agenda of political issues by choosing among the great variety of themes, problems, and issues dealt with by political and social forces and by magnifying them for the public. Finally, television now provides the arena for national electoral campaigns, largely displacing mass rallies and meetings.

Confidence in various sources of political information varies among different groups. Young people and shopkeepers are most confident in radio and television information, while managers are more confident in the written press than television for political information.

Until 1982 all radio and television stations that originated programs on French territory were owned by the state and operated by personnel whom the state appointed and remunerated. Since then the system of state monopoly gradually has been dismantled. As a first and quite important step, the Socialist government authorized private radio stations. This move attempted to regularize and regulate more than a thousand existing pirate radio stations. Inevitably, this vast network of 1,600 stations was consolidated by private entrepreneurs who provide programming services and in some instances control of a large number of local stations.

The 1982 legislation also reorganized the public television system. It granted new rights of reply to government communications and allotted free time to all political parties during electoral campaigns. During the following years, however, even greater changes were produced by a process of gradual privatization and globalization of television broadcasting. Today as many as 900 television channels from throughout the world are available to French viewers (depending on the system that they choose), compared with 3 in 1980 and 30 in 1990.

## RECRUITMENT AND STYLE OF ELITES

Until the Fifth Republic, Parliament provided the core of French decisionmakers. Besides members of Parliament, elected officers of municipalities or departments, some local party leaders, and a few journalists of national renown are counted among what is known in France as the **political class**. Altogether they comprise not more than 15,000 or 20,000 people. All gravitated toward the halls of the National Assembly or the Senate. From about 1879 on, professionals (lawyers, doctors, and journalists) dominated the Chamber of Deputies, now called the National Assembly. The vast majority were local notables, trained in law and experienced in local administration.

A substantial change in political recruitment occurred during the Fourth Republic, when the percentages of self-employed and farmers became a minority. The steadily diminishing share of blue- and white-collar workers during the Fifth Republic is due partially to the professionalization of parliamentary personnel, as well as to the decline of the Communist Party.

Strikingly, a large number of legislators now come from the public sector: almost half the deputies in the 1980s and 32 percent after the victory of the right in 2007. The number of top civil servants in the National Assembly has risen constantly since 1958, and the left landslide of 1981 accentuated this process. Although the majority of high civil servants usually lean toward parties of the right, more than half of those who sat in the National Assembly elected in 2007 were part of the Socialist group.

Even more important than their number is the political weight that these deputy-bureaucrats carry in Parliament. Some of the civil servants who run for election to Parliament have previously held positions in the political executive, either as members of the ministerial staffs or as junior ministers. Not surprisingly, they are frequently candidates for a post in the Cabinet.

More than in any other Western democracy, the highest ranks of the civil service are the training and recruitment grounds for top positions in both politics and industry. Among the high civil servants, about 3,400 are members of the most important administrative agencies, the five **grands corps**, from which the vast majority of the roughly 500 administrators engaged in political decisionmaking are drawn.[19] The recruitment base of the highest levels of the civil service remains extremely narrow. The knowledge and capability required to pass the various examinations give clear advantages to the children of senior civil servants. As a result, the ranking bureaucracy forms something approaching a hereditary class. Past attempts to develop a system of more open recruitment into the higher civil service have been only marginally successful.

The **École Nationale d'Administration (ENA)** and the **École Polytechnique,** together with the other grandes écoles, play an essential role in the recruitment of administrative, political, and business elites. Virtually all the members of the grands corps are recruited directly from the graduating classes of the ENA and the Polytechnique. What differentiates the members of the grands corps from other ranking administrators is their general competence and mobility. At any one time, as many as two-thirds of the members of these corps might be on leave or on special missions to other administrative agencies or special assignments to positions of influence.

They might also be engaged in politics as members of Parliament (thirty-seven in the National Assembly elected in 2007), local government, or the executive. Twelve of the eighteen prime ministers who have served since 1959 were members of a grand corps and attended a grande école. The percentage of ministers in any given government who belong to the grands corps has varied between 10 and 60 percent. When Jean-Pierre Raffarin became prime minister in April 2002, he was widely described as an "outsider," in part because his political career had been primarily in the provinces and in part because he had *not* been a student at the ENA. One study calculates that 40 percent of those who graduated from the ENA between 1960 and 1990 served as ministerial advisors. Thus, the grandes écoles–grands corps group, though small in membership, produces a remarkable proportion of the country's political elite.

The same system is increasingly important in recruiting top-level business executives. Members of the grands corps can move from the public sector to the private sector because they can go on leave for years, while they retain their seniority, their pension rights, and the right to return to their job. (Few who leave do in fact return to serve as civil servants.)[20] In 2007, 75 percent of the members of the executive boards of the 40 largest companies in France were graduates of a grande école. In the early 1990s, 17 percent of all ENA graduates were working in French industry. Moreover,

though the number of ENA graduates is small (about 170 a year), it is three times larger now than in the early 1960s.

The relationship between the grandes écoles and the grands corps, on the one hand, and politics and business, on the other hand, provides structure for an influential elite and survives changes in the political orientation of governments. While this system is not politically monolithic, the narrowness of its recruitment contributes to a persistent similarity of style and operation and to the fairly stable—at times rigid— value system of its operators.

For outsiders this tight network is difficult to penetrate. Even during the 1980s—the period when industrial restructuring and privatization of state-run enterprises encouraged a new breed of freewheeling businesspeople in the United States and in Britain—a similar process had a very limited impact on the recruitment of new elites in France.

## The Importance of Gender

The representation of women among French political elites is almost the lowest in Western Europe. Women make up well over half the electorate, but were barely 18.5 percent of the deputies in the National Assembly in 2007 and only 18.2 percent of Senate members in 2008. Women fare better at the local level, where they made up 32 percent of the municipal councilors and 12 percent of the mayors elected in 2001, 50 percent more than six years before.

Political parties structure access to political representation far more in France than in the United States. The left has generally made a greater effort to recruit women than has the right. Thus, when the Socialists and Communists gained a substantial number of seats in the 1997 legislative elections, the proportion of women in the National Assembly almost doubled.

In contrast to the United States, political advancement in France generally requires a deep involvement in political parties, with a bias in favor of professional politicians and administrators. However, relatively few women have made this kind of long-term commitment to political life.

One woman who has is **Ségolène Royal**. A graduate of the ENA and a member of the Council of State (one of the five grands corps), she has also been a Socialist government minister, a deputy in the National Assembly, and president of one of the regions of

France. She was the (defeated) Socialist candidate for the presidential elections in 2007. In addition, the present national secretary (and 2007 presidential candidate) of the French Communist Party is a woman, as is the president of the employers' confederation, the Mouvement des Enterprisès de France (MEDEF).

Periodically, governments and the political parties recognize this dearth of women in representative institutions, but little has been done about it. The Constitutional Council has rejected some remedies, and some proposed reforms have challenged accepted institutional norms. By the 1990s leaders of all political parties favored amending the constitution to permit positive discrimination to produce greater gender parity in representative institutions. Thus, with support of both the president of the Republic and the prime minister and without dissent, the National Assembly passed an amendment in December 1998 stipulating that "the law [and not the constitution] determines the conditions for the organization of equal access of men and women to electoral mandates and elective functions." Enforcement legislation requires greater gender parity, at least in the selection of candidates. This is a significant departure for the French political system, which has resisted the use of quotas in the name of equality. As a result of this parity legislation, the number of women in the 2007 National Assembly actually increased modestly, from 10.2 percent in 2000 to 18.5 in 2007.

Perhaps the most important change in the political behavior of French women is in the way they vote. During the Fourth Republic, a majority of women consistently voted for parties of the right. However, as church attendance among women has declined, their political orientation has moved from right to left. In every national election between 1986 and 1997, a clear majority of women voted for the left. By 2002, however, the pattern of voting among women changed. In both 2002 and 2007, women supported both Chirac and Sarkozy more than men, even though Sarkozy's opponent in 2007 was a woman. On the other hand, women have given far less support than men to the extreme right.[21]

## INTEREST GROUPS

### The Expression of Interests

As in many other European countries, the organization of French political life is largely defined within the historical cleavages of class and religious traditions.

Interest groups have therefore frequently shared ideological commitments with the political parties with which they have organizational connections.

Actual memberships in most economic associations have varied considerably over time by sector, but they are generally much smaller than comparable groups in other industrialized countries. In 2005 no more than 8 percent of workers belonged to trade unions (the largest decline in Western Europe over the past twenty-five years). About 50 percent of French farmers and 75 percent of large industrial enterprises belong to their respective organizations.[22]

Historically, many of the important economic groups have experienced a surge of new members at dramatic moments in the country's social or political history. But membership then declines as conditions normalize, leaving some associations with a membership too small to justify their claims of representativeness.

Many groups lack the resources to employ a competent staff, or they depend on direct and indirect forms of state support. The modern interest group official is a fairly recent phenomenon that is found only in certain sectors of the group system, such as business associations.

Interest groups are also weakened by ideological division. Separate groups defending the interests of workers, farmers, veterans, schoolchildren, and consumers are divided by ideological preferences. The ideological division of representation forces each organization to compete for the same clientele in order to establish its representativeness. Consequently, even established French interest groups exhibit a radicalism in action and goals that is rare in other Western democracies. For groups that lack the means of using the information media, such tactics also become a way to put their case before the public at large. In such a setting, even the defense of purely economic, social, or cultural interests takes on a political color.

### The Labor Movement

The French labor movement is divided into national confederations of differing political sympathies, although historical experiences have driven labor to avoid direct organizational ties with political parties.[23] Union membership has declined steeply since 1975, but there are indications that the decline has leveled off. Although union membership is declining in almost every industrialized country, it is now the lowest by far in France (see Figure 3.1 in Chapter 3). The youngest salaried workers virtually deserted the trade union movement in the 1990s. Although the decline in membership has slowed slightly in recent years, recruitment of young workers has lagged. In addition, after 1990, candidates supported by nonunion groups in various plant-level elections have attracted more votes than any of the established union organizations.[24] In fact, unions lost members and (electoral) support at the very time when the French trade union movement was becoming better institutionalized at the workplace and better protected by legislation.

Despite these clear weaknesses, workers still maintain considerable confidence in unions to defend their interests during periods of labor conflict. Support for collective action and confidence in unions and their leadership of strike movements remain strong. Indeed, during the massive strikes—strikes of truckers and taxi drivers in 2000 and strikes against changes in civil service pensions in 2003, youth contracts in 2006 and long strikes in education in 2009—public support for the strikers was far higher than confidence in the government against which the strikes were directed.[25] However, even though there are occasional massive strikes in France, strike levels have declined over the past thirty years.

French labor has had the most difficulty dealing with ideological fragmentation. Indeed, the decline in union membership has not encouraged consolidation rather, it has produced more fragmentation (as we will see in the following discussion). Unlike workers in the United States, French workers in the same plant or firm may be represented by several union federations. As a result, there is constant competition among unions at every level for membership and support. Even during periods when the national unions agree to act together, animosities at the plant level sometimes prevent cooperation.

Moreover, the weakness of union organization at the plant level—which is where most lengthy strikes are called—means that unions are difficult bargaining partners. Unions at this level maintain only weak control over the strike weapon. Union militants are quite adept at sensitizing workers, producing the preconditions for strike action, and channeling strike movements once they begin. However, the unions have considerable difficulty in effectively calling strikes and ending them. Thus, unions depend heavily on the general environment, what they call the "social climate," in order to support their positions at the bargaining table. Because their ability to mobilize workers at any given moment is an essential criterion of their representativeness, union ability to represent workers is frequently in question.

The left government passed legislation in 1982–1983 (the Auroux laws) to strengthen the unions' position at the plant level. By creating an "obligation to negotiate" for management and by protecting the right of expression for workers, the government hoped to stimulate collective negotiations. In fact, this act brought about important changes in industrial relations and stimulated collective negotiations. However, given their increasing weakness, unions have not taken full advantage of the potential benefits of the legislation. This law refocused French industrial relations on the plant level without necessarily increasing the effectiveness of unions.

The oldest and the largest of the union confederations is the **Confédération Générale du Travail (CGT)** (General Confederation of Labor). Since World War II, the CGT has been identified closely with the Communist Party, with which it maintains a considerable overlap of leadership. Yet by tradition and by its relative effectiveness as a labor organization, it enrolls many non-Communists among its members. Its domination diminished in the 1990s, however, mostly because the CGT lost more members and support than all other unions.

The second largest labor organization in terms of membership is now the **Confédération Française Democratique du Travail (CFDT)** (French Democratic Confederation of Labor). In many ways the CFDT is the most original and the most interesting of all labor movements in Western Europe. An offshoot of a Catholic trade union movement, the CFDT's earlier calls for worker self-management (*autogestion*) were integrated into the Auroux laws. The leaders of the CFDT see the policy of the confederation as an alternative to the oppositional stance of the CGT. The CFDT now offers itself as a potential partner to modern capitalist management.

This movement to the right created splits within several CFDT public service unions and resulted in the establishment of a national rival, the *Solidaire Unitaire et Democratique (SUD)* (Solidarity United and Democratic), in 1989. The split was further accentuated by the CFDT's opposition to the massive public service strike of 1995. The SUD, in turn, was integrated into a larger group of twenty-seven militant autonomous civil service unions, **G-10** (le Groupe des dix), in 1998.

The third major labor confederation, **Force Ouvrière (FO)** (Workers' Force), was formed in 1948 in reaction to the Communist domination of the CGT. Although its membership is barely half that of the two other major confederations, the FO made gains in the 1990s. As the state moved to cut back benefits for civil servants, teachers, and railway workers, FO leadership adopted a more confrontational position with the state. During the strike movements of 1995 and 1996, FO leadership strongly supported the more radical elements of striking workers. Trotskyist elements of the left continue to hold considerable influence in the organization.

One of the most important and influential of the "autonomous" unions is the **Fédération de l'Education Nationale (FEN)** (Federation of National Education), the teachers' union. At the end of 1992, as a result of growing internal conflict and declining membership, the FEN split. The core FEN group continued. The rump of the FEN joined with other independent unions to form the *Union Nationale des Syndicats Autonomes (UNSA)* (National Union of Autonomous Unions). In October 1994 the UNSA was officially recognized by the government. In legal terms this means that the government placed the UNSA on the same level as the other national confederations. Nevertheless, by 1996 the FEN (and the UNSA) was substantially weakened when the rival *La Fédération Syndicale Unitaire (FSU)* (United Union Federation)—which is close to the Communist Party—gained greater support in social elections (elections for shop stewards, shop committees and union representatives), support that has been reaffirmed since then.

In addition to the fragmentation that results from differences within existing organizations, there are challenges from the outside. In 1995 the National Front organized several new unions. When the government and the courts blocked these initiatives, the extreme-right party began to penetrate existing unions.

Thus, at a time when strong opposition to government action seems to give union organizations an opportunity to increase both their organizational strength and their support, the trade union movement is more fragmented than ever. As in the past, massive strike movements have accentuated divisions and rivalries, rather than provoking unity.

## Business Interests

Since the end of World War II, most trade associations and employers' organizations have kept within one dominant and exceptionally well staffed confederation, renamed in 1998 the **Mouvement des Entreprises de France (MEDEF)** (Movement of French Business). However, divergent interests, differing economic concepts, and conflicting ideologies frequently prevent the national organization from acting forcefully. At times this division hampers its representativeness in negotiations with government or trade unions. Nevertheless, the MEDEF weathered the difficult years of the **nationalization** introduced by the Socialists and the restructuring of social legislation and industrial relations without lessening its status as an influential interest group.

Since the MEDEF is dominated primarily by big business, shopkeepers and the owners of many small firms feel that they are better defended by more movement-oriented groups.[26] As a result, a succession of small business and shopkeeper movements has challenged the established organization and has evolved into organized associations in their own right.

## Agricultural Interests

The defense of agricultural interests has a long record of internal strife. However, under the Fifth Republic, the **Fédération Nationale des Syndicats Agricoles (FNSEA)** (National Federation of Agricultural Unions) is the dominant group among several farm organizations. The FNSEA has also served as an effective instrument for modernizing French agriculture.

The rural reform legislation of the 1960s provided for the "collaboration of the professional agricultural organizations," and from the outset real collaboration was offered only to the FNSEA. From this privileged position, the federation gained both patronage and control over key institutions that were transforming agriculture. It used these instruments to organize a large proportion of French farmers. After establishing its domination over the farming sector with the support of the government, it then periodically demonstrated opposition to government policy with the support of the vast majority of a declining number of farmers.[27]

The principal challenges to the FNSEA in recent years are external, rather than internal. The agricultural sector has suffered from the fruits of its own productive success. Under pressure from the EU, France agreed in 1992 to major reforms of the Common Agricultural Policy (CAP) that took substantial amounts of land out of production and replaced some price supports with direct payments to farmers. That same year the EU reached an agreement with the United States that the EU would reduce subsidized grain exports and cut back cultivation of oilseed products. France is the largest exporter of these products in the EU. FNSEA protests (some of them violent) were joined by farm unions from throughout the EU. This ultimately resulted in a face-saving General Agreement on Tariffs and Trade (GATT) accord in 1994. The enlargement of the EU toward the East has heightened pressures to further reduce the budget of CAP. The substantial opposition in France (and other parts of Europe) to the importation of genetically modified agricultural products has increased the tensions within the World Trade Organization (WTO) (formerly GATT).

However, the more substantial issue for the WTO is agreement on the reduction of export subsidies for European and American agricultural products. Poorer countries have demanded the reduction of such subsidies for a long time. In 2007 and again in 2008, the Doha Round of trade negotiations broke down in part over this issue, the first time such multilateral trade negotiations have failed since World War II. The breakdown has been blamed on several factors, but specifically on the influence of agricultural groups in both France and the United States.

French organized interests are expressed through an impressive range of different kinds of organizations, from the weak and fragmented trade union movement to the well-organized FNSEA. Overall, what seems to differentiate French groups from those of other industrial countries is their style of expression and their forms of activity.

## Means of Access and Styles of Action

In preceding regimes organized interests saw Parliament as the most convenient means of access to political power. During the Third and Fourth Republics, the highly specialized and powerful parliamentary committees often seemed to be little more than institutional facades for interest groups that frequently substituted bills of their own design for those submitted by the government.

Among the reasons given in 1958 for reforming and rationalizing Parliament was the desire to reduce the role of organized interests in the legislative process. By and large this has been accomplished. But interest groups have not lost all influence on rulemaking and policy formation. To be effective groups now use the channels that the best-equipped groups have long found most rewarding, channels that give them direct access to the administration. The indispensable collaboration between organized private interests and the state is institutionalized in advisory committees that are attached to most administrative agencies. These committees are composed mainly of civil servants and group representatives. Nonetheless, tendencies toward privileged access, sometimes called **neocorporatism** (democratic corporatism) (see Chapter 3), have, except in the areas of agriculture and big business, remained weak in France.

The weak organization of labor and small business means that these organizations are often regarded as unreliable partners. Organized interests also attempt to pressure the political executive. The ministerial staffs—those circles of personal collaborators who support every minister—are an important target. The strengthened position of the political executive enables both the prime minister and the president to function more effectively as arbiters between competing claims and to exercise stricter control over many agencies and ministries.

It is not surprising that some interests have easier access to government bureaus than others. An affinity of views between group representatives and public administrators might be based on common outlook, common social origin, or education. The official of an important trade association or its national association who sorts out the raw demands of constituents and submits them in rational fashion easily gets a more sympathetic hearing than the official of an organization that defends atomistic interests by mobilizing latent resentment.

High civil servants tend to distinguish between "professional organizations," which they consider serious enough to listen to, and "interest groups," which should be kept at a distance. The perspectives of interest representatives tend to reflect their own strength, as well as their experience in collaborating with different parts of the state and government. Trade union representatives acknowledge their reliance on the social climate (essentially the level of strike activity) to bargain effectively with the state. Representatives of business rely more on contacts with civil servants. Agricultural interests say that they rely more on contacts at the ministerial level.[28]

Central to the state interest group collaboration described as neocorporatism is the notion that the state plays a key role in both shaping and defining the legitimacy of the interest group universe. The state also establishes the rules by which the collaboration takes place. The French state, at various levels, strongly influences the relationship among groups and even their existence in key areas through official recognition and subsidies. Although representative organizations may exist with or without official recognition, this designation gives them access to consultative bodies, the right to sign collective agreements (especially important in the case of trade unions), and the right to obtain certain subsidies. Therefore, recognition is an important tool that both conservative and Socialist governments have used to influence the group universe.

The French state subsidizes interest groups, both indirectly and directly. By favoring some groups over others in these ways, the state seems to conform to neocorporatist criteria. However, in other ways the neocorporatist model is less applicable in France than in other European countries. Neocorporatist policy-making presumes close collaboration between the state administration and a dominant interest group (or coalition of groups) in major socioeconomic sectors. Yet, what stands out in the French case is the unevenness of this pattern of collaboration.[29]

If the neocorporatist pattern calls for interest group leaders to control organizational action and coordinate bargaining, the French interest groups' mass actions—such as street demonstrations, "wildcat" strikes, and attacks on government property—are often poorly controlled by group leadership. Indeed, it can be argued that group protest is more effective in France (at least negatively) than in other industrialized countries because it is part of a pattern of group-state relations.

Protests are limited in scope and intensity, but the government recognizes them as a valid expression of interest. In April 2006 half of those surveyed said that they were prepared to take part in such direct action. This explains why governments backed by a majority in Parliament frequently make concessions to weakly organized interest groups. In the spring of 2006, for example, legislation that created a new labor contract was passed by Parliament and signed by the president, but withdrawn after weeks of growing protests and occupations by students that threatened the stability of the government (see Box 9.1).[30]

## Protest in France                                                    BOX 9.1

During the Socialist governments of the 1980s, more and more people—farmers, artisans, people in small businesses, truckers, doctors, medical students—took to the streets to protest impending legislation, often out of fear for their status. The demonstrations frequently led to violence and near riots. The same scenario took place later under conservative governments. Demonstrations by college and high school students forced the withdrawal of a planned university reform in 1987. A planned imposition of a "youth" minimum wage in 1994, ostensibly to encourage more employment of young people, was dropped when high school students opposed it in the streets of Paris and other large cities. After a month of public service strikes and massive demonstrations in 1995, the new Chirac government abandoned a plan to reorganize the nationalized railway system and revised a plan to reorganize the civil service. A year later striking truckers won major concessions from a still weakened government. In the autumn of 2000, a protest led by truckers and taxi drivers (that spread to England) against the rising price of oil and gasoline forced the government to lower consumer taxes on fuel. Finally, in 2006 the government passed legislation to establish a work contract (one among many) meant to encourage employers to hire young people under the age of 25 by making it easier to fire them during the first two years of their employment. After a three-month struggle of street demonstrations and school occupations by many of the same young people who were supposed to be the beneficiaries of the law (which was supported by all of the major trade unions and the major parties of the left—at least initially), the law was withdrawn.

# POLITICAL PARTIES

## The Traditional Party System

Some analysts of elections see a chronic and seemingly unalterable division of the French into two large political families, each motivated by a different mood or temperament and usually classified as the right and the left. If we view elections from this perspective, political alignments have remained surprisingly stable over long periods of history. As late as 1962, the opposition to de Gaulle was strongest in departments where republican traditions had a solid foundation for more than a century. The alignments in the presidential contest of 1974 and the parliamentary elections of 1978 mirrored the same divisions. Soon thereafter, however, the left's inroads into formerly conservative strongholds changed the traditional geographic distribution of votes. Majorities changed at each legislative election between 1981 and 2002, and few departments now remain solid bastions for either the right or the left.

The electoral system of the Fifth Republic favors a simplification of political alignments. In most constituencies runoff elections result in the confrontation of two candidates, each typically representing one of the two camps. A simple and stable division could have resulted long ago in a pattern of two parties or coalitions alternating in having power and being in opposition—and hence giving valid expression to the voters' opinions. Why has this not occurred?

Except for the Socialists and the Communists, and more recently the RPR (Rally for the Republic—now the UMP—see below), French political parties have mostly remained weakly organized. French parties developed in a mainly preindustrial and preurban environment, catering at first to upper-middle-class and later to middle-class voters. Their foremost and sometimes only function was to provide a framework for selecting and electing candidates for local, departmental, and national offices. Even among the better organized parties, party organization has been both fragmentary at the national level and local in orientation, with only modest linkage between the two levels.

This form of representation and party organization survives largely because voters support it. An electorate that distrusts authority and wants protection against arbitrary government is likely to be suspicious of parties organized for political reform. For all their antagonism, the republican and antirepublican traditions have one thing in common: their aversion to well-established and strongly organized parties.

Party membership has always been low except during short and dramatic situations. As late as the 1960s, no more than 2 percent of registered voters were party members. In Britain and Germany, for example, some parties have had more than a million members, a membership level never achieved by any French political party. Organizational weakness contributes to the endurance of a multiparty system.

In a two- or three-party system, major parties normally move toward the political center in order to gain stability and cohesion. But where extreme party plurality prevails, the center is unable to become a political force. In France centrist coalitions were an effective, if limited, means of maintaining a regime in the Third and Fourth Republics, but an ineffective means of developing coherent policy.

The Fifth Republic created a new political framework that has had a major, if gradual and mostly unforeseen, influence on all parties and on their relationships to each other. The emerging party system, in turn, influenced the way that political institutions actually worked.[31] The strengthening of parliamentary party discipline in the 1970s gave meaning to the strong executive leadership of president and prime minister and stabilized the political process. The main political parties also became the principal arenas in which to develop and debate alternative policies.

The main political parties still dominate the organization of parliamentary work and the selection of candidates, but they have become far less important as mass membership organizations. In 2002 at least seventy-nine parties or groups presented 8,424 candidates for 577 seats in the National Assembly, a record for the Fifth Republic. In 2007 the four main parties were supported by 78 percent of the electorate, with the National Front and the Greens attracting an additional 15 percent. If we include the National Front and the Greens, less than 10 percent of the electorate supported an array of issue-based and personality-based parties in 2007, a sharp decline compared with 2002. Nine parties are represented in the National Assembly in four parliamentary groups, two in the right majority, two allied in the left opposition.

## The Main Parties: The Right and Center

*Union for a Popular Movement*    The **Union for a Popular Movement (UMP)** is the most recent direct lineal descendant of the Gaullist party. The original Gaullist party was hastily thrown together after de

Gaulle's return to power in 1958. Only weeks after its birth, it won almost 18 percent of the vote and about 38 percent of the seats in the first Parliament of the new Republic in 1958.

In several respects the new Gaullist party differed from the traditional conservative parties of the right. It appealed directly to a broad coalition of groups and classes, including a part of the working class. The party's leadership successfully built a membership that at one time reached several hundred thousand. Yet the membership's role was generally limited to appearing at mass meetings and assisting in propaganda efforts at election time. An important novelty was that the party's representatives in Parliament followed strict discipline in voting on policy. Electoral success increased with each contest until the landslide election—held after the massive strikes and student **demonstrations of May–June 1968**—enabled the Gaullists to hold a majority in the National Assembly. This achievement was never before attained under a republican regime in France.

For sixteen years (from 1958 to 1974) both the presidency and the prime ministership were in Gaullist hands. In 1974, after the death of both Charles de Gaulle and Georges Pompidou, Valéry Giscard-d'Estaing was elected president. He was a prominent conservative who was not a Gaullist; thus, the Gaullist party's status deteriorated and electoral support declined.

For a time Jacques Chirac reversed the party's decline by restructuring it and renaming it the **Rally for the Republic (RPR)**. In fact, the RPR was quite different from its Gaullist predecessors. Although Chirac frequently invoked Gaullism as his inspiration, he avoided the populist language that had served the movement at its beginnings. The RPR appealed to a restricted, well-defined constituency of the right, similar to the classic conservative clientele. Its electorate overrepresented older, wealthier voters, as well as farmers (now included as the dominant part of the UMP electorate in Table 9.1). Its voters were most likely to define themselves as being on the right, antileft, positive toward business and parochial schools, more likely to vote for personality than for ideas, and least supportive of a woman's right to abortion. After presiding over a government that dubbed itself neoliberal and that engaged in a round of privatization of previously nationalized industries between 1986 and 1988, Chirac set out to assure those who feared change.

The party's electoral level remained more or less stagnant in the 1980s. Even in the massive electoral victory for the right in 1993, when the conservative coalition gained 80 percent of the parliamentary seats, the RPR just edged out its conservative rivals with less than 20 percent of the vote in the first round of the elections. In 1997 its vote declined to 16.8 percent, less than 2 percentage points more than the National Front. Nevertheless, with an estimated 100,000 members in 1997 (relatively low by European standards), the RPR was the largest party in France.[32]

By 2002 the RPR was a long way from the party once dominated with a firm hand by Gaullist "barons" and defined by the organizing discourse of Gaullism. Jacques Chirac's victory in the 1995 presidential elections should have given him an opportunity to rebuild the RPR as a party of government. However, a seemingly unending series of political crises after the summer of 1995 and the disastrous losses in the June 1997 legislative elections only intensified the divisions within the party and with its partners. In 1999 Chirac (still president of the Republic) lost control over the party when his chosen candidate was defeated in an election for party president.

In the fall of 2000, Chirac's candidacy for reelection in 2002 seemed to be undermined by dramatic new evidence of massive corruption in the Paris party machine that directly implicated the president (and former mayor of Paris). However, the unexpected match against Jean-Marie Le Pen (leader of the National Front—see below) in the presidential race of 2002 gave both Chirac and the party a new lease on life.

Chirac's massive victory in the second round of the 2002 presidential election created the basis for the organization of the UMP, a new successor to the RPR. (The UMP was originally called the Union for a Presidential Majority in 2002.) The party included deputies from the RPR, some from the **Union for French Democracy (UDF)**, and some from other small parties of the right. With more than 60 percent of the new National Assembly, the UMP united the fragmented groups of the right behind the victorious president. By 2006 Chirac's detested rival within the party, **Nicolas Sarkozy**, had become party leader, minister of the interior, and virtually unchallenged party candidate for the presidency in 2007.

***Union for French Democracy (UDF)*** Valéry Giscard d'Estaing's foremost concern was to prevent the center's exclusion from power in the Gaullist Republic. His

## Voting Patterns in the 2007 Legislative Elections

**TABLE 9.1**

Leftist parties disproportionately gain support from the young and white-collar employees, while UMP/UDF draw more votes from older voters and the bourgeoisie

| | PS/PC/Greens + Other Left | UMP/UDF + Other Right | Extreme Right FN/MNR |
|---|---|---|---|
| **Sex** | | | |
| Men | 36% | 50% | 7% |
| Women | 38 | 56 | 2 |
| **Age** | | | |
| 18–29 | 43 | 49 | 1 |
| 30–49 | 39 | 52 | 5 |
| 50+ | 32 | 56 | 6 |
| **Profession** | | | |
| Shopkeepers, craftsmen, and businesspeople | 21 | 62 | 1 |
| Executives, professionals, and intellectuals | 41 | 44 | 1 |
| Middle management | 45 | 47 | 1 |
| White-collar | 39 | 49 | 6 |
| Workers | 32 | 48 | 16 |
| Unemployed | 43 | 40 | 15 |
| **Level of Education** | | | |
| No degree | 34 | 52 | 9 |
| Vocational degree | 36 | 55 | 6 |
| High School (academic) | 45 | 49 | 3 |
| Higher education | 38 | 55 | 2 |
| **All Voters** | 37 | 53 | 4 |

Source: CSA–CISCO, *Les Elections Legislatives: Explication du Vote et Perspectives Politiques, Sondage Jour du vote*, June 2007, p. 10.

small party, the Independent Republican Party (RI), was the typical party, or rather nonparty, of French conservatism. It came into existence in 1962, when Giscard and a few other conservative deputies opposed de Gaulle's strictures against European unity and his referendum on direct elections for the presidency.

From that time on, the group provided a small complement for the conservative majority in Parliament. Giscard himself, a scion of families long prominent in business, banking, and public service, was finance minister under both de Gaulle and Pompidou before his election to the presidency in 1974. His party derived its political strength from its representatives in Parliament, many of whom held Cabinet posts, and from local leaders who occupied important posts in municipal and departmental councils.

To increase the weight of the party (the name was changed to the Parti Républicain [PR] in 1977), President Giscard chose the path that parties of the right and center have always found opportune: a heterogeneous alliance among groups and personali-

ties organized to support the president in the 1978 legislative elections. The result was the Union for French Democracy (UDF). In addition to Giscard's Republicans, it included remnants of a Catholic party (CDS), the once militant anti-Catholic radicals, and some former Socialists. It is estimated that all of the parties of the UDF combined had no more than 38,000 members as the party moved into the 2002 elections.

After 1981 the UDF and the RPR generally cooperated in elections. As the National Front gained in electoral support after 1983, the UDF and the RPR presented more joint candidates in the first round of parliamentary elections to avoid being defeated by the National Front. Nevertheless, even combined, they were incapable of increasing their vote percentage beyond 45 percent. Still, they won majorities in Parliament in 1986, 1993, and 2002 (see Figure 9.4). The two governments organized after Chirac's election in 1995 under Prime Minister **Alain Juppé** were double coalitions: first, coalitions of factions within the RPR

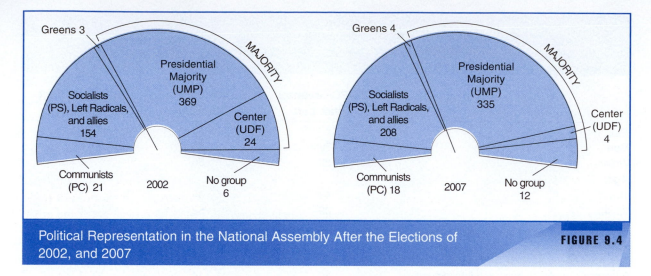

**Political Representation in the National Assembly After the Elections of 2002, and 2007**     FIGURE 9.4

and the UDF and, second, coalitions between the RPR and the UDF. Thus, the representatives of the UDF exercised considerable influence over the policymaking process, both as members of the Cabinet and as chairs of three of the six permanent committees of the National Assembly. The government in 2002 was also a double coalition. Prime Minister Jean-Pierre Raffarin (who served until 2005) was a long-time member of the UDF. With the integration of most of the UDF deputies into the UMP, the UDF as a party lost most of its independent influence.

*National Front* Divisions within the right result in part from different reactions to the electoral rise of the **National Front (FN)**. **Jean-Marie Le Pen** founded the FN in 1972. Until the 1980s it was a relatively obscure party of the far right. In none of the elections before 1983 did the FN attract more than 1 percent of the national vote. In the 1984 European Parliament elections, the FN built on support in local elections and attracted almost 10 percent of the vote, to the consternation of the established parties of the right and the left.

Then, in the parliamentary elections of 1986, the FN won almost 10 percent of the vote (about 2.7 million votes—and in metropolitan France, more votes than the Communists). This established it as a substantial political force. Two-thirds of the FN's votes came from voters who previously supported established parties of the right, but the remainder came from some former left voters (mostly Socialists) or from new voters and former abstainers.

Profiting from the change to proportional representation elections in 1986, thirty-five FN deputies entered Parliament. In the 1993 legislative elections, FN candidates attracted almost 13 percent of the vote in the first round. Because the electoral system was once again based on single-member districts, the party elected no deputies. With over 15 percent of the vote in the first round of the 1997 legislative elections, the FN sent a record number of candidates into the second round. However, only one of these candidates was elected.

Nevertheless, the FN seemed well on its way to developing a network of local bases. In 1992 the right depended on the party for its majority in fourteen out of twenty-two regions. In 1998 this dependency was translated into a political breakthrough when five UDF regional leaders formally accepted FN support to maintain their regional presidencies. In 1995, for the first time, the FN won municipal elections in three cities and gained some representation in almost half of the larger towns in France. It gained one additional city in a special election in 1997.

The ability of Le Pen to come in second—with 17 percent of the vote in the first round of the presidential elections of 2002—was a considerable shock to the political system. The FN results in the legislative elections two months later (11 percent) were far lower, but a confirmation that the party—and not simply Le Pen—remained a political force.

The National Front is often compared to the shopkeeper movement (the Poujadist movement), which attracted 2.5 million votes in the 1956 legislative elections and then faded from the scene.[33] But the

FN draws its electoral and organizational support from big-city, rather than small-town, voters. Its supporters come more from transfers from the right than did those of Poujade. In addition, the FN has been far more successful than the Poujadist movement in building a strong organizational network.

Because of the electoral system, the FN never had more than one deputy in the National Assembly after 1988. But it has hundreds of elected representatives on the regional, departmental, and local levels (as well as in the European Parliament). By 1998 it was estimated that the FN had 50,000 members (compared with 10,000 in 1985).

The National Front was seemingly given new life by Le Pen's success in 2002, success that was generally confirmed by the results of the regional and European parliamentary elections in 2004. In addition, the process of party development has affected voters of all parties, especially those who would normally vote for the right and young workers who had formerly been mobilized by the Communist Party.

Approval of the FN's issues increased dramatically among *all* voters in the 1980s and, after mid-1999, increased again. Moreover, the dynamics of party competition have forced other political parties to place FN issues high on their political agenda. Thus, Nicolas Sarkozy, in an attempt to attract FN supporters, used his position as minister of the interior to confront illegal immigration and deal with issues of law and order.

Although this strategy had been tried before, Sarkozy's efforts showed some indications of success. In fact, it proved to be remarkably successful in the presidential elections of 2007. Jean-Marie Le Pen received 800,000 fewer votes than in 2002, and almost all of them went to Sarkozy. This stunning loss weakened the party, as confirmed by the local election results in March 2008.

## The Left

*Socialist Party* In comparison with the solid social-democratic parties in other European countries, the French **Socialist Party (PS)** lacked muscle almost since its beginnings in 1905. Slow and uneven industrialization and reluctance to organize not only blocked the development of labor unions, but also deprived the PS of the working-class strength that other European labor parties gained from their trade union affiliations.

Unlike the British Labour Party, the early PS also failed to absorb middle-class radicals, the equivalent of the Liberals in England. The Socialist program, formulated in terms of doctrinaire Marxism, prevented inroads into the electorate of the left-of-center middle-class parties for a long time. The pre–Fifth Republic party was never strong enough to assume control of the government by itself. Its weakness reduced it to being, at best, one of several partners in the unstable coalition governments of the Third and Fourth Republics.

The emergence of the French Communist Party in 1920 effectively deprived the Socialists of core working-class support. Most of the Socialists' working-class following was concentrated in a few regions of traditional strength, such as the industrial north and urban agglomeration in the center. However, the party had some strongholds elsewhere—among the winegrowers of the south, devotees of republican ideals of anticlericalism, and producers' cooperatives. The proportion of civil servants, especially teachers, and people living on fixed incomes has been far higher among Socialist voters than in the population at large.

The party encountered considerable difficulties under the changed conditions in the Fifth Republic. After several false starts, the old party dissolved, and a new Socialist Party emerged in 1969. The new party successfully attracted new members and reversed its electoral decline. Incipient public disenchantment with conservative governments combined with the strong party leadership of François Mitterrand brought about this reversal in party fortunes. Compared with the past, the party membership reached respectable heights in the 1980s (about 180,000 by 1983), though it was still not comparable to the large labor parties of Britain and the Continent.

The new members came predominantly from the salaried middle classes, the professions, the civil service, and especially the teaching profession. Workers rallied to the PS in large numbers in the 1970s, but they were still sparsely represented in the party's leadership. In the 1970s the PS did what other European Socialist parties were unable to do: It attracted leaders of some of the new social movements of the late 1960s—among them, ecologists and regionalists, as well as leaders of small parties of the non-Communist left.[34]

Mitterrand reaped the benefits of the elections of 1981. With Mitterrand as president of the Republic and a Socialist majority in Parliament (but also supported by the Communists), the PS found itself in a situation it had never known—and for which it was ill-prepared. The following years of undivided power affected the party's image and outlook. The years in office between 1981 and 1986 were an intense, and painful, learning experience for the PS at all levels. Under pressure from Mitterrand and a succession of Socialist governments, the classical socialist ideology was dismantled. What the German Social Democrats had done by adopting a new program at Bad Godesberg in 1959 the French PS did in the early 1980s by its daily practice.

Indeed, by most measures the Socialist Party was to the 1980s what Gaullists were to the 1960s: a party of government with broad support among most social groups throughout the country. When reelected for a second seven-year term in 1988, Mitterrand carried seventy-seven of the ninety-six departments of metropolitan France. The Socialists made inroads in the traditionally conservative western and eastern areas of the country. However, this nationalization of Socialist electoral strength meant that the party's legislative majority depended on constituencies where voter support was far more conditional. In the legislative elections of 1993, the PS lost a third of its electorate, compared with 1988, but far more than that in areas outside of its traditional bastions.

Social trends favored the left for a time. The decline of religious observance, urbanization, the growth of the salaried middle classes (technicians, middle management, etc.) and the service sector of the economy, and the massive entry of women into the labor market all weakened the groups that provided the right's stable strength. This included farmers, people in small businesses, the traditional bourgeoisie, and the nonemployed housewives.

However, the party loyalty of large numbers of voters, especially younger voters, was evolving during the 1980s. Voter loyalty became more related to individual attitudes toward specific issues than to collective loyalties based on group or class. Thus, rising unemployment rates, the growing sense among even Socialist voters that the party leadership was worn out, and the mobilization of large numbers of traditional Socialist voters against the government during the campaign for the Maastricht referendum all undermined Socialist support between 1992 and 1994.

During ten years as a governing party (broken by two years of opposition from 1986 to 1988), Socialist leadership cohesion depended on the prerogatives of power. If the Fifth Republic became normalized during the 1980s—in the sense that the left and the right alternated in government with each legislative election—

the PS became like other governing parties in its dependence on governing power. One index of this normalization was the increased incidence of political corruption within the party. Accusations, investigations, and convictions for corruption swept all parties beginning in the late 1980s. For the Socialists, however, this corruption undermined the party's image and contributed to the voters' desertion of the party. Estimated membership dropped to about 100,000 by 1995.

Under these circumstances PS leader **Lionel Jospin** was a remarkably effective presidential candidate in 1995, winning the first round before being defeated in the second round by Chirac. After the elections the PS gained in the municipal elections, performed well in by-elections, and made significant gains in the (indirect) 1995 Senate elections. The real test for Socialist leadership came when President Chirac called surprise legislative elections in April 1997.

Although Jospin and his colleagues were clearly unprepared for the short campaign, they benefited from Chirac's rapidly deteriorating popularity and the lack of efficacy of his majority, as well as from the electorate's tendency to vote against the majority in power. Jospin put together a thirty-one-seat majority (called the *plural left*), became prime minister, and formed the first cohabitation government of the left in June 1997.

The government passed a set of important, but controversial reforms, including a thirty-five–hour workweek, domestic partnership legislation, and a constitutional amendment requiring parity for women candidacies for elective office. Finally, there were major structural reforms: The presidential term was reduced to five years (with the agreement of the president), and a process began to radically alter the relationship between Corsica and the French state.

Although the government's popularity had been declining, the elimination of Jospin in the first round of the 2002 presidential elections (by less than 1 percent) was entirely unexpected. It largely resulted from the defection of PS voters to marginal candidates of the left alliance. Jospin quickly resigned as party leader, leaving the PS without effective leadership. This resulted in the left's defeat in the legislative elections that followed, as PS representation was cut in half.

Following a well-established rhythm, the Socialists— together with their allies on the left—rebounded two years later and swept the regional elections in 2004. They won control of all but one of the twenty-two regional governments in France. They accomplished this impressive victory without strong leadership at the national level. The victory represented profound public disappointment with—and opposition to—the right, which had used the majority it had gained in 2002 to push through cuts in welfare state benefits.

Without strong leadership, however, the PS appeared engaged in a self-destructive struggle to choose a presidential candidate for the elections of 2007. In this environment Ségolène Royal initiated a well-orchestrated and well-financed campaign for the nomination a full year and a half before the elections. The campaign was to convince members of the party—who would select her by a large majority in the fall of 2006—that her candidacy was a *fait accompli*. What made her campaign interesting is that it was directed toward the voters, rather than the party members who vote for the nominee.

Royal, the first woman candidate for a major political party, was a well-established political leader of the Socialist Party. A graduate of the ENA, she rose through the party ranks, first as a deputy, then with various ministerial posts, and then as president of the Poitou-Charentes region. Her campaign substantially increased the membership of the PS. With a claimed membership of 133,000 in December 2005, the PS's paid membership increased by 54,000 in three months; membership in Paris alone doubled during this period. Therefore, it was even more disappointing when Royal lost the election to Nicolas Sarkozy in May 2007, once again leaving the party without leadership.

*French Communist Party* Until the late 1970s, the **French Communist Party (PCF)** was a major force in French politics. This was so despite the fact that, except for a short interlude after World War II (1944–1947), the party was rejected as a coalition partner in national government until 1981.

During most of the Fourth Republic, the PCF received more electoral support than any other single party (with an average of just over 25 percent of the electorate). During the Fifth Republic, the party remained, until 1978, electorally dominant on the left, although it trailed the Gaullists on the right. In addition to its successes in national elections, the party commanded significant strength at the local level until the early 1980s. Between 1977 and 1983, Communist mayors governed in about 1,500 towns in France, with a total population of about 10 million people.

Over several decades the party's very existence constantly impinged nationally, as well as locally, on the rules of the political game and thereby on the system itself. The seemingly impressive edifice of the Communists and of its numerous organizations of sympathizers was badly shaken, however—first by the rejuvenation of the PS under Mitterrand's leadership in the 1970s and then by the collapse of international communism and the Soviet Union in the 1980s.

The PCF fielded its leader, **Georges Marchais,** as a candidate in the first ballot of the presidential election of 1981 with disastrous results: With 15 percent of the vote, the PCF lost one-fourth of its electorate. In the parliamentary elections that followed, the number of its deputies was cut in half. The party's defeats in 1981 were only the beginning of a tailspin of electoral decline.[35] The voters who left the party in 1981 never came back.

By 2007 its presidential candidate attracted a mere 2 percent of the vote (about half that of far-left candidate Olivier Besancenot) and just 2 percent of the working-class vote. In the legislative elections that followed, the PCF was clearly marginal to the left. To win elections, it has grown increasingly dependent on continued (and often difficult) cooperation with the Socialists, as well as on the personal popularity of some of its long-established mayors. Nineteen of the twenty-four Communist deputies, and those associated with them, elected in 2007 were municipal council members. In 2003 the party selected **Marie-George Buffet** as its national secretary.

Although the party's claimed membership remains large by French standards, more than 200,000—but certainly less—its organization is increasingly divided, ineffective, and challenged by successive waves of dissidence from within.

What does the marginalization of the PCF mean for the French party system? It has healed the division that had enfeebled the left since the split of the Socialist Party in 1920, in the wake of the Bolshevik seizure of power in Russia. But a price has been paid: This has weakened political representation of the French working class. Although the fortunes of the PCF have fallen in inverse relation to the PS's rising electoral strength, the proportion of workers actually voting for both parties combined has declined by 30 percent since the 1970s. Perhaps most important, it appears that many young workers, who previously would have been mobilized by Communist militants, are now being mobilized to vote for the National Front.

## PATTERNS OF VOTING

Although France is a unitary state, elections are held with considerable frequency at every territorial level. Councilors are elected for each of the more than 36,000 **communes** in France, for each of the 100 departments (counties), and for each of the twenty-two regions. Deputies to the National Assembly are elected at least once every five years, and the president of the Republic is elected (or reelected) every five years (since 2002—every seven years before that). In addition, France elects representatives to the European Parliament every five years.

France was the first European country to enfranchise a mass electorate, and France was also the first European country to demonstrate that a mass electorate does not preclude the possibility of authoritarian government. The electoral law of 1848 enfranchised all male citizens over age 21. However, within five years this same mass electorate had ratified Louis Napoléon's *coup d'état* and his establishment of the Second Empire. Rather than restricting the electorate, Napoléon perfected modern techniques for manipulating it by gerrymandering districts, skillfully using public works as patronage for official candidates, and exerting pressure through the administrative hierarchy.

From the Second Empire to the end of World War II, the size of the electorate remained more or less stable. It suddenly more than doubled when women age 21 and older were granted the vote in 1944. After the voting age was lowered to 18 in 1974, 2.5 million voters were added to the rolls. By 2007 there were more than 42 million voters in France.

### Electoral Participation and Abstention

Voting participation in elections of the Fifth Republic has undergone a significant change and fluctuates far more than during previous republics. Abstention tends to be highest in referendums and European elections and lowest in presidential contests, with other elections falling somewhere in between (see Table 9.2). In the presidential election of 2007, a trend toward growing abstention was broken when 84 percent of registered voters voted in the first round.[36] The elections for the European Parliament always attract relatively few voters, but in 2004 more than 57 percent of the registered voters stayed home (slightly more than in 1999). For referendums a new record was set in 2000: Almost 70 percent of the registered voters chose not to vote in a (successful) referendum to reduce the presidential term from seven to five years (after the elections of 2002).

Rising abstention seems linked to a larger phenomenon of change in the party system. Since the late 1970s, voters' confidence in all parties has declined, and the highest abstention rates are usually among those voters who express no preference between parties of the right and left. Nevertheless, in contrast with the United States, among the 90 percent of the electorate that is registered to vote, individual abstention appears to be cyclical and there are few permanent abstainers.[37] In this sense it is possible to see abstention in an election as a political choice (42 percent of them in 2002 said that they abstained because they had no confidence in politicians).[38] Nevertheless, as in other countries, the least educated, the lowest income groups, and the youngest and oldest age groups vote less frequently.

### Voting in Parliamentary Elections

France has experimented with a great number of electoral systems and devices without obtaining more satisfactory results in terms of government coherence. The stability of the Fifth Republic cannot be attributed to the method of electing National Assembly deputies, for the system is essentially the same one used during the most troubled years of the Third Republic.

As in the United States, electoral districts (577) are represented by a single deputy who is selected through two rounds of elections. On the first election day, candidates who obtain a majority of all votes cast are elected to Parliament. This is a relatively rare occurrence (less than 20 percent in 2007) because of the abundance of candidates. Candidates who obtain support of less than 12.5 percent of the registered voters are dropped from the "second round" a week later. Other candidates voluntarily withdraw in favor of a better-placed candidate close to their party on the political spectrum. For instance, preelection agreements between Communists and Socialists (and, more recently, the Greens) usually lead to the withdrawal of the weaker candidate(s) after the first round. Similar arrangements have existed between the UMP and other parties of the center-right. As a result, generally three (or at most four) candidates face each other in the second round, in which a plurality of votes ensures election.

**TABLE 9.2**

## Parliamentary Elections in the Fifth Republic

Shifting party vote shares and parliamentary seats since 1981—percentage of votes cast, first ballot

|  | 1981 | | 1986ᵃ | | 1988 | | 1993 | | 1997 | | 2002 | | 2007 | |
|---|---|---|---|---|---|---|---|---|---|---|---|---|---|---|
| Registered voters (in millions) | 35.5 | | 36.6 | | 37.9 | | 37.0 | | 39.2 | | 41.0 | | 43.9 | |
| Abstentions (%) | 29.1 | | 21.5 | | 34.3 | | 31.0 | | 32.0 | | 35.6 | | 39.6 | |
| **Party Seats** | **%** | **Seats** | **%** | **Seats** | **%** | **Seats** | **%** | **Seats** | **%** | **Seats** | **%** | **Seats** | **%** | **Seats** |
| Communists (PCF) | 16.2 | 44 | 9.7 | 35 | 11.3 | 27 | 9.1 | 24 | 10.0 | 37 | 4.8 | 21 | 4.6 | 18ʰ |
| Socialists (PS) | 37.6 | 267 | 31.6 | 208 | 34.8 | 274 | 19.2 | 61 | 23.7 | 245 | 25.3 | 141 | 27.7 | 201ʰ |
| *Left Radicals | — | 14 | 3.0 | 2 | 1.1 | 2 | — | 8 | 1.5 | 13 | — | 8 | — | 7 |
| Majority (UMP) | — | — | — | — | — | — | — | — | — | — | 33.3ᶠ | 362ᶠ | 45.5 | 335ʰ |
| *UDF (RI and other centrists) | 19.2 | 63 | — | 129 | 18.5 | 130 | 18.8 | 207 | 14.8 | 109 | 4.9 | 22 | 7.7 | 4 |
| Gaullists (RPR) | 20.8 | 87 | 42.0 | 145 | 19.2 | 128 | 19.7 | 242 | 16.8 | 140 | — | — | — | — |
| National Front (FN) | — | — | 9.9 | 35 | 9.8 | 1 | 12.7 | 0 | 15.1 | 1 | 11.3 | — | 4.7 | — |
| Others | 6.2 | 16 | 6.6 | 23 | 5.3 | 15 | 20.5ᵇ | 37ᶜ | 18.7ᵈ | 32ᵉ | 16.3ᵍ | 13 | 6.3 | 12ᵍ |

*Votes for the Left Radicals in 1981, 1993, 2002, and 2007 are included with those of the Socialists; votes for the UDF in 1986 are included with those of the Gaullists.

ᵃ The 1986 election was by proportional representation.

ᵇ Includes the three Green parties, which received 10.9 percent of the vote.

ᶜ Includes 36 unaffiliated deputies of the right.

ᵈ Includes the Green parties' vote of 6.3 percent, as well as votes for smaller movements of the right and the left.

ᵉ Includes eight ecologists (Greens), seven dissident Socialists, and other unaffiliated deputies.

ᶠ UMP (Union of the Presidential Majority—new center-right party organized for the 2002 legislative election).

ᵍ Includes ecologists (Greens) and dissidents of the right and left, as well as the extreme right party (MNR) in 2002.

ʰ Includes affiliated independent deputies.

Source: Official results from the Ministry of the Interior, found on www.assemblee-nationale.fr/elections.

This means that the first round is similar to American primary elections except that in the French case the primary is among candidates of parties allied in coalitions of the left or center-right. There is considerable pressure on political parties to develop electoral alliances, since those that do not are at a strong disadvantage in terms of representation.

The National Front has been more or less isolated from coalition arrangements with the parties of the center-right in national elections (though less so at the subnational level). Consequently, in 2007, with electoral support of 4.4 percent, none of the FN candidates was elected. In comparison, the Communist Party benefited from an electoral agreement with the Socialists: With the same 4.4 percent of the vote, fifteen of their candidates were elected. Not surprisingly, the leading party (or coalition of parties) generally ends up with a considerably larger number of seats than is justified by its share in the popular vote.

## Voting in Referendums

Between 1958 and 1969, the French electorate voted five times on referendums (see Table 9.3). In 1958 a vote against the new constitution might have involved the country in a civil war, which it had narrowly escaped a few months earlier. The two **referendums** that followed endorsed the peace settlement in the Algerian War. In 1962, hardly four years after he had enacted by referendum his "own" constitution, General de Gaulle asked the electorate to endorse a constitutional amendment of great significance: to elect the president of the Republic by direct popular suffrage. Favorable attitudes toward the referendum and the popular election of the president, however, did not prevent the electorate from voting down another proposal submitted by de Gaulle in 1969, thereby provoking his resignation.

Since 1969 there have been only five referendums (see Table 9.3). President Georges Pompidou called a

## Election Results
### French Presidential Elections (second round) and Referendums

TABLE 9.3

| Date | Present Abstained (%) | Voted for: Winner (%) | Winning Candidate | Losing Candidate |
|------|------------------------|------------------------|-------------------|------------------|
| **Presidential Elections** | | | | |
| 12/19/65 | 15.4 | 54.5 | de Gaulle | Mitterrand |
| 6/15/69 | 30.9 | 57.5 | Pompidou | Poher |
| 5/19/74 | 12.1 | 50.7 | Giscard d'Estaing | Mitterrand |
| 5/10/81 | 13.6 | 52.2 | Mitterrand | Giscard d'Estaing |
| 5/8/88 | 15.9 | 54.0 | Mitterrand | Chirac |
| 5/7/95 | 20.1 | 52.6 | Chirac | Jospin |
| 6/5/02 | 20.3 | 82.2 | Chirac | Le Pen |
| 5/10/07 | 16.0 | 53.1 | Sarkozy | Royal |

| Date | Abstained | %Voted Yes | Outcome |
|------|-----------|------------|---------|
| **Referendums** | | | |
| 9/28/58 | 15.1 | 79.2 | Constitution passed |
| 1/8/61 | 23.5 | 75.3 | Algeria settlement |
| 4/8/62 | 24.4 | 90.7 | Algeria settlement |
| 10/28/62 | 22.7 | 61.7 | Direct election of president |
| 4/18/69 | 19.6 | 46.7 | Defeat reform package |
| 4/23/72 | 39.5 | 67.7 | Britain joins Common Market |
| 11/6/88 | 63.0 | 80.0 | New Caledonia agreement |
| 9/20/92 | 28.9 | 50.8 | Maastricht Treaty |
| 9/24/00 | 69.7 | 73.2 | Reduction of presidential term |
| 5/29/05 | 30.7 | 45.3 | Defeat EU Constitution |

Source: Official results from the Ministry of the Interior for each election and referendum: http://www.interieur.gouv.fr/misill/sections/a_votre_service/elections/resultats/accueil-resultats/view

BOX 9.2

## French Parties: The Maastricht Referendum of 1992 and the European Constitution Referendum of 2005

The loss of the referendum on the European Constitutional Treaty in 2005 was in many ways a repeat of what had happened in 1992, but with a key difference. In 1992 the president of the Republic, the leaders of the Socialist Party, most (but not all) of the leaders of the conservative opposition, and (before the summer) two-thirds of the electorate supported the referendum. It would establish the European Union, with European citizenship and (within a decade) a single European currency. It was expected to achieve an impressive majority and give a boost of support for the Socialist president and government in anticipation of the 1993 legislative elections. The results were far different. The proposed treaty split the electorates of each of the major political parties in unanticipated ways, and the summer campaign proved particularly bitter. The Gaullist opposition to the treaty was partly a revolt against the leadership of Jacques Chirac, and it was supported by a majority of RPR deputies and voters.

Within the left the Communists were weak, but bitter opponents to the approval of the treaty, and Socialist leaders were less than enthusiastic proponents. The National Front was united in its opposition. In the end the treaty was approved by a slim majority of the voters, but the results were a political disaster for those who won. For each of the major parties, their "natural" electorates split badly, and the results—in which opposition to the treaty was concentrated among the less privileged voters and in the poorest regions of the country—were widely viewed as a broad rejection of established political leadership, particularly that of the governing coalition. In 1992, with the exception of the Communists, the voters of the left strongly supported the "yes" vote, while the voters of the right generally voted "no." In 2005 the French electorate rejected the proposed new European "constitution." This time, however, the pattern was the reverse—voters of the right strongly voted "yes," while those of the left generally voted "no."

---

referendum for the admission of Britain to the Common Market. The first referendum during the Mitterrand period, in 1988, dealt with approval for an accord between warring parties on the future of New Caledonia; the referendum was a condition of the agreement. Sixty-three percent of the voters stayed home, but the accord was approved. The electorate was far more extensively mobilized when the question of ratifying the **Maastricht Treaty** on the European Union was submitted to referendum in 1992. The results were far more significant for the future of French political life (see Box 9.2). The 2000 referendum—on the reduction of the presidential term from seven to five years—was overwhelmingly approved (by 73 percent of those who voted), but the referendum was most notable for the record number of abstentions—almost 70 percent.

In contrast, the most recent referendum, in 2005 on a European constitutional treaty, attracted far more voter interest. As in a similar referendum in 1992 on the Maastricht Treaty, the campaign deeply divided both the right and the left (although the largest parties of both supported the "yes" vote), and abstention was relatively low. In contrast with 1992, however, the gov-

ernment decisively lost its gamble, and the majority voted no. When the Netherlands also rejected the document a few days later, the treaty was effectively killed.

Public opinion polls indicate that the electorate is positive toward the referendum as a form of public participation. It ranked just behind the popularly elected presidency and the Constitutional Council, among the most highly approved institutional innovations of the Fifth Republic. In one of its first moves, the new government under President Jacques Chirac in 1995 passed a constitutional amendment that expanded the use of the referendum in the areas of social and economic policy.

### Voting in Presidential Elections

Presidential elections are for French voters the most important expressions of the general will. After the presidential elections of 1965, it was evident that French voters got great satisfaction from knowing that, unlike in past parliamentary elections, national and not parochial alignments were at stake and that they could pronounce themselves on such issues. The traditional

## The Accidental President

BOX 9.3

On May 5, 2002, Jacques Chirac was reelected president of France by the largest majority ever obtained by a presidential candidate in a popular election during the Fifth Republic. Yet, when the results of the first round of the presidential elections were tabulated two weeks before, this victory was wholly unexpected. Chirac's first term was marked by the largest strike movement since 1968 and then by an ill-conceived decision to call early legislative elections in 1997, which were won by the left. After 1997 his leadership of the RPR was challenged by fragmentation and then by loss of control of the party machine (eventually to his rival, Nicolas Sarkozy). This was followed by revelations of dramatic new evidence of massive corruption in the Paris party machine that directly implicated the president (the former mayor of Paris). He appeared to be headed for likely defeat in 2002.

Then came the "divine surprise" of April 2002. With the worst result of any outgoing president in the first round (less than 20 percent of the vote), Chirac edged out his Socialist rival, Lionel Jospin. But Jospin himself was edged out by the resurgent candidate of the extreme right, Jean-Marie Le Pen. With sixteen candidates in the first round, Le Pen's considerable achievement was due in part to an accident of the electoral system and in part to the inability of leftist voters to anticipate the consequences of their dispersed votes. As a result, the shocked and leaderless left rallied to the support of Chirac to block Le Pen. Confronted with an unhappy choice between a candidate who had been accused of corruption and a candidate of the extreme right, more than 82 percent of the electorate voted for the former.

and once deeply rooted attitude that the only useful vote was against the government no longer made sense when people knew that the task was to elect an executive endowed with strong powers. Accordingly, turnout in presidential elections, with one exception, has been the highest of all elections (84 percent in 2007).

The nomination procedures for presidential candidates make it very easy to put a candidate on the first ballot, far easier than in presidential primaries in the United States. So far, however, no presidential candidate, not even de Gaulle in 1965, has obtained the absolute majority needed to ensure election on the first ballot. In runoffs, held two weeks after the first ballot, only the two most successful candidates face each other. All serious candidates are backed by a party or a coalition of parties. Nevertheless, with a record number of candidates in 2002 (sixteen—twelve in 2007), this proposition was stretched to the limit.

Because the formal campaigns are short and concentrated, radio, television, and newspapers grant candidates, commentators, and forecasters considerable time and space. The televised duels between the presidential candidates in the last four elections—patterned after debates between presidential candidates in the United States, but longer and of far higher quality— were viewed by at least half of the population.

Informal campaigns, however, are long and arduous. The fixed term of the French presidency means that, unless the president dies or resigns, there are no snap elections for the chief executive. As a result, even in the absence of primaries, the informal campaign gets quite intense years before the election. In many ways the presidential campaign of 2007 began soon after the elections of 2002.

Just as in the United States, coalitions that elect a president are different from those that secure a legislative majority for a government. This means that any candidate for the presidency who owes his nomination to his position as party leader must appeal to an audience broader than a single party. Once elected, the candidate seeks to establish political distance from his party origins. François Mitterrand was the first president in the history of the Fifth Republic to have been elected twice in popular elections. Jacques Chirac accomplished this same achievement, but served two years less because of the reduction in the length of the presidential term. (See Box 9.3).

Although the 2002 presidential election deeply divided all of the major parties, the process of coalition-building around presidential elections has probably been the key element in political party consolidation and in the development of party coalitions since 1968.

The prize of the presidency is so significant that it has preoccupied the parties of both the right and the left. It influences their organization, their tactics, and their relations with one another.

## POLICY PROCESSES

### The Executive

As we have seen, the French constitution has a two-headed executive. As in other parliamentary regimes, the prime minister presides over the government. But unlike in other parliamentary regimes, the president is far from being a figurehead. It was widely predicted that such an arrangement would necessarily lead to frequent political crises. Each of the four presidents of the Fifth Republic, and each of the prime ministers who have served under them, left no doubt that the executive has only one head: the president.

The exercise of presidential powers in all their fullness was made possible not so much by the constitutional text as by a political fact: Between 1958 and 1981, the president and the prime minister derived their legitimacy from the same Gaullist majority in the electorate—the president by direct popular elections, the prime minister by the majority support in the National Assembly. In 1981 the electorate shifted its allegiance from the right to the left, yet for the ensuing five years, the president and Parliament were still on the same side of the political divide.

The long years of political affinity between the holders of the two offices solidified and amplified presidential powers and shaped constitutional practices in ways that appear to have a lasting impact. From the very beginning of the Fifth Republic, the president not only *formally appointed* to Parliament the prime minister proposed to him (as the presidents of the previous republics had done, and as the queen of England does), but also *chose* the prime minister and the other **Cabinet** ministers. In some cases the president also dismissed a prime minister who clearly enjoyed the confidence of a majority in Parliament.

Hence, the rather frequent reshuffling of Cabinet posts and personnel in the Fifth Republic is different from similar happenings in the Third and Fourth Republics. In those systems the changes occurred in response to shifts in parliamentary support and frequently in order to forestall, at least for a short time, the government's fall from power. In the present system, the president or the prime minister—depending on the circumstances—may decide to appoint, move, or dismiss a Cabinet officer on the basis of his or her own appreciation of the member's worth (or lack of it). This does not mean that considerations of the executive are merely technical. They may be highly political, but they are exclusively those of the executive.

Since all powers proceeded from the president, the government headed by the prime minister became essentially an administrative body until 1986, despite constitutional stipulations to the contrary. The prime minister's chief function was to provide whatever direction or resources were needed to implement the policies conceived by the president. The primary task of the government was to develop legislative proposals and present an executive budget. In many respects the government's position resembled that of the Cabinet in a presidential regime such as the United States, rather than that of a government in a parliamentary system such as Britain and the earlier French republics.

Regardless of the political circumstances, weekly meetings of the Cabinet are chaired by the president and are officially called the **Council of Ministers**. They are not generally a forum for deliberation and confrontation. Although Cabinet decisions and decrees officially emanate from the council, in fact real decisions are made elsewhere.

The prime minister is more than first among equals in relation to Cabinet colleagues. Among the prime minister's many functions is the harnessing of a parliamentary majority for presidential policies, since according to the constitution, the government must resign when a majority in Parliament adopts a motion of censure or rejects the government program. This provision distinguishes France from a truly presidential regime, such as the United States or Mexico.

The relationship between president and the prime minister, however, has operated quite differently during the periods of so-called cohabitation. From 1986 to 1988 and from 1993 to 1995, a conservative majority controlled Parliament, and the president was a Socialist. From 1997 to 2002, the left held a parliamentary majority, and the president was from a conservative party. Without claiming any domain exclusively as his own, the president (Mitterrand in the first two cases and Chirac from 1997 to 2002) continued to occupy the foreground in foreign and military affairs, in accordance with his interpretation of his mandate under the constitution. The prime minister became the effective leader of the executive and pursued government objectives, but avoided interfering with presidential prerogatives.

In part because of the experiences of cohabitation, the president's role is now less imposing than it had been before 1986. Even during the interlude of Socialist government between 1988 and 1993, the Socialist prime minister was largely responsible for the main options for government action, with the president setting the limits and the tone. The relationship between President Sarkozy and his prime minister, François Fillion, indicates a reassertion of presidential prerogatives.

Another limit to executive power became clear in the spring of 2006. The effective authority of both the president and the prime minister was diminished by important policy failures (the loss of the referendum in May 2005, the urban riots the following fall, and strikes in the spring of 2006). Support for the government within the large parliamentary majority began to fray. The minister of the interior, Nicolas Sarkozy, introduced policy proposals often opposed by President Chirac and Prime Minister de Villepin, but sometimes supported by parliamentary leaders.

Thus, after the 1990s the relationship between the president and the prime minister was more complicated than during the earlier period of the Fifth Republic and varied according to the political circumstances in which each had assumed office. By 2006 the relationship between the executive and the parliamentary majority showed signs of changing as well.

Since the early days of the de Gaulle administration, the office of the chief of state has been organized to maximize the ability of the president to initiate, elaborate, and frequently execute policy. In terms of function, the staff at the Elysée Palace, the French White House, composed of a general secretariat and the presidential staff, is somewhat similar to the Executive Office staff of the U.S. president. Yet it is much smaller, comprising only forty to fifty people, with an additional support staff of several hundred people.

As the president's eyes and ears, his staff members are indispensable for the exercise of presidential powers. They are in constant contact not only with the prime minister's collaborators, but also directly with individual ministries. Through these contacts the president can initiate, impede, interfere, and assure himself that presidential policies are followed.

The prime minister has a parallel network for developing and implementing policy decisions. The most important method is the so-called interministerial meetings, regular gatherings of high civil servants attached to various ministries. The frequency of these sessions, chaired by a member of the prime minister's personal staff, reflects the growing centralization of administrative and decisionmaking authority within the office of the prime minister and the growing importance of the prime minister's policy network in everyday policymaking within the executive.

As we have seen, two different patterns exist for the sharing of executive power. When the presidential and parliamentary majorities are identical (as has been the case since 2008), the prime minister is clearly subordinate to the president.[39] Even in this case, however, the president's power is limited because he does not control the administrative machinery directly and must work through the prime minister's office and the ministries. Cooperation between the two is thus essential for effective government.

## Parliament

The constitution severely and intentionally curtails the powers of Parliament both as a source of legislation and as an organ of control over the executive. The fact that both houses of Parliament were initially confined to sessions of no more than six months in a calendar year severely reduced effectiveness. In 1995 maximum sessions were increased to nine months, opening new possibilities for parliamentary leadership to exercise initiative and control.

Despite restrictions on parliamentary activity, the legislative output of the Parliament in the Fifth Republic has been quite respectable. The average of only 98 laws per year enacted during the years of the Fifth Republic (125 per year during the reform period between 1981 and 1986) is much lower than that during the Fourth Republic. However, it is double the British average for the same period. Although either the government or Parliament may propose bills, almost all legislation is proposed by the government. The government effectively controls the proceedings in both houses and can require priority for those bills that it wishes to see adopted (see Figure 9.5). Article 44 of the

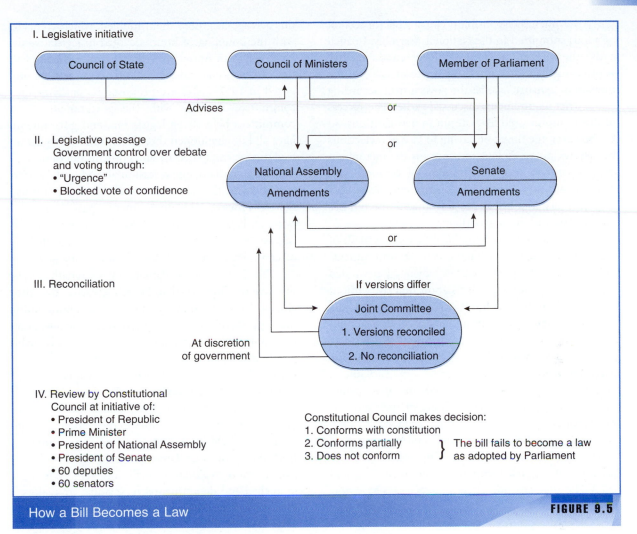

I. Legislative initiative

**Council of State**     **Council of Ministers**     **Member of Parliament**

Advises                              or

II.  Legislative passage
Government control over debate
and voting through:
• "Urgence"
• Blocked vote of confidence

                                 or

**National Assembly**          **Senate**

**Amendments**               **Amendments**

                                 or

III. Reconciliation                          If versions differ

**Joint Committee**

1. Versions reconciled

At discretion
of government                  2. No reconciliation

IV. Review by Constitutional
Council at initiative of:
• President of Republic
• Prime Minister              Constitutional Council makes decision:
• President of National Assembly   1. Conforms with constitution
• President of Senate          2. Conforms partially        } The bill fails to become a law
• 60 deputies                  3. Does not conform          } as adopted by Parliament
• 60 senators

How a Bill Becomes a Law                        **FIGURE 9.5**

Constitution empowers the government to force Parliament by the so-called **blocked vote** to accept a bill in its entirety with only the amendments agreed to by the government. In recent years the government has used the blocked vote to maintain discipline within the majority, rather than to impose the will of the executive over a chaotic Parliament. Its use has become an index of conflict within the governing party or coalition.[40] Now the amendments of 2008 have constrained the use of the blocked vote, and its use has been linked to the parliamentary majority.

Article 38 invites Parliament to abandon "for a limited time" its legislative function to the government if the government wishes to act as legislator "for the implementation of its program." Once Parliament votes a broad enabling law, the government enacts legislation by way of so-called **ordinances**. The government used this possibility of executive lawmaking twenty-two times between 1958 and 1986—often for important legislation and sometimes simply to expedite the legislative process. Decisions of the Constitutional Council have limited the use of enabling laws, requiring that the enabling act spell out the limits of executive lawmaking with some precision.

Another constitutional provision gives the government a unique tool to ensure parliamentary support for any bill that it introduces. According to Article 49, Section 3, the prime minister may pledge the "government's responsibility" on any bill (or section of a bill) submitted to the National Assembly. In such a case, the bill is automatically "considered as adopted," without further vote, unless the deputies succeed in a **motion of censure** against the government according to the strict requirements discussed earlier. The success of this motion would likely result in new elections. So far, however, the threat of having to face new elections has always put sufficient pressure on the incumbent deputies not to support a motion of censure. As a consequence, whenever the government pledges its responsibility to a bill it has introduced, the bill has become law without any parliamentary vote.

Earlier in the Fifth Republic, little use was made of this provision. Between 1981 and 1986, the governments of the left used it for reasons of expediency. It permitted them to enact important legislation quickly, without laying bare conflicts within the ranks of the governing majority. After 1986 governments of both the right and the left resorted to this procedure with considerable frequency when they needed to overcome the precariousness of their majorities in Parliament. During the five years between 1988 and 1993, prime ministers engaged the responsibility of their governments thirty-nine times, nine times each year in 1990 and 1991 alone. Between June 1997 and the election of a new parliament in 2002, this procedure was not used, but it was used three times between 2002 and 2007. The 2008 amendments to finance laws have now limited its use.

Other devices for enhancing the role of Parliament have become somewhat more effective over the years, even before the 2008 amendments. In the 1970s the National Assembly instituted a weekly question period that is similar to the British (and German) version. Two days a week the party groups submit a dozen or more written questions an hour in advance, in rough proportion to the membership of each group, and then the relevant minister answers them. This process has been expanded by the amendments of 2008. The presence of television cameras in the chamber (since 1974) creates additional public interest and records the dialogue between the government representatives and the deputies.

By using its power to amend, Parliament has vastly expanded its role in the legislative process during the past decades. During the 1980s proposed amendments averaged almost 5,000 a year. Since 1990

this average has more than doubled, which coincides with the doubling of hours devoted to legislative debate each year. About two-thirds of the amendments that are eventually adopted (33 percent of those proposed in 1997–2002) are proposed by parliamentary committees working with the government. Thus, committees help shape legislation, and governments have all but abandoned their constitutionally guaranteed prerogative to declare amendments out of order.[41] The long parliamentary session introduced in 1995 has enhanced the role of committee leaders in the legislative process. The amendments passed in 2008 bring parliamentary committees directly into the legislative process by making the legislation reported out of committees the basis for parliamentary approval.

Finally, the role of Parliament is strengthened by the general support that French citizens give their elected deputies. Better organized parties both add to the deputy's role as part of a group and somewhat diminish his or her role as an independent actor, capable of influencing the legislative process merely for narrow parochial interests. Nevertheless, individual deputies still command a considerable following within their constituencies. This pattern is enhanced because more than 87 percent of the deputies in the National Assembly in 2008 held local office, most of them municipal councilors or mayors. Large numbers were also on departmental or regional councils, and some were both municipal and departmental or regional councilors.[42] In 2001, when confidence in political parties was at 24 percent, confidence stood at 36 percent for deputies and 70 percent for mayors (see again Figure 9.3).

Because the electoral college that elects the members of the Senate is composed almost entirely of people selected by small-town elected officials, the parties of the center that are most influential in small towns are best represented in the upper house. Not surprisingly, 61 percent of senators also held local office in 2008. In 2008 the Senate was dominated by the governing majority party, the UMP, which is dependent, however, on the UDF for its majority. The Socialists are the second largest group, a result of the PS's strong roots at the local level. The Communists continue to be well represented for the same reason. Although the right remains dominant in the upper house, the Senate has not always been on the right of the political spectrum. Its hostility to social and economic change is balanced by a forthright defense of traditional republican liberties and by a stand against demagogic appeals to latent antiparliamentary feelings.

The Senate, in the normal legislative process, can do little more than delay legislation approved by the government and passed by the National Assembly. However, there are several situations in which the accord of the Senate is necessary. The most important is that any constitutional amendment needs the approval of either a simple or a three-fifths majority of senators (Article 89). In 2000 lack of support in the Senate forced the president (and prime minister) to withdraw an amendment to create an independent judiciary and to modify the amendment on parity for women (that was passed).

Some legislation of great importance—such as the nuclear strike force, the organization of military tribunals in cases involving high treason, the reorganization of local government in Corsica, and the change in the system of departmental representation—was enacted in spite of senatorial dissent. Nonetheless, until 1981 relations between the Senate and the National Assembly were relatively harmonious. The real clash with the Senate over legislation came during the years of Socialist government between 1981 and 1986, when many key bills were passed over the objections of the Senate. However, leftist government bills that dismantled some of the "law and order" measures enacted under de Gaulle, Pompidou, and Giscard were supported by the Senate. The upper house also played an active role when it modified the comprehensive decentralization statute passed by the Socialist majority in the Assembly. Most of the changes were accepted in joint committee.

Criticism of the Senate as an unrepresentative body and proposals for its reform have come from Gaullists and Socialists alike (most recently in 2008). All of these proposals for reforming the Senate have failed, though some minor modifications in its composition and mode of election have been passed.

## Checks and Balances

France has no tradition of judicial review. As in other countries with civil law systems, the sovereignty of Parliament has meant that the legislature has the last word. A law enacted in a constitutionally prescribed form is not subject to further scrutiny.

This principle seemed to be infringed upon when the Constitution of 1958 brought forth an institutional novelty, the Constitutional Council. The council in certain cases must, and in other cases may upon request, examine legislation and decide whether it conforms to the constitution. A legal provision declared unconstitutional may not be promulgated.

The presidents of the National Assembly and Senate each choose three of the council's members, and the president of the Republic chooses another three for a (nonrenewable) nine-year term. Those who nominate the council's members were, until 1974, together with the prime minister, the only ones entitled to apply to the council for constitutional scrutiny. In 1974 an amendment to the constitution made it possible for sixty deputies or sixty senators to submit cases to the Constitutional Council. Since then, appeals to the council by the opposition, and at times by members of the majority, have become a regular feature of the French legislative process.

Whichever side is in opposition, conservative or Socialist, routinely refers all major (sometimes minor) pieces of legislation to the council. In a given year, as many as 28 percent of laws passed by Parliament have been submitted for review. A surprisingly high percentage of appeals lead to a declaration of unconstitutionality. Few decisions declare entire statutes unconstitutional, and those that declare parts of legislation unconstitutional (sometimes trivial parts) effectively invite Parliament to rewrite the text in an acceptable way.

The Constitutional Council's decisions have considerable impact and have sometimes modified short-term, and occasionally long-term, objectives of governments. The council assumes the role of a constitutional court. By doing so, it places itself at the juncture of law and politics, in a way similar to the U.S. Supreme Court when it reviews the constitutionality of legislation.

In a landmark decision rendered in 1971, the council declared unconstitutional a statute adopted by a large majority in Parliament that authorized the prefects to refuse authorization to any association that they thought might engage in illegal activities. According to the decision, to require any advance authorization violated the freedom of association, one of "the fundamental principles recognized by the laws of the

Republic and solemnly reaffirmed in the preamble of the Constitution." The invocation of the preamble greatly expanded the scope of constitutional law, since the preamble incorporated in its wording broad "principles of national sovereignty," the "attachment to The Declaration of Rights of Man," and an extensive bill of rights from the Fourth Republic constitution. For introducing a broad view of judicial review into constitutional law, the decision was greeted as the French equivalent of the U.S. Supreme Court decision in *Marbury v. Madison.*

Some of the Constitutional Council's most important decisions—such as those on the nationalization of private enterprises (under the Socialists), on the privatization of parts of the public sector (under the conservatives), and on government control over the media (under both)—conform to an attitude that in the United States is called judicial restraint. A few decisions can be qualified as activist, since they directly alter the intent of the law. But as a nonelected body, the council generally avoids interference with the major political choices of the government majority. In recent years the council has nevertheless reviewed 10 percent or more of legislation that is passed each year. On average it has found 50 percent of this legislation at least partially violates the constitution. In 2007 almost 80 percent of the laws that came before the council were declared unconstitutional in part.

In a period in which alternation of governments has often resulted in sharp policy changes, the council decisions have helped to define an emerging consensus.

By smoothing out the raw edges of new legislation in judicial language, it often makes changes ultimately more acceptable (see Box 9.4).

The approval of the council's activities by a large sector of public opinion (52 percent in 2001, as shown in Figure 9.3) has encouraged the council to enlarge its powers. These efforts were partially successful in 2008, as an amendment gave the council a role in the judicial system. Cases in which the defendant claims that a law violates "rights and liberties" guaranteed by the constitution can now be appealed to the Constitutional Council, once the appeal is vetted by either the appeals court or the Conseil d'Etat.

Thus, the judicial appeal and the development of a judicial check on policymaking enhance the role of the much older **Council of State**, which in its present form dates back to 1799. The government now consults this council more extensively on all bills before they are submitted to Parliament and, as it has always done, on all government decrees and regulations before they are enacted. The council also gives advice on the interpretation of constitutional texts. While its advice is never binding, its prestige is so high that its recommendations are seldom ignored.

Unlike the Constitutional Council, the Council of State provides recourse to individual citizens and organized groups who have claims against the administration. The judicial section of the Council of State, acting either as a court of appeal or as the court of first instance, is the apex of a hierarchy of administrative courts. Whenever the council finds

---

## Judicial Review in France and the United States

**BOX 9.4**

Judicial review has become part of the French legislative process, but in a way it is still quite different from judicial review in of the United States. Direct access is limited, although citizens will have the right to bring appeals based on some constitutional issues before the Constitutional Council after 2008. The council, unlike the U.S. Supreme Court, considers legislation before it is promulgated. Since 1981 virtually all constitutional challenges have been initiated by legislative petition, a process that does not exist in the United States. A time element precludes the possibility of extensive deliberation: Rulings must be made within a month and, in emergency situations, within eight days. This is surely speedy justice, but the verdicts cannot be as explanatory as those rendered by constitutional courts in other countries. Dissenting opinions are never made public.

[See CPT9 for example of layout, this new table begins in 1981 adds 2007 election].

official acts to be devoid of a legal basis, whether those of a Cabinet minister or a village mayor, the council will annul them and grant damages to the aggrieved plaintiff.

## THE STATE AND TERRITORIAL RELATIONS

Since the First Republic in the eighteenth century, when the Jacobins controlled the revolutionary National Assembly, the French state has been characterized by a high degree of centralized political and administrative authority. Although there have always been forces that have advocated *decentralization* of political authority, as well as deconcentration of administrative authority, the French unitary state remained (formally) "one and indivisible."[43] Essentially, this meant that subnational territorial units (communes, departments, and regions) had little formal decisionmaking autonomy. They were dominated by political and administrative decisions made in Paris. Both state action and territorial organization in France depended on a well-structured administration, which during long periods of political instability and unrest kept the machinery of the state functioning.

France is divided into 100 **departments** (including four overseas departments), each about the size of an American county. Each is under the administrative responsibility of a **prefect** and has a directly elected general council. Since 1955 departments have been grouped into twenty-two **regions**, each with its own appointed prefect (in addition to the departmental prefects). Since 1986, each region has an elected assembly and president as well as a prefect (see Figure 9.6).

Centralization has always been more impressive in its formal and legal aspects than it has been in practice. The practical and political reality has always been more complex. Although France is renowned for its centralized state, what is often ignored is that political localism dilutes centralized decisionmaking (see Box 9.5).

The process of decentralization initiated by the government of the left between 1982 and 1986 was undoubtedly the most important and effective reform passed during that period. The reform built on the long-established system of interlocking relationships between central and local authorities, as well as on the previous patterns of change. The reform altered the formal roles of all the local actors, but the greatest change was that it formalized the previously informal power of these actors.[44]

These powers are based on a system of mutual dependency between local actors and the prefects, as well as field services of the national ministries. The administrators of the national ministries had the formal power to implement laws, rules, and regulations at the local level. However, they needed the cooperation of local officials, who had the confidence of their constituents, to facilitate the acceptance of the authority of the central state and to provide information to operate the administration effectively at the local level. Local officials, in turn, needed the resources and aid of the administration to help their constituents and keep their political promises.[45] As in any relationship based on permanent interaction and on cross-functioning controls, it was not always clear who controlled whom. Both the autonomy and the relational power of municipalities were conditioned by the extent of the mayor's contacts within the political and administrative network. These contacts were reinforced by the linkage to national decisionmaking that mayors had established through **cumul des mandats**—the ability to hold several electoral offices at the same time (since 2000 deputies are prohibited from holding a local executive office, including mayor of a larger city).

The decentralization legislation transferred most of the formal powers of the departmental and regional prefects to the elected presidents of the departmental and regional councils. In March 1986 *regional councils* were elected for the first time (by a system of proportional representation). In one stroke the remnants of formal prefectural authorization of local government decisions were abandoned in favor of the decisions of local officials. The department presidents, elected by their department councils, are now the chief departmental executive officers, and they, rather than the prefects, control the department bureaucracy.[46]

What then is left of the role of the central bureaucracy in controlling the periphery? The greatest loss of authority has probably been that of the prefects. Their role now seems limited to security (law and order) matters, to the promotion of the government's industrial policies, and to the coordination of the state bureaucracy at the departmental level.

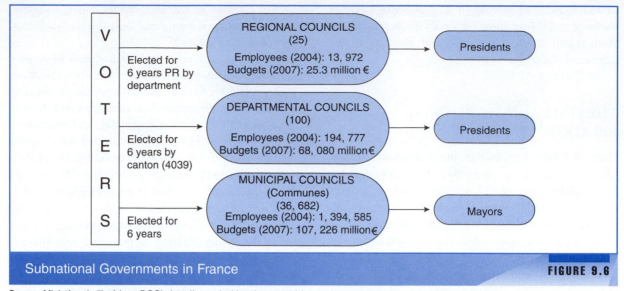

**Subnational Governments in France**

**FIGURE 9.6**

Source: Ministère de l'Intérieur, DGCL: http://www.dgcl.interieur.gouv.fr/

In matters of financing, the principal mechanisms through which the state influences local government decisions (financial dependency and standards) have been weakened, but have not been abandoned. There is still overall financial dependence of subnational governments on the state. Particularly at the commune level, local taxes provide only 40 percent of the annual budget (collected by the state). The price for financial assistance from above is enforced compliance with standards set by the state. In areas in which the state retains decisionmaking power—police, education, a large area of welfare, and social security, as well as a great deal of construction—administrative discretion and central control remain important.

Decentralization in the 1980s, combined with the system of *cumul des mandats,* gave a new impetus to local officials to expand what they previously had done in a more limited way: to trade influence for private money, to direct kickbacks into party funding operations, and to use their public office for private advantage. The pressures that led to corruption also led to more expensive political campaigns and an often poorly demarcated frontier between the public and private arenas in a country in which people who

## The Political Durability of Local Governments

**BOX 9.5**

One manifestation of the political importance of local government in France has been the ability of local units to endure. It is no accident that even after recent consolidations there are still 36,551 communes (the basic area of local administration), each with a mayor and council, or about as many as in the original six Common Market countries and Britain together. Almost 33,000 French communes have fewer than 2,000 inhabitants, and of these more than 22,000 have fewer than 500. What is most remarkable, however, is that since 1851 the number of communes in France has been reduced by only 400. Thus, unlike every other industrialized country, the consolidation of population in urban areas has resulted in almost no consolidation of towns and villages.

emerge from the grandes écoles–grands corps system move easily between the two.

## PERFORMANCE AND PROSPECTS

### A Welfare State

The overall performance of democracies can be measured by their commitment and ability to distribute the benefits of economic growth. France has a mediocre record for spreading the benefits of the postwar boom and prosperity among all its citizens. In terms of income and of wealth, discrepancies between the rich and the poor remain somewhat less in France than in other countries in Europe (see also Table 1.2 in Chapter 1). In 2001 the percentage of income earners in the top 10 percent of incomes (25 percent) was higher than in Sweden, but lower than in Germany, the United Kingdom, or the United States.[47] The percentage in the lowest 10 percent of incomes was lower than in Germany or Sweden, but slightly higher than in the United Kingdom or the United States. The income gap narrowed significantly between 1976 and 1981, and then even more during the first year of Socialist government. Yet, subsequent austerity measures, especially the government's successful effort to hold down wages, have widened the gap again.

The emergence of long-term unemployment (about 40 percent of those unemployed in 2004) has increased the number of the new poor, who are concentrated among those who are poorly trained for a rapidly evolving employment market. As opposed to the past, the majority of the lowest income group is no longer the elderly and retired and the heads of households with marginal jobs. Particularly since 1990, the unemployed are younger people, many of them long-term unemployed, especially younger single parents. Although youth unemployment rates have come down during the past decade, they remain double the national average.

Since large incomes permit the accumulation of wealth, the concentration of wealth is even more conspicuous than the steepness of the income pyramid. In the 1970s the richest 10 percent controlled between 35 and 50 percent of all wealth in France; the poorest 10 percent owned not more than 5 percent. In the 1990s it is estimated that the richest 10 percent of the families in the country owned 50 percent of the wealth, while the richest 20 percent owned 67 percent.[48]

In spite of some assertions to the contrary, it is not true that the French economy is burdened with higher taxes than other countries of similar development. Overall tax rates in 2008 were higher than those in the United Kingdom or the United States, but lower than those in Sweden or Germany. What is special about France is the distribution of its taxes. The share of indirect taxes—such as the value-added tax (VAT) and excise taxes—remains far higher in France than in other industrialized countries. Indirect taxes not only drive up prices, but also weigh most heavily on the poor. The percentage of revenue collected through regressive indirect taxation was the same in 1986, after five years of Socialist government, as it had been in 1980, and remains about the same now (77 percent in 2004).

The French welfare state is most effective in the area of social transfers. These transfers are at about the same level as in Germany and Denmark, but ahead of most other European democracies, and far ahead of the United States. A comprehensive health and social security system, established after World War II and extended since then, and a variety of programs assisting the aged, large families, persons with disabilities, and other such groups, disburses substantial benefits (Figure 9.7). When unemployment benefits, the cost of job-training programs, and housing subsidies are added in, total costs are as high as the remainder of the public budget, with three-fourths of them borne by employers and employees.

The effectiveness of the French welfare state is most evident in the relatively low poverty rates—slightly higher than in Sweden, but lower than in Germany, and far lower than in the United Kingdom and the United States. France has also maintained a high level of quality medical services and public services. High spending for welfare programs has also cushioned the worst impact of the economic crisis in 2008-2009. Much of the ad hoc stimulus spending in the United States is already built into the way the welfare state functions in France.

In contrast with the United States, there have been fewer cutbacks in welfare state programs in France in recent years—even after the cutbacks of pension benefits in 2003. Indeed, the population covered by health insurance has expanded, but financing for these programs has been at the heart of government concerns since 1995 (see Table 9.4). Although spending on social

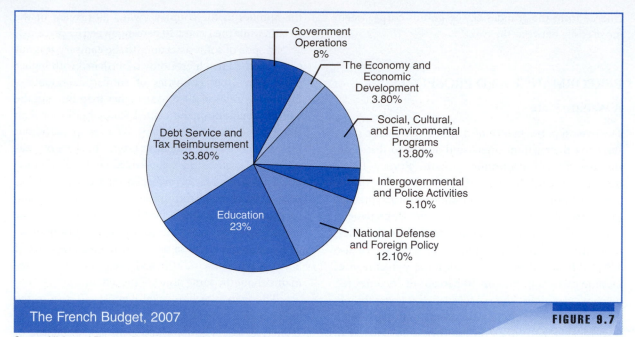

**The French Budget, 2007**

**FIGURE 9.7**

Source: Ministry of Finance, Projet de loi de finances, 2008, *Tableau de comparaison, à structure 2008, par mission et programme, des crédits proposés* pour 2008 à ceux votés pour 2007.

programs has remained stable as a percentage of the gross national product (GNP) since 1984, the government cut public spending to reduce its budget deficit in a successful effort to conform to criteria for the common European currency.

In addition, some important gaps in benefits remain. As in other systems where outcomes have been compared with socioeconomic status, studies of the French system indicate that there are important inequalities in France in access to services and in health

**Welfare State Spending**

**TABLE 9.4**

France ranks relatively high in government spending as a share of the GDP and social service programs

| | General Government Expenditure as Percentage of GDP 2006 | Government Employment as Percentage of Total Employment 1996–2000 | State Contributions to Protection Programs as Percentage of GDP 2001 | State Health Expenses as Percentage of GDP | |
|---|---|---|---|---|---|
| | | | | 1994–1995 | 2005–2006 |
| Britain | 45.0 | 18.7 | 27.2 | 5.2 | 8.4 |
| France | 53.4 | 20.1 | 30.0 | 6.6 | 11.1 |
| Germany | 45.7 | 12.3 | 29.8 | 6.3 | 10.6 |
| Italy | 50.1 | 20.5 | 25.6 | 5.3 | 8.9 |
| Spain | 38.5 | 11.6 | 20.6 | 4.7 | 8.2 |
| Sweden | 55.5 | 6.6 | 31.3 | 8.1 | 9.1 |
| United States | 36.6 | 15.6 | 16.0 | 13.3 | 15.3 |

Source: OECD 2008 (www.oecd.org), French Ministry of Finance, 2004 (www.finances.gouv.fr), Eurostat, 2004(http://epp.eurostat.ec.europa.eu/portal/), OECD Public Sector Pay and Employment Database (www.oecd.org).

outcomes. These disparities have grown since 1980, even as financial barriers to health care have diminished.[49] High levels of unemployment, social problems, and problems of homelessness create pressures to expand social programs, while diminishing the revenue base that finances them. Since 1998 the French government has confronted many of the same social service problems facing the United States, but resistance to the American-type solutions is widespread. In 1999, for example, as part of the campaign to fight "social exclusion" in France, the Socialist government passed legislation instituting universal medical coverage. This means-tested, tax-financed, and targeted health insurance program represents a departure from the tradition of social insurance in France.

In reaction to the riots of November 2005 in the "suburbs" of large French cities (the equivalent of inner-city neighborhoods), the government vowed to increase social spending in these areas and to increase employment and educational opportunities for youth. These promises were placed on hold, however, until after the presidential and legislative elections of 2007, and several years later still remain on hold.

## Nationalization and Regulation

Government-operated business enterprises have long existed in France in fields that are under private ownership in other Western European countries. After several waves of nationalization in the 1930s and after the end of World War II, the government owned and operated all or part of the following: railroads, energy production (mining, electricity, nuclear energy), telecommunication (radio and television), air and maritime transport, the aeronautic industry, 85 percent of bank deposits, 40 percent of insurance premiums, one-third of the automobile industry, and one-third of the housing industry. All this was in addition to the old state monopolies of mail services, telephone, telegraph, tobacco, match manufacture, and various less important activities.

By the 1970s public enterprises accounted for about 11 percent of the GNP. Fifteen percent of the total active population, or 27 percent of all salary and wage earners (excluding agricultural labor), were paid directly by the state as civil servants, either as salaried workers or on a contractual basis. Their income came close to one-third of the total sum of wages and salaries.

Legislation enacted during the first governments of the left in 1981–1982 completed the nationalization of the banking sector and expanded state ownership to thirteen of the twenty largest firms in France and controlling interest in many other firms in such fields as machine tools, chemistry (including pharmaceutical products), glass, metals, and electrical power. In addition, the government obtained majority control of two important armaments firms and several ailing steel companies.

The conservative government that held power in 1986–1988 substantially altered the structure of the nationalized sector in France, accelerating a trend of partial privatization begun during the previous government of the left. Its ambitious plans for **privatization** were halted (40 percent completed) only a year after their implementation began, partially because of the stock market collapse in 1987.[50] Thus some, but not all, of the companies that were nationalized by the Socialist government in 1982 were returned to private stockholders. The conservative government also privatized some companies that the state had long controlled. However, both the companies that were privatized and those that remained in the hands of the state were quite different from what they had been a few years before. Recapitalized, restructured, and modernized, for the most part, they were, in 1988, the leading edge of the French industrial machine.[51]

After the wave of privatization, the percentage of salary and wage earners receiving their checks directly or indirectly from the French state was reduced to about 22 percent in 1997. While this was high compared with the U.S. percentage, it was not out of line with other European countries. If one out of five French citizens depended on the state for his or her paychecks in the 1990s, so did about the same proportion of British and Italian citizens (see again Table 6.4). Moreover, under pressure of EU directives on competition and globalization trends, privatization is a continuing process, which is most controversial in the service sector. The state maintains only small minority interests in France Télécom and Air France, and discussions continue about selling off the few remaining state monopolies (notably the railroads and gas and electricity).

For the actual operation of French business, the move toward deregulation of the economy begun by the Socialists and continued by conservative governments was probably more important than privatization. The deregulation of the stock market, the banking system, telecommunications, and prices fundamentally changed the way business is conducted in both the private and public sectors.[52] The combination of budgetary rigor, pressures from the EU, and state disengagement meant a real reduction of aid to industry. Sectors in difficulty—including steel, chemicals, shipbuilding, and automobile manufacturing—were therefore forced to accelerate their rationalization plans and their cutbacks in workers.

As a result, the interventionist and regulatory weight of the state in industry is less important now than it was before the Socialists came to power in 1981. The old issue of nationalization and ownership has been bypassed and replaced by more subtle issues of control and regulation in the context of global competition.

In other areas, the regulatory weight of the state has not diminished, but has changed during the past twenty-five years. During the 1970s France expanded individual rights by fully establishing the rights to divorce and abortion. Under the Socialist governments of the 1980s, capital punishment was abolished, the rights of those accused of crimes were strengthened, and detention without trial was checked by new procedures. After much wrangling, in 1994 the Parliament replaced the obsolete Criminal Code dating from the time of Napoléon. The new code is generally hailed as expressing a consensus across the political spectrum on questions of crime and punishment. Moreover, individual rights in France must now conform to the decisions of the European courts under the general umbrella of the EU. Finally, in conformity with the Maastricht Treaty, citizenship rights of EU residents in France have increased during the 1990s, and in 2006 a right to the presumption of innocence in criminal cases was created under French law.

Finally, in still other areas, the regulatory weight of the state has increased. One of the most obvious is environmental controls. Beginning in the 1990s, the French state made its first significant efforts to regulate individual behavior that has an impact on the environment. The first limitations on smoking, for example, came into effect in the late 1980s and expanded after that. In February 2007 smoking was banned in most public spaces and was extended to restaurants and bars in December 2007.

In an effort to deal with the politics of immigration, particularly after 1993, the state increased the regulation of all residents of foreign origin in ways that have diminished individual rights. In 2004 France moved to regulate "ostentatious" religious symbols worn by students in public schools in response to the wearing of Islamic head scarves.

The "war on terror" had begun in France more than a decade before the September 11, 2001, attacks in the United States. However, a group of investigating judges controls the process. Although actions by the police are therefore scrutinized by judges and are undertaken under law, the challenge to civil liberties remains important nevertheless.

## Outlook: France and the New Architecture of Europe

The main concerns that dominate French politics have changed dramatically from three decades ago. In the 1980s, a coalition of Socialists and Communists was promising a "rupture" with capitalism, and the ideological distance between left and right appeared to be enormous. Today none of the major parties—including the National Front—is proposing dramatic change in society or the political system. As in the United States, political parties are making their commitments as vague and as flexible as possible (with the exception of the National Front). After an experiment with socialism, followed by a reaction of conservative neoliberalism, political parties appear to lack fresh ideas on how to deal with the major problems of the French economy and society. The transition away from a smokestack economy has been difficult and painful, and the resulting unemployment continues to dominate public concerns.

Political cleavages based on new conflicts are emerging, even if their outlines are still unclear. Indeed, the issues of the first decade of the twenty-first century may very well be more profound and untenable than those of the past. The political stakes have moved away from questioning the nature of the regime: They are focused much more intensely on the nature of the political community. Between 1986 and the present, this has become evident in a variety of ways.

Immigration has given way to ethnic consciousness, particularly among the children of immigrants from North Africa. Unlike most of the immigrant communities in the past, those of today are more reluctant to assume French cultural values as their own. This, in turn, leads to questioning the rules of naturalization for citizenship, integration into French society, and (in the end) what it means to be French.[53] During the 1980s, the National Front gave a political voice to growing ethnic tensions, which mobilized voters and solidified support based on racist appeals. In part because of the growing role of the FN, ethnic consciousness and diversity have grown in France and altered the context of French politics.

Twenty years ago the Cold War and the division of Europe were the basis for much of French foreign, defense, and, to some extent, domestic policy. The Cold War is long over. As a result, Eastern European ethnic consciousness and conflicts previously held in check by Soviet power, and in any case insulated from Western Europe by the Iron Curtain, now have been suddenly liberated. The disintegration of the Soviet Communist experiment (and the Soviet Union) has also undermined the legitimacy of classic socialism and has thus removed from French (and European) politics many of the issues that have long separated left from right. Parties of the right have lost the anti-Communist glue that contributed to their cohesiveness, but parties of the left have lost much of their purpose.

Coincidentally, the disintegration of the Communist bloc has occurred at the same time that the countries of the European Union have reinvigorated the process of European enlargement and integration, with France in the lead. Membership in the EU shapes almost every aspect of policy and provides the context for the expansion and restructuring of the economy during the Fifth Republic.[54]

At the beginning of his presidency in the early 1980s, François Mitterrand expressed his satisfaction with the existing structures of the Common Market. Having experienced their weakness, however, he increasingly felt that some form of federalism—a federalist finality—was necessary to enable Western Europe to use its considerable resources more effectively. Thus, during the Mitterrand presidency, France supported a larger and a more tightly integrated Europe. This included efforts to increase the powers of European institutions and the establishment of a European monetary and political union as outlined in the Maastricht Treaty, approved somewhat reluctantly in 1992. French commitment to a common European currency generated plans to cut public spending, plans that many French citizens ferociously resisted. Nevertheless, in 1998 France met all key requirements for and is now firmly part of the European Monetary Union.

The opening of French borders, not only to the products of other countries, but increasingly to their people and values (all citizens of the EU had the right to vote and run for office in the French local elections in 2001), feeds into the more general uneasiness about French national identity.

The integration of French economic and social institutions with those of its neighbors will progressively remove key decisions from the French government acting alone. In the past the French economy reacted to joint decisions made in Brussels. In the future, a broader range of institutions will be forced to do the same. Rumblings of resistance are no longer limited to the fringe parties (the parties of the extreme right and the Communists). Opposition exists within all of the major political parties, especially the UMP. Here, too, there is considerable potential for new political divisions.

The rejection of the European Constitutional Treaty in 2005 was what one scholar has called "an event waiting to happen." It reflected a deep questioning of two aspects of European development. First, the enlargement of Europe, particularly the candidacy of Turkey, has raised questions of both French and European identity, particularly among voters of the center-right. Second, the rapidly growing regulatory power of the EU and its liberal use of this power have deeply troubled voters of the left. The divisions evoked by the referendum of 2005 were not new, but reflected the same ones revealed in the 1992 Maastricht referendum.

Nevertheless, this chapter, completed at the end of the first year of the presidency of Nicolas Sarkozy, presents a story of a strong and stable political system with an increasingly volatile and unstable party system. The forces destabilizing the party system are the major challenges now confronting all of the members of the European Union: the problem of identity in an expanding European Union and an independent world; the problem of democratic legitimacy among voters who are less ideologically committed, and an increasing skepticism of government and politicians, by those who expect more from government.

## KEY TERMS

baccalauréat

blocked vote

Bonaparte, Napoléon

Buffet, Marie-George

Cabinet

Chirac, Jacques

communes

Confédération Française Democratique du Travail (CFDT)

Confédération Générale du Travail (CGT)

Constitution of 1958

Constitutional Council

Council of Ministers

Council of State

cumul des mandats (accumulation of electoral offices)

de Gaulle, Charles

departments

demonstrations of May–June 1968

Ecole Nationale d'Administration (ENA)

Ecole Polytechnique

European Union (EU) (European Community before 1992)

Fédération de' l'Education Nationale (FEN)

Fédération Nationale des Syndicats Agricoles (FNSEA)

Fifth Republic

Force Ouvrière (FO)

Fourth Republic

French Communist Party (PCF)

G-10

grands corps

grandes écoles

Jospin, Lionel

Juppé, Alain

Le Pen, Jean-Marie

Maastricht Treaty

Marchais, Georges

Mitterrand, François

motion of censure

Mouvement des Entreprises de France (MEDEF)

Muslims

National Assembly

National Front (FN)

nationalization

neocorporatism

new immigrants

political class

prefect

president of the Republic

prime minister

privatization

Rally for the Republic (RPR)

referendums

regions

Royal, Ségolène

Sarkozy, Nicolas

Senate

Socialist Party (PS)

Union for French Democracy (UDF)

Union for a Popular Movement (UMP)

## SUGGESTED READINGS

Ambler, John, ed. *The Welfare State in France.* New York: New York University Press, 1991.

Baumgartner, Frank R. *Conflict and Rhetoric in French Policymaking.* Pittsburgh, PA: University of Pittsburgh Press, 1989.

Bleich, Erik. *Race Politics in Britain and France: Ideas and Policymaking Since the 1960s.* Cambridge, England: Cambridge University Press, 2003.

Bowen, John. *Why the French Don't Like Headscarves: Islam, the State and Public Space.* Princeton, NJ: Princeton University Press, 2007.

Chapman, Herrick, Mark Kesselman, and Martin Schain. *A Century of Organized Labor in France.* New York: St. Martin's Press, 1998.

Culpepper, Pepper D., Peter Hall, and Bruno Palier. *Changing France: The Politics That Markets Make.* Basingstoke, England: Palgrave, 2006.

Gordon, Philip, and Sophie Meunier. *The French Challenge.* Washington, DC: Brookings Institution Press, 2001.

Hollifield, James. *Immigrants, Markets, and States: The Political Economy of Postwar Europe.* Cambridge: Harvard University Press, 1992.

Keeler, John T. S. *The Politics of Neocorporatism in France.* New York: Oxford University Press, 1987.

Keeler, John T. S., and Martin A. Schain, eds. *Chirac's Challenge: Liberation, Europeanization, and Malaise in France.* New York: St. Martin's Press, 1996.

Lewis-Beck, Michael. *The French Voter Before and After the 2002 Elections.* Basingstoke, England: Palgrave 2004.

Perrineau, Pascal, ed. *Le Vote Européen, de l'Élargissement au Référendum Français.* Paris: Presses de Sciences-Po, 2005.

Schain, Martin. *The Politics of Immigration in France, Britain and the United States: A Comparative Analysis.* New York: Palgrave-Macmillan, 2008.

Schmidt, Vivien A. *From State to Market: The Transformation of Business and Government.* New York: Cambridge University Press, 1996.

Smith, Rand W. *Crisis in the French Labor Movement: A Grassroots Perspective.* New York: St. Martin's Press, 1988.

Stone, Alec. *The Birth of Judicial Politics in France: The Constitutional Council in Comparative Perspective.* New York: Oxford University Press, 1992.

Suleiman, Ezra. *Elites in French Society.* Princeton, NJ: Princeton University Press, 1978.

———. *Private Power and Centralization in France.* Princeton, NJ: Princeton University Press, 1987.

Wilson, Frank L. *Interest Group Politics in France.* New York: Cambridge University Press, 1987.

## INTERNET RESOURCES

Office of the President: **www.elysee.fr/ang/index.shtm**

National Assembly: **www.assemblee-nat.fr**

Senate: **www.senat.fr**

Collection of websites to French institutions: **www.assemblee-nationale.fr/liens.asp**

Embassy of France in the United States: **www.info-france-usa.org**

## ENDNOTES

1. Claire Guéland, "La France s'enfonce dans une recession d'une ampleur jamais vue," *Le Monde*, March 21, 2009, p. 12.

2. The best book in English on the Constitutional Council is Alec Stone, *The Birth of Judicial Politics in France* (New York: Oxford University Press, 1992).

3. Laurence Wylie, "Social Change at the Grass Roots," in *In Search of France*, ed. Stanley Hoffmann, Charles Kindleberger, Laurence Wylie, Jesse R. Pitts, Jean-Baptiste Duroselle and François Goguel (Cambridge: Harvard University Press, 1963), p. 230.

4. See Olivier Duhamel, "Confance institutionnelle et *défiance* politique: *la démocratic* française," in Sofres, *L'État de l'opinion 2001* (Paris: Seuil, 2001), p. 75.

5. Interesting data on religious practice can be found in Sofres, *L'Etat de l'opinion 1994* (Paris: Seuil, 1994), pp. 179–199. These data are taken from an unpublished exit poll dated 26 May 1997.

6. See Sylvain Brouard and Vincent Tiberj, *Français comme les autres? Enquête sur les citoyens d'origine maghrébine, africaine et turque* (Paris: Presses de Sciences-Po, 2006).

7. See the Pew Global Attitudes Project, 6 July 2006. Retrieved July, 2006 from pewglobal.org/reports.

8. One important study found greater spontaneous class consciousness among French workers in the 1970s than among comparable groups of British workers. Duncan Gallie, *Social Inequality and Class Radicalism in France and Britain* (London: Cambridge University Press, 1983), p. 34.

9. Annick Percheron, "Socialization et tradition: transmission et invention du politique," *Pouvoirs* 42 (1988): 43.

10. Edgar Morin, *The Red and the White* (New York: Pantheon Books, 1970), discusses the noisy revolution of the teenagers and the silent one of women.

11. See Janine Mossuz-Lavau and Mariette Sineau, *Les Femmes françaises en 1978: Insertion sociale, Insertion politique* (Paris: Centre de Documentation Sciences Humaine de CNRS, 1980). The authors also found that women who were previously employed were likely to express opinions closer to those of working women than of nonworking women.

12. Annick Percheron and M. Kent Jennings, "Political Continuities in French Families: A New Perspective on an Old Controversy," *Comparative Politics* 13, no. 4 (July 1981): 421–436.

13. Ronald Inglehart, *Culture Shift* (Princeton, NJ: Princeton University Press, 1990), chs. 1–3 and tab. 2.4; Michele Tribalat, *Faire France* (Paris: La Découverte, 1995), pp. 93–98; Sylvain Brouard and Vincent Tiberj, *Français com les autres?*

*Enquête sur les citoyens d'origine maghrébine, africaine, et turque* (Paris: Presses de Sciences-Po, 2006), pp. 30–32.

14. See Laurence Haeusler, "Le monde associatif de 1978–1986," in *Données Sociales 1990*, ed. INSEE (Paris: INSEE, 1990), pp. 369–370. See also Henry Ehrmann and Martin Schain, *Politics in France,* 5th ed. (New York: HarperCollins, 1992), tab. 3.6.

15. Institut national de la statistique et des études économiques, *Tableaux de l'économie française* (Paris: INSEE, 2008).

16. John Ambler, "Constraints on Policy Innovation in Education: Thatcher's Britain and Mitterrand's France," *Comparative Politics* 20, no. 1 (October 1987): 85–105. See also John Ambler, "Conflict and Consensus in French Education," in *Chirac's Challenge: Liberalization, Europeanization, and Malaise in France*, ed. John T. S. Keeler and Martin A. Schain (New York: St. Martins Press, 1996).

17. The restrictive recruitment of the grandes écoles is confirmed by a study: "Le recruitment social de l élite scholaire depuis quarante ans," *Education et Formations* 41 (June 1995). Which institutions qualify as grandes écoles is controversial. But among the 140 or so designated as such in some estimates, only 15 or 20, with an enrollment of 2,000 to 2,500, are considered important, prestige schools. The number of private engineering and business schools that are generally considered to be grandes écoles has increased in recent years. Therefore, the total enrollment of all these schools has increased significantly to well over 100,000.

18. These results are taken from Russell J. Dalton, *Citizen Politics in Western Democracies*, 5th ed. (Washington, DC: CQ Press, 2008), ch. 2. See Sofres, *L'Etat de l'opinion 1994*, p. 232.

19. There is no legal definition for a grande école, although it is widely alluded to by citizens, journalists, and scholars. On these issues, see J.-T. Bodiguel and J.-L. Quermonne. *La Haute fonction publique sous la Ve République* (Paris: PUF, 1983), pp. 12–25, 83–94. The figures given here for grands corps (the elite administrative agencies) are approximations, based on a series of articles in *Les Echos,* 20–22 June 2006.

20. See *le Figaro*, March 25, 2008.

21. Janine Mossuz-Levau, "Les Femmes," in *Presidentielle 2007: Atlas électoral*, ed. Pascal Perrineau (Paris: Presses de Sciences Po, 2007), pp. 75–78.

22. These percentages are only approximations, since interest groups in France either refuse to publish membership figures or publish figures that are universally viewed as highly questionable. For estimates of interest group memberships, see Peter Hall, "Pluralism and Pressure Politics," in *Developments*

*in French Politics,* rev. ed., ed. Peter Hall, Jack Hayward, and Howard Machin (London: Macmillan, 1994). For recent estimates of trade union membership, see Antoine Bevort, "Les effectifs syndiqués à la CGT et à la CFDT 1945–1990," *Communisme* 35–37 (1994): 87–90. See also the recent study by Dominique Andolfatto and Dominique Labbé, *Histoire des Syndicats* (Paris: Seuil, 2006).

23. Herrick Chapman, Mark Kesselman, and Martin Schain, *A Century of Organized Labor in France* (New York: St. Martin's Press, 1998).

24. Mark Kesselman, "Does the French Labor Movement Have a Future?" in *Chirac's Challenge,* ed. Keeler and Schain. The reports of the congresses of the two largest union confederations in 2006 confirm that less than 5 percent of their members are under age 30. See *Le Monde,* 12 June 2006.

25. See Martin A. Schain, "French Unions: Myths and Realities," *Dissent* (Summer 2008), pp. 11–15.

26. The most interesting recent study is Sylvie Guillaume, *Le Petit et moyen patronat dans la nation française, de Pinay a Rafferin, 1944–2004* (Pessac, France: Presses Universitaires de Bordeaux, 2004). An earlier study by Henry W. Ehrmann. *Organized Business in France* (Princeton, NJ: Princeton University Press, 1957), presents case studies about the contacts between the administration and the employers' organizations, but it is now dated.

27. John Keeler, *The Politics of Neocorporatism in France* (New York: Oxford University Press, 1987).

28. Frank Wilson, *Interest-Group Politics in France* (New York: Cambridge University Press, 1987), pp. 151, 153, 162, and 164.

29. John T. S. Keeler, "Situating France on the Pluralism-Corporatism Continuum," *Comparative Politics* 17 (January 1985): 229–249. On subsidies, see "Patronat et organizations syndicales: un système a bout de soufflé," dossier special, *Le Monde,* 30 October 2007.

30. See the articles by John Ambler, Frank Baumgartner, Martin Schain, and Frank Wilson in *French Politics and Society* 12 (Spring/Summer 1994).

31. For a good survey of party developments between 1958 and 1981, see Frank L. Wilson, *French Political Parties Under the Fifth Republic* (New York: Praeger, 1982).

32. See Colette Ysmal, "Transformations du militantisme et déclin des partis," in *L'Engagement Politique, déclin ou mutation?* ed. Pascal Perrineau (Paris: Presses de la FNSP, 1994), p. 48. See also *L'Etat de la France* (Paris: La Découverte, 1997), pp. 521–526.

33. Stanley Hoffmann, *Le Mouvement Poujade* (Paris: A. Colin, 1956).

34. D. S. Bell and Byron Criddle, *The French Socialist Party: The Emergence of a Party of Government,* 2nd ed. (Oxford, England: Clarendon, 1988).

35. For an analysis of the decline of the Communist vote, see Martin Schain, "The French Communist Party: The Seeds of Its Own Decline," in *Comparative Theory and Political Experience,* ed. Peter Katzenstein, Theodore Lowi, and Sidney Tarrow (Ithaca, NY: Cornell University Press, 1990). Also see Jane Jenson and George Ross, *View from the Inside: A French Communist Cell in Crisis* (Berkeley: University of California Press, 1984), pt. 5.

36. It must be noted—and this is true for all figures on electoral participation throughout this chapter—that French statistics calculate electoral participation based on registered voters, while American statistics take as a basis the total number of people of voting age. About 9 percent of French citizens entitled to vote are not registered. This percentage must therefore be added to the published figures when one wishes to estimate the true rate of abstention and to compare it with the American record.

37. See Françoise Subileau and Marie-France Toinet, *Les chemins de l'abstention* (Paris: La Découverte, 1993), and Marie-France Toinet, "The Limits of Malaise in France," in *Chirac's Challenge,* ed. Keeler and Schain, pp. 289–91.

38. *Le Monde,* 15 June 2002, p. 8.

39. John T. S. Keeler and Martin A. Schain, "Presidents, Premiers and Models of Democracy in France," in *Chirac's Challenge,* ed. Keeler and Schain.

40. One of the very few analyses of the use of the blocked vote, as well as the use by the government of Article 49.3, is found in John Huber, "Restrictive Legislative Procedures in France and the United States," *American Political Science Review* 86, no. 3 (September 1992): 675–687. Huber also compares such tools with similar procedures in the U.S. Congress.

41. Didier Maus, "Parliament in the Fifth Republic: 1958–1988," in *Policy-Making in France.* ed. Paul Godt (New York: Pinter, 1989), 17; Didier Maus, *Les grands textes de la pratique institutionelle de la Ve République* (Paris: La Documentation Française, 1992).

42. These figures are taken from *cumul des mandates* presented by a committee of the French National Assembly: "Rapport fait au nom de la Commissions des lois constitutionnelles, de la legislation et de l'administration générale de la République sur le projet de loi organiques (no. 827) *limitant le* cumul *des* mandats électoraux *et* fonctions électives," par M. Bernard Roman. 2008 figures were retrieved 3 January 2009 from www. assemblée-nationale.

43. This description refers to the first article of the Constitution of 1793, which proclaims: "The French Republic is one and indivisible." The Constitution of the Fifth Republic repeats it.

44. Vivien A. Schmidt, *Democratizing France* (New York: Cambridge University Press, 1990).

45. The now classic statement of this relationship was written by Jean-Pierre Worms, who years later had major responsibilities for developing the decentralization reforms for the government of the left. See "Le Préfet et ses notables," *Sociologie du Travail* 8, no. 3 (1966): 249–275.

46. Mark Kesselman, "The Tranquil Revolution at Clochemerle: Socialist Decentralization in France," in *Socialism, the State, and Public Policy in France,* ed. Philip G. Cerny and Martin A. Schain (New York: St. Martin's Press, 1985), p. 176.

47. *OECD Factbook 2008* (Washington, DC: OECD, 2008), pp. 248–249.

48. See *Le Monde,* 7 October 1999, p. 6.

49. Victor Rodwin and Contributors, *Universal Health Insurance in France: How Sustainable?* (Washington, DC: Embassy of France, 2006), p. 187.

50. As a result, the number of workers paid indirectly by the state declined. Nevertheless, the proportion of the workforce paid directly by the state (government employment) remained stable at about 23 percent, about a third higher than in the United States, Germany, and Italy, but lower than in the Scandinavian countries. See Vincent Wright, "Reshaping the State: The Implications for Public Administration," *West European Politics* 17, no. 3 (July 1994).

51. They were also controlled by the same people as when they were nationalized. None of the newly privatized firms changed managing directors. See Michel Bauer, "The Politics of State-Directed Privatization: The Case of France 1986–1988," *West European Politics* 11, no. 4 (October 1988): 59.

52. Philip G. Cerny, "The 'Little Big Bang' in Paris," *European Journal of Political Research* 17, no. 2 (1989).

53. Martin A. Schain, *The Politics of Immigration in France, Britain and the United States: A Comparative Study* (New York: Palgrave-Macmillan, 2008).

54. See Alain Gayomarch, Howard Machin, and Ella Ritchie, *France and the European Union* (New York: St. Martin's Press, 1998).

# POLITICS IN GERMANY

*Russell J. Dalton*

## Country Bio

**Population**
82.4 million

**Territory**
137,803 square miles

**Year of Independence**
1871

**Year of Current Constitution**
1949

GERMANY

**Head of State**
President Horst Köhler

**Head of Government**
Chancellor Angela Merkel

**Languages**
German

**Religion**
Protestant 34%, Roman Catholic 34%, Muslim 4%, unaffiliated or other 28%

The unusual outcome of the 2005 elections has shaped contemporary German politics. The election results were so close that even the next day it was unclear who "won" the election. This began a protracted process of coalition-building. Neither of the largest two parties had a majority of votes, and in such cases, one party normally forms a coalition with a smaller party. But after weeks of negotiation and false starts, a new solution appeared. The two major parties—Christian Democrats and Social Democrats—would form a Grand Coalition with **Angela Merkel** becoming Germany's newest chancellor.

This result is unusual because these two parties were rivals in the just-completed election. It was as if the Democratic Party and the Republican Party in the United States decided to govern as partners despite their policy differences. The logic was that the two German parties could unite to address some of the nation's political problems that required a broad political agreement. But this meant the parties forming the government held three-quarters of the seats in the parliament and the opposition held only a quarter of the seats.

At another level Merkel's selection as chancellor was an important result. She had never held a major elective office. Having grown up in East Germany, she had been a member of the Communist Youth League. Instead of seeking a political career, she worked as a chemist until the collapse of the Berlin Wall. Further, she was a woman in a society that had always been governed by men. Merkel's election represents how much Germany has changed. Communism now seems like a memory from the distant past, and traditional social norms that shaped gender roles and political roles have changed.

The major achievement of contemporary German politics is the creation of a unified, free, and democratic nation in the short period since the unification of West Germany—the **Federal Republic of Germany (FRG)**—and East Germany—the **German Democratic Republic (GDR)**—occurred in 1990. A unified, democratic Germany has contributed to the political stability of Europe and has given millions of Eastern Germans their freedom and new opportunities. Now the challenge facing the government is to maintain the social and economic vitality of the nation, to enact reforms to ensure that the German economy and political system continue to function effectively, and to build a policy consensus on the reforms to achieve these goals.

## CURRENT POLICY CHALLENGES

What political problems do Germans typically read about when they open the daily newspaper or watch their favorite television newscast—and what political problems preoccupy policymakers in Berlin? Often the answer is the same as in most other industrial democracies. News reports analyze the state of the economy, report on crime, and generally track the social and economic health of the nation.

Economic issues are a recurring source of political debate. Germany still faces a series of economic and social problems that emerged from unification. Because the economic infrastructure of the East lagged far behind that of the West, the Eastern economy has struggled to compete in the globalized economic system. Eastern plants lacked the technology and management of Western firms, Eastern workers lacked the training and experience of their Western counterparts, and the economic infrastructure of the East was crumbling under the Communist regime. Consequently, government agencies and the **European Union (EU)** have invested more than 1,000 billion euros (€) in the East since unification—raising taxes for all Germans in the process. Still, the nightly news routinely chronicles the continuing economic difficulties in the East, which still affect the entire nation (see Box 10.1).

The economic challenges have worsened with the worldwide recession that began in late 2008. In the mid 2000s, Germany's export-oriented economy benefited from global economic expansion and domestic economic reforms. However, when the recession decreased international trade and consumption within Europe, this created new economic strains. Merkel's government has moved very cautiously, enacting two modest stimulus bills in early 2009. The recession (and a looming election in 2009) ended plans for broad structural reforms of the economic system and social programs. The Federal Republic faces greater economic uncertainty than perhaps at any other time in its history. Germany has joined with other EU member states to strengthen the banking and credit system and now faces economic slowdown with an unreformed economic system. This will be a major challenge for the new government elected in 2009.

Social services represent another source of policy debate. Health, pension, and other social welfare costs have spiraled upward, but there is little agreement on how to manage these costs. As the German population ages, the demands being placed on the social welfare system are predictably increasing. Few economists believe that the present system of social benefits is sustainable in the future, especially as Germany competes in a global economic system and works to improve conditions in the East. As the federal elections approach in fall 2009, it is likely that partisan differences on economic or social services policy will widen between the governing partners and little policy reform will occur.

The challenges of becoming a multicultural nation create another new source of political tension. Germany already had a sizeable foreign-born population because of its foreign worker programs of the 1960s and 1970s. During the 1990s there was a large

---

### The Curse of Unification?

**BOX 10.1**

Germany's attempt to rebuild its once Communist East has been an unmitigated disaster, and the massive financial transfers from the West endanger the entire nation's economy, according to a government-commissioned report.

A panel of thirteen experts, headed by former Hamburg Mayor Klaus von Dohnanyi, was charged with examining the reconstruction of Germany's eastern states. The panel concluded that the estimated €1.25 trillion ($1.54 trillion) in aid has done little to help the economically depressed region.

Perhaps even more worrying, the experts fear the €90 billion spent by the government each year is slowly destroying the economy of western Germany, as growth stagnates and the eastern states fail to revive fourteen years after German reunification.

Source: *The Deutsche Welle Report,* April 4, 2004, p. 62.

influx of refugees from the Balkan conflict, asylum seekers, and ethnic Germans from East Europe. Some people argue that "the boat is full" and new immigration should be limited, while others claim that immigration is essential for the nation's future. Policy reforms in the 1990s restricted further immigration, and the government changed citizenship laws in 2000 and reformed immigration legislation in 2002. However, the public is divided on the appropriate policies. Like much of the rest of Europe, Germany now struggles to address these issues, which are particularly difficult because of the legacy of Germany's past.

Finally, foreign policies are another source of public debate. The EU is an increasingly visible part of political reporting, and Germans are trying to determine their desired role in an expanding EU (see Chapter 12). Germany has been a prime advocate of the expansion of EU membership to include Eastern Europe, even though this may dilute Germany's influence within the EU. However, EU policies, such as monetary union and the development of a European currency, are creating internal divisions over the nation's relationship to the EU. The economic downturn in 2008 was exceptionally hard in Eastern Europe, prompting calls for Germany and other affluent western economies to support the new EU members in the East. This creates a joint economic and foreign policy challenge.

In addition, Germany is trying to define its role in the post–Cold War world. For the first time since World War II, German troops took part in a military action outside of German territory: in Kosovo in 1999 and in Afghanistan in 2001. However, Germany actively opposed the U.S. invasion of Iraq in 2003, and the current government remains critical of the U.S. actions in Iraq. Merkel, however, has worked to strengthen Germany's ties to the United States through the North Atlantic Treaty Organization (NATO) military alliance and other foreign policy activities.

The Federal Republic is one of the most successful and vibrant democracies in the world today. It has made substantial progress in improving the quality of life of its citizens, strengthening democracy, and developing a secure nation, and it has become an important member of the international community. But the continuing burdens of German unification and the lack of consensus on future policy directions mean that the current government has managed the current policy challenges, but has not taken decisive action to fully address them. These policy challenges will thus carry over to the new government elected in 2009.

## THE HISTORICAL LEGACY

The German historical experience differs considerably from that of most other European democracies. The social and political forces that modernized the rest of Europe came much later in Germany and had a less certain effect. By the nineteenth century, when most nations had defined their borders, German territory was still divided among dozens of political units. Although most European states had developed a dominant national culture, Germany was split by sharp religious, regional, and economic divisions. Industrialization generally was the driving force behind the modernization of Europe, but German industrialization came late and did not overturn the old feudal and aristocratic order. German history, even to the present, represents a difficult and protracted process of nation-building.

### The Second German Empire

Through a combination of military and diplomatic victories, Otto von Bismarck, the Prussian chancellor, enlarged the territory of Prussia and established a unified Second German Empire in 1871.[1] The empire was an authoritarian state, with only the superficial trappings of a democracy. Political power flowed from the monarch—the **Kaiser**—and the government at times bitterly suppressed potential opposition groups, especially the Roman Catholic Church and the Social Democratic party. The government expected little of its citizens: They were to pay their taxes, serve in the army, and keep their mouths shut.

The central government encouraged national development during this period. Industrialization finally occurred, and German influence in international affairs grew steadily. The force of industrialization was not sufficient to modernize and liberalize society and the political system, however. Economic and political power remained concentrated in the hands of the bureaucracy and traditional aristocratic elites. The authoritarian state was strong enough to resist the democratic demands of a weak middle class. The state was supreme: Its needs took precedence over those of individuals and society.

Failures of government leadership, coupled with a blindly obedient public, led Germany into World War I (1914–1918). The war devastated the nation. Almost 3 million German soldiers and civilians lost their lives, the economy was strained beyond the breaking point, and the government of the empire collapsed under the weight of its own incapacity to govern. The war ended with Germany a defeated and exhausted nation.

## The Weimar Republic

In 1919 a popularly elected constitutional assembly established the new democratic system of the **Weimar Republic**. The constitution granted all citizens the right to vote and guaranteed basic human rights. A directly elected parliament and president held political power, and political parties became legitimate political actors. Belatedly, the Germans had their first real experience with democracy.

From the outset, however, severe problems plagued the Weimar government. In the Versailles peace treaty ending World War I, Germany lost all its overseas colonies and a large amount of its European territory. The treaty further burdened Germany with the moral guilt for the war and the financial cost of postwar reparations to the victorious Allies. A series of radical uprisings threatened the political system. Wartime destruction and the reparations produced continuing economic problems that finally led to an economic catastrophe in 1923. In less than a year, the inflation rate was an unimaginable 26 billion percent! Ironically, the Kaiser's government, which had produced these problems, was not blamed for these developments. Instead, many people criticized the empire's democratic successor—the Weimar Republic.

The fatal blow came with the Great Depression in 1929. The Depression struck Germany harder than most other European nations or the United States. Almost a third of the labor force became unemployed, and people were frustrated by the government's inability to deal with the crisis. Political tensions increased, and parliamentary democracy began to fail. **Adolf Hitler** and his **National Socialist German Workers' Party (the Nazis)** were the major beneficiaries. Their vote share grew from a mere 2 percent in 1928 to 18 percent in 1930 and 33 percent in November 1932.

Increasingly, the machinery of the democratic system malfunctioned or was bypassed. In a final attempt to restore political order, President Paul von Hindenburg appointed Hitler chancellor of the Weimar Republic in January 1933. This was democracy's death knell.

Weimar's failure resulted from a mix of factors.[2] The lack of support from political elites and the public was a basic weakness of Weimar. Democracy depended on an administrative and military elite that often longed for the old authoritarian political system. Elite criticism of Weimar encouraged similar sentiments among the public. Many Germans were not committed to democratic principles. The fledgling state then faced a series of severe economic and political crises. Such strains might have overloaded the ability of any system to govern effectively. These crises further eroded public support for Weimar and opened the door to Hitler's authoritarian and nationalistic appeals. The institutional weaknesses of the political system contributed to Weimar's political vulnerability. Finally, most Germans drastically underestimated Hitler's ambitions, intentions, and political abilities. This underestimation, perhaps, was Weimar's greatest failure.

## The Third Reich

The Nazis' rise to power reflected a bizarre mixture of ruthless behavior and concern for legal procedures. Hitler called for a new election in March 1933 and then suppressed the opposition parties. Although the Nazis failed to capture an absolute majority of the votes, they used their domination of the parliament to enact legislation granting Hitler dictatorial powers. Democracy was replaced by the new authoritarian "leader state" of the **Third Reich**.

Once entrenched in power, Hitler pursued extremist policies. Social and political groups that might challenge the government were destroyed, taken over by Nazi agents, or coopted into accepting the Nazi regime. The powers of the police state grew and choked off opposition. Attacks on Jews and other minorities steadily became more violent. Massive public works projects lessened unemployment, but also built the infrastructure for a wartime economy. The government enlarged and rearmed the military in violation of the Versailles treaty. The Reich's expansionist foreign policy challenged the international peace.

Hitler's unrestrained political ambitions finally plunged Europe into World War II in 1939. After initial victories a series of military defeats beginning in 1942 led to the total collapse of the Third Reich in May 1945. A total of 60 million lives were lost worldwide in the war, including 6 million European Jews who were murdered in a Nazi campaign of systematic genocide.[3] Germany lay in ruins: Its industry and transportation systems were destroyed, its cities were rubble, millions were homeless, and even food was scarce. Hitler's grand design for a new German Reich had instead destroyed the nation in a Wagnerian *Götterdämmerung*.

## The Occupation Period

The political division of postwar Germany began as foreign troops advanced onto German soil. At the end of the war, the Western Allies—the United States, Britain, and France—controlled Germany's Western zone, and the Soviet Union occupied the Eastern zone. This was to be an interim division, but growing frictions between Western and Soviet leaders increased tensions between the regions.

In the Western zone, the Allied military government began a denazification program to remove Nazi officials and sympathizers from the economic, military, and political systems. The occupation authorities licensed new political parties, and democratic political institutions began to develop. These authorities also reorganized the economic system along capitalist lines. Currency and market economy reforms in 1948 revitalized the economic system of the Western zone, but also deepened divisions between the Eastern and Western zones.

Political change followed a much different course in the Eastern zone. The new **Socialist Unity Party (SED)** was a mechanism for the Soviets to control the political process. Since they saw capitalism as responsible for the Third Reich, the Soviets tried to destroy the capitalist system and construct a new socialist order in its place. By 1948 the Eastern zone was essentially a copy of the Soviet political and economic systems.

As the political distance between occupation zones widened, the Western allies favored creation of a separate German state in the West. In Bonn, a small university town along the banks of the Rhine, the Germans began to create a new democratic system. In 1948 a parliamentary council drafted an interim constitution that was to last until the entire nation was reunited. In May 1949 the state governments in the Western zone agreed on the **Basic Law (Grundgesetz)** that created the FRG, or West Germany.

These developments greatly worried the Soviets. The Soviet blockade of Berlin in 1948, for example, partially sought to halt the formation of a separate West German state—though it actually strengthened Western resolve. Once it became apparent that West Germany would follow its own course, preparations began for a separate East German state. A week after the formation of the FRG, the People's Congress in the East approved a draft constitution. On October 7, 1949, the GDR, or East Germany, was formed. As in earlier periods of German history, a divided nation was following different paths (see Figure 10.1). It

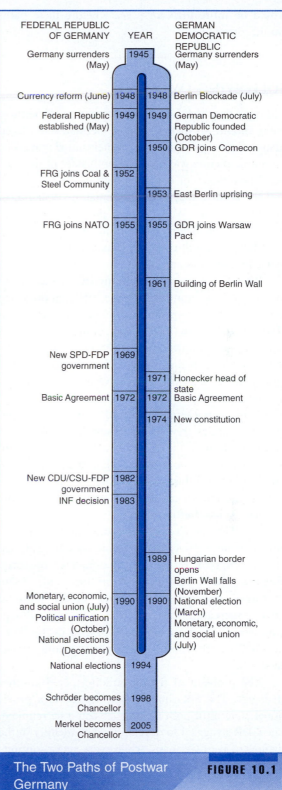

| FEDERAL REPUBLIC OF GERMANY | YEAR | GERMAN DEMOCRATIC REPUBLIC |
|---|---|---|
| Germany surrenders (May) | 1945 | Germany surrenders (May) |
| Currency reform (June) | 1948 | Berlin Blockade (July) |
| Federal Republic established (May) | 1949 | German Democratic Republic founded (October) |
| | 1950 | GDR joins Comecon |
| FRG joins Coal & Steel Community | 1952 | |
| | 1953 | East Berlin uprising |
| FRG joins NATO | 1955 | GDR joins Warsaw Pact |
| | 1961 | Building of Berlin Wall |
| New SPD-FDP government | 1969 | |
| | 1971 | Honecker head of state |
| Basic Agreement | 1972 | Basic Agreement |
| | 1974 | New constitution |
| New CDU/CSU-FDP government | 1982 | |
| INF decision | 1983 | |
| | 1989 | Hungarian border opens Berlin Wall falls (November) |
| Monetary, economic, and social union (July) Political unification (October) National elections (December) | 1990 | National election (March) Monetary, economic, and social union (July) |
| National elections | 1994 | |
| Schröder becomes Chancellor | 1998 | |
| Merkel becomes Chancellor | 2005 | |

**The Two Paths of Postwar Germany**    **FIGURE 10.1**

The history of the Federal Republic and the German Democratic Republic since 1949 would be more than forty years before these paths would converge.

## FOLLOWING TWO PATHS

Although they had chosen different paths (or had these paths chosen for them), the two German states faced many of the same challenges in their initial years. The economic picture was bleak on both sides of the border. Unemployment remained high in West Germany, and the average wages were minimal. In 1950 almost two-thirds of the West German public felt they had been better off before the war, and severe economic hardships were still common. The situation was even worse in East Germany.

West Germany was phenomenally successful in meeting this economic challenge.[4] Relying on a free enterprise system championed by the **Christian Democratic Union (CDU)**, the country experienced sustained and unprecedented economic growth. By the early 1950s, incomes had reached the prewar level, and growth had just begun. Over the next two decades, per capita wealth nearly tripled, average hourly industrial wages increased nearly fivefold, and average incomes grew nearly sevenfold. By most economic indicators, the West German public in 1970 was several times more affluent than at any time in its pre–World War II history. This phenomenal economic growth is known as West Germany's **Economic Miracle (Wirtschaftswunder)**.

East Germany's postwar economic miracle was almost as impressive. Its economic system was based on collectivized agriculture, nationalized industry, and centralized planning.[5] From 1950 until 1970, industrial production and per capita national income increased nearly fivefold. Although still lagging behind its more affluent relatives in the West, the GDR was the model of prosperity among socialist states.

The problem of nation-building posed another challenge. The FRG initially was viewed as a provisional state until both Germanies could be reunited. The GDR struggled to develop its own identity in the shadow of West Germany, while expressing a commitment to eventual reunification. In addition, the occupation authorities retained the right to intervene in the two Germanies even after 1949. Thus, both states faced the challenge of defining their identity—as separate states or as parts of a larger Germany—and regaining national sovereignty.

West Germany's first chancellor, **Konrad Adenauer**, steered a course toward gaining national sovereignty by integrating the FRG into the Western alliance. The Western Allies would grant greater autonomy to West Germany if it was exercised within the framework of an international body. For example, economic redevelopment was channeled through the European Coal and Steel Community and the European Economic Community. West Germany's military rearmament occurred within NATO.

The Communist regime in the GDR countered the FRG's integration into the Western alliance with calls for German unification. And yet, the GDR was simultaneously establishing itself as a separate German state. In 1952 the GDR transformed the boundary between East and West Germany into a fortified border; this restricted Western access to the East and limited Easterners' ability to go to the West. The GDR integrated its economy into the Soviet bloc through membership in the Council for Mutual Economic Assistance (COMECON), and it was a charter member of the Warsaw Pact military alliance. The Soviet Union recognized the sovereignty of the GDR in 1954. The practical and symbolic division of Germany became official with the GDR's construction of the Berlin Wall in August 1961. More than a physical barrier between East and West, it marked the formal existence of two separate German states.

Intra-German relations took a dramatically different course after the Social Democratic Party (SPD) won control of West Germany's government after the 1969 elections. The new SPD chancellor, Willy Brandt, followed a policy toward the East (**Ostpolitik**) that accepted the postwar political situation and sought reconciliation with Eastern European nations, including the GDR. West Germany signed treaties with the Soviet Union and Poland to resolve disagreements dating back to World War II and to establish new economic and political ties. In 1971 Brandt received the Nobel Peace Prize for his actions. The following year the two Germanies adopted the Basic Agreement, which formalized their relationship as two states within one nation. To the East German regime, *Ostpolitik* was a mixed blessing. On the one hand, it legitimized the GDR through its recognition by the FRG and the normalization of East-West relations. On the other hand, economic and social exchanges increased East

Germans' exposure to Western values and ideas, which many GDR politicians worried would undermine their closed system. The eventual revolution of 1989 seemingly confirmed their fears.

After reconciliation between the two German states, both spent most of the next two decades addressing their internal needs. SPD policy reforms in the West expanded social services and equalized access to the benefits of the Economic Miracle. Total social spending nearly doubled between 1969 and 1975. As global economic problems grew in the mid-1970s, Helmut Schmidt of the SPD became chancellor and slowed the pace of reform and government spending.

The problems of unrealized reforms and renewed economic difficulties continued into the 1980s. In 1982 the CDU enticed the **Free Democratic Party (FDP)** to form a new government under the leadership of **Helmut Kohl**, head of the Christian Democratic Union. The new government wanted to restore the FRG's economy, while still providing for social needs. Kohl presided over a dramatic improvement in economic conditions. The government also demonstrated its commitment to the Western defense alliance by accepting new NATO nuclear missiles. The public returned Kohl's coalition to office in the 1987 elections.

Worldwide economic recession also buffeted the GDR's economy starting in the late 1970s. The cost competitiveness of East German products diminished in international markets, and trade deficits with the West grew steadily. Moreover, long-delayed investment in the country's infrastructure began to show in a deteriorating highway system, an aging housing stock, and an outdated communications system. Although East Germans heard frequent government reports about the nation's economic success, their living standards evidenced a widening gap between official pronouncements and reality.

In the late 1980s, East German government officials were concerned with the winds of change rising in the East. Soviet President Mikhail Gorbachev's reformist policies of *perestroika* and *glasnost* seemed to undermine the pillars supporting the East German system (see Chapter 10). At one point an official GDR newspaper even censored news from the Soviet Union in order to downplay Gorbachev's reforms. Indeed, the stimulus for political change in East Germany came not from within, but from the events sweeping across the rest of Eastern Europe.

In early 1989 the first cracks in the Communist monolith appeared. Poland's Communist government accepted a series of democratic reforms, and the Hungarian Communist Party endorsed democratic and market reforms. When Hungary opened its border with neutral Austria, a stream of East Germans vacationing in Hungary started leaving for the West. East Germans were voting with their feet. Almost 2 percent of the East German population emigrated to the FRG over the next six months. The exodus also stimulated mass public demonstrations against the regime within East Germany.

Gorbachev played a crucial role in directing the flow of events in Germany. He encouraged the GDR leadership to undertake internal reforms with the cautious advice that "life itself punishes those who delay." Without Soviet military and ideological support, the end of the old GDR system was inevitable. Rapidly growing public protests increased the pressure on the government, and the continuing exodus to the West brought the East's economy to a near standstill. The government did not govern; it barely existed, struggling from crisis to crisis. In early November the government and the SED Politburo resigned. On the evening of November 9, 1989, a GDR official announced the opening of the border between East and West Berlin. In the former no-man's-land of the Berlin Wall, Berliners from East and West joyously celebrated together.

Once the euphoria of the Berlin Wall's opening had passed, East Germany had to address the question of "What next?" The GDR government initially tried a strategy of damage control, appointing new leaders and attempting to court public support. However, the power of the state and the vitality of the economy had already suffered mortal wounds. Protesters who had chanted "We are the people" when opposing the Communist government in October took up the call for unification with a new refrain: "We are one people." The only apparent source of stability was unification with the FRG, and the rush toward German unity began.

In March 1990 the GDR had its first truly free elections since 1932. The Alliance for Germany, which included the eastern branch of the Christian Democrats, won control of the government. Helmut Kohl and Lothar de Maiziere, the new GDR leader, both forcefully moved toward unification. On July 1 an intra-German treaty gave the two nations one currency and essentially one economy. Soviet concessions on the terms of union opened the road to complete unification. On October 3, 1990, after more than four decades of separation, the two German paths again converged.

Unification largely occurred on Western terms. In fact, Easterners sarcastically claim that the only trace of the old regime is one law kept from the GDR: Automobiles can turn right on a red light in the East. Otherwise, the Western political structures, Western interest groups, Western political parties, and Western economic and social systems were simply exported to the East.

Unification was supposed to be the answer to a dream, but during the next few years, it must have occasionally seemed like a nightmare. The Eastern economy collapsed with the end of the GDR; at times unemployment rates in the East exceeded the worst years of the Great Depression. The burden of unification led to inflation and tax increases in the West and weakened the Western economy. The social strains of unification stimulated violent attacks against foreigners in both halves of Germany. At the end of 1994, Kohl's coalition won a razor-thin majority in national elections.

Tremendous progress had been made by 1998, but the economy still struggled and necessary changes in tax laws and social programs languished. When the Germans went to the polls in 1998, they voted for a change and elected a new government headed by **Gerhard Schröder** and the Social Democrats in alliance with The Greens (*Die Grünen*). The new governing coalition made some progress on addressing the nation's major policy challenges—such as a major reform of the tax system and continued investments in the East—but not enough progress. The coalition won the 2002 election, but with a reduced margin.

After cumulative losses in state elections and deepening dissatisfaction with the government, Schröder called for early elections in 2005. After an intense campaign, both the SPD and the Christian Democratic Union/Christian Social Union (CDU/CSU) gained the same share of the vote. The closeness of the vote showed the divisions on how the nation should deal with its current policy challenges. Merkel eventually convinced a Schröder-less SPD to join the CDU/CSU in forming a Grand Coalition. Analysts hoped that this alliance could enact significant economic and policy reforms, but the divisions within the coalition have led to a cautious style of government with little major policy change.

## SOCIAL FORCES

The new unified Germany is the largest state in the European Union. It has about 82 million people, 68 million in the West and 14 million in the East, located in Europe's heartland. The total German economy is also Europe's largest. The combined territory of the new Germany is also large by European standards, although it is small in comparison to the United States—a bit smaller than Montana.

The merger of two nations is more complex than the simple addition of two columns of numbers on a balance sheet, however. Unification created new strengths, but it also redefined and potentially strains the social system that underlies German society and politics. The merger of East and West holds the potential for reviving some of Germany's traditional social divisions.

Young people from East and West Berlin celebrate the opening of the Berlin Wall in November 1989.

Lionel Cironneau/AP Images

## Economics

Postwar economic growth occurred at different rates in the West and East and followed different paths. In the FRG, the service and technology sectors grew substantially, and government employment more than doubled during the later twentieth century. Although we often think of Germany as an industrial society, barely a quarter of those in the labor force describe themselves as blue-collar workers; two-thirds say they have a white-collar occupation. In contrast, the GDR's economic expansion was concentrated in heavy industry and manufacturing. In the mid-1980s about half of the Eastern labor force worked in these two areas, and the service-technology sector was a small share of the economy.

By the mid-1980s the FRG's standard of living ranked among the highest in the world. By comparison, the average East German's living standard was barely half that of a Westerner. Basic staples were inexpensively priced in the East, but most consumer goods were more expensive, and so-called luxury items (color televisions, washing machines, and automobiles) were beyond the reach of the average family. In 1985 about a third of the dwellings in East Germany lacked their own bathroom. GDR residents lived a comfortable life by East European standards, although far short of Western standards.

German unification meant the merger of these two different economies: the affluent Westerners and their poor cousins from the East; the sophisticated and technologically advanced industries of the FRG and the aging rust-belt factories of the GDR. At least in the short run, unification worsened the economic problems of the East. By some accounts, Eastern industrial production fell by two-thirds between 1989 and 1992—worse than the decline during the Great Depression. The government sold Eastern firms, and often the new owners began by reducing the labor force. Even by mid-2008, a sixth of the Eastern labor force was still unemployed.

During the unification process, politicians claimed that the East would enjoy a new economic miracle in a few years. This claim was overly optimistic. The government assumed a major long-term role in rebuilding the East's economic infrastructure and encouraging investment in the East. Only massive social payments by the FRG initially maintained the living standards in the East. And many young Easterners moved to the West to find a job. While economic conditions have improved in the East, many Easterners remain skeptical about their economic future. The persisting economic gap between East and West creates a basis for social and political division in the new Germany. Even after significant economic growth in recent years, in 2008 Germans felt they have benefited little from this growth and worried that inflation is eroding their living standard.[6]

## Religion

The postwar FRG experienced a moderation of religious differences, partly because there were equal numbers of Catholics and Protestants and partly because elites made a conscious effort to avoid the religious conflicts of the past. Secularization also gradually reduced the public's religious involvement. In the East the Communist government sharply limited the political and social roles of the churches.

German unification has shifted the religious balance in the new Federal Republic. Catholics make up two-fifths of Westerners, but less than a tenth of Easterners. Thus, Protestants now slightly outnumber Catholics in unified Germany. There is also a small Muslim community that accounts for about 4 percent of the population. Even more dramatic, most Easterners claim to be nonreligious, which may decrease support for policies that benefit religious interests. A more Protestant and secular electorate should change the policy preferences of the German public on religiously based issues, such as abortion, and may potentially reshape electoral alliances.

## Gender

Gender roles are another source of social differentiation. In the past the three K's—*Kinder* (children), *Kirche* (church), and *Küche* (kitchen)—defined the woman's role, while politics and work were male matters. Attempts to lessen role differences have met with mixed success. The FRG's Basic Law guarantees the equality of the sexes, but the specific legislation to support this guarantee has been lacking. Cultural norms changed only slowly; cross-national surveys show that males in the West are more chauvinist than the average European and that women in the West feel less liberated than other European women.[7]

The GDR constitution also guaranteed the equality of the sexes, and the government aggressively protected this guarantee. However, East German women were one of the first groups to suffer from the unification process.

Eastern women lost rights and benefits that they had held under East German law. For instance, in 1993 the Constitutional Court resolved conflicting versions of the FRG and GDR abortion laws and essentially ruled for the FRG's more restrictive standards. The GDR provided child-care benefits for working mothers that the FRG did not. The greater expectations of Eastern women moved gender issues higher on the FRG's political agenda after unification. The government passed new legislation on job discrimination and women's rights in 1994. Most Eastern women feel they are better off today than under the old regime because they have gained new rights and new freedoms that were lacking under the GDR. Merkel's selection as chancellor in 2005 is stimulating further changes in gender norms and policies in Germany.

## Minorities

A new social cleavage involves Germany's growing minority of foreigners.[8] When the FRG faced a severe labor shortage in the 1960s, it recruited millions of workers from Turkey, Yugoslavia, Italy, Spain, Greece, and other less developed countries. German politicians and the public considered this a temporary situation, and the foreigners were called **guest workers** (**Gastarbeiter**). Most of these guest workers worked long enough to acquire skills and some personal savings, and then they returned home.

A strange thing happened, however. Germany asked only for workers, but they got human beings. Cultural centers for foreign workers emerged in many cities. Some foreign workers chose to remain in the FRG, and they eventually brought their families to join them. Foreigners brought new ways of life, as well as new hands for factory assembly lines.

From the beginning the foreign worker population has faced several problems. They are concentrated on the low rung of the economic ladder. Foreigners—especially those from Turkey and other non-European nations—are culturally, socially, and linguistically isolated from mainstream society. The problems of social and cultural isolation are especially difficult for the children of foreigners. Foreigners also were a target for violence in reaction to the strains of unification, and there is opposition to further immigration.

The nation has struggled with the problem of becoming a multicultural society, but the solutions are still uncertain. The Federal Republic revised the Basic Law's asylum clause in 1993 (making it closer to U.S. immigration policy), took more decisive action in combating violence, and mobilized the tolerant majority in German society. The government changed the citizenship laws in 2000 to better integrate foreign-born residents into German society. However, the gap between native Germans and Muslim immigrants seems to be widening. Attempts to liberalize naturalization of citizenship are linked to programs to educate the new citizens about German language, culture, and political norms. Addressing the issues associated with permanent racial/ethnic minorities (roughly 6 percent of the population) will be a continuing feature of German politics.

## Regionalism

Regionalism is another potential social and political division. Germany is divided into sixteen states (*Länder*), ten states in the West and six new states created in the East, including the city-state of Berlin. Many of the *Länder* have their own distinct historical traditions and social structure. The language and idioms of speech differentiate residents from the Eastern and Western halves of the nation. No one would mistake a northern German for a Bavarian from the south—their manners and dialects are too distinct.

Unification greatly increased the cultural, economic, and political variations among the states because of differences between West and East. It is common to hear of "a wall in the mind" that separates *Wessies* (Westerners) and *Ossies* (Easterners). Easterners still draw on their separate traditions and experiences when making political decisions, just as Westerners do. Regional considerations thus are an important factor in society and politics.

The decentralized nature of society and the economy reinforces these regional differences. Economic and cultural centers are dispersed throughout the country, rather than being concentrated in a single national center. There are more than a dozen regional economic centers, such as Frankfurt, Cologne, Dresden, Düsseldorf, Munich, Leipzig, and Hamburg. The mass media are organized around regional markets, and there are even several competing "national" theaters.

These various social characteristics—economic, religious, gender, ethnicity, and regionalism—are politically relevant for many reasons. They define differing social interests, such as the economic needs of the working class versus those of the middle class, that are often expressed in policy debates. Social groups also are a source of political and social identity that links individuals to interest groups and political parties. Voting patterns, for instance, typically show clear group differences in party support. Thus, identifying the important group differences in German society provides a foundation for understanding parts of the political process.

# THE INSTITUTIONS AND STRUCTURE OF GOVERNMENT

When the Parliamentary Council met in Bonn in 1948–1949, its members faced a daunting task. They were supposed to design a new political structure for a new democratic Germany that would avoid the problems that led to the collapse of the Weimar Republic.[9] If they failed, the consequences might be as dire as the last collapse of German democracy.

The Basic Law they crafted is an exceptional example of political engineering—the construction of a political system to achieve specific goals:

- Develop a stable and democratic political system,
- Maintain some historical continuity in political institutions (which, for Germany, meant a parliamentary system of government),
- Re-create a federal structure of government,
- Avoid the institutional weaknesses that contributed to the collapse of Weimar democracy, and
- Establish institutional limits on extremist and antisystem forces.

The framers wanted to establish clearer lines of political authority and to create a system with extensive checks and balances in order to prevent the usurpation of power that occurred during the Third Reich. The new system created a parliamentary democracy that involves the public, encourages elite political responsibility, disperses political power, and limits the influence of extremists.

The Basic Law was supposedly temporary until both halves of Germany were united. In actuality, the GDR's rapid collapse in 1990 led to its incorporation into the existing constitutional and economic systems of the Federal Republic. In September 1990 the FRG and the GDR signed a treaty to unify their two states, and the government amended the Basic Law to include the states in the East. Thus, the political system of the unified Germany functions according to the Basic Law. This section describes the key institutions and procedures of this democratic system.

## A Federal System

One way to distribute political power and to build checks and balances into a political system is through a federal system of government. The Basic Law created one of the few federal political systems in Europe (see Figure 10.2). Germany is organized into sixteen states (*Länder*). Political power is divided between the federal government (*Bund*) and the state governments. The federal government has primary policy responsibility in most policy areas. The states, however, have jurisdiction in education, culture, law enforcement, and regional planning. In several other policy areas, the federal government and the states share responsibility, although federal law takes priority. Furthermore, the states can legislate in areas that the Basic Law does not explicitly assign to the federal government.

The state governments have a unicameral legislature, normally called a *Landtag*, which is directly elected by popular vote. The party or coalition that controls the legislature selects a minister president to head the state government. Next to the federal chancellor, the minister presidents are among the most powerful political officials in the Federal Republic.

The federal government is the major force in the legislation of policy, and the states are primarily responsible for policy administration. The states enforce most of the domestic legislation enacted by the federal government, as well as their own regulations. The state governments also oversee the operation of the local governments.

One house of the bicameral federal legislature, the Bundesrat, is comprised solely of representatives appointed by the state governments. State government officials also participate in selecting the federal president and the justices of the major federal courts. This federal system thus decentralizes political power by balancing the power of the state governments against the power of the federal government.

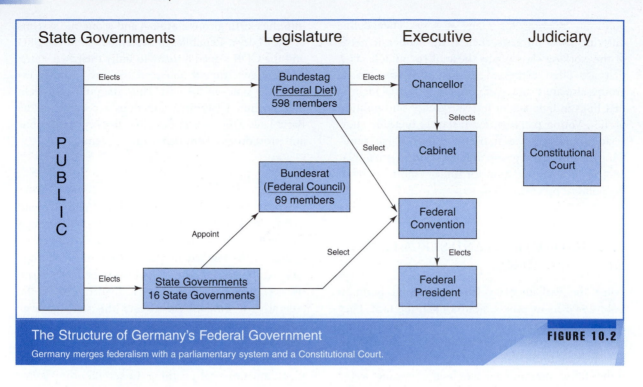

**The Structure of Germany's Federal Government**

Germany merges federalism with a parliamentary system and a Constitutional Court.

**FIGURE 10.2**

## Parliamentary Government

The central institution of the federal government is the parliament, which is bicameral: The popularly elected Bundestag is the primary legislative body; the Bundesrat represents the state governments at the federal level.

*The Bundestag* The 598 deputies of the **Bundestag (Federal Diet)** are the only national government officials who are directly elected by the German public.[10] Elections to select parliamentary deputies normally occur every four years.

The Bundestag's major function is to enact legislation; all federal laws must receive its approval. The initiative for most legislation, however, lies in the executive branch. Like other modern parliaments, the Bundestag primarily evaluates and amends the government's legislative program. Another important function of the Bundestag is to elect the federal chancellor, who heads the executive branch.

Through a variety of mechanisms, the Bundestag is a forum for public debate. Its plenary sessions discuss the legislation before the chamber. Debating time is allocated to all party groupings according to their size; both party leaders and backbenchers normally participate. The Bundestag televises its sessions, including live broadcasts on the Internet, to expand the public audience for its policy debates.[11]

The Bundestag also scrutinizes the actions of the government. The most common method of oversight is the "question hour" adopted from the British House of Commons. An individual deputy can submit a written question to a government minister: Questions range from broad policy issues to the specific needs of one constituent. Government representatives answer the queries during the question hour, and deputies can raise follow-up questions at that time. Bundestag deputies posed more than 15,000 oral and written questions during the 1998–2002 term of the Bundestag.

The Bundestag boasts a strong set of legislative committees that strengthen its legislative and oversight roles. These committees provide expertise to balance the policy experience of the federal agencies; the committees also conduct investigative hearings in their area of specialization. Their oversight function is further strengthened because opposition parties chair a proportionate share of these committees, a very unusual pattern for democratic legislatures.

The opposition parties normally make greatest use of these oversight opportunities; about two-thirds

The beginning of a new nation: Chancellor Helmut Kohl addresses the first meeting of the all-German parliament (Bundestag) held in the Berlin Reichstag building in October 1990.

dpa/Newscom

of the questions posed during the 1994–1998 term came from the opposition parties. Rank-and-file members of the governing parties also use these devices to make their own views known.

Overall, the Bundestag's oversight powers are considerable, especially for a legislature in a parliamentary system. Legislative committees can collect the information needed to understand and question government policymakers. Bundestag members can use the question hour and other methods to bring attention to political issues and challenge the government. And through its votes, the Bundestag often prompts the government to revise its legislative proposals to gain passage.

*The Bundesrat* The second chamber of the parliament, the **Bundesrat (Federal Council)**, reflects Germany's federal system. The state governments appoint its sixty-nine members to represent their interests. The states normally appoint members of the state cabinet to serve jointly in the Bundesrat; the chamber thus acts as a permanent conference of state officials. Each state receives Bundesrat seats in numbers roughly proportionate to the state's population, from three for the least populous states to six seats for the most. Each state delegation casts its votes in a bloc, according to the instructions of the state government.

The Bundesrat's role is to represent state interests. It does this in evaluating legislation, debating government policy, and sharing information between federal and state governments. The Bundesrat is an essential part of the German federal system.

In summary, the parliament mainly reacts to government proposals, rather than taking the policy initiative. However, in comparison to other European parliamentary systems, the Bundestag exercises more autonomy than the typical parliament. Especially if one includes the Bundesrat, the German parliament has considerable independence and opportunity to revise government proposals and to exercise oversight on the government. By strengthening the power of the parliament, the Basic Law sought to create a check on executive power. Experience shows that the political system has met this goal.

## The Federal Chancellor and Cabinet

A weakness of the Weimar system was the division of executive authority between the president and the chancellor. The Federal Republic still has a dual executive, but the Basic Law substantially strengthened the formal powers of the **federal chancellor (Bundeskanzler)** as the chief executive office. Moreover, the incumbents of this office have dominated the political process and symbolized the federal government by their personalization of power. The chancellor plays such a central role in the political system that some observers describe the German system as a "chancellor democracy."

The Bundestag elects the chancellor, who is responsible for the conduct of the federal government. The chancellor wields substantial power. She represents a majority of the Bundestag and normally can count on their support for the government's legislative proposals. The chancellors usually have led their own party, directing party strategy and leading the party at elections. Each chancellor also brings a distinct personality to the office. Schröder was a doer who governed with a strong personality; Merkel prefers a more consultative and cooperative decisionmaking style, while still shaping the course of her government.

Another source of the chancellor's authority is her control over the Cabinet. The federal government now consists of fourteen departments, each headed by a minister. The Cabinet ministers are formally appointed, or dismissed, by the federal president on the recommendation of the chancellor (Bundestag approval is not necessary). The Basic Law also grants the chancellor the power to decide the number of Cabinet ministers and their duties.

The federal government functions in terms of three principles described in the Basic Law. First, the *chancellor principle* says that the chancellor defines government policy. The formal policy directives issued by the chancellor are legally binding on the Cabinet and the ministries. Thus, in contrast to the British system of shared Cabinet responsibility, the German Cabinet is formally subordinate to the chancellor in policymaking.

The second principle, *ministerial autonomy,* gives each minister the authority to direct the ministry's internal workings without Cabinet intervention as long as the policies conform to the government's guidelines. Ministers are responsible for supervising the activities of their departments, guiding their policy planning, and overseeing the administration of policy within their jurisdiction.

The *cabinet principle* holds that when conflicts arise between departments over jurisdictional or budgetary matters, the Basic Law calls for the Cabinet to resolve them.

The actual working of the federal government is more fluid than the formal procedures listed in the Basic Law. The number and choice of ministries for each party are major issues in building a multiparty government coalition after each election. Cabinet members also display great independence on policy despite the formal restrictions of the Basic Law. Ministers are appointed because of their expertise in a policy area. In practice, ministers often identify more with their role as department head than with their role as agent of the chancellor; their political success is judged by their representation of department interests.

The Cabinet thus serves as a clearinghouse for the business of the federal government. Specific ministers present policy proposals originating in their departments in the hope of gaining government endorsement. The chancellor defines a government program that reflects a consensus of the Cabinet and relies on negotiations and compromise within the Cabinet to maintain this consensus.

## The Federal President

Because of the problems associated with the Weimar Republic's divided executive, the Basic Law changed the office of **federal president (Bundespräsident)** into a mostly ceremonial post. The president's official duties involve greeting visiting heads of state, attending official government functions, visiting foreign nations, and carrying out similar tasks.[12] To insulate the office from electoral politics, the president is selected by the Federal Convention, composed of all Bundestag deputies and an equal number of representatives chosen by the state legislatures. The president is supposed to remain above partisan politics once elected.

The reduction in the president's formal political role does not mean that an incumbent is uninvolved in the policy process. The Basic Law assigns several legal functions to the president, who appoints government and military officials, signs treaties and laws, and has the power of pardon. In these instances, however, the chancellor must countersign the actions. The president also nominates a chancellor to the Bundestag and can dissolve parliament if a government bill loses a no-confidence vote. In both instances the Basic Law limits the president's ability to act independently.

Potentially more significant is the constitutional ambiguity over whether the president must honor certain government requests. The legal precedent is unclear on whether the president has the constitutional right to veto legislation, to refuse the chancellor's recommendation for Cabinet appointments, or even to reject a request to dissolve the Bundestag. Analysts see these ambiguities as another safety valve built into the Basic Law's elaborate system of checks and balances.

The office of the federal president also has political importance that goes beyond the articles of the Basic Law. An active, dynamic president can influence the political climate through his speeches and public activities. The president is the one political figure who can rightly claim to be above politics and who can work to extend the vision of the nation beyond its everyday concerns. Horst Köhler was elected president in 2004 after serving as director of the International Monetary Fund.

## The Judicial System

The ordinary courts, which hear criminal cases and most legal disputes, are integrated into a unitary system. The states administer the courts at the local and state levels. The highest ordinary court, the Federal Court of Justice, is at the national level. All courts apply the same national legal codes.

A second set of administrative courts hear cases in specialized areas. One court deals with administrative complaints against government agencies, one handles tax matters, another resolves claims involving social programs, and one deals with labor-management disputes. Like the rest of the judicial system, these specialized courts exist at both the state and the federal levels.

The Basic Law created a third element of the judiciary: the independent **Constitutional Court**. This court reviews the constitutionality of legislation, mediates disputes between levels of government, and protects the constitutional and democratic order.[13] This is an innovation for the German legal system because it places one law, the Basic Law, above all others. This also implies limits on the decisionmaking power of the parliament and the judicial interpretations of lower court judges. Because of the importance of the Constitutional Court, its sixteen members are selected in equal numbers by the Bundestag and Bundesrat and can be removed only for abuse of the office.

The creation of a body to conduct constitutional review is another successful institutional innovation of the Federal Republic. The Constitutional Court provides another check on the potential excesses of government and gives citizens additional protection for their human rights. It has become a third pillar of contemporary German democracy.

## The Separation of Powers

One of the Basic Law's secret strengths is avoiding the concentration of power in the hands of any one actor or institution. The framers wanted to disperse political power so that extremists or antidemocrats could not overturn the system; democracy would require a consensus-building process. Each institution of government has strong powers within its own domain, but a limited ability to force its will on other institutions.

For instance, the chancellor lacks the authority to dissolve the legislature and call for new elections, something that normally exists in parliamentary systems. Equally important, the Basic Law limits the legislature's control over the chancellor. In a parliamentary system, the legislature typically can remove a chief executive from office by a simple majority vote. During the Weimar Republic, however, extremist parties used this device to destabilize the democratic system by opposing incumbent chancellors. To address situations where parliament might desire to remove the chancellor, the Basic Law created a **constructive no-confidence vote**.[14] In order for the Bundestag to remove a chancellor, it simultaneously must agree on a successor. This ensures continuity in government and an initial majority in support of a new chancellor. It also makes it more difficult to remove an incumbent; opponents cannot simply disagree with the government—a majority must agree on an alternative. The constructive no-confidence vote has been attempted only twice—and has succeeded only once. In 1982 a majority replaced Chancellor Schmidt with a new chancellor, Helmut Kohl.

The Constitutional Court is another check on government actions, and it has assumed an important role as the guarantor of citizen rights and the protector of the constitution. The distribution of power and policy responsibilities between the federal and state governments is another moderating force in the political process. Even the strong bicameral legislature ensures that multiple interests must agree before making public policy.

This structure complicates the governing process—compared with a unified system, such as that in Britain, the Netherlands, or Sweden. However, democracy is often a complicated process. This system of shared powers and of checks and balances has enabled German democracy to grow and flourish. This is a very successful example of how constitutional engineering helped democratize the nation.

## REMAKING POLITICAL CULTURES

Consider for a minute what the average German must have thought about politics as World War II was ending. Germany's political history was hardly conducive to good democratic citizenship. Under the Kaiser the government expected people to be subjects, not active participants in the political process; this style nurtured feelings of political intolerance. The interlude of the

Weimar Republic did little to change these values. The polarization, fragmentation, and outright violence of the Weimar Republic taught people to avoid politics, not to be active participants. Moreover, democracy eventually failed, and national socialism arose in its place. The Third Reich then raised another generation under an intolerant, authoritarian system.

Because of this historical legacy, the Federal Republic's development was closely linked to the question of whether its political culture was congruent with its democratic system. Initially, there were widespread fears that West Germany lacked a democratic political culture, thereby making it vulnerable to the same problems that undermined the Weimar Republic. Postwar opinion polls in the West presented a negative image of public opinion that was probably equally applicable to the East.[15] West Germans were politically detached, accepting of authority, and intolerant in their political views. A significant minority of them were unrepentant Nazis, sympathy for many elements of the Nazi ideology was widespread, and anti-Semitic feelings remained commonplace.

Perhaps even more amazing than the Economic Miracle was the transformation of West Germany's political culture in little more than a generation. Confronted by an uncertain public commitment to democracy, the government undertook a massive political reeducation program. The schools, the media, and political organizations were mobilized behind the effort. The citizenry itself also was changing—older generations raised under authoritarian regimes were gradually being replaced by younger generations socialized during the postwar democratic era. The successes of a growing economy and a relatively smoothly functioning political system also changed public perceptions. These efforts created a new political culture more consistent with the democratic institutions and process of the Federal Republic.

With unification Germany confronted another serious cultural question. The Communists had tried to create a rival culture in the GDR that would support their state and its socialist economic system. Indeed, the efforts at political education in the East were intense and extensive; they aimed at creating a broad "socialist personality" that included nonpolitical attitudes and behavior.[16] Young people were taught a collective identity with their peers, a love for the GDR and its socialist brethren, acceptance of the Socialist Unity Party, and a Marxist-Leninist understanding of history and society.

German unification meant the blending of these two different political cultures, and at first the consequences of this mixture were uncertain. Without scientific social science research in the GDR, it was unclear if Easterners had internalized the government's propaganda. At the same time, the revolutionary political events leading to German unification may have reshaped even long-held political beliefs. What does a Communist think after attending communism's funeral?

Unification thus created a new question: Could the FRG assimilate 16 million new citizens with potentially different beliefs about how politics and society should function? The following sections discuss the key elements of German political culture and how they have changed over time.

## Orientations Toward the Political Community

A common history, culture, territory, and language created a sense of a single German community long before Germany was politically united. Germany was the land of Schiller, Goethe, Beethoven, and Wagner, even if the Germans disagreed on political boundaries. The imagery of a single *Volk* binds Germans together despite their social and political differences.

Previous regimes had failed, however, to develop a common political identity to match the German social identity. Succeeding political systems were short lived and did not develop a popular consensus on the nature and goals of German politics. Postwar West Germany faced a similar challenge: building a political community in a divided and defeated nation.

In the early 1950s, large sectors of the West German public identified with the symbols and personalities of previous regimes.[17] Most people felt that the Second Empire or Hitler's prewar Reich represented the best times in German history. Substantial minorities favored a restoration of the monarchy or a one-party state. Almost half the population believed that if it had not been for World War II, Hitler would have been one of Germany's greatest statesmen.

Over the next two decades, these ties to earlier regimes gradually weakened, and the bonds to the new institutions and leaders of the Federal Republic steadily grew stronger (see Figure 10.3). The number of citizens who believed that Bundestag deputies represent the public interest doubled between 1951 and 1964; public respect shifted from the personalities of

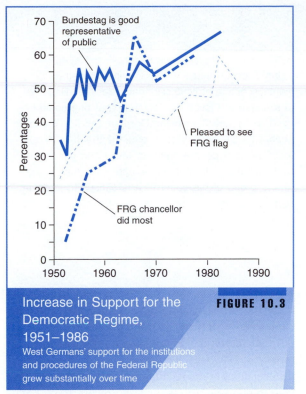

**Increase in Support for the Democratic Regime, 1951–1986**

**FIGURE 10.3**

West Germans' support for the institutions and procedures of the Federal Republic grew substantially over time

Source: Russell J. Dalton, *Politics in Germany,* 2nd ed. (New York: HarperCollins, 1993), p. 121.

prior regimes to the chancellors of the Federal Republic. By the 1970s an overwhelming majority of the public felt that the present was the best time in German history. West Germans became more politically tolerant, and feelings of anti-Semitism declined sharply. The public displayed a growing esteem for the new political system.[18]

Even while Westerners developed a new acceptance of the institutions and symbols of the Federal Republic, something was missing, something that touched the spirit of their political feelings. The FRG was a provisional entity, and "Germany" meant a unified nation. Were citizens of West Germany to think of themselves as Germans, West Germans, or some mix of both? In addition, the trauma of the Third Reich burned a deep scar in the Western psyche, making citizens hesitant to express pride in their nation or a sense of German national identity. Because of this political stigma, the FRG avoided many of the emotional national symbols that are common in other nations. There were few political holidays or memorials, one seldom heard the national

anthem, and even the anniversary of the founding of the FRG received little public attention. This legacy means that even today Germans are hesitant to openly express pride in the nation (see Box 10.2).

The quest for a national identity also occurred in the East. The GDR claimed to represent the "pure" elements of German history; it portrayed the FRG as the successor to the Third Reich. Most analysts believe that the GDR had created at least a sense of resigned loyalty to the regime because of its political and social accomplishments. Thus, a 1990 study found that Eastern youth most admired Karl Marx (followed by the first president of the GDR), while Western youth were most likely to name Konrad Adenauer, the first chancellor of the FRG.[19] Once socialism failed, however, the basis for a separate East German political identity also evaporated.

Unification began a process by which the German search for a national political identity could finally be resolved. The opening of the Berlin Wall created positive political emotions that were previously lacking. The celebration of unification, and the designation of October 3 as a national holiday, finally gives Germans a positive political experience to celebrate. Citizens in East and West remain somewhat hesitant to embrace an emotional attachment to the nation, and Easterners retain a lingering tie to their separate past. Yet, the basic situation has changed. For the first time in over a century, nearly all Germans agree where their borders begin and end. Germany is now a single nation—democratic, free, and looking toward the future.

## Orientations Toward the Democratic Process

A second important element of the political culture involves citizen attitudes toward the political process and system of government. In the early years of West Germany, the rules of democratic politics—majority rule, minority rights, individual liberties, and pluralistic debate—did not fit citizens' experiences. To break this pattern, political leaders constructed a system that formalized democratic procedures. Citizen participation was encouraged and expected, policymaking became open, and the public gradually learned democratic norms by continued exposure to the new political system. Political leadership provided a generally positive example of competition in a democratic setting. Consequently, a popular consensus slowly developed in support of the democratic political system. By

## Can One Be Proud and German?

**BOX 10.2**

Could anyone imagine a French president or a British prime minister or indeed just about any other world leader refusing to say he was proud of his nationality? Yet, this is a contentious statement in Germany because expressions of nationalism are still linked by some to the excessive nationalism of the Third Reich. Thus, when in 2001 the general secretary of the Christian Democratic Union declared: "I am proud to be German," he set off an intense national debate. A Green member of the Social Democratic Party–Green

Cabinet replied that this statement demonstrated the mentality of a right-wing skinhead. President Rau tried to sidestep the issue by declaring that one could be "glad" or "grateful" for being German, but not "proud." Then Chancellor Schröder entered the fray: "I am proud of what people have achieved and our democratic culture. . . . In that sense, I am a German patriot who is proud of his country." It is difficult to imagine such exchanges occurring in Washington, D.C., or Paris.

Source: *The Economist*, March 24, 2001, p. 62.

the mid-1960s there was nearly unanimous agreement that democracy was the best form of government. More important, the Western public displayed a growing commitment to democratic procedures—a multiparty system, conflict management, minority rights, and representative government.[20]

Political events occasionally have tested popular commitment to democratic values in West Germany. For instance, during the 1970s a small group of extremists attempted to topple the system through a terrorist campaign.[21] In the early 1980s, the Kohl government faced a series of violent actions by anarchic and radical ecology groups. In recent years new threats from international terrorists and jihadist extremists have threatened the nation. In these instances, however, the basic conclusion was that the political system could face the onslaughts of political extremists and survive with its basic procedures intact—and without the public losing faith in the democratic process.

The propaganda of the East German government also stressed a democratic creed. In reality, however, the regime tried to create a political culture that was compatible with a communist state and a socialist economy. The culture drew on traditional Prussian values of obedience, duty, and loyalty: The government again told people that obedience was the responsibility of a good citizen and that support of the state (and the party) was an end in itself. Periodically, political events—the 1953 East Berlin uprising, the construction of the Berlin Wall, and the expulsions of political dissidents—

reminded East Germans of the gap between the democratic rhetoric of the regime and reality.

One reason the popular revolt may have grown so rapidly in 1989 was that citizens no longer supported the principles of the regime, even if they might be hesitant to publicly express such sentiments under a Stasi police state. For instance, studies of young Easterners found that identification with Marxism-Leninism and belief in the inevitable victory of socialism dropped off dramatically during the mid-1980s.[22] At the least, the revolutionary changes that swept through East Germany as the Berlin Wall fell nurtured a belief in democracy as the road to political reform. A 1990 public opinion survey found nearly universal support for basic tenets of democracy among both West and East Germans.[23]

The true test of democracy, of course, occurs in the real world. Some studies suggest that Easterners' initial understanding of democracy was limited, or at least different from that of Westerners.[24] Yet, Easterners in 1989 were markedly more supportive of democracy than were Germans in 1945. Rather than remaking this aspect of the East German culture, the greater need was to transform Eastern support for democracy into a deeper and richer understanding of the workings of the process and its pragmatic strengths and weaknesses. And now, almost two decades after unification, with an Easterner as the chancellor, the principles of democracy are becoming engrained in the political culture—both West and East.

## Social Values and the New Politics

Another area of cultural change in West Germany involves a shift in public values produced by the social and economic accomplishments of the nation. Once West Germany addressed traditional social and economic needs, the public broadened its concerns to include a new set of societal goals. New issues—such as the environment, women's rights, and increasing citizen participation—attracted public attention.

Ronald Inglehart explained these political developments in terms of the changing value orientations of Westerners.[25] He maintains that a person's value priorities reflect the family and societal conditions that prevail early in life. Older generations, socialized before the post–World War II transformation, have experienced uncertain economic and political conditions, which lead them to still emphasize economic security, law and order, religious values, and a strong national defense—despite the economic and political advances of the past half century. In contrast, because younger generations grew up in a democratic and affluent nation, they were shifting their attention toward **New Politics** values. These new values emphasize self-expression, personal freedom, social equality, self-fulfillment, and quality of life.

Although only a minority of Westerners hold these new values, they represent a "second culture" embedded within the dominant culture of FRG society. These values are less developed among Easterners. Still, the evidence of political change is apparent. Public interest in New Politics issues has gradually spread beyond its youthful supporters and developed a broader base. Even in the East, many of the early demonstrations for democracy had supporters calling for *"Freiheit und Umwelt"* (freedom and the environment).

## Two Peoples in One Nation?

Citizens in the East and West share a common German heritage, but forty years of separation created cultural differences that now are blended into a single national culture.

Because of these different experiences, the broad similarities in many of the political beliefs of Westerners and Easterners are surprising. Easterners and Westerners both espouse support for the democratic system and its norms and institutions. There is also broad acceptance of the principles of Germany's social

Greenpeace Germany protests against nuclear power and the nuclear recycling plant at Sellafield.

AP Images/Fabian Bimmer

market economy. Thus, the Federal Republic's second transition to democracy features an agreement on basic political and economic values that is markedly different from the situation after World War II.

Yet, other aspects of cultural norms do differ between regions. For instance, although residents in both the West and the East endorse the tenets of democracy, it is harder to reach agreement on how these ideals translate into practical politics. The open, sometimes confrontational style of Western politics is a major adjustment for citizens raised under the closed system of the GDR. In addition, Easterners endorse a broader role for government in providing social services and guiding social development than is found among Westerners.[26]

There are also signs of a persisting gap in regional identities between East and West. The passage of time and harsh postunification adjustments created a nostalgia for some aspects of the GDR among its former residents. Easterners do not want a return to communism or socialism, but many miss the slower and more predictable style of their former lives. Even while expressing support for Western capitalism, many Easterners have difficulty adjusting to the idea of unemployment and to the competitive pressures of a market-based economy. There is a nostalgic yearning for symbols of these times, ranging from the Trabant automobile to consumer products bearing Eastern labels. The popularity of the 2003 movie *Goodbye Lenin!* is an indication of these sentiments—and a good film for students interested in this phase of German history. In fact, Easterners have developed a regional identity that is similar to the feelings of Southerners in the United States. Moreover, even though Easterners favor democracy, only 41 percent in 2007 were satisfied with how it functions in the Federal Republic, compared with more than two-thirds among Westerners.[27] Easterners still feel that the political system overlooks their needs.

Unification may have also heightened New Politics conflicts within German society. The GDR had struggled to become a materialist success, while the West enjoyed its postmaterial abundance. Consequently, Easterners give greater weight to such goals as higher living standards, security, hard work, and better living conditions. Most Easterners want first to share in the affluence and consumer society of the West before they begin to fear the consequences of this affluence. The clash of values within West German society is now joined by East-West differences.

Germans share a common language, culture, and history—and a common set of ultimate political goals—although the strains of unification may magnify and politicize the differences. The nation's progress in blending these two cultures successfully will strongly affect the course of the new Germany.

## POLITICAL LEARNING AND POLITICAL COMMUNICATION

If a congruent political culture helps a political system to endure, as many political experts maintain, then one of the basic functions of the political process is to create and perpetuate these attitudes. This process is known as *political socialization*. Researchers normally view political socialization as a source of continuity in a political system, with one generation transmitting the prevailing political norms to the next. In Germany, however, the socialization challenges for the past half century have been to change the culture inherited from the Third Reich and then to change the culture inherited from the GDR.

### Family Influences

During their early years, children have few sources of learning comparable to their parents—normally the major influence in forming basic values. Family discussions can be a rich source of political information and one of the many ways that children internalize their parents' attitudes. Basic values acquired during childhood often persist into adulthood.

In the early postwar years, family socialization did not function smoothly on either side of the German border. Many parents did not discuss politics with their children for fear that the child would ask, "What did you do under Hitler, Daddy?" The potential for parental socialization grew steadily as the political system of the FRG began to take root, however.[28] The frequency of political discussion increased in the West, and family conversations about politics became commonplace. Moreover, young new parents raised under the system of the FRG could pass on democratic norms held for a lifetime.

The family also played an important role in the socialization process of the GDR. Family ties were especially close in the East, and most young people claimed to share their parents' political opinions. The family was one of the few settings where people could openly discuss their beliefs, a private sphere where individuals could be free of the watchful eyes of others. Here one could express praise for—or doubt about—the state.

Despite the growing socialization role of the family, there is often a generation gap in political values in both West and East. Youth in the West are more liberal than their parents, more oriented toward noneconomic goals, more positive about their role in the political process, and more likely to challenge prevailing social norms.[29] Eastern youth are also a product of their times, now being raised under the new democratic and capitalist systems of the Federal Republic. Under the GDR, conformity was mandated; imagine what Eastern parents think when their teenagers adopt hiphop or punk lifestyles. Clearly, young people's values and goals are changing, often putting them in conflict with their elders.

## Education

The educational system was a major factor in the creation of a democratic political culture in the FRG. As public support for the FRG's political system increased, this decreased the need for formal instruction in the principles of democracy and the new institutions of the political system. The content of civics instruction changed to emphasize an understanding of the dynamics of the democratic process—interest representation, conflict resolution, minority rights, and the methods of citizen influence. The present system tries to prepare students for their adult roles as political participants.

In the East the school system also played an essential role in political education, although the content was very different. The schools tried to create a socialist personality that encompassed a devotion to communist principles, a love of the GDR, and participation in state-sponsored activities. Yet, again, the rhetoric of education conflicted with reality. The textbooks told students that the GDR endorsed personal freedom, but then they stared from their school buses at the barbed wire strung along the border. Many young people accepted the rhetoric of the regime, but the education efforts remained incomplete.

Another cornerstone of the GDR's socialization efforts was a system of government-supervised youth groups. Nearly all primary school students enrolled in the Pioneers, a youth organization that combined normal social activities—similar to those in the Boy Scouts or Girl Scouts in the United States—with a heavy dose of political education. At age 14 about three-fourths of the young joined the Free German Youth (FDJ) group, which was a training and recruiting ground for the future leadership of East Germany. Like other communist states, the GDR staged mass sporting events that included an opportunity for political indoctrination and used the Olympic medal count as a measure of the nation's international status. In short, from a school's selection of texts for first-grade readers to the speeches at a sports awards banquet, the values of the GDR regime touched everyday life. This changed, of course, with German unification,

so that the schools teach about common values across the nation.

*Social Stratification* Another important effect of education involves its consequences for the social stratification of society. The secondary school system in the Federal Republic has three distinct tracks. One track provides a general education that normally leads to vocational training and working-class occupations. A second track mixes vocational and academic training. Most graduates from this program are employed in lower middle-class occupations. A third track focuses on academic training at a Gymnasium (an academic high school) in preparation for university education.

In selecting students for different careers, these educational tracks reinforce social status differences within society. The schools direct students into one track after only four to six years of primary schooling, based on their school record, parental preferences, and teacher evaluations. At this early age, family influences are still a major factor in the child's development— your future career choices are largely determined at age 10. This means that most children in the academic track come from middle-class families, and most students in the vocational track are from working-class families. Sharp distinctions separate the three tracks. Students attend different schools, so that social contact across tracks is minimized. The curriculums of the three tracks are so different that once a student is assigned, he or she would find it difficult to transfer. The Gymnasia are more generously financed and recruit the best-qualified teachers. Every student who graduates from a Gymnasium is guaranteed admission to a university, where tuition is free.

Reformers have made numerous attempts to lessen the class bias of the educational system. There is a clear tendency for middle-class children to benefit under the tracked educational system. Some states have a single, comprehensive secondary school that all students may attend, but only about 10 percent of Western secondary school students are enrolled in these schools. Reformers have been more successful in expanding access to the universities. In the early 1950s, only 6 percent of college-aged youths pursued higher education; today this figure is over 30 percent. The Federal Republic's educational system retains an elitist accent, though it is now less obvious.

The socialist ideology of the GDR led to a different educational structure. Students from different social backgrounds and with different academic abilities attended the same school—much like the structure of public education in the United States. The schools emphasized practical career training, with a heavy dose of technical and applied courses in the later years. Those with special academic abilities could apply to the extended secondary school during their twelfth year, which led to a university education. Ironically, the Eastern system provided more opportunities for mobility than did the educational system in the FRG.

At first, the Eastern states attempted to keep their system of comprehensive schools after German union. However, unification has generally led to the expansion of the West's highly tracked educational system to the East, rather than to reforms to liberalize the German system of secondary education to lessen social biases and grant greater opportunity to all.

## Mass Media

The mass media have a long history in Germany: The world's first newspaper and first television service both appeared on German soil. Under previous regimes, however, political authorities frequently censored or manipulated the media. National socialism showed what a potent socialization force the media could be, especially when placed in the wrong hands.

The mass media of the Federal Republic were developed with the goal of avoiding the experience of Nazi propaganda and contributing to a new democratic political culture.[30] The Federal Republic began with a new journalistic tradition, committed to democratic norms, objectivity, and political neutrality.

The German media are also highly regionalized. The Federal Republic lacks an established national press like that of Britain or France. Instead, each region or large city has one or more newspapers that circulate primarily within that locale. Of the several hundred daily newspapers, only a few—such as the *Frankfurter Allgemeine Zeitung, Welt, Süddeutsche Zeitung,* and *Frankfurter Rundschau*—have a national following.

The electronic media in the Federal Republic are also regionally decentralized. Public corporations organized at the state or regional level manage the public television and radio networks. These public broadcasting networks still are the major German television channels. To ensure independence from commercial pressures, the public media are financed mostly by taxes assessed on owners of radios and television sets. But new technologies of cable and satellite television have undercut the government's media monopoly. These new media have eroded the government's control of the information flow and increased pressures to cater to consumer preferences. Many analysts see these new media offerings as expanding the citizens' choice and the diversity of information, but others worry that the quality of German broadcasting has suffered as a result. Once one could not even watch soccer matches on television because government planners considered it inappropriate. Now cable subscribers can watch a previously unimaginable range of social, cultural, political, and sports programming.

The mass media are a primary source of information for the public and a communications link between elites and the public. The higher-quality newspapers devote substantial attention to domestic and international reporting, although the largest circulation newspaper, *Bild Zeitung*, sells papers through sensationalist stories. The public television networks are also strongly committed to political programming; about one-third of their programs deal with social or political issues.

Public opinion surveys show that Germans have a voracious appetite for the political information provided by the mass media. A 2005 survey found that 52 percent of the public claimed to read news in the newspaper on a daily basis, 56 percent listened to news on the radio daily, and 70 percent said they watched television news programs daily.[31] These high levels of media usage indicate that Germans are attentive media users and well informed on the flow of political events.

## CITIZEN PARTICIPATION

In the In the 1950s the Western public did not participate in the new political process; they acted like political spectators who were following a soccer match from the grandstand. Previous German history certainly had not been conducive to developing widespread public involvement in politics. The final step in remaking the political culture was to involve citizens in the process—to have them come onto the field and participate.

From the start both German states encouraged their citizens to be politically active, but with different expectations about what was appropriate. The democratic procedures of West Germany induced many people to at least vote in elections. Turnout reached up to 90 percent for some national elections. Westerners became well informed about the political system and developed an interest in political matters. After continued democratic experience, people began to internalize their role as participants. Most Westerners think their participation can influence the political process—people believe that democracy works.

The public's changing political norms led to a dramatic increase in involvement. In the 1950s almost two-thirds of the West German public never discussed politics; today about three-quarters claim they talk about politics regularly. Expanding citizen interest created a participatory revolution in the FRG as involvement in campaigns and political organizations increased. Perhaps the most dramatic example of rising participation levels was the growth of **citizen action groups (Bürgerinitiativen)**. Citizens interested in a specific issue form a group to articulate their political demands and influence decisionmakers. Parents organize for school reform, homeowners become involved in urban redevelopment projects, taxpayers complain about the delivery of government services, or residents protest the environmental conditions in their locale. These groups expanded citizen influence significantly beyond the infrequent and indirect methods of campaigns and elections.

The GDR system also encouraged political involvement, but people could be active only in ways that reinforced their allegiance to the state. For example, elections offered the Communist leadership an opportunity to educate the public politically. More than

90 percent of the electorate cast ballots, and the government parties always won nearly all the votes. People were expected to participate in government-approved unions, social groups (such as the Free German Youth or the German Women's Union), and quasi-public bodies, such as parent-teacher organizations. However, participation was a method not for citizens to influence the government, but for the government to influence its citizens.

Although they draw on much different experiences, Germans from both the East and the West have been socialized into a pattern of high political involvement (see Figure 10.4).[32] Voting levels in national elections are among the highest of any European democracy. Almost 80 percent of Westerners and almost 75 percent of Easterners turned out at the polls in the 2005 Bundestag elections. This turnout level is very high by U.S. standards, but it has declined from nearly 90 percent in FRG elections of the 1980s. High turnout partially reflects the belief that voting is part of a citizen's duty. In addition, the electoral system encourages turnout: Elections are held on Sunday when everyone is free to vote, voter registration lists are constantly updated by the government, and the ballot is always simple—there are at most two votes to cast.

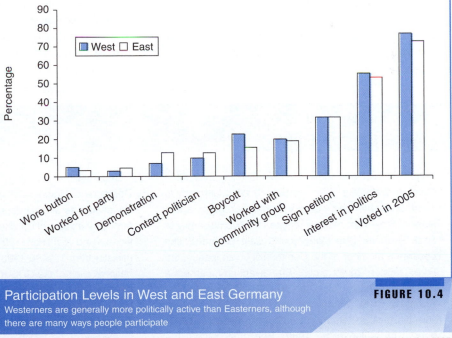

**Participation Levels in West and East Germany**
Westerners are generally more politically active than Easterners, although there are many ways people participate

**FIGURE 10.4**

Source: 2004 European Social Survey (ess.nsd.uib.no); voter turnout is from government statistics for the 2005 election.

Beyond the act of voting, many Germans participate in other ways. A survey conducted after the 2004 European election illustrates the participation patterns of Easterners and Westerners (see again Figure 10.4). Almost a third of the public in West and East had signed a petition in the previous year, and a fifth had boycotted some product on political grounds. These are high levels by cross-national standards.

The pattern of working with political parties and citizen action groups is also interesting. A significant proportion of Westerners (3 percent) and Easterners (4 percent) said they had worked for a political party during the 2004 election, and about the same percentages said they had displayed a campaign sticker or button. Yet, participating in a legal demonstration or working with others on a community problem was much more common than campaign activity in both regions. A substantial proportion of the public had also written or contacted a politician during the past year. This indicates the expansion of political involvement to new modes of action.

Thus, Germans on both sides of the former border are now actively involved in politics. Moreover, participation extends beyond the traditional role of voting in elections to include a wide range of political activities. The spectators have become participants.

## POLITICS AT THE ELITE LEVEL[33]

The Federal Republic is a representative democracy. This means that above the populace is a group of a few thousand political elite who manage the actual workings of the political system. Elite members, such as party leaders and parliamentary deputies, are directly responsible to the public through elections. Civil servants and judges are appointed, and they are at least indirectly responsible to the citizenry. Leaders of interest groups and political associations participate as representatives of their specific clientele groups. Although the group of politically influential elites is readily identifiable, it is not a homogeneous power elite. Rather, elites in the Federal Republic represent the diverse interests in German society. Often there is as much heterogeneity in policy preferences among the political elites as there is among the public.

Individuals may take numerous pathways to elite positions. Party elites may have exceptional political abilities; administrative elites are initially recruited because of their formal training and bureaucratic skills; interest group leaders are selected for their ability to represent their group.

One feature of elite recruitment that differs from American politics is the long apprenticeship period before one enters the top elite stratum. Candidates for national or even state political office normally have a long background of party work and officeholding at the local level. Similarly, senior civil servants spend nearly all their adult lives working for the government. Chancellor Merkel's biography is an unusual example because she did not follow the typical model of a long career or party and political positions (see Box 10.3).

---

### The Atypical Chancellor                                        BOX 10.3

Angela Merkel has the most unlikely biography for a German chancellor. She was born in West Germany in 1954, and when she was a year old, her father, a left-leaning Protestant minister, chose to move his family to East Germany. Like many young East Germans, she became a member of the Communist youth league, the Free German Youth group. She eventually earned a Ph.D. in chemistry from the East Berlin Academy of Sciences in 1989. Merkel pursued a career as a research scientist until the German Democratic Republic (GDR) began to collapse in 1989. She first joined the Democratic Awakening and then the Christian Democratic Union (CDU) and was elected to the Bundestag as a CDU deputy in 1990. She rose quickly through the ranks of CDU leaders, serving as minister for women and youth from 1991 to 1994 and as environment minister from 1994 to 1998. In 2000 Merkel became the national chair of the CDU. With her election in 2005, she became the first woman, and the first former citizen of the GDR, to head the German federal government. In 2008 *Forbes* magazine ranked Chancellor Merkel as number 1 on their list of the 100 most powerful women in the world.

A long apprenticeship means that political elites have extensive experience before attaining a position of greatest power; elites also share a common basis of experience built up from interacting over many years. National politicians know each other from working together at the state or local level; the paths of civil servants frequently cross during their long careers. These experiences develop a sense of trust and responsibility in elite interactions. For instance, members of a chancellor's Cabinet are normally drawn from party elites with extensive experience in state or federal government. Until Merkel was elected, chancellors since the 1960s had previously served as the minister president of their state. Seldom can top business leaders or popular personalities use their outside success to attain a position of political power quickly. This also contributes to the cohesion of elite politics.

Because they represent different political constituencies, elites differ in many of their policy priorities. For instance, SPD elites and officials from labor unions are more likely to emphasize the need for greater social and economic equality, social security, and the integration of foreigners.[34] Church officials stress moral and religious principles, while CDU/CSU and business representatives typically have a distinct economic position. Green activists have their own distinct alternative agenda. This method of representation gives citizens a voice in the decisions made by elites, and the clearer the link, the more direct the voice.

## INTEREST GROUPS

Interest groups are an integral part of the German political process, even more so than in the United States. Some specific interests may be favored more than others, but interest groups are generally welcomed as necessary participants in the political process.

German interest groups are connected to the government more closely than are such groups in the United States. Doctors, lawyers, and other self-employed professionals belong to professional associations that are established by law and receive government authorization of their activities, making them quasi-public bodies. These associations, which date back to the medieval guilds, enforce professional rules of conduct.

Interest groups also participate in a variety of governmental commissions and bodies, such as that managing public radio and television. Some groups receive financial or administrative support from the government to assist them in carrying out policy-related activities, such as the administration of a hospital or the monitoring of environmental conditions. Federal administrative law requires that ministry officials contact the relevant interest groups when formulating new policies that may affect them. These consultations ensure that the government can benefit from the groups' expertise.

In some instances the pattern of interest group activity approaches the act of governance. For example, when the government sought structural reform in the steel industry, it assembled interest group representatives from the affected sectors to discuss and negotiate a common plan. Group officials attempted to reach a consensus on the necessary changes and then implemented the agreements, sometimes with the official sanction of the government. Similar activities have occurred in other policy sectors.

This cooperation between government and interest groups is described as **neocorporatism**, a general pattern having the following characteristics:[35]

- Social interests are organized into virtually compulsory organizations.
- A single association represents each social sector.
- Associations are hierarchically structured.
- Associations are accepted as formal representatives by the government.
- Associations may participate directly in the policy process.

Policy decisions are reached in discussions and negotiations between the relevant association and the government—then the agreements are implemented by government action.

This neocorporatist pattern solidifies the role of interest groups in the policy process. Governments feel that they are responding to public demands when they consult with these groups, and the members of these interest groups depend on the organization to have their views heard. Thus, representatives of the major interest groups are important actors in the policy process. Neocorporatist relations also lessen political conflict; for instance, strike levels and political strife tend to be lower in neocorporatist systems.

Another advantage of neocorporatism is that it makes for efficient government; the involved interest groups can negotiate on policy without the pressures of public debate and partisan conflict. However, efficient government is not necessarily the best government, especially in a democracy. Decisions are reached in conference groups or advisory commissions, outside of the representative institutions of government decisionmaking. The "relevant" interest groups are involved, but this assumes that all relevant interests are organized and that only organized interests are relevant. Decisions affecting the entire public are often made through private negotiations, as democratically elected representative institutions—state governments and the Bundestag—are sidestepped and interest groups deal directly with government agencies. Consequently, interest groups play a less active role in electoral politics, as they concentrate their efforts on direct contact with government agencies.

Interest groups come in many shapes and sizes. This section describes the large associations that represent the major socioeconomic forces in society. These associations normally have a national organization, a so-called **peak association**, that speaks for its members.

## Business

Two major organizations represent business and industrial interests. The **Federation of German Industry (BDI)** is the peak association for thirty-five separate industrial groupings. The BDI-affiliated associations represent nearly every major industrial firm, forming a united front that speaks with authority on matters affecting their interests.

The **Confederation of German Employers' Associations (BDA)** includes even more business organizations. Virtually every large- or medium-sized employer in the nation is affiliated with one of the sixty-eight employer and professional associations of the BDA.

The two organizations have overlapping membership, but they have different roles in the political process. The BDI represents business on national political matters. Its officials participate in government advisory committees and planning groups, presenting the view of business to government officials and members of parliament. In contrast, the BDA represents business on labor and social issues. The individual employer associations negotiate with the labor

unions over employment contracts. At the national level, the BDA represents business on legislation dealing with social security, labor legislation, and social services. It also nominates business representatives for a variety of government committees, ranging from the media supervisory boards to social security committees.

Business interests have a long history of close relations with the Christian Democrats and conservative politicians. Companies and their top management provide significant financial support for the Christian Democrats, and many Bundestag deputies have strong ties to business. Yet both the Social Democrats and the Christian Democrats readily accept the legitimate role of business interests within the policy process.

## Labor

The **German Federation of Trade Unions (DGB)** is the peak association that incorporates eight separate unions—ranging from the metalworking and building trades to the chemical industry and the postal system—into a single organizational structure.[36] The DGB represents more than 7 million workers. Union membership has declined, however, and today barely a third of the labor force belongs to a union. The membership includes many industrial workers and an even larger percentage of government employees.

As a political organization, the DGB has close ties to the Social Democratic Party, although there is no formal institutional bond between the two. Most SPD deputies in the Bundestag are members of a union, and about one-tenth are former labor union officials. The DGB represents the interests of labor in government conference groups and Bundestag committees. The large mass membership of the DGB also makes union campaign support and the union vote essential parts of the SPD's electoral base.

In spite of their differing interests, business and unions have shown an unusual ability to work together. The Economic Miracle was possible because labor and management implicitly agreed that the first priority was economic growth, from which both sides would prosper. Work time lost through strikes and work stoppages has been consistently lower in the Federal Republic than in most other Western European nations.

This cooperation is encouraged by joint participation of business and union representatives in government committees and planning groups. Cooperation also extends into industrial decisionmaking through **codetermination** (**Mitbestimmung**), a federal policy requiring that employees elect half of the board of directors in large companies. The system was first applied to the coal, iron, and steel industries in 1951, and in 1976 it was extended a modified form to large corporations in other fields. Initially, there were dire forecasts that codetermination would destroy German industry. The system generally has been successful, however, in fostering better labor-management relations and thereby strengthening the economy. The Social Democrats also favor codetermination because it introduces democratic principles into the economic system.

## Religious Interests

Religious associations are the third major organized interest. Rather than being separated from politics, as in the United States, church and state are closely related. The churches are subject to the rules of the state, and in return they receive formal representation and support from the government.

The churches are financed mainly through a church tax collected by the government. The government adds a surcharge (about 10 percent) to an employee's income tax, and the government transfers this amount to the employee's church. A taxpayer can officially decline to pay that tax, but social norms discourage this. Catholic primary schools in several states receive government funding, and the churches accept government subsidies to support their social programs and aid to the needy.

The churches are often directly involved in the policy process. Church appointees regularly sit on government planning committees that deal with education, social services, and family affairs. By law the churches participate on the supervisory boards of the public radio and television networks. Members of the Protestant and Catholic clergy occasionally serve in political offices, as Bundestag deputies or as state government officials.

The Catholic and Protestant churches receive the same formal representation by the government, but the two churches differ in their political styles. The Catholic Church has close ties to the Christian Democrats and at least implicitly encourages its members to support this party and its conservative policies.

The Catholic hierarchy is not hesitant to lobby the government on legislation dealing with social or moral issues and often wields an influential role in policymaking.

The Protestant community is a loose association of mostly Lutheran churches spread across Germany. Church involvement in politics varies with the preferences of local pastors, bishops, and their respective congregations. In the West the Protestant churches are not very involved in partisan politics, although they are seen as favoring the Social Democrats. Protestant groups also work through their formal representation on government committees or function as individual lobbying organizations.

Protestant churches played a more significant political role in the GDR because they were one of the few organizations that was autonomous from the state. Churches were places where people could freely discuss the social and moral aspects of contemporary issues. As the East German revolution gathered force in 1989, many churches acted as rallying points for opposition to the regime. Religion was not the opiate of the people, as Marx had feared, but one of the forces that swept the Communists from power.

Declining church attendance in both West and East marks a steady secularization of German society. About one-tenth of Westerners claim to be nonreligious, as are nearly half the residents in the East. The gradual secularization of German society suggests that the churches' popular base will continue its slow erosion.

Germany's growing Muslim community represents a new aspect of religious interests. These communities have built mosques across Germany, often facing resistance from the local population. The mosques then receive tax support, just like the Catholic and Protestant churches. Some activists have demanded that schools teach the Koran and that they provide instruction in languages other than German. As more foreign residents become German citizens, this community is likely to become a more vocal participant in the political process.

## New Politics Movement

During the late twentieth century, new citizen groups emerged as part of the New Politics movement. Challenging business, labor, religion, agriculture, and other established socioeconomic interests, these new organizations have focused their efforts on the lifestyle and quality-of-life issues facing Germany.[37] Environmental groups are the most visible part of the movement. Following the flowering of environmental interests in the 1970s, antinuclear groups popped up like mushrooms around nuclear power facilities, local environmental action groups proliferated, and new national organizations formed. The women's movement is another part of the New Politics network. That movement developed a dualistic strategy for improving the status of women: changing the consciousness of women and reforming the laws. A variety of associations and self-help groups at the local level nurture the personal development of women, while other organizations focus on national policymaking.

Different New Politics groups have distinct issue interests and their own organizations, but they are also part of a common movement unified by their shared interest in the quality of life for individuals, including the quality of the environment, the protection of human rights, and peace in an uncertain world. They draw their members from the same social base: young, better educated, and middle-class citizens. These groups also are more likely to use unconventional political tactics, such as protests and demonstrations.

New Politics groups do not wield the influence of the established interest groups, although their combined membership now exceeds the formal membership in the political parties. These groups are important and contentious actors in the political process. Moreover, the reconciliation of women's legislation in the united Germany and the resolution of the East's environmental problems are likely to keep these concerns near the top of the political agenda.

## THE PARTY SYSTEM

Political parties are an essential part of a democratic government, and they perform a variety of functions within the political process. Moreover, political parties in Germany play a larger and more active role than do political parties in the United States. Germany is often described as a system of party government.

Following World War II, the Western Allies created a new democratic, competitive party system in the West. The Allies licensed a diverse set of parties that were free of Nazi ties and committed to democratic procedures. The Basic Law requires that parties support the constitutional order and democratic methods of the FRG. Because of these provisions, the FRG developed a strong system of competitive party politics that is a mainstay of the democratic order. Elections focused on the competition between the conservative Christian Democrats and the leftist Social Democrats, with the smaller parties typically holding the balance of power. When New Politics issues entered the political agenda in the 1980s, a new political party, the Greens, formed to represent these concerns. A small extreme-right party, the **Republikaner (REP)**, formed in the late 1980s as an advocate of nationalist policies and antiforeigner propaganda.[38]

The GDR supposedly had a multiparty system and elections, but this presented only the illusion of democracy—the Socialist Unity Party (SED) firmly held political power. When the GDR collapsed, the SED and other Communist front parties also collapsed. Support for the SED plummeted, and the party remade itself by changing its name to the **Party of Democratic Socialism (PDS)**. Although many opposition groups competed in the 1990 democratic elections in the East, the West German parties largely controlled the electoral process, taking over the financing, tactics, organization, and substance of the campaign. Today the party system of unified Germany largely represents an extension of the Western system to the East.

### Christian Democrats

The creation of the **Christian Democratic Union (CDU)** in postwar West Germany signified a sharp break with the tradition of German political parties. The CDU was founded by a mixed group of Catholics and Protestants, businesspeople and trade unionists, conservatives and liberals. Rather than representing narrow special interests, the party wanted to appeal to a broad segment of society in order to gain government power. The party sought to reconstruct West Germany along Christian and humanitarian lines. Konrad Adenauer, the party leader, developed the CDU into a conservative-oriented catchall party (*Volkspartei*)—a sharp contrast to the fragmented ideological parties of Weimar. This strategy succeeded; within a single decade, the CDU emerged as the largest party, capturing 40 to 50 percent of the popular vote (see Figure 10.5).

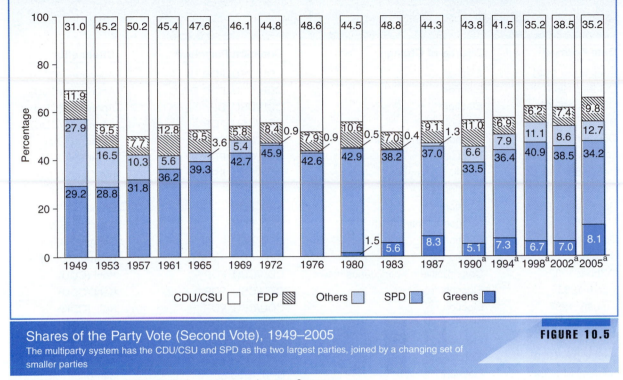

**Shares of the Party Vote (Second Vote), 1949–2005**          FIGURE 10.5
The multiparty system has the CDU/CSU and SPD as the two largest parties, joined by a changing set of smaller parties

a1990–2005 percentages combine results from western and eastern Germany.

The CDU operates in all states except Bavaria, where it allies itself with the Bavarian **Christian Social Union (CSU)**, whose political philosophy is more conservative than that of the CDU. These two parties generally function as one (CDU/CSU) in national politics, forming a single parliamentary group in the Bundestag and campaigning together in national elections.

The CDU/CSU's early voting strength allowed the party to control the government, first under Adenauer (1949–1963) and then under Ludwig Erhard (1963–1966), as shown in Table 10.1. In 1966, however, the party lost the support of its coalition partner, the Free Democrats, and formed a Grand Coalition with the Social Democrats. Following the 1969 election, the Social Democrats and Free Democrats formed a new government coalition; for the first time in the history of the FRG, the CDU/CSU was the opposition party.

In the early 1980s, a weakening economic situation increased public support for the party and its conservative policies. In 1982 the Christian Democrats and the Free Democrats formed a new conservative government through the first successful constructive

no-confidence vote, which elected Helmut Kohl as chancellor. Public support for Kohl's policies returned the governing coalition to power following the 1983 and 1987 elections.

The collapse of the GDR in 1989 provided a historic opportunity for the CDU and Kohl. While others looked on the events with wonder or uncertainty, Kohl embraced the idea of closer ties between the two Germanies. Thus, when the March 1990 GDR election became a referendum in support of German unification, the Christian Democrats were assured of victory because of the party's early commitment to German union. Kohl emerged victorious from the 1990 Bundestag elections, but his government struggled with the policy challenges produced by German unification. The governing coalition lost seats in the 1994 elections, but Kohl retained a slim majority. By the 1998 elections, the accumulation of sixteen years of governing and the special challenges of unification had taken their toll on the party and Helmut Kohl. Many Germans looked for a change. The CDU/CSU fared poorly in the election, especially in the Eastern Länder, which were frustrated by their persisting

## Composition of Coalition Governments
### A listing of government parties and chancellors of the Federal Republic

TABLE 10.1

| Date Formed | Source of Change | Coalition Partners[a] | Chancellor |
|---|---|---|---|
| September 1949 | Election | CDU/CSU, FDP, DP | Adenauer (CDU) |
| October 1953 | Election | CDU/CSU, FDP, DP, G | Adenauer (CDU) |
| October 1957 | Election | CDU/CSU, DP | Adenauer (CDU) |
| November 1961 | Election | CDU/CSU, FDP | Adenauer (CDU) |
| October 1963 | Chancellor retirement | CDU/CSU, FDP | Erhard (CDU) |
| October 1965 | Election | CDU/CSU, FDP | Erhard (CDU) |
| December 1966 | Coalition change | CDU/CSU, SPD | Kiesinger (CDU) |
| October 1969 | Election | SPD, FDP | Brandt (SPD) |
| December 1972 | Election | SPD, FDP | Brandt (SPD) |
| May 1974 | Chancellor retirement | SPD, FDP | Schmidt (SPD) |
| December 1976 | Election | SPD, FDP | Schmidt (SPD) |
| November 1980 | Election | SPD, FDP | Schmidt (SPD) |
| October 1982 | Constructive no-confidence vote | CDU/CSU, FDP | Kohl (CDU) |
| March 1983 | Election | CDU/CSU, FDP | Kohl (CDU) |
| January 1987 | Election | CDU/CSU, FDP | Kohl (CDU) |
| December 1990 | Election | CDU/CSU, FDP | Kohl (CDU) |
| October 1994 | Election | CDU/CSU, FDP | Kohl (CDU) |
| September 1998 | Election | SPD, Greens | Schröder (SPD) |
| September 2002 | Election | SPD, Greens | Schröder (SPD) |
| September 2005 | Election | CDU/CSU, SPD | Merkel (CDU/CSU) |

[a] CDU: Christian Democratic Union; CSU: Christian Social Union; DP: German Party; FDP: Free Democratic Party; G: All-German Bloc Federation of Expellees and Displaced Persons; SPD: Social Democratic Party.

second-class status. The CDU's poor showing in the election was a rebuke to Kohl, and he resigned the party leadership.

The CDU made some gains after the election and seemed poised to win several state elections in 1999 and 2000—and then lightning struck. Investigations showed that Kohl had accepted illegal campaign contributions while he was chancellor. Kohl's allies within the CDU were forced to resign, and the party's electoral fortunes suffered. To change its popular image, in 1999 the CDU selected a party leader who was nearly the opposite of Kohl: Angela Merkel.

The CDU/CSU chose Edmund Stoiber, the head of the Christian Social Union, as its chancellor candidate in 2002. Stoiber's campaign stressed the struggling German economy, and the CDU/CSU gained the same vote share as the Social Democrats and nearly as many seats in the Bundestag (see Figure 10.6). However, an SPD-led coalition retained control of the government.

When early elections were called in 2005, the CDU/CSU selected Merkel as its chancellor candidate. Merkel and the party ran ahead of the SPD throughout the campaign, and most observers expected a CDU victory. But the party, and Merkel, faltered late in the campaign. The election ended as a dead heat between the CDU/CSU and the SPD—and both Merkel and Schröder declared victory. After weeks of negotiation and the exploration of potential coalitions, the CDU/CSU and a Schröder-less SPD agreed to form a Grand Coalition, which was similar to the U.S. Democrats and Republicans sharing control of the government. Government positions, including Cabinet posts, were split between the two parties. It was hoped that this collaboration between the two large parties would enable the government to undertake the difficult reforms needed to reenergize the economy and society. In actuality, the differences in political philosophies between the two large parties led to limited policy change. Merkel's style of modernization and compromise kept

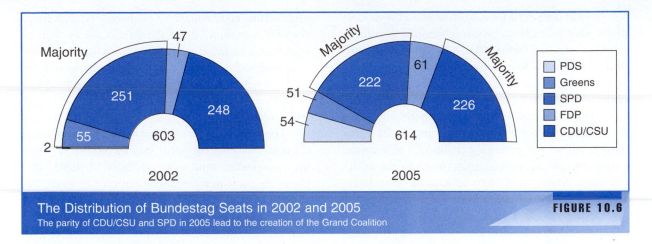

**The Distribution of Bundestag Seats in 2002 and 2005**
The parity of CDU/CSU and SPD in 2005 lead to the creation of the Grand Coalition

**FIGURE 10.6**

the coalition together, but little more. Thus, many of the challenges the government faced in 2005 will still face the new government elected in 2009.

## Social Democrats

The postwar **Social Democratic Party (SPD)** in West Germany was constructed along the lines of the SPD in the Weimar Republic—an ideological party, primarily representing the interests of unions and the working class.[39] In the early postwar years, the Social Democrats espoused strict Marxist doctrine and consistently opposed Adenauer's Western-oriented foreign policy. The SPD's image of the nation's future was radically different from that of Adenauer and the Christian Democrats.

The SPD's poor performance in early elections (see again Figure 10.5) generated internal pressures for the party to broaden its electoral appeal. At the 1959 Godesberg party conference, the party renounced its Marxist economic policies and generally moved toward the center on domestic and foreign policies. The party continued to represent working-class interests, but by shedding its ideological banner, the SPD hoped to attract new support from the middle class. The SPD transformed itself into a progressive catchall party that could compete with the Christian Democrats.

An SPD breakthrough finally came in 1966 with the formation of the Grand Coalition (see again Table 10.1). By sharing government control with the CDU/CSU, the SPD decreased public uneasiness about the party's integrity and ability to govern. Political support for the

party also grew as the SPD played an active part in resolving the nation's problems.

Following the 1969 election, a new SDP–FDP government formed with Willy Brandt (SPD) as chancellor. After enacting an ambitious range of new policies, a period of economic recession let to Brandt's replacement by Helmut Schmidt in 1974 and a new focus on the faltering economy. The SPD retained government control in the 1976 and 1980 elections, but these were trying times for the party. The SPD and the FDP frequently disagreed on economic policy, and political divisions developed within the SPD.

These policy tensions eventually led to the breakup of the SPD-led government in 1982. Once again in opposition, the SPD faced an identity crisis. In one election it tried to appeal to centrist voters and in the next election to leftist/Green voters—but neither strategy succeeded. In 1990 the SPD campaign was overtaken by events in the East.

Perhaps no one (except perhaps the Communists) was more surprised than the SPD by the course of events in the GDR in 1989–1990. The SPD had been normalizing relations with the SED as a basis of intra-German cooperation, only to see the SED ousted by the citizenry. The SDP stood by quietly as Kohl spoke of a single German *Vaterland* to crowds of applauding East Germans. The party's poor performance in the 1990 national elections reflected its inability either to lead or to follow the course of the unification process. Germans were frustrated by the nation's policy course after unification; they came to the brink of voting the SPD into office in 1994—and then pulled back.

In 1998 the Social Democrats selected the moderate Gerhard Schröder to be their chancellor candidate. Schröder attracted former CDU/CSU and Free Democratic voters who were dissatisfied with the government's performance. The SPD vote share increased in 1998, and the party formed a new coalition government with the Green Party. Schröder pursued a middle course, balancing the centrist and leftist views existing within the governing coalition. For instance, the government allowed German troops to play an active role in Kosovo and Afghanistan, while mandating the phasing out of nuclear power.

During the 2002 election, Schröder vocally opposed U.S. policy toward Iraq to win support from leftist voters. This strategy succeeded, and the SPD-Green government returned to office with a narrow majority, but this strained relations between Germany and the United States.

The SPD-Green government was criticized by some for doing too much to reform the economy and by others for not doing enough. As the economy stagnated, the party lost important state elections, and its popularity declined further. Schröder was a gambler, and instead of struggling on until the next election, in early 2005 he called for early elections. At first, few gave him a chance to win—but by the end of the campaign, he had matched Merkel in the final vote tally. This was Schröder's last hurrah, and he left the party to new faces.

The SPD now shares governing responsibilities with the CDU/CSU, with Frank-Walter Steinmeier of the SPD serving as vice chancellor and foreign minister. In 2008 the party selected Steinmeier as its chancellor candidate for 2009. His election would return Germany to many of the policies of the Schröder era, although winning a majority in the election appears to be very difficult. Certainly, he and Merkel would offer distinctly different choices for Germany's future in the election.

## Free Democratic Party

Although the **Free Democratic Party (FDP)** is far smaller than the CDU/CSU or the SPD, it has often held enough seats to have a pivotal role in forming a government coalition. This has given the FDP a larger political role than its small size would suggest.

The FDP was initially a strong advocate of private enterprise and drew its support from the Protestant middle class and farmers. Its economic policies made the FDP a natural ally of the CDU/CSU in difficult economic times (see again Table 10.1). Its liberal foreign and social programs have opened the way for coalition with the SPD when the these issues dominate the agenda. This led to a coalition with the SPD from 1969 until 1982.

The FDP has generally been a moderating political influence, limiting the leftist leanings of the SPD and the conservative tendencies of the CDU/CSU. This places the party in a precarious position, however, because if it allies itself too closely with either major party, it may lose its political identity. The party struggled with this problem for the past several elections.

In January 2001 Guido Westerwelle became party leader. The party fared poorly in 2002 because of internal divisions, which kept the conservative CDU/CSU–FDP coalition from winning a majority. After 2005 it became the largest party on the opposition benches. The party's hope is that it will hold the balance of power after the 2009 election and reenter the government to pursue its mix of economic conservativism and social liberalism.

## The Greens

The Greens *(Die Grünen)* are literally a party of a different color.[40] The party addresses a broad range of New Politics issues: opposition to nuclear energy and Germany's military policies, commitment to environmental protection, support for women's rights, and further democratization of society. The party also was synonymous with an unconventional political style. The Greens initially differed so markedly from the established parties that one Green leader described them as the "antiparty party."

The party won its first Bundestag seats in 1983, becoming the first new party to enter parliament since the 1950s. Using this political forum, the Greens campaigned vigorously for an alternative view of politics, such as stronger measures to protect the environment, gender equality, and staunch opposition to nuclear power. The Greens also added a bit of color and spontaneity to the normally staid procedures of the political system. The typical dress for Green deputies was jeans and a sweater, rather than the traditional business attire of the established parties; their desks in parliament often sprouted flowers, rather than folders of official-looking documents.

Angela Merkel celebrates victory after the 2005 federal elections.

Peer Grimm/DPA/epa/Corbis

received a majority in the election, and for the first time, the Greens became part of the national government. It is difficult to be an outsider when one is inside the establishment, however. The antiparty party struggled to balance its unconventional policies with the new responsibilities of governing—and steadily gave up its unconventional style. For instance, the party supported military intervention into Kosovo, despite its pacifist traditions; it supported tax reform that lowered the highest rates in exchange for a new environmental tax. It pressed for the abolition of nuclear power, but agreed to wait thirty years for this to happen. The Greens ran a 2002 campaign heavily based on the personal appeal of their leader, Joschka Fischer, and their success returned the SPD-Green government to power.

The Greens faired well in 2005, but the coalition math did not include them in the government. And with a new strong rival in the *Die Linke,* their future identity and electoral fortunes have blurred. The Greens have become a conventional party in terms of their style, now pursuing unconventional and reformist policies as a critique of the CDU/CSU–SPD alliance.

## Communists to *Die Linke*

The Communist Party was one of the first parties to form in postwar Germany, and its history reflects Germany's two postwar paths. In the West the Communist Party (KPD) suffered because of its identification with the Soviet Union and the GDR. The party garnered a shrinking sliver of the vote in the early elections, and then in 1956 the Constitutional Court banned the KPD because of its undemocratic principles. A reconstituted party began contesting elections again in 1969, but never attracted a significant following.

The situation was obviously different in the East. As World War II was ending, Walter Ulbricht returned to Berlin from exile in Moscow to reorganize the Communist Party in the Soviet military zone. In 1946 the Soviets forced a merger of the Eastern KPD and SPD into a new Socialist Unity Party of Germany (SED), which became the ruling institution in the East. The SED controlled the government apparatus and the electoral process, party agents were integrated into the military command structure, the party supervised the infamous state security police (*Stasi*), and party membership was a prerequisite to positions of

The party's loose and open internal structure stood in sharp contrast to the hierarchic and bureaucratized structure of the established parties. Despite initial concerns about the Greens' impact on the political system, most analysts now agree that the party brought necessary attention to political viewpoints that previously were overlooked.

German unification caught the Greens unprepared. To stress their opposition of Western hegemony, the Western Greens refused to form an electoral alliance with the Eastern Greens in the 1990 elections. The Eastern Greens/Alliance '90 won enough votes to enter the new Bundestag, but the Western Greens fell short of the 5 percent hurdle and won no seats. The Greens' unconventional politics had caught up with them. After this loss the Greens charted a more moderate course for the party. They remained committed to the environment and an alternative agenda, but they tempered the unconventional style and structure of the party. The party reentered the Bundestag in 1994.

By 1998 moderates controlling the Green Party asked voters to support a new Red-Green coalition of SPD and the Greens. This Red-Green coalition authority and influence. The state controlled East German society, and the SED controlled the state.

The SED's power collapsed in 1989 along with the East German regime. Party membership plummeted, and local party units abolished themselves. The omnipotent party suddenly seemed impotent. To save the party from complete dissolution and to compete in the upcoming democratic elections, the party changed its name to the Party of Democratic Socialism (PDS). The old party guard was ousted from positions of authority, and new moderates took over the leadership.

The PDS has campaigned as the representative of those who opposed the economic and social course of German unity. In the 1990 Bundestag elections, the PDS won 11 percent of the Eastern vote, but captured only 2 percent of the national vote. The PDS was successful in winning Bundestag seats in the 1994 and 1998 elections, but failed to surmount the electoral threshold in 2002.

The PDS suffered in 2002 partly because of internal party divisions and partly because the SPD consciously sought support from former PDS voters. The party's popular leadership was also aging, and the PDS seemed destined to be a regional party of the East. Then the early elections in 2005 prompted a change in party history. Oscar Lafontaine, a former SPD chancellor candidate, orchestrated a coalition of leftist interests in the West, *Die Linke,* and the PDS in the East. This new party drew the support of Western leftists who were disenchanted by Schröder's government and PDS voters from the East. They nearly doubled the PDS vote over the previous election and gained more than fifty Bundestag seats. The party's success precluded the formation of either an SPD-Green or a CDU/CSU–FDP government.

In 2007 the two parties formally merged, and now will compete under the label **Die Linke.**[41] This is likely to inject new ideological debate into the political process and make it more complicated to form a majority coalition in national and state governments.

## THE ROLE OF ELECTIONS

The framers of the Basic Law had two goals in mind when they designed the electoral system. One was to create a **proportional representation (PR)** system that allocates legislative seats based on a party's percentage of the popular vote. If a party receives 10 percent of the popular vote, it should receive 10 percent of the

Bundestag seats. Other individuals saw advantages in the system of single-member districts used in Britain and the United States. They thought that this system would avoid the fragmentation of the Weimar party system and ensure some accountability between an electoral district and its representative.

To satisfy both objectives, the FRG created a mixed electoral system. On one part of the ballot, citizens vote for a candidate to represent their district. The candidate with the most votes in each district is elected to parliament.

On a second part of the ballot, voters select a party. These second votes are added nationwide to determine each party's share of the popular vote. A party's proportion of the second vote determines its total representation in the Bundestag. Each party receives additional seats so that its percentage of the combined candidate and party seats equals its percentage of the second votes. These additional seats are distributed to party representatives according to lists prepared by the state parties before the election. Half of the Bundestag members are elected as district representatives and half as party representatives.[42]

An exception to this PR system is the 5-percent clause, which requires that a party win at least 5 percent of the national vote (or three district seats) to share in the distribution of party-list seats.[43] The law aims to withhold representation from the type of small extremist parties that plagued the Weimar Republic. In practice, however, the 5-percent clause handicaps all minor parties and lessens the number of parties represented in the Bundestag.

This mixed system has several consequences for electoral politics. The party-list system gives party leaders substantial influence on who will be elected to parliament by the placement of people on the list. The PR system also ensures fair representation for the smaller parties. The FDP, for example, has won only one direct candidate mandate since 1957 and yet it receives Bundestag seats based on its national share of the vote. In contrast, Britain's district-only system discriminates against small parties; in 2005 the British Liberal Democrats won 22.1 percent of the national vote but less than 10 percent of the parliamentary seats. The German two-vote system also affects campaign strategies. Although most voters cast both their ballots for the same party, the smaller parties encourage supporters of the larger parties to "lend" their second votes to the smaller party.

Because of its mixed features, the German system is sometimes described as the ideal compromise in building an electoral system.[44]

## The Electoral Connection

Democratic elections are about making policy choices in the form of a future government, and Germans have a rich set of parties and policy programs from which to choose. Think of how the United States would be different if there were some communists and environmentalists elected to the House of Re presentatives, as well as the two major parties and a traditional European liberal party. One of the essential functions of political parties in a democracy is interest representation, and this is especially clear in the case of Germany elections.

The voting patterns of social groups reflect the ideological and policy differences among parties. Although social differences in voting have gradually narrowed, voting patterns in 2005 reflect the traditional social divisions in German society and politics (see Table 10.2).[45]

The CDU/CSU's electoral coalition draws more voters from the conservative sectors of society, with greater support from seniors, residents of rural areas and small towns, and the middle class. Catholics and those who attend church frequently also give disproportionate support to the party.

The SPD now forms a coalition with the CDU/CSU in the government, but its voter base contrasts with that of the CDU/CSU: A large share of SPD votes comes from nonreligious voters and blue-collar workers, although the middle class provides most of the party's voters. In some ways the SPD has suffered because its traditional voter base—blue-collar workers—has declined in size and it has not established a new political identity that draws a distinct voter clientele.

The Greens' electoral base is heavily drawn from groups that support New Politics movements: the new middle class, the better educated, the nonreligious, and urban voters. A large proportion of Green voters (42.5 percent) are under age 40. However, this youth vote has steadily declined over time, partially because the party and its leadership are aging.

The FDP's voter base in 2005 illustrates the party's ambiguous electoral appeal. The FDP voters still include a high percentage of the self-employed, but for many other characteristics, it mirrors the general population. It no longer clearly appeals to the

better educated, Protestants, and urban voters, which were its traditional voter base.

Perhaps the most distinct voter bloc is the Linke/PDS. This is first an East-oriented party, with 46.9 percent of its vote coming from the East. The PDS's Communist roots also appear in its appeal to blue-collar workers and the nonreligious. The Linke/PDS has the most distinctly male electorate. It is a party for those frustrated with the economic and political path Germany has followed since unification.

In recent elections these social group differences have generally narrowed, as fewer voters make their decisions based on class, religious, or other cues. Instead, more voters are deciding based on their issue opinions or evaluations of the candidates. Yet, the ideology and clientele networks of the parties still reflect these traditional group bases, so they have a persisting influence on the parties.

## PARTY GOVERNMENT

Political parties in Germany deserve special emphasis because they are such important actors in the political process, perhaps even more important than in most other European democracies. Some observers describe the political system as government for the parties, by the parties, and of the parties.

The Basic Law is unusual because it specifically refers to political parties (the U.S. Constitution does not). Because the German Empire and the Third Reich suppressed political parties, the Basic Law guarantees their legitimacy and their right to exist if they accept the principles of democratic government. Parties are also designated as the primary institutions of representative democracy. They act as intermediaries between the public and the government and function as a means for citizen input on policy preferences. The Basic Law takes the additional step of assigning an educational function to the parties, directing them to "take part in forming the political will of the people." In other words, the parties should take the lead and not just respond to public opinion.

The parties' centrality in the political process appears in several ways. There are no direct primaries that would allow the public to select party representatives in Bundestag elections. Instead, a small group of official party members or a committee appointed by the membership nominates the district candidates.

## Electoral Coalitions in 2005

Voting patterns show the conservative social base of the CDU/CSU and the liberal base of the SPD, Greens, and Linke

**TABLE 10.2**

| | CDU/CSU | SPD | Greens | FDP | Linke/PDS | Total Public |
|---|---|---|---|---|---|---|
| **Region** | | | | | | |
| West | 78.3% | 82.3% | 84.0% | 81.6% | 53.2% | 81.1% |
| East | 21.7 | 17.7 | 16.0 | 18.4 | 46.9 | 18.9 |
| **Occupation** | | | | | | |
| Worker | 20.1% | 23.8% | 19.3% | 16.8% | 29.7% | 22.0% |
| Self-employed | 13.7 | 4.9 | 16.1 | 17.8 | 9.5 | 10.7 |
| White-collar/government | 66.3 | 71.3 | 64.6 | 65.4 | 60.8 | 67.4 |
| **Education** | | | | | | |
| Basic | 49.5% | 45.0% | 28.9% | 34.0% | 33.3% | 42.5% |
| Medium | 30.5 | 31.4 | 26.0 | 43.2 | 44.9 | 33.5 |
| Advanced | 20.0 | 23.6 | 45.3 | 22.8 | 21.8 | 24.0 |
| **Religion** | | | | | | |
| Catholic | 44.2% | 34.0% | 20.4% | 35.3% | 12.8% | 35.3% |
| Protestant | 39.5 | 45.3 | 45.3 | 40.3 | 32.1 | 41.4 |
| Other, none | 16.3 | 20.7 | 34.3 | 24.3 | 55.1 | 24.0 |
| **Church Attendance** | | | | | | |
| Never | 24.2% | 39.2% | 43.6% | 35.4% | 60.3% | 36.2% |
| Occasionally | 53.8 | 50.1 | 47.0 | 51.9 | 33.3 | 49.8 |
| Frequently | 22.0 | 10.7 | 9.4 | 12.6 | 6.4 | 14.0 |
| **Size of town** | | | | | | |
| Less than 50,000 | 30.0% | 21.3% | 13.7% | 21.8% | 26.4% | 24.0% |
| 50,001–100,000 | 24.1 | 23.7 | 29.7 | 23.3 | 23.7 | 24.2 |
| 100,001–500,000 | 24.8 | 24.8 | 26.4 | 30.6 | 25.0 | 25.9 |
| More than 500,000 | 21.1 | 20.1 | 30.2 | 24.3 | 25.0 | 26.0 |
| **Age** | | | | | | |
| Under 40 | 28.4% | 34.3% | 42.5% | 37.9% | 29.5% | 33.4% |
| 40–59 | 32.9 | 32.9 | 36.9 | 34.5 | 47.4 | 34.5 |
| 60 and over | 38.8 | 32.7 | 21.0 | 27.7 | 23.1 | 32.2 |
| **Gender** | | | | | | |
| Male | 46.7% | 46.8% | 47.0% | 54.9% | 57.1% | 47.9% |
| Female | 53.3 | 53.2 | 53.0 | 45.1 | 42.9 | 52.3 |

Note: Some percentages may not total 100 because of rounding.
Source: Comparative Study of Electoral Systems Survey, Germany, Postelection September 2005 conducted by the Bernhard Wessels, Wissenschaftszentrum Berlin für Sozialforschung (weighted N = 2,018).

State party conventions select the party-list candidates. Thus, the leadership can select list candidates and order them on the list. This power can be used to reward faithful party supporters and discipline party mavericks; placement near the top of a party list virtually ensures election, and low placement carries little chance of a Bundestag seat.

Political parties also dominate the election process. Most voters view the candidates merely as party representatives, rather than as autonomous political figures. Even the district candidates are elected primarily because of their party ties. Bundestag, state, and European election campaigns are financed by the government; the parties receive public funds for each vote they get. The government provides free television time for a limited number of campaign advertisements, and these are allocated to the parties, not the individual candidates. Government funding for the parties also continues between elections, to help them perform their informational and educational functions as prescribed in the Basic Law.

Once an election is completed, the parties then shift to forming a government. Since no party has a majority, a group of parties with a majority of the votes must agree to form a coalition government. Often such agreements are made before the election, but sometimes they wait until the votes are counted. Because of the closeness of the vote in 2005, it took months for the eventual governing parties to agree on a coalition and the program that the new CDU/CSU–SPD government would follow.

Within the Bundestag, the parties are also central actors. The Bundestag is organized around party groups (*Fraktionen*), rather than individual deputies. The important legislative posts and committee assignments are restricted to members of a party Fraktion. The size of a Fraktion determines its representation on legislative committees, its share of committee chairs, and its participation in the executive bodies of the legislature. Government funds for legislative and administrative support are distributed to the Fraktion, not to the deputies.

Because of these factors, the cohesion of parties within the Bundestag is exceptionally high. Parties caucus before major legislation to decide the party position, and most legislative votes follow strict party lines. This is partially a consequence of a parliamentary system and partially a sign of the pervasive influence parties have throughout the political process.

As a result of these many factors, political parties play a larger role in structuring the political process in Germany (and many other parliamentary systems) than they do in the United States. Parties are more distinctive in their policy positions, more unified in their views, and more decisive in their actions. Representative democracy works largely through and by political parties as the means to connect voters to the decisions of government.

## THE POLICYMAKING PROCESS

The policymaking process may begin with any part of society—an interest group, a political leader, an individual citizen, or a government official. These elements interact in making public policy. This makes it difficult to trace the true genesis of any policy idea. Moreover, once a new policy is proposed, other interest groups and political actors are active in amending, supporting, or opposing the policy.

The pattern of interaction among policy actors varies with time and policy issues. One set of groups is most active on labor issues, and these groups use the methods of influence that are most successful for their cause. A very different set of interests may attempt to affect defense policy and use far different methods of influence. This variety makes it difficult to describe policymaking as a single process, although the institutional framework for enacting policy is relatively uniform in all policy areas.

The growing importance of the European Union has also changed the policymaking process for its member states.[46] Now, policies made in Brussels often take precedence over German legislation. Laws passed by the German government must conform to EU standards in many areas. The European Court of Justice also has the power to overturn laws passed by the German government. Thus, policymaking is no longer a solely national process.

This section describes the various stages of the policy process and clarifies the balance of power among the institutions of the German government.

### Policy Initiation

Most issues reach the policy agenda through the executive branch. One reason for this predominance is that the Cabinet and the ministries manage the affairs of government. They are responsible for preparing the budget, formulating revenue proposals, administering existing policies, and conducting the other routine activities of government. The nature of a parliamentary democracy further strengthens the policymaking influence of the chancellor and the Cabinet. The chancellor is the primary policy spokesperson for the government and for a majority of the Bundestag deputies. In speeches, interviews, and formal policy declarations, she sets the policy agenda for the government. It is the responsibility of the chancellor and Cabinet to propose new legislation to implement the government's policy promises. Interest groups realize the importance of the executive branch, and they generally work with the federal ministries—rather than Bundestag deputies—when they seek new legislation.

The executive branch's predominance means that the Cabinet proposes about two-thirds of the legislation considered by the Bundestag. Thirty members of the Bundestag may jointly introduce a bill, but only about 20 percent of legislative proposals begin in this manner. Most of the Bundestag's own proposals involve private-member bills or minor issues. State governments also can propose legislation in the Bundesrat, but they do so infrequently.

The Cabinet generally follows a consensual decisionmaking style in setting the government's policy program. Ministers seldom propose legislation that is not expected to receive Cabinet support. The chancellor has a crucial part in ensuring this consensus. The chancellor's office coordinates the legislative proposals drafted by the various ministries. If the chancellor feels that a bill conflicts with the government's stated objectives, she may ask that the proposal be withdrawn or returned to the ministry for restudy and redrafting. If a conflict on policy arises between two ministries, the chancellor may mediate the dispute. Alternatively, interministerial negotiations may resolve the differences. Only in extreme cases is the chancellor unable to resolve such problems; when such stalemates occur, policy conflicts are referred to the full Cabinet.

The chancellor also plays a major role in Cabinet deliberations. The chancellor is a fulcrum, balancing conflicting interests to reach a compromise that the government as a whole can support. This leadership position gives the chancellor substantial influence as she negotiates with Cabinet members. Very seldom does a majority of the Cabinet oppose the chancellor. When the chancellor and Cabinet agree on a legislative proposal, they have a dominant position in the legislative process. Because the Cabinet also represents the majority in the Bundestag, most of its initiatives are eventually enacted into law. In the fifteenth Bundestag (2002–2005), almost 90 percent of the government's proposals became law; in contrast, about 40 percent of the proposals introduced by Bundestag members became law. The government's legislative position is further strengthened by provisions in the Basic Law that limit the Bundestag's authority in fiscal matters. The parliament can revise or amend most legislative proposals. However, it cannot alter the spending or taxation levels of legislation proposed by the Cabinet. Parliament cannot even reallocate expenditures in the budget without the approval of the finance minister and the Cabinet.

## Legislating Policy

When the Cabinet approves a legislative proposal, the government sends it to the Bundesrat for review (see Figure 10.7). After receiving the Bundesrat's comments, the Cabinet formally transmits the government's proposal to the Bundestag. The bill receives a first reading, which places it on the agenda of the chamber, and it is assigned to the appropriate committee.

Much of the Bundestag's work takes place in these specialized committees. The committee structure generally follows the divisions of the federal ministries, such as transportation, defense, labor, or agriculture. Because bills are referred to the committee early in the legislative process, committees have real potential for reviewing and amending their content. Committees evaluate proposals, consult with interest groups, and then submit a revised proposal to the full Bundestag. Research staffs are small, but committees also use investigative hearings. Government and interest group representatives testify on pending legislation, and committee members themselves often have expertise in their designated policy area. Most committees hold their meetings behind closed doors. The committee system thus provides an opportunity for frank discussions of proposals and negotiations among the parties before legislation reaches the floor of the Bundestag.

When a committee reports a bill, the full Bundestag examines it and discusses any proposed revisions. At this point in the process, however, political positions already are well established. Leaders in the governing parties took part in developing the legislation. The parties have caucused to decide their official position. Major revisions during the second and third readings are infrequent; the government generally is assured of the passage of its proposals as reported out of committee.

Bundestag debate on the merits of government proposals is thus mostly symbolic. It allows the parties to present their views to the public. The successful parties explain the merits of the new legislation and advertise their efforts to their supporters. The opposition parties place their objections in the public record. Although these debates seldom influence the outcome

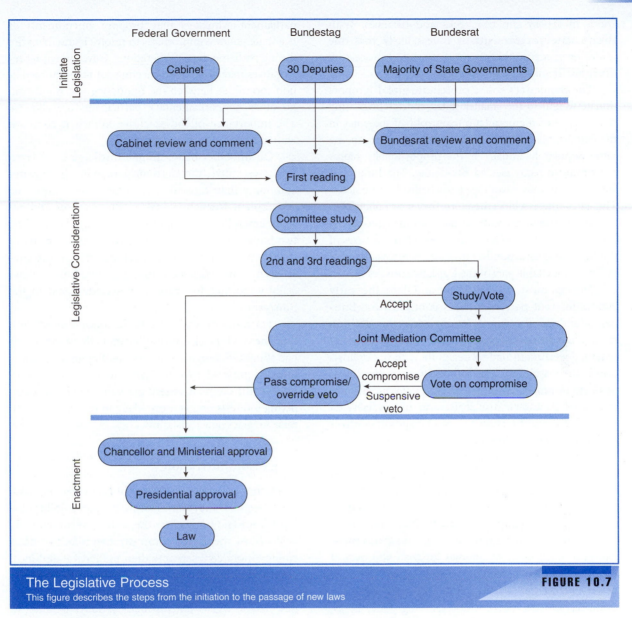

Federal Government          Bundestag          Bundesrat

**Initiate Legislation**

Cabinet    30 Deputies    Majority of State Governments

Cabinet review and comment ⟷ Bundesrat review and comment

First reading

**Legislative Consideration**

Committee study

2nd and 3rd readings

Study/Vote

Accept

Joint Mediation Committee

Accept compromise

Pass compromise/override veto ⟵ Vote on compromise

Suspensive veto

**Enactment**

Chancellor and Ministerial approval

Presidential approval

Law

**The Legislative Process**                                      **FIGURE 10.7**
This figure describes the steps from the initiation to the passage of new laws

of a vote, they are nevertheless an important part of the Bundestag's information function.

A bill that passes the Bundestag is transmitted to the Bundesrat, which represents the state governments in the policy process. As in the Bundestag, much of the Bundesrat's work is done in specialized committees where bills are scrutinized for both their policy content and their administrative implications for the states. The legislative authority of the Bundesrat equals that of the Bundestag in areas where the states share concurrent powers with the federal government or administer

federal policies. In these areas the Bundesrat's approval is necessary for a bill to become law. In the policy areas that do not involve the states directly, such as defense or foreign affairs, Bundesrat approval of legislation is not essential. Historically, about two-thirds of legislative proposals required Bundesrat approval.[47]

The sharing of legislative power between the state and federal governments has mixed political consequences. State leaders can adapt legislation to local and regional needs through their influence on policy-making. This division of power also provides another check in the system of checks and balances. With strong state governments, it is less likely that one leader or group could control the political process by usurping the national government.

The Bundesrat's voting procedures give disproportionate weight to the smaller states; states representing only a third of the population control half the votes in the Bundesrat. Thus, the Bundesrat cannot claim the same popular legitimacy as the proportionally represented and directly elected Bundestag. The Bundesrat voting system may encourage parochialism by the states. The states vote as a bloc; therefore, they view policy from the perspective of the state, rather than the national interest or party positions. The different electoral bases of the Bundestag and Bundesrat make such tensions over policy an inevitable part of the legislative process.

During most of the 1990s and into the early 2000s, different party coalitions controlled the Bundestag and the Bundesrat. In one sense this division strengthened the power of the legislature because the federal government had to negotiate with the opposition in the Bundesrat, especially on the sensitive issues of German union. However, divided government also prevented necessary new legislation in a variety of areas. The current CDU/CSU–SPD coalition controls both houses of parliament.

If the Bundesrat approves of a bill, it transmits the measure to the chancellor for her signature. If the Bundesrat objects to the Bundestag's bill, the representatives of both bodies meet in a joint mediation committee and attempt to resolve their differences.

The mediation committee submits its recommendation to both legislative bodies for their approval. If the proposal involves the state governments, the Bundesrat may cast an absolute veto and prevent the bill from becoming a law. In the remaining policy areas, the Bundesrat can cast only a suspensive veto. If the Bundestag approves of a measure, it may override a suspensive veto and forward the proposal to the chancellor. The final step in the process is the promulgation of the law by the federal president.

There are several lessons from this process. On the one hand, the executive branch is omnipresent throughout the legislative process. After transmitting the government's proposal to the Bundestag, the federal ministers work in support of the bill. Ministry representatives testify before Bundestag and Bundesrat committees to present their position. Cabinet ministers lobby committee members and influential members of parliament. Ministers may propose amendments or negotiate policy compromises to resolve issues that arise during parliamentary deliberations. Government representatives may also attend meetings of the joint mediation committee between the Bundestag and Bundesrat; no other nonparliamentary participants are allowed. The importance of the executive branch is common with most parliamentary systems.

On the other hand, despite this large role played by the executive, the German parliament has greater autonomy than most parliamentary legislatures. The government frequently makes compromises and accepts amendments proposed in the legislature. The two houses of parliament often reflect different party coalitions and different political interests, so the government must take these into account. This is especially important for state interests advocated in the Bundesrat.

Thus, the process reflects the autonomy of both branches and the checks and balances that the framers had sought in designing the Federal Republic's institutions. Compared to other parliamentary systems in Europe, the German system gives more voice to competing interests and is more likely to require compromise to enact new legislation.

## Policy Administration

In another attempt to diffuse political power, the Basic Law assigned the administrative responsibility for most domestic policies to the state governments. As evidence of the states' administrative role, the states employ more civil servants than the federal and local governments combined.

Because of the delegation of administrative duties, federal legislation normally is fairly detailed to ensure that the actual application of a law matches the government's intent. Federal agencies may also supervise state agencies, and in cases of dispute, they may apply sanctions or seek judicial review.

Despite this oversight by the federal government, the states retain discretion in applying most federal legislation. This is partially because the federal government lacks the resources to follow state actions closely. Federal control of the states also requires Bundesrat support, where claims for states' rights receive a sympathetic hearing. This decentralization of political authority provides additional flexibility for the political system.

## Judicial Review

As in the United States, legislation in Germany is subject to judicial review. The Constitutional Court can evaluate the constitutionality of legislation and void laws that violate the provisions of the Basic Law.[48]

Constitutional issues are brought before the court by one of three methods. The most common involves constitutional complaints filed by individual citizens. Individuals may appeal directly to the court when they feel that a government action violates their constitutional rights. More than 90 percent of the cases presented to the court arise from citizens' complaints. Moreover, cases can be filed without paying court costs and without a lawyer. The court is thus like an ombudsman, assuring the average citizen that his or her fundamental rights are protected by the Basic Law and the court.

The Constitutional Court also hears cases based on "concrete" and "abstract" principles of judicial review. Concrete review involves actual court cases that raise constitutional issues and are referred by a lower court to the Constitutional Court. In an abstract review, the court rules on legislation as a legal principle, without reference to an actual case. The federal government, a state government, or one-third of the Bundestag deputies can request review of a law. Groups that fail to block a bill during the legislative process sometimes use this legal procedure. In recent years various groups have challenged the constitutionality of the unification treaty with the GDR (upheld), the abortion reform law (overturned), the involvement of German troops in United Nations peacekeeping roles (upheld), the new citizenship law (upheld), and several other important pieces of legislation. Over the last two decades, the court received an average of two or three such referrals a year.[49] Judicial review in the abstract expands the constitutional protection of the Basic Law. This directly involves the court in the policy process and may politicize the court as another agent of policymaking.

In recent years the judicial review by the European Court of Justice (ECJ) has added a new dimension to policymaking in Germany and the other EU states.[50] Petitioners can challenge German legislation that they believe violates provisions of certain EU policies. Hundreds of German laws are reviewed each year, and anticipation of ECJ review also now influences the legislative process of the parliament.

## POLICY PERFORMANCE

By most standards, the two Germanies could both boast of their positive records of government performance since their formation. The FRG's economic advances in the 1950s and early 1960s were truly phenomenal, and the progress in the GDR was nearly as remarkable. By the 1980s the FRG had one of the strongest economies in the world, and other policies improved the education system, increased workers' participation in industrial management, extended social services, and improved environmental quality.

The GDR had its own impressive record of policy accomplishments, even though it lagged behind the West. It developed a network of social programs, some of which were even more extensive than in the West. The GDR was the economic miracle of the Eastern bloc and the strongest economy in COMECON. Unification created new challenges of maintaining the advances in the West and improving conditions in the East.

The integration of two different social and political systems created strains that are still one of Germany's major policy challenges. In addition, the nation faces many of the same policy issues as other European democracies: competing in a global economic system, dealing with the new issues of multiculturalism, and charting a foreign policy course in a changing world. This section describes the present policy programs and outputs of the Federal Republic. Then we discuss the policy challenges currently facing the nation.

### The Federal Republic's Policy Record

For Americans who hear politicians rail against "big government" in the United States, the size of the German government gives greater meaning to this term. Over the past half century, the scope of German government has increased both in total public spending and in new policy responsibilities. Today government spending accounts for almost half of the total economy, and government regulations touch many areas of the economy and society. Germans are much more likely than Americans to consider the state responsible for addressing social needs and to support government policy activity. In summary, total public expenditures—federal, state, local, and the social security system—have increased from less than €15 billion in 1950 to €269 billion in 1975 and over €1 trillion for a united Germany in 2006, which is nearly 50 percent of the gross domestic product. That is big government.

Public spending in Germany flows from many different sources. Social security programs are the largest part of public expenditures; however, they are managed in insurance programs that are separate from the government's normal budget.

In addition, the Basic Law distributes policy responsibilities among the three levels of government. Local authorities provide utilities (electricity, gas, and water), operate the hospitals and public recreation facilities, and administer youth and social assistance programs. The states manage education and cultural policies. They also hold primary responsibility for public security and the administration of justice. The federal government's responsibilities include foreign policy and defense, transportation, and communications. Consequently, public expenditures are distributed fairly evenly over the three levels of government. In 2006 the federal budget's share was 28.3 percent, the state governments spent 25.9 percent, and the local governments spent 15.6 percent (plus the social insurance spending and other miscellaneous programs).

Figure 10.8 describes the activities of government, combining public spending by local, state, and federal governments, as well as the expenditures of the social insurance systems in 2002. Public spending on social programs alone amounted to €555.3 billion, more than was spent on all other government programs combined. Because of these extensive social programs, analysts often describe the Federal Republic as a welfare state—or more precisely, a social services state. A compulsory social insurance system includes nationwide health care, accident insurance, unemployment compensation, and retirement benefits. Other programs provide financial assistance for the needy and individuals who cannot support themselves. Finally, additional programs spread the benefits of the Economic Miracle regardless of need. For instance, the government provides financial assistance to all families with children and has special tax-free savings plans and other savings incentives for the average wage earner. The unemployment program is a typical example of the range of benefits available (see Box 10.4). For much of the FRG's early history, politicians competed to expand the coverage and benefits of such programs. Since the 1980s the government has tried to scale back social programs, but the basic structure of the welfare state has endured.

Unification has put this system (and the federal budget) to an additional test. Unemployment, welfare, and health benefits provided for basic social needs in the East during the difficult economic times following unification. However, this effort cost several hundred billion Deutschmarks (DM; now euros) and placed new strains on the political consensus in support of these social programs, as well as the government's ability to provide these benefits (as discussed in the following section).

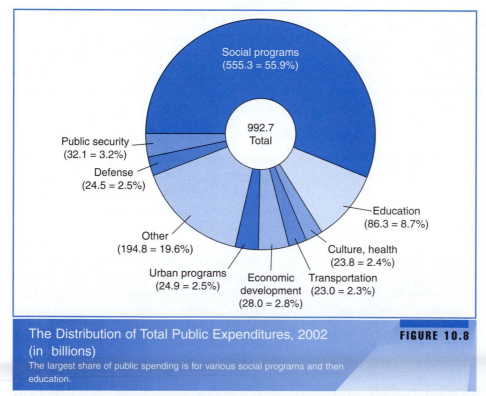

**The Distribution of Total Public Expenditures, 2002 (in billions)**    **FIGURE 10.8**

The largest share of public spending is for various social programs and then education.

Source: *Statistisches Jahrbuch für die Bundesrepublik Deutschland* (Berlin: Statistiches Bundesamt, 2005), p. 565.

## German Unemployment Benefits

BOX 10.4

An unemployed worker receives insurance payments that provide up to 67 percent of normal pay (60 percent for unmarried workers and those without children) for up to two years. After that, unemployment assistance continues at a reduced rate for a period that depends on one's age. The government pays the social insurance contributions of individuals who are unemployed, and government labor offices help the unemployed worker find new employment or obtain retraining for a new job. If the worker locates a job in another city, the program partially reimburses travel and moving expenses. These benefits are much more generous than those typically found in the United States and may be a factor in the higher unemployment rate in Germany.

The federal government is also involved in a range of other policy activities. Education, for example, is an important concern of all three levels of government, accounting for about one-tenth of all public spending (see again Figure 10.8). The federal government is deeply involved in communications and transportation; it manages public television and radio, as well as owning the railway system.

In recent years the policy agenda has expanded to include new issues; environmental protection is the most visible example. Several indicators of air and water quality show real improvements in recent decades, and Germany has a very ambitious recycling program. The Green Dot system recycles about 80 percent of bottles used in commercial packaging, compared to about 20 percent in the United States. The SPD-Green government developed stronger policies for environmental protection, such as phasing out nuclear power, encouraging renewable energy, and initiating programs to limit global warming.

Defense and foreign relations are also important activities of government. More than for most other European nations, the FRG's economy and security system are based on international interdependence. The Federal Republic's economy depends heavily on exports and foreign trade; in the mid-1990s over one-fourth of the Western labor force produced goods for export, a higher percentage than for most other industrial economies.

The FRG's international economic orientation makes the nation's membership in the European Union (EU) a cornerstone of its economic policy. The FRG was an initial advocate of the EU and has benefited considerably from its EU membership. Free access to a large European market was essential to the success of the Economic Miracle, and it still benefits the FRG's export-oriented economy. Germany's integration into the EU has gradually grown over recent decades, as illustrated by the currency shift from the DM to the euro in 2002. The Federal Republic has also strongly advocated expanding the policy responsibilities and membership of the EU. At the same time, participation in EU decisionmaking gives the Federal Republic an opportunity to influence the course of European politics on a transnational scale.

The Federal Republic is also integrated into the Western military alliance through its membership in the North Atlantic Treaty Organization (NATO). Among the Europeans the Federal Republic makes the largest personnel and financial contributions to NATO forces, and the German public supports the NATO alliance. In the post–Cold War world, however, the threats to Germany's national security no longer come from the Warsaw Pact in the East. This has led to a reduction in overall defense spending to less than 3 percent of total public spending.

Public expenditures show the policy efforts of the government, but the actual results of this spending are more difficult to assess. Most indicators of policy performance suggest that the Federal Republic is relatively successful in achieving its policy goals. Standards of living have improved dramatically, and health statistics show similar improvement. Even in new policy areas such as energy and the environment, the government has made real progress. The opinions of the public reflect these policy advances (see Figure 10.9). In 2004 most Westerners were satisfied with most aspects of life that might be linked to government performance: housing, living standards, work, income, and education. Eastern evaluations of their lives lag behind those of the West, but still represent a marked improvement from the years immediately after unification.

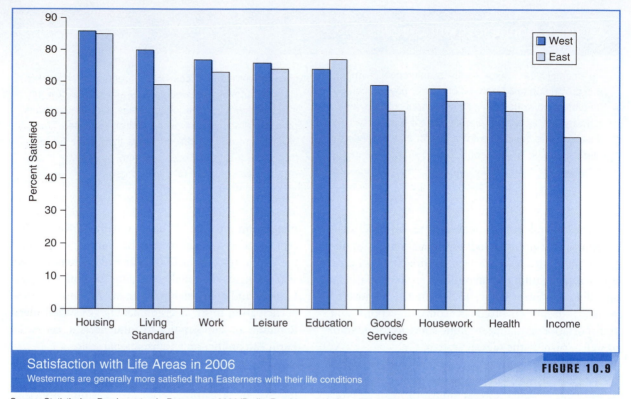

**Satisfaction with Life Areas in 2006**
Westerners are generally more satisfied than Easterners with their life conditions

**FIGURE 10.9**

Source: Statistisches Bundesamt, ed., *Datenreport 2006* (Berlin: Bundeszentrale für politische Bildung, 2006), pp. 443–444.

## Paying the Costs

The generous benefits of government programs are not, of course, due to government largesse. Individual and corporate taxes and financial contributions provide the funds for these programs. Therefore, large government outlays inevitably mean an equally large collection of revenues by the government. These revenues are the real source of government programs.

Three different types of revenue provide the bulk of the resources for public policy programs.[51] Contributions to the social security system represent the largest source of public revenues (see Figure 10.10). The health, unemployment, disability, retirement, and other social security funds are primarily self-financed by employer and employee contributions. For example, contributions to the pension plan amount to about 20 percent of a worker's gross monthly wages; health insurance is about 13 percent of wages; and unemployment is 6.5 percent. The various insurance contributions are divided between contributions from the worker and from the employer.

The next most important source of public revenues is direct taxes—that is, taxes that are directly assessed by the government and paid to a government office. One

of the largest portions of public revenues comes from a personal income tax that the federal, state, and local governments share. The rate of personal taxation rises with income level, from a base of 15 percent to a maximum of 45 percent for high-income taxpayers (plus a solidarity surcharge to benefit the East). Even after the recent reforms of the tax rates, the German rates are still significantly higher than those in the United States. Corporate profits are taxed at a lower rate than personal income to encourage businesses to reinvest their profits in further growth.

The third major source of government revenues is indirect taxes. Like sales and excise taxes, indirect taxes are based on the use of income, rather than on wages and profits. The most common and lucrative indirect tax is the **value-added tax (VAT)**—a charge that is added at every stage in the manufacturing process and increases the value of a product. The standard VAT is 19 percent for most goods and 7 percent for basic commodities such as food. Other indirect taxes include customs duties and liquor and tobacco taxes. In 1999 the government introduced a new energy tax on the use of energy to create incentives for conservation and

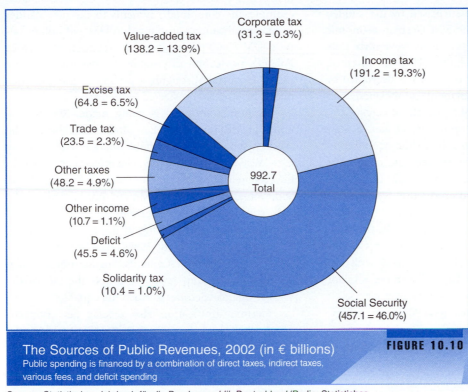

Corporate tax
(31.3 = 0.3%)

Value-added tax
(138.2 = 13.9%)

Excise tax
(64.8 = 6.5%)

Trade tax
(23.5 = 2.3%)

Other taxes
(48.2 = 4.9%)

Other income
(10.7 = 1.1%)

Deficit
(45.5 = 4.6%)

Solidarity tax
(10.4 = 1.0%)

Income tax
(191.2 = 19.3%)

992.7
Total

Social Security
(457.1 = 46.0%)

**The Sources of Public Revenues, 2002 (in € billions)**
Public spending is financed by a combination of direct taxes, indirect taxes, various fees, and deficit spending

**FIGURE 10.10**

Source: *Statistisches Jahrbuch für die Bundesrepublik Deutschland* (Berlin: Statistiches Bundesamt, 2005), p. 571.

borrowing—to maintain the level of government services. The costs of unification inevitably increased the flow of red ink. A full accounting of public spending would show deficits averaging more than €50 billion a year since union.

The German taxpayer seems to contribute an excessive amount to the public coffers, and Germans are no more eager than other nationalities to pay taxes. Yet, the current CDU/CSU–SPD government has further decreased corporate taxes, while raising income taxes on the highest earners. Still, the question is not how much citizens pay, but how much value is returned for their payments. In addition to normal government activities, Germans are protected against sickness, unemployment, and disability; government pension plans furnish livable retirement incomes. Moreover, the majority of the public expects the government to take an active role in providing for the needs of society and its citizens.

## ADDRESSING THE POLICY CHALLENGES

The last decade has been a time of tremendous policy change and innovation for the Federal Republic as it has adjusted to its new domestic and foreign policy circumstances. While a government faces policy needs in many areas, we discuss three prominent issues. The first is to accommodate the remaining problems flowing from German unification. The second is to reform the German economic and social systems. And the third is to define a new international role for Germany.

### The Problems of Unification

Some of the major policy challenges facing contemporary Germany flow from the unification of East and

to provide additional government revenue. Altogether, indirect taxes account for about two-fifths of all public revenues. Indirect taxes—one of the secrets to the dramatic growth of government revenues—are normally "hidden" in the price of an item, rather than explicitly listed as a tax. In this way people are not reminded that they are paying taxes every time they purchase a product; it is also easier for policymakers to raise indirect taxes without evoking public awareness and opposition. Indirect taxes are regressive, however; they weigh more heavily on low-income families because a larger share of their income goes for consumer goods.

The average German obviously has deep pockets to fund the extensive variety of public policy programs; U.S. taxation levels look quite modest by comparison. On average German workers pay about half of their income for taxes and social security contributions, compared with a rate of about 40 percent in the United States.

Even with these various revenue sources, public expenditures repeatedly have exceeded public revenues in recent years. To finance this deficit, the government draws on another source of "revenue"—loans and public

West. Most observers were surprised by the sudden and dramatic collapse of the East German economic and social systems in the wake of the November 1989 revolution. During the first half of 1990, for instance, the gross domestic product of the GDR decreased by nearly 5 percent, unemployment skyrocketed, and industrial production fell off by nearly 60 percent.[52]

The most immediate economic challenge after unification was the need to rebuild the economy of the East, integrating Eastern workers and companies into the West's social market economy. The GDR's impressive growth statistics and production figures often papered over a decaying economic infrastructure and outdated manufacturing facilities. Similarly, the GDR was heavily dependent on trade with other COMECON nations. When COMECON ended with the collapse of communism in Eastern Europe, a major portion of the GDR's economy was destroyed.

The Currency Union in July 1990 was an experience in "cold turkey capitalism"—overnight the Eastern economy had to accept the economic standards of the Federal Republic. Even with salaries one-third lower in the East, productivity was still out of balance. Matching the Western economy against that of the East was like racing a Porsche against the GDR's antiquated two-cylinder Trabant—a race in which the outcome is foreordained.

The Federal Republic took several steps to rebuild the economy of the East and then raise it to Western standards. The government-directed Trust Agency (*Treuhandanstalt*) privatized the 8,000 plus firms that the GDR government had owned. All of these firms were sold off or closed by 1994, when the Treuhand itself was disbanded. However, privatization did not generate capital for investment as had been planned, and disputes about property ownership further slowed the pace of development. The sale of the GDR's economic infrastructure generated a net loss for the nation.

German unification had multiple economic byproducts. The high levels of unemployment placed great demands on the Federal Republic's social welfare programs. Unemployed Eastern workers drew unemployment compensation, retraining benefits, and relocation allowances—without having made prior contributions to these social insurance systems. The FRG also took over the pensions and health insurance benefits of Easterners. The government spent massive amounts: from rebuilding the highway and railway systems of the East, to upgrading the telephone system, to moving the capital from Bonn to Berlin. In 1991, for

example, the combined payments to the new Länder from official sources amounted to DM 113 billion (almost DM 7,000 per capita); this was more than twice Poland's per capita disposable income for the same year.[53] Even today, roughly 4 percent of the gross domestic product is transferred to the East.

Economic progress is being made. Recent economic growth rates in the East often exceed those in the Western states by a comfortable margin. However, the East-West gap is still wide. Unemployment rates in the East are still more than double the rates in the West, and even after years of investment, productivity in the East still lags markedly behind that of the West. Although standards of living in the East have rapidly improved since the early 1990s, they remain significantly below Western standards. Furthermore, even if the Eastern economy grows at double the rate of the West, it will take decades to reach full equality.

German unification also creates new noneconomic challenges. For example, the GDR had model environmental laws, but these laws were not enforced. Consequently, many areas of the East resembled an environmentalist's nightmare: Untreated toxic wastes from industry were dumped into rivers, emissions from power plants poisoned the air, and many cities lacked sewage treatment plants. The unification treaty called for raising the environmental quality of the East to Western standards. The cost of correcting the GDR's environmental legacy competes against economic development projects for government funding. Thus, unification intensified the political debate on the trade-offs between economic development and environmental protection.

Thus, despite the real progress that has been made since 1990, a real policy gap still exists between West and East. At the same time, Germans still pay an extra "solidarity surcharge" on their income tax that funds part of the Eastern reconstruction. Equalizing living conditions across regions remains a national goal, but it is a goal that will demand continuing resources and take decades more to accomplish.

## Reforming the Welfare State

The *Wirtschaftswunder* (Economic Miracle) is a central part of the Federal Republic's modern history—but these miraculous times are now in the distant past. Contemporary Germany faces a series of new problems as its economy and social programs strain to adjust to a new global economic system.

For instance, business interests repeatedly criticize the uncompetitiveness of the German economy in a global economy. Labor costs are higher than in many other European nations and dramatically higher than labor costs in Eastern Europe and other regions. The generous benefits from liberal social services programs come at a cost in terms of employee and employer contributions. Other regulations impede the creation of new jobs or temporary employment. A recent report claimed that some German firms are mired in a spider web of government bureaucracy; they must provide sixty-two different datasets to government offices, file seventy-eight reports for social insurance, supply another sixty forms for tax purposes, and complete no less than 111 more to comply with labor laws. Thus, German unemployment remains relatively high, productivity has not grown as rapidly as experts might expect, and Germany faces pressures to change these public policies.

A related issue is the economic viability of Germany's social service programs. A rapidly aging population means that the demand for health care and pension benefits will steadily increase over time, but there are fewer employed workers to contribute to social insurance programs. For instance, in the 1950s there were roughly four employees for every person receiving a pension; by 2010 there will be fewer than two employees for every pensioner. Similar demographic issues face Germany's other social programs. As the population ages, health care costs have also increased.

The Schröder government commissioned a series of studies and blue-ribbon commissions to formulate policy reforms. In 2004 the government enacted a new reform program known as Agenda 2010. One set of measures reformed the labor market by easing employment rules, reducing the nonwage labor costs, and reforming the unemployment system. A second set of reforms reduced benefits in the pension and health care systems. The third set of reforms was to restructure the tax system.

While these reforms moved in a positive direction, many experts claimed that more was needed. The economy stagnated during Schröder's second term, which contributed to the government's loss in the 2005 elections. The economy began to grow in 2005, partially as a result of earlier reforms. The gross domestic product increased by 10 percent from 2005 to 2008, and unemployment edged downward.

Many analysts hoped the Grand Coalition of CDU/CSU and SPD would undertake a new round of reforms that would be even more far-reaching and reap even greater returns. However, Merkel has pursued a cautious course. Modest economic and social services reforms changed policies at the margins without dealing with the fundamental policy challenges. Then the German economy suffered as part of the global recession that began in 2008. The immediate economic priorities took precedence over longer term economic reforms. In addition, the citizens and the elites lack a political consensus on what policies are most desirable. Thus, these policy challenges will still face the new German government that forms after the 2009 Bundestag elections.

## A New World Role

Paralleling its domestic policy challenges, the new Germany is redefining its international identity and its foreign policy goals. The Federal Republic's role in international politics is linked to its participation in the NATO alliance and the European Union. Both relationships are changing because of German unity.

In mid-1990 Russia agreed to continued German membership in NATO in return for concessions on the reduction of combined German troop levels; the definition of the GDR territory as a nuclear-free zone; and Germany's continued abstention from the development or use of atomic, biological, and chemical weapons. With unification, Germany became a fully sovereign nation and now seeks its own role in international affairs.

The new Germany will likely play a different military and strategic role because of these agreements and the changing international context. NATO existed as a bulwark of the Western defense against the Soviet threat; the decline of this threat will lessen the military role of the alliance. Moreover, Germany wants to be an active advocate for peace within Europe, developing its role as a bridge between East and West. The Federal Republic thus was among the strongest proponents of the recent expansion of EU membership to several East European nations.

The new Germany is also assuming a larger responsibility in international disputes outside the NATO region. In 1993 the Constitutional Court interpreted the Basic Law to allow German troops to serve outside of Europe as part of international peacekeeping activities. In 1998 Schröder survived a no-confidence vote on sending German soldiers into former Yugoslavia, which changed the course of German foreign policy. In mid-2008 German troops served in twelve nations as part of international peacekeeping efforts.

After Schröder's disagreements with the United States over the Iraq war, Merkel worked to restore Germany's relationship with the United States. Even in the case of Iraq, Germany assists the reconstruction through training and support programs that do not require a military presence in Iraq. There may be more disagreements between Merkel and her SPD foreign minister Frank-Walter Steinmeier than between her and American foreign policy. But regardless of the outcome of the 2009 election, the Federal Republic will likely exercise a more independent foreign policy, within a framework of partnership with its allies.

Unification is also reshaping the Federal Republic's relationship to the European Union.[54] The new Germany outweighs the other EU members in both its population and its gross national product; thus, the parity that underlies the consensual nature of the EU will change. Germany has been a strong advocate of the EU, but this has sometimes made other Western members uneasy. For instance, Germany had pushed for the eastward expansion of the EU and strongly supported the euro, while other nations favor a slower course. And now with the new EU constitution on hold and difficult issues of further expansion of EU membership on the table, the debates on the future of the EU will intensify. At the least, it is clear that a united Germany will approach the process of European integration based on a different calculus than that which guided its actions for the previous forty years.

## AFTER THE REVOLUTION

Revolutions are unsettling, both to the participants and to the spectators. Such is the case with the German revolution of 1989. Easterners realized their hopes for freedom, but they also have seen their everyday lives change before their eyes, sometimes in distressing ways. Westerners saw their hopes for German union and a new peace in Europe answered, but at a substantial political and economic cost to the nation. The Federal Republic is now forging a new social and political identity that will shape its domestic and international policies. Many Germans on both sides of the former border are hopeful about, but still uncertain of, what the future holds for their nation. The Federal Republic's neighbors wonder what role the new Germany will play in European and international affairs. Addressing these questions will test the strength of the Federal Republic and its new residents in the East.

Unification has clearly presented new social, political, and economic challenges for the nation. One cannot merge two such different systems without experiencing problems. However, these strains were magnified by the inability or unwillingness of elites to state the problems honestly and to deal with them in a forthright manner. As seen in the 2005 elections, Germans are divided on the direction they want the government to follow. To make further progress, Germany must reforge the social and political consensus that was a foundation for the Federal Republic's past accomplishments.

Unification has created a new German state linked to Western political values and social norms. Equally important, unity was achieved through a peaceful revolution (and the power of the DM), not blood and iron. The trials of the unification process are testing the public's commitment to these values. The government's ability to show citizens in the East that democracy and the social market economy can improve the quality of their lives is the best way to consolidate the political gains of unification and to move the nation's social development forward.

## KEY TERMS

Adenauer, Konrad

Basic Law (*Grundgesetz*)

Bundesrat (Federal Council)

Bundestag (Federal Diet)

Christian Democratic Union (CDU)

Christian Social Union (CSU)

citizen action groups (*Bürgerinitiativen*)

codetermination (*Mitbestimmung*)

Confederation of German Employers'

Associations (BDA)

Constitutional Court

constructive no-confidence vote

Economic Miracle (*Wirtschaftswunder*)

European Union (EU)

federal chancellor (*Bundeskanzler*)

federal president (*Bundespräsident*)

Federal Republic of Germany (FRG)

Federation of German Industry (BDI)

Free Democratic Party
(FDP)

German Democratic
Republic (GDR)

German Federation of
Trade Unions (DGB)

The Greens

guest workers
(*Gastarbeiter*)

Hitler, Adolf

Kaiser

Kohl, Helmut

*Die Linke*

Merkel, Angela

National Socialist German
Workers' Party (the
Nazis)

neocorporatism

New Politics

Ostpolitik

Party of Democratic
Socialism (PDS)

peak association

proportional
representation (PR)

Republikaner
(REP)

Schröder, Gerhard

Social Democratic Party
(SPD)

Socialist Unity Party
(SED)

Third Reich

value-added tax
(VAT)

Weimar Republic

## SUGGESTED READINGS

Anderson, Christopher, and Karsten Zelle, eds. *Stability and Change in German Elections: How Electorates Merge, Converge, or Collide.* Westport, CT: Praeger, 1998.

Ash, Timothy Garton. *In Europe's Name: Germany in a Divided Continent.* New York: Random House, 1993.

Bark, Dennis, and David Gress. *A History of West Germany.* 2 vols. 2nd ed. London: Blackwell, 1993.

Childers, Thomas, and Jane Caplan, eds. *Reevaluating the Third Reich.* New York: Holmes and Meier, 1993.

Fulbrook, Mary. *Anatomy of a Dictatorship: Inside the GDR, 1949–1989.* New York: Oxford University Press, 1995.

———. *History of Germany, 1918–2000.* Oxford, England: Blackwell, 2002.

Gellner, Winand, and John Robertson, eds. "The Berlin Republic: German Unification and a Decade of Changes," special issue of *German Politics* 11, no. 3 (December 2002).

Kershaw, Ian. *Hitler: A Biography.* New York: Norton, 2008.

Kolinsky, Eva. *Women in Contemporary Germany.* New York: Berg, 1993.

Kopstein, Jeffrey. *The Politics of Economic Decline in East Germany, 1945–1989.* Chapel Hill: University of North Carolina Press, 1997.

Krisch, Henry. *The German Democratic Republic: The Search for Identity.* Boulder, CO: Westview Press, 1985.

Langenbocher, Eric. *Launching the Grand Coalition: The 2005 Election and the Future of German Politics.* New York: Berghahn Books, 2006.

McAdams, James. *Germany Divided: From the Wall to Unification.* Princeton, NJ: Princeton University Press, 1993.

———. *Judging the Past in Unified Germany.* New York: Cambridge University Press, 2001.

Merkl, Peter, ed. *The Federal Republic at Fifty: The End of a Century of Turmoil.* New York: New York University Press, 1999.

Orlow, Dietrich. *A History of Modern Germany.* 5th ed. Englewood Cliffs, NJ: Prentice Hall, 2001.

Padgett, Stephen. *Organizing Democracy in Eastern Germany.* Cambridge, England: Cambridge University Press, 2000.

Padgett, Stephen, William Patterson, and Gordon Smith, eds. *Developments in German Politics 3.* London: Palgrave, 2003.

Rohrschneider, Robert. *Learning Democracy: Democratic and Economic Values in Unified Germany.* New York: Oxford University Press, 1999.

Sheehan, James. *German History 1770–1866.* New York: Oxford University Press, 1989.

Sinn, Gerlinde, and Hans-Werner Sinn. *Jumpstart: The Economic Unification of Germany.* Cambridge, MA: MIT Press, 1992.

Sinn, Hans-Werner. *Can Germany Be Saved? The Malaise of the World's First Welfare State.* Cambridge, MA: MIT Press, 2007.

Spielvogel, Jackson. *Hitler and Nazi Germany: A History.* 5th ed. Englewood Cliffs, NJ: Prentice Hall, 2005.

Turner, Henry. *Germany from Partition to Unification.* New Haven, CT: Yale University Press, 1992.

Vanberg, Georg. *The Politics of Constitutional Review in Germany.* New York: Cambridge University Press, 2005.

## INTERNET RESOURCES

Bundestag: **www.bundestag.de**

Federal government: **www.bundesregierung.de**

German Information Center: **www.germany-info.org**

*Politics in Germany* (online textbook edition): **www.socsci.uci.edu/
~rdalton/Pgermany.htm**

## ENDNOTES

1. The First German Empire was formed in the ninth century through the partitioning of Charlemagne's empire. See Kurt Reinhardt, *Germany: 2000 Years,* vol. 1 (New York: Ungar, 1986).

2. Karl Dietrich Bracher, *The German Dictatorship* (New York: Praeger, 1970); Martin Broszat, *Hitler and the Collapse of Weimar Germany* (New York: St. Martin's Press, 1987).

3. Raul Hilberg, *The Destruction of the European Jews,* 3rd. ed. (New York: Holmes and Meier, 2003); Deborah Dwork and Robert Jan van Pelt, *Holocaust: A History* (New York: Norton, 2002).

4. Karl Hardach, *The Political Economy of Germany in the Twentieth Century* (Berkeley: University of California Press, 1980); Eric Owen Smith, *The German Economy* (London: Routledge, 1994).

5. Gregory Sandford, *From Hitler to Ulbricht: The Communist Reconstruction of East Germany, 1945-1946* (Princeton, NJ: Princeton University Press, 1983).

6. Forschungsgruppe Wahlen, *Politbarometer, June 2008* (Mannheim, Germany: Forschungsgruppe Wahlen, 2008).

7. Eva Kolinsky, *Women in Contemporary Germany* (New York: Berg, 1993); Pippa Norris and Ronald Inglehart, *A Rising Tide* (New York: Cambridge University Press, 2003); Russell Dalton, *Citizen Politics, 5th ed.* (Washington, DC: CQ Press, 2008), ch. 6.

8. Ruud Koopmans, Paul Statham, Marco Giugni, and Florence Passy, *Contested Citizenship: Immigration and Cultural Diversity in Europe* (Minneapolis: University of Minnesota Press, 2005); Richard Alba, Peter Schmidt, and Martina Wasmer, eds., *Germans or Foreigners? Attitudes Toward Ethnic Minorities in Post-reunification Germany* (New York: Palgrave Macmillan, 2003).

9. The Allied occupation authorities oversaw the drafting of the Basic Law and held veto power over the final document. See Peter Merkl, *The Origins of the West German Republic* (New York: Oxford University Press, 1965).

10. In 2002 the membership of the Bundestag was reduced from its previous size of 656. This resulted from redistricting to equalize the number of voters in each district.

11. The URL for the Bundestag is: www.bundestag.de.

12. Ludger Helms, "Keeping Weimar at Bay: The German Federal Presidency Since 1949," *German Politics and Society* 16 (Summer 1998): 50–68.

13. Donald Kommers, *Constitutional Jurisprudence of the Federal Republic* (Durham, NC: Duke University Press, 1989); Donald Kommers, "The Federal Constitutional Court in the German Political System," *Comparative Political Studies* 26 (1994): 470–491.

14. A second type of no-confidence vote allows the chancellor to attach a no-confidence provision to a government legislative proposal. If the Bundestag defeats the proposal, the chancellor may ask the federal president to call for new Bundestag elections. This tool was used by Kohl in 1983 and Schröder in 2005 to call for early elections.

15. Anna Merritt and Richard Merritt, *Public Opinion in Occupied Germany* (Urbana: University of Illinois Press, 1970); Ralf Dahrendorf, *Society and Democracy in Germany* (New York: Doubleday, 1967).

16. Christiane Lemke, "Political Socialization and the 'Micromilieu,'" in *The Quality of Life in the German Democratic Republic,* ed. Marilyn Rueschemeyer and Christiane Lemke (New York: M. E. Scharpe, 1989).

17. Gabriel Almond and Sidney Verba, *The Civic Culture* (Princeton, NJ: Princeton University Press, 1963); David Conradt, "Changing German Political Culture," in *The Civic Culture Revisited,* ed. Gabriel Almond and Sidney Verba (Boston: Little Brown, 1980).

18. Conradt, "Changing German Political Culture," pp. 229-231; Kendall Baker, Russell J. Dalton, and Kai Hildebrandt, *Germany Transformed: Political Culture and the New Politics* (Cambridge: Harvard University Press, 1981).

19. Deutsches Jugendinstitut, *Deutsche Schüler im Sommer 1990* (Munich: Deutsches Jugendinstitut, 1990).

20. Conradt, "Changing German Political Culture."

21. Gerald Braunthal, *Political Loyalty and Public Service in West Germany* (Amherst: University of Massachusetts Press, 1990).

22. Walter Friedrich and Hartmut Griese, *Jugend und Jugend forschung in der DDR* (Opladen, Germany: Westdeutscher Verlag, 1990).

23. Russell Dalton, "Communists and Democrats: Democratic Attitudes in the Two Germanies," *British Journal of Political Science* 24 (1994): 469–493; Frederick Weil, "The Development of Democratic Attitudes in Eastern and Western Germany in a Comparative Perspective," in *Democratization in Eastern and Western Europe,* ed. Frederick Weil (Greenwich, CT: JAI Press, 1993).

24. Richard Hofferbert and Hans-Dieter Klingemann, "Democracy and Its Discontents in Post-wall Germany," *International Political Science Review* 22 (2001): 363-378; Robert Rohrschneider, *Learning Democracy: Democratic and Economic Values in Unified Germany* (New York: Oxford University Press, 1999).

25. Ronald Inglehart, *Modernization and Postmodernization* (Princeton, NJ: Princeton University Press, 1997); Ronald Inglehart, *Culture Shift in Advanced Industrial Society* (Princeton, NJ: Princeton University Press, 1990).

26. See Chapter 3; Dalton, *Citizen Politics,* ch. 6.

27. Commission of the European Union, *Eurobarometer 67* (Brussels: European Union, 2007).

28. Christiane Lemke, "Political Socialization and the 'Micromilieu.'"

29. Meredith Watts et al., *Contemporary German Youth and Their Elders* (New York: Greenwood, 1989); Elizabeth Noelle-Neumann and Renate Köcher, *Die verletze Nation* (Stuttgart: Deutsche Verlag, 1987); Deutsches Jugendinstitut, *Deutsche Schüler im Sommer* 1990.

30. Peter Humphreys, *Media and Media Policy in Germany: The Press and Broadcasting Since 1945,* rev. ed. (New York: Berg, 1994).

31. Commission of the European Union, *Eurobarometer 63.4.*

32. Achim Koch, Martina Wasmer, and Peter Schmidt, eds., *Politische Partizipation in der Bundesrepublik Deutschland: Empirische Befunde und theoretische Erklärungen.* (Opladen, Germany: Leske and Budrich, 2001).

33. Wilhelm Bürklin, Hilke Rebenstorf, et al. *Eliten in Deutschland: Rekrutierung und Integration* (Opladen,

Germany: Leske and Budrich, 1997); Dietrich Herzog, Hilke Rebensstorf, and Bernhard Wessels, eds., *Parliament und Gessellschaft:* (Opladen, Germany: Westdeutscher Verlag, 1993).

34. Wilhelm Bürklin, "Einstellungen und Wertorientierungen ost- und westdeutscher Eliten 1995," in *Einstellungen und politisches Verhalten in Transformationsprozess,* ed. Oskar Gabriel (Opladen, Germany: Leske and Budrich, 1996); Rohrschneider, *Learning Democracy.*

35. Also see Chapter 4; Volker Berghahn and Detlev Karsten, *Industrial Relations in West Germany* (New York: Berg, 1989); Claus Offe, "The Attribution of Political Status to Interest Groups," in *Organizing Interests in Western Europe,* ed. Suzanne Berger (New York: Cambridge University Press, 1981), pp. 123–158.

36. Kathleen Thelen, *Union in Parts: Labor Politics in Postwar Germany* (Ithaca, NY: Cornell University Press, 1991).

37. Ruud Koopmans, *Democracy from Below: New Social Movements and the Political System in West Germany* (Boulder, CO: Westview Press, 1995).

38. The Republikaner and other small right-wing parties have not won Bundestag seats, but they have won seats at the state and local levels. See Hans-Joachim Veen, Norbert Lepszy, and Peter Mnich, *Die Republikaner Party in Germany: Right-Wing Menace or Protest Catchall?* (Westport, CT: Praeger, 1993); and Pietro Ignazi, *Extreme Right Parties in Western Europe* (Oxford, England: Oxford University Press, 2006).

39. Gerard Braunthal, *The German Social Democrats Since 1969,* 2nd ed. (Boulder, CO: Westview Press, 1994).

40. Thomas Poguntke, *Alternative Politics: The German Green Party* (Edinburgh: University of Edinburgh Press, 1993); Margit Mayer and John Ely, eds., *The German Greens: Paradox Between Movement and Party* (Philadelphia: Temple University Press, 1998).

41. Dan Hough, Michael Koss, and Jonathan Olsen, *The Left Party in Contemporary German Politics* (London: Palgrave, 2007).

42. If a party wins more district seats in a state than it should have based on its proportion of the second vote, the party is allowed to keep the additional seats and the size of the Bundestag is increased. In 2005 the actual Bundestag membership was 614.

43. A party that wins at least three district seats also shares in the PR distribution of seats. In 1994 and 1998, the PDS won four district seats in East Berlin, which earned it additional seats through the PR distribution. In 2002 the PDS won only two district seats.

44. Matthew Shugart and Martin Wattenberg, eds., *Mixed-Member Electoral Systems: The Best of Both Worlds?* (Oxford, England: Oxford University Press, 2001). Also see Chapter 4.

45. For voting patterns in prior elections, see Christopher Anderson and Karsten Zelle, eds., *Stability and Change in German Elections: How Electorates Merge, Converge, or Collide* (Westport, CT: Praeger, 1998); and Russell Dalton, "Voter Choice and Electoral Politics" in *Developments in German Politics 3,* Stephen Padgett, William Patterson, and Gordon Smith, eds. (London: Palgrave, 2003).

46. Vivien Schmitt, *The Futures of European Capitalism* (Oxford, England: Oxford University Press, 2002); Alec Stone Sweet, Wayne Sandholtz, and Neil Fligstein, eds., *The Institutionalization of Europe* (Oxford, England: Oxford University Press, 2001).

47. A constitutional reform in 2006 has changed the Bundesrat's legislative role. In exchange for greater state autonomy in several policy areas, the Bundesrat's approval is no longer required for the passage of various administrative proposals. Analysts predict that under the new system only 30–40 percent of legislation will now require Bundesrat approval.

48. The European Court of Justice also has the power to evaluate German legislation against the standards of the EU agreements.

49. Alec Stone, "Governing with Judges: The New Constitutionalism," in *Governing the New Europe,* ed. Jack Hayward and Edward Page (Oxford, England: Polity Press, 1995).

50. Karen Alter, *Establishing the Supremacy of European Law: The Making of an International Rule of Law in Europe* (Oxford, England: Oxford University Press, 2001).

51. Arnold Heidenheimer, Hugh Heclo, and Carolyn Adams, *Comparative Public Policy,* 3rd ed. (New York: St. Martin's Press, 1990), ch. 6.

52. Gerlinde Sinn and Hans-Werner Sinn, Jumpstart: *The Economic Unification of Germany* (Cambridge, MA: MIT Press, 1992).

53. Sinn and Sinn, *Jumpstart,* pp. 24-25.

54. Maria Cowles, Thomas Risse, and James Caporaso, eds., *Transforming Europe* (Ithaca, NY: Cornell University Press, 2001); Desmond Dinan, *Ever Closer Union? An Introduction to the European Community,* 2nd ed. (Boulder, CO: Lynne Rienner, 1999).

# JAPAN

HOKKAIDO

HOKKAIDO

Sapporo

Hakodate

PACIFIC
OCEAN

0   50   100   150   200   250 Miles

0   50   100   150   200   250 Kilometers

Sea
of
Japan

AOMORI

AKITA

IWATE

YAMAGATA   MIYAGI

Sendai

NIGATA   FUKUSHIMA

HONSHU

ISHIKAWA   TOYAMA   TOCHIGI

Kanazawa   GUMMA   IBARAKI

NAGANO   SAITAMA

TANEGA SHIMA

FUKUI   GIFU   YAMANASHI   TOKYO   TOKYO

YAKU SHIMA

OKI   YAMANASHI   Yokohama   CHIBA

KAGOSHIMA

TOTTORI   SHIGA   KYOTO   AICHI   KANAGAWA

SHIMANE   KYOTO   HYOGO   Kyoto   Nagoya

OKAYAMA   Kobe   NARA   MIE

AMAMI O SHIMA

HIROSHIMA   Osaka   WAKAYAMA

TOKUNO SHIMA

YAMAGUCHI   KAGAWA

Kitakyushu   TOKUSHIMA

FUKUOAKA   EHIME   KOCHI

SHIKOKU

Naba   OKINAWA

SAGA   OITA

Philippine

OKINAWA

GOTO   NAGASAKI

Sea

Nagasaki   KUMAMOTO

East China   MIYAZAKI   KYUSHU

Sea   KAGOSHIMA

SEE INSET

RYUKU ISLANDS

ISHIGAKI
SHIMA   MIYAKO JIMA

0   50   100   150   200   250 Miles

IRIOMOTE
JIMA   0   50   100   150   200   250 Kilometers

# POLITICS IN JAPAN

*Frances Rosenbluth and Michael F. Thies*

## Country Bio

**JAPAN**

**Population**
127.1 million

**Territory**
145,882 square miles

**Year of Independence**
660 B.C.

**Year of Current Constitution**
1947

**Head of State**
Emperor Akihito

**Head of Government**
Prime Minister Taro Aso

**Language**
Japanese

**Religion(s)**
Observe both Shinto and Buddhist 84%, other 16% (including Christian 0.7%)

At first glance, almost everything about Japan appears to set it apart from other countries. Japan is the only long-lived democracy in East Asia. It was the first advanced industrial state in Asia. Japan's rapid economic growth after World War II has fascinated outside observers, not least because of the disadvantages of its dearth of natural resources and its overcrowded population. Japan is the tenth most populous country in the world, with 127.1 million people living in an archipelago less than 90 percent as large as the U.S. state of California, and arable land constitutes less than 20 percent of that area. Understanding how Japan developed the second largest economy in the world has become an important field of study. Interested parties include not only academic political scientists and economists, but also other governments curious about Japan's "secrets," and businesspeople interested in Japan's products and markets. The governments of South Korea, Taiwan, and several Southeast Asian countries have sought to emulate the "Japanese model" of rapid development. In that model, government is seen as playing an important economic role, but debate still rages as to the nature of

that role. Japan's prolonged recession in the 1990s tarnished its image as a model to emulate, but it remains the world's second largest economy nonetheless. Beyond the business-government relationship, Japan's educational system, corporate culture, manufacturing strategies, and trade policies have all come under intense scrutiny.

Japan is a democracy, but its political institutions, like its economy, are considered by many to be somehow atypical and perhaps even suspect. The advent of postwar democracy was in the form of a constitution imposed on Japan by the U.S.-led occupation authorities in 1946. And while the Japanese have never seen fit to amend that constitution, many believe that its foreign origin and alien ideals cause it to be undermined by actual political practices in the country. Stories abound of inveterate corruption among politicians and of domination of policymaking by autonomous and powerful bureaucrats. Do Japan's political institutions function differently from institutions in other democracies? Does the Liberal Democratic Party's uninterrupted dominance of government for nearly four decades reveal undemocratic practices? How has Japan maintained such a high level of political stability?

In the past several years, this political stability has vanished, at least temporarily. Japan's political party system, dominated by the center-right Liberal Democratic Party (LDP) from 1955 to 1993, has fragmented, leaving a trail of ever-realigning parties in its wake. The seven parties that formed the first post-LDP coalition included parties that had been around for much of the postwar era, splinter groups from the LDP, and newcomers to national politics. This coalition enacted a change in the electoral rules to combat endemic political corruption and to loosen the LDP's grip on the central government.

## CURRENT POLICY CHALLENGES

For the two decades prior to the 1990s, the description most commonly associated with "Japan" was "economic miracle." After the devastation of World War II, in which most of its industrial base was destroyed, the Japanese economy skyrocketed in just over a generation to the point that Japanese and western pundits alike predicted the imminent Japanese domination of the world economy. As American cultural icons from Columbia Pictures and Rockefeller Center to Pebble Beach were gobbled up by Japanese investors (to say nothing of an enormous share of U.S. government debt), many worried that nothing (short of war, perhaps) could stop *Pax Nipponica*.

How quickly things change. Since the beginning of the 1990s, Japan has reeled from one recession to the next, from bad economic straits to worse. Fiscal year 1997 became Japan's first full year of negative economic growth since 1975 (which was a temporary blip in the aftermath of the first oil shock). A banking crisis emerged from the bursting of the stock and property bubbles of the late 1980s, producing mountains of unrecoverable loans. Deflation, unemployment, and bankruptcies, all unheard of for decades, have stagnated the economy and shocked the national psyche. Compounding Japan's economic woes is a widening budget deficit brought about by large government spending programs meant to jump-start the stalled economy. A succession of Japanese governments have been slow to deal with the slumping economy. When the economy appeared to be taking a turn for the

better in 1996, the Japanese government implemented a tax increase to reduce its budget deficit. The result was renewed economic slowdown. In the early 2000s, the economy showed signs of sustainable recovery, only to be knocked backward again by the global financial crisis of 2008–2009. Fiscal deficits are worse than ever.

On the heels of the recent economic crises, Japan must focus on an important problem in its near future—its rapidly aging population. For most of the postwar era, the proportion of Japanese over age 65 has been lower than in all other advanced industrial countries. The percentage of Japanese age 65 or older was 12.1 percent, but that percentage jumped to 14.5 by 1995, and 18.0 by 2001.[1] Government projections expect this age group to account for nearly a quarter of the population by 2025, and almost a third by 2050.[2] This demographic change, coupled with extremely low birth rates (currently below 1.4 children per woman), will reduce the relative size of the labor force, reduce government tax revenue, and increase expenditures on pensions and health care. Accommodating this trend's impact will be another formidable task.[3] The government took one important step in 1988, by instituting the first national consumption tax, while simultaneously reducing income taxes. The idea here was to shift the government away from its dependence on **direct taxes** toward greater reliance on **indirect taxes,** an important change as the share of the income-earning population declines in an aging society: retirees may stop earning, but they continue to spend.

Since the 1950s, exports have been fueling Japan's economic growth, but the country's own relatively closed domestic markets have exasperated its trading partners. Since the mid-1980s, Japan has come under fire from the United States and countries in Western Europe for its protectionist policies, and other practices deemed by those countries to be "unfair." Over the last decade, the Japanese government has taken down many of the troublesome trade barriers, and it has faced the wrath of its own farmers and small retailers for doing so. But many Japanese markets remain closed, and the persistent trade surplus may prove especially difficult for the Japanese government to try to reduce without sending the economy back into recession.

Related to both trade policy and domestic economic troubles is the need for Japan to deregulate much of its economy. The heavy-handed government intervention and cozy government-sponsored collusion in many economic sectors are cited by domestic and foreign critics alike as causes of trade friction and economic slowdown. But dismantling these arrangements, cutting loose inefficient firms that the government has kept afloat, and allowing the expansion of competition are policy decisions easier advocated than implemented. Even if deregulation might help the Japanese economy (not to mention the world economy) in the long run, it could cause massive economic disruption in the short run, and those hurt have strong incentive to flex their political muscles to forestall reforms. So the government has delayed and compromised, only to see the problems deepen and multiply.

Along with deregulation of domestic economic markets, Japan is also facing the need to modernize its immigration policies. As we will discuss later in this chapter, one challenge of globalization for Japan, especially given its own internal demographic pressures, will be to accept the influx of unskilled workers from poorer parts of the world. For any country, immigration is a disruptive phenomenon, both economically and culturally, but for a country like Japan—literally closed to the world for over 250 years, and with high protectionist barriers ever since—a lack of experience with immigration is likely to create an even trickier policy minefield for the government to negotiate. **Community building,** never a difficult problem in a relatively homogeneous society such as Japan's, may become a policy challenge sooner rather than later.

Finally, security policy provides new challenges with the end of the Cold War. Since its surrender in 1945, Japan has played the role of junior partner in the regional security policy scheme overseen by the United States. But now the U.S. government is less willing to spend as much money and manpower on Cold War-era concerns, and the possibility of a power vacuum in East Asia has forced Japan to face new choices. Before, simply providing bases for U.S. troops sufficed; now the issues include the extent to which Japan will participate in multilateral peacekeeping operations, fights against international terrorism, nonproliferation, and the like. Recently, North Korea has begun to appear more threatening. In 1998, its firing of a missile over Japanese airspace raised Japanese concerns, and several confrontations between Japanese coast guard ships and North Korean spy ships over the last few years have further increased tensions. Most recently, North Korea's announcement that it has produced

nuclear bombs and its test firing of several missiles in July 2006 have caused even greater concern among Japanese citizens and policymakers. China also remains an unpredictable threat, as its economy grows at breakneck speed, and it rattles its sabres not just at Taiwan, but at Japan as well, over the control of several long-disputed islands.

It seems clear that Japan's neighbors—for whom a militant Japanese foreign policy before and during World War II remains a bitter memory—are not anxious for it to assume a more active security posture in the region. And while Japan's own national trauma over the memory of its failed past as a military power is not as acute as it was a generation ago, only a minority of Japanese citizens and leaders desire significant changes in foreign policy.

Despite these concerns, the Japanese remain among the wealthiest and longest-lived people in the world, and there is little danger that the "economic miracle" will somehow be reversed. For now, Japan's neighborhood is stable, and the alliance with the United States is strong. But it is equally clear that the economic rhetoric and expectations of the late 1980s were vastly overblown, and that the Japanese government has a lot of difficult work to do before the current "economic malaise" is ended. Meanwhile, the rise of China and the unpredictability of North Korea combine to make geopolitics more challenging than ever before in the postwar period.

This chapter analyzes politics in Japan by placing the competing explanations for how things work in the context of the popular impressions of Japanese culture, the historical path Japan has taken, and the political institutions that channel and constrain political behavior. Many scholars have found that studying Japan's culture and history is the key to understanding Japanese political behavior. Others argue that understanding Japan's political institutions is more important. They contend that political behavior is best understood as being driven by the incentives built into the institutions that govern the activities of political actors.

Perhaps the wisest path is that of Nobel Laureate Douglass North,[4] who proposes that both formal rules and cultural norms matter, precisely because societal norms constrain and shape political behavior just as surely as do the rules codified in the constitution: they are "informal institutions." Whether formal or informal, the "rules of the game" shape behavior not primarily by affecting individual or group values, but rather by affecting their calculations. Consequently, any understanding of political behavior must begin with an exposition of those rules.

Much of this chapter demonstrates how the strategies political actors have created to deal with Japan's political institutions, particularly the electoral rules, have impacted the relative power of competing groups and, ultimately, policy decisions. Because the old Lower House electoral system (used until 1994) produced intraparty competition, it created incentives for the ruling LDP to favor organized groups that could provide consistent votes and/or money for LDP members to use to compete against one another. Competition over policy was less useful in battles against fellow party members, so the LDP offered its members incentives to avoid it.

The result of these political incentives was to promote government complicity in collusive economic behavior. Many domestic Japanese economic sectors—particularly agriculture, distribution, finance, and retail—became quite inefficient and, where feasible, cartelized. Vested economic interests were able to gain LDP acquiescence to, and even assistance for, regulatory protection from economic competition. In effect, heavy bureaucratic oversight assisted these economic sectors by thwarting entry of new competitors (including foreign competitors) and by setting prices to ensure profits for even the most inefficient firms. The LDP's long rule was a testament to its ability to balance and nurture these interests, creating considerable inertia against policy change.

The notion that electoral rules affect the calculations—and hence the policy decisions—of politicians has led some observers and practitioners to hold out hope that the new electoral system—adopted in 1994—might break this inertia. The new electoral rule should alter the relative power of the various competing interest groups for two reasons. First, it ended intraparty competition—no longer do members of the same party have to spend money and favors to compete with each other. Second, since 300 of the Lower House's 480 members are now elected from single-member districts, politicians should face an incentive to appeal to a broader array of interests within their constituencies, at the expense of the narrow particularistic interests that had been favored under the old electoral rules. This development should increase the efforts of politicians to combat the inefficiencies and rents desired by economic actors in favor of diffuse

interests, such as consumer interests, even though most voters are likely to remain less well coordinated for political action than will business interests. As of 2007, the new electoral system has been used four times (in 1996, 2000, 2003, and 2005), so the postreform structure of Japanese politics is beginning to take form. We shall discuss this in detail later on in the chapter. We begin now by setting the historical stage for Japan's postwar political and economic development.

## HISTORICAL ORIGINS OF THE MODERN JAPANESE STATE[5]

The first inhabitants of Japan were most likely hunter-gatherers from the Asian mainland. The introduction of a new culture, known as Jomon, began in about 11,000 B.C. Artifacts suggest that from about 300 B.C. a rather abrupt shift from the Jomon culture occurred, possibly the result of invasions or waves of migration from the mainland through the Korean peninsula. The new culture, known as Yayoi, was characterized by the use of bronze and iron including weaponry, and the development of wet-field rice agriculture. The Yayoi people spread from the southern island of Kyushu through Shikoku and much of main island (Honshu) by the third century A.D. During the next era (known as the Kofun period, A.D. 300–710), the most powerful clan, the Yamato, eventually asserted political control over much of the country. The Japanese court sponsored Buddhism, began to write histories using Chinese characters, wrote a constitution, and promulgated legal codes. In 794, the capital was moved from Nara to Kyoto, which served as the home of the imperial court until the nineteenth century. The court lacked an effective centralized military system, however, and warrior clans (later known as samurai) gradually began to assume more power. In the ensuing centuries, political control by the Imperial Court in Kyoto waned as power became decentralized under competing—and often warring—samurai families.

In 1600, the **Tokugawa clan** finally managed to achieve preeminence and a considerable degree of national unity. The Tokugawa family ruled from Edo, present-day Tokyo, from 1600 to 1868. Under Tokugawa rule, the feudal structure of Japanese society that had been evolving for several centuries took on a rigid, systematic form. Confucian doctrine informed the rigid class system that was constructed during this period.

The Tokugawa government also closed Japan to contact with the outside world.

After over 250 years of virtual isolation, a U.S. naval officer, **Commodore Matthew C. Perry,** sailed a small fleet into what is now known as Tokyo Bay in 1853. Perry delivered a letter from U.S. President Millard Fillmore demanding that the Tokugawa government open Japan's ports to trade with the United States. The ease with which Perry's fleet intimidated the government exposed the weakness of the Tokugawa regime, the cost of so long an isolation from outside influences. This action emboldened regional barons—largely from fiefdoms in Kyushu, Shikoku, and southwestern Honshu—to depose the Tokugawa clan and "restore" the emperor to power. The **Meiji Restoration** (1868), as this transition is called, was named for the young Emperor Meiji, who was nominally installed as the supreme political and religious leader. But the new regime in fact gave the emperor little real power. The samurai who subverted the Tokugawa regime used the imperial institution as a symbol to unify the nation to further their own political ends. These ends entailed a centralization of political power beyond any previous experience in Japan. They established a national tax system based on land and eliminated the system of samurai stipends. But the major goals of the Japanese government during the Meiji era were to catch up with the imperialist powers of the West, by promoting industrial development and ridding itself of "unequal treaties" that had been forced upon Japan when its isolation was ended so abruptly.[6] These treaties had given the foreign powers trade rights that were not reciprocal and secured extraterritoriality (immunity from local laws) for citizens of these countries. Many in the Japanese government felt these treaties might be a precursor to western colonization of Japan.

Although the new **oligarchs** had no intention of democratizing politics on any mass level, they did relent to the establishment of a constitution with an elected legislature. The government established the **Diet,** a bicameral legislative body, on the model of European parliamentary democracy. But the Diet did not control the cabinet. Instead, the oligarchs managed to control cabinet decisionmaking by choosing the prime minister and the ministers of the various government bureaucracies. Still, the 1889 constitution had given the Diet the ability to reject certain governmental actions (specifically the budget), so that the cabinet had to bargain with nascent political parties on many issues. Parties became sufficiently obstreperous that they were able to increase their influence over time.

This creeping democratization reached its prewar apex from 1918 to 1932, which became known as the **"Taisho Democracy."** (Emperor Taisho succeeded his father, Meiji, in 1912.) During this period, cabinets were dominated by the political parties that controlled the parliament. The remaining oligarchs felt it necessary to select prime ministers from among the party leaders in order to gain the Diet's cooperation. Throughout the 1920s, party-controlled cabinets became the norm.

How powerful did prewar party cabinets actually become? Despite a ban on firing bureaucrats, personnel rosters show that cabinets manipulated the civil service by selectively promoting and demoting at will. Both large parties used the mechanisms of government to favor their respective constituents, but over time both parties became increasingly beholden to the *zaibatsu* (Japan's prewar industrial conglomerates) that funded their expensive electoral campaigns.

By 1932, endemic political corruption, *zaibatsu* favoritism, and an ambitious military had eroded public support for the parties. After the assassination of Prime Minister Tsuyoshi Inukai by ultranationalists, the military took over the government with little visible public opposition. Along with the end of civilian government came a rapid increase in spending on munitions. The military's proportion of the budget rose from 28.5 percent in 1928 to 38.7 percent in 1933.[7] Military spending grew even more rapidly after 1937, when the army began a full-scale war against China. When the U.S. government blockaded oil shipments to Japan in response to Japanese aggression in China, the Japanese navy responded by attacking sources of oil in Southeast Asia (in particular Indonesia) as well as U.S. warships and aircraft at Pearl Harbor. It was not until Japan's surrender in August 1945, and its subsequent occupation by the Allied powers, that the military's role in politics was ended and civilian democracy was allowed to flourish.

## THE OCCUPATION

The **Allied Occupation of Japan** was administered by the **Supreme Commander for the Allied Powers (SCAP),** under the direction of U.S. **General Douglas MacArthur.** Its initial objectives were to demilitarize and democratize Japan, to render Japan unable and unwilling to wage war ever again. This idealism was discarded rather quickly in the face of Communist advances in China and increasing conflict between the United States and the Soviet Union. But in the early phase of the Occupation, SCAP efficiently demobilized the army and navy and repatriated 3.3 million Japanese troops still left abroad at the end of the war. SCAP also implemented wide-ranging measures to uproot the old elite and its basis of power. In early 1946, it ordered the creation of the International Military Tribunal for the Far East, better known as the Tokyo War Crimes Trial. Twenty-five men were tried as class "A" war criminals: seven were given death sentences, with the others receiving prison terms varying from seven years to life. For supposed complicity during the war, 200,000 more were purged from politics, business, and the media. Holding companies, which owned and coordinated the *zaibatsu*, were outlawed. This action forced the dissolution and decentralization of ownership control over much of the industrial economy.[8] The trials and the purges struck many Japanese as a show of victors' justice. They created a sense of sympathy for the defendants and did not necessarily represent the great education in democracy that SCAP had intended. After the Occupation ended in 1952, those still imprisoned were released, and those purged were allowed to return to their previous careers.

An even broader attempt at political reform involved the implementation of a new constitution. At SCAP's prompting, the new cabinet proposed a draft constitution. SCAP rejected that draft for, among other shortcomings, retaining the sovereignty of Japan in the emperor and allowing the Diet to restrict the individual freedoms supposedly guaranteed elsewhere in the constitution.[9] Within a matter of days, SCAP submitted its own draft, which added an extensive bill of rights. These rights include guarantees for individual liberties, social equality, and gender equality.

Perhaps the best known provision of the Japanese Constitution is **Article 9,** the "Peace Clause," in which Japan renounces the right to wage war or even to maintain a military capability (see Box 11.1). Conservative governments and courts have interpreted the provision flexibly (to say the least) to allow for a defensive capability. Many conservatives take umbrage at Article 9, arguing that it compromises Japanese sovereignty. During the 1960s, public opinion tipped overwhelmingly against any amendment to the Constitution that would dismantle Article 9. That has begun to change, however, as the share of the population that remembers the devastation of the war dwindles, and as Japan has emerged from its postwar geopolitical shell, participating in international peacekeeping operations, and even sending troops to Iraq in early 2004. Discussions are ongoing, but both major parties now support some constitutional revision for the first time.

Land reform represented the other major aim of the Occupation, and arguably was one of its greatest successes. At the time of the Japanese surrender, 70 percent of farmers were either full tenants or at least had to rent some land to supplement what they owned.[10] Many SCAP officials believed that poverty had been a significant factor in breeding right-wing radicalism and militarism in the 1930s. The creation of broad land ownership was intended to reduce these tendencies. Under the 1946 Farm Land Reform Law, 4.3 million farmers purchased new land at extremely low prices, often with the aid of low-interest government loans. A further aim of this reform was to instill farmers with an interest in politics that SCAP thought would coincide with land ownership. The success of

---

## Article 9 of the Constitution of Japan

**BOX 11.1**

### ARTICLE 9. RENUNCIATION OF WAR

Aspiring sincerely to an international peace based on justice and order, the Japanese people forever renounce war as a sovereign right of the nation and the threat or use of force as means of settling international disputes.

2. In order to accomplish the aim of the preceding paragraph, land, sea, and air forces, as well as other war potential, will never be maintained. The right of belligerency of the state will not be recognized.

this aim is evident in the large role farming interests came to play in postwar political competition. In the prewar period, agrarian interests had been neglected.

SCAP also undertook to create an independent trade-union movement, protected from harassment by government and business. Under SCAP pressure, the Diet passed a series of liberal labor laws. Article 28 of the Constitution and the Trade Union Law of 1945 guaranteed the right to strike and bargain collectively. It provided for labor relations boards at the national and prefectural levels.

The Occupation oversaw several structural changes in the bureaucracy. The Home Ministry, the largest and most powerful prewar agency, was broken up and its functions were dispersed among the Prime Minister's Office, the National Police Agency, the Labor Ministry, the Construction Ministry, the Health and Welfare Ministry, the Education Ministry, the Local Autonomy Ministry, and others. Education was made compulsory until the ninth grade and textbooks were purged of nationalistic myths and militaristic virtues. Much of the bureaucracy remained untouched, as much by need as by design. SCAP had inadequate resources to rule directly, so it relied on many of the wartime bureaucratic agencies to implement its decisions. These agencies were managed, for the most part, by the same bureaucrats who had controlled them before and during the war.[11]

As already suggested, the priorities of SCAP shifted from the demilitarization of Japan to securing Japan as a reliable ally in the Cold War. The consolidation of Soviet influence in Eastern Europe and North Korea, and the strengthening of the communist grip on China, convinced the U.S. Department of State that Japan should become a "bulwark against Communism" and a vital link in the new U.S. policy of "containment."[12] Toward this end, SCAP worked with the conservative government of **Shigeru Yoshida** to crack down on labor unrest. A general strike, planned for February 1, 1947, was disallowed, and business organizations were given the upper hand in dealing with left-wing-backed unions. Also, antitrust measures taken to protect against a future return of the *zaibatsu* were relaxed. Now looking at Japan as an ally in the Pacific, the United States switched its objectives to economic stabilization and growth.

In September 1951, Japan signed a general peace treaty in San Francisco with all Allied powers except the Soviet Union,[13] formally ending the Occupation

and ceding Japan's postwar autonomy. At the same time, the **U.S.–Japan Mutual Security Treaty** was signed. This treaty allowed the United States to station troops in Japan and to continue to occupy Okinawa as a military base, a vital link in the U.S. anticommunist "containment strategy" during the Cold War (discussed later in this chapter).

At the close of the Occupation—aided by the "Korean War Boom"—Japan's economy had recovered enough to match its prewar high, but a decade of growth had been lost amidst the devastation of the war.[14] The political system was functioning smoothly, but the party system remained somewhat fragmented. Japan was once again a sovereign nation about to embark on a remarkable period of its history.

## POLITICAL INSTITUTIONS

Postwar Japanese politics is chock-full of fascinating personalities and episodes, but four watershed events stand out. The first was the promulgation of the postwar Constitution in 1947, which established Japan's political institutions and specified their relative shares of political power. The second was the 1955 party merger that resulted in the formation of the Liberal Democratic Party (LDP), which was to govern Japan for the next four decades. The third was the 1960 U.S.–Japan Mutual Security Treaty crisis, which both crystallized the foreign policy cleavage that persisted until the end of the Cold War and induced the government to downplay such issues and instead place economic growth squarely on the front burner. The fourth was the temporary fall of the LDP from power in 1993, and the subsequent adoption of new electoral rules in 1994. Although the LDP remains the largest party in the Diet, it no longer governs alone; it now faces a new, big partisan rival, operating under these new rules of the game. This section describes Japan's political institutions, followed in the next three sections by detailed examinations of the Japanese electoral and party systems, and of the Japanese policymaking process.

### The National Diet

Japan's system of government is parliamentary, bicameral, and, despite the existence of elected local governments, nonfederal (see Figure 11.1). Article 41 of the

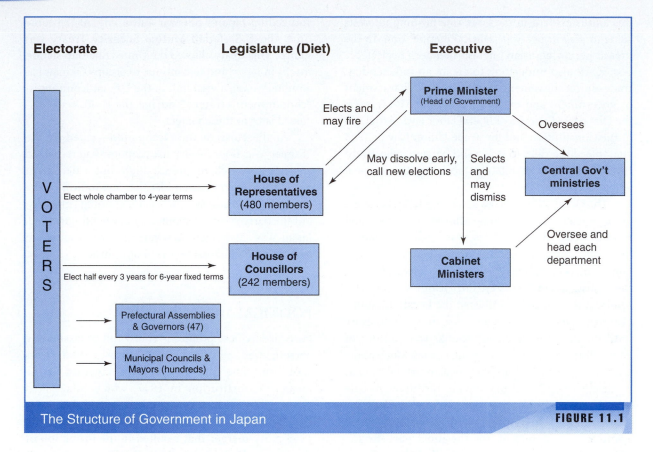

**Electorate**  **Legislature (Diet)**  **Executive**

VOTERS

Elect whole chamber to 4-year terms

Elect half every 3 years for 6-year fixed terms

**House of Representatives** (480 members)

**House of Councillors** (242 members)

Prefectural Assemblies & Governors (47)

Municipal Councils & Mayors (hundreds)

**Prime Minister** (Head of Government)

Elects and may fire

May dissolve early, call new elections

Selects and may dismiss

Oversees

**Central Gov't ministries**

Oversee and head each department

**Cabinet Ministers**

The Structure of Government in Japan    **FIGURE 11.1**

Constitution specifies that the parliament, the National Diet, "shall be the highest organ of state power, and shall be the sole law-making organ of the State." Thus, there is no separately elected executive with whom the Diet must share policymaking authority. The Diet consists of two legislative chambers: the **House of Representatives** (the Lower House) and the **House of Councillors** (the Upper House). Both chambers must pass a bill in identical form for it to become law, with three important exceptions: the House of Representatives alone chooses the prime minister, passes the budget, and ratifies treaties. In these three areas, arguably the most important tasks for any government, the Upper House may offer an opinion or counterproposal, but it cannot compel the Lower House to pay any attention (as stipulated in Articles 59 and 60 of the Constitution). For all other legislation, however, the Lower House must accommodate the preferences of the Upper House, unless the Lower House can muster a two-thirds majority to override an Upper House veto. Thus, the Japanese Upper House is among the world's strongest.

As in all parliamentary systems, the first business that any new parliament must conduct (after an election) is to elect one of its members to serve as prime minister. The person elected is usually, but not always, the leader of the largest party in the Lower House. During the LDP's long reign as majority party, the LDP leader always won that prize (see Table 11.1). The Upper House may offer its own nominee, but Article 67 specifies that if the two chambers disagree, the choice of the Lower House prevails. The new prime minister then appoints a cabinet, at least half of whose members must be legislators (Article 68). These appointees head up the cabinet-level ministries and agencies that comprise the central government bureaucracy.

### Local Government

Japan is divided administratively into forty-seven **prefectures,** each of which elects its own governor and legislature. The country's hundreds of municipalities elect their own mayors and city councils as well. Nevertheless, Japan is not a federal system: all local

| TABLE 11.1 | | |
|---|---|---|
| **Japanese Prime Ministers Since 1945** | | |
| **Prime Minister** | **Selection Date** | **Partisan Support** |
| Norihiko Higashikuni | August 8, 1945 | Nonpartisan |
| Kijiro Shidehara | October 9, 1945 | Nonpartisan |
| Shigeru Yoshida | May 22, 1946 | Liberal Party+Progressive Party |
| Tetsu Katayama | May 24, 1947 | JSP+DP+NCP |
| Hitoshi Ashida | February 23, 1948 | JSP+DP+NCP |
| Shigeru Yoshida | October 15, 1948 | Liberal Party[a] |
| Shigeru Yoshida | February 16, 1949 | Liberal Party+Democratic Party |
| Shigeru Yoshida | October 30, 1952 | Liberal Party |
| Ichiro Hatoyama | December 10, 1954 | Democratic Party[a] |
| Ichiro Hatoyama | November 22, 1955 | LDP |
| Tanzan Ishibashi | December 23, 1956 | LDP |
| Nobusuke Kishi | July 10, 1957 | LDP |
| Hayato Ikeda | July 19, 1960 | LDP |
| Eisaku Sato | June 3, 1965 | LDP |
| Kakuei Tanaka | July 7, 1972 | LDP |
| Takeo Miki | December 9, 1974 | LDP |
| Takeo Fukuda | December 24, 1976 | LDP |
| Masayoshi Ohira | December 7, 1978 | LDP |
| Zenko Suzuki | July 17, 1980 | LDP |
| Yasuhiro Nakasone | November 11, 1982 | LDP (+NLC)[b] |
| Noboru Takeshita | October 31, 1987 | LDP |
| Sosuke Uno | June 3, 1989 | LDP |
| Toshiki Kaifu | August 10, 1989 | LDP |
| Kiichi Miyazawa | November 5, 1991 | LDP |
| Morihiro Hosokawa (JNP) | August 9, 1993 | JNP+JRP+NPH+JSP+DSP+SDF+Komeito |
| Tsutomu Hata (RP) | April 29, 1994 | JNP+JRP+DSP+SDF+Komeito |
| Tomiichi Murayama (JSP) | June 30, 1994 | LDP+JSP+NPH |
| Ryutaro Hashimoto (LDP) | January 11, 1996 | LDP+JSP+NPH |
| Ryutaro Hashimoto | November 7, 1996 | LDP[c] |
| Keizo Obuchi | July 30, 1998 | LDP+Komeito+LP |
| Yoshiro Mori | April 5, 2000 | LDP+Komeito+CP |
| Junichiro Koizumi | April 26, 2001 | LDP+Komeito (+CP)[d] |
| Shinzo Abe | September 30, 2006 | LDP+Komeito |
| Yasuo Fukuda | September 26, 2007 | LDP+Komeito |
| Taro Aso | September 24, 2008 | LDP+Komeito |

[a] Minority government.
[b] From 1983 until 1986. When it merged back into the LDP, the New Liberal Club received one cabinet seat.
[c] Started as a minority government, but the LDP added enough new members to gain a majority.
[d] The CP dissolved after the November 2003 General Election, with its remaining members joining the LDP.

*Party Abbreviations*: Komeito-*Komeit* or Clean Government Party; CP-Conservative Party; DP-Democratic Party; DSP-Democratic Socialist Party; JNP-Japan New Party; JRP-Renewal Party; JSP-Japan Socialist Party; LDP-Liberal Democratic Party; NCP-National Cooperative Party; NLC-New Liberal Club; NPH-New Party Harbinger; SDF-Social Democratic Federation.

government authority is delegated, and may be retracted, by the national government. In Japan, delegation to prefectural and municipal governments is extensive, and subnational governments account for about two-thirds of all government spending. However, it is interesting to note that they raise only about one-third of all tax revenues. Thus, on average, half of subnational government budgets are allocated to them at the

Prime Minister Taro Aso took office in September, 2008.

Kazuhiro Nogi/AFP/Getty Images

discretion of the House of Representatives, which compiles the national budget annually.[15] Recently, some steps have been taken to delegate a little more fiscal and regulatory discretion to local governments, but as of 2007, decentralization was still very limited.

Still, local politics matters. Local frustration with national policy decisions often leads to the election of populist or progressive prefectural governors or mayors. These officials can be thorns in the side of the central government, loudly expressing their constituents' dissatisfaction. In some cases, this dissatisfaction signals to the party or coalition in control of the national government the political prudence of a change in policy. After all, the same voters who elect "protest candidates" to municipal or prefectural office might choose to vote similarly in the next round of national elections. So the national government is wise to keep abreast of trends in local politics. Perhaps the best example of the importance of this mechanism came in 1970, when the LDP-dominated Diet undertook a drastic change in policy by passing a slew of antipollution measures championed by progressive local governments that had used that issue to beat local LDP

incumbents. More recently, local governments have signaled their displeasure on all manner of national policies, from airport development to public works projects to waste disposal issues.[16] These protests do not *compel* the national government to change policy, but the national government is unwise to dismiss local complaints out of hand.

## The Judiciary

The Japanese legal system ostensibly features the same degree of judicial independence that courts in the United States enjoy. Such independence is guaranteed in the Constitution (Articles 76–81). Nonetheless, independence does not appear to be the reality in Japan. Political domination and manipulation of the courts have arisen from a combination of the LDP's long reign and its ability to use appointment powers and bureaucratic mechanisms to avoid putting courts into positions where they might render decisions anathema to LDP interests. We hasten to point out that this is common in parliamentary democracies. A prominent reason for de facto judicial independence in the United States is the sharing of political power by separately elected legislative and executive branches, not to mention the conflicts of interest between federal and state levels of government. In this sense, the U.S. Supreme Court acts as an arbiter between the various branches and levels of government, interpreting the Constitution and common law in order to iron out differences among competing institutions. In a unitary parliamentary system, especially one with a long-tenured majority party, there are fewer checks and balances, and hence fewer conflicts for courts to mediate, other things equal.

The Cabinet directly appoints the fifteen members of the Supreme Court, and indirectly, through the administrative apparatus of the Supreme Court, helps to determine all lower court appointments as well. The LDP made it a practice to appoint to the highest court only elderly judges, near the mandatory retirement age of 70. This way, it already had a clear idea of how the appointees would behave, based on decisions those judges made during their careers. If it turned out that the Cabinet made a "poor" selection (by promoting a judge who then ruled against the LDP's interests), forced retirement would be just around the corner. In the meantime, there would be fourteen other Supreme Court members to keep any regrettable appointments in check. It will be interesting to see if this practice changes now that LDP control over government is less secure. Will it follow recent American practice and appoint younger judges, in case it is not still in power to appoint their replacements?

The Supreme Court, through its Secretariat, controls the career paths of lower court judges. Evidence of LDP manipulation is easy to find in the career paths of judges. Judges who have ruled against LDP interests have been punished by relegation to the low-profile backwaters of the judiciary and have seen their promotion to higher levels of the judiciary slowed to a crawl. There are several examples of judges seemingly on the fast track to the Supreme Court who have had their careers derailed and ended up in some rural family court because they made an impolitic decision. However, these are the exceptional incidents: just as Diet rejection of bills is rare because the bureaucracy and the Cabinet do not bother to submit doomed legislation, political punishment of judges is rare, because judges know the consequences of annoying the LDP. If a judge has moved up the ranks quickly enough to have an opportunity to be appointed to the Supreme Court, it is a safe bet that he has not ruled against LDP interests on any important matter.[17]

What has the LDP's indirect manipulation of judicial appointments bought them? Two infamous examples of judicial review show that the Supreme Court will overrule lower courts that decide cases against the preferences of LDP governments. First, in 1983 a district court determined that the **malapportionment** in House of Representatives' elections had grown so large as to be unconstitutional. Since the LDP wins a considerable proportion of its support from overrepresented rural areas, a forced reapportionment of Lower House seats would have been detrimental to the party. The Supreme Court intervened, and while not throwing out the lower court's ruling of unconstitutionality, it did not attempt to establish a strict rule for reapportionment either. Most importantly, it did not void the election results, which would have been damaging to the LDP. This allowed the LDP to make narrow changes toward reapportionment without threatening its hold on power.

Second, the Supreme Court consistently has upheld the LDP's position that Article 9 of the Constitution allows the maintenance of armed forces for self-defense, as well as the LDP's definition of self-defense. Opponents contend—and judges in regional courts have ruled on several occasions—that a literal reading of Article 9 reveals Japan's Self-Defense Forces (SDF) to be unconstitutional, as a Sapporo district court ruled in 1973. The Sapporo High Court reversed this decision the same year. The Supreme Court refused to hear an appeal in the case in 1982, effectively supporting the LDP's position. Not coincidentally, the district court judge who ruled against the government saw his career prospects take a turn for the worse.[18]

## ELECTORAL SYSTEMS AND ELECTORAL COMPETITION

Electoral rules determine the nature of competition among politicians for office. Such details as the size and location of electoral districts, the number of seats up for grabs, and the number and partisanship of competitors determine how politicians must behave in order to win. Also important, of course, are the particular configurations of voters' interests, and the rules concerning what sorts of campaign activities are allowed and disallowed. Since voters care about what politicians do once they are elected, electoral rules also have had profound consequences for policy.

The two chambers of the National Diet use different electoral rules (see Tables 11.2A and Table 11.2B). The rules for the more powerful House of Representatives were changed in 1994, but since only four elections have been held under the new rules, we begin by focusing on the rules that shaped political competition up until the 1994 reform. We then discuss the new electoral rules, and their consequences, before turning to a brief discussion of the House of Councillors.

### The Old Electoral Rules—House of Representatives

According to the Constitution, members of the House of Representatives are elected to four-year terms, but these terms usually end early, as the prime minister may dissolve the chamber and call elections at any time. Two basic changes were instituted for the first postwar election, held in 1946: (1) women were granted the right to vote, enabling all Japanese age 20 years and older to vote in national and local elections; and (2) the Communist Party was legalized. A new electoral system using proportional representation

| TABLE 11.2A | | |
|---|---|---|
| **Japanese Electoral Rules: Lower House, 1947–Present** | | |

| Time Period | 1947–1994 | 1994–Present | |
|---|---|---|---|
| | | 1994–Present | |
| Election rule | SNTV | SMD | Closed-list PR |
| Number of districts | ~129 | 300 | 11 |
| Number of seats | ~511 | 300 | 180§ |
| Average district size | 4 | 1 | 16.4 |
| *Intraparty competition* | *Always* | *No* | *No\** |

| TABLE 11.2B | | |
|---|---|---|
| **Japanese Electoral Rules: Upper House, 1947–Present** | | |

| | Prefectural Districts | | National List | | |
|---|---|---|---|---|---|
| Time Period | 1947–1998 | 2001–Present | 1947–1980 | 1983–1998 | 2001–Present |
| Election rule | STNV (SMD) | | SNTV | Closed-List PR | Open-List PR |
| Number of districts | 47 | 47 | | 1 | |
| Number of seats | 76/76 | 73/73 | | 50/50 | 48/48 |
| Average district size | 1.6 | 1.55 | | 50 | 48 |
| *Intraparty competition* | *Rarely* | *Rarely* | *Some* | *No\** | *Some* |

\*Under closed-list PR, candidates competed for the favor of party leaders in order to secure favorable list positions. But there was no intraparty competition in front of voters (since voters cast votes for parties, not individuals).

§The 1994 reform created 200 PR seats, but this number was reduced to 180 before the 2000 election.

(PR) in prefecturewide districts was instituted by Japanese politicians eager to conduct an election before the Occupation administration was up and running. The new system produced a plethora of new parties, and the Socialist Party performed best of all. In 1947, SCAP insisted that another election be held to ratify the new Constitution; and this time the conservative parties managed to readopt the **Single Non-Transferable Vote (SNTV) system** that had been used since 1925.[19] The return to SNTV made sense because the large parties could not agree among themselves on a new electoral rule, but all had an interest in establishing a system that restricted the role of small parties. With SCAP pushing for a quick decision, reverting to the old rules was the easiest solution.

The number of electoral districts and the overall number of seats in the Lower House have increased over time. In the last election held under the SNTV rules in 1993, 511 Lower House members were elected from 129 electoral districts, which ranged in size from two to six seats. Each voter cast a single vote for an individual, not a party or party list. The vote was nontransferable; so if candidates received more votes than necessary for victory (or too few to win a seat), their unneeded votes could not be transferred to the voters' second-choice candidates. In effect, this system was much like the single-member district plurality rule used for legislative elections in the United States, Britain, and Canada, except for one crucial difference: instead of only the top single vote-getter receiving a seat, the top two to six vote-getters (depending on the number of seats available in a district) each received a seat in the House of Representatives. So in, say, a five-seat district, coming in fifth place was good enough to win a seat.

This combination of a nontransferable vote with multiseat districts created a variety of incentives and consequences to which parties and candidates had to respond. Any party seeking a parliamentary majority would have to win at least 256 seats, or an average of almost exactly two seats per district (256 seats/129 districts). It follows that it had to nominate an average of *at least* two candidates per district, and probably more, since it could not expect every candidate to win. Furthermore, each voter could vote for only one candidate, which meant that the candidates from the same party had to compete directly with each other for the favor of the same voters. Indeed, a candidate's most bitter rivals were not members of other parties, but candidates in the same party.

How did candidates convince their party's voters to favor them over their co-partisan rivals? How did they differentiate themselves from one another, despite the same party platform, and more or less the same ideology? One possible answer is that a party's several candidates might have staked out different policy positions. For example, one might have run on a hawkish foreign policy platform, one as a dove, and the third as a moderate. But the party did not want its candidates fighting with each other over policy in front of voters, because doing so would have confused voters as to what the party stood for. In the United States, these sorts of intraparty policy battles occur only in primary elections. But once a party's candidate has been chosen, the public intraparty squabbles stop (more or less) so that the party can present a united front against its equally united opponent. One way to look at the dilemma for Japanese politicians under SNTV would be to imagine that the primary and general election campaigns were taking place at the same time.

The LDP solved this vote-division problem by allowing its candidates to create decentralized campaign organizations. Individual LDP candidates targeted groups in their districts, through either geographic or professional relationships, and specialized in distributing political favors to those groups. LDP members used the money raised from the groups they assisted to build up loyal personal support bases. The party abetted its candidates' efforts by doling out pork-barrel projects for which candidates could claim credit and by enforcing a policy-specialization scheme. The party also saw to it that its two or three or four candidates within a given district specialized in *different* areas of policy. This way, they could differentiate themselves from each other by pointing to exclusive influence over "their" policy turf. Each would thereby have a natural group of supporters within the district that was protected from competing claims by co-partisan rivals. One member would cultivate small retailers in a district, another farmers, and a third manufacturers, for example.[20]

The LDP's response to the need to divide the vote also had consequences for political competition. This system produced huge entry barriers for challengers, especially non-LDP challengers. Since politics centered on the distribution of private goods, the party that controlled access to these resources always had the upper hand. Thus, to implement this strategy successfully, the LDP relied on its ability to control the national budget.[21]

As another consequence, the system for political competition lowered the electoral salience of issues. Since politicians of the dominant LDP barraged their supporters with political favors, the opposition parties could not respond in kind. Corruption scandals (see Box 11.2) or other issues occasionally afforded the opposition a chance to excite the public, but it was difficult for voters to pass up the tangible favors LDP members offered them in exchange for electoral support. Voting for the opposition, even when the opposition espoused policies closer to their own preferences, might never pay off.

A final distinctive feature of the Japanese electoral system is its restrictive rules for campaigning, most of which survived the electoral reform of 1994. Until the reform, candidates were not allowed to advertise on television or the radio, with the exception of two five-minute spots on the government-controlled public broadcasting system. Since 1994, the use of media (including the Internet) has expanded dramatically. Door-to-door canvassing, however, was and still is prohibited. The official campaign period begins with the call for Lower House elections and lasts for only twelve days. (This was shortened from 30 days to 25 days in 1952, to 20 days in 1958, 15 days in 1983, 14 days in 1992, and finally to 12 days in 1994.) Any campaigning outside of that period is (officially) illegal. The law, moreover, limits how much money candidates are permitted to spend on their campaigns.

The net effect of all of these restrictions is to give an advantage to incumbents at the expense of challengers. In Japan's personalistic pre-1994 electoral system, name recognition and personal relationships with voters were of paramount importance, and these campaign restrictions made it hard for newcomers to establish themselves.[22] Moreover, and perhaps more subtly, the rules also advantaged the LDP at the expense of opposition parties (and not only because the majority-LDP always had the most incumbents). These rules made it very difficult for candidates to appeal to large groups of voters at once. Televison and

**BOX 11.2**

## Electoral Incentives, Political Scandals, and the LDP

Numerous scandals have plagued the Liberal Democratic Party (LDP) during its thirty-eight-year reign. Money-intensive campaign strategies have made Japanese elections perhaps the most expensive in the world. Businesses, small and large, have been consistent LDP contributors in exchange for a variety of favorable policies, from agricultural subsidies to protective regulatory regimes. Here are brief summaries of three of the most infamous episodes.

- In 1976, former Prime Minister Kakuei Tanaka was arrested for having accepted, while in office, a bribe from the U.S. airplane-maker Lockheed, in exchange for facilitating the sale of aircraft to Japan's major domestic airline. Actually, Tanaka had been forced from office two years earlier, after a series of other financial misdeeds were exposed in the popular journal *Bungei Shunju*. The Lockheed scandal dragged on for several years before Tanaka was finally convicted in 1983.
- The most extensive scandal, both in terms of the amount of money involved and the number of

recipients, was the Recruit scandal (1988–1989). The president of Recruit Cosmos Corporation (an employment information and property management firm) sold Recruit shares to various politicians and a few bureaucrats during 1985 and 1986 at far below their actual value. When Recruit shares were offered to the public in 1986, their value skyrocketed, giving those in the loop enormous windfall profits. When the scandal came to light, Prime Minister Noboru Takeshita and four other cabinet ministers were forced to resign from government.

- In the early 1990s, Sagawa Kyubin, a package delivery company, donated illegally large sums of money to powerful LDP members in hopes of obtaining favorable changes in trucking regulation. The highlight of this scandal came when prosecutors raided the home of party kingpin Shin Kanemaru and found millions of dollars in gold and cash hidden in his basement. The public outrage at this corruption contributed to the party split that finally cost the LDP its legislative majority.

---

radio would be the easiest ways to issue broad-based appeals, but they were disallowed. This was fine for LDP candidates who were too preoccupied with intraparty competition to be concerned with broad-based, partisan appeals. But opposition parties, especially those that ran only one candidate per district, would have benefited enormously from the ability to present their platforms to a mass audience via television and radio advertising. The easiest restrictions to circumvent—because they were the most difficult to enforce—were the spending limits and the canvassing ban. These were precisely the areas in which the LDP maintained distinct advantages.[23]

### The New Electoral Rules— House of Representatives

In January 1994, several months after wresting power from the LDP, a seven-party coalition government enacted a major restructuring of the Lower House electoral rules. The new rules set the size of the House

of Representatives at 500 seats, later reduced to 480. Of these, 300 are elected on the basis of equal-sized **single-member districts,** and 180 (originally 200) are elected from eleven regional districts by **proportional representation (PR).** Each voter casts two votes: one for a candidate in the single-member district, and one for a party in the PR region. As in Germany and New Zealand (among other places), which use similar systems, a candidate may run in a district *and* appear on the corresponding party list in the larger region; so unsuccessful district candidates can be "saved" by the list. The Japanese press was quick to dub such politicians "*zombies,*" inasmuch as they seemed to be revivified despite their district demise, and Japanese voters are not terribly fond of this aspect of the new rules.

The key improvement that this system was expected to produce was the elimination of intraparty competition. No longer do members of the same party have to compete against one another (at least in front of the voters—they still have to compete within the party for district endorsements and good spots on party lists). Instead, electoral contests now focus on competition among parties. Another major expectation, arising from the introduction of single-member districts, is movement toward a two-party system. Of course, the PR component of the electoral rule will ensure that some small parties continue to survive, but they should fade away in the single-member districts, where only large parties have a realistic chance of winning. (Interestingly, the Conservatives and Komeito, both small parties, managed to win a handful of single-member districts because the LDP, which needed both parties to form a governing coalition, agreed to endorse their candidates in those races instead of running its own candidates.) In fact, the postreform elections and the party reorganizations that have been ongoing since the reform suggest that two large parties may well arise as the major sources of power under the new rule. The LDP, so far, has maintained its position as one of those parties, and recently, the Democratic Party has been the LDP's challenger in most single-member districts nationwide.

## The Electoral Rules—House of Councillors

Members of Japan's Upper House (see again Table 11.2B) serve fixed six-year terms, with half elected every three years. Each voter has two votes: one cast in the prefectural SNTV district for an individual candidate, and the second cast for a party in the national district (with each party receiving a share of the 50 PR seats that matches the share of the vote it receives). Unlike the new, two-tiered Lower House system, however, candidates may not run in both tiers in the Upper House simultaneously.

Just before the 2001 election, two changes were made to the Upper House electoral system. First, the number of PR seats available was reduced from fifty to forty-eight, and the number of SNTV seats from seventy-six to seventy-three. A similar reduction for the 2004 election meant an overall elimination of ten Upper House seats. Second, and more importantly, the PR tier was changed from closed-list to open-list. Under closed-list PR, parties rank their candidates, and voters are asked only to choose their favorite party. If a party wins enough votes for, say, fifteen PR seats, then the party's fifteen top-ranked candidates get those seats. Under open-list PR, voters may, if they wish, choose an individual candidate within a party. Before seats are allocated, then, each party's candidates are reranked

according to how many preference votes they received. So who gets into that top fifteen depends on the voters, not the party leaders. This might seem a more democratic way to do things, but that is not why the LDP pushed for the change. Instead, in light of the party's flagging popularity at the time, it hoped that some of its individual candidates (mostly celebrities that it placed at the top of the national list) would be more attractive than the party as a whole, and that this would earn the LDP extra votes, and hence extra seats.

Despite the use of SNTV for the Upper House districts, there is not very much intraparty competition. Of the forty-seven prefectural districts, more than half (twenty-seven) are single-seat constituencies, in which there is no reason for a party to nominate more than one candidate. Even in the fifteen two-seat districts, it is uncommon for a party to nominate more than one candidate. So the possibility of intraparty competition—and hence the need to divide the vote, as in the Lower House—is limited primarily to the five districts that send three or four members to the Diet.[24] In the national PR district, the 2001 switch to open lists raises the specter of intraparty competition again, as candidates within a party now must compete with each other to win enough preference votes to rise on the party's list, but with a nationwide constituency, any concern about personalism dominating partisanship (as in the pre-1994 Lower House strategies) is likely unfounded.

Thus, the primary focus in Upper House elections is on parties, not individuals, so it is no coincidence that Upper House elections feature more in the way of issue-based campaigning, and less in the way of money politics. Personal support groups play a lesser role. This has made the LDP more vulnerable to the mood of the electorate in Upper House elections over unpopular policies or scandals than it is in Lower House elections. This fact was brought home in 1989, when the LDP lost its Upper House majority, apparently as a result of a recently enacted sales tax and a flurry of scandals. More recently, the LDP did well in the 2001 election due to the popularity of Junichiro Koizumi, but faltered in 2004. Then, in 2007, the party suffered a massive defeat when Shinzo Abe's government proved inept and out of touch.

Electoral rules have had a profound impact on the party system, political competition, and party organization. The next section describes the evolution of the Japanese party system over the postwar era.

## THE JAPANESE PARTY SYSTEM

For most of the postwar era, the Japanese party system has been unusual in that it has combined multipartism with the sustained dominance of one majority party, the LDP. The most logical way to trace the postwar history of the party system is to subdivide it into three distinct periods. The first, which lasted throughout the Occupation and a few years beyond, was a rather volatile period, in which no party or coalition of parties stayed on top for very long; it was characterized by the appearance of new parties, the disappearance of existing ones, party splits, and party mergers. The second period began in 1955, with the formation (through mergers) of the LDP and its chief rival for the next four decades, the Japan Socialist Party. From 1955 until 1993, these parties remained the two largest in the Diet, with the LDP consistently enjoying about twice the strength of the Socialists. This second period saw the formation of two small, but important, centrist parties, which managed to win some seats from both large parties, though never enough to deprive the LDP of its Diet majority. Finally, the third (current) period began with the split of the LDP in 1993, followed by a change in the electoral system that sent the rest of the party system into flux. Today, the LDP remains by far the largest political party, but governs in coalition with a former rival, and now faces a new lead opposition party currently led by an LDP defector. In this section, we examine each of these three periods. As you read this section, Figures 11.2, 11.3, and 11.4 should help you keep the party names (and acronyms) straight. Throughout, we concentrate on the more important House of Representatives.

### The Party System, 1946–1955

In the immediate aftermath of World War II, the Japanese political party system was somewhat chaotic. Two major conservative parties, two major socialist parties, a newly legalized communist party, and a handful of micro-parties dotted the landscape, encouraged by the permissive attitude of the early Occupation and by the fractionalizing incentives of the proportional representation electoral system used in 1946. With the reintroduction of the SNTV electoral system in 1947, most of the small parties disappeared, but it was not until 1955 that the party system really began to consolidate in earnest.

The Liberal Party and the Democratic Party spent most of the pre-1955 period competing with one another, each trying to take the lead as the standard bearer of conservative politics. Between them, they held a majority of seats in the Diet, but they were unable to devise a mechanism for shared control of government.

The largest force on the left, the Japan Socialist Party, was untainted by militarism and appealed to the strong pacifist sentiment in postwar Japan by defending Article 9 of the Constitution and vilifying conservatives who wished to remove the "Peace Clause." It called for a foreign policy characterized by "unarmed neutrality" and opposed Japan's **Self-Defense Forces** as unconstitutional. The party maintained complete opposition to the acquisition of nuclear weapons and even opposed the production of nuclear power as too dangerous.

The Socialist Party was for a time the largest force in the Diet, and even participated in a couple of coalition governments, with a Socialist (Tetsu Katayama) as prime minister briefly in 1947. By the early 1950s, however, the Socialists were split into two warring camps, the "Left Socialists" (who were backed by public sector labor) and the "Right Socialists" (whose adherents were to be found primarily in the urban, private sector). Moreover, the far left end of the ideological spectrum was held down by the **Japan Communist Party (JCP)**. The JCP had formed back in 1922, but had been driven underground in the prewar era when many of its leaders were imprisoned for radicalism. SCAP legalized the party in 1945, but it garnered only small vote shares early on. The JCP's platform is antiemperor, anticapitalism, and antimilitary. Although it has resolved to work within the democratic political system, it ritualistically opposes the policies of the LDP. As the only party entirely untainted by money politics, the JCP generally leads the way in excoriating the LDP for its frequent scandals and in calling for political reform.

This first period of postwar Japanese party politics ended in 1955. In October of that year, the two Socialist parties remerged to form the **Japan Socialist Party (JSP).** The Socialists continued to find most of their support in the burgeoning labor movement. Unions provided votes, campaign finance, and candidates for the party. In return, the party championed workers' rights and redistributive economic policies. But the merger did not end (but merely internalized) the battles between moderates and radical leftists that had split the party into Left and Right.

In response to the Socialist merger, the Liberals and Democrats merged a month later to form the **Liberal Democratic Party (LDP),** which immediately enjoyed a large majority of Diet seats. Suddenly, the chaos of the early postwar years had been replaced by what became known as a "One-and-a-Half Party System" (also called the "1955 system"). The top row of Figure 11.2 shows the endpoint for the first period of postwar Japanese party politics, and the beginning of the second period (note that the parties are arrayed from left to right, according to the standard ideological spectrum). In 1955, the LDP was the single largest party, and the JSP controlled approximately half as many seats. The JCP represented the only clear third party, but won just 2 percent of the vote and an even smaller share of seats. Many believed that Japan was headed toward the formation of a two-party system in which alternation in power between the LDP and JSP would become the norm.[25]

### The Party System, 1955–1993

The most important characteristic of the second period was that the LDP remained firmly in control of both Diet chambers. But true two-party politics never took hold in Japan. Instead, the party system refragmented somewhat during the next thirty-eight years, with new parties siphoning support from both the LDP and the JSP. This expansion can be traced in part to the SNTV electoral system, and in part to the emergence of a group in Japanese society that felt its needs could not be represented by any of the existing parties. Because most electoral districts sent three to five "winners" to the Diet, potential candidates knew that the number of votes they would need to win was not that large—in many districts, even finishing in fifth place was good enough to win a seat. This meant that when the going got rough in an existing party, the formation of a new party was certainly a feasible alternative. It also meant that a grassroots organization dissatisfied with the platforms of existing parties might choose to form a new party from scratch rather than try to change the platform of an existing party from within. The period between 1955 and 1993 saw the formation of important new parties for both of these reasons.

*The 1960s* In 1960, the U.S.–Japan Mutual Security Treaty came up for renewal. Protests (even riots) against renewal broke out, led by the Japan Communist Party but supported broadly by the left. The public sector unions, the largest backers of the JSP, led work stoppages. Chaos reigned in the Diet. Opposition party members barricaded the Speaker of the House of Representatives in his office to prevent the calling of a vote on treaty renewal. Diet police were obliged to drag them out of the building. Though this event was said to have reduced popular support of the JSP, it probably also reinforced the support of its true believers, thereby both narrowing the JSP's range of support and anchoring its ideological position.

Also in 1960, the JSP's right wing defected to form the **Democratic Socialist Party (DSP).** Until its dissolution in 1994, the DSP's platform resembled closely that of the JSP, with the important exception that the DSP strongly supported the U.S.–Japan Mutual Security Treaty and the Self-Defense Forces. The 1960 Socialist split coincided with a split in the labor movement. A federation of private industry labor unions arose to support the DSP, while the main public-sector unions continued to back the JSP. In both cases, union support gave the parties a steady share of votes, but both were unable to expand their bases of support much further. The DSP peaked with 8.8 percent of the Lower House vote in the 1960 election and drew slightly smaller vote shares thereafter.

The next important change in the "1955 system" came in 1964, with the formation of the **Komeito** (sometimes known by its awkward English translation, the **Clean Government Party).** The Komeito formed as the political arm of a lay Buddhist organization called **Soka Gakkai.** The group, together with the party, grew in urban areas as postwar Japan underwent rapid urbanization. Soka Gakkai "blocks" act as a neighborhood basis for party organization. They provide money, a volunteer labor force, and loyal, active voters. The Komeito's high degree of organization and concentration of supporters in urban areas allows it to maximize its seat shares. The Komeito's platform is based on "humanitarian socialism," but it remains fiercely anticommunist. The party opposes revision of Article 9, but has come to support the U.S.–Japan alliance in recent years. However, the Komeito's connection to the Soka Gakkai has prevented the party from extending its support base much beyond Soka Gakkai devotees. Unable to grow, the Komeito resorted to coordinating with other centrist parties in many districts during the 1970s and 1980s.

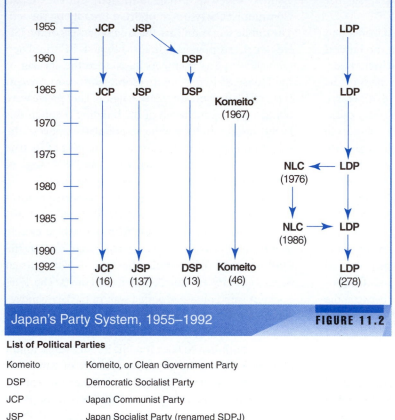

Japan's Party System, 1955–1992      **FIGURE 11.2**

**List of Political Parties**

| | |
|---|---|
| Komeito | Komeito, or Clean Government Party |
| DSP | Democratic Socialist Party |
| JCP | Japan Communist Party |
| JSP | Japan Socialist Party (renamed SDPJ) |
| LDP | Liberal Democratic Party |
| NLC | New Liberal Club |

*Note: The Komeito supported candidates in the Upper House as early as 1956, but did not endorse Lower House candidates until 1967.

decade of rapid economic growth. The LDP's reward, of course, was continued control of government.

With tremendous economic growth came dramatic demographic change. Japan's rapid postwar urbanization and industrialization reduced the size of groups that were key parts of the LDP's support base, specifically agricultural workers and small retailers.[26] The rise of a new urban class, and of the urban blights of industrialization (for example, pollution and overcrowding), fueled dissatisfaction with the LDP, and the party's legislative majorities decreased steadily. From 1958 to 1969, the LDP's vote share declined from 57.8 percent to 47.6 percent. Nonetheless, the LDP was able to maintain its majority of seats by virtue of electoral **malapportionment,** its more efficient nomination strategies, and its continued control over government purse strings. Despite the chinks in the LDP armor, however, the JSP was unable to capitalize on the situation. Instead, the Komeito, DSP, and JCP took votes away from both large parties (see Figure 11.3).

As the largest opposition party in the Diet, the JSP often led the charge against LDP policies, but its perpetual minority status meant that it could do little to stop the LDP from working its will on policy. Instead it fell back on two strategies. The first was to employ extraparliamentary tactics, such as boycotts and obstructionism, to call public attention to LDP actions in the hope that the LDP would be shamed into modifying its policies somewhat. The second tactic was to work behind the scenes to force the LDP to moderate certain bills, holding out the threat of obstructionism as a bargaining chip.

The Socialists suffered a steady decline in vote shares over the postwar era, its decline paralleling the steady decline in union membership. The LDP had impeded public-sector unions through harassment, as it did with the teachers' union Nikkyoso, and, in the 1980s, through privatization, as with Japan National Railways and Nippon Telegraph and Telephone.[27]

Throughout the 1960s, the party system remained somewhat polarized around the issues of Article 9 and the U.S.–Japan Mutual Security Treaty. The Socialists and Communists stood firmly for retention of the former and against the latter. However, after the turmoil surrounding the renewal of the Security Treaty in 1960 forced Prime Minister **Nobusuke Kishi** from office, the LDP resolved to avoid a repetition of such events. Under the new prime minister, **Hayato Ikeda,** the LDP began to downplay security and defense issues and focus instead on the goal of economic growth. Ikeda made his famous "income doubling" pledge that year, promising to double Japan's per capita gross national product (GNP) by the end of the 1960s. In fact, Japan's economy far surpassed this objective. Pursuit of this goal diminished other policy areas in relative importance, with the payoff for the public being more than a

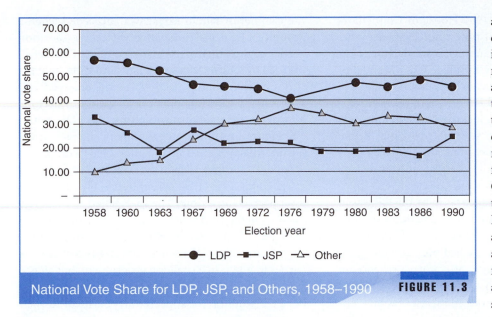

National Vote Share for LDP, JSP, and Others, 1958–1990    **FIGURE 11.3**

able each time to add enough conservative independent winners to reestablish its majority and keep sole control of the government. Prior to the 1976 election, a band of young, urban LDP members defected to form the New Liberal Club (NLC), a new party that denounced the LDP's persistent scandals and demanded electoral and campaign finance reform. The NLC managed to win seventeen seats in the election.

The LDP's slide bottomed out in 1980, when the purposeful abstention by several party members allowed a no-confidence measure to pass the Diet. Heading into the subsequent election campaign, the party's prospects looked pretty grim, and the possibility of coalition governments seemed greater than at any time since 1955.

Why did the JSP not alter its platform to mirror changing public sentiment? By the late 1960s, both the Security Treaty and the Self-Defense Forces enjoyed overwhelming public support, but the JSP's rhetoric did not keep pace. With the right wing of the party having split off to form the DSP, the remaining moderates in the JSP were weakened. This situation allowed the party's left-wing activists to prevail against intraparty competitors. Watering down the party's rhetoric would have alienated the core of the party's support.

**The 1970s** By the end of the 1960s, the party system had crystallized. There were five political parties: one dominant and four in opposition (see again Figure 11.2). But the 1970s brought two crises that threatened the LDP's stranglehold on political power. First, the oil shock of late 1973 brought Japan's heady high-growth era to an abrupt halt. For years, economic expansion had afforded the LDP the politically popular luxury of increasing government spending while lowering income taxes every year. After 1974, the LDP had to resort to larger and larger government budget deficits just to keep spending at comparable levels. The second crisis for the LDP concerned money scandals. In 1974, public outrage over a collection of campaign finance scandals forced Prime Minister Kakuei Tanaka from office.

The LDP failed to win a majority of Lower House seats outright in the 1976 and 1979 elections, but was

**The 1980s** The LDP won its largest victory to date in 1980—a surprising result usually attributed to two factors. First, the sudden death of Prime Minister (and LDP leader) **Masayoshi Ohira** only ten days before the election brought out a huge wave of sympathy votes for the party. Second, the 1980 election was the first in which both Diet chambers were chosen simultaneously. This further increased turnout, which hurt the JCP and Komeito (which do best when overall turnout is low) and allowed the LDP to win back many of the seats it had lost during the previous decade.[28] Moreover, the 1976 election proved to have been the New Liberal Club's peak year, and it posed no threat to the LDP in 1980.

As Figure 11.2 shows, the structure of the Japanese party system changed very little in the 1980s (the one exception was the reintegration of the few remaining NLC members into the LDP), although party fortunes waxed and waned. The LDP had a bad election in 1983, but rebounded again in 1986 (see again Figure 11.3).

In 1989, the JSP seemed poised to reverse its three decades as an also-ran. Through a combination of fortunate circumstances, a popular policy stance, and some savvy electioneering, the party was able to win a plurality of seats in the 1989 House of Councillors election and, for the first time since 1955, deny the LDP control of one of Japan's legislative chambers. For the JSP, the fortunate circumstance was a scandal of unprecedented proportions—the "Recruit" scandal—that ripped through the LDP, and even into the supposedly untouchable bureaucracy. This ignominy was compounded by a sex scandal involving Prime Minister Sosuke Uno (who, ironically, had been chosen as party leader because he was not tainted by Recruit) just before the election.

The popular policy stance taken by the JSP was in opposition to the introduction of a nationwide consumption tax, which took effect in April 1989. The LDP and Ministry of Finance had been struggling for ten years over how to reduce the country's reliance on income taxes, and had finally settled on a 3 percent levy on the final sales of goods and services as the solution. Although the new tax was implemented along with massive income tax cuts (making the net revenue effect roughly a wash), it was extremely unpopular. And for once, the JSP found itself on the popular side of an issue. Finally, Socialist leader **Takako Doi,** the first woman to lead a major political party in Japan, took advantage of the particular outrage of female voters at both the scandals and the consumption tax by nominating a record number of female candidates for the 1989 Upper House poll. The tactic was successful, and the JSP won more seats than the LDP for the first time ever.

As it turned out, the JSP's 1989 triumph was more of a last gasp than a herald of Socialist resurgence. The LDP rebounded from its devastating 1989 Upper House defeat with a strong showing only a few months later in the 1990 Lower House election, and the JSP fell off even further. However, dissension among—and even within—the LDP's factions was planting the seeds of a party split.

## The Party System Since 1993

With corruption scandals mounting, calls for electoral and campaign finance reform increased within the LDP as well as among the opposition parties. But many within the LDP were wary of changing a system that they had mastered so well for so long. Individual party members had no way of knowing how a new system might affect their own chances for reelection. Finally, in June 1993 a vote of no-confidence against

the Cabinet of **Kiichi Miyazawa** succeeded when a group of LDP legislators voted with the opposition parties against their party's government. This defection, led by **Ichiro Ozawa** and **Tsutomu Hata,** split the LDP, and the ensuing election saw the emergence of several new parties into political competition. Electoral reform was the main issue prompting the LDP split.

Figure 11.4 illustrates the many changes in the Japanese party system in and after 1993, with parties arrayed left to right. Clearly the stability that had characterized the 1955–1992 period (especially since 1965) disappeared for a time. The LDP failed to achieve a majority in the 1993 general election, winning only 223 seats out of 511, but it remained far and away the largest party. The LDP tried to convince two of the new parties to join it in a coalition government, but all had run on political reform platforms, and an alliance with the LDP would have appeared hypocritical to their supporters. The result was an unwieldy seven-party coalition government that included every party *except* the LDP and the Communists. The coalition came together under the leadership of **Morihiro Hosokawa,** the leader of the small, centrist Japan New Party.

The coalition's only stated policy objective was to complete the reform of the electoral system that the LDP had failed to accomplish. The parties that entered power in 1993 were united in their desire for an electoral reform that would diminish the LDP's grip on power and reduce the political corruption engendered by the insatiable appetite for campaign funds. But similar objectives do not necessarily dictate similar solutions. Some parties, in particular the JSP, favored a greater emphasis on proportionality, while others (who hoped to merge into a large catch-all party) preferred a greater reliance on single-member districts. In an ironic twist of fate, the eventual compromise required the support of the now-opposition LDP for passage, because the JSP found unpalatable the new government's plan to rely heavily on single-member districts.

Once the electoral reform passed, the next issue on the coalition's agenda was tax reform, but on this matter, the JSP's preferences were diametrically opposed to those of other coalition members. The JSP pulled its members out of the coalition, and the government fell after only eight months in office. It was followed by a minority cabinet led by the Japan Renewal Party's Tsutomu Hata. After only two months, Hata's government collapsed, and a new coalition came together that no one expected. The LDP moved back into government in partnership with its former nemesis, the Japan Socialist Party, as well as the tiny New Party Harbinger (Shinto Sakigake). In exchange for the JSP's partnership, the LDP allowed JSP leader **Tomiichi Murayama** to assume the prime ministership. From June 30, 1994 to January 11, 1996, Murayama governed as Japan's first Socialist prime minister since 1947.

In general, single-member districts tend to produce two-party competition, while proportional representation elections allow the survival of several parties. The new Japanese electoral system (as we saw earlier in this chapter) contains both of these elements. What has been the effect on the party system?

There has already been some movement toward party system consolidation in Japan, with the LDP as one of the main parties. But the formation of a second major party has proceeded in fits and starts, and it may never manage to encompass all LDP opponents. As Figure 11.4 shows, in December 1994, the JRP, JNP, Komeito, DSP, and a few other splinter groups (not shown) merged to form the **New Frontier Party (NFP)** (Shinshinto). In its first electoral test in the 1995 Upper House election, the NFP solidified its

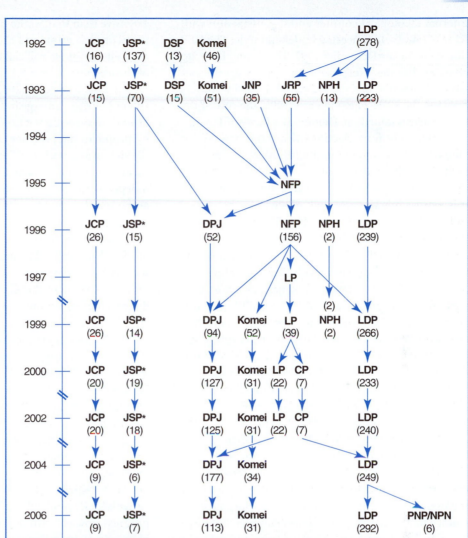

**Japan's Party System, 1992–2006**    **FIGURE 11.4**

Political Parties: Komei-Komeito or Clean Government Party; CP-Conservative Party; DPJ-Democratic Party of Japan; DSP-Democratic Socialist Party; JCP-Japan Communist Party; JNP-Japan New Party; JRP-Japan Renewal Party; JSP-Japan Socialist Party*; LDP-Liberal Democratic Party; NFP-New Frontier Party; NPH-New Party Harbinger; PNP/NPN: People's New Party/New Party Nippon

*The JSP changed its name to Social Democratic Party in the early 1990s, but we retain the old name for purposes of clarity. Parties are arranged ideologically left to right (relative placement of DPJ and Komeito is tricky, with the DPJ more to the left due to its inclusion of many JSP refugees and the Komeito's long-standing coalition with the LDP).

Note: Numbers in parentheses are the number of Lower House seats that each party held at several points in time. There were also 20 independents and two vacant seats as of 2007.

position as the major opposition force, even outpolling the LDP in the PR portion of the election, 31 percent to 27 percent. It was also the second largest party in the 1996 Lower House election, but by that time had already begun to splinter as a result of internal ideological conflict and dissatisfaction with Ichiro Ozawa's domineering leadership style. The NFP disbanded in late December 1997. The former Komeito reemerged as the "New Komeito." Some Ozawa loyalists formed the Liberal Party, while a few others rejoined the LDP. Then, in early 1998, the rest of the NFP refugees joined the **Democratic Party of Japan.**

After only four elections using the new Lower House electoral system, and with many of the same politicians still on the scene, it is too early to conclude that the party system has finished shifting around, but it is worthwhile to take stock of what has happened since 1993 (see again Figure 11.4). The main similarities between the 2006 party system and the 1992 version are the LDP, which is still on top, and the Communists and Komeito, with their small but loyal followings. The LDP's longtime nemesis but short-time partner, the Japan Socialist Party, has all but disappeared, and the Democrats, who have married much of the former JSP labor-support base to the largest group of LDP defectors, have emerged as the main competitor for the LDP. Before its dramatic defeat in the snap September 2005 election, the Democrats held just over 70 percent as many seats as the LDP (see Figure 11.5). The temporary emergence of the Liberal Party and the Conservative Party ended when the former merged with the Democrats, and the latter with the LDP.

In sum, the effect of the electoral reform on the party system has been to move the primary locus of the opposition rightward along the ideological spectrum. The Democratic Party looks considerably more "centrist" and moderate than did the JSP when it led the opposition. But the changes have been more extensive than that, in the nature of campaigns, intraparty organization, and the advent of coalition government. A simple roll call of parties is merely the tip of the iceberg.

The main reason that a stable, two-party system is still not likely to emerge in Japan is that 180 of the 480 Lower House seats are now filled from large districts by proportional representation. This component of the new system offers incentives for small parties to eschew mergers, in favor of continuing to compete independently. The Communists and Komeito, as well as the Socialists, now survive almost completely due to the PR tier.

The split in the LDP, and the subsequent coalition of LDP defectors and former opposition parties, was a momentous event in postwar Japanese politics. The resulting change in the electoral rule has already produced changes in the way political competition is structured both between and within parties. The LDP's traditional practice of dampening competition through a strategy of private goods distribution should prove less successful in the future (and in July 2002, Prime Minister Koizumi seemed to confirm this by calling for cutbacks in public works spending, despite the ongoing recession). Further, the internal organization of the political parties, in particular the LDP, is changing—today's LDP is different in many ways from the party that dominated Japanese politics for thiry-eight years. The party system, already convulsed by multiple splits and mergers, should progress toward two large parties battling it out in the single-member districts (right now, the LDP and the Democrats), and a couple more (small) parties (currently, the Komeito and Communists) surviving in the Upper House and in the Lower House's PR section.

Finally, it is important to note that the LDP has not been able to recapture control of the House of Councillors since 1989. With the LDP's historic defeat in the 2007 election, it declined to the number two party in that chamber, which is now controlled by the Democrats and their

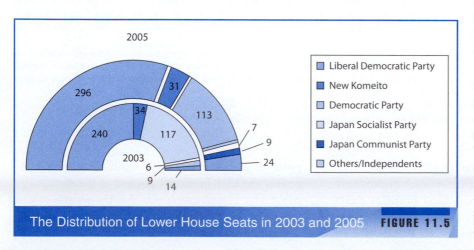

2005

296
31
34
113
240
117
7
9
2003
6
24
9
14

| | Liberal Democratic Party |
| | New Komeito |
| | Democratic Party |
| | Japan Socialist Party |
| | Japan Communist Party |
| | Others/Independents |

**The Distribution of Lower House Seats in 2003 and 2005**   **FIGURE 11.5**

allies. The LDP's inability to deal with persistent economic stagnation and financial turmoil contributed to the defeat, with only a halting recovery after a decade of economic travails. And, as we will describe later, despite the LDP's remarkable victory in the 2005 Lower House election, the party's dominance there is tenuous as well. Another party split—with some members gravitating toward the ideological center, and others toward the more conservative pole—is far from impossible.

## POLITICAL PARTICIPATION AND VOTING BEHAVIOR

By international standards, the political involvement of ordinary Japanese is low. Voters generally identify with political parties based on personal identification with a candidate or association with a party-affiliated interest group.[29] Since the SNTV electoral rule generated intraparty competition for parties that endorsed multiple candidates in a single district, LDP candidates could not use the LDP label as a sufficient cue for voters. A voter might support the LDP's platform, but if there were two or three LDP candidates running in the district, how could the voter decide *which* LDP candidate to support? To deal with this problem, LDP candidates constructed *koenkai*—personal support coalitions based on services the candidate provided for constituents or involvement in policy areas salient to aligned groups. A national party organization would have offered to the LDP no method for internal party vote division. Instead, LDP supporters were tied to individual LDP candidates. This fact may have reduced voters' identification with the party, but that was an acceptable tradeoff for the LDP. This strategy certainly contributed to the LDP's long-term dominance. It allowed the party to appeal to a variety of communities with often-contradictory interests. In this way the LDP remains a catch-all party, casting its net in all directions in search of support.

*Koenkai* consist of influential district members who gather votes from their economic or geographic communities based on personal relationships with voters. This strategy has worked best in rural areas where communities are long established and close-knit. Support was given to LDP members in exchange for past or future benefits. Rapid urbanization, however, created complications for this strategy. Urban

communities are amorphous, offering little geographic basis for vote appeals. Urban voters are younger on average, have much more diverse interests, and perhaps most importantly, do not work in the same district in which they reside (and therefore generally do not work with their neighbors). This has been a factor leading to increased campaign costs for LDP candidates. The clearest result has been the larger number of parties in urban areas. Rural districts have been dominated by the LDP, and to a lesser extent, JSP candidate machines. From the 1960s through 1993, however, there was far greater party competition in urban areas. Indeed, the Komeito is an entirely urban organization (as was the Democratic Socialist Party), and the Communists, though they run a candidate in every district, gain most of their support in urban areas as well.

With the end of intraparty competition, the nature of the *koenkai* is changing. Most often, *koenkai* have transformed themselves into the district party organization, since there is now at most one party candidate per district. Since most campaign contributions are now directed to district party offices, it was natural for *koenkai* to undertake this transformation in order to maintain their control over the flow of resources.[30]

During the long LDP reign, opposition parties lacked access to government services and money accorded to those in control of government, and therefore had to follow more traditional methods of voter involvement. Being tied to particular interest groups with ideological foundations supplied a steady stream of voter support. It also anchored parties to specific policy principles that could be abandoned only at risk of the party's survival—a conjecture that seems confirmed by the near disappearance of the JSP under the new electoral rules.

Only two parties have strong party organizations at the local level: the Japan Communist Party and the Komeito. The JCP is an ideological party whose support base is predictable. Because JCP voters rarely fail to turn out on election day, low *overall* voter turnout translates into increased JCP vote shares. On occasion, the JCP's ideological and antagonistic approach to political competition makes it the home for "protest votes" when the LDP angers the general public. Similarly, the Komeito does better in elections with low overall turnout, because its supporters (well mobilized by the Soka Gakkai) almost always show up at the polls.

Voter turnout at election time has been declining steadily on a nationwide basis. Recently, party identification has declined as well, as self-proclaimed "independents" now make up the largest group of respondents in public opinion polls. Though many commentators express dismay over this decline, it is unclear whether it represents a worrisome new political alienation or whether it is simply a sign that Japanese democracy has matured, now that Japanese voters seem as apathetic and complacent about politics as their counterparts in other advanced democracies. It is probably some of each, and more clearly identifiable party platforms may reignite some interest in party politics. Recent studies do indicate that Japanese voter turnout is determined by the same factors that drive turnout in other countries. Specifically, turnout tends to increase when elections are competitive, when the weather is good, and in districts with older voters, among a variety of other demographic variables.[31]

## INTEREST GROUPS

In Japan, well-organized producer groups that are able to coordinate their actions with relative ease have done well promoting their interests over those of less well-organized groups. The most important of these interest groups are farmers, big business, and, sometimes, small retailers and small manufacturers as well. In contrast with other industrialized countries, however, labor unions have been relatively weak and ineffective in postwar Japan.[32] Least successful of all have been the diffuse interests, especially consumers, who have borne the burden of government support for the former groups.

The most important interest groups are discussed in the following sections. The first three groups—big business, small manufacturers and retailers, and agriculture—all prospered under LDP rule. Though their preferences did not always converge, for most of the postwar era the interests of these groups have not been in direct conflict. This is changing. With the end of rapid economic growth, these groups increasingly find themselves in conflict, a trend that party competition under the new electoral rules may exacerbate.

### Big Business

Japanese firms—thanks in part to the long-term dominance of a conservative, pro-producer, pro-growth party and the close relationship between business and government—have prospered in the postwar period. Many Japanese firms have become household names throughout the world. Firms such as Sony, Toyota, Mitsubishi, and Matsushita have become dominant players in economic markets across the globe. The government has helped many of these firms through protection against foreign competition, through the formation and maintenance of research cartels, and through massive subsidies and tax incentives. (It is important to note, however, that some firms, most notably Sony, Pioneer, and Honda, have prospered despite government antagonism.) Large firms are often linked to one another in industrial groupings known as **keiretsu.** The United States claims that the cross-shareholding and vertical integration among *keiretsu* member firms constitute informal trade barriers that should be prohibited under Japanese antitrust laws. But the close LDP-business relationship has protected these groups from scrutiny until recently.

In the past, big business had little choice but to accept the LDP's attention to backward, inefficient sectors (such as farmers and small retailers) because the LDP was the only party clearly committed to business interests. In recent years, however, big business has become dissatisfied with the heavy expense of financing the LDP's electoral campaigns and of paying high taxes to underwrite the generous budget subsidies reserved for farmers and inefficient small firms. The new electoral rule, because it eliminated intra-party competition, should produce less costly electoral contests. The impetus for the rule change, and the LDP's acquiescence and assistance in the change, in part reflect the desires of business for reduced campaign spending. With the split in the LDP in 1993, the opposition included parties with similar preferences to the LDP, which allowed big business to hedge its bets for the first time. Consequently, the possibility of the LDP losing an election is now less troublesome for big business. It is likely that any new governing party would be satisfactory in the eyes of these large firms.

### Small- and Medium-Sized Businesses

Though from the outside it appears that large firms dominate the Japanese economy, small- and medium-sized businesses (defined as firms with fewer than 300 employees) make up a surprisingly large part of the economy. As of 2001, seven out of every ten workers in manufacturing, retail, wholesale, and other service industries worked for small or medium-sized firms, and small firms collectively produced 51.1 percent of all manufactured goods.[33] In both manufacturing and retail sales, these well-organized firms have pursued their political objectives with great success. They have gained considerable support from LDP policies over the post-war era. In return, these sectors are a good source of campaign funds (similar to big business) and, perhaps more importantly, offer a steady supply of votes for the LDP.

The benefits that have accrued to small- and medium-sized businesses have varied across sectors. Small manufacturers have enjoyed a variety of tax breaks and direct subsidies. Furthermore, financial policies have provided access to credit for small businesses even at the expense of big business. In the retail sector, small firms have been protected from competition by larger firms that would have threatened their existence. For example, the infamous Large Scale Retail Store Law protected "mom and pop" shops by limiting the entry of larger, more efficient retailers. Reduced competition allowed small retailers to remain profitable even as they became increasingly uncompetitive. Similar policies propped up small, inefficient banks.[34] More recently, many of these protective measures have been rolled back. The Large Scale Retail Store Law has been weakened substantially, and the Ministry of Finance (MOF) has begun to allow some insolvent banks to go under, after decades of issuing subsidies and engineering profit-padding regulatory protections to assure that this would never happen. While some of this liberalization preceded the electoral reform, it has accelerated since 1994, especially in the financial sector.[35]

## Agriculture

Agricultural interests are well organized politically, similar to big business, and they direct a significant and geographically concentrated vote bloc to the LDP electoral cause. Most farmers belong to local agricultural cooperatives whose national peak organization (Nogyo Kyodo Kumiai, or **Nokyo**) bargains with the government on their behalf.[36] Nokyo performs many quasi-governmental tasks, implementing programs that in other countries are controlled directly by government agencies. Local Nokyo offices function as monopoly providers of farming inputs (such as fertilizer, pesticides, and machinery), as monopsony purchasers of farm products (which they then resell), and as insurers and banks for farming communities. All

these roles are sanctioned by the government. This degree of autonomy speaks volumes for the effectiveness of agriculture's political lobbying efforts.

Farmers have been a significant source of votes for the LDP. Though the number of rural voters has declined precipitously in response to postwar urbanization, the malapportionment of the previous electoral system's districts that overrepresented agricultural interests benefited the LDP and farmers. Support from local agricultural cooperatives was at least as important for LDP candidates as was the party endorsement—and in many cases was necessary even to get that endorsement. In return for their electoral support, farmers received tariff and quota protection from competing imported products, price supports, and minimal taxation. Nonetheless, the LDP cannot take the farm vote for granted. This became clear to everyone in 2007, when the DPJ actually trounced the LDP in rural districts in that year's Upper House election.

## Organized Labor

Because Japanese labor unions are organized on the basis of workplace rather than occupation, craft, or economic sector, they are called **enterprise unions.** Nonmanagerial employees of a firm are all members of that firm's union. But ties between the workers of rival firms within a sector (say, for example, between Toyota workers and Nissan workers) are much weaker than in any other industrial democracy. Not surprisingly, this setup has reduced the tension between management and labor *within* firms (at the expense, many would argue, of worker welfare).[37] Cooperative management-labor relations have not led to similarly cordial relations with the government. The major union federations have had adversarial relationships with the succession of LDP governments.

Unionization levels have dropped over the past couple of decades in Japan, as has been true in Western Europe and North America. Never as numerous as in the highly unionized workforces of countries such as Germany and Britain, today fewer than 25 percent of Japanese workers are union members.[38] Remember, much Japanese economic activity takes place in small- and medium-sized firms. Employees in these firms typically are not unionized.

In the pre-reform party system, public-sector unions were tied closely to the Japan Socialist Party, while private-sector unions backed the Democratic

Japanese farmers rally in Tokyo to protest proposals to open Japanese markets to imported rice.

Masaharu Hatano/Reuters/Landov

Socialist Party. In 1989, seventeen public-sector unions and twenty-one private-sector unions together formed **Rengo,** the Japan Trade Union Confederation. At its inception, Rengo represented 65 percent of organized workers, but the subsequent fragmentation of the political party system has caused the demise of its erstwhile partisan advocates.[39]

## POLITICAL CULTURE AND ISSUE CLEAVAGES

Japanese culture has held significant sway as an explanation for Japanese political behavior and policy. Early social scientists, such as Max Weber, considered the Confucianist principles common in much of East Asia to be detrimental to political and economic development.[40] This viewpoint has been challenged by the rise of Japan and the subsequent economic growth throughout most of East Asia. Indeed, Lucian Pye has stood Weber on his head, arguing that varieties of "Confucian Authority" explain much of East Asia's economic success.[41]

Much of Japanese political behavior has been attributed to Japan's culture. Postwar Japanese democracy emerged from a history of authoritarianism. Those who have characterized Japan as a second-rate democracy often draw on the pre-Meiji-era history of feudalism and Confucianism to explain Japanese political behavior. They are quick to point out, moreover, that foreigners established Japan's postwar democratic institutions.

In discussions of Japanese political culture, the concepts of hierarchy, homogeneity, and conformity to group objectives take center stage.[42] For example, Japan's feudal experience, during which it cut itself off from the outside world, is argued to have been influential in establishing the importance of hierarchy. Meiji leaders, apparently thinking along the same lines as Weber, sought to westernize their nation. The fervent nationalism associated with prewar and wartime Japan may have been in part a backlash to Western influences. In the postwar era, renewed emphasis on westernization as a path toward industrial growth was also tempered, as Japan's world-beating industrialization success led many to return to the ingredients of Japanese culture to explain the country's newfound fortune.

Social hierarchy governs most Japanese relationships. In the family, in the workplace, and in politics, the hierarchical traits of loyalty and obligation can be found. Superiors do not simply dominate those below them. They are obliged to tend to their subordinates' needs as well. Such relationships are common in politics. Some see intraparty factions as simply a political version of the typical Japanese hierarchical relationship, where the factional leader acts as the elder with the followers as subordinates.[43] Relationships within factions are based on seniority. Seniority within LDP faction's made members reasonably sure when they would progress into gradually higher committee positions, party positions, and government posts.

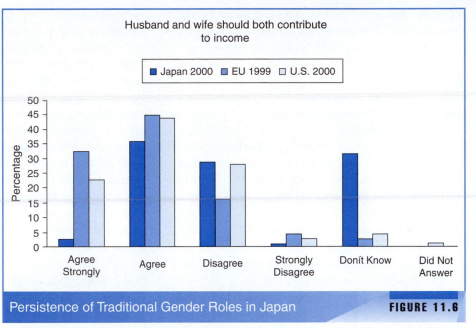

Husband and wife should both contribute to income

Persistence of Traditional Gender Roles in Japan    **FIGURE 11.6**

Note: EU data do not include Austria, Cyprus, or Ireland.

Source: European Values Study Group and World Values Survey Association. European and World Values Surveys Four-Wave Integrated Data File, 1981–2004, v.20060423, 2006. Aggregate File Producers: Análisis Sociológicos Económicos y Políticos (ASEP) and JD Systems (JDS), Madrid, Spain/Tilburg University, Tilburg, The Netherlands. Data Files Suppliers: Análisis Sociológicos Economicos y Políticos (JDS), Madrid, Spain/Tillburg University, Tillburg, The Netherlands/Zentralarchiv fur Empirische Sozialforschung (ZA), Cologne, Germany. Aggregate File Distributors: Análisis Sociológicos Económicos y Políticos (ASEP) and JD Systems (JDS), Madrid, Spain/Tillburg University, Tilburg, The Netherlands/Zentralarchiv fur Empirische Sozialforschung (ZA), Cologne, Germany.

## Women: At Home and in the Workplace

Another manifestation of the emphasis on social hierarchy and order in Japan is the halting change in gender roles in the postwar period. Although women's opportunities are improving, prospects for women in Japanese politics and in the workplace remain limited. The traditional role of "good wives and wise mothers" (*ryosai kenbo*) has been little altered by either evolving social values or legal prescription.[44]

Although the Constitution contains language guaranteeing equal rights for women, the judiciary has not been active in enforcing those rights. In June 2006, the Diet approved revision to the **Equal Employment Opportunity Law** that was passed in the mid-1980s to bar discrimination in the workplace. The initial passage of the law did lead to an influx of women into the paid workforce, but prior to the 2006 revision, there was nothing to prevent discriminatory hiring practices based on such factors as physical appearance, and the "glass ceiling" was low and mostly impenetrable.

As a result, employment opportunities for women are inadequate in scope and duration. Women are commonly expected to find employment after completing school that serves only as a transition to marriage and childcare (see Figure 11.6). Few opportunities exist for secure employment so, unsurprisingly, most women follow the established path. Statistics show that about 70 percent of women will quit their jobs upon becoming mothers,[45] while only 13 percent of women will find new jobs a year and a half after giving birth.[46]

Government has done little to assist the integration of women, either into the workplace or into politics. The Japanese welfare state is much less extensive than those in Europe (especially Scandinavia). Partly as a result, it is very difficult to find appropriate childcare or elderly care services that would help women to balance family and career. One unintended, but understandable consequence of this is that Japanese women now marry later and bear fewer children than their counterparts in nearly any other advanced country. This has exacerbated the rapid aging of the population, probably the most pressing problem that the Japanese government will face over the next few decades.

Finally, and not coincidentally, although the representation of women in government has improved in recent years, it is still the lowest among industrialized democracies—currently only forty-five of 480 Lower House seats (9 percent) are held by women. Women have fared somewhat better in the Upper House, with, at present, forty-three of 242 seats (18 percent). In each chamber, as expected, more female members enter via the proportional representation tier than by winning district seats.

Two changes may improve opportunities for women in both the political and economic arenas. The electoral rule change now selects nearly two-fifths of the Lower House from regional PR elections. At least one major political party has already stated that it will endorse more women on its party lists in the PR elections.[47] Though this might be simply a strategy to elicit support from female voters and might not result in any immediate changes in male domination of political parties, it should increase the number of women in the Diet. In the longer run, especially if female MPs gain seniority, this might matter for policy outputs as well.

A second trend that bodes well for women's opportunities in the workplace is demographic. The aging of Japanese society, in combination with declining birth rates, means that the Japanese population will begin to decline very soon, if it hasn't begun already. The Japanese workforce will decline even faster, absent other changes. The simplest way to stem the tide and forestall a decline in economic output would be to grant women a more prominent role in the workplace. Doing this would require (and produce) changes in cultural attitudes and expectations, and would not be easy or unopposed. The only alternative is to allow more immigration, likely a solution with even less support in Japan.

## Ethnic Homogeneity vs. Immigration

Japanese political behavior and economic success have also been attributed, at least in part, to ethnic and cultural homogeneity. This homogeneity has been credited with allowing Japan to focus in a unified manner on national goals—the foremost being economic growth. But Japan is not completely homogeneous, and the few minority groups that do exist face significant discrimination. **Koreans** make up Japan's largest ethnic minority. Brought to Japan as laborers during the war, Koreans are still treated poorly today. A few become naturalized Japanese citizens (citizenship does not come with birth in Japan) and manage to assimilate more or less fully. Those who do not may not vote or hold government jobs, and discrimination in the private-sector workforce is widely recognized. Until recently, those refusing the onerous demands of Japanese citizenship, including the taking of a Japanese name, were fingerprinted and required to carry alien registration identification.

The **Ainu** are another ethnic minority in Japan, an indigenous group who were pushed to the northern parts of the Japanese islands as the frontier was extended by the people now considered to be ethnic Japanese. Today there are estimated to be fewer than 17,000 Ainu surviving, most living in the northernmost island, Hokkaido. Finally, **Burakumin,** though ethnically Japanese, are descendents of a feudal outcast class that performed jobs considered impure by the Buddhist elite. Although it is illegal, discrimination over employment and housing against members of this group continues. The Buraku Liberation League has fought resolutely for better treatment by the government and society.

An understanding of why the Japanese feel confident that they are homogeneous may be found in the lack of strong issue cleavages. In many countries, there are a variety of societal cleavages over which politics is contested—language, religion, region, and race, to name the most prominent. But these sorts of issues rarely if ever arise in Japan. Indeed, one reason the LDP was so successful for so long at implementing a campaign strategy that downplayed issues in favor of the distribution of private goods was the simple absence of many common issue cleavages.

This might not be the case for much longer, however. As Japan's economy becomes ever more integrated with those of its Asian neighbors and more distant trade partners, new immigrants—mostly from South and Southeast Asia, but also including South Americans of Japanese descent—are arriving in greater numbers, many or even most illegally. These immigrants bring with them new demands on government services, as well as their own sets of cultural values and social practices, which are seen by Japanese as certainly foreign and potentially incompatible with Japanese culture. Japan is in dire need of younger workers ready to take up the jobs that its own citizens are no longer willing to perform. Indeed, since Japanese society is aging even more quickly than most of its counterparts, and given that its native population is projected to shrink by nearly a sixth in the next few decades,[48] its need for immigration to keep the economy growing and pay the pension and health care costs of so many retired citizens is that much more acute. But Japan is not accustomed to accepting immigrants, so the blending of Japanese society and culture with those of its new arrivals will likely create new and challenging problems both for its people and its government. Already, local governments and the national government have run into obstacles over health care benefits, access to housing and education, and even the relatively simple matter of producing administrative documents in languages other than Japanese, to say nothing of naturalization and citizenship rights such as voting. Clearly, the list of policy challenges at the start of this chapter will expand to include these sorts of issues in the very near future.

Nevertheless, and despite the persistence of the foreign policy disagreements described earlier in this chapter, the primary political cleavage in Japan, as embodied in the party system, remains the debate over economic growth versus economic redistribution. The opposition parties have been, to varying degrees, in favor of more thorough and equitable redistribution

of the wealth Japan produced during the postwar era. For most of the era of high economic growth, however, even the poorest segments of Japanese society saw their standards of living improve rapidly. This reduced the salience of redistributive issues to the general public with the consequence of reducing popular opposition to the pro-growth policies of the LDP. Japan's low levels of economic growth in the decade-plus since 1990 may lead eventually to an increased desire for redistributive policies and perhaps even a more thoroughgoing welfare state.

Studies of Japanese culture also stress the Japanese emphasis on conformity—the belief that individual goals should be sublimated to the objectives of the group.[49] Conformity to the good of the whole is sacrosanct; undermining the group by attention to one's own goals is not tolerated. This trait has been given much credit for Japan's postwar economic recovery and the vitality of Japanese firms, particularly manufacturers[50] (but see Box 11.3).

Certainly, cultural homogeneity and a respect for hierarchy have not stifled dissent or dissatisfaction with government in modern Japan. Just as might be

---

**BOX 11.3**

## The Myth of the Reluctant Litigant

The popular impression that Japanese are loathe to resort to the courtroom to settle their differences is widely acknowledged. Japanese and non-Japanese authors have found the basis for this reluctance in a cultural predisposition toward "informal, mediated settlements of private disputes." Support for this proposition is grounded, supposedly, in Japanese attitudes that favor compromise and disdain public confrontations. Observations of postwar litigiousness seem to support this contention. The number of civil cases initiated in Japanese courts is far lower than in the United States and remains on par or lower than for most other industrialized democracies.

John Owen Haley has demolished this claim, making his argument in two ways. First, he examines *prewar* rates of civil case initiation and shows that such figures are dramatically larger than in the *postwar* era, exceeding even American figures for the same period. How, he asks, could a cultural predisposition toward

compromise explain this dramatic change in the behavior of ordinary Japanese? How is it that litigation has declined as Japan has westernized?

Second, Haley argues, a variety of roadblocks were constructed by the *postwar* government to make civil contestation time-consuming, expensive, predictable, and, consequently, less profitable. In 1974 the number of cases assigned to a typical Japanese judge exceeded fivefold the number given to an American federal judge, so civil cases move at a seemingly glacial pace. Simple trials last an average of two years. Appeals can drag a trial out for five or even ten years. Even cases that would almost certainly result in victory easily produce expenses that exceed any conceivable court-awarded compensation. The result is that prospective plaintiffs turn to various forms of civil mediation or simply do not pursue any civil litigation. Hence, it is not "un-Japanese" to sue; it is merely unprofitable.

Source: John Owen Haley, "The Myth of the Reluctant Litigant," *Journal of Japanese Studies*, 4, no. 2 (Summer 1978), 359–390.

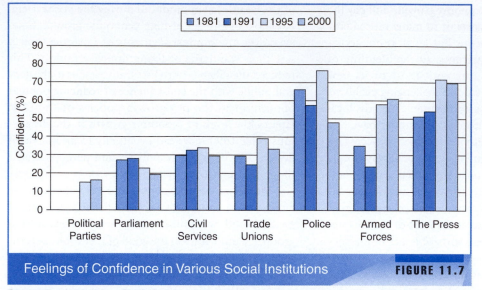

**Feelings of Confidence in Various Social Institutions**

Legend: 1981 | 1991 | 1995 | 2000

**FIGURE 11.7**

Source: European Values Study Group and World Values Survey Association. European and World Values Surveys Four-Wave Integrated Data File, 1981–2004, v.20060423, 2006. Aggregate File Producers: Análisis Sociológicos Económicos y Políticos (ASEP) and JD Systems (JDS), Madrid, Spain/Tilburg University, Tilburg, The Netherlands. Data Files Suppliers: Análisis Sociológicos Económicos y Políticos (ASEP) and JD Systems (JDS), Madrid, Spain/Tillburg University, Tillburg, The Netherlands/Zentralarchiv fur Empirische Sozialforschung (ZA), Cologne, Germany. Aggregate File Distributors: Análisis Sociológicos Económicos y Políticos (ASEP) and JD Systems (JDS), Madrid, Spain/Tillburg University, Tillburg, The Netherlands/Zentralarchiv fur Empirische Sozialforschung (ZA), Cologne, Germany.

is in the U.S. Congress as well, and in neither country is the norm inviolable. Indeed, violations of seniority seem most common for the post of prime minister, as several recent prime ministers have not even been faction leaders.

In the 1980s, the popular press invented a new term for the study of the uniqueness of Japanese culture: "*nihonjinron*," or "the theory of Japaneseness." It is in fact less of a theory than a pastiche of self-images, but we can say for certain that the Japanese have emerged from centuries of contact with other civilizations— first the Chinese and

expected in any country, public opinion surveys reveal widespread dissatisfaction, and not only due to the poor economic environment of the late 1990s. Figure 11.7 shows that citizens' trust of various institutions has fluctuated over time, but has been consistently low for politicians and even civil servants.

Clearly Japanese culture affects the behavior of Japanese political actors just as any culture constrains those operating within its sphere. But by itself, reference to culture cannot explain many things that are interesting about Japanese politics. For example, factions within parties might be simply a political manifestation of the Japanese propensity to form hierarchical groups in all areas of social interaction. But such a cultural generalization cannot explain why the number of LDP factions declined from twelve to five over the 1955–1980 period, why patterns of factional organization and behavior are different in the Upper and Lower Houses of the Diet (which are equally "Japanese"),[51] why JSP factions were divided among ideological lines while LDP factions were not, or why factional organization and behavior have changed since the 1994 electoral reform. Similarly, seniority rule is a common norm in awarding Diet posts, but it

then the West—with some agreement about what it means to be culturally Japanese. The Japanese like to think of themselves as a people who value the group over the needs and wants of individuals. They value hard work, particularly when directed to the common cause, and are leery of people who seek to display extraordinary talent or native ability ("the nail that stands up is the one that is hammered down"). They view themselves as being hierarchically organized and status-conscious. They believe they are unlike westerners in that they seek to avoid conflict whenever possible and in their preference for settling disputes through intermediaries rather than directly or adversarially through courts of law. In contrast to the Chinese supposed love of excitement (*renao*) embodied by the color red, Japanese aesthetics are spare and understated, matched by the value they place on quiet dignity, self-control, patience, and the ability to anticipate the needs of others.

A quick review of Japan's colorful history, including literally hundreds of years of civil wars (1335–1600) and unending political upheavals, of vainglorious samurai warriors with shifting loyalties of convenience—even in the midst of a battle (Conlan 2004), and of the often violent chafing of lower castes at the impositions of feudal hierarchy (Souyri 2003), should be sufficient to dispel the most romantic versions of Japanese traditions and values. Nonetheless, a large part of political culture is the anthology of myths that societies build about themselves, and while these might not always be historically accurate, they still inform political socialization and political behavior in modern times.

So, Japanese culture channels and constrains the behavior of politicians and voters, and a lot of the political behavior we can observe is "typically Japanese." But culture does not *determine* behavior, and it is not sufficient to explain all that we want to know. One must go beyond culture to explain the details of politics and policy. Japan is a democracy comparable to those in the United States and Europe, where political competition is fueled by high levels of political participation, free speech, and a watchdog media. There are many subtle ways in which Japan is uniquely Japanese, to be sure, but we suggest that these affect the choreography more than the substance of politics.

## POLITICAL SOCIALIZATION

### The Family

Political socialization begins, of course, at home, where values are transmitted from one generation to the next. Japan has largely transitioned from an agrarian society, in which multigenerational families live together for the sake of preserving the homestead, to an urban society with nuclear families. Over half of Japanese working-age women work outside the home, at least part time, although the percentage is somewhat lower than other economies at comparable levels of development. In the typical family, a woman will work until her children are born, and then quit work until the youngest child is in kindergarten, returning then to the labor market in part-time jobs. Given the expectation that females will interrupt their careers for child-rearing, it is not surprising that families socialize their daughters to prepare as much for the marriage market as for careers in the labor market.

### Education

Japanese elementary and high school students consistently score toward the top of international league tables in math and science, far outpacing their American counterparts (third out of forty-one countries in eighth grade math, for example, compared with America's seventeenth out of forty-one). Sixty percent of Japanese students also go to "cram schools" (*juku*) after school for supplemental lessons to get a leg up in the competition for getting into better schools.[52] What accounts for that level of exam anxiety is that top Japanese corporations hire workers disproportionately from the top colleges, and because many of those jobs in Japan are for life, which school one attends is of supreme importance.

The Japanese education system gets high marks for teaching basic skills, but the university system is in sorry shape. Entrance exams are extremely difficult, and students study obsessively in order to gain acceptance at the most prestigious schools. Once they have matriculated, however, it is the exception rather than the rule that a student learns much while a university student. During Japan's period of rapid growth, big businesses and even the vaunted central government ministries preferred things this way. The entrance exams would sort out the brightest and hardest working students, who would then be unspoiled by the liberal ideas of postsecondary education, and could, after a four-year respite, move on to their new (and for the elite, permanent) employers, who would start by providing the necessary job-specific training that they would not have received in college anyway.

Lately, after the economic crunch of the 1990s meant fewer job openings than college graduates for the first time in generations, the government, firms, and universities have begun to rethink the wisdom of this educational model. Increasingly, competition among universities has begun to focus more on the educational value added for students, and less on the prestige value of a high entrance-exam score alone. In particular, the government has engaged in considerable soul searching as to whether the educational system produces students with enough creativity to succeed in the world's new software economy. Based on the international success of Japanese video game software, it is obvious that the educational system is not stamping out native creativity, but it is not necessarily the top schools that are producing these software engineers. Another problem is that high levels of teen unemployment have discouraged many students from staying in school.[53] "School refusal syndrome" is a widespread problem among junior high and high school students.

From the standpoint of Japan's neighbors, a more pressing issue concerns the earlier stages of education, specifically the way that Japan's role in the 1937–1945 war against China is presented in the government-sanctioned textbooks. Saburo Ienaga (1913–2002) was a pacifist historian who spent much of his adult life suing the Japanese Ministry of Education for censoring his description of Japanese chemical and medical experiments on Chinese prisoners of war. One of the cases finally made its way to the Supreme Court in 1997, which ruled that, while the textbook authorization system itself was constitutional, the Ministry had censored too aggressively, and ordered the Japanese government to compensate Ienaga all of 400,000 yen (about $3,700). China's government continuously protests that the Japanese government remains insufficiently penitent for the depredations of the Japanese army against China, and Japanese textbooks remain a battlefield in this debate. At least as it affects Japanese attitudes toward foreign policy, this clearly is one area in which the effects of (arguably incomplete) education affect political socialization in important ways.

Figures 11.8A and 11.8B offer two snapshots of age differences in political attitudes. The youngest voters (the voting age is 20) are the least interested in politics, and interest peaks in middle age. But perhaps the most important lesson from Figure 11.8A is that nearly all Japanese express at least some interest in politics. Figure 11.8B is a little more striking. Clearly, 20-somethings have the most cavalier (or perhaps complacent) attitude toward the simplest form of participation in politics, with fewer than one in five answering that voting is a duty of citizenship. Citizens in their sixties and seventies, those born before or during the war, feel the most duty-bound to vote.

One thing that these snapshots cannot tell us is whether today's 60-year-olds felt the same way forty years ago as today's 20-year-olds do now. But there is good reason to believe that the relative complacency of today's youth is a reflection more of the times than of their youthfulness. The disruptions in the economy discussed earlier in this chapter and the uncertainty that recent college graduates (not to mention their nongraduate contemporaries) feel about whether they missed

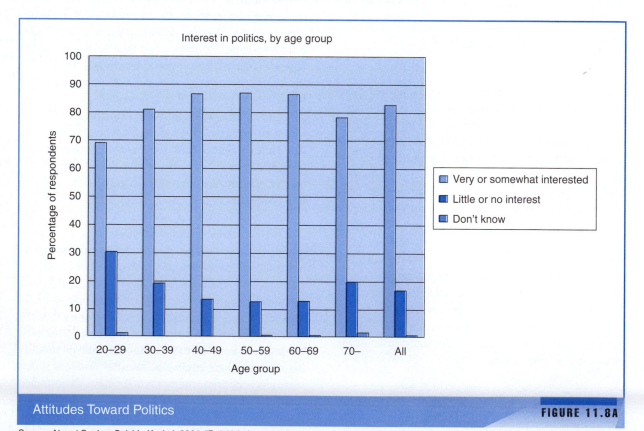

**Attitudes Toward Politics**

**FIGURE 11.8A**

Source: Akarui Senkyo Suishin Kyokai, 2001. "Dai 19 kai sangi-in tsujo senkyo no jittai," http://www.akaruisenkyo.or.jp/search/19/19qa.html

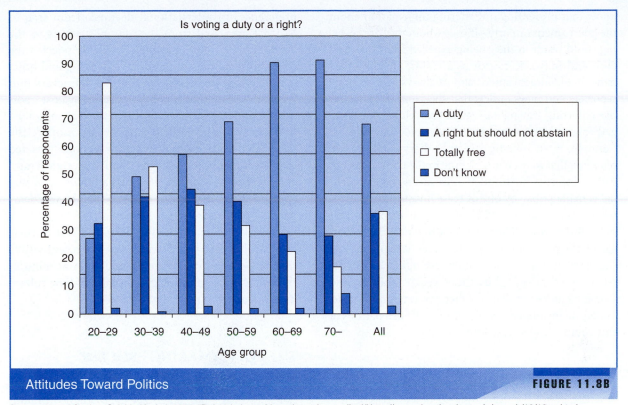

**Is voting a duty or a right?**

Legend:
- A duty
- A right but should not abstain
- Totally free
- Don't know

Y-axis: Percentage of respondents (0–100)
X-axis: Age group (20–29, 30–39, 40–49, 50–59, 60–69, 70–, All)

**Attitudes Toward Politics**     **FIGURE 11.8B**

Source: Akarui Senkyo Suishin Kyokai, 2001. "Dai 19 kai sangi-in tsujo senkyo no jittai," http://www.akaruisenkyo.or.jp/search/19/19qa.html

out on the economic miracle have created high levels of angst and even resentment about the broken promises of their elders that likely spill over into political attitudes. If the economy really is out of the woods, and the job market continues to improve, it will be interesting to see if Figure 11.8B looks different in a decade's time, when the next group of new voters arrives, having been socialized *after* the notorious lost decade of the 1990s.

## Mass Media

The Japanese media play a highly visible role in public life, comparable to that in the United States. Newspaper readership is the highest in the world, and the newspapers have national reach compared with the largely regional U.S. newspaper business. The top three Japanese newspapers, *Yomiuri*, *Asahi*, and *Mainichi*, have a combined circulation of over 50 million readers, compared with less than 10 million for the *Wall Street Journal*, the *New York Times*, and the *Washington Post*. That is not to say that the Japanese are more likely to read *any* newspaper than Americans (and it takes no

account of the Internet), but it does indicate that it is more likely they are reading the *same* paper regardless of where they live. The three main papers cover a range of political space, with the *Asahi* taking a center-left position against the *Yomiuri*'s centrism and *Mainichi*'s more conservative stance.

Television media are also widespread in Japan. Rare is the Japanese home without multiple televisions, and many homes have cable or satellite access to the same bewilderingly large number of channels as in the United States. Political commentary in Japan is a popular sport, particularly on weekends, when representatives of various parties face off each other on issues of the day, or face interviewers seeking a new angle.

Some observers have questioned the independence of the established press in Japan, because the "press club" system seems to entail a swap of information for docility. Government agencies and political parties each house a press club on their premises, in which reporters from various news media have desks, attend news briefings, and write their reports each day. Media reporters know that presenting unflattering information about the government or party officials whom they are covering could result in their being expelled from the press club and may self-censor as a result. On the other hand, media organizations almost always have separate reporters and news outlets that specialize in investigative reporting, leaving the regular press club reporters to gather routine information in peace. *Shukan Asahi*, for example, is an investigative subsidiary of the *Asahi Shimbun* that may be unwelcome in the press clubs but gathers information through other means. Once a scandal is made public by one of these investigative outlets, reporters at the press clubs are free to abandon their polite forbearance. The sensational and relentless coverage by the press of every political scandal since at least the Recruit case of the 1980s (see again Box 11.2) has been spearheaded by these weekly tabloids, and would be quite familiar to American veterans of post-Watergate investigative journalism, or British patrons of that country's aggressive fourth estate.

### Transforming Political Culture

Japanese political culture today is in a process of dramatic transformation from relational to policy voting. Once of paramount value was candidates' personal qualities and their ability to provide constituents with personal favors. Michio Watanabe, a former faction leader in the Liberal Democratic Party, is famous for admitting that he kept a white tie in one pocket for funerals, a black tie in the other for weddings, and lots of money in both pockets to make his visits memorable. It is possible to draw parallels between the use of money in electoral campaigns and the highly developed sense of reciprocity that the Japanese exercise in everyday life. Under the new electoral rules in which district-based politicians must build coalitions large enough to win a plurality, however, money is of less marginal benefit. More important now is the ability to present convincing arguments about policy issues, because these can reach a wider swath of the voting population more effectively.

Another example of how political culture can change quickly is the phenomenon of **Junichiro Koizumi,** Japan's prime minister from 2001 through most of 2006 (see Box 11.4). Koizumi has been the most persistently popular prime minister in the postwar period, not despite, but *because* of his public image as an iconoclast. He boldly asserted Japanese

preferences in international dealings, from Iraq to North Korea, and from the United Nations to the World Trade Organization. He explicitly rejected the conformist politics of factional balancing and quiet deal-making, frequently baiting his detractors into very public battles over policy. He railed against traditional political practices and more often than not, he not only won these fights, but, perhaps more to the point, his popularity grew each time he poked a sacred cow. Koizumi embodied the "nail that stands up," and contrary to the theory of Japaneseness, he was applauded considerably more often than he was denigrated for his audacity.

Social expectations are sticky and transformations of this kind occur slowly, but the recent visible shifts in both electoral strategies and in prime ministerial politics in Japan provide examples of how culture itself can adapt to new circumstances.

## THE POLICYMAKING PROCESS

As discussed in the earlier section on political institutions, Japan is a parliamentary democracy, with both houses of the National Diet directly elected, and with the prime minister and the cabinet chosen by, and accountable to, the Lower House (see again Figure 11.1). In practice, the Diet, like all parliaments, tends to leave the proposal of legislation to the Cabinet, reserving the right to pass, reject, or amend those proposals as it sees fit. The Cabinet, in turn, delegates the task of drafting legislation—everything from regulation to the budget—to policy experts in the bureaucracy. The Cabinet ministers oversee this process in the broadest sense, but most of the expertise resides, and most of the action takes place, in the various bureaus and departments of the government ministries and agencies.

### The Basics: How a Bill Becomes a Law

Members of either house of the Diet may submit legislation, and they do so quite often. But these "member bills" are almost always exercises in grandstanding for the sponsors' constituencies, where the proposal itself is the point, and they rarely have any hope of passing into law. Therefore, the typical path for new legislation proceeds as follows. A ministry drafts legislation for some policy change in its jurisdiction and

**BOX 11.4**

## Junichiro Koizumi—Prime Minister as Celebrity?

Junichiro Koizumi, prime minister of Japan from April 2001 to September 2006, was a forceful and charismatic leader who broke with the long-standing pattern of relatively colorless prime ministers whose main job was to broker relations among the LDP's powerful factions.* Koizumi ignored factions in his cabinet line-up and sought systematically to undermine the electoral support networks of LDP politicians who opposed his reformist agenda. He sought and won Diet agreement to send Japanese troops to help the rebuilding of Iraq and became the first Japanese leader to travel to North Korea. He attacked two sacred cows of traditional LDP governance, calling for sharp restrictions on the quasi-corrupt practice of *amakudari* (discussed in text) and cutting back on pork-barrel public works spending, despite his colleagues' instinct to buy back support lost in the midst of the long recession that began in 1990. Indeed "reform, with no sacred cows" was one of his slogans, along with the even more provocative "reform Japan by destroying the LDP." How did he get away with staying on top by attacking his own party?

Koizumi is quirky by Japanese standards. Apart from his blow-dried looks and his much-advertised fondness for all things Elvis, he is a divorceé in a country that still stigmatizes marital breakups, and sometimes seems more a celebrity than a political leader. His insistence on (some say "obsession with") breaking up the Postal Savings System has been a long-standing passion, rare among LDP politicians, who have a collective reputation of being opportunistic about policies rather than committed against all odds. Even before he rose to the party leadership, Koizumi had bucked the status quo by forming a cross-factional group of younger party members dedicated to reform. This did not endear him to party elders, and it is fair to say that his ascendancy occurred despite their objections, and due to his own personal popularity among voters. Consistently, Koizumi would rail against the conservatives who were stifling his reforms. When the old guard joined the opposition parties to defeat his postal savings reform package in July 2005, Koizumi raised the stakes by dissolving the Diet and calling for general parliamentary elections, thus putting many political lives including his own at risk. He expelled the thirty-seven LDPers who had voted against his reform bills, and assigned the party nominations in their districts to hand-picked candidates, known as "Koizumi's assassins." It was a stunning sign of Koizumi's goodwill with voters that many of the assassins won, even against senior politicians who were battling for political survival using all of the personal electoral machinery (*koenkai*) at their disposal. Koizumi had managed to convince most voters that this election was only about reform, and he led the LDP (minus those who were expelled) to a huge electoral mandate.

This is not to suggest that political figures as colorful and decisive as Koizumi are likely to become the norm in Japan. Koizumi's first two successors, Abe and Fukuda, each projected a more traditional image of staid dignity and caution. The current Prime Minister Taro Aso, swept to office on a wave of popular sentiment, due in part to his outspokenness and a playboy image, but that popularity has evaporated as he has proved an indecisive leader.

*Koizumi had to step down in September 2006, despite his continued popularity, because the constitution of the Liberal Democratic Party stipulates a maximum of two terms as party president.

submits the bill to the Cabinet. The Cabinet may send the bill back, reject it, or amend it in any way it wishes, but if and when it is satisfied, it submits the bill to the Diet. The Diet may then do whatever it wants with the bill. Normal legislation must be passed in identical form by both houses, unless the Lower House can muster a two-thirds majority to override Upper House objections (this has happened only once). Again, if the bill is the annual budget, or a treaty to be ratified, then only the Lower House need pass it; the Upper House may delay that passage for up to thirty days, but it may not stop it.

Any bill passed by the Diet becomes the law of the land. There is no separately elected president who may veto Diet actions, and Diet laws supersede any local laws that might conflict. The Supreme Court may declare a law unconstitutional, but as we explained earlier, this is exceedingly rare.

The Diet Building, which houses Japan's two parliamentary chambers in the heart of Tokyo, pictured here in 1936 just after its completion.

AP Images

The final steps in the process involve implementation. The Diet can pass legislation, but it delegates to the bureaucracy the job of implementing and enforcing the new rules. Indeed, laws are often so vague that the bureaucrats must do considerably more than robotically carry out the Diet's orders. This is true in most countries—legislators are not experts in every policy area, and they cannot foresee every circumstance under which the new law might apply. So bureaucrats are also given resources and discretion with which to make the day-to-day decisions and rulings necessary to administer the laws passed by the Diet.

The circle is completed at the next election. Voters might have some idea of what goes on in the Diet, in the Cabinet, and in the halls of the government agencies, but their best view of policy is at the implementation stage. Do they approve of the policies they see being administered? Do they believe themselves to be better off or worse off? Voters make these judgments, and then reward or punish incumbent legislators and parties by voting either to retain or replace them at the next election.

Naturally, the actual policy process is more complex, given the rules that govern the Diet and bureaucracy. Even the internal decisionmaking process

of the ruling party or coalition has an impact on policy outcomes. The following sections will demonstrate in greater detail some of this complexity.

## The Bureaucracy

The Japanese bureaucracy is probably more ballyhooed than any other bureaucracy in the world; at least it was until the "lost decade" of the 1990s. Its prestige and difficult entrance examinations allow it to recruit the best and brightest of Japan's college graduates. Once they enter their respective ministries, bureaucrats put in long days for very little compensation. These "elite" bureaucrats are often credited with having played a crucial role in the remarkable success of the postwar Japanese economy, coordinating action among players in a given industry, choosing new industries to promote, and regulating the economy much more extensively and competently than in most countries.

However, the heavy involvement of bureaucrats in policymaking should not be taken as an indication that they have usurped power from the politicians in the Diet and the Cabinet. Indeed, the common characterization of Japanese bureaucrats as exceptionally important is largely a function of comparison with the United States, where a system of separated powers obliges members of Congress to become much more deeply involved in the details of policymaking. In Japan, as in any parliamentary democracy in which a single party controls government for a long time, politicians need not worry that writing vague laws that delegate a great deal of discretion to bureaucrats will allow bureaucrats to run amok. Remember, in a parliamentary government, the executive branch (the cabinet, which oversees the day-to-day workings of the administrative bureaucracy) is accountable to the legislature. Legislators can always write more specific laws later if they discover any problems in the way that bureaucrats are choosing, interpreting, or implementing policy. If need be, they may even "fire" the cabinet at any time. In a presidential system, by contrast, the legislature must be more careful in delegating, because it cannot be sure that the president will acquiesce in later efforts to overturn decisions made by executive bureaucracies headed by the president's own appointees, and it cannot threaten the president's job for failing to yield to congressional demands.

Nonetheless, it is true that Japanese bureaucrats are exceptionally talented, so the question of why the best and brightest would choose to work so hard under such stressful conditions (often putting in eighty-hour workweeks) and for such little compensation is an interesting one. The private sector would compensate them more handsomely. Devotion to public service and the prestige of government jobs undoubtedly play a role, but another key factor is early retirement and the prospect of a lucrative second career. A new bureaucrat enters his ministry with a cohort of those who passed the entrance examination at the same time. For several years, the entire cohort advances in lock-step, each individual rotating through a series of one- or two-year appointments in various bureaus within the ministry. After several years, however, the cohort hits the level at which there are fewer jobs than candidates, and some do not get promoted. At each successive round of promotions, the cohort is whittled down. At the apex, only one person will make it to the post of administrative vice minister, the top civil service job in the ministry (or, the cohort might be passed over altogether for the top post, to make way for more talented prospects in younger classes). Those who are not promoted at each round are obliged to resign from the ministry. Thus, every year, a group of smart, experienced 40- to 55-year-old former bureaucrats are looking for work in the private sector.

Some former bureaucrats try their hand at politics, but most, in a practice known as **amakudari** (literally, "descent from heaven"), move into cushy positions in the firms they used to regulate. And, generally speaking, the salary and authority of their new positions vary directly with how far they advanced in the ministry before retiring. After all, seniority in the meritocratic ministry is a signal of talent and of variety of experience and contacts, and the firms that hire these individuals do so precisely to take advantage of these qualifications.[54]

So part of the answer to the puzzle of the noble bureaucrats would appear to be that they work hard today for a better reward tomorrow. In terms of their full careers, compensation is not inadequate, it is merely loaded at the back end. The better they perform in their early years, the better they are compensated in their second careers.

In addition to the constitutional point that bureaucrats are subject to political control, those who see Japanese bureaucrats as autonomous economic miracle workers face another difficulty as well, namely the economic depression of the 1990s. Nothing changed in or around 1990 in terms of patterns of recruitment, bureaucratic organization, career patterns, or compensation. Bureaucrats were still the "best and brightest." So did they suddenly forget how to run an economy and start making bad decisions instead of good ones? Also notable is the fact that the image of Japanese bureaucrats as incorruptible has taken a beating of late. The last few corruption scandals in Japan (going back to the "Recruit" scandal in the late 1980s—see again Box 11.2) have implicated bureaucrats along with the normal panoply of politicians.

While we do see heavy-handed government regulation as a contributing factor to the creation and bursting of the economic bubble, we place the blame for those policies on the bureaucrats' political overseers, namely the LDP, not on the bureaucrats themselves. Bureaucrats were simply carrying out the economic mandate of politicians, whose short-term electoral interests demanded policies (such as trade protectionism, heavy subsidies for numerous inefficient industries and bailouts for individual firms, mountains of "pork-barrel" spending on unnecessary construction projects, and a bloated and insufficiently regulated financial system) that allowed stock- and land-price bubbles to form and then burst, stagnated growth, and entrenched special interests with good reason to oppose reforms.

Whatever the true responsibility of bureaucrats for Japan's postwar economic miracle or its postmiracle economic malaise, "bureaucrat-bashing" became fashionable in the press and in political circles in the 1990s. In January 2001, the government undertook a major reorganization of the central bureaucracy, consolidating over twenty separate departments into only ten ministries and two agencies. Since this reshuffling changed very little in terms of responsibilities or powers, it appears to have been more window-dressing than substance, merely relabeling and combining agencies and ministries instead of reforming them in any systematic way. Of potentially greater significance was an effort headed by Prime Minister Junichiro Koizumi to rein in *amakudari*. He announced in July 2002 his intention to end the practice of mandatory early retirement. His main purpose was to allow political leaders more discretion to retain talented and loyal senior bureaucrats, and not have to cycle through them just because the time comes to promote the next cohort. Not surprisingly, Koizumi's plan elicited howls of protest from bureaucrats, particularly younger officials who joined the bureaucracy with regular promotions and eventual *amakudari* in mind.[55]

## The Diet: Rubber Stamp or Sovereign?

Comparative studies of the world's legislatures typically characterize the Japanese Diet as a weak, ineffectual institution. Observers point out that the Diet rarely rejects Cabinet-submitted bills, or even amends them, and that debate is brief and apparently *pro forma*. Moreover, Japanese laws are much shorter and much more vague than those in the United States. Bureaucrats are delegated a great deal more discretion than in the United States, and while they seem to have the skills to use that discretion to produce good policies for the country, the idea of bureaucratic government strikes many as somehow undemocratic. On the other hand, Article 41 of the Constitution declares that the Diet is all-powerful—the Cabinet is its appointee and the bureaucracy merely a staff of experts. How can we explain this paradox?

The key to the answer is the LDP's long reign as a majority party. The continued control of the Diet and the Cabinet by the same political party, and the expectation, right up to the end, that this control would continue into the future, allowed the *formal* legislative process to become routinized and tranquil. This explains both the relative inactivity of the Diet and the extensive reliance on the bureaucracy.

First, the LDP internalized the policymaking process with its own committee system (the so-called Policy Affairs Research Committees) that paralleled, then subdivided, the jurisdictions of Diet committees. Thus, policy battles were fought out "in house," without the nuisance of opposition party tactics or public scrutiny. Once the party had come to a decision, it simply had its leaders (who controlled the Cabinet) submit those bills to the Diet, where the party could use its majority to approve its own proposals. And in that sense, it is typical of parliamentary systems with single-party majority control. When a single party can work its will, there is no need to air internal discussions or squabbles publicly. The public portion of majoritarian politics *should* be boring and uneventful. A parliament that does not actively initiate or amend draft legislation, and rarely rejects government proposals, is not necessarily weak or ineffectual. Any majority party in any country could do (and probably does) what the LDP has done, getting all its ducks in a row before submitting actual legislation for parliamentary "scrutiny." What was unusual about Japan until 1993 was that the same party was in control for so long that this "in-house" decisionmaking became institutionalized through formal LDP-only committees.

It is important to note that bureaucrats do not present bills to the Cabinet without having first run them past the LDP's policy committees. Instead, bureaucrats consult regularly, and work together with the relevant committees and subcommittees within the party to refine draft legislation and remove politically objectionable provisions. This way, the Cabinet knows that any bill presented to it by a ministry has already been scrutinized at lower levels in the party. For similar reasons, party committees replaced the Diet committees in their oversight roles. During the period of LDP hegemony, then, the formal activities of the Diet itself were pro forma because the LDP's majority allowed it to make them so—it could use its control of the Diet to simply make official what it had already decided internally. In both Diet committees and on the floor of the House, when these bills were "debated," LDP members typically would sit quietly (or even sleep!) while the opposition party representatives aired their disapproval, and then, once the (LDP) chairperson banged the gavel and called for a vote, the LDP majority would simply outvote the combined opposition and approve the bill they had already agreed to before it was ever submitted. Anything that the ruling party could not agree about internally never made it as far as formal submission to the Diet.

Thus, for most of the postwar era, the most interesting steps of the policy process were hidden within the policy apparatus of the LDP to protect the party from unpleasant public scrutiny. No wonder the legislation that made it as far as official submission to the Diet almost always passed quickly and quietly. Of course, if the LDP were to lose power, or have to share it with another political party or parties, the policy process would become considerably less routinized and tranquil, and activity in the Diet would increase. As soon as an in-house LDP decision became insufficient to guarantee Diet passage, the formal processes of the Diet might begin to matter more. The Diet as a legislative body would not become any more powerful, but the fact that its power would have to be shared by more than one party would cause it to become more active and interesting.

In fact, in 1989, the LDP did lose control of the Upper House, and its need to build coalitions with other parties in that chamber led to very public horse-trading—most famously over the post-Gulf War decision to allow Japanese troops to participate in United Nations-sponsored peacekeeping operations. Then, in 1993, the LDP finally lost its Lower House majority as well. After a year in opposition, the LDP returned to govern, but always in coalition with other parties. So how has this affected the policy process? To forestall the unpredictability of wide-open Diet debates, the LDP endeavors to strike deals with its coalition partners before submitting draft legislation (again, this is typical among coalition governments in Western Europe). If the LDP splits again, or shrinks through electoral losses to the point that it does not tower over its coalition partners, we might begin to see more regularized and structured cross-party policy discussions. Similarly, if looser, more frequently shifting cabinet coalitions were to become the norm (as in, say, pre-reform Italy), then it might become more and more difficult to keep all policy debates and decisionmaking in-house and the formal committee structures of the Diet would have to decide issues, instead of merely

ratifying decisions made elsewhere. Diet proceedings would become, in that sense, more "interesting," but not because of any sort of enhancement of the quality of democracy.

## POLICY PERFORMANCE

The LDP's long period of dominance was built on a series of policy successes that produced social and economic stability that kept the voting public content. Economic growth raised real incomes at a rapid pace, increasing the affluence of all levels of Japanese society. Beyond private financial gain, democracy had instilled a variety of civil rights—including freedom of speech and of the press—that have constrained the government's ability to interfere in the practice of individual liberties. The Japanese government has provided for high levels of law and order, boasting some of the lowest rates of crime in the industrialized world. Though sometimes criticized for emphasizing conformity over creativity, education policy has produced one of the best trained labor forces in the world. This section surveys several policy areas, some important to maintaining LDP hegemony and some neglected because they were located outside the winning political coalition.

### Industrial Policy and the Economic Miracle

Perhaps the most well-known aspect of postwar Japanese history has been the country's remarkable economic development. At the time of surrender in 1945, Japan's economy had been devastated by the war. Its cities lay in ruins from Allied bombing, its industrial capacity all but destroyed, many of its people starving. Looking at the Japanese economy in the 1990s, it is difficult to believe that the country was ever in such dire straits. The economy grew at an average rate of 10 percent between 1950 and 1973, and from 1973 to 1988, despite the oil shocks, it still grew at 5 percent per year, faster than any other advanced industrial democracy.[56] Along the way, Japan officially joined the ranks of advanced industrial economies, with its admission to the General Agreement on Tariffs and Trade (GATT), the International Monetary Fund, the World Bank, and later the World Trade Organization, and as the leading donor to the Asian Development Bank. By 2001, per capita income had risen to $36,300, slightly higher than that of the United States.[57]

In the late 1980s, Japan displaced the United States as the world's leading donor of aid to developing nations (although it has fallen back to number two as a result of its own recent economic troubles). Its firms have established dominant positions in such industries as automobiles, consumer electronics, semiconductors, and high-technology ceramics. To citizens and shopkeepers in countries worldwide, the term "rich Japanese tourist" seemed redundant. As the first industrial democracy in East Asia, Japan has been looked to as a model for other industrializing countries in the region.

Arguments over who should receive credit for Japan's economic growth have raged for years, with three major theories contending. The role of government intervention in the economy is at the center of each of these explanations. The first theory stresses the role that market fundamentals have played in directing Japanese economic growth. Japan's high postwar growth is simply a result of returning to the growth path established before World War II, but interrupted by the devastation of the war. According to this argument, growth rates were so high in part because the base (beginning in 1945) was so low. Blessed with a well-educated but low-cost labor force, and an open world market, Japanese firms converted to peacetime production with a vengeance. This theory discounts any positive role for interventionist government policy in explaining Japan's economic miracle.[58]

A second theory, widely subscribed to both inside and outside Japan, contends that Japan's government (or more precisely its well-trained bureaucrats) is the source of economic success. In this account, skillful use of government in providing firms with access to capital was crucial to Japan's economic rebirth. Further, the Ministry of International Trade and Industry (MITI—since renamed), the bureaucratic agency in charge of **industrial policy** decisionmaking, used its administrative authority to point firms in fruitful directions. Government is also credited with retreating intelligently and carefully from declining economic sectors, such as coal, that were unlikely to prove beneficial in the future. This view argues that MITI was adept at picking industries that would become profitable, and discarded losing economic sectors to enhance the economy as a whole.[59]

A third view suggests that Japan has maintained a form of "strategic capitalism" requiring cooperation between the firms in an economic sector and the government over the type and depth of government involvement.[60] Government is most involved in economic decisionmaking when firms can agree to limit competition among themselves. Firms acquiesce to this involvement because they benefit.[61] Reduced competition from other established firms and restrictions on new entrants bring higher profits to firms in a given sector. But these cartels can function only so long as all participants consent. When members leave, there are few tools available to other members or government to enforce compliance. During the 1950s and 1960s, MITI was able to restrict access to domestic investment capital and to foreign exchange through the Foreign Exchange Control Law. To the extent that firms required outside investment or foreign exchange to purchase industrial inputs, they were obligated to accede to the wishes of MITI and the other firms in their sector. Firms with their own sources of capital or foreign exchange had to be coaxed back in rather than being coerced. By the 1980s, MITI's grip on these financial resources had loosened, giving firms even greater autonomy.

The latter two theories agree that government intervention in the economy has been a key factor in Japanese economic development, and differ only on the question of who was controlling this government intervention. The third theory rejects the second theory's emphasis on heroic, autonomous bureaucrats, and points instead to the political logic of government-business interaction, and why it varies in intensity, scope, and success, industry by industry.

In light of the heavy-handed regulation in the Japanese domestic market, how can we explain the highly competitive Japanese firms we see around the world? The answer is that competition was not proscribed in all sectors of the economy nor, indeed, was it completely eradicated in cartelized sectors. In automobiles and consumer electronics, the most important Japanese export sectors, competition has always been fierce. Even in highly cartelized sectors, such as financial services, competition remains among firms, although it is based more on service than on price. Also, the "cooperative capitalism" of domestic cartels did not extend into export markets, so Japanese firms that relied on export markets were disciplined by those markets.

To recapitulate, evidence seems to defy the common view that government and business work closely together in Japan because of the dictates of bureaucratically determined industrial policy. To turn this old argument on its head, close government-business relations, stemming from the LDP's probusiness electoral stance, are what made industrial policy possible in the first place (and what made confronting economic decline difficult). The government facilitates bargaining and cooperation among firms but can do so easily only when the firms themselves want that cooperation. It is worth noting that none of the theories predicted Japan's economic downturn in the 1990s. And only the third theory sheds light on why the Japanese government has been unable to deal forcefully with economic stagnation. After all, the political deals that held the postwar system together could not be easily undone without causing the ruling LDP electoral harm. New deals required a new political logic.

## Trade Policy

Exports have been the fuel powering Japan's economic growth, but the relatively closed domestic marketplace with its "cooperative capitalism" has exasperated Japan's trading partners. The basis for economic expansion in Japan was success in export markets; for the first few postwar decades, the United States was Japan's largest foreign customer. This worked well for Japan as the United States subordinated trade matters to security concerns. The United States indulged Japan in its quest for export markets just as Japan bowed to the American desire for preeminence on security issues.

The Japanese strategy has provided a model of export-led growth, subsequently followed by South Korea, Taiwan, Singapore, and Hong Kong.[62] Today numerous other Asian and Latin American countries have begun to follow Japan's lead. Export-led growth represents an economic strategy of protecting one's home markets in order to nurture emerging industries and offering those industries incentives to compete in export markets.[63] Japan's steel producers, for example, had quotas for selling steel abroad. Those who met and exceeded their quotas were rewarded with licenses for expanded production. Such policies came under attack as Japanese manufacturers began to displace their competitors in their own markets.

As Japanese products improved in quality, exports increased. The oil crisis brought about two results that soured U.S.–Japan trade relations. First, it compelled the Japanese to increase their export efforts to pay for rising fuel costs. Second, it made fuel-efficient Japanese automobiles attractive to U.S. and European consumers, now hit by the high costs of operating inefficient gas guzzlers (the second oil shock, in 1979–1980, accelerated these trends). The U.S.–Japan trade imbalance, which had already attracted the attention of U.S. policymakers in 1969 when it passed $1 billion, soared to over $10 billion in 1978.[64]

A pattern has arisen in lockstep with Japan's increased trade surplus with the United States: the United States charges Japan with "unfair" regulatory policy or corporate collusion. Japan generally denies the charges or insists the arrangements have no anticompetitive results. U.S. pressure forces negotiations over the issue. Japan stalls, but agreement eventually is reached, and the effects of removal of the "unfair" practice are minimal or nonexistent. This process has repeated itself over a variety of economic sectors—from machine tools to rice and from product distribution to retail establishments.

It is easy to understand Japan's reluctance to alter its protectionist economic policies, given the LDP's electoral reliance on the protected economic sectors. Japanese firms that flourish outside Japan would rather avoid angering the governments of countries in whose economies they profit. On the other hand, the farmers and small firms that would be most hurt by foreign competition form the backbone of LDP support. Thus, each U.S. demand for policy change forces the LDP to balance the clashing interests of important constituents. Increasingly, over the last decade, Japan has opened many of its markets and faced the wrath of farmers and small retailers for doing so. And now, in the Doha Round of world trade negotiations, Japan finds itself on the same side of the table as the United States and (especially) the European Union, jointly resisting calls by developing countries to jettison remaining farm subsidies and market protections once and for all.

## Security and Foreign Policy

Japan's postwar security and foreign policy have focused on maintaining a close relationship with the United States. Bargaining from a position of weakness, Japan has been on the receiving end of most U.S. foreign policy decisions. With the end of the Cold War, Japanese voters have become more ambivalent about the alliance. Increasing U.S. emphasis on economic issues over security issues has made many Japanese feel more vulnerable despite the end of the Cold War.

Shigeru Yoshida, prime minister from 1946 to 1947 and again from 1948 to 1954, is generally credited with the doctrine that balanced the benefits of the U.S. security relationship with concern for the economy and popular pacifism. The Self-Defense Forces (SDF) were created and the U.S.–Japan Mutual Security Treaty was promulgated during his tenure as prime minister. In 1960, revision and renewal of the treaty engendered a domestic political crisis that shook the LDP and pushed the party to avoid popular suspicion of Japan's defense policy by focusing the public on economic gains. The strategy worked so well (and the economy grew so quickly) that by 1970 when renewal of the treaty again became necessary, it went through without major incident. Most recently, the 2000 treaty renewal caused no uproar, despite the fact that it actually expanded Japan's commitment to assist the United States in East Asian military operations outside Japan.

With national security taken care of by the treaty, the Japanese government was able to focus its foreign policy on economic matters. Sustaining the trade relationship with the United States was always a high priority, as was continued access to the raw materials—especially fuel—that Japan lacks. The United States reciprocated by favoring security over economic issues even as the U.S. trade deficit grew and evidence of restrictive Japanese trade practices mounted.

Japan's low-profile foreign policies have served the economy well. By one estimate, Japan's GNP in 1970 would have been 30 percent lower had the government spent as much on defense as had the United States.[65] Recently, however, Japan has been obliged to pay for a large share of the U.S. defense commitment to all of East Asia. Japan now pays fully 50 percent of all costs of deploying U.S. troops on Japanese soil.[66]

The end of the Cold War has seen Japan extend its military presence by agreeing to allow SDF personnel to participate in UN peacekeeping operations. Though the policy change was not very popular domestically, it was pursued to quiet international critics' complaints that Japan was a free rider on world security provided by others. This criticism reached its peak when Japan was the only U.S. ally to send no troops to assist in the Gulf War, although the Japanese government did contribute $13 billion to pay for the war (more than any country other than Saudi Arabia). Because Japan's efforts generally have come only after much foot dragging, it gets little international credit for its contributions.

The ability and willingness of the United States to project military power to East Asia are declining relative to the growing strength of regional powers and the growing importance of domestic economic concerns on Washington's agenda. It is unclear whether Japan will be asked (and, if asked, whether it will be willing) to fill this vacuum by increasing its own military expenditures. Certainly most of Japan's neighbors would be opposed to such a shift. Indeed, visits by sitting prime ministers to the Yasukuni Shrine, dedicated to Japanese soldiers killed in war (and including the remains of several convicted war criminals), never fail to inflame tensions between Japan and its neighbors, especially China and South Korea.

Early in his administration, Prime Minister Koizumi surprised even many within his own party when he made the first visit by a Japanese prime minister to North Korea. Other than some symbolic gestures regarding Japanese citizens who had been kidnapped by North Korean agents in the 1970s, in exchange for a Japanese acceptance of responsibility for Korean suffering before and during World War II, not much was accomplished by this visit. Nevertheless it may signal the advent of a more assertive, independent Japanese foreign policy in years to come. It is interesting to note that Koizumi's popularity at home, which had been flagging due to popular frustration with his government's failure to revive the economy, jumped considerably after his historic trip to Pyongyang.

Over the past few years, Japan has joined the United States, China, Russia, and South Korea in pressuring North Korea to give up its self-proclaimed nuclear weapons in exchange for economic and humanitarian incentives. But when North Korea launched a series of (unarmed) missiles toward Japan in a widely condemned test in 2006, some in the Japanese government speculated openly about the possibility (and constitutionality) of retaliating with a strike against North Korean missile bases. This reaction, though not official, was interesting in at least two ways. First, it was the boldest call for the projection of Japanese military power since 1945. Second, it was also pure bluster: Japan does not possess the offensive military capability even to carry out such an action. The statement was simultaneously jarring for its aggressive tone and sobering for its sheer impracticality.

## Environmental Pollution Policy

Environmental policy has been counted among the real successes of the LDP, even if only due to duress. Despite much hesitation, the LDP moved decisively toward introducing strict environmental regulations in the early 1970s. This episode is an important example of how the LDP was capable of moving quickly once consensus within the party had been established, and of how the LDP balances the competing interests of its constituents.

High economic growth naturally led to high levels of pollution. As a densely populated country, high concentrations of pollution had by the 1960s led to several cases of pollution-related disease. The most noted of these was the mercury poisoning that occurred in **Minamata,** a small fishing town in Kumamoto Prefecture on the southern island of Kyushu. The Minamata incident produced severe mental and physical disabilities in the newborn children of area residents who had eaten fish containing the contaminant. Although a team of scientists at Kyushu University pointed to pollution as the source of this "mysterious disease," the government squelched evidence for many years for fear of hurting the business climate for manufacturing in Japan. Eventually the information became public and citizens around the country were livid. This and other notorious pollution tragedies led popular opinion toward favoring increased regulation, but the LDP's business constituency found such policies anathema to its interests.

Meanwhile, the opposition parties began to use the issue to attack and defeat the LDP in numerous local elections throughout Japan. Fearful that these local political setbacks would be replicated on the national stage, the LDP moved to forestall this challenge with a special legislative session now known as the "Pollution Diet." Fourteen laws were enacted in the single Diet session, including a provision of jail terms for polluters who exceeded established pollutant limits. This made Japan the first country to criminalize such activities. For a time, Japan, despite its conservative pro-growth and pro-business policies, had the strictest pollution controls in the world.[67]

After thus calming popular discontent, however, the LDP has done little to strengthen pollution controls in subsequent years. With popular pressure defused, the LDP reverted readily to pro-producer policies. Consequently, environmental problems persist, abetted by loose regulation and lax oversight. Dioxin resulting from trash incineration has recently arisen as a serious pollution problem that was never seriously regulated because it would have been too costly for LDP supporters. Until 1999, Japanese dioxin standards allowed 80–800 times more emissions than most advanced industrialized nations and many incinerators exceed these standards. Other pollutants related to electronics manufacturing have come to light, demonstrating how far Japan has fallen beneath international pollution level standards since the early 1970s.[68]

## Welfare Policy: Health Care and Pensions

Health care in Japan is universally covered through a government-administered, single-payer program that requires all individuals to pay a health insurance premium based on income level. Standards of service are below what is commonly found in the U.S. private system, but the coverage ensures widespread access to basic health services. Despite many failings, the benefits of Japan's health care system are clear. Infant mortality, at four per 1,000 live births, is the lowest among industrialized nations, and life expectancy is the highest, now age 85.5 years for women and 78.6 for men. The Japanese accomplish this even though public spending on health care constitutes a smaller percentage of GNP in Japan (5.7 percent) than in the United States (6.6 percent), Britain (5.8 percent), France (8.0 percent), or Germany (8.2 percent).[69]

On pension policies, the Japanese government has been much less active. Public and private pensions are meager. In the early 1970s, as welfare became a prominent issue, the LDP set out on a program of building an advanced welfare state, but the oil crisis of 1973 put a brake on creating new welfare programs, extinguishing this political strategy. Nonetheless, overall welfare spending has grown steadily as Japanese society has aged. Figure 11.9 shows the shares of general account spending

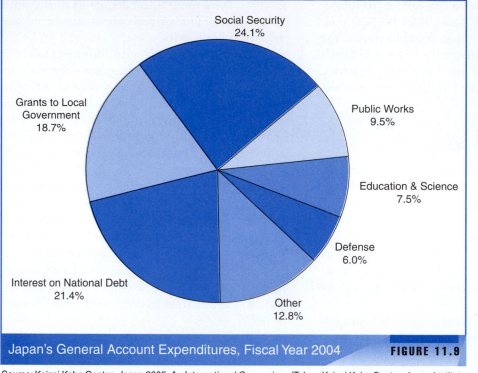

Social Security
24.1%

Public Works
9.5%

Grants to Local
Government
18.7%

Education & Science
7.5%

Defense
6.0%

Interest on National Debt
21.4%

Other
12.8%

**Japan's General Account Expenditures, Fiscal Year 2004**    **FIGURE 11.9**

Source: Keizai Koho Center, *Japan 2005: An International Comparison* (Tokyo: Keizai Koho Center, Japan Institute for Social and Economic Affairs, 2005) 35.

the extent that it reduces the need for campaign funding and increases politicians' incentives to satisfy broad constituencies. This, in turn, means that politicians should begin appealing more to consumer, as opposed to producer, interests. One way to do so is to move away from personalistic appeals based on pork-barrel spending and toward the provision of public goods. These goods might be lower prices, better infrastructure, better land and housing policies, stricter environmental standards, and a stronger welfare state.[70]

devoted to various categories in fiscal year 2004. Slowed economic growth expanded the government budget deficit (by reducing tax revenues) more than it actually impinged on continued welfare programs.

An **aging society** in Japan will exacerbate the costs of present welfare benefits and increase the political desirability of expanding such programs. In 1950, only 4.9 percent of Japanese were over age 65. In 2000, the figure was 17.2 percent, and population projections suggest that the figure will reach 32.3 percent in 2050. The Japanese government recently increased co-payments on medical benefits in order to increase revenue and decrease overuse of the service. Such reductions of existing benefits may become more common as the government strives to keep up with the demographic changes that increase the number of people demanding assistance.

## Policy Implications of Political Reform

The new electoral system alters the political incentives facing politicians. This has policy implications to

Of course, if politicians from all parties are promising voters that they will finally reap the benefits of Japan's wealth, the question remains as to what will become the basis of interparty competition under the new regime. Since the 1993 election, the LDP and its top competitor (first the New Frontier Party and now the Democratic Party) have both been centrist parties. At present, it appears that the issues most likely to define political competition will involve levels and scope of economic regulation. As the LDP struggles to balance the interests of its efficient big business constituents with those of its less efficient small business and farming constituents, even while trying to woo consumers, there will be room for rival parties to exploit these internal tensions and to champion one group or another. So far, the opposition parties do seem to covet the identity of consumer advocates, demanding deregulation and urban welfare, but they have not convinced enough voters to leave the LDP yet.

Deregulation is proceeding most visibly in the financial sector. Spurred on by a series of bank failures, corruption in the financial sector, and a flagging economy, the LDP-led government has announced plans to open the traditionally cartelized banking, securities, and insurance industries. The banking sector has gradually been shedding enormous quantities of non-performing loans, leading to improved profit margins, though it still lags behind its major European and American competitors in profitability. Other sectors undergoing market liberalization include air travel, electric power production, and telecommunications. Until now, postwar Japan's political economy had prevented market competition in any of these sectors. Gradually, however, market competition is becoming more common in the Japanese economy.

## CONCLUDING THOUGHTS ABOUT JAPANESE POLITICS

The less we understand something, the more likely we are to subject it to unrealistic caricature. No wonder, then, that common labels for Japan during the 1970s and 1980s—"the successful state-led economy" and "Japan, Inc."—have given way to radically different classifications in the wake of Japan's financial crisis of the 1990s. This chapter has provided a more nuanced and textured picture of how Japan works. The most important lesson is that the Japanese policy process has been, and continues to be, supremely *political*—even if, on the surface, it seems that an insulated army of smart bureaucrats is calling all the shots.

Another central goal of this chapter has been to place Japan's "unique" political culture in comparative and analytical perspective. Certainly, Japanese politics is not identical to politics anywhere else—in that sense, every country is unique. But that does not imply that Japanese politics cannot be studied in the same fashion as politics elsewhere. We can ask the same questions about Japanese politicians, voters, bureaucrats, parties, committees, courts, and businesses as we ask about those groups in any democracy, although some of the answers will differ. So Japanese politics is not unique in the strong sense that it is "incomparable" to politics elsewhere. Japan's parliamentary system of government, its SNTV electoral rules, and the LDP's long hold on power have combined to create a political environment distinct from those of other democracies, yet understandable in more general and comparative terms.

A major theme of this chapter has been how institutional incentives shape political motivations and influence policy outcomes. The particularistic nature of Japanese elections, the discretionary powers of the bureaucracy, and the reticence of Japanese citizens to use courts to seek redress all stem, at least in part, from Japan's particular political institutions. To take just one specific example, Japan's close government-business relations helped to fuel the country's spectacular postwar economic growth. But protectionist trade policies, motivated by politicians' desire for campaign support, contained the seeds of future failures. Politicians had an electoral interest in helping even their weakest constituents survive, but in the process, weakened the ability of significant parts of Japan's economy to survive international economic competition.

Finally, the new electoral system provides different political incentives for Japanese politicians. At the time of this writing, fifteen years and four elections have passed since the LDP's hold on power was interrupted and since the abandonment of the SNTV electoral system. Not surprisingly, the areas most changed in this short time have been the organization of the party system, the internal structure of parties, and the nature of electoral campaigns. But it is still too soon to expect the policy effects of electoral reform to have played themselves out completely. Until politicians sort themselves into parties that make programmatic sense (a process that will require another LDP split to progress further), the LDP will continue to muddle through, trying to keep its business supporters as happy as possible even at the expense of the general public.

In 2001, the LDP chose Junichiro Koizumi to be party leader and prime minister (see again Box 11.4). Ironically, Koizumi's record-high popularity came as a consequence of his public rejection of the LDP's old policies and practices. Abetted fecklessly by old-guard LDP stalwarts who opposed his reform efforts at every turn, he managed to stay on top for five years by running against his own party. Thus, while Koizumi saw many (but not all) of his reform ideas stymied by his conservative LDP colleagues, he remained personally popular. He was able to purge some opponents from the party, and to leave another reformer in charge. But his successors have let reform stall, as remaining conservatives have dug in their heels. Comprehensive reform will still take some time, and may require a new party in government. Whatever happens, it will certainly be interesting to watch.

## KEY TERMS

Abe, Shinzo

aging society

Ainu

Allied Occupation of Japan

*amakudari*

Article 9

Aso, Taro

Burakumin

Clean Government Party (*Komeito*)

community building

Democratic Party of Japan

Democratic Socialist Party (DSP)

Diet

direct taxes

Doi, Takako

enterprise unions

Equal Employment Opportunity Law

Hata, Tsutomu

Hosokawa, Morihiro

House of Councillors (Upper House)

House of Representatives (Lower House)

Ikeda, Hayato

indirect taxes

industrial policy

Japan Communist Party (JCP)

Japan Socialist Party (JSP)

*keiretsu*

Kishi, Nobusuke

*koenkai*

Koizumi, Junichiro

Koreans (in Japan)

Liberal Democratic Party (LDP)

MacArthur, General Douglas

malapportionment

Meiji Restoration

Minamata

Miyazawa, Kiichi

Murayama, Tomiichi

New Frontier Party (Shinshinto)

*nokyo*

Ohira, Masayoshi

oligarchs

Ozawa, Ichiro

Perry, Commodore Matthew C.

prefectures

proportional representation (PR)

Rengo

Self-Defense Forces

single-member districts

single non-transferable vote (SNTV) system

Soka Gakkai

Supreme Commander for the Allied Powers (SCAP)

Taisho Democracy

Tokugawa clan

U.S.–Japan Mutual Security Treaty

Yoshida, Shigeru

*zaibatsu*

## SUGGESTED READINGS

Beason, Dick, and Dennis Patterson. *The Japan That Never Was: Explaining the Rise and Decline of a Misunderstood Country.* Albany, NY: SUNY Press, 2004.

Brinton, Mary. *Women and the Economic Miracle.* Berkeley: University of California Press, 1993.

Calder, Kent E. *Crisis and Compensation.* Princeton, NJ: Princeton University Press, 1988.

Campbell, John C. *How Policies Change: The Japanese Government and the Aging Society.* Princeton, NJ: Princeton University Press, 1992.

Cowhey, Peter F., and Mathew D. McCubbins, eds. *Structure and Policy in Japan and the United States.* New York: Cambridge University Press, 1995.

Curtis, Gerald L. *The Japanese Way of Politics.* New York: Columbia University Press, 1988.

———. ed. *Japan's Foreign Policy After the Cold War: Coping with Change.* New York: Sharpe, 1993.

Doi, Takeo. *The Anatomy of Dependence.* Translated by John Bester. Tokyo: Kodansha International, 1971.

Flanagan, Scott et al. *The Japanese Voter.* New Haven, CT: Yale University Press, 1991.

Haley, John O. *Authority Without Power: Law and the Japanese Paradox.* Oxford: Oxford University Press, 1991.

Hayao, Kenji. *The Japanese Prime Minister and Public Policy.* Pittsburgh, PA: University of Pittsburgh Press, 1993.

Hrebenar, Ronald J. *Japan's New Party System.* Boulder, CO: Westview, 2000.

Ito, Takatoshi. *The Japanese Economy.* Cambridge: MIT Press, 1992.

Itoh, Hiroshi. *The Japanese Supreme Court.* New York: Marcus Weiner, 1989.

Jain, Purnendra, and Takashi Inoguchi, eds. *Japanese Politics Today: Beyond Karaoke Democracy?* New York: St. Martin's Press, 1997.

Kohno, Masaru. *Japan's Postwar Party Politics.* Princeton, NJ: Princeton University Press, 1997.

Miwa, Yoshiro, and J. Mark Ramseyer. *The Fable of the Keiretsu: Urban Legends of the Japanese Economy.* Chicago: University of Chicago Press, 2006.

Nakane, Chie. *Japanese Society.* Berkeley: University of California Press, 1970.

Ozawa, Ichiro. *Blueprint for a New Japan.* Tokyo: Kodansha International, 1994.

Ramseyer, J. Mark, and Frances Rosenbluth. *Japan's Political Marketplace.* Cambridge: Harvard University Press, 1993.

Samuels, Richard J. *The Business of the Japanese State: Energy Markets in Comparative and Historical Perspective.* Ithaca, NY: Cornell University Press, 1987.

Scheiner, Ethan. *Democracy Without Competition in Japan: Opposition Failure in a One-Party Dominant State.* New York: Cambridge University Press, 2006.

Schoppa, Leonard. *Bargaining with Japan: What American Pressure Can and Cannot Do*. New York: Columbia University Press, 1997.

Souyri, Pierre. *The World Turned Upside Down: Medieval Japanese Society*. New York: Columbia University Press, 2003.

Upham, Frank K. *Law and Social Change in Postwar Japan*. Cambridge: Harvard University Press, 1987.

Uriu, Robert. *Troubled Industries: Confronting Economic Change in Japan*. Ithaca, NY: Cornell University Press, 1996.

## INTERNET RESOURCES

University-maintained websites with links on Japanese politics:

Harvard's Reischauer Institute maintains links to Japanese government, institutions, media, and myriad other sites: **www.fas.harvard.edu/~rijs/resources/politics.html**

Stanford University offers links to sites covering interest groups, the Supreme Court, and regional governments. **jguide.stanford.edu/site/government_politics_16.html**

"Japanese Politics Central" archives data on elections and public opinion polls: **jpcentral.virginia.edu**

The UCLA library offers links to sites covering social sciences, humanities, and government sources of data: **http://www.library.ucla.edu/libraries/eastasian/6569.cfm**

Periodicals: Asahi Shimbun, **www.asahi.com/english/english.html**; Japan Times, **www.japantimes.co.jp/**; Yomiuri Shimbun, **www.yomiuri.co.jp/index-e.htm**; Japan Echo, **www.japanecho.co.jp**

## ENDNOTES

1. Japan, Statistics Bureau and Statistics Center, Ministry of Public Management, Home Affairs, Posts and Telecommunications. "Population Census," 2001. http://www.stat.go.jp/english/data/jinsui/2001np/index.htm.

2. Japan, Ministry of Health and Welfare, *Annual Report on Health and Welfare*, 1999. http://www.mhlw.go.jp/english/wp/wp-hw/vol1/p2c1s1.html.

3. Europe's population is aging rapidly as well. Among advanced industrial countries, the United States is an outlier for its continued (or more accurately, "renewed") youthfulness. Due to both much greater immigration and higher fertility rates, the U.S. population should keep growing rapidly for the forseeable future. "Half a Billion Americans? *The Economist*, 24 August, 2002, 20–22.

4. Douglass C. North, *Institutions, Institutional Change, and Economic Performance* (New York: Cambridge University Press, 1990).

5. For more thorough treatments of modern Japanese history, see Peter Duus, *The Rise of Modern Japan* (Boston: Houghton Mifflin, 1976); and Mikiso Hane, *Modern Japan: A Historical Survey* (Boulder, CO: Westview, 1986).

6. Akira Iriye, *Pacific Estrangement* (Cambridge: Harvard University Press, 1972).

7. William W. Lockwood, *The Economic Development of Japan* (Princeton, NJ: Princeton University Press, 1968), 292.

8. Kazuo Kawai, *Japan's American Interlude* (Chicago: University of Chicago Press, 1960), 22–24; Hans H. Baerwald, *The Purge of Japanese Leaders Under the Occupation* (Berkeley: University of California Press, 1959), 97; and T. A. Bisson, *Zaibatsu Dissolution in Japan* (Berkeley: University of California Press, 1954), 97–104.

9. Supreme Commander for the Allied Powers, Government Section, *Political Reorientation of Japan*, vol. 1 (Washington, DC: U.S. Gov't Printing Office, 1949), 98–109.

10. Hane, *Modern Japan*, 347–48.

11. Chalmers Johnson, *MITI and the Japanese Miracle* (Stanford, CA: Stanford University Press, 1982).

12. John Lewis Gaddis, *Strategies of Containment: A Critical Appraisal of Postwar American National Security Policy* (Oxford: Oxford University Press, 1982), 75.

13. A dispute over the four small "Kurile" islands north of Hokkaido—which the Soviet Union annexed at the end of the war, and which post-Soviet Russia still controls—still holds up the formal normalization of relations between the two countries.

14. Lockwood, *Economic Development of Japan*, 594.

15. Home Affairs Ministry, *Chiho zaisei no shikumi to sono unei jitai* (Tokyo: Home Affairs Ministry, 1987); see also, Hiromitsu Ishi, *The Japanese Tax System* (Oxford: Oxford University Press, 1989), 11.

16. "The Day of the Governors," *The Economist*, 16 June, 2001: 41–42.

17. J. Mark Ramseyer and Frances McCall Rosenbluth, *Japan's Political Marketplace* (Cambridge: Harvard University Press 1993), 142–60.

18. John Owen Haley, *Authority without Power: Law and the Japanese Paradox* (New York: Oxford University Press, 1991), 189; and Ramseyer and Rosenbluth, *Japan's Political Marketplace*, 162.

19. Masaru Kohno, *Japan's Postwar Party Politics* (Princeton, NJ: Princeton University Press, 1997), 38–44. For a historical account of the choice of SNTV in the prewar years, see Masao Soma, *Nihon senkyo seido shi [The History of the Japanese Electoral System]* (Fukuoka, Japan: Kyushu Daigaku Shuppan-kai, 1986).

20. Mathew D. McCubbins and Frances Rosenbluth, "Party Provision for Personal Politics: Dividing the Vote in Japan," in Peter F. Cowhey and Mathew D. McCubbins, eds., *Structure and Policy in Japan and the United States* (Cambridge: Cambridge University Press, 1995), 35–55.

21. Ethan Scheiner, *Democracy Without Competition: Opposition Failure in a One-Party Dominant State* (New York: Cambridge University Press, 2006).

22. Ronald J. Hrebenar, *The Japanese Party System*, 2nd ed. (Boulder, CO: Westview 1992), 47–48.

23. Gary W. Cox and Michael F. Thies, "The Costs of Intraparty Competition: The Single, Nontransferable Vote and Money Politics in Japan," *Comparative Political Studies* 31, no. 3 (June 1998): 267–91.

24. Gary W. Cox, Frances M. Rosenbluth, and Michael F. Thies, "Electoral Rules, Career Ambitions, and Party Structure: Comparing Factions in Japan's Upper and Lower Houses," *American Journal of Political Science* 44, no. 1 (January 2000): 115–22.

25. Robert A. Scalapino and Junnosuke Masumi, *Parties and Politics in Contemporary Japan* (Berkeley: University of California Press, 1962), 41–53.

26. Michael F. Thies, "When Will Pork Leave the Farm? Institutional Bias in Japan and the United States," *Legislative Studies Quarterly* 23, no. 4 (November 1998): 467–92.

27. Ramseyer and Rosenbluth, *Japan's Political Marketplace*, 43.

28. High turnout is bad for the JCP and CGP precisely because they have the most loyal and consistently active supporters. The "sometime" voters whose participation causes overall turnout to rise are not JCP or CGP supporters. Thus, the relative impact of those parties' loyalists goes down when overall participation rates increase.

29. Thomas R. Rochon, "Electoral Systems and the Basis of the Vote: The Case of Japan," in John C. Campbell, ed., *Parties, Candidates, and Voters in Japan: Six Quantitative Studies* (Ann Arbor: Center for Japanese Studies, University of Michigan, 1981), 1–28.

30. Sasaki Takeshi et al., eds. *Daigishi to kane: Seiji shikin zenkoku chosa hokoku [Diet Members and Money: A National Investigative Report on Political Finance]* (Tokyo: Asahi sensho, 1999); and Steven R. Reed and Michael F. Thies, "The Consequences of Electoral Reform in Japan," in Matthew Soberg Shugart and Martin P. Wattenberg, eds., *Mixed-Member Electoral Systems: The Best of Both Worlds?* (New York: Oxford University Press, 2000).

31. Ikuo Kabashima, *Seiji sanka [Political Participation]* (Tokyo: Tokyo University Press, 1988); Gary W. Cox, Frances M. Rosenbluth, and Michael F. Thies, "Mobilization, Social Networks, and Turnout: Evidence From Japan," *World Politics* 50, no. 3 (April 1998): 447–74.

32. T. J. Pempel and Keiichi Tsunekawa, "Corporatism Without Labor? The Japanese Anomaly," in Philippe C. Schmitter and Gerhard Lehmbruch, eds., *Trends Toward Corporatist Intermediation* (London: Sage, 1979), 231–70.

33. This percentage was calculated by the Small and Medium Enterprise Agency of the Ministry of Economics, Trade, and Industry from data compiled by the Ministry of Public Management, Home Affairs, Posts and Telecommunications, Establishment and Enterprise Census of Japan (2001), available at www.chusho.meti.go.jp/sme_english/outline/07/01.html.

34. Frances McCall Rosenbluth, *Financial Politics in Contemporary Japan* (Ithaca, NY: Cornell University Press, 1989).

35. Leonard J. Schoppa, *Bargaining with Japan: What American Pressure Can and Cannot Do* (New York: Columbia University Press, 1997): and Ross D. Schaap, *The Electoral Determinants of Regulatory Change: Explaining Japan's 'Big Bang' Financial Liberalization* (unpublished Ph.D. dissertation, University of California, Los Angeles, 2002).

36. Kent E. Calder, *Crisis and Compensation*, ch. 5 (Princeton, NJ: Princeton University Press, 1988).

37. Ronald Dore, *British Factory–Japanese Factory: The Origins of National Diversity in Industrial Relations* (Berkeley: University of California Press, 1973).

38. Keizai Koho Center, *Japan 1994: An International Comparison* (Tokyo: Keizai Koho Center, 1993).

39. Yutaka Tsujinaka, "Rengo and Its Osmotic Networks," in Gary D. Allinson and Yasunori Sone, eds., *Political Dynamics in Contemporary Japan* (Ithaca, NY: Cornell University Press, 1993), 200; and Lonny E. Carlile, "Party Politics and the Japanese Labor Movement: Rengo's New Political Force," *Asian Survey*, 34, no. 7 (July 1994), 606–20.

40. H. H. Gerth and C. Wright Mills, *From Max Weber: Essays in Sociology* (New York: Oxford University Press, 1958).

41. Lucian Pye, *Asian Power and Politics: The Cultural Dimensions of Authority* (Cambridge: Belknap-Harvard Press, 1985).

42. Thomas C. Smith, *The Agrarian Origins of Modern Japan* (Stanford, CA: Stanford University Press, 1959).

43. Chie Nakane, *Japanese Society* (Berkeley: University of California Press, 1970).

44. Sharon Sievers, "Feminist Criticism in Japan Politics in the 1880s: The Experience of Kishida Toshiko," *Signs* 6, no. 4 (1981): 602–16.

45. Anna Cock, "Where Men Are Men and Still Born to Rule," *Sunday Telegraph*, 26 March 2006.

46. Mari Yamaguchi, "Japanese Government Report Urges Job Training and Business Money for Working Mothers," Associated Press Newswires, 9 June 2006.

47. "DPJ Seeks to Use Gender-Based Quotas in Fielding Candidates," *The Japan Times*, 26 January 1998.

48. Keizai Koho Center, *Japan 2005: An International Comparison* (Tokyo: Keizai Koho Center, 2004), 12.

49. Bradley M. Richardson, *The Political Culture of Japan* (Berkeley: University of California Press, 1974), 3.

50. Dore, *British Factory–Japanese Factory.*

51. Cox, Rosenbluth, and Thies, "Electoral Rules, Career Ambitions, and Party Structure."

52. Steve Bossy, "Academic Pressure and Impact on Japanese Students," *McGill Journal of Higher Education* 35, 1 (2000), 79–81; and Keiko Hirao, "Privatized Education Market and maternal Employment in Japan," in Frances Rosenbluth, ed., *Political Economy of Low Fertility: Japan in Comparative Perspective*, (Stanford, CA: Stanford University Press, 2007), 170–197.

53. Mary Brinton, "Trouble in Paradise: Institutions in the Japanese Economy and the Youth Labor Market," in Victor Nee and Richard Swedberg, eds., *The Economic Sociology of Capitalism* (Princeton, NJ: Princeton University Press, 2005), 419–44.

54. B. C. Koh, *Japan's Administrative Elite* (Berkeley: University of California Press, 1989), 232–40.

55. *Nikkei Net Interactive*, http://www.nni.nikkei.co.jp/ (17 July 2002).

56. Takatoshi Ito, *The Japanese Economy* (Cambridge: MIT Press, 1992), 61–79.

57. Note, however, that Japan's high prices weakened the purchasing power of Japan's high per capita income, making real incomes somewhat lower than those in the United States. In

fact, the 2001 purchasing power parity value of per capita GNP was only $25,600, well below the U.S. value of $36,000. Keizai Koho Center, *Japan 2002: An International Comparison*, (Tokyo: Keizai Koho Center, 25 December 2001), 15.

58. Hugh Patrick and Henry Rosovsky, "Japan's Economic Performance: An Overview," in Hugh Patrick and Henry Rosovsky, eds., *Asia's New Giant: How the Japanese Economy Works* (Washington, DC: Brookings Institution, 1976).

59. Johnson, *MITI and the Japanese Miracle.*

60. Kent E. Calder, *Strategic Capitalism: Private Business and Public Purpose in Japanese Industrial Finance* (Princeton, NJ: Princeton University Press, 1993).

61. Richard J. Samuels, *The Business of the Japanese State: Energy Markets in Comparative Historical Perspective* (Ithaca, NY: Cornell University Press, 1987).

62. Johnson, "Political Institutions and Economic Performance: The Government-Business Relationship in Japan, South Korea, and Taiwan," in Frederic C. Deyo, *The Political Economy of the New Asian Industrialism*, 136–64.

63. Richard E. Barrett and Soomi Chin, "Export-Oriented Industrializing States in the Capitalist World System: Similarities and Differences," in Frederic C. Deyo, *The Political Economy of the New Asian Industrialism*, 23–43.

64. Keizai Koho Center, *Japan 1992: An International Comparison* (Tokyo: Keizai Koho Center, 1991), 34.

65. Patrick and Rosovsky, "Japan's Economic Performance," 45.

66. Joseph P. Kettl, Jr., *The Politics of Defense in Japan* (Armonk, NY: Sharpe, 1993), 173–205.

67. Frank K. Upham, *Law and Social Change*, in *Postwar Japan* (Cambridge. Harvard University Press, 1987), 18–19, 28–77.

68. "Toxic Waste in Japan: The Burning Issue," *The Economist*, 25 July 1998, 60–61. For an excellent account of the daunting obstacles that citizens groups encounter when tackling local pollution problems, see Jeffrey Broadbent, *Environmental Politics in Japan* (New York: Cambridge University Press, 1998). See also Frances M. Rosenbluth and Michael F. Thies, "The Political Economy of Japanese Pollution Regulation," *The American Asian Review* 20, 1 (Spring 2002): 1–32.

69. World Bank, *World Bank Development Report*, 1998–99 (New York: Oxford University Press, 1999), 202–03. For an in-depth look at medical as well as pension issues, see John C. Campbell, *How Policies Change* (Princeton, NJ: Princeton University Press, 1992).

70. Peter F. Cowhey and Mathew D. McCubbins, "Conclusion," in Cowhey and McCubbins, eds., *Structure and Policy in Japan and the United States*, 253–60.

# POLITICS IN RUSSIA

*Thomas F. Remington*

## Country Bio

RUSSIA

**Population**
142.2 million

**Territory**
6,593,000 square miles

**Year of Independence**
1991

**Year of Current Constitution**
1993

**Head of State**
President Dmitrii Anatol'evich Medvedev

**Head of Government**
Premier Vladimir Vladimirovich Putin

**Language(s)**
Russian, other languages of ethnic nationalities

**Religion**
Russian Orthodox 70–80%, other Christian 1–2%, Muslim 14–15%, Buddhist 0.6%, Jewish 0.3%; other or non-religious 5–15%

## ENSURING CONTINUITY OF POWER

On May 7, 2008, **Dmitrii Anatol'evich Medvedev** took the oath of office as president of the Russian Federation. The solemn ceremony—attended by his predecessor, Vladimir Putin, and the Russian Orthodox Patriarch of Russia, Alexii II—signaled that the leadership was united around the choice of the new president. Elsewhere in the former Soviet Union, the succession from one president to another has sometimes triggered a struggle for power among contending political forces, leading to popular uprisings with unpredictable outcomes.[1] The Russian authorities were determined not to allow a similar disruption in the transfer of power from one president to the next.

The succession was smooth, but hardly democratic. Although a presidential election had been held on March 2, every detail was closely controlled so that no serious challenge to Medvedev could arise. Once Putin had decided that Medvedev would succeed him—a choice he announced the previous December—the Kremlin took no chances on the outcome. The state-controlled mass media, regional governors, big business, and the election commission all fell in line. The manipulated election process demonstrated to the world and to any would-be opponents that Medvedev was backed by a united front of all the authorities.

Adding to the display of continuity was the fact that Vladimir Putin himself stayed on in power as prime minister. Medvedev's first act as newly inaugurated president was to name Putin as head of government. This neat exchange—Putin made Medvedev his successor, Medvedev kept Putin in power—solved several problems. Putin's exceptional popularity among the public and the authorities' fear of a destabilizing split among the ruling elite made it desirable to find a postpresidency role for Putin that would ensure continuity and legitimate the new president. At the same time, the authorities deemed it important to observe the niceties of constitutional law, which require that a president serve no more than two consecutive terms. Putin's move therefore allowed the leadership to comply with the constitution, while retaining power.

Yet, this improvised arrangement of shared power opened up huge uncertainty. No one in the political elite could be certain whether Putin was really still in charge and Medvedev was just a figurehead, whether Putin really intended to give up near-autocratic power and turn his attention instead to the details of managing the government, or whether this was a fragile temporary truce that would result in one or the other of the two men ultimately triumphing over the other. Observers noted that the constitution makes the prime minister first in line to succeed the president. So if Medvedev decided to step down prematurely or met with an unfortunate accident, Putin would automatically succeed him and become acting president (much as Putin had become acting president eight years before when Yeltsin resigned the presidency six months ahead of time). Then Putin could presumably be elected to a new term as president in his own right—the constitution only bars a president from serving more than two *successive* terms. No one could be sure what would happen next, but few thought that the duo of Putin as prime minister and Medvedev as president could last long: Most expected that sooner or later one or the other of them would be forced out.

The peculiarity of the situation arose from the fact that Russia's constitution, like that of France and many other countries, provides both for a directly elected president and a prime minister who must enjoy the confidence of parliament. France under the constitution of the Fifth Republic has demonstrated that a president of one party can coexist tolerably well with a prime minister of an opposing party so long as they agree on how to divide responsibilities and do not fight too openly. But Russia has never had successful experience with the sharing of power between two leaders, one with overall responsibility for guiding the state and the other in charge of the government. As Boris Yeltsin once put it, "in Russia, only one person can be number one." Under Communist rule (which lasted from the Bolshevik Revolution in 1917 until the collapse of the Soviet Union in 1991), the regime worked out a division of power between the Communist Party and the government. The party's leader was always the supreme leader in the country, and the head of government was always subordinate. If a similar logic prevails now, Putin, as prime minister, will have to content himself with managing the economy, and Medvedev, as president, will have final say in all policy matters at home and abroad. Whatever happens, by ensuring a seamless succession from Putin to Medvedev, Russia has launched yet another constitutional experiment, the outcome of which is highly uncertain.

## CURRENT POLICY CHALLENGES

Dmitrii Medvedev took over as president at a particularly auspicious point. After a decade of calamitous economic decline in the 1990s following the breakdown of the Soviet regime, Russia's economy has entered a sustained period of recovery. Russia's role as a leading world exporter of fuels and metals (Russia is second only to Saudi Arabia as a world exporter of oil) means that the high world prices for oil, gas, and other commodities have brought prosperity. Until the financial crisis of 2008, the gross national product grew annually in the range of 7–8 percent since 1999, and the government initiated major programs to rebuild schools, hospitals, housing, and agricultural infrastructure. Wages and pensions have risen significantly, while poverty and unemployment have plummeted. Public opinion surveys suggest that the population is pleased with the current trends: 60 percent of the population believes the country is headed in the right direction. Compare that with the nadir of the troubles of the 1990s: For example, in early 1999, only 6 percent thought the country was going the right way. in ___, 73 percent of the country expressed approval of Medvedev's performance as president.[2] However, the rapidity and severity of the economic crisis that unfolded in 2008–2009 pose a grave challenge to the Putin-Medvedev leadership.

A question debated actively in Russia and abroad is how much credit Vladimir Putin and his authoritarian style of rule deserve for Russia's turnaround (Box 12.1). Behind this question lie two widespread beliefs: First, after a turbulent political transition, a spell of authoritarian rule is often the only way that a country can make a decisive turn toward economic growth and prosperity, with democracy possible only once the institutions of market capitalism are firmly installed (many point to China as a case in point). Second is the idea that whatever the experience of other countries, Russia can only be governed autocratically.

An alternative view is that Putin's actions as leader had relatively little to do with Russia's success. Skeptics argue that any country where oil and gas make up over 60 percent of exports would have realized a huge windfall from the sharp increase in world oil prices. (From 1999 to 2008, the average price of a barrel of crude oil on world markets rose tenfold—from $10 to $100.) From that standpoint, Putin was not so much clever as lucky.

**BOX 12.1**

## Vladimir Putin

Vladimir Vladimirovich Putin was born on October 7, 1952, in Leningrad (called St. Petersburg since 1991). In 1970 he entered Leningrad State University and specialized in civil law. Upon graduation in 1975, Putin worked for the KGB and was first assigned to counterintelligence and then to the foreign intelligence division. Proficient in the German language, he was sent to East Germany in 1985. In 1990, after the Berlin Wall fell, Putin went back to Leningrad, working at the university, but in the employ of the KGB. When a former professor of his, Anatolii Sobchak, became mayor of Leningrad in 1991, he went to work for Sobchak.

In 1996 Putin took a position in Yeltsin's presidential administration. He rose rapidly. In 1998 Yeltsin named Putin head of the FSB (the Federal Security Service—successor to the KGB) and in March 1999 secretary of the Security Council. In August 1999

Yeltsin appointed him prime minister. Thanks to his decisive handling of the military operation in Chechnia, Putin's popularity ratings soared. On December 31, 1999, Yeltsin resigned, making Putin acting president. Putin ran for the presidency and, on March 26, 2000, won with an outright majority of the votes.

Over time, Putin's political persona grew clearer. Uncomfortable with the give and take of public politics, he prefers the hierarchical style of organization used in the military and police. He is a pragmatist with no particular affection for either the Soviet or the tsarist order. Capable of projecting an affable, relaxed demeanor on some occasions, on others he can be brusque, even crude. Like many previous Russian rulers, he has made the consolidation of his own political power his first priority.

But whichever perspective is right, the fact remains that Medvedev faces serious challenges over the longer run. He and Putin have both repeatedly warned that Russia must not allow itself to become economically dependent on its petroleum resources for economic growth, but must instead generate technological innovation and continuing productivity improvements. "The main problem of the Russian economy today is its extreme inefficiency," Putin declared shortly before stepping down as president. "Labor productivity in Russia remains unacceptably low. We have the same expenditures of labor as in the most developed countries but in Russia they bring several times less return. And that is doubly dangerous in conditions of growing global competition and rising costs for skilled labor and energy."[3] The plunge in world energy prices at a time of sharp worldwide recession in 2008–2009 has confirmed Putin's warning.

Both Putin and Medvedev are well aware of the dangers of the "resource curse": that is, the idea that in countries with windfall revenues from natural resources, the leaders avoid investing in the skills and knowledge of the population, and the societies wind up with lower levels of development than in resource-poor countries.[4] Russia's leaders have worked to invest

the oil revenues in projects intended to improve the country's living standard and educational level, stimulate the development of small business, and invest in new and promising technologies.

At the same time, they have frankly acknowledged the grim demographic realities: Russia's population is declining each year as a result of the excess of deaths over births, and the economy is becoming increasingly dependent on migrant labor from China, Central Asia, and elsewhere. Inequality across regions and social groups is rising. A recent National Human Development Report written by a team of Russian experts noted that some regions of Russia live at a level of human development comparable to that of Central Europe, while others are closer to an African level.[5]

But while Russian leaders have admitted the gravity of the problems the country faces, they have been unable to break through the obstacles standing in the way of solving them. Three in particular have proven to be stumbling blocks: the long experience of Russian bureaucrats in defeating any reforms that weaken their power; the vast physical span of the country, which impedes efforts to unite groups in society around broad common interests; and the legacy of the Soviet development model, which concentrated resources in giant state-owned enterprises—often located in remote, harsh regions—that are difficult, if not impossible, to convert into competitive, viable capitalist firms operating in a global market. Therefore, while Russia has enjoyed a substantial economic recovery in the 2000s, thanks to its reserves of natural resources, the sustainability of its progress over the longer term remains in doubt.

## HISTORICAL LEGACIES

### The Tsarist Regime

The Russian state traces its origins to the princely state that arose around Kiev (today the capital of independent Ukraine) in the ninth century. For nearly a thousand years, the Russian state was autocratic. That is, it was ruled by a hereditary monarch whose power was unlimited by any constitutional constraints. Only in the first decade of the twentieth century did the Russian tsar agree to grant a constitution calling for an elected legislature—and even then, the tsar soon dissolved the legislature and arbitrarily revised the constitution.

In addition to autocracy, the historical legacy of Russian statehood includes absolutism, patrimonialism, and Orthodox Christianity. *Absolutism* means that the tsar aspired to wield absolute power over the subjects of the realm. *Patrimonialism* refers to the idea that the ruler treated his realm as property that he owned, rather than as a society with its own legitimate rights and interests.[6] This concept of power continues to influence state rulers today. Finally, the tsarist state identified itself with the *Russian Orthodox Church*. In Russia, as in other countries where it is a dominant religious tradition, the Orthodox Church ties itself closely to the state, considering itself a national church. Traditionally, it has exhorted its adherents to show loyalty and obedience to the state in worldly matters, in return for which the state treated it as the state church. This legacy is still manifested in the present-day rulers' efforts to associate themselves with the heritage of the church and in many Russians' impulse to identify their state with a higher spiritual mission.

Absolutism, patrimonialism, and orthodoxy have been recurring elements of Russian political culture. But alternative motifs have been influential as well. At some points in Russian history, the country's rulers have sought to modernize its economy and society. Russia imported Western practices in technology, law, state organization, and education in order to make the state competitive with other great powers. Modernizing rulers—such as Peter the Great (who ruled from 1682 to 1725) and Catherine the Great (from 1762 to 1796)—had a powerful impact on Russian society, bringing it closer to West European models. The imperative of building Russia's military and economic potential was all the more pressing because of Russia's constant expansion through conquest and annexation of neighboring territories and its ever-present need to defend its borders. The state's role in controlling and mobilizing society rose with the need to govern a vast territory. By the end of the seventeenth century, Russia was territorially the largest state in the world. But for most of its history, Russia's imperial reach exceeded its actual grasp.

Compared with other major powers of Europe, Russia's economic institutions remained backward well into the twentieth century. However, the trajectory of its development, especially in the nineteenth century, was toward that of a modern industrial society. By the time the tsarist order fell in 1917, Russia had a large industrial sector, although it was concentrated in a few cities. The country had a sizeable middle class, although it was greatly outnumbered by the vast and impoverished peasantry and the radicalized industrial working class. As a result, the social basis for a peaceful democratic transition was too weak to prevent the Communists from seizing power in 1917.

The thousand-year tsarist era left a contradictory legacy. The tsars attempted to legitimate their absolute power by appealing to tradition, empire, and divine right. They treated law as an instrument of rule, rather than a source of authority. The doctrines that rulers should be accountable to the ruled and that sovereignty resides in the will of the people were alien to Russian state tradition. Throughout Russian history, state and society have been more distant from each other than in Western societies. Rulers and populace regarded one another with mistrust and suspicion. This gap has been overcome at times of great national trials, such as the war against Napoleon and later World War II. Russia celebrated victory in those wars as a triumphant demonstration of the unity of state and people. But Russia's political traditions also include a yearning for equality, solidarity, and community, as well as for moral purity and sympathy for the downtrodden. And throughout the Russian heritage runs a deep strain of pride in the greatness of the country and the endurance of its people.

## The Communist Revolution and the Soviet Order

The tsarist regime proved unable to meet the overwhelming demands of national mobilization in World War I. Tsar Nicholas II abdicated in February 1917 (March 1917, by the Western calendar). He was replaced by a short-lived provisional government, which, in turn, fell when the Russian Communists—Bolsheviks, as they called themselves—took power in October 1917 (November, by the Western calendar). Their aim was to create a socialist society in Russia and, eventually, to spread revolutionary socialism throughout the world. Socialism, the Russian Communist Party believed, meant a society without private ownership of the means of production, one where the state owned and controlled all important economic assets and where political power was exercised in the name of the working people. **Vladimir Ilyich Lenin** was the leader of the Russian Communist Party and the first head of the Soviet Russian government. (Figure 12.1 lists the Soviet and post-Soviet leaders since 1917.)

Under Lenin's system of rule, the Communist Party controlled all levels of government. At each level of the territorial hierarchy of the country, full-time Communist Party officials supervised government. At the top, final power to decide policy rested in the Communist Party of the Soviet Union (CPSU) Politburo. Under **Joseph Stalin**, who took power after Lenin's death in 1924, power was even further centralized. Stalin instituted a totalitarian regime intent on building up Russia's industrial and military might. The state survived the terrible test of World War II, ultimately pushing back the invading German army all the way to Berlin. But the combined cost of war and terror under Stalin was staggering. The institutions of rule that Stalin left behind when he died in 1953 eventually crippled the Soviet state. They included personalistic rule, insecurity for rulers and ruled alike, heavy reliance on the secret police, and a militarized economy. None of Stalin's successors could reform the system without undermining Communist rule itself.

As vast as the Soviet state's powers were, their use was frustrated by bureaucratic immobilism. As in any organization, overcentralization undermined the leaders' actual power to enact significant policy change—or even to recognize when serious policy change was needed. The center's ability to coordinate bureaucratic

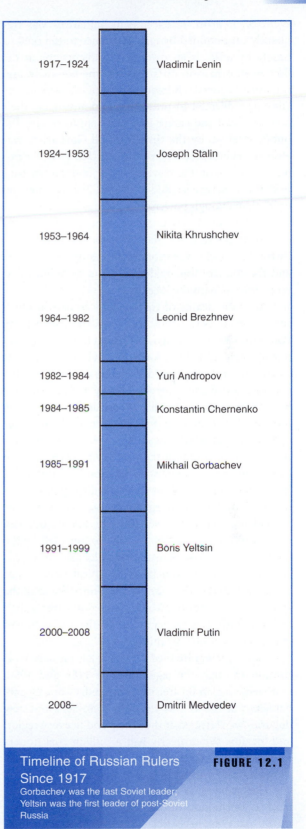

| | |
|---|---|
| 1917–1924 | Vladimir Lenin |
| 1924–1953 | Joseph Stalin |
| 1953–1964 | Nikita Khrushchev |
| 1964–1982 | Leonid Brezhnev |
| 1982–1984 | Yuri Andropov |
| 1984–1985 | Konstantin Chernenko |
| 1985–1991 | Mikhail Gorbachev |
| 1991–1999 | Boris Yeltsin |
| 2000–2008 | Vladimir Putin |
| 2008– | Dmitrii Medvedev |

**Timeline of Russian Rulers Since 1917**    **FIGURE 12.1**

Gorbachev was the last Soviet leader; Yeltsin was the first leader of post-Soviet Russia

agencies in order to execute its initiatives was frequently undermined by tacit resistance to the center's orders by officials at lower levels, distortions in the flow of information up and down the hierarchy, and the force of inertia. Bureaucratic officials were generally more devoted to protecting and advancing their own personal and career interests than to serving the public interest. By the time **Mikhail Gorbachev** was elected General Secretary of the CPSU in 1985, the political system of the Soviet Union had grown top-heavy, unresponsive, and corrupt. The regime had more than enough power to crush any political opposition. However, it was unable to modernize the economy or improve living standards for the population. By the early 1980s, the economy had stopped growing, and the country was unable to compete militarily or economically with the West.

After the deaths of three elderly leaders in quick succession in 1982, 1984, and 1985, the ruling party Politburo turned to a vigorous young (54-year-old) reformer named Mikhail Gorbachev to lead the country. Gorbachev quickly grasped the levers of power that the system granted the general secretary. He moved both to strengthen his own political base and to carry out a program of reform.[7] Emphasizing the need for greater openness—**glasnost'**—in society, Gorbachev stressed that the ultimate test of the party's effectiveness lay in improving the economic well-being of the country and its people. Gorbachev not only called for political democratization, but also legalized private enterprise for individual and cooperative businesses and encouraged them to fill the many gaps in the economy left by the inefficiency of the state sector. He welcomed the explosion of new informal social and political associations. He made major concessions to the United States in the sphere of arms control, which resulted in a treaty that, for the first time in history, called for the destruction of entire classes of nuclear missiles.

Gorbachev railroaded his proposals for democratization through the legislature. In 1989 and 1990, Gorbachev's plan for free elections and a working parliament was realized as elections were held and new deputies were elected at the center and in every region and locality. When nearly half a million coal miners went on strike in the summer of 1989, Gorbachev declared himself sympathetic to their demands.

Gorbachev's radicalism received its most dramatic confirmation through the astonishing developments of 1989 in Eastern Europe. All the regimes making up the Communist bloc collapsed and gave way to multiparty parliamentary regimes in virtually bloodless popular revolutions. The Soviet Union stood by and supported the revolutions. The overnight dismantling of communism in Eastern Europe meant that the elaborate structure of party ties, police cooperation, economic trade, and military alliance that had developed with Eastern Europe after World War II vanished. Divided Germany was allowed to reunite.

In the Soviet Union itself, the Communist Party faced a critical loss of authority. The newly elected governments of the national republics making up the Soviet state one by one declared that they were sovereign. The three Baltic republics declared their intention to secede from the union. Between 1989 and 1990, throughout the Soviet Union and Eastern Europe, Communist Party rule crumbled.

## Political Institutions of the Transition Period: Demise of the Soviet Union

Gorbachev's reforms had consequences he did not intend. The 1990 elections of deputies to the supreme soviets in all fifteen republics and to local soviets stimulated popular nationalist and democratic movements in most republics. In the core republic of Russia itself, Gorbachev's rival Boris Yeltsin was elected chairman of the Russian Supreme Soviet in June 1990. As chief of state in the Russian Republic, Yeltsin was well positioned to challenge Gorbachev for preeminence.

Yeltsin's rise forced Gorbachev to alter his strategy. Beginning in March 1991, Gorbachev sought terms for a new federal or confederal union that would be acceptable to Yeltsin and the Russian leadership, as well as to the leaders of the other republics. In April 1991 he reached an agreement on the outlines of a new treaty of union with nine of the fifteen republics, including Russia. A weak central government would manage basic coordinating functions. But the republics would gain the power to control the economies of their territories.

Gorbachev had underestimated the strength of his opposition. On August 19, 1991, a conspiracy of senior officials placed Gorbachev under house arrest and seized power. In response, thousands of citizens in Moscow and St. Petersburg rallied to protest the coup attempt. The coup collapsed on the third day, but

Gorbachev's power had been fatally weakened. Neither the union nor the Russian power structures heeded his commands. Through the fall of 1991, the Russian government took over the union government, ministry by ministry. In November 1991 President Yeltsin issued a decree formally outlawing the Communist Party of the Soviet Union. In December Yeltsin and the leaders of Ukraine and Belarus formally declared the Union of Soviet Socialist Republics dissolved. On December 25, 1991, Gorbachev resigned as president and turned the powers of his office over to Boris Yeltsin.[8]

## Political Institutions of the Transition Period: Russia 1990–1993

Boris Yeltsin was elected president of the Russian Federation in June 1991. Unlike Gorbachev, Yeltsin was elected in a direct, popular, competitive election, which gave him a considerable advantage in mobilizing public support against Gorbachev and the central Soviet Union government (see Box 12.2).

Like Gorbachev before him, Yeltsin demanded extraordinary powers from parliament to cope with the country's economic problems. Following the August 1991 coup attempt, parliament delegated to him emergency decree powers to cope with the economic crisis. Yeltsin formed a government led by a group of young, Western-oriented reformers determined to carry out a decisive economic transformation. The new government's economic program took effect on January 2, 1992. Their first results were felt immediately as prices skyrocketed. Quickly, many politicians began to distance themselves from the program: Even Yeltsin's vice president denounced the program as "economic genocide." Through 1992 opposition to the reforms grew stronger and more intransigent. Increasingly, the political confrontation between Yeltsin and the reformers on the one side and the opposition to radical economic reform on the other became

---

## Boris Yeltsin: Russia's First President

**BOX 12.2**

Boris Yeltsin, born in 1931, graduated from the Urals Polytechnical Institute in 1955 with a diploma in civil engineering and worked for a long time in construction. From 1976 to 1985, he served as first secretary of the Sverdlovsk *oblast* (provincial) Communist Party organization.

Early in 1986 Yeltsin became first secretary of the Moscow city party organization, but he was removed in November 1987 for speaking out against Mikhail Gorbachev. Positioning himself as a victim of the party establishment, Yeltsin made a remarkable political comeback. In the 1989 elections to the Congress of People's Deputies, he won a Moscow at-large seat with almost 90 percent of the vote. The following year he was elected to the Russian republic's parliament with over 80 percent of the vote. He was then elected its chairman in June 1990. In 1991 he was elected president of Russia, receiving 57 percent of the vote. Thus, he had won three major races in three successive years. He was reelected as president in 1996 in a dramatic, come-from-behind race against the leader of the Communist Party.

Yeltsin's last years in office were notable for his lengthy spells of illness and for the carousel of prime ministerial appointments. The entourage of family members and advisors around him, dubbed colloquially "the Family," seemed to exercise undue influence over him. Yet, infirm as he was, he judged that Russia's interests and his own would be safe in Vladimir Putin's hands. Yeltsin's resignation speech was full of contrition for his failure to bring a better life to Russians. After retiring, Yeltsin stayed out of the public eye. He died of heart failure on April 23, 2007, and was buried in Moscow with full honors.

Yeltsin's legacy is mixed. He was most effective when engaged in political battle, whether he was fighting for supremacy against Gorbachev or fighting against the Communists. Impulsive and undisciplined, he was gifted with exceptionally keen political intuition. He regarded economic reform as an instrument in his political war with the Communist opposition and used privatization to make it impossible for any future rulers to return to state socialism. Imperious and willful, he also regarded the adoption of the 1993 constitution as a major achievement and willingly accepted the limits on his presidential power that it imposed.

centered in the two branches of government. President Yeltsin demanded broad powers to carry out the reforms, but parliament refused to go along. In March 1993 an opposition motion to remove the president through impeachment nearly passed in the parliament.

On September 21, 1993, Yeltsin decreed the parliament dissolved and called for elections for a new parliament. Yeltsin's enemies barricaded themselves inside the parliament building. After a ten-day standoff, the dissidents joined with some loosely organized paramilitary units outside the building and attacked the Moscow mayor's offices adjacent to the Russian White House. They even called on their followers to "seize the Kremlin." Finally, the army agreed to back Yeltsin and suppress the uprising by force, shelling the parliament building in the process.

The violence of October 1993 cast a long shadow over subsequent events. Yeltsin's decree meant that national elections were to be held for a legislature that did not constitutionally exist, since the new constitution establishing these institutions was to be voted on in a referendum held in parallel with the parliamentary elections. Yet for all the turmoil, the constitution approved in the December referendum has remained in force since then.

## THE CONTEMPORARY CONSTITUTIONAL ORDER

### The Presidency

Yeltsin's constitution combined elements of presidentialism and parliamentarism. (See Figure 12.2 for a schematic overview of the Russian constitutional structure.) Although it provided for the separation of the executive, legislative, and judicial branches and for a federal division of power between the central and regional levels of government, it gave the president wide power. The president is directly elected for a six-year term and may not serve more than two consecutive terms. The president names the prime minister to head the government. Yet, the government must have the confidence of parliament to remain in power. Although the constitution does not call the president the head of the executive branch, he is so in fact by virtue of his power to appoint the prime minister and the rest of the government and his right to issue **presidential decrees** with the force of law. (The

decree power is somewhat limited in that decrees may not violate existing law and can be superseded by legislation.)

Over the years since the constitution was approved, some informal practices have come to govern the exercise of central power. For example, the president and government divide executive responsibility. The government, headed by the prime minister, is primarily responsible for economic and social policy. The president directly oversees the ministries and other bodies directly concerned with coercion, law enforcement, and state security—the "power ministries." These include the Foreign Ministry, Defense Ministry, Ministry of Internal Affairs (which controls the regular police and security troops), Federal Security Service (FSB—formerly the KGB), and several other security and intelligence agencies. The president and his staff set overall policy in the foreign and domestic domains, and the government develops the specific proposals and rules carrying out this policy. In practice, the government answers to the president, not parliament. The government's base of support is the president, rather than a particular coalition of political forces in parliament. This arrangement appears to be continuing under the duo of President Medvedev and Prime Minister Putin, although it may not last.

Despite the pronounced presidential tilt to the system, the parliament does have some potential for independent action. Its ability to exercise its rights, however, depends on the composition of political forces represented in parliament and the cohesiveness of the majority. Parliament's approval is required for any bill to become law. The State Duma (the lower house of parliament) must confirm the president's nominee for prime minister. If, upon three successive votes, the Duma refuses to confirm the nomination, the president must dissolve the Duma and call new elections. Likewise, the Duma may vote to deny confidence in the government. If a motion of no confidence carries twice, the president must either dissolve parliament or dismiss the government. During Yeltsin's tenure as president, the Duma was able to block some of Yeltsin's legislative initiatives. Since 2003, however, it has largely been a rubber stamp. The constitution allows for a variety of types of relationships among the president, government, and parliament, depending on the degree to which the president dominates the political system.

In addition to these powers, the president has a number of other formal and informal powers in his

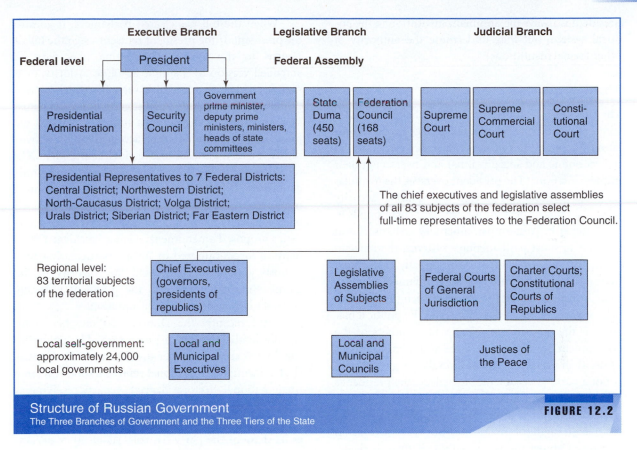

**Structure of Russian Government**
The Three Branches of Government and the Three Tiers of the State

**FIGURE 12.2**

constitutional capacity as "head of state," "guarantor of the constitution," and commander in chief of the armed forces. He oversees a large presidential administration, which supervises the federal government and keeps tabs on regional governments. Informally, the administration also manages relations with the parliament, the courts, big business, the media, political parties, and major interest groups.

The president also oversees many official and quasi-official supervisory and advisory commissions, which he creates and directs using his decree power. One is the **Security Council**, chaired by the president. Besides the president, the Security Council consists of a permanent secretary, the heads of the power ministries and other security-related agencies, the prime minister, and the chairs of the two chambers of parliament. Its powers are broad, but shadowy. Putin used it to formulate policy proposals not only in matters of foreign and defense policy, but also on selected issues having to do with the organization of the executive branch.

Another prominent advisory body is the **State Council**, which comprises the heads of the regional governments and thus parallels the Federation Council. Still another is the **Public Chamber**, which is made up of 126 members from selected civic, sports, artistic, and other nongovernmental organizations (NGOs). Its purpose is to deliberate on matters of public policy, make recommendations to parliament and the government on pending policy issues, and link civil society with the state. Like the State Council, it is a quasi-parliamentary deliberative body that the president can consult at will. All three bodies duplicate some of the deliberative and representative functions of parliament—and therefore weaken parliament's role. They illustrate the tendency, under both Yeltsin and Putin, for the president to create and dissolve new structures answering directly to the president. These improvised structures can be politically useful for the president as counterweights to constitutionally mandated bodies (such as parliament), as well as providing policy advice and feedback. They help ensure that the president is always the dominant institution in the political system, but they undermine the authority of other formal institutions.

## The Government

The *government* refers to the senior echelon of leadership in the executive branch. It is charged with formulating the main lines of national policy (especially in the economic and social realms) and overseeing their implementation. (The president oversees the formulation and execution of foreign and national security policy.) In this respect the government corresponds to the Cabinet in Western parliamentary systems. But in contrast to most parliamentary systems, the makeup of the Russian government is not directly determined by the party composition of the parliament. Indeed, there is scarcely any relationship between the distribution of party forces in the Duma and the political balance of the government. Nearly all members of the government are career managers and administrators, rather than party politicians. Overall, the government is not a party government, but reflects the president's calculations about how to weigh considerations such as personal loyalty, professional competence, and the relative strength of major bureaucratic factions in selecting Cabinet ministers. Although there is recurrent discussion of the idea that the party that forms the majority in the Duma should have the right to name the head of the government, no president has been willing to move toward instituting this model—no doubt out of fear that it would reduce his freedom of action in governing.

## The Parliament

The parliament—called the Federal Assembly—is bicameral. The lower house is called the **State Duma**, and the upper house, the **Federation Council**. Legislation originates in the Duma. As Figure 12.3 shows, upon passage in the State Duma, a bill goes to the Federation Council for consideration. The Federation Council can only pass it, reject it, or reject it and call for the formation of an agreement commission (consisting of members of both houses) to iron out differences. If the Duma rejects the upper house's proposed changes, it can override the Federation Council by a two-thirds vote and send the bill directly to the president for his signature.

When the bill has cleared parliament, it goes to the president. If the president refuses to sign the bill, it returns to the Duma. The Duma may pass an amended version by a simple absolute majority, or it may override the president's veto, for which a two-thirds vote is required. The Federation Council must then also approve the bill by a simple majority if the president's amendments are accepted or by a two-thirds vote if it chooses to override the president. On rare occasions the Duma has overridden the president's veto; it has overridden the Federation Council more frequently. In other cases the Duma has passed bills rejected by the president after accepting the president's proposed amendments. Under President Yeltsin political forces opposed to Yeltsin, particularly Communists and nationalists, held the majority in the Duma. But parliament and the president generally worked to head off major confrontations.

Until recently the Duma's 450 members were equally divided between deputies elected by a plurality rule in 225 single-member districts and 225 deputies elected through proportional representation (PR) in a single national electoral district. A party receiving at least 5 percent of the vote on the party-list ballot was entitled to as many of the party-list seats in the Duma as its share of the party-list vote. As in other PR systems, votes cast for parties that fail to clear the barrier are redistributed to winning parties. Since the 2007 Duma election, all 450 deputies are elected proportionally from party lists in a single nationwide district, and the threshold for winning seats rose to 7 percent.[9]

The parties clearing the 7 percent threshold form their own factions in the Duma. According to newly amended Duma rules, deputies may not switch faction membership (those who leave or are expelled lose their seats). Faction leaders are represented on the governing body of the Duma, the Council of the Duma. Factions are the main site of political discussion in the Duma and give members a channel for proposing bills to the chamber.

Since the December 2003 elections, the Kremlin has enjoyed the support of a commanding majority in the Duma, where the **United Russia** party holds two-thirds of the seats. United Russia holds twenty-six of the thirty-two committee chairmanships and eight of the eleven seats of the Council of the Duma, which is the steering body for the chamber. Since United Russia deputies vote with a high degree of discipline, the Duma consistently delivers the president solid legislative majorities. Other

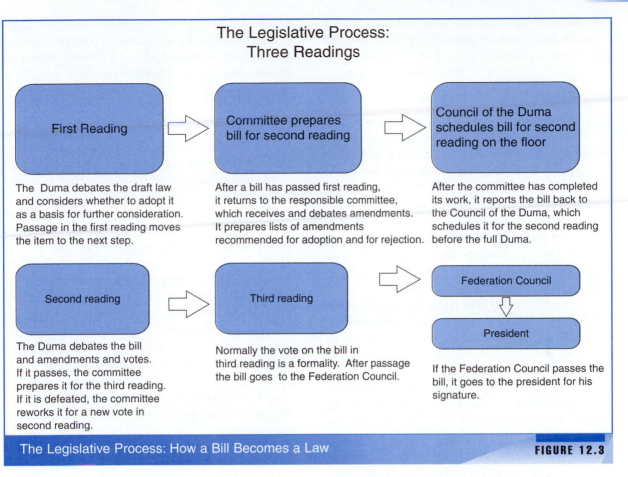

## The Legislative Process: Three Readings

**First Reading**

The Duma debates the draft law and considers whether to adopt it as a basis for further consideration. Passage in the first reading moves the item to the next step.

**Committee prepares bill for second reading**

After a bill has passed first reading, it returns to the responsible committee, which receives and debates amendments. It prepares lists of amendments recommended for adoption and for rejection.

**Council of the Duma schedules bill for second reading on the floor**

After the committee has completed its work, it reports the bill back to the Council of the Duma, which schedules it for the second reading before the full Duma.

**Second reading**

The Duma debates the bill and amendments and votes. If it passes, the committee prepares it for the third reading. If it is defeated, the committee reworks it for a new vote in second reading.

**Third reading**

Normally the vote on the bill in third reading is a formality. After passage the bill goes to the Federation Council.

**Federation Council**

**President**

If the Federation Council passes the bill, it goes to the president for his signature.

**The Legislative Process: How a Bill Becomes a Law**    **FIGURE 12.3**

factions have very little opportunity to influence the agenda, let alone the outcomes of legislative deliberations. Therefore, United Russia's control over the agenda and voting has turned the Duma into a rubber stamp for the executive branch.

Each deputy is a member of one of thirty-two standing committees. Bills submitted to the Duma are assigned to committees according to their subject matter. The committees collect and review proposed amendments before reporting out the bills for votes by the full chamber with the committee's recommendations.

The Federation Council is designed as an instrument of federalism in that (as in the U.S. Senate) every constituent unit of the federation is represented by two representatives. Thus, the populations of small ethnic-national territories are greatly overrepresented, compared with more populous regions. The Federation Council has important powers. Besides acting on bills passed by the lower house, it approves presidential nominees for high courts, such as the Supreme Court

and the Constitutional Court. It must approve presidential decrees declaring martial law or a state of emergency and any acts altering the boundaries of territorial units. It must consider any legislation dealing with taxes, budget, financial policy, treaties, customs, and declarations of war.

Until a major reform was pushed through by President Putin in the spring of 2000, the Federation Council's members were the heads of the executive and legislative branches of each constituent territory of the federation. Now, however, each governor and each regional legislature names a representative to the Federation Council to serve on a full-time basis. The governors name their representatives, who are then confirmed by the legislatures. The regional legislatures elect their delegates and can recall them.

There is considerable dissatisfaction over the current role of the Federation Council. Many believe that the chamber's members should be popularly elected. This must be reconciled, however, with the constitutional rule that the two members of the chamber from each of Russia's territorial subjects must represent its executive and legislative branches.

## Executive-Legislative Relations

Relations between president and parliament during the 1990s were often stormy. The first two Dumas, elected in 1993 and in 1995, were dominated by the Communist and other leftist factions hostile to President Yeltsin and the policies of his government. This was particularly true in areas of economic policy and privatization. On other issues, such as matters concerning federal relations, the Duma and president often reached agreement—sometimes against the resistance of the Federation Council, whose members fought to protect regional prerogatives.

The 1999 election produced a Duma with a pro-government majority. President Putin and his government built a reliable base of support in the Duma for their legislative initiatives made up of a coalition of four centrist political factions. The 2003 election produced a still wider margin of support for the president in the Duma and an overwhelming majority for the United Russia party—which means that the president does not need to expend much effort in bargaining with the Duma to win its support for his policies. The Fifth Duma, elected in December 2007, is also dominated by the United Russia party and has continued to give its loyal support to the Medvedev-Putin team.

Although the level of voting discipline within the majority party is similar to that in a Westminster-style parliament, as is the practice of reliably supporting the government's initiatives, the relationship between the Duma and the government is somewhat different. In a Westminster-type setting, the government needs to maintain a majority in parliament. If it loses its majority, it must face the voters in a new election. Majority Members of Parliament would prefer to hold onto their seats as long as possible and vote for the government's proposals so as to avoid a parliamentary dissolution and new election. By the same token, the government is normally unwilling to face a revolt on the floor of Parliament and the possible loss of its majority. Thus, the government and the majority party need each other. In Russia the parliamentary deputies have almost no political resources outside the party, so the government has a much stronger hand in instructing them how to vote. A deputy who defies party discipline can be expelled and has very few alternatives. A major shift in the alignment of political forces in society, however, could lead to a different relationship between executive and legislative power.

## The Constitutional Court

The 1993 constitution provides for judicial review by the **Constitutional Court**. Its nineteen members are nominated by the president, but are subject to confirmation by the Federation Council. The court is empowered to consider the constitutionality of actions of the president, the parliament, and lower-level governments. The court has carefully avoided issuing any decisions restricting presidential powers in any significant way. However, it has decided a number of thorny constitutional issues, including the relations between the two chambers of parliament and the delineation of powers between the central and regional governments. It has consistently defended the rights of individual defendants in the criminal justice system against actions of federal and regional authorities. The court has also tended to uphold the sovereignty of federal law over the rights of the constituent territories of the federation.

Since Putin took office in 2000, the court has taken care to avoid crossing the president. Nevertheless, even the possibility that it might exert a measure of independent political influence led Putin to move the seat of the court to St. Petersburg in 2008. This may have been intended as a means to distance the court from the tight web of governing bodies located in Moscow and thus to marginalize it politically. Conceivably, however, it might wind up increasing the court's independence.

## Central Government and the Regions

Following the breakup of the Soviet Union, many Russians feared that Russia would also dissolve into a patchwork of independent fiefdoms. Certainly, Russia's territorial integrity was subjected to serious strains. Under President Yeltsin the central government granted wide autonomy to regional governments in return for political support. Yeltsin went so far as to sign a series of bilateral treaties with over forty regions to codify the respective rights and responsibilities of the federal government and the individual regional governments. Under Putin, however, the pendulum of federal policy swung back sharply toward centralization.

The demographic factor is one reason that Russia did not break up. Eighty percent of Russia's population is ethnically Russian. None of its ethnic minorities accounts for more than 4 percent of the total (the Tatars form the largest of the ethnic minorities, constituting about 5.5 million of Russia's total population of 142 million). Rebuilding national community in post–Soviet Russia has been helped by Russia's thousand-year history of statehood. Yet, until 1991 Russia was never constituted as a nation-state: Under the tsars it was a multinational empire, and under Soviet rule it was nominally a federal union of socialist republics. State policy toward nationality has also varied over the centuries. In some periods Russia recognized a variety of distinct ethnic-national communities and tolerated cultural differences among them. In other periods the state pressured non-Russian groups to assimilate to Russian culture.

Russia was formally established as a federal republic under the Soviet regime. In contrast to the Soviet Union, of which it was the largest component, only some of Russia's constituent members were ethnic-national territories.[10] The rest were pure administrative subdivisions, populated mainly by Russians. The non-Russian ethnic-national territories were classified by size and status into autonomous republics, autonomous provinces, and national districts. In many of them, the indigenous ethnic group constituted a minority of the population. As of 2008 Russia comprises 83 constituent territorial units, officially termed "subjects of the federation." They represent six different types of units. Republics, autonomous districts (all but one of them located within other units), and the one autonomous *oblast* give formal political representation to ethnic minorities; *oblasts* (provinces), *krais* (territories), and two cities of federal status (Moscow and St. Petersburg) are treated as ordinary administrative subdivisions with no special constitutional status.

One of the centralizing measures President Putin pursued is the absorption of smaller ethnic districts into larger surrounding units. In most of these cases, the smaller ethnic district was impoverished and hoped for better living standards as part of a consolidated territory.[11] The mergers also reduced the patronage rights and political voice that came with an ethnic district's status as a constituent unit of the federation.[12]

The ethnic republics jealously guard their special status. From 1990 to 1992, all the republics adopted declarations of sovereignty, and two made attempts to declare full or partial independence from Russia. Only one, however, the Chechen Republic (**Chechnia**), resorted to arms to back up its claim. Chechnia is one of a belt of predominantly Muslim ethnic republics in the mountainous region of the North Caucasus, between the Black and Caspian seas. Chechnia's president declared independence from Russia in 1991, an act Russia refused to recognize, but did not initially attempt to overturn by force. When negotiations failed, however, in December 1994 Russian forces attacked the republic directly, subjecting its capital city, Groznyi, to devastating bombardment. This forced tens of thousands of Chechen and Russian residents to flee and led to a protracted, destructive war. Fighting ceased in the summer of 1996, but resumed in 1999. Federal forces had established control over most parts of Chechnia by early 2000, but Chechen guerrillas continue to carry out ambushes and suicide attacks against federal units.

In the mid-1990s, a radical fundamentalist form of Islam replaced national independence as the guiding ideology of the Chechen rebel movement. The guerrillas have resorted to terrorist attacks against civilian targets both in the North Caucasus region and in Moscow. One of the most shocking of these incidents was the seizure of a school in the town of Beslan, near Chechnia, in September 2004 (see Box 12.3). The brutal methods used by federal forces to suppress the uprising have fueled continuing hatred on the part of many Chechens against the federal government, which, in turn, facilitates recruitment by the terrorists. With time, order has been restored under the sometimes brutal rule of Ramzan Kadyrov, and much of Groznyi has been rebuilt. Attacks and reprisals continue to occur occasionally, however, especially in ethnic republics neighboring Chechnia, where unemployment and poverty are severe.

Chechnia, fortunately, was an exceptional case. In the other twenty ethnic republics, Moscow reached an accommodation granting the republics a certain amount of autonomy in return for acceptance of Russia's sovereign power. All twenty-one ethnic republics have the constitutional right to determine their own form of state power so long as their decisions do not contradict

BOX 12.3

## Beslan

September 1 is the first day of school each year throughout Russia. Children, accompanied by their parents, often come to school bringing flowers to their teachers. A group organized by the Chechen warlord Shamil Basaev chose September 1, 2004, to carry out a horrific attack. A group of heavily armed militants stormed a school in the town of Beslan, located in the republic of North Ossetia, next door to Chechnia. They took over 1,000 schoolchildren, parents, and teachers hostage. The terrorists crowded the captives into the school gymnasium, which they filled with explosives to prevent any rescue attempt. The terrorists refused to allow water and food to be brought into the school. Negotiations over the release of the hostages failed.

On the third day of the siege, something triggered the detonation of one of the bombs inside the school. In the chaos that followed, many of the children and adults rushed to escape. The terrorists fired at them. Federal forces stormed the school, trying to rescue the escaping hostages and to kill the terrorists. Many of the bombs planted by the terrorists exploded. Ultimately, about 350 of the hostages died, along with most of the terrorists.

The media covered the events extensively. The Beslan tragedy had an impact on Russian national consciousness comparable to that of September 11 in the United States. While there had been a number of previous attacks tied to Chechen terrorists, none had cost so many innocent lives.

Putin claimed that the terrorists were part of an international terrorist movement aimed ultimately at the dismemberment of Russia itself and avoided linking the incident to Russian policy in Chechnia. In response to the crisis, Putin called for measures to reinforce national security. He also demanded increased centralization of executive power, including an end to the direct election of governors. Most observers assumed that Putin had wanted to make these changes anyway and that the Beslan tragedy simply gave him a political opening to enact them. Beslan was a tragic indication that the insurgency that began in Chechnia is spreading throughout the North Caucasus region.

---

federal law. All twenty-one have established presidencies. In many cases the republic presidents have constructed personal power bases around appeals to ethnic solidarity and the cultural autonomy of the indigenous nationality. Often they have used this power to establish personalistic dictatorships in their regions.

President Putin made clear his intention to reassert the federal government's authority over the regions. The reform of the Federation Council in 2000 was one step in this direction. Another was Putin's decree of May 13, 2000, which created seven new "federal districts." He appointed a special presidential representative to each district who monitors the actions of the regional governments within that district. This reform sought to strengthen central control over the activity of federal bodies in the regions. Often, in the past, local branches of federal agencies had fallen under the influence of powerful governors.

Still another very important measure was the abolition of direct popular election of governors, including the presidents of the ethnic republics. Before 2005 regional chief executives were chosen by direct popular election. Since 2005, however, the president nominates a candidate to the regional legislature, which then approves the nomination (no legislature has dared to oppose one of Putin's appointments). Many citizens supported this change, believing that the institution of local elections had been discredited by corruption and fraud and that elections were more often determined by the influence of wealthy insiders than by public opinion. Critics of the reform accused Putin of creating a hypercentralized, authoritarian system of rule. Putin clearly hoped that appointed governors would be more accountable and effective, but past experience suggests that centralizing power by itself is unlikely to improve governance in the regions in the absence of other mechanisms for monitoring government performance and for enforcing the law.

Below the tier of regional governments are units that are supposed to enjoy the right of self-government—municipalities and other local government units. Under new legislation the right of local self-government has been expanded to a much larger set of units—such as urban and rural districts and small settlements—raising the total number of local self-governing units to 24,000. In principle, local self-government is supposed to permit substantial policymaking autonomy in the spheres of housing, utilities, and social services (and to reduce the federal government's burden in providing such services). However, the new legislation—which is being phased in gradually—provides no fixed, independent sources of revenue for these local entities. They thus depend for the great majority of their budgets on the regional governments. For their part the regional governments resist allowing local governments to exercise any significant powers of their own. In many cases, the mayors of the capital cities of regions are political rivals of the governors of the regions. Moscow and St. Petersburg are exceptional cases because they have the status of federal territorial subjects like republics and regions. Other cities lack the power and autonomy of Moscow and St. Petersburg, and they must bargain with their superior regional governments for shares of power.

Russia's postcommunist constitutional arrangements are still evolving. The political system allows considerable room for the arbitrary exercise of power and even, as under President Putin, the evisceration of democracy. Both Yeltsin and Putin interpreted their presidential mandates broadly, and although President Medvedev has called for adherence to the rule of law, it is likely that he will also find it expedient on occasion to push the limits of presidential power.

The constitutional arrangements established under President Yeltsin have the potential to evolve toward democracy or to be used for authoritarian rule, depending on the inclinations of the leaders and the balance of forces in the country. Russia's future political evolution depends on more than its formal institutional arrangements. The informal traditions and understandings surrounding formal rules strongly shape the way officeholders wield power and determine how effectively institutions hold leaders accountable for their actions. Informal rules can be far more important than formal rules. If rulers can circumvent formal limits on their power, constitutional structures may become irrelevant to the actual exercise of power.

Under Vladimir Putin Russia's system of rule became a hybrid regime that includes elements of democracy within a largely authoritarian framework. In this system elections are held regularly, and opposition forces are allowed a small, marginal role. The ruling authorities decide how much freedom to allow opposition groups to organize and campaign, and they exercise substantial control over television and radio, although allowing much greater freedom to the print and Internet media. Business is given wide sway to pursue its economic interests, but may not finance a political challenge to the authorities. Above all, elections are not allowed to result in a loss of power for the ruling authorities. There is still considerable room for the articulation of interests and the discussion of policy alternatives. At the same time, corruption is rampant, and occasional murders of outspoken journalists and politicians go unpunished. The suppression of democratic freedoms is far more effective at pushing political opposition to the sidelines than at giving the authorities an independent means of controlling the bureaucracy.

Over the eight years of his presidency, Putin reversed the disarray of the early postcommunist period by constructing a hybrid democratic/authoritarian regime. Without explicitly violating any constitutional limits on his power and without abolishing elections or other formal democratic rights, Putin effectively negated the constitutional constraints on executive power. Putin stands in sharp contrast to Yeltsin in terms of the use of presidential power. Yeltsin used his presidential powers erratically and impulsively. But Yeltsin respected certain limits on his power: He did not suppress media criticism, and he tolerated political opposition. Faced with an opposition-led parliament, Yeltsin was willing to compromise with his opponents to enact legislation. However, Yeltsin grew dependent on a small group of favored **oligarchs** (business magnates with strong connections to government) for support and allowed them to accumulate massive fortunes and corrupt influence. Likewise, Yeltsin allowed regional bosses to flout federal authority with impunity because he found it less costly to accommodate them than to fight them.

The loss of state capacity under Yeltsin illustrates one danger of an overcentralized political system. When the president does not effectively command the powers of the office, power drifts to other centers of power. Putin's presidency illustrates the opposite danger. When Putin took over, he was faced with the task of reversing the breakdown of political control and responsibility that had accelerated under Yeltsin. Although he publicly called for a system based on respect for the rule of law, he steadily restored authoritarian methods of rule. Although Dmitrii Medvedev often refers to freedom and democracy as necessary for Russia, it is likely that any moves he makes toward liberalizing the system will be modest and gradual.

Boris Berezovsky was one of the most prominent oligarchs of the Yeltsin era. Today he lives in exile in Great Britain and faces criminal charges if he returns to Russia.

Borys Bierezowsky/East News/Getty Images

## RUSSIAN POLITICAL CULTURE IN THE POST-SOVIET PERIOD

Russian political culture is the product of centuries of autocratic rule, rapid but uneven improvement of educational and living standards in the twentieth century, and rising exposure to Western standards of political life. The resulting contemporary political culture is a contradictory bundle of values: A sturdy core of belief in democratic values is accompanied by a firm belief in the importance of a strong state and sharp disillusionment with the results of the reforms of the late 1980s and early 1990s. In a 2005 survey, 66 percent of Russians agreed that "Russia needs democracy," but 45 percent said that the kind of democracy Russia needs is "a completely special kind corresponding to Russian specifics."[13] A survey shortly before the December 2007 election found that almost two-thirds of the public did not believe the elections would be free or fair; yet, a majority believed that their lives would improve thanks to the elections.[14] Asked whether they believed they could have any influence on policy decisions in the country, 83 percent said no.[15] But two-thirds of voters thought that democratic elections are at least somewhat important to the country, and a majority said that as president, Dmitrii Medvedev would pursue policies that would strengthen democracy.[16] Can such contradictory beliefs about democracy be reconciled?

In interpreting such results, we must remember that Russians judge political principles such as democracy according to their effect on preserving the integrity of the state. Many Russians cannot forgive Gorbachev and Yeltsin for pursuing policies that resulted in the breakup of the Soviet state, widespread poverty, the amassing of great wealth by a few individuals using unscrupulous methods, and the loss of status as a great world power. Many associate concepts such as "democracy" and the "market economy" with misguided or malevolent efforts to remold Russia along Western lines. The restoration of the state's power and prestige, therefore, is a criterion for judging the worth of principles such as freedom and democracy. That helps explain why many Russians praise Putin for strengthening democracy and hope Medvedev will continue his policies. Far from seeing "freedom" and "order" as necessary enemies, many recognize that freedom is only possible in an ordered society. But if forced to choose between freedom and order, Russians divide rather evenly. For example, in an international survey conducted under the auspices of the British Broadcasting Company, 47 percent of Russians (compared with 40 percent internationally) said that stability and peace are more important concerns than freedom of the press, whereas 39 percent (versus 56 percent globally) gave priority to press freedom.[17]

We can understand these competing influences on Russian political culture when we consider the long-term forces (such as the rapid rise in educational levels of the population in the Soviet period) shaping it, as well as the impact of recent history.

The reforms of the late 1980s and early 1990s raised expectations that Russia would enjoy a significant rise in living standards once it got rid of communism. The sharp fall in living standards that followed the collapse of the old regime dispelled any notion that changing that political and economic system could turn the country around overnight.

Still, the years of economic recovery and political stability after 1999 have tempered some of the sharp disappointment that Russians felt with the change in regime and have erased much of the nostalgia for the old Soviet order. Both optimism and personal happiness have risen significantly in recent years. In December 2007, 40 percent of Russians reported that they were looking ahead to 2008 with optimism; a year before only 30 percent expressed optimism about the coming year.[18] Over the past ten years, the number of people considering themselves happy rose from 60 percent to 77 percent, while the number reporting that they are unhappy fell from 25 percent to 15 percent.[19] More people are willing to look back and say that the radical reforms of the economy beginning in 1992 brought greater good than harm (43 percent said more good than harm, while 35 percent said more harm than good in a December 2007 poll).[20] Russians even have more faith in the ruble as a currency after long preferring the dollar or the euro to the ruble: In April 2008, 61 percent (compared with 37 percent in July 2002) said they had more confidence in the ruble than in the dollar or the euro.[21] A similar number—61 percent—now believe that it was a good thing that Russia became independent of the Soviet Union. Ten years before, only 27 percent thought so.[22]

One reason Russians are willing to sacrifice democratic rights for political security is the widespread view that political order is fragile, a view that the authorities have worked hard to keep alive. Russians have long been taught that a weakening of the internal cohesion of the state invites predation from outside powers, and many episodes of Russian history bear out this belief. The Putin leadership pointed to the popular uprisings in Ukraine, Georgia, and elsewhere not as signs of a democratic spirit in the face of attempted election fraud by local strongmen, but as proof that outside powers (such as the U.S. Central Intelligence Agency and other Western intelligence services) were fomenting unrest in order to overthrow the legitimate state authorities. Asked what they consider the main internal threat facing Russia today, Russians expressed fear about political instability connected with political succession (16%), struggle among competing factions in power (12%), loss of control by the central government over the regions (9%), separatism in the North Caucasus (4%), and loss of control over the regions in the Far East located near China (4%).[23]

Surveys also show that citizens have little faith in most present-day political institutions, although, as Figure 12.4 shows, they have a good deal of confidence in the president and government. Confidence in elective bodies such as the parliament is low, and in the law enforcement and security organs, it is even lower, while it is higher in local and regional government and higher still in the Orthodox Church.

Some of Putin's popularity rubbed off on the state's political institutions. Still, Russians distinguish between the constitutional framework of the state and the personalities of the leaders. Few Russians thought that power should transfer with Putin from the presidency to the prime ministership; two-thirds preferred maintaining a system of "strong presidential power."[24] Neither did most Russians want to see presidential power increased.[25] As Figure 12.5 shows, by a wide margin Russians believe that there should be a political opposition to the authorities. Russians exhibit a strong sense of skepticism about and mistrust of most institutions of the state; yet, by a two-to-one margin, most Russians believe they cannot solve their problems without it.[26] Most accept that the state requires firm guidance by a capable president and give Putin credit for having restored order and purpose to the state. Therefore, although there continues to be a strong foundation of support for democratic values, that support is contingent on whether these values will help hold the country together or pull it apart.

The political culture thus combines contradictory elements. Russians do value democratic rights, but experience has taught them that under the banner of democracy, politicians can abuse their power to the detriment of the integrity of the state and the well-being of society. They also feel powerless to affect state policy. Little wonder that a leader such as Putin can

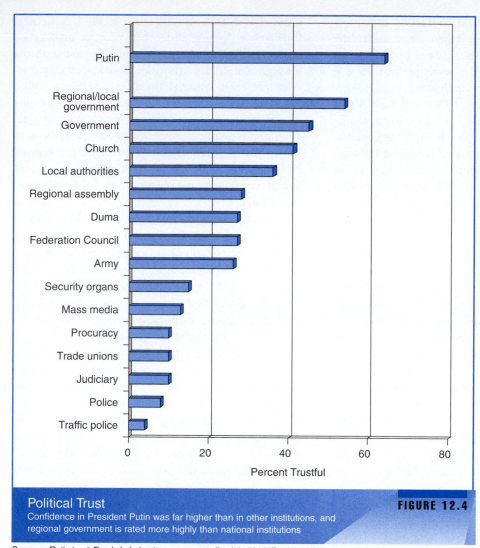

**Political Trust**
Confidence in President Putin was far higher than in other institutions, and regional government is rated more highly than national institutions

**FIGURE 12.4**

Sources: Putin trust: Fond obshchestvennogo mneniia, July 2008. Retrieved July 11, 2008 from bd.fom.ru/report/map/projects/dominant/dom0826/d082621#Abs3. All other items: Fund for Public Opinion, May 2007. Retrieved July 11, 2008 bd.fom.ru/report/cat/power/pow_rei/d071901.

United States, Russians believe that the state is responsible for providing a just moral and social order, with justice being understood more as social equality than as equality before the law. This pattern reflects the lasting influence of traditional conceptions of state and society on Russian political culture. Still, few would support the reestablishment of Soviet rule or a reversion to a military dictatorship.

Political culture is also shaped by slower acting, but more lasting influences, including the succession of generations, rising educational levels, and urbanization.[28] These are mutually reinforcing changes as new generations of young people are exposed to fundamentally different influences than those to which their parents were exposed, while the older generations tend to have lower levels of education and less exposure to the more cosmopolitan way of life of cities.

## Political Socialization

The Soviet regime devoted enormous effort to political indoctrination and propaganda. The regime controlled the content of school curriculums, mass media, popular culture, political education, and nearly every other channel by which values and attitudes were formed. The heart of Soviet doctrine was the Marxist belief that the way in which a society organizes economic production—feudalism, capitalism, socialism,

command such widespread support despite the general mistrust Russians have for the post-Soviet political institutions. Russians see him as restoring order following a protracted period of social and political breakdown. As Richard Rose and his colleagues argued, the reason Russians generally approved of the Putin regime was not because they considered it to be ideal, but because it improved economic well-being and in any case they saw little prospect for changing it.[27]

Surveys also reveal considerable continuity with the past in support for the idea that the state should ensure society's prosperity and the citizens' material security. More so than residents of Western Europe or the

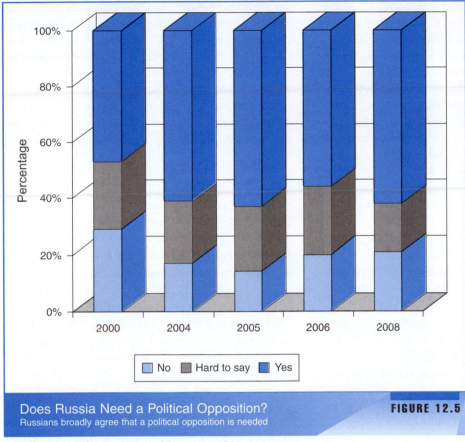

**Does Russia Need a Political Opposition?**
Russians broadly agree that a political opposition is needed

**FIGURE 12.5**

Note: Percentages are percentages of those responding.
Source: Levada Center, "Politicheskaia oppozitsiia v Rossii," July 2008. Retrieved July 11, 2008, from www.levada.ru/press/2008073102.html

Historical figures who in the Communist era were honored as heroes of the struggle of ordinary people against feudal or capitalist masters are now held up as great representatives of Russia's national culture.[29] Schoolbooks and mass media place heavy emphasis on loyalty to Russia as a state. This theme underlies Russia's effort to create a new sense of national community within the country's post-Soviet state boundaries.

The authorities have also turned to the Orthodox Church as an aid in political socialization. They regard the Church as a valuable ally in building patriotic loyalty, national pride, and a framework of ethical values. The Church, in turn, seeks to protect its

and so forth—determines the structure of values and beliefs prevalent in the society. The idea was that the ruling class in each society determines the basic ideology of the society. Therefore, Soviet propaganda and indoctrination emphasized that Soviet citizens were part of a worldwide working-class movement to overthrow capitalism and replace it with socialism, in which there would be no private property. Needing to knit together a highly diverse multinational state, the Soviet regime downplayed national feeling and replaced it with a sense of patriotic loyalty to the Soviet state and to the working class's interests in the worldwide class struggle.

Today the ideological content of Russian education has changed significantly, and there is much less overt political control over the formation of attitudes and values. In place of the idea of the class struggle and the international solidarity of the working class, textbooks stress love for the Russian national heritage.

traditional status as Russia's state church, enabling it to block other Christian denominations from proselytizing in Russia. As of the fall of 2006, a course on the fundamentals of Orthodox culture had been introduced into the school curriculum in nearly twenty regions, and about 20,000 Orthodox priests were serving as chaplains in the armed forces.[30] The Church's rising influence in the schools has prompted a backlash among many intellectuals, who protest that teaching religion in the schools violates the constitutional provision that Russia is a secular state.[31] But many people, whether religious or not, deplore the decay of morals in society and the relentless rise of consumerism and materialism as Russia opens itself to the global capitalist system. They see the Church, with its long history of partnership with the state, as a way of restoring traditional moral values in society.

In the 1990s the regime generally respected media freedom. Under Putin, the authorities moved to set limits on the media (particularly television), but did not institute an elaborate political socialization system such as the Soviet state employed. Nevertheless, the authorities have used the media to build support for their foreign and domestic policies. The overall political line under Putin and Medvedev has been that Russia is rejecting totalitarian communism on the one hand and unbridled oligarchic capitalism on the other and is restoring continuity with the best traditions of Russia's political history. Both, however, have repeatedly insisted that Russia must make use of democracy and capitalism, although in its own way.

The media system is stratified. Television reaches almost everyone and is by far the most important source of news for the population. Accordingly, it is subjected to the tightest political control by the authorities, who give the editors of the main broadcast programs regular guidance on what to cover and what not to cover. Print and Internet media are allowed much more freedom, but they reach a far smaller audience, so they are of less immediate concern to the authorities.[32] Aware of the stultifying effects of the old Soviet system of ideological control over communications, the authorities' strategy is defensive, in that they want to prevent organized groups from challenging their claim to power, rather than being overtly ideological.

Russian political socialization is therefore much less subject to direct state control than it was in the Soviet era, and even then, awareness of the political and economic standards of the outside world filtered into the consciousness of the Soviet population. Today's authorities want to use schools and communications media to build loyalty to the state and its leaders, confidence in the future, and acceptance of a centralized regime, while at the same time spurring Russians to modernize the economy.

## POLITICAL PARTICIPATION

In a democracy citizens take part in public life both through direct forms of political participation (such as voting, engaging in party work, organizing for a cause, demonstrating, and lobbying) and through indirect forms of participation (such as holding membership in civic groups and in voluntary associations). Both kinds of participation influence the quality of government. By means of collective action, citizens signal to policymakers what they want government to do. Through these channels of participation, activists rise to positions of leadership. But, despite the legal equality of citizens in

democracies, levels of participation in the population vary with differences across groups in resources, opportunities, and motivations. The better off and the better educated are disproportionately involved in political life everywhere, but in some societies, the disproportion is much greater than in others. And where deep inequalities in the distribution of wealth and income reinforce differentials in political voice between rich and poor, democracy itself is at risk.[33]

## The Importance of Social Capital

A healthy fabric of voluntary associations has long been recognized as an important component of democracy. Participation in civic life builds social capital—reciprocal bonds of trust and obligation among citizens that facilitate collective action. Where social capital is significant, people treat one another as equals, rather than as members of social hierarchies. They are more willing to cooperate in ways that benefit the society and improve the quality of government by sharing the burden of making government accountable and effective.[34] For example, where people feel less distance from and mistrust toward government, governments are better able to float bonds to provide improvements to community infrastructure. People are more willing to pay their taxes, so that government has more revenue to spend on public goods—and less ability and less incentive to divert it into politicians' pockets. Both capitalism and democratic government rest on people's ability to cooperate for mutual benefit.

In Russia, however, social capital has historically been scarce, compared with West European societies, and participation in civic activity has been extremely limited. Moreover, state and society have generally been separated by mutual mistrust and suspicion. State authorities have usually stood outside and above society, extracting what resources they needed from society, but not cultivating ties of obligation to it. The Communist regime further depleted the stock of social capital by coopting associations useful for the state and repressing those that threatened its interests. Therefore, social capital not only in Russia, but also throughout the former Communist bloc, is significantly lower than in other parts of the world.[35]

The weakness of intermediate associations linking political elites to ordinary citizens widens the felt distance between state and society. Thus, although Russians turn out to vote in elections in relatively high numbers, participation in organized forms of political activity is low. Opinion polls show that most people believe that their involvement in political activity is futile, and they have little confidence that they can influence government policy through their participation. Although there was an intense surge in political involvement in the late 1980s and early 1990s when controls over political expression and association were lifted, it ebbed substantially over the 1990s.

Membership in voluntary associations in contemporary Russia is extremely low. According to survey data, 91 percent of the population does not belong to any sports or recreational club, literary or other cultural group, political party, local housing association, or charitable organization. Four percent belong to sports or recreation groups, and 2 percent each say that they belong to a housing bloc, neighborhood association, or cultural group. Only half a percent reports being a member of a political party. About 9 percent report attending church at least once a month, and about 20 percent say that they are members of trade unions. Attending religious services and being a member of a trade union are very passive forms of participation in public life. Yet, even when these and other types of participation are taken into account, almost 60 percent of the population still is outside any voluntary public associations.[36] For example, today some 87 percent of Russian Orthodox believers are not members of a congregation, going to church only occasionally.[37]

This is not to say that Russian citizens are *psychologically* disengaged from public life or that they are socially isolated. Half of the Russian adult population reports reading national newspapers "regularly" or "sometimes," and almost everyone watches national television "regularly" (81%). Sixty-nine percent read local newspapers "regularly" or "sometimes." Sixty-six percent discuss the problems of the country with friends "regularly" or "sometimes," and 48 percent say that people ask them their opinions about what is happening in the country. A similar percentage of people discuss the problems of their city with friends.[38] Russians do vote in high proportions in national elections—higher in fact than those of their American counterparts.[39]

Moreover, Russians prize their right *not* to participate in politics. Today's low levels of political participation are a reflection of the low level of confidence in political institutions and the widespread view that ordinary individuals have little influence over government. In the 2003 Duma elections, 4.7 percent of the voters expressed their dissatisfaction with the array of choices offered by checking the box marked "against all" on the party-list ballot.[40] But the authorities worried that this was too attractive a means of expressing disaffection and eliminated the option from later elections.

## Elite Recruitment

Elite recruitment refers to the institutional processes in a society by which people gain access to positions of influence and responsibility. Elite recruitment is closely tied to political participation because it is through participation in community activity that people take on leadership roles, learn civic skills (such as organization and persuasion), develop networks of friends and supporters, and become interested in pursuing political careers.

In the Soviet regime, the link between participation and elite recruitment was highly formalized. The Communist Party recruited the population into a variety of officially sponsored organizations—such as the Communist Party, youth leagues, trade unions, and women's associations. Through such organizations the regime identified potential leaders and gave them experience in organizing group activity. The party reserved the right to approve appointments to any positions that carried high administrative responsibility or that were likely to affect the formation of public attitudes. The system for recruiting, training, and appointing individuals for positions of leadership and responsibility in the regime was called the **nomenklatura** system. Those individuals who were approved for the positions on nomenklatura lists were informally called "the nomenklatura." Many citizens regarded them as the ruling class in Soviet society.

The democratizing reforms of the late 1980s and early 1990s made two important changes to the process of elite recruitment. First, the old nomenklatura system crumbled along with other Communist Party controls over society. Second, although most members of the old ruling elites adapted themselves to the new circumstances and stayed on in various official capacities, the wave of new informal organizations and popular elections brought many new people into elite positions. Today the contemporary Russian political elite consists of a mixture of career types: those who worked their way up through the state bureaucracy and those who entered politics through other channels, such as elective politics or business.

Today some of the old Soviet institutional mechanisms for recruitment are being restored. In the Communist regime, the party maintained schools to train

President Medvedev and
Prime Minister Putin
confer at the Kremlin.

Anatoly Maltsev/epa/Corbis

political leaders, where rising officials received a combination of management education and political indoctrination. Today most of those schools serve a similar function as academies for training civil servants and are overseen by the presidential administration. The authorities are working to systematize the selection and training of officials in order to ensure that a competent and politically reliable cadre is available for recruitment not only to state bureaucratic positions, but even for management positions in major firms.[41]

There are two major differences between elite recruitment in the Communist regime and that in the present. The nomenklatura system of the Soviet regime ensured that in every walk of life, those who held positions of power and responsibility were approved by the party. They thus formed different sections of a single political elite and owed their positions to their political loyalty and usefulness. Today, however, there are multiple elites (political, business, professional, cultural, etc.), reflecting the greater degree of pluralism in post-Soviet society.

Second, there are multiple channels for recruitment to today's *political* elite. Many of its members come from positions in the federal and regional executive agencies. Putin relied heavily on the police (the regular police and the security services) and the military as sources of personnel for his senior-level appointments.[42] He also turned to colleagues he had worked with closely in St. Petersburg in the 1990s; an

example is President Dmitrii Medvedev. Medvedev has worked closely with Putin since 1990 when he became an advisor to Putin, who was serving as a deputy to the mayor. Medvedev then moved with Putin to Moscow in 1999 when Putin was made deputy head of the presidential administration under Yeltsin. Putin gave him ever broader responsibilities, first as head of the presidential administration and then as first deputy chairman of the government. This pattern of close patron-client relations, where a rising politician brings members of his "team" with him each time he moves up the career ladder, is a common feature of elite recruitment in Russia. One effect is to generate competition between rival groups of clients, sometimes called "clans." In Russia's case there has been persistent behind-the-scenes rivalry between two such clans, both composed of associates of Putin. One is close to the security services, while the other, with a slightly more liberal cast, is made up of trained lawyers. When Putin chose Medvedev as his anointed successor, it was seen as a serious blow against the first group.[43]

The Soviet elite recruitment system produced many of today's successful businesspeople as old guard bureaucrats discovered ways to cash in on their political contacts and get rich quickly. Money from the Communist Party found its way into the establishment of many new business ventures, including several of the first commercial banks. Insiders took advantage of their contacts to obtain business licenses, office space, and exclusive contracts with little difficulty. Some bought (at bargain basement prices) controlling interests in state firms that were undergoing privatization and a few years later became millionaires.

Today's business elite is closely tied to the state both because state officials keep business on a short leash and because business provides material and political benefits to officials. In some cases bureaucratic factions form around particular enterprises and industries such as the oil or gas industry. Businesses need licenses, permits, contracts, exemptions, and other benefits from government. Political officials, in turn, need financial contributions to their campaigns, political support, favorable media coverage, and other benefits that business can provide. In the 1990s the close and collusive relations between many businesses and government officials nurtured widespread corruption and the meteoric rise of a small group of business tycoons, or oligarchs. They took advantage of their links to Yeltsin's administration to acquire control of some of Russia's most valuable companies. The prominence of the newly rich fed a public backlash that made it politically viable for Putin to suppress some of them and destroy their business empires by police methods. And in many cases the state takeover of private firms ended up concentrating wealth and power in the hands of well-connected state officials (often from the security services) who have treated the firms as private fiefdoms, rather than increasing their productivity or accountability.[44]

## INTEREST ARTICULATION: BETWEEN STATISM AND PLURALISM

The political and economic changes of the last two decades in Russia have had a powerful impact on the way social interests are organized. A diverse spectrum of interest associations has developed. The pattern of interest articulation, however, reflects the powerful impact of state control over society, as well as the sharp disparities in wealth and power that formed during the transition period. A few organizations have considerable influence in policymaking, while other groups have little.

The Communist regime did not tolerate the open pursuit of any interests except those authorized by the state. Interest organizations—such as trade unions, youth groups, professional societies, and the like—were closely supervised by the Communist Party. Glasnost' upset this statist model of interest articulation by setting off an explosion of political expression. This, in turn, prompted new groups to form and to make political demands. It is hard today to imagine how profound the impact of glasnost' was on Soviet society. Almost overnight, it opened the floodgates to a growing stream of startling facts, ideas, disclosures, reappraisals, scandals, and sensations. In loosening the party's controls over communication sufficiently to encourage people to speak and write freely and openly, the regime also relinquished the controls that would have enabled it to rein in political expression when it went too far.

As people voiced their deep-felt demands and grievances, others recognized that they shared the same beliefs and values and made common cause with them, sometimes forming new, unofficial organizations. Therefore, one result of glasnost' was a wave of participation in "informal"—that is, unlicensed and uncontrolled—public associations. When the authorities tried to limit or prohibit such groups, they generated still more frustration and protest. Associations of all sorts formed, including groups dedicated to remembering the victims of Stalin's terror, ultranationalists who wanted to restore tsarism, and nationalist movements in many republics. The explosion of the nuclear reactor at Chernobyl in 1986 had a tremendous impact in stimulating the formation of environmental protest, linked closely to nationalist sentiment in Belarus and Ukraine.[45]

The elimination of the state's monopoly on productive property resulted in the formation of new interests, among them those with a stake in the market economy. Now groups can form to represent a diversity of interests, compete for access to influence and resources, and define their own agendas. The Justice Ministry estimates that there are nearly half a million NGOs, although probably no more than a quarter of them are active at any given time.[46]

In some cases NGOs are the successors of recognized associations of the old regime, such as official trade unions. Often these groups cling to their inherited organizational assets and continue to seek "insider" access to the state. Other groups sprang up during the glasnost' period or later, but must cooperate with local authorities in order to gain access to meeting places and media attention.

There were elements of corporatism in the state's relations with interest groups under Putin because of the regime's preference for dealing directly with controllable umbrella organizations representing particular segments of society. An example is the formation of the Public Chamber to create a state-approved platform for the activity of selected NGOs. Operating within the limits set by the regime, the Public Chamber has been able to serve to some extent as a channel of communication between the public and the authorities.[47] Similar chambers have been created in many regions. Overall, however, the pattern of interest group activity is more pluralist than corporatist because in most cases interest associations are too numerous, too weak internally, and too competitive for corporatism to succeed. But under Putin, interest articulation did become more statist as the regime gradually increased political controls on nongovernmental associations.

A law enacted at the beginning of 2006 imposed new restrictions on NGOs, making it easier for the authorities to deny them registration and to shut them down. At the same time, the authorities warned that foreign intelligence services were sponsoring Russian NGOs for the purposes of intelligence gathering and subversion. The political atmosphere for NGOs became considerably chillier.

Let us consider three examples of associational groups: the **Russian Union of Industrialists and Entrepreneurs (RUIE)**, the **League of Committees of Soldiers' Mothers**, and the **Federation of Independent Trade Unions of Russia (FITUR)**. They illustrate different strategies for organization and influence and different relationships to the state.

## The Russian Union of Industrialists and Entrepreneurs

Most formerly state-owned industrial firms are now wholly or partly privately owned. More and more industrial managers respond to the incentives of a market economy, rather than to those of a state socialist economy. Under the old regime, managers were told to fulfill the plan regardless of cost or quality. Profit was not a relevant consideration.[48] Now most managers seek to maximize profits and increase the value of their firms. Although many still demand subsidies and protection from the state, more and more want an environment where laws and contracts are enforced by the state, regulation is reasonable and honest, taxes are fair (and low), and barriers to foreign trade are minimized. These changes are visible in the political interests of the association that represents the interests of big business in Russia, the Russian Union of Industrialists and Entrepreneurs (RUIE). The RUIE

is the single most powerful organized interest group in Russia. Its membership comprises both the old state industrial firms (now mostly private or quasi-private) and new private firms and conglomerates.

In the early 1990s, the RUIE's lobbying efforts were aimed at winning continued state support of industrial firms and planning for a slow transition to a market economy. The RUIE also helped broker agreements between business and labor, and it was a source of policy advice for government and parliament. In 2000 the Putin administration let it be known that it wanted the oligarchs to join the RUIE and the RUIE to become the unified voice of big business. The Putin leadership also sponsored two other business associations to articulate the interests of small and medium-size business.

Over time the RUIE's role has changed according to the opportunities and limits set by the state authorities. In the 2000s it has been a loyal source of policy advice and political support for the government. It has expanded its in-house capacity for working with the government in drafting legislation. On a number of issues, such as tax law, pension policy, bankruptcy legislation, regulation of the securities market, and the terms of Russia's entry to the World Trade Organization, the RUIE has been active and influential in shaping policy. For the most part, it works behind the scenes to lobby for its interests, but occasionally, if it feels its voice has been ignored, it applies pressure more publicly.[49]

Yet the limits of RUIE's power as the collective voice of big business are clear. When the Putin regime began its campaign to destroy the Yukos oil firm starting in July 2003 (see Box 12.4), the RUIE confined itself to mild expressions of concern. Its members, evidently fearful of crossing Putin, chose not to defend Yukos's head, Mikhail Khodorkovsky, or to protest the use of police methods to destroy one of Russia's largest oil companies. Instead, they promised to meet their tax obligations and to do more to help the country fight poverty. Perhaps if big business had taken a strong and united stand, they could have influenced state policy. But the desire by each individual firm to maintain friendly relations with the government and the fear of government reprisals undercut big business's capacity for collective action.

## The League of Committees of Soldiers' Mothers

The Soviet regime sponsored several official women's organizations, but these mainly served propaganda purposes. During the glasnost' period, a number of unofficial women's organizations sprang up. One

BOX 12.4

## Mikhail Khodorkovsky and the Yukos Affair

One of the most widely publicized episodes of the Putin era was the state takeover of the powerful private oil company, Yukos, and the criminal prosecution of its head, Mikhail Khodorkovsky. At the time of his arrest in October 2003, Khodorkovsky was the wealthiest of Russia's new postcommunist magnates. His career began in the late 1980s when he started a bank. Later he acquired—at a bargain basement price—80 percent of the shares of the Yukos oil company when the government privatized it. At first, like some other newly wealthy tycoons, Khodorkovsky sought to squeeze maximum profit from the firm by stripping its assets. Soon his business strategy changed, and he began to invest in the firm's productive capacity. He made Yukos the most dynamic of Russia's oil companies. As he improved the efficiency and transparency of the firm, the share prices rose and, with them, Khodorkovsky's own net worth. At its peak in 2002, the company's assets were estimated at about $20 billion, of which Khodorkovsky owned nearly $8 billion.

Seeking to improve his public image, Khodorkovsky created a foundation and launched several charitable initiatives. He recruited some distinguished international figures to his foundation's board. He became active in Russian politics, helping to fund political parties and sponsoring the election campaigns of several Duma deputies. Critics accused him of wanting to control parliament and even of wanting to change the constitution to turn it into a parliamentary system. There was talk that he intended to seek the presidency.

By spring 2003, the Putin administration decided that Khodorkovsky and Yukos had grown too independent. In a series of actions, several top figures in Yukos and associated companies were arrested and charged with fraud, embezzlement, tax evasion, and even murder. In December 2003, the government began issuing claims against the company for billions of dollars in back taxes and froze the company's bank accounts as collateral against the claims. When Yukos failed to pay the full tax bill, the government seized its main production subsidiary and auctioned it off to a firm that, three days later, sold it to Russia's only state-owned oil company, Rosneft'. In October 2003 Khodorkovsky was arrested and charged with fraud and tax evasion. In May 2004 he was sentenced to nine years' imprisonment and sent to a prison camp in Siberia. In 2006 the last remnants of the company were forced into bankruptcy.

Whatever the regime's motives—political, economic, or both—the Yukos affair shows that the authorities are willing to manipulate the legal system for political purposes when it suits them and that the fight to redistribute control of Russia's natural resource assets remains a driving force in politics.

---

such group was the Committee of Soldiers' Mothers. It formed in the spring of 1989 when some 300 women in Moscow rallied to protest the end of student deferments from military conscription. Their protest came hard on the heels of Gorbachev's withdrawal of Soviet forces from the decade-long war in Afghanistan, where over 13,000 Soviet troops were killed in bitter and demoralizing fighting. In response to the Soldiers' Mothers' actions, Gorbachev agreed to restore student deferments. Since then the Soldiers' Mothers' movement has grown, with local branches forming in hundreds of cities and joining together in the League of Committees of Soldiers' Mothers. Their focus has expanded somewhat, but remains centered on the problems of military service. The league presses the military to end the brutal hazing of recruits, which results in the deaths (in many cases by suicide) of hundreds of soldiers each year. The league also advises young men on how to avoid being conscripted.[50]

The onset of large-scale hostilities in Chechnia in 1994–1996 and 1999–2000 stimulated a new burst of activity by the league. It helped families locate soldiers who were missing in action or captured by the Chechen rebel forces. It sent missions to Chechnia to negotiate for the release of prisoners and to provide proper burial for the dead. It collected information about the actual scale of the war and of its casualties. It also continued to lobby for decent treatment of recruits. Through the 1990s it became one of the most sizeable and respected civic groups in Russia. It can call on a network of thousands of active volunteers for its work. These volunteers visit wounded soldiers in hospitals and help military authorities identify casualties. One of the movement's greatest assets is its members' moral authority as mothers defending the interests of their children. This stance makes it hard for their opponents to paint them as unpatriotic.

The league plays both a public political role (for instance, it lobbied to liberalize the law on alternative civil service for conscientious objectors, and it fights for an end to the brutality in the treatment of servicemen[51]) and a role as service provider. Much of its effort is spent on helping soldiers and their families deal with their problems.

Like many NGOs, the League of Committees of Soldiers' Mothers cultivates ties with counterpart organizations abroad, and it has won international recognition for its work. For some groups such ties are a source of dependence, as organizations compensate for the lack of mass membership with aid and know-how from counterpart organizations abroad. However, the league enjoys a stable base of public support in Russia. Its international ties have also probably helped protect the group in the face of the sometimes hostile attitude of the authorities.[52]

## The Federation of Independent Trade Unions of Russia

The Federation of Independent Trade Unions of Russia (FITUR) is the successor of the official trade union federation under the Soviet regime. Unlike the RUIE, however, it has poorly adapted itself to the postcommunist environment, even though it inherited substantial organizational resources from the old Soviet trade union organization. In the Soviet era, virtually every employed person belonged to a trade union. All branch and regional trade union organizations were part of a single labor federation, called the All-Union Central Council of Trade Unions. With the breakdown of the old regime, some of the member unions became independent, while other unions sprang up as independent bodies representing the interests of particular groups of workers. Nonetheless, the nucleus of the old official trade union organization survived in the form of the FITUR. It remains by far the largest trade union federation in Russia. Around 95 percent of all organized workers belong to unions that are, at least formally, members of the FITUR. The independent unions are much smaller. By comparison with big business, however, the labor movement is fragmented, weak, and unable to mobilize workers effectively for collective action.

The FITUR inherited valuable real estate assets from its Soviet-era predecessor organization, including thousands of office buildings, hotels, rest homes, hospitals, and children's camps. It also inherited the right to collect workers' contributions for the state social insurance fund. Control of this fund enabled the official trade unions to acquire enormous amounts of income-generating property over the years. These assets and income streams give leaders of the official unions considerable advantages in competing for members. But the FITUR no longer has centralized control over its regional and branch members. In the 1993 and 1995 parliamentary elections, for instance, member unions formed their own political alliances with parties. Thus, internal disunity is another major reason for the relative weakness of the FITUR as an organization. Much of its effort is expended in fighting independent unions to win a monopoly on representing workers in collective bargaining with employers, rather than in joining with other unions to defend the interests of workers generally.[53]

The ineffectiveness of the FITUR is also illustrated by the tepid response of organized labor to the severe deterioration in labor and social conditions in the 1990s, when there was much less labor protest than might have been expected. There were some strikes and protests, mainly over wage arrears. Surveys found that in any given year in the 1990s three-quarters of all workers received their wages late at least once.[54] Teachers were particularly hard hit by the problem of unpaid wages. Waves of strikes by teachers shut down thousands of schools in the late 1990s. After 1999 strikes subsided as the economy began to recover. Recent research shows that much of the labor protest was actually organized not by the unions, but by governors seeking to pressure the central government for more money.[55]

Why are unions so weak? One reason is that workers depend on the enterprises where they work for a variety of social benefits that are administered through the enterprise, such as housing, recreation facilities, and medical and day care services.[56] Another, however, is the close relationship between the leadership of the FITUR and government authorities. As a result, it is very difficult for labor to mount collective actions. Workers generally feel unrepresented by their unions.[57]

## New Sectors of Interest

In a time when people's interests are changing rapidly, interest groups search for new roles. Some old groups decline, while new organizations form. In Russia many new associations have formed around the interests of new categories of actors. Bankers, political consultants, realtors, mayors of small cities, mayors of large cities, judges, attorneys, auditors, television broadcasters, political consultants, and numerous other professional and occupational groups have formed associations to seek favorable policies or set professional standards. Environmental groups, women's organizations, human rights activists, and many other cause-oriented groups have organized. Most of these operate in a particular locality, but a few have national scope.

The rules of the game for interest articulation changed sharply after the Soviet regime fell and are continuing to change as the postcommunist regime redefines the framework for relations between state and society. In the Yeltsin period, lobbying frequently took corrupt forms, including bribery of parliamentary deputies and government officials. By the end of the 1990s, more collective action by business and other sectors of interest was evident, and there was more open bargaining over the details of policy. In the 2000s, however, policymaking is more centralized again, and interest groups are more dependent on the goodwill of the authorities for their ability to operate. The authorities have created corporatist structures such as the Public Chamber for consultation between the state and civil society and have tightened controls over NGOs. Still, interest articulation is mainly pluralistic, with tens of thousands of nonstate associations competing to voice their interests through the mass media, the parliament, and the government. Despite the political controls, public pressure expressed through interest groups does have some impact on policymaking.

## PARTIES AND THE AGGREGATION OF INTERESTS

Interest aggregation refers to the process by which the demands of various groups of a society are pooled to form programmatic options for government. Although other institutions also aggregate interests, in most countries political parties are the quintessential structure performing this vital task. How well parties aggregate interests, define choices for voters, and hold politicians accountable is of critical importance to democracy.

Although Russia's party system in the 1990s was fluid and fragmented, a clear structure has emerged in the 2000s in which the United Russia party dominates, while other parties are marginal. In the 1990s there was considerable turnover in the parties from one election to the next. Voters had little sense of attachment to parties and more often associated them with particular politicians' personalities than with specific ideological stances. Most parties had very weak roots in society, although parties guided the work of the State Duma through their parliamentary factions.[58]

Russia's party system has undergone a major transformation in the 2000s. The authorities have succeeded in creating a single party that dominates elections. Russians term such a party a **party of power**, indicating that the party serves the collective interests of those holding office: For them it is a vehicle for career advancement, while for the voters it is the electoral face of the state. In the 1990s there were several short-lived attempts to form parties of power, but in the 2000s the United Russia party has become *the* unquestioned party of power. United Russia presently casts such a long and commanding shadow over the political system that some observers believe that the Kremlin seeks to turn it into a replica of the ruling Communist Party of the Soviet era.

Political parties tend to be prominent in national and regional legislative elections, but much less so in presidential elections. Because Russia's presidential system encourages the president to avoid making commitments to parties, presidential races usually concentrate attention on the candidates' personalities, rather than on their policy programs. Moreover, the fact that the winning party in parliament does not form the government tends to undercut politicians' loyalty to parties. Instead, the Kremlin uses parties to control politicians' careers and to build legitimacy for its power by winning elections.

### Elections and Party Development

Table 12.1 indicates the official results of the party-list voting in the 1993, 1995, 1999, 2003, and 2007 elections. The table groups parties into five categories that have characterized party identities since the early 1990s: *democratic* (those espousing liberal democratic principles), *leftist* (those advocating socialist and statist values), *centrist* (those mixing leftist and liberal democratic appeals), *nationalist* (those highlighting ethnic nationalism, patriotism, and imperialism), and *parties of power.*

## Patry-List Vote in Duma Elections Since 1993                    TABLE 12.1

Support for United Russia has grown at the expense of support for democratic, Communist, and nationalist parties

| Party | 1993 | 1995 | 1999 | 2003 | 2007 |
|---|---|---|---|---|---|
| **Democratic Parties** | | | | | |
| Russia's Choice | 15.5 | 3.9 | — | — | — |
| Union of Rightist Forces (SPS) | — | — | 8.5 | 4.0 | 0.9 |
| Yabloko | 7.8 | 6.8 | 5.9 | 4.3 | 1.5 |
| Party of Russian Unity and Concord (PRES) | 6.7 | — | — | — | — |
| Democratic Party of Russia (DPR) | 5.5 | — | — | 0.2 | 0.1 |
| **Centrist Parties** | | | | | |
| Women of Russia | 8.1 | 4.6 | 2.0 | — | — |
| Civic Union[a] | 1.9 | 1.6 | — | — | — |
| **Parties of Power** | | | | | |
| Our Home Is Russia | — | 10.1 | 1.2 | — | — |
| Fatherland—All Russia (OVR) | — | — | 13.3 | — | — |
| Unity/United Russia[b] | — | — | 23.3 | 38.2 | 64.3 |
| A Just Russia | — | — | — | — | 7.7 |
| **Nationalist Parties** | | | | | |
| Liberal Democratic Party of Russia (LDPR)[c] | 22.9 | 11.2 | 5.9 | 11.6 | 8.1 |
| Congress of Russian Communities (KRO)[d] | — | 4.3 | 0.6 | — | — |
| Motherland (Rodina) | — | — | — | 9.2 | — |
| **Leftist Parties** | | | | | |
| Communist Party of the Russian Federation (CPRF) | 12.4 | 22.3 | 24.2 | 12.8 | 11.5 |
| Agrarian Party | 7.9 | 3.8 | — | 3.6 | 2.3 |
| Other parties failing to meet 5% threshold | 10.9 | 26.8 | 12.5 | 11.1 | 2.1 |
| Against all[e] | 4.3 | 2.8 | 3.3 | 4.7 | — |

[a]In 1995 the same alliance renamed itself the Bloc of Trade Unionists and Industrialists.
[b]In 2003 Unity ran under the name United Russia, following a merger with the Fatherland party.
[c]In 1999 the LDPR party list was called the Zhirinovsky bloc.
[d]In 1999 this party was called Congress of Russian Communities and Yuri Boldyrev Movement.
[e]In 2007 the "Against all" option was not available.
Source: Compiled by author from reports of Central Electoral Commission. See http://cikrf.ru.

Figure 12.6 shows how the election results translated into the distribution of seats in the Duma to various party factions following the 1999, 2003, and 2007 elections. Note how the spectrum of parliamentary parties has dwindled as United Russia has come to occupy a dominant position. It has been aided by some strategic engineering of the electoral system that has included tightening the rules for party registration, raising the threshold for representation from 5 percent to 7 percent, switching to an all-PR Duma, and prohibiting deputies from leaving their factions without losing their seats. Above all, the increasing use of electoral fraud to ensure overwhelming victories for United Russia has padded its margin. In the nearly twenty years since contested elections first were held, the party system has evolved from being one with many weakly supported parties to an authoritarian dominant party system.[59]

## From the Multiparty System to the Dominant Party Regime

The multiparty system arose with the elections under Gorbachev to the reformed Soviet and Russian Republic parliaments. Democratically oriented politicians coalesced to defeat Communist Party officials in the 1989 and 1990 elections and, once elected, formed

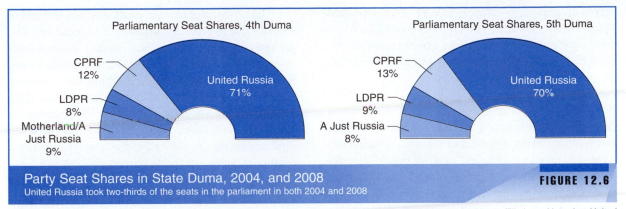

Party Seat Shares in State Duma, 2004, and 2008
United Russia took two-thirds of the seats in the parliament in both 2004 and 2008

**FIGURE 12.6**

Notes: Figures taken as of May 2004 and January 2008. Percentages shift with time as members change factional affiliations. Note that United Russia was the result of a merger of the Fatherland Pary and United and that. A Just Russia formed in 2006 from the merger of Motherland, the Pensioners' Party, and the Party of Life.

Source: Compiled by author from reports of State Duma.

legislative caucuses in parliament. There they fought with Communist, nationalist, and agrarian groups. These parliamentary factions became the nuclei of political parties in the parliamentary election of December 1993.

***Polarization and the Party System*** Elections in the late 1980s and early 1990s were aligned around two poles, one associated with Yeltsin and the forces pushing for democracy and a market economy, the other fighting to preserve the old system based on state ownership and control of the economy. Other parties positioned themselves in relation to these poles. For instance, Vladimir Zhirinovsky's nationalistic **Liberal Democratic Party of Russia (LDPR)** claimed to offer an alternative to both the democrats and the Communists, appealing to xenophobia, authoritarianism, and the nostalgia for empire. The party's unexpectedly strong showing in the 1993 election was a signal of widespread popular discontent with the Yeltsin economic reforms.

The main anchor of the left (statist and socialist) pole of the spectrum has been the Communists (**Communist Party of the Russian Federation**, or **CPRF**), who are the heirs of the old ruling Communist Party of the Soviet Union and who espouse a mixture of communist and nationalist principles.

On the right, or pro-market and pro-democracy, side of the spectrum have been several parties whose fortunes have fallen dramatically since the 1990s. One of these is *Yabloko*. Yabloko has consistently defended democratic principles and a social democratic policy

in the economy and has opposed some of the policies pursued by Yeltsin and Putin that have sought to dismantle most of the old state supports and controls in the economy. It is no longer represented in the Duma because it has failed to attract enough votes to clear the 7 percent threshold.

Elections in the early to mid-1990s reflected the polarization between democrats and Communists, but also tended to produce a fragmented field of parties. In the 1993 and 1995 Duma elections, neither pro-democracy parties nor Communists won a clear majority, although democrats were in the minority, while Communists, nationalists, and their allies had a majority of seats. Except for a few parties (the CPRF, the LDPR, and Yabloko), most parties had shallow roots and tended to spring up shortly before elections. Many sought to avoid taking a clear programmatic stance, instead claiming to be "centrists" and pragmatists who would steer between the opposing poles of the democrats and Communists.

Presidential elections have not tended to stimulate party development as much as parliamentary elections have because they have revolved more around the personalities of the candidates. When Boris Yeltsin ran for reelection in 1996, he started out with an approval rating in the single digits (and even considered canceling the election at one point), but ultimately rallied his strength and succeeded in persuading voters that the election was about a choice between him and a return to communism. Yeltsin's displays of vigor during the campaign, his lavish promises to voters, and his domination of the media all contributed to a surge in popularity and a victory over Gennadii Ziuganov, his Communist rival (see Table 12.2).[60] The campaign took its toll on Yeltsin, however. Soon afterward he had major heart surgery, and for much of his second term, he was in poor health.

***Building the Party of Power*** The 1999 election was dominated by the question of who would succeed Yeltsin as president. Many federal and regional officeholders wanted to rally around a new "party of power" in order to protect their jobs. A group of backroom Kremlin strategists formed a movement called Unity in the late summer of 1999. They wanted to create an electoral bloc that state officials throughout the country could rally around in the race for the Duma. They also intended it to serve as a political vehicle for Vladimir Putin, whom Yeltsin had just named prime minister and anointed as his successor. Conveniently for Putin, within days of Unity's formation and Putin's appointment, Chechen rebels launched raids into the neighboring region of Dagestan. Bombings of apartment buildings—officially blamed on Chechen terrorists—also occurred in Moscow and other cities. Putin's decisive handling of the military operations against the Chechen guerrillas gave him and the Unity movement a major boost in popularity. Unity, which had not even existed until late August, won 23 percent of the party-list vote in December.

The presidential election of 2000 occurred ahead of schedule due to President Yeltsin's early resignation. Under the constitution the prime minister automatically succeeds the president if the president leaves office early, but new elections must be held within three months. Accordingly, the presidential election was scheduled for March 26, 2000. The early election gave the front-runner and incumbent, Putin, an advantage because he could capitalize on his popularity and the country's desire for continuity. Putin ran the Russian equivalent of a "rose garden" campaign, preferring to be seen handling the normal daily business of a president, rather than going out on the hustings and asking for people's votes. He counted on the support of officeholders at all levels, a media campaign that presented a "presidential" image to the voters, and the voters' fear that change would only make life worse. His rivals, moreover, were weak. Several prominent politicians prudently chose not to run against him. Putin's strategy worked brilliantly: He won an outright majority in the first round (see Table 12.3).

***The 2003 and 2004 Elections*** Under Putin the ideological divide between Communists and democrats that had marked the transition era disappeared. The political arena was dominated by the president and his supporters. The loyal pro-Putin party Unity was renamed United Russia after it absorbed a rival party, Fatherland (headed by Moscow mayor Yuri Luzhkov). United

---

**Presidential Election, 1996**    **TABLE 12.2**

Yeltsin edged out the Communist candidate in the first round and then won decisively in the second round.

|  | First Round (June 16, 1996) | Second Round (July 3, 1996) |
|---|---|---|
| Boris Yeltsin | 35.2% | 53.8% |
| Gennadii Ziuganov | 32.0 | 40.3 |
| Alexander Lebed | 14.5 | — |
| Grigorii Yavlinskii | 7.3 | — |
| Vladimir Zhirinovsky | 5.7 | — |
| Svyatoslav Fedorov | 0.9 | — |
| Mikhail Gorbachev | 0.5 | — |
| Martin Shakkum | 0.3 | — |
| Yurii Vlasov | 0.2 | — |
| Vladimir Bryntsalov | 0.1 | — |
| Aman Tuleev | 0.0 | — |
| Against all candidates | 1.5 | 4.8 |

---

**Russian Presidential Elections in the 2000s**    **TABLE 12.3**

Putin and Medvedev won in the first round by wide margins in each race

|  | 2000 | 2004 | 2008 |
|---|---|---|---|
| Vladimir Putin | 52.9 | 71.3 | — |
| Gennadii Ziuganov (CPRF) | 29.2 | — | 17.7 |
| Vladimir Zhirinovsky (LDPR) | 2.7 | — | 9.3 |
| Grigorii Yavlinskii (Yabloko) | 5.8 | — | — |
| Nikolai Kharitonov (CPRF) | — | 13.7 | — |
| Dmitrii Medvedev | — | — | 70.2 |
| Andrei Bogdanov (DPR) | — | — | 1.3 |
| Other | 6.5 | 10.7 | — |
| Against all candidates | 1.8 | 3.4 | — |

Legend: CPRF: Communist Party of the Russian Federation; LDPR: Liberal Democratic Party of Russia; DPR: Democratic Party of Russia.

Note: The "Against all candidates" option was not available on the 2008 ballot.

Gennadii Ziuganov rallies the Communist Party faithful under a portrait of Vladimir Lenin at a November 1998 anniversary celebration of the October Revolution.

Alexander Natruskin/Reuters

Russia held a near monopoly in the party spectrum, squeezing other parties to the margins. A series of changes in the electoral law made it increasingly difficult for all but a few parties to compete in elections, while the Kremlin mounted a major effort to pressure regional governors and big business to back United Russia.

The Kremlin's success in making United Russia the dominant party was demonstrated vividly in the 2003 parliamentary election. United Russia won 38 percent of the party-list vote and wound up with two-thirds of the seats in the Duma. The Communists suffered a severe blow, losing almost half their vote share, and the democrats did even worse. For the first time, none of the democratic parties won seats on the party-list vote. The result underscored Putin's drive to eliminate any meaningful political opposition. Such an impressive showing for United Russia assured Putin's reelection as president. The March 2004 race was a landslide. Putin

won easily with 71.3 percent of the vote, while his Communist rival received less than 14 percent of the vote (see Table 12.3). European observers commented that the elections were "well administered," but hardly constituted "a genuine democratic contest" in view of the president's overwhelming control of media coverage of the race and the absence of genuine competition.[61]

United Russia's dominance was confirmed in the 2007 Duma election. Shortly before the election, Putin declared that he would head the party's list (though he said he would not join the party and he did not intend to take his Duma seat).[62] This indicated that Putin intended to use the party as a basis for his power even after he left the presidency. Even though the Kremlin created a second party of power (called A Just Russia) as a mechanism to siphon off some votes on the left side of the spectrum and to offer an alternative outlet for some politicians who could not be accommodated in United Russia, United Russia's overwhelming success was never in doubt, and it went on to win 64.3 percent of the vote. The authorities used a variety of methods to manipulate the election, ranging from grossly unequal access to the media for the parties to outright falsification of results in many regions (in some districts, the reported vote for United Russia was greater than 100 percent of the registered voters).[63]

Similarly, the authorities took no chances in the 2008 presidential election. Again, they violated numerous provisions of the law in order to guarantee the desired outcome—for example, by disqualifying potentially serious opposition candidates, pouring large resources from the state budget into Medvedev's campaign, giving Medvedev disproportionate media coverage, and ignoring challenges brought by opposition groups and election rights NGOs over violations of the election law. Medvedev would probably have won in any case, but the large-scale manipulation of the election signaled to voters and opponents alike that the authorities were in complete control of the succession. The authorities managed the outcome so successfully that Medvedev officially won over 70 percent of the vote—about 1 percentage point below Putin's reported margin in 2004 (see Table 12.3).

The establishment of the dominant party regime has changed the way parties represent different social groups. In the 1990s there were some systematic links between particular social groups and particular parties. For instance, younger and better educated voters tended to support the democratic parties, while older and less educated voters supported Communist and nationalist parties. But as the United Russia party has gained dominance, it has appealed to all parts of the society. As a result, social structure has become less and less significant as an influence on voting, while voters' attitudes toward the authorities in general and toward Putin in particular have become the most important predictor of voting preferences.

Table 12.4 indicates that voters of all camps tend to see United Russia as the embodiment of President Putin's political legacy. The challenge for United Russia in the future will be to establish a basis of support that goes beyond simply its identification with Putin. The party will need to cultivate more lasting attachments based on its ability to deliver policy benefits to the voters. Putin and other Kremlin officials have warned the party that it cannot hope to feed off the Kremlin's life-support system forever—though they are unwilling to cut it loose.

For other parties the 2007–2008 elections confirmed the new reality that United Russia is likely to enjoy a dominant position for years to come. Other parties have been relegated to playing a small, marginal role in national politics and concentrating their efforts on winning seats in regional parliaments.

## THE POLITICS OF ECONOMIC REFORM

### The Dual Transition

Russia's postcommunist transition was wrenching because the country had to remake both its *political* and its *economic* institutions following the end of communism. The move to a market economy created opportunities for some—and hardships for many more. Democratization opened the political system to the influence of groups that could organize to press for exclusive economic benefits for themselves. Many people who had modest, but secure livelihoods under the Soviet regime were ruined by inflation and unemployment when the planned economy broke down. A smaller number took advantage of opportunities for entrepreneurship or exploited their connections with government to amass sizeable fortunes. One reason Vladimir Putin was so popular was that people gave him credit for restoring growth and prosperity to the economy and cracking down on some of the tycoons who had amassed great fortunes by dubious means.

*Stabilization* Russia pursued two major sets of economic reforms in the early 1990s, macroeconomic

| Grounds for Support of United Russia — Support for United Russia strongly reflects attitudes toward Vladimir Putin | TABLE 12.4 |
| --- | --- |
| Wanted to support Putin | 46% |
| I like this party, I trust it | 32 |
| I don't especially like this party, but the others are even worse | 3 |
| I wanted to vote the same way as everyone else | 2 |
| I was forced to vote for it but I didn't especially want to | <1 |
| Other | <1 |
| Hard to answer | 15 |

Source: All-Russian Center for the Study of Public Opinion (VTsIOM), "Political Attitudes and the Vote for United Russia," Press Release No. 840, December 19, 2007. Retrieved July 11, 2008, from wciom.ru/arkhiv/tematicheskii-arkhiv/item/single/9406.html (survey conducted December 8–9, 2007; N = 1,600).

stabilization and privatization. Stabilization, which in Russia came to be called **shock therapy**, is a program intended to stop a country's financial meltdown. This required a painful dose of fiscal and monetary discipline by slashing government spending and squeezing the money supply. Structural reform of this kind always lowers the standard of living for some groups of the population in the short run.

Initially, many expected that the greatest enemies of stabilization would be those whose living standards suffered as a result of the higher prices and lower incomes, such as workers in state enterprises and pensioners. In practice, however, those who benefited from the early steps to open the economy and privatize state assets proved to be the greatest obstacles to further reform because they exploited their privileged access to the authorities to lock in their own gains and to oppose any subsequent measures to expand competition. Among these were officials who acquired ownership rights to monopoly enterprises and then worked to shut out potential competitors from their markets, state officials who benefited from collecting "fees" to issue licenses to importers and exporters or permits for doing business, and entrepreneurs whose firms dominated the market in their industry.[64] A fully competitive market system, with a level playing field for all players, would have posed a threat to their ability to profit from their privileged positions.

***From Communism to Capitalism*** Communist systems differed from other authoritarian regimes in ways that made their economic transitions more difficult. This was particularly true for the Soviet Union and its successor states. For one, the economic growth model followed by Stalin and his successors concentrated much production in large enterprises. This meant that many local governments were entirely dependent on the economic health of a single employer. The heavy commitment of resources to military production in the Soviet Union further complicated the task of reform in Russia, as does the country's vast size. Rebuilding the decaying infrastructure of a country as large as Russia is staggeringly expensive.

The economic stabilization program began on January 2, 1992, when the government abolished most controls on prices, raised taxes, and cut government spending sharply. Almost immediately, opposition to the new program began to form. Economists and politicians took sides. The shock therapy program was an easy target for criticism, even though there was no consensus among critics about what the alternative should be. It became commonplace to say that the program was all shock and no therapy.

By cutting government spending, letting prices rise, and raising taxes, the stabilization program sought to create incentives for producers to increase output and find new niches in the marketplaces. But Russian producers did not initially respond by raising productivity. As a result, society suffered from a sharp, sudden loss in purchasing power. People went hungry, bank savings vanished, and the economy fell into a protracted slump. Firms that were politically connected were able to survive by winning cheap credits and production orders from the government, which dampened any incentive for improving productivity. Desperate to raise operating revenues, the government borrowed heavily from the International Monetary Fund (IMF) and issued treasury bonds at ruinously high interest rates. IMF loans came with strings attached—the government pledged to cut spending further and step up tax collections as a condition of accepting IMF assistance, which fueled the depression further. Communists and nationalists got a rise out of audiences by depicting the government as the puppet of a malevolent, imperialist West.

***Privatization*** Stabilization was followed shortly afterward by the mass **privatization** of state firms. In contrast to the shock therapy program, privatization enjoyed considerable public support, at least at first.

Privatization transfers legal title of state firms to private owners. Under the right conditions, private ownership of productive assets is usually more efficient for society as a whole than is state ownership because in a competitive environment owners are motivated by an incentive to maximize their property's ability to produce a return. Under the privatization program, every Russian citizen received a voucher with a face value of 10,000 rubles (around $30 at the time). People were free to buy and sell vouchers, but they could be used only to acquire shares of stock in privatized enterprises or shares of mutual funds investing in privatized enterprises. The program sought to ensure that everyone became a property owner instantly. Politically, the program aimed to build support for the economic reforms by giving citizens a stake in the outcome of the market transition. Economically, the government hoped that privatization would eventually spur increases in productivity by creating meaningful property rights. Beginning in October 1992, the program distributed 148 million privatization vouchers to citizens. By June 30, 1994, when the program ended, 140 million vouchers had been exchanged for stock out of the 148 million originally distributed. Some 40 million citizens were, in theory, share owners. But these shares were often of no value because they paid no dividends and shareholders exercised no voting rights in the companies.

The next phase of privatization auctioned off most remaining shares of state enterprises for cash. This phase was marked by a series of scandalous sweetheart deals in which banks owned by a small number of Russia's wealthiest tycoons wound up with title to some of Russia's most lucrative oil, gas, and metallurgy firms for bargain basement prices. The most notorious of these arrangements became known as the **loans for shares** scheme. It was devised in 1995 by a small group of business magnates with strong connections to government who persuaded Yeltsin to auction off management rights to controlling packages of shares in several major state-owned companies in return for loans to the government. If the government failed to repay the loans in a year's time, the shares would revert to the banks that made the loans. The government, as expected, defaulted on the loans, letting a small number of oligarchs acquire ownership of some of Russia's most valuable companies.[65]

***Consequences of Privatization*** On paper, privatization was a huge success. By 1996 privatized firms produced about 90 percent of industrial output, and about two-thirds of all large and medium-sized enterprises had been privatized.[66] In fact, however, the actual transfer of ownership rights was far less impressive than it appeared. For one thing, the dominant pattern was for managers to acquire large shareholdings of the firms they ran. As a result, management of many firms did not change. Moreover, many nominally private firms continued to be closely tied to state support, such as cheap state-subsidized loans and credits.[67]

The program allowed a great many unscrupulous wheeler-dealers to prey on the public through a variety of financial schemes. Some investment funds promised truly incredible rates of return. Many people lost their savings by investing in funds that went bankrupt or turned out to be simple pyramid schemes. The Russian government lacked the capacity to protect the investors. Privatization was carried out before the institutional framework of a market economy was in place. Markets for stocks, bonds, and commodities were small in scale and weakly regulated. The legal foundation for a market economy has gradually emerged, but only after much of the economy was already privatized. For much of the 1990s, the lack of liquidity in the economy meant that enterprises failed to pay their wages and taxes on time, trading with one another using barter.

The government fell into an unsustainable debt trap. Unable to meet its obligations, it grew increasingly dependent on loans. As lenders became increasingly certain that the government could not make good on its obligations, they demanded ever higher interest rates, deepening the trap. Ultimately, the bubble burst. In August 1998, the government declared a moratorium on its debts and let the ruble's value collapse against the dollar. Overnight the ruble lost two-thirds of its value, and credit dried up.[68] The government bonds held by investors were almost worthless. The effects of the crash rippled through the economy. The sharp devaluation of the ruble made exports more competitive and gave an impetus to domestic producers, but also significantly lowered people's living standards.

As Table 12.5 shows, economic output in Russia fell for a decade before beginning to recover in 1999. The recovery was not due to a structural reform of the economy. There has not been a substantial overhaul of the banking system or of the way industry is managed. The economy is still vulnerable to a downturn in the international economic situation because Russia remains highly dependent on exports of natural resources: Oil and gas make up over half of Russian exports and a fifth of Russian gross domestic product (GDP).[69] Still, a number of branches besides energy are showing real vigor—among them, construction and retail trade. Following the 1998 crash, several sectors (such as agriculture) got a boost from the drop in the ruble's exchange value as their prices became competitive and imported products became more expensive. As the economy revived, enterprises were able to pay off arrears in back wages and taxes. In turn, these taxes allowed government to meet its own obligations, in turn allowing consumer demand for industry's products to rise, and so on. These trends have raised living standards noticeably.

Unemployment has fallen since the August 1998 crisis, and the number of people living in poverty has declined by over one-third, from over 30 percent to under 20 percent. The leaders have expressed satisfaction with the favorable trends in the economy, but warn that they are not sufficient to achieve sustained and balanced development. Both Putin and Medvedev have called for reducing the economy's reliance on natural resource exports and increasing its capacity for innovation. However, some of Putin's actions—such as the renationalization of a number of firms and the creation of large state-owned holding companies—tended to

---

## Russian Annual GDP Growth and Price Inflation Rates, 1991–2007    TABLE 12.5
Russa has enjoyed sustained growth in the 2000s, after a dismal decade in the 1990s

|  | 1991 | 1992 | 1993 | 1994 | 1995 | 1996 | 1997 | 1998 | 1999 | 2000 | 2001 | 2002 | 2003 | 2004 | 2005 | 2006 | 2007 |
|---|---|---|---|---|---|---|---|---|---|---|---|---|---|---|---|---|---|
| GDP | −5 | −14.5 | −8.7 | −12.6 | −4.3 | −6 | 0.4 | −11.6 | 3.2 | 7.6 | 5 | 4 | 7.3 | 7.1 | 6.4 | 7.4 | 8.1 |
| Inflation | 138 | 2323 | 844 | 202 | 131 | 21.8 | 11 | 84.4 | 36.5 | 20.2 | 18.6 | 15.1 | 12 | 11.7 | 10.9 | 9 | 11.9 |

Note: GDP is measured in constant market prices. Inflation is measured as the percentage change in the consumer price index from December of one year to December of the next.

Source: Press reports of Russian State Statistical Service (www.gks.ru).

undermine incentives for raising productivity. The narrowness of the foundation on which Russia's recovery was based became acutely evident when the world economic crisis struck in 2008–2009. Russia's stock market lost three-quarters of its value in half a year. Credit markets froze up and industrial production plummeted. Unemployment rose. Revenues from energy exports fell sharply. Fears of social unrest spread. The crisis demonstrated how vulnerable Russia was to changes in world financial and energy markets.

*Social Conditions* Living standards fell sharply during the 1990s. A small minority became wealthy, and some households improved their lot modestly. Most people, however, suffered a net decline in living standards as a result of unemployment, lagging income, and nonpayment of wages and pensions.

Income inequality grew sharply both during the period of economic decline in the 1990s and again during the period of economic recovery in the 2000s. This has been caused by many factors. In the 1990s it was the result of the lag of wage increases behind price inflation, the sharp rise in unemployment, the deterioration of the pension and other social assistance systems, and the concentration of vast wealth in the hands of a small number of people. In the 2000s poverty has decreased significantly, along with unemployment, and pension levels have risen. Yet, inequality continues to rise as a result of large disparities in wage levels (two workers in the same occupation and in the same region might have widely different wages depending on where they work),[70] the extremely high earnings of managers in industries such as energy and finance, and the Putin regime's shift to a flat (13%) income tax and abolition of estate taxes. As a result of both government policy and current economic trends, therefore, economic prosperity is benefiting those at the upper end of the income distribution much more than it is those at the lower end. This helps explain the sharp rise in the number of Russian billionaires. According to *Forbes Magazine*'s list, the number of billionaires in Russia shot up from 60 to 110 between 2007 and 2008.[71] Something like twelve of them have seats in the Federation Council.[72]

One commonly used measure of inequality is the Gini index, which is an aggregate measure of the total deviation from perfect equality in the distribution of wealth or income. In Russia the Gini index nearly doubled during the early 1990s, rising from 26 in 1987–1990 to 48 in 1993–1994. Inequality in Russia was higher than in any other postcommunist country except for Kyrgyzstan.[73] As the economy began to recover and poverty fell, the Gini index declined slightly, to just under 40, before creeping back up in the mid-2000s to over 40 (approximately equal to the level of income inequality in the United States). In 2006 the richest tenth of the population in Russia received 15.3 times as much income as did the poorest tenth, up from 14 times in 2002. The actual level of income inequality is probably considerably greater than the official figure because of the large scale of unreported, "off-book" income due to tax evasion.

The continuing rise in inequality and the absence of a growing middle class constitute a matter of some concern to Russian leaders. In his address to the State Council on February 8, 2008, President Putin declared that the current level of income inequality was "absolutely unacceptable" and should be reduced to more moderate levels; he called for measures that would bring about an expansion of the middle class. Its share of the population, he declared, should reach 60 or even 70 percent by 2020.[74]

An especially disturbing dimension of the social effects of transition has been the erosion of public health. Although public health had deteriorated in the late Communist period, the decline worsened after the regime changed. Mortality rates have risen sharply, especially among males. Life expectancy for males in Russia is at a level comparable to that in poor and developing countries. At present, life expectancy at birth for males is just under fifty-nine years and for females seventy-two years. The disparity between male and female mortality—enormous by world standards—is generally attributed to the higher rates of abuse of alcohol and tobacco among men. Other demographic indicators are equally grim. Prime Minister Fradkov told a Cabinet meeting in July 2006 that only 30 percent of newborn children "can be described as healthy" and that "there are more than 500,000 disabled children in need of various forms of treatment, and also some 730,000 orphans or abandoned children."[75] Rates of incidence of HIV and other infectious diseases, murders, suicides, drug addiction, and alcoholism are rising.

Russia's leaders consider the demographic crisis to pose a grave threat to the country's national security both because of the growing shortage of labor in some regions (experts believe that there are 12 or 14 million illegal immigrants in Russia, about the same number as in the United States) and because of the army's inability to recruit enough healthy young men.[76] Every year Russia's population declines by about three-quarters of a million people due to the excess of deaths over births. Demographers estimate that Russia's population could fall by over one-third by 2050. In his 2006 message to parliament, President Putin called for a series of measures to raise birthrates, reduce mortality, and stimulate immigration.

Setting the country on a path of self-sustaining economic growth, where workers and investors are confident in their legal rights, requires a complete overhaul of the relationship of the state to the economy. The Soviet state used central planning to direct enterprises on what to produce and how to use resources. Much of the economy was geared to heavy industry and defense production, and government ministries directly administered each branch of the economy. The postcommunist state must have an entirely different relationship to the economy in order to stimulate growth. It must set clear rules for economic activity, regulate markets, enforce the law, supply public goods and services, and promote competition. Shifting the structure of the state bureaucracy and the attitudes of state officials has been a Herculean task.

We can get some idea of the legacy of the communist system in the way the state was intertwined with the economy by looking at the structure of the state budget. Figure 12.7 shows the breakdown of spending for the 2007 federal budget. Total spending was set at 5.4 trillion rubles, or about US$220 billion. The share spent on national defense (at 15%) probably understates the actual amount. The shares of spending on general administration (15%), law enforcement (12%), and subsidies to various regional development funds (34%) are high, compared with other countries, and indicate how substantial the central government's role is in state and society. Over half the government's revenues come from oil and gas revenues, a degree of dependence on resource rents that Russia's government knows to be unhealthy over the long term.[77]

The government also recognizes that the oil- and gas-fueled budget surpluses pose a serious danger of creating inflationary pressures in the economy. For this reason, like some other oil-rich states, Russia has created a "stabilization fund" that removes some of the revenues generated by high world energy prices from circulation and uses them to pay off external debt. In

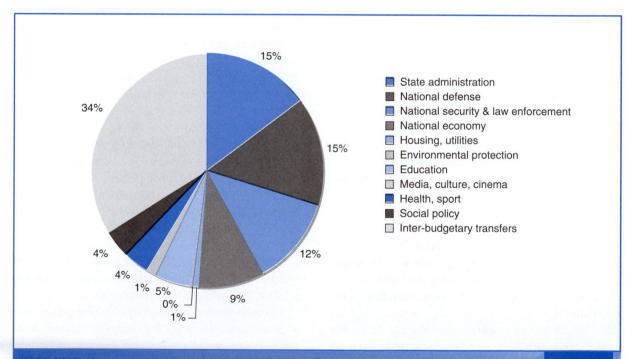

**Legend:**
- State administration
- National defense
- National security & law enforcement
- National economy
- Housing, utilities
- Environmental protection
- Education
- Media, culture, cinema
- Health, sport
- Social policy
- Inter-budgetary transfers

**2007 Russian Federal Budget**
Nearly half the budget goes to state administration and transfers to other levels of government

**FIGURE 12.7**

Source: Russian Ministry of Finance www.minfin.ru

2007 the government divided the stabilization fund into two portions, one called the reserve fund, to be used in the event of a serious fall in government revenues, and the other called a national welfare fund, to be used mainly to shore up the pension system. By the beginning of 2008, the reserve fund held about $120 billion in assets and the national welfare fund about $30 billion. The Putin and Medvedev governments have held firm in the face of mounting political pressure to spend down these funds, conscious of the serious risk of wrecking the country's finances through inflation if they do so. The country's fiscal surplus has made it possible, however, for the government to launch ambitious programs of spending on four high-priority projects to improve conditions in education, health care, housing, and agriculture. The reserve fund became crucial in enabling Russia's government to cover its deficits as its revenues dropped and its social spending obligations rose when the 2008–2009 financial crisis struck. If the crisis lasts beyond 2009, however, the fiscal situation may become untenable.

## RULE ADJUDICATION: TOWARD THE RULE OF LAW

### The Law-Governed State

One of the most important goals of Gorbachev's reforms was to make the Soviet Union a **law-governed state (pravovoe gosudarstvo),** rather than one in which state bodies and the Communist Party exercised power arbitrarily. Since 1991 the Russian leaders have asserted that the state must respect the primacy of law over politics—even when they took actions grossly violating the constitution. The difficulty in placing law above politics testifies to the lingering legacy of the old regime's abuse of the legal system. Presidents Putin and Medvedev have repeatedly declared their commitment to the principle of the rule of law (in a strange, but memorable phrase, Putin once called for the "dictatorship of law"), even when their actions have flagrantly infringed on the independence of the judiciary.

The struggle for the rule of law began well before Gorbachev. After Stalin died, his successors ended mass terror and took significant steps to reduce the use of law for political repression. Still, throughout the late Soviet era, the Communist Party and the KGB often used legal procedures to give the mantle of legal legitimacy to acts of political repression. Although the prosecution of political dissidents has ended, the use of the legal system for political purposes by state authorities continues. Reforms in the 1990s took some steps toward making the judiciary independent of the authorities, but in the 2000s, political control over the legal system has increased.

The major institutional actors in the legal system are the **procuracy**, the courts (judiciary), and the bar. Each has undergone substantial change in the post-communist period.

*The Procuracy* Russia's legal system traditionally vested a great deal of power in the procuracy, which was considered to be the most prestigious branch of the legal system. The procuracy is comparable to the system of federal and state prosecuting attorneys in the United States, but has more wide-ranging responsibilities and is organized as a centralized hierarchy headed by the procurator-general. The procuracy is charged with fighting crime, corruption, and abuses of power in the bureaucracy. It seeks to ensure that all state officials and public organizations observe the law. It investigates criminal charges and prosecutes cases in court. The procuracy has traditionally been the principal check on abuses of power by state officials. But it is inadequately equipped to meet the sweeping responsibilities assigned to it because of the difficulty of effectively supervising the vast state bureaucracy. Although the procuracy is nominally independent of the executive, the president names the procurator-general (subject to confirmation by the Federation Council) and informally supervises any politically significant cases.

*The Judiciary* In contrast to the influence that the procuracy has traditionally wielded in Russia, the bench has been relatively weak. Trial judges are usually the least experienced and lowest paid members of the legal profession—and the most vulnerable to external political and administrative pressure. In a few instances, judges have been murdered when they attempted to take on organized crime. Many judges have left their positions to take higher-paying jobs in other branches of the legal profession, and caseloads have risen substantially.

State officials pay lip service to the principle of judicial independence, but often violate it in practice by pressuring judges to render particular judgments in politically sensitive matters. At the same time, many reforms since the end of communism are intended to make the administration of justice more effective, and some increase the rights of defendants in criminal cases.

For example, in the 1990s, trial by jury in major criminal cases was introduced in several regions on an experimental basis and since then has spread throughout the country in serious criminal cases. The goal of adopting the jury system was to make the judicial system more adversarial, so that the prosecution and the defense have equal status in the courtroom and the judge becomes a neutral arbiter between them.[78] In a number of high-profile cases, juries have acquitted defendants when they found the procuracy's case unconvincing.

The Russian judiciary is a unitary hierarchy. All courts of general jurisdiction are federal courts. There are also other specialized types of courts in addition to federal courts of general jurisdiction—among them, the commercial courts, the constitutional courts of ethnic republics, the local municipal courts (equivalent to justices of the peace), and the military courts. Most criminal trials are held in district and city courts of general jurisdiction, which have original jurisdiction in most criminal proceedings. Higher-level courts, including regional and republic-level courts, hear appeals from lower courts and have original jurisdiction in certain cases. At the pinnacle of the hierarchy of courts of general jurisdiction is the Russian Supreme Court, which hears cases referred from lower courts and also issues instructions to lower courts on judicial matters. The Supreme Court does not have the power to challenge the constitutionality of laws and other official actions of legislative and executive bodies. The constitution assigns that power to the Constitutional Court. Under the constitution, the judges of the Supreme Court are nominated by the president and confirmed by the Federation Council.

There is a similar hierarchy of courts hearing cases arising from civil disputes between firms or between firms and the government called **commercial courts (arbitrazhnye sudy)**. Like the Supreme Court, the Supreme Commercial Court is both the highest appellate court for its system of courts and the source of instruction and direction to lower commercial courts. As with the Supreme Court, the judges of the Supreme Commercial Court are nominated by the president and confirmed by the Federation Council. In recent years the Supreme Commercial Court has handed down a number of major decisions that clarify the rules of the economic marketplace.

The Ministry of Justice oversees the court system and provides for its material and administrative needs. Its influence over the legal system is limited, however, because it lacks any direct authority over the procuracy.

**The Bar** Change of another sort has been occurring among those members of the legal profession who represent individual citizens and organizations in both criminal and civil matters: advocates (*advokaty*). They are comparable to barristers in Great Britain and litigating attorneys in the United States. Their role has expanded considerably with the spread of the market economy. They have long enjoyed some autonomy through their self-governing associations, through which they elect officers and govern admission of new practitioners. In the past their ability to use their rights was limited, but in recent years their opportunities have risen markedly. Private law firms are proliferating. The profession is attractive for the opportunities it provides to earn high incomes. A number of lawyers have become celebrities by taking on high-profile cases.

**Constitutional Adjudication** One of the most important reforms in postcommunist Russia's legal system is the establishment of a court for constitutional review of the official acts of government. The Constitutional Court has authority to interpret the constitution in a variety of areas. It has ruled on several ambiguous questions relating to parliamentary procedure. It has overturned some laws passed by national republics within Russia and has struck down several provisions of the Russian Criminal Code that limited individual rights. Generally, in disputes between individuals and state authorities, the court finds in favor of individuals, thus reaffirming the sphere of individual legal rights. It has consistently upheld the sovereignty of the federal constitution over regional governments.

The most important challenge for the court, however, is the huge domain of presidential authority. The court has been reluctant to challenge the president. One of its first and most important decisions concerned a challenge brought by a group of Communist parliamentarians to President Yeltsin's decrees launching the war in Chechnya. The court ruled that the president had the authority to wage the war through the use of his constitutional power to issue decrees with the force of law. In other, less highly charged issues, the court established legal limits to the president's authority. For instance, the court ruled that Yeltsin could not refuse to sign a law after parliament had overridden his veto. However, in the more authoritarian climate of the 2000s, the court has not issued any rulings restricting the president's powers. Generally, the court is sensitive to the political climate surrounding it and takes care not to issue a ruling that would be ignored or opposed by the president.

A family in Chechnia surveys the damage to their home from the war.

Malcolm Lintron/Getty Images

## Obstacles to the Rule of Law

Movement toward the rule of law continues to be hampered by the abuse of legal institutions by the political authorities and by endemic corruption in state and society.

In the post-Soviet state, the security police continue to operate autonomously. In the Soviet period, the agency with principal responsibility for maintaining domestic security was called the KGB (State Security Committee). The KGB exercised wide powers, including responsibility for both domestic and foreign intelligence. Since 1991 its functions have been split up among several agencies. The main domestic security agency is called the Federal Security Service (FSB). Although the structure and mission of the security agencies have changed, they have never undergone a thorough purge of personnel. No member of or collaborator with the Soviet-era security services has been prosecuted for violating citizens' rights. In contrast to Eastern Europe, there has been no review of officials' records for past collaboration with the secret police. This is one of several ways in which post-Soviet Russia has still not put its Communist past behind it.

The security police are regarded as one of the more professionally competent and uncorrupted state agencies. However, despite being assigned new tasks, such as fighting international narcotics trafficking and terrorism, they still demonstrate a Soviet-style preoccupation with controlling the flow of information about the country. For example, in 2001 the security police sent a directive to the Academy of Sciences demanding that scholars report all contacts with foreigners. Many similar Soviet-era police practices have been revived under Putin.

President Putin also resumed the Soviet-era practice of using the legal system to suppress potential political opposition. An example is the series of legal maneuvers taken against the owners of independent media in the early 2000s. These included police harassment and criminal prosecution, as well as civil actions such as bankruptcy proceedings. For example, the owners of two television companies were forced to divest themselves of their media holdings and transfer ownership to companies loyal to the administration. As a result, Russia's two relatively autonomous national television companies lost their political independence, one respected liberal newspaper was shut down, and the entire media establishment was sent a strong signal that it would be wise to avoid crossing the current administration. Today only a small number of print media have retained a measure of political independence.

In the 1990s the bankruptcy laws were often used by businesses to drive rivals into bankruptcy in order to take them over; today state companies use civil and criminal laws for the same purpose—to force a private company to sell out at a bargain price so that it can then be taken over and its assets stripped. For example, the state used charges of tax evasion and theft to force the Yukos oil firm into bankruptcy so that its most profitable elements could be sold at a low price to the state oil company, Rosneft'. These forced hostile takeovers are called *reiderstvo* (raiding).[79]

*Corruption*  Another obstacle to the rule of law is endemic corruption. Corruption increased substantially after the Soviet period. It is widespread both in everyday life and in dealings with the state. A large-scale survey by a Moscow research firm gives some indication of the nature and scale of corruption. At least half the population of Russia is involved in corruption in daily life. For instance, the probability that an individual will pay a bribe to get an automobile inspection permit is about 60 percent. The likelihood of paying a bribe to get one's child into a good school or college or to get good grades is about 50 percent. There is a 26 percent chance of paying a bribe to get a favorable ruling in a court case. The areas where the largest sums are spent are health care, education, courts, and automobile inspections; these alone account for over 60 percent of the money paid in bribes.[80]

President Medvedev has declared fighting corruption to be a top priority of his administration. As a result, the topic has been given increasing public attention. Experts believe that the scale of corruption grew considerably in the 2000s, no doubt because of the flood of oil revenues into the country. One estimate is that the total volume of corrupt transactions doubled between 2006 and 2008, from $240 billion (approximately equal to the total national budget) to $480 billion (approximately one and one-half times the size of the national budget).[81]

Corruption is hardly unique to Russia or to the former Communist world. However, it is especially widespread in Russia and the other former Soviet states. Corruption on this scale imposes a severe drag on economic development, both because it diverts resources away from public needs and because it undermines people's willingness to invest in productive activity.[82] Moreover, much corruption is tied to organized crime, which bribes government officials for protection and drives out legal businesses. The corruption of the police and courts ensures that many crimes go unpunished and forces legal businesses to compete in the corruption market with illegal ones.

Corruption in Russia has deep roots, and many Russians assume that it is ineradicable. Comparative studies of corruption demonstrate, however, that a culture of corruption can be changed by changing the expectations of the public and the government.[83] The key is for the political leadership to make a serious effort to combat corruption and to back up this commitment with institutional reform and sustained attention to the problem.

Since the early 1990s, there have been a number of reforms, such as the adoption of trial by jury and the creation of the Constitutional Court, that have the potential to strengthen the judiciary's independence from both political pressure and corruption. However, the authorities' habitual use of the procuracy and the courts for political purposes and the powerfully corrosive effect of corruption continue to subvert the integrity of the legal system. In the long run, movement toward the rule of law will require that power be sufficiently dispersed among groups and organizations in the state and society so that neither private nor state interests are powerful enough to subordinate the law to their own purposes.

## RUSSIA AND THE INTERNATIONAL COMMUNITY

Russia's thousand-year history of expansion, war, and state domination of society has left behind a legacy of autocratic rule and a preoccupation with defending national borders. The collapse of the Soviet regime required Russia to rebuild its political institutions, economic system, national identity, and relations with the outside world. During the Soviet period, state propaganda used the image of an international struggle between capitalism and socialism to justify its repressive control over society and its enormous military establishment. Now the country's leaders recognize that only through international integration can Russia hope to prosper. Today's leaders aim to capture the benefits of economic integration with the developed capitalist world, while at the same time building an authoritarian political order at home featuring direct state control of the strategically important sectors of the economy.

Gorbachev, Yeltsin, Putin, and Medvedev all asserted that the integration of Russia into the community of developed democracies is strategically important for Russia. Gorbachev was willing to allow Communist regimes to fall throughout Eastern Europe for the sake of improved relations with the West. Yeltsin accepted the admission of East European states into the North Atlantic Treaty Organization as a necessary condition for close relations with the United States and Europe. Putin repeatedly emphasized that he regarded

Russia's admission to the World Trade Organization as critical for Russia's long-term economic success. Following the September 11, 2001, terrorist attacks on the United States, Putin immediately telephoned U.S. President George W. Bush to offer his support. Putin clearly saw an advantage for Russia in aligning itself with the United States against Islamic terrorism, which it identified as an immediate threat to its own security. Putin cited Russia's own war in Chechnia as part of the global struggle against Islamic terrorists.

At the same time, Russia has not accepted the constraints of international law. It has expanded its military presence in several former Soviet republics, pressuring them to become satellites of Russia. In August 2008 it launched a well-prepared military invasion of independent, pro-Western Georgia after Georgia attempted to use force to take back control over a Russia-backed breakaway region, South Ossetia. The overwhelming Russian response was clearly intended to subjugate Georgia to Russia's interest in preserving a buffer of subordinate states in the territory of the former Soviet Union.

Likewise, in its brutal military campaigns in Chechnia from 1994 to 1996 and then again from 1999 to 2006, Russia refused to allow international human rights organizations to monitor Russian practices, which included mass bombardment of civilian areas. In 2007 Russia resumed the Cold War–era practice of sending its strategic bombers on long-distance missions over the Atlantic, Pacific, and Arctic oceans to demonstrate the global reach of its military power. As its economic and military power has revived, Russia has attempted to establish itself as a counterweight to American power and to rebuild Russian influence in the former Soviet region.

Russia's quasi-imperial behavior in parts of the former Soviet Union and its refusal to be bound by democratic principles have kept it from becoming fully integrated into the international community. Yet, it is far more open than it was under Soviet rule, and its leaders recognize that they cannot retreat into isolation and autarky. They are also aware of the grave vulnerabilities Russia faces—its declining population, aging infrastructure, dependence on immigrant labor, and overreliance on natural resources for state revenues. Thus, while they seek to be a hegemonic power in the territory of the former Soviet Union, they also do not want to resurrect Russia's role as the United States's enemy in the bipolar world; they would prefer that Russia be one of several major powers in a multipolar world.

Russia's vast territory, weak government capacity, and tradition of state domination over society make it likely that the primary objective of its leaders for the foreseeable future will be to strengthen the state, in both its internal and its international dimensions. The end of the Communist regime and the dissolution of the Soviet Union damaged the state's capacity to enforce the laws, protect its citizens, and provide basic social services. Favorable economic conditions in the 2000s enabled the state to rebuild its power at home and abroad, but the crisis of 2008–2009 revealed Russia's susceptibility to trends in international financial and energy markets. In the long run, self-sustaining economic development will require the rule of law and effective institutions for articulating and aggregating social interests. The viability of Russia's postcommunist state will ultimately depend on how responsive and adaptive its institutions are to the demands of Russia's citizens in a globalized and interdependent world.

## REVIEW QUESTIONS

- How did Yeltsin's "shock therapy" program contribute to the constitutional crisis of 1993?

- What effects did the constitutional struggles of 1992–1993 have on the features of the 1993 constitution?

- How did President Putin go about strengthening the power of the central government vis-à-vis regional governments? What were his reasons for shifting the balance of power in this way?

- What are the main similarities and differences between the channels of elite recruitment under the Soviet system and today?

- Most Russians evaluate the pre-Gorbachev Soviet system favorably, yet would prefer not to bring it back. How would you explain this apparent contradiction?

- Why has United Russia been so successful as a "party of power"?

- What are the main obstacles to the rule of law in Russia? What changes in the political system would be required to overcome them?

## KEY TERMS

Chechnia

commercial courts
(*arbitrazhnye sudy*)

Communist Party of the
Russian Federation
(CPRF)

Constitutional Court

Federation Council

Federation of
Independent Trade
Unions of Russia
(FITUR)

glasnost'

Gorbachev, Mikhail

law-governed state
(*pravovoe gosudarstro*)

League of Committees of
Soldiers' Mothers

Lenin, Vladimir Ilyich

loans for shares

Medvedev, Dmitrii
Anatol'evich

Nomenklatura

oligarchs

party of power

presidential decrees

privatization

procuracy

Public Chamber

Russian Union of
Industrialists and
Entrepreneurs (RUIE)

Security Council

shock therapy

Stalin, Joseph

State Council

State Duma

United Russia

## SUGGESTED READINGS

Aslund, Anders. *Russia's Capitalist Revolution: Why Market Reform Succeeded and Democracy Failed*. Washington, DC: Peterson Institute for International Economics, 2007.

Baker, Peter, and Susan Glasser. *Kremlin Rising: Vladimir Putin's Russia and the End of Revolution*. New York: Scribner, 2005.

Breslauer, George W. *Gorbachev and Yeltsin as Leaders*. Cambridge, England: Cambridge University Press, 2002.

Colton, Timothy J. *Yeltsin: A Life*. New York: Basic Books, 2008.

Fish, M. Stephen. *Democracy Derailed in Russia: The Failure of Open Politics*. Cambridge, England: Cambridge University Press, 2005.

Hale, Henry. *Why Not Parties in Russia? Democracy, Federalism, and the State*. Cambridge, England: Cambridge University Press, 2006.

Hellman, Joel S. "Winners Take All: The Politics of Partial Reform in Postcommunist Transitions." *World Politics* 50, no. 1 (1998): 203–234.

Hill, Fiona, and Clifford Gaddy. *The Siberian Curse: How Communist Planners Left Russia Out in the Cold*. Washington, DC: Brookings Institution, 2003.

McFaul, Michael. *Russia's Unfinished Revolution: Political Change from Gorbachev to Putin*. Ithaca, NY: Cornell University Press, 2001.

Rose, Richard, William Mishler, and Neil Munro. *Russia Transformed: Developing Popular Support for a New Regime*. Cambridge, England: Cambridge University Press, 2006.

Sakwa, Richard. *Putin: Russia's Choice*. London: Routledge, 2004.

Shleifer, Andrei, and Daniel Treisman. *Without a Map: Political Tactics and Economic Reform in Russia*. Cambridge, MA: MIT Press, 2000.

White, Stephen, Richard Rose, and Ian McAllister. *How Russia Votes*. Chatham, NJ: Chatham House, 1997.

## INTERNET RESOURCES

The main institutions of the federal government—the president, the parliament, and the government: **www.gov.ru/index.html** (Most of the content accessible through this site is in Russian, but some resources are in English.)

An e-mail newsletter containing news stories and commentary: **www.cdi.org/russia/johnson**

A wide range of political resources: **www.politicalresources.net/russia.htm**

The University of Pittsburgh links to resources on Russia: **www.ucis.pitt.edu/reesweb**

A joint Internet project by a team of Russians and Americans: **www.friends-partners.org**

The *Moscow Times* is an English-language daily newspaper primarily for expatriates: **www.themoscowtimes.com**

The University of Strathclyde's Center for the Study of Public Policy provides public opinion and electoral information from Russia: **www.RussiaVotes.org**

# ENDNOTES

1. Hale, Henry E. "Regime Cycles: Democracy, Autocracy and Revolution in Post-Soviet Eurasia." *World Politics* 58 (2005): 133–165.

2. From surveys conducted by Russia's premier polling organization, the Levada Center. The "right/wrong direction" survey was posted on April 2, 2008, to their website: www.levada.ru/press/2008040201.html. Results of the survey on approval of the president available at www.levada.ru/press/2008061102.html.

3. Putin's address to the State Council, February 8, 2008. Retrieved from the presidential website: president.kremlin.ru/text/appears/2008/02/159528.shtml.

4. The resource curse has also been linked to the perpetuation of autocracy, since rulers in resource-rich countries prefer to receive revenues from extractive industries, rather than building up a broad base of tax revenues in exchange for political representation by the citizens. On the "resource curse," see Jeffrey D. Sachs and Andrew M. Warner, "Natural Resource Abundance and Economic Growth," NBER Working Paper no. 5398, December 1995; and Michael L. Ross, "The Political Economy of the Resource Curse," *World Politics* 51, no. 2 (1999): 297–322.

5. United Nations Development Programme_Russia. *National Human Development Report, Russian Federation 2006/2007: Russia's Regions: Goals, Challenges, Achievements* (Moscow: United Nations Development Programme, 2007), 8.

6. Richard Pipes, *Russia Under the Old Regime,* 2nd ed. (New York: Penguin Books, 1995).

7. Archie Brown, *The Gorbachev Factor* (New York: Oxford University Press, 1996).

8. For a comparison of the leadership styles of Gorbachev and Yeltsin, see George W. Breslauer, *Gorbachev and Yeltsin as Leaders* (Cambridge, England: Cambridge University Press, 2002); see also Archie Brown and Lilia Shevtsova, eds., *Gorbachev, Yeltsin, and Putin: Political Leadership in Russia's Transition* (Washington, DC: Carnegie Endowment for International Peace, 2001); Lilia Shevtsova, *Putin's Russia* (Washington, DC: Carnegie Endowment for International Peace, 2003); and Richard Sakwa, *Putin: Russia's Choice* (London: Routledge, 2004).

9. Many observers agreed that the point of the reform was to weaken the influence of local interests on Duma deputies, further centralizing power in the executive.

10. On nationality policy in the Soviet Union, see Terry Martin, *The Affirmative Action Empire: Nations and Nationalism in the Soviet Union, 1923–1939* (Ithaca, NY: Cornell University Press, 2001).

11. Julia Kusznir, "Russian Territorial Reform: A Centralist Project That Could End Up Fostering Decentralization?" *Russian Analytical Digest* no. 43 (June 17, 2008). Retrieved from www. res. ethz. ch/ analysis/ rad.

12. J. Paul Goode, "The Push for Regional Enlargement in Putin's Russia," *Post-Soviet Affairs* 20, no. 3 (July–September 2004): 219–257.

13. From a survey conducted by the widely respected Levada Center in June 2005.

14. Brian Whitmore, "RFE/RL Poll Finds Russians Skeptical About Elections, Hopeful for Future," *RFE/RL Newsline,* November 16, 2007.

15. L. D. Gudkov, B. V. Dubin, and Yu. A. Levada, *Problema <elity> v segodniashnei Rossii: Razmyshleniia nad rezul'tatami sotsiologicheskogo issledovaniia* (Moscow: Fond Liberal'naia missiia, 2007), 136.

16. Whitmore, "RFE/RL Poll"; *RFE/RL Newsline,* March 14, 2008.

17. Reported in Polit.ru, December 10, 2007; full report in BBC World Service Poll, "World Divided on Press Freedom." Retrieved December 10, 2007, from www.globescan.com/news_archives/bbc75. Thirteen other countries from the developed and developing worlds were surveyed.

18. *RFE/RL Newsline,* December 28, 2007.

19. Retrieved May 22, 2008, from Kommersant.ru.

20. Retrieved January 11, 2008, from Polit.ru.

21. *RFE/RL Newsline,* April 14, 2008.

22. *Nezavisimaia gazeta,* June 11, 2008.

23. Levada Center. Retrieved February 14, 2008, from www.levada.ru/press/2008020800.html

24. *RFE/RL Newsline,* March 31, 2008.

25. *RFE/RL Newsline,* September 18, 2007.

26. *RFE/RL Newsline,* October 3, 2007.

27. Richard Rose, Neil Munro, and William Mishler, "Resigned Acceptance of an Incomplete Democracy: Russia's Political Equilibrium," *Post-Soviet Affairs* 20, no. 3 (2004): 195–218.

28. Donna Bahry, "Society Transformed? Rethinking the Social Roots of Perestroika," *Slavic Review* 52, no. 3 (1993): 512–554.

29. Elena Lisovskaya and Vyacheslav Karpov, "New Ideologies in Postcommunist Russian Textbooks," *Comparative Education Review* 43, no. 4 (1999): 522–532.

30. *RFE/RL Newsline,* February 15, 2006; August 31, 2006.

31. Some 1700 scientists and other professionals sent an open letter to President Putin calling for an end to religion courses in state schools. See Polit.ru, April 16, 2008.

32. On television, see Ellen Mickiewicz, *Television, Power, and the Public in Russia* (Cambridge, England: Cambridge University Press, 2008); on the regime's media policies more generally, see Sarah Oates, "The Neo-Soviet Model of the Media," *Europe-Asia Studies* 59, no. 8 (2007): 1279–1297; on the Internet, see Marcus Alexander, "The Internet and Democratization: The Development of Russian Internet Policy." *Demokratizatsiiya* 12 (2004): 607–627, and Anton Troianovski, "Playing by New Rules: Soft Power and the Fight for Russian Cyberspace" (senior thesis, Harvard University, 2008).

33. Daron Acemoglu and James A. Robinson, *Economic Origins of Dictatorship and Democracy* (Cambridge, England: Cambridge University Press, 2006); for studies of the effects of inequality on democracy in the United States, see Theda Skocpol and Lawrence R. Jacobs, *Inequality and American Democracy: What We Know and What We Need to Learn* (New York: Russell Sage, 2005).

34. Robert D. Putnam, *Making Democracy Work: Civic Traditions in Modern Italy* (Princeton, NJ: Princeton University Press, 1993).

35. Marc Morje Howard, *The Weakness of Civil Society in Post-Communist Europe* (Cambridge, England: Cambridge University Press, 2003).

36. Richard Rose and Neil Munro, *Elections Without Order: Russia's Challenge to Vladimir Putin* (Cambridge, England: Cambridge University Press, 2002), 224–225; Richard Rose, *Getting Things Done with Social Capital: New Russia Barometer VII* (Glasgow: Center for the Study of Public Policy, University of Strathclyde, 1998), 32–33.

37. Emil' Pain, "Ot vlasti avtoriteta k vlasti normy," *Nezavisimaia gazeta,* May 20, 2008.

38. Rose, *Getting Things Done.*

39. Turnout for the December 2003 parliamentary elections was reported to be 55.45 percent and for the presidential election in March 2004, 64.4 percent. In the United States, turnout of the voting-age population for the closely contested presidential election in 2000 was 51.3 percent.

40. A reform sponsored by President Putin and the United Russia Party has moved to eliminate the "against all" option from future elections. Although the goal is to force voters to support one of the given parties, many observers—including the chairman of the Central Election Commission—warn that this change will reduce electoral turnout.

41. Eugene Huskey, *Nomenklatura Lite? The Cadres Reserve (Kadrovyi reserv) in Russian Public Administration* (NCEEER Working Paper) (Washington, DC: National Council for Eurasian and East European Research, 2003).

42. Olga Kryshtanovskaya and Stephen White, "Putin's Militocracy," *Post-Soviet Affairs* 19, no. 4 (2003): 289–306.

43. Another feature of this rivalry is that the *siloviki*—the group of security types, headed by Igor' Sechin, a former military intelligence (GRU) official—is tied to the state oil company, Rosneft'. Sechin is chairman of the Rosneft' board. The rival clan of "liberals" has ties to Gazprom (until he became president of Russia, Medvedev was chairman of the board of Gazprom). Gazprom and Rosneft' have fought openly over control of oil and gas assets.

44. William Tompson, "Back to the Future? Thoughts on the Political Economy of Expanding State Ownership in Russia," *Les Cahiers Russie–The Russia Papers* (6) (2008).

45. Jane I. Dawson, *Eco-nationalism: Anti-nuclear Activism and National Identity in Russia, Lithuania, and Ukraine* (Durham, NC: Duke University Press, 1996).

46. *RFE/RL Newsline,* April 18, 2006.

47. For example, in July 2008, the Public Chamber issued a report on the state of freedom of speech in two Russian regions, as well as a handbook on the rules for military conscription. Kommersant.ru, July 2, 2008; Leonid Fedorov, "Svobodu slova postavili na uchet," *Nezavisimaia gazeta,* July 1, 2008.

48. In a system where all prices were set by the state, there was no meaningful measure of profit in any case. Indeed, relative prices were profoundly distorted by the cumulative effect of decades of central planning. The absence of accurate measures of economic costs is one of the major reasons that Russia's economy continues to be so slow to restructure.

49. A sore point has been fire safety inspections. Businesses regularly complain that these are usually shakedown efforts by state officials whose inspections invariably discover numerous violations of fire safety rules—which can be resolved by a bribe. The RUIE has pushed openly to reduce the powers of the fire safety inspectors.

50. Article 59 of the constitution provides that young men of conscription age who are conscientious objectors to war may do alternative service, rather than being called up to army service. Legislation specifying how this right may be exercised finally passed in 2002.

51. The chairwoman of Soldiers' Mothers recently estimated that some 3,500 servicemen lose their lives each year as a result of "various accidents and suicides." *RFE/RL Newsline,* February 14, 2008.

52. Several authors have examined the effect of Western aid on NGOs in Russia and other post-Communist countries. See Sarah L. Henderson, *Building Democracy in Contemporary Russia: Western Support for Grassroots Organizations* (Ithaca, NY: Cornell University Press, 2003); Thomas Carothers and Marina Ottaway, eds., *Funding Virtue: Civil Society Aid and Democracy* (Washington, DC: Carnegie Endowment for International Peace, 2000); and Sarah E. Mendelson and John K. Glenn, eds., *The Power and Limits of NGOs: A Critical Look at Building Democracy in Eastern Europe and Eurasia* (New York: Columbia University Press, 2002).

53. The FITUR reached a Faustian bargain with the government over the terms of a new labor relations code, which was adopted in 2001. Under the new legislation, employers no longer have to obtain the consent of the unions to lay off workers. But collective bargaining will be between the largest union at each enterprise and the management unless the workers have agreed on which union will represent them. Thus, the new labor code favors the FITUR at the expense of the smaller independent unions.

54. Richard Rose, *New Russia Barometer VI: After the Presidential Election* (Studies in Public Policy no. 272) (Glasgow: Center for the Study of Public Policy, University of Strathclyde, 1996), 6; and Rose, *Getting Things Done,* 15.

55. Graeme B. Robertson, "Strikes and Labor Organizations in Hybrid Regimes," *American Political Science Review* 101, no. 4 (2007): 781–798.

56. Linda J. Cook, *Labor and Liberalization: Trade Unions in the New Russia* (New York: Twentieth Century Fund Press, 1997), 76–77.

57. A recent survey in Nizhnii Novgorod found that 81 percent of workers said their interests were either not protected at all or protected insufficiently; 85 percent did not consider themselves members of a trade union, but 58 percent said they desired to belong to a union that would actually defend their interests. Ol'ga Morozova, "Profsoiuzy ne pomogaiut," Vedomosti.ru, July 8, 2008.

58. Two recent books detail the obstacles to the formation of a stable competitive party system: Henry Hale, *Why Not Parties in Russia?* (Cambridge, England: Cambridge University Press, 2006); and Regina Smyth, *Candidate Strategies and Electoral Competition in the Russian Federation: Democracy Without Foundation* (Cambridge, England: Cambridge University Press, 2006).

59. Ora John Reuter and Thomas F. Remington, "Dominant Party Regimes and the Commitment Problem: The Case of United Russia." *Comparative Political Studies* 42:4 (2009), pp. 501–526;; Smyth. *Candidate Strategies and Electoral Competition*; Hale, *Why Not Parties in Russia?*

60. Stephen White, Richard Rose, and Ian McAllister, *How Russia Votes* (Chatham, NJ: Chatham House, 1997), 241–270.

61. Quoted from a press release of the election observer mission of the Organization for Security and Cooperation in Europe, posted to its website immediately following the election, as reported by *RFE/RL Newsline,* March 15, 2004.

62. In all, 108 candidates on the United Party list declined to take their seats in parliament. Such candidates were used as "locomotives"—they were used to attract votes, but had no intention of serving in the Duma once the party won.

63. On the scale of fraud in recent Russian elections, see Mikhail Myagkov, Peter C. Ordeshook, and Dmitri Shakin, *The Forensics of Election Fraud: Russia and Ukraine* (Cambridge: Cambridge University Press, 2009).

64. Joel S. Hellman, "Winners Take All: The Politics of Partial Reform in Postcommunist Transitions," *World Politics* 50, no. 1 (1998): 203–234.

65. An excellent account of the "loans for shares" program, based on interviews with many of the participants, is Chrystia Freeland, *Sale of the Century: Russia's Wild Ride from Communism to Capitalism* (New York: Crown, 2000), 169–189.

66. Joseph R. Blasi, Maya Kroumova, and Douglas Kruse, *Kremlin Capitalism: Privatizing the Russian Economy* (Ithaca, NY: Cornell University Press, 1997), 50.

67. Blasi, Kroumova, and Kruse, *Kremlin Capitalism;* Michael McFaul, "State Power, Institutional Change, and the Politics of Privatization in Russia," *World Politics* 47 (1995): 210–243.

68. Thane Gustafson, *Capitalism Russian-Style* (Cambridge, England: Cambridge University Press, 1999), 2–3, 94–95.

69. Organization for Economic Co-operation and Development, *OECD Economic Survey of the Russian Federation, 2004: The Challenge of Sustaining Growth* (Paris: OECD, 2004). Retrieved from www.oecd.org/document/62/0,2340,en_2649_201185_32474302_1_1_1_1,00.html.

70. Simon Clarke, "Market and Institutional Determinants of Wage Differentiation in Russia," *Industrial and Labor Relations* 55, no. 4 (2002): 628–648.

71. Nikolaus von Twickel, "Rich Get Richer as Poor Get Poorer," *Moscow Times,* August 8, 2008.

72. Heidi Brown, "Russia: The World's Richest Government." Retrieved April 2, 2008, from www.forbes.com/2008/03/28/russia-billionaires-duma-biz-cz_hb_0401russiapols_print.html.

73. World Bank, *Transition: The First Ten Years—Analysis and Lessons for Eastern Europe and the Former Soviet Union* (Washington, DC: World Bank, 2002), 9.

74. Quoted from Vladimir Putin's address to an expanded session of the State Council, February 8, 2008, "On the Strategy of Development of Russia to 2020." Retrieved from president.kremlin.ru/text/appears/2008/02/159528.shtml.

75. *RFE/RL Newsline,* July 20, 2006.

76. Russian military commanders reported that one-third of the men they had called up in the fall of 2004 were unfit to serve as a result of health problems. Polit.ru, December 9, 2004.

77. *RFE/RL Newsline,* August 18, 2006.

78. A vivid portrait of a recent jury trial in Moscow is presented by Peter Baker and Susan Glasser, *Kremlin Rising: Vladimir Putin's Russia and the End of Revolution* (New York: Scribner, 2005), 231–250.

79. The use of police intimidation to force private owners to sell to state companies was described in a revealing newspaper interview in late 2007. Maksim Kvashe, "Partiiu dlia nas olitsetvoriaet silovoi blok, kotoryi vozglavliaet Igor' Ivanovich Sechin." *Kommersant,* November 30, 2007, 20.

80. G. A. Satarov, *Diagnostika rossiiskoi korruptsii: Sotsiologicheskii analiz* (Moscow: Fond INDEM, 2002), 16–17.

81. Nikita Krichevskii, "Aktual'nye predlozheniia na vechnuiu temu: kak dolzhna stroit'sia strategiia bor'by s korruptsiei," *Nezavisimaia gazeta,* June 11, 2008.

82. Joel S. Hellman, Geraint Jones, and Daniel Kaufmann, "*Seize the State, Seize the Day": State Capture, Corruption, and Influence in Transition* (Policy Research Working Paper no. 2444) (Washington, DC: World Bank Institute, September 2000).

83. Susan Rose-Ackerman, *Corruption and Government: Causes, Consequences and Reform* (Cambridge, England: Cambridge University Press, 1999), 159–174.

CHINA

Urūmqi

XINJIANG

GANSU
Yumen

QINGHAI

Xining

Lanzhou

TIBET

Lhasa

SICHUAN
Chengdu

CHONGQING

YUNNAN
Kunming

GUIZHOU
Guiyang

GUANGXI

Nanning

INNER
MONGOLIA

HEILONGJIANG
Qiqihar

Harbin

Changchun

JILIN

Shenyang

LIAONING

Sea
of
Japan

HEBEI
Hohhot        BEIJING ★
              TIANJIN      Dalian

Yellow
Sea

Taiyuan    Shijiazhuang
           Jinan    Qingdao
SHANXI     SHANDONG

Yinchuan

NINGXIA

Huang He

Xi'an
SHAANXI

Zhengzhou

HENAN

Hefei

JIANGSU

Nanjing    SHANGHAI

East

China

Sea

Wuhan
HUBEI

ANHUI

Hangzhou

ZHEJIANG

Chang Jiang

Changsha

HUNAN

Nanchang

JIANGXI

Fuzhou

FUJIAN

GUANGDONG
Guangzhou

Pearl River

HONG KONG
MACAO

Zhanjiang

Haikou

HAINAN

South China

Sea

0    200    400    600 Miles

0    200    400    600 Kilometers

# POLITICS IN CHINA

*Melanie Manion*

## Country Bio

**CHINA**

**Population**
1,307.56 million

**Territory**
3,705,386 square miles

**Year of PRC Inauguration**
1949

**Year of Current Constitution**
1982

**Head of Party and State**
Hu Jintao

**Head of Government**
Wen Jiabao

**Languages**
Standard Chinese or Mandarin (Putonghua, based on the Beijing dialect), Yue (Cantonese), Wu (Shanghaiese), Minbei (Fuzhou), Minnan (Hokkien-Taiwanese), Xiang, Gan, Hakka dialects, minority languages

**Religions**
Daoism (Taoism), Buddhism, Muslim 2–3%, Christian 1% (est.). Note: officially atheist.

On October 1, 1949, Mao Zedong, the peasant revolutionary who had led the Chinese communists in war against the Japanese and in civil war, pronounced a basic communist victory, proclaimed a new regime, and promised a new era for China. From the centuries-old Gate of Heavenly Peace in Beijing, Mao formally inaugurated the People's Republic of China (PRC). For nearly three decades after, until his death in 1976, Mao was the chief architect and agitator for a comprehensive project of revolutionary transformation designed to lead a largely backward agrarian people to modernization, prosperity, and (ultimately) communist utopia. A few years after Mao's death, his successors officially and publicly rejected most of the premises, strategies, and outcomes of this revolutionary project, essentially declaring it a failure. They launched a new era of reform, ongoing today. Economic reform in post-Mao China is nearly as radical and dramatic as the revolutions that toppled most of the world's communist regimes in 1989 and 1990. The resulting transformation is awesome.

Without publicly abandoning the ultimate goal of communism, Mao's successors have defined their current quest mainly in pragmatic economic terms, rather than utopian ideological terms. They have identified economic growth as the nation's highest priority and the Communist Party's main assignment. To achieve this objective, the communist party-state has largely retreated from thirty years of direct administration of the economy. Openly acknowledging the superiority of the capitalist experience, Chinese reformers are promoting a **"socialist market economy,"** with a place for foreign investors, private entrepreneurs, and stock markets. More than anything else, Chinese leaders have staked their legitimacy on the performance of this new economy.

While embracing economic markets, Chinese leaders have repeatedly rejected political pluralism. The communist party-state was in clear evidence in Beijing on June 4, 1989, when the People's Liberation Army employed its tanks and machine guns to clear the streets and main public square of thousands of protesters. The regime tolerates no open challenge to the Communist Party's monopoly on political power.

For most of the 1.3 billion ordinary Chinese, political reform is mainly reflected in a new official acceptance of a private sphere and a new official tolerance of political apathy. Compared with the Maoist years, when a taste for the music of Beethoven signified dangerous "bourgeois decadence," much less in daily life today is considered political. Moreover, under the new regime, ordinary citizens need not necessarily demonstrate active support for official policies and the political system—so long as they do not engage in active opposition. Chinese leaders have not charted a road toward liberal democracy, at least not purposefully. Instead, the political system has become merely authoritarian in its limited reach, rather than pervasively totalitarian.

Yet, post-Mao reform is more than the retreat of the state from the economy and the imposition of fewer demands on citizens politically. A project of institutionalization is underway in China, to create an infrastructure promoting more transparency, stability, and responsiveness. In large part, this is to encourage investment and innovation, to support the goal of economic growth. At the same time, Mao's successors are also committed to political institutionalization for political reasons: to safeguard against the arbitrary dictatorship and disruptive politics of the Maoist past. The effort has included better-crafted laws and a new legality, more assertive representative assemblies, and popularly elected grassroots leaders.

Much of China's transformation in the past quarter-century is only partly a direct result of the various policies that constitute reform. It is at least as much a by-product of these policies. Reform has set in motion processes of economic, political, and social change that appear now largely beyond the control of leaders at the political center. Consider a few examples. Eased restrictions on population movement have created a "floating population" of more than 100 million internal migrants, most of them from the countryside and seeking work in towns and cities, many of them unregistered squatters, all of them reflecting a new relationship between state authority, social welfare, and market opportunity. Local governments, empowered by a new fiscal federalism, pursue local economic growth with less and less heed to central guidelines. Growth in individual wealth and a telecommunications revolution have produced an astonishing 298 million Internet users in China, linking Chinese to one another and to the outside world in ways that are nearly impossible to control.

## CURRENT POLICY CHALLENGES

Meeting with the president of the United States in late 2005, China's President Hu Jintao frankly acknowledged that problems of political corruption, rural unrest, a growing wealth gap, and severe pollution consume nearly all his time.[1] Some of these problems represent new policy challenges for Chinese leaders; others are not new, but their magnitude and impact have only recently been understood. The new and ongoing policy challenges arise very significantly from China's economic successes in the past quarter-century.

Since 1978, Chinese leaders have agreed to be judged mainly by their ability to foster economic growth and deliver a better material life for Chinese citizens. China's development has in fact been very impressive. Its economy has grown at a rate of nearly 10 percent per year since 1980, a record of sustained growth comparable only to Japan and Korea in the latter half of the twentieth century. In terms of purchasing power parity, China is now the world's second largest economy (after the United States) and third largest recipient of foreign direct investment (largest among developing countries). In 2006, it overtook Japan as the world's biggest holder of foreign exchange reserves.

Economic success has not been costless. It has provided more opportunities to pursue private gain, legally and also illegally through the abuse of public office. Despite decades of anticorruption efforts, year after year, ordinary citizens tell pollsters that corruption is one of China's most serious problems. In the cities, Chinese poke fun at the perceived insincerity of the anticorruption reforms: "not daring *not* to fight corruption, not daring to fight corruption seriously." In the countryside, villagers rise up to protest abuses of power by "local emperors" imposing illegal fees and excessive taxes.

In recent years, the requisition, rezoning, and sale of agricultural land by local governments has provoked rural riots, usually suppressed with great violence. Land is not privately owned, but contracted for agricultural use by Chinese farmers. Local governments have seized on more lucrative opportunities for land use provided by real estate and industrial development. Farmers tend to be poorly compensated in these instances of eminent domain for local economic development (and local government profit). Top

Chinese leaders have condemned these actions, not least of all because arable land is already scarce.

The growing wealth gap fuels the perceptions of official abuse. Chinese policymakers have promoted a policy that "some get rich first." One result is rapidly rising inequality. Rural incomes are about 30 percent of urban incomes, and coastal regions have been advantaged over the interior. Urban Chinese in modern Shanghai enjoy annual incomes exceeding $2,000, while rural Chinese in backward Guizhou province make do with $200. Poorer Chinese deeply resent the newly conspicuous economic inequalities of the socialist market economy. While some struggle for a basic livelihood, there are also Chinese entrepreneurs and venal officials who travel in luxury sedans, do business on cellular phones, and feast ostentatiously at expensive restaurants. In 2006, Chinese authorities admitted to a Gini coefficient of 0.46, mostly reflecting a gap between urban and rural residents.[2] As the wealth gap has exploded within a single generation, it has great potential to impact social stability.

According to the Ministry of Public Security, in 2005, China experienced 87,000 "public disturbances," both urban and rural—up 7 percent from the previous year. Land takings, economic distress, and political corruption certainly provoked much of this unrest. A nontrivial number of rural "disturbances" are directed against pollution, which has displaced tens of millions of farmers.

Although the Chinese have developed a significant legal and organizational infrastructure of environmental protection in the past decade, environmental pollution and degradation have increased at a rate that far outpaces the capacity of the state to protect the environment. This reflects developmental priorities: indeed, as late as the mid-1990s, Chinese leaders routinely articulated the principle of "first development, then environment." The World Bank estimates that annually 300,000 Chinese die prematurely from air pollution. Children breath in the equivalent of smoking two packs of cigarettes per day. Sixteen of the world's twenty most polluted cities are Chinese cities—including Beijing, the site of the 2008 Olympic Games. The expanding ownership of private automobiles by the new middle class exacerbates the problem: Chinese domestically designed and manufactured automobiles emit ten to twenty times more pollutants than American or Japanese models.

As Chinese leaders confront their domestic challenges, they do so in a global context that they now actively engage. The U.S. government now uses the term "stakeholder" to describe the new role of China in the world. This has much to do with China's accession to the World Trade Organization (WTO) in 2001, which has further opened the economy, subjecting it to a new discipline of global competition and pushing development of the economic legal infrastructure. WTO accession agreements require China to fully open its banking sector to foreign investors in 2007—and this will accelerate an already rapid process of economic reform. China is not only an economic player, however. It has also shown its willingness to play a role in helping to resolve international crises, such as the production and testing of nuclear weapons by North Korea. As the only country with political influence over North Korea, China organized the six-party talks, bringing the United States to the negotiating table in a multilateral situation.

China has thoroughly abandoned the strictures of communist ideology, has experienced an awesome economic revolution, and is taking its place as an important world power. Yet, unlike most other communist regimes, which toppled in the face of popular uprisings, China has experienced no second political revolution. Today, it is still a communist party-state. Chinese policymakers have promoted limited liberalization, sometimes as an antidote to corruption at the grassroots. While they have opened up political processes to more diversified inputs, they have also firmly suppressed organized challenges to the Communist Party. A handful of leaders at the very top still monopolize the authority to choose what sorts of inputs from what sorts of groups are acceptable, and the decision rules are not always transparent.

Strikingly little remains of Mao's grand revolutionary schemes. Viewed from the perspective of the 1970s, the magnitude and pace of change in China in the past quarter-century are practically unimaginable. Chinese politics today is "post-Mao" politics in the sense that there is a new regime, not simply a change of leaders—and, given its dynamics, there appears to be no turning back. Of course, without a grasp of China's rich political history, it is not only impossible to appreciate what has (and has not) changed, but also impossible to understand the crucial context of post-Mao reform: what has been rejected.

## HISTORICAL SETTING

When ordinary Chinese today are asked about what it is they, as Chinese, are most proud, many respond: "our long history." Chinese civilization emerged more than six thousand years ago. As a polity, imperial China was the longest-lived major system of governance in world history, enduring as a centralized state ruled with little change in political philosophy or bureaucratic organization for more than two millennia until the fall of the Qing, the last dynasty, in 1911.[3]

Traditional China was governed by an emperor and a unique bureaucracy of scholar-officials at the capital and in the localities, who gained their positions meritocratically through examinations that tested knowledge of the Confucian classics. Anyone was eligible to participate in the examinations, but successful performance required a classical education, usually through a private tutor, not available to most ordinary Chinese. **Confucianism** was basically a conservative philosophy. It conceived of society and the polity in terms of an ordered hierarchy of harmonious relationships. At the top of the hierarchy was the emperor, who maintained social order through his conduct as a moral exemplar. Confucianism blurred the distinction between state and society: it saw harmony (not conflict) as the natural social order; this harmony resulted because the virtuous emperor provided an example of correct conduct. Loyalty to the emperor was the highest principle in the hierarchy of relationships entailing mutual obligations throughout society.

### Imperial Order to the Founding of the PRC

This remarkable imperial order began to crumble in the mid-nineteenth century, when Qing rulers proved unable to uphold their political authority and maintain territorial integrity in the presence of large-scale domestic rebellion and foreign economic and military encroachment. The republic founded in 1912 did not restore order or sovereignty to China, but effectively collapsed within a few years, as dozens of Chinese regional warlords ruling with personal armies competed for control of territory.[4] Nearly four decades of political upheaval and continuous warfare ensued, as the Chinese sought solutions to the problems of governance that had brought down the Qing.

The dominant problems were the struggle for national sovereignty and the struggle for peasant livelihood. The former involved two sorts of claims:

cession of Chinese territory in treaties imposed forcibly by Western powers beginning in the nineteenth century, and outright military invasion and occupation by the Japanese in the 1930s. As to the Chinese peasantry, poverty in the countryside due to socioeconomic conditions of exorbitant taxes, high rents, and usurious credit was aggravated by frequent floods and droughts, which usually brought ruin. An observer compared the condition of the Chinese peasant to a man standing up to his neck in water: one ripple would drown him.[5]

These two struggles were played out in the context of a competition to unify the country. By the 1920s, the **Nationalist Party** and army had emerged as the most prominent political and military force in the country. The Nationalists had their strongest social base in the urban areas; in the countryside, they were mainly dependent on the support of the landlord class. This largely explains Nationalist reluctance to implement land and social reforms to resolve the problems of Chinese peasants. Peasant poverty was exacerbated by absentee landlordism and the replacement of ties of mutual obligation with economic ties enforced by managing agents. Land distribution was not part of the Nationalist agenda; nor were tax controls or provision of cheap credit effectively implemented.

Between 1924 and 1927, the Nationalists allied with the communists in a battle to eliminate regional warlords and to unify China. By the late 1920s, the Nationalists had practically realized this aim. In 1927, they broke their alliance with the communists in a violent massacre that reduced the Communist Party from nearly 58,000 to 10,000 members. The break inaugurated a new civil war. In the end, the Nationalists were forced to retreat to the island of Taiwan in 1949.

By contrast with the Nationalists, the intellectual revolutionaries who founded the **Chinese Communist Party** in 1921 were unlikely contenders for power. The rise and eventual victory of the communists owe much to historic opportunities in the 1930s and 1940s. These opportunities were available for other forces to exploit too, but the communists exploited them best.[6] **Mao Zedong** emerged as leader of the communists in the mid-1930s, consolidating his leadership in the early 1940s.[7]

After the Nationalist attack in 1927, many communists retreated to the countryside. Mao had already reported on the spontaneous impulse for radical social change among the peasantry and had proposed a revolutionary strategy different from that suggested by communist theory or Russian experience. Mao rejected the idea that the Chinese communists could win power through a revolution of the small urban working class in China. Instead, he argued, a communist victory could be achieved only by providing leadership for a nascent rural revolution and building a guerrilla Red Army to surround the cities with the countryside. From a base in southeastern China, Mao and other communists implemented a program of political education and social change, including land redistribution. In 1934, a major Nationalist offensive forced them on a strategic retreat, the historic Long March, that ended at the caves of Yanan in China's northwest, where Mao and his communist forces, their numbers literally decimated, established their headquarters. From Yanan, they built on the strategy of rural revolution to further develop support in the countryside.

The second indispensable component in communist victory was the 1937 Japanese invasion of central China, beyond territory in the northeast that the Japanese had occupied since 1931.[8] Mao seized the strategic initiative to call for a truce in the civil war so that Chinese could unite to resist Japanese aggression. Nationalist leaders were initially wary. This combination of Nationalist reluctance and strong anti-Japanese sentiment in the cities and countryside earned the communists enormous popularity as the true nationalist resistance to foreign aggression. From 1937 to 1945, the communists grew in force from 40,000 to more than a million. Japanese defeat in World War II ended the alliance between Nationalists and communists. A new civil war began.[9] In four years, the communists won victory, as peasant revolutionaries and Chinese nationalists. Once in power, they turned their energies to the construction of socialism.

## History of the PRC

The history of the People's Republic of China (PRC) can be divided into three major periods. In the first, between 1949 and 1957, the Chinese adopted a "lean to one side" strategy, emulating the experience of the first and most powerful communist state, the Soviet Union. The second period began in 1958, when the Chinese introduced their own model of revolutionary development. Except for a few years at the beginning of the 1960s, this Maoist model prevailed until Mao's

death in 1976. A short transitional period ensued, during which immediate problems of policy orientation and leadership succession were resolved with the arrest and trial of key radical leaders. In December 1978, the third period, a new era of reform, ongoing today, was inaugurated with a Central Committee declaration favoring learning from practical experience and rejecting the ideological constraints of Maoism—or any theory.[10] **Deng Xiaoping,** China's new "paramount leader," charted and presided over the reforms. In the same sense that Chinese politics in the two decades ending in 1976 are appropriately characterized as the Maoist years, the last two decades of the twentieth century belong most to Deng—despite important differences in the power of these two leaders and how they wielded it.

*"Lean to One Side"* The Chinese communists had won power largely by ignoring Soviet advice. Once in power, however, they looked to the Soviet Union for a plan to build socialism. They concluded a treaty of friendship and alliance in 1950. Soviet financial aid to China in the 1950s was not large. Mainly, aid was given in a massive technology transfer: over 12,000 Soviet engineers and technicians were sent to work in China; over 6,000 Chinese studied in Soviet universities, tens of thousands more in Soviet factories on short-term training courses. With this Soviet assistance, the Chinese developed heavy industry, establishing a centralized bureaucracy of planning agencies and industrial ministries to manage the economy according to five-year plans. They nationalized private industry. In the early 1950s, they sent communists down to the grassroots to instigate and organize land reform, a violent "class struggle." Each peasant household was classified according to land holdings, and land seized from landlords was redistributed to poor peasants, the majority of the peasantry.[11] Agricultural collectivization followed. This process was also essentially coercive, especially in its later stages, but not as violent as land reform.

The "lean to one side" period did feature some Maoist strategies, especially in political participation and socialization. The Chinese implemented many policies by mobilizing the masses in intensive campaigns, with essentially compulsory participation. For the Chinese communists, potential regime opponents—such as intellectuals and capitalists—were capable of being politically transformed through practices such as "thought reform." Communist leaders were sufficiently confident about the results of political education and regime accomplishments to invite nonparty intellectuals to voice criticism in the Hundred Flowers Campaign in 1957. When criticism was harsh, revealing weak support for the communist system, the leaders quickly reversed themselves. They launched an Anti-Rightist Campaign, which discovered more "poisonous weeds" than "blooming flowers." About a half million people, many of them intellectuals, were persecuted as "rightists" in a campaign that effectively silenced political opposition for twenty years.[12] Mass campaigns, political education, and political labeling were all coercive measures that resulted in the persecution of millions. To some extent, this coercion had a characteristic Maoist (and Confucian) element: fundamentally, it rejected the Stalinist version of political purge as physical liquidation, because it viewed the individual as malleable and ultimately educable. Yet, "enemies of the people" were not spared: one million to three million landlords and "counterrevolutionaries" were persecuted to death in the early 1950s alone.

In 1956, frictions in relations with the Soviet Union began to develop. Tensions increased throughout the 1950s, resulting in the withdrawal of aid and advisers and a Sino-Soviet split that shocked the world in 1960. Major irritants included Soviet reluctance to support efforts to "liberate" Taiwan, Soviet unwillingness to aid China's nuclear development, and a relaxation of Soviet hostility toward the United States. At about the same time, Mao was reconsidering his view of the Soviet model of development and developing his own radical model of building communism.

**Great Leap Forward** The first five-year plan had invested in heavy industry, not agriculture. Following the Soviet model, central planners had not diverted resources from industry to promote agricultural growth. In 1958, Mao proposed a strategy of simultaneous development of industry and agriculture to be achieved in two ways: (1) the labor-intensive mass mobilization of peasants to increase agricultural output by building irrigation facilities, and (2) the organization of primitive production processes to give inputs to agriculture (such as small chemical fertilizer plants and primitive steel furnaces to make tools) without taking resources from industry. A crucial element of Mao's solution was an increase in size of the collective

farms. In order to build irrigation facilities, local communist officials needed to control a labor force of large numbers of peasants, larger than the current collectives that grouped together a few hundred households. By combining several collectives into one gigantic farm, Mao hoped to realize economies of scale. In 1958, with prodding from above, the people's communes were born, grouping together thousands of households in one unit of economic and political organization managed by Communist Party officials.

The Maoist model was not simply an economic development strategy. It was fundamentally a political campaign, a point exemplified in the main slogan of the **Great Leap Forward:** "politics in command."[13] The Great Leap Forward abandoned most material rewards for moral incentives. By 1958, in Mao's view, Chinese peasants had demonstrated tremendous enthusiasm and were ready to leap into communism, if properly mobilized by local leaders. In the politically charged climate, economic expertise was denigrated and caution criticized as lack of faith in the masses. Leaders in Beijing set output targets high, demanding that local leaders believe in the ability of the Chinese people to accomplish miracles. By implication, failure to achieve high targets could be due only to poor leadership. A dangerous vicious cycle was set in motion: local leaders competed to demonstrate their political correctness; when communes failed to meet targets set in Beijing, local leaders calculated output imaginatively to report targets had been met or exceeded; production results were increasingly exaggerated as reports went to higher and higher levels; the response from Beijing to the falsely reported leap in output was a further leap in targets.

In 1958, dislocation associated with forming the communes and peasant mobilization to help meet high steel output targets by making steel in primitive furnaces was so great that the autumn harvest was not all gathered. That year too, a false belief in excess production led to reduction in areas sown in grain. Even with reduced acreage, peasant contributions to agricultural labor were decreasing due to physical exhaustion, weak material rewards, and the abolition of private plots (and, in some cases, private property for complete communization). In 1959, when top Chinese leaders met to consider these problems, the Minister of National Defense criticized radicalism in policy implementation. In response, Mao accused the minister of factionalism, turned the meeting into a referendum on his leadership, and challenged others to dare to attack the Leap's radical principles.

The meeting was a terrible turning point. With political correctness reasserted, radicalism returned. Moreover, just as the 1957 antirightist campaign had silenced opposition outside the party, Mao's 1959 accusations and threats effectively silenced opposition in the top echelons of party leadership.[14] That same year, large parts of China suffered from severe drought, others from severe flooding, in one of the worst natural disasters experienced in decades.

**Retreat from the Leap**  Over the next three years, the famine cost an estimated 27 million lives.[15] China retreated from Maoist radicalism. Mao retreated from day-to-day management of public affairs, but continued in his position as Communist Party chairman. In the early 1960s, the communes ceased to be relevant to agricultural production. Instead, peasant households contracted with the state for production, selling the surplus in newly established free markets. In industry, there was a renewed reliance on material incentives, technical expertise, and profitability as the standard to judge performance. The education system emphasized the creation of a knowledgeable and highly skilled corps of managers and leaders. Policy processes took into account advice by experts, rather than reliance on mass miracles.

**Cultural Revolution**  By the mid-1960s, Mao had further developed his radical critique of the Soviet model and extended it to the Chinese experience. In China, Mao saw a "new class" of economic managers and political officials, privileged by elitist policies that increased social antagonisms. In 1966, Mao argued that many communist leaders (notably, China's head of state, Liu Shaoqi, but also others, including Deng Xiaoping) were corrupt "capitalist roaders" who opposed socialism and must be thrown out of power. He launched the Great Proletarian Cultural Revolution, yet another exercise in radical excess. The **Cultural Revolution** was simultaneously a power struggle, an ideological battle, and a mass campaign to transform culture. Compared with the Great Leap Forward, its impact on the Chinese economy was minor; its impact on society was devastating.

For Mao, the enemy of socialism was within the Communist Party. Unable to rely on the party to correct

Defense Minister Lin Biao sits beside Chairman Mao Zedong and Premier Zhou Enlai during the Cultural Revolution. PLA soldiers wave the Little Red Book of quotations from Chairman Mao, a reflection of the cult of Mao that Lin helped to build.

SV Bilderdienst/The Image Works

its mistakes, Mao instructed secondary school and university students to overturn "bourgeois culture" and "bombard the headquarters." The Communist Party became effectively powerless as an organization. For the first time since 1949, Chinese were free to organize politically. Unconstrained by the party, Chinese engaged in political action legitimated by their own interpretations of Mao Zedong Thought. Students formed radical Red Guard groups to criticize and persecute victims, often chosen quite arbitrarily or for reasons more personal than political. In schools, factories, and government agencies, those in power were criticized and persecuted. Persecution was frequently physical. It was not uncommon for victims to be held in makeshift prisons, forced to do harsh manual labor, and subjected to violent public "struggle sessions" to force them to confess their crimes. Many were "struggled" to death, and many others committed suicide. Factional fighting was inevitable, as rival Red Guard groups fought for power, each faction claiming true representation of Mao Zedong Thought.[16]

In 1967, the country was near anarchy. The schools had been shut down; most party and government offices no longer functioned; transportation and communications were severely disrupted; factional struggles were increasingly violent contests, some of them armed confrontations. Having unleashed social conflict, Mao had been able to manipulate it—but not to control it. Mao called on the army to restore order, a process that began in 1969.

The 1970s were years of more moderate conflict, mostly played out as a struggle at the apex of power rather than in society generally. Radical leaders (including Mao's wife) who had risen to power in the Cultural Revolution supported a continuation of radical policies. Other leaders, reinstated by Mao to balance the power of the radicals, supported policies of economic modernization. The conflict was ongoing at the time of Mao's death in 1976. Within two years, the economic modernizers had won. China embarked on a new course of reform, different from anything in the experience of any communist system.

## SOCIAL CONDITIONS

Chinese society has changed in various ways since the communists came to power. These changes include social structural transformations engineered by the regime, especially in the early decades. This section focuses on basic features that make up the social environment for Chinese politics that have not undergone fundamental transformation but have changed only in degree, if at all.

First among these is China's huge population. When the communists came to power in 1949, China's population was 540 million. Today China remains the world's most populous country, with a population of 1.3 billion. As in the 1950s, most Chinese live in the countryside, although the proportion has been changing more rapidly in recent years. In the 1950s, about 85 percent of Chinese lived in the countryside; by 1980 that proportion had decreased only slightly, to 82 percent. More than two decades of economic reform produced significant transformation. De facto relaxation of rural to urban migration restrictions liberated the underemployed farming population to seek work in cities. Rural industrialization and the growth of towns also changed the situation. By 2005, only 57 percent of Chinese lived in the countryside. An increasing proportion of this rural population work at least part-time in industry. Before economic reforms in the 1980s, state-owned enterprises dominated industry in China. Today, rural collective industry, in the form of township and village enterprises under the direction of local governments, is the most dynamic industrial sector.

The second basic feature involves geography. Although China is the world's second largest country in area, the population is concentrated in the eastern third of the land. This is largely because only about a quarter of China's land is arable. Population growth and reduction in cultivated area have greatly exacerbated the land shortage. Despite efforts to preserve arable land for farming, China's leaders have been unable to reverse the reduction in cultivated area. In part, this is a result of agricultural decollectivization and a return to household farming: land is used for property borders, burial grounds, and bigger houses. In recent years, local government land requisitions for lucrative residential and industrial development have further reduced arable land and provoked much rural unrest. The basic problem of feeding China's large population can be expected to continue to loom large as more Chinese grow prosperous and change their diet: eating more, and eating more meat and less grain.

The third feature is that China is a multiethnic state. At least 92 percent of Chinese are ethnically Han, but there are fifty-five recognized **ethnic minorities,** ranging in number from a few thousand to more than 16 million. Although minorities make up only a fairly small proportion of China's population, areas in which minorities live comprise more than 60 percent of China's territory, and much of this is in strategically important border regions.[17] This includes Tibet (bordering India) and Xinjiang (bordering three new post-Soviet states), which have experienced fairly continuous minority unrest over the decades. The Chinese have maintained considerable armed forces in these areas to quell secessionist efforts.

Finally, Han Chinese share the same Chinese written language, a unifying force in China for more than two millennia, practically defining what it is to be Chinese. The same written language is spoken in many different dialects, however, often making communication difficult. Mandarin, based on the dialect of the Beijing locality, is the official language promoted by the communist regime through the education system and mass media.

## STRUCTURE OF THE PARTY-STATE

From top to bottom, Chinese politics has changed noticeably since the Maoist period. Yet, the essential form of the Chinese political system retains an organizational design borrowed decades ago from the Soviet Union and developed nearly a century ago in Russia by Lenin—the design of the communist **party-state.**

### Design Features

Lenin viewed political legitimacy in ways that justify a monopoly of power by a communist party elite that is not popularly elected. He believed that ordinary citizens do not understand their own real interests and that larger interests of society are not best advanced by aggregating interests that citizens articulate. According to Lenin, as ordinary citizens typically lack revolutionary consciousness and knowledge of communist theory, they are incapable of making the correct choices that will lead from capitalism to socialism and toward communism—a utopia characterized by a high level of economic prosperity, an absence of social conflict, and a minimal role for government. Lenin proposed a solution to this problem: a political party and political system built on the principles of guardianship and hierarchy.[18] To these two principles, Chinese leaders

added the idea of the mass line, formulated by Mao in the 1940s. Guardianship and hierarchy define the communist party-state. The mass line adds another dimension, which moderates guardianship.

**Guardianship** describes the main relationship between the Communist Party and society. The party bases its claim to legitimate rule not on representation of the expressed preferences of a majority but on representation of the "historical best interests" of all the people. In theory, as most ordinary citizens do not know their best interests, society is best led by an elite vanguard party with a superior understanding of the historical laws of development. The Communist Party is therefore an exclusive organization—in China, membership is about 5 percent of the population—not a mass political party with membership open to all. The notion of Communist Party leadership is explicitly set forth in each of the four Chinese constitutions promulgated since 1949, as is some version of the notion of dictatorship. Currently, the constitution describes the political system as a socialist state under the "people's democratic dictatorship." As the Communist Party is the only organization with the politically correct knowledge to lead society, it is the authoritative arbiter of the interests of the people. In effect, dictatorship in the name of the people is Communist Party dictatorship. Party leaders today are more informed of public opinion than in the past, but there is no place in the Chinese political system (or in Leninist theory) for organized opposition to Communist Party leadership.

Chinese Communist Party guardianship is, in theory, informed by the practice of the **mass line.** The party leads, but its leadership is not isolated from the opinions and preferences of the mass public. The degree to which mass preferences actually find expression in public policy depends on their fit with larger goals determined by party leaders. Party leaders at all levels (but especially at the grassroots) are supposed to maintain a close relationship with ordinary citizens so that the party organization can transform the "scattered and unsystematic ideas" of the masses into "correct ideas" and propagate them "until the masses embrace them as their own." In this way, policy is supposed to flow "from the masses to the masses."[19]

*Party Organization*    The internal organization of the Communist Party is organized around a hierarchy of party congresses and committees extending from the top of the system down to the grassroots. Lower party organizations are subordinate to higher party organizations, and individual party members are subordinate to the party as an organization. Inner-party rules for decisionmaking are based on the Leninist principle of **democratic centralism.**

In democratic centralism, democracy refers mainly to consultation. It requires that party leaders provide opportunities for discussion, criticism, and proposals in party organizations (often including lower party organizations) as part of the normal process of deciding important issues or making policy.

Centralism requires unified discipline throughout the party: top-level official party decisions are binding on party organizations and members. Centralism is never sacrificed to democracy. Party members are allowed to hold personal views contrary to party decisions and to voice them through proper party channels, but they are not free to act in ways that promote these views. According to the Communist Party constitution, the formation of "factions" or any sort of "small group activity" within the party is a punishable violation of organizational discipline. Communist Party hierarchy and the requirement that party members observe party discipline are designed as organizational guarantees that the party, in exercising leadership over society, acts as a unified force, responsive to the leadership of the highest level of party organization.

Ideology is today both less prominent and less coherent in Chinese politics than it was in the past. The principles of guardianship, hierarchy, and the mass line are not inconsequential abstractions, however. They have concrete practical implications, evident throughout the Chinese political system. Change in the system is evident too, of course, both as a product and by-product of policies of reform in the past two decades. Yet, while the political reforms of recent decades are not trivial, they do not add up to fundamental systemic change. For now, as in the past, the design of the communist party-state is a fair model of the organization of political power in China.

*Two Hierarchies, with Party Leadership*  The design of the communist party-state is perhaps most evident in the organization of power in two hierarchies of political structures, illustrated in Figure 13.1. The focus in this section is politics at the national level, what the Chinese refer to as the political center of the system, but government structures are more or less duplicated at each level of the political system by Communist Party structures. In principle, there is a division of labor between party and government structures. In practice, the two often perform similar functions, with party structures and party officials exercising leadership over parallel government structures and government officials. This section on political structures distinguishes the party from the government, while elaborating on the variety of mechanisms the party uses to exercise control over officials in party and government structures. The following sections on policymaking and policy implementation emphasize that, because of the interconnectedness of party and government, distinctions between party and government are of only limited use in understanding decisionmaking in China. Both party and government structures have changed since 1949. The description in the following section focuses on the system that emerged in the reform era.

## Government Structures

At the political center in Beijing, the key government structures are the **National People's Congress (NPC),** which is China's legislature, and the **State Council,** which exercises executive functions. Under the State Council are government ministries and commissions, which have ranged in number from thirty-two to 100 since 1949. Below the political center, government structures extend downward in a five-tiered hierarchy consisting of 31 provinces, 333 large cities, 2,862 counties, 41,636 townships, and 629,000 villages. Local government structures (local people's congresses, local governments, and government departments) are found at the provincial, municipal, county, and township levels. The provincial level includes four megacities (Beijing, Shanghai, Tianjin, and Chongqing). As shown in Figure 13.1, Chinese voters elect delegates to township and county people's congresses only. Municipal, provincial, and national congress delegates are elected by congresses one level down. At all five levels, congress delegates elect their governments. Villages are popularly elected self-governing rural grassroots organizations, not part of the formal government hierarchy.

*National People's Congress*  According to the constitution, the highest organization of state authority is the NPC.[20] The NPC and its permanent body, the NPC Standing Committee, exercise legislative functions.

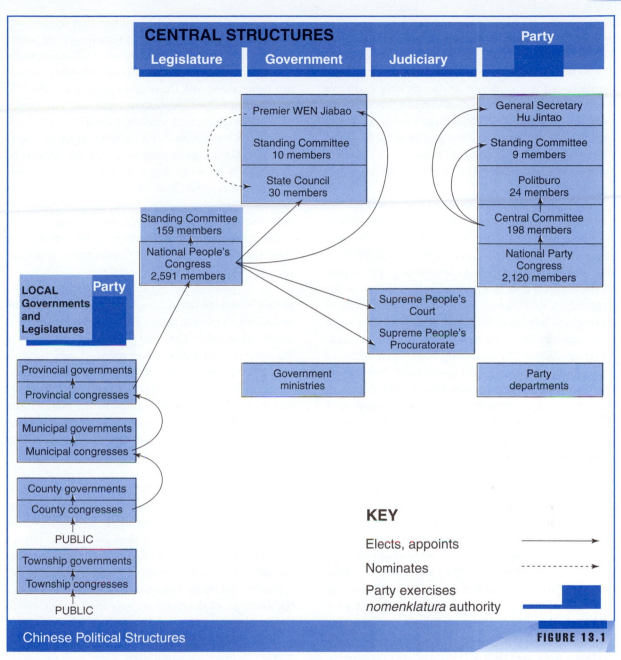

CENTRAL STRUCTURES
Party

Legislature    Government    Judiciary

Premier WEN Jiabao

Standing Committee
10 members

State Council
30 members

General Secretary
Hu Jintao

Standing Committee
9 members

Politburo
24 members

Central Committee
198 members

National Party
Congress
2,120 members

Standing Committee
159 members

National People's
Congress
2,591 members

LOCAL
Governments
and
Legislatures

Party

Supreme People's
Court

Supreme People's
Procuratorate

Provincial governments

Provincial congresses

Government
ministries

Party
departments

Municipal governments

Municipal congresses

County governments

County congresses

PUBLIC

KEY

Township governments

Township congresses

PUBLIC

Elects, appoints

Nominates

Party exercises
*nomenklatura* authority

Chinese Political Structures

**FIGURE 13.1**

NPC delegates are elected for five-year terms by delegates in provincial-level congresses and the armed forces. Normally, NPC delegates assemble once annually for a plenary session of about two weeks (although they did not meet at all between 1965 and 1975). The number and composition of delegates are prescribed by law, but the NPC has always been huge. In 1986, the law set a ceiling of 3,000 delegates, which is about the number elected to each congress since 1983. By law, urban Chinese are overrepresented: a 1995 law set the ratio of rural to urban Chinese per NPC delegate at 4:1—already less unequal than in previous years, due to legal change as well as urbanization.

Formally, the NPC has extensive powers, including amendment of the constitution, passage and amendment of legislation, approval of economic plans and government work reports, and appointment of top state and government leaders. For most of the year, when the NPC is not in session, its Standing Committee of about 150 members, who reside in Beijing and meet regularly throughout the year, serves as the working legislative assembly. The 1982 constitution considerably strengthened the role of the NPC Standing Committee. It now exercises all but the most formal powers of the NPC and prepares the agenda for the annual NPC plenary sessions, when the full NPC typically ratifies its interim legislative actions.

Is the NPC (and its Standing Committee) a "rubber stamp" assembly? For the Maoist years, the answer is clearly "yes." In recent decades, however, the NPC has become more assertive, and its Standing Committee has assumed a greater role in law making. This is part of the political reform undertaken in response to the extreme institutional nihilism of the Cultural Revolution. NPC assertiveness is evident in an increase in delegate motions (by an order of magnitude) and, more significantly, in dissenting votes. The practice of unanimous approval, once automatic, has ended, sometimes with embarrassing results. In 1998, 45 percent of NPC delegates demonstrated their disapproval of the government's failure to control corruption by abstaining or voting against the work report of the chief procurator. While this high level of dissent remains unusual for votes on work reports, economic plans, and official appointments, dissenting votes of 20 to 30 percent on draft laws are not uncommon. Actual failure to pass legislation submitted to the NPC has occurred twice: a draft of the controversial Enterprise Bankruptcy Law was voted down in 1986, and a very restrictive draft of the Law on Public Demonstrations was voted down not long after the crushing of the 1989 mass protests. Both laws were sent back for substantial revision before securing the requisite majority approval in the NPC. A dramatic example of the new view of NPC authority occurred in 1989, when Hu Jiwei circulated a petition among fellow NPC Standing Committee members to call an emergency meeting of the NPC to exercise its constitutional power to repeal martial law.

The full NPC cannot be expected to function routinely as a credible legislature because it is too large and meets too infrequently and briefly. More important is the lawmaking role of the less cumbersome NPC Standing Committee. In the early 1980s, many party and government elders retired from important positions in central and provincial administration to the NPC Standing Committee. Instead of retreating from political life, these elders used the Standing Committee as a channel for political influence. Their enhanced role was institutionalized with the establishment of a Legislative Affairs Committee (with significant staff) and eight permanent specialized legislative committees to consider draft legislation. With these changes, the NPC (and its Standing Committee) can no longer be dismissed as a rubber stamp. The legislature remains institutionally weak, however, for two main reasons (discussed later in this chapter): the practice of executive-led government (which does not distinguish the Chinese system from parliamentary systems in other countries) and the practice of Communist Party leadership (which is more fundamental).

*State Council* In lawmaking, the State Council is the center of government activity, although this role too is newly enhanced.[21] The State Council is composed of the premier, who is head of government, and his cabinet of vice-premiers, state councillors, ministers, auditor general, and secretary general (currently thirty-six members, all formally nominated by the premier and appointed by the NPC). In 2003, Wen Jiabao became premier. The State Council has its own Standing Committee, which meets twice weekly, with members reporting on work in their assigned portfolios. As in parliamentary systems, the bulk of legislation is drafted by specialized ministries and commissions under the direction of the cabinet. Also, however, as most Chinese laws are drafted in general and imprecise language, they require detailed "implementing regulations" to have any effect. These regulations are typically drafted by State Council ministries (under the direction of the newly reestablished State Council Legislation Bureau) and promulgated by the ministries or State Council without consideration by the NPC or its Standing Committee.

*Communist Party Leadership* The Communist Party exercises direct leadership over government and legislative functions in a variety of ways. Before the NPC assembles, party leaders convene a meeting of all delegates who are members of the Communist Party (73 percent of NPC delegates in 2006). At these meetings, leaders discuss the NPC agenda and offer "hopes" of the party leaders for the forthcoming session, including suggestions about the tone (how open or restrained

NPC debate should be, for example). Also, NPC powers of appointment are effectively nullified by party control over candidate nomination and the usual practice of an equal number of candidates and positions. For example, although the NPC formally appoints the president, vice president, premier, and cabinet members, there has never been more than one nominee for these positions and candidate nomination is decided at the party meeting convened before the NPC assembles. The only positions for which NPC elections have ever featured choice are the 1988 and 1998 elections to the NPC Standing Committee. Those elections featured no choice for positions of leadership, however, and only limited choice for regular NPC Standing Committee membership (about 6 percent more candidates than positions).

As to lawmaking, Communist Party leaders have veto power over all legislation of consequence. The system of party review of legislation that emerged in the early 1990s rejects party micromanagement of the State Council or NPC Standing Committee work. Nonetheless, all important laws, constitutional amendments, and political laws submitted to the NPC or its Standing Committee must have prior approval by the party center. In short, the Chinese system is executive-led government, but with an important difference having to do with the role of the Communist Party.

The president of the PRC is head of state. This is a purely ceremonial office, held by **Hu Jintao.** Hu is also head of the Communist Party organization and of the Central Military Commission, in which leadership of military forces is formally vested. The commission was established as a government structure only in 1982, but its Communist Party counterpart functioned long before then and remains in existence, with the same membership in party and government structures.

*Judiciary* Judicial authority rests with the Supreme People's Court at the center and with local people's courts below. Formally, the Supreme People's Court is responsible to the NPC. Courts at lower levels are responsible to the people's congresses at their respective levels and also take direction from courts above them.

The Supreme People's Procuratorate, restored in 1978 after decades of neglect, is the central prosecutorial agency. It sits at the top of a hierarchy of procuratorates extending down to the county level, each

formally responsible to a local people's congress and each also under the direction of the procuratorate above. The Supreme People's Procuratorate is responsible to the NPC.

Procuratorates act as a bridge between public security agencies and the courts. They supervise criminal investigations, approve arrests, and prosecute cases. Beginning in the mid-1980s, the most important role of the procuratorates has been investigation and prosecution of corruption. In each new congress session, the NPC appoints the chief justice of the Supreme People's Court and the chief procurator.

## Party Structures

At the political center in Beijing, the key party structures are the National Party Congress and its Central Committee, the Politburo, and the Politburo Standing Committee. In addition, party departments are organized under a secretariat. Below the center, down to the township level, are local party congresses and local party committees.

*National Party Congress* As in the government hierarchy, while the formal power of Communist Party structures is directly proportional to size, actual impact on policy is inversely proportional to size. The Communist Party constitution vests supreme authority in the **National Party Congress,** but this structure is too big and meets too infrequently to play a significant role in political decisionmaking. The Central Committee determines the number of congress delegates and the procedures for their election. Since 1949, National Party Congresses have ranged in size from one to two thousand delegates, with recent congresses at about two thousand delegates. In the past, the congresses met irregularly, but party constitutions since 1969 have stipulated that congresses are normally convened at five-year intervals. This has been more or less the practice since 1969 and has been strictly observed in the post-Mao years, as shown in Table 13.1. The seventeenth party congress met in October 2007.

National Party Congress sessions are short, about a week or two at most. A main function is to ratify important changes in broad policy orientation already decided by more important smaller party structures. Although party congresses yield no surprises, these changes receive their highest formal endorsement at

| TABLE 13.1 Chinese Communist Party Congresses and Growth of Party Membership, 1921–2007 | | |
|---|---|---|
| **Congress** | **Year** | **Party Members** |
| 1st | 1921 | More than 50 |
| 2nd | 1922 | 123 |
| 3rd | 1923 | 432 |
| 4th | 1925 | 950 |
| 5th | 1927 | 57,900[a] |
| 6th | 1928 | 40,000 |
| 7th | 1945 | 1.2 million |
| **Founding of the PRC, 1949** | | |
| 8th | 1956 | 11 million |
| 9th | 1969 | 22 million |
| 10th | 1973 | 28 million |
| 11th | 1977 | 35 million |
| 12th | 1982 | 40 million |
| 13th | 1987 | 46 million |
| 14th | 1992 | 51 million |
| 15th | 1997 | 58 million |
| 16th | 2002 | 66 million |
| 17th | 2007 | 74 million |

[a] Communist party membership dropped from 57,900 to 10,000 after April 1927, when the Nationalists broke the "united front" with the communists in a massacre that decimated communist forces and ignited civil war.

Source: *Beijing Review*, 41, no. 8 (1998): 22; *People's Daily*, 2 September 2002, and 19 June 2006; Xinhua, 2 July 2008.

the party congresses. Therefore, the sessions have the public appearance of major historic events. A second function of the National Party Congress is to elect the **Central Committee,** which exercises the powers of the congress between sessions. Official candidates for Central Committee membership are determined by the Politburo before the congress meets. According to the 1982 party constitution, elections to the Central Committee are by secret ballot, and wide deliberation and discussion of candidates precedes them. Of course, centralism prevails: elections rarely offer choice (or much choice) among candidates.

**Central Committee** The Central Committee is the Chinese political elite, broadly defined: it is a collection of the most powerful several hundred political leaders in the country. All Central Committee members hold some major substantive position of leadership, as ministers in the central state bureaucracy or provincial party leaders, for example. Membership on the Central Committee reflects this political power—it does not confer it. In this sense, the Central Committee is less important intrinsically as a political structure than extrinsically, for the different sorts of interests and constituencies represented by its members.

Although the Central Committee does not initiate policy, changes in policy or leaders at the political center must be approved by it. This is done fairly routinely at plenary sessions now convened at least annually. Party leaders at the top rely on the bureaucratic and regional elites on the Central Committee to ensure that the "party line" is realized in practice. Central Committee membership brings these elites into the process as participants and, in effect, guarantors: in endorsing party policy, members also take on responsibility for its realization.

*Politburo* The Central Committee elects the **Politburo,** the Politburo Standing Committee, and the party general secretary—all of whom are also Central Committee members. These leaders are at the very apex of the political system. The composition of these structures is determined by party leaders before the party congress, and elections are mainly ceremonial, featuring no candidate choice. The Politburo is the top political elite, usually no more than two dozen leaders, most of whom have responsibility for overseeing policymaking in some issue area. Its inner circle is the Politburo Standing Committee, typically no more than a half-dozen leaders, who meet about once weekly, in meetings convened and chaired by the party general secretary. Members of the Politburo and its Standing Committee are the core political decision-makers in China, presiding over a process that concentrates great power at the top.

*Top Leader and the Succession Problem* Since the abolition of the position of party chairman in 1982, the top party leader is the general secretary, a position held by Hu Jintao since 2002 (see Box 13.1). The change in terminology reflects the effort to promote collective leadership, a reaction against norms of past years when Mao presided as nearly all-powerful chairman of the party until his death in 1976. Yet, if general secretaries in the 1980s and 1990s have been less powerful than Chairman Mao, this has mainly to do with the unusual elite politics of the post-Mao

**BOX 13.1**

## Hu Jintao and the "Fourth Generation" of Leaders

In November 2002, Jiang Zemin relinquished to Hu Jintao the office of Communist Party general secretary. This event marked the first time in PRC history that the transfer of party leadership occurred as a regular matter at a party congress, rather than as a result of the death or political purge of the incumbent. Hu succeeded Jiang in his other offices in the years that followed: the presidency of the PRC in 2003, the chairmanship of the party Central Military Commission in 2004, and the chairmanship of the government Central Military Commission in 2005. Hu is a technocrat: he graduated in hydraulic engineering at the prestigious Qinghua University, which is known as China's MIT. He is typical of the "fourth generation" of Chinese leaders, the least dogmatic cohort to accede to top offices in Chinese politics. As president of the Central Party School in the 1990s, Hu supported bold studies of political reform, including reform of the party. However, as party leader, Hu has been less bold—promoting increased supervision of the mass media and strengthening control of Internet content, for example.

transition period and especially the role of Deng Xiaoping.[22]

In communist systems, the death of the top leader creates a succession crisis: there is no formal or generally acknowledged position of second-in-command and no regularized mechanism to choose a new top leader. Mao's death ushered in a power struggle at the top, won by Deng and his fellow modernizers. Deng, already in his seventies at the time of Mao's death, chose to eschew top formal leadership of party or government in the interest of resolving the problem of succession.

In the late 1970s, Communist Party elders who had formerly held important positions of power were reinstated after years of forced retirement during the Cultural Revolution. Within a few years, however, many of them retired (or semiretired) to the "second line," to serve as advisers and involve themselves only in major policy issues or broad strategy.

At the very top, a half-dozen elders, all senior communist revolutionaries in their eighties or nineties, continued to play key roles in decisionmaking and occupy formal positions of leadership, although not the top party or government positions. The best example, of course, was "paramount leader" Deng himself. Deng never held the top formal position of leadership in party or government, although he was on the Politburo Standing Committee until 1987 and chaired the Central Military Commission until 1989. Just below this very small group at the top, elders retired to advisory positions on a Central Advisory Commission, set up in 1982. Other elders "retired" to formal positions on the NPC. Younger leaders were promoted to the top positions on the "first line," to allow them to develop their own bases of support and authority, with the support of their elder patrons.

This arrangement did not provide a solution to the succession problem, however. In principle, elders on the second line used their prestige and informal power to support younger leaders in top executive positions. In practice, younger leaders on the first line, in the effort to establish their own authority, sometimes adopted positions at odds with the views of elder patrons. Friction with party elders resulted in two purges of top party executives in the 1980s: Hu Yaobang was dismissed as party general secretary in 1987 and his successor Zhao Ziyang was dismissed in 1989 (see Figure 13.2). The situation today is different: by the mid-1990s, most of the elders at the very top, including Deng, had "gone to see Marx," and the Central Advisory Commission had been dismantled, having served its purpose of easing leaders into retirement. After a dozen years as party secretary and beneficiary of Deng's support until Deng's death in 1997, Jiang Zemin stepped down in 2002, lending his support to Hu Jintao.

**Party Bureaucracy** The party has its own set of bureaucratic structures, managed by the Secretariat. The Secretariat provides staff support for the Politburo, transforming Politburo decisions into instructions for subordinate party departments. Compared with their government counterparts, party departments are fewer in number and have more broadly defined areas of competence.

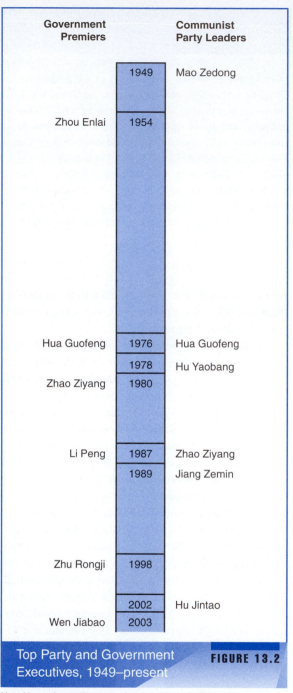

| Government Premiers | | Communist Party Leaders |
|---|---|---|
| | 1949 | Mao Zedong |
| Zhou Enlai | 1954 | |
| Hua Guofeng | 1976 | Hua Guofeng |
| | 1978 | Hu Yaobang |
| Zhao Ziyang | 1980 | |
| Li Peng | 1987 | Zhao Ziyang |
| | 1989 | Jiang Zemin |
| Zhu Rongji | 1998 | |
| | 2002 | Hu Jintao |
| Wen Jiabao | 2003 | |

**Top Party and Government Executives, 1949–present**    **FIGURE 13.2**

Note: Year refers to the year a leader assumed office.

## People's Liberation Army

The **People's Liberation Army (PLA),** which includes the navy, air force, and army, has played a major role in Chinese politics. Party and army were practically inseparable until 1949. After 1949, the PLA participated in important nonmilitary functions, such as economic construction. In the Cultural Revolution, the PLA was brought more directly into politics to resolve violent factional struggles in society, at a time when party and government structures had been shattered. In 1989, the PLA was instrumental in crushing the mass protests.

The PLA does not dictate policy to party leaders, but it is the self-appointed guardian of Chinese sovereignty and nationalism, with a particular interest in preventing Taiwan's independence.[23] This issue has the greatest potential to spark military confrontation, and it is a matter the Chinese claim is completely domestic. Since the mid-1980s, the PLA has engaged in a program of military modernization and professionalization, increasing defense expenditures, procuring new weapons systems and technologies, and streamlining forces to realize a "smaller but stronger" force of 2.5 million. Despite these efforts, the military gap between China and the West is not narrowing, but widening, as western military technological advances continue at an increasingly rapid pace. The PLA is at least a decade behind in almost all weapons systems and remains predominantly a land force.

## Party Dominance

Party and government structures from top to bottom are staffed by more than 40 million officials on state salaries. One important mechanism of party leadership, described earlier in this chapter, is the structural arrangement: the duplication of political structures and the dominance of party structures and leaders over government structures and leaders. The Chinese Communist Party exercises leadership in political structures in other ways too. Among the most important are overlapping directorships, "party core groups," party membership penetration, and the *nomenklatura* system. Mechanisms of party leadership specific to policymaking are discussed later in this chapter.

*Nomenklatura System* The **nomenklatura system** is the most important mechanism by which the Communist Party exerts control over officials. In some sense, it is the linchpin of the political system. It refers to the management of all party and government officials in positions of even moderate importance by party committees. Party committees exercise authority over all major personnel decisions (such as appointment, promotion, transfer, and removal from office). Management authority is organized hierarchically and specified in lists of official positions. Any official at or above the rank of section chief is on such a list.[24] This amounted to about 8 million officials in the late 1980s, and the number must be considerably higher now.

Today, party committees, through their organization departments, directly manage all officials in positions one level down in the administrative hierarchy. At the top of the system, the Politburo exercises direct management authority over all officials at the provincial level in the territorial hierarchy and at the ministerial level in the bureaucratic hierarchy—about 7,000 officials in all (including the entire NPC Standing Committee, for example).

The extension of management authority downward in a hierarchy of dyadic relationships that are known to officials has important implications. Party leaders have a means of ensuring that the real constituency of every important official is the superior party committee—and ultimately the Central Committee and its Politburo. In looking ahead to career advancement, then, even officials who owe their positions formally to elections must look upward to "selectorates" of party committees rather than only (if at all) downward to electorates of congress deputies and ordinary citizens. Otherwise, they can be penalized. For example, for his effort in 1989 to assert NPC authority to repeal martial law, Hu Jiwei was expelled from the NPC Standing Committee.

**Party Membership** Another means by which the Communist Party exercises leadership over officials is in party membership penetration in political structures. The vast majority of officials in political structures (including government structures and positions filled by elections) are Communist Party members. At their places of work, officials are members of party committees, general branches, or branches located in a hierarchy of basic-level party organizations. They meet regularly to participate in party "organizational life," which is quite apart from their professional work. They are obliged to observe the inner-party discipline of democratic centralism. The routine activities of party branches in government offices are supervised by departments specially assigned to ensure that the Communist Party remains an active force in government structures. Because the party monopolizes opportunities to get along and ahead in the Chinese political system, the organizational hierarchy and party discipline designed to guarantee unified party leadership over society also promote party leadership in political structures.

**Party Core Groups** Separate from the basic-level party organizations that bring party members in all workplaces under the Communist Party hierarchy are party core groups, formed in government structures only and composed of a handful of party members who hold the most senior positions.[25] The head of the party core group is normally also the head of the structure (for example, government ministers typically head party core groups of their respective ministries). Party core groups are appointed by the party committees one level up, and they answer to these party committees. While basic-level party organizations are mechanisms to promote unity and discipline under party leadership within political structures overall, party core groups are mechanisms to promote party leadership over leaders in their government host structures. Between 1987 and 1988, the system of party core groups was formally abolished (and many were actually dismantled) as part of a brief reform effort to separate party and government functions. Party core groups were quickly revived in 1989, however, after the purge of Zhao Ziyang, the leader most closely associated with the reform.

**Overlapping Directorships** Finally, the structural distinctions illustrated in Figure 13.1 mask some overlap of directorates in party and government structures. Hu Jintao is concurrently head of state, head of the party, and chairman of the Central Military Commission of both government and party. The practice of "wearing two hats" (party and government) has always been common. Premier Wen Jiabao is also at the apex of party power, as a member of the Politburo Standing Committee. Wu Bangguo, who chairs the NPC Standing Committee, is also a member of the Politburo Standing Committee. Overlapping directorships were much more extensive in the past than they are now. Membership of local party committees and their parallel governments used to be indistinguishable. In the 1980s, overlapping directorships were retained at the political center, but practically eliminated at lower levels. There is some evidence that they are returning.

*Elite Recruitment*  Some key features of elite recruitment emerge from the discussion earlier in this chapter. First, membership in the Communist Party is a prerequisite for political elite status. Over the decades, the party has changed its focus of recruitment in society, reflecting larger changes in policy orientation. In the 1950s, for example, the party recruited most intensely among industrial workers, to build a more traditional Communist Party from a largely peasant base. In the Cultural Revolution of the 1960s and 1970s, radical leftist standards dominated—and recruitment was directed toward the less educated and less well-connected. In the 1980s and 1990s, the party focused its recruitment effort on intellectuals, professionals, and (more ambivalently) private entrepreneurs—all social groups identified as important for China's development as a prosperous nation (see Box 13.2).

Second, the party controls not only accessibility to this fundamental prerequisite for elite status, but also possesses a powerful organizational mechanism to recruit and promote elites: the *nomenklatura* system. Both appointed and elected leaders are vetted for office, level by level, such that a party committee at some level is the real constituent for leaders below. Beijing has not relinquished this key power, despite significant economic decentralization in recent decades.

What determines who gets along and ahead in the Chinese political system? That is, what criteria have leaders at higher levels viewed as most important for promotion? While much is made of the role of informal politics in China, a systematic study of provincial leaders from 1949 to 1998 shows that economic performance is the most important determinant of elite promotion in the post-Mao era of reform.[26] Leaders in provinces with higher economic growth or revenue contributions to the center during their tenure are less likely to be demoted or retired from office. In short, to win the support of their real constituents in Beijng, provincial leaders have to "deliver the goods." This is not surprising, considering that leaders in Beijing have staked their claim to legitimacy on precisely this outcome.

## Rule by Law

The principle of "rule of law" is traditionally associated with liberal democratic ideals. It implies a particular relationship between individuals and the state, the essence of which is protection of individual rights by limitations on arbitrary state power. Such limitations are enshrined in the law and in legal institutions. This notion makes no sense in traditional communist ideology: law is a weapon of the state to use in exercising dictatorship. In 1978, however, Chinese leaders began to revive and develop important ideas and institutions of legality that had flourished for a brief period in the

---

## "Red Capitalists"                                          BOX 13.2

In the mid-1980s, many party and government officials plunged into the private sector economy, shedding their offices but not their Communist Party membership. With little fanfare, the party also began to recruit private entrepreneurs as new members—a practice that reflected the party's commitment to economic growth, but met strong opposition from many as an abandonment of basic communist tenets. How could millionaire exploiters represent Chinese workers and peasants? When private entrepreneurs lent their support to protesters in 1989, leaders imposed a ban on their recruitment into the party. More than a decade later, in 2000, party leader Jiang Zemin introduced a convoluted new formula to justify welcoming them

back: the "three represents," added in 2004 to China's constitution. In this formula, the party does not simply represent workers and peasants, but represents the developmental needs of the advanced social productive forces, the promotion of advanced culture, and the fundamental interests of the greatest majority of the people. In 2001, on the party's eightieth anniversary, Jiang proposed lifting the ban on recruitment of private entrepreneurs into the party. His proposal was soon implemented. Today, one-third of private entrepreneurs are party members. Even though "red capitalists" still account for only a very small proportion of party members, their inclusion reflects a highly significant policy.

1950s. The new Chinese legality acknowledges **rule by law.**[27] Briefly, this means: there are laws, and all are equally subject to them. As the second principle is often violated, this may seem a trivial advance. It is not. The ongoing effort to establish rule by law in China has already changed the way Chinese act and think, in important ways.

***Socialist Legality*** The initial Chinese experiment with "socialist legality" began with the promulgation of the first constitution in 1954 and ended in 1957 with the Anti-Rightist Movement. Legalistic perspectives were rejected as examples of "bourgeois rightist" thinking. Legal scholars and legal professionals were criticized and labeled as "rightists." Work on development of criminal law stopped. Legal training and legal scholarship practically ceased. Defense lawyers disappeared from the legal process. Party committees took direct control of legal proceedings. The abandonment of law reached a peak during the Cultural Revolution, when violent "class struggle" and "mass justice" substituted for any regularized procedures to resolve social conflicts. This degree of radical lawlessness was not characteristic of the entire Maoist period, but a general official hostility to law prevailed from the late 1950s.

***Legal Reform*** Legal reform began in 1978. The legal system, barely functioning at the time, required urgent action for a number of reasons. First, there was an immediate need to establish legitimacy by righting past wrongs: investigating and reversing verdicts of dubious legality issued during the Cultural Revolution were a high priority. Second, Deng Xiaoping and other leaders wanted not only to restore public order and stability after years of chaos and uncertainty, but also to express their commitment to system building as a substitute for arbitrary political rule. Finally and not least of all, Chinese leaders hoped that the new legality would encourage economic investment and growth by promoting predictability—through transparent rules and impartial rule adjudication.

Rule by law requires laws. Nearly thirty years after the founding of the PRC, there was no criminal law. In 1978, Chinese leaders appointed committees of legal specialists to pick up work set aside for decades and to draft criminal codes for immediate promulgation. In 1979, the NPC passed the first criminal law and criminal procedure law. In the years that followed, as government agencies issued interim regulations that amended and clarified the hastily drafted laws, the NPC Legislative Affairs Committee worked on legal revisions. In 1996 and 1997, the NPC passed substantially amended and more precise versions of the laws. The 1997 amended criminal law takes into account changes in the Chinese economy that have created opportunities for economic crimes almost unimaginable in 1979 (such as insider securities trading). It abolishes the vaguely defined crimes of "counterrevolution." The 1996 amended criminal procedure law grants the accused the right to seek counsel (a right rejected in the 1950s) at an early stage of legal proceedings.

Rule by law implies equality before the law. This idea stands in sharp contrast to both the politicized view of law in communist ideology and routine practices in the Maoist years. In 1978, the NPC restored the procuratorates, which had been abolished in the 1960s. A new important role of procuratorates in the 1980s and 1990s became the investigation and prosecution of official crimes, for which procuratorates have full independent responsibility, according to law. Chinese leaders have regularly and prominently voiced a commitment to equality before the law, stating that officials who abuse public office and violate laws must be punished. Equality before the law, labeled "bourgeois" in the 1950s, is featured in the 1982 constitution—which also, for the first time, subjects the Communist Party (not only party members) to the authority of the law. At the same time, as described later in this chapter, there has been an explosion of corruption in recent years. In practice, the Communist Party, through its political-legal committees and its system of discipline inspection committees, routinely protects officials from equality before the law in cases involving abuses of power.

At the end of the 1970s, most Chinese were ignorant of laws and mistrustful of legal channels, a reasonable position when politics routinely superceded law. In the 1980s, the authorities launched a number of campaigns to educate ordinary citizens about the content of important laws and about certain ideas, such as equality before the law. Developing legal norms when legality has been actively denounced (not merely neglected) for decades has been difficult. Yet, ordinary Chinese do use law to pursue their interests. One indicator of the effect of the legal education effort is the growth in lawsuits against government agencies and officials under the administrative litigation law. The

Cyber cafés are popular with urban Chinese youth. Even with some 50,000 cyber-police, it is impossible to fully monitor Internet activity.

AP Images/Greg Baker

number of such lawsuits processed in the legal system has increased steadily since passage of the law in 1989. Even in cases not won outright in court, out-of-court settlements that favor plaintiffs have become sufficiently common to make lawsuits worthwhile.[28]

*Criticism of Legal Practices*  Legal reform has provoked criticism of Chinese law and legal practices outside China.[29] Three examples illustrate. First, Chinese criminal law stipulates the death penalty in "serious circumstances" of smuggling, rape, theft, bribery, trafficking in women and children, and corruption. In periodic intensive efforts to "strike hard" at crime, the authorities have resorted widely to capital punishment. Critics argue that capital punishment is excessively harsh for these crimes. Second, by design, criminal proceedings are inquisitorial (not adversarial), focused on determination of punishment (not guilt). As cases are prosecuted only after sufficient evidence has been collected to demonstrate guilt, most prosecutions result in guilty verdicts. The right to seek counsel at an early stage of proceedings is recognized in the law, but the requirement is only that a public defender be assigned no later than ten days before trial. By that time, the case has been prepared for prosecution and usually a confession (for which the law promises leniency) has already been obtained. This practice of "verdict first,

trial second" has been questioned and debated inside China and criticized outside China. Finally, despite abolition of specifically political crimes of counter-revolution, the Chinese authorities acknowledge "several thousand" political prisoners. While human rights groups estimate the number to be much larger, all critics view the situation as essentially inconsistent with the new law.

Nonetheless, the new legality has produced significant change. Today more than ever before, the Chinese state is more constrained by laws, while Chinese citizens are freer from political arbitrariness because of laws. Abuse of authority is acted on differently from before. The law is a weapon, because the regime has invested heavily in it. To the extent that, in practice, a double standard for citizens and officials persists, the law is a political weapon, which ordinary citizens can take up against perceived injustice. The official effort to build rule by law, by making law salient, has produced a basis for "rightful resistance" to hold the regime accountable to its own proclaimed standards.

## POLITICAL SOCIALIZATION

One result of the economic policy of opening up to the outside is that Chinese leaders today cannot control information as in the Maoist years.[30]

*Mass Media* Ordinary Chinese are now routinely exposed to news and opinions about public affairs in their country through access to Hong Kong (which maintains relatively free and critical mass media) and the outside world in newspapers, books, radio and television broadcasts, and the Internet. Moreover, Chinese connect with one another to transmit information as never before: in blogs, bulletin boards, e-mail, telephone, and text messages. China imported its first mobile phone facilities in 1987; by mid-2006, the country had more than 420 million mobile phone subscribers, the largest number in the world. One result of the telecommunications explosion and the opening to the outside world is the dilution in importance of the state-dominated mass media. In 1978, there were fewer than 900 periodicals and 200 newspapers with a provincial circulation in China; today, there are nearly 9,500 periodicals and nearly 2,000 newspapers.

To be sure, not all messages in the media are acceptable. Yet, most of the new media outlets do not touch on politics, offering instead the latest perspectives on sports, fashion, music, and movie stars. New academic journals carry lively scholarly discussions about the economy, law, and politics, however. Moreover, Chinese journalists expose government wrongdoings and thwart official efforts to suppress news of disasters.

At the same time, Chinese leaders reserve the right to shut down publications that in their view go too far. A government watchdog department monitors the media, focusing especially on coverage of Taiwan, party leaders, major political events, and the interpretation of party history—all explicitly defined in regulations as politically sensitive topics "of importance to state security and social stability." Media content has been scrutinized more carefully in recent years. At the same time, the most effective censorship the authorities can exercise in the new context is self-censorship—which generally operates fairly well. This is especially the case with Internet chat rooms and bulletin boards, which are otherwise nearly impossible to monitor, despite a force of some 50,000 cyber-police.

*Education System* The new content and style of political socialization are clearly evident in the education system. Mao's successors inherited an educational system designed to build communist values—and fundamentally at odds with the priority of economic growth. During the Cultural Revolution, high school graduates were sent to factories or farms to acquire work experience and learn from the masses. University entrance examinations were replaced with recommendations by grassroots leaders, focusing on revolutionary political credentials. With the persecution of scholars and denigration of expert knowledge in the

China is no longer a bicycle nation. Chinese-designed and manufactured automobiles emit ten to twenty times more pollution than American or Japanese models.

Justin Guariglia/The Image Works

universities, the content of university education was redesigned to include more politics in every specialization. Graduates were more "red" than expert. An entire decade was lost. The generation that missed out on an education during this decade is known today as the "lost generation."

Today, with the return of the university entrance examinations and huge numbers of Chinese studying in foreign universities, the respect for expertise is thoroughly restored. Indeed, in fall 2006, on instructions from top party and government departments, colleges across the country reduced the seven compulsory courses on political ideology and party history to four, in the first major curricular change in twenty-five years.

## POLITICAL CULTURE

Older and middle-aged Chinese have experienced not only the radicalism of the Maoist years, but also more than two decades of "reform and opening" to the outside world. Young Chinese have only the personal experience of the relatively open post-Mao years, including the decade of the 1990s that saw the "third wave" of democratization, with the triumph of democracy in nearly every communist country. When asked about the most memorable event in their lifetime, Chinese of all ages talk mainly about recent events, such as the post-Mao reforms.[31] Surely recent changes, both inside and outside China, have left their imprint on the way Chinese view their government and their relationship to political authorities.

Because Maoist-era leaders regarded social science with great suspicion, we have no good baseline of public opinion data by which to assess change over time in the beliefs of ordinary Chinese. We can say something about the Chinese political culture today, however, based on survey research in China, including surveys organized and conducted by political scientists based in the United States. What is the orientation toward politics of ordinary Chinese? In particular, to what extent do the beliefs of Chinese seem conducive to political change in the direction of further democratization?

***Political Knowledge*** An important building block for democracy is a citizenry knowledgeable about politics and interested in public affairs, so as to be able to monitor the performance of representatives and leaders. Most ordinary Chinese follow public affairs at least weekly, mainly through radio or television programs and somewhat less through newspapers, but politics is not something that is a regular topic of discussion in China. A majority say they *never* talk about politics with others, a stark reflection of lack of active interest.

Political knowledge and interest are not uniformly distributed in China, of course. A more active knowledge and interest are seen among men, the more highly educated, and Chinese with higher incomes, which is not so different from what we observe in other countries. Not surprisingly, Chinese in Beijing are much more interested in politics than Chinese overall; in fact, they discuss politics very frequently. Yet, even if we consider the situation of Chinese overall, which includes the relatively less knowledgeable and less interested rural population, political knowledge in China today is higher than in Italy in the early 1960s and political discourse higher than in Italy or Mexico in the early 1960s.[32]

***Political Values*** How do the Chinese view their communist government? With the increased availability of information on other countries, including liberal democracies, do the Chinese see their relationship with political authorities differently? Moreover, does the Chinese political culture reflect traditional values—the influence of Confucianism, which conceived of legitimacy to rule in moral terms?

Perhaps the most interesting perspective on contemporary Chinese political culture is a comparative one that considers its fate across three different Chinese political systems. An extraordinary survey of a representative sample of Chinese in mainland China, Hong Kong, and Taiwan, conducted in 1993 and 1994, provides this perspective and helps to sort out different influences of traditional culture, political system, and socioeconomic development.[33] Figure 13.3 compares responses of ordinary Chinese in the PRC, Hong Kong, and Taiwan to questions about political relationships. Two questions tap orientations to popular accountability and political liberty. Another frames relationships in traditional Confucian terms of virtuous leadership. Altogether, these questions probe Chinese support for values commonly associated with liberal democracy. The responses reveal a fairly consistent, easily interpretable, and striking pattern.

First, there seems to be a strong impact due to political system. A majority of Chinese in the PRC reject every democratic value, and support for democratic values is generally lowest in the PRC. This is not surprising. By the early 1990s, when this survey was conducted, Taiwan's process of democratization was well underway. Hong Kong, while still under British colonial rule, had enjoyed very significant civil liberties for decades and was taking initial steps to increase electoral competition.

Second, the influence of non-Chinese political socialization is evident. The traditional Confucian orientation to the moral state is least evident in Hong Kong: nearly three-fourths of Hong Kong Chinese reject the view that everything should be left up to virtuous leaders. By contrast, this view finds strong support in the PRC. Chinese in Taiwan are somewhere in the middle, perhaps reflecting rule by a Chinese government but a society long open to outside influences.

Third, and perhaps most interesting of all for speculation about support for democratization in the PRC, the responses show an impact of socioeconomic development. This is most evident in a comparison of responses in the PRC overall with those in urban China only. Urban Chinese are much more supportive of democratic values than are mainland Chinese generally.

In sum, traditional Chinese orientations to moral leadership appear to prevail in the PRC, and high proportions of the population have orientations unfavorable to democratization.[34] Barring the introduction of very major political change by the leaders themselves, popular disgruntlement about the performance of the government appears unlikely to transform itself into collective action for regime change. Overall, the responses suggest that mainland Chinese are "elitist

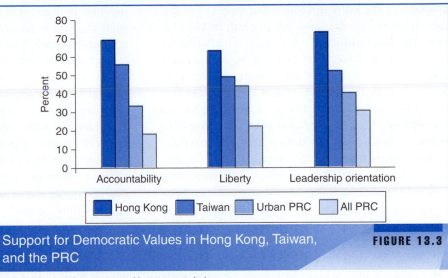

**FIGURE 13.3**

Support for Democratic Values in Hong Kong, Taiwan, and the PRC

Percent expressing *disagreement* with statements below.

Accountability:  "Top government officials are like the heads of a big family. We should follow all their decisions on national issues."

Liberty:  "The government should have the power to decide which opinions (perspectives) are to be circulated in a society and which are not."

Leadership orientation:  "We can leave everything to morally upright leaders."

Source: Yun-han Chu and Yu-tzung Chang, "Culture Shift and Regime Legitimacy: Comparing Mainland China, Taiwan, and Hong Kong," in Shiping Hua, ed., *Chinese Political Culture, 1989–2000* (Armonk, NY: M. E. Sharpe, 2001), 332–33. Based on surveys conducted in 1993 and 1994.

and authority-oriented," and this contributes to the stability of the communist regime.[35]

## POLITICAL PARTICIPATION

In the communist party-state, political participation, interest articulation, and interest aggregation differ from the processes normally found in liberal democratic systems. The source of difference is, of course, different conceptions of the relationship between leaders and citizens: the notion of guardianship is fundamentally incompatible with liberal democratic notions of representation. The Communist Party organization claims to represent the interests of all society. It rejects, as unnecessary and unacceptable, political parties other than itself. While there has been change in political processes in recent decades, the "officially acceptable" forms of political participation, interest articulation, and interest aggregation in the Chinese political system continue to reflect the relationship of guardianship between party and society. This section discusses political participation; the next section explores interest articulation and aggregation.

*Changes in the Rules*  An important aspect of political reform undertaken after Mao's death in 1976 has been the redefinition of what constitutes "officially acceptable" political participation in the Chinese system. Guidelines for the new political participation are evident in three categories of rule changes that have routinized participation and reduced its burden for ordinary Chinese. The changes reflect an official reaction against the disruption that characterized mass participation in the Maoist years (especially during the Cultural Revolution), an official assumption that economic growth is predicated on order and stability, and an official recognition that changes in economic relationships require adjustments in political relationships.

The first category of rule changes involves political participation, which has become essentially optional for ordinary Chinese since the early 1980s. In the first thirty years of communist rule, for a broad range of political activities, failure to participate was considered tantamount to opposition to the communist regime. Today, politics intrudes far less in the lives of ordinary Chinese. The scope and demands of politics have shrunk. The single most important measure signifying this change is the official removal, in 1979, of all class and political labels. After thirty years, the Chinese are no longer formally identified by class background or past "political mistakes." Not only does politics no longer dominate daily life, but in the diminished sphere of political activities, political apathy is no longer risky for ordinary Chinese.

The second category has been the assiduous avoidance by the regime of rousing the mass public to realize policy objectives. In the Maoist years, by contrast, the quintessential form of political participation was the **mass mobilization campaign**—intensive, large-scale, disruptive group action, implemented by grassroots leaders. The Great Leap Forward launched in 1958 and the Cultural Revolution launched in 1966 were essentially mass campaigns, on a gargantuan scale. Typically in mass campaigns, grassroots party leaders, responding to signals from the political center, roused ordinary Chinese to achieve regime goals of various sorts, often aimed at identified categories of enemies—such as "counterrevolutionaries" in 1950–1951; the "landlord class" in 1950–1952; the "rightists" in 1957; and the "unclean cadres" in 1962–1963. Mass-campaign

methods were adopted for nonpolitical objectives too, such as the ill-conceived and ecologically harmful effort to eradicate "four pests" (sparrows, rats, flies, and mosquitoes) in 1956. Participation in campaigns was virtually compulsory. Only three years after Mao's death, Chinese leaders issued an official rejection of mass campaigns as a mode of political participation. Many leaders who emerged at the top echelons of power in the late 1970s had themselves been victims of persecution in the Cultural Revolution. The social disorder of campaigns was rejected as antithetical to the new priority of economic growth.

The third category is the rejection of mass mobilization as the dominant mode of political participation. Chinese leaders have instead encouraged ordinary citizens to express their opinions and participate in politics through a variety of regular official channels, some new, others newly revived: offices to receive complaints, centers and telephone hotlines to report abuses of power, and letters to newspaper editors, for example.[36] Not least of all, the authorities have introduced important reforms in elections. As a consequence, political participation in China is varied and extensive in scope. Table 13.2 shows findings from a survey conducted in Beijing in the 1980s and 1990s. The extent of citizen participation in a wide range of activities is quite remarkable, not at all the picture of Maoist mobilization.

Elections and an electoral connection between citizens and leaders are integral to liberal democratic conceptions of representation. For this reason, governments and nongovernmental organizations in liberal democracies have paid close attention to electoral reforms in China.

*Local Congress Elections*  Elections to local people's congresses in the Maoist years were political rituals, featuring no candidate choice and no secret ballot. Voters directly elected deputies to township-level congresses only; at higher levels, deputies were elected by congresses at the level immediately below. Such elections served as vehicles of regime legitimation, popular education, and political socialization, but they did not really allow ordinary citizens to choose representatives.

In 1979, a new election law introduced direct election of deputies to county-level congresses, mandated secret ballots rather than public displays of support,

**TABLE 13.2**

## Political Participation in Beijing  (percent reporting having participated in political act)

| Political Act | 1988 | 1996 |
|---|---|---|
| Voting for deputies in 1988 local congress elections | 71.5 | 81.0 |
| Contacting leaders of workplace | 51.2 | 54.2 |
| Complaining through bureaucratic hierarchy | 43.0 | 47.5 |
| Voting for leaders in workplace | 34.8 | 16.1 |
| Complaining through trade unions | 18.9 | 24.4 |
| Using connections (*guanxi*) | 15.5 | 16.6 |
| Complaining through political organizations | 15.0 | 17.7 |
| Slowing down on the job | 12.6 | 9.3 |
| Writing letters to government officials | 12.5 | 15.3 |
| Persuading others to attend campaign meetings for congress deputies | 8.9 | 13.0 |
| Complaining through congress deputies | 8.6 | 14.1 |
| Persuading others to attend campaign or briefing meetings at workplace | 7.7 | 5.4 |
| Organizing others to fight against leaders | 7.6 | 3.0 |
| Writing letters to newspaper editors | 6.8 | 8.3 |
| Persuading others to vote for certain leaders in workplace elections | 5.7 | 3.5 |
| Whipping up public opinion against workplace leaders | 5.1 | 1.7 |
| Persuading others to vote for certain deputies in congress elections | 4.7 | 8.0 |
| Giving gifts in exchange for help | 4.6 | 8.0 |
| Persuading others to boycott unfair workplace elections | 4.6 | 2.9 |
| Reporting to complaint bureaus | 4.0 | 8.1 |
| Persuading others to boycott unfair congress elections | 3.7 | 6.8 |
| Bringing cases to court | 1.2 | 4.5 |
| Participating in strikes | 0.9 | 2.6 |
| Participating in demonstrations | 0.4 | 1.4 |

Source: Tianjian Shi, "Mass Political Behavior in Beijing," in Merle Goldman and Roderick MacFarquhar, eds., *The Paradox of China's Post-Mao Reforms* (Cambridge: Harvard University Press, 1999), 155.

and required the number of candidates to be one and a half times the number of deputies to be elected.

Although local Communist Party organizations continue to play a key leadership role in election committees, essentially vetting candidates, not all candidates can win under current rules. Some officially nominated candidates lose elections. Indeed, some candidates officially designated for government office lose elections. A growing number of candidates who are not Communist Party members have competed and won in elections. A smaller number of government executives nominated by deputies are not official candidates and win without official endorsement.[37] An electoral victory signifies some degree of popular support, while losing signifies a problematic relationship with the mass public. At a minimum, the new rules are a means for the Communist Party organization to gauge popular views about local officials, diversify the pool from which leaders are recruited, and monitor local leaders. To be sure, the new rules have not produced radical change. Nor can such an outcome be expected without further change in rules: no platform of opposition to the Communist Party is permissible.

*Village Committees* China also now has nearly two decades of experience with rural grassroots democratization, formally approved in November 1987 when the NPC, after over a year of debate, passed a provisional version of the Organic Law on Village Committees. A final revised version was passed in November 1998.

The law defines **village committees** as "autonomous mass organizations of self-government," popularly elected in elections featuring choice among candidates for three-year terms and accountable to a village council comprised of all adult villagers.

The introduction of popularly elected village committees in 1987 was designed to strengthen state capacity to govern in the aftermath of agricultural decollectivization. In the early 1980s, the people's communes had been dismantled and replaced with township governments. Land and other production inputs were divided among peasant households to manage on their own, free markets were opened, most obligatory sales to the state were abolished, and private entrepreneurship was promoted.[38] The results of these reforms were successful by most economic standards, but disastrous in their consequences for rural leadership. As villagers gained greater economic initiative and autonomy, the power of the Chinese party-state to exact compliance was enormously weakened. By the mid-1980s, village leadership had seriously atrophied. Leaders were enriching themselves at the expense of the community, and villagers were resisting their efforts to implement unpopular policies. Violent conflicts between villagers and village leaders had become common. The revitalization of village committees in 1987 was designed to make the countryside more governable by increasing accountability. Presumably, villagers would be more responsive to leaders elected from below rather than those imposed from above as before.

In 1998, when the NPC affirmed the experience of village elections, most villages had undergone at least three rounds of elections, with enormous local variation in implementation. In many villages, the village Communist Party branch controlled candidate nomination, there was no candidate choice for the key position of village committee director, and voting irregularities were common. Even in villages that made serious progress—with genuinely competitive elections, widespread popular participation in candidate nomination, and scrupulous attention to voting procedure—real managerial authority often resided not with the popularly elected village committee but with the village Communist Party branch. Even today, too little is known to generalize about overall progress in village elections, its determinants, or its consequences.[39] Certainly, to the degree that the practices of grassroots democracy acquire the force of routine and expectations accumulate, however slowly, among nearly 750 million Chinese in more than 600,000 villages, political participation in the countryside will change profoundly.

***"Unacceptable" Political Participation***   More dramatic than the reforms that have redefined officially acceptable political participation has been the political action of ordinary Chinese in city streets and squares beginning in the late 1970s. With strikes, marches, posters, petitions, and occupation of public spaces, ordinary citizens have acted as if political reform comprehended or condoned mass political action and public disorder. The official record suggests the contrary, however.

In 1980, the right to post "big-character posters" (usually criticisms of leaders, written by individuals or groups and posted on walls), introduced during the Cultural Revolution, was removed from the Chinese constitution. In 1982, the constitutional right to strike was rescinded. As for mass protests, the official view was made clear in 1979 with the introduction of the "four fundamental principles" that political participation must uphold: (1) the socialist road, (2) Marxism-Leninism-Mao Zedong Thought, (3) the people's democratic dictatorship, and (4) the leadership of the Communist Party. Of these principles, only the last is necessary to restrict political participation effectively, as the content of the first three has become what party leaders make of it. Participants (especially organizers) face real risks of physical harm and criminal punishment. Why then did ordinary citizens engage in mass protests with increasing frequency in the 1970s and 1980s? Why did urban worker and peasant unrest increase in the 1980s and 1990s?

Different sorts of "officially unacceptable" political participation have different explanations, but none can be explained without reference to the post-Mao reforms. On the one hand, economic reforms have produced some socially unacceptable outcomes: more (and more visible) inflation, unemployment, crime, and corruption, for example. Rural unrest has typically been triggered by local corruption and exaction of excessive (often illegal) taxes and fees. Urban unrest—strikes, slowdowns, and demonstrations—has increased too, as state enterprises struggle to survive in the socialist market economy. A number of enterprises have been closed down; many have engaged in massive layoffs; others have been unable to pay bonuses and pensions. For the first time since

1949, many urban Chinese have been living on fixed incomes, no incomes, or unpredictable incomes as the cost of living increases.

***Protesters and Reformers*** In 1989, a different sort of urban unrest captured the attention of the world news media and, consequently, of the world. The demonstration that brought a million people to Tiananmen Square was the third major political protest movement since Mao's death. The first was in 1978–1979, the second in 1986–1987. All three were officially unacceptable, all were linked in some important way to official reforms and reformers, and all ended in failure for mass protesters (and resulted in setbacks to official reforms too).[40]

Despite links between protesters and official reformers, the post-Mao movements were not mass mobilization campaigns. As they were not explicitly initiated by the regime, once underway they could not be easily stopped with an official pronouncement from the political center. Instead, the authorities turned to coercive force wielded by the police, the armed police, and ultimately the army to terminate the protests with violence.

Protests are officially unacceptable mainly because of their form of expression. The official consensus since December 1978 has been that the most important priority for China is economic growth, with social order and stability as prerequisites for growth. Mass protests are distinctly disorderly. Further, as a form of political participation, mass protests are a symptom of regime failure in two senses. By turning to the streets to articulate their demands, protesters demonstrate that official channels for expressing critical views are not working and that they do not believe the Communist Party's claim that it can correct its own mistakes. Further, protesters are clearly not alienated from politics: while they reject official channels of participation, they are not politically apathetic; indeed, they articulate explicitly political demands despite serious risks and the difficulty associated with organizing outside the system. In short, political protests signify that mass political participation can neither be contained within official channels nor deterred with a better material life.

For the most part, despite some radical elements, the protests have not been blatantly antisystem in their demands. This does not appear to be merely strategic. Rather, the protests are something of a rowdy mass counterpart to the official socialist reform movement, exerting more pressure for more reform, and (while officially unacceptable) often linked with elite reformers.

In the **Democracy Movement** of 1978–1979, Deng Xiaoping publicly approved many of the demands posted on Democracy Wall and published in unofficial journals, which called for a "reversal of verdicts" on individuals and political events. The demands were an integral part of the pressure for reform that surrounded the meetings of top leaders in

In 1989, ordinary Chinese participated in the largest spontaneous protest movement the communists had ever faced. A lone protester shows defiance of regime violence in his intransigent confrontation with a Chinese tank.

AP Images/Jeff Widener

**BOX 13.3**

## Wei Jingsheng and the "Fifth Modernization"

In late 1978, in an atmosphere of great change that included official "reversals of verdicts" of the Cultural Revolution, many Chinese began to gather regularly at a large wall close to Beijing's Tiananmen Square to post, read, and discuss political posters. One of the boldest posters to appear on Democracy Wall was an essay by Wei Jingsheng. It argued that the ambitious new program to modernize agriculture, industry, national defense, and science and technology could not succeed without a "fifth modernization"—democracy. Wei wrote: "The hated old political system has not changed. Are not the people justified in seizing power from the overlords?" Wei published even more critical

essays in his unofficial journal *Explorations,* one of more than fifty such journals circulating at the time. In March 1979, he posted an attack on Deng Xiaoping, asking: "Do we want democracy or new dictatorship?" Wei was tried and convicted of "counterrevolutionary crimes" and "leaking state secrets" to foreigners. Some fifteen years later, Wei was released from prison, only to be rearrested for dissident activities. In 1997, after years of pressure from human rights groups and governments outside China, China's most famous political dissident was released and exiled to the United States, where he continues to criticize the Chinese authorities.

---

late 1978, allowing elite reformers to argue for major changes in policy and political orientation. The poster campaign and unofficial journals were tolerated. To be sure, when a bold dissidenter named Wei Jingsheng demanded a "fifth modernization," by which he meant democracy of a sort never envisaged by the communists, the Chinese authorities promptly sentenced him to a fifteen-year prison term (ostensibly for revealing state secrets) and introduced the "four fundamental principles" to establish the parameters of acceptable debate[41] (see Box 13.3).

When the Communist Party congress convened in late 1987, party leader Zhao Ziyang acknowledged conflicts of interest in society at the current time. The years 1988 and 1989 were high points for political liberalization. The political criticism expressed in Tiananmen Square in 1989 largely echoed public views of elite reformers in the party and government. From the perspective of communist authorities, the real danger in 1989 was not the content of mass demands but the organizational challenge: students and workers organized their own unions, independent of the party, to represent their interests.

The challenge was exacerbated by an open break in elite ranks when Zhao Ziyang voiced his support for the protesters and declared his opposition to martial law. Other party and government leaders and retired elders, including Deng Xiaoping—many of whom had been victims of power seizures by youths in the Cultural Revolution—viewed the problem as a basic

struggle for the survival of the system and their own positions. The movement was violently and decisively crushed with tanks and machine guns in the **Tiananmen massacre** of June 4, 1989.[42]

All three protests ended in defeat for the participants: prison for the main protest organizers in 1979, expulsion from the Communist Party for intellectual leaders in 1987, and prison or violent death for hundreds in 1989. The defeats extended beyond the mass protest movement to encompass setbacks to the official reform movement too. When demands for reform moved to the city streets, more conservative leaders attributed the social disorder to an excessively rapid pace of reform. The result was a slower pace or postponement of reforms. Twice, the highest party leader was dismissed from office as a result of the mass protests (Hu Yaobang in 1987 and Zhao Ziyang in 1989), and the official reform movement lost its strongest proponent.

## INTEREST ARTICULATION AND AGGREGATION

Most ordinary citizens engage in interest articulation without interest aggregation. This takes the form of personal contacts to articulate individual concerns about the effects of policies on their lives. Much of this interest articulation takes place at the workplace. As shown earlier in Table 13.2, more than 50 percent of those surveyed in Beijing in the 1980s and 1990s had engaged in precisely this sort of low-level politics. And more than 15 percent of those surveyed had made use of personal connections. For the most part, the function of interest aggregation is monopolized by the Communist Party, although the party's role in interest aggregation is being diluted and the methods it employs have also evolved.

***Organizations under Party Leadership***  Under the formal leadership of the Communist Party are eight "satellite parties," a legacy of the communist pre-1949 strategy of provisional cooperation with noncommunist democratic parties.[43] These parties have no real role in policymaking, but they are represented (with prominent nonparty individuals) in the Chinese People's Political Consultative Conference. In 1989 the Central Committee proposed greater cooperation with the noncommunist parties by regular consultation with their leaders on major policies—or at least a stronger effort to inform the parties of Communist Party policies. Of course, this proposal referred only to the eight officially tolerated parties. In 1998, the authorities arrested, tried, and imprisoned a veteran of the 1978–1979 Democracy Movement who attempted to register a fledgling China Democracy Party.

The other older formal organizations that aggregate like interests in the Chinese political system are the "mass organizations," extensions of the Communist Party into society, nationwide in scope and organized hierarchically. The All-China Federation of Trade Unions and the Women's Federation remain active and important mass organizations today. Mass organizations are led by Communist Party officials, who are specially assigned to these positions and who take direction from party committees. The main function of these organizations is not to aggregate and represent group interests for consideration in the policymaking process, but to facilitate propagation of party policy to the relevant groups. Essentially, mass organizations represent the interests of the Communist Party to the organized "interest groups" it dominates, not vice versa. The classic description of this relationship refers to mass organizations as "transmission belts" for the Communist Party.

***NGOs and GONGOs***  A very different set of associations emerged in the late 1980s with official encouragement. These "social organizations," over 170,000 in number, range widely in form and focus. In form, they include genuine nongovernmental organizations (NGOs) and government-organized nongovernmental organizations (**GONGO**s). Some GONGOs are essentially front organizations for government agencies, set up to take advantage of the interest of foreign governments and international NGOs to support the emergence of Chinese civil society. Other GONGOs have strong and mutually beneficial relationships with NGOs, acting as a bridge to government agencies. In focus, GONGOs and especially NGOs cover a wide range of interests and activities.

Among the most interesting GONGOs are the business associations set up to organize firms: the Self-Employed Laborers Association, the Private Enterprises Association, and the Federation of Industry and Commerce. The Federation of Industry and Commerce, which organizes the largest Chinese firms, has independent resources that have permitted it to create a separate organizational network (chambers of commerce), a national newspaper, and a financial institution to provide credit to members.

Among NGOs, the 250 organizations that focus on environmental issues are at the vanguard of NGO activity.[44] The largest, best funded, and best organized environmental NGOs focus primarily on species and nature conservation and environmental education. With strong support from the media, these NGOs often work with central authorities to expose and counter local government failure to implement environmental laws and policies. One environmental NGO trains lawyers to engage in enforcement of laws, educates judges about the issues, and litigates environmental cases.

Individual environmental activists have also organized to influence political decisions. A good example is the independent publication of *Yangtze! Yangtze!*, a collection of papers by scientists and environmentalists critical of the world's biggest and most controversial hydroelectric project, the Three Gorges Dam. The study was released in early 1989 with the aim of influencing the widely publicized NPC vote to approve dam construction. Although it failed to halt approval, nearly a third of NPC delegates voted against the project or abstained—prompting the government to postpone dam construction until the mid-1990s (see Box 13.4).

Considering the "Leninist organizational predisposition" to thwart organizational plurality, the

## The Three Gorges Dam

BOX 13.4

The Three Gorges Dam, essentially completed in May 2006, is the biggest, most costly, and most controversial hydropower station ever built. It was conceived to regulate the flow of the Yangtze, the third most powerful river in the world. Three times in the past century, the river has flooded, killing hundreds of thousands of people. The new dam will supply an estimated 10 percent of China's electric power, for industrial production and "basic electrification" of the countryside. Building it displaced more than a million people. Environmentalist opponents of the dam are concerned about damage to the ecosystem and endangerment of some species of fish and birds. Other critics are concerned about flooding more than 100 significant archeological sites. Opposition to the dam also focuses on safety issues: problems of sedimentation may cause floods upstream and weaken foundations of cities built on silt downstream. Most opponents suggested building several smaller dams, rather than one mega-dam. Central to these concerns are doubts that the government sufficiently considered expert advice in designing the project—which was a dream of Chinese leaders since 1919 and took on meaning as a political accomplishment.

encouragement of NGO emergence and activity in the Chinese context seems puzzling.[45] It is explained by the closure of many state enterprises and the downsizing of government at all levels, in the 1980s and 1990s, creating a need for the growth of social organizations to take on some former government functions, especially social welfare functions. Essentially, this change shifts the burden from government to society. The 1998 plan to downsize the central government bureaucracy explicitly noted that many functions "appropriated by government" must be "given back" to society and managed by new social associations. This plan opened the political space for the emergence of NGOs. The authorities also recognize that NGOs can help the center monitor local government policy implementation; this is the role that environmental NGOs have played most prominently, for example.

For the most part, NGO activity is in fact well within the parameters of officially acceptable political participation. Most groups do not seek autonomy from the state, but rather seek "embeddedness" within the state. To be autonomous is to be outside the system and relatively powerless, unable to exercise influence. In sum, for the most part, the emerging Chinese civil society aggregates and articulates its interests without challenging the state.

To be sure, the authorities have taken measures to guarantee that NGOs work with (not against) them. An elaborate set of regulations requires social organizations to affiliate with a sponsor that is responsible for their activity, to register with the government, and to have sufficient funding and membership. The regulations also prohibit the coexistence of more than one organization with the same substantive focus at the national level or in any particular locality. This preserves the monopoly of the official mass organizations to represent the interests of women and workers, for example.

In practice, however, it is simply impossible really to control NGO activity: some NGOs register as businesses, others thrive as Internet-based virtual organizations, and government sponsors cannot monitor the organizations registered as their affiliates. For example, the All-China Women's Federation is responsible for more than 3,000 social organizations dealing with women's issues. In this context, Chinese NGOs can be expected to continue to grow.

It is important to note that one significant social group lacks a legitimate organizational channel (even a mass organization) that aggregates its interests: farmers. To the extent that Chinese farmers engage in collective action to articulate their interests, it is largely through petitions and protests.

## POLICYMAKING AND IMPLEMENTATION

Today, it is inconceivable that a scheme such as the Great Leap Forward could be launched and implemented as it was in the 1950s. Controversial policies are no longer adopted at the whim of a single leader;

experts play a significant role in policy formulation; experimentation in selected localities precedes widespread implementation; and local authorities no longer slavishly sacrifice local development goals to meet unrealistic campaign targets dictated by the center.

The single most important difference distinguishing policy processes of the 1950s from those of the 1990s and after, however, is the recent greater reliance on consultation and consensus building among a wider range of bureaucratic, local, and economic players. This change is partly due to economic reforms that provide increased opportunities and incentives for players to devote resources to projects outside the state plan rather than to state-mandated projects. In discussing policy processes, the Chinese often refer to the following expression: "The top has its policy measures; the bottom has its countermeasures." Having renounced campaigns and purges, policymakers at the top have instead worked to forge agreements with a variety of players at the political center and in the localities so that policies adopted are implemented, not ignored or radically reshaped in the course of implementation. At the apex of the system, consultation has become even more important, because no leader possesses either the experience or the personal prestige of a Mao Zedong or a Deng Xiaoping.

The political structures described at the beginning of this chapter are essential points of reference for the description of policymaking and policy implementation here. However, key features of policy processes are not well illustrated by consideration of these formal structures alone. As elaborated below, the formal distinction between party and government structures is less relevant than it appears; at least one key structure does not appear on formal organizational charts; and authority is more fragmented and less well-bounded than formal structure suggests.

## Policymaking

Policymaking in China today is less concentrated and more institutionalized than ever before. It involves three sets of institutional players: the party, the government, and the legislature, shown in Figure 13.4. It is also useful to distinguish three tiers in the policymaking process. Different party, government, and legislative structures at different tiers interact at different stages of the process. Moreover, a number of individual players overlap, appearing in more than one set of institutions. This section traces the process by which major policies emerge and are eventually formalized as laws. It is worth noting, however, that many important policy decisions do not go through the legislature at all. For example, the State Council has the power to issue administrative regulations, decisions, instructions, orders, and measures to local governments; central government ministries issue their own departmental regulations, clarifications, and responses to respective local government departments; and the Communist Party Politburo and individual party departments have their own separate systems of regulations, decisions, instructions, orders, and measures issued to counterparts in the localities and lower levels of the party bureaucracy.

***Three Tiers in Policymaking***   At the very top tier are the leaders at the apex of the party: in the Politburo and its Standing Committee. The party generalists at this tier are each typically responsible for at least one broad policy area. As a group, they make all major policy decisions. Formally, the Politburo has the ultimate authority to determine major policies, but it probably meets in plenary session only about once monthly for a morning to ratify policies already approved by the Politburo Standing Committee. It is useful to recall here that the leaders at the top of the party hierarchy include not only party leaders but also the prime minister and the NPC chairman. Overlapping directorships help coordinate major decisionmaking across the three sets of institutions.

The most thorough consideration of policy options and shaping of policy decisions occur at the second tier—within **leading small groups (LSGs),** which are defined by broad policy areas.[46] LSGs are headed by leaders at the top tier of the party, although deputy heads are likely to be outside the top tier. LSGs have sweeping mandates to preside over policy research, formulation of policy proposals, sponsorship of policy experiments in the localities, and drafting of policy documents. LSGs bring together all the senior officials with responsibility for different aspects of a policy area.[47] They exercise leadership as policies emerge onto an initial agenda, and they make specific recommendations to the Politburo Standing Committee once policies are ready to move onto the legislative agenda. They are a crucial coordinating mechanism in the policymaking process, linking top

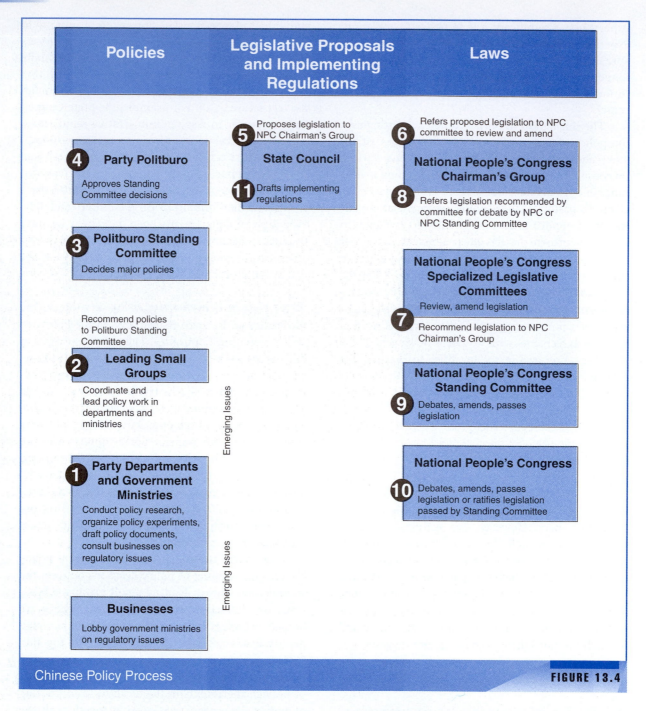

| Policies | Legislative Proposals and Implementing Regulations | Laws |

**4** Party Politburo
Approves Standing Committee decisions

**5** Proposes legislation to NPC Chairman's Group
State Council
**11** Drafts implementing regulations

**6** Refers proposed legislation to NPC committee to review and amend
National People's Congress Chairman's Group
**8** Refers legislation recommended by committee for debate by NPC or NPC Standing Committee

**3** Politburo Standing Committee
Decides major policies

National People's Congress Specialized Legislative Committees
Review, amend legislation
**7** Recommend legislation to NPC Chairman's Group

Recommend policies to Politburo Standing Committee
**2** Leading Small Groups
Coordinate and lead policy work in departments and ministries

National People's Congress Standing Committee
**9** Debates, amends, passes legislation

**1** Party Departments and Government Ministries
Conduct policy research, organize policy experiments, draft policy documents, consult businesses on regulatory issues

National People's Congress
**10** Debates, amends, passes legislation or ratifies legislation passed by Standing Committee

Businesses
Lobby government ministries on regulatory issues

Emerging Issues

**Chinese Policy Process**

**FIGURE 13.4**

decisionmakers to bureaucracies and bridging institutional systems.

Coordinating mechanisms are particularly important to policymaking in the Chinese system because authority is formally structured so as to require the cooperation of many bureaucratic units, nested in separate chains of authority. The fragmentation of formal authority and its resolution by formal and informal coordinating mechanisms at the top of the system have led some scholars to characterize the Chinese system as one of **fragmented authoritarianism.**[48]

In what ways is formal authority fragmented? The best example is the system of dual subordination. On the one hand, authority is organized in systems of vertical bureaucracies in hierarchies that extend from ministries at the center to lower-level departments in the localities. Each ministry under the State Council is at the top of a hierarchy of subordinate departments that exist at the provincial, county, and township levels of government. On the other hand, the central ministry and subordinate departments are all government departments and, as such, are subordinate to their respective governments too. The Chinese refer to the two structural arrangements as "lines" and "pieces." Authoritative communications are channeled from top to bottom (vertically, in lines) and also from governments to their departments (horizontally, in pieces). The two sorts of authority come together only at the center, at the level of the State Council. Simply put, then, all local government departments have two bosses in their formal authority relationships—not to mention their relationships with party departments in the same issue area and party committees with *nomenklatura* authority over them. In Chinese terminology, there are "too many mothers-in-law." This structure of formal authority routinely creates blockages in policy processes. Many policy issues cannot be resolved at lower levels but must be pushed up to a sufficiently high level, such as an LSG, that spans many authority structures and can overcome bureaucratic impasses below.

Below leading small groups, at the third tier, are the relevant party departments and government ministries. As LSGs have little staff of their own, the research centers and staff in departments and ministries at the third tier do the actual work of gathering information and drafting policy documents. Increasingly, with a high proportion of policy related to economic matters, government ministries play a key role—but at this tier it is the specific policy area that determines which bureaucratic players are most involved.

*From Agenda Setting to Implementing Regulations* There are five main stages in policymaking and lawmaking: agenda setting; inter-agency review; Politburo approval; NPC review, debate, and passage; and the drafting of implementing regulations.[49] The two stages that have the most impact on substance are interagency review and drafting of implementing regulations. The State Council dominates both these stages.

LSGs provide leadership and coordination among party departments and government ministries, from which draft proposals emerge. Leaders of departments and ministries are continuously considering relevant policy issues and waiting for (or creating) opportunities to push proposals onto the agenda. A draft proposal is on the agenda when it is assigned to interagency review.

Interagency review is usually a very prolonged process, still at the third tier, initially involving only the most relevant ministries but gradually incorporating a wider group of departments, localities, and other players. At some point, either the State Council Legislation Bureau or the Legislative Affairs Work Committee approves a drafting group for the law. The last phase of interagency review is opinion solicitation. By then, most of the law's content has already been decided. This does not imply that relevant nonbureaucratic players are shut out of the policy process, however—at least in economic policymaking.

New case studies of the government–business relationship in China show that marketization has prompted Chinese firms to take an active interest in the many industrial policies and regulations that impact their competitiveness.[50] Businesses interact regularly with government departments on midrange policies, such as industry standards, tax rates, prices, and international competition—mostly regulatory issues that do not go through the legislative process. Interacting takes two forms: consultation and lobbying. On the one hand, government departments now routinely take the initiative to consult with relevant businesses before drafting industrial policies and regulations, calling meetings of key players or inviting them to formal hearings, for example. Similarly, business executives, including foreign business executives, now routinely lobby government officials to influence policy in favor of the firm or industry. Larger firms have the most direct and regular access to government officials, although large state-owned enterprises (SOEs) appear to have more access than large foreign firms, perhaps a legacy of interaction under central planning or the enormous importance of these players to social stability. Businesses lobby all departments relevant to policies that impact them, with one unsurprising exception: despite the influence of environmental regulations on industry competitiveness, businesses typically ignore the State Environment Protection Agency (SEPA)—reflecting an assumption that environmental protection is at odds with economic profits.

For policies that will involve passage of legislation, after interagency review, a draft proposal is included on the Legislation Bureau's or Legislative Affairs Work Committee's annual legislative plan. Politburo approval precedes NPC passage of any major piece of political, economic, or administrative legislation, although this practice is not formally required in any legal document.

Officially, legislation may be proposed by the State Council, its ministries, or groups of NPC delegates. Not surprisingly in this quasi-parliamentary system, the overwhelming majority of legislation is proposed by the State Council and its ministries at the third tier. Although it is unusual for laws to pass through NPC review without amendment, a bill approved in principle by the Politburo is not normally opposed in the NPC.

The NPC review stage begins with referral (by the NPC Chairmen's Group) of the draft legislation to a specialized legislative NPC standing committee for review and amendment. The structure that links party and legislative institutions at this stage is the NPC Standing Committee party group. After draft legislation is recommended by an NPC legislative committee, the party group (acting officially through the NPC Chairmen's Group) decides whether the draft will be debated in the NPC Standing Committee or the full NPC. It is common for the NPC Standing Committee to debate and revise draft legislation many times before voting on passage. When draft legislation encounters significant opposition in the NPC, a vote is usually postponed to avoid a public show of opposition.

After a law is passed, implementing regulations are drawn up, usually by the State Council Legislation Bureau. Implementing regulations transform laws into language that can be applied by local governments and subordinate departments throughout the country. Through implementing regulations, the State Council regains design control over policy before releasing it for implementation.

## Policy Implementation

Although the state has partially retreated from direct control over many aspects of the economy, politics, and society in recent decades, the proportion of decisions affecting all three spheres that is made at the political center in China remains higher than that in liberal democracies. Considering this scope, the fragmented structure of authority, and the size and regional diversity of the country, policymakers are seriously constrained in their efforts to elicit effective policy implementation, despite the recent trend toward greater consultation and consensus building to bring relevant departments and localities into the policy process at an earlier stage.

This section discusses problems of policy implementation in China. It is worth pointing out here, however, that despite problems and their consequences for unsuccessful policy implementation, the Chinese authorities have achieved impressive policy success in two areas designated as vitally important for the country's development: promoting economic growth and controlling population growth. They have been less successful in another policy area: environmental protection. These examples of policy performance are discussed at length later in this chapter. Here, the focus is on general issues in policy implementation.

*Monitoring* The major issue of policy implementation is the monitoring problem, especially serious in China because of the constraints noted earlier.[51] How do China's policymakers ensure that central-level decisions are translated into actions at lower levels? Central authorities have a very limited capacity to monitor the many aspects of the economy, politics, and society affected by their policies. To cope, they adopt fairly simplistic performance indicators. Not only are these problematic as accurate measures of compliance, but also they can produce unanticipated results. Additionally, policymakers rely mainly on departments and localities, which have their own particular interests to pursue, for much of the information on which to base evaluations of performance. Leaders at the political center have attempted in recent years to develop channels of information independent of ministries and local governments. The National Bureau of Statistics has been given more resources and responsibilities to gather and compile information relevant to policymaking and assessment of policy performance. Research institutes and public opinion polls have also played a greater role in channeling different sorts of information to leaders at the political center. The State Auditing Administration and the Ministry of Supervision, both newly established in recent years, are designed to improve central capacity to measure and monitor implementation. Nonetheless, central authorities are unable to verify most reports independently. As a result, information is routinely distorted to make policy implementers appear compliant. Policymakers appear to take this bias into consideration when assessing implementation.

*Policy Priorities*  As policymakers routinely communicate multiple (and conflicting) policy objectives downward through several channels, local authorities must arrive at a reasonable ordering of policy priorities. In deciding priorities, local objectives as well as the apparent priorities of the political center are considered. Local governments and parallel party committees are multitask agencies. Policy priorities communicated in documents channeled down from Beijing in the functionally specialized line hierarchies of government may not be treated as policy priorities by local governments. Policies appear more likely to be implemented in conformity with central directives when signals from the center indicate that top leaders have reached a consensus among themselves and are paying attention. This sort of signal is generally communicated through documents issued by executive organizations (not simply central ministries) of the Communist Party (not simply the government). Party executives may also signal their attention to the implementation of policy issues by speaking at work conferences convened to assess progress in particular areas or establishing an ad hoc leading small group to manage a particular policy problem.

*Adapting Policy to Local Conditions*  Chinese politics presents no electoral incentives for top leaders to line up public policy with the expressed preferences of special interest groups or ordinary voters. To be sure, policymakers consult the players they view as relevant to policy outcomes. Yet, with restrictions on investigation or criticism by the mass media and the prohibition on organized opposition groups, policymakers face relatively little routine outside pressure in formulating policies. Despite increased consultation of players below the top tiers, the policymaking process is relatively closed compared with liberal democracies. In a structural context that limits widespread input and provides no electoral connection to policymakers at the top, reshaping policy in the course of policy implementation is often the most effective way for officials

to influence policy outcomes. Leaders at the political center accept a certain amount of "adaptation of central policy to local conditions"—indeed, this is a stock phrase of Chinese politics.

## Corruption

Economic reform has produced unprecedented growth and prosperity, but also the conditions for new forms of **corruption.** Since the early 1980s, the economy, no longer centrally planned but not fully marketized, has provided opportunities for officials to gain privately from abuse of their control over resources, contracts, and permissions. On the one hand, the new opportunities for corruption may have eased resistance by officials with the most to lose from economic reform. On the other, abuse of public office to pursue private gain has grown in scope, scale, volume, and severity to become one of the gravest challenges facing the regime, even threatening the Chinese armed forces.[52] In public opinion polls conducted over the years, Chinese citizens consistently view corruption as a serious social problem, often the most serious problem. The huge 1989 mass protests, as much about corruption as about democracy, reflected and aired this view.

Chinese leaders are alarmed about corruption, recognizing the threat to regime legitimacy and political stability. Since 1982, they have waged a nearly continuous corruption control effort. While corrupt officials have been prosecuted and punished, the battle against corruption suffers from a basic contradiction between Communist Party leadership and rule by law in China. In principle, as described earlier, equality before the law is a core component of the new legality. In practice, the Chinese legal system has not been used to full effect to control corruption. An important obstacle is a structural one, reflecting a more basic political obstacle. In 1978, party leaders reinstated discipline inspection committees, specialized departments subordinate to party committees at each level of the party hierarchy. Discipline inspection committees investigate misconduct and enforce ethical and political standards for party members. As the preponderance of officials are party members, discipline inspection committees investigate corruption. Regulations require the transfer of criminal cases to procuratorates, but party investigations and party punishments generally precede criminal investigations. Procuratorates routinely encounter obstacles in their efforts to prosecute such cases, not only because officials call up networks of cronies for support but also because successful prosecution is botched when officials have sufficient time to destroy evidence. In principle, the system holds Communist Party members to a higher standard of conduct than ordinary citizens. In practice, exemption from prosecution and substitution of disciplinary action for criminal punishment are very common for officials (but not for ordinary citizens). Public cynicism about corruption control is understandable. In the instances that high-ranking officials are removed from office and sentenced through the legal system, many interpret it as the outcome of a political power struggle.

The problem of corruption and corruption control reflects a basic contradiction between the principles of Communist Party leadership and rule by law. If law is supreme, then the party is subordinate to law and under supervision by procuratorates and courts, not vice versa. So long as party leaders cannot commit to supervision by an impartial legal system, the building of a legal infrastructure will not amount to rule by law. Yet, to commit to such supervision calls into question party leadership and the foundations of the communist party-state.

## POLICY PERFORMANCE

In late 1978, China's leaders defined economic growth as the most important policy priority for decades to come. Despite disagreement about the appropriate pace and scope of economic reform, there has been consensus on a broad strategy of retreat from direct state intervention. The Chinese state has been achieving more by directly controlling less. This strategy has applied not only to economic goals but also to most other policy goals in the reform era. This includes environmental protection, which is less well suited to such a strategy. The important exception has been population control, which Chinese leaders identified as a major policy priority in the late 1970s. The one-child family policy introduced in 1978 features the Chinese state in a more directly interventionist role in population control than ever before.

This section examines the performance of policies of economic reform, environmental protection, and compulsory family planning, focusing on the role of the state in achieving policy goals.

## Economic Growth

Although the Chinese have moved only slowly on political reforms, they have been bold in economic reforms. Since 1978, Chinese leaders have staked their political legitimacy on economic growth, more than anything else. For the most part, the gamble has succeeded. Chinese economic growth, illustrated in Table 13.3, has averaged just under 10 percent per year since 1980.[53] Real per capita income has grown rapidly, to more than $1,700 in 2005 or nearly $6,000 in purchasing power parity (PPP). Although China is still very much a developing country, it is the world's second largest economy in PPP terms. Economic reform has been a remarkable success story. It has been achieved through three major strategies: opening up the economy to the world outside; marketizing the economy; and devolving authority downward to create incentives for local governments, enterprises, households, and individuals to pursue their own economic advancement.

In the late 1970s, Chinese leaders rejected the economic autarky of Maoist "self-reliance," instead opening up the country to foreign trade and investment. As shown in Table 13.4, China had become a major trading economy, moving toward a trade surplus in 1990. The favorable trade balance has allowed China to amass one of the world's largest foreign exchange reserves. It has also created frictions with the United States and some other trading partners. Foreign-invested firms are responsible for much of China's

| | | **TABLE 13.3** |
|---|---|---|
| Economic Performance, 1980–2005   (in constant yuan) | | |
| | **GDP (billion yuan)** | **GDP per Capita (yuan)** |
| 1980 | 452 | 460 |
| 1985 | 898.9 | 853 |
| 1990 | 1,859.8 | 1,634 |
| 1995 | 5,749.5 | 4,854 |
| 2000 | 8,825.4 | 7,086 |
| 2005 | 18,232.1 | 14,025 |
| | U.S. $2,279 billion | U.S. $1,753 ($6,800 PPP) |

Sources: State Council Information Office, China Internet Information Center at http://www.china.org.cn; National Bureau of Statistics of China, Statistical Communique, 28 February 2006 at http://www.stats.gov.cn; 2005 PPP figure is from Central Intelligence Agency, *World Factbook* at http://www.cia.gov/cia/publications/factbook/.

| Foreign Trade, 1978–2005 (in U.S. billion constant dollars) | | | **TABLE 13.4** |
| :--- | :--- | :--- | :--- |

| Year | Trade Volume | Imports | Exports |
| :--- | ---: | ---: | ---: |
| 1978 | 20.64 | 10.89 | 9.75 |
| 1979 | 29.33 | 15.67 | 13.66 |
| 1980 | 38.14 | 20.02 | 18.12 |
| 1981 | 44.03 | 22.02 | 22.01 |
| 1982 | 41.61 | 19.29 | 22.32 |
| 1983 | 43.62 | 21.39 | 22.23 |
| 1984 | 53.55 | 27.41 | 26.14 |
| 1985 | 69.60 | 42.25 | 27.35 |
| 1986 | 73.85 | 42.91 | 30.94 |
| 1987 | 82.65 | 43.21 | 39.44 |
| 1988 | 102.79 | 55.27 | 47.52 |
| 1989 | 111.68 | 59.14 | 52.54 |
| 1990 | 115.44 | 53.35 | 62.09 |
| 1991 | 135.70 | 63.79 | 71.91 |
| 1992 | 165.53 | 80.59 | 84.94 |
| 1993 | 195.70 | 103.96 | 91.74 |
| 1994 | 236.62 | 115.61 | 121.01 |
| 1995 | 280.86 | 132.08 | 148.78 |
| 1996 | 289.88 | 138.83 | 151.05 |
| 1997 | 325.16 | 142.37 | 182.79 |
| 1998 | 323.95 | 140.24 | 183.71 |
| 1999 | 360.63 | 165.70 | 194.93 |
| 2000 | 474.29 | 225.09 | 249.20 |
| 2001 | 509.65 | 243.55 | 266.10 |
| 2002 | 620.77 | 295.17 | 325.60 |
| 2003 | 850.99 | 412.76 | 438.23 |
| 2004 | 1,154.55 | 561.23 | 593.32 |
| 2005 | 1,421.90 | 659.95 | 761.95 |

Source: National Bureau of Statistics of China, *2006 China Statistical Abstract* (Beijing: China Statistics Press, 2006), 169.

exports, reflecting the country's appeal—through preferential policies, cheap labor, and a potentially huge market—as a destination for foreign direct investment (FDI). China attracts more FDI than any other developing nation; overall, it is the world's third largest recipient of FDI. The role of FDI in promoting economic growth through exports has compensated for the weakness of Chinese private capital as the country emerged from its socialist economic past.

Post-Mao leaders inherited a centrally planned economy, organized according to a Stalinist model borrowed from the Soviet Union in the 1950s. They did not initially set out with a stated goal or program to create a socialist market economy. Indeed, the goal to create a market system was not officially affirmed until 1993. Rather, economic reform proceeded incrementally, in a process often described as "crossing the river by groping for stones." Initially, some top party leaders envisaged only a small secondary role for the market economy, as a "bird in a cage" of the planned economy. By the mid-1990s, however, the Chinese economy had basically "grown out" of the plan.[54] In 1998, the Chinese approved a "shareholding system" that is essentially privatization, thinly disguised to maintain ideological orthodoxy.

The emergence of scarcity prices, reflecting market supply and demand, to replace prices determined bureaucratically by central authorities is a good example of this incrementalism. Initially, the government pursued a "two-track" pricing system: it maintained bureaucratic prices for some key industrial inputs, but allowed scarcity to determine prices of other commodities. Some scarcity prices were determined fully by market forces; others were allowed to rise and fall within a range. Over time, the number of commodities with bureaucratic prices was steadily decreased. By the mid-1990s, two-track prices were a thing of the past.

Finally, a key economic reform strategy has been decentralization. Leaders in Beijing have devolved authority to empower local governments, enterprises, households, and individuals. Agricultural decollectivization in the early 1980s was the first such reform, replacing collective farming with household farming. Individual entrepreneurs emerged at about the same time, engaging in small-scale production or providing services (such as transportation of commodities to markets) long ignored under central planning. Existing rural enterprises were allowed to expand into practically any product line, rather than being restricted to "serving agriculture," as before. Most of these industries were organized as "collective enterprises," with formal ownership by the township or village community and with strong direct involvement of local government in management. These small-scale township and village enterprises (TVEs) proved themselves adaptable to the demands of the new market environment. They drove much of China's rapid growth in the 1980s and into the 1990s. Fiscal arrangements negotiated in the mid-1980s also favored local governments, at the expense of the center; in a renegotiation in the mid-1990s, the central government gained back some revenues, but without removing incentives for local economic initiative.

The reform of the state-owned enterprise (SOE) system began in the mid-1980s. Initial reforms created incentives to boost production by replacing government appropriation of all SOE profits with a system of taxing profits—allowing SOEs to retain a portion of profits. Of course, until prices reflected scarcity, the incentives remained weak. More important, SOEs employed (and employ) a very high proportion of urban workers. This effectively put SOEs on a "soft budget constraint": as local governments feared worker unrest, unprofitable SOEs did not fear bankruptcy; they could count on state banks to bail them out. In 1993, the Chinese authorities announced that one-third of SOEs were loss-making and one-third barely breaking even. In 1994, the Company Law was passed to provide a legal framework for corporatization. A strategy of "targeting the large, releasing the small" emerged: Beijing continued to nurture about 1,000 large SOEs, encouraging them to form giant conglomerates, assisting them with loans but imposing greater financial discipline; the smaller SOEs were left to confront market forces and reorganize themselves through mergers, takeovers, conversion into shareholding companies, or outright closure. This dual process of corporatization and reorganization continues today, with increasing privatization through conversion to shareholding and greater political toleration of SOE closures and sales, including sales to foreign partners.

## Environmental Degradation

China's rapid economic growth has resulted in serious environmental damage. Environmental pollution and degradation have increased at a rate that outpaces the capacity of the Chinese state to protect the environment.[55] Township and village enterprises contribute more than half of pollutants of all kinds, dumping their untreated waste directly into rivers and streams and relying heavily on coal for energy. Use of coal, a major source of air pollution but a vital contributor to energy supply (see Box 13.5), has doubled since the economic reforms. Water scarcity poses a major challenge: prices do not reflect scarcity because most water is directed toward agriculture for irrigation, and local governments fear rural unrest will erupt with meaningful water price increases. Integration into the global economy

has made China a global market for resource-intensive goods, such as paper and furniture—producing a massive drop in forest coverage with increases in logging by Chinese and multinational businesses. China has also become a destination of choice for some of the world's most environmentally damaging industries.

Environmental economists at the World Bank and other organizations estimate the cost to the Chinese economy of environmental degradation and resource scarcity at 8 to 12 percent of GDP annually. This includes health and productivity losses associated with air pollution and water scarcity costs in lost industrial output. Even so, through the mid-1990s, leaders and the Chinese media continued to articulate the principle of "first development, then environment." The ideal of sustainable development, prominent in official

The policy of "first development, then environment" has taken a heavy toll. Pollution far outpaces the government's capacity for environmental protection.

Topham/The Image Works

**BOX 13.5**

## Shutting Down 5,000 Coal Mines

China depends on coal for more than 65 percent of its growing energy needs, but in 2005 the central government ordered more than 5,000 coal mines shut down. China's mines are the most dangerous in the world: in that year alone, nearly 6,000 Chinese coal miners died in mining accidents, almost 80 percent of the world's total mining fatalities. The mines ordered closed were both unsafe and illegal. Many were lucrative small-scale mines, managed as township or village enterprises. Others were privately owned, often with local officials holding private (strictly illegal) shares. Mine managers routinely flout safety standards, taking local government acquiescence for granted. The miners generally resign themselves to the high risks, because mining pays better than alternative employment in agriculture. In such conditions, despite laws, orders, and rhetoric on industrial safety, dangerous mines will continue to operate. Undoubtedly, they include many mines shut down in 2005.

rhetoric today, was incorporated into the economic planning process only in 1992.

Over the past decade, China has erected a legal and bureaucratic infrastructure of environmental protection. In 1984, the State Council established a central government department responsible for environmental matters; in 1989, the NPC adopted an environmental protection law; and in 1993, a specialized legislative environmental protection and natural resources committee was established in the NPC.

Nonetheless, in the policymaking process, the environmental bureaucracy is weak in negotiations with the many ministries with developmental priorities. The problem is even more serious at the local level. The laws that emerge tend to be too diluted and general to provide useful guidelines for enforcement.

The Chinese tally a great number of enforcement successes over the past decade: the resolution of more than 75,000 environmental law violation cases, the closure of more than 16,000 enterprises for illegal discharge of pollutants, and the issuance of more than 10,000 warnings to environment polluters.[56] Yet, the devolution of authority to local governments, a strategy that unlocked economic growth, constitutes a fundamental obstacle to enforcement.

Although local environmental protection bureaus (EPBs) are nominally accountable to both the State Environmental Protection Agency (SEPA) in Beijing and their local governments, they depend on local governments for their growth and survival—budgets, career advancement, staff size, and allocation of resources, such as vehicles and office buildings. Local government developmental priorities practically always dominate efforts to enforce environmental standards, especially when enterprises are collective enterprises or firms with a large number of workers. Pollution discharge fees are routinely not collected (or not fully collected), and legal requirements to improve pollution control capacity are routinely waived. The 2006 policy decision to consider environmental protection performance, including energy use, in evaluating local governments may have some impact, but its importance is unlikely to trump economic growth in the near future.

Environmental protection is also underfunded. The five-year plan adopted in March 2006 budgeted 1.6 percent of GDP for environmental protection—an increase over past years but nonetheless an amount that Chinese scientists believe is well below what is needed to produce notable improvements. At the same time, the Chinese set an ambitious policy goal: 10 percent of their energy needs to be supplied by environmentally friendly renewable sources by 2010.

### Population Control

While reducing state intervention to promote economic growth, policymakers have increased their intervention involving a new policy priority: population control. For most of the Maoist years, population planning was not actively promoted. In 1978, with the population close to a billion and amid rising concern about meeting economic goals and ensuring basic livelihood, employment opportunities, and social security support at the current rate of population growth, China's leaders declared population control a major policy priority. State-sponsored family planning was added to the constitution, and an ideal family size of one child was endorsed as national policy. According to this policy, most couples are required to stop childbearing after one or two births. Married couples in urban areas, with few exceptions, are restricted to one child. In rural areas, married couples are subject to rules that differ across provinces. In some provinces, two children are normally permitted; in others, only one child is permitted; in most provinces, a second child is permitted only if the first is a girl.

*One-Child Family Policy* The **one-child family policy** is inherently difficult to implement in China, particularly in the countryside, where nearly 60 percent of Chinese live.[57] There, the population is relatively poorly educated and has poor access to public health facilities—circumstances that do not facilitate an effective family planning program. Traditional views about the family prevail: as in most agrarian societies, big families and many sons are viewed as ideal. Moreover, in China, a married daughter joins the household of her husband, while a married son

remains in the household to support aging parents. Decollectivization and the return to household farming in the early 1980s enhanced the value of sons compared to daughters, for their labor power. The dismantling of the commune system has also left the state less able to monitor compliance, just as the new economic independence of peasants has left the state less able to enforce compliance. Finally, population control involves the state as the dominant decisionmaker in choices that are traditionally viewed, in China as elsewhere, as private family matters.

Despite the inherent difficulties, the Chinese have succeeded in curbing population growth dramatically, as is illustrated in Figure 13.5. A population structure normally resembles a pyramid: with relatively unchanged rates of births and deaths, the proportion of population from top to bottom is progressively bigger. The population pyramid in Figure 13.5 deviates from this form in a few places. The first, located at about the middle of the pyramid, reflects fewer births as well as differentially more deaths among the young in the disaster following the Great Leap Forward, in the cohort aged 45–49 in 2005. The second, evident beginning with the cohort aged 25–29 in 2005, reflects the impact of

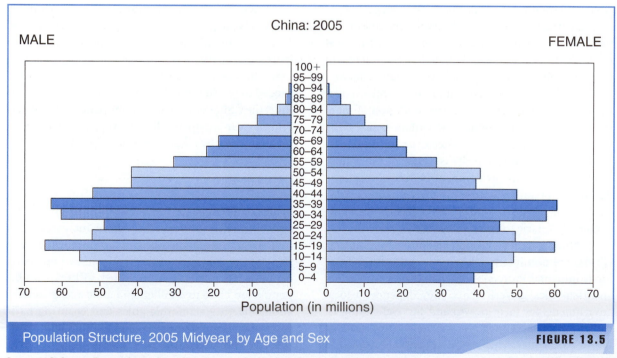

Population Structure, 2005 Midyear, by Age and Sex

**FIGURE 13.5**

Source: U.S. Census Bureau, International Data Base at http://www.census.gov/ipc/www/idbpyr.html.

family planning policies introduced in the 1970s. Variation in policy emphasis by leaders at the political center is reflected in variation in number of births, beginning in the mid-1970s. Implementation of the one-child family policy began in 1979. In 1983, responding to concerns at the political center, implementation became more coercive. From 1984 through the late 1980s, the policy was relaxed and implementation in the countryside faltered due to difficulties associated with decollectivization. Births rose immediately. From 1989 to the present, policy implementation has been stringent. Urban-rural outcomes differ significantly, however. In the cities, the one-child family appears to be the accepted norm. In the countryside, however, any relaxation of policy has been reflected in immediate big increases in births.[58]

**Policy Implementation** Policy implementation has taken a number of forms: a legal requirement of late marriage, a requirement of insertion of an intrauterine device after a first birth, and a requirement of sterilization of one partner after a second birth. There are incentives to sign a one-child family certificate after the first birth, including priority in entrance to schools and funding for health fees for the child. Fines are imposed on the family for policy violations. Birth planning workers at the grassroots are given birth quotas from higher levels, which they allocate on the basis of family circumstances. From the perspective of leaders at the political center, abortion is a sign of failure, not success, in policy implementation. At the grassroots, from the perspective of birth planning workers, however, the obvious fact is that abortions do not add above-plan births. Undeniably, birth planning workers have incentives to encourage abortions and face few disincentives for doing so.

**Perverse Outcomes** In recent years, policymakers have expressed concern about a perverse result of compulsory family planning: the shortage of young girls, compared with boys. Recent figures show atypical birth disparities: a national average of 118 newborn boys to 100 newborn girls in 2005. These figures compare with an international average of about 106 boys to 100 girls.

The shortage of girls reflects the traditional Chinese preference for male children in the context of compulsory family planning. Traditional practices of female infanticide as well as abandonment and severe neglect of girls beyond infancy have led to excess female infant mortality. Not least of all, missing girls are increasingly the result of sex-selective abortion, made possible with the widespread use of ultrasound technology in the early 1980s. These practices prompted top legislators to consider criminalizing such abortions, although ultimately they decided against it.

China's success in reducing population growth has strong supporters and detractors outside the country. The official Chinese response to criticism from human rights advocates has focused on "economic rights" that the government argues would be denied to all Chinese in the decades to come if population growth is not brought under control.

## HONG KONG

In 1842 and 1860, the island of **Hong Kong** and adjacent territory on the Chinese mainland were ceded by treaty to Britain in perpetuity. In 1898, more adjacent territory was ceded in a ninety-nine-year lease. These cessions were largely the outcome of British victory in wars fought to impose trade on China. For nearly a century, Hong Kong (including the adjacent territories) was a British colony, ruled by a governor appointed in London. Hong Kong flourished economically, with a disciplined labor force of Chinese immigrants, a free-market economy, and a government commitment to rule of law and civil liberties but not elected government.

In 1984, the Chinese communist authorities elaborated the principle of **"one country, two systems,"** applicable to Hong Kong after 1997. China and Britain signed a joint declaration: Hong Kong would revert to Chinese sovereignty in 1997, but would continue to enjoy "a high degree of autonomy." The Chinese agreed that Hong Kong would enjoy economic, financial, and monetary autonomy, maintaining its capitalist system, legal system, and way of life for fifty years. At midnight on June 30, 1997, Hong Kong became a special administrative region of communist-ruled China.

The British had made little effort to democratize politics in Hong Kong through the 1980s. The governor had consulted business elites and other key constituencies on policy affairs, but there had been no elected legislature or government. Nor had political parties really developed in such an environment. All this changed in 1989.

The Tiananmen massacre galvanized Hong Kong Chinese and British expatriates into efforts to accelerate the pace of political democratization before 1997. In 1991, in the first direct elections to the Legislative Council, only a third of the legislative deputies were directly elected. In 1995, a controversial electoral reform bill introduced by Governor Christopher Patten guided elections: for the first time, ordinary Hong Kong citizens elected all deputies in the Legislative Council. Hong Kong's most liberal democratic parties won overwhelmingly in geographic voting districts. Openly pro-Beijing forces did poorly.

Communist authorities rejected the elections and the legislature as violations of the Basic Law, Hong Kong's miniconstitution passed in China's National People's Congress in 1990. They supervised selection of a chief executive and provisional legislature in 1996. At the moment of the historic handover, this chief executive and provisional legislature officially replaced the governor and the legislature elected in 1995.

Since the handover, Beijing authorities have been less heavy-handed than feared. Hong Kong today enjoys most of the same civil liberties as under British rule. Human rights organizations and pro-democracy organizations that monitor and support progress in the PRC have bases in Hong Kong. Hong Kong newspapers provide information about politics in the PRC and are critical in ways not permitted on the mainland. Chinese communist authorities hope that success in implementing "one country, two systems" in Hong Kong will woo Taiwan back to the PRC too.

## TAIWAN

**Taiwan,** governed by the Nationalists as the **Republic of China** since 1945, lies a mere 100 miles off the east coast of the Chinese mainland. Communist "liberation" of Taiwan became moot when the United States sent its Seventh Fleet to the Taiwan Strait, declaring an American interest in the security of Taiwan after the outbreak of the Korean War in the 1950s. For the next three decades, the Chinese routinely bombarded

offshore islands of Taiwan and continued to threaten liberation by military force. For the most part, however, it was a cold war—and until the 1970s, Taiwan was the clear winner, enjoying international recognition as the sole legitimate representative of China.

In the 1970s, two major events affected Taiwan's status. In 1971, Taiwan lost its membership in the United Nations and its seat on the Security Council to China. In 1979, the United States recognized China diplomatically, downgrading the relationship with Taiwan to one of unofficial liaison. Today, fewer than thirty countries recognize Taiwan. These events have put China in a position of relative strength.

The two sides have engaged in negotiations on and off over the years. Since democratization in the late 1980s, Taiwan's leaders are more constrained than ever to represent majority public opinion, which does not support unification with the mainland. The election of a pro-independence party candidate to the presidency in 2000 exacerbated friction across the Taiwan Strait.

## CHINA'S POLITICAL FUTURE

Two main themes have run through this study of Chinese politics today. First, despite very significant economic liberalization and a nascent political institutionalization, Chinese politics takes place within the boundaries of what is still essentially a communist party-state. Second, the dramatic changes sweeping the Chinese economy, polity, and society, many of which now seem beyond the control of political leaders, are as much a by-product of reform as a direct product of reform policies. The first theme cautions against liberal democratic optimism when considering China's political future. The second reminds us that the script of the political future will not be written by Chinese communist leaders alone.

In this new century, China must confront a number of key issues that will significantly determine its development. Can structures and processes that bolster and foster economic growth safeguard against the threat of more significant political liberalization and eventual democratization—which remain unacceptable to the Chinese authorities?

Around the world, political change in recent decades has created an age of democratization—the result, in many countries, of revolutions that toppled communist regimes older than the Chinese regime. Will the "third wave" of world democratization reach China early in the twenty-first century?

Certainly, liberal democratic ideals and practices are quite alien to Chinese culture. Chinese history provides no examples of democratic rule, and the Chinese cultural tradition expresses no concerns to protect individuals by checking state power. Past experience and cultural tradition, then, offer little encouragement to those looking for the seeds of democratization in China.

Yet, authoritarianism has not survived intact with economic modernization in many East Asian countries that have a similar lack of historical and cultural foundations for democracy. To be sure, even with continued economic growth, China will differ

from these countries for many years to come. It will be bifurcated in its development: middle-class prosperity is emerging in the big cities and coastal regions, but Chinese in the countryside will remain relatively poor for some time.

With reform, for most ordinary Chinese, the party has demanded less and delivered more in recent decades. Unlike communist parties that gained (and held) power with the aid of Soviet troops and tanks, the Chinese Communist Party has indigenous and nationalist roots. Barring a major economic crisis, it is less likely to collapse in the face of the sort of mass discontent that toppled communist regimes in Eastern Europe. More likely, in the medium term at least, the party will continue to transform China in the years to come and to transform itself in order to continue to rule.

## KEY TERMS

Central Committee
Chinese Communist Party
Confucianism
corruption
Cultural Revolution
Democracy Movement
democratic centralism
Deng Xiaoping
ethnic minorities
fragmented
    authoritarianism

GONGOs
Great Leap Forward
guardianship
Hong Kong
Hu Jintao
leading small groups
    (LSGs)
Mao Zedong
mass line
mass mobilization
    campaign

Nationalist Party
National Party Congress
National People's
    Congress (NPC)
*nomenklatura* system
one-child family policy
one country, two systems
party-state
People's Liberation Army
    (PLA)
Politburo

Republic of China
rule by law
socialist market economy
State Council
Taiwan (Republic of
    China)
Tiananmen massacre
village committees

## SUGGESTED READINGS

Bianco, Lucien. *Origins of the Chinese Revolution, 1915–1949.* Stanford, CA: Stanford University Press, 1971.

Chang, Jung. *Wild Swans: Three Daughters of China.* New York: Anchor, 1991.

Economy, Elizabeth C. *The River Runs Black: The Environmental Challenge to China's Future.* Ithaca, NY: Cornell University Press, 2004.

Goldman, Merle, and Roderick MacFarquhar, eds. *The Paradox of China's Post-Mao Reforms.* Cambridge: Harvard University Press, 1999.

Gries, Peter Hays, and Stanley Rosen, eds. *State and Society in 21st-century China: Crisis, Contention, and Legitimation.* New York: RoutledgeCurzon, 2004.

Lieberthal, Kenneth. *Governing China: From Revolution Through Reform.* 2d ed. New York: Norton, 2004.

Nathan, Andrew J. *Chinese Democracy.* Berkeley: University of California Press, 1986.

Spence, Jonathan D. *The Search for Modern China.* New York: Norton, 1990.

Weston, Timothy B., and Lionel Jensen, eds. *China Beyond the Headlines.* Lanham, MD: Rowman & Littlefield, 2000.

Wong, Jan. *Red China Blues.* Sydney, Australia: Doubleday, 1996.

## INTERNET RESOURCES

**www.china.org.cn/english.** China Internet Information Center, State Council Information Office. Authorized website of Chinese government, link to National People's Congress. Access to government White Papers, news, statistical data.

**www.stats.gov.cn/english/.** National Bureau of Statistics. Official monthly and yearly statistics, including downloadable Excel files.

**www.chinadaily.com.cn.** *China Daily.* News from China directed toward external readership.

**http://english.peopledaily.com.cn/.** *People's Daily.* Official newspaper of Communist Party of China.

**www.scmp.com.** *South China Morning Post.* News about Hong Kong and mainland China, from Hong Kong.

**www.wws.princeton.edu/~lynn/chinabib.pdf.** Contemporary China bibliography, Professor Lynn White, Princeton University.

**www.uschina.org.** United States–China Business Council. Analysis and advocacy of policy issues of interest to U.S. corporations engaged in business relations with China.

## ENDNOTES

1. *New York Times,* 17 April 2006.

2. Lou Jiwei, Deputy Minister of Finance, *People's Daily* online, 22 June 2006. Bai Jinfu, a former deputy director of a research center under the State Council, estimates the Gini coefficient to be 0.50. See *South China Morning Post* online, 11 July 2006.

3. For a good, very readable discussion of Chinese history beginning with the late Ming (seventeenth century) and extending into the 1980s, see Jonathan D. Spence, *The Search for Modern China* (New York: Norton, 1990). Other good historical overviews include Charles O. Hucker, *China's Imperial Past: An Introduction to Chinese History and Culture* (Stanford, CA: Stanford University Press, 1975); and Immanuel C. Y. Hsu, *The Rise of Modern China*, 5th ed. (New York: Oxford University Press, 1995).

4. See Hsi-sheng Chi, *Warlord Politics in China, 1916–1928* (Stanford, CA: Stanford University Press, 1976); and Edward A. McCord, *The Power of the Gun: The Emergence of Modern Chinese Warlordism* (Berkeley: University of California Press, 1993).

5. R. H. Tawney, *Land and Labour in China* (London: Allen & Unwin, 1932).

6. See especially Lucien Bianco, *Origins of the Chinese Revolution, 1915–1949* (Stanford, CA: Stanford University Press, 1971). See also Benjamin Schwartz, *Chinese Communism and the Rise of Mao* (Cambridge: Harvard University Press, 1951).

7. The classic political biography of Mao is Edgar Snow, *Red Star Over China* (New York: Grove Press, 1968). Of the many excellent studies by Stuart R. Schram, see especially *The Political Thought of Mao Tse-tung,* rev. ed. (New York: Praeger, 1969); *The Thought of Mao Tse-tung* (Cambridge: Cambridge University Press, 1989), and his biography of Mao, *Mao Tse-tung,* rev. ed. (Harmondsworth: Penguin, 1967). After Mao's death, scholars appraised Mao and his legacy from a variety of perspectives in Dick Wilson, ed., *Mao Tse-tung in the Scales of History: A Preliminary Assessment* (Cambridge: Cambridge University Press, 1977).

8. See Chalmers A. Johnson, *Peasant Nationalism and Communist Power: The Emergence of Revolutionary China* (Stanford, CA: Stanford University Press, 1962).

9. See Suzanne Pepper, *Civil War in China: The Political Struggle, 1945–1949* (Berkeley: University of California Press, 1978).

10. For a good selection of essays offering a comprehensive overview of PRC history, see Roderick MacFarquhar, ed., *The Politics of China: The Eras of Mao and Deng,* 2nd ed. (Cambridge: Cambridge University Press, 1997). Other good discussions of post-Mao history are found in Richard Baum, *Burying Mao: Chinese Politics in the Age of Deng Xiaoping* (Princeton, NJ: Princeton University Press, 1994); and Harry Harding, *China's Second Revolution: Reform After Mao* (Washington, DC: Brookings Institution, 1987). Good discussions of particular topics of reform are found in Merle Goldman and Roderick MacFarquhar, eds., *The Paradox of China's Post-Mao Reforms* (Cambridge: Harvard University Press, 1999).

11. The classic account is by William Hinton, who observed land reform before 1949 in *Fanshen: A Documentary of Revolution in a Chinese Village* (New York: Viking, 1966).

12. Roderick MacFarquhar, ed., *The Hundred Flowers Campaign and the Chinese Intellectuals* (New York: Praeger, 1960); and Fu-sheng Mu, *The Wilting of the Hundred Flowers Movement: Free Thought in China Today* (London: Heinemann, 1962).

13. See Dali L. Yang, *Calamity and Reform in China: State, Rural Society, and Institutional Change Since the Great Leap Famine* (Stanford, CA: Stanford University Press, 1996).

14. See Frederick C. Teiwes, *Politics and Purges in China: Rectification and the Decline of Party Norms, 1950–1965* (Armonk, NY: M. E. Sharpe, 1979); and Frederick C. Teiwes, *Leadership, Legitimacy, and Conflict in China: From a Charismatic Mao to the Politics of Succession* (Armonk, NY: M. E. Sharpe, 1984).

15. See Jasper Becker, *Hungry Ghosts: Mao's Secret Famine* (New York: Free Press, 1996).

16. Some of the best accounts of the Cultural Revolution are biographical or autobiographical. See, for example, Gordon A. Bennett and Ronald N. Montaperto, *Red Guard: The Political Biography of Dai Hsiao-ai* (Garden City, NY: Doubleday, 1971); Jung Chang, *Wild Swans: Three Daughters of China* (New York: Anchor, 1991); Yuan Gao, *Born Red: Chronicle of the Cultural Revolution* (Stanford, CA: Stanford University Press, 1987); Liang Heng and Judith Shapiro, *Son of the Revolution* (New York: Knopf, 1983); Anne F. Thurston, *Enemies of the People: The Ordeal of the Intellectuals in China's Great Cultural Revolution* (Cambridge: Harvard University

Press, 1988); Daiyun Yue and Carolyn Wakeman, *To the Storm: The Odyssey of a Revolutionary Chinese Woman* (Berkeley: University of California Press, 1985); and Nien Cheng, *Life and Death in Shanghai* (New York: Grove Press, 1986).

17. See Dru C. Gladney, *Muslim Chinese: Ethnic Nationalism in the People's Republic* (Cambridge: Council on East Asian Studies, Harvard University, 1991); and Stevan Harrell, ed., *Cultural Encounters on China's Ethnic Frontiers* (Seattle: University of Washington Press, 1995).

18. An excellent discussion of guardianship is found in Robert A. Dahl, *Democracy and Its Critics* (New Haven, CT: Yale University Press, 1989), ch. 4. On Leninism in general, see especially Alfred G. Meyer, *Leninism* (Cambridge: Harvard University Press, 1957).

19. Mao Zedong, "Some Questions Concerning Methods of Leadership," in *Selected Works of Mao Tse-tung*, vol. 3 (Peking: Foreign Languages Press, 1965), 117–22.

20. On the changing role of the NPC, see Murray Scot Tanner, *The Politics of Lawmaking in Post-Mao China: Institutions, Processes, and Democratic Prospects* (New York: Oxford University Press, 1999); and "Breaking the Vicious Cycles: The Emergence of China's National People's Congress," *Problems of Post-Communism* 45, no. 3 (1998): 29–47. For an historical perspective, see Kevin J. O'Brien, *Reform Without Liberalization: China's National People's Congress and the Politics of Institutional Change* (Cambridge: Cambridge University Press, 1990).

21. See Murray Scot Tanner, "How a Bill Becomes a Law in China: Stages and Processes of Lawmaking," *China Quarterly*, no. 141 (1995): 39–64.

22. See the selection of essays in David Shambaugh, ed., *Deng Xiaoping: Portrait of a Chinese Statesman* (New York: Oxford University Press, 1995).

23. Tai Ming Cheung, "The Influence of the Gun: China's Central Military Commission and Its Relationship With the Military, Party, and State Decision-Making Systems," in David M. Lampton, ed., *The Making of Chinese Foreign and Security Policy in the Era of Reform* (Stanford, CA: Stanford University Press, 2001), 61–90; and Michael D. Swaine, "Chinese Decision-Making Regarding Taiwan, 1979–2000," in *The Making of Chinese Foreign and Security Policy in the Era of Reform*, 289–336. On military modernization, see David Shambaugh and Richard H. Yang, eds., *China's Military in Transition* (Oxford: Clarendon Press, 1997); and David Shambaugh, "The People's Liberation Army and the People's Republic at 50: Reform at Last," *China Quarterly*, 159 (1999): 660–72.

24. See Melanie Manion, "The Cadre Management System, Post-Mao: The Appointment, Promotion, Transfer, and Removal of Party and State Leaders," *China Quarterly*, 102 (1985): 203–33; John P. Burns, *The Chinese Communist Party's Nomenklatura System* (Armonk, NY: M. E. Sharpe, 1989); and "Strengthening Central CCP Control of Leadership Selection: The 1990 *Nomenklatura*," *China Quarterly*, 138 (1994): 458–91.

25. See Hsiao Pen, "Separating the Party From the Government," in Carol Lee Hamrin and Suisheng Zhao, eds., *Decision-Making in Deng's China: Perspectives from Insiders* (Armonk, NY: M. E. Sharpe, 1995), 153–68.

26. See Zhiyue Bo, *Chinese Provincial Leaders: Economic Performance and Political Mobility Since 1949* (Armonk, NY: M. E. Sharpe,

2002). For an earlier discussion of elite recruitment and mobility, based on case studies, see David M. Lampton, *Paths to Power: Elite Mobility in Contemporary China* (Ann Arbor: Center for Chinese Studies, University of Michigan, 1986).

27. For an overview of the change, see Richard Baum, "Modernization and Legal Reform in Post-Mao China: The Rebirth of Socialist Legality," *Studies in Comparative Communism* 19, no. 2 (1986): 69–103. For notions underlying the change, see Carlos W. H. Lo, "Deng Xiaoping's Ideas on Law: China on the Threshold of a Legal Order," *Asian Survey* 32, no. 7 (1992): 649–65. For a description of the law in practice in post-Mao China, see James V. Feinerman, "Economic and Legal Reform in China, 1978–91," *Problems of Communism* 40, no. 5 (1991): 62–75; Pitman B. Potter, ed., *Domestic Law Reforms in Post-Mao China* (Armonk, NY: M. E. Sharpe, 1994); "The Chinese Legal System: Continuing Commitment to the Primacy of State Power," *China Quarterly*, no. 159 (1999): 673–83; and Stanley B. Lubman, *Bird in a Cage: Legal Reform in China After Mao* (Stanford, CA: Stanford University Press, 1999).

28. See Minxin Pei, "Citizens v. Mandarins: Administrative Litigation in China," *China Quarterly*, 152 (December 1997): 832–62.

29. See, for example, Donald C. Clarke and James V. Feinerman, "Antagonistic Contradictions: Criminal Law and Human Rights in China," *China Quarterly*, 141 (1995): 135–54.

30. See the account of "thought work" in Daniel Lynch, *After the Propaganda State: Media, Politics, and "Thought Work" in Reformed China* (Stanford, CA: Stanford University Press, 1999).

31. M. Kent Jennings and Ning Zhang, "Collective Memories in the Chinese Countryside" (paper presented at the Annual Meeting of the International Society of Political Psychology, July 2002, Berlin). Chinese who were adolescents during the Cultural Revolution also recall that event as memorable, more so than do Chinese in other age groups.

32. See Tianjian Shi, "Cultural Values and Democracy in the People's Republic of China," *China Quarterly*, 162 (2000): 540–59; and Yang Zhong, Jie Chen, and John Scheb, "Mass Political Culture in Beijing: Findings From Two Public Opinion Surveys," *Asian Survey* 38, no. 8 (1998): 763–83. For a comparative perspective, see Gabriel A. Almond and Sidney Verba, *Civic Culture: Political Attitudes and Democracy in Five Nations* (Princeton, NJ: Princeton University Press, 1963).

33. Yun-han Chu and Yu-tzung Chang, "Culture Shift and Regime Legitimacy: Comparing Mainland China, Taiwan, and Hong Kong," in Shiping Hua, ed., *Chinese Political Culture, 1989–2000* (Armonk, NY: M. E. Sharpe, 2001), 320–47. See also Tianjian Shi, "Cultural Values and Political Trust: A Comparison of the People's Republic of China and Taiwan," *Comparative Politics* 33, no. 4 (2001): 401–19.

34. This is the conclusion of Tianjian Shi, based on analysis of the same survey data. See "Cultural Values and Democracy in the People's Republic of China." See also Andrew J. Nathan and Tianjian Shi, "Cultural Requisites for Democracy in China: Findings from a Survey," *Daedalus* 122, no. 2 (1993): 95–123.

35. Two independent sets of surveys, including surveys of the more politically knowledgeable and interested Beijing population, conclude this in almost exactly the same words. See Shi, "Cultural Values and Democracy in the People's Republic of China"; and Zhong, Chen, and Scheb, "Mass Political Culture in Beijing."

36. See the excellent discussion of forms of political participation in Tianjian Shi, *Political Participation in Beijing* (Cambridge: Harvard University Press, 1997), ch. 2.

37. On the Maoist period, see James R. Townsend, *Political Participation in Communist China* (Berkeley: University of California Press, 1967). On post-Mao elections, see Andrew Nathan, *Chinese Democracy* (Berkeley: University of California Press, 1985); Robert E. Bedeski, "China's 1979 Election Law and Its Implementation," *Electoral Studies* 5, no. 2 (1986): 153–65; Barrett L. McCormick, *Political Reform in Post-Mao China* (Berkeley: University of California Press, 1990); J. Bruce Jacobs, "Elections in China," *Australian Journal of Chinese Affairs*, 25 (1991): 171–200; and Melanie Manion, "Chinese Democratization in Perspective: Electorates and Selectorates at the Township Level. Report from the Field," *China Quarterly*, 163 (2000): 133–51.

38. On rural decollectivization, see especially Daniel Kelliher, *Peasant Power in China: The Era of Rural Reform, 1979–1989* (New Haven, CT: Yale University Press, 1992); and Kate Xiao Zhou, *How the Farmers Changed China: Power of the People* (Boulder, CO: Westview Press, 1996).

39. See Melanie Manion, "The Electoral Connection in the Chinese Countryside," *American Political Science Review* 90, no. 4 (1996): 736–48; Tianjian Shi, "Economic Development and Village Elections in Rural China," *Journal of Contemporary China* 8, no. 22 (1999): 433–35; Anne F. Thurston, *Muddling Toward Democracy: Political Change in Grassroots China* (Washington, DC: United States Institute of Peace, 1999); and Lianjiang Li, "Elections and Popular Resistance in Rural China," *China Information* 16, no. 1 (2002): 89–107.

40. On protest movements in the 1970s and 1980s, see especially Andrew J. Nathan, *Chinese Democracy* (Berkeley: University of California Press, 1985); Jeffrey N. Wasserstrom and Elizabeth J. Perry, eds., *Popular Protest and Political Culture in Modern China: Learning From 1989* (Boulder, CO: Westview, 1992); and Gregor Benton and Alan Hunter, *Wild Lily, Prairie Fire: China's Road to Democracy, 1942–1989* (Princeton, NJ: Princeton University Press, 1995).

41. James D. Seymour, ed., *The Fifth Modernization* (Stanfordville, NY: Human Rights Publishing Group, 1980).

42. On the 1989 protests, see Michel Oksenberg, Lawrence R. Sullivan, and Marc Lambert, eds., *Beijing Spring, 1989: Confrontation and Conflict, The Basic Documents,* (Armonk, NY: M. E. Sharpe, 1990); Han Minzhu and Hua Sheng, eds., *Cries for Democracy: Writings and Speeches From the 1989 Chinese Democracy Movement* (Princeton, NJ: Princeton University Press, 1990); Tony Saich, ed., *The Chinese People's Movement: Perspectives on Spring 1989* (Armonk, NY: M. E. Sharpe, 1990); Jonathan Unger, ed., *The Pro-Democracy Protest in China: Reports From the Provinces* (Sydney: Allen & Unwin, 1991); and Craig Calhoun, *Neither Gods Nor Emperors: Students and the Struggle for Democracy in China* (Berkeley: University of California Press, 1995).

43. See James D. Seymour, *China's Satellite Parties* (Armonk, NY: M. E. Sharpe, 1987).

44. See Fengshi Wu, *New Partners or Old Brothers? GONGOs in Transnational Environmental Advocacy in China*, China Environmental Series, no. 5 (Washington, DC: Woodrow Wilson Center Press, 2002); and Elizabeth C. Economy, *The River Runs Black: The Environmental Challenge to China's Future* (Ithaca, NY: Cornell University Press, 2004), 129–76.

45. For good discussions of NGOs and their relationship to the state, see especially Tony Saich, "Negotiating the State: The Development of Social Organizations in China," *China Quarterly*, 161 (2000): 124–41; and Bruce Dickson, *Red Capitalists in China: The Party, Private Entrepreneurs, and Prospects for Political Change* (Cambridge: Cambridge University Press, 2003), 1–28.

46. The most thorough description and thoughtful analysis of leading small groups is by Carol Lee Hamrin, "The Party Leadership System," in Kenneth G. Lieberthal and David M. Lampton, eds., *Bureaucracy, Politics, and Decision Making in Post-Mao China* (Berkeley: University of California Press, 1992), 95–124. See also David M. Lampton, ed., *The Making of Chinese Foreign and Security Policy in the Era of Reform* (Stanford, CA: Stanford University Press, 2001), especially the contribution by Lu Ning, "The Central Leadership, Supraministry Coordinating Bodies, State Council Ministries, and Party Departments," 39–60.

47. These areas are defined in very comprehensive terms, such as party affairs, national security and military issues, foreign affairs, legal issues, personnel, finance, and the economy.

48. See Kenneth Lieberthal and Michel Oksenberg, *Policy Making in China: Leaders, Structures, and Processes* (Princeton, NJ: Princeton University Press, 1988).

49. See Murray Scot Tanner, "How a Bill Becomes a Law in China: Stages and Processes in Lawmaking," *China Quarterly*, 141 (1995): 39–64; and *The Politics of Lawmaking in China: Institutions, Processes, and Democratic Prospects* (Oxford: Oxford University Press, 1999).

50. Scott Kennedy, *The Business of Lobbying in China* (Cambridge: Harvard University Press, 2005).

51. See David M. Lampton, ed., *Policy Implementation in Post-Mao China* (Berkeley: University of California Press, 1987); and Yasheng Huang, "Administrative Monitoring in China," *China Quarterly*, 143 (1995): 828–43.

52. See especially Ting Gong, "Forms and Characteristics of China's Corruption in the 1990s: Change with Continuity," *Communist and Post-Communist Studies* 30, no. 3 (1997): 277–88; Xiaobo Lu, "Booty Socialism, Bureau-preneurs, and the State in Transition," *Comparative Politics* 32, no. 3 (2000): 273–94; Yan Sun, "Reform, State, and Corruption: Is Corruption Less Destructive in China Than in Russia?" *Comparative Politics* 32, no. 1 (1999): 1–20; and James Mulvenon, *Soldiers of Fortune: The Rise and Fall of the Chinese Military-Business Complex, 1978–1998* (Armonk, NY: M. E. Sharpe, 2001).

53. This (economic growth rate) is based on official Chinese statistics, which probably overstate real growth rates. One estimate suggests average annual rate of gross domestic product (GDP) growth in the 1980s and 1990s may have been as low as 7.9 percent rather than the official figure of 9.9 percent. Of course, this estimate would still have made China one of the five most rapidly growing economies in the world. See Nicholas R. Lardy, *China's Unfinished Economic Revolution* (Washington, DC: Brookings Institution, 1998). More recently, Thomas G. Rawski has ignited controversy with his significantly lower estimates of growth for 1998–2001 (i.e., annual growth rates ranging from 2.5 to 4.0 percent), based on low energy consumption. See "How Fast Is China's Economy Really Growing?" *China Business Review* 29, no. 2 (2002): 40–43.

54. See Barry Naughton, *Growing Out of the Plan: Chinese Economic Reform, 1978–1993* (Cambridge: Cambridge University Press, 1996).

55. Two excellent recent sources on the environment are Elizabeth C. Economy, *The River Runs Black: The Environmental Challenge to China's Future* (Ithaca, NY: Cornell University Press, 2004); and Kristen A. Day, ed., *China's Environment and the Challenge of Sustainable Development* (Armonk, NY: M. E. Sharpe, 2005).

56. State Council Information Office, 2006 White Paper on the Environment, "Environmental Protection in China (1996–2005)."

57. See Susan Greenhalgh, Zhu Chuzhu, and Li Nan, "Restraining Population Growth in Three Chinese Villages, 1988–93," *Population and Development Review* 20, no. 2 (1994): 365–95.

58. See the excellent study by Judith Banister, "China: Population Dynamics and Economic Implications," in Joint Economic Committee, U.S. Congress, *China's Economic Future: Challenges to U.S. Policy* (Armonk, NY: M. E. Sharpe, 1997), 339–60. On coercion in implementation, see John Aird, *Slaughter of the Innocents: Coercive Birth Control in China* (Washington, DC: AEI Press, 1990).

**MEXICO**

Tijuana

BAJA CALIFORNIA

SONORA

Ciudad
Juárez

Rio Grande

CHIHUAHUA

Chihuahua

Conchos R.

Yaqui R.

Gulf of California

BAJA CALIFORNIA SUR

COAHUILA

Rio Bravo del Norte

SINALOA

DURANGO

Monterrey
NUEVO
LEÓN

ZACATECAS

TAMAULIPAS

Gulf of Mexico

NAYARIT

AGUAS-
CALIENTES

SAN LUIS
POTOSÍ

Tampico

Panuco R.

PACIFIC
OCEAN

Lerma R.

GUANAJUATO
León

QUERÉTARO

Querétaro

HIDALGO

Mérida
YUCATÁN

QUINTANA
ROO

Guadalajara

JALISCO

MEXICO
CITY

MICHOACÁN

TLAXCALA
Veracruz

MORELOS

Puebla

PUEBLA

VERACRUZ

Bay of
Campeche

CAMPECHE

COLIMA

Balsas R.

TABASCO

MEXICO

GUERRERO

OAXACA

CHIAPAS

Gulf of
Tehuantepec

| 0 | 100 | 200 | 300 Miles |
|---|-----|-----|-----------|
| 0 | 100 | 200 | 300 Kilometers |

# POLITICS IN MEXICO

*Wayne A. Cornelius and Jeffrey A. Weldon*

## Country Bio

### MEXICO

**Population**
107 million

**Territory**
761,602 square miles

**Year of Independence**
1810

**Year of Current Constitution**
1917

**Head of State**
President Felipe Calderón Hinojosa

**Head of Government**
President Felipe Calderón Hinojosa

**Languages**
Spanish, various Mayan, Nahuatl, Zapotec, and other regional indigenous languages

**Religions**
nominally Roman Catholic 89%, Protestant 7%

---

It is election night. Friends and family gather around televisions to watch the returns, as computer-generated graphics showing vote trends flash on and off the screen. Mirroring the final preelection surveys, exit poll results show a presidential race that is too close to call. A few hours after the polls close, both major candidates appear on television to claim victory. More than a month passes, but the election outcome remains in doubt. Millions of votes are recounted. Election officials are accused of incompetence and bias in the vote-counting. It would be up to the lawyers and the courts to determine who will be the country's next president. More than two months after the election, the court finally declares a winner.

What is striking about this picture is that it occurred not in the United States (2000, Bush v. Gore), but in Mexico (2006, Calderón v. López Obrador). For more than six decades, the outcomes of Mexican presidential elections had been known the moment that the ruling **Partido Revolucionario Institucional (PRI)** announced its nominee. Since the hotly contested but fraud-ridden presidential election of 1988, however, Mexico has experienced a remarkable passage from a political system in which systematic manipulation of elections by the ruling party was condoned by senior

political leaders and cynically accepted by the general public to one in which government respect for voters' preferences is expected—indeed, demanded. This and other key elements of modern democratic politics have become routinized in Mexico.

Recurrent economic crises (1976–1977, 1982–1989, 1994–1996) were among the most powerful catalysts for this revolution in citizen expectations. The vast majority of Mexicans suffered severe economic pain during these two decades, directly attributable to government mismanagement of the national economy. Millions of jobs were lost, real wages were stagnant or declining in all but a few years of the period, savings and businesses were decimated by inflation and currency devaluations, and government benefits for the middle and lower classes were slashed in the austerity budgets necessitated by the economic crises.

The 1988 presidential election brought a tidal wave of antigovernment protest voting, with the PRI's candidate eking out a bare majority victory.[1] The government could contain the discontent and keep the PRI in power because it completely dominated the machinery of elections as well as the mass media. In the 1994 election, the PRI rode the coattails of the still highly popular

President Carlos Salinas, and took advantage of public anxieties created by the Zapatista rebellion in Chiapas.

In the 2000 election, however, voters were furious at having been deceived twice by their government, first during the oil boom era of 1977–1981 and then during the Salinas presidency (1988–1994), periods when the government created an illusion of prosperity and boundless future economic gains. Salinas was almost universally blamed for the economic crisis that engulfed Mexico within weeks after he left office. For the first time in 71 years, the voters soundly rejected the presidential candidate of the PRI, turning to Vicente Fox, a maverick former Coca Cola executive-turned-politician who ran under the banner of **Partido Acción Nacional (PAN).**

Public confidence that a vote for some alternative to the PRI would actually be respected by the authorities had been boosted significantly by several rounds of reforms in the federal electoral law in the 1990s—changes that the government proposed and the PRI endorsed, under strong pressure from citizens and the opposition parties. These procedures added so many procedural safeguards into the conduct of elections that the worst, old-style forms of vote fraud (stuffing ballot boxes or stealing them, falsifying vote tallies, etc.) became virtually impossible. Most importantly, the law created a new federal elections agency independent of government and PRI authority and made it responsible for organizing all phases of the electoral process, giving all parties access to the media, allocating public funds for campaigns, recruiting and training citizens to run the polling places, counting votes, and certifying the results.

The results of the 1997 elections for Congress had been a stunning setback for the PRI, which lost 112 of 300 single-member districts. For the first time since 1929, the PRI had to surrender control of the Chamber of Deputies (the lower house of Congress) to a coalition of four opposition parties. The PRI also lost its two-thirds majority in the Senate, which is needed to approve constitutional amendments. In the 2000 elections, the PRI lost the presidency for the first time and continued to lose ground in Congress. In 2006, the PRI finished in a distant third in the race for president, and its delegation in Congress was reduced to about a fifth of the lower chamber.

While its 2006 presidential candidate was trounced, the PRI retained control of over half of the state governorships (see Figure 14.1). All of these factors exemplify Mexico's shift toward a much more competitive, pluralistic political system, in which no single party is dominant throughout the country but each of the three major parties has regional strongholds.

Beyond the division of power that has prevailed at the federal level since 1997, divided governments at the state level have become commonplace. During the 1989–1997 period, for example, seven states had legislatures controlled by a party different from that of the state's governor. Mexicans elected non-PRI candidates as governors in ten (out of thirty-two) states during this period; prior to 1989 no opposition party victory at the state level had been recognized by the government.

The presidential election of 2006 featured three strong candidates and a highly divided electorate. Late

Shortly after taking office in 2006, President Felipe Calderón launched an all-out effort to break the power of Mexico's drug cartels. Seen here are Mexican army soldiers patrolling Reynosa, a northern border city wracked by drug-related violence.

Adriana Zehbrauskas/The New York Times/Redux Pictures

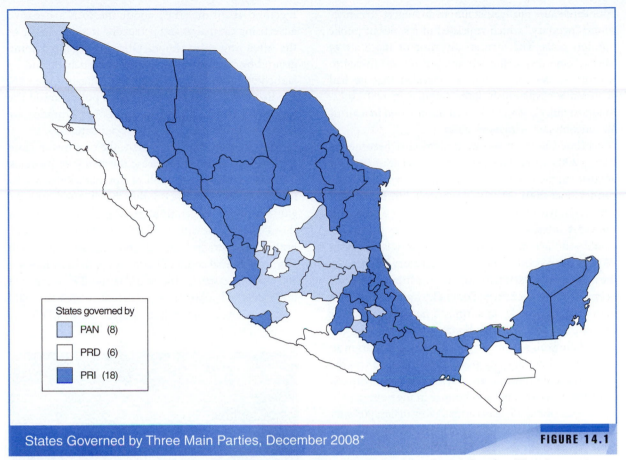

**States Governed by Three Main Parties, December 2008\***          FIGURE 14.1

States governed by
- PAN (8)
- PRD (6)
- PRI (18)

*\*PAN-governed states* were Aguascalientes, Baja California, Guanajuato, Jalisco, Morelos, Queretaro, San Luis Potosí, and Tlaxcala.
*PRD-governed states* were Baja California Sur, Chiapas, Distrito Federal, Guerrero, Michoacan, and Zacatecas.
*PRI-governed states* were Campeche, Chihuahua, Coahuila, Colima, Durango, Hidalgo, Mexico, Nayarit, Nuevo León, Oaxaca, Puebla, Quintana Roo, Sinaloa, Sonora, Tabasco, Tamaulipas, Veracruz, and Yucatán.

polling showed a very close race, with the two leading candidates within the margin of statistical error.

The PRD's candidate, Andrés Manuel López Obrador—the mayor of Mexico City from 2000 to 2005—had been leading in the polls for most of the preceding two years. In 2004, the federal attorney general's office began investigating López Obrador, who was accused of violating a court order arising from a land-use dispute in Mexico City. Because he was an elected official, he had the benefit of immunity from prosecution, and a ruling by the federal Chamber of Deputies was required to remove that immunity. After the attorney general formally sought an indictment against López Obrador, in April 2005, the chamber voted to remove his immunity (the PRI and the PAN voted in favor and the **Partido de la Revolución Democrática (PRD)** against). People who are under indictment or are serving sentences after convictions are ineligible to run for federal office, so the removal of his immunity made López Obrador ineligible to run for president. His supporters claimed that the true rationale for the indictment was to remove the leading candidate from the presidential race. His opponents claimed that the charges were genuine and demonstrated his lack of respect for the separation of powers.

Responding to mounting domestic and international criticism of the López Obrador indictment, President Fox fired the attorney general and dismissed the charges against the mayor. This episode increased the popularity of López Obrador, who portrayed himself as the victim of a conspiracy organized by the Fox government, the PAN, the PRI, and the private sector. He returned to his job as Mexico City mayor, resigning a few months later to run for president.

When the PRI lost power in 2000, Roberto Madrazo, the party's president (2002–2005), became the leading candidate for that party's 2006 presidential nomination. However, not all PRIistas favored Madrazo.

Four candidates ran against him in an August 2005 first-round "primary," which consisted of a series of public opinion polls. The former governor of the State of Mexico emerged as the winner, but he was forced to withdraw after media reports revealed that he had acquired a suspiciously large fortune in real estate. Madrazo quickly gained the PRI nomination in a virtually uncontested primary election.

Felipe Calderón was an underdog to become the PAN's 2006 candidate. Santiago Creel, the Interior Minister in the Fox administration, had been the front-runner since 2001. The PAN scheduled three regional primaries, with the rule that the candidate who won the most votes, summing across the three primaries, would win the nomination. The primary was limited to PAN members and "adherents" (a category invented by the party to allow sympathizers to vote in some internal primaries). The race turned out to be more competitive than expected. Calderón surprised nearly everyone by winning the first primary by ten points. He won the second and third primaries by a sufficient margin to win an absolute majority of votes. Because he was the only candidate nominated in a competitive primary, Calderón received a healthy bounce in the polls.

López Obrador began campaigning in fall 2005 with a considerable lead; Calderón started out in third place in most polls, but within striking distance of the PRI candidate. After lengthy negotiations, the candidates agreed on two nationally televised debates, in April and June. López Obrador hoped to sit on his lead and declined to participate in the first debate. He also began to ridicule the still highly popular President Fox, calling him a "*chachalaca*" (a large, wild bird that screeches loudly) and telling him to "shut up." Many Mexicans took this as an insult to the presidency and were offended.

At this point, the Calderón campaign "went negative," running a series of ads comparing López Obrador with leftist/populist Venezuelan President Hugo Chávez. Some of the spots showed both Chávez and López Obrador ridiculing President Fox. Their message: López Obrador, like Chávez, was a dangerous authoritarian. The ads also claimed that López Obrador would increase public debt to finance his expensive social welfare and public works projects, which would push Mexico toward another economic crisis. At the end of each spot, the PAN claimed that López Obrador was a "Menace to Mexico."

By early April, Calderón, who had beaten Madrazo in the first televised debate, had overtaken López Obrador in most polls, with the PRI's Madrazo in third place. López Obrador complained to the Federal Electoral Institute (IFE) about the PAN's negative advertising campaign and persuaded it to ban many of the offending spots. López Obrador regained some ground by participating in the second debate, and by launching his own highly negative ads against the PAN candidate. By the end of June, most polls showed the race tied between Calderón and López Obrador, or with small advantages for either candidate.

On election day, July 2, 2006, the race was so close that the IFE declined to release the results of its quick count (essentially an exit poll, except that it sums results from a sample of precincts rather than a sample of individual voters). The computerized preliminary results showed Calderón with a small lead (about 1 percent). Both López Obrador and Calderón claimed victory. On July 5, the formal count of the votes began in each of the 300 electoral districts. The next day, the IFE announced that Calderón had won by 0.58 percent, or about 244,000 votes out of nearly 42 million cast (see Table 14.1).

Felipe Calderón, presidential candidate of the PAN, celebrates his razor-thin election victory on July 5, 2006.

Wesley Bocxe/The Image Works

| TABLE 14.1 | | |
|---|---|---|
| Votes for President of Mexico in 2006 (official district counts, including voters abroad) | | |
| **Candidate** | **Votes** | **% of Valid Votes** |
| Felipe Calderón (PAN) | 15,019,300 | 36.70 |
| Andres Manuel López Obrador (PRD-PT-Convergencia) | 14,767,438 | 36.09 |
| Roberto Madrazo (PRI-PVEM) | 9,302,801 | 22.73 |
| Patricia Mercado (PASC) | 1,129,737 | 2.76 |
| Roberto Campa (Nueva Alianza) | 401,932 | 0.98 |
| Nonregistered candidates | 298,018 | 0.73 |
| Invalid votes | 937,735 | |
| Total votes | **41,856,961** | **100.00** |

Source: Instituto Federal Electoral (http://www.ife.org.mx), 2006.

The election results divided Mexico in two, with the PAN winning most of the northern states (except Zacatecas and Baja California Sur, both governed by the PRD). The PRD won every state to the south, except Yucatán (governed by the PAN) and Puebla (where the PRI governor was under the clouds of scandal). Calderón and López Obrador each won sixteen states. Madrazo, incredibly, won not a single state (see Figure 14.2).

López Obrador and the PRD immediately claimed that there had been electoral fraud, orchestrated by the PAN, the PRI, the Federal Electoral Institute, and the business community. They initially claimed that the fraud was achieved through lines of code in the computer program that added up the votes on election night (although the votes were counted by hand in the precincts and with calculators and standard spreadsheets in the electoral districts). Eventually, the PRD dropped the computer-fraud argument and charged instead that there had been "old-fashioned" fraud in the precincts, with poll workers adding votes for Calderón and invalidating votes for López Obrador. The PAN and the IFE pointed out that the PRD's polling place representatives had not complained of fraud on election day. López Obrador responded that his party's representatives must have been bribed.

The PRD asked the Federal Electoral Tribunal to order a nationwide recount of votes. The court refused this request and instead ordered recounts in about 9 percent of the 130,000 precincts—those where there had been arithmetical inconsistencies in the reported vote. The PRD then argued that if the recount did not turn the outcome in López Obrador's favor, the entire election should be annulled. The PRD's case for annulment was based on the claim that government had intervened improperly in the electoral process, through President Fox's criticism of López Obrador during the campaign and his open support of Calderón's candidacy.

To pressure the electoral tribunal to order a complete recount, the PRD launched a civil disobedience campaign in Mexico City. Hundreds of thousands of López Obrador's followers demonstrated in the Zócalo (the central plaza). Then thousands of protesters set up

Andrés Manuel López Obrador, presidential candidate of the PRD, refuses to concede electoral defeat in July 2006.

AP Images/Eduardo Verdugo

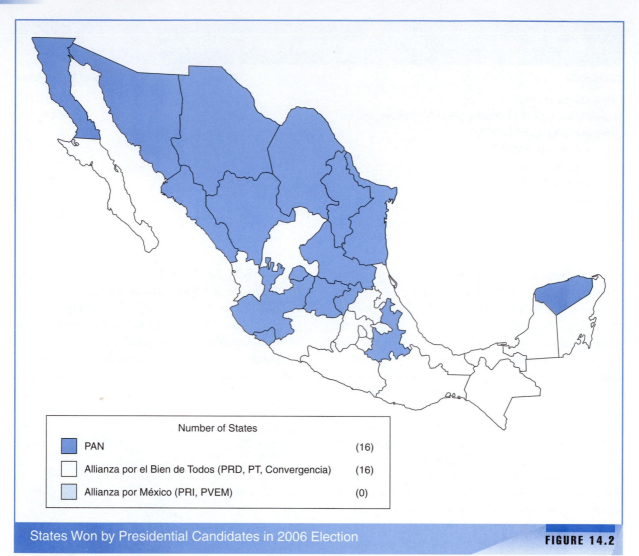

Number of States

| | | |
|---|---|---|
| ■ | PAN | (16) |
| □ | Allianza por el Bien de Todos (PRD, PT, Convergencia) | (16) |
| ▨ | Allianza por México (PRI, PVEM) | (0) |

States Won by Presidential Candidates in 2006 Election    **FIGURE 14.2**

tents on Paseo de la Reforma (the principal boulevard) and the Zócalo, blocking all traffic in the heart of Mexico City. The partial recount and the subsequent nullification of some disputed precincts shifted about 14,000 votes to López Obrador—not enough to extrapolate a change in the outcome had all votes been recounted. Calderón's victory was certified by the electoral tribunal in early September. But López Obrador refused to recognize the "spurious president," and in November 2006 inaugurated himself as "the legitimate president of Mexico" before 100,000 of his supporters in the Zócalo. He vowed to lead "years of resistance" throughout the country and to pressure the Calderón government into adopting his legislative proposals, including measures for breaking up business monopolies and creating a universal health care system. Indeed, during the first two years of the Calderón administration, López Obrador engaged in a permanent campaign of rallies and demonstrations.

## CURRENT POLICY CHALLENGES

Mexico had entered the twenty-first century with huge social and economic problems: an economy that produces far too few jobs to accommodate the young people entering the labor market each year; an educational system sorely in need of modernization; a growing impoverished population, with at least half of all Mexicans living below the official poverty line; a highly unequal distribution of income; a huge developmental gap between the affluent, urbanized, economically modern northern states and the poor, rural, heavily indigenous south; acute environmental problems that damage the health of both rural and urban

López Obrador's
supporters demonstrate
in Mexico City's Zócalo
(central plaza),
August 2006.

Imelda Medina/epa/Corbis

dwellers; and a criminal justice system that barely functions, routinely violates the human rights of citizens, and is heavily corrupted by drug trafficking. The PRI lost its grip on the Mexican political system in large part because it had failed to deal effectively with these problems. It remains to be seen whether the democratic "opposition," now in power, can manage them with conspicuously greater success.

Several emerging policy challenges will be no less daunting. As a developing country, Mexico has to play catch-up with its international trade partners and competitors. It must modernize its agricultural sector to allow it to survive competition from the United States and Canada, where subsidies and more efficient methods make agricultural goods cheaper. This vulnerable sector was further challenged when trade barriers were eliminated completely in 2008. Mexico needs to replace its antiquated and inefficient labor law with new statutes that both protect workers and encourage job creation. It must renovate the energy sector—oil, electricity, and natural gas— either by increasing government spending or by allowing more private or foreign investment, which would require controversial constitutional amendments. An unfamiliar demographic problem is beginning to emerge—an aging population—and the Mexican people must soon bolster the funding of private and government-sponsored pension plans. Finally, the government must expand the tax base to provide the resources needed to address all of these challenges.

On the political front, additional changes in electoral rules are needed to close loopholes concerning the financing of campaigns, to make it more difficult for elected officials to use government resources to promote their party's candidates, and to allow the immediate reelection of legislators, which would make them more responsive and accountable to their constituents. But in terms of consolidating a fully democratic system, these refinements may be less important than the rapidly spreading belief that alternation in power among Mexico's main parties, at all levels of governance, is both desirable and achievable. In short, most Mexicans seem to have concluded that it is time to get on with the business of modern democracy.

## HISTORICAL PERSPECTIVES

### Colonialism and Church-State Relations

Long before Hernán Cortés landed in 1519 and began the Spanish conquest of Mexico, its territory was inhabited by numerous Indian civilizations. Of these, the Maya in the Yucatán peninsula and the Toltec on the central plateau had developed the most complex political and economic organizations. Both of these civilizations had disintegrated, however, before the Spaniards arrived. Smaller Indian societies were decimated by diseases introduced by the invaders or were vanquished by the sword. Subsequent grants of land and Indian labor by the Spanish Crown to the

**BOX 14.1**

## Key Political Events in Mexico

| | |
|---|---|
| **1810–1821** | War of Independence against Spain |
| **1846–1848** | War between Mexico and the United States |
| **1910–1920** | Mexican Revolution |
| **1917** | New constitution issued, incorporating Revolutionary goals and ideals |
| **1924–1928** | Presidency of Plutarco Elías Calles |
| **1927–1929** | Cristero Rebellion (Catholic Church vs. State) |
| **1928** | Alvaro Obregón elected president, assassinated a few months later |
| **1928–1934** | "Jefe Máximo" Plutarco Elías Calles rules from behind the scenes, under several provisional presidents (the "Maximato" period) |
| **1929** | Plutarco Elías Calles establishes Partido Nacional Revolucionario (PNR) |
| **1934–1940** | Presidency of Lázaro Cárdenas |
| **1938** | President Cárdenas reorganizes PNR, which becomes the Partido de la Revolución Mexicana (PRM); Cárdenas nationalizes oil industry |
| **1939** | Partido Acción Nacional (PAN) founded |
| **1940–1946** | Presidency of Manuel Avila Camacho |
| **1946–1952** | Presidency of Miguel Alemán |
| **1946** | PRM is restructured, renamed the Partido Revolucionario Institucional (PRI) |
| **1952–1958** | Presidency of Adolfo Ruiz Cortines |
| **1958–1964** | Presidency of Adolfo López Mateos |
| **1964–1970** | Presidency of Gustavo Díaz Ordaz |

| | |
|---|---|
| **1968** | Student protest movement challenges the government and is violently repressed (the "Tlatelolco massacre") |
| **1970–1976** | Presidency of Luis Echeverría |
| **1976–1982** | Presidency of José López Portillo; period of the oil export boom |
| **1981–1982** | Drop in world oil prices and rising interest rates cause economic collapse; Mexico unable to service its external debt |
| **1982–1988** | Presidency of Miguel de la Madrid |
| **1988–1994** | Presidency of Carlos Salinas de Gortari |
| **1994** | North American Free Trade Agreement (NAFTA) goes into effect; peasant rebellion erupts in the state of Chiapas; PRI presidential candidate Luis Donaldo Colosio assassinated and replaced by Ernesto Zedillo; peso sharply devalued, provoking a deep economic crisis |
| **1994–2000** | Presidency of Ernesto Zedillo |
| **1997–2000** | PRI loses majority control in the Chamber of Deputies |
| **2000** | PRI loses the presidency for the first time in 71 years |
| **2000–2006** | Presidency of Vicente Fox |
| **2006** | PAN wins the presidency again and a plurality in both houses of Congress; closeness of the presidential result provokes large-scale protests and a partial recount |
| **2006–2012** | Presidency of Felipe Calderón |

colonists further isolated the rural Indian population and deepened their exploitation.

The combined effects of attrition, intermarriage, and cultural penetration of Indian regions have drastically reduced the proportion of Mexico's population culturally identified as Indian. By the 1990 census figures, 7.9 percent of the nation's population spoke an Indian language.[2] The Indian minority has been persistently marginal to the national economy and political system. Today, the indigenous population is heavily concentrated in rural communities that the government classifies as the country's most economically depressed and service-deprived, located primarily

in the southeast and the center of the country. They engage in rainfall-dependent subsistence agriculture, using traditional methods of cultivation, are seasonally employed as migrant laborers in commercial agriculture, or produce crafts for sale in regional and national markets. The Indian population is an especially troubling reminder of the millions of people who have been left behind by uneven development in twentieth-century Mexico.

The importance of Spain's colonies in the New World lay in their ability to provide the Crown with vital resources to fuel the Spanish economy. Mexico's mines provided gold and silver in abundance until the wars of independence began in 1810. After independence, Mexico continued to export these ores, supplemented in subsequent eras by hemp, cotton, textiles, oil, and winter vegetables.

Since the Spanish conquest, the Roman Catholic Church has been an institution of enduring power in Mexico. Priests joined the Spanish invaders in an evangelical mission to convert the Indians to Catholicism, and individual priests have continued to play important roles in national history. Father Miguel Hidalgo y Costilla helped launch Mexico's war of independence in 1810, and Father José María Morelos y Pavón replaced Hidalgo as spiritual and military leader of the independence movement when the Crown executed Hidalgo in 1811.

During Mexico's postindependence period, institutional antagonisms between the church and the central government have occasionally flared into open confrontations on such issues as church wealth, educational policy, the content of public school textbooks, and political activism by the church. The Constitutions of 1857 and 1917 formally established the separation of church and state and defined their respective domains. Constitutional provisions dramatically reduced the church's power and wealth by nationalizing its property, including large agricultural landholdings. The 1917 Constitution also made church-affiliated schools subject to the authority of the federal government, denied priests the right to vote or speak publicly on political issues, and gave the government the right to limit the number of priests who can serve in Mexico. Government efforts during the 1920s to enforce these constitutional provisions led to a civil insurrection that caused 100,000 combatant deaths, uncounted civilian casualties, and economic devastation in a large part of central Mexico. The settlement of this "Cristero rebellion" established, once and for all, the church's subordination to the state, in return for which the government relaxed its restrictions on church activities in nonpolitical arenas.

This accord inaugurated a long period of relative tranquility in church-state relations, during which the government and the church ignored many of the anticlerical provisions of the 1917 Constitution (such as the prohibition on church involvement in education). The central church hierarchy—among the most conservative in Latin America—cooperated with the government on a variety of issues, and the church posed no threat to the ruling party's hegemony.

## Revolution and Its Aftermath

The nationwide civil conflict that erupted in Mexico in 1910 is often referred to as the first of the great "social revolutions" that shook the world early in the twentieth century. Mexico's upheaval, however, originated within the country's ruling class. The revolution did not begin as a spontaneous uprising of the common people against an entrenched dictator, Porfirio Díaz, and against the local bosses and landowners who exploited them. Even though hundreds of thousands of workers and peasants ultimately participated in the civil strife, most of the revolutionary leadership came from the younger generation of middle- and upper-class Mexicans who had become disenchanted with three and a half decades of increasingly heavy-handed rule by the aging dictator and his clique. These disgruntled members of the elite saw their future opportunities for economic and political mobility blocked by the closed group surrounding Díaz. Their battle cry was "effective suffrage, no reelection"—the end of self-perpetuating dictatorship made possible by sham elections.

Led by Francisco I. Madero, whose family had close ties with the ruling group, these liberal middle-class reformers were committed to opening up the political system and creating new opportunities for themselves within a capitalist economy whose basic features they did not challenge. They did not seek to destroy the established order. Instead, they sought to make it work more in their own interest, rather than that of the foreign capitalists who dominated key sectors of Mexico's economy during the Porfirian dictatorship.

Of course, some serious grievances had accumulated among workers and peasants. Once the rebellion against Díaz got underway, leaders who appealed to the disadvantaged masses pressed their claims against the central government. Emiliano Zapata led a movement of peasants in the state of Morelos; they were bent on regaining the land they had lost to the rural aristocracy by subterfuge during the Porfiriato. In the north, Pancho Villa led an army of jobless workers, small landowners, and cattle hands, whose main interest was steady employment. As various revolutionary leaders contended for control of the central government, the political order that had been created and enforced by Díaz disintegrated into warlordism—powerful regional gangs led by revolutionary *caudillos* (political-military strongmen) who aspired more to increasing their personal wealth and social status than to leading a genuine social revolution.

The first decade of the revolution produced a new, remarkably progressive constitution, replacing the Constitution of 1857. The young, middle-class elite that dominated the constitutional convention of 1916–1917 "had little if any direct interest in labor unions or land distribution. But it was an elite that recognized the need for social change. . . . By 1916, popular demands for land and labor reform were too great to ignore."[3] The Constitution of 1917 established the principle of state control over all natural resources, subordination of the church to the state, the government's right to redistribute land, and rights for labor that had not yet been secured even by the labor movement in the United States. Even so, nearly two decades passed before most of these constitutional provisions began to be implemented.

Many historians today stress the continuities between prerevolutionary and postrevolutionary Mexico. The processes of economic modernization, capital accumulation, state building, and political centralization that gained considerable momentum during the Porfiriato were interrupted by civil strife from 1910 to 1920. They resumed once a semblance of order had been restored. During the 1920s, the central government set out to eliminate or undermine the most powerful and independent-minded regional *caudillos* by co-opting the local power brokers, known as **caciques.** These local political bosses became, in effect, appendages of the central government, supporting its policies and maintaining control over the population in their communities. By the end of this period, leaders with genuine popular followings (like Zapata and Villa) had been assassinated and control had been seized by a new postrevolutionary elite bent on demobilizing the masses and establishing the hegemony of the central government.

The rural aristocracy of the Porfiriato had been weakened but not eliminated; its heirs still controlled large concentrations of property and other forms of wealth in many parts of the country. Most of the large urban firms that operated during the Porfiriato also survived, further demonstrating that the revolution was not an attack on private capital per se. Except during the years of most intense violence (1914–1917), the revolution had surprisingly minor effects on private investment and economic growth.

## The Cárdenas Upheaval

Elite control was maintained during the 1930s, but this was nevertheless an era of massive social and political upheaval in Mexico. During the presidency of Lázaro Cárdenas (1934–1940), peasants and urban workers succeeded for the first time in pressing their claims for land and higher wages; in fact, Cárdenas actively encouraged them to do so. The result was an unprecedented wave of strikes, protest demonstrations, and petitions for breaking up large rural estates.

Most disputes between labor and management during this period were settled, under government pressure, in favor of the workers. The Cárdenas administration also redistributed more than twice as much land as that expropriated by all of Cárdenas's predecessors since 1915, when Mexico's land reform program was formally initiated. By 1940, the country's land tenure system had been fundamentally altered, breaking the traditional domination of the large haciendas and creating a large sector of small peasant farmers (*ejidatarios*)—more than 1.5 million of them—who had received plots of land under the agrarian reform program. The Cárdenas government actively encouraged the formation of new organizations of peasants and urban workers, grouped the new organizations into nationwide confederations, and provided arms to rural militias formed by the *ejidatarios.* Even Mexico's foreign relations were disrupted in 1938 when the Cárdenas government nationalized oil companies that had been operating in Mexico under U.S. and British ownership.

Mexican intellectuals frequently refer to 1938 as the highwater mark of the Mexican revolution as measured by social progress; they characterize the period since then as a retrogression. Certainly, the distributive and especially the redistributive performance of the Mexican government declined sharply in the decades that followed, and the worker and peasant organizations formed during the Cárdenas era atrophied and became less and less likely to contest either the will of the government or the interests of Mexico's private economic elites. De facto reconcentration of landholdings and other forms of wealth occurred as the state provided increasingly generous support to the country's new commercial, industrial, and financial elites during a period of rapid industrialization.

The Cárdenas era fundamentally reshaped Mexico's political institutions. The presidency became the primary institution of the political system, with sweeping powers exercised during a constitutionally limited six-year term with no possibility of reelection; the military was removed from overt political competition and transformed into one of several institutional pillars of the regime; and an elaborate network of government-sponsored peasant and labor organizations provided a mass base for the official political party and performed a variety of political and economic control functions, utilizing a multilayered system of patronage and clientelism.

By 1940, a much larger proportion of the Mexican population was nominally included in the national political system, mostly by their membership in peasant and labor organizations created by Cárdenas. No real democratization of the system resulted from this vast expansion of "political participation," however. Although working-class groups did have more control over their representatives in the government-sponsored organizations than over their former masters on the haciendas and in the factories, their influence over public policy and government priorities after Cárdenas was minimal and highly indirect. Policy recommendations, official actions, and nominations for elective and appointive positions at all levels still emanated from the central government and official party headquarters in Mexico City, filtering down the hierarchy to the rank and file for ratification and legitimation.

## The Era of Hegemonic Party Rule

The political system shaped by Lázaro Cárdenas proved remarkably durable. From 1940 until the late 1980s, Mexico's official party-government apparatus was the most stable regime in Latin America. It had a well-earned reputation for resilience, adaptability to new circumstances, a high level of agreement within the ruling elite on basic rules of political competition, and a seemingly unlimited capacity to co-opt dissidents, both within and outside of the ruling party. As late as 1990, the celebrated Peruvian novelist Mario Vargas Llosa could plausibly describe Mexico's regime as "the perfect dictatorship," combining stability, legitimacy, and durability in a way that even the former Soviet Union and Castro's Cuba had never achieved.[4]

With the fall of the Communist Party of the Soviet Union in 1991, the PRI became the world's longest continuously ruling political party. Since 1929, when the "official" party was founded, both political assassination and armed rebellion had been rejected as routes to the presidency by all contenders for power. A handful of disappointed aspirants to the ruling party's presidential nomination mounted candidacies outside the party (in the elections of 1929, 1940, 1946, 1952, and 1988), but even the most broadly supported of these breakaway movements were successfully contained through government-engineered vote fraud and intimidation.

In the early 1970s concerns had been raised about the stability of the system, after the bloody repression of a student protest movement in Mexico City by President Gustavo Díaz Ordaz on the eve of the 1968 Olympic Games. The student massacre marked the opening of a "dirty war" in which the army and police forces are believed to have executed, without trial, more than 700 alleged enemies of the state. Many analysts at that time suggested that Mexico was entering a period of institutional crisis, requiring fundamental reforms in both political arrangements and strategy of economic development.

But the discovery of massive oil and natural gas resources during the late 1970s gave the incumbent regime a new lease on life. Continued support of the masses and the elites was purchased with an apparently limitless supply of petro-pesos, even without major structural reforms. The government's room for maneuver was abruptly erased by the collapse of the oil boom in August 1982, owing to a combination of adverse international economic circumstances (falling oil prices, rising interest rates, recession in the United States) and fiscally irresponsible domestic policies. Real wages and living standards for the vast majority of Mexicans plummeted, and the government committed itself to a socially painful restructuring of the economy, including a drastic shrinkage of the sector owned and managed by the government itself.

The economic crisis of the 1980s placed enormous stress on Mexico's political system. In the July 6, 1988, national elections, the PRI suffered unprecedented reverses in both the presidential and congressional races. The vote share officially attributed to Carlos Salinas was more than 20 percentage points below that of PRI presidential candidate Miguel de la Madrid in the 1982 election. Ex-PRIista Cuauhtémoc Cárdenas, son of the much-revered former President Lázaro Cárdenas, heading a hastily assembled coalition of minor leftist and nationalist parties, was officially credited with 31.1 percent of the presidential vote—far more than any previous opposition candidate but probably much less than he actually received if the vote count had been honest.[5] A diminished PRI delegation still controlled the Congress, but the president's party had lost the two-thirds majority needed to approve constitutional amendments.

Carlos Salinas breathed new life into the creaking PRI apparatus. His brand of strong presidential leadership and his accomplishments—especially the toppling of corrupt labor union bosses, a sharp reduction in inflation, and the National Solidarity Program, a new-style antipoverty and public works program that increased government responsiveness to lower-class needs—sufficed to rebuild electoral support for the PRI and to paper over the cracks within the ruling political elite. Salinas opened the Mexican economy to foreign trade and investment, and privatized hundreds of inefficient state-owned companies. Mexico at last seemed poised to make a giant leap from Third World to First World status. While political liberalization had proceeded slowly and unevenly under Salinas, far behind the pace of his sweeping free-market economic reforms, Mexico appeared to be coasting inexorably toward a transfer of power to yet another PRI national government in 1994.

The illusion of proximate economic modernity and political inevitability was shattered on New Year's Day 1994, by a "postmodern" peasant revolt in Chiapas, Mexico's most underdeveloped and politically backward state. An estimated 2,000 primitively armed but well-disciplined Indian rebels seized control of four isolated municipalities and declared war on the central government—something that had not happened since 1938. Their demands for social justice and democracy resonated throughout Mexico, long after the initial skirmishes with the Mexican army had claimed at least 145 lives and a cease-fire had been negotiated. Suddenly, middle- and upper-class Mexicans, as well as foreign governments and investors, were reminded of the persistence of political repression, human rights violations, extreme poverty, and inequality in Mexico. The impoverished Indians who took up arms against the state in Chiapas symbolized the many millions of Mexicans who had been left behind in the drive for economic modernity and internationalism.

Less than three months after the Chiapas rebellion erupted, President Salinas's hand-picked successor, Luis Donaldo Colosio, was assassinated while campaigning in Tijuana. The crime has never been solved. With a last great exertion of presidential will, Carlos Salinas imposed on the PRI another hand-picked successor, economist-technocrat Ernesto Zedillo, to replace the slain Colosio. In August 1994, in a high-turnout election that was judged by most independent observers at the time to be the cleanest in Mexico's postrevolutionary history, the opposition parties were soundly defeated. Not only did the PRI retain control of the presidency (albeit with just a plurality of 48.8 percent of the total votes cast), it also maintained an ample majority in the federal Congress.[6]

## The End of PRI Dominance

The appearance of restored stability created by the ruling party's impressive performance in the August 1994 elections was short-lived. In December 1994, a militarily insignificant renewal of the Zapatista rebels' activities in Chiapas, followed immediately by a sustained speculative attack on the overvalued peso by short-term foreign and domestic investors, opened a Pandora's box of economic and political troubles. What began as a currency and financial liquidity crisis quickly evolved into a massive capital flight and a deep recession. After publicly criticizing Zedillo and his cabinet ministers for provoking the economic crisis by mishandling the devaluation of the peso, ex-President Salinas went into de facto exile in Ireland. The Zedillo administration in turn made Salinas the scapegoat for the financial collapse.

By the late 1990s, the PRI once again appeared to be in a state of accelerated decomposition. Divisions within the party were deeper than at any time since the mid-1930s. With the defeat of its presidential candidate in 2000, the PRI lost control of the vast patronage resources of the central government, which were crucial to keeping it in power for more than seven decades. After its disastrous, third-place finish in the 2006 presidential election, the PRI seemed to be retreating into its regional strongholds, with its status as a national party in jeopardy.

## International Environment

Since independence, Mexico's politics and public policies have always been influenced by proximity to the United States. Porfirio Díaz is widely reputed to have exclaimed, "Poor Mexico! So far from God and so close to the United States." Indeed, this proximity has made the United States a powerful presence in Mexico. A wide array of factors—the 2,000-mile land border between the two countries; Mexico's rich supplies of minerals, labor, and other resources needed by U.S. industry; and Mexico's attractiveness as a site for U.S. private investment—has made such influence inevitable.

Midway through the nineteenth century, Mexico's sovereignty as a nation was directly threatened when the U.S. push for territorial and economic expansion met little resistance in northern Mexico. Emerging from a war for independence from Spain and plagued by chronic political instability, Mexico was highly vulnerable to aggression from the north. By annexing Texas in 1845 and instigating the Mexican-American War of 1846 to 1848 (Ulysses S. Grant later called it "America's great unjust war"), the United States seized half of Mexico's national territory: disputed land in Texas; all of the land that is now California, Nevada, and Utah; most of New Mexico and Arizona; and part of Colorado and Wyoming. This massive seizure of territory, along with several later military interventions and meddling in the politics of "revolutionary" Mexico that extended throughout the 1920s, left scars that have not healed. Even today, the average Mexican suspects that the United States has designs on Mexico's remaining territory, its oil, even its human resources.

The lost territory includes the U.S. regions that have been the principal recipients of Mexican immigrant workers in this century. This labor migration, too, was instigated mainly by the United States. Beginning in the 1880s, U.S. farmers, railroads, and mining companies, with U.S. government encouragement, obtained many of the workers needed to expand the economy and transport systems of the Southwest and Midwest by sending labor recruiters into northern and central Mexico.

By the end of the 1920s, the economies of Mexico and the United States were sufficiently intertwined that the effects of the Great Depression were swiftly transmitted to Mexico, causing unemployment to rise and export earnings and gross national product (GNP) to plummet. In response to these economic shocks, Mexico tried during the 1930s to reduce its dependence on the United States as a market for silver and other exports. The effort failed. By 1940, Mexico was more dependent than before on the flow of goods, capital, and labor to and from the United States.

After 1940, Mexico relied even more heavily on U.S. private capital to help finance its drive for industrialization. The United States also experienced severe shortages of labor in World War II, and Mexico's dependence on the United States as a market for its surplus labor became institutionalized through the so-called *bracero* program of importing contract labor. Operating from 1942 to 1964, this program brought more than 4 million Mexicans to the United States to work in seasonal agriculture. After the demise of the *bracero* program, migration to the United States continued, with most new arrivals entering illegally. By 2005, 6.2 million Mexicans had taken up residence in the United States illegally, and as many as 400,000 new unauthorized migrants continued to arrive each year.[7]

The U.S. stake in Mexico's continued political stability and economic development has increased dramatically since World War II. In recent years, Mexico has been one of the three largest trading partners of the United States (with Canada and Japan). Employment for hundreds of thousands of people in both Mexico and the United States depends on this trade. In 1982, when U.S. trade with Mexico fell by 32 percent because of Mexico's economic crisis, an estimated 250,000 U.S. jobs were lost. Largely because of the 1994 peso devaluation, which made Mexico's exports cheaper in the United States and U.S. products unaffordable to most Mexican consumers, the overall U.S. trade deficit soared to record levels in the first quarter of 1995.

Despite the sharp fluctuations in its economy since the early 1980s, Mexico is one of the preferred sites for investments by U.S.-based multinational corporations, especially for investments in modern industries (such as petrochemicals, pharmaceuticals, food processing, machinery, transportation, and athletic footwear). In recent years, 55 percent of total foreign direct investment in Mexico has come from the United States. Subsidiaries of U.S. companies produce half of the manufactured goods exported by Mexico. Firms in Mexico's own private sector have actively sought foreign capital to finance new joint ventures and expand plant facilities.

Mexico's external economic dependence is often cited by both critics and defenders of the Mexican system as an all-encompassing explanation for the country's problems. In fact, economic ties between Mexico and the United States usually explain only part of the picture. And these linkages do not necessarily predetermine the choices of policy and development priorities that are set by Mexico's rulers. But Mexico's increasingly tight linkage to the U.S. economy limits the range of choices that can be made by Mexican officials, and economic fluctuations in the United States are a large source of uncertainty in Mexico's planning and policymaking.

The international environment of Mexico's political system was transformed fundamentally by the signing of the North American Free Trade Agreement (NAFTA) in 1993. NAFTA made Mexico a much more attractive investment site for U.S. firms seeking low-cost labor and for Asian and European firms seeking privileged access to the U.S. market. While Carlos Salinas opposed such an agreement during his 1988 presidential campaign (because "there is such a different economic level between the U.S. and Mexico"), he soon found himself with no alternative to pursuing increased economic integration with the United States. With about one million new job seekers entering its labor force each year, Mexico desperately needed to increase its rate of economic growth. The only way to do that while containing inflation was to stimulate a massive new infusion of investment capital from abroad. By 1998, thanks to NAFTA, Mexico had surpassed Japan to become the United States' second most important trading partner (after Canada).

Less than a year after NAFTA was implemented, the implications of the much closer linkage between the U.S. and Mexican economies became painfully clear when a new financial crisis erupted in Mexico. While there was virtually no political constituency within the United States for a U.S. government "bailout" of Mexico, and no enthusiasm among Mexicans for taking on more foreign loans and using the country's oil revenues to collateralize them (just one of the stringent conditions imposed by the United States), neither government had any realistic alternative to such a rescue. A Mexican default on repayment of nearly $30 billion in *tesobonos* (short-term bonds issued by the Mexican treasury) held mostly by U.S. pension funds, mutual funds, and other institutional investors would have threatened the assets of many millions of American households whose money had been invested in the high-yielding Mexican government bonds. Moreover, a meltdown of the Mexican economy could have caused a dramatic surge in illegal immigration to the United States. Consequently, a nearly $50 billion multilateral package of loan guarantees and credit line swaps—including $20 billion from a U.S. government currency stabilization fund—was made available to Mexico in January 1995.

The net macroeconomic impact of NAFTA has been positive for Mexico, as well as for the United States and Canada. However, NAFTA has not reduced the U.S.-Mexico income gap. Gross domestic product (GDP) has risen in Mexico, but it has risen much faster in the United States (see Figure 14.3). Today, annual U.S.

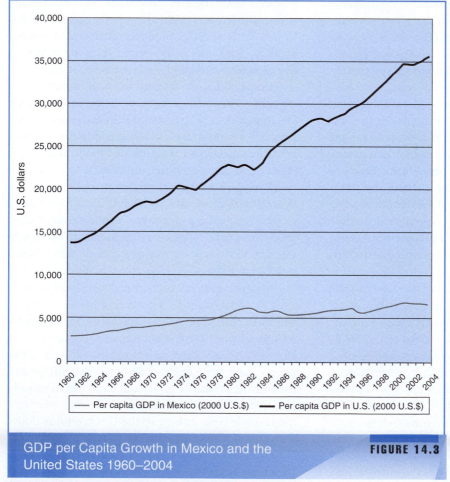

**GDP per Capita Growth in Mexico and the United States 1960–2004**

**FIGURE 14.3**

Source: Instituto Nacional de Estadística, Geografía e Informática, www.inegi.gob.mx, 2006.

GDP per capita is more than six times that of Mexico. If anything, NAFTA has increased illegal migration to the United States and made Mexico's economy more dependent on money remitted by its citizens working in the United States, who sent an estimated $24 billion home in 2006. NAFTA created jobs in Mexico's manufactured-export sector, but competition from cheaper U.S. imports has put millions of small farmers out of work, and the nonagricultural jobs that have been created under NAFTA do not pay enough to lift most Mexican families out of poverty.

## POLITICAL CULTURE AND SOCIALIZATION

Most of what we know empirically about Mexican political culture is based on research completed during the period of sustained economic growth and virtually unchallenged one-party rule in Mexico, from 1940 through the mid-1970s. The portrait of Mexican political culture that emerges from these studies can be summarized as follows: Mexicans are highly supportive of the political institutions that evolved from the Mexican Revolution, and they endorse the democratic principles embodied in the Constitution of 1917. However, they are critical of government performance, especially in creating jobs, reducing social and economic inequality, fighting crime, and delivering basic public services. Most government bureaucrats and politicians are viewed as distant, elitist, and self-serving, if not corrupt. Mexicans traditionally have been pessimistic about their ability to affect election outcomes, anticipating fraud and regarding attendance at campaign rallies and voting as ritualistic activities.

On the surface, this combination of attitudes and beliefs seems internally contradictory. How could Mexicans support a political system that they see as unresponsive or capricious at best, in which they are mere "subjects" rather than true participants? Historically, popular support for the Mexican political system derived from three sources: the revolutionary origins of the regime, the government's role in promoting economic growth, and its performance in distributing concrete, material benefits to a substantial proportion of the Mexican population since the Cárdenas era. Each of these traditional sources of support has been undermined to some extent since 1976.

The official interpretation of the 1910 revolution stressed symbols (or myths), such as social justice, democracy, the need for national unity, and the popular origins of the current regime. The government's identification with these symbols was constantly reinforced by the mass media, public schools, and the mass organizations affiliated with the official party. Over the years, the party's electoral appeals were explicitly designed to link its candidates with agrarian reform and other revered ideals of the revolution, with national heroes like Emiliano Zapata and Lázaro Cárdenas, and with the national flag. (The PRI emblem conveniently has the same colors, in the same arrangement.) However, President Salinas broke decisively with so many tenets of "revolutionary ideology" (strict church-state separation, land reform, economic nationalism, etc.) that the PRI's claim to the revolutionary mantle became tenuous. Indeed, since the late 1980s, that mantle has been claimed by the PRD.

Relatively few Mexicans based their support for the system primarily on its revolutionary origins or symbolic outputs, however. For most sectors of the population, symbols were supplemented with particularistic material rewards: plots of land or titles to land that had been occupied illegally, schools, low-cost medical care, agricultural crop price supports, government-subsidized food and other consumer goods, and public sector jobs. For more than forty years, the personal receipt of some material "favor" from the official party-government apparatus, or the hope that such benefits might be received in the future, ensured fairly high levels of mass support for the system. Even now, Mexicans' concept of democracy emphasizes economic and social outputs rather than procedural liberties.[8]

In the 2006 election, many voters were attracted to PRD candidate López Obrador by his performance as Mexico City mayor, delivering high-visibility public works and monthly payments to senior citizens. PAN candidate Felipe Calderón promised to reduce social inequality through a major expansion of Oportunidades, a federal welfare program already benefiting 5 million low-income families. While not on a par with traditional vote-buying by the PRI—trading specific material payoffs for votes at the individual level—such campaign strategies clearly resonate with an electorate whose concept of democracy is still largely distributive.

Despite their growing distrust of key political institutions (especially Congress and the political parties), a plurality of Mexicans have remained "system loyalists." Indeed, Mexicans' pride in their country still seems rooted largely in their nation's political institutions. Survey data collected during the 1980s and 1990s consistently revealed the Mexican people's fundamental aversion to notions of radical transformation, especially if violence might result.[9] Nevertheless, most Mexicans today do not hesitate to criticize the way in which their government functions, and many more feel free to demonstrate their dissatisfaction by voting to throw the rascals out. In 1998, for example, the PAN lost control of the governorship of Chihuahua, partly because of the previous PANista governor's lackluster record in crime-fighting.

Historically, most Mexicans tolerated corruption in government as a price to be paid in order to extract benefits from the system or to deal with police harassment. But the unbridled corruption of the López Portillo and the Salinas administrations drastically reduced such tolerance, and an upsurge in drug-related corruption in the 1990s—reaching into the highest levels of the government bureaucracy and the national security apparatus—angered many Mexicans. They feared that their government had been taken over by "*narco-políticos*"—public officials in league with corrupt police and drug lords. The slowness of the Vicente Fox administration to root out government and police corruption, despite its independence from the structure of corruption created under PRI rule, was a source of public anger by the end of Fox's term.

Despite much more competition in the electoral system since the 1980s, the average Mexican remains relatively uninterested in politics. At the beginning of the bitterly fought presidential election campaign of 2006, two-thirds of the interviewees in a national survey expressed little or no interest in politics, and 55 percent said they rarely or never discussed politics with other people. These percentages are essentially unchanged since the 2000 presidential campaign.[10]

In the last two national elections, however, Mexicans have shown themselves to be sensitive to short-term campaign stimuli, such as presidential candidates' debates, negative television ads, and "straight news" media coverage. In fact, Mexicans appear more susceptible to persuasive campaign appeals than voters in the United States and other established democracies. Relatively more Mexicans change their party identification during the course of a campaign.[11] While such findings may indicate the absence of a core set of stable political beliefs, they reveal that Mexicans are paying close attention to the options provided by political competitors, at least during hard-fought national election campaigns.

## Mass Political Socialization

How do Mexicans form their attitudes toward the political system? In addition to the family, the schools and the Catholic Church are important sources of preadult political learning. All schools, including church-affiliated and lay private schools, must follow a government-approved curriculum and use the same set of free textbooks, written by the federal Ministry of Education. Although the private schools' compliance with the official curriculum is often nominal, control over the content of textbooks gives the government an instrument for socializing children to a formal set of political values.

Under PRI rule, school-based political learning stressed the social and economic progress accomplished under postrevolutionary governments. The president was depicted as an omnipotent authority figure whose principal function is to maintain order in the country. Thus, despite the many egregious failures of presidential leadership that Mexicans have witnessed since the mid-1970s, many continue to express a preference for strong presidentialist government. However, mass public education has increased criticism of partisan politics and poor government performance. Higher levels of education are also associated with stronger support for the right to dissent and other democratic liberties.

The Catholic Church has been another key source of values affecting political behavior in Mexico. Church-run private schools have proliferated in recent decades. Along with secular private schools, they provide education for a large portion of children from middle- and upper-class families. Religious schools and priests have criticized anticlerical laws and policies, promoted individual initiative (as opposed to governmental action), and preached against abortion and gay marriage. They have also stressed the need for moral Christian behavior in public life.

As adults, Mexicans learn about politics from their personal encounters with government functionaries and the police. They also learn from participating in local community-based organizations and popular movements that seek collective benefits or redress of grievances from the government. There has been an impressive proliferation of popular movements in Mexico since 1968, when the student protest movement was violently repressed. The catalysts for this new wave of popular movements included gangsterism in government-affiliated labor unions, increasingly blatant PRI vote fraud in state and local elections during the 1980s, environmental disasters, and the implementation of neoliberal economic policies that adversely affected low- and middle-class segments of the society.

While most of these popular movements are quite localized in scope and concerns, a few have grown to embrace thousands of Mexicans in many different states. For example, the Civic Alliance—a coalition of hundreds of nongovernmental organizations, independent labor unions, and popular movements—has mobilized tens of thousands of Mexican citizens and hundreds of foreign observers to scrutinize the conduct of every national election since 1994 and publish reports on election irregularities. Nevertheless, nongovernmental organizations remain heavily concentrated in the Mexico City metropolitan area, where nearly 30 percent of the country's NGOs are registered. By contrast, the state of Chiapas hosts only 0.3 percent.

For seven decades, the PRI-government apparatus systematically used the mass media as an agent of political socialization. Although the government did not often directly censor the media, there were significant economic penalties for engaging in criticism or investigative reporting that seriously embarrassed the president. For example, government advertising—a major source of revenue for most newspapers and magazines—could be withheld from offending publications. The Salinas administration ended the long-standing practices of bribing reporters to get favorable treatment and threatening to cut off newsprint to troublesome periodicals.

Since the PRI lost control of the presidency in 2000, the mass media have been much more openly critical of government performance. Many newspapers and news magazines retain their PRI partisan bias and energetically criticize the president and other PANista officials. The independent media have kept up

their intense scrutiny of the executive branch and are also highly critical of what they see as incompetence and inefficiency in Congress.

The print media reach only a tiny fraction of the Mexican population (even the largest Mexico City newspapers have circulations under 100,000). Until recently, television was virtually monopolized by a huge private firm, Televisa, which had a notoriously close working relationship with the PRI-government apparatus and invariably defended the incumbent president's performance. One consequence of the Salinas administration's privatization program was the breakup of Televisa's virtual monopoly. A formerly government-owned television channel in Mexico City has grown quickly into a rival network, TV Azteca, and Televisa itself has adjusted to the competition by giving much more coverage to opposition voices. In 2006, Congress approved a bill that would end government discretion in the awarding of specific parts of the television broadcasting spectrum. The Interior Ministry had in the past used its control of these concessions to guarantee positive media treatment of the government. The television spectrum would be auctioned off to the highest bidders. Opponents criticized this reform, claiming that it would exacerbate Televisa's monopoly because the corporation could often end up being the highest bidder. In 2007, the Supreme Court ruled that the new law unconstitutionally abdicated the State's authority over telecommunications. It became a question of weighing pluralism in the government against pluralism in the market.

Moreover, electoral system reforms enacted in 1996 require the Federal Electoral Institute to systematically monitor campaign coverage by the national and local electronic media in order to determine whether they favor one party over another. Consequently, exposure to the mass media no longer socializes the Mexican public to a particular set of political orientations sanctioned by incumbent authorities.

## Political Participation

Traditionally, most political participation in Mexico has been of two broad types: (1) ritualistic, regime-supportive activities (for example, voting, attending campaign rallies); and (2) petitioning or contacting of public officials to influence the allocation of some public good or service. By law, voting is obligatory in

Mexico, though there are no civil penalties for not voting. Evidence of having voted in the most recent election has sometimes been required to receive public services. People participate in campaign rallies mostly because attending might have a specific material payoff (a free meal, a raffle ticket, a T-shirt), or because failure to do so could have personal economic costs. In the past, as they went to the polls, Mexicans knew that they were not selecting those who would govern but merely ratifying the choice of candidates made earlier by the PRI-government hierarchy. Some voted because they regarded it as their civic duty, others because they wished to avoid difficulty in future dealings with government agencies. Some voted in response to pressures from local *caciques* and PRI sector representatives. And some, especially in rural areas, freely sold their votes in return for handouts from local officials.

As elections have become moments of genuine political confrontation in most parts of Mexico, the ritualistic quality of voting and participating in campaign activities has diminished. Since 1994 Mexico has experienced an explosion in political participation,

evidenced not only by the virtually nonstop protests of citizens' movements of all types, but also by a sharp rise in turnout in federal elections. The turnout of registered voters rose from 49 percent in the 1988 presidential election, to 61 percent in the midterm 1991 elections, to 78 percent in the 1994 presidential election (see Figure 14.4). In the highly competitive 2006 presidential election, over 41,800,000 Mexicans cast their votes, a turnout rate of 59 percent. The total included 33,131 Mexicans abroad who were permitted to vote absentee in the presidential election for the first time.

Unfortunately, valid comparisons with electoral participation rates in the pre-1988 period are impossible, since the 1988 presidential election was the first for which reasonably accurate turnout figures were made public. In all previous national elections, the government inflated turnout statistics in an effort to convince Mexicans and the outside world that it had succeeded in relegitimating itself in impressive fashion.

The closeness of the 2006 presidential vote and the PRD's accusations of bias and manipulation temporarily damaged the credibility of the Federal

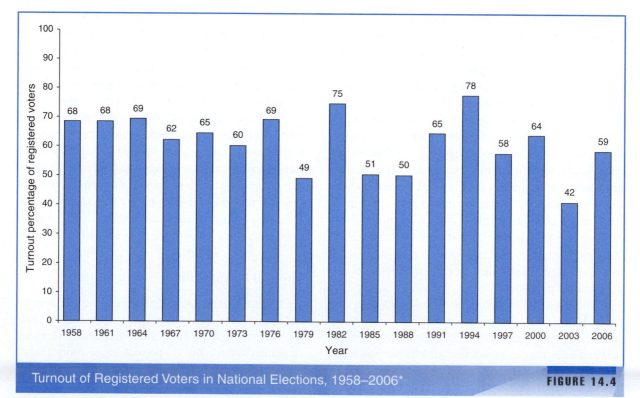

Turnout of Registered Voters in National Elections, 1958–2006*    FIGURE 14.4

*Beginning in 1970, the legal voting age was lowered from 21 to 18.

Source: Data from Comisión Federal Electoral for 1958–1991; from Instituto Federal Electoral for 1994–2006.

Electoral Institute, but over half of the public interviewed in postelection surveys thought the vote count had been clean. As long as electoral politics remain as competitive as in the period since 1988, and potential voters continue to believe in the security of the electoral system, we can expect further, gradual movement toward a genuinely participant political culture in Mexico.

## POLITICAL STRUCTURE AND INSTITUTIONS

Mexican politics has long defied easy classification. In the 1950s and 1960s some U.S. political scientists depicted the regime as a one-party democracy that was evolving toward "true" (North Atlantic-style) democracy. They recognized certain imperfections, but in the view of these analysts, political development in Mexico was simply incomplete. After the government's massacre of student protesters in 1968 and 1971, most analysts described the system as authoritarian, but even this characterization was subject to qualification.

By the 1990s, Mexico seemed to belong to a rapidly expanding category of hybrid, part-free, part-authoritarian systems that did not conform to classical typologies. Such labels as "selective democracy," "hard-line democracy," *democradura* (a Spanish contraction of "democracy" and "dictatorship"), and "modernizing authoritarian regime" have been applied to such systems. These are characterized by partly competitive (though not necessarily fair and honest) elections that install governments more committed to maintaining political stability and labor discipline than to expanding democratic freedoms, protecting human rights, or mediating class conflict.

Since the democratic breakthrough election of 2000, tolerance of undemocratic practices (for example, electoral fraud, selective repression of dissidents, and heavy-handed control of mass media) has declined dramatically. The functioning of all political institutions is scrutinized intensely, and they are held to much higher standards than ever before. The political design issue is no longer regime transition but how to improve democratic institutions already in place, especially to eliminate the structure of corruption that still supports abuses of authority and the electoral process at the local level in some parts of the country.

On paper, the Mexican government is structured much like the U.S. government: a presidential system, three autonomous branches of government (legislative, executive, and judicial) with checks and balances, and federalism with considerable autonomy at the local (municipal) level (see Figure 14.5). Until the late 1990s, however, Mexico's system of government was in practice far removed from the U.S. model. Decisionmaking was highly centralized. The president, operating with relatively few restraints on his authority, completely dominated the legislative and judicial branches. Supreme Court justices were presidentially appointed and confirmed by a simple majority of the PRI-dominated Senate. Each incoming president replaced most justices, which made the judges agents of the executive branch. Until 1997, the ruling PRI continuously controlled both houses of the federal legislature. Opposition party members could criticize the government and its policies vociferously; but their objections to proposals initiated by the president and backed by his party in Congress rarely affected the final shape of legislation. Courts and legislatures at the state level normally mirrored the preferences of the state governors, many of whom themselves were hand-picked by the incumbent president.

Until the late 1990s, the overwhelming majority of those elected to public office in Mexico were, in effect, political appointees—named to their positions by higher-ups within the PRI-government apparatus. Selection as a candidate of the PRI was tantamount to election, except in a handful of municipalities and congressional districts where opposition parties were so strong that they could not be ignored. Since reelection to office is prohibited at all levels of government, those elected on the PRI ticket were accountable and responsible not primarily to the people who elected them, but also to their political patrons within the regime. Nominating conventions—if held at all—were attended only by party activists, whose role was to ratify the choices made in private by officials at higher levels.

In 1988 the ruling party's control of the Congress was weakened significantly, setting the stage for a new era in executive-legislative relations. In that year's national elections, 66 PRI district-level candidates for seats in the lower house of Congress were defeated—nearly as many as the total of ruling party candidates defeated in all elections between 1946 and 1985. Between 1988 and 1991, the PRI was reduced to a bare

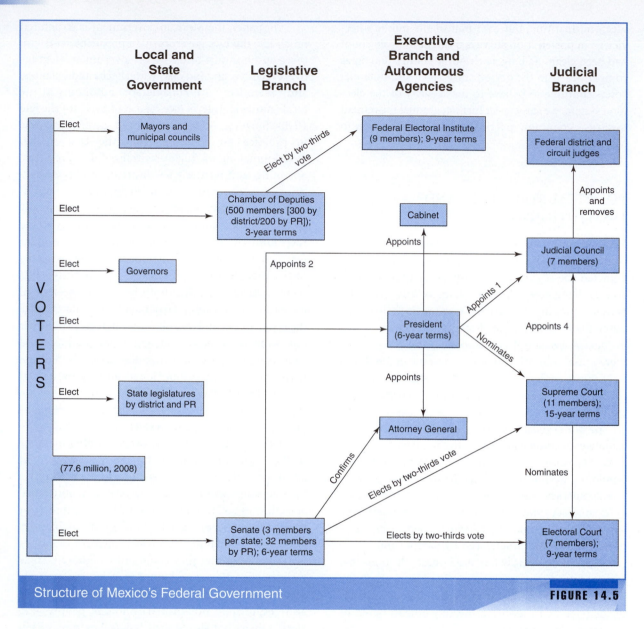

**Local and State Government** — **Legislative Branch** — **Executive Branch and Autonomous Agencies** — **Judicial Branch**

VOTERS

Elect → Mayors and municipal councils

Elect → Chamber of Deputies (500 members [300 by district/200 by PR]); 3-year terms

Elect by two-thirds vote → Federal Electoral Institute (9 members); 9-year terms

Federal district and circuit judges

Elect → Governors

Appoints 2

Appoints → Cabinet

Elect → President (6-year terms)

Appoints → Judicial Council (7 members)

Appoints 1 → Judicial Council

Appoints and removes

Appoints 4 → Supreme Court (11 members); 15-year terms

Nominates → Supreme Court

Elect → State legislatures by district and PR

Appoints → Attorney General

(77.6 million, 2008)

Elect → Senate (3 members per state; 32 members by PR); 6-year terms

Confirms

Elects by two-thirds vote → Supreme Court

Elects by two-thirds vote → Electoral Court (7 members); 9-year terms

Nominates → Electoral Court

**Structure of Mexico's Federal Government**    **FIGURE 14.5**

working majority in the Chamber of Deputies (260 out of 500 seats), and for the first time since the ruling party was founded in 1929, opposition party candidates were elected to the Senate (four out of sixty-four seats). Because the PRI no longer commanded a two-thirds majority in the lower house, President Salinas had to negotiate with the opposition party delegations (he chose to deal mostly with the PAN) to secure passage of key legislation amending the Constitution.[12] Moreover, the Congress had ceased to function as a reliable instrument for internal distribution of power and its perks with the ruling

party. With the recognition of so many opposition victories for congressional seats in 1988, aspiring PRIistas had to face the reality that nomination by their party was no longer equivalent to election. The tradition of the *carro completo* (clean sweep) by PRI candidates had ended.

The electoral law reform of 1993 further transformed the Congress by greatly increasing the representation of opposition parties in the Senate. The Senate was doubled in size (the current rules call for three senators per state, plus thirty-two senators elected by proportional representation in a closed national list). The reforms guaranteed that the opposition parties, combined, would control at least one-third of the Senate seats, compared with less than 5 percent during the 1988–1993 period. The 1993 reforms also expanded the opposition parties' presence in the Chamber of Deputies, guaranteeing that no party could have more than 300 out of 500 seats.

As part of an overall strategy to broaden the base of support for his administration, President Zedillo offered to share power with the Congress in several key areas. He proposed congressional approval of all major judicial appointments as well as oversight of all federal spending by a new auditing agency under congressional control.

The Congress, including the PRI's delegation, responded to Zedillo's challenge. In March 1995, after some fifty PRI deputies threatened to vote against a key element of the government's postdevaluation austerity plan—an increase in the value-added tax, which is levied on virtually all goods and services, from 10 percent to 15 percent—Zedillo found it necessary to aggressively lobby the congressional leaders of his own party to secure approval of the much-despised tax increase. Only Zedillo's arm twisting, combined with PRIistas' fears that the president would begin working directly with the opposition party members if his own party split on this crucial vote, prevented a wholesale breakdown of party discipline. The tax increase, combined with voter resentment over the 1995–1996 recession, led to the PRI's "defeat" in the 1997 midterms, when the party won only 239 seats in the Chamber of Deputies—twelve short of a majority.

Since 1997, the government has lacked a majority in either or both chambers of Congress. President Vicente Fox had to lobby and negotiate with Congress on a routine basis to pass legislation, as does President Felipe Calderón. The era when Congress's sole functions were to serve as a debating arena for the opposition parties (and for factions within the ruling party until the whips were applied) and as a rubber stamp for decisions already taken by the president has clearly ended.

## Federalism

Despite the federalist structure of government that is enshrined in the 1917 Constitution and legal codes, with their emphasis on the *municipio libre* (the concept of the free municipality, able to control its own

affairs), in practice the Mexican political system has usually functioned in a manner classified as **political centralism.**

From the 1920s through the Salinas presidency, the concentration of decisionmaking power at the federal level in most policy areas was continuous. Control over the preparation, conduct, and validation of elections—placed entirely at the municipal and state levels by the initial postrevolutionary electoral code, enacted in 1918—also passed to agencies that were part of the federal government apparatus or state-level entities controlled by federal authorities. A high degree of political centralism has been considered one of the main factors underlying Mexico's long-term political stability, although research at the state and local levels has demonstrated that political control by the center has been far less complete than is commonly assumed.[13]

Mexico is divided into thirty-one states and the Federal District, each one divided into *municipios*—politico-administrative units roughly equivalent in size and governmental functions to county governments in the United States. The *municipio* is governed by an *ayuntamiento*, or council, headed by a *presidente municipal* (mayor). Municipal officials are elected every three years. Each successive layer of government in Mexico is significantly weaker, less autonomous, and more impoverished than the levels above it. The federal government now controls about 90 percent of total public revenues—one of the highest degrees of fiscal centralization in Latin America.[14]

All of Mexico's seven most recent presidents entered office pledging to renew the "struggle against centralism," but serious efforts to decentralize have been made only since 1984. Under de la Madrid and Salinas, a limited form of revenue sharing was implemented, and the federal Constitution was amended to enhance the capacity of local governments to raise their own revenues. Partially successful efforts were also made to shift decisionmaking authority over public education and health care from the federal government to the states.[15] At the same time, the Salinas administration's National Solidarity Program (PRONASOL)—its principal social program, reaching into more than 95 percent of the country's 2,378 municipalities—was structured and administered to reinforce highly centralized presidential rule.

More assertively than any of his predecessors, President Zedillo vowed to reduce centralism. He went so far as to sign an agreement with the country's state governors and mayors calling for constitutional amendments that would provide the legal framework for "a new Mexican federalism." Zedillo promised a more equitable distribution of federal funds to the states and devolution of some functions that had been usurped by the federal government. But some federal ministries, especially the Treasury Department, have resisted further revenue sharing with municipal governments on the grounds that they lack the administrative capacity to make effective use of additional resources.

The state governors represent another potential obstacle to the "new federalism." The governors retain control over all resources transferred from the federal government, and effective administrative decentralization down to the municipio level would require them to relinquish a major portion of their political power—something that they have successfully resisted. It is clear that, even under a president strongly committed to redistributing resources and sharing power with subnational units of government, movement toward U.S.-style federalism in Mexico will meet with opposition from many different quarters, including federal government agencies and the states themselves.

## The Legislative Branch

Mexico's political system has been commonly described as presidentialist or presidentially centered. Nonetheless, these characterizations were based on observed practices in a dominant-party regime, in which the institutional rules of the party had overwhelmed the formal constitutional rules. A careful examination of the Mexican Constitution reveals a president who is among the more constitutionally constrained in Latin America and a Congress with strong, sometimes dominant powers over the other branches of government. The difference between the informal and formal institutions is the history of the PRI government.

The federal Congress has two houses: a 128-member upper chamber, the Senate; and a 500-member lower house, the Chamber of Deputies. Both chambers employ a so-called mixed-member system in which some of the members are elected by plurality vote in single-member districts, while others are elected by a system of compensatory proportional representation on closed-party lists.[16] The current electoral rules for the Senate, dating to 1996, call for plurality elections in each of the thirty-two states whereby each party

nominates a slate of two Senate candidates. The party that wins a plurality elects both candidates from the slate to the Senate. The party that places second sends the first candidate on the list to the upper chamber. Furthermore, thirty-two senators are elected by proportional representation on closed national lists, so that each party that wins at least 2 percent of the national vote elects its proportional share of the thirty-two list senators. The rules prevent any party from winning more than two-thirds of the seats in the Senate except under extraordinary circumstances (a party would have to place first in every state and win more than two-thirds of the national vote).

For the Chamber of Deputies, 300 members are elected by plurality in single-member districts, and an additional 200 deputies are elected by proportional representation in five regional closed lists. Each party that wins at least 2 percent of the national vote is entitled to its proportional share of the list deputies with a few restrictions. First, no party can ever have more than 300 total seats, which restricts the largest party to less than the two-thirds majority required for constitutional reforms. Second, no party's share of the total number of seats can exceed by more than 8 percent its share of the national vote. This means that in order to win a majority in the lower chamber, a party must win more than 42 percent of the vote and a sufficient margin of victory over the second-place party (usually around four percentage points) to win enough districts.

The mixed-member system directly affects the party system. Usually, plurality systems lead to two-party systems, as the voters find that it is better to coordinate their votes toward one of the two leading parties rather than waste them on third-party candidates. Proportional representation systems tend to create multiparty systems, because votes for the larger minority parties are not wasted. In Mexico, the mixed-member system has yielded a three-party system, in which most regions now have two-party systems (respecting the tendencies of the plurality system) but nationally the vote is split into three main blocs. The three parties with significant representation in the Mexican Congress in the 60th Legislature (2006–2009) are the PAN (with 41 percent of the seats), the PRD (with 25 percent), and the PRI (with 21 percent). The low threshold allows small parties to attain representation in the Chamber of Deputies, as well: five small parties won seats in the 60th Legislature (see Table 14.2).

## Composition of the Mexican Congress, 2006–2009

TABLE 14.2

| | Seats Won by Plurality Vote | Seats Won by P. R. System | Total | Percentage |
|---|---|---|---|---|
| **Chamber of Deputies** | | | | |
| Partido Acción Nacional (PAN) | 137 | 69 | 206 | 41.2 |
| Partido de la Revolución Democrática (PRD)[1] | 90 | 36 | 126 | 25.2 |
| Partido Revolucionario Institucional (PRI)[2] | 63 | 41 | 104 | 20.8 |
| Partido Verde Ecologista de México (PVEM)[2] | 2 | 17 | 19 | 3.8 |
| Convergencia[1] | 5 | 11 | 16 | 3.2 |
| Partido del Trabajo (PT)[1] | 3 | 13 | 16 | 3.2 |
| Nueva Alianza | 0 | 9 | 9 | 1.8 |
| PASC | 0 | 4 | 4 | 0.8 |
| Total | 300 | 200 | 500 | 100 |
| **Senate** | | | | |
| Partido Acción Nacional (PAN) | 41 | 11 | 52 | 40.6 |
| Partido Revolucionario Institucional (PRI)[2] | 27 | 6 | 33 | 25.8 |
| Partido de la Revolución Democrática (PRD)[1] | 23 | 6 | 29 | 22.7 |
| Partido Verde Ecologista de México (PVEM)[2] | 2 | 4 | 6 | 4.7 |
| Convergencia[1] | 3 | 2 | 5 | 3.9 |
| Partido del Trabajo (PT)[1] | 0 | 2 | 2 | 1.6 |
| Nueva Alianza | 0 | 1 | 1 | 0.8 |
| Total | 96 | 32 | 128 | 100 |

[1]Alianza por el Bien de Todos
[2]Alianza por México

Source: Instituto Federal Electoral (http://www.ife.org.mx), 2006.

The mixed-member system complicates creating majorities in either chamber. Since the 8-percent rule on maximum overrepresentation was established in the lower house, no party has been able to achieve a majority. The Senate rules went into effect fully for the first time in the 2000 elections. Now, when the race is close between the first- and second-place parties, it is also unlikely that a majority party will emerge in the Senate. This means that the party of the president will rarely have a majority in Congress, thus creating a situation of divided government.

Like the U.S. Constitution, the 1917 Mexican Constitution lists the legislative branch first. The Congress is primarily responsible for enacting nearly all public policy, with only a few exceptions. The president has constitutional decree powers only over questions of land reform (expropriation decrees) and tariffs and quotas in international trade (in which he can unilaterally adjust tariffs and quotas if the circumstances call for modifications). All regular legislation

must be approved by both chambers in the same form, and then submitted to the president for publication. The president must publish the bill within ten days or return the bill to the chamber of origin (see Box 14.2).

A presidential veto can take two forms: one is a regular veto, in which the president expresses his rejection of a bill; the second is a corrective veto, in which the president requests that Congress amend the bill, usually because of technical errors in the text. In either case, Congress can insist on the original text of the bill by a two-thirds vote, after which the president must publish the legislation. In case of corrective vetoes, Congress often modifies the bill as requested and sends it back to the president for promulgation.

Each of the two chambers has exclusive powers and areas of specialization. The Chamber of Deputies specializes in fiscal legislation. All revenue bills must originate in the lower chamber. The Chamber of Deputies first approves the revenue and tax legislation, sending it to the upper chamber for Senate approval.

BOX 14.2

## How a Bill Becomes a Law in Mexico

- Bills can be introduced by federal deputies, senators, the president, or the state legislatures. All revenue bills, regardless of the sponsor, must be introduced in the Chamber of Deputies. Therefore, the president's annual economic package is sent to the Chamber of Deputies. However, senators can introduce revenue legislation directly in the Chamber of Deputies. All other legislation can begin in either the Chamber of Deputies or the Senate. The federal bureaucracy assists the president in preparing executive bills for introduction.

- All bills are sent to committees. There are twenty-nine committees in the Chamber of Deputies and thirty in the Senate. Committees amend most legislation before reporting it to the floor (87 percent in the Chamber of Deputies, and 75 percent in the Senate). The federal bureaucracy often sends commentary on pending legislation to the relevant committees. The legislators are not required to heed these opinions.

- All legislation reported by committee is voted on the floor. The chamber can amend legislation from committees, but only 34 percent of the legislation is amended on the floor in the Chamber of Deputies, and only 24 percent on the floor of the Senate. If a bill is approved by the first chamber, it is sent to the other chamber for approval.

- In the second chamber, bills are sent to committee. Routine legislation is usually reported to the floor without amendment. Important bills are usually amended in committee. If the second chamber approves the bill on the floor without amendment, it is sent to the president; if the bill is amended, it is sent back to the first chamber for approval. Bills can be considered twice by each chamber before a final version is settled on.

- The president must sign or veto a bill within ten days, unless Congress has ended its session. In those cases, the president must dispatch the bills before the next session begins. The federal bureaucracy usually makes recommendations to the president on whether to sign or veto a bill. If the president vetoes a bill, it is sent to the first chamber for reconsideration. If the first chamber rejects the veto by a two-thirds vote, it is sent to the other chamber. If the second chamber also rejects the veto by a two-thirds vote, the president must publish the law. The president also has a corrective veto, in which he can return a bill to the first chamber, suggesting amendments. Each chamber may accept these amendments by a majority vote, or reject the amendments by a two-thirds vote.

- The annual appropriations bill is considered by only the Chamber of Deputies. The president sends the appropriations bill to the chamber by September 8. The chamber must approve the bill, with or without amendments, by November 15, sending the bill back to the president. If the president vetoes the bill, the Chamber of Deputies can accept his suggestions by a majority vote or reject them by a two-thirds vote. The Senate never considers appropriations.

However, only the Chamber of Deputies approves the appropriations legislation. This gives the Chamber of Deputies extraordinary influence over the federal public administration. Likewise, the lower chamber has exclusive powers over budgetary oversight and approves the public accounts.

The Senate has exclusive power to oversee foreign affairs. The Mexican president is supposed to conduct foreign relations under seven constitutionally specified doctrines: self-determination, nonintervention, the peaceful solution of conflicts, the prohibition on the international use of force, legal equality among countries, international cooperation toward development, and the pursuit of peace and international security. The upper chamber has the power to monitor foreign affairs, and it approves treaties submitted by the president by a majority vote.

The Senate also has the power to remove state governors and depose state legislatures. The Constitution allows the Senate to topple state governments when it recognizes that the state can no longer provide for domestic security. This requires a vote of the upper chamber; afterwards, the president proposes a list of three candidates from which the Senate elects the interim governor by a two-thirds vote. Prompted by PRI presidents, the Senate deposed many governors during the twentieth century, though usually for political reasons rather than for security motives. The Senate also regulates pacts between the federal and state governments concerning revenue-sharing and program administration.

Federal deputies and senators have shown extraordinary levels of party discipline in recent years. For example, during the last two years of the 57th Legislature (1997–2000), on average 99.6 percent of the PRIista deputies voted together on party bills. Party cohesion for the PANista deputies in the 57th Legislature was about 92 percent, and for PRDista deputies, 93 percent. During the 58th Legislature (2000–2003), cohesion among PAN deputies increased to 95 percent, and hit 98 percent after 2003, nearly equaling the levels of PRI discipline when it held the presidency. Meanwhile, PRI discipline declined to 91 percent during the first two terms in which it did not control the executive branch, but recovered to 95 percent after 2006 (see Table 14.3).

High party discipline in Mexico has two main sources.[17] First, consecutive reelection for deputies and senators is prohibited. This nearly eliminates accountability of the representatives to their constituents. Voters can neither reward their legislators for good performance nor punish them for bad representation. Since federal legislators are not required to seek cues from their electorate, they look elsewhere for guidance, and the party leadership is more than

willing to provide it. Second, nomination procedures in each of the parties are relatively closed. The leadership traditionally has selected candidates directly in the PRI and the PRD, while PANista candidates are nominated in closed (but often competitive) conventions of party activists. This further focuses the legislators on party leadership, because without the support of the party elite their political futures would be dismal.

Each party generally votes as a bloc in Congress, which creates incentives for the leaders of each of the parties to negotiate bills among themselves rather than allow the rank-and-file members to work out compromises in committee. Other rules of Congress grant extensive authority to the coordinators of the parties (such as the power to assign members to committees and dole out office space and expense accounts to the deputies). Together, these institutions create a highly centralized legislative branch. When the president was recognized as the natural leader of the majority party in the Congress, the centralized tendencies in that branch allowed him to rule as a near dictator without changing any constitutional norms.

## The Executive Branch

Despite the constitutionally limited powers of the executive branch, no one would dispute that the president was the dominant political actor in Mexico for the greater part of the twentieth century. In addition to his rather modest constitutional powers, the

**TABLE 14.3**

Party Cohesion in the Chamber of Deputies: Party Votes, 1998–2008 (percentages)

| | | PRI | PAN | PRD | PVEM | PT |
|---|---|---|---|---|---|---|
| 57th Legislature | Mean | 99.6 | 92.2 | 92.8 | 97.5 | 88.9 |
| (1997–2000) | s.d. | 1.3 | 12.6 | 13.9 | 8.0 | 16.4 |
| 58th Legislature | Mean | 90.8 | 95.1 | 91.7 | 95.0 | 96.9 |
| (2000–2003) | s.d. | 13.0 | 11.7 | 15.1 | 10.8 | 11.0 |
| 59th Legislature | Mean | 90.9 | 98.4 | 95.2 | 96.4 | 95.3 |
| (2003–2006) | s.d. | 11.8 | 5.9 | 9.1 | 9.7 | 12.3 |
| 60th Legislature | Mean | 95.2 | 98.6 | 90.7 | 98.7 | 94.9 |
| (2006–2009) | s.d. | 7.8 | 5.7 | 14.5 | 5.6 | 11.5 |

Note: Data for the 57th Legislature begins October 8, 1998; data for the 60th Legislature ends December 11, 2008. Party votes are roll calls in which at least one party dissented from the rest. Party cohesion is the percentage of the party voting with the majority of that party; "s.d." is the standard deviation.

Source: For the 57th Legislature, Jeffrey A. Weldon, "Institutional and Political Factors in Party Discipline in the Chamber of Deputies, 1998–2002," presented at the First Latin American Political Science Congress, Salamanca, Spain, July 2002. Data for the last three legislatures calculated by Weldon from the *Diario de los Debates* and the *Gaceta Parlamentaria* of the Chamber of Deputies.

Mexican president possessed a broad range of unwritten but generally recognized "metaconstitutional" powers that traditionally ensured his dominance over all of the country's other political institutions.[18] Mexicans use the term *presidencialismo* to connote this extraordinary concentration of powers, formal and informal, in the hands of the president, and the implication that incumbents frequently abuse these powers in pursuit of personal and political ends.

On any issue of national political significance, the federal judiciary would take its cue from the incumbent president. Until very recently, the Supreme Court never found presidential decisions or legislation enacted at the behest of the president to be unconstitutional, and Congress never challenged presidential appointments to the federal judiciary. The president had the informal power to seat and unseat state governors, mayors, and members of Congress. For example, during President Salinas's term, seventeen state governors resigned, most under pressure from Los Pinos (the residence of the Mexican president). From 1929 through 1994, the president also functioned as the "supreme head" of the official party, choosing its leaders, dictating his legislative proposals to the PRI delegation in Congress, shaping the party's internal governance, imposing his personal choices for the PRI's gubernatorial and congressional candidates, and—most importantly—controlling the selection of the party's next presidential nominee.

The absence of a rigid, fully elaborated political ideology made it possible for a Mexican president to have a pragmatic, flexible program and style of governance. The so-called ideology of the Mexican Revolution was never more than a loosely connected set of goals or symbols. The only "revolutionary" ideology that has been scrupulously observed is the constitutionally mandated no-reelection principle for the presidency: the president is limited to a single six-year term.[19]

During the PRI's seven decades of rule at the national level, three factors were required to create strong presidentialism.[20] First, the president's party had to have a majority in both chambers of Congress. Under **divided government,** the opposition majorities in Congress are unlikely to follow the dictates of the president. Second, there must be high levels of discipline in the majority party of Congress. This was achieved by the mechanisms described earlier. If there is insufficient discipline, the Mexican president would look more like most U.S. presidents, because the members of Congress act as free agents. Third, the president must be considered the leader of his party. In the 1930s, the first two factors were in place, but the leader of the party, Plutarco Elías Calles, received all of the benefits of the disciplined party, not the president. After Cárdenas reorganized the official party along lines of authority that led directly to himself, strong *presidencialismo* was finally achieved.

All three key ingredients of strong presidentialism were generally in place from 1946 to 1994. Even a bare 52-percent PRI majority in the 54th Legislature (1988–1991) was sufficient to maintain a strong presidency for Salinas. His successor, Ernesto Zedillo, adhered to a very different model of presidential leadership. Most importantly, Zedillo refused to assume the president's traditional role as leader of the PRI. He publicly pledged to refrain from interfering in internal party matters, including candidate selection. He also assured that, unlike his predecessors, he would not involve himself in adjudicating disputed elections, thereby serving notice to the PRI that the president could no longer be relied on to be the ultimate guarantor of the party's electoral victories.

The most important test of Zedillo's resolve to recast the institution of the presidency came as his term was ending. Tradition dictated that, at that point, he would exercise his metaconstitutional power as incumbent president to select his own successor, with minimal input from other key actors in the ruling coalition. (In September 1990, Luis Echeverría became the first former president to publicly acknowledge this crucially important, unwritten rule of the Mexican political system.) In the presidential succession of 2000, PRI leaders—with President Zedillo's blessing—opted to hold a nationwide primary election in November 1999 to determine the party's 2000 presidential candidate. Four veteran PRI politicians entered the race, campaigned actively for the nomination, and debated each other on national television. The winning candidate, Francisco Labastida, was widely considered to be Zedillo's favorite. The primary was considered a great success by the media and the party, and after some counseling from the president, the losers accepted defeat. However, seven months after the first open PRI primary for the presidency, the PRI candidate himself had to accept defeat in the general election.

In the 2006 succession, the outgoing president had even less influence. The PAN maintained some distance between itself and the presidency during the entire Fox administration, and the president had no influence in the selection of PANista candidates for state or congressional offices. Vicente Fox's preferred candidate for the PAN's 2006 presidential nomination was soundly defeated in the party's primary elections by Felipe Calderón, who during his campaign criticized errors of political management by the Fox team.

## Executive-Legislative Relations

The dynamics of executive-legislative relations in Mexico used to be determined by the metaconstitutional powers of the president. The operation of the three key factors outlined earlier—unified government, high party discipline in the ruling party, and the recognition of the president as the de facto head of the party—explained a compliant Congress. Today, now that the first and third factors no longer hold, executive-legislative relations follow constitutional rather than partisan norms, and Mexico either enjoys or suffers from the everyday republican conflicts of separation of powers.

Comparing the levels of productivity of the last six legislatures allows us to evaluate the executive's influence over the legislative branch under varying conditions of the metaconstitutional conditions listed earlier, as well as the relative strength of the president's party in the lower chamber (see Table 14.4). During the 54th Legislature (1988–1991), the first half of the Salinas presidency, the PRI held a small majority of 52 percent of the lower chamber. Despite the marginal majority, 98.6 percent of the executive's public bills were approved. Of the 110 bills approved during the 54th Legislature, nearly two-thirds had originated in the executive branch. The 55th Legislature (1991–1994) gave the PRI and Salinas a large majority in the Chamber of Deputies, around 63 percent. Again, 98.5 percent of the president's public bills were approved. More than three out of every five bills that were eventually approved in the lower chamber had been introduced by the executive. During both legislatures, the three conditions for metaconstitutional power were strongly in place.

During the 56th Legislature (1994–1997), the first half of President Zedillo's term, the president was no longer functioning as de facto leader of his party: Zedillo had promised to keep a healthy distance between himself and the PRI. Nevertheless, the lower chamber approved 98.9 percent of his bills, thanks to the three-fifths majority held by the ruling party. Nearly three-quarters of all of the bills approved by the chamber had originated in the executive branch. Although the president had claimed that he was no longer interested in being the head of the PRI, it appears that the party was not yet listening.

In the 57th Legislature (1997–2000), divided government prevailed for the first time since 1928. The PRI held just under 48 percent of the seats in the lower chamber, while the PAN and the PRD each had about a quarter of the seats. Thus, the first of the conditions for metaconstitutional power—unified government—was eliminated. Under divided government, 90 percent of the president's bills were approved—a decline of nine percentage points from the previous legislature. In fact, two executive-introduced bills were defeated: the revenue law for 1998 (a substitute bill was subsequently approved) and a bank bailout bill. Since 1928, a majority of the bills that the Chamber of Deputies approved had originated in the executive branch. In the 57th Legislature, this trend was abruptly reversed: only 31 percent of the bills approved in the term had been introduced by the executive, while nearly 60 percent had been sponsored by deputies.

By the time that the 58th Legislature had convened in 2000, metaconstitutional presidentialism had ended. The first condition—unified government—remained unfulfilled. President Fox's PAN held only 41 percent of the seats in the lower chamber. Nor was Fox treated as the head of his party. The PAN delegation occasionally voted against the preferences of the president, as they did in 2001 when they opposed allowing representatives of the Zapatista rebels to speak from the podium of the Chamber of Deputies. Nearly 90 percent of Fox's bills were approved during the 2000–2003 term, an achievement no different from Zedillo's under divided government. However, nearly every bill that Fox had sent to Congress had been extensively amended in at least one of the chambers. Never before has a higher percentage of executive bills been amended, either in committee or on the floor.

In the 2003 midterm election, the PRI ended up with nearly 45 percent of the seats, while the PAN won only 30 percent. The PRD also increased its size in the lower chamber, winning nearly one-fifth of the seats, mostly due to district victories in the Federal District.

| Sponsorship and Approval of Public Bills in the Chamber of Deputies, 1988–2006 | | | | TABLE 14.4 |

| Legislature | % of Deputies from President's Party | Sponsor* | % of Total New Bills Introduced | % of Total Bills Approved | % of Sponsor's Bills Approved |
|---|---|---|---|---|---|
| 54th (1988–1991) | 52 | Executive | 22.8 | 65.1 | 98.6 |
|  |  | Deputies | 77.2 | 34.9 | 15.6 |
|  |  | Other | 0.0 | 0.0 | — |
|  |  | Total | 100.0 | 100.0 | 34.5 |
| 55th (1991–1994) | 63 | Executive | 42.4 | 62.6 | 98.5 |
|  |  | Deputies | 56.3 | 36.5 | 38.5 |
|  |  | Other | 1.3 | 0.9 | 50.0 |
|  |  | Total | 100.0 | 100.0 | 50.0 |
| 56th (1994–1997) | 60 | Executive | 33.8 | 74.2 | 98.9 |
|  |  | Deputies | 61.7 | 24.2 | 16.2 |
|  |  | Other | 4.5 | 1.7 | 16.7 |
|  |  | Total | 100.0 | 100.0 | 42.7 |
| 57th (1997–2000) | 48 | Executive | 10.1 | 31.0 | 90.0 |
|  |  | Deputies | 81.9 | 59.6 | 20.8 |
|  |  | Other | 7.9 | 9.4 | 32.2 |
|  |  | Total | 100.0 | 100.0 | 28.6 |
| 58th (2000–2003) | 41 | Executive | 6.8 | 23.7 | 89.9 |
|  |  | Deputies | 77.3 | 57.7 | 18.4 |
|  |  | Other | 15.8 | 18.6 | 30.0 |
|  |  | Total | 100.0 | 100.0 | 24.9 |
| 59th (2003–2006) | 30 | Executive | 2.8 | 8.6 | 73.2 |
|  |  | Deputies | 85.8 | 72.0 | 19.6 |
|  |  | Other | 11.4 | 19.4 | 38.0 |
|  |  | Total | 100.0 | 100.0 | 23.3 |

*"Other" includes bills introduced by state legislatures, revenue bills presented in the lower chamber by senators, and bills that originated in the Senate that had been introduced there by senators. Executive bills that originated in the Senate are classified under the "Executive" category.

Source: *Diario de los Debates* and the *Gaceta Parlamentaria* of the Chamber of Deputies. Data compiled at ITAM under the direction of Jeffrey Weldon.

During the 59th Legislature (2003–2006), only 73.2 percent of the president's bills were approved, and a mere 8.6 percent of the bills approved by the Chamber of Deputies originated in the executive branch. However, overall productivity in the lower chamber reached an all-time high. The deputies approved more bills than any previous legislature, more than doubling the record set in 1937–1940 during the Cárdenas reform era.

Mexico's first "opposition" president had difficult relations with a Congress in which the opposition parties—when united—had majority control. In March 2001, Fox introduced a major tax reform that would have placed a 15-percent value-added tax (VAT) on food, medicines, books, and private school tuition. Opposition legislators in the Chamber of Deputies, led by the PRI and the PRD, strongly opposed this provision, and the PAN deputies were reluctant to join what appeared to be a lost cause in support of their president. After several months of intense debate, the VAT proposal was killed. In April 2002, with the PRI and

PRD members again leading the pack, the Senate denied Fox permission to make a trip to several U.S. and Canadian cities, to demonstrate its opposition to various elements of his foreign policy. The trip was cancelled.

Executive-legislative relations worsened during the second half of Fox's term. The proposal to raise the VAT was reintroduced in the fall of 2003, but the Chamber of Deputies narrowly defeated the bill on the floor. In the fall 2004 term, the opposition coalition in the Chamber of Deputies amended Fox's revenue bill, increasing dependence on oil sources as a part of expected federal revenue and raising the deficit target. The opposition also modified considerably the federal appropriations bill, decreasing or eliminating a number of federal programs and increasing pork-barrel expenditures for PRI and PRD states. Fox vetoed the appropriations bill; this was the first budget veto cast by a president since 1933. The Chamber of Deputies disputed the veto by filing a suit in the Supreme Court, claiming that the president did not have the constitutional power to veto the budget (despite the fact that there had been forty-five vetoes of the budget between 1917 and 1933, none of which had been challenged on constitutional grounds by Congress). The Supreme Court suspended the expenditures to which the president had objected, and later ruled that the budget veto was indeed constitutional. Such tests of will between the executive and legislative branches are increasingly common in Mexico's era of divided government, with the judicial branch assuming an increasingly important role as arbiter between the two branches.

During the first two years of the Calderón administration, the president has enjoyed legislative success despite divided government, accomplished by *logrolling* legislation with the PRI. For example, Calderón and the PAN won a major victory in tax reform, through the creation of two new taxes. An alternative minimum tax on business income complements the regular income tax and thwarts common routes of tax evasion. The new tax on cash deposits in banks targets the informal economy. Both have increased revenue, allowing for greater public investment. Simultaneously, the PRI won an electoral reform to its liking. Party influence over the electoral authorities was increased, campaign financing was reduced, and officeholders can no longer promote themselves while in office. Negative campaign advertising (even if truthful) was banned. The law prohibits parties from buying TV or radio time for their spots, instead using free media time allocated by the electoral authorities (this was opposed by the private television networks). However, no other person or organization can buy time to promote political ideas or candidates at any time.

Another reform pushed by both the PRI and the PRD ends the presidential practice of delivering his state-of-the-union message in Congress, which diminishes the pomp and circumstance surrounding the speech, and permits Congress to avoid embarrassing itself by the recent antics of some of the opposition legislators (frequent interrupting, donning masks, and turning their backs to the president). In return, the president is now permitted to leave the country for up to seven days without the consent of Congress (Fox had been denied twice). The president also won a series of major reforms in public security and police and judicial procedures.

Calderón also won a reform long yearned for by both Presidents Zedillo and Fox—a comprehensive energy reform. The president had asked for new interpretations of the laws prohibiting private investment in the oil industry, though he insisted that neither PEMEX nor any part of the process would be privatized. After instructions from López Obrador, deputies from the PRD, Convergencia, and PT closed down Congress for two weeks in April 2008. The other parties convened sessions in alternate sites, but ceded to the PRD in granting a summer-long series of hearings on the issue. The committee report in October was a watered down version of Calderón's bill, but the PAN and PRI passed the law, along with part of the PRD.

## RECRUITING THE POLITICAL ELITE

What kinds of people gain entry into Mexico's national political elite, and who makes it to the top? At least since the days of the Porfiriato, the Mexican political elite has been recruited predominantly from the middle class. The 1910 revolution did not open up the political elite to large numbers of people from peasant or urban laborer backgrounds. That opening occurred only in the 1930s, during the Cárdenas **sexenio (six-year term),** and then mainly at the local and state levels rather than the national elite level. By 1989, only 8.3 percent of all state governors, senators, cabinet, and subcabinet members had peasant or working-class origins; in a sample of 1,113 federal government bureaucrats, only 0.7 percent said that their fathers were peasants while 0.9 percent described them as workers.[21]

In the last three PRI-dominated administrations (1982–2000), the national political elite was drawn heavily from the ranks of *capitalinos*—people born or raised in Mexico City. By the 1980s more than half of the presidential cabinet had been born in Mexico City and an even higher percentage had been raised there.[22] Postgraduate education, especially at elite foreign universities and in disciplines like economics and public administration, became much more important as a ticket of entry into the national political elite. Over half of the cabinet members appointed by Presidents de la Madrid, Salinas, and Zedillo had studied economics or public administration, and over half of those who received training in these subjects at the graduate level did so in the United States. The economic cabinets of these three presidents were filled with recipients of Ph.D.s from universities such as Harvard, MIT, Stanford, Yale, and the University of Chicago. Typically, the PRIista *técnicos* (technocrats)spent their entire career within the government bureaucracy, especially the financial and planning agencies, never engaging in partisan politics. The economic policy debacles presided over by technocrat presidents and cabinet ministers in the 1990s discredited this breed of Mexican officials in the eyes of the public as well as the party leaderships. Significantly, a national PRI assembly in 1996 removed most technocrats from the line of presidential succession by requiring the party's future presidential nominees to have previously held elective office.

Relatively few card-carrying technocrats found their way into the cabinet of Vicente Fox, who favored persons with nongovernmental experience, a bachelor's or master's degree in business administration, educated in Mexico—like himself. Nearly half (45 percent) of Fox's top fifty-two appointees—many of them recruited through professional head-hunting firms—had no previous public-sector experience. The involvement of persons with private-sector experience in the Fox administration (46 percent) was far greater than in any of the PRI governments since 1929. Fox also broke with his PRI predecessors in recruiting more top officials from outside of Mexico City (60 percent of his top officials were from the provinces), and more who had received their undergraduate education in private rather than public universities (54 percent).

Most strikingly, 75 percent of Fox's original top fifty-two appointees had no known political party affiliation. Fewer than one-fifth were recruited from the PAN.[23] Only four members of Fox's original cabinet had a history of militancy in the PAN, and the dearth of card-carrying PANistas was even more conspicuous at the subcabinet level. Some ministries were nearly devoid of PANistas.

Fox's reluctance to call on experienced PAN partisans until late in his term was consistent with his "independent" campaign for the presidency—not dependent on the PAN apparatus and even opposed by significant segments of it—and with his professed insistence on building a team of the "best and brightest" managers, regardless of partisanship. But Fox's extreme distancing from his own party in staffing his administration contributed to tense relations with the PAN's congressional delegation and made it more difficult for him to achieve some policy goals. During the second half of the Fox *sexenio*, the president increased substantially the number of PANistas in his cabinet, and party loyalty to the president in Congress consequently improved.

In terms of professional background, Fox's successor, Felipe Calderón, is something of a throwback to the late technocratic PRI presidents. Calderón earned Master's degrees in economics and public administration (the latter from Harvard University's Kennedy School of Government). However, in contrast to the last five PRI presidents, Calderón also had extensive experience in party politics and elective office. He was twice elected to a seat in Congress and once to the legislative body of Mexico City, and like the other two major presidential candidates in 2006, Calderón also served as his party's national chairman. He later served as director of BANOBRAS, a federal development bank, and as Secretary of Energy in Fox's cabinet. Calderón's own economic cabinet is dominated by technocrats holding doctoral degrees from U.S. universities, including Chicago, Columbia, MIT, and the University of Pennsylvania.

Since the 1970s, kinship ties have become more important as a common denominator of those who attain top positions of political power. Increasingly, such people are born into politically prominent families that have already produced state governors, cabinet ministers, federal legislators, and even presidents. Two of the three major presidential candidates in 2006 exemplify this pattern. Felipe Calderón's father was one of the founders of the PAN; Roberto Madrazo's father had been national chairman of the PRI. Only López Obrador was not born into a politically influential family.

These political families are increasingly interconnected: At least one-third of the government officials and politicians interviewed by one researcher for several books on the Mexican political elite were related to other officials, not counting those related through marriage and the traditional rite of *compadrazgo* (becoming a godparent to a friend's child).[24] Family connections can give an aspiring political leader a powerful advantage over rivals.

The growing importance of kinship ties and other indicators of increasing homogeneity in personal backgrounds causes some observers to worry that Mexico's political elite is becoming more closed and inbred. While its social base may indeed be narrowing, the modern Mexican political elite still shows considerable fluidity; the massive turnover of officeholders every six years is proof of that. This factor helps to explain why in Mexico—unlike other postrevolutionary countries, such as China and (until recently) the Soviet Union—the regime did not become a gerontocracy. In fact, the median age of cabinet members and presidential aspirants in Mexico has been dropping; in recent *sexenios,* most have been in their late 30s or early 40s. Exemplifying this trend, Felipe Calderón was 44 years old when elected to the presidency.

## INTEREST REPRESENTATION AND POLITICAL CONTROL

In Mexico's presidentialist system, important public policies used to be initiated and shaped by the inner circle of presidential advisers before they were even presented for public discussion. Thus, most effective interest representation took place within the upper levels of the federal bureaucracy. The structures that aggregate and articulate interests in Western democracies (the ruling political party, labor unions, and so on) actually served other purposes in the Mexican system: limiting the scope of citizens' demands on the government, mobilizing electoral support for the regime, helping to legitimate it in the eyes of other countries, and distributing jobs and other material rewards to select individuals and groups. For example, the PRI typically had no independent influence on public policymaking; nor did the opposition parties, except where they controlled state or local governments.

From the late 1930s until the PRI's defeat in 2000, Mexico had a **corporatist** system of interest representation in which each citizen and societal segment was expected to relate to the state through a single structure "licensed" by the state to organize and represent that sector of society (peasants, urban unionized workers, businesspeople, teachers, and so on). The official party

itself was divided into three **sectors:** (1) the Labor Sector, (2) the Peasant Sector, and (3) the Popular Sector, a catch-all category representing various segments of the middle class (government employees, other white-collar workers, small merchants, private landowners) and residents of low-income urban neighborhoods. Each sector in the PRI is dominated by one mass organization; other organizations are affiliated with each party sector, but their influence is dwarfed by that of the "peak" organization. Thus, the **Confederación de Trabajadores de México (CTM)** has dominated the Labor Sector; the **Confederación Nacional Campesina (CNC)** the Peasant Sector; and the **Confederación Nacional de Organizaciones Populares (CNOP)** the Popular Sector.

A number of powerful organized interest groups—foreign and domestic entrepreneurs, the military, the Catholic Church—were not formally represented in the PRI. These groups often dealt directly with the government elite, often at the presidential or cabinet level. They did not need the PRI to make their preferences known. They also had well-placed representatives within the executive branch who could be counted on to articulate their interests. In addition, the business community was organized into several government-chartered confederations. Since the Cárdenas administration, all but a small minority of the country's industrialists were required by law to join one of these employers' organizations, which channeled business interests into a few, well-controlled outlets. These confederations still exist, but the Supreme Court ruled in 1999 that compulsory membership was an unconstitutional restriction on the freedom of association.

Because the ruling party and the national legislature did not effectively aggregate interests in the Mexican system, individuals and groups seeking something from the government often circumvented their nominal representatives in the PRI sectoral organizations and the Congress, and sought satisfaction of their needs through personal contacts within the government bureaucracy. These **patron-client relationships** compartmentalized the society into discrete, noninteracting, vertical segments that served as pillars of the regime. Within the lower class, for example, unionized urban workers were separated from nonunion urban workers; *ejidatarios* from small private landholders and landless agricultural workers. The middle class was compartmentalized into government bureaucrats, educators, health care professionals, lawyers, economists, and so forth. Thus competition among social classes was replaced by highly fragmented competition within classes.

The articulation of interests through patron-client networks assisted the PRI regime by fragmenting popular demands into small-scale, highly individualized or localized requests that could be granted or denied case by case. Officials were rarely confronted with collective demands from broad social groupings. Rather than having to act on a request from a whole category of people (slum dwellers, *ejidatarios,* teachers), they had easier, less costly choices to make (as between competing petitions from several neighborhoods for a paved street or a piped water system). The clientelistic structure thus provided a mechanism for distributing public services and other benefits in a highly selective, discretionary if not always arbitrary manner. This system put the onus on potential beneficiaries to identify and cultivate the "right" patrons within the government bureaucracy. The prohibition on consecutive reelection prevented local elected officials from taking on the role of patron. As they could be neither punished nor rewarded for their performance, elected politicians abdicated this responsibility, and it was only natural that the bureaucracy would replace them in the role of patron.

After the dismal performance of the sectoral organizations in delivering votes to Carlos Salinas in the 1988 presidential election, the dysfunctional nature of the corporatist system of interest representation became a matter of urgent concern for the government elite. Salinas and PRI leaders chose to deemphasize, if not eliminate, the role of the discredited sectors in interest articulation and aggregation. They decided that ossified corporatist structures should be supplemented with territorially based "movements" and committees, led by new cadres who could distance themselves (and, implicitly, the PRI itself) from the detested bosses who ran the sectoral organizations and foster a more direct relationship between the PRI and individual citizens.

Unquestionably, the PRI's vaunted political control capabilities were weakened by the economic and political crises of recent *sexenios.* Nevertheless, the traditional instruments of control—patron-client relationships, *caciquismo* (local-level boss rule), the captive labor movement, and selective repression of dissidents by government security forces—are still effective in some PRI-controlled states.

In many of the states and localities where the PAN has come to power since the 1980s, officials have attempted to implement very different models of state-society relations, aimed at increasing civic participation in public administration and placing greater reliance on public-private partnerships. For example, the Citizen Wednesday program, pioneered by the PANista mayor of León, Guanajuato, "encouraged citizens to make their particular needs and concerns known to the local government through weekly, one-on-one sessions with the heads of municipal departments for public lighting, paving, sewerage, water, public safety, and social welfare. . . . The program soon became the principal point of access between citizens and the government in León. It was quickly adopted by other PAN governments throughout Mexico."[25]

In other places, however, the limited success of PAN administrations in solving high-salience public security and urban development problems has undermined attempts to build new, enduring state-society relationships. For example, in 2004, disillusioned voters in key northern border city of Tijuana turned out the PAN after three terms, installing as mayor a traditional PRI politician with a reputation for corruption and authoritarianism. He quickly set about restoring the corporatist networks that his PANista predecessors had labored to dismantle.

## POLITICAL PARTIES

### The Partido Revolucionario Institucional

The Partido Revolucionario Institucional (PRI) was founded in 1929 by President Plutarco Elías Calles to serve as a mechanism for reducing violent conflict among contenders for public office and for consolidating the power of the central government, at the expense of the personalistic, local, and state-level political machines of the decade following the 1910–1920 revolution. Between 1920 and 1929, there had been four major rebellions against the national executive by these subnational political machines. As historian Lorenzo Meyer has observed, the PRI was a party born not to fight for power, nor to share it with the opposition, "but rather to administer it."[26]

For more than half a century, the ruling party served with impressive efficiency, as a mechanism for resolving conflicts, for co-opting newly emerging interest groups into the system, and for legitimating the regime through the electoral process. Potential defectors from the official party were deterred by the government's manipulation of electoral rules, which made it virtually impossible for any dissident faction to bolt from the party and win the election. Dissident movements did emerge occasionally, but before the neo-Cardenista coalition contested the 1988 election, no breakaway presidential candidacy had been able to garner more than 16 percent of the vote (by official count).

In 1938 President Lázaro Cárdenas transformed the official party from a mechanism for elite conflict resolution and co-optation into a mass-based political party that could be used explicitly to build popular support for government policies and mobilize participation in elections. Cárdenas accomplished this by merging into the official party the local-, state-, and national-level organizations of peasants and urban workers that had been created during his presidency. This reorganization established the party's claim to be an inclusionary party—one that would absorb the diverse economic interests and political tendencies represented in Mexican society. By including lower income sectors, it reinforced the revolutionary credentials of the party, as well. The official party and its affiliated mass organizations occupied so much political space that opposition parties found it difficult to recruit supporters.

From the beginning, the official party was an appendage of the government itself, especially of the presidency. It was never a truly independent arena of political competition. A handful of nationally powerful party leaders, such as Fidel Velázquez, the patriarch of the PRI-affiliated labor movement until his death in 1997, occasionally constrained government actions, but the official party itself never determined the basic directions of government economic and social policies. Indeed, one of the key factors underlying the erosion of party unity and discipline since the late 1980s and the PRI's overwhelming defeats in state-level elections beginning in 1995, leading to its loss of the presidency in 2000, was the party's inability to distance itself from the unpopular austerity policies made by the technocrats in the federal government.

The official party traditionally enjoyed virtually unlimited access to government funds to finance its campaigns. No one knew how much was actually being siphoned from government coffers to the PRI, because Mexico had no laws requiring the reporting of campaign income and expenditures. When a PANista government took power in the state of Baja California in 1989, it found bank and legal records showing that more than $10 million in government funds had been channeled to the PRI for its 1989 gubernatorial campaign in that state. Reforms to the federal electoral code between 1993 and 1994 established minimal public reporting requirements for campaign income and expenditures, as well as Mexico's first-ever limits on individual and corporate contributions to electoral campaigns.

In the 1993–1994 electoral code reforms, ceilings on private contributions were set very high—the equivalent of $650,000 for an individual contribution. With its privileged access to financing from big business, the PRI continued to outspend its opponents by a huge margin, even without cash from government sources. In 1994, the PRI legally spent $44 million on its presidential campaign. It had even more money to spend on its campaigns, at all levels, than ever before, despite the contribution limits included in the electoral code reforms. In the same year, Roberto Madrazo, the PRI candidate for governor in the state of Tabasco (and 2006 presidential candidate), spent in excess of $50 million on his campaign—many times the limit for a gubernatorial race.

Yet another round of electoral reforms, passed by Congress in 1996, limited total private contributions to any party to 10 percent of the total amount of regular public financing to all parties, and no individual can contribute more than 0.05 percent of the total regular public financing. Also, the reforms greatly increased public funding for all parties. (In the 2006 presidential campaign, the three main candidates received and spent more than $200 million in public funds.) The law also added a new prohibition on "the use of public resources and programs to benefit any political party or electoral campaign."

Campaign finance abuses did not disappear, however. After the 2000 presidential election, the federal internal auditor discovered that the government-owned oil company, PEMEX, had made a $140 million loan to the oil-workers' union, one of the two most important PRI-affiliated labor unions. These funds were subsequently donated to the campaign of PRI candidate Francisco Labastida.

As the party in power, the PRI profited from a vast network of government patronage through which small-scale material benefits could be delivered to large segments of the population. The president himself controlled a large slush fund ("*la partida secreta*"), authorized each year by Congress as part of the federal government budget, that could aid PRI officials and finance the party's campaigns as needed. By the late 1990s, in the context of an increasingly competitive electoral system, such "incumbency advantages" were being intensely criticized by the opposition parties and the media. Responding to this pressure, Ernesto Zedillo virtually eliminated the presidential "secret budget."

Historically, the official party's most potent advantage over the competition was its ability to commit electoral fraud with relative impunity. A wide variety of techniques were used: stuffing the ballot boxes; disqualifying opposition party poll watchers; relocating polling places at the last minute to sites known only to PRI supporters; manipulating voter registration lists, padding them with nonexistent or nonresident PRIistas, and/or *rasurando* (shaving off) those who are expected to vote for opposition parties; issuing multiple voting credentials to PRI supporters; buying, "renting," or confiscating opposition voters' credentials, often in return for material benefits; organizing *carruseles* (flying brigades) of PRI supporters transported by truck or van to vote at several different polling places; and so forth.

Moreover, until 1996, the PRI held majority representation in all of the state and federal government entities that controlled vote counting and certification. The PRI could count on these bodies to manipulate the tallies to favor its candidates or, in cases where the opposition vote got out of control, nullify the unfavorable election outcomes. Adding votes to the PRI column, rather than taking them away from opposition parties, was the most common form of electoral fraud. In some predominantly rural districts, this practice led to election results in which the number of votes credited to the PRI candidate exceeded the total number of registered voters, or even the total number of adults estimated from the most recent population census.

In a successful effort to build up domestic and international credibility for the 1994 national elections, the Salinas government introduced a number of important safeguards against fraud. New, high-tech, photo-identification voter credentials were issued to the entire electorate. The Federal Electoral Institute (IFE) was greatly strengthened and given greater autonomy. The PRI and its government representatives were denied a majority on the IFE's decisionmaking board. A new system of independent electoral tribunals was established to adjudicate election disputes, and a special prosecutor's office was established to investigate alleged violations of the electoral laws. The law defined a broad range of electoral offenses—not previously subject to prosecution—as electoral crimes (though the special

prosecutor was appointed by the president and reported to the federal attorney general, who was unlikely to bring charges against important PRI leaders or government officials). The role of independent, Mexican citizen observers in monitoring the casting and tallying of votes was formally recognized, and the presence of foreign electoral observers (euphemistically termed "international visitors") was legalized. Exit polls of voters and "quick counts" of the actual vote in sample precincts by the IFE as well as private organizations were authorized and publicly announced on election night.

Taken together, these innovations, which cost the Mexican taxpayers more than $1 billion, represented a major advance toward improving the security, professionalism, and fairness of the Mexican electoral system. However, various types of irregularities—especially violations of ballot secrecy and efforts by local bosses to induce voters to support the PRI—were still widespread in the more isolated, rural areas. Subsequent state and local elections in various parts of the country have demonstrated that subnational PRI leaders continue to use direct threats and other forms of intimidation, particularly against peasant voters.

The 1996 electoral reform greatly increased the institutional autonomy of the IFE. The Interior Minister was removed as president of the IFE and replaced by a nonpartisan president and eight nonpartisan commissioners. These electoral commissioners are elected for a nine-year term by a two-thirds vote of the Chamber of Deputies. Since no party can control more than 60 percent of the seats in the lower chamber, the IFE commissioners are elected by consensus of all of the parties. In the national elections from 1997 through 2006 there was very little evidence of systematic fraud. Since the IFE controls most of the process in a nonpartisan manner (for example, all poll workers are chosen at random from voter registration lists, as jurors are selected in the United States), the remaining sources of electoral fraud are vote-buying (still common in some states, especially in the Southeast) and the buying or renting of voter credentials. Both practices are illegal, but neither is easy for federal electoral authorities to police.

The share of the vote claimed by the PRI had been declining for three decades, but until recently the erosion was gradual and did not threaten the party's grasp on the presidency and state governorships (see Figure 14.6). In the 1980s and 1990s, however, Mexican elections became much more competitive. The proportion of electoral districts dominated to varying degrees by the PRI dropped dramatically, from 70 percent in 1979

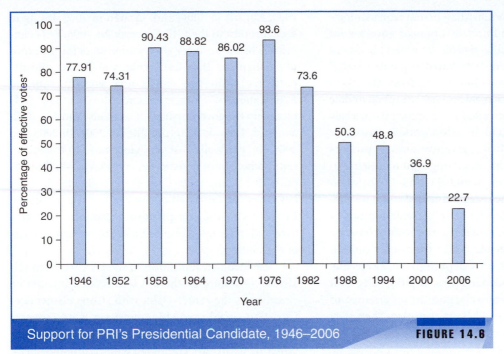

Support for PRI's Presidential Candidate, 1946–2006    **FIGURE 14.6**

*Percentage base includes annulled votes and those cast for independent candidates.

Note: The 1976 PRI candidate, José López Portillo, ran virtually unopposed because the PAN failed to nominate a candidate. The only other significant candidate was Valentín Campa, representing the Communist Party, which was not legally registered to participate in the 1976 election. More than 5 percent of the votes were annulled.

Source: Data from Comisión Federal Electoral, 1946–1988; and Instituto Federal Electoral, 1994–2006.

The PRI is significantly weaker in cities with 100,000 or more inhabitants, where more than half of the Mexican population now lives. Mexico City has been a particular disaster area for the PRI in recent elections. The PRI lost the mayoral races in Mexico City by large margins in 1997, 2000, and 2006. Including elections for mayor, congressional seats, ward presidents, and local assembly seats, the PRI has won only one out of 330 majority races in the last four electoral cycles in Mexico City. Even in rural areas, however, the PRI's formerly safe vote continues to erode. While the PRI still gets a higher share of the vote in rural areas than any other party, the average vote for PRI candidates in rural precincts fell markedly from 1982 through 2006.[27]

The PRI has had to adjust from being an official party—a political machine based on incumbency advantages—to being a party out of power. PRI legislators for the first time have had to figure out how to vote without presidential leadership. The whole party has had to define its ideology as a political party, not as an instrument of power. During the Fox *sexenio*, the main issues that distinguished the PRI from the government were taxes (the PRI wanted less), spending (the PRI wanted more), and reform of the government-owned electrical energy industry.

### The Partido Acción Nacional

The Partido Acción Nacional (PAN) was established in 1939, largely in reaction to the leftward drift of public policy under President Lázaro Cárdenas, particularly his policies in support of socialist public education. Its founders included prominent Catholic intellectuals

to 1 percent in 2000. The "Soviet-style" precincts that regularly delivered 98 to 100 percent of their votes to PRI candidates have disappeared.

In the four elections prior to 2006, the PRI did best among older voters, the less educated, and low-income people. It has also held the loyalty of a plurality of union members. However, the corporatist vote in general is no longer a dependable source of support for the PRI, and the low mobilization of these voters was one of the major reasons for its defeat in the 2000 elections.

Another key factor accounting for the long-term decline in the PRI's effectiveness as a vote-getting machine is the massive shift of population from rural to urban areas that has occurred in Mexico since 1950. In that year, 57 percent of the population lived in isolated rural communities of fewer than 2,500 inhabitants. By 1990 less than 29 percent lived in such localities. This massive rural-to-urban migration is reflected in occupational statistics: In urban Mexico, authoritarian control mechanisms are less efficacious. Education and income levels are higher, and the middle classes—which provide a considerable share of the opposition vote—are larger. A smaller proportion of the population is subject to pressures from local-level bosses.

who espoused an early Christian democratic ideology, and the party has traditionally opposed government restrictions on church activities. The party attacked political centralism and advocated expanded states' rights long before it was fashionable to do so. The PAN's principal constituency has always been the urban middle class, but is has also attracted votes among the socially conservative peasants and the urban working class.

Between 1964, when a primitive form of proportional representation increased opposition presence in the Chamber of Deputies, and the mid-1990s, when the PAN was governing many municipal and state governments, the focus of PANista representation was in the federal Congress, especially the lower chamber (the first PANista was elected to the Senate only in 1991). In these years, PAN deputies would typically begin their congressional terms fighting electoral fraud from the previous election, in an attempt to increase the number of PANista deputies. Then they would settle in and begin to propose legislation. Until the Salinas years, these bills would almost always be ignored in the chamber at the time of introduction; but eventually most of the PAN's legislative proposals were adopted by the federal executive and reintroduced and approved by Congress.

Among the PANista ideas later embraced by PRI governments were increased proportional representation in both chambers of Congress, autonomous electoral courts and electoral agencies, the permanent voting credential, increased municipal autonomy, increased autonomy and authority for the Supreme Court, increased self-governance for the Federal District (Mexico City), federal revenue-sharing with the states, liberalization of the social security systems, a national consumer protection agency, and profit-sharing with employees.

The PAN's regional strongholds include the North, the Center-West, and some of the large municipalities of the states of México and Veracruz. Between 1989 and 2001, the PAN won gubernatorial elections in nine states (Baja California, Chihuahua, Guanajuato, Jalisco, Nuevo León, Querétaro, Aguascalientes, Morelos, and Yucatán), and it managed to create a de facto two-party system with the PRI in most of these states.

In 1995, the PAN retained control of the governorship of Baja California, thereby accomplishing something that no opposition party had previously done: the transfer of power from one elected opposition governor to another. The PAN failed to retain the governorship of Chihuahua in 1998, Nuevo León in

2003, Nayarit in 2004, and Yucatán in 2007, losing in each instance to the PRI. However, by 2006, PAN candidates had won three consecutive races for governor in Guanajuato, Baja California, and Jalisco, and the party had won two consecutive governorships in Aguascalientes, Querétaro, and Morelos. The PAN picked up the governorships of San Luis Potosí in 2003, and took Tlaxcala from the PRD in 2004. In 2003 and 2004, the party also lost very close races to the PRI in Campeche, Sonora, Veracruz, and Oaxaca—all previously PRI strongholds. Over the last decade, the PAN has governed nearly all of the twenty largest cities in Mexico, with the conspicuous exception of Mexico City, and it has also governed most of the capital cities of the country.

The ideological position of the PAN has been relatively constant over the last six decades. It could be classified as the center-right, with strong elements of Christian socialism (which covers a wide range of policies, from center-left on labor issues to right-of-center on abortion), combined with traditional liberal attitudes on trade, municipal decentralization, and general democratization. The party is affiliated with international Christian Democratic organizations. The PAN's relative position on the ideological spectrum has depended mostly on the positioning of the PRI, whose pendulum has shifted to positions clearly to the left of the PAN (as in the 1970s) or to the right of the PAN (as was the case from 1988 to 2000).

Statistical analysis of roll-call votes in the 57th Legislature (1997–2000) placed the PAN at the center of the political spectrum, to the left of the PRI. Although roll calls are not available for earlier years, congressional debates suggest that the PAN held a similar position for most of the Salinas and Zedillo years. Despite the nationalist and populist background of their party, PRI deputies found themselves voting to the right of the PAN because they had to support the neoliberal economic policies and austerity measures of PRI presidents. However, since 2001, under a PANista president, PAN members generally vote to the right of the PRI. Now it is the PAN deputies who must support the austerity programs of their president, while PRI deputies are liberated to vote their conscience and constituencies rather than take cues from the president.

The PAN has worked long and hard to develop a strong network of grassroots militants. While clearly the leader today among Mexico's parties in terms of organizational strength, the PAN is a party with several major weaknesses. Since the mid-1970s it has been divided into moderate-progressive and militant-conservative ("neo-PANista") factions, which have jockeyed for control of the party machinery and carried out purges of opposing faction members when they were in power.

Vicente Fox's ideology was closer to the moderate-progressives than to the neo-PANistas. This helped the PAN gain control of the presidency in 2000, by attracting an ideologically diverse group of voters, united mainly by their desire to remove the PRI from power.[28] In recent years, the PAN has continued its evolution toward a catch-all party, while still embracing with greater enthusiasm than its rivals the free-market, pro-foreign investment policies favored by the country's business community.[29]

## The Partido de la Revolución Democrática

Before 1988, the Mexican left had spawned political parties like the Partido Popular Socialista (PPS), which for decades served as a home for socialists and other left-of-center politicians willing to collaborate with the government and even to endorse the PRI's presidential candidates, in exchange for a seat in Congress. The more independent left—that is, those who did not cooperate openly with the ruling party—was traditionally represented by the Partido Comunista Mexicano (PCM). The Communists were allowed to compete legally in elections during the presidency of Lázaro Cárdenas, but their party was subsequently outlawed and did not regain legal representation until 1979, when its congressional candidates won 5 percent of the vote.

During most of the 1980s, even in the face of Mexico's gravest economic crisis since the 1910 Revolution, and despite a series of party mergers intended to reduce the fractionalization of the leftist vote, the parties on the left lost ground electorally. They were hampered by constant internal squabbling (motivated mostly by personalistic rivalries, and to a lesser extent to ideological cleavages), an inability to do effective grassroots organizing, and an identification with discredited, statist economic policies.

The key to the left's rejuvenation in 1988 was a split within the PRI leadership—the most serious since the early 1950s. In August 1986 a number of nationally prominent PRI figures, all members of the party's center-left wing, formed a dissident movement within the PRI known as the Corriente Democrática (CD). They were led by Porfirio Muñoz Ledo (former

head of the PRI, runner-up candidate for the party's presidential nomination in 1976, former secretary of labor and secretary of education) and Cuauhtémoc Cárdenas, who was just finishing his term as governor of the state of Michoacán. The CD criticized the de la Madrid administration's economic restructuring program and sought a renewed commitment by the PRI to traditional principles of economic nationalism and social justice. Most urgently, CD adherents called for a top-to-bottom democratization of the PRI, beginning with the elimination of the *dedazo* (the unilateral selection by the outgoing president) as the mechanism for determining the party's presidential candidate. The CD's proposals were widely interpreted as a last-ditch attempt by the PRI's traditional politicos to recover leadership of the party by influencing the outcome of the 1987–1988 presidential succession. The CD's demands for reform were resoundingly rejected by the PRI hierarchy, and its leaders formally split from the party in October 1987.

Confronted with the defeat within the PRI, Cárdenas accepted the presidential nomination of the Partido Auténtico de la Revolución Mexicana (PARM), a conservative, nationalist party established by another group of dissident PRIistas in 1954. Later, four other parties—all on the left and including the remnants of the old Mexican Communist Party—joined the PARM to form a coalition, the Frente Democrático Nacional (FDN), to contest the 1988 presidential election, with Cárdenas as their candidate. Soon after the 1988 elections, however, the left's long-standing ideological and personalistic cleavages reasserted themselves, and by 1991, when midterm elections were held, most of Cárdenas's 1988 coalition partners had gone their separate ways, leaving the newly constituted PRD as the principal standard-bearer of the left. Even within the PRD, serious disagreements emerged over such issues as the degree of democracy in internal party governance and strategies for dealing with the government (dialogue and collaboration on certain issues versus permanent confrontation).

The left's problems in the early 1990s were not all self-inflicted. Under Salinas, the government showed no inclination to negotiate seriously with the Cardenista left. Salinas showed much greater willingness to recognize electoral victories of the PAN than those claimed by the PRD. And when the PRD's victories (all at the municipal level) were recognized, the city governments under its control were punished and starved for resources by PRI state governors. Conflicts between PRD militants and local PRI *caciques* were bitter, with hundreds of PRD activists murdered during the first five years of the party's existence.

President Zedillo opened a new chapter in PRD-government relations, recognizing Cuauhtémoc Cárdenas's overwhelming victory in the 1997 mayoral race in Mexico City. In 1998–1999, the PRD won gubernatorial elections in the states of Zacatecas, Tlaxcala, and Baja California Sur. In 2000, it picked up the state of Chiapas, and again won the Mexico City mayoralty. In 2001, the PRD finally won Cárdenas's home state of Michoacán, after nominating his son, Lázaro, for governor. In all of these early victories, except for Mexico City and Michoacán, the PRD candidates were defectors from the PRI who had been passed over for the party's gubernatorial nomination.

These outcomes illustrate a key advantage for the PRD in Mexico's current three-party competition: in places where the PRI organization is fractured by internal rivalries, where the local factions are unable to reach consensus on a candidate, the PRD is usually the main beneficiary. For PRIistas whose political aspirations are thwarted by their own party, the PRD—the party run by ex-PRIistas—is a natural new home.

Since 2003, the PRD lost the governorship of Tlaxcala to the PAN but picked up the state of Guerrero (where Acapulco is located); retained the governorships of Baja California Sur, Michoacán, and Zacatecas; and won the Federal District (the Mexico City mayoralty) for the third consecutive time.

Until 2000, the PRD continued to take policy positions to the left of the ruling party on some issues (for example, arguing against the use of any taxpayer money to bail out bankers who made bad loans during the Salinas *sexenio*). Its differences with most recent government policies were matters of degree, pacing, and how much was being done to ameliorate the social costs of these policies, rather than their basic direction. During the 57th Legislature (1997–2000), when for the first time the PRI lost majority control of the lower chamber, the PRD tended to vote with the PAN and against the PRI on issues of political reform and to enhance the oversight of the legislative branch over the federal executive. On most economic issues, the PAN and the PRI voted together, with the PRD often voting against.

In the 58th Legislature (2000–2003), the PRD took a more radical stance on policy issues and was more intransigent in its relations with the other parties. In part this is due to the diminished presence of the party in the Congress—about 60 percent smaller than the PRD delegation in the 1997–2000 period. It introduced bills that, taken together, amounted to a sweeping restructuring of the Mexican political system, designed to weaken the federal executive. One bill would have introduced a parliamentary system with an elected president, akin to the presidential-premier system in France. In the 59th Legislature (2003–2006), the much larger PRD delegation increased its opposition to the federal government's economic policies. Once the party realized that it could win the presidency in 2006, it backed off pressing its bills to weaken the executive branch and to foment a parliamentary system.

In its early years, the PRD did a poor job of mobilizing previously uncommitted voters. It had retained many of the urban working-class voters who traditionally supported the parties of the independent left, but it was not very successful in establishing ties with the popular movements that had developed outside of the PRI-affiliated corporatist structures. However, its ties to the rural areas were underdeveloped, and the PRD had been dominated by Mexico City-based politicians and intellectuals for whom the provinces hardly existed. Central party leaders often shortchanged local organizers in their allocation of party funds. This trend was reversed in the 2006 election, when the PRD under López Obrador proved much more effective at mobilizing rural voters.

## The Shifting Social Bases of Mexico's Parties

The social bases of political support for the parties shifted dramatically in the 2006 election (see Table 14.5). Before 2006, the PRI's most dependable base was the rural voter. It also did relatively well with women and older voters. In 2006, the PRD's López Obrador did best among rural voters, and Madrazo of the PRI finished third among such voters, even behind Calderón (PAN). As in 2000, the PAN did best among urban voters, but the PRD finished ahead of the PRI for the urban vote in 2006.

There was a sizable gender gap in the 2000 election, with the PAN doing particularly well among male voters and the PRI relatively better among women. In 2006, the PRD took the male vote by a small margin, but Calderón did much better among women. In both cases, women tended to support the candidate who appeared to pose less of a threat to economic stability.

| TABLE 14.5 | | | |
|:---|:---|:---|:---|
| **Party Choice in 2006 Presidential Election, by Demographic Attribute (percentages)** | | | |
| | **PAN** | **PRI** | **PRD** | **Others** |
|:---|:---:|:---:|:---:|:---:|
| **Type of Locality** | | | | |
| Urban | 40 | 20 | 35 | 5 |
| Rural | 31 | 28 | 36 | 3 |
| **Region** | | | | |
| North | 43 | 27 | 24 | 6 |
| Center-West | 46 | 20 | 27 | 4 |
| Center | 34 | 15 | 44 | 7 |
| South | 27 | 29 | 40 | 4 |
| **Gender** | | | | |
| Male | 36 | 22 | 37 | 2 |
| Female | 38 | 23 | 32 | 4 |
| **Age** | | | | |
| 18–29 | 38 | 21 | 34 | 6 |
| 30–49 | 38 | 21 | 35 | 4 |
| 50 | 34 | 26 | 37 | 2 |
| **Education** | | | | |
| None and Primary | 34 | 29 | 33 | 3 |
| Secondary | 37 | 21 | 35 | 5 |
| University | 42 | 14 | 38 | 5 |
| **Annual Income (dollars)** | | | | |
| Under $2,161 | 31 | 30 | 34 | 4 |
| $2,162–$4,321 | 32 | 24 | 39 | 4 |
| $4,322–$7,021 | 36 | 21 | 37 | 5 |
| $7,022–$9,938 | 43 | 16 | 36 | 4 |
| Above $9,939 | 50 | 14 | 30 | 5 |

Source: Nationwide exit poll conducted by *Reforma* newspaper (Mexico City), 3 July 2006.

In 2000, the PAN did best among voters below age 50, while the PRI was preferred by older voters. This was probably because this segment of the electorate remembered the social benefits and economic growth achieved in the better years of PRI rule. In 2006, the PAN again carried younger voters, but now voters over age 50 chose the PRD, possibly because, as mayor of Mexico City, López Obrador had introduced a pension plan for senior citizens.

In 2000, the PRI did better among voters with lower education, taking the vote among those with less than a secondary education. The PAN did best, by a large margin, among voters with higher levels of education. In 2006, education mattered less in determining the vote. Calderón attracted the most votes at all levels of education, and López Obrador placed second. López Obrador did relatively well among higher educated voters because of the strong support that he received from public university students.

In 2006, the PRD did best among the poor and the lower middle class. Both López Obrador and Madrazo promised reforms that would increase the spending power of voters with incomes below about U.S. $10,000 per year (the PRD through subsidies, and the PRI through income tax cuts). The PAN did much better among higher income voters, who were attracted by its pro-business platform and frightened by the populism of López Obrador.

In general, however, social class was not nearly as important to voters' choices in 2006 as was the region in which they live. The PRD was weak in most of the northern and central states but had strong support in the Mexico City metropolitan area and the South, while the PAN's support was concentrated in the North and center of the country. In 2006, region was as powerful a predictor of party preference as all other demographic variables combined (age, gender, income, education, skin color, urban vs. rural residence). Thus, the dominant cleavage in Mexico's electorate today is not social class but region—especially the North-South split.[30]

## GOVERNMENT PERFORMANCE

### Promoting Economic Growth and Reducing Poverty

There is little debate about the importance of the state's contribution to the economic development of Mexico since 1940. Massive public investments in infrastructure (roads, dams, telecommunications, electrification) and generous, cheap credit provided to the private sector by Nacional Financiera and other government development banks made possible a higher rate of capital accumulation, stimulated higher levels of investment by domestic entrepreneurs and foreign corporations, and enabled Mexico to develop a diversified production capacity second only within Latin America to that of Brazil.

From 1940 until well into the 1970s, a strong elite consensus prevailed on the state's role in the economy. The state facilitated private capital accumulation and protected the capitalist system by limiting popular demands for consumption and redistribution of wealth; it established the rules for development; and it participated in the development process as the nation's largest single entrepreneur, employer, and source of investment capital. The state served as the "rector" (guiding force) of this mixed economy, setting broad priorities and channeling investment (both public and private) into strategic sectors. Acting through joint ventures between private firms and state-owned enterprises, the government provided resources for development projects so large that they would have been difficult or impossible to finance from internal (within-the-firm) sources or through borrowing from private banks.

The result, from the mid-1950s to the mid-1970s, was the much-touted "Mexican miracle" of sustained economic growth at annual rates of 6 to 7 percent, coupled with low inflation (5 percent per annum

between 1955 and 1972). By 1980, the gross national product had reached $2,130 per capita, placing Mexico toward the upper end of the World Bank's list of semi-industrialized or "middle-developed" countries. As sole proprietor of PEMEX, the state oil monopoly, the government was responsible for developing the crucial oil and natural gas sector of the economy. By the end of the oil boom (1978–1981), oil was generating more than $15 billion a year in export revenues and fueling economic growth of more than 8 percent per year—one of the world's highest growth rates.

It is the distributive consequences of this impressive performance in economic development and the manner in which it was financed by the PRI governments of the 1970s and 1980s that have been harshly criticized in retrospect. From Miguel Alemán (1946–1952) to the present, all but one or two of Mexico's presidents and their administrations reflected the private sector's contention that Mexico must first create wealth and then worry about redistributing it—the belief being that the state would quickly be overwhelmed by popular demands that it could not satisfy. By the early 1970s, however, there was convincing evidence that an excessively large portion of Mexico's population was being left behind in the drive to become a modern, industrialized nation.

This is not to say that some benefits of the development process did not trickle down to the poor. From 1950 to 1980, poverty in absolute terms declined. The middle class expanded to an estimated 29 percent of the population by 1970. From 1960 to 1980, illiteracy dropped from 35 to 15 percent of the population, infant mortality was reduced from 78 to 70 per 1,000 live births, and average life expectancy rose from 55 to 64 years. Clearly, the quality of life for many Mexicans—even in isolated rural areas—did improve during this period, although several other Latin American countries (Chile, Colombia, Costa Rica, Cuba, Ecuador, El Salvador, and Venezuela) achieved higher rates of improvement on indicators of social well-being than did Mexico during the same period.

There was, however, a dark side to Mexico's economic miracle. From 1950 to the mid-1970s, ownership of land and capital (stocks, bonds, time deposits) became increasingly concentrated. Personal income inequality also increased, at a time when, given Mexico's middle level of development, the national income distribution should have been shifting toward greater equality, according to classical economic development theory. Indeed, Mexico apparently had a higher overall concentration of income in the mid-1970s than in 1910, before the outbreak of the revolution. By 1977, the poorest 70 percent of Mexican families received only 24 percent of all disposable income, while the richest 30 percent of families received 76 percent of income. With only brief interruptions, the trend toward greater income inequality continued in the 1980s and 1990s.

Other social indicators mirrored the pattern of personal income distribution. By 1989, more than one-quarter of Mexican children under age 5 in rural areas were malnourished; the incidence of severe malnutrition among such children had risen by 100 percent during the preceding ten years. While 78 percent of Mexico's elementary school-age children were enrolled in 1990, only 54 percent of those starting primary school finished it. Among the dwellings included in the 1990 census, 57 percent had no sewerage connections, 50 percent had no piped water inside the dwelling, and 13 percent had no electricity.

By every indicator of economic opportunity and social well-being, there are vast disparities among Mexico's regions and between rural and urban areas. Unemployment and underemployment are concentrated overwhelmingly in the rural sector, which contains at least 70 percent of the population classified as living in extreme poverty. The rate of infant mortality in rural areas is nearly 50 percent higher than the national average. Interregional disparities in social well-being are equally extreme. In 2000, the percentage of persons with incomes lower than two minimum salaries (a bare subsistence level) ranged from 22 percent in Baja California to 76 percent in Chiapas. A composite index of social well-being in 2000 shows the Federal District (Mexico City) and the northern border states as being the most privileged, and the southern states (especially Chiapas, Oaxaca, and Guerrero) as the most marginalized (see Figure 14.7). This pattern of extreme spatial inequalities has remained essentially unchanged for several decades.

The policies and investment preferences of Mexico's postrevolutionary governments contributed much to the country's highly inegalitarian development. At minimum, the public policies pursued since 1940 failed to counteract the wealth-concentrating effects of private market forces. Evidence is strong that some government investments and policies actually reinforced these effects. For example, during most of

the post-1940 period, government tax and credit policies worked primarily to the advantage of the country's wealthiest agribusiness and industrial entrepreneurs. Government expenditures for social security, public health, and education remained relatively low by international standards. By the late 1970s, Mexico was still allocating a smaller share of its central government budget to social services than some countries, such as Bolivia, Brazil, Chile, and Panama. The slowness with which basic social services were extended to the bulk of the population in Mexico was a direct consequence of the government's policy of keeping inflation low by concentrating public expenditures on subsidies and infrastructure for private industry, rather than on social programs and subsidies to consumers.

Even during the period between 1970 and 1982, when populist policies were allegedly in vogue and government revenues were expanding rapidly because of the oil export boom, public spending for programs like health and social security remained roughly constant, in real per capita terms. The economic crisis that erupted in 1982, after an unprecedented run-up in Mexico's domestic and externally held debt, made it impossible to maintain even that level of government commitment to social well-being. By 1986, debt service was consuming over half of the total federal government budget, necessitating deep cuts in spending for health, education, consumer subsidies, and job-creating public investments. Social welfare expenditures per capita fell to 1974 levels.

Mexico's macroeconomic adjustment program was considerably more severe than those in other major Latin American countries that also experienced debt crises during the 1980s. The severity of the adjustment is reflected particularly in minimum real wages, which fell by two-thirds between 1980 and 1989. Despite a modest resurgence of economic growth in the early 1990s, by the end of the Salinas *sexenio* real wages for most Mexicans had still not recovered their levels of 1981. The economic crisis of the mid-1990s caused most Mexicans to lose whatever ground they had gained during the Salinas years. By 2002, half of Mexico's population was living at or below the World Bank's official poverty level, and one-fifth were living in extreme poverty.

Under Mexico's four most recent presidents, the government has implemented a **neoliberal economic development model** stressing the need to give much freer rein to market forces. The primary objective of this

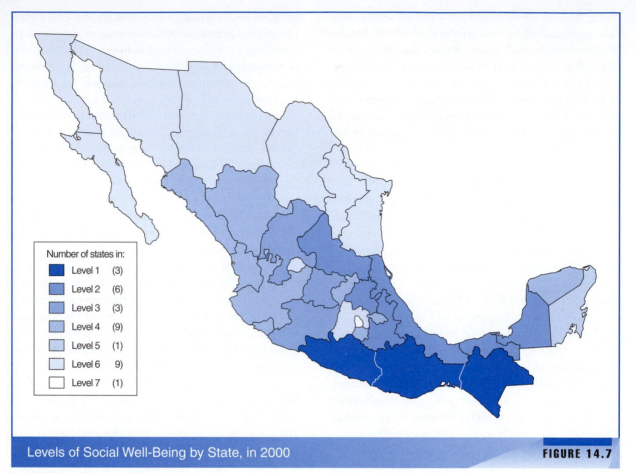

**Levels of Social Well-Being by State, in 2000**

**FIGURE 14.7**

Number of states in:

- Level 1  (3)
- Level 2  (6)
- Level 3  (3)
- Level 4  (9)
- Level 5  (1)
- Level 6  9
- Level 7  (1)

Level 1: Chiapas, Guerrero, Oaxaca
Level 2: Campeche, Hidalgo, Puebla, San Luis Potosí, Tabasco, Veracruz
Level 3: Guanajuato, Michoacán, Zacatecas
Level 4: Colima, Durango, Jalisco, Morelos, Nayarit, Querétaro, Sinaloa, Tlaxcala, Yucatán
Level 5: Quintana Roo
Level 6: Aguascalientes, Baja California, Baja California Sur, Coahuila, Chihuahua, México, Nuevo León, Sonora, Tamaulipas
Level 7: Distrito Federal

Note: Level of social well-being is measured by characteristics of dwellings (have electricity, refrigerator, television, concrete vs. dirt floors, sewerage connection, private bathroom; number of rooms; use something other than firewood or coal for cooking) and population characteristics (percentage economically active; literate; 6–19-year-olds who attend school; receive health care; live in urban area; average number of children born to women over age 12).

Source: Instituto Nacional de Estadística, Geografía e Informática, www.inegi.gob.mx.

"technocratic free-market revolution" has been to attract more private investment (especially foreign capital) and thereby push up Mexico's rate of economic growth. While drastically shrinking the public sector of the economy through a sweeping privatization program and opening up nearly all sectors of the economy to private investment (including those formerly reserved to the state), the technocrats were unwilling to completely surrender the government's traditional "rectorship" role in the economy. "The new [government] elite did not

believe that the market, left to its own devices, would resolve all problems through invisible hands."[31]

This concern is reflected in the considerable spending by the last three administrations on social welfare initiatives, like Salinas's National Solidarity Program, Zedillo's PROGRESA program, and Fox's Oportunidades program—all efforts to construct a minimal safety net for the millions of low-income Mexicans who were the short-term "losers" from neoliberal economic policies and trade liberalization under the

North American Free Trade Agreement (NAFTA). But these carefully targeted social programs were not sufficient to offset the structural impoverishment caused by falling real wages, the elimination of millions of jobs, and the slashing of most consumer subsidies.

During the Fox administration, the government implemented a new health care program known as the **Seguro Popular** (Popular Health Insurance), designed to provide health services to people who were not covered by the Social Security Institute's health programs. Social Security in Mexico provides health coverage for salaried persons, but the unemployed, the self-employed, and many rural workers are excluded from the system. The Seguro Popular program requires beneficiaries to enroll in the program and pay relatively affordable premiums. The poorest Mexicans (the bottom 20 percent) do not have to pay premiums. The goal of the Seguro Popular is to achieve universal health insurance coverage by 2010.

It is clear that the market-oriented development model of the past two decades has exacerbated—not alleviated—Mexico's poverty and inequality problems, even when the model was apparently working well in macroeconomic terms (that is, from 1989 through 1992).[32] Moreover, Mexico's experience with rapid economic growth during the "miracle" years of the 1950s and 1960s and the oil boom of the late 1970s and early 1980s suggests that without strong, sustained government action to correct for market failures and improve human capital endowments through education and job training, income concentration and related social problems will continue unabated.

Net job creation in Mexico under neoliberal economic policies since the late 1980s has been anemic, despite a huge influx of foreign capital. This dismal performance can be explained in part by the fact that well over half of the foreign funds received by Mexico during this period were invested in stocks, short-term government-issued bonds, and other financial instruments, rather than in job-creating, direct investment projects. Equally important, the government's strategy of promoting export-led development has induced many private firms to become more competitive in the global marketplace by shedding labor and becoming more capital-intensive.

Thus it has yet to be proved that economic liberalization and free trade can yield significantly higher rates of job creation, especially jobs that pay enough to lift Mexican families above the poverty line. There is a growing consensus that the government will have to do much more to upgrade workers' skills through vocational education and subsidized, on-the-job training if Mexico is to realize a greater return from its painful shift to an open, market-oriented development strategy. A fundamental reform of the country's public education system will be necessary to achieve a better distribution of the gains from NAFTA.

## Financing Development and Controlling Inflation

From 1940 to 1970, Mexico's public sector acquired an international reputation for sound, conservative monetary and fiscal policies. This conservative style of economic management, coupled with Mexico's long record of political stability, gave the country an attractive investment climate. By 1982, this image had been shattered; the public sector (and much of the private sector) was suffering from a deep liquidity crisis, and inflation had reached levels unheard of since the first decade of the Mexican Revolution, when paper currencies lost most of their value. What happened?

The basic difficulty was that the government had attempted to spend its way out of the social and economic problems that had accumulated since 1940, without paying the political cost that sweeping redistributive policies would have entailed. Instead, it attempted to expand the entire economic pie by enlarging the state's role as banker, entrepreneur, and employer. Since 1940, and especially after 1970, Mexico's public sector expanded steadily while its revenue-raising capability lagged. The result was ever-larger government deficits, financed increasingly by borrowing abroad.

For most of the post–World War II period, Mexico's tax effort—its rate of taxation and its actual performance in collecting taxes—was among the lowest in the world. Officials feared that any major alteration in the tax structure would drive domestic and foreign capital out of the country. Two modest attempts at tax reform, in 1964 and 1972, failed because of determined opposition from the business community. When the private sector refused to accede to higher taxes, the Echeverría administration opted for large-scale deficit financing, external indebtedness, and a huge increase in the money supply. The public sector itself was vastly enlarged, increasing the number of state-owned enterprises from eighty-four in 1970 to 845 in 1976. Fiscal restraint was finally forced on the government by depletion of its currency reserves in 1976.

Echeverría's successor, José López Portillo, at first attempted to reverse the trend toward larger government deficits, but the effort was abandoned when the treasury began to swell with oil export revenues. Again, the temptation was to address basic structural problems by further expanding the state sector, and López Portillo found it impossible to resist. Oil revenues seemed to be a guaranteed, limitless source of income for the government. Mexico borrowed heavily from abroad, anticipating a steady rise in oil prices. When world oil prices declined in 1981 and 1982, the government was forced to suspend repayment of the foreign debt and negotiate a long-term reduction in interest rates—the first of several debt "restructurings," the most recent of which was completed in 1990.

Deficit financing, especially in the context of the overheated economy of the oil boom years, also touched off a burst of inflation. The average annual inflation rate rose from 15 percent during Echeverría's presidency (nearly triple the average rate between 1940 and 1970), to 36 percent under López Portillo and 91 percent during the de la Madrid *sexenio* (159 percent in 1987; see Figure 14.8). Both the de la Madrid and Salinas

administrations made reducing the inflation rate their top economic priority, but Salinas was much more effective in bringing inflation under control than his predecessor. His principal instrument was price and wage controls, enforced by a formal, trilateral government-business–organized labor "pact" that was renewed six times, with some adjustments, at twelve- to eighteen-month intervals. This form of shock therapy brought the inflation rate down to single digits by 1994.

The other key to Salinas's success in fighting inflation was deep cuts in spending to reduce and eventually eliminate the public deficit, coupled with unprecedented steps to boost federal government revenues. These measures included the sale or closure of hundreds of state-owned enterprises, vigorous enforcement of the tax laws (only two individual tax evaders had been caught and imprisoned between 1921 and 1988), and the introduction of a 2 percent annual tax on total business assets, intended to reduce manipulations that had previously enabled 70 percent of Mexico's businesses to evade paying any taxes.

Even after the Salinas administration's "successful" tax reform, however, the federal government still obtained most of its revenues (over 60 percent) from socially regressive indirect taxes, primarily the value-added tax levied on about 70 percent of all goods and

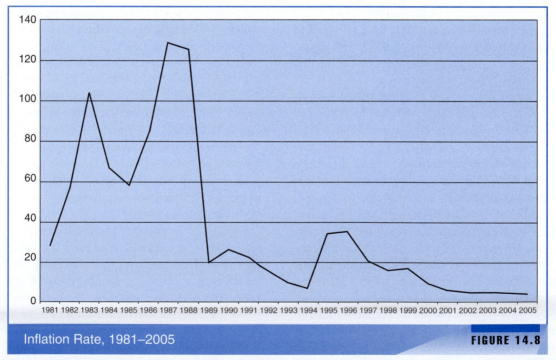

Inflation Rate, 1981–2005

**FIGURE 14.8**

Source: Instituto Nacional de Estadística, Geografía e Informática, www.inegi.gob.mx, 2006.

services. Personal income tax rates for the wealthiest Mexicans were actually reduced from 50 percent in 1988 to 35 percent in 1990, and a proposed tax on capital gains by individual investors in the stock market was shelved. "As on previous occasions, the government decided it was too risky to tax the savings of the richest Mexicans. The threat of capital flight . . . remained a powerful constraint on the government's taxing powers."[33]

The deep financial crisis that erupted in the first month of Ernesto Zedillo's presidency raised serious questions about the wisdom of the Salinas administration's obsessive pursuit of one-digit inflation, as well as its decision to "live with" a seriously overvalued peso until after the August 1994 national elections—indeed, until after President Salinas had left office. An earlier, staged devaluation would have boosted inflation and interest rates at a politically inopportune moment, but it could have prevented the financial panic and massive capital flight that followed the sudden, mega-devaluation of December 20, 1994. More than $10 billion in investment capital fled Mexico within a week; the peso had to be sharply devalued, eventually losing more than half of its value against the U.S. dollar; and the government came within a few days of insolvency as its foreign currency reserves were depleted.

Salinas and his financial ministers were also justly criticized for creating illusions of prosperity by financing a huge current accounts deficit (resulting mostly from a flood of consumer imports) with short-term, highly speculative capital. That "hot money"—mostly from large, U.S. institutional investors—flowed into *tesobonos,* the high-yielding, U.S. dollar-denominated bonds with maturities ranging from twenty-eight to 180 days that were issued by the Mexican Treasury in prodigious quantities beginning in 1989. By the end of 1994, Mexico's debt in *tesobonos* had grown to almost $30 billion, and with the central bank's reserves virtually depleted by its efforts to fend off six speculative attacks on the peso during 1994, there was no way to pay off these bonds as they matured. Only massive financial assistance from the United States prevented a default and a general collapse of the Mexican economy.

How could a technocratic government that had earned worldwide respect for its skillful management of the economy, even in the midst of the political shocks of 1994, have erred so grievously? Most likely, a combination of political and personal factors led to the debacle: the government's need to paper over the financial cracks that were developing in order to achieve a decisive PRI

victory in the 1994 elections; Carlos Salinas's desire to protect his image in the midst of a difficult and ultimately unsuccessful campaign to become head of the World Trade Organization after he left the presidency; and the ineptitude and inexperience of President Zedillo's newly installed economic team in dealing with skittish private investors. In any case, the Mexican government suffered a severe loss in credibility abroad, and the average Mexican has paid—and will continue to pay—a high price for the politically motivated manipulation of macroeconomic policy.

Under President Fox, macroeconomic stability was maintained through a combination of fiscal restraint and good fortune; government revenues were boosted by rising oil prices in global markets, and the U.S. market for Mexico's exports was strong after the U.S. economy recovered from the 2001–2002 recession. The absence of a major, end-of-*sexenio* economic crisis—for the first time since 1970—was a key factor in Felipe Calderón's victory in 2006. Calderón could plausibly claim that he was better equipped than his opponents to continue the economic policies that had averted such crises under Fox.

## Establishing the Rule of Law

The one area of performance in which the Mexican government has been failing most conspicuously, especially since the mid-1990s, is the administration of justice. From the poorest urban workers to middle-class professionals to the richest business tycoons, Mexicans are appalled and incensed that the government seems totally incapable of dealing effectively with street crime—armed robberies, muggings, kidnappings, rapes, and homicides. Surveys in the late 1990s found that virtually every resident of Mexico City had either been a crime victim or had a close relative or friend who had suffered the same fate in recent years.

Nationally, homicide rates rose by nearly 20 percent in the 1990s, and by far more in many of the states (for example, 230 percent in Guerrero; 211 percent in Chihuahua). Statistics on street crime (robberies, assaults, muggings) showed an even steeper increase in the mid-1990s. In Mexico City, the total number of crimes reported to police doubled from 1993 to 1997. And official crime statistics have understated the magnitude of the problem because of widespread underreporting. Three-quarters of crimes go unreported due to citizens' low expectation that the perpetrators will be caught and punished, and to fears of reprisals by either criminals or the police.[34]

The swelling public clamor to establish the rule of law in Mexico encompasses a broad range of demands: make the system of justice work more efficiently (that is, actually solve crimes, try and jail the perpetrators); reduce police corruption and brutality; ensure that people accused of crimes are treated fairly, respecting their constitutionally guaranteed rights and liberties, regardless of social class or political connections; make the system of justice equally accessible to citizens seeking redress of grievances; make elected officials accountable, legally, for their actions ("end impunity"); and increase the independence of the judiciary, especially vis-à-vis the executive branch.

President Zedillo began tackling the rule of law problem by addressing the last of these demands. In his first significant official act upon taking office in December 1994, he replaced all but two of the incumbent Supreme Court justices and reduced the size of the Supreme Court from twenty-four to eleven justices. He changed the terms of the justices from six-year periods, coinciding with the six-year presidential term, to fixed, fifteen-year terms. He also changed the requirement for confirmation of Supreme Court justices by the Senate, from a simple majority to two-thirds of the Senate. This means that the president's nominees must attract at least some votes from the opposition parties; they cannot be rubber-stamped by a PRI majority. Finally, Zedillo expanded the judicial review powers of the Supreme Court by explicitly granting the Court the ability to declare acts of Congress and other federal government actions unconstitutional.

The 1994 reforms made it possible for the opposition parties to bring various laws and government actions forward to the Supreme Court for constitutional review. For example, the cases brought in 1995 and 1996 included challenges to an increase in the federal sales tax that the Congress (then under PRI control) had approved in 1995. Demands for investigations of human rights violations, such as a massacre of unarmed peasant political activists by state police in Guerrero, also came before the Court. Another case challenged the president's use of the military to deal with the Zapatista rebellion in Chiapas, without first declaring an official state of emergency. Several of these cases were dismissed on legal technicalities. In other cases, a 6-to-5 majority of the justices ruled against the federal government's position, but under the 1994

judicial reforms it would have taken a *supermajority* of eight out of eleven justices to strike down a law or official action as unconstitutional, so the Court's decision had no practical impact in these cases.

These outcomes illustrate a major limitation of Zedillo's 1994 judicial reforms: The requirement that laws can be declared unconstitutional only with a supermajority ruling of Supreme Court justices is a very high threshold, one that can stymie the Court in dealing with the most sensitive political issues rulings.[35] In short, while Zedillo was willing to expand the Supreme Court's powers of judicial review and thereby reduce its subordination to the executive, he wanted to keep the Court on a fairly short leash.

Another major limitation of the 1994 reforms is that they apply only to the top level of the federal judiciary: state-level courts continue to function as before, and the federal Supreme Court must still rely on state-level officials to implement its rulings. In the campaign spending and human rights violation cases mentioned earlier, PRI-dominated state legislatures simply ignored or overturned the Supreme Court's rulings. Until Court decisions based on abstract principles of law cannot be undermined by political actors whose interests could be damaged by those rulings, the goal of a "government of laws, not men" will remain elusive in Mexico.

To the average citizen, what matters most is being liberated from the constant preoccupation with matters of personal security: how to avoid becoming a victim of violent crime. The causes of rising crime rates in Mexico are not difficult to identify. In the 1990s, Mexico became an increasingly important conduit for illegal drugs destined for the U.S. market. In states where drug trafficking is concentrated (Baja California, Chihuahua, Sinaloa, Jalisco), a high percentage of violent crime is related to the operations of drug cartels. Drug trafficking has also contributed mightily to the corruption of police, prosecutors, judges, and military personnel.

The police forces—federal, state, and local—themselves are a major source of Mexico's crime problem. Not only are they corruptible (because of low pay and low professionalization), they actually commit a sizable portion of crimes, especially in large cities. In recent years, most of the kidnappings of urban residents, carried out to extort money from them and their relatives, have involved former or active-duty police officers. A remarkably large number of Mexican

Former New York City Mayor Rudolph Giuliani (center) and Mexico City Mayor Marcelo Ebrard (left) tour the main plaza of Mexico City.

Famed for reducing crime in New York in the 1990s with his "zero tolerance" policy, Giuliani was hired in 2001 as a $4.3 million consultant by a group of prominent Mexican businessmen to produce a plan for reducing the capital's crime rate.

AP Images/Guillermo Arias

police officers are actually wanted for crimes, but the warrants for their arrest never get served because the offenders are protected by corrupt superior officers. Simply firing criminal elements in the police forces is not the solution, since they only return to the street as civilians, committing crimes with impunity.

Social and economic factors have also contributed powerfully to the recent epidemic of crime in Mexico. The rise in violent crime in the mid-1990s coincided with a sharp increase in the number of people living in poverty and the number of unemployed and severely underemployed people—all consequences of the deep economic crisis that erupted in 1994. In a quantitative analysis of homicide rates in a national sample of 1,750 *municipios* in Mexico, a general index of poverty was, by far, the single most important predictor of homicide rates at the local level. Other indicators of economic distress—the unemployment rate and the degree of income inequality in a *municipio*—were also significant predictors. So were certain demographic variables, like the percentage of single mothers.[36] The frequency of female-headed households is an indicator of the breakdown of the Mexican family structure, which is strongly related to adverse economic conditions and the necessity for household heads to migrate to the United States for long periods to supplement the family's income.

Finally, the inefficiency or malfunctioning of the criminal justice system is a major contributor to crime in Mexico. The actual probability of being caught, convicted, and serving substantial prison time

is far too low to serve as a significant deterrent to crime. For example, out of every 100 crimes committed in Mexico in 2001, only twenty-five were reported to police, only 1.2 went to trial, and only 0.4 cases resulted in a jail sentence of more than two years.[37]

Potential remedies for Mexico's dysfunctional criminal justice system include implementing tighter screening, testing, and monitoring of law enforcement personnel; increasing the pay and improving the training for police; making criminal proceedings more transparent and efficient by introducing oral argument; giving public prosecutors greater autonomy to prevent undue interference from politicians; standardizing sentencing guidelines nationwide; making the corrections system more humane and effective in rehabilitation; and funding more ambitious crime prevention programs aimed at young people. None of these possible remedies is a panacea, and most experts believe that real progress in reducing public insecurity will depend on addressing the root causes, including joblessness and extreme income inequality.

## MEXICO'S POLITICAL FUTURE

In the months following Vicente Fox's victory in the 2000 presidential elections there was a major debate among Mexican intellectuals and the political elite over whether the country had successfully completed its transition to democracy, with the alternation of power in the presidency, or whether further and deeper structural reforms would be necessary before Mexico should be classified as a democratic republic. In the aftermath of the 2006 election, particularly because of the disputed presidential result, precisely the same debates are being rehashed.

It is certain that elections in Mexico at the federal level are now as democratic and transparent as nearly any other country in the Americas. Electoral law reforms have ended most forms of fraud that were typical in the past. The Federal Electoral Institute has a strong record as a guardian of democracy. Campaign finance regulation is still deficient (disclosure rules for private contributions are very weak; the IFE can impose fines for violations only after the election), but with generous public financing of all parties' campaigns, the playing field has been leveled. Considering that the PRI-government apparatus functioned as a political machine—in which maintaining power in the executive branch was absolutely necessary to maintain the incentive structure for the rest of the political elite—the end of PRI domination of the presidency arguably has concluded the authoritarian era of Mexican politics. At the same time, many argue that a mere alternation in power is insufficient to consolidate a democratic transition. They claim that structural reforms, especially a comprehensive state reform, are required before the transition to democracy can be completed. In the first months after Mexico's 2000 election, there was a major movement to replace the 1917 Constitution, creating a system with a weaker president and stronger Congress, courts, and state governments. There was talk of changing the electoral formulas once again (though, of course, each party proposed formulas that were variously more or less proportional, according to their relative electoral strengths).

The political strategies that follow from these two concepts of Mexico's transition are very different. The notion that the political transition was completed with the alternation in power in 2000 leads to political actors facing up to the problem of divided government, accepting that the electorate gave mixed signals on election day, and allowing each branch of government to make the best of the situation considering the constitutional powers that it holds. Therefore, the Congress should not consider executive bills to be untouchable (and considering the frequency with which they are amended in the chambers, this certainly seems to be the case). The president should use his constitutional decree powers and his veto as he sees fit, and not worry that their use be considered an affront to the legislative branch. The Supreme Court should arbitrate. Both the president and the parties in Congress should use publicity in the press to get their message out and pressure the other branch to give in.

The opposing camp calls for national political accords and consensus on all basic matters of governance. They believe that the constitutional boundaries between the branches must be redefined, again by consensus. Proponents of this plan in the executive branch want to create a strong, flexible presidency, while those in the opposition parties want congressional dominance or even parliamentary government.

There is little doubt that Mexico should now be classified as a democracy in terms of electoral transparency and even personal freedoms. Despite all of the sound and fury between the executive and legislative branches under divided government, there is little doubt that Mexico now has one of the best-functioning democratic political systems in Latin America—certainly closer to Chile and Costa Rica than to Brazil, Argentina, or Venezuela. While the PRI's abysmal performance in the 2006 election moved Mexico closer to a two-party system, the overall results of the election suggest that the three-party system that took shape in the late 1980s will endure for at least another *sexenio*.

Electoral shenanigans still take place in some states, but at the national level, when the attention of all of the major parties is closely focused on the process, recent elections have been remarkably clean. International election observers, hundreds of whom have been present for each of these elections, and academic analysts have found no evidence of systematic fraud.[38]

The large-scale civil disobedience campaign carried out by losing candidate López Obrador in an attempt to overturn the 2006 election result severely tested Mexico's new democratic institutions. López Obrador's party now faces a fundamental choice: admit electoral defeat and work within the Congress to push legislative remedies to the social problems that the PRD has highlighted, or engage in a sustained resistance campaign aimed at destabilizing the government and blocking its policy initiatives. The latter choice could end up weakening Mexico's fragile democracy, and it would make the PRD an antisystem party, working outside of the institutional framework. Such parties often receive considerable media attention, but they are less likely to be able to influence public policy.

## REVIEW QUESTIONS

- How does political recruitment in the PAN differ from traditional forms of recruitment in the PRI? What explains these differences?

- What is metaconstitutional presidentialism? What are the conditions that bring it about? Was Vicente Fox able to govern without the benefit of metaconstitutional powers?

- What explains the shift in party preferences between 2000 and 2006? Which parties benefit and which lose out in this change in public preferences?

- How much of the political and public policy legacy of Lázaro Cárdenas survives intact today?

- Have the judicial reforms of recent years achieved the desired effect in terms of division of powers, corruption, and public security? What are the main obstacles to progress in this issue area?

- Have the 1996 electoral reforms been successful in stemming electoral fraud? Have they achieved general public acceptance of electoral returns? What further reforms could improve the results in either case?

- What are the effects of the prohibition of immediate reelection of federal legislators? What are the effects of the absolute prohibition of reelection of the president?

## KEY TERMS

*caciques*

*Cardenismo*

Confederación de Trabajadores de México (CTM)

Confederación Nacional Campesina (CNC)

Confederación Nacional de Organizaciones Populares (CNOP)

corporatism/corporatist

divided government

*municipios*

neoliberal economic development model

Partido Acción Nacional (PAN)

Partido de la Revolución Democrática (PRD)

Partido Revolucionario Institucional (PRI)

patron-client relationships

political centralism

*presidencialismo*

sectoral organizations sectors (of the PRI)

sectors

Seguro Popular

*sexenios*

*técnicos*

## SUGGESTED READINGS

Babb, Sarah. *Managing Mexico: Economists From Nationalism to Neoliberalism.* Princeton, NJ: Princeton University Press, 2001.

Bruhn, Kathleen. *Taking on Goliath: Mexico's Party of the Democratic Revolution.* University Park, PA: Pennsylvania State University Press, 1997.

Camp, Roderic A. *Generals in the Palacio: The Military in Modern Mexico.* New York: Oxford University Press, 1992.

———. *Crossing Swords: Politics and Religion in Mexico.* New York: Oxford University Press, 1997.

———. *Mexico's Mandarins: Crafting a Power Elite for the Twenty-First Century.* Berkeley: University of California Press, 2002.

Centeno, Miguel Angel. *Democracy Within Reason: Technocratic Revolution in Mexico,* 2nd ed. University Park: Pennsylvania State University Press, 1997.

Chambers, Edward J., and Peter H. Smith, eds. *NAFTA in the New Millennium.* La Jolla and Edmonton: Center for U.S.-Mexican Studies, University of California-San Diego and University of Alberta Press, 2002.

Chand, Vikram K. *Mexico's Political Awakening.* Notre Dame, IN: University of Notre Dame Press, 2001.

Cornelius, Wayne A. et al., eds. *Subnational Politics and Democratization in Mexico.* La Jolla: Center for U.S.-Mexican Studies, University of California-San Diego, 1999.

Cornelius, Wayne A., and Jessa M. Lewis, eds. *Impacts of Border Enforcement on Mexican Migration: The View From Sending Communities.* Boulder, CO: Lynne Rienner Publishers, 2006.

Cornelius, Wayne A., and David A. Shirk, eds., *Reforming the Administration of Justice in Mexico.* Notre Dame, IN: University of Notre Dame Press, 2007.

Díaz-Cayeros, Alberto. *Federalism, Fiscal Authority, and Centralization in Latin America.* Cambridge: Cambridge University Press, 2006.

Domínguez, Jorge I., and James A. McCann. *Democratizing Mexico: Public Opinion and Elections.* Baltimore, MD: Johns Hopkins University Press, 1995.

Domínguez, Jorge I., and Chappell Lawson, eds. *Mexico's Pivotal Democratic Election.* Stanford, CA and La Jolla: Stanford

University Press and Center for U.S.-Mexican Studies, University of California-San Diego, 2003.

Domínguez, Jorge I., James A. McCann, and Alejandro Poiré, eds. *Toward Mexico's Democratization: Parties, Campaigns, Elections, and Public Opinion.* New York: Routledge, 1999.

Eisenstadt, Todd A. *Courting Democracy in Mexico: Party Strategies and Electoral Institutions.* Cambridge: Cambridge University Press, 2004.

Knight, Alan. *The Mexican Revolution,* 2 vols. Lincoln: University of Nebraska Press, 1990.

Krauze, Enrique. *Mexico—Biography of Power: A History of Modern Mexico, 1810–1996.* New York: HarperCollins, 1997.

Lawson, Chappell. *Building the Fourth Estate: Democratization and the Rise of a Free Press in Mexico.* Berkeley: University of California Press, 2002.

Levy, Daniel C., Kathleen Bruhn, and Emilio Zebadúa. *Mexico: The Struggle for Democratic Development.* Berkeley: University of California Press, 2001.

MacLeod, Dag. *Downsizing the State: Privatization and the Limits of Neoliberal Reform in Mexico.* University Park: Pennsylvania State University Press, 2004.

Magaloni, Beatriz, *Voting for Autocracy: Hegemonic Party Survival and Its Demise in Mexico.* Cambridge: Cambridge University Press, 2006.

Peschard-Sverdrup, Armand B., and Sara R. Rioff, eds. *Mexican Governance: From Single-Party Rule to Divided Government.* Washington, D.C.: Center for Strategic and International Studies, 2005.

Rodríguez, Victoria E., ed. *Women's Participation in Mexican Political Life.* Boulder, CO: Westview, 1998.

Rubin, Jeffrey. *Decentering the Regime: Ethnicity, Radicalism, and Democracy in Juchitán, Mexico.* Durham, NC: Duke University Press, 1997.

Shirk, David A. *Mexico's New Politics: The PAN and Democratic Change.* Boulder, CO: Lynne Rienner Publishers, 2005.

Smith, Peter H. *Labyrinths of Power: Political Recruitment in Twentieth-Century Mexico.* Princeton, NJ: Princeton University Press, 1979.

Snyder, Richard. *Politics After Neoliberalism: Reregulation in Mexico.* Cambridge: Cambridge University Press, 2001.

Ward, Peter M. *Mexico City,* 2nd ed. New York: Wiley, 1998.

Ward, Peter M., and Victoria E. Rodríguez. *Bringing the States Back In: New Federalism and State Government in Mexico.* Austin: Lyndon B. Johnson School of Public Affairs, University of Texas-Austin, 1999.

## INTERNET RESOURCES

President's Office: **www.presidencia.gob.mx**

Chamber of Deputies: **www.diputados.gob.mx**

Senate: **www.senado.gob.mx**

National Statistical Institute: **www.inegi.org.mx**

National Population Council: **www.conapo.gob.mx**

Federal Electoral Institute: **www.ife.org.mx**

## ENDNOTES

1. PRI candidate Carlos Salinas de Gortari was credited with 50.74 percent of the valid votes cast. However, if the 695,042 "spoiled" ballots and 14,333 votes cast for nonregistered presidential candidates are included in the calculation, Salinas won by a plurality of only 48.7 percent.

2. This percentage represents an undercount, since the census identifies as Indians only people over age 50. Indians of all ages constitute an estimated 15 percent of the total population.

3. Peter H. Smith, "The Making of the Mexican Constitution," in William O. Aydelotte, ed., *The History of Parliamentary Behavior* (Princeton, NJ: Princeton University Press, 1977), 219.

4. Quoted in Denise Dresser, "Five Scenarios for Mexico," *Journal of Democracy* 5, no. 3 (July 1994): 57.

5. The actual extent of irregularities in the 1988 presidential vote will never be determined. Within a few hours after the polls closed, with early returns showing Cárdenas ahead by a significant margin, top authorities ordered the computerized count to be suspended. When results for a majority of the country's polling places were announced six days later, Salinas had won. There is no corroborating evidence from exit surveys of voters,

because the government denied permission for such surveys in 1988. The PRI-controlled Congress later ordered the ballots stored in its basement to be burned, thereby eliminating any possibility of challenging the election outcome. Study of the partial, publicly released results and preelection polling data has led most analysts to conclude that Salinas probably did win but that his margin of victory over Cárdenas was much smaller than the 19-point spread indicated by the official results.

6. According to statistics of the IFE, Zedillo won 50.18 percent of the valid votes (i.e., excluding "spoiled" ballots and write-in votes cast for unregistered candidates). However, if the calculation is based on total votes cast (including those annulled by electoral authorities), his share of the vote declines to 48.77 percent.

7. Jeffrey S. Passel, "The Size and Characteristics of the Unauthorized Migrant Population in the U.S." (Research Report, Pew Hispanic Center, Washington, DC, 7 March 2006).

8. See Roderic A. Camp, *Citizen Views of Democracy in Latin America* (Pittsburgh, PA.: University of Pittsburgh Press, 2001).

9. For illustrative survey data from the early 1990s, see Jorge I. Domínguez and James A. McCann, *Democratizing Mexico:*

*Public Opinion and Electoral Choices* (Baltimore, MD: Johns Hopkins University Press, 1996), 29–47.

10.  James A. McCann and Chappell Lawson, "An Electorate Adrift?—Public Opinion and the Quality of Democracy in Mexico," *Latin American Research Review*, 38 no. 3., (2003): 60–81; and Francisco Flores-Macías and Chappell Lawson, "Mexican Democracy and Its Discontents," *Review of Policy Research*, forthcoming, 2006.

11.  McCann and Lawson, "An Electorate Adrift?"; and Jorge I. Domínguez and Chappell Lawson, eds., *Mexico's Pivotal Democratic Election* (Stanford and La Jolla: Stanford University Press/Center for U.S.-Mexican Studies, University of California–San Diego, 2003).

12.  Constitutional reforms are very common in Mexican law because regular statutory reforms or new policy programs frequently require constitutional sanction before they can be enacted. Therefore, constitutional reforms in Mexico are not only questions of basic structural or political reform, but also matters of public policy.

13.  See Alan Knight, "Historical Continuities in Social Movements," in Joe Foweraker and Ann L. Craig, eds., *Popular Movements and Political Change in Mexico* (Boulder, CO: Lynne Rienner, 1990), 78–102; Jeffrey W. Rubin, *Decentering the Regime: Ethnicity, Radicalism, and Democracy in Juchitán, Mexico* (Durham, NC: Duke University Press, 1997); and Wayne A. Cornelius, Todd Eisenstadt, and Jane Hindley, eds., *Subnational Politics and Democratization in Mexico* (La Jolla: Center for U.S.-Mexican Studies, University of California–San Diego, 1999).

14.  Alberto Díaz-Cayeros, *Federalism, Fiscal Authority, and Centralization in Latin America* (Cambridge: Cambridge University Press, 2006), 8, 143–47.

15.  See Victoria E. Rodríguez, *Decentralization in Mexico: From Reforma Municipal to Solidaridad to Nuevo Federalismo* (Boulder, CO: Westview, 1997); and Peter M. Ward and Victoria E. Rodríguez, *Bringing the States Back In: New Federalism and State Government in Mexico* (Austin: Lyndon Baines Johnson School of Public Affairs, University of Texas-Austin, 1999).

16.  For a recent discussion of mixed-member electoral systems in general, and comparisons between Mexico's electoral regime with similar systems, see *Mixed-Member Electoral Systems: The Best of Both Worlds?* Matthew Soberg Shugart and Martin P. Wattenberg, eds. (Oxford: Oxford University Press, 2001).

17.  See Jeffrey A. Weldon, "Political Sources of *Presidencialismo* in Mexico," in Scott Mainwaring and Matthew Soberg Shugart, eds., *Presidentialism and Democracy in Latin America* (New York: Cambridge University Press, 1997), 225–58.

18.  For a conventional interpretation of the powers of the Mexican president, see Luis Javier Garrido, "The Crisis of *Presidencialismo*," in Wayne A. Cornelius, Judith Gentleman, and Peter H. Smith, eds., Mexico's *Alternative Political Futures* (La Jolla: Center for U.S.-Mexican Studies, University of California–San Diego, 1989), 417–34.

19.  The purported rationale for this principle, applied to the president in the 1917 Constitution and extended to members of Congress in 1933, was to ensure freedom from self-perpetuating, dictatorial rule in the Porfirio Díaz style. However, the real reason for prohibiting the consecutive reelection of deputies and senators was probably to cut the ties between local political bosses and their federal legislators, at a time that the ruling party was seeking greater centralization of authority.

20.  See Weldon, "The Political Sources of *Presidencialismo* in Mexico."

21.  Miguel Angel Centeno, *Democracy Within Reason: Technocratic Revolution in Mexico*, 2nd ed. (University Park: Pennsylvania State University Press, 1997), 112.

22.  Centeno, *Democracy Within Reason.*

23.  David A. Shirk, *Mexico's New Politics: The PAN and Democratic Change* (Boulder, CO: Lynne Rienner Publishers, 2005), 191–94.

24.  Unpublished data from Roderic A. Camp. See also Roderic A. Camp, "Family Relationships in Mexican Politics," *Journal of Politics* 44 (August 1982): 848–62; and Peter H. Smith, *Labyrinths of Power: Political Recruitment in Twentieth-Century Mexico* (Princeton, NJ: Princeton University Press, 1979), 307–10.

25.  Shirk, *Mexico's New Politics*, 181.

26.  Lorenzo Meyer, "La Democracia Política: Esperando a Godot," *Nexos* 100 (April 1986): 42.

27.  Joseph L. Klesner, "Electoral Competition and the New Party System in Mexico," *Latin American Politics and Society*, 47, no. 2 (2005): 103–42; and Klesner, "Social and Regional Factors in the 2006 Presidential Election" (unpublished paper, Dept. of Political Science, Kenyon College, August 2006).

28.  Alejandro Moreno, *El votante mexicano* (México, DF: Fondo de Cultura Económica, 2003).

29.  As Joseph Klesner has shown, both the PAN and the PRD now exhibit catch-all characteristics, driven by the dealignment of the electorate from the PRI and the desire of its rivals to broaden their constituencies by capturing these "delinked" voters. Klesner, "Electoral Competition and the New Party System."

30.  Chappell Lawson, "Blue States and Yellow States: Preliminary Findings From the Mexico 2006 Panel Study" (unpublished paper, Dept. of Political Science, Massachusetts Institute of Technology, 27 July, 2006).

31.  Centeno, *Democracy Within Reason*, 194.

32.  A wealth of statistical data demonstrating these trends can be found in Enrique Dussel Peters, *Polarizing Development: The Impact of Liberalization Strategy* (Boulder, CO: Lynne Rienner, 2000).

33.  Carlos Elizondo, "In Search of Revenue: Tax Reform in Mexico Under the Administrations of Echeverría and Salinas," *Journal of Latin American Studies* 26, no. 1 (February 1994): 159–90.

34.  Guillermo Zepeda Lecuona, "Criminal Investigation and the Subversion of the Principles of the Justice System in Mexico," in Wayne A. Cornelius and David A. Shirk, eds., *Reforming the Administration of Justice in Mexico* (Notre Dame, IN: University of Notre Dame Press, 1997).

35.  Sara Schatz, "A Neo-Weberian Approach to Constitutional Courts in the Transition From Authoritarian Rule: The Mexican Case, 1994–1997," *International Journal of the Sociology of Law* 26 (1998): 217–44.

36.  Andrés Villarreal, "Structural Determinants of Homicide in Mexico" (paper presented at the annual meeting of the American Sociological Association, 5 January, 1999).

37.  Zepeda Lecuona, "Criminal Investigation."

38.  Regarding the 2006 election, see Luis Estrada and Alejandro Poiré, "La Evidencia del Fraude," *Reforma*, 13 August 2006 (Enfoque supplement), 12–13.

**BRAZIL**

0 100 200 300 400 500 Miles

0 500 Kilometers

*ATLANTIC OCEAN*

*ATLANTIC OCEAN*

Boa Vista

*Negro R.*

AMAPÁ

Macapá

*Amazon R.*

Belém

São Luis

Manaus

AMAZONAS

*Madeira R.*

PARÁ

MARANHÃO

Fortaleza

CEARÁ

Teresina

RIO GRANDE
DO NORTE

Natal

*Purus R.*

*Tapajos R.*

*Xingu R.*

PARAÍBA

João
Pessoa

PIAUI

PERNAMBUCO

Recife

ACRE

Porto Velho

*Araguaia R.*

*Tocantins R.*

ALAGOAS

Maceió

Rio
Branco

RONDÔNIA

MATO

GROSSO

TOCANTINS

Palmas

BAHIA

SERGIPE

Aracaju

*São Francisco R.*

Salvador

GOIÁS

BRASÍLIA ★

Goiânia F.D.

Cuiabá

MINAS
GERAIS

MATO GROSSO

Campo
Grande

DO SUL

*Parana R.*

SÃO PAULO

Belo
Horizonte

ESPÍRITO
SANTO

Vitória

RIO DE
JANEIRO

São Paulo

Rio de
Janeiro

PARANÁ

Curitiba

SANTA
CATARINA

Florianópolis

RIO GRANDE
DO SUL

Porto Alegre

# POLITICS IN BRAZIL

*Frances Hagopian*

## Country Bio

**BRAZIL**

**Population**
187.1 million

**Territory**
3,286,470 square miles

**Year of Independence**
1822

**Year of Current Constitution**
1988

**Head of State**
President Luiz Inácio Lula da Silva

**Head of Government**
President Luiz Inácio Lula da Silva

**Language**
Portuguese

**Religions**
Roman Catholic 70%, Protestant 15%

In 2002, after the two-term presidency of Fernando Henrique Cardoso—whose administration delivered stable prices, a more open economy, rising levels of school enrollments, and a more efficient administration of many public services—Brazilians boldly handed the presidency in a landslide to Luiz Inácio da Silva. "Lula," as he is known in Brazil, is a former metalworker and leader of Latin America's largest party of the left. The voters imagined a country with a more representative, honest, and accountable democratic government, one that could adequately house, feed, educate, and protect its people. In short, they loudly proclaimed themselves to be in favor of a fairer and more equitable society.

The first Lula government may have disappointed supporters anxious for the prompt delivery of social justice, but its fiscal conservatism, deep economic reforms, and steady if gradual progress in social policy pleasantly surprised many foreign and domestic creditors and investors. Any gains, however, were overshadowed by a major corruption scandal involving top leaders of the Workers' Party and President Lula's closest political advisers. Though Lula was untouched by the scandal, it nonetheless shattered the faith those across the political spectrum held in the integrity of government leaders. Observers now wonder whether Lula's second administration can recover and meet the challenges facing Brazilian society.

## CURRENT POLICY CHALLENGES

Brazilians share a common identity, allegiance to their government, and political community. There is no serious religious conflict, no large linguistic minority, and the last armed confrontation between any region and the central government was in 1932, when São Paulo went to war with the Brazilian federation.

Brazil is challenged to compensate for past racial discrimination and exclusion, improve educational and employment opportunities, and provide the full rights of citizenship to its small indigenous and substantial Afro-Brazilian populations—communities that clearly form part of the larger Brazilian community. The other two broad challenges identified in Chapter 1—fostering development and deepening democracy—are still pressing.

Successive Brazilian governments have been reasonably successful at generating sporadic growth, and Lula's government has been no exception. Although political uncertainty surrounding the 2002 election initially caused the currency value and the São Paulo stock index to fall, the currency and stock market rebounded quickly on strong signals from the Lula camp that investors and creditors would have little to fear. Exceeding expectations, the new administration adhered to a tight monetary policy, which produced a budget surplus, brought inflation back down to manageable levels, allowed Brazil to pay off foreign loans ahead of schedule, and reduced the public debt as a share of the gross domestic product (GDP). Growth rates lagged during much of the first Lula administration, but rebounded strongly in 2005 and 2006.

These accomplishments, however, have come largely at the price of high taxes, high interest rates, and low levels of government investment. Brazil's tax-to-GDP ratio, which rose sharply after 1995, today (at 37 percent) is twice as high as the rest of Latin America and close to the average of the countries in the Organization for Economic Cooperation and Development (OECD). Such a high rate in a middle-income country typically either drives economic activity underground or dampens it altogether. Many feel Brazil needs to lower rates and to overhaul its tax structure by unifying disparate state taxes on goods and services and creating a single value-added tax (VAT). In the absence of such reform, the government has controlled inflation through monetary policy; that is, with very high interest rates. High rates, in turn, have choked private investment, discouraged job creation, and constrained public-sector investment. Most critically, with the government unable to invest even in maintaining the country's transportation system, physical infrastructure is crumbling.

The government's priority for economic stability has also relegated other economic and social development problems to the back burner. Brazilians are looking for better access to health and education, and an end to grotesque poverty. The public health care system that primarily services the poor has long been underfunded and inefficient. Brazil's educational system has been improved in recent years, but nonetheless Brazil has a population that is less literate and less well schooled than many of its neighbors. Clearly, this is not only an injustice but also a constraint on economic development. The poverty rate, though steadily declining, remains stubbornly high at 31 percent.

Brazil has one of the most unequal distributions of income in the world. Brazilian society is stratified by region, gender, and race. Increasingly, Brazilians are beginning to understand that their country faces the challenge of greater economic and social inclusion for Brazilians of color, who represent nearly half of the population.

Other policy areas also require attention. Environmental protection is an important challenge not merely because of the need to develop the Amazonian region's natural resources in a sustainable way, but also because many years of lax controls have compromised air and water quality. Another challenge is to provide agricultural land for the tiller, dramatized in recent years by Brazil's movement of landless workers.

Now that Brazil is the second largest consumer of illegal drugs (after the United States), Brazilians are also acutely worried about the impact of drugs and the criminal drug trade on public security. The government faces the task of enforcing public order and reducing a violent crime rate so high that it has driven the rich to build higher fences, travel in helicopters, and contract private security; and the poor to administer mob justice.

In attempting to meet the public security challenge, however, the government faces perhaps an ever greater one: guaranteeing civil rights and the rule of law for all its citizens, male or female, black or white, rich or poor. After reestablishing democratic rule, Brazil saw an erosion of human rights and civil liberties. The murder rate (37,000 per year) is unacceptably high. The judicial system is overwhelmed. Torture, especially against poor criminal suspects in order to extract confessions, is routine. Extrajudicial killings by the police are disguised as shootouts with dangerous criminals. Violence against women and children is common. Freedom House has charged that "Brazil's police are among the world's most violent and corrupt," and that "human rights, particularly those of socially marginalized groups, are violated with impunity on a massive scale."[1]

Is Brazil's political system up to meeting these challenges? On the one hand, democracy is stronger than at any time in Brazil's history. On the other hand, political institutions do not function as smoothly as they might.

A new party law that took effect in 2006 should reduce the age-old problem of a fragmented party system. Political reformers have set their sights on strengthening party loyalty, establishing a mixed-district voting system, and reforming the system by which election campaigns are financed.

Brazil's democracy was rocked in 2005 by the revelation of a corruption scandal that engulfed the government and the **Workers' Party (PT).** The scandal was taken so seriously because Brazilians believed the PT represented a new kind of politics, in which politicians did not steal from the public purse, buy votes at the ballot box, or buy votes on the floor of Congress. When Brazilians learned that the PT had engaged in these activities (see Figure 15.1), the scandal reverberated throughout the political system. Trust in Congress, political parties, and politicians are at an all-time low.

Whether the Brazilian government can sustain growth, reduce poverty, redress inequality, improve public services, and clean up government corruption—or whether it will fail to develop its vast economic potential and remain an elite-dominated polity that neglects and represses its poor—is still uncertain. We must understand the economic, social, and political conditions that created Brazil's current policy challenges to understand its prospects for the future.

## HISTORICAL PERSPECTIVES

Brazil has a legacy of political order and several decades of competitive government, but genuine democracy is relatively recent. Brazil gained its independence from Portugal in 1822 not by insurrection, as in Spanish America, but by fiat of the Portuguese emperor's son. For seven decades, Brazil was governed as an "empire," and successive emperors exercised strong central authority. This type of rule prevented the fragmentation of territory and provided a unique degree of order and political stability in the New World.

Brazil became a republic in 1889, one year after slavery was finally abolished. The empire fell swiftly and suddenly when disgruntled military and agrarian elites separately withdrew their support. The military wanted to replace the empire with a strong central government committed to "order and progress"—a motto still emblazoned on the Brazilian flag. By 1891,

however, civilian elites from the largest and economically strongest states had wrested control of the new republic from the military. They favored a decentralized federalism and framed a constitution that accorded the states even wider latitude than did U.S. federalism, from which it drew its inspiration. The "Old Republic," as it was called, was dominated by the regional oligarchies of the strongest states. The overwhelming majority of Brazilians were without the effective legal rights, levels of literacy, or socioeconomic conditions of citizenship.

In 1930, a combination of labor unrest and protest from young army officers, the world depression, the crisis in Brazil's coffee economy, and regional rivalries brought down the Old Republic and spawned a "revolution" that brought a southern politician, Getúlio Vargas, to the presidency. Vargas quickly strengthened the central government at the expense of the state and local governments, and enhanced bureaucratic autonomy. In 1937, impressed by the political and social organization of fascist Italy, he reneged on a promise to hold elections and instead exercised dictatorial powers in a regime he called the *Estado Nôvo* (New State).

### Postwar Democracy

With the defeat of the Axis powers and the collapse of the prestige of fascism in 1945, Vargas reluctantly restored democracy. With the growth of new social classes, the political system was opened to broader political participation and competition. Voters as a percentage of the population rose from 6 percent in 1930, to 13 percent in 1945, to 18 percent in 1960. Many of these new participants, especially from the urban areas of the South and Southeast, were incorporated into the political system through loose associations with populist leaders, parties, and institutions. Populist politicians nominally claimed to represent the interests of the urban middle and working classes. In practice, however, the urban lower classes were well controlled and the rural lower classes were excluded from political life altogether. Their interests were not represented through any political party, they were not allowed to organize rural unions, and most rural workers, who were illiterate, could not vote.

In the next two decades, several political parties competed for power at the national level, although political bosses still exerted much local control.

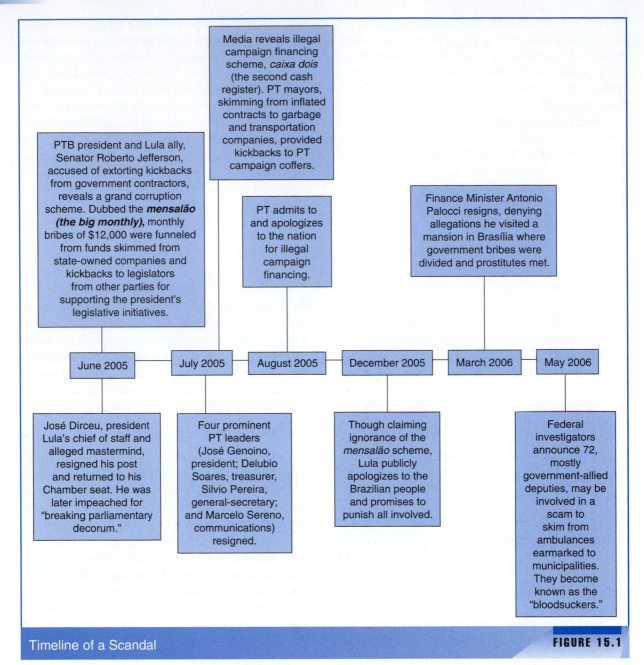

Timeline of a Scandal

**FIGURE 15.1**

The country prospered, especially during the late 1950s when physical infrastructure was laid. Foreign auto plants settled in São Paulo, and a new capital, Brasília, was built in the interior.

In the early 1960s, however, Brazil's political system began to strain. With thirteen political parties in the Chamber of Deputies and the share of seats won by small parties on the rise, the party system was so fragmented that Congress was ineffective and no president could count on a stable base of support. Elites became threatened by the mobilization of peasant leagues, the electoral advance of the populist **Brazilian Labor Party (PTB),** and the leftist rhetoric of João Goulart, who assumed the presidency in 1961 (see Figure 15.2). In March 1964, amid high inflation and a stagnating economy, Goulart advocated revolutionary change in the countryside and the Congress. He supported the mutiny of a group of enlisted sailors

| Year | Nature of Government | President |
|------|---------------------|-----------|
| 1946 | Civilian* | Eurico Dutra (PSD/PTB) |
| 1951 | Civilian | Getúlio Vargas (PTB/PSP) |
| 1954 | Civilian** | João Café Filho (PSP) |
| 1956 | Civilian | Juscelino Kubitchek (PSD/PTB) |
| 1961 | Civilian | Jânio Quadros (UDN/PDC/PL/PTN) |
| 1961 | Civilian** | João Goulart (PTB) |
| 1964 | Military | Humberto Castelo Branco |
| 1967 | Military | Artur Costa e Silva |
| 1969 | Military | Emilio Garrastazú Médici |
| 1974 | Military | Ernesto Geisel |
| 1978 | Military | João Figueiredo |
| 1985 | Civilian** | José Sarney (PFL/PMDB) |
| 1990 | Civilian | Fernando Collor de Mello (PRN) |
| 1992 | Civilian** | Itamar Franco |
| 1995 | Civilian | Fernando Henrique Cardoso (PSDB) |
| 1999 | Civilian | Fernando Henrique Cardoso (PSDB) |
| 2003 | Civilian | Luis Inácio Lula da Silva (PT) |
| 2007 | Civilian | Luis Inácio Lula da Silva (PT) |

*Dutra, a general, was directly elected as a candidate of the PSD and headed a civilian government.
**Not directly elected.

**Brazilian Administrations Since 1945**

**FIGURE 15.2**

against naval officers. Brazilian military officers, who had come to view movements of the left as threats to national security and economic instability as well as a breeding ground for subversive ideologies, interpreted these events as a signal that Brazil had entered a dangerous phase of an internal war. Believing that civilian politicians were ill equipped to contain such a threat, they concluded that they themselves should assume an expanded role in government and in politics.

## The Military Steps In

In April 1964, the Brazilian military deposed President Goulart and instituted direct military rule. In order to tackle inflation, attract foreign investment, and stimulate economic development, the military centralized economic policymaking. It strengthened the Executive Branch by permitting it exclusive powers over the budget and the authority to rule by decree. It also replaced politicians with military officers and civilian economists, engineers, educators, and professional administrators. After one year in power, it abolished existing political parties and cancelled future elections for state governors and mayors of state capitals and "national security" areas.

The regime turned harshly repressive when "hard-line" military factions gained power in 1967, especially toward the labor and student movements. It suspended habeas corpus; it imposed a state of siege; and like other Latin American militaries of this period, it subjected enemies—real and imagined—to arbitrary detention, torture, exile, and even death. Nonetheless, even at the height of the repression, Brazil's military regime was more moderate than those of its neighbors. Military courts handed down some not-guilty verdicts, only about 500 politicians lost their right to hold office (compared with 15,000 in Uruguay), and the government was responsible for "only" 333 deaths from 1964 to 1981. This death toll in per capita terms was 100 times lower than that of neighboring Argentina and fifty times lower than Chile after military coups.

Moreover, unlike other dictatorships in the region, the Brazilian military did not eliminate elections and representative institutions altogether. It created a pro-government party—the National Renovating Alliance (ARENA)—and an official opposition known as the Brazilian Democratic Movement (MDB) to replace the parties it had abolished. It permitted these parties to contest elections for members of the national and state legislatures mayors of most cities and towns, and local councils. The Congress remained in session throughout military rule for all but two brief periods. Of course, victories for ARENA were all but ensured by manipulation of electoral law, and legislators and other elected officials were divested of meaningful powers by the 1967 Constitution. Nonetheless, the veil of legality, a two-party system, and elections ultimately laid the conditions for Brazil's particular path to democratization in the 1980s.

Political liberalization began within the military itself. In early 1974, General Ernesto Geisel, the new, "soft-line" military president, signaled that he would "relax" military rule by easing up on press censorship, allowing a freer expression of ideas, and permitting slightly freer elections. Geisel hoped that more political freedom would check the power of military hard-liners, and that more competitive elections would bring down abstention rates and enhance regime legitimacy.

Having every reason to be confident of victory— Brazil had experienced seven years of impressive economic performance and the opposition was so dispirited and disorganized that it had contemplated disbanding—the government held new elections only to suffer a stinging defeat. The opposition MDB won sixteen of the twenty-two contested seats in the senatorial elections, increased its share of the seats in the Chamber of Deputies from 28 percent to 44 percent, and took control of five additional state legislatures. This stunning victory was largely due to an effective media campaign protesting bread-and-butter economic issues. Although the military regime from that point on limited party access to television and appointed one-third of the Senate in order to secure its advantage in Congress, the regular staging of elections allowed the regime's opponents to mobilize and pressure the government to stay the course of its *abertura política* (political opening).

The regime also faced an invigorated civil society. The political opening allowed the Catholic Church and several segments of elite opinion (including the press, bar associations, and the business community) to express grave reservations about military authoritarianism. As the political space opened, nonelite groups that had either been silenced (such as the labor movement) or not previously organized politically (such as the women's movement) pressed for their specific interests as well as for greater political freedom.

## Democracy Restored

The military regime finally came to an end in March 1985. Amid rising inflation and unemployment and popular disenchantment with the military, many of its civilian supporters abandoned it. Regime supporters and opponents together negotiated a series of political deals that paved the way for a smooth road to a democratic regime. A civilian opposition leader, Tancredo Neves, was elected president in an "electoral college" of elite officeholders. After his untimely death, vice president-elect José Sarney, the former president of the promilitary party, was sworn in as president. The franchise was extended to illiterate adults in 1985, and congressional elections followed in 1986.

A new constitution, which expunged many authoritarian laws and guaranteed basic political and social rights, was promulgated in 1988. By 1989, when Brazilians went to the polls to vote for president for the first time since 1961, most people considered Brazil to have established a democratic regime.

## ECONOMY AND SOCIETY

In the past sixty years Brazil has undergone a socioeconomic transformation as profound as any country has ever experienced—from a nation that bore the obvious imprint of having been an agricultural colony and a slave society to one of the world's major industrial countries. In large part, the state orchestrated that transformation. Today, Brazil seeks to sustain its economic expansion by scaling back the scope of the state's economic intervention and allowing a greater role for market forces. At the same time, it aims to eradicate hunger, illiteracy, and the other bitter vestiges of inequality.

### Economy

Until 1930, plantation agriculture organized Brazil's economy and society. Large-scale sugar estates along the northeastern coast relied on slave labor well into the 1800s. In the early 1850s, between 25 and 30 percent of Brazil's population of 7.5 million were slaves.

After the sugar economy declined, new fortunes were made further south in the mid-nineteenth century in the cultivation of coffee. The Brazilian state subsidized immigrant laborers from Southern

Europe, and coffee planters grew rich and politically powerful.

When the bottom fell out of the coffee economy with the stock market crash of October 1929, the Brazilian state, like many others in Latin America at the time, led an industrialization drive. It protected markets for nascent industries, subsidized energy, manipulated exchange rates to make imported industrial inputs cheaper, and controlled the labor force. This model, called "import-substituting industrialization," produced growth in the 1950s, but it strained in the early 1960s when investment dropped and inflation rose.

Under military rule, the state promoted industrialization to an even greater degree. The Brazilian military had long dreamed of developing Brazil's vast mineral and agricultural resources and hydroelectric potential in order to make Brazil a great power. Unlike in Chile, where the military government pursued a radical free-market economic experiment, the Brazilian military government increased the state's revenue base, controlled wages and prices, and ran hundreds of profitable public-sector enterprises in the mining, petroleum, public utilities, and transportation sectors.

Under the military, Brazil also successfully attracted significant foreign investment in such sectors as automobiles and petrochemicals which required large capital investments and sophisticated technologies. From 1968 to 1974, the model produced an "economic miracle." Gross national product doubled as the economy grew on average by 11 percent per year, industry by 13 percent, and the motor vehicle industry by as much as 35 percent. But the fruits of growth did not trickle down to much of the population. Some, like World Bank President Robert McNamara, criticized the Brazilian government for neglecting its poor. Finance Minister Delfim Netto defended the model, arguing that growth had to come first, or else "you'll end up distributing what doesn't exist."

Growth rates finally slowed in 1974. Dependent for 80 percent of its energy needs on imported petroleum, Brazil was hit hard by soaring oil prices brought on by the Arab oil embargo and production cutbacks by the Organization of Petroleum Exporting Countries (OPEC). Military rulers borrowed from abroad to keep the economy growing and to pay the bills, a strategy that backfired as oil prices continued to climb. Rising interest rates and a recession that closed the markets for Brazil's exports drove the foreign debt up to $71 billion in 1980 and, at its peak in 1987, to $123 billion.

Brazil's indebtedness dramatically changed the country's economic prospects. Payments on the debt's interest and principal averaged 43 percent of Brazil's export earnings from 1985 to 1989. Interest payments on the debt exceeded 4 percent of gross national product (GNP) in 1985 and 1988. Servicing the debt plunged the nation into a deep recession for much of the 1980s. Inflation soared to four-digit annual rates. Brazil finally renegotiated the terms of its debt with its creditors in 1993.

By the early 1990s, then, the model of the heavily indebted producer-state—which governed a protected and regulated market and produced high fiscal deficits and inflation—had revealed itself to be unsustainable. The government began to dismantle trade protection and deregulate prices and financial services. Brazil's stubborn inflation was finally tamed in 1994 by a currency reform known as the **Real Plan** (named for the new currency it introduced). This gradually de-indexed the economy and converted all prices to an index pegged to the U.S. dollar. In the year immediately prior to the Real Plan, *monthly* inflation had averaged 39 percent; after the plan, *annual* rates fell to single digits. Policymakers expected that foreign investment and privatization would accelerate new growth, and the victory over inflation would be consolidated through public-sector reform.

In fact, barriers to direct foreign investment were removed in 1995, and foreign direct investment poured into Brazil. From 1996 to 2000, Brazil attracted an annual average of $21 billion in investment. The only emerging market to receive more foreign investment in this period was China. The sale of several key state enterprises (the state mining company, several electricity companies, a number of ports) and a series of major concessions (in the telecommunications sector) after 1997 brought in $103 billion.[2] Yet reform of the public sector was slow in coming, and Brazil's inability to reduce the state's financial commitments jeopardized the positive results that currency reform, foreign investment, and privatization had had on stability and growth. With reform incomplete, the lid was kept on inflation with high real interest rates; in 1995 short-term interest rates exceeded 50 percent. Such high rates slowed the economy and left an overvalued currency vulnerable in foreign financial markets.

When the Asian financial crisis hit in 1997, the Brazilian government had to devalue the real. A recovery in 2000 was derailed in 2001 by a severe drought, by the September 11 terrorist attacks in the United States, and by a political crisis in neighboring Argentina. The Cardoso administration made slow progress on relaxing job tenure for employees in the state administration (thus enabling the federal government to reduce its payroll) and partially gained control of social security obligations, but it failed to reform the tax code.

One of Cardoso's most significant accomplishments may have been to lay the foundation for limiting the deficit spending of the subnational governments. After years of hard negotiations, the federal government assumed the hefty debts of the state governments, which were given thirty years to repay them. In return, the state governments agreed to privatize their state banks and many state enterprises, and limit their spending, especially on the state payroll. Because the reforms were only partial, the Cardoso government kept interest rates high (about 25 percent until 2001). More ominously, shortfalls were covered by foreign and especially domestic debt. Public debt as a percentage of GDP rose from 30 percent in 1994, just before Cardoso assumed office, to 63 percent by the end of his term. Inflation rates creeped back into double digits, reaching 13 percent in 2002.

With little room for maneuver, Lula's government, too, had to keep interest rates high. Inflation fell steadily each year until it bottomed out at 4 percent in 2005. Though it has not tackled tax reform, Lula's administration did reform the pension system for public-sector workers, toughening the requirements for retirement and reducing benefits. In all, the government impressively produced a fiscal surplus of 4.25 percent of GDP, voluntarily exceeding the budget surplus target of 3.75 percent of GDP recommended by the International Monetary Fund. Its frugality allowed it to pay off its foreign public debt ahead of schedule and reduce long-term debt from $210 billion in 2000 to $171 billion in 2004. Moreover, investments in oil drilling in the Atlantic Ocean by Petrobras, the state oil company, and an innovative alternative fuel program have made Brazil energy self-sufficient.

## Society

*A Modern Society* The rapid economic growth of recent decades has fundamentally altered Brazilian society. In 1940, when Brazil was predominantly a rural, agrarian society, 68 percent of the population lived in rural areas. Today, only about 17 percent of Brazilians remain in the countryside, and there are least thirty-six cities with more than half a million residents. Equal percentages of the work force (19 percent) are employed in industry and agriculture (most—62%—work in commerce and services). Agricultural workers are no longer primarily sharecroppers and renters; they are wage laborers on some of the most modern and

Pumps for alcohol and gasoline are offered at service stations in Brazil. Brazil is a major producer of alternative fuels.

John Maier, Jr./The Image Works

productive farms in the world. In addition, women entered the labor force en masse in the 1970s and 1980s. In the three decades from 1970 to 2000, women's participation in the labor force rose from 18.5 to 44 percent.[3]

Brazilians also have greater exposure to modern means of communication. In 2005, nine in ten households had televisions, for the first time exceeding the number with radios. Also for the first time in 2005, the percentage of households with cell phone service (60 percent) exceeded the number with fixed-line service (48 percent). Thirty-seven percent of all Brazilians now have personal cell phones, and just over a fifth in all and one-third of youths aged 15 to 17 has Internet access.

The modernization of society, however real, is incomplete. Adult illiteracy stands at 11 percent of the population, and about a quarter of Brazilians over age 10 have completed three years of formal schooling or less. Just over half of the work force pays into the social security system, and though that is the highest rate ever, one quarter who work in the informal sector and another quarter that is self-employed are left outside the system. Seventy percent of the labor force works more than forty hours per week (19 percent work forty-nine hours or more); 28 percent earn less than the minimum wage.

*An Unequal Society*  Brazil has long been known as one of the countries with the most unequal distribution of wealth in the world. The share of the national income captured by the richest 10 percent of the population climbed steadily from 40 percent in 1960 to 52 percent in 1989, when the poorest 20 percent received only 2 percent. The Gini coefficient (a standard measure of inequality with 0 as perfect equality and 1 as perfect inequality) reached a high of .64.[4] Today, the share of the wealthiest 10 percent has dropped to 45 percent, and the Gini coefficient has fallen slowly every year since 1989 to .54 in 2005. Nonetheless, despite recent improvements, income inequality stubbornly persists and permeates virtually every aspect of society from school quality to access to justice.

Inequality is reproduced across regions, which have developed unevenly. According to convention, Brazil has five regions: (1) the Northeast, (2) North, (3) Southeast, (4) South, and (5) Center-West. The nine states comprising the desperately poor and drought-plagued Northeast (Maranhão, Piauí, Ceará,

Rio Grande do Norte, Paraíba, Pernambuco, Alagoas, Sergipe, and Bahia) now contain 29 percent of Brazil's population. Yet, in 2003 the region contributed only 14 percent of the GDP (see Figure 15.3). The North, comprising Brazil's Amazon region, and the Center-West (Brazil's frontier) are relatively less populated and developed than the coastal regions. São Paulo, perhaps the most industrialized center of the Third World, is part of the Southeast (along with states of Minas Gerais, Rio de Janeiro, and Espírito Santo). The Southeast is home to 44 percent of the population but generates 55 percent of national economic activity and wealth.

Living standards vary dramatically across regions. In 2004, the adult illiteracy rate in the Northeast (22 percent) was double the national average of 11 percent. The Northeast's poverty rate was nearly three times that of the more developed Southeast (56 percent of the region's population live below the poverty line). The infant mortality rate in the Northeast, while dropping dramatically from eighty-eight per 1,000 live births in 1990 to forty-three in 2001, stubbornly remained at more than twice the level of the Southeast and South.

Brazilian society is stratified by color as well as by class and region. Brazilians classified as "black" by the 2000 census are estimated as 6 percent of the population, with another 39 percent categorized as *parda* or *mulata* (of mixed black and white blood), *mestiça* or *mameluca* (of white and Indian blood), *cafuza* (of black and Indian blood), or simply of Indian descent. With 75 million Afro-Brazilians, Brazil is the country with the second largest black population in the world behind Nigeria. Nonwhites make up 70 percent of the population of Brazil's Northeast, about 36 percent of the Southeast region, and about 15 percent of the South. Although less than 1 percent of the Brazilian population is of Asian origin, São Paulo has one of the largest ethnic Japanese communities in the world outside of Japan.

Black Brazilians are poor, suffer harsh treatment at the hands of the police, and find their promotions blocked in public and private life. They are more than twice as likely to be illiterate, and they earn considerably less than their white counterparts. In 2003, the average monthly salary for white men was 931 reais, for white women, 554, for black men, 428, and for black women, 279. Thus, black men earned less than half as much as white men, and black women, less than

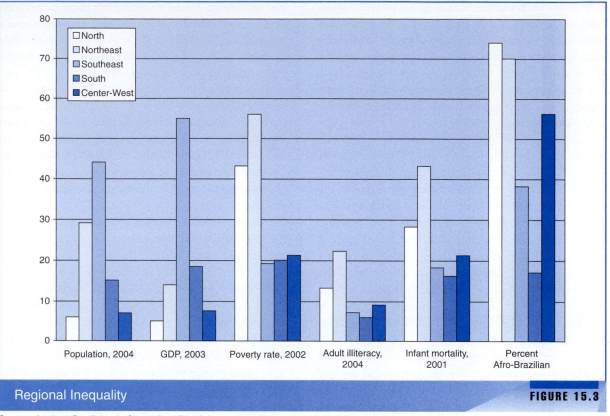

**Regional Inequality**

**FIGURE 15.3**

Sources: Instituto Brasileiro de Geografia e Estatística; Instituto Nacional de Seguridade Social.

one-third. Put another way, while Afro-Brazilians constitute over 46 percent of the population, they account for 60 percent who earn the monthly minimum wage, 63 percent of those who are inadequately nourished, and 72 percent of those who are "seriously" hungry. Racial discrimination, moreover, extends into the judicial system. Black defendants in cases of violent crimes are more likely than their white counterparts to be held in custody pending trial, to rely on public defenders, to be convicted, and to be severely punished.

Like the black population, Brazil's Indians have been seriously disadvantaged from Portuguese colonial days to the present. Portuguese settlers and their descendants coveted Indian labor, lands, and more recently, the timber and minerals on Indian lands. They also threatened the very survival of Indian culture through various schemes to integrate Indians into Brazilian society.

It was not until 1988 that the collective rights of Indians—including the right to hold lands necessary for production, preservation of the environment, and their physical and cultural reproduction—were constitutionally guaranteed. In contrast to the huge population of African descent, today Brazil has more than 200 Indian groups, located mainly in the Amazon region, but these groups together have fewer than a quarter of a million members.

## INSTITUTIONS AND STRUCTURES OF GOVERNMENT

Since the establishment of the republic in 1889, the Brazilian state has been federal and presidential, with three branches of government—executive, legislative, and judicial. However, the distribution of power, the limits on state and governmental authority, and how policy is framed and executed have changed substantially with each regime and constitution.

The *Estado Nôvo* and military dictatorships centralized decisionmaking and expanded state authority; civilian elites have, as reactions to authoritarianism, attempted to decentralize administration and deconcentrate power. The framers of the 1988 Constitution were highly motivated to check the unrestrained exercise of state power. In order to eliminate the excessive centralization of the authoritarian period and the domination of the state and of society by the Executive Branch, they strengthened the fiscal base of the subnational governments, the powers of the national Congress, and individual and collective civil and political rights.

## Federalism: The Union, States, and Local Governments

Brazil is one of the most decentralized federations in the world. Its federal system has three tiers of autonomous governing bodies: (1) the central government, in Brazil called the Union; (2) the state governments; and (3) local governments called *municípios*, which are roughly equivalent to U.S. counties (see Figure 15.4).

Each of Brazil's twenty-six states elects a governor, lieutenant governor, and representatives to a unicameral state legislature, known as the Legislative Assembly, who all serve four-year terms. The Federal District also elects its governor and a District Assembly. Brazil's 5,564 *municípios* are governed by elected mayors, vice mayors, and local councils of from nine to twenty-one representatives (*municípios* with more than 1 million inhabitants have substantially larger councils).

Throughout Brazil's history as a republic, there has been a tension between the centralizing ambitions of the central government and the states' aspirations for greater autonomy. Under military rule, the central government collected most taxes, dictated the rates on the ones state and local governments were allowed to levy, and restricted the use of federal revenue-sharing funds intended to supplement state and local taxes.

With redemocratization, the Union restored substantial fiscal resources and autonomy to subnational governments. Regional politicians succeeded in writing a "new federalism" into the 1988 Constitution, which required that 21.5 percent of the income tax and the industrial products tax be returned to the states and 22.5 percent to the municipal governments, with no strings attached. The automatic transfers generated by this provision, which increased in fifteen years by over 200 percent, resulted in a dramatic increase in the share of total expenditure by state and local governments. This grew from 32 percent in 1980

to over 40 percent in 2000, a figure comparable to U.S. levels. Local governments in particular gained in comparison with the 1960s and 1970s. From 1975 to 1995, the share of total national expenditures of Brazilian municipalities nearly doubled.[5]

In May 2000, the government passed the **Fiscal Responsibility Law,** which sets strict spending limits for all levels of government and prohibits the central government from refinancing subnational debt. It incorporated the guidelines of the *Camata law*, which limited all state government payrolls to 60 percent of total state revenues. After the Fiscal Responsibility Law came into effect, the share of total government expenditures accounted for by state and municipal levels of government declined, in 2003, to 15 and 11 percent, respectively.

## The Executive Branch

The president is both the head of state and the head of government. The president and vice president are elected jointly for four-year terms (Figure 15.4). Since 1997 they can be immediately reelected once. The military regime broadly amplified the powers of the Executive Branch. The democratic constitution only partially reinstituted congressional authority in many of these areas. Today, the president has ample legislative powers, including the exclusive power to initiate budget legislation and to issue emergency decrees.

## The Legislative Branch

The national Congress is made up of two houses that form a system of "balanced bicameralism" in that one house does not clearly dominate the other. Both can initiate legislation, and they share the power to review the national budget.

The upper house, the Senate, has three senators from each state and the Federal District, for a total of eighty-one. Senators serve staggered eight-year terms; elections are held every four years alternately for one-third and two-thirds of the Senate.

The lower house, the Chamber of Deputies, has grown in recent decades along with the addition of more states. It now comprises 513 representatives from twenty-six states and the Federal District. Deputies serve four-year terms. The size of each state's delegation is determined in proportion to its population—but the Constitution establishes a minimum of eight

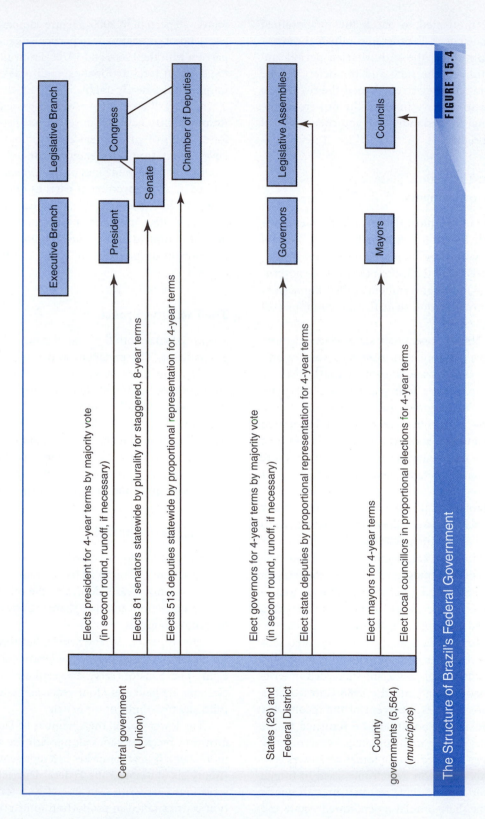

**FIGURE 15.4**

The Structure of Brazil's Federal Government

Executive Branch   Legislative Branch

Central government (Union)

President — Congress — Senate — Chamber of Deputies

Elects president for 4-year terms by majority vote (in second round, runoff, if necessary)

Elects 81 senators statewide by plurality for staggered, 8-year terms

Elects 513 deputies statewide by proportional representation for 4-year terms

States (26) and Federal District

Governors   Legislative Assemblies

Elect governors for 4-year terms by majority vote (in second round, runoff, if necessary)

Elect state deputies by proportional representation for 4-year terms

County governments (5,564) (*municípios*)

Mayors   Councils

Elect mayors for 4-year terms

Elect local councillors in proportional elections for 4-year terms

Brazilian President Lula,
during the 2002 campaign.

AP Images/Marcelo Hernandez

and a maximum of seventy deputies for each state. These constitutional limits especially underrepresent residents of the densely populated southeastern and southern states. Whereas one deputy represents approximately 40,000 residents in the Amazonian state of Roraima and 60,000 in Amapá, each deputy in São Paulo represents 530,000 citizens. While democracies often overrepresent underpopulated regions in *upper chambers* in order to safeguard the interests of all federal units (as in the U.S. Senate), the malapportionment of Brazil's *lower house*, exacerbated by the military to advantage its supporters in the Northeast and the Amazon, is unusual.

Congress is no longer the rubber stamp it was during the military regime. Today it can initiate legislation, review the budget, approve or reject emergency laws, and override presidential vetoes. It conducts public hearings on proposed legislation and summons ministers of government.

With the approval of one-third of both the Chamber of Deputies and the Senate, Congress can set up **Parliamentary Commissions of Inquiry (CPIs).** In the 1990s, CPIs inquired into the financial crisis in the state enterprises and severe breaches of public ethics, including the 1992 allegations of corruption against President Collor de Mello and his campaign treasurer, the 1993 congressional budget scandal, and the 1997 controversy surrounding state government bonds. In all, there were nineteen CPIs convened during the 51st Congress (1999–2002) and ten in the first three and one-half years of the 52nd Congress (2003–2006). Among the most notable inquiries were those reviewing the role of the National Economic and Social Development Bank (BNDES) in the privatization of the electrical energy sector; the PT campaign finance scandal in 2005; and the corruption scandal involving the so-called bloodsuckers, dozens of members of Congress implicated in skimming off the sales of ambulances at inflated prices.

## The Judiciary

The Judicial Branch is comprised of the Supreme Court, the Superior Court, five regional federal appeals courts, labor courts, electoral courts, military courts, and state courts. The Constitution stipulates criteria for entry into judicial service (by means of a competitive examination), promotion (by seniority and merit), and mandatory retirement at the age of 70 or after thirty years of service. Eleven justices, or "ministers," are named by the president to the Supreme (constitutional) Court—**Supremo Tribunal Federal (STF)**—and approved by the Senate, as are thirty-three ministers to the Superior (civil) Court.

The electoral courts constitute a subsystem of the federal judicial system. The Superior Electoral Court—**Tribunal Superior Eleitoral (TSE)**—came into being in 1932 to check the rampant electoral fraud in the Old Republic. Today, electoral courts at all levels rule on a variety of areas relating to party registration, the mandates of elected members of Congress, the admissibility of candidacies, procedures for counting ballots, and even the constitutionality of legislation governing these areas.

The labor courts were created by the Consolidated Labor Code of 1943. Once the primary venue in which grievances between labor and management were settled, today superior and regional labor courts arbitrate disputes between private-sector workers and employers and public-sector workers and governmental authorities when they cannot come to an agreement through collective bargaining.

The military justice system was also retained in the 1988 Constitution, but its reach has been scaled back since the dictatorship, when military courts had the jurisdiction to try civilians for crimes against "national security." Today, federal and state military courts try military crimes. These include most crimes committed by military police, which are responsible for patrolling the streets (civilian police are investigators). Cases of intentional homicide by the military police against civilians are now tried before civilian judges and juries. Ordinary state courts enforce state constitutions and state laws.

The courts today are stronger than ever before. The 1988 Constitution notably expanded judicial power, broadened individual rights, and expanded access to the courts at all levels of the federal judiciary. It also enhanced judicial independence by guaranteeing judicial budget autonomy, establishing professional procedures of appointment, and maintaining stable terms for judges. As a result, judges enjoy a good deal of independence even from superiors.

While most of these reforms have had salutary effects, there have also been drawbacks. Most notably, the federal court system is clogged and has been used to stall or block policy. To give a comparative sense of the federal courts' workload, Brazil has three-fifths the population of the United States, but in 2001 Brazil's Supreme Constitutional Court heard more than 110,000 cases, the STJ nearly 185,000, and five Regional Federal Tribunals another 545,500. The number of cases before Brazil's Supreme Court rose again in 2002 to 160,000. In contrast, in 2001 the U.S. Supreme Court ruled on 7,852 cases and twelve U.S. Courts of Appeal ruled on another 57,464.[6]

There are several reasons why the docket of Brazil's federal courts is so overloaded. For one, because lower courts' decisions are not binding or final, cases are appealed repeatedly until they finally reach the STF. Second, a legal instrument known as a **direct action of unconstitutionality** (ADIN) allows plaintiffs (the president, leaders of the Senate and Chamber, state governors, the organization of Brazilian lawyers, political parties with representation in Congress, and national union or class associations) to question the constitutionality of a policy directly at the STF without going through the lower courts. Not surprisingly, most constitutional challenges come from a select group of political actors—state governors (27 percent), class associations (26 percent), and political parties (21 percent)—not ordinary citizens.[7]

When political actors do use the lower courts for constitutional complaints, they do so in a strategic manner, to benefit from the delay of decisions. Judicial autonomy has promoted broad judicial activism, which has benefited groups with privileged access to the court system seeking to stall or block policies coming out of the Executive or Legislative branches. The Brazilian judiciary has been active in recent years in tax, pension, and land reform issues, often ruling against the Executive and Congress. Many judicial rulings may have negatively impacted the economy. During his presidential campaign in 2006, opposition candidate Gerardo Alckmin highlighted judicial insecurity as an impediment to private-sector investment and growth.[8]

## Limitations on Governmental Authority

Elevating their symbolic importance, the opening paragraphs of the 1988 Constitution exalt the principles of sovereignty, citizenship, human dignity, social values, and political pluralism. Substantively, the Constitution extends the traditional guarantees of individual rights to social groups and prohibits discrimination against minorities. It also grants parties, unions, and civic associations legal recourse against the actions of other social actors and permits them to challenge before the Supreme Court the constitutionality of legislation and administrative rulings. Individual rights are inviolable, and articles stipulating the federal form of the state, the direct, secret, universal, and regular periodic vote, and the separation of powers cannot be amended. Other articles can be amended by initiative of one-third of the Chamber of Deputies or the Senate, the president, or by a relative majority of the state Legislative Assemblies. Successful passage of constitutional amendments requires a three-fifths vote of both houses, on two separate occasions.

The Brazilian executive must observe limits when invoking a state of siege in order to restore public order (the president may declare an unlimited state of siege in wartime). A state of siege must be approved by an absolute congressional majority, not exceed 30 days, and is renewable only once. In cases of war or public disturbance, the government can suspend the right of free assembly and institute procedures of search and seizure. However, it cannot lift the immunity of federal deputies and senators, and its ability to censor the press, telecommunications, and private correspondence is limited.

Each tier of the court system is vested with the power of judicial review. Traditionally, Brazilian courts had the power to review legislation only on a case-by-case basis. Today, with the broader power of abstract review, courts may assume a more activist bent. The Supreme Court is charged to review the constitutionality of legislation, as well as to try the president and members of Congress for common crimes. With the power to determine the constitutionality of electoral legislation, the Superior Electoral Court constitutes another check on government.

An important, newly redesigned institution is the **Ministério Público (Public Prosecution).** It became formally independent of the Executive and Judicial branches of government with the 1988 Constitution (under military rule, it was part of the Executive Branch). The Public Prosecution is responsible for defending the constitutional interests of citizens and society at large, safeguarding the environment, protecting consumers, guaranteeing minority rights, and monitoring public administration at both the federal and state levels. It can take to court any person or entity for any breaches of collective rights or the artistic and cultural autonomy of the nation. The independence of its more than 300 federal and nearly 1000 state-level members, who enter through a civil service exam, is safeguarded through life tenure.

Since it came into existence, hundreds of mayors and ex-mayors have been charged and convicted for the misuse of public funds, and even members of Congress have been investigated for corruption. The Public Prosecution has received high marks from the most respected newspapers in Brazil for providing a "new sense of hope that we can end public impunity."[9]

Additionally, the **Tribunal de Contas,** a federal court of accounts, though formally part of the Legislative Branch of government (six of its nine members are appointed by Congress), acts more like an independent agency overseeing accounts rendered by the president for administration of the Brazilian government. It has broad oversight powers, and it can investigate even congressional accounts. Crucially, its members, like those of the Ministério Público, have job tenure.

## POLITICAL CULTURE

Most observers would agree that Brazil's politics are elite-dominated, a consequence of a centuries-long pattern of socioeconomic inequality and the country's political inheritance. Although general laws exist for all citizens, Brazilian society confers advantages on those who are "somebody." As one noted Brazilian anthropologist put it, social differentiation before the law means that the "somebodies" are above and beyond the reach of the law, but the masses are subject to and victims of the law. The "somebody" can say to "the people," "*Você sabe com quem está falando?*" ("Do you know with whom you are speaking?").[10]

Brazil also has a legacy of patrimonialism, a traditional system of domination of society by a strong state with a centralized bureaucracy. For most of the twentieth century, Brazilians from the left to the right of the political spectrum looked to the state for solutions. Both right and left became disenchanted with statism during the dictatorship. For the right, the state was too interventionist and impermeable to societal interests; for the left, the dream of an egalitarian state was turned into a nightmare of violence and repression. Many Brazilians henceforth began to view their trust in the state as folly and looked instead to civil society to lead the way toward change.

## Civil Society

During the military regime, ordinary citizens came together in independent organizations for social solidarity, to petition government for better services, and to oppose authoritarian rule. Brazilian civil society witnessed an unprecedented spate of associational activity among new social movements—of neighborhood associations, women, blacks, ecologists, and grassroots Catholics. These new social movements, some have contended, contributed to the democratization of political culture by socializing the women, religious workers, and slum dwellers who joined them into the norms of participatory democracy. Since the transition to democracy, membership in these organizations has only grown.

*Religion and Political Culture*  Brazil is a Catholic nation, and the country with the largest number of Catholics in the world. Nevertheless, religious observance has traditionally been low, and unlike many other predominantly Latin and Catholic countries, the church did not exercise significant influence in the educational system. Religion was not an important factor in elections. Before 1964 the church had a conservative orientation, and was generally supportive of the state and the dominant elites, but it did not attempt to impose a radically conservative order.

After 1964, the Brazilian Catholic Church earned the reputation of being one of the most progressive in the world. Much of the hierarchy shared with parish priests, nuns, and the laity a vision of a "popular" church committed to the poor. During the military regime, the church became an important and effective opponent of authoritarian rule. It provided a safe haven for the victims of state repression of various faiths and their families, and in the late 1970s it sheltered striking workers. Members of the popular church helped to organize the labor movement and supported the Workers' Party. Political action and a commitment to working for social justice and a redistribution of power and wealth were encouraged by **liberation theology,** which, exhorting the faithful to embrace the poor as implied in the Gospels, gained widespread adherence in Brazil and other parts of Latin America in the 1970s. Even today, church groups continue to play an active role in helping to organize social movements in defense of the material as well as moral interests of their poor parishioners.

Perhaps the most important initiative of the popular church and the one with a direct bearing on the transformation of political culture in Brazil was the promotion of **ecclesial base communities (CEBs)**— small, relatively homogeneous, grassroots groups of ten to forty people who gather regularly to read the Bible and reflect on their daily lives in light of the Gospel. Brazil's bishops actively promoted the creation of CEBs in the spirit of the Vatican II reforms, which sought to energize the church by making participation less ritualistic and more meaningful for the faithful, and as a response to the shortage of priests. The CEBs handed the study of the Bible directly to the people, who had previously relied on priests to interpret the message of the Gospel for them, thereby transforming the attitudes of their members toward hierarchy and authority, within and outside the church. CEB members also gained from their participation in these local church groups the personal confidence and leadership skills that were necessary to broaden their participation in community affairs, neighborhood and women's movements, and eventually politics. Today, there are more than 100,000 of these grassroots communities across Brazil, and in one national survey, 40 percent of women and 31 percent of men reported belonging to one.[11]

The message carried by CEBs has recently changed, and the scope of their activities has narrowed. Since the mid-1980s, papal leadership has restrained liberation theologians, appointed several conservative bishops, and reduced the influence of progressive bishops in the **National Conference of Brazilian Bishops (CNBB).**

Competition from other religions has also refocused church leadership on evangelization and spirituality. The Catholic Church has long shared the fealty of many Brazilians with such religions of the African Diaspora. Today, its religious hegemony is especially challenged by Pentecostal Protestantism, which has made inroads among those in the Brazilian population who are usually poorer, less literate, and seeking faith healing and personal redemption. Brazil's Catholics have converted to Protestant sects on a massive scale. Whereas 90 percent of the population was at least nominally Catholic in 1950, only 74 percent of Brazilians self-identified as Roman Catholic in the 2000 Census. Traditional and Pentecostal Evangelicals constituted 15 percent of the population; 2 percent reported practicing spiritism, Umbanda, and Candomblé; and 7 percent declared themselves to have no religion.

Has participation in religious organizations changed Brazil's political culture? In Brazil as elsewhere, people who participate in church groups also tend to join voluntary associations and participate more actively in politics. Though there is a large Protestant electoral and legislative presence, there is no appreciable difference in political participation rates, outlooks, and voting patterns among Catholics and Protestants. Catholic members of CEBs, however, are more likely to support the Workers' Party than are Catholics associated with conservative movements within the church, such as the Catholic Charismatic Renewal.[12]

**Gender Relations** As a Latin American country, Brazil has not been immune from the cultural influences of *machismo*—which familiarly refers to an aggressive and virile form of masculinity—and *marianismo,* the cult of the Virgin Mary and the feminine counterpart of *machismo,* which views Latin American women as morally superior to men and the force that holds together the family and brings up the children.

Across Latin America, these traditional images and self-images of women contributed to their political conservatism. This factor, in turn, was exploited by parties of the right in the period of competitive party politics and later by the region's militaries to justify their interventions and policies. In Brazil, women voted in larger numbers for candidates of the right than did men. In 1964, they mobilized against "communism," "subversion," and the leftist government of João Goulart in favor of the "family," "God," and "freedom."

Under military rule, the traditional image and orientations toward politics of women began to change. For the middle and upper classes, political opportunity followed educational and occupational opportunities. The number of girls graduating from secondary school soared from 9 percent in 1950 to 25 percent in 1970 and nearly half in 1980, and just in the six-year period from 1969 to 1975, the number of women attending Brazilian universities increased fivefold (while the number of men doubled). By 1980, more women than men were enrolled in Brazil's universities, and the number of women earning master's and doctoral degrees exploded.

Authoritarianism, coincidentally, also exercised an important economic impact on poor women. With the drop in the value of the minimum wage and the lack of adequate social services and urban infrastructure, these women found it increasingly more difficult to perform their ascribed feminine roles of securing the welfare of their families and communities. As wives and mothers, they assumed the lead in their communities' struggles for health care and sanitation, and even against the rising cost of living.

With the political liberalization of the mid-1970s, women's movements were formed. The regime at first viewed women's movements as apolitical and allowed them greater political space than traditional labor movements. Eventually during the 1970s and 1980s as many as 400 feminist organizations were formed, turning the Brazilian women's movement into one of Latin America's most powerful. Women's movements injected into the national political debate several issues that had previously been considered private: reproductive rights, violence against women, and daycare.

Several recent policy developments signal a change in the attitudes of Brazilians about gender and politics. Political parties adopted many concerns of the women's movement in their party programs, and the Constitution substituted the concept of *pater familiae*—which attributes greater authority to the man as the head of a married couple—with the concept of equal and shared authority. To combat violence against women, city governments created police precincts staffed entirely by female police officers to process complaints of rape and domestic violence. In 1991, the law absolving men of the murder of their wives when in the "legitimate defense of their honor" was abrogated. Under pressure from feminists, more than a dozen public hospitals in Brazil introduced legal abortion services (for victims of rape). In 2001, the Brazilian Congress approved a new civil code granting men and women equality in marriage and rendering children equal in rights and obligations regardless of the circumstances of their birth. Debate has begun on extending the conditions under which legal abortions may be performed.

Underlying these changes are shifts in attitudes among both women and men. The combination of exposure to secondary and higher education, workplace experience, and political activity visibly and measurably altered the political attitudes of women. Women who worked outside the home and who were well educated were much more likely to express an interest in politics, want to vote, watch an electoral campaign, and identify with a political party (particularly one on the left of the political spectrum).[13]

A gender gap nonetheless remains. In 2006, 64 percent of men but only 58 percent of women voted for Lula in the second round presidential election. Nonetheless, Brazilians hold favorable attitudes toward women holding office. In 2001, a majority of Brazilians believed that women in senior government posts are more honest, responsible, trustworthy, and competent than men.[14] As we shall see later in this chapter, more women have been recruited into politics and high elective office in recent years than ever before.

*Race and Racial Politics* Until recently, few Brazilians acknowledged that Brazil had a "race problem." For decades, they believed the official myth that compared with the United States, beset by bigotry and race-related violence, Brazil had a "racial democracy." Drawing from Gilberto Freyre's classic 1933 thesis that Portuguese masters viewed their African slaves more favorably, and treated them less harshly, than in North America,[15] the myth claimed that widespread miscegenation had blurred the boundaries of racial identification and prevented the development of conflict based on a polarized racial consciousness. Brazilians believed that the absence of state-sponsored segregation and the social recognition of intermediate racial categories made their postemancipation society more racially and culturally accommodating than other multiracial societies. Following from this analysis, they also believed that disadvantage was based on class, not race.

The myth notwithstanding, racial prejudice in Brazil is pervasive and not as subtle as many Brazilians believe. Although the white middle class believes in equal opportunities for mulattoes and blacks, they accept most stereotypes of blacks and mulattoes (including sexual promiscuity and an aversion to thrift, work, and trustworthiness) and would not marry a black or mulatto. A group of United Nations experts concluded after an October 2005 mission to Brazil that "racial discrimination is deeply rooted in Brazil and has influenced the structure of the entire society for the last five centuries," and that "traveling in Brazil is like moving simultaneously between two different planets, from that of the lively colored and mixed races of the streets to that of the almost all-white corridors of political, social, economic and media power."[16]

Cultural movements of black Brazilians date back to the 1940s, but racial prejudice, disadvantage, and outright repression during the military regime sparked the formation of new black movements during the political opening. The Unified Black Movement Against Racial Discrimination—the **Movimento Negro Unificado**—formed in 1978 to call attention to racism and the poor quality of life of Brazil's nonwhite population. Although it initially lacked the political success of other movements, in part due to the disparate nature of the black movement and even police repression, it did raise a new racial consciousness among Brazil's black population. A quarter century after its formation, it has campaigned for affirmative action quotas and for an end to extrajudicial police killings of black youth (see Box 15.1).

## How Democratic Are Brazilians?

Have the expansion of civil society, the presence of new subcultures, and other factors added up to any palpable changes in the national political culture of Brazil? In particular, is there any evidence that Brazil is developing a more democratic political culture (also see Chapter 3)?

On the one hand, Brazilians are less tolerant of authoritarianism than ever before. Whereas in the early 1970s the Brazilian population was generally accepting of the military's participation in politics, by the late 1980s Brazilians expressed a clear preference for democracy over dictatorship.

On the other hand, if mass attitudes shifted in favor of democracy, Brazilians did not share a single vision of what *kind* of democracy they supported. In the early 1980s, better-educated, middle-class Brazilians (who held democracy in higher esteem than those with only a primary school education) favored restoring civilian democratic institutions but were less likely to believe that people were capable of voting wisely or to support enfranchising illiterates. Conversely, less well-educated, working-class Brazilians desired universal suffrage without necessarily being committed to civilian governmental institutions.[17] This picture essentially has not changed. Even today, the poor support democracy conditionally, and value it more for its substantive promise than its procedures. Tellingly, in one recent poll, when asked, "What is the principal meaning of democracy?" 26 percent of

**BOX 15.1**

## Brazil's Controversial Racial Quotas

At the World Conference on Racism in South Africa in September 2001, Brazil's government report recommended the adoption of quotas to expand the access of black students to public universities. Soon thereafter, the state governments of Rio de Janeiro and Bahia announced they would reserve 40 percent of the places in their state universities for Afro-Brazilians (a lower quota of 20 percent was set in Minas Gerais). In early 2003, the Foreign Ministry (Itamaraty) launched an affirmative action program that provides scholarship support for up to twenty black candidates to help them study for the public service entrance exam. Legislation has been introduced to extend the quotas to the federal university system, and a debate has begun on establishing quotas for professors.

While the facts of racial disadvantage are no longer in dispute in Brazil, the desirability of a quota system is controversial. Quotas are popular among the poor, regardless of race, but not among the well-off.

Overall, 65 percent of Brazilians in a nationwide poll in mid-2006 favored racial quotas in university admissions. However, those earning less than two times the minimum wage were 1.8 times as likely to support racial quotas as those earning more than ten times the minimum.

Supporters of quotas argue that blacks and mulattos, who make up almost half of the population, are the poorest, least well educated, and most severely disadvantaged in Brazilian society, and that only a strong affirmative action program will lift them from poverty. Opponents charge that quotas exacerbate prejudice, lead to reverse discrimination, insult blacks by presuming they cannot compete on their own merits, and fail to address the causes of black exclusion. Critics of quotas also question how easy it would be to identify just who is black in Brazil. Activists counter that if self-identification does not work, when in doubt, "call a policeman, who always knows."

Sources: Mala Htun, "From 'Racial Democracy' to Affirmative Action: Changing State Policy on Race in Brazil," *Latin American Research Review*, 39, no. 1 (2004): 60–89; and FolhaOnline, 23 July 2006.

Brazilians surveyed cited "freedom" and 15 percent cited "elections" (compared with the Latin American averages of 38 and 26 percent, respectively), but 37 percent answered "an economy that assures one an honorable wage," well above the Latin American mean of 21 percent (see Figure 15.5).

If Brazilians are more committed to democracy today, they distrust politicians, political parties, and democratic institutions more than in the recent past. Immediately after the 1989 election, 39 percent of respondents expressed confidence in Congress and 41 percent in the office of the president. In 2000, only 19 percent still trusted Congress, and only 25 percent trusted the president.[18] In 2005, public confidence had slid even farther; a mere 10 percent retained trust in political parties and 8 percent in politicians (down from 15 and 12 percent, respectively, in 1999).[19] Less than half of Brazilians believed that without Congress, there could be no democracy.

Do Brazilians distrust democratic institutions today more than other Latin Americans? The short

answer is yes. In 2005, 62 percent of all Latin Americans but only 56 percent of Brazilians expressed the view that they would not support a military government under any circumstances. Moreover, only 37 percent of Brazilians expressed support for the democratic regime (well below the Latin American average of 53 percent), and only 22 percent of Brazilians were satisfied with how democracy works (compared with 31 percent across the region).

Brazilians were also less aware of their civic rights and responsibilities than most Latin Americans; in 2005, only a quarter reported that they knew at least something about the country's Constitution. Finally, Brazilians also did not trust each other: only about 3 percent agreed that "you can trust most people." In their level of interpersonal trust, which many political scientists consider to be essential to democracy, Brazilians scored the lowest of any Latin American nation.

Such responses may lead one to believe that Brazil's democratic political culture is weak. Yet, in

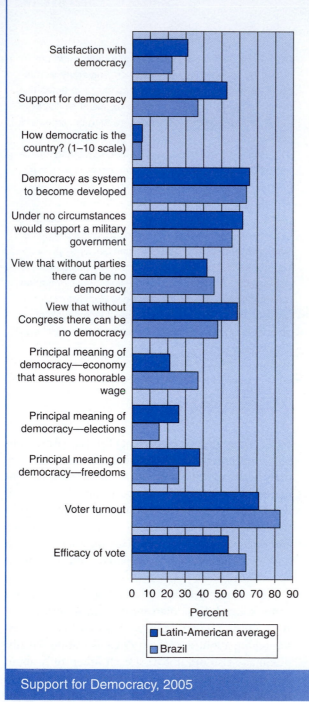

Key:

Q. In general, would you say that you are very satisfied, somewhat satisfied, not very satisfied, or not satisfied at all with the functioning of democracy in Brazil? Here "very satisfied" and "somewhat satisfied."

Q. Democracy is preferable to any other form of government. In some circumstances, an authoritarian government can be preferable to a democratic one. For people like me, it doesn't matter whether the regime is democratic or nondemocratic. Percent agreeing that "democracy is preferable to any other form of government."

Q. On a scale from 1 to 10, where 1 is "not democratic" and 10 is "totally democratic," where would you put Brazil? (Mean response.)

Q. Are you very much in agreement, in agreement, in disagreement, or very much in disagreement with the following statement: "Democracy is the only system under which Brazil can become developed." Here "very much in agreement and "in agreement."

Q. Would you support a military government as a replacement for the democratic government, if things became very difficult, or would you not support a military government under any circumstance? Here "under no circumstance would I support a military government."

Q. There are people who say that without parties there can be no democracy, while other people say that democracy can function without parties. Which phrase comes closer to your view?

Q. There are people who say that without a national Congress there can be no democracy, while other people say that democracy can function without a national Congress. Which phrase comes closer to your view?

Q. People often have different points of view on what are the most important characteristics of democracy. Choose only one characteristic, that to you, is the most essential feature of a democracy: regular, free, and fair elections; an economy that assures a just wage; freedom of expression to be openly critical; a judicial system that treats everyone equally; respect for minorities; government of the majority; members of a parliament that represent their voters; a competitive party system; don't know, no response.

**Support for Democracy, 2005**                          **FIGURE 15.5**

Source: *Informe Latinobarómetro 2005* (available at www.latinobarometro.org).

other ways, Brazilians *behave* in more democratic ways than their lukewarm responses to these questions might imply. They turn out to vote at higher rates and believe their vote matters more than on average across Latin America. Three in ten speak of politics, a quarter try to convince others of their political positions, and Brazilians join civic organizations in larger numbers than in other emerging democracies.

Moreover, in a salutary trend for strengthening the fabric of Brazilian democracy, Brazilian tolerance for corruption may have run out even before the 2005 scandal. Contrary to the longstanding belief that Brazilians view favorably politicians or a party that "robs, but gets things done," in 2002, 65 percent of respondents to the National Election Study disagreed with the assertion "it doesn't matter if a politician robs, as long as he gets done things that the population needs" (see Figure 15.6). As if to anticipate the PT's campaign finance scandal, moreover, 85 percent disagreed that a politician that delivers good government should be able to divert public money to finance his electoral campaign.

In sum, there is little doubt that political culture in Brazil has changed in the past quarter century. Brazilians generally have grown more skeptical of hierarchy, less tolerant of corruption, and more supportive of democracy in practice, if not always in surveys. But this transformation is incomplete. Alongside the religious, feminist, and racial groups of civil society that have contributed to the democratization of civil society, other citizens who have not participated in these groups have been socialized in more traditional ways.

## SOCIALIZATION AND MASS COMMUNICATION

### Political Learning

In most countries, there is a consensus that a good deal of political learning takes place in such key social institutions as schools, the family, churches, and community groups. In Brazil, traditionally, the first two of these institutions were generally only weak agents of political socialization. In contrast with countries with higher levels of educational attainment, Brazilian schools were poorly staffed and attended, and until recently, much of the population did not stay in school past the third grade. In a context of extremely weak partisanship, moreover, families did not generally transmit political loyalties.

Religious, neighborhood, and workplace associations have served as more significant sources of political socialization, especially in recent decades. The diversity of Brazil's religious denominations, beliefs, and experiences had produced multiple paths of political socialization. Whereas the intense discussions about party platforms and policies that concern the poor in the Roman Catholic grassroots ecclesial communities and "faith and politics" groups have profoundly shaped the political worldviews of their poor participants in a more progressive direction, the Charismatic Catholic Renewal and various Pentecostal Protestant sects have, to a lesser degree, socialized their members in more traditionally conservative ways. Political discussion within social networks and neighborhood contexts has also helped to form political opinions, especially during election campaigns.[20]

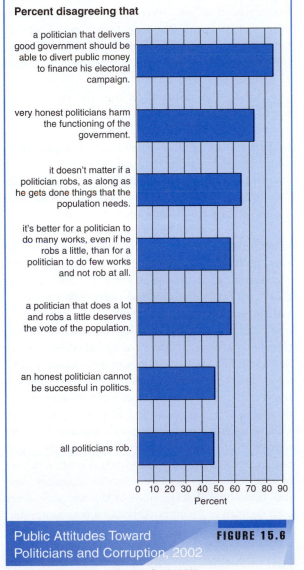

**Percent disagreeing that**

- a politician that delivers good government should be able to divert public money to finance his electoral campaign.
- very honest politicians harm the functioning of the government.
- it doesn't matter if a politician robs, as along as he gets done things that the population needs.
- it's better for a politician to do many works, even if he robs a little, than for a politician to do few works and not rob at all.
- a politician that does a lot and robs a little deserves the vote of the population.
- an honest politician cannot be successful in politics.
- all politicians rob.

Percent

**Public Attitudes Toward Politicians and Corruption, 2002**    **FIGURE 15.6**

Source: Brazilian National Election Study, 2002.

## Mass Media

Political scientists generally believe that in modern society institutions such as the mass media have taken the place of political parties and other traditional institutions in shaping the formation of the political culture, political attitudes, and even voting propensities. They particularly believe this is true in countries like Brazil where parties do not have deep roots in the electorate. Given low levels of educational attainment, it is not surprising that 95 percent of the population says it watches television regularly and levels of newspaper readership are comparatively low. Brazil's daily newspaper circulation rate is forty-six per 1,000 inhabitants, compared with sixty in India, ninety-four in Mexico, and 105 in Russia (see Table 7.4 in Chapter 7). By contrast, the prevalence of televisions (369 per 1,000) is far greater than in India and Mexico.

Analysts claim that television has influenced the political attitudes of Brazilians in at least three ways. First, it brings politics into Brazilian homes via the *horário gratuito*, free television time set aside during election campaigns for the political parties to advertise their candidates and messages.

Second, individual candidates and parties receive coverage during television news and any televised debates. Free television time for candidates, televised debates, and television news shape voters' perceptions to a degree surpassed only by conversations with family and friends.[21]

Third, *telenovelas* (prime-time soap operas) project themes that subtly influence the ways in which people view politicians and institutions.

In a context in which the media holds such influence, it is noteworthy that the ownership of television and radio stations in Brazil is extremely concentrated. Brazil's powerful Globo network, one of the largest networks in the world, commands the lion's share of the national audience, though its nearest rival, the STB (Brazilian Television System), has been gaining ground in recent years. Most observers believe that the media, and particularly the Globo network, played a strong role in promoting the successful presidential candidacies of Fernando Collor de Mello in 1989 and Fernando Henrique Cardoso in 1994. Locally, the Ministry of Communications notoriously awarded licenses for television and radio stations in return for political support. Politicians still use media empires in their home states to influence their coverage on local television and radio news and in major newspapers they own or control. In some states, more than half of the local congressional delegation owns a television station, a ratio station, or both.

## POLITICAL RECRUITMENT AND POLITICAL PARTICIPATION

### Politics at the Elite Level

*Elite Recruitment* Traditionally, Brazilian politics was elite-dominated. Within the elite, recruitment took place within a small circle of political families. Typically, leading politicians were from landed families, schooled in law, served several terms of elective office as local councillor, state deputy, and eventually federal deputy, and built up their power base by joining the state cabinet or becoming president of the state Legislative Assembly.

During the military regime, the structure of opportunity improved for the middle and upper-middle classes. Technical credentials and competence became a more broadly applied criteria for advancement, especially in the national cabinet, federal and state bureaucracies, and public-sector companies. The "technocrats" were by and large educated in engineering and economics in a few select universities.

With the political liberalization of the late authoritarian period and especially since the return to democracy, political recruitment patterns changed again. Technocratic expertise was still prized in the economic ministries, but politicians played a larger role in the political and social service ministries. Politics is now more open to representatives from diverse educational and class backgrounds, as evidenced by Lula's election (see Box 15.2). Five percent of the deputies elected in 2002 were educators; 7 percent were entrepreneurs in industry, commerce, or finance; 8 percent were economists, engineers, or agronomists; and 10 percent were physicians or other medical professionals, but only 1 percent were blue-collar workers (see Table 15.1). Nearly 20 percent identified a political post—such as senator, deputy, or local councillor—as their principal occupation, and the "traditional" backgrounds of law and agriculture both declined to 2 percent. Although it is no longer necessary to belong to or be allied with an elite family to run for elective office, in some parts of Brazil and on some party labels, family connections can still be most helpful.

## From Metalworker to Chief Executive: President Lula

BOX 15.2

Luiz Inácio "Lula" da Silva, a metalworker, was born in rural Pernambuco and migrated to São Paulo as a child with his family. Formally, he graduated only from primary school (though he earned a high school equivalency degree and enrolled in a technical training school). At age 14, he went to work in a screw factory. He ran for his first union post in 1968, and by 1975 had become president of the Metalworkers' Union of São Bernardo and Diadema. This post catapulted him to national and international prominence in the late 1970s. He cofounded the Workers' Party and served as its standard-bearer in every presidential election since its inception. In the 2002 presidential elections, he won a resounding victory with 52.8 million votes, 61.3 percent of the more than 86 million valid votes cast. The U.S. Ambassador to Brazil at the time, Donna Hrinak, characterized Lula's rise from such humble origins to the Brazilian presidency as emblematic of the "American success story."

Lula has been a steadfast voice for economic nationalism and social justice. In the 2002 election, he donned a suit and tie, trimmed (but did not shave) his beard, and moved his party and his electoral platform closer toward the political center. He moderated his tone on Brazil's international commitments, including its agreements with the International Monetary Fund, its foreign debt obligations, and its stance on a hemispheric trade zone and economic liberalization, but not on hunger, health, and social justice.

### Backgrounds of Brazilian Deputies, 2003–2007 (percentage)

TABLE 15.1

| Occupational Experience | Percentage |
| --- | --- |
| Politics (Senator, Deputy, Councillor) | 29.0 |
| Lawyer/Judge | 15.0 |
| Physician/Dentist | 10.0 |
| Technical (Engineer, Agronomist, Economist) | 8.0 |
| Industrialist, Merchant, Entrepreneur | 7.0 |
| Professor/Teacher | 5.0 |
| White Collar (Manager, Accountant) | 3.0 |
| Rural Property Owner | 2.0 |
| Journalist, Broadcaster | 2.0 |
| Government Employee | 2.0 |
| Military/Police | 1.0 |
| Blue Collar | 1.0 |
| Religious | 2.0 |
| Student | .5 |
| Retired | .5 |
| Other | 12.0 |

Source: Tribunal Superior Eleitoral (TSE) (available at http://www.tse .gov.br).

In running for reelection, incumbent deputies in Brazil have more of an advantage than in many Latin American countries but far less so than in the United States. The turnover rates—that is, the percentage of deputies who did not occupy a seat in the previous Congress—was 47 in 2002.[22] Only about a quarter serve more than two consecutive terms. About a quarter of the deputies elected in 1990 had been cabinet secretaries in their respective states.[23] Deputies are nonetheless fairly adept at retaining their seats if they choose to run again. In 1995, 70 percent of the members of Congress sought reelection; of these, 62 percent won back their seats.[24] The level and type of political experience of members of Congress also vary considerably along with their party label, reflecting their party's proximity to power.

How open is entry to the exclusive club of the Brazilian Congress? Women have gained many more seats than in earlier decades, when one or two at most were elected to the Congress, but progress has nonetheless been slow. In 1994, a breakthrough year, thirty-two women were elected as federal deputies and eighty-two as state deputies. Also, Roseana Sarney of Maranhão, the daughter of former president José Sarney, became the first woman to be elected a state governor in Brazil. That same year, five women were elected to the Senate. One of them, Marina Silva, a 36-year-old who was illiterate and had worked as a maid at age 16, had gone on to earn a university degree in history and organize against the destruction of rubber trees in the Amazon. Another, Benedita Da Silva, the daughter of a laundrywoman, eventually became governor of the state of Rio de Janeiro.

Since then, however, although there have been flashes of success in the recruitment of women to high office, overall progress in female representation in the corridors of political power has been slow. In 2002, Rita Camata, a deputy of the Party of the Brazilian Democratic Movement (PMDB) from the state of Espírito Santo, was chosen to be José Serra's vice presidential running mate, and in 2006, three women were elected state governors. Yet, only four women gained Senate seats in 2006 (joining seven other incumbents for a total of 14 percent), and forty-five won election to the Chamber of Deputies (representing 9 percent of the total). In all, of the 2,498 women running for federal and statewide offices in 2006, only 175, or 7 percent of the total, were elected. The presence of Brazilian women in elective office is also low compared with several other Latin American countries that have adopted effective quota laws and other affirmative action measures. Brazil quotas have set targets, but they have resulted in only minimal gains in women's representation.

Women are also underrepresented in top Executive Branch decisionmaking posts, the judicial system, and the diplomatic corps. In 2000, Brazil was one of only three Latin American countries to have no female ministers in the Cabinet. During his entire presidency, Cardoso (1994–2002) appointed only two women to serve in Cabinet positions (one for a very short time). Although Lula appointed three women as ministers of government, and one federal secretary (Women's Rights), that still amounted to only about 11 percent of the Cabinet. Women hold up to one-quarter of the Cabinet posts in El Salvador, Honduras, Panama, and Venezuela, and nearly half of the Colombian and Chilean Cabinets. In 2000, a woman was appointed to the Supreme Court for the first time in Brazilian history, despite the fact that 29 percent of candidates who pass public examinations to become judges are women. In 2000, there were six women at the top rank of the diplomatic corps, and eighteen at the second-highest rank.[25]

Consistent with the characterization of the United Nations' Special Rapporteur on Racial Disadvantage of the "almost all-white corridors of political power," only nine deputies (2 percent of the Congress) self-identified as black in 2003.[26] To deliberately open the process of elite political recruitment, Lula named four Afro-Brazilians to his Cabinet, appointed the country's first Afro-Brazilian Supreme Court justice, and pledged that Afro-Brazilians should make up at least one-third of the federal government within five years. The Supreme Court and the Ministry of Justice have introduced quotas for black employees.

***Elite Orientations***  The Brazilian elite is generally not divided along economic, religious, or ethnic lines. It is more "moderate" than its counterparts elsewhere in Latin America. The business community supported the military coup of 1964 in an unstable economy. In the 1970s, facing a regime that concentrated decisionmaking and restricted freedom, many business leaders preferred a return to democracy. In the 1990s, most military and business leaders, public administrators, and members of the press identified themselves as "centrist" in their ideological orientation. They gave the democratic regime from 1985 to 1990 higher marks for establishing a viable political structure for the country, and they downgraded military governments for failing to raise the international prestige of the country, promote educational development, and reduce regional and social inequalities.[27]

Elites are predictably far less preoccupied with unemployment, health care, and drugs than respondents earning the minimum salary. They are, however, the *most* concerned about education and income concentration. In 2002, those with a college education were more than twice as worried about education and four and a half times more concerned about income concentration as the average Brazilian. Those earning more than ten times the minimum salary were more than three times more likely than the national average to rank income inequality as one of the three most important problems facing the country.[28]

## Politics at the Mass Level

***Citizen Politics***  During the latter part of the military regime, Brazilians began to associate in the realm of civil society as they never had before. The combination of the easing of repression and the increased freedom of information, together with the continued authoritarian nature of decisionmaking and the lack of genuine representation from formal political institutions and political parties, helped these new social movements flourish. Prominent among these were the hundreds of women's movements and at least 100,000 grassroots church groups discussed earlier.

In addition, thousands of neighborhood associations emerged in the 1970s as the most explicitly political of all social movements in the waning years of the military dictatorship.

Neighborhood associations had existed in the past. In the 1950s, a handful of nonpartisan middle-class associations in Rio de Janeiro monitored policy, but were disengaged from larger ideological concerns, and had little concern for participation and for working out democratic norms at the local level. These associations essentially disbanded in the early 1960s, although associations in poorer urban shantytowns survived even the most repressive period of military rule.

The approximately 8,000 associations that blossomed in the late 1970s, by contrast, demanded state regulation of real estate firms in their neighborhoods, state goods and services, and selective state nonintervention. Their demands were generally satisfied.[29] In just the southern city of Porto Alegre, 540 neighborhood associations and fifty-one housing cooperatives emerged within a decade.[30]

In the early 1990s, only about one-third of Brazilians did *not* belong to a voluntary association; one-fifth belonged to three or more. Many of these associations were not formally political (most common were grassroots religious groups, athletic clubs, labor unions, and neighborhood associations). In 2002, 19 percent of respondents to the National Election Study reported belonging to a labor union and 13 percent to professional associations, rates that were much higher than in other countries in Latin America. Membership had declined in neighborhood associations, but still ran high in religious organizations.

Citizens have also organized movements around various identities, single issues, and political and social rights, most notably those to protect indigenous peoples, the environment, and human rights, and to gain land for the landless. To advance their goals, these movements have employed a variety of strategies, including participating in government, enlisting international allies, and engaging in direct action.

Indian organizations in Brazil are but one example of citizen groups to emerge around the globe in the late twentieth century on the basis of identity—that is, organized around who people *are* rather than what they *produce*. After military development projects threatened the extinction of several of Brazil's indigenous tribes, these tribes organized nearly fifty citizen groups in the 1980s; most were in the North, with twenty-three of them in the state of Amazonas.[31] Their efforts won constitutional protections for Indian lands and the collective rights of Indian nations, an impressive accomplishment given the small number of Indians in Brazil and their fragmentation into different tribes.

Citizens' groups to protect the environment have also been effective at enlisting international allies. Local and regional environmental organizations which date back to the 1970s mobilized in the late 1980s to influence the new Constitution and the 1992 global summit on the environment held in Rio de Janeiro. Brazil's environmental movement has scored important achievements in the areas of controlling pesticides, nuclear waste and production, and the emission of chlorofluorocarbons. Somewhat paradoxically, environmental organizations have been slower to appear, less active, and less visible in the Amazon region than in the rest of Brazil. Rather, the ball on environmental issues of the Amazon region has been carried by indigenous groups and rubber tappers. Using tactics of direct confrontation, they have effectively influenced international lenders, such as the World Bank, to establish environmental protection as a condition for aid.[32]

The tactics of direct confrontation are perhaps best illustrated by the **Movement of Landless Rural Workers (MST),** one of the most vibrant social movements in Latin America today. One of the most effective strategies used by MST members has been the seizure of government-owned or unproductive private land (the organization's slogan is "Agrarian reform—by law or by disorder"). Because participating families become the beneficiaries of land if the occupations are successful, the incentives to join these actions among the landless are high. In 1998, there were 608 such occupations. After a brief period around the 2002 election when it decelerated land occupations as a sign of good faith in the new Lula government (which had promised to step up land distribution), the MST resumed these tactics to protest slower than anticipated progress toward land reform. In 2004, the MST staged 496 occupations involving nearly 80,000 families.[33]

The MST has also pressured the formal political system, including the courts (where it seeks legal title to land), and pursued a strategy of staging disruptive and sometimes spectacular protests. Its members

A group of 2,800 landless peasant families celebrate a May 1996 decree expropriating an estate along the banks of the São Francisco River, in the state of Sergipe. The families had pitched and maintained for several months a precarious settlement at the entrance of the estate.

Sebastião Salgado/Contact Press Images

have occupied federal and state government buildings and roads in as many as twenty states; these actions have surpassed the number of land occupations every year. The MST has also staged highly visible demonstrations, beginning with a march on Brasília in 1997 to commemorate the one-year anniversary of the April 1996 massacre by state police in the state of Pará of nineteen landless peasants occupying a road. In another daring action, the MST invaded President Cardoso's farm in 2002. In 2004, nationwide demonstrations involved more than half a million people.

Brazilians are generally sympathetic to the occupation of land as a legitimate tactic to combat hunger and misery when it is carried out without violence. Of late, although they blame the government (more than landowners and the MST) for rural violence and favor moving agrarian reform to the purview of the federal government, they generally believe that land invasions have a negative impact on agrarian reform negotiations and weaken democracy.[34]

Today, perhaps the most important avenues of citizen political participation are through nongovernmental organizations (NGOs). A worldwide phenomenon, NGOs are private groups, normally well funded and institutionalized, that often assume public functions. They may help implement health care, investigate ways

to privatize national pension systems, press for civil rights for Afro-Brazilians, and monitor government compliance with environmental accords. Brazil's nearly 5,500 NGOs receive $400 million annually from international sources; most enjoy some kind of partnership with government agencies. Brazilian NGOs reportedly influence or control $1.2 billion in funds administered by the Ministry of the Environment, the Ministry of Social Security and Welfare, and international banks.[35]

***Mass Political Participation*** The sheer numbers of Brazilians participating in politics today is staggering, especially compared with earlier in the twentieth century when less than 5 percent of adults voted in presidential elections. In 1960, only 19 million people voted for president. In 1989, after the enfranchisement of illiterates in 1985 and the award of the franchise to 16-year-olds in 1988, an electorate of 82 million elected Fernando Collor de Mello president. In 2006, the Brazilian electorate numbered 126 million people.

Ordinary Brazilian citizens participate in elections at fairly robust rates. In 2006, turnout was 82 percent. This rate is high when compared with that in the United States, where less than half the electorate routinely votes. Although voting in Brazil is compulsory, and though there are potential penalties for noncompliance, these are rarely enforced, and participation rates are still higher than in other countries with compulsory voting.

One way that scholars gauge disinterest in elections is by monitoring the so-called blank (without the name of a candidate or party) and null (spoiled) ballots. In 1990, 31.5 percent of those who voted cast blank or null ballots, a rate comparable to that registered in 1970 during the most repressive phase of the military dictatorship. Voter interest has since recovered. In 2006, in the first round of presidential balloting only 2.7 percent of ballots cast were blank and 5.7 percent were spoiled.

Since the 1990s, one of the most important forms of citizen political involvement is through **participatory budgeting.** Launched by the local PT administration, participatory budgeting began as an experiment in local government in 1989 in Porto Alegre, the capital of Rio Grande do Sul. It has since been copied in over 140 cities and six states in Brazil and in several cities worldwide.

Participatory budgeting is a process in which hundreds of thousands of citizens meet in a series of open, public assemblies before the legislative budget cycle begins in order to establish spending priorities. Elected delegates negotiate the budget with state bureaucrats and monitor the previous year's spending and continuing investment priorities. The idea is to allocate public resources to districts taking into account population size, the status of specific public services, and local priorities as defined by citizens directly, not by the political criteria of a notoriously clientelistic political system.

The results are very promising. In Porto Alegre, the percentage of the public budget available for investment rose almost immediately from 2 percent in 1989 to 20 percent in 1994. Municipal services, such as running water and sewerage, were also quickly extended to 98 percent of all city residences. Participatory budgeting earned high marks from international agencies for enhancing the transparency of the budgeting process and for creating institutions of good governance. Students of democracy have also praised it for encouraging popular participation (particularly among the poor), strengthening civil society, and ultimately, enhancing democracy in Brazil.

In short, there has been a proliferation of citizens' groups concerned with issues ranging from environmental protection to protecting indigenous rights and human rights more broadly. Nongovernmental organizations, moreover, serve as important watchdogs of public policy and thereby increase the transparency of government. Whether or not they have contributed to a broader pattern of more extensive, informed, and widespread political participation that may complement or even supplement political parties and long-established interest groups, however, is a far more complicated question.

## INTEREST GROUPS

Traditionally, political interests in Brazil have been organized and represented differently from those in liberal democracies, where plural and voluntary groups serve as the basic unit of interest group activity. In Brazil, interest groups came under state control during the Vargas era in a system known as **corporatism.**[36] Under corporatist law, modeled after the labor codes of fascist Italy, interest groups were defined in economic terms, recognized and funded by the state, and granted a representational monopoly in their area of competence. But in return, the state could remove their leaders and prohibit strikes.

For labor unions, cooperation with state authorities initially gained them recognition and benefits for their members that they had been unable to secure independently in confrontation with owners. The Consolidated Labor Code of 1943 created labor courts, established procedures for resolving disputes between capital and labor, and charged unions with providing social services and legal representation for members. But labor soon discovered that the military regime could use those same structures to remove and replace the elected leaders of union organizations and shackle their organizations. Many labor leaders were jailed; many more were sacked by their employers. Strikes were brutally repressed for a decade.

During the period of military rule, changes within Brazil's unions began to break down these corporatist structures. In the 1970s, a new generation of union leaders who came from the shop floor shunned the strategies of cultivating good working relationships with state officials that older union leaders had depended on for their power and to secure benefits for their members. Instead, these new leaders adopted a more combative stance toward the state, and with the support of their own rank and file, toward their employers as well. The most famous of these leaders was Lula (see again Box 15.2). As the head of the São Bernardo metalworkers union, he led a half million workers in six states and the Federal District on strike in 1978 for higher wages. And again in 1979, he led more than 3 million workers all over Brazil. The "new" unions were willing to forgo state financing and protection in exchange for the right to bargain collectively with their employers.

Business associations were also formally organized into state federations of industry and commerce. Unlike labor, during the dictatorship private-sector elites enjoyed informal access to the president, Cabinet heads in the economic ministries, and the heads of state-owned industries and banks. When entrepreneurs found their access was closed, the business community became convinced that a reduction in state authority was necessary, just as labor became convinced it needed to stand on its own two feet when the state abandoned it.

The creation of new independent interest groups and the transformation of old ones from instruments of authoritarian social control to pressure groups in a democratic society are as important as any change in Brazilian politics of the last quarter century. Alongside labor unions and business and agrarian associations, single-issue interest groups have become effective lobbies for environmental and consumer protection.

## Labor Unions

With the transition to democracy, labor lobbied to have its interests represented in the Constitution, with great success. Article 8 grants freedom of union association. Public employees won the right to form unions, and workers were guaranteed the right to strike. Lifting the lid on union formation led to a proliferation of union organizations, in no sector more rapidly than among agricultural workers. Membership in rural unions rose from 2.9 million members in 1974 to 7.8 million in 1990. In all, trade union membership has increased by over tenfold since 1960. Professional white-collar workers had unionized at an even faster rate: only 40,491 were union members in 1960, but 549,680 were in 1992, a thirteenfold increase.[37]

The IBGE's (Brazilian Institute of Geography and Statistics) 2005 household survey estimated that a record high 18.3 percent of the labor force was now unionized, up from 16.2 percent a decade earlier.[38]

With the right to strike officially sanctioned, the pattern of labor militancy evident at the close of the authoritarian regime continued. General strikes were staged by labor in 1986, 1987, and 1989. Since then, corporatism has continued to erode in the Brazilian labor movement. The Constitution maintained the obligatory union tax, which critics charge ties the unions to the state. In practice, however, unions rely on it less and on voluntary member dues more, although the proportion of voluntary dues to the state-collected union tax is much higher in the urban sector than in the rural. Since the mid-1980s, labor unions have attempted to press the interests of their members through central organizations, or peak unions, which have eclipsed their corporatist predecessors. These central organizations advocate union independence from state authorities and direct collective bargaining with employers, either at the firm level or with employers' associations. The most important of these by far is the **Central Única dos Trabalhadores (CUT),** formed in 1983. It endorses a militant form of the "new unionism," as well as combative strategies, such as strikes and the occupation of factories. The CUT draws much of its strength from the metalworkers unions (which include the autoworkers) and white-collar and public-sector workers; geographically, it draws from the industrial heartland of the Southeast.

In the past fifteen years, unions, and especially those representing service-sector workers, have grown more powerful than ever. Unions are estimated to have a combined budget of $1.2 billion. The largest union in the country, the Union of Metallurgical Workers of the state of São Paulo, has an annual budget of $80 million and net assets of $45 million. The Union of Bank Workers of the state of São Paulo has a radio station and one of the five largest newspapers in São Paulo. The labor lobby, the **Departamento Intersindical de Assessoria Parlamentar (DIAP),** is one of the most powerful lobbies in Brasília. Even more a sign of the changing times, the unions had a "block" of thirty-five deputies in Congress in the late 1990s, which was larger than the delegations of eleven political parties. Middle-class labor unions, especially those in the public sector, occupy a central place in the battles over state reform.

## Business Associations

Since 1985, business leaders have engaged in several types of interest group activity—most notably election campaigns, lobbying, and collective bargaining—that they had abandoned during two decades of military rule. Like labor, industrialists attempted to influence the outcome of the 1986 congressional elections. With a reported war chest of $600 million, they succeeded in electing 211 members, short of their goal of 300 but a significant delegation nonetheless.

What is curious given the size of the delegation that can be claimed to have represented them and the smaller number of workers' representatives is that business generally failed to have many of its concerns addressed in the Constitution. The 1988 Constitution severely restricted foreign investment and granted generous labor rights and privileges (although the restrictions on foreign investment were lifted in 1995). It also provided a 120-day paid maternity leave, a paternity leave, paid holidays, and the bonus known as the thirteenth-month salary. Most observers, including those who might applaud strengthening the rights of workers and working-class families, agree that the Constitution imposed financial burdens on employers and the state that Brazil could not afford.

Why Brazil's business organizations weakly represented business interests, especially relative to labor, may be due to the fact that business was slower to reform its constraining corporatist structures. In one rare case in which the business lobby was successful—stopping the proposed job security provisions in the Constitution—the ball was carried by the National Front for Free Enterprise. The FNLI was formed outside the official corporatist system. In later years, the business community did not enter the debate on fiscal decentralization, although it did attempt to back the efforts at fiscal reform, to little avail.[39]

Since the late 1980s, business has created new organizations and has begun to turn its corporatist associations, including some 1,565 urban employers' unions, into interest groups to better promote and protect the economic interests of the private sector. Business associations have also shifted tactics, turning their lobbying efforts from the Executive to the Legislative branch. The powerful National Confederation of Commerce (CNI), for instance, formed an advisory group for legislative affairs that circulates information about the legislative agenda in business outlets.[40] Another business lobby group, the Informal Business Forum (UBE), comprises sixty business federations and 200 private firms and has on its executive council the presidents of the CNI, the National Confederation of Agriculture, the National Confederation of Transportation, and the National Federation of Banking.[41] A third group, the Institute for Studies of Industrial Development (IEDI), brings together the thirty largest and most powerful members of the business community.

Business has also tried to transform its most powerful federations that represent specific sectors of the economy to become more effective pressure groups for favorable tax, trade, and pension policies. These include the Brazilian Association for Infrastructure and Basic Industry (ABDIB), the National Organization of the Petroleum Industry (ONIP), and the giant **Federation of Industries of the State of São Paulo (FIESP),** which represents 100,000 firms employing 2 million workers.[42]

Despite these initiatives, Brazil's business lobbies have not been entirely effective in defending members' interests in such areas as reducing corporate tax levels. Brazilian economic elites also seek political alliances. They do not predominantly rely on one or two political parties of the right to defend their interests, as they might in other countries. Rather, they diversify their political alliances and almost always support individual candidates and politicians.[43]

## Agrarian Elites

Traditionally, associations of landowners were the most powerful in Brazil. Rural societies all over the country remain independent of the state. Agricultural elites also have a network of sectoral federations—such as the Federation of Sugar Industries—that are integrated into the official system of interest representation. The representatives of these associations have gradually been added to the boards of state agencies charged with overseeing public policy, such as the Institute for Sugar and Alcohol, which helped to design Brazil's ambitious program to substitute cane-derived alcohol for imported petroleum.

During the debates in the Constituent Assembly over land reform, agrarian elites mobilized in the National Confederation of Agriculture and a new independent, radical right-wing group, the Ruralist Democratic Union (UDR), to lobby Congress. To defeat a government proposal to push ahead with agrarian reform, large landowners organized public demonstrations. They mounted an antireform campaign in the press; attempted to influence members of the major political parties, the president, and the military; and committed much violence in the countryside. They defeated an amendment to the Constitution that would have enacted a national program of agrarian reform, and instead, the issue was thrown back to the states. In most state legislatures, where the power of agrarian elites was even stronger, the matter appeared to have died a quiet death, at least until the Landless Movement forced it back onto the political agenda in the mid-1990s and the banner of agrarian reform was taken up by the "Agrarian Delegation" (Bancada Agraria) in Congress.

Since then, landowners have been effectively represented in Congress by the "Rural Delegation" (Bancada Ruralista); with nearly 90 members, it was the third largest caucus in Congress. Caucus members were effective in securing for large landowners the favorable rescheduling of agricultural credits from public banks in the late 1990s. In recent years, they have ushered legislation through Congress that has slowed the review of occupied property (a prerequisite to expropriation), speeded compensation for expropriated lands, made more stringent the size and productivity thresholds for expropriation, and classified land occupation as a "heinous crime and act of terrorism."[44]

### The Consumer Lobby

A relatively new Brazilian lobby is concerned with consumer rights. A web of civic organizations in various states have worked for consumer rights by raising public awareness of consumer issues, conducting research, monitoring legislative activity, and lobbying regulatory agencies, government ministries, Congress, the president's office, and the Public Prosecution. They have also taken judicial action.

The most prominent of these organizations is the Brazilian **Institute for the Defense of the Consumer.**

**IDEC** has been active in a number of areas, including public services and utilities. Since 1999, it has sought to strengthen consumer participation in the process of privatizing electric energy, telephones, and sanitation services. It has been particularly active in monitoring rate hikes in the energy sector. Its most notable success has come in the area of genetically modified food. Brazil became the first country in the world to prohibit the planting and marketing of genetically modified foods. This decision was most significant in the case of the soybean crop (as Brazil is the world's second largest producer of soy behind the United States), and both the United States and Argentina (its nearest competitor) permit the planting of genetically modified soy.

### The Military

Paradoxically, the military is the most powerful but one of the least effective interest groups in Brazil today. Upon exiting from government, it retained more prerogatives—and conceded less civilian authority to supervise its expenditures, arms procurements, and control over its internal affairs—than most other militaries in the world. It also succeeded in keeping, without debate, Article 142 of the Brazilian Constitution. Article 142 authorizes the armed forces to "guarantee the constitutional powers and, by initiative of any of these, law and order," which the military interprets as authorizing it to depose elected governments when law and order are threatened.

For at least a decade, many politicians and ordinary citizens still feared the potential of a military coup, and one was even rumored to have been a possibility in 1992 during the impeachment scandal of President Collor de Mello. During the 1994 presidential campaign, the leftist Workers' Party promised the military the prerogative to develop nuclear power as a means of softening its expected resistance to a PT-led government.

Despite its past capacity to frighten civilians, the military appears to be less and less capable of defending its interests. In the early 1990s, armed with a powerful mandate as Brazil's first elected president in nearly three decades and backed by emboldened legislators, Fernando Collor de Mello significantly trimmed military spending from its 1990 level (20.5 percent of the budget) to just over 14 percent.[45] Three years later, Brazil spent a smaller percentage of its gross national product on its military—1.7 percent in 1995—than the United States, China, and France (5.3, 5.0, and 3.4 percent, respectively), as well as other Latin American countries such as Chile (2.7 percent). Salaries fell, equipment aged, and morale sagged. Many officers moonlight to get by.

The capacity of the military to influence national policy on claims of national security also appears to have waned. For decades, military organization, training, and ideology were shaped by the Cold War and the perceived need to fight subversion within its own borders. With redemocratization, the military tried to reorient its mission toward external defense, particularly of Brazil's northern borders and the Amazon's natural resources. Fearing the "internationalization of the Amazon," it built military airstrips, garrisons, and outposts, as well as roads and conducted agricultural and colonization projects along a vast stretch of the Amazon region as part of a project known as Calha Norte. For a while, the military also resisted national and international pressure to reserve a continuous and uninterrupted stretch of land along the Venezuelan border for the Yanomami Indians. It also resisted external assistance that required foreign monitoring of Brazilian compliance in such schemes as "debt-for-nature" swaps (in which international environmental groups would buy a portion of a country's debt in world financial markets, and then forgive this debt in exchange for a commitment to set aside matching funds for a particular environmental project). Eventually the Brazilian government reserved 94 million hectares for the Yanomami, left virtually unfunded the Calha Norte project, and reversed Brazil's opposition to debt-for-nature swaps.[46]

A further sign of the erosion of military influence occurred in 1998 when a Special Commission on the Political Killed and Disappeared identified 280 individuals who had been killed or disappeared under the military regime. It indemnified family members in 265 of these cases. The decision to compensate the victims' families was anathema to many active duty officers, but it was nonetheless accepted by the military leadership. In 1999, Fernando Henrique Cardoso abolished the three separate service ministries and named a civilian to head a new ministry of defense. One of the first acts of Lula's government, arguing that the money could be better used to relieve hunger, was to suspend a $760 million purchase of a dozen new jet fighter planes for its air force. Showing how far Brazil has traveled from the days of military tutelage over the political system, Air Force Commander General Luiz Carlos Bueno publicly accepted the decisions, remarking, 'We are working with the government, not against it.'[47]

## Conclusion

The proliferation of citizens' groups and the strengthening of interest groups and their growing autonomy from the state may be just what are necessary in Brazil to diminish arbitrary state authority and the underlying foundations of authoritarianism. But the advance of civil society has carried a tradeoff and a danger. The tradeoff is that the gains of *participatory* democracy have been achieved at the price of a decline of *representative* democracy. The danger is that citizen groups, NGOs, and organized interest groups may have outstripped the capacity of Brazil's political institutions to process their demands, or they may at least cast that impression. If the increase in participatory democracy is to be welcomed for the partnership between government and civil society that it brings, Brazil's former president Fernando Henrique Cardoso nonetheless admonished in a 1996 speech at Stanford University, "direct participation is no substitute for representation." And when society advances more rapidly, in political terms, than the state does, Cardoso continued, "disorganized pressures from society on the state can create the impression of a government adrift."[48] In the sections that follow, we examine the institutions of representative democracy.

## POLITICAL PARTIES AND ELECTIONS

Traditionally, political parties in Brazil have been ephemeral, lacking in cohesion and discipline, and the party system has been highly fragmented. Until recently, traditional local bosses and the practice of clientelism dominated most parties, and few had ideologies or even programs of government. Politicians changed parties frequently and with impunity, eroding accountability. Not surprisingly, the parties did not lay deep roots in the electorate, and voters often cast ballots for different parties from one election to the next.

Many politicians and analysts claim weak parties are at the core of many governance problems in Brazil

Angry protestors carry effigies of President Lula and his top advisers in the PT. The effigies are dressed in prison garb, not so subtly hinting that they deserved to be jailed for acts of government and party corruption.

Antonio Scorza/AFP/Getty Images

today. But others contend that in the 1990s, the party system stabilized, party discipline rose, and parties across the political spectrum developed distinctive ideological orientations and positions on a range of policy issues.[49] The one party that everyone agreed was truly different, the Workers' Party, fell victim in 2005 to a corruption scandal that rocked the party and shook public faith in the entire political system.

## Historic Strains of Clientelism and Personalism

Brazil's parties were traditionally elite-dominated and formed around personalities, not particular issues. In the early twentieth century when elites in other Latin American countries were organizing competition within their own ranks, elites in each Brazilian state had their own republican party and intrastate monopolies on power. State oligarchies were supported by powerful local bosses, usually the largest landowners, who had their own militias, controlled local judicial officials, and shepherded their followers to the polls on the back of farm trucks and told them for which candidate to vote. In exchange for delivering votes to the state elite, the local boss secured for his municipality roads, employment, and other resources, and for himself, the power that came from the exclusive right to appoint all powerful posts in his jurisdiction. This system of traditional clientelism was known as **coronelismo** (for the *coroneis*, or colonels, whose forebears once held the rank of local commander in the National Guard).

The postwar party system divided along pro- and anti-Vargas lines. Vargas supporters formed the elite

Social Democratic Party (PSD) and the mass-based Brazilian Labor Party (PTB). Vargas's opponents joined the National Democratic Union (UDN). The PTB espoused a vague platform of nationalism and populism, but generally, parties lacked guiding ideologies. Party organizations represented loose agglomerations of patronage networks headed by state and local politicians. Local political bosses used the control of public appointments and urban-based political machines to hold onto power when people moved from the countryside to the cities. The growth of the electorate, as well as the expansion of the state into new areas of regulation and distribution, made clientelism even more pervasive than it had been before 1930.

In 1965, the military transformed the fragmented, multiparty system it inherited into a two-party system. Most UDN and PSD politicians joined the progovernment ARENA; most PTB representatives joined the opposition MDB. The two-party system worked for a while. But once voters began to identify more closely with the opposition beginning with the 1974 election, the military stepped up spending for agricultural credit, low-income housing, and basic sanitation programs, and trusted their delivery to traditional politicians.[50] In 1979, the regime eased the restrictions on the formation of political parties in order to split the advancing MDB. ARENA leaders formed the Democratic Social Party (PDS), and MDB leaders formed the **Party of the Brazilian Democratic Movement (PMDB).** Other smaller parties were formed by competing currents within the opposition. After the transition to democracy, Brazil's communist parties were legalized and many more parties were formed.

## Brazil's Contemporary Party System

The party system today is broadly representative of a wider range of ideological positions than perhaps ever before. Parties of the left, which won only 9 percent of the legislative seats in 1986, elected 31 percent of Congress in 2006. Members of the centrist and rightist parties won 42 and 27 percent of the seats, respectively (see Figure 15.7).

Until 2006, Brazil's party system was highly fragmented. No minimum percentage of the vote, or threshold, was required to gain seats in the legislature. Thus in 2002, for example, there were twenty-nine registered political parties, of which seventeen were represented in Congress, but only eight (the PT, PMDB, PFL, PSDB, PP, PTB, PL, and PSB) had won at least 5 percent of the seats in the Chamber of Deputies.

This picture changed with the elections of 2006, the first in which the **"barrier clause,"** passed as part of the 1995 party law, took effect.[51] Under the terms of the barrier clause, parties must receive 5 percent of the valid vote nationwide and a minimum of 2 percent of the vote in at least nine states in order to elect leaders who participate in the internal governing bodies of the legislature, name members of congressional committees, and enjoy free television time during election campaigns. Only seven parties surpassed the barrier, prompting several declining and minor parties to merge. Also in 2006, a new law made it more difficult for parties to fashion ad hoc electoral alliances in local and state races.

## The Left

The most important leftist party is the Workers' Party (PT). For two decades, the PT was perceived as a genuine labor party and a genuinely different party on the Brazilian political landscape. Its representatives voted the party line, did not switch to other parties, and did not promise to be brokers of clientelistic benefits. The party's congressional delegation was composed largely of intellectuals and workers. Lula's victory in the 2002 presidential election helped to elect three governors and ninety-one deputies and fourteen senators, making the PT the largest party in Congress.

Although a significant proportion of PT members consider themselves to be radicals (up to 30 percent), the party has moved beyond its initial base in the industrial unions of São Paulo, the landless rural workers' movement, and Catholic activists, toward the political center. Nonetheless, not all members were happy with the turn of events. Some members of Congress,

Party Representation in the Brazilian Congress, 2007–2010    **FIGURE 15.7** like Senator Heloísa Helena, spoke out against government policies and were expelled for their rebellion. Others resigned their party membership, especially after the cash-for-votes scandal came to light, reducing the PT delegation to eighty-one. Even after defections and corruption scandals, the PT won eighty-three seats in the Chamber of Deputies and held ten in the Senate in 2006, as well as five state governorships (see Table 15.2).

**TABLE 15.2**

### Election Results, 2006

| Parties | Chamber of Deputies (seats) | | Senate (seats)[a] | | Congress | | | Governors' Races | State Assemblies (seats) | |
|---|---|---|---|---|---|---|---|---|---|---|
| | # | % | # | % | #[b] | Cumulative | % | # | # | % |
| **PMDB** Party of the Brazilian Democratic Movement | 89 | 17.3 | 4 | 14.8 | 18 | 107 | 18 | 7 | 164 | 15.8 |
| **PT** Workers' Party | 83 | 16.2 | 2 | 7.4 | 10 | 93 | 34 | 5 | 126 | 12.2 |
| **PFL** Party of the Liberal Front | 65 | 12.7 | 6 | 22.2 | 18 | 83 | 48 | 1 | 119 | 11.5 |
| **PSDB** Party of Brazilian Social Democracy | 65 | 12.7 | 5 | 18.5 | 13 | 78 | 61 | 6 | 152 | 14.7 |
| **PP** Progressive Party | 42 | 8.2 | 1 | 3.7 | 1 | 43 | 68 | 1 | 53 | 5.1 |
| **PSB** Brazilian Socialist Party | 27 | 5.3 | 1 | 3.7 | 3 | 30 | 73 | 3 | 60 | 5.8 |
| **PDT** Democratic Labor Party | 24 | 4.7 | 1 | 3.7 | 5 | 29 | 78 | 2 | 66 | 6.4 |
| **PR** Party of the Republic | 26 | 5.0 | 1 | 3.7 | 3 | 29 | 83 | 0 | 58 | 5.6 |
| **MD** Democratic Mobilization | 26 | 5.0 | 1 | 3.7 | 1 | 27 | 88 | 2 | 81 | 7.8 |
| **PTB** Brazilian Labor Party | 23 | 4.3 | 3 | 11.1 | 4 | 27 | 91 | 0 | 50 | 4.8 |
| **PC do B** Communist Party of Brazil | 13 | 2.5 | 1 | 3.7 | 2 | 15 | 94 | 0 | 12 | 1.2 |
| **PV** Green Party | 13 | 2.5 | 0 | — | 0 | 13 | 96 | 0 | 34 | 3.3 |
| **PSC** Christian Social Party | 9 | 1.8 | 0 | — | 0 | 9 | 98 | 0 | 27 | 2.6 |
| Minor parties[c] | 8 | 100 | 1 | 3.7 | 3 | 11 | 100 | 0 | 33 | 3.2 |
| Total | 513 | | 27 | | | | 100 | 27 | 1,035 | 100 |

[a]One-third of the Senate, or 27 seats, were up for election in 2006.
[b]Total congressional delegation, comprising all senators, including those not up for election in 2006, plus all deputies elected.
[c]PSOL (Socialism and Liberty Party); PTC (Christian Labor Party); PRB (Brazilian Republican Party); PRTB (Brazilian Labor Renewal Party)

Source: Tribunal Superior Eleitoral (available at www.tse.gov.br).

In 2005, Helena and other defectors formed the Socialism and Liberty Party (PSOL). The PSOL favors a sharp change in course, including slashing interest rates. It won only three seats in the lower house. Other parties of the left include the **Brazilian Socialist Party (PSB),** which won thirty seats in Congress and three governorships in 2006, and the **Democratic Labor Party (PDT),** which won twenty-nine seats in the Chamber and Senate and the governorships of two states.

## The Center

In the center of the political spectrum lies the PMDB (Party of the Brazilian Democratic Movement). A quintessential catch-all, centrist party, the PMDB is the largest party in Brazil with eighty-nine deputies, eighteen senators, and seven governors. The **Party of Brazilian Social Democracy (PSDB)** broke off from the PMDB in 1988. Formed by several respected leaders of the PMDB, including Cardoso, the party began as a center-left party. When the party was in government, however, it advanced an agenda of market reforms and moved to the right. In 1998, its best election, the PSDB elected the second largest congressional delegation, the largest number of state governors, and the president. Today, it is the fourth largest party in Congress, and six states are led by PSDB governors. Two new centrist blocs were formed in the aftermath of the 2006 election from parties that failed to surpass the barrier. On the center-left, the Democratic Mobilization (MD) wedded the leftist Popular Socialist Party (PPS) to the smaller centrist Party of National Mobilization (PMN) and the Humanistic Solidarity Party (PHS). On the center-right, the new Party of the Republic (PR) resulted from the merger of three parties: the Liberal Party (PL), once a probusiness party that later allied with the PT government and suffered from the corruption scandal that engulfed the government, the rightist Party for the Reconstruction of National Order (PRONA), and the newer, smaller Labor Party of Brazil (PTdoB).

## The Right

The largest party on the right of the Brazilian political spectrum is the **Party of the Liberal Front (PFL).** It was formed in 1985 by defectors from the PDS—former supporters of the military regime. In 2006, it elected

only one state governor, but it had the third largest delegation in Congress with eighty-three members.

The second significant conservative party is the **Progressive Party (PP),** a probusiness, proeconomic reform party also with roots in the PDS. The PTB, which was re-formed in the wake of the 1979 party reform law, has seen its vote totals slide steadily over the years to 4 percent in legislative elections. It absorbed two minor parties after the 2006 election. Several very small parties on the right remain, including some ultraconservative ones.

Parties of the right have opposed agrarian reform and the liberalization of abortion laws. Whereas combined parties of the left increased their share of the vote from 20 percent in 1995 to 31 percent in 2006, parties of the right have seen their share decrease in the same period from nearly 45 percent to 27 percent.

## Social Cleavages and Voting

For several years, the most important social cleavage in Brazil was territorial. Brazil had two electorates: one resided in the large, metropolitan areas of the Southeast and South and was more aware of the issues and more likely to vote for candidates on the basis of party program. The other was in the smaller, poorer, less industrialized, predominantly rural counties of the interior, especially in the Northeast and Center-West, and voted according to personalistic and patronage criteria. The poor and the poorly educated residents of remote areas of Brazil generally voted for candidates of the right. Those who had higher levels of education and income favored the center-left PSDB and especially the leftist PT, as did younger voters.

This cleavage was evident in the 2002 presidential election, when the most significant divide was county size and type. Residents of large metropolitan areas, capital cities, and the Southeast heavily preferred Lula. Inhabitants of smaller counties, counties of the interior, and counties in the Northeast voted for the candidate of the PSDB. Lula split evenly the support of the lowest and highest income brackets with his opponent.

In 2006, the territorial cleavage faded and the income/education divide became more salient. Lula drew votes equally from the urban periphery and the interior counties. Reversing the earlier trends, voters in

| Social Bases of Voting in Brazil, 2006* | | | | TABLE 15.3 |

| | Luiz Inácio Lula da Silva (PT) | Gerardo Alckmin (PSDB) | Others | (blank/null/none, don't know) |
|---|---|---|---|---|
| Gender | | | | |
| Male | 54 | 44 | 11 | 10 |
| Female | 44 | 26 | 14 | 15 |
| Age | | | | |
| 16–24 | 47 | 28 | 15 | 9 |
| 25–34 | 50 | 26 | 15 | 12 |
| 35–44 | 51 | 23 | 11 | 14 |
| 45–59 | 47 | 25 | 12 | 15 |
| More than 60 | 50 | 25 | 11 | 14 |
| Education | | | | |
| Elementary | 55 | 22 | 9 | 14 |
| Secondary | 45 | 28 | 15 | 12 |
| College | 32 | 31 | 24 | 13 |
| Region | | | | |
| North/Center West | 50 | 23 | 14 | 13 |
| Northeast | 65 | 13 | 9 | 13 |
| Southeast | 43 | 30 | 15 | 13 |
| South | 37 | 34 | 13 | 13 |
| County Type | | | | |
| Capital | 46 | 25 | 17 | 12 |
| Periphery | 51 | 22 | 15 | 13 |
| Interior | 50 | 26 | 11 | 12 |
| Household Income (in minimum salaries) | | | | |
| Up to 2 | 55 | 21 | 10 | 14 |
| 2–5 | 45 | 29 | 15 | 11 |
| 5–10 | 40 | 31 | 19 | 9 |
| More than 10 | 36 | 35 | 16 | 13 |
| Brazilian Average | 49 | 25 | 12 | 13 |

*Voting intentions for first round presidential election revealed in nationwide sample of 6,279 adults.

Source: DataFolha, PO 3351, 22 August 2006 (downloaded from http://datafolha.folha.uol.com.br/).

the Northeast favored the PT standard-bearer by a five-to-one margin (see Table 15.3). Moreover, as Lula lost middle-class votes over revelations of corruption, he cemented his support among those with only a primary school education as well as among those earning less than two times the minimum salary. As one Brazilian scholar put it, "Increasing support for Lula among the popular sectors is not the result of populism or irrationality, but because the poor are better off than they were before he took office."[52]

## The Electoral System

Brazil employs three different electoral systems. The president, state governors, and mayors of cities with at least 200,000 voters are elected by majority vote. In the event that no candidate captures 50 percent of the vote in a first round, a runoff election is held between the top two vote-getters. In 1989 and 2002, a runoff election was held for president; in 1994 and 1998, presidents were elected on the first ballot. In 2006, seventeen governors were elected in the first round; in ten states a second-round runoff election was required. Senators and mayors of cities with less than 200,000 voters are elected by a second system called "first past the post"—that is, they need only win a plurality of the vote to gain office and no runoff election takes place.

Federal and state deputies and local councillors are elected by yet a third system, **open-list proportional representation** with multimember districts. More than one representative is elected per district, which in federal and state races is the state itself. Seventy deputies are elected to represent the state of São Paulo in the federal Congress, for example, and they draw votes from all over the state. Voters choose one candidate from any one of several party lists. Each party's list may contain up to one and a half times the number of candidates as the number of seats to be filled. The system works similarly for council elections, except that the municipality is the district, and each party may nominate up to three times the number of candidates as there are seats to be filled.

In a proportional representation system, the number of seats in a legislature or local council awarded to each party is based on the proportion of the total vote that the candidates for each party receive. In most electoral systems in which seats are awarded according to proportional representation, the list is "closed." Party leaders determine the order of the names on the party ballot. They can ensure the election of deputies needed as Cabinet ministers or some other capacity as well as protect loyal deputies by placing them high on the party list. They can just as easily punish deputies who might have been unfaithful in a key vote in Congress by placing that deputy so low on the party list that reelection is improbable. In Brazil's open-list proportional representation system, by contrast, voters determine which candidates on the party list will represent the party in the legislature.

Critics contend that electoral systems like the Brazilian system—which give more weight to popular voting than to the party organization in determining who is elected—undermine political parties and encourage individualistic behavior among politicians.[53] Running in huge, statewide districts, deputies have greater incentive to campaign against members of their own party than they do against their opponents in other parties. The system rewards pork-barrel politics and undermines adherence to a party platform. Politicians enjoy broad autonomy from their party leaders in state and national legislatures. Weak party discipline, in turn, cripples the ability of governments to pass necessary legislation. Crucial policy reforms sometimes pass only after wavering representatives are guaranteed substantial pork from state coffers for their constituents.

Electoral rules have obviously contributed to the fragmentation of Brazil's party system. This factor adds to the comparative lack of party cohesion in the legislature, and the lack of institutionalization of parties in the electorate. Yet the PT, the PSDB, and other parties are reasonably disciplined and programmatically oriented, and they have secured prominent places in Brazil's party system. Moreover, there are more changes on the horizon, which raise the question of whether or not Brazil's parties should still be considered weak.

## Are Brazil's Parties Still Weak?

Brazil's political parties have traditionally been regarded as weak because they are unable to count on the loyalty of either their representatives in the legislature or the voters. Is this still the case? More specifically, do party legislative delegations lack cohesion and discipline? Is Brazil's party system still fragmented? Do parties lack roots in the electorate?

*Parties in Congress* Brazilian parties traditionally exhibited comparatively low levels of party cohesion, or the propensity of representatives to adopt similar positions on key legislative votes. And party discipline (that is, the ability of party leaders to direct their representatives how to vote in the legislature) was also weak. According to conventional wisdom, representatives of most parties in the legislature break party ranks to vote to serve the interests of their states, a particular interest group, or even their own careers. This is problematic, because setting aside party programs in favor of securing patronage resources for their states and districts reinforces personalism, clientelism, and regionalism, and weakens party identities and accountability. In the extreme, the representatives switch parties.

In fact, Brazil's parties *are* less disciplined than their counterparts elsewhere in Latin America.

Nonetheless, party discipline in the legislature is stronger than sometimes claimed. From 1989 to 1999, party leaders won 94 percent of congressional votes on which they issued recommendations.[54]

Brazilian politicians also change parties frequently, not because of philosophical differences with their party, but to advance their personal electoral prospects by joining the party group they perceive will win the next election. In the 1980s and 1990s, hundreds of members of Congress switched parties at least once: 260 deputies elected in 1990 (52 percent of the Chamber) defected from the party on whose label they stood for election, as did 167 (27 percent) of those elected in 1995.[55]

Yet, shallow party loyalty is an affliction of many but not all of Brazil's parties. Parties of the left evoke strong loyalty among their elite members, and their congressional delegations are more likely to remain faithful to their parties and their parties' positions than their counterparts on the right. In a survey conducted of the Brazilian Congress in 1988, more than 70 percent of deputies from conservative parties reported that when there is a conflict between the needs of their states and the positions of their parties, they would favor the interests of their state.[56] In contrast, 75 percent of representatives of the left parties would put their party's interests first.

Recently, some of these general trends may have been reversed. First, the rate of party switching has slowed modestly. As of 2002, approximately ninety-two of 513 deputies elected to the Chamber of Deputies in 1998 switched parties.[57] Survey evidence also suggests that members of Congress value their party's label more today than a decade ago. The percentage of deputies who would place the interests of their state ahead of their party fell from 56 to 45 percent between 1988 and 2000.[58] Also, in 1990, 82 percent of members believed they were elected mostly or almost exclusively due to their personal effort (as opposed to because of their party label or a combination of their party label and individual effort), but more recently, only 56 percent did. Perhaps following from this perception, deputies today are more willing to concede greater authority to party congressional leaders. In 1988, two-thirds of all respondents believed that a member of Congress who changed

party affiliation should *not* lose her seat,[59] but in 2000, 63 percent believed she *should* lose her mandate for switching. And whereas in 1990, 27 percent of Congress favored moving to a closed-list proportional representation system—a reform that would clearly strengthen party leaders by handing them control of the ballot—in 2000, 37 percent favored such a change.[60] Finally, recent surveys suggest that the members of the congressional delegations of many Brazilian parties, especially the PT and the PSDB, have developed cohesive preferences on a series of major economic policy issues.

***Parties in the Electorate*** Brazilian parties are also considered weak because they lack deep roots in the electorate. In 2002, only 35.2 percent of voters identified with a party, a level that is typical of emerging democracies but low when compared with industrial democracies (in which nearly half of voters identify with a party). Not surprisingly, the PT has the strongest partisans; two-thirds of Brazilians who identify with any party do so with the PT. Another 10 percent identify with the PMDB and PSDB.[61]

Citizens, moreover, do not really actively participate in Brazil's traditional parties. Party "members," usually about twenty per municipality, are actually members of local governing bodies called directorates whose only say in state- and national-level party decisions is to elect delegates to nominating conventions. Ordinary citizens may be "affiliates" of local parties, a status that carries no rights or responsibilities. Only about 7 percent reported in the 2005 Latinobarometro survey that they work for their party.

Because survey respondents are sometimes reluctant to express support for a particular party, political scientists also consider how deeply or superficially voters are attached to party labels by the stability of party vote shares. By the measure of electoral volatility—the turnover of votes from one party to its competitors from one election to the next—Brazilian parties have grown stronger in the electorate. In the 1980s, Brazil had one of the most volatile party systems in Latin America, but rates fell in the 1990s. In federal legislative elections, electoral volatility declined from 45 percent in 1990 to 16 percent in 1998. In 2002, it remained around 15 percent despite the presidential swing vote to the PT candidate. Brazil's ratio of electoral volatility now matches the levels of some of the most institutionalized party systems in Latin America, including Mexico (15 percent) and Argentina (13 percent).[62]

Moreover, the relationship between parties and voters may be changing. Today, Brazilian politicians and political parties still practice clientelism, but it is getting harder to do. Though politicians still control many public-sector jobs and distribute public works projects and social services to reward politically loyal districts and individuals, state patronage jobs are scarcer thanks to the Camata law. This law reduces pork-barrel projects by limiting budget amendments that individual members of Congress can sponsor. Vote-buying has been legally proscribed and practically rendered less useful by conditional cash transfer programs. Public tolerance for clientelism and vote-buying is also diminishing. In 2002, a majority of Brazilians believed people should not sell their vote, even for food for a hungry family or medicine for a sick child. Parties in the future will have to compete not merely on program, but also on performance.

## THE POLICYMAKING PROCESS

Policy in Brazil is generally framed and implemented through either the legislative process or the Executive Branch—including the Cabinet and bureaucracy. Although the legislature has gained in stature and strength since the military constitution was discarded in 1988, the Executive in practice still dominates the policymaking process.

### The Legislative Process

"Ordinary" and "complementary" laws may be initiated by any member of the Chamber of Deputies or Senate, by the president, by ministers of the Supreme Court, by the attorney general, or by citizens. Popular initiative requires 1 percent of the national electorate, representing no less than 0.3 of a percent of the electors in at least five states, to launch the legislative process. Debate on proposed legislation initiated outside of Congress begins in the Chamber of Deputies. The first law to be passed in this fashion was the 1999 bill, initiated by Catholic activists, to make vote-buying a crime punishable by loss of mandate.

A bill sponsored by a member of Congress can be introduced in either chamber (Figure 15.8). If it is introduced in the Chamber of Deputies, it is first examined by the **mesa directiva** ("the board"), or the lower house leadership (the president, two vice presidents, and four secretaries). Where possible, chamber leaders are awarded positions on the *mesa* to reflect the strength of their parties in Congress. The president, for instance, normally comes from the largest party. A second important leadership body is the **College of Leaders.** It consists of the president of the Chamber of Deputies, the majority and minority leaders, leaders of parties who (beginning in 2007) have at least 6 percent of the seats in the Chamber, and leaders of legislative "blocks." In practice, it organizes the legislative agenda on behalf of the *mesa*. In Brazil, committee chairs do not enjoy the degree of autonomy from the congressional leadership in setting their agendas as committee chairs do in the U.S. Congress.

Once a bill passes the leadership of the Chamber, it is directed to the appropriate legislative committees for review. There are fourteen permanent technical committees in the Chamber of Deputies, six in the Senate, and a joint Senate-Chamber budget committee. All proposed legislation is first reviewed by the judiciary committee for its constitutionality. If it passes this test, it is then sent to the specific technical committee or committees with jurisdiction in its area. An economic bill, for instance, would be reviewed by the economy committee and the finance committee.

If three committees approve a bill, it is sent directly to the Senate for consideration. If approved by two committees, or if it fails to secure the approval of a committee, it goes to the floor of the Chamber. Once approved in the Chamber, it must similarly be reviewed by the Senate judiciary and economic affairs committees. If approved by the full Senate, it is sent to the president, who may either sign it into law or veto it in whole or in part. An absolute majority of both houses is required to override a veto. A bill that originates in the Senate must also pass the Chamber of Deputies. Two of the most important types of Executive-initiated bills—appropriations and emergency measures—are taken up by the legislature in joint session (see again Figure 15.8). Constitutional reform bills must be

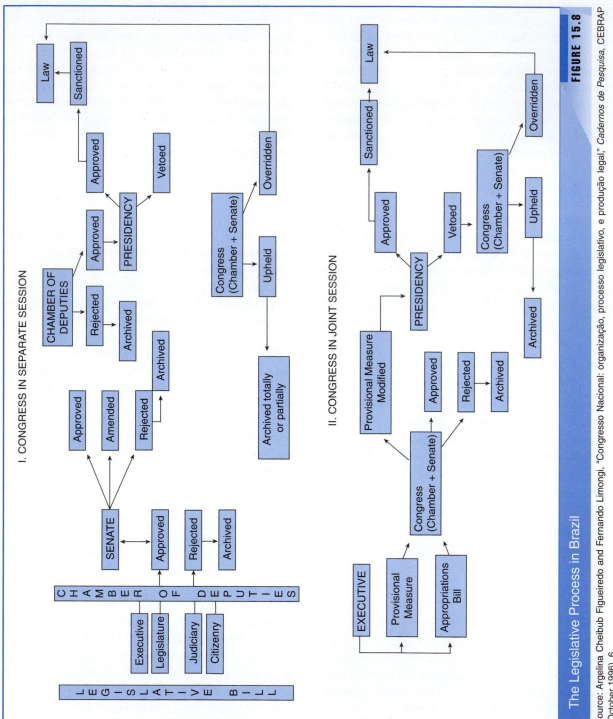

I. CONGRESS IN SEPARATE SESSION

II. CONGRESS IN JOINT SESSION

The Legislative Process in Brazil

Source: Argelina Cheibub Figueiredo and Fernando Limongi, "Congresso Nacional: organização, processo legislativo, e produção legal," *Cadernos de Pesquisa*, CEBRAP (October 1996), 6.

**FIGURE 15.8**

passed by supermajorities—three-fifths of both chambers of Congress—on two separate occasions within the same legislature.

In practice, most laws originate from the Executive Branch, especially those in the economic and administrative areas. From 1989 to 1994, four-fifths of all legislative output in Brazil was initiated by the president. Only 14 percent of successful bills were initiated within Congress itself (these pertained mostly to social issues) and 7 percent by the judiciary. In fact, the president's legislative powers are expansive.

## Presidential Legislative Powers

The Brazilian president dominates the legislative process through various prerogatives and measures. One of the most important is the exclusive right the Constitution gives to the Executive Branch to set the legislative process in motion in several important areas. Only the president can initiate legislation fixing or modifying the size of the armed forces, creating public posts and reorganizing the Cabinet, or setting pay levels for public employees. Most crucially, the Executive has the exclusive right to initiate appropriations measures. Nearly nine in ten of the laws that the president submits to Congress are passed in the same year, in contrast to fewer than two in ten of those initiated by Congress.[63]

The Brazilian president also can enact **provisional measures,** which take effect immediately upon issue. The provisional measures are a carryover from the infamous "decree laws" of the military period, which the framers of the 1988 Constitution intended to be exercised in exceptional and temporary circumstances. If Congress did not approve provisional measures within thirty days, they would fail to become law. In practice, Brazilian presidents made frequent recourse to these emergency measures, and they circumvented the requirement for congressional consent by reissuing decrees that failed to win approval. In a little more than a decade, four presidents had issued sixty decrees and reissued 5,491, a monthly mean of 78.4.

Seeking to restrain presidential power and reclaim its agenda-setting power, Congress amended the Constitution in 2001 to restrict presidents to a single reissue of a lapsed decree. The reform backfired.

Cardoso in his second term and Lula in his first stepped up the rate at which they issued provisional measures. (In his first three years in office, Lula issued decrees at a rate 50 percent higher than the average of his predecessors from 1998–2001.) Moreover, presidents were more, not less, successful at dominating the legislative agenda. With the restriction on the Executive's authority to reissue a decree, Congress agreed to move to the top of its agenda any measure on which it had not acted within forty-five days of issue. Finally, after the reform, 79 percent of provisional measures became law (compared with 43 percent before the reform).[64]

In addition to those areas in which the president has exclusive authority, he may also significantly alter the legislative agenda by requesting that Congress act on proposed legislation "urgently." During the life of a Congress, the president may designate more than a hundred pieces of legislation as urgent. Finally, the president enjoys veto power, which is a powerful instrument of Executive authority. The president has recourse to veto congressional legislation in whole (a *full* veto) or in part (a *partial* veto), and only rarely has Congress overridden a presidential veto.

## The Cabinet and Bureaucracy

The third essential rung of the policymaking process is the bureaucracy. By the close of military rule, the Brazilian bureaucracy and the weight of bureaucratic regulation had grown so large that Brazil's last military president, João Figueiredo, established a "Debureaucratization" Ministry to reduce it.

In making Cabinet appointments, presidents balance their needs for technical competence with those for partisan and regional political support in Congress. With the exception of the Foreign Ministry, the state-owned oil company Petrobrás and a handful of economic agencies, appointments to much of the Brazilian bureaucracy have been controlled by politicians of the party in power seeking to maximize their power through patronage.

The military explicitly disdained the politicized nature of decisionmaking and especially what it perceived to be a lack of resolve in carrying through tough but correct programs. It proceeded to "depoliticize" policy, to hand over important decisions to neutral, technically qualified persons who, it believed, would not be subject to the same sorts of political pressures that made politicians vulnerable. Under the military-technocratic alliance, important decisions were taken out of the hands of Congress. Civilian "technocrats" achieved a degree of power and prestige perhaps unprecedented in Brazil and the world.

Civilian governments continued the practice of closed policymaking in democracy's early years. Although economic policy today remains in the hands of technocrats, elected politicians play a more major role in the Cabinet, especially heading portfolios that manage social policy and political administration, and policy proposals are debated in Congress.

Despite the growth in its professionalism by some highly dedicated and talented public servants in recent years, the bureaucracy has remained highly politicized. During the Sarney administration (1985–1990), there was a virtually unprecedented expansion of public employment, patronage, and clientelism. State administrative reform in the late 1990s, especially the Camata law restricting the payrolls of state governments to 60 percent of net revenue, has made a dent in reducing the public payroll and improving the efficiency of state services.

## POLICY PERFORMANCE

Brazil's policy performance has been uneven. On the one hand, the state has effectively increased its own extractive and regulatory capacities and marshalled resources for economic growth and development. On the other, it has been woefully ineffective, to an extraordinary degree in comparative terms, in providing basic social welfare, ameliorating racial inequality, and combating crime.

After decades of slow progress, governments since the mid-1990s have made great strides in reforming the economy, delivering social services more efficiently, and even better distributing the fruits of economic growth and reducing inequality of opportunity and in the law. The government must still sustain noninflationary growth, provide employment, equitably distribute national wealth and income, and enact fiscal reform. At the same time, it must work to eradicate hunger, improve educational levels, provide adequate housing and health care, and guarantee public security by effectively combating

drug-related and other crime and establishing the rule of law. It has finally made a start.

### The Economic Record

The most dramatic success of Brazilian policy for many decades was economic growth. The state was immensely effective in regulating economic activity, setting wages and prices, doling out agricultural credit, restricting imports, and controlling foreign currency transactions. Brazil grew at an average rate of 7 percent per year for more than three decades across democratic and military regimes. By contrast, growth rates after 1985 were modest at best, averaging less than 3 percent per year. Civilians were disadvantaged at first by a less favorable international climate, as foreign investment and trade opportunities lagged relative to the 1960s and 1970s. During the 1980s, known across Latin America as the "lost decade," onerous service on the foreign debt contracted by military governments severely constrained the ability of their democratic successors to invest in economic growth and social services, and living standards declined.

The most dramatic economic failure of successive Brazilian regimes was their inability to control inflation. Though the military immediately attacked inflation (which was running at 90 percent in 1964), after 1967 it accepted as livable annual inflation rates in the 20 percent range and accorded all priority to growth. Rising world oil prices and interest rates undoubtedly contributed to driving Brazil's inflation rates to triple and then quadruple digits. But soaring government budget deficits (including those of the state governments) in the late 1980s and early 1990s also contributed to skyrocketing prices. In the first decade of civilian rule, inflation *averaged* over 1,000 percent per year, and was more frequently measured in monthly, not annual, terms.

No administration seemed capable of stemming the tide until 1994, when Cardoso introduced the Real Plan. Ultimately, the pegged exchange rate was difficult to sustain, and Brazil was forced to set the real free to float in January 1999. Rising inflation after the democratic transition eroded the purchasing power of the poor even more than it had already fallen during military rule. It was only after the price stabilization of the Real Plan that the real value of the minimum wage began to recover.

Brazil's progress toward liberalizing its economy was slower than in neighboring Chile, Peru, and Argentina. In the early 1990s trade protection was dismantled and a handful of state-owned steel companies were sold. But otherwise, reform efforts stalled. Scholars contended that much needed economic reform was slowed by the problem of too many "veto players," that is, the individual and collective actors (such as members of the Executive branch, congressional leaders, governors, and political party leaders) that have to agree to a change.

The pace of reform quickened with the Cardoso administration. In 1995, Cardoso won support in Congress for constitutional amendments to eliminate state monopolies in the gas, telecommunications, and petroleum industries, and to end constitutionally based discrimination against foreign investment. These legislative victories, in turn, provided the foundation for the privatization program. In 1997–1998, the government auctioned shares of the giant public mining company (the CVRD), sold a series of public power utilities, attracted private investment to modernize Brazil's ports, and opened the lucrative telecommunications companies to private investors.

Other reforms of the state sector deemed crucial for the successful consolidation of the stabilization program were slower to pass in Congress. Two key reforms for reducing the state's financial obligations—administrative reform and pension reform—required constitutional reform. Streamlining a public administration bloated by patronage in the preceding decade was made difficult because civil-sector workers enjoyed constitutional protection from dismissal on any grounds other than demonstrated instances of graft or corruption. And the social security system was strained by the ratio of workers to retirees (2 to 1), and especially by the timing of retirement determined by years of service rather than age (public-sector workers, in effect, could retire by age 50). Administrative reform and a revision of the social security system for private-sector workers were eventually passed, but only after grave financial crises had debilitated the currency and much time and political capital had been spent. Even with these reforms, state pension obligations created an annual deficit equivalent to 5 percent of GDP.[65]

One of the most significant long-term policy successes of the Cardoso government was in reforming the financial relationship between the subnational (state and county) and central governments. Free-spending state and local governments not only spent what the Constitution awarded them but also in the late 1980s and the 1990s mounted staggering debts; total state government debt in 1999 exceeded $90 billion. Much of this spending was directed to political patronage. In the late 1980s, the salaries and wages of public employees in several states of the Northeast accounted for over 100 percent of government revenues.[66] After dragging their feet on state reform and pressing the central government to roll over state government debt for years, state governors and legislative delegations finally agreed to privatize state banks, limit state payrolls, and repay the federal government.

In contrast to these successful reforms, little government initiative and even less progress was made toward deregulating financial and labor markets, which are generally regarded as fettered. Pension reform for public-sector workers, as well as fiscal reform, was left to Lula. In 2003, the government pressed ahead with a pension reform bill that raised the retirement age for civil servants and realigned benefits based on workers' ages and length of contributions, with caps for highest earners. Previously, the system had awarded public-sector workers benefits equal to their last (and highest) salary.

The Brazilian state has as much extractive capacity as any Latin American state, and perhaps of any developing country. Today, Brazil's gross tax burden (tax revenue as a percentage of GDP) stands at 37 percent. The largest single source of public revenue comes from employer and worker contributions to social security (these amounted to 19.7 percent of the total in 2003 (see Figure 15.9). Taxes on income, by contrast, generate a small percentage of government revenues: the personal income tax represents 5 percent of public revenue, and corporate income and profit taxes together account for only another 10 percent. Taxes on assets, such as the property (building and land) tax levied by municipal governments and an excise tax on automobile ownership, amounted to another 7.2 percent. The largest category of taxes is indirect taxes, assessed on the production and circulation of goods and services. The most important of these taxes is the **Tax on the Circulation of Goods and Services (ICMS),** which is collected by the state governments and accounted for 16.8 percent of public revenues in 2003. A series of other taxes on goods and services, some targeted to stabilize social security or education spending, represent another 18.7 percent of public revenues.

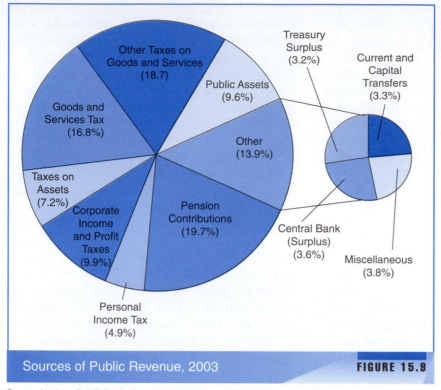

Other Taxes on
Goods and Services
(18.7)

Treasury
Surplus
(3.2%)

Current and
Capital
Transfers
(3.3%)

Public Assets
(9.6%)

Goods and
Services Tax
(16.8%)

Other
(13.9%)

Taxes on
Assets
(7.2%)

Corporate
Income
and Profit
Taxes
(9.9%)

Pension
Contributions
(19.7%)

Central Bank
(Surplus)
(3.6%)

Miscellaneous
(3.8%)

Personal
Income Tax
(4.9%)

**Sources of Public Revenue, 2003**    **FIGURE 15.9**

Source: Instituto Brasileiro de Geografia e Estatística (IBGE), "Finanzas Públicas do Brasil 2002–2003"
(available at www.ibge.gov.br).

the problem. As if to reinforce this point, in his January 2003 inaugural address as Finance Minister, Antônio Palocci decried, "We spend a lot . . . although we spend even more as time goes by, we do not benefit that share of the population that really needs public aid. . . . [T]oday we face the same degree of income distribution inequality that we had in 1970." Indeed, Brazil spends as much, or more, as a proportion of its wealth on social welfare as many other countries in the world. In 2002–2003, 12 percent of all government spending was devoted to education (more than in Britain, France, Germany, and Japan; see Table 7.4 in Chapter 7) and health care expenditures accounted for just under 8 percent of GDP (see Table 7.3 in Chapter 7).

For years, much social policy was badly designed and inefficiently administered. The federal government spent over $5 billion a year on public universities—the best in the country—which charge no tuition.[67] While such a policy made free education theoretically accessible to all, in practice it diverted funds from basic education for the poorer segments of society. In effect, this policy subsidized the higher education of children of the upper-middle and even upper classes, who can afford to pay. The effectiveness of Brazilian social policy also suffered from bureaucratic appointments and resource allocations being made on the basis of political clientelism rather than merit. Clientelism was cited as the "single most effective impediment to redistributive reform in health care."[68]

In the past decade, Brazil has made significant progress in social policy. Literacy rates have increased, the infant mortality rate has decreased, and indigence rates are falling (see Table 15.4). This success can be attributed at least in part to administrative decentralization and more efficiently targeted funding. It also can be seen as the result of the

Governments in the past decade have been unable to enact a fiscal reform that would change the tax structure. The ICMS is considered particularly problematic because each of Brazil's twenty-six states and the Federal District can set separate rates for various goods and services, and compete with one another to attract industry by offering tax incentives. Today, there are fifty-five rates. Reformers have set their sights on passing a single federal law that might set as few as five rates across Brazil. Similarly, they wish to unify all taxes on consumption into a single value-added tax (VAT). This is considered important in order to eliminate distortions in the tax structure and comparatively high payroll taxes that contribute significantly to raising the international price of Brazil's goods.

## Social Welfare Outputs

The record of successive Brazilian governments in the area of social policy was disappointing for many years. Comparative data suggest that spending alone was not

## The Rising Performance of Brazilian Governments

**TABLE 15.4**

| | Sarney-Collor-Franco 1988–1994 | Cardoso 1995–2002 | Lula 2003–2006 |
|---|---|---|---|
| **Economy** | | | |
| Growth[a] | 1.43 | 2.33 | 2.50 |
| Inflation[b] | 1365.60 | 9.25 | 7.50 |
| Real Minimum Wage[c] | −26% | +42% | +44% |
| Income Inequality—Gini coefficient[d] | .60 | .59 | .57 |
| **Welfare** | | | |
| Percentage Minimally Literate[e] | 82.00 | 84.00 | 89.00 |
| Average Years of School[f] | — | 5.30 | 6.70 |
| Infant Mortality Rate[g] | 45.10 | 30.10 | 26.60 |
| Percent Indigent[h] | 20.00 | 14.00 | 11.00 |
| **Liberty**[i] | | | |
| Political Freedom | 2.10 | 2.60 | 2.00 |
| Civil Liberties | 3.10 | 3.60 | 2.70 |

[a] Average annual percent change in gross domestic product; Lula government through 2005.
[b] Annual average increase in extended consumer price index; Lula government through 2005.
[c] Percent change over period; Lula administration through September 2006.
[d] Latest year available for each administration: 1993, 2002, and 2005.
[e] Figures are for the population age 15 and older, 1990, 2000, and 2005.
[f] Figures are for 1995 and 2005.
[g] Figures are for 1991, 2000, and 2004.
[h] Latest year available for each administration: 1993, 2002, and 2005.
[i] As rated by Freedom House, averaged for years 1988–1994, 1995–2002, and 2003–2006 (1 - most free, 7 - not free).

Sources: Instituto de Pesquisa Econômica Aplicada (IPEA) (downloaded from www.ipeadata.gov.br); Instituto Brasileira de Geografia e Estatística (IBGE), "Pesquisa Nacional por Amostra de Domicílios, Síntese de indicadores sociais 2005" (available at www.ibge.gov.br); Freedom House, FH Country Ratings (available at www.freedomhouse.org).

priority accorded to social policy by three successive governments.

The Cardoso government's most notable welfare gains were scored in education. It reorganized and decentralized the delivery of crucial social services. It also stepped up agrarian reform efforts. More than 600,000 landless peasant families were settled on homesteads during Cardoso's two terms, three times as many as in the preceding thirty years. But it left much to be done.

Lula placed early priority on eradicating hunger for the 15 percent of Brazil's population that goes hungry, in a social program known as "Zero Hunger." The symbolism of the program's launch by Brazil's first president to have experienced hunger firsthand as a child was enormous, but insufficient to make the program a success.

Learning from its early missteps, the Lula government consolidated several conditional cash transfer (CCT) and other social welfare programs into a single program known as **Bolsa Familia.** Bolsa Familia, the Lula administration's flagship social program, comprises four previously existing programs, including the Cardoso era Bolsa Escola and the Lula administration's failed Zero Hunger. Lula created the new Ministry of Social Development to oversee the program, which today reaches a quarter of the Brazilian population and is the world's largest CCT program (see Box 15.3). These programmatic reforms have produced tangible results in key areas of social policy.

*Education* The Cardoso government inherited a dismal educational system. Government spending on education had declined as a percentage of total

## Out of Poverty? Bolsa Familia

**BOX 15.3**

Social policy analysts have decried that many expensive social insurance programs in poor countries, including Brazil, disproportionately benefit the middle class. Brazil has innovated a new approach to poverty, known generically as conditional cash transfers. These CCTs target the poor with cash payments to meet specific policy objectives.

How does it work? Parents, ideally mothers (who are more apt than fathers to use the money for their children) are given 95 reais ($52) for a family of five or more. In return, they must ensure that their children see a doctor regularly, receive their vaccinations, and stay in school. For very poor families, cash provides emergency assistance and allows them to forgo the earnings they would have received from their children's employment. In terms of economic development, the program makes long-term investments in human capital, which ideally will help to break the cycle of poverty.

The program appears to be working: almost four-fifths of children from beneficiary families are now attending classes. And the cost is modest. Bolsa Familia costs the federal government a mere .36 percent of gross domestic product (GDP). Even extending the program to 11.2 million families (44 million people)—the government's short-term goal—would represent only .5 percent of GDP and 2.5 percent of total government spending.

Sources: *Economist,* 15 September 2005; Kathy Lindert, "Brazil: Bolsa Familia Program–Scaling-up Cash Transfers for the Poor," Managing for Development Results, *Principles in Action: Sourcebook on Emerging Good Practices* (March 2006), 67–74 (www.mdar.org/sourcebook.html).

expenditure from 1988 to 1993. The average number of years spent in school in Brazil was only 3.8. Sixty-five percent of children did not complete primary school (in northeastern Brazil, the dropout rate was over 70 percent), and of those who did, only 3 percent were able to do so in the normal eight years. Most failed and were forced to repeat several grades; it took students on average 11.2 years to complete primary school. Only 1 percent of the Brazilian population reached university, the same percentage as in the 1960s.[69]

The Cardoso administration increased spending on education—to 5.2 percent of gross domestic product in 1998—but most significantly, it redistributed educational resources to favor primary education and sought to reduce regional inequalities in funding. The new **Basic Federal Law on Education Finance (FUNDEF)** specifically earmarked a percentage of federal funds for primary education, set a national minimum to be spent per student in grades one through eight, and required the federal government to make up the shortfall in states too poor to meet the minimum. Between 1998 and 2000, annual spending per pupil grew by 48.5 percent nationwide, but by 117.5 and 90 percent, respectively, in the poorer Northeast and North.[70] The law also encouraged a substantial increase in teachers' salaries.

The efforts of the Cardoso government to improve teacher training and graduation rates met with considerable success. Between 1991 and 1999, school enrollment among 7- to 14-year-olds (for whom school attendance is mandatory) rose from 86 to 97 percent, and from 1994 to 2001, the number of students in primary school rose from 31.1 to 35.3 million, a 13.5 percent increase, but the most dramatic increase came in secondary school enrollments, which rose from 4.4 to 8.4 million, an increase of 90 percent. From 1991 to 2000, the proportion of adults who had not completed three years of schooling had dropped from 41 to 31 percent.

*Health*  The delivery of public health also constitutes a major challenge. The 1988 Constitution mandated a single, unified health system, replacing the previous system in which only formal sector workers had health care coverage. Although every citizen has been entitled to medical treatment in public or contracted private facilities since 1988, in practice, access to the health care system is uneven and policy outputs in this area have been disappointing.

A Brazilian classroom. More children are in school today than ever before, thanks to a program that pays families a monthly stipend to keep their children in school. The federal government has also created a foundation to fund primary education.

John Maier, Jr./The Image Works

In recent years, an administrative decentralization of health care to local governments and increased federal spending have raised the quality of health care in Brazil. Access to primary health care improved significantly when José Serra, who became Health Minister in 1998, managed to triple federal transfers to the states and municipalities for this purpose. After 2001, a constitutional amendment obliged all levels of government to increase their earmarks for spending on health care.[71]

These modest changes have improved policy outputs in the health sector. Life expectancy at birth has risen from 67 years in 1991 to 72 years in 2004. While Brazil's infant mortality rate (the number of deaths of babies of less than one year of age per 1,000 live births) is still higher than China's, Mexico's, and Russia's (30, 23, and 16 percent, respectively), it dropped from 48 in 1990 to 33 in 2003 (though its child mortality rate—the number of deaths per 1,000 children under age 5—remains one of the highest in the world at 50) (see again Table 7.3). Moreover, the percentage of the population that lacked access to safe water and sanitation also diminished markedly from 1990, when these rates were 17 and 30 percent, respectively, to 2002, when they fell to 11 and 25 percent (see again Table 7.2). Another notable success of the

Brazilian government, for which it has gained international acclaim, is its policy to combat the spread of AIDS (see Box 15.4).

*Racial Equality* Signaling a new priority, Lula created the **Special Secretariat for the Promotion of Racial Equality (SEPPIR)** in 2003 to advance the cause of racial equality in Brazil. SEPPIR has not produced many tangible policy results, in no small part because it is, as one Afro-Brazilian leader put it, "a minister without a ministry, and a secretariat without a budget," but symbolically, Brazil has taken a step forward.

The centerpiece of the government's program, initiated during the Cardoso administration, is to promote racial quotas in the higher education system as well as in several branches of government. The use of quotas to promote racial equality has been controversial (see again Box 15.1). With public opinion generally behind the use of quotas, a statute of racial equality is winding its way through the Brazilian Congress. Even if it passes, however, it has not always been easy to fill the quotas set aside for Afro-Brazilians. In the state of Paraná, for example, although 20 percent of places at the Federal University were reserved for Afro descendents, only 8 percent of the class entering in 2006 consisted of black students.

**BOX 15.4**

## Fighting AIDS: A Brazilian Success Story

Brazil has one of the most effective programs to combat the spread of AIDS in the world. In the 1990s, the cost of treating patients, the numbers dying from the disease, and the incidence of new cases all fell dramatically. In 2002, there were 630,000 confirmed cases of AIDS, half the 1.2 million that the World Bank projected it would have in 2000. Brazil's program stands on two pillars: reducing the cost of treating patients infected with the HIV virus, and expanding prevention programs.

In 2001, the Brazilian government announced that it would produce locally generic versions of the anti-retroviral medications to treat HIV patients if the international pharmaceutical companies holding the patents on these drugs did not lower their prices. It argued that in cases of "abusive prices," patent law should not supersede fundamental human rights. The United States filed a complaint against Brazil with the World Trade Organization, but withdrew it when Brazil was supported by the United Nation's Human Rights Commission and the World Health Organization. Brazil

had won the "patent war," and now manufactures its own generic drugs at a much lower cost.

The Brazilian government also has an impressive campaign to treat infected patients and prevent new cases. It distributes free medicine to 120,000 patients, which has reduced the incidence of related diseases, such as tuberculosis. The Health Ministry also encourages the use of condoms to check the spread of new cases. The government distributed close to 200 million condoms free of charge in 2002. It intends to open a state-run condom factory, and to distribute a billion free condoms in 2007. The government steps up its condom distribution at Carnival time when sexual activity rises sharply. The Catholic Church in Brazil is caught between fighting to defend church teaching on artificial contraception and to defend life. When the president of Brazil's National Conference of Catholic Bishops was asked in February 2005 about the church's position on the free condom distribution during Carnival, he said only, "The church does not want to arm wrestle with the government."

## Crime, the Law, and Civil Liberties

Economic deprivation and the lack of an effective government policy to deal with Brazil's "social problem" have fueled an increase in crime, which itself has been driven by the surge in drug use. Drugs and crime are cited as among the most important problems facing Brazil by 41 and 35 percent of the population, respectively; only unemployment and health are considered more pressing. Drug lords rule in many neighborhoods, perhaps nowhere as dramatically as in Rio de Janeiro, where there are estimated to be 10,000 heavily armed combatants, leading President Itamar Franco in 1994 to call in the army to restore order in the city. Police say that most violent crime—perhaps as much as 70 to 80 percent—in the country is related, directly or indirectly, to the illegal drug trade. An estimated 200,000 Brazilians are employed in the narcotics business, with at least 5,000 heavily armed gang members working for different drug-trafficking groups in Rio de Janeiro alone. In 2001, Brazil suffered from an

unprecedented wave of kidnappings, which authorities say was largely the work of organized crime groups. The murder rate has doubled since the mid-1980s; in 2000, it reached twenty-eight per 100,000. In the five-year period from 1995 to 2000, homicides in São Paulo increased by over 40 percent, to 3,249. Across Brazil, 37,000 people are murdered each year. According to the United Nations, Brazil has the highest rate of homicides caused by firearms for any country not at war—more than 70 percent.[72] The wealthy have responded by resorting to private security. In 2001, there were 1.4 million private security guards in the country, more than twice the number of police. The poor often take the law into their own hands, with hundreds of reported lynchings and mob executions.

The failure of the Brazilian government to reduce crime is part of a broader failure since the transition to democracy to guarantee civil liberties and enforce the rule of law. Violence against peasants, rural workers, and their advocates is widespread and goes virtually unpunished. According to the Pastoral Land Commission of the Catholic Church, as of 1992, only twenty-nine cases of 1,730 such killings from 1964 through 1992 had been brought to trial, and only eighteen had resulted in convictions. This is hardly surprising given that many areas of intense rural conflicts have no judge or public prosecutor, and they are particularly rare in the northern and northeastern states.[73] The federal police (which investigate crimes involving corruption, contraband, and human rights violations) has fewer than 5,000 agents, most of whom are in Brasília. Clientelism has also undermined the efficient functioning of the law enforcement agencies. In the North and Northeast of Brazil, most police commissioners are political appointees of the state governors, and in practice, the requirement that they hold a law degree is often circumvented.[74]

Even more glaring is the state's failure to control the violence of its own military and police forces. Police officers themselves join death squads that murder street children and frequently torture common criminals. From December 1995 to August 1996, 300 police officers were indicted for torture, but none were actually punished. The state civilian police (who are responsible for conducting investigations) justify their routine use of illegal methods of investigation and see the rule of law as an obstacle to social control. The state military police (who are in charge of patrolling and preventing crime) have been reported to commit blatant human rights violations, including summary executions of suspects. In July 1993, the Rio military police opened fire on seventy homeless children and youths sleeping near the Candelária church in downtown Rio de Janeiro, killing eight. In the state of São Paulo members of the military police murdered 1,450 people in 1992; in 1997, the number declined—there were 435 such deaths.[75] Military and police repression of prisoners is notorious in Brazil. The prison system, with 200,000 incarcerated (nearly half in São Paulo), is overwhelmed. In October 1992, the military police of São Paulo massacred 111 inmates in the Carandiru prison. In 2001, fifteen prisoners were killed in São Paulo's biggest-ever prison uprising, several apparently the victims of summary executions by police who were called in to restore order. In the same year, twenty-seven police officers were accused of being involved in kidnapping rings in Rio de Janeiro.

Brazilian police are systematically underpaid (at the lower ranks, officers earn only the minimum wage) and lack training.

The Cardoso government tried to address this huge public policy challenge. Cardoso created a ministerial rank secretariat charged with defending human rights, launched a national plan of action for human rights, upgraded the crime of torture from a misdemeanor to a serious crime punishable by up to sixteen years in prison, and proposed making all rights violations federal crimes, thus moving their investigation from the jurisdiction of state civil and military police forces. Nonetheless, by the end of his term, only one high-security federal jail had been built and a 1999 gun control bill sent to Congress got nowhere.

Lula created the National Coordination for the Protection of Human Rights Defenders, made up of government officials and civil society representatives, in 2003. In 2004, it put into place a telephone hotline service that people can use to report rights abuses. Yet, there is clearly much to be done before violence is curbed and justice established in Brazil.

## INTERNATIONAL RELATIONS

Brazil has long had a professional foreign service, but not until the Cardoso government did it begin to assume a position of respect on the world stage as a major player in international and regional affairs. Brazil has aimed to cooperate with other countries on nuclear nonproliferation, environmental protection (especially implementing the Rio and Kyoto protocols), advancing human and women's rights, and reducing drug trafficking. Under Lula's first government, the explicit aims of Brazil's foreign policy were to reduce the gap between rich and poor nations, promote equality among peoples, and democratize the international system. Lula himself became a voice on the world stage for developing nations.

Yet, the fears of some observers that under Lula Brazil might lurch dangerously to the political left turned out to be unfounded. Lula's rise in the polls in 2002 caused grave concern over whether or not Brazil would honor its international financial obligations, though throughout the campaign, Lula sought to calm investors by committing himself to honoring Brazil's external obligations. In December 2005, Lula kept his word, as Brazil paid off its $15.5 billion loan (contracted in 2002) two years ahead of schedule. Moreover, Lula has not joined forces with such Latin American leaders as Hugo Chávez in Venezuela, who routinely condemn the United States in international forums, and in fact, its relations with Bolivia suffered in 2006 when the Morales government threatened Brazilian investments in Bolivian natural gas. Brazil has steered its own course in hemispheric affairs.

Trade is one of the most important issues for Brazil's international relations, and Brazil is especially keen to open markets for its exports. Brazil is a member of the South American regional trading bloc, **Mercosur,** the Common Market of the South (Argentina, Paraguay, and Uruguay; Chile and Bolivia are associate members). Mercosur, which came into being in 1991, eliminated tariffs on 95 percent of the goods traded among its member countries, created a market of 220 million people with a GDP of $1.3 trillion, and in its first six years expanded regional trade by more than 400 percent. The 1997 Asian crisis, the January 1999 devaluation of the real, and the 2001 Argentine crisis slowed the momentum of intraregional trade; nonetheless, about 11 percent of Brazil's exports (by value) are still traded within the Mercosur region.

Meanwhile, Brazil has deliberately dragged its feet in multilateral negotiations to create the **Free Trade Area of the Americas (FTAA),** which began a decade ago with the goal of concluding an agreement by 2005. The United States, Mexico, and Chile all favor hastening the FTAA; Venezuela and Bolivia oppose any further integration with the United States; Brazil contends that it will make concessions on intellectual property rights, financial regulation, and market access, and sign the agreement only when the United States provides fair access to its market for Brazil's farmers. At issue are billions of dollars of agricultural subsidies that the United States pays its farmers. Brazil's approach has been to work for global trade reform through the World Trade Organization (WTO) and the Doha round before establishing the FTAA. In fact, Brazil has joined forces with many smaller African nations in a movement to end the rich world's agricultural subsidies (the European Union, too, pays out billions of dollars worth of price supports to its farmers). In 2004, Brazil took the United States to World Trade Court and won a ruling (see Box 15.5).

Commensurate with its status as one of the world's largest countries in terms of territory, population, and economic activity, Brazil aspires to occupy a seat on the United Nations Security Council. It is a member of the so-called G–4, a group that includes Germany, Japan, and India. These nations want to enlarge the UN Security Council to "reflect the 21st century's new balance of forces." In 2005, they proposed adding six

---

## Brazil vs. the U.S.: The Case of Cotton Subsidies

**BOX 15.5**

Agricultural subsidies and farm supports paid by rich countries amount to $300 billion a year. The United States and the European Union defend the subsidies, arguing that they do not violate international trade rules and do no harm to global markets. Brazil and other developing countries contend that the subsidy programs increase production, destroy markets for their exports, and undermine the livelihood of their farmers. World Bank economists agree that 144 million people could be lifted out of poverty if rich countries reduced or eliminated these subsidies and supports.

In 2004 Brazil won a preliminary ruling at the World Trade Organization that subsidies worth $3 billion paid by the U.S. government to American cotton farmers each year, as well as $1.7 billion in subsidies to American agribusiness and manufacturers to buy American cotton, violated international trade rules. Brazil estimated that without the subsidies, U.S. cotton production would fall 29 percent and U.S. cotton exports would drop 41 percent, which would lead to a rise in international cotton prices of 12.6 percent. The WTO agreed.

Source: "W.T.O. Rules Against U.S. on Cotton Subsidies," *New York Times,* 27 April 2004.

new seats that would be nonveto-wielding permanent seats, to be allotted to these four and two states from Africa. The proposal, though endorsed by Britain and France, has faltered due to divisions within the African Union, Chinese opposition to Japan's ascension, and U.S. opposition to any enlargement of the Council at this time.

## PROSPECTS FOR THE FUTURE

While Brazilians have long been ambivalent about their democracy, and have become ever more distrustful of political parties and institutions, the Brazilian people have not given up on their country's leaders, economy, and future prospects. In 2005, 67 percent of Brazilians believed their children would live better than they had lived (well above the Latin American average of 54 percent).[76] Despite a grave political scandal in his party, Brazilians last October handed Lula a reelection victory.

A good deal of this optimism undoubtedly has followed from better government performance, especially in those areas that correspond to the greatest human need. As the head of a government of the modern left, Lula met several challenges: soothing the fears of foreign investors and creditors, producing a fiscal surplus, gaining control of the public debt, and turning in positive growth rates. The recovery of the nation's fiscal health and prosperity, moreover, enabled the recovery of living standards and social development. But Brazilians learned in 2005 and 2006 that some of those gains had come at a high political cost.

After a string of presidents who lacked the support of either the public or Congress, and several corruption scandals involving public officials, the two-term Cardoso presidency provided Brazil with much needed political stability. That stability, perhaps real, perhaps illusory, was shattered by the illegal campaign finance, cash-for-votes, and "bloodsucker" scandals that exposed PT mayors and members of Congress, once believed to be uniquely honest, to be just as corrupt as those against whom they had railed while in opposition. No fewer than seventy-two members of Congress running for reelection in 2006 were under investigation by federal authorities, the Public Prosecution, and Congress' own Parliamentary Commission of Inquiry. Only time will tell whether or not the damage wrought by this scandal will offset the enhanced prestige and effectiveness of Brazil's parties marked by increased cohesion, discipline, and ideological range.

Can Brazilians retain their optimism, buoyed up four years ago by Lula's election and his promises to eradicate hunger, redress inequality, and forge a decent society, amid one of the worst corruption scandals in the nation's history? Can Lula govern in a second term? Can he get bills through an opposition-controlled Congress but now without the benefit of kickbacks and side payments? Lula's apparent options are to reach out to forge a broad governing coalition (something he did not do in his first administration) or scale back the ambition of his government. In the days after his reelection, he promised to do the former. Brazil's prospects for the future depend on his ability to govern broadly.

## KEY TERMS

barrier clause

Basic Federal Law on Education Finance (FUNDEF)

Bolsa Familia

Brazilian Labor Party (PTB)

Brazilian Socialist Party (PSB)

Central Única dos Trabalhadores (CUT)

College of Leaders

*coronelismo*

corporatism

Democratic Labor Party (PDT)

Departamento Intersindical de Assessoria Parlamentar (DIAP)

direct action of unconstitutionality (ADIN)

ecclesial base communities (CEBs)

Federation of Industries of the State of São Paulo (FIESP)

Fiscal Responsibility Law

Free Trade Area of the Americas (FTAA)

*horário gratuito*

Institute for the Defense of the Consumer (IDEC)

liberation theology

Mensalão (the big monthly)

MERCOSUR

*mesa directiva*

Ministério Público (Public Prosecution)

Movement of Landless Rural Workers (MST)

Movimento Negro Unificado

National Conference of Brazilian Bishops (CNBB)

open-list proportional representation

Parliamentary Commissions of Inquiry (CPIs)

participatory budgeting

Party of the Brazilian Democratic Movement (PMDB)

Party of Brazilian Social Democracy (PSDB)

Party of the Liberal Front (PFL)

Progressive Party (PP)

provisional measures

Real Plan

Special Secretariat for the Promotion of Racial Equality (SEPPIR)

Supremo Tribunal Federal (STF)

Tax on the Circulation of Goods and Services (ICMS)

Tribunal Superior Eleitoral (TSE)

Tribunal de Contas

Workers' Party (PT)

## SUGGESTED READINGS

Abers, Rebecca. *Inventing Democracy.* Boulder, CO: Lynne Rienner, 2000.

Alvarez, Sonia E. *Engendering Democracy in Brazil: Women's Movements in Transition Politics.* Princeton, NJ: Princeton University Press, 1990.

Ames, Barry. *Political Survival: Politicians and Public Policy in Latin America.* Berkeley: University of California Press, 1987.

———. *The Deadlock of Democracy in Brazil.* Ann Arbor: University of Michigan Press, 2001.

Burdick, John. *Looking for God in Brazil: The Progressive Catholic Church in Urban Brazil's Religious Arena.* Berkeley: University of California Press, 1993.

Caldeira, Teresa. *City of Walls: Crime, Segregation, and Citizenship in São Paulo.* Berkeley: University of California Press, 2000.

Geddes, Barbara. *Politician's Dilemma: Building State Capacity in Latin America.* Berkeley: University of California Press, 1994.

Hagopian, Frances. *Traditional Politics and Regime Change in Brazil.* Cambridge: Cambridge University Press, 1996.

Hanchard, Michael George. *Orpheus and Power: The Movimento Negro of Rio de Janeiro and São Paulo, Brazil, 1945–1988.* Princeton, NJ: Princeton University Press, 1994.

Hochstetler, Kathryn, and Margaret E. Keck. *Greening Brazil: Environmental Activism in State and Society.* Durham, NC: Duke University Press, 2007.

Hunter, Wendy. *Eroding Military Influence in Brazil: Politicians Against Soldiers.* Chapel Hill: University of North Carolina Press, 1997.

Keck, Margaret E. *The Workers' Party and Democratization in Brazil.* New Haven, CT: Yale University Press, 1992.

Kingstone, Peter R. *Crafting Coalitions for Reform: Business Preferences, Political Institutions, and Neoliberal Reform in Brazil.* University Park: Pennsylvania State University Press, 1999.

Kingstone, Peter R., and Timothy J. Power, eds. *Democratic Brazil: Actors, Institutions, and Processes.* Pittsburgh, PA: University of Pittsburgh Press, 2000.

Kinzo, Maria D'Alva Gil, and James Dunkerley, eds. *Brazil Since 1985: Politics, Economy, and Society.* London: Institute of Latin American Studies, 2003.

Luna, Francisco Vidal, and Herbert S. Klein. *Brazil Since 1980 (The World Since 1980).* Cambridge: Cambridge University Press, 2006.

Mainwaring, Scott. *The Catholic Church and Politics in Brazil, 1916–1985.* Stanford, CA: Stanford University Press, 1986.

———. *Rethinking Party Systems in the Third Wave of Democratization: The Case of Brazil.* Stanford, CA: Stanford University Press, 1999.

McDonough, Peter. *Power and Ideology in Brazil.* Princeton, NJ: Princeton University Press, 1981.

Payne, Leigh A. *Brazilian Industrialists and Democratic Change.* Baltimore, MD: Johns Hopkins University Press, 1994.

Pereira, Anthony W. *The End of the Peasantry: The Rural Labor Movement in Northeast Brazil, 1961–1988.* Pittsburgh, PA: University of Pittsburgh Press, 1997.

Power, Timothy J. *The Political Right in Postauthoritarian Brazil: Elites, Institutions, and Democratization.* University Park: Pennsylvania State University Press, 2000.

Samuels, David. *Ambition, Federalism, and Legislative Politics in Brazil.* Cambridge: Cambridge University Press, 2003.

Schmitter, Philippe C. *Interest Conflict and Political Change in Brazil.* Stanford, CA: Stanford University Press, 1971.

Schneider, Ben Ross. *Politics Within the State: Elite Bureaucrats and Industrial Policy in Authoritarian Brazil.* Pittsburgh, PA: University of Pittsburgh Press, 1991.

Skidmore, Thomas E. *The Politics of Military Rule in Brazil, 1964–85.* New York: Oxford University Press, 1988.

Stepan, Alfred. *The Military in Politics: Changing Patterns in Brazil.* Princeton, NJ: Princeton University Press, 1971.

———. *Rethinking Military Politics: Brazil and the Southern Cone.* Princeton, NJ: Princeton University Press, 1988.

Stepan, Alfred, ed. *Authoritarian Brazil: Origins, Policies, and Future.* New Haven, CT: Yale University Press, 1973.

———. *Democratizing Brazil: Problems of Transition and Consolidation.* New York: Oxford University Press, 1989.

Von Mettenheim, Kurt. *The Brazilian Voter: Mass Politics in Democratic Transition 1974–1986.* Pittsburgh, PA: University of Pittsburgh Press, 1995.

Weyland, Kurt. *Democracy Without Equity: Failures of Reform in Brazil.* Pittsburgh, PA: University of Pittsburgh Press, 1996.

## INTERNET RESOURCES

General informational websites on Brazil: **www.lanic.utexas.edu/ la/; cfdev.Georgetown.edu/pdba/countries/**

Government website: **www.brasil.gov.br**

Legislature website: **www.senado.gov.br; www.camara.gov.br**

Census bureau website: **www.ibge.gov.br**

Planning Ministry's research arm: **www.ipea.gov.br**

Electoral tribunal website: **www.tse.gov.br**

## ENDNOTES

1. Freedom House, *Freedom in the World, Brazil (2005)* (available at www.freedomhouse.org).

2. "October Poll Puts Country on Hold," *Financial Times Survey: Brazil*, 3 July 2002, 1.

3. Instituto Brasileiro de Geografia e Estatística (IBGE), *Annuário Estatístico do Brasil 1976* (Rio de Janeiro: Fundação IBGE), 62; *Annuário Estatístico do Brasil 1987*, 105; and *Censo Demográfico 2000* (available at www.ibge.gov.br).

4. Fernando Henrique Cardoso, "Associated-Democratic Development and Democratic Theory," in Alfred Stepan, ed., *Democratizing Brazil: Problems of Transition and Consolidation* (New York: Oxford University Press, 1989), 306; and IBGE, *Annuário Estatsítico do Brasil 1993*, 2–61 and 2–62.

5. David Samuels, *Ambition, Federalism, and Legislative Politics in Brazil* (Cambridge: Cambridge University Press, 2003), 161, 171, 175.

6. Matthew M. Taylor, "Veto and Voice in the Courts: Policy Implications of Institutional Design in the Brazilian Judiciary," *Comparative Politics*, 38, no. 3 (April 2006).

7. Mariana Sousa, "Judicial Roles in the Policy-Making Process and Public Policy in Latin America" (paper presented at the annual meeting of the American Political Science Association, 31 August–3 September 2006, Philadelphia), 21, 34.

8. In an interview with the *Financial Times*, 11 July 2006.

9. Maria Tereza Sadek and Rosângela Batista Cavalcanti, "The New Brazilian Public Prosecution: An Agent of Accountability," in Scott Mainwaring and Christopher Welna, eds. *Democratic Accountability in Latin America* (Oxford: Oxford University Press, 2003), 209, 210–11, 213–15, 225.

10. Roberto Da Matta, *Carnavais, Malandros e Heróis: Para uma Sociologia do Dilema Brasileiro* (Rio de Janeiro: Zahar, 1978).

11. Peter McDonough, Doh C. Shin, and José Álvaro Moisés, "Democratization and Participation: Comparing Spain, Brazil, and Korea," *Journal of Politics* 60 (November 1998): 925.

12. Antônio Flávio Pierucci and Reginaldo Prandi, "Religiões e Voto: A Eleição Presidencial de 1994," *Opinião Pública*, 3, no. 1 (1994): 25.

13. Lúcia Avelar, *O Segundo Eleitorado: Tendências do Voto Feminino no Brasil* (Campinas: Unicamp, 1989), 105–28.

14. Mala Htun, "Puzzles of Women's Rights in Brazil," *Social Research* 69, no. 3 (Fall 2002):733–51 (2003).

15. Gilberto Freyre, *The Masters and the Slaves* (New York: Knopf, 1946).

16. "Racism, Racial Discrimination, Xenophobia, and All Forms of Discrimination," United Nations Commission on Human Rights, Addendum, Mission to Brazil (17–26 October 2005), 18.

17. Thomas R. Rochon and Michael J. Mitchell, "Social Bases of the Transition to Democracy in Brazil," *Comparative Politics* 21, no. 3 (April 1989): 315–18; and José Alvaro Moisés, "Elections, Political Parties, and Political Culture in Brazil: Changes and Continuities," *Journal of Latin American Studies* 25, no. 3 (October 1993): 597.

18. Marta Lagos, Latinobarómetro 2000 (paper presented at Inter-American Dialogue, Washington, DC, 10 November 2000) (available at www.latinobarometro.org).

19. IBOPE Opinião, "Confiança nas Instituições," 6 September 2005 (available at www.ibope.com.br).

20. Andy Baker, Barry Ames, and Lucio R. Renno, "Social Context and Campaign Volatility in New Democracies: Networks and Neighborhoods in Brazil's 2002 Elections." *American Journal of Political Science* 50, no. 2 (April 2006): 382–99.

21. Respondents to a survey during the 1989 presidential campaign reported that their choice of candidate was much less frequently influenced by newspapers, radio news, neighborhood associations, the Catholic Church, union activists, and public opinion polls. Joseph Straubhaar, Organ Olsen, and Maria Cavaliari Nunes, "The Brazilian Case: Influencing the Voter," in Thomas E. Skidmore, ed., *Television, Politics, and the Transition to Democracy in Latin America* (Baltimore/Washington, DC: Johns Hopkins University Press/Woodrow Wilson Center Press, 1993), 123, 127–28, 133.

22. *Folha* Online, 2002 election special (available at www. folha .uol.com.br).

23. Câmara dos Deputados, *Deputados Brasileiras, 49a Legislatura, 1991–1995 Repertório Biográfico* (Brasília, 1991).

24. Scott Morgenstern, "Explaining Legislative Politics in Latin America," in Scott Morgenstern and Benito Nacif, eds., *Legislative Politics in Latin America* (Cambridge: Cambridge University Press, 2002), 416.

25. Htun, "Puzzles of Women's Rights in Brazil."

26. Mala Htun, "From 'Racial Democracy' to Affirmative Action: Changing State Policy on Race in Brazil," *Latin American Research Review* 39, no. 1 (2004): 63.

27. Amaury de Souza and Bolívar Lamounier, *As Elites Brasileiras e a Modernização do Setor Público: Um Debate* (São Paulo: IDESP/Sumaré, 1992).

28. IBOPE, OPP 570/December 2002 (retrieved from www .ibope.com.br).

29. Renato Boschi, "Social Movements and the New Political Order in Brazil," in John D. Wirth, Edson de Oliveira Nunes, and Thomas E. Bogenschild, eds., *State and Society in Brazil: Continuity and Change* (Boulder, CO: Westview, 1987), 180, 187–88, 197.

30. Gianpaolo Baiocchi, "Participation, Activism, and Politics: The Porto Alegre Experiment and Deliberative Democratic Theory," *Politics and Society* 29 (March 2001): 55.

31. Carlos Frederico Marés de Souza, Jr., "On Brazil and its Indians," in Donna Lee Van Cott, ed., *Indigenous Peoples and Democracy in Latin America* (New York: Inter-American Dialogue/St. Martin's Press, 1994), 218–21, 230–31.

32. Kathryn Hochstetler, "The Evolution of the Brazilian Environmental Movement and Its Political Roles," in Douglas A. Chalmers, eds. et al., *The New Politics of Inequality in Latin America: Rethinking Participation and Representation* (Oxford: Oxford University Press, 1997), 204–07, 209, 211–12.

33. Patricia M. Rodriguez, "The Participatory Effectiveness of Land-Related Movements in Brazil, Ecuador, and Chile: 1990-2004," Ph.D. Dissertation, University of Notre Dame, 2009, 79.

34. February 2006 poll, IBOPE Opinião (retrieved from www .ibope.com.br on 7 August 2006).

35. According to the respected Brazilian newspaper, *Folha de São Paulo*, as cited in Kathryn Hochstetler, "Democratizing Pressures From Below? Social Movements in the New Brazilian Democracy," in Peter R. Kingstone and Timothy J. Power, eds., *Democratic Brazil: Actors, Institutions, and Processes* (Pittsburgh, PA: University of Pittsburgh Press, 2000), 179.

36. This is different from the *neocorporatism* system described in Chapter 4 that presumes a democratic relationship between government and interest groups.

37. Timothy J. Power and J. Timmons Roberts, "A New Brazil? The Changing Sociodemographic Context of Brazilian Democracy," in Kingstone and Power, *Democratic Brazil,* 254.

38. Instituto Brasileiro de Geografia e Estatistica (IBGE), Pesquisa Nacional por Amostra de Domicilios, Sintese de Indicadores 2005 (www.ibge.gov.br).

39. Samuels, *Ambition, Federalism, and Legislative Politics,* 167.

40. Eli Diniz, "Empresariado, Estado y Políticas Públicas en Brasil: Nuevas Tendencias en el Umbral del Nuevo Milenio," in Vicente Palermo, ed., *Política Brasileña Contemporánea: De Collor A Lula en Años de Transformación* (Buenos Aires: Instituto Di Tella/Siglo XXI, 2003), 462–63.

41. Leigh Payne, *Brazilian Industrialists and Democratic Change* (Baltimore, MD: Johns Hopkins University Press, 1994), 114.

42. Peter R. Kingstone, *Crafting Coalitions for Reform: Business Preferences, Political Institutions, and Neoliberal Reform in Brazil* (University Park: Pennsylvania State University Press, 1999), 111–48.

43. Scott Mainwaring, Rachel Meneguello, and Timothy J. Power, "Conservative Parties, Democracy, and Economic Reform in Contemporary Brazil," in Kevin J. Middlebrook, ed., *Conservative Parties, the Right, and Democracy in Latin America* (Baltimore: Johns Hopkins University Press, 2000), 216–17.

44. Rodriguez, "Mobilization," 23–26.

45. Wendy Hunter, *Eroding Military Influence in Brazil: Politicians Against Soldiers* (Chapel Hill: University of North Carolina Press, 1997), 112–13.

46. Hunter, *Eroding Military Influence,* 123–24, 129–32.

47. *New York Times,* 4 January 2002, A3.

48. Fernando Henrique Cardoso, "In Praise of the Art of Politics," *Journal of Democracy* 7, no. 3 (July 1996): 12, 14–15.

49. Among the former are Scott Mainwaring, *Rethinking Party Systems in the Third Wave of Democratization: The Case of Brazil* (Stanford, CA: Stanford University Press, 1999); and Barry Ames, *The Deadlock of Democracy in Brazil* (Ann Arbor: University of Michigan Press, 2001). Those who argue that parties have grown stronger include Argelina Cheibub Figueiredo and Fernando Limongi, *Executivo e Legislativo na nova ordem constitucional* (Rio de Janeiro: Editora FGV, 1999); and Celso Ricardo Roma, "Atores, Preferências e Instituição na Câmara dos Deputados" (Ph.D. dissertation, University of São Paulo, 2004).

50. Barry Ames, *Political Survival: Politicians and Public Policy in Latin America* (Berkeley: University of California Press, 1987), 204–06.

51. The law allowed for a transitional period of two full electoral cycles before the clause would take effect, presumably allowing time for parties to adjust.

52. Maria Herminia Tavares de Almeida, quoted in the Woodrow Wilson International Center for Scholars, Brazilian Institute Special Report No. 2 (Washington, DC, September 2006), 3.

53. Scott Mainwaring, "Politicians, Parties, and Electoral Systems: Brazil in Comparative Perspective," *Comparative Politics* 24, no. 1 (October 1991): 24.

54. Figueiredo and Limongi, *Executivo e Legislativo,* 112.

55. Mainwaring, *Rethinking Party Systems,* 143–45; and Carlos Ranulfo Felix de Melo, "Partidos e Migração na Câmara dos Deputados," *Dados* 43, no. 2 (2000); 207–239.

56. Mainwaring, *Rethinking Party Systems,* 160.

57. Calculated from biographical data of individual deputies available at the website of the Brazilian Chamber of Deputies (www.camara.gov.br).

58. The earlier data are reported in Mainwaring, *Rethinking Party Systems* (page 160), and the recent data are from author's surveys.

59. Mainwaring, "Politicians, Parties, and Electoral Systems," 33, 36.

60. Survey data for 1990 are from Timothy J. Power, *The Political Right in Postauthoritarian Brazil* (University Park: Pennsylvania State University Press, 2000), 126–32. Recent survey data are from author's surveys.

61. David Samuels, "Sources of Mass Partisanship in Brazil," *Latin American Politics and Society* 48, no. 3 (Summer 2006), 5, 7.

62. Kenneth M. Roberts and Erik Wibbels, "Party Systems and Electoral Volatility in Latin America: A Test of Economic, Institutional, and Structural Explanations," *American Political Science Review* 93, no. 3 (1999): 577.

63. Figueiredo and Limongi, *Executivo e Legislativo,* 105.

64. Carlos Pereira, Timothy J. Power, and Lucio Rennó, "From Logrolling to Logjam: Agenda Power, Presidential Decrees, and the Unintended Consequences of Reform in the Brazilian Congress" (Working Paper No. CBS 71–06, Centre for Brazilian Studies, University of Oxford, 2006).

65. "Can Lula Finish the Job?" *Economist,* 5 October 2002, 25.

66. Mainwaring, *Rethinking Party Systems,* 205.

67. Power and Roberts, "A New Brazil," 252.

68. Kurt Weyland, *Democracy Without Equity: Failures of Reform in Brazil* (Pittsburgh: University of Pittsburgh Press, 1996), 182.

69. *Exame,* September 1997, 10.

70. Sônia M. Draibe, "Federal Leverage in a Decentralized System: Education Reform in Brazil," in Robert R. Kaufman and Joan M. Nelson, eds., *Crucial Needs, Weak Incentives: Social Sector Reform, Democratization, and Globalization in Latin America* (Washington, DC/Baltimore: Woodrow Wilson Center Press/Johns Hopkins University Press, 2004), 395–402.

71. Marta Arretche, "Toward a Unified and More Equitable System: Health Reform in Brazil," in Kaufman and Nelson, eds., *Crucial Needs, Weak Incentives,* 178–79.

72. Freedom House, *Freedom in the World 2000–2001* (available at www.freedomhouse.org).

73. Paulo Sérgio Pinheiro, "Popular Responses to State-Sponsored Violence," in Chalmers, ed. et al., *The New Politics of Inequality in Latin America,* 271–72.

74. Pinheiro, "Popular Responses to State-Sponsored Violence," 272.

75. Anthony W. Pereira, "An Ugly Democracy? State Violence and the Rule of Law in Postauthoritarian Brazil," in Kingstone and Power, *Democratic Brazil,* 234.

76. Informe Lafinobarómetro 2005 (available at www.latino barometro.org).

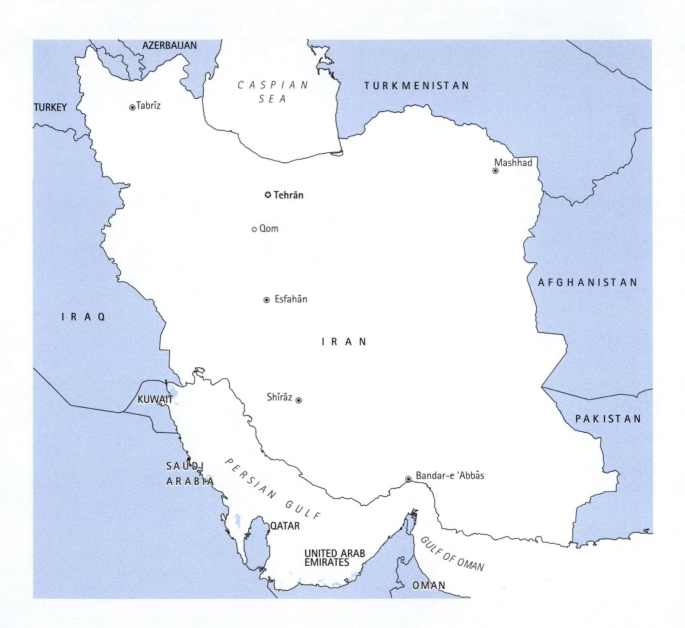

# POLITICS IN IRAN

*H. E. Chehabi and Arang Keshavarzian*

## Country Bio

**IRAN**

**Population**
66.3 million

**Territory**
636,296 square miles

**Year of Independence**
550 B.C.

**Year of Current Constitution**
1979, amended in 1989

**Head of State**
Ali Khamenei

**Head of Government**
Mahmud Ahmadinejad

**Languages**
Persian, regional languages

**Religions**
Twelver Shiite Muslim 90%, Sunni Muslim 10%, non-Muslims less than 1%

The Islamic Republic of Iran is the world's only **theocracy,** a form of government in which ideally all laws are grounded in religion and express the will of God, and a clergy exercises supreme power. While Islamic law has always been applied to varying degrees in Muslim states, it has almost always been complemented by some sort of nonreligious customary law. Moreover, various sultans, shahs, sheikhs, and, since the twentieth century, presidents or prime ministers have traditionally exercised political power in the Muslim world. Genuine theocracies have been very rare. Although the **ulema,** as religious scholars are called in the Muslim world, have been critical of rulers who strayed from the path of Islam, they almost never aspired to exercise power directly as they do in Iran today. Therefore, far from being a manifestation of Islamic conservatism, Iran's current theocratic regime constitutes a break with Muslim tradition. The only other Muslim theocracy of the twentieth century was that of the Taliban in Afghanistan (1996–2001), who, unlike the ulema of Iran, never gained control over the entire country and whose regime was generally not recognized by the international community.

The Islamic Republic of Iran was established in 1979, a few months after a popular revolution uniting poor and middle-class, religious and secular people overthrew **Mohammad-Reza Shah Pahlavi** (r. 1941–1979), the last ruler of the country's ancient monarchy. **Ruhollah Khomeini,** a charismatic clerical leader who had authored a blueprint for theocratic government in the early 1970s, led the 1979 revolution. In this blueprint, Khomeini opposed democracy on religious grounds. Sovereignty, he argued, belongs to God alone. Divine law, known as the *shari'a,* as interpreted and applied by the ulema, takes precedence over laws made by human legislators. In spite of its beginnings as a clerical dictatorship, Iran developed a very lively political system after Khomeini's death in 1989. Presidential, parliamentary, and local elections offer the citizens a choice of candidates advocating differing policies. The emergence of limited democratic practices and institutions under a regime founded on the negation of democracy is only one of many paradoxes to be found in Iran. Most Third World dictatorships pay lip service to democracy while routinely violating its spirit and undermining its practice.

## CURRENT POLICY CHALLENGES

As long as **Islamists**—by which we mean people who consider the religion of Islam a political ideology that addresses issues of private and public life—are in political opposition, it is easy for them to blame the shortcomings of the society on inadequate attention to the teachings of Islam and the "blind following of Western models." Islamists promise a society characterized by social justice and moral propriety in which an "authentic" Muslim culture can flourish uncontaminated by Western "decadence." Iran is the first country in which Islamists have had to deliver on these promises.

During the first decade of the Islamic Republic some redistribution of wealth did indeed take place, as the government expropriated much of the property of the old prerevolutionary elite. The new leadership came mostly from humble or middle-class backgrounds and adopted populist policies that somewhat bettered the lot of the poorest. For instance, the new regime invested heavily in rural development, including in health, women's education, and roads. However, the postrevolutionary reality is far from ideal, and poverty, inequality, and underemployment continue to be major public grievances. Possessing the world's second largest oil and gas reserves, the public expects its government to improve the lot of ordinary Iranians and establish the basis for long-term and sustainable development. However, transforming natural wealth into income and long-term investment has proven difficult. In the ideological climate of the Islamic Republic, industrial entrepreneurs are seen as exploiters, and so private investment tends to go into speculation and rent seeking rather than long-term industrial investment aimed at enhancing exports and creating sustainable development. Consequently, job creation has been very inadequate.

The need to increase economic output in order to provide employment for a rapidly growing labor force is perhaps the greatest challenge facing the government. Iran's population grows by about one million every year (see Figure 16.1). Although the government has been quite successful in bringing down the birth rate, the effects of the lower population growth rate will not be felt for many years. In 2002, 59 percent of the total population was under age 25.[1] Even under the best circumstances it would be difficult to provide employment for the 800,000 men and women who enter the labor market every year, but Iran's antientrepreneurial outlook as well as its unattractiveness to foreign investment mean that the situation is even worse. Regional conflicts and the continuing tension between Iran and the United States discourage both foreign and domestic investment. At the same time, a vastly expanded educational system means that many of the young unemployed hold an academic degree, which adds to their frustration and discontent. This discontent has produced massive migration. In recent years 200,000 Iranians have been leaving per year, causing one of the most massive brain-drains in the world. One in four Iranians with a higher education degree lives abroad.[2] The Islamists' anti-Western stance notwith-

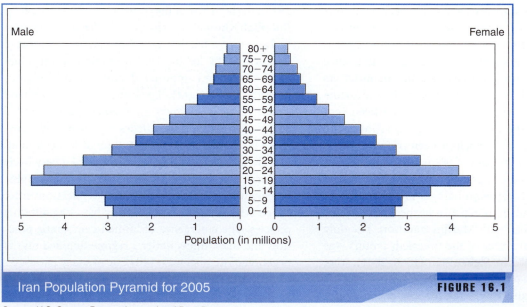

Male                                    Female

80+
75−79
70−74
65−69
60−64
55−59
50−54
45−49
40−44
35−39
30−34
25−29
20−24
15−19
10−14
5−9
0−4

5    4    3    2    1    0    0    1    2    3    4    5
Population (in millions)

**Iran Population Pyramid for 2005**    **FIGURE 16.1**

Source: U.S. Census Bureau, International Data Base.

standing, millions of young Iranians dream of moving to the West.

The presence of a large Iranian diaspora in the United States, Canada, and Europe has made life in the West familiar for Iranians. Even poorer Iranians often have a friend or relative in Los Angeles ("Tehrangeles") or Toronto ("Tehranto"). Thanks to cheap telephone cards and the Internet they can stay in touch with their relatives and friends abroad. When they compare the opportunities Iran offers them with those their cousins enjoy "on the other side," they find them terribly wanting.

Corruption makes matters even worse. The print media increasingly report about corruption, and it is debated in Parliament and by politicians. As many Iranians struggle to find gainful employment and make ends meet, a new elite has made fortunes by exploiting personal connections to the officials who control access to hard currency, import licenses, and tax shelters. The relatives of former president **Ali-Akbar Hashemi Rafsanjani** are often cited as examples of the wealth nourished by privileged access and information.

For all these reasons, the promises of the Islamic revolutionaries concerning a more just and more moral society ring hollow with many Iranians, half of whom are too young to recall the corruption, political repression, and inequality under the Shah. As a result, the theocratic model of government has suffered a massive loss of legitimacy. While the people may still be religious, the ulema no longer command their deference and respect. In addition, Islam itself is developing in new directions that question the right of the ulema to rule.

A new challenge concerns dissatisfaction with the status quo among some of Iran's ethnic minorities, who live mostly in the country's peripheral areas. Azeris live in the northwest, Kurds in the west, Arabs in the southwest, Turkomans in the northeast, and Baluchis in the southeast.[3] All these minorities have ethnic kin on the other side of the border. Until recently, this did not matter much, since they constituted minorities on the other side as well. With the breakup of the Soviet Union, however, independent Azerbaijan exerts a certain attraction for Azeris in Iran. The consolidation of a semi-independent Kurdish state in Iraq plays a similar role for Kurds in Iran (and Turkey). Iran's Arabs, until now loyal to the Iranian state because they are mostly Shiites, may

become less certain of their national affiliation if Shiites gain the upper hand in neighboring Iraq. For the time being, such challenges to Iran's territorial integrity are relatively weak compared with neighboring states, such as Iraq and Turkey. But these challenges are growing, partly because the government is seen as favoring the Persian-speaking majority and partly because they are subtly encouraged by outside powers.

Like other Third World countries, Iran faces general challenges of community and development. Iran's leaders are confronted with the daunting tasks of integrating large groups of disaffected citizens (the young, the unemployed, and ethnic minorities) and producing enough economic development to improve living conditions for these groups. The Islamic regime's failure to address these issues has dented its legitimacy considerably.

## HISTORICAL LEGACY

Iran, like China and Japan, is one of a handful of non-Western states that were never formally colonized by Europeans. Iran's borders were not drawn artificially by colonial powers but result from the historical balance of power between its shahs and their neighboring rulers. The Iranian state tradition is over twenty-five centuries old, but the current Iranian state was set up in the early sixteenth century by the Safavid dynasty. The dynasty's most lasting impact was the establishment of **Twelver Shiism** as the official state religion and the conversion of most Iranians who had been **Sunnis** to Shiism. Historically, the shrine cities of Iraq had been the cradle of this branch of Islam, but with the establishment of a powerful Shiite state in Iran, Iran became the political center of the Shiite world.

### Twelver Shiism

The split between Sunnis (who constitute about 90 percent of all Muslims) and the Shiites came about after the death of the founder of Islam, the Prophet Muhammad. Muhammad was not only the founder of a new religion but also a political leader. Therefore, after he died in 628 C.E. the nascent Muslim community had to find a leader to succeed him. A minority of believers, who later came to be known as Shiites, deemed the descendants of the Prophet to be his only rightful successors. Shiites call these hereditary successors to the Prophet *Imams*. Of particular importance is the Third Imam, Husayn, whose martyrdom in 680 C.E. symbolizes for Shiites the struggle of the just against the unjust. This event is still commemorated yearly in emotional processions that acquire a political dimension in times of political crisis.

While some small Shiite sects believe in an unbroken line of Imams all the way to the present, the vast majority believe that the twelfth was the last of the Imams, hence their name. According to these Shiites, the twelfth Imam disappeared from view as a child in 874 C.E., but did not die. He is alive (rather like Elijah in the Jewish tradition) and will come forth and show himself to establish a just rule at the end of time. In other words, he is a messiah-like figure. From the moment the Twelfth Imam disappeared from public view, therefore, Twelver Shiite political thought faced a dilemma. The only figure who could exercise legitimate rule over the community of believers was not physically present, and no one knew when he would reveal himself. Most of the time this dilemma did not matter in practice, because Shiites were a minority lacking political power, making their political theology inconsequential.

With the establishment of a Twelver Shiite state by the Safavid dynasty in sixteenth century, the unavailability of the one truly legitimate ruler became an existential problem. In the absence of the Twelfth Imam, who had the right to rule in practice? Most ulema were willing to accord this right to the secular rulers, the shahs, so long as they ruled justly and in accordance with Islam. By the end of the seventeenth century, however, a minority of ulema argued that for the rule of a shah to be legitimate, he had to have the ulema's explicit endorsement. After the fall of the Safavids in 1722 Iran was in the grip of civil wars as various short-lived dynasties succeeded each other. The Qajar dynasty finally emerged victorious in 1796.

During this troubled century the ulema established themselves as an institution independent of the state. Since the state was in disarray much of the time, believers' tithes were increasingly paid to the ulema directly, assuring them of financial independence. Moreover, the center of Twelver Shiism, the city of Najaf, lay in Ottoman Iraq, outside the control of Iran's worldly authorities. Beginning in the nineteenth century, therefore, the ulema had greater social, political, and religious prominence in Iran than in the Sunni world. They had their own sources of income and were beyond the control of the state. Without this legacy the establishment of a theocracy would not even have been conceivable in the 1970s.

In some ways the role and function of the ulema resemble that of a clergy in Christian countries. However, while the Shiite ulema form a loose hierarchy, they are not organized in a pyramidal structure like the Roman Catholic Church. There is no equivalent of the pope, and no one leader can define dogma in a way that is binding for everyone else. Consequently, the ulema have often disagreed among each other on political and even minor religious matters, a state of affairs that, as we will see, has not ended with the creation of an Islamic state.

## Constitutionalism in Iran

Iran's geographic location between the Russian empire in the north and the British empire in the south allowed it to survive the heyday of European imperialism as an independent state. Both empires allowed it to remain a neutral buffer between their respective domains. Nevertheless educated Iranians recognized the fragility of their country's sovereignty. As they became more familiar with Europe in the nineteenth century, they became more aware of their own backwardness. As long as Iran was less developed than Europe, it would forever remain vulnerable to imperialist encroachment. Consequently, "catching up with the West" became the major goal of Iran's intellectual and political elite. They believed that the rule of law was the secret of European superiority, whereas arbitrary rule prevailed in Iran. They concluded that constitutional government had to be introduced to strengthen the nation. Japan's victory over Russia in the war of 1905 confirmed Iranian constitutionalists in their view. For the first time an Asian power had vanquished a European one, and Iranians argued that this reversal of fortunes occurred because Japan was the only constitutional power in Asia and Russia was the only autocracy among the major European powers.

In 1905 widespread dissatisfaction with the way the country was governed led to a popular movement that eventually wrested a constitution from the shah in December 1906. Shiite ulema played a major role in the constitutionalist movement. Until a few years earlier the Iranian state had been characterized by an implicit contract between worldly and spiritual authorities. The shah upheld the official religion, and the ulema legitimated the shah's rule. But by the early twentieth century many politically active ulema shared the views of merchants and Western-educated intellectuals: that the powers of the monarchy needed to be curtailed. They believed that the citizenry had the right to elect a representative parliament; that the shah could name a prime minister only in agreement with parliament; and that parliament could hold the government accountable. These very European ideas were criticized by conservative ulema for being alien to Islam, but constitutionalist ulema found ways to justify them in Islamic terms. Most famously, Ayatollah Muhammad-Husayn Na'ini argued that a despotic shah violated the rights of the Twelfth Imam and those of the people, whereas rule by the people violated only the rights of the Twelfth Imam. He concluded that while neither form of government was ideal, the latter was the lesser evil and thus preferable to the former.[4] This argument implied the novel idea that as long as the Twelfth Imam chose to remain in hiding, the believers themselves were his deputies. This elegant formulation reconciled Shiism's core beliefs with modern notions of constitutionalism and is a legacy that the revolutionaries of 1979 could not ignore as they set out to create an Islamic state.

## The Pahlavi Monarchy

The Constitution of 1906 did not bring the hoped-for progress, however. In a 1907 secret agreement Britain and Russia divided Iran into two spheres of influence. During World War I, belligerents repeatedly violated Iran's neutrality and fought each other on Iranian territory, causing much hardship to the population. By the end of the war, local warlords were challenging the authority of the central government in peripheral regions.

In 1921, a *coup d'état* put an end to the rule of the old establishment. The commander of the troops, Reza Khan, lost no time in extending government control over rebellious provinces and began an ambitious modernization program to develop and centralize state authority. By 1925, he ousted the ruling Qajar dynasty and had Parliament proclaim him the new ruler as Reza Shah Pahlavi. From his coronation in 1926 until his ouster by the British in the wake of the Allied occupation of Iran in 1941, he ruled as dictator, although he left the Constitution formally in place. Reza Khan initially enjoyed the support of most of the clergy. But in the 1930s his relations with the ulema deteriorated after he implemented reforms that reduced their social functions and aimed at westernizing the daily culture of Iranians, such as prohibiting women's veiling. With his departure into exile politics opened up again. His 21-year-old son and successor, Mohammad-Reza Shah Pahlavi, did not have the authority yet to continue his father's ways (see Figure 16.2).

Between 1941 and 1953 Iran's political system included three main camps. First, the pro-Western conservative establishment, including the Shah and the landlords, was supported tacitly by most of the ulema. Second was the pro-Soviet communist **Tudeh**

| Year | Head of State | President | Prime Minister |
|------|---------------|-----------|----------------|
| 1941 | Shah: Mohammad-Reza Pahlavi | — | —Various cabinets |
| 1951 | — | — | Mohammad Mossadegh (51–53) |
| — | — | — | —Various cabinets |
| 1965 | — | — | Amir-Abbas Hoveyda |
| 1977 | — | — | Jamshid Amuzegar |
| 1979 | Leader: Ruhollah Khomeini | — | Mehdi Bazargan |
| 1980 | — | Abolhasan Banisadr | — |
| 1981 | — | Ali Rajai, Ali Khamenei | Mir-Hosein Musavi |
| 1989 | Ali Khamenei | Ali-Akbar Hashemi Rafsanjani | Position abolished |
| 1997 | — | Mohammad Khatami | — |
| 2005 | — | Mahmud Ahmadinejad | — |

**Iranian Regimes**                                            **FIGURE 16.2**

**party.** Third was the neutralist National Front, which aimed at establishing the full rule of law within the country and consolidating its standing among nations. As the National Front saw it, the nation's sovereignty was compromised by British control over Iran's oil resources through the British-owned Anglo-Iranian Oil Company(AIOC). The Iranian government had no say in the company, not even the right to see its books. From 1945 to 1950, the total net profits of the AIOC were £250 million after deducting high British taxes, royalties, and exaggerated depreciation figures; at the same time, royalties paid to Iran for its oil amounted to merely £90 million.[5]

The leader of the National Front was **Mohammad Mossadegh,** who advocated nationalizing the Iranian oil industry. This was accomplished in March 1951, and soon thereafter Mossadegh was elected prime minister by Parliament. Subsequent negotiations between the Iranian and British governments to resolve the oil dispute failed. Consequently, the British began plotting Mossadegh's overthrow, which was accomplished with the help of the U.S. Central Intelligence Agency (CIA) in August 1953.[6]

Iran's political system reverted to royal autocracy as the second ruler of the Pahlavi dynasty increasingly asserted himself, taking full command of the country in January 1963. He launched a reform program that became known as the "White Revolution," which included land reform and the granting of the suffrage to women. In the 1950s the Shah had enjoyed the support of the clerical hierarchy, but by the early 1960s his dictatorial methods and westernizing policies elicited the anger of religious traditionalists. These traditionalists rioted in June 1963 in support of a new oppositional member of the ulema, Ruhollah Khomeini. The riots were suppressed with bloodshed, and Khomeini was arrested and exiled. He finally settled in the Shiite shrine city of Najaf in Iraq; he remained there until October 1978, when he was expelled by Saddam Hussein and sought refuge in Paris until his triumphant return to Iran on February 1, 1979.

Until 1963, opposition to royal autocracy was carried out in the name of the Constitution of 1906, which the two Pahlavi shahs were criticized for not respecting. Free elections were the opposition's main demand. After 1963, however, opponents of the Shah, increasingly driven underground or abroad, despaired of ever attaining constitutional rule by peaceful means and became radicalized. Gradually the Constitution

itself suffered a loss of legitimacy. Opponents of the Shah demanded the abolition of the monarchy and its replacement by a new regime. Given the Shah's suppression of civil society and of the secular opposition, mosques and religious circles became the only places where one could speak one's mind. Thus, religion became a more prominent political force, despite the secularist policies of the state. By the 1970s Shiite activists, many of them students or followers of Khomeini, were arguing about the shape of the ideal Islamic state.

While the Shah's regime was increasingly contested at home, it continued to receive support from the West in general and the United States in particular. Since the Shah's rule had been made possible through the direct intervention of the CIA, his opponents thought of him as an American puppet whose policies were designed to benefit the United States rather than Iran. Opposition to the Shah thus logically entailed opposition to the United States and Israel, with which the Shah had contracted a strategic alliance directed against radical Arab states, such as Egypt, Iraq, and Syria. In recent years, evidence has appeared suggesting that at the height of his power in the early 1970s the Shah, far from being manipulated by the United States, was actually successful in manipulating U.S. policymakers to achieve his ends.[7]

Although Iran's first revolution failed to produce a constitutional state based on the rule of law, during the seven decades of its life Iran acquired the trappings of a modern nation-state. The government acquired a monopoly on the use of force; introduced unified legal codes; developed a functioning civil service, including a territorial administration that extended the writ of the state into distant provinces; and secured the country's international borders. These accomplishments gave the new theocracy the form of an Islamic *republic* in the aftermath of the revolution of 1978–1979.

## The Islamic Revolution

In 1977 Jimmy Carter became president of the United States and U.S. foreign policy began emphasizing respect for human rights by American allies.[8] Unbeknownst to the public, the Shah had terminal cancer. To ensure a smooth transition to his heir at a time when U.S. support could no longer be taken for granted, he began liberalizing Iran's political system in 1977. Amir-Abbas Hoveyda, who had been prime minister since 1965 and embodied the cabinet's subservience to the Shah, was replaced with former finance minister Jamshid Amuzegar. But various dissident and social groups with grievances took advantage of this liberalization to push for greater reforms. From late 1977 to early 1979 the calls for greater liberalization snowballed into a call for the abolition of the monarchy by a largely urban coalition. This coalition consisted of intellectuals, university and high school students and teachers, bazaar merchants, politically active clerics and seminarians, industrial workers, and, in the final stage, state employees and white-collar workers.[9] The popular movement against the regime's despotism, corruption, and alliances with the United States and Israel united such diverse ideological factions as liberal adherents of the 1906 Constitution, Marxist-Leninist leftists, and Islamists. The latter comprised democrats whose reading of Islam was decidedly liberal and noncoercive, leftists who stressed the egalitarian aspects of Islam, and direct followers of Khomeini who championed an Islamic state supervised by clerics. These activists organized massive meetings, demonstrations, and strikes, and they distributed antiregime pamphlets in a largely peaceful manner.[10] In his reaction, the Shah vacillated between repressing the movement with force and making belated concessions to it. The result was that the activists became ever more radicalized during 1978, finally driving him and his family into exile in January 1979.[11]

In the course of the revolutionary uprising and immediately after the departure of the Shah's family,

Khomeini's followers were the best-organized and most united force, and they rapidly sidelined the nonclerical currents in their coalition. The organizational power of Khomeini and his followers was enhanced by their access to independent sources of revenue, as traditionally observant Shiites pay their tithes directly to the ulema. In 1970 Khomeini had revived the strain in Twelver Shiite thought that called for clerical oversight of government and carried it to its logical conclusion. In a treatise titled "Islamic Government" he argued that God had revealed his laws to humankind, not so that they would be ignored until the moment the Twelfth Imam revealed himself, but in order to apply them here and now. Khomeini further observed that the people most suited to rule in accordance with divine law are those who know it best, namely the ulema themselves. This principle came to be known as **velayat-e faqih,** which is best translated as "guardianship of the jurisprudent"[12] (see Box 16.1).

Given Khomeini's charismatic leadership of the revolution, his followers succeeded in late 1979 to enshrine this principle in the new Iranian Constitution. However, in deference to the preexisting constitutional tradition and to placate the many non-Islamists and moderate Islamists who had participated in the revolution, the Constitution maintained a parliament elected by universal suffrage. The shah was replaced with an elected president. The Islamic Republic was thus born with a mixed political system that is informed by both a version of Twelver Shiite political doctrine and Western notions of popular sovereignty and division of powers.[13]

## Velayat-e Faqih

**BOX 16.1**

*Velayat-e faqih*—the lynchpin of Iran's theocratic Constitution—is best translated as "guardianship of the jurisprudent." Ayatollah Ruhollah Khomeini described this while he was in exile in 1970 in Iraq. Khomeini argued that since God revealed the laws according to which Muslims should live and organize their community, Muslims should apply these laws in practice rather than just debate them theoretically. The most qualified people to supervise the application of these laws in the state, he wrote, are those who know them best (that is, the clerics who specialize in jurisprudence). He

concluded that such a cleric must therefore be the head of state. In 1979 this principle was enshrined in the Constitution of the Islamic Republic of Iran, and Khomeini himself became the ruling jurisprudent, referred to henceforth as "Leader." For the first time in Iranian history, religious and worldly authorities were fused. *Velayat-e faqih* is not strongly grounded in scripture, and most Twelver Shiite clerics disagree with the principle. They see the task of the Shiite clergy as being that of guiding the believers and advising rulers, as can be seen in post-Saddam Iraq.

From 1979 to June 1981 secular moderates, leftists, moderate Islamists, and radical Islamists inspired directly by Khomeini competed for power. As time went on, the confrontation between adherents of *velayat-e faqih* and their opponents became ever more implacable and violent. In fact, far more people were killed in confrontations among the revolutionaries than had died as a result of the Shah's half-hearted efforts to suppress the revolutionary mass movement. By the summer of 1981 the supporters of Khomeini gained the upper hand and began instituting Islamic law in all spheres of public life. Their suppression of all who opposed them was facilitated by the war that was now raging with neighboring Iraq.

## Iran–Iraq War

Soon after the revolution, Khomeini began calling for the overthrow of the Iraqi president, Saddam Hussein. This provoked Saddam Hussein to attack Iran in September 1980. The war that ensued lasted until 1988 and ended in a stalemate.

Officially termed the "imposed war" or the "sacred defense" in Iran, the war was a major watershed. Over two million Iranians were mobilized, with over one million killed and injured, many due to Iraq's use of chemical weapons.[14] The war enabled the revolutionary regime to consolidate its hold on power by calling for national unity in the face of a foreign invasion. The war became a means to suppress dissent and public debate. At the level of society, the conflict created a "war generation" of young men who were shaped as much by their experiences at the front as by the revolution. Now many of these soldiers and officers are in their forties and fifties, and some are demanding a bigger say in national and local politics. These veterans have tended to call for more "social order" and a greater state role in providing for the lower classes, who volunteered and perished in the war in disproportionately large numbers.

## The Legacy of Oil Wealth: A Rentier State

Like other nations enriched by large amounts of natural resources such as oil or diamonds, the Iranian state has particular characteristics that shape its relations with society. The export of petroleum products has made the Iranian state dependent on the world economy for the bulk of its budget. This revenue is rent, which is a windfall accruing directly to the treasury.

Since the 1960s, Iran's budget has not depended on domestic revenues (taxes or borrowing), which has made the state largely autonomous from society.[15] Unlike most states that must bargain with social groups to generate revenue for public projects, to pay public employees, and to fight wars, **rentier states** like Iran can sustain themselves independently of social pressures and powerful interest groups. At the same time, the state is particularly susceptible to fluctuations in the world oil market, making long-term planning more difficult. The massive revenue from petroleum exports has often been cited as a major reason for the Iranian state's unresponsiveness to social demands, and even its authoritarianism.[16] Thus, what was initially thought of as a blessing is now often seen as a curse (we will discuss interest aggregation later in this chapter).

# INSTITUTIONS OF THE ISLAMIC REPUBLIC

Two types of institutions coexist in the political system of the Islamic Republic of Iran: appointed and elected offices. This dualism reflects the attempted synthesis between divine and popular sovereignty enshrined in the Constitution. The institutional structure of Iran is further complicated by the existence of what is known as **multiple power centers,** institutions created by the revolutionaries to supplement the activities of the traditional state institutions, with which they share overlapping responsibilities.

## Leader

The highest authority in the Islamic Republic is the **Leader,** who combines religious and temporal authority in accordance with the theocratic principle of *velayat-e faqih.* The position was tailor-made for Khomeini himself, who was both a high-level member of the ulema and a charismatic political leader. For his succession, the Constitution provided for a popularly elected **Assembly of Experts,** consisting of ulema who would choose the Leader from among the most learned ulema. By 1989, however, none of the ulema who had the requisite learning shared his notions of theocratic rule. Consequently, in April 1989 Khomeini appointed an assembly to revise the Constitution to relax the religious requirements of the office. Khomeini died on June 3, 1989. The Assembly of Experts chose **Ali Khamenei,** who had been president for eight years but was a low-level cleric, to be the new Leader. From the outset, much of the clerical hierarchy contested Khamenei's religious authority, reopening the split between state and "church" that the Islamic Republic had supposedly closed with its fusion of worldly and spiritual authorities.

The Leader sets the overall policies of the state and appoints some of its key figures, such as the head of the Judiciary, half the members of the **Council of Guardians,** the members of the **Expediency Council,** the director of the state radio and television broadcasting monopoly, and the commanders of the various military forces. He also oversees the numerous parastatal economic foundations and organizations that were formed after the revolution out of the expropriated companies belonging to the previous economic elite. These organizations are ostensibly oriented toward charity and bear such names as the Foundation of the Disinherited and War Injured and the Martyr's Foundation. In fact, they are major holding companies that benefit from state resources and subsidies without being accountable to and regulated by the elected government. Khamenei has used these "nonprofit" organizations as a means to distribute patronage[17] (see Box 16.2).

In theory, the Assembly of Experts, which is elected every ten years by universal suffrage, is more powerful than the Leader. It elects him and can dismiss him if he can no longer assume the responsibilities of his office or proves unworthy of it. However, candidacies to the Assembly of Experts are subject to the approval of the Council of Guardians, whose members are chosen by the Leader, who thus maintains his supremacy in practice.

## President

The president is elected by universal suffrage every four years. He must be a Twelver Shiite and a male. However, a number of women have tried, always unsuccessfully, to become presidential candidates. Until 1989 the office was largely ceremonial and the

---

**BOX 16.2**

## The Martyr's Foundation

Among the most powerful **parastatal foundations** is the Martyr's Foundation (Bonyad-e Shahid) established in 1979. Its original mandate was to provide for the needs of families of those who were martyred and the disabled in the Islamic Revolution and the Iran–Iraq war. The foundation provides support to 188,000 people by giving aid, priority admission for education, in-kind transfers, housing services to relatives of martyrs and disabled veterans, and other benefits. These services are funded by assets formerly belonging to supporters of the shah that were expropriated, allocations from the state budget and the office of the Leader, and profits from the operation of the foundation's various firms. In the mid-1980s it was reported that the Martyr's Foundation owned $3.3 billion in capital reserves, including sixty-eight industrial factories, seventy-five commercial firms, twenty-one construction companies, and many farms and pieces of urban property.

To administer this large and diverse economic conglomerate, the Martyr's Foundation employs 30,000 people and has a whole host of subdivisions, such as the International Relations Office and the Marriage Bureau for Widows of Wartime Martyrs. The foundation also puts out a magazine that spreads the early revolutionary ideology. In 1993, the foundation established the Shahid Investment Company in order to pool the savings of surviving relatives of the martyrs and invest them. By 2000 shareholders were complaining that the investment company never disclosed its accounts to the shareholders. Mehdi Karrubi was the president of the foundation from 1980 to 1992. Karrubi became speaker of the Sixth Parliament (2000–2004). He ran for president in 2005 on a pro-welfare and distribution platform and came in third only narrowly behind Hashemi-Rafsanjani and Ahmadinejad in the first round.

Sources: Ali A. Saeidi, "The Accountability of Para-governmental Organizations (*bonyad*s): The Case of Iranian Foundation," *Iranian Studies* 37, no. 3 (September 2004), 488; and Wilfried Buchta, *Who Rules Iran? The Structure of Power in the Islamic Republic* (Washington, DC: Washington Institute, 2000), 75.

Executive Branch of government was headed by a prime minister chosen by Parliament. In the course of the 1989 constitutional revision the office of prime minister was abolished and the presidency became an executive one. The president heads the Executive except in matters reserved for the Leader, signs bills into law once they have been approved by the legislature, and appoints the members of the cabinet and provincial governors, subject to parliamentary approval. He can be impeached by Parliament, at which point the Leader can dismiss him. The president does not have to be a cleric, but between 1981 and 2005 three different members of the ulema held the office for two consecutive terms each, reflecting the hegemony of that group in the Islamic Republic. The June 2005 election of Mahmud Ahmadinejad, a lay (that is, a nonulema) Islamist and a veteran of the Iran–Iraq war, may herald the partial replacement of the clergy by the "war generation," men who risked their lives in the revolution and the war and feel that it is time that they reap the benefits of their sacrifices.

## Parliament

Iran's unicameral Parliament, the **Majles,** comprises about 290 members elected by universal suffrage for four-year terms. Members have to be Muslims, but the Constitution provides for five members of Parliament (MPs) to represent Christians (three), Jews (one), and Zoroastrians (one).

The Majles has law-making powers, but its legislative output must not contravene the Constitution or Islam, as determined by the Council of Guardians (as we will discuss shortly). It has the right to investigate affairs of state, to approve or reject the presidents' cabinet appointments, and to call ministers to account and subject them to votes of no-confidence.

In his treatise on Islamic government, Khomeini assigned little importance to Parliament, arguing that Islam had already laid down laws for most matters. A legislative assembly's task was to draw up rules and regulations for minor issues not dealt with in Islamic jurisprudence. Since 1979, however, the Majles has shown remarkable dynamism and initiative. For one, the traditional corpus of Islamic law proved to be woefully inadequate for the purpose of governing a modern state, requiring Parliament to fill some of the gaps. Furthermore, the legislative deputies have vigorously debated state business and held government officials accountable, the office of the Leader excepted.

In the first Parliament of the Islamic Republic almost half of all deputies were clerics. Under the Shah no free elections had taken place, so few people had enough name recognition at the local level to get themselves elected to Parliament. Consequently, in many places voters chose the local cleric. But over time, the percentage of clerics in the Majles has declined, as can be seen in Table 16.1. Although the ulema had generally opposed female suffrage in 1963, the founders of the Islamic Republic maintained women's active and passive suffrage in spite of their patriarchal disposition. Since 1980 every legislature has included female deputies, who have often spoken out on women's rights. Table 16.1 shows the evolution of the number of women who have held seats in the Parliament of the Islamic Republic.

Nonetheless, two features of the political system seriously limit the Majles's legislative role. First, many policies, rules, and regulations are set by unelected specialized bodies; second, all its bills are subject to the

## Women in Parliament — TABLE 16.1

| | Female MPs | Clerical MPs | Total MPs |
|---|---|---|---|
| First Majles (1980–1984) | 4 | 131 | 263 |
| Second Majles (1984–1988) | 4 | 122 | 269 |
| Third Majles (1988–1992) | 4 | 77 | 267 |
| Fourth Majles (1992–1996) | 9 | 65 | 270 |
| Fifth Majles (1996–2000) | 10 | 53 | 274 |
| Sixth Majles (2000–2004) | 13 | 35 | 278 |
| Seventh Majles (2004–2008) | 12 | 42 | 281 |

veto of the Council of Guardians. Under the Islamic Republic, the Majles has been a forum where policies are discussed and proposals aired, and where some state officials are taken to account.[18]

## Council of Guardians

The Constitution of 1906 provided for a committee of five Majles deputies who were members of the ulema to examine legislation for its compatibility with Islam. This committee was never constituted, however. In order to forestall any possibility for compromising the Islamic character of the state, the 1979 Constitution instituted an altogether separate body for ensuring the conformity of legislation with Islam: the Council of Guardians.

The body consists of six members of the ulema and six lay Muslim lawyers. The ulema are appointed by the Leader; the lawyers are nominated by the head of the Judiciary (who is himself appointed by the Leader) but approved by Parliament. The compatibility of laws with Islam is determined by the six ulema members only; their compatibility with the Constitution by the entire council. Through the years the Council of Guardians has rejected numerous bills because it interpreted them as violating the Constitution and/or Islamic law.

The Council of Guardians also "supervises" the elections to the Assembly of Experts, the presidency, and Parliament. It has interpreted this provision of the Constitution to signify that it can vet candidacies. It uses this self-ascribed power to limit citizens' choice at elections by not allowing candidates of whose views it disapproves to run. When in 1991 the Majles passed a law stripping the council of these powers, the latter, unsurprisingly, declared the law to be contrary to the Constitution.

## Expediency Council

Disagreement between Parliament and the Council of Guardians has been endemic in the Islamic Republic, resulting in legislative gridlock. As long as Khomeini was alive, he acted as the ultimate arbiter when a protracted stalemate arose, as all involved deferred to him. In early 1988 Khomeini set up a new collective body to arbitrate in such cases, and it was aptly called the "Council for the determination of what is in the interest of the regime," an unwitting admission that conformity to the teachings of Islam now took a back seat to political expedience. Indeed, official Iranian documents render the name of this body in English as "Expediency Council." Its existence was anchored in the constitutional revision of 1989.

The Leader directly appoints over thirty members of this body, who are chosen mainly from among top government officials, key cabinet members and military leaders, the ulema members of the Council of Guardians, and ulema chosen for their personal prestige. In addition to arbitrating conflicts between the Majles and the Council of Guardians, the Expediency Council has the constitutional mandate of advising the Leader in formulating overall state policy.

## An Honestly Undemocratic Constitution

As our discussion shows, the authority of the elective offices of the Islamic Republic, essentially the presidency and Parliament, is systematically circumscribed by unelected bodies. To be sure, the Leader is chosen by an elected body, the Assembly of Experts, but there is no limit on his term, making him for all intents and purposes an unremovable leader with vast powers. By appointing the head of the judiciary and the commanders of the police, army, and **Islamic Revolutionary Guard Corps (Pasdaran),** he, rather than the president and Parliament, controls the coercive apparatus of the state.

The limited authority of the president and Parliament became startlingly blatant when reformists bent on liberalizing Iranian politics and society won a string of elections in the late 1990s. They gained control of the presidency in 1997 and 2001 with the election of **Mohammad Khatami,** and of Parliament in 2000. However, Leader Ali Khamenei openly sided with antireformist conservatives, whom he chose as the head of the Judiciary and as the members of the Council of Guardians. When the lawyers proposed by the Judiciary to fill vacant seats on the Council of Guardians failed to gain the endorsement of the reformist Parliament in 2001, the Leader simply refused to schedule the swearing-in ceremony of the reformist president, who had just been reelected with 77.9 percent of the popular vote. In the end, the lawyers took their seats without gaining majority support in Parliament, after which the Leader consented to swear in the president.

Although the reformists tried to bring about change by legal and constitutional means, the fact that they were ultimately stymied by the leader, the Council of Guardians, and the Judiciary, using powers granted to them by the Constitution, shows that this Constitution is, if not liberal and democratic, at least honest: its provisions need not be violated to prevent democratic governance.

The same can be said for citizens' rights. Although freedom of speech and association and the safety of the person are guaranteed, these are usually qualified by the clause "within the criteria of Islam," leaving the authorities considerable leeway to abridge them. The same is true for the equality of citizens. Christian, Jewish, and Zoroastrian Iranians are accorded some legal recognition and can practice their religion freely. However, Iran's largest non-Muslim minority, the adherents of the Baha'i faith, are considered heretics and systematically discriminated against; to this day they may not attend university, for instance. Even Sunni Muslims, representing about 10 percent of the total population, are systematically discriminated against in the civil service and are not allowed to maintain a mosque of their own in Tehran. In the words of a prominent exiled Iranian human rights lawyer, in the Islamic Republic "the rights of the clerics do not equal those of nonclerics, the rights of Twelver Shiites do not equal those of non-Twelver Shiites, the rights of Shiites do not equal those of Sunnis, the rights of Muslims do not equal those of non-Muslims, the rights of 'recognized religious minorities' do not equal those of other 'minorities,' and the rights of men do not equal the rights of women."[19] The explicit denial of legal equality to citizens found throughout Iran's Constitution and legal system stands in sharp contrast to the universalist language of many other Third World regimes.

## Multiple Power Centers

When the revolutionaries took over the state in 1979, they inherited an administrative bureaucracy whose commitment to the new ideology they did not trust. Not content with purging state institutions of individuals they deemed counterrevolutionary, they built new ones whose competency overlapped with the old established ones. The idea was that the old institutions would more or less carry on with business as usual, while the new institutions would actively pursue the realization and defense of the new Islamic order (see Figure 16.3). Examples include the Construction Jihad, which sent young people to the rural areas to help develop them in parallel to the ministry of

agriculture, the office of the revolutionary prosecutor (paralleling the ministry of justice), and the *komitehs* (paralleling the police). The most important example is the Islamic Revolutionary Guard Corps, known in Persian as *Pasdaran*, whose original function was to safeguard the revolution but which in time developed into a parallel army and even acquired an air force and a navy. These revolutionary institutions prevented the provisional government, which had taken over the Shah's administrative apparatus, from gaining control of the country.[20]

As hardliners consolidated their rule in the mid-1980s, they attempted to merge state and revolutionary organizations. However, these attempts were mostly unsuccessful and the revolutionary organizations are still active. In the late 1990s, as some state institutions came under the control of the reformists, conservatives created new parallel institutions under the aegis of the office of the Leader. Thus, when the ministry of information, as the secret police is called, came to be staffed mainly by reformists, the Judiciary, whose head is named by the Leader, proceeded to set up a parallel secret police (which even maintains a prison system for political prisoners). These multiple power centers complicate policymaking considerably, as we shall see.

With these caveats about the relative importance of Iran's republican institutions in mind, let us now turn to elections and parties.

## ELECTIONS AND PARTIES

### The Prerevolutionary Legacy

With the brief exception of the 1940s, between 1906 and 1979 competitive elections were rarely held in Iran. In 1963 the Shah gave women the active and passive suffrage. This action did not mean much in practice because there were no free elections for the remainder of his reign, but it did establish standards that could not be undone. Although much of the ulema had vehemently opposed the extension of the suffrage to women in 1963, the mobilization of women in the course of the revolution was so important that it was simply not possible to deprive them of the right to vote again. In fact, the electorate was enlarged by fixing the minimum voting age at 15.

Under the monarchy political parties were mostly weak and ephemeral. After World War II, two

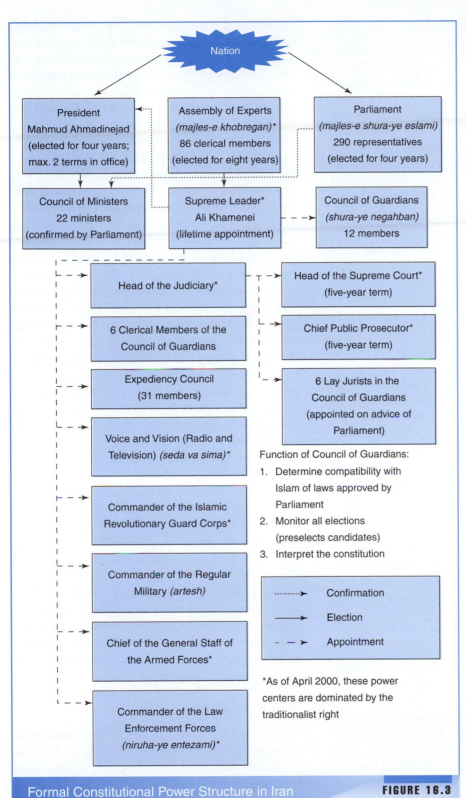

**Figure 16.3** Formal Constitutional Power Structure in Iran

Nation

President
Mahmud Ahmadinejad
(elected for four years;
max. 2 terms in office)

Assembly of Experts
(majles-e khobregan)*
86 clerical members
(elected for eight years)

Parliament
(majles-e shura-ye eslami)
290 representatives
(elected for four years)

Council of Ministers
22 ministers
(confirmed by Parliament)

Supreme Leader*
Ali Khamenei
(lifetime appointment)

Council of Guardians
(shura-ye negahban)
12 members

Head of the Judiciary*

Head of the Supreme Court*
(five-year term)

6 Clerical Members of the
Council of Guardians

Chief Public Prosecutor*
(five-year term)

Expediency Council
(31 members)

6 Lay Jurists in the
Council of Guardians
(appointed on advice of
Parliament)

Voice and Vision (Radio and
Television) (seda va sima)*

Function of Council of Guardians:

1. Determine compatibility with
   Islam of laws approved by
   Parliament

Commander of the Islamic
Revolutionary Guard Corps*

2. Monitor all elections
   (preselects candidates)

3. Interpret the constitution

Commander of the Regular
Military (artesh)

········▶  Confirmation

─────▶  Election

─ ─ ─▶  Appointment

Chief of the General Staff of
the Armed Forces*

*As of April 2000, these power
centers are dominated by the
traditionalist right

Commander of the Law
Enforcement Forces
(niruha-ye entezami)*

Source: Adapted from Wilfried Buchta, *Who Rules Iran?* (Washington, DC: Washington Institute for Near East Policy, 2000). © Wilfried Buchta, Rabat 2000.

groupings succeeded in establishing a lasting societal presence: the Communist Tudeh party and the nationalist National Front of Mohammad Mossadegh. These two were revived in the course of the revolution of 1978. However, they were overshadowed by more radical leftist or Islamist groups that had emerged from the armed struggle against the Shah, such as the Marxist-Leninist Fada'iyan-e Khalq and the leftist Islamist Mojahedin-e Khalq. Initially, the Liberation Movement of Iran (LMI), a moderate Islamist offshoot of the National Front founded in 1961, fared somewhat better. Its leaders largely staffed the provisional government of Prime Minister Mehdi Bazargan that administered the country from February to November 1979, when they resigned in protest over radical students' seizure of American diplomats as hostages. In 1981 the National Front, the Fada'iyan-e Khalq, and the Mojahedin-e Khalq were banned for advocating policies that contradicted the basic premise of the Islamic Republic. In 1983 the Tudeh party was disbanded and its leaders jailed for having spied for the Soviet Union. The LMI, for its part, has managed to maintain low-level activity within the country.

## Postrevolutionary Parties

In early 1979 a group of loyal followers of Khomeini, including later President Rafsanjani and Leader Khamenei, founded a new party to work toward the realization of their version of an Islamic state: the Islamic Republican Party (IRP). Soon, however, different factions crystallized within the IRP around different economic, social, and foreign policy agendas. Factionalism having rendered the party dysfunctional, Rafsanjani and Khamenei announced the dissolution of the IRP in a letter to Khomeini in June 1987. They said that the party had achieved its goal, the establishment of *velayat-e faqih*, and had thus ceased to have a *raison d'être*.

But the underlying reasons for the factionalism did not go away. Some regime figures advocated more state intervention in the economy on the grounds that Islam is the religion of social justice and that therefore an Islamic government must look after the interests of the poor. Others argued that Islam protects the sanctity of private property, and that therefore more laissez-faire policies were in order as long as everybody adhered to the rules that Islamic jurisprudence established for the conduct of economic activity. As the leaders of the Islamic Republic grappled with the problem of translating Islam into a political ideology that provides guidance for the solution to all problems, it became clear that divergent policy options could be derived from Islamic principles. In 1987 the Speaker of Parliament Rafsanjani admitted that there were "two powerful wings" within the Islamic Republic, adding that "basically they represent two unorganized parties. Indeed when they describe the positions they hold, they are two parties, not two wings."[21] The tensions came out into the open in 1988 when the Society of Militant Clergy, a pro-*velayat-e faqih* group, split in two as some less conservative members, including future President Mohammad Khatami, left to form the Association of Militant Clerics.

As long as Khomeini was alive, he acted as the ultimate arbiter among the factions. When government figures turned to him to break a factional deadlock over a policy, he would normally urge all to cooperate. But when pressed, more often than not Khomeini came out against the conservatives. After Khomeini's death in 1989, the fact that the leadership of the Islamic Republic included no high-ranking ulema combined with the rivalry of opinions among the ulema allowed many policy disagreements to remain unresolved. These disagreements were channeled into the political system and became the basis of electoral competition, as different candidates espoused opposing views for which they sought people's votes. This factor has given Iranian elections a poignancy they lack in other nondemocratic states.

Ideological differences became the basis of factional politics among three broad clusters in the political elite: conservatives, pragmatists, and radicals. The conservatives were clerics and lay politicians who favored stricter social rules (such as gender segregation in public places) and called for greater authority to be given to the Leader at the expense of elected bodies, while simultaneously (and confusingly) supporting freer, market-oriented economic policies. Pragmatists, including Rafsanjani and many technocrats who staffed the ministries in the 1990s, were more accommodating on social issues and supported economic liberalization and the privatization of state-owned and parastatal companies. Moreover, they toned down support for exporting the revolution and were somewhat more conciliatory regarding U.S.–Iranian relations. Finally, the radicals were the younger Islamist revolutionaries and clerics who were influenced by leftist and anti-imperialist politics. In the 1980s and the early 1990s they called for increased state control of the economy to ensure greater social justice and were active in supporting Islamist struggles in the Middle East. Beginning in the mid-1990s, these radicals modified their positions and became more liberal (as we will discuss later).[22]

As a result of the political liberalization linked to the election of Mohammad Khatami, a number of political parties appeared on the scene. With the possible exception of the Islamic Iran Participation Front, the leading component of the reformist coalition that backed Khatami's policies, most are vehicles for one man's political ambitions and lack any grassroots organization. Since strong parties are absent, journals, newspapers, and increasingly websites play a key role as vehicles for discussing, formulating, and disseminating ideological alternatives.

## Presidential Elections

In January 1980 Iran held its first ever presidential election, resulting in the victory of a lay Islamist, Abolhasan Banisadr. But Banisadr was impeached by Parliament and deposed by Khomeini in June 1981. His more pliant successor together with the prime minister were killed two months later by a bomb attack. The next four elections had predictable results, as close companions of Khomeini—Ali Khamenei in 1981 and 1985 and Ali-Akbar Hashemi Rafsanjani in 1989 and 1993—easily won contests in which the other candidates were minor figures. Consequently, the participation rate went steadily down, as can be seen in Figure 16.4 on electoral participation.

The pattern seemed to repeat itself in 1997. Although Rafsanjani would have liked to run again, he could not because the Constitution provides for only one immediate reelection. The mere fact that the term limit was respected shows to what an extent constitutional norms had finally come to govern Iranian politics. The speaker of Parliament, conservative cleric

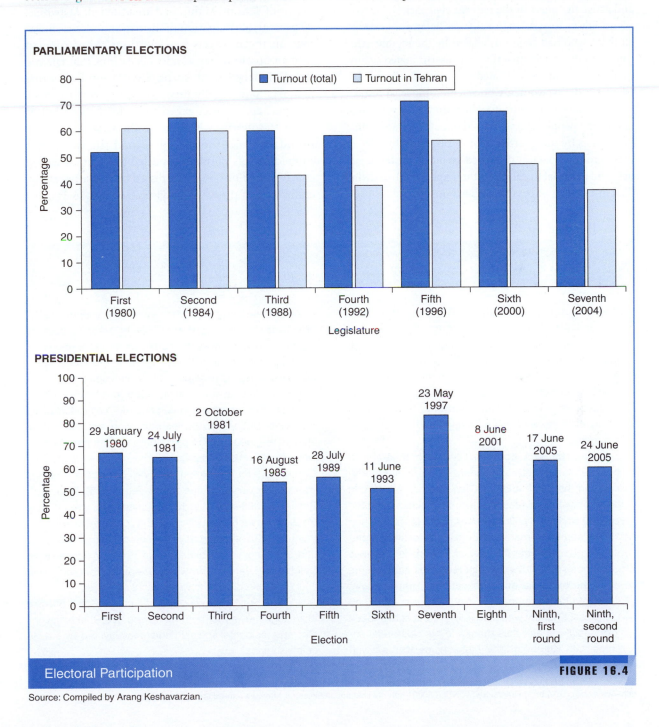

**PARLIAMENTARY ELECTIONS**

Legend: Turnout (total), Turnout in Tehran

**PRESIDENTIAL ELECTIONS**

Electoral Participation

**FIGURE 16.4**

Source: Compiled by Arang Keshavarzian.

Ali-Akbar Nateq Nuri, was endorsed by most of the government and the politically active ulema, including the Leader, and most observers expected him to win. Instead Mohammad Khatami, a moderate cleric who had resigned as minister of culture in 1992 after conservatives gained control over Parliament, ran a modern and effective campaign by reaching out to university students and active members of the nascent civil society. He won a landslide victory. As an "outsider," Khatami appealed to all those who had been humiliated by the regime: educated people who felt that the state discriminated against them in favor of less educated but ideologically reliable Islamic activists, women who resented the legal restrictions and discriminations to which they were subjected, and young people who were tired of being harassed on a daily basis by the guardians of public morality. To all these groups Khatami promised greater cultural openness and personal freedoms. Although his reforms dwindled in 1999, he was easily reelected in 2001.

For the first time since 1981, there was no official government candidate in the 2005 presidential elections. Three allies of Khatami, four conservatives, and Rafsanjani ran for the highest elective office. No candidate having gained a majority, for the first time there was a second round, runoff election, pitting Rafsanjani against the arch-conservative mayor of Tehran, Mahmud Ahmadinejad. At around 60 percent, participation in the two rounds was lower than in the previous two elections. Ahmadinejad won an upset victory amidst allegations that Islamic Revolutionary Guard Corps (IRGC) and Basij commanders had illegally urged troops to vote for him, and perhaps even engaged them in stuffing ballot boxes to increase his share of the vote in the first round in which he placed second. In any event, Ahmadinejad's message appealed to the poor whose concerns had not been addressed by the cultural liberalization of the Khatami years (see Box 16.3).

## Biography of Two Presidents and Two Generations

**BOX 16.3**

The biographies of Iran's last two presidents—Mohammad Khatami (1997–2005) and Mahmud Ahmadinejad (2005–present)—illustrate the changing face of Iran's political elite, from an older generation formed by the struggle against the shah and the revolution to a younger one shaped largely by the events of the postrevolutionary era. Moreover, the socioeconomic differences between Khatami and Ahmadinejad are telling.

Khatami was born in 1943 into a family of notable clerics and landowners. He is a cleric educated in the seminaries of Qom and holds a B.A. in philosophy from a secular university. He has authored several works on philosophy, is fluent in Arabic, and knows some German and English. After the revolution, he became the Minister of Culture and Islamic Guidance (1982–1992), which regulates and censors all forms of media and publications. There he was known to be a supporter of freedom of speech and the press. Khatami was able to carve out some space for his cultural activities thanks to his close relationships with Khomeini and his son, as well as with

journalists and students who would later support his presidency. Nonetheless, after growing pressure from hard-line conservatives, Khatami was forced to resign in 1992 and became the director of the National Library until he successfully ran for president.

Ahmadinejad was born in 1956 to a blacksmith and moved to Tehran at a young age. He is a product of the prerevolutionary secular education system and studied engineering. He participated in the Iran–Iraq war as a member of the Islamic Revolutionary Guard Corps. He later performed very well during his three years as governor of the newly established Ardabil Province (1993–1996). In 1997 Ahmadinejad earned a Ph.D. from a technical university and continued to teach there. In 2003 he was part of the new conservative faction of younger politicians known as the Alliance of Builders of Islamic Iran, which swept the Tehran city council elections, and he was elected as mayor.

What brings these disparate profiles and outlooks together is that both men were overwhelmingly elected president—against candidates favored by the establishment.

Sources: Wilfried Buchta, *Who Rules Iran? The Structure of Power in the Islamic Republic* (Washington, DC: The Washington Institute, 2000), 30; http://www.bbc.co.uk/persian/iran/story/2005/08/050801_pm-mv-khatami-profile.shtml; http://www.mardomyar.com/aspx2/aboutme.aspx.

Mahmud Ahmadinejad,
left; Mohammad Khatami,
right.

AP Images/Hasan Sarbakhshian

## Parliamentary Elections

For the purpose of parliamentary elections, Iran is divided into multimember constituencies, the largest being Tehran with thirty MPs. Each voter can write down the names of as many candidates as there are seats in a constituency. The top vote-getters in each constituency are elected provided they receive over 50 percent of the total vote. If a constituency has more seats than candidates who passed the 50 percent barrier, a second round determines the remaining MPs from among the runners-up. In the second round the number of candidates is twice that of the seats that remain to be filled. In the absence of organized political parties, candidacies tend to be endorsed by a number of different political, religious, and cultural associations. This factor makes it difficult to deduce accurate figures about the relative popularity of different political groupings from the election results.

In the first legislative elections of 1980, a few National Front, LMI, and regionalist candidates were elected to Parliament. Since 1984 only candidates unequivocally committed to *velayat-e faqih* have been allowed to run. Radicals formed the majority in the second (1984–1988) and third Parliaments (1988–1992), but after Khomeini's death the conservative-dominated

Council of Guardians arrogated to itself the right to vet candidacies and proceeded to invalidate the candidacies of most radicals. Consequently, conservatives dominated the fourth and fifth Parliaments (1992–2000) with pragmatist supporters of Rafsanjani forming the minority. In the wake of Mohammad Khatami's surprise victory in the presidential election of 1997, however, a record number of reformists became candidates. Since they were unknown to the Council of Guardians, they were allowed to run for office in 2000. They swept the elections, gaining around 70 percent of the vote. Where did these reformists suddenly come from?

In the course of the 1990s many of the radicals of the 1980s had a change of heart and moderated their views. Their evolution had a number of reasons. For one, the experience of being barred from entering Parliament in 1992 brought home the importance of fair elections and political pluralism. Furthermore, the collapse of communism in the Soviet Union and Eastern Europe delegitimized the statecentric approach to social and political organization. At the same time, a group of Muslim intellectuals, some of them ulema themselves, challenged both the traditional jurisprudential approach to religion that led to the preeminence of the ulema and the survival of obsolete rules and regulations, and the ideologization of religion that led to the loss of spirituality and totalitarian government. This more liberal approach to religion created a tentative connection between Islamic reformists and social groups that had hitherto not participated in politics, boosting participation rates at elections.

For the parliamentary elections of 2004, however, the Council of Guardians disallowed about 2,000 reformist candidates, including about eighty sitting MPs, which was unprecedented. Thereupon many reformist personalities and associations called for a boycott of the elections. Although participation diminished, 50 percent of the population still went to the polls. The reason is that in many areas outside the main cities voters do not judge candidates by their ideology but by what they can do (or have done) to further the interests of their constituents. Figure 16.4 shows the evolution of electoral participation.

## Local Elections

Although the Constitution of 1906 provided for elected local government councils, these bodies were never actually constituted. The similar provisions of the 1979 Constitution were first put into action in 1999, when Iranians for the first time went to the polls to elect city, town, and village councils.

Reformists won control over most councils, including Tehran. With the conservatives stymieing the reformist camp, apathy overtook voters in the new decade. Voting came to be seen by many as a futile exercise, since ultimately power rests with unelected bodies. In the second local elections in 2003 only 15 percent of the eligible voters in Tehran, mostly conservatives, bothered to vote, even though these were the freest elections in Iranian history. For the first time the Council of Guardians had not vetted candidates, and even avowed secularists were allowed to run. Consequently the nation's capital, home to about 15 percent of its total population, got a uniformly conservative city council, which elected as mayor the man who would two years later use his position as a springboard for a successful bid for the presidency. Elsewhere in the country, however, campaigns were more centered on concrete problems and participation was thus higher, testifying to a relatively high level of civic engagement of the citizenry.[23] In December 2006 the third local elections were held. Participation sharply increased, and supporters of President Ahmadinejad won only a few seats. As if to

rebuke him for his incompetent management of the economy, his supporters won only three out of fifteen seats on Tehran's municipal council. They were led by his sister, Parvin Ahmadinejad.

## POLITICAL CULTURE

To a large extent Iran's political culture results from its place in the international system. Iran survived the age of imperialism as a nominally sovereign state, but this independence did not prevent outside powers, mainly Great Britain and Russia, from meddling in Iran's domestic affairs and controlling its economy.[24] Their country having been a long-standing member of the international society of nations, Iranians have tended to compare themselves more readily with the dominant countries of the West than with other Third World nations; nevertheless, transforming their country's formal independence into genuine sovereignty has always been a key concern of politically conscious Iranians.

One result of foreign meddling in Iranian affairs has been the Iranians' propensity to believe in conspiracies and to interpret politics in the light of conspiracy theories (that is, theories that purport to prove that politics is dominated by the ill-intentioned and conspiratorial machinations of small groups whose aims and values are profoundly opposed to those of the rest of society).[25] Belief in conspiracies as a motor force in history is common in the rest of the Middle East as well.[26] But in the Iranian case, the plausibility of such theories is enhanced by the fact that Iran *has* indeed been the victim of conspiracies, most recently in 1953 when the U.S. and British governments conspired with Iranian conservatives to install the Shah as ruler of the country. The main reason why the seizure of the American hostages in November 1979 was so popular at the time was that it symbolically ended the era of foreign interference in Iranian affairs by allowing Iranians to occupy what most believed to be the epicenter of all conspiracies: the U.S. embassy.

## System Level

Iran is not a country whose borders and statehood are a bequest of European colonialism, which helps explain why the modern polity enjoys considerable historic legitimacy among Iranians, in spite of their ethnic diversity: Iranians with different mother tongues have lived with each other for centuries. The

Iranian nationalism propagated by the Pahlavi shahs included pride in the glories of ancient Persia and in a continuous "national" history of 2,500 years. This history was interpreted as conferring upon Iranians an intrinsic nobility that neighboring peoples and states cannot match.

This intense national pride survived the revolution but changed garb. While the glories of pre-Islamic Iran are now much less emphasized than before, the new authorities and their supporters considered Iran to be the vanguard of the Islamic world's struggle against Western domination. This position fuses commitment to Islam with Iranian nationalism. In recent years, however, Pahlavi-type ethnic Persian nationalism has been making a comeback among Iranians who are disenchanted with theocratic rule.

By the same token, ethnic nationalism has become stronger among Iran's non-Persian populations. This is particularly noticeable among the predominantly Sunni Kurds, who resent not only the poverty of the Kurdish areas but also discrimination on sectarian grounds. In the most recent presidential election, for instance, a candidate who expressly addressed Sunni grievances carried the largely Sunni province of Sistan and Baluchistan. At the same time, an Azeri who emphasized his ethnicity carried the three largely Azeri-speaking provinces of northwestern Iran. In theory, there is no reason why this new ethnic assertiveness should not be compatible with a strong sense of Iranian civic nationalism, but that depends on how the central government will manage it. Repressive measures are likely to erode the identification with the Iranian state in the ethnic periphery.

One time-honored way governments shore up their legitimacy is by appealing to feelings of patriotism. In Iran the issue around which the government has recently hoped to unite Iranians is the development of nuclear technology. The Iranian leaders' insistence that Iran has a "right" to develop nuclear energy has struck a sympathetic chord among ordinary Iranians, even among many of those who oppose Islamist rule. If Americans, Europeans, Chinese, and even Indians and Pakistanis have nuclear weapons, many people ask, why should Iranians not have them too?

## Process Level

One indisputable result of the Islamic revolution was the dramatic increase in the number of citizens who participated in politics. The millions of Iranians who poured into the streets to demand the departure of the Shah throughout 1978 refused to become mere subjects of a theocratic state after the revolution was over. The same cannot be said for those who opposed either the revolution or the Islamic state to which it ultimately gave rise. Many emigrated, and those who remained behind tended to consider the "Association of Militant Clerics" and the "Society of Militant Clergy" little more than Tweedledum and Tweedledee. It was these passive subjects of the Islamic Republic that Khatami had in mind when he repeatedly asserted that he wanted to be the president of *all* Iranians. They participated for the first time since the inception of the new regime, carrying electoral participation rates to new heights. In the elections of 2004 and 2005, however, many of them boycotted the elections, feeling that their participation had not brought the country nearer to a more republican and less theocratic form of government.

Another key feature of Iran's political culture is extreme individualism and lack of trust. Most observers impute this to the country's long history of despotism, which never developed a state of law that made life predictable and governed by rules rather than personal connections. The conspiracy belief mentioned earlier added to this absence of trust. Political opponents tend to accuse each other of being in league with foreign powers, making compromise (necessary for deliberative politics) very difficult, for one cannot compromise or negotiate with a "traitor." In the Islamic Republic the fact that the revolutionary credentials of the leaders of the various factions are equally strong has led to a certain mutual tolerance among those political leaders who remain faithful to *velayat-e faqih*. But even now, dissidents who question the system itself are invariably accused of doing the bidding of foreign (read: hostile) powers. The most consistent victims of this propensity to believe in conspiracies are religious minorities, especially Baha'is, who have been widely presented as agents of "Zionism." This charge is motivated by the fact that the world center of the Baha'i faith is located in Israel, which is a historic accident.

Distrust not only permeates the political elite, but is also evident among citizens. Recent results of the World Value Survey suggest that Iranians, like Egyptians, do not trust government (see Figure 16.5).[27]

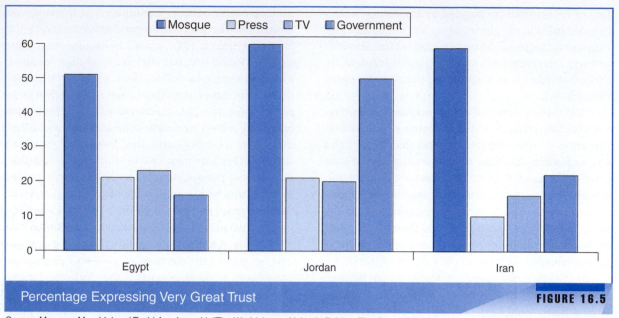

Percentage Expressing Very Great Trust

**FIGURE 16.5**

Source: Mansoor Moaddel and Taghi Azadarmaki, "The Worldviews of Islamic Publics: The Case of Egypt, Iran, and Jordan," in Ronald Ingelhart, ed., *Human Values and Social Change: Findings From the Values Survey* (Leiden: Brill, 2003), 81.

Since television channels are state-run and much of the press is owned by the state or heavily monitored by it, the low levels of trust in these institutions also illustrate a lack of trust in government. Meanwhile, the relatively high level of trust in the "mosque" should be interpreted with caution. As we will soon see, "the mosque" is far from a homogeneous entity and does not necessarily reflect a particular political agenda or culture.

This individualism and lack of trust are underlying causes for the absence of true political parties and the constant splits that the few parties that did come into existence have undergone. While all Iranians bemoan their inability to cooperate, it is this very inability that saved Iran from becoming a totalitarian state in the 1980s. If the ulema had the discipline and centralist organization of either the Roman Catholic Church or a Communist party, their rule would have become far more totalitarian and monolithic, and factionalism would never have been institutionalized.

A final consequence of the individualism and conspiracy belief prevalent in Iran's political culture is the periodic appearance of charismatic leaders. These leaders embody the yearning of the citizenry for overcoming the current order and the source of all problems—imperialists and autocrats. Mohammad Mossadegh, Ayatollah Khomeini, and even (to a much lesser extent) Mohammad Khatami exemplify this tendency. Some have argued that Twelver Shiism, with its expectation of the Twelfth Imam, predisposes Iranians to put their hopes in a charismatic savior figure.

## Policy Level

Given the fact that the Iranian state derives most of its income from oil, Iranians have tended to expect the state to provide welfare and material well-being for everybody and alleviate the gap between rich and poor. In other words, they want their share of the oil wealth. Part of the delegitimation of the Shah's regime occurred because people thought that not enough wealth trickled down to the poorer strata.

Corruption has been endemic in Iran, and fighting it has been an aspiration of Iranians of all political persuasions. Its persistence has been blamed on the regime, which has thereby lost some legitimacy, just like the Pahlavi regime in the 1960s and 1970s.

A noteworthy feature of Iran's contemporary political culture is the suspicion of private enterprise in the industrial sector. Beginning under Reza Shah (r. 1925–1941), the state took a leading role in the development of industry. Under Reza Shah's son, this statism was supplemented by an emerging class of capitalists who contributed considerably to Iran's industrialization in the 1960s and 1970s. But they were closely connected to the Shah and his relatives, they cooperated with foreign companies whose activities were suspicious for the mere reason that they were foreign, and some of them were members of religious minorities. Consequently, both the Islamists and leftists who carried the revolutionary movement opposed them and the mode of economic development they represented, calling them exploiters. The legacy of this opposition is visible in Iran's Constitution, which puts heavy limits on foreign investment.

The populism propagated by the revolutionaries has intensified opposition to conspicuous consumption and privately owned large-scale economic activity. This has not affected rich bazaar merchants, who engage mostly in trade rather than production. Their activity is less immediately visible than that of an industrialist, as a merchant can deal in millions armed with nothing but a cell phone and sitting behind a desk in a small shop in the bazaar. In contrast, the factory and offices of an industrialist attract immediate attention.[28] The result of this general distrust of industrialists has been that citizens expect the state to be the main purveyor of development and increased living standards. The election of Mahmud Ahmadinejad in 2005 is partly due to the timid privatization carried out under his two predecessors, which aggravated income inequality.

While many Iranians thus expect the state to alleviate poverty and unemployment, others expect the state to provide an environment in which individual talent and creativity can flourish. Collectivism and individualism are both present in Iranian society, and the result is that Iran's political culture is highly conflictual. The citizenry is sharply divided over the very essence of the regime, with many, especially among the more educated, considering Islamic theocracy, if not the Islamic Republic, to be an anachronistic form of government.

## POLITICAL SOCIALIZATION

The political socialization of citizens is a process simultaneously driven from above by state institutions and from below by social practices. In Iran, state-controlled institutions—such as the education system and the military—transmit many of the basic political values and norms in society and also establish the framework for debating their meaning. Meanwhile, through their everyday practices as members of their family, neighborhood, or social group, Iranians negotiate, challenge, and even sometimes undermine these norms.

As in many postrevolutionary and postcolonial regimes, state-sanctioned political socialization in Iran has aimed at generating national unity and masking political, ethnic, and socioeconomic cleavages. Under the Pahlavi monarchy national unity was championed in the mission of creating a modern, industrial, and Western society. Under this vision the nation was presented as secular, classless, and thoroughly Persian in identity. The schools, for instance, were the primary means to educate the entire Iranian population in the official language of Persian, a critical means to distance the significant numbers of Azeri (roughly 25 percent), Kurdish (8–10 percent), and Arabic (2–5 percent) speakers from their local and ethnic loyalties. The calls for greater economic equality, ethnic inclusion, and religious observance during the Islamic revolution dramatically questioned both the notion of national homogeneity and the perception that the Iranian nation accepted this image of itself. Under the Islamic Republic, the content of the official discourse and normative agenda has changed. However, the methods of socialization and the overwhelming elite desire to limit input from citizens and ignore the pluralistic nature of society remain quite similar to the prerevolutionary regime.

## Education System

The school system has been the principal "agent of socialization" for creating good Islamic citizens out of young Iranians. The school system was one of the first institutions to be Islamicized by the new regime. School curricula were changed to include a heavy dose of religious studies, yearly classes on the Islamic revolution, and an increased number of mandatory Arabic language courses. Meanwhile, textbooks were rewritten to present a state-sanctioned history of Iran, which highlighted the role of the clergy in all "popular uprisings," erased or distorted any role played by nonreligious forces (such as liberal nationalists or leftist parties), and presented the Pahlavi monarchy (and all monarchs) as equally and continually oppressive and immoral. Textbooks also depicted the state's image of the family.

Unlike the prerevolutionary textbooks that showed Iranian women as unveiled, families eating around a table, and children with non-Arabic and nonreligious names, the postrevolutionary textbooks depicted all women as veiled (even inside the home), families sitting cross-legged around a simple spread on the floor, and children with Islamic names.[29] Schoolchildren also received revolutionary doctrine by reciting chants and poems praising the greatness of Khomeini and the regime, while denouncing the Baathist regime in Iraq as well as "the imperialists," most commonly the United States.

The authorities initially emphasized the role of primary and secondary schools for creating loyal and mobilized supporters. However, a group of Islamist activists and scholars also led a charge to "cleanse" the universities of "counterrevolutionary" elements by reviewing both the faculty and the curriculum. This "Cultural Revolution" was headed by what is now known as the Supreme Council for the Cultural Revolution. University campuses being the epicenter of antiregime activism, the Cultural Revolution closed all universities for three years (1980–1983) and worked to develop links between the universities and the religious seminaries. When the universities were reopened, strict entrance requirements were established, including religious examinations, to give greater opportunities to those the regime expected would be more supportive of its ambitions. In addition, war veterans and relatives of those killed in the revolution and the Iran–Iraq war were allotted special quotas in all universities. In the meantime, the regime established new institutions to create a new set of technocrats and teachers to staff the ministries and the universities. For instance, Imam Sadeq University (on the campus of a former business school affiliated with Harvard Business School) was fashioned to produce technocrats. Another new aspect of the university system was the establishment of the "Islamic Open University," with autonomous campuses all over the country, including small towns. This university was to provide higher education to Iranians living outside of the main population centers and to provide opportunities for students who fail to pass the highly competitive entrance examination for the elite national universities or whose families would not let them move to the larger cities.

The content of higher education was transformed by the Islamic Republic with the regime promoting and funding attempts to elaborate contain fields, such as "Islamic Economics" and "Islamic Sciences," as ways to compete with what some viewed as the fundamentally distorted and anti-Islamic nature of Western social and natural sciences. Over the years, the regime has also sponsored the establishment of pro-regime volunteer organizations (**Basij**) to monitor the political activities of students and faculty and mobilize students for pro-regime activities on the campuses.

The Islamic Republic's efforts to create obedient and loyal citizens out of the "children of the revolution" seem far from successful. Many of the investigative journalists exposing government abuses and incompetence or the staunchest supporters of reform and the burgeoning civil society (such as arts organizations and women's nongovernmental organizations) are products of the state school system and its post-Cultural Revolution higher education establishments. In fact, the university that the state tried so hard to control in the wake of the revolution is again full of students publishing political journals and declarations, organizing talks challenging the regime, and flaunting and mocking the social mores and the state's policies regarding gender relations. The large student demonstrations of 1999 and 2003 are indicative of the inability of the regime to fully manage this politicized space.

## The Military

Military conscription has also been a fundamental mechanism for creating national unity, at least for young men. The shared experience of basic training and interacting with the military bureaucracy was augmented by the experience of the long war with Iraq. The war was a critical historical juncture that shaped a large number of Iranian men and their families. With approximately four million to five million Iranians serving in the armed forces during the eight-year war, a very large percentage of Iranian families were directly affected by it.[30] Various public commemorations and war murals, as well as stories in cinema and fiction, act to foster emotional bonds between the war generation and those who preceded and followed it.

Politically, however, the war has been divisive, with part of the ruling establishment questioning the policy to continue the war even after the Iraqi army was driven off Iranian soil in 1982.[31] Moreover, Iran's military includes the Islamic Revolutionary Guard Corps and the Basij, which have become distinct institutions with growing political influence. In the parliamentary election of 2004, over 100 former members of the Revolutionary Guards won seats, and in 2005 a former member won the presidency. These institutions, largely autonomous from the regular army and police force, are under the direct supervision of the Leader, and have acquired significant economic holdings.

## Religion and Religious Institutions

While most Iranians consider themselves religious and consider religious matters and practices as important aspects of their lives, results from the 2000–2001 World Value Survey project suggest a more nuanced view.[32] Table 16.2 and Figure 16.6 show that many Iranians consider themselves religious, believe religion is very important in life, and participate in religious services but at lower rates than in Jordan and Egypt. Moreover, while surveyed Iranians more often characterize themselves as "above all a Muslim" than as "above all a nationalist," about a third put nationalism first, far more than in either Egypt or Jordan.

Notwithstanding these aggregate findings, under the Islamic Republic religion and religious practice have played a more divisive than unifying role. On the surface, religion permeates daily life. Official speeches and pronouncements are peppered with religious

| Percentage of People Describing Self as "a Religious Person" | TABLE 16.2 |
|---|---|
| Egypt | 98 |
| Nigeria | 94 |
| Jordan | 85 |
| Iran | 82 |
| United States | 82 |
| India | 80 |
| Turkey | 75 |
| Spain | 75 |
| Mexico | 65 |
| Russia | 64 |
| Germany | 50 |
| Sweden | 33 |
| Japan | 24 |

Source: Mansoor Moaddel and Taghi Azadarmaki, "The Worldviews of Islamic Publics: The Case of Egypt, Iran, and Jordan," in Ronald Ingelhart, ed., *Human Values and Social Change: Findings From the Values Survey* (Leiden: Brill, 2003), 75.

expressions and quotations, the calendar is full of religious holidays, and religious observance is often public and conspicuous. Shiite Islam plays a central role both in official discourse and as a means to regulate who can gain high office in the state. Friday congregational prayers and commemorations of religious anniversaries are state-regulated events that bring people from all walks of life together at neighborhood public spaces. As if to underline the emasculation of Tehran University as the center of secular opposition to the Islamic regime, Tehran's official Friday congregational prayers are held on what used to be the campus's soccer field. On these occasions leading members of the government give sermons in which they passionately weave together religious and moral issues and the pressing political problems of the day.

In staging these public and mass religious meetings, the state consciously attempts to mobilize citizens in support of the regime and also to transmit political messages. These events and state-owned radio and television are dominated by the well-versed and symbolic Shiite language of martyrdom and self-sacrifice, as exemplified by the Third Imam, in the name of justice and standing up to the great powers who usurp the rights of the innocent and faithful.

It is difficult, however, to monopolize the symbols, interpretations, and ephemeral beliefs that make up a religion. Over the years the Islamic Republic has had difficulty controlling members of the political elite and clergy, let alone the hearts and minds of its citizens. Given the absence of a Shiite "pope," Iran's theocratic state has never been able fully to impose its politicized vision of Shiite Islam within Iran, let alone across the Shiite world. With the death of Khomeini and the appointment of the less religiously erudite and charismatic Khamenei, fundamental disagreements have emerged over the meaning of Islamic government and the role of religion in public life. For instance, the political faction commonly described as "reformists" has stressed the republican dimensions of the Constitution and the revolution. In contrast, the conservatives have highlighted the centrality of clerical authority and its right of oversight over the popular will. Meanwhile, lay religious intellectuals (such as Abdol-Karim Soroush) and clerics (such as Hassan Eshkevari) have called for a reformulation of the relationships among God, the individual, and political authority that explicitly challenges the basic assumptions of the current interpretation of *velayat-e faqih*.

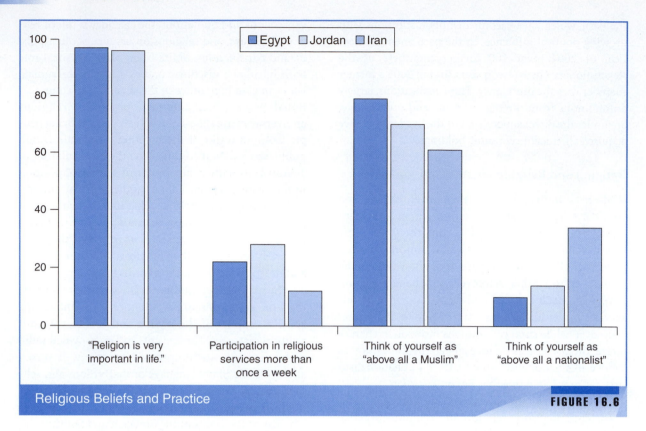

**Religious Beliefs and Practice**

**FIGURE 16.6**

These debates have not only percolated in the intellectual environments of the universities, seminaries, and magazines, but have also begun to shape more public discussions regarding the relationship between religion and politics and resonate with the philosophical and political debates of ordinary Iranians too.[33]

Finally, in more organizational terms, religious observance has always had a localized flavor. Numerous neighborhood and guild-based Koranic reading groups and religious associations cater to the spiritual needs of men and women of different regional, ethnic, and class backgrounds. These informal meetings act as grassroots and independent forums for religious practice, which by definition escape the watchful eye of those clerics who are affiliated with the regime. Sometimes escaping the attention of observers is the tension between the clerical state and the seminaries in the cities of Qom and Mashhad. With the vast majority of clergy historically shying away from politics and the seminary system historically maintaining financial independence, Khomeini's political innovation of clerical-led government has reconfigured "church"–state relations. For instance, job opportunities and

income are available for clerics in the judicial system and in the ministries, and as Friday prayer leaders, the last being appointed by the office of the Leader. While the ulema, especially former students of Khomeini, have been prominent in the higher reaches of the regime, the actual running of the state has never been dominated by seminary graduates, and their presence has declined over the last quarter century. One indication is the decline in the number of clerics in the Parliament. In the very first Majles almost half of the MPs were clerics, but by the late 1990s clerics constituted less than 20 percent of MPs.

For the vast majority of clerics—who remain in the seminaries to teach, study, and interpret religious texts—the regime has in fact been intrusive. The authorities in Tehran have tried to monitor teaching in the seminaries by dictating curricula and identifying texts to be taught in Qom. In addition, the Leader has used his office and funds to support seminaries and teachers who are deemed to be "militant" and sympathetic to the regime's interpretations of Islam. The upshot is that while the mosque and state are perfectly aligned in theory, in practice the state can never be sure that the seminaries are producing appropriate clergy for the government or socializing Iranians in the official doctrine. Mosque and state remain distinct entities despite the infusion of religion and seminarians into the Constitution of the state.

## Mass Media

The media play both a unifying and a divisive role in socializing Iranians. Radio and television are monopolized by the state and are one of the major means to transmit the official doctrine and to mobilize Iranians for elections and rallies across the country. Since the head of the Radio and Television Organization is directly appointed by the Leader, in recent years it has also reflected the interests of the conservative wing of the regime. The strong bias of state television was clearly demonstrated during the presidency of Mohammad Khatami (1997–2005), when news broadcasts either ignored or misrepresented many of the raging political debates.

In recent years, as satellite television has grown and the dishes have become less expensive, antiregime Persian language programming from abroad and foreign news outlets (CNN and BBC) provide greater diversity for the viewing public. In response, the state has repeatedly tried to outlaw private use of satellite dishes, although the law has not been applied consistently. The dishes can be seen on rooftops in major cities and even small towns.

The printed press has been the most diverse and fascinating form of media in postrevolutionary Iran. In the first decade of the revolution, newspapers and journals became increasingly uniform in their coverage. But as the regime began to feel more consolidated and elite competition became more open after the passing away of Khomeini, a growing number of independent newspapers and magazines appeared on the scene. These newspapers and magazines reflected specific schools of thought and critical views from intellectuals on the right and left and the more republican and the more authoritarian wings of the regime. A flourishing nonstate press and burgeoning investigative journalism constituted the backbone of Khatami's surprising election victory in 1997 and underpinned the enormous popularity of the reformist movement in his first term. The critics of the government (many of whom were part of the revolutionary establishment) and the many young journalists writing critical articles presented a new political language of accountability, civil society, and participation to the educated, urban, and young population of Iran. In doing so, these newspapers both reflected and produced deep cleavages among the ruling establishment.

During the authoritarian backlash against the reformist movement since 2000, the conservative-controlled Judiciary has gone a long way in clamping down on the most vibrant aspects of this press. Currently, journalists have turned to the Internet to distribute their reports and publish their commentaries in online newspapers or in the mushrooming collection of weblogs. Today, Persian is the fourth most widely used language in terms of numbers of bloggers, after English, French, and Portuguese. In Iran today, journalists and newspaper editors, some of whom have been imprisoned or physically attacked, have become the new political heroes of many of the youth.

## The Family and Social Groups

Political socialization takes place in the private sphere as well as in the public sphere. This is particularly the case in more authoritarian contexts. In Iran, both under the monarchy and the Islamic Republic, the home has been a relatively free place to discuss politics by recounting the unofficial history of the country or debate current events with family members and friends. While patriarchy (and sometimes matriarchy) does prohibit unfettered debate in the family setting, the memory of key political episodes—such as the 1953 coup or the events leading up to the overthrow of the Shah in 1979—is transmitted in these settings. By retelling stories from earlier eras or speculating about the conspiracies behind them, older family members indoctrinate the family's younger generation in a political memory and culture that have not been sanctioned by the state and that are at variance with the official story, as contained in school textbooks and official rhetoric.

But with greater numbers of Iranians completing high school and attending universities, the family dynamic appears to have changed. Young men and women now have a certain authority as they are the first generation in their families to graduate from high school and university. It is they who are interpreting politics for their relatives by explaining differences between political factions and bringing campus politics into their homes. Over the last ten years, greater political freedoms, or at least a less fearful setting, has allowed for many of these types of discussions to take place while one waits for oven-fresh bread outside the local bakery, peruses headlines at the newspaper kiosk, or shares a collective taxi with total strangers. These ritualistic acts of resistance prevent the state from fully dominating politics, but at the same time they do not challenge the bases of regime power.

In short, political socialization under the Islamic Republic has shifted from being solely the responsibility of the state to one that is contested by counterelite and popular voices. The early revolutionary message of unity and mobilization in the name of revolutionary Islam once taught in school textbooks and recounted in Friday sermons and newspaper pages has given way to greater pluralism and contestation, intriguingly by many of the same people who read those school texts and wrote those newspaper articles in the 1980s. Whether the regime will be able to accommodate and represent pluralistic discourse or impose the single voice of unity is very much the question facing Iran's authorities. Their decision and capacity in this regard will determine whether Iran will move toward more democratic politics or authoritarianism.

## RECRUITING THE POLITICAL ELITE

What kinds of people govern Iran? Under the Shah, the small class of educated and secular Iranians who could demonstrate personal loyalty to the monarch gained access to political offices. Many of the ministers came from land-owning families and attended Western high schools and universities.[34] The Shah, however, carefully monitored his court in order to prevent the rise of potential competitors with a strong personality or independent bases of support. For instance, highly competent policymakers and administrators—such as the Abol-Hasan Ebtehaj, who headed the Plan and Budget Organization—were muscled out of office as soon as the Shah sensed they were growing in stature.[35] This policy produced a highly dependent inner circle, whose members were unwilling to challenge the Shah and preferred to censor information and opinions in order not to offend His Imperial Majesty. This passive and dependent nature of the political elite prevented the Shah from

acting in a timely and decisive manner as the revolts and political challenges of 1977 and 1978 snowballed into the revolution.[36]

Under the Islamic Republic personalism has also played an important role, but in a broader sense. In the early years, political elites came from various backgrounds, but their most fundamental credentials were their revolutionary pedigrees. Those who could point to active participation in the Islamic revolution, and in particular the various groups associated with Khomeini and his students, leveraged this past experience into positions in ministries, the parastatal economic foundations, the Islamic Revolutionary Guard Corps, and various other institutions with access to state revenue. Thus, the new political elite that came to power immediately after the revolution was younger and less cosmopolitan; they were from more middle-class and lower-middle-class backgrounds, often hailing from the provinces rather than the capital.

In general, the state has expanded since the revolution. From 1976 to 1986, the number of employees in the public sector more than doubled, reaching more than 30 percent of all employed Iranians. In the 1980s, four-fifths of all new jobs created were in the public sector, and by 1986 public-sector employment accounted for 31 percent of total employment.[37] This expansion was due to a number of reasons, including the requisites of the war effort, the state-led economic development program, and the revolutionary agenda to restructure and Islamicize society from above.

Initially the clergy that were recruited into the state were trained in the seminaries in Najaf and Qom where Khomeini and his students taught during the 1960s and 1970s. The principal seminary that produced these new judges and ministers was the Fayziyeh Seminary in Qom. Over time, the Haqqani Seminary in Qom has grown in importance, in part because many of its alumni include staunch conservatives who have dominated the Judiciary, the Council of Guardians, and the security apparatus. The so-called Haqqani circle has included important figures in the conservative backlash against Khatami's attempts to institutionalize political reform and encourage active participation by civil society. In the recent parliamentary and presidential elections, the Haqqani alumni in conjunction with some elements of the Islamic Revolutionary Guard Corps have both supported social conservatives and opposed moderate conservatives and reformists.

Nonclerical parliamentarians and ministers tend to emerge from educational and military institutions. First, many attend the newly Islamicized universities, such as Imam Sadeq University or Tarbiat Modarres University. In the 1990s, think tanks and research centers were important in recruiting and producing political elites. Many of the reformists who dominated the Sixth Parliament and supported President Khatami were based in the Center for Strategic Studies. These younger elites often are too young to have significant revolutionary credentials, but their studies in these universities and institutes give them technical know-how, intellectual credentials, and the social networks to gain access to various government and state institutions.

More recently, many of the new elite have come from the ranks of the Islamic Revolutionary Guard Corps and the Basij. The current president, Ahmadinejad, the mayor of Tehran, Mohammad-Baqer Qalibaf, and many of the ministers all were military figures from these corps or worked for the research institutes connected to the IRGC. It is worth noting that the regular army, navy, and air force have not had much influence in politics. This growing militarization of politics is a new phenomenon in modern Iranian history. Unlike neighboring Pakistan, Turkey, and Iraq, which have had numerous military coups and governments headed by generals, the Iranian political establishment was overwhelmingly civilian throughout the twentieth century.

Kinship ties are commonly used to gain political and economic power. Many of the sons and brothers, and on some rare occasions, daughters and sisters, of government officials use their family ties to gain access to the state. Often their contacts are used as means for rent seeking (receiving subsidized hard currency, special import licenses, or securing subsidized loans) and personal enrichment. In addition, marriage is used as a powerful way to cement political alliances and create bonds between prominent families. For instance, President Khatami's brother, Mohammad-Reza Khatami—who was a member of the Sixth Parliament and the secretary general of the reformist Islamic Iran Participation Front—is married to Zahra Eshraqi, a granddaughter of Khomeini. Meanwhile, the daughter of the current speaker of the Parliament, Gholam-Ali Haddad-Adel, is married to the son of Ali Khamenei, the Leader. These and other kinship relations thus help integrate the elite and distinguish them from ordinary citizens.

# INTEREST ARTICULATION AND AGGREGATION

The mix of electoral politics and authoritarian powers generates multiple and competing forms of interest articulation and aggregation under the Islamic Republic. The most institutionalized forms are regular presidential, parliamentary, and local elections, as discussed earlier. The least institutionalized, but probably the most prevalent and effective, is the use of personalistic ties and patron-client relations. As a consequence, representation under the Islamic Republic is highly fragmented, fluid, and contentious, although not fully pluralistic, competitive, and democratic.

## Noninstitutional Forms of Interest Articulation and Aggregation

The principal means of interest aggregation in contemporary Iran is clientelism and the forging of relationships between political figures and citizens through patron-client networks. Given the state's access to external sources of revenue from the world oil market, Iranian political figures have exchanged political loyalty and support for access to such resources as subsidies, hard currency, subcontracts, and secure government jobs. This system of patronage can take a very direct form where parliamentarians, ministers, or bureaucrats dole out these resources to kin, schoolmates, and people from the same city or province. Special access to powerful figures in the office of the Leader, state-owned banks, and economic foundations have benefited these clients, while ensuring their dependence, if not loyalty, to the political system that plays more of a distributive, rather than an extractive, role. Since patron-client relations are based on the goods that the patron provides the client, if the patron loses power then so do his clients.

In a less targeted manner, the Islamic Republic distributes large subsidies to ensure the loyalty of large portions of the population. Food and medicine are subsidized at an annual rate of about $2 billion and particularly to benefit the urban poor. By contrast, the annual $10 billion energy subsidy for gasoline and electricity is quite regressive because it benefits the middle and upper classes that own automobiles, homes, and electrical equipment. Obviously, this form of political aggregation undermines pretensions of institutional impartiality and meritocracy that are essential principles behind equal citizenship and participation.

## Institutionalized Forms of Interest Articulation and Aggregation: Voting

Elections are regularized political events, but they do not provide complete pluralism nor necessarily entail a shift in power and policies, since the powers of the representative institutions are quite limited. Elections tend to function more as an act and measurement of regime legitimacy, and only secondarily as a means for citizens to express their interests by selecting among diverse sets of candidates with specified policy positions. Thus, except for the most recent elections, there has been more discussion about election turnout than candidates. The turnout in the nine presidential elections averaged around 63 percent (see again Figure 16.4, presidential elections) and for the seven parliamentary elections, about 60 percent.

Both the 1997 and 2005 presidential elections, however, indicated that under certain conditions elections can be moments of interest articulation and offer information regarding the preferences of citizens. In 1997, it was quite clear that the regime candidate was Ali-Akbar Nateq-Nuri, the sitting speaker of the Parliament and close confidant of the Leader. However, thanks in part to the burgeoning civil society and his low government profile, Mohammad Khatami, as "the outsider" and "nonregime" candidate, swept to victory with a surprising 70 percent of the vote. In somewhat similar fashion, although with a very different political agenda and significance, Mahmud Ahmadinejad surprised many pundits by defeating Ali-Akbar Hashemi Rafsanjani, who has been one of the cornerstones of the Islamic Republic since its establishment. These surprising outcomes indicate that in spite of the limited nature of elections in the Islamic Republic, voters are able to express their views, and these preferences can matter even when they go against the wishes of the ruling establishment or the expectations of political experts.

Given the weakness of party organizations, as mentioned earlier, political parties play no major role. The factions that contend for power and influence in Iran have not formed a clearly defined party system that would act as a mechanism for representing and aggregating the interests of constituents. Parties and political associations, such as the Society of Combatant Clergy or the Islamic Iran Participation Front, are groupings of members of the political elite that become active during elections, yet until now they have been unable to maintain party discipline with direct and formalized links to the citizenry.

## Institutional Groups and Professional Organizations

While political parties are less developed, groups based in state organizations have a more corporate identity and a greater ability to shape policy, in much the same manner as controlled interest group systems. The Islamic Revolutionary Guard Corps and the volunteer mobilization corps (Basij), consisting of 120,000 and 90,000 men, respectively,[38] are two of the most prominent arms of the state that directly represent their interests in various policymaking areas, although they were established to mobilize support for the regime. These ostensibly military and security forces have also played a role in the economy through their business subsidiaries, which are involved in large-scale construction projects as well as allegedly importing consumer goods. Since the 2003 local council elections, the IRCG and Basij have taken a more visible role in politics. A number of their high-ranking figures have run for local offices, Parliament, and, most recently, the presidency. Finally, since they are in direct communication with the Leader, and not the president and Parliament, they have the ability to influence policy.

Iran does have a host of associations representing the interests of labor, business, professional groups, and industrial sectors. However, the House of Labor or the Iranian Chamber of Commerce, Industries, and Mines and other such organizations operate more as a means for state officials to manage these corporate entities rather than as vehicles to represent specific interest and shape policymaking. Only in very recent elections have professional organizations endorsed different candidates, which may signal the emergence of an independent role for these corporate groups in political competition.

In the course of the struggle against the Shah and in the years following his overthrow, neighborhood councils and guild associations sprang up all over the country as grassroots initiatives to address ordinary citizens' needs during the revolution and the war years. Over time they have become integrated into the patron-client system, and today they are either mere appendages of state officials or means for the state to penetrate society.[39] Hence, there is no clear separation between interest groups and government officials. Moreover, since the revolution the government has encouraged workers, merchants, and students to establish Islamic associations in universities, factories, and guilds as the principal means of aggregating the interests of these groups.

Nonetheless, in the 1990s and especially during the relatively less repressive administration of President Khatami, a large number of genuinely autonomous associations representing strata of society that had been largely sidelined by the revolutionary regime emerged. For instance, various women's organizations of both secular and reformist Islamist persuasion came into being and started initiatives seeking to change discriminatory laws, provide services, and raise general consciousness regarding women's issues. (Most notable is the 2003 Nobel Peace Prize Winner, **Shirin Ebadi.** She was the first woman to become a judge under the Shah, but she lost her job when women were barred from that position following the revolution. Ebadi was active in a host of legal organizations championing and defending the rights of women, children, and political dissidents.) Simultaneously, students and secular intellectuals took advantage of these opportunities to establish or reactivate associations and publications that were independently minded and represented alternative visions of politics.

## Nonassociational Social Groups

Many social strata in Iran exist without independent associations aggregating and representing their interests. Among the historically and politically important social groups without corporate representation, it is worth mentioning the bazaari merchants. Among the more recent social groups, the war veterans and the relatives of those killed in the war (referred to as "martyrs") stand out as well.

Bazaari merchants based in the historic covered bazaars of Iran, ranging from retailers and brokers to wholesalers and even international traders, have played a central role in various political episodes from the Constitutional Revolution (1905–1911) to the Oil Nationalization Movement (1951–1953) to the Islamic Revolution. Even though important differences have existed among bazaaris in terms of socioeconomic

status, political persuasion, and position in the international and national economies, they have developed a sense of solidarity because of the well-defined and vibrant physical space of the bazaar, which ensures socially embedded and crosscutting relations. Their political significance is enhanced both by their economic power and their close relationship with the ulema. Since the revolution, bazaari economic interests have been threatened by the state's domination of the economy, while the homogeneity of bazaari interests has been undermined by key pro-Khomeini bazaari families being co-opted by the new regime.

War veterans, the families of the martyrs, and those disabled in the Iran–Iraq war make up a large and politically important social group. They are ostensibly represented by various organizations and political groups, such as the Martyr's Foundation, the Foundation of the Disinherited, the Society of the Devotees of the Islamic Republic, and the Headquarters of the POWs. But these organizations have proved unable to address adequately the everyday demands of many of their constituents, and they have moved away from their original mandate of providing services to war veterans and their families. The state has also provided for this important constituency by setting up all kinds of affirmative action schemes (ranging from easier access to higher education to priority in flight reservations) and subsidizing consumer goods for veterans and relatives of both veterans and "martyrs" in order to enhance their socioeconomic standing. Yet these measures have not always worked adequately to both address the needs of this social group and suppress challenges. Some prominent war veterans and former members of the IRGC have aligned themselves with the reformist faction, calling for greater political participation and freedoms. Others have accused the regime of turning its back on the wartime principles of self-sacrifice and justice. For much of the postwar era there have been growing complaints by some war veterans that the memory of the war and respect for the sacrifices of the war generation have faded, while the veterans and relatives of the martyrs have not been sufficiently provided for. This position was given voice by some ultraconservative newspapers, certain filmmakers engaged in producing war films, and outspoken figures of a group called Ansar-e Hezbollah (Partisans of the Party of God) who have taken it upon themselves to combat moral, political, and economic corruption.

## Demonstrations and Public Protests

Given the closed nature of institutional interest representation and aggregation, many social groups and political tendencies have turned to civil disobedience to express their grievances. The relatively fresh memory of the demonstrations and strikes that constituted the revolution of 1978–1979 are a model for workers, students, activist women, and the urban poor to use public collective action to make their claims. Throughout the 1990s, industrial workers, for instance, protested against privatization policies, the selling of state-owned factories, and nonpayment of their wages. One high-profile tactic has workers blocking the main expressway connecting Tehran to the industrial satellite city of Karaj. These protesters have succeeded on several occasions in blocking the selling of state-owned factories to private business interests they suspected of planning to lay off workers. Teachers and government pensioners in recent years have protested in front of the Parliament to draw attention to their inadequate income. On the eve of the 2005 presidential election, women's groups united to organize protests against the male bias enshrined in the Constitution. Ethnic political groups, especially Kurdish and Arab activists on the Iran–Iraq border, have vocally called for greater distribution of wealth and local authority in their provinces. Since 2003, these tensions have flared up with mysterious bombings taking place and the Iranian security forces and IRGC responding brutally.

The most dramatic protests, however, have been based in the universities and spearheaded by students. During the summers of 1999 and 2003, student organizations staged sit-ins and demonstrations to protest against authoritarian measures by the regime. In the first case they challenged the closure of a prominent reformist newspaper and in the second case the sentencing of an outspoken intellectual who had questioned clerical rule. These protests were originally based in Tehran University, but they spread to other cities and university campuses and persisted for several days. With little support or protection from reformist parties and other social groups (such as workers, bazaaris, and teachers), the volunteer forces (Basij) and police violently suppressed the demonstrators and prevented the movement from escalating.

Although these and other events demonstrate that Iranian society is not completely passive in the face of government policies, the inability of these disparate groups to unite or coordinate their localized organizational capabilities is an indication of the overwhelming social atomization in contemporary Iran. Given the pervasive use of patron-client relations and lack of trust among Iranians, collective action and alliance-building is particularly difficult. Moreover, these non-institutional forms of politics reflect the lack of efficacy of institutional politics and the belief on the part of many Iranians that their political voice cannot be heard unless it is in this form.

## POLICY FORMULATION

In the Islamic Republic of Iran state policy is set by a number of bodies, some of them explicitly mentioned in the Constitution, some not. Given the mixed nature of the political system, overlaps, duplications, and even contradictions abound, and it is not rare for different policymaking bodies to work at cross-purposes.

## State Institutions Mentioned in the Constitution

As befits a theocracy in which, at least in theory, no state policy may contradict Islam, those who determine what does and does not contradict Islam have a preponderant voice in setting policy. In the Islamic Republic this means first and foremost the Leader. The first Leader, Ruhollah Khomeini, on numerous occasions used his authority to determine state policy by issuing religious edicts (*fatwa*s). On a few occasions these edicts broke with established religious tradition, which is not astonishing given the charismatic nature of his leadership.[40] One of the earliest examples was his ruling on caviar. According to Shiite (and Jewish) dietary laws, a fish can be eaten only if it has scales. The sturgeon, however, has no scales and traditionally its meat and, by extension, its roe (caviar) were not deemed permissible. But caviar is one of Iran's main exports, and so the matter was revisited. A specially appointed state commission concluded that the sturgeon does indeed have scales, but that they are of a peculiar shape. Taking note of this finding, in November 1983 Khomeini issued a *fatwa* declaring that caviar could be eaten. In 1988 he broke with other time-honored legal traditions by authorizing the playing of chess, provided no bets were made on the outcome, betting and gambling being forbidden in Islam. He also liberalized the early republic's stifling cultural life by relaxing the rules pertaining to music and television programming.[41]

Khomeini's interventions in the state's policy-making were often made necessary by continued deadlock between Parliament and the Council of Guardians, as mentioned earlier. To avoid paralysis, in January 1988 Khomeini amended his doctrine of *velayat-e faqih*, guardianship of the jurisprudent, by issuing an edict that gave the state, as embodied by its Leader, authority to override religious law when that is expedient. This "absolute dominion of the jurisprudent" (*velayat-e motlaqeh-ye faqih*), he averred, was the "most important of divine commandments and has priority over all derivative divine commandments . . . even over prayer, fasting, and the pilgrimage to Mecca."[42] This reinterpretation of the theocratic principle was enshrined in the Constitution when that document was revised in 1989.

Needless to say, most traditional Muslims and most members of the ulema were horrified by this subordination of religion to reason of state, as the whole purpose of setting up an Islamic state had been the exact opposite. Moreover, no person other than Khomeini could conceivably get away with disregarding religion when it was expedient for the state to do so, and as a result shortly before his death Khomeini invested the newly established Expediency Council with the authority to advise the Leader on invoking the absolute authority. As president (1981–1989), Khamenei had been a member of the conservative faction, and in his first years as Leader he more or less tried to give the impression of remaining above the fray, but with the onset of the Khatami presidency in 1997 he abandoned all pretense of neutrality and became the de facto leader of the conservatives who did their best to stymie the reformist zeal of the elected officials.

The Expediency Council has emerged as the institution in which the most vital policies of the nation are decided. For instance, in Iran's negotiations with Britain, France, Germany, and the International Atomic Energy Commission (IAEC) about its nuclear program, the top Iranian negotiator, Hasan Rowhani, did not come from the foreign ministry or the Atomic Energy Organization of Iran, but was an engineer-turned-cleric who was the secretary of the National Security Council, where

foreign policy is made, and as such a member of the Expediency Council. Politically identified with Hashemi Rafsanjani, he resigned from his position as chief negotiator after the election of Mahmud Ahmadinejad to the presidency in June 2005. With Ahmadinejad's election, the old establishment became apprehensive about the new president's ultraconservative and populist policies, policies that threaten not only the domestic status quo but also Iran's security.[43] And so in October 2005 the chairman of the Expediency Council since 1997, none other than Ali-Akbar Hashemi Rafsanjani, managed to extract a letter from the Leader that granted the Expediency Council broad supervisory powers over all three branches of government. Whether this move will have a moderating effect on the new administration's policymaking is impossible to tell at this point, but it shows that rivalries among institutions over policymaking powers have not disappeared now that both the presidency and Parliament are dominated by conservatives.

In the course of the 1988 revision of the Constitution, a body formed some years earlier was added to the official institutional structure: the National Security Council, whose members include the heads of the three branches of government, top military commanders, the foreign minister, the minister of information (that is, intelligence), and a few other figures named by the Leader. It has emerged as the nation's highest policymaking body in matters of foreign and security policy, which, in the case of the Islamic Republic, includes the struggle against what is officially called "Western cultural aggression."

The Council of Guardians does not have a major policymaking role, but its six lay members are present in Parliament when it is in session and have at times attempted to work with sympathetic MPs to introduce legislation. As for Parliament itself, it has been largely emasculated as a policymaking body by the unelected bodies mentioned earlier. Legislative proposals come before it either from the cabinet or from a minimum of twenty-five MPs, and while successive Parliaments have tried to create frameworks for conducting economic policies and changing the penal and civil codes, much of their activities have been stymied by the Council of Guardians.

Areas where the executive branch of government (prime minister until 1989, president since then) and Parliament have had an impact on state policy include setting the state budget, providing and regulating social and welfare services, and handling territorial administration, which includes redrawing provincial borders. Beginning in the mid-1980s, for instance, the MPs of the northwestern city of Ardabil campaigned for the creation of a new province around their city. Young men from Ardabil having died in disproportionate numbers in the Iran–Iraq war, the people of the city used the moral leverage that their sacrifices gave them to renew their demands with greater fervor after the war ended in 1988. All sorts of civic associations mobilized for the demand, which was expressed inside Parliament by the MPs. In the end, the administration of President Hashemi Rafsanjani introduced a bill in Parliament providing for the new province. The bill was hotly debated, and it finally passed in a secret vote in early 1993.[44]

The extensive powers of the Leader and the existence of such unelected decisionmaking bodies as the Council of Guardians, the Expediency Council, and the National Security Council severely limit the policymaking role of the elected officials: the president, the individual cabinet members named by him and approved by Parliament, and Parliament itself. Popular sovereignty is thus severely undermined.

## State Institutions Not Mentioned in the Constitution

The role of elected officials is further limited by councils that are not mentioned expressly in the Constitution and that were established for the express purpose of formulating state policy in a particular field. The most prominent of these is the Supreme Council for the Cultural Revolution, which was set up by order of Khomeini in 1986 to perpetuate the policies unleashed during the Cultural Revolution of the early 1980s that purged universities of leftists and secularists. Its tasks include determining not only state policies in the realms of culture, education, and research, but also "the spread and reinforcement of the influence of Islamic culture in all areas of society." Its supremacy over Parliament can be seen from the fact that in recent years the Council of Guardians has at times vetoed legislation on the grounds that it contradicted policies determined by the Supreme Council for the Cultural Revolution, the latter having the approval of the Leader.

## Power Centers and the Difficulty of Policy Coordination

Given the existence of multiple power centers, policies are often not coordinated, as some state institutions make and implement their own policies independently of the relevant ministries. This includes the Judiciary, which does not limit itself to implementing the law but in fact takes it into its own hands, and the Revolutionary Guards, who wage their own struggle against dissent and pursue a foreign policy independent of that of the foreign ministry and even the National Security Council.

The impact of these inconsistencies became particularly apparent under President Khatami, when the dispute between reformists and conservatives added an ideological dimension to the diffuse, ill-defined, and overlapping competencies of many state bodies. A few examples will illustrate this.

Under Khatami, who had been a liberalizing minister of culture between 1982 and 1992, the ministry of culture, which controls censorship and issues licenses for newspapers and journals, adopted more liberal policies, inaugurating a period of press freedom and diversity. But the Judiciary, headed by a conservative ally of the Leader, used its powers to close down newspapers and indict and jail reformist journalists and editors who had incurred the displeasure of conservatives. For every newspaper that was closed down, the ministry of culture would issue a new license and the newspaper would appear under a new name.[45] But by 2000 the most critical voices had been silenced by the Judiciary and its allies in the armed forces.

Another example comes from the security apparatus. In late 1998, six months after the commander of the Revolutionary Guards had threatened violence against opponents of the regime, a number of opposition politicians, journalists, and writers were killed in what became known as the "chain murders." Khatami insisted on an investigation and persuaded Khamenei to give his consent. Soon it became clear that the murders had been carried out by members of the ministry of information. This led to a purge in the ministry, which operates under the authority of the president and of Parliament.[46] While the ministry of information subsequently became more tolerant of dissent and respectful of the law, the Revolutionary Guards and the Judiciary proceeded to set up their own parallel intelligence organizations, replete with prosecutors and prisons, to pursue the conservatives' agenda of suppressing dissent.[47]

A final example is from foreign policy. Beginning at the end of the 1980s, a number of foreign ministry officials began calling for a policy that would privilege Iran's national interest in light of *realpolitik* rather than the pursuit of worldwide revolution. Tirelessly arguing their case and demonstrating the cost for Iran of remaining on the margins of world diplomacy, they managed to inflect foreign policy with a number of countries, except the United States and Israel. But while government officials engaged in diplomacy denied that Iran meddled in the internal affairs of other countries, various state or parastatal institutions pursued separate activist foreign policy agendas. Thus, when in 1998 the ministry of foreign affairs reached an agreement with Britain to the effect that Iran would do nothing to carry out the death penalty imposed by Khomeini in 1988 on British author Salman Rushdie, the parastatal Second of Khordad Foundation immediately increased the $2 million bounty it had put on the author's head in 1989. Although the director of this foundation is appointed by the Leader, its administrative and financial autonomy from the government enabled the latter to claim that the foundation was not a state entity.[48] Likewise, while the foreign ministry under Khatami repeatedly stated that Iran would do nothing to impede the Arab-Israeli peace process, which the Iranian government deemed doomed in advance anyway, various organizations (such as the IRGC) continue to channel funds to the Palestinian Islamic Jihad organization, which carries out suicide attacks on targets in Israel and the occupied territories. These inconsistencies have seriously damaged Iran's credibility on the international scene, as Iranian negotiators seem unable to deliver on their commitments.

## Economic Policymaking

One of the most contentious topics in the postrevolutionary era is economic policymaking. From the very outset, the founders of the Islamic Republic and the new elite in the ministries and parastatal organizations had fundamentally differing views on what the best approach was to foster economic development. Initially, those who favored a more state-centered approach to development dominated policymaking through the Parliament, ministries, and such institutions as the Construction Jihad. In the 1980s the state played a critical role in rationing hard currency, setting prices for consumer goods, and using the public banking system to distribute loans to key sectors of the economy. The logic of state control found support at the time in large part due to the requirements of war, the political necessity of redistributing the assets of the numerous industrialists who had been forced into exile, and the fact that international investment had come to a standstill.

A liberal approach to development that placed greater emphasis on the private sector and market mechanisms began to dominate policymaking circles in the late 1980s. This was encouraged by the conclusion of the Iran–Iraq war and the global rise of neoliberal development agendas in the wake of the Soviet Union's demise. The major impetus to redirect economic policies, however, was the general economic recession and poor performance of the economy (see Figure 16.7 and discussion later in this chapter). Thus, both the Rafsanjani and Khatami administrations tried to restructure Iran's economy by selling state-owned assets, lifting trade restrictions, and encouraging private and foreign investment. These policy initiatives have had mixed results. Iran liberalized its trade regime, with ministries and procurement boards now playing a less pronounced role. Furthermore, private banks and industries take advantage of incentives to export goods. Nonetheless, the deregulation of the economy has also led to hardship and has therefore faced opposition. On the one hand, many state employees and those who rely on state subsidies have been hurt by economic insecurity and inflation. Many of these Iranians were probably receptive to Ahmadinejad's pro-welfare and anti-inequality message, a message that harkened back to the economic approaches of the 1980s. On the other hand, the government's attempt to reform the economy has challenged the economic powers and vested interests of the large economic foundations that control large portions of Iran's commercial, industrial, and agricultural sectors, and that are largely unaccountable to the Parliament, the central bank, and development policymaking bodies.

Khatami's and the reformists' attempt to introduce greater transparency and competition into the economy was limited by the economic foundations' and parastatal organizations' autonomous and privileged access to resources and markets. Thus, any

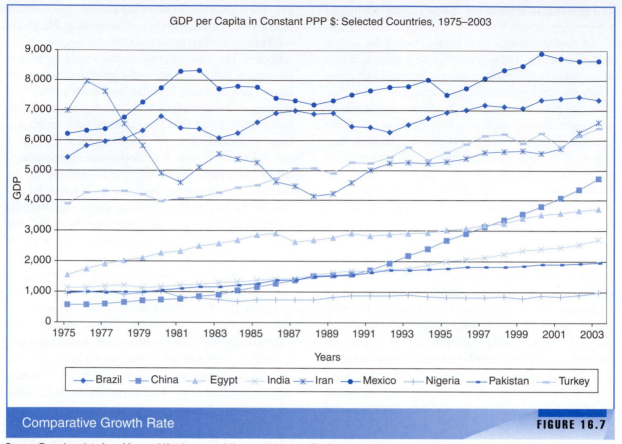

GDP per Capita in Constant PPP $: Selected Countries, 1975–2003

Comparative Growth Rate

**FIGURE 16.7**

Source: Based on data from Massoud Karshenas and Hassan Hakimian, "Oil, Economic Diversification and the Democratic Process in Iran," *Iranian Studies* 38, no. 1 (March 2005), 67–90.

attempt to reform the economy, boost productivity, or direct investment toward exports must address the inequality and inconsistencies of the parallel economy controlled by these organizations. To date, those who favor liberalizing Iran's economy have been unable to limit the power of the parastatals or even persuade large numbers of Iranians that such an economic reform would benefit them, and this policy bottleneck thus remains unaddressed in practice.

## POLICY OUTCOMES

### Incoherent Policies

The result of the multiplicity of policymaking bodies is frequent incoherence and sometimes paralysis. On a positive note, this incoherence has prevented the system from becoming totalitarian, as the overlapping spheres of activity of various state institutions have

made centralized control of public life well nigh impossible. To illustrate this point, let us look at one example from cultural policy, which is of supreme importance for a regime dedicated to changing the nation's culture.

Traditionally, the ulema have frowned on music, fearing that it will whet listeners' appetites for illicit pleasures, such as wine and fornication—an association not unknown in the West, as the triad "wine, women, and song" attests. After the revolution, most forms of music were officially banned in Iran. But given the impossibility of suppressing music entirely, Khomeini relaxed the prohibitions in a series of edicts. Inside the ministry of culture—whose official name is Ministry of Culture and Islamic Guidance—a general directorate for music has the task of defining guidelines for what musicians can do in public. Officially, for instance, the 6/8 rhythm, the basis of most Iranian dances, is outlawed; women may not sing solo in front of an audience that includes men; and certain poems by some of Iran's greatest poets, such as Hafez of Shiraz (1326–1390), that castigate the bigotry of the religious classes may not be sung at concerts. When musicians produce a tape, this directorate has the task of granting or withholding a license to have it distributed commercially. This arrangement would seem to give the ministry total authority over musical life, except that another organization, the Islamic Propaganda Organization operating under the auspices of the Leader, has an arts section that also contains a music department. This department issues licenses for recordings independently of the ministry of culture and operates a state-of-the-art recording studio that musicians can rent. Paradoxically, it is more liberal than its ministerial counterpart, rumor having it that the Leader is secretly a lover and connoisseur of classical Persian music. Moreover, the state radio and television monopoly maintains its own music bureaucracy, which decides independently of the other two what can be broadcast. The result is that musicians can play one bureaucracy against the other, enhancing their chances of getting around restrictions.[49]

## Spreading Progress and Prosperity

The chief complaint of the revolutionaries had been that the Shah's policies failed to benefit the majority of Iranians. While succeeding administrations in the Islamic Republic have been on the whole indifferent to the interests of the educated upper middle class, they have tried to adopt policies that will improve the lot of the poor.

The state educational system is astonishingly good, given the limitations imposed by the political system. Iranian students regularly win medals at international science olympiads, and literacy rates have continued rising, reaching 84 percent for men and 70 percent for women by 2000, up from 48 percent and less than 25 percent, respectively, in 1970.[50]

After pronatalist policies in the 1980s, the government realized that birth rates had to be brought down, and it inaugurated a multifaceted policy of facilitating birth control. All forms of contraception are widely distributed and subsidized both in cities and in villages, everywhere clinics offer free sterilization to men and women, and the state actively encourages couples to have "only two children, be they boys or girls." All

over Iran couples do indeed have fewer children than their parents' generation. But for the foreseeable future Iran's population will keep rising, as the very numerous Iranians born in the 1980s are beginning to have children of their own. The current growth rate of the Iranian population is 1.3 percent, one of the lowest in the Middle East.

Health care is another area of considerable progress. Small clinics staffed by paramedics serve many villages, and there is no shortage of physicians. While the quality of medical care may not always be very high, its availability to the general population is respectable even when compared with rich Western countries. These rural social and economic development programs are successful partly because they have been spearheaded by the local communities rather than by experts from distant urban areas who typically are unaware of the local needs or social and cultural conditions.

Much effort has gone into improvements in the countryside. Paved roads now connect all towns and many villages, and many villages have clean water and electricity. But in spite of the state's efforts to create a welfare state financed by oil income, most Iranians struggle to make ends meet. To some extent this is because the middle class has grown tremendously. People whose parents were illiterate and poor peasants now aspire to a middle-class lifestyle; they expect to eat meat every day, send their children to good schools, and have decent housing. Table 16.3 compares some basic human development indicators for the year 2003 of Iran with those of a few comparable countries.[51]

The provision of basic services to the general population has been quite successful. Obviously, more than three decades of high oil income have made a difference, for in many ways the indicators for Iran are closer to those of Turkey than to those of Egypt or Pakistan. However, many Iranians are unwilling to credit the government for this, and impute it to the natural development of a country with a large oil income. It is often argued that with better planning, more competent management, and an acceptance of Saddam Hussein's offer to end the Iran–Iraq war in 1982, the situation might be much better still. Moreover, as Figure 16.7 reveals, over the last three decades Iran's overall macroeconomic performance has fallen behind the newly developing countries in Latin America or East Asia. The per capita growth rates have not kept pace with the emerging economic

**TABLE 16.3**

## Comparison of Development Indicators, 2003

| Country | Population | Population Growth | Life Expectancy | Infant Mortality (before age 1) | Access to Sanitation (%) |
|---|---|---|---|---|---|
| Iran | 66 million | 1.3 | 69 | 33 | 84 |
| Turkey | 70 million | 1.5 | 69 | 33 | 83 |
| Egypt | 67 million | 1.8 | 69 | 33 | 68 |
| Pakistan | 148 million | 2.4 | 64 | 74 | 54 |
| India | 1 billion | 1.5 | 63 | 63 | 30 |
| China | 1.3 billion | 0.6 | 71 | 30 | 44 |
| Mexico | 102 million | 1.4 | 74 | 23 | 77 |
| Nigeria | 136 million | 2.4 | 45 | 98 | 38 |

| Country | Literacy/Men | Literacy/Women | Education as Part of GNP | GNP/Capita $ | GNP/PPP $ |
|---|---|---|---|---|---|
| Iran | 84 | 70 | 4.9 | 2,010 | 7,000 |
| Turkey | 94 | 79 | 3.7 | 2,240 | 6,710 |
| Egypt | 67 | 44 | ? | 1,390 | 3,940 |
| Pakistan | 57 | 28 | 1.8 | 520 | 2,040 |
| India | 68 | 45 | 4.1 | 540 | 2,880 |
| China | 95 | 87 | ? | 1,100 | 4,980 |
| Mexico | 93 | 89 | 5.2 | 6,230 | 8,980 |
| Nigeria | 74 | 59 | ? | 350 | 900 |

PPP: Purchasing Power Parity.

powers of China and India.[52] In fact, Iran's growth indicators have been quite volatile, with a rather extended period of depression in the 1980s due to war, sanctions, high birth rates, and deficient economic policies. Even with the gradual improvement in per capita gross domestic product (GDP) since the early 1990s, which was largely due to the rise in oil prices, unemployment remains the number-one worry for young people, and the growth rate of the economy is not nearly enough to absorb the growing population. In fact, youth unemployment increased from 14.8 percent in 1996 to 27.5 percent in 2001.[53]

### Islamicization of Society

Another motivation of much policymaking is the desire to roll back secularism and spread Islamic moral values among the population. Since the early 1980s alcohol consumption is banned except for the non-Muslim minorities; veiling is enforced in public spaces; the state is in theory committed to minimizing contact between unrelated men and women; the religious content of education is vastly expanded; and gruesome physical punishments chastise adulterers, homosexuals, and other offenders of religious morality.[54] Divine law, as interpreted by the state, also allows capital punishment, and in 2004 the number of death penalties carried out in Iran (159) was second only to China (3,400), Iran coming before Vietnam (64) and the United States (59).[55]

Outwardly, the Islamicization of society has been a success. Women cover their hair in public, people are in general more familiar with religious doctrine than before the revolution, the country has more mosques, Friday congregational prayers are routine in towns and cities, and all flights of Iran Air (the national flag carrier) begin with a prayer. Even the best hotels serve no alcohol, even to foreign guests. Underneath the surface, however, the situation is more complicated. Prostitution is rife, driven by poverty. Over two million Iranians are drug addicts. Bootlegging flourishes, often with the connivance of the forces of order, who get a cut. As education has become longer and the marriage age has gone up, young people are much more likely to have premarital sex than their parents' generation, at least in Tehran. Corruption operates at almost all levels, from the petty official who will do his job only if he is paid a bribe to the relatives of the top leaders who have enriched themselves by controlling economic life.

All of this should not be construed to mean that Iranians have become irreligious. But religious practice has become more private, as the influence of clerics over religious life has declined. One study, comparing data gathered in 1975 and in 2001, demonstrates that while levels of personal religiosity (such as frequency of prayer) have remained relatively constant, participation in organized religion (such as attendance of congregational Friday prayers) has declined, reflecting a growing ambivalence toward state-sponsored public religious practices.[56]

Iranian Islam has always contained an anticlerical strain, as believers have always criticized clerics for their greed and hypocrisy. The ulema's assumption of power in the Islamic Republic has given a new fillip to this tendency. Taxi drivers are known not to stop for clerics, many of whom have taken to wearing civilian clothes in public. Foreign observers are often astonished by how few turbaned clerics one sees in the streets of Tehran.

The rise of anticlericalism has led some of the more thoughtful members of the Shiite clergy to revisit the relations between "church" and state and to call for a separation of the two. They do so not because they advocate secularism, but out of concern for the collective reputation of the ulema. In the Muslim world advocates of the separation of "church" and state had always been secularists. In Iran for the first time *religious* arguments are being made for that separation on the grounds that coercively imposed religion harms spirituality.[57] One may even wonder whether at least some of the pious people who voted for Mahmud Ahmadinejad in the last presidential election did so in order to rebuke the ulema, many of whom—such as the losing candidate, Hashemi Rafsanjani—have joined the country's ruling class and are seen to have been corrupted by power.

## Gender Relations

One of the key reproaches that Islamists addressed to the Shah's regime before the revolution was that its promotion of Western lifestyles turned women into sex objects and was generally conducive to moral corruption and sexual depravity. Hence the effort to reorder gender relations and place them on an authentic Islamic footing.

Looked at from a Western perspective, the legal status of women improved under the Pahlavi monarchy, whereas the majority of society remained more conservative than the laws governing it. After the revolution much of the legislation that reduced the gender gap was repealed. According to the Islamic penal code introduced in 1981, the value of a woman's life is half that of a man's, in the sense that the law of the talion ("an eye for an eye") instituted by that code explicitly states that the blood-money of a woman is half of that of a man.[58] In practice, this means that if a man kills another man, the relatives of the victim can either ask for the execution of the murderer or accept a legally fixed blood-money. But if a man kills a woman, her relatives can ask for the murderer's execution only if they pay half a man's blood-money. By the same token, in courts of law the testimony of one man is worth that of two women. In some cases (such as adultery, murder), a woman's testimony does not count at all. A man can easily divorce his wife, whereas in principle a woman can initiate divorce proceedings only under exceptional circumstances; polygamy is recognized under the law. To travel abroad, a wife needs the formal permission of her husband, but the latter can leave the country as he pleases. The foreign wife of an Iranian man can easily acquire Iranian citizenship, whereas an Iranian woman cannot obtain Iranian citizenship for her foreign husband and her children from that husband.[59]

In addition to these legal restrictions on women's rights, the Islamic Republic has instituted all sorts of ad hoc discriminations. Many fields of study, such as agronomy and mining engineering, were closed to female students at the universities on the assumption that they were too rough for women. Women's sports were severely restricted because the attire worn by female athletes is incompatible with veiling. This differential treatment of men and women is in stark violation of the International Convention on Civil and Political Rights, an international treaty that prohibits discrimination on religious and gender grounds. Iran acceded to the Convention in 1975 and remained a party after its regime changed. But from the point of view of theocracy, divine law obviously supercedes obligations incurred under international law.

In spite of these legal restrictions, Iranian women have continuously increased their participation in public life and their presence in the public sphere since strict Islamic law began to be enforced in the early 1980s.[60] At the same time they have challenged the logic of patriarchy. There are a number of reasons for this seemingly paradoxical development. The widespread participation of women in the mass anti-Shah demonstrations of 1978 made it unlikely that their interest in public affairs would end once the revolution was over. After the war against Iraq broke out in 1980 and millions of men were serving at the front, this situation forced many women to do jobs hitherto performed by men. Many women became their families' main breadwinners. Furthermore, the aspiration to a middle-class existence awakened by the revolution, coupled with the slow growth of the economy, has meant that women increasingly supplement their husbands' income by joining the labor force. And given the strictly enforced rules on veiling and gender interaction in the public sphere, more traditional women have felt more at ease entering the public sphere. In addition, more traditional men are less reluctant to let their wives, daughters, or sisters work outside the house. Restrictions that are deeply annoying to nontraditional women have thus had a liberating effect on religiously observant women—and these constitute, after all, a majority of the female population.

The relative strength of the antitraditional attitude toward women's roles in society is reflected in the comparative results of the World Value Survey. For instance, while only 4 percent of Egyptians and 12 percent of Jordanians disagree with the statement that "marriage has become an outdated institution," 17 percent of surveyed Iranians agree.[61] A plurality of surveyed Iranians disagree with the statement that "women need to have children in order to feel satisfied," whereas only 12 percent of Egyptians and 9 percent of Jordanians disagree with it.[62] Finally, 40 percent of Iranians agreed with the statement that "a working mother can develop intimate relationships with her children just like a nonworking mother," a rate that is double that of surveyed Egyptians and Jordanians.[63] Thus, despite the regime's initial attempts to inculcate a traditional image and role for women in the family and society, Iranian men and women seem to hold a less narrow view of women.

The visitor to today's Iran encounters women everywhere: they staff government agencies, work in offices, sell goods in shops, own and run businesses. Most dramatically, women now constitute over 60 percent of the student body at the universities, restrictions on what they can study having been gradually lifted throughout the 1990s to the point where none remain. In Persian literature, the traditional emphasis on poetry has given way to a boom in the writing of novels—and most novelists are women. In sports, a daughter of then-President Hashemi Rafsanjani took over women's sports in the early 1990s. Using her father's clout, she instituted a system whereby women compete under international rules and in normal athletic gear but at locations to which no men are admitted. This change led, incidentally, to many more women becoming coaches, referees, paramedics, and state sports officials.[64] Even veiling is now enforced less strictly, and the partial covering of the head that hardliners call "mal-veiling" has spread. None other than Khomeini's granddaughter complained in an interview with an American journalist about the state's intrusiveness in this regard.[65]

The widening gap between women's growing participation in public life and the legal system governing their society, and the many-voiced debates to which this discrepancy has given rise, have had repercussions for Islam itself in Iran. Given the impossibility of criticizing any state of affairs from a secular perspective, feminists couch their arguments in Islamic terms. This has led to the emergence of "Islamic feminism," which is espoused by both truly observant Muslim women and by secular women who have no other way of articulating their demands. Given the continued religiosity of Iranians in general, Islamic feminism has been arguably more effective in raising the gender consciousness of the average woman than secular feminism would have been. These Islamic feminists are discreetly supported by a few sympathetic clerics who have helped them to contest discriminatory policies or laws by proposing ways to circumvent them or even suggesting alternative readings of the relevant scriptural passages and legal principles. Small gains have thus been made. Take the issue of divorce. According to Islamic law, marriage is a contract whose clauses have to be agreed on freely by both husband and wife. A woman has always had the right to ask that her marriage contract include a clause giving her the right to initiate divorce proceedings, but this clause had to be added on to the standard contract issued by the state. Very few bridegrooms consented to it. Since the early 1980s, however, the standard contract includes the clause, meaning that for the woman not to get the right to divorce, bride and bridegroom have to ask for its removal—to which nowadays few educated women consent.

The greater success of women in higher education and the fact that the vast majority of Iranian drug addicts are men, coupled with the continued existence of domestic violence against women, have led Shirin Ebadi, the woman who more than any other personifies women's struggles and occasional successes, to quip that Iran does not have a "women's question" but a "men's question."

## Foreign Policy

Under the Shah, Iran was an ally of the United States, but the Islamic revolution dramatically changed the foreign policy orientation of the country. Like the French, Russian, Chinese, and Cuban revolutionaries before them, Iran's Islamic revolutionaries saw themselves as the vanguard of a vast revolutionary wave that would encompass other countries as well. According to the preamble of the Constitution of 1979, the role of the army and the IRGC is not limited to "securing the borders" of the country but includes "struggling to spread the rule of divine law in the world." Managing the inherent tension between an ideological commitment to helping to overthrow or weaken other governments on the one hand, and dealing with these governments on a daily basis on the other, has posed a tremendous challenge.

Beginning in the early 1990s, "national interest" rather than "export of the revolution" came to dominate the foreign policy agenda. The best example of this trend is the discreet support Iran gave to Christian Armenia in its conflict with Muslim (and predominantly Shiite) Azerbaijan in the war that followed the breakup of the Soviet Union in the mid-1990s. But, as elsewhere in the world, there is little consensus as to what constitutes a nation's national interest, and many in Iran argue that Iran's national interest demands the solidification of its ties with the rest of the Islamic world.

Ultimately, the foreign policy of the Islamic Republic is driven by a "Third Worldist" desire to escape the hegemony of the Western world. In the parlance of Iran's leaders, Western hegemony is referred to as "world arrogance." In its struggle against "world arrogance," Iran has sought alliances, and these can be conceptualized in terms of three concentric circles. The outermost circle consists of Third World nations and in the beginning even included such groups as the Irish Republican Party (IRA) that fought British rule in Northern Ireland. The middle circle is made up of Muslim countries and movements, and the innermost one is constituted by the Shiites in West and South Asia (Lebanon, Iraq, Bahrain, Afghanistan, Pakistan).

In many Third World countries the revolution of 1979 was greeted with sympathy. However, the subsequent triumph of hard-line Islamists put a damper on pro-Iranian sympathies in non-Muslim nations. For instance, then-President Ali Khamenei's refusal to shake hands with female officials, as strict Islamic norms dictated, while on a state visit in Zimbabwe in 1986 caused a diplomatic incident. Sunni Islamists, for their part, were divided over support for revolutionary Iran. As the *Shiite* nature of the *Islamic* Republic became ever more apparent, and as Khomeini refused to accept Saddam Hussein's offer to end the Iran–Iraq war, thus causing continued intra-Muslim bloodshed, most Sunni Islamists turned away from Iran. This estrangement was encouraged by Saudi Arabia, because the Wahhabi version of Sunni Islam dominant in that country is hostile to Shiism. With American connivance, Saudi money helped create a Sunni *cordon sanitaire* around Iran to contain the spread of revolutionary Shiism in such countries as Afghanistan and Pakistan. Thus, the second Islamic state in the region, that of the Taliban in Afghanistan, was implacably hostile to the Islamic Republic of Iran. This hostility reached the point where a number of Iranian diplomats in that country were actually killed.[66] Today Iran maintains very few client movements among Sunnis, most notably the Palestinian Islamic Jihad.

This leaves Twelver Shiites as the only group among which Iranian efforts to spread the revolution have been somewhat successful. The founding of Lebanon's Hizballah in the early 1980s was facilitated by Iran, and Iran continues to support the party and its social welfare activities financially. Iran also sponsored formation in Iran of the Supreme Council for the Islamic Revolution of Iraq (SCIRI), a party that, ironically, has come to play a major role in Iraq thanks to the American intervention that led to the ouster of the Saddam Hussein regime.

In the aftermath of September 11, 2001, Iran has found itself surrounded by U.S.-installed governments in Afghanistan and Iraq and by U.S. troops and military bases in the countries to its north and south. At the same time, Al-Qaeda and other anti-Shiite groups pose a threat to the Islamic Republic's claim to constitute the vanguard of a worldwide Islamic revolution. Even within the world of Twelver Shiism, however, the Iranian theocracy may yet lose some influence. If Iraq stabilizes under Shiite hegemony, Najaf could conceivably regain its centrality and independence as a center of Shiite learning, thereby attracting Shiite scholars who do not share Khomeini's notion of *velayat-e faqih*, including even Iranians.

In its relations with the West and the Soviet bloc, the early Islamic Republic had as its motto "Neither East nor West." Iran was an American ally under the Shah, but after the revolution it joined the nonaligned movement. In practice, however, Iran's foreign policy, like that of many other Third World "nonaligned" countries, was far more anti-Western than anti-Soviet. In the case of the Islamic Republic, this stance reflects the revolutionaries' mistrust of a West that had supported the hated Shah, and the geographic proximity of the Soviet Union, whose occupation of neighboring Afghanistan in December 1979 was a constant reminder of the need for caution. The Islamic Republic has maintained cordial relations with the Soviet Union and Russia, but Iran has not had diplomatic relations with the United States since the United States severed them in response to the seizure of American diplomats as hostages in November 1979. Iranians have paid a heavy price for their government's hostility to the West. In the last stages of the war against Iraq, most Western powers discreetly assisted the Iraqi side. The United States has maintained an economic embargo on Iran. For instance, Iranian airlines have difficulty purchasing a sufficient number of modern passenger aircraft and adequate spare parts for the old ones, forcing them to keep flying old Russian planes or Boeing jets purchased before the revolution. As a result, "Iran's civil aviation sector suffers from one of the world's highest rates of accidents and incidents."[67]

After Khomeini's death, presidents Hashemi Rafsanjani and Khatami tried to lessen Iran's diplomatic isolation. Relations with Arab countries, most of which had supported Iraq in the war, improved, and Iran made an effort to mend its ties with Europe and Japan. In the 1990s, the European Union embarked on a policy of "critical dialogue" with Iran, which offered Iran concessions in exchange for improvement in the field of human rights. During the Khatami years the policies of the government did indeed become less repressive, but given the overall control of unelected bodies none of these liberalizing measures could be institutionalized.

The main issue confronting current Iranian diplomacy in its relations with the West is Iran's nuclear program. Since the days of the Shah, successive Iranian governments have declared that they are not interested in developing nuclear weapons. The official line of the government of the Islamic Republic is that all weapons of mass destruction are contrary to Islamic ethics. Iran is a signatory of the Nuclear Nonproliferation Treaty, whose Article IV grants its signatories the "inalienable right" to "research, develop, produce, and utilize" nuclear technology for peaceful purposes. On that basis, the Iranian government has embarked on a vast program to develop a self-sufficient nuclear industry by mastering the fuel cycle in which uranium is enriched to produce the fuel needed to power reactors. Western countries worry that this knowledge would also allow Iran to produce highly enriched uranium or plutonium that could be used to produce nuclear weapons. What lends this worry a certain plausibility is Iran's development of long-distance missiles to which nuclear warheads could be fitted, and the fact that some nuclear facilities and experiments were kept secret until an exiled opposition group revealed their existence in 2002. At that point, the Iranian government allowed IAEA inspectors to visit them. Britain, France, and Germany have negotiated with Iran in the hope of getting the government to suspend its enrichment program, while the IAEA has not declared Iran to be in violation of its treaty obligations. As of early 2007, the negotiations were continuing.

# CONCLUSION

Iranian politics in the twentieth century were tumultuous. The century started with a constitutionalist movement seeking to make a monarchy more accountable, and ended with a reformist movement striving to make a theocracy more republican. In between these two bookends, nationalist, religious, secular, and Marxist ideologies competed for followers, while social relations were restructured by processes associated with modernization. The Pahlavi monarchy promised to usher Iran into the modern industrial age, and because of both its successes and failures in doing so, the Shah was overthrown by a mass revolution that established a republic, but one that, unlike other revolutionary regimes, incorporated the clergy.

To manage the many objectives of the revolutionaries, the Islamic Republic has created a bewildering set of institutions and organizations, many of which compete with one another and occasionally work at cross purposes. The regime has been in continuous conflict with the United States and some regional powers, such as Israel. It has provided social welfare to many of its citizens, which has resulted in outcomes that were unintended by the establishment, whose authority has increasingly been challenged. By the admission of many of its own leaders, "the economy is sick" and "social pathologies" tarnish all layers of society. Unlike most other states in the region, which have almost completely muzzled dissent, contestation is pervasive and sometimes public even among state officials.

How has a regime that faces so many challenges survived for a quarter of a century, and what are the prospects for significant change? The irony is that the same institutions that have created contestation and allowed a degree of pluralism in Iran have also contributed to the regime's survival and ability to withstand opposition.[68] The fragmented nature of the state enables differences to emerge and persist, but it is this very fragmentation that prevents the aggregation of interests. Thus, even though many of the founders of the Islamic Republic have defected from the regime or called for quite fundamental changes, they have not had the leverage to restructure the regime. Elite politics in Iran today is factional politics, not party politics encompassing debates over specific policies and specified platforms and visions of the future. Factionalism is endemic to the system: although the presidency and Parliament have been controlled by the same party since June 2005, Parliament refused to confirm the first three of the president's nominees for the important post of minister of oil.

Meanwhile, a myriad of patron-client networks, in conjunction with a robust coercive apparatus and an individualist political culture, creates a fragmented state with divisions at all levels of society. Corporate and associational interests are ill defined and undermined by personalism, and even ideologically similar groups often battle with one another over access to assets. State-society relations as they are constituted now hinder coordination and alliance-building, which are essential for mass mobilization, and prevent the emergence of public deliberation and consensus-building.

The problems faced by the Islamic Republic have reopened the debate on the proper relation between religion and politics in Iran. Going farther than revisiting Islamic law, some reformist Muslims are questioning whether religious law is as central to Islam as, say, ethics or personal experience of transcendence. These reformers impute the current preoccupation with Islamic law, *shari'a*, in Muslim governance to the prominence of the ulema in Muslim society, pointing out that the ulema are, after all, merely legal scholars. This new tendency reconnects with other important traditions within Islam, as exemplified by the beloved Persian poet Hafez of Shiraz, who wrote:

> Do what you want, but don't hurt anyone
> For that is the only sin in our *shari'a*

As we said at the beginning of this chapter, Iran was the first state in which Islamists got to exercise political power. The problems they have faced, the forces they have unleashed, and the responses they have elicited from society could have profound implications for political Islam in the rest of the world. In practice, however, Iran's experience remains of limited relevance to Islamists elsewhere. Given the Shiite nature of the Iranian state, Sunni Islamists can always brush aside the intellectual and social impasses encountered by Iran's regime in its effort to institute Islamic law in all spheres of social life by claiming that they are due to Iranians' sectarian deviation from "true" Islam.

## KEY TERMS

Assembly of Experts

Basij

Council of Guardians

Ebadi, Shirin

Expediency Council

Islamists

Hashemi Rafsanjani,
Ali-Akbar

Khamenei, Ali

Khatami, Mohammad

Khomeini, Ruhollah

Leader

Majles

Mossadegh,
Mohammad

multiple power centers

Pahlavi, Mohammad-Reza
Shah

parastatal foundations

*Pasdaran* (Islamic
Revolutionary Guard
Corps)

rentier states

*shari'a*

Sunnis

theocracy

Twelver Shiism

Tudeh party

ulema

*velayat-e faqih*

## SUGGESTED READINGS

Abrahamian, Ervand. *Iran Between Two Revolutions*. Princeton; NJ: Princeton University Press, 1982.

Adelkhah, Fariba. *Being Modern in Iran*. New York: Columbia University Press, 2000.

Amir Arjomand, Said. *The Turban for the Crown: The Islamic Revolution in Iran*. New York: Oxford University Press, 1988.

Amuzegar, Jahangir. *Iran's Economy Under the Islamic Republic*. London: I.B. Tauris, 1997.

Ansari, Ali M. *Iran, Islam and Democracy: The Politics of Managing Change*. London: Royal Institute for International Affairs, 2000.

Ashraf, Ahmad. "The Appeal of Conspiracy Theories to Persians." *Princeton Papers* 5 (Winter 1997): 57–88.

Ashraf, Ahmad, and Ali Banuazizi. "The State, Classes and Modes of Mobilization in the Iranian Revolution." *State, Culture, and Society* 1, no. 3 (Spring 1985): 3–39.

Atabaki, Touraj. *Azerbaijan: Ethnicity and Autonomy in Twentieth-Century Iran*. London: British Academic Press, 1993.

Azimi, Fakhreddin. *Iran: The Crisis of Democracy 1941–1953*. New York: St. Martin's, 1989.

Bakhash, Shaul. *The Reign of the Ayatollahs: Iran and the Islamic Revolution*. New York: Basic Books, 1984.

———. "The Politics of Land, Law, and Social Justice in Iran." *Middle East Journal* 43, no. 2 (1989): 186–201.

Baktiari, Bahman. *Parliamentary Politics in Revolutionary Iran: The Institutionalization of Factional Politics*. Gainesville: Florida University Press, 1996.

Bayat, Assef. *Street Politics: Poor People's Movements in Iran*. New York: Columbia University Press, 1997.

Bill, James A. *The Eagle and the Lion: The Tragedy of American-Iranian Relations*. New Haven, CT: Yale University Press, 1988.

Binder, Leonard. *Iran: Political Development in a Changing Society*. Berkeley: University of California Press, 1964.

Buchta, Wilfried. *Who Rules Iran? The Structure of Power in the Islamic Republic*. Washington, DC: Washington Institute for Near East Policy, 2000.

Chehabi, H. E. "Religion and Politics in Iran: How Theocratic Is the Islamic Republic?" *Daedalus* 120, no. 1 (Summer 1991): 69–91.

———. "The Political Regime of the Islamic Republic of Iran in Comparative Perspective." *Government and Opposition* 36, no. 1 (Winter 2001): 48–70.

Gasiorowski, Mark J. *U.S. Foreign Policy and the Shah: Building a Client State in Iran*. Ithaca, NY: Cornell University Press, 1991.

Hoogland, Eric, ed. *Twenty Years of Islamic Revolution: Political and Social Transformation in Iran Since 1979*. Syracuse, NY: Syracuse University Press, 2002.

Karshenas, Massoud. *Oil, State, and Industrialization in Iran*. Cambridge: Cambridge University Press, 1990.

Keddie, Nikki R. *Modern Iran: Roots and Results of Revolution*. New Haven, CT: Yale University Press, 2003.

Keshavarzian, Arang. "Contestation Without Democracy: Elite Fragmentation in Iran." In Marsha Pripstein Posusney and Michelle Penner Angrist, eds., *Authoritarianism in the Middle East: Regimes and Resistance*. Boulder, CO: Lynne Rienner, 2005.

———. *Bazaar and State in Iran: The Politics of the Tehran Marketplace*. Cambridge: Cambridge University Press, 2007.

Kurzman, Charles. *The Unthinkable Revolution in Iran*. Cambridge: Harvard University Press, 2004.

Maloney, Suzanne. "Agents or Obstacles? Parastatal Foundations and Challenges for Iranian Development." In Parvin Alizadeh, ed., *The Economy of Iran: Dilemmas of an Islamic State*. London: I.B. Tauris, 2000.

Martin, Vanessa. *Islam and Modernism: The Persian Revolution of 1906*. London: I.B. Tauris, 1988.

Menashri, David. *Post-Revolutionary Politics in Iran: Religion, Society, and Power*. Portland, OR: Frank Cass, 2001.

Milani, Mohsen. *The Making of Iran's Islamic Revolution: From Monarchy to Islamic Republic*. 2nd ed. Boulder, CO: Westview, 1994.

Moin, Baqer. *Khomeini: Life of the Ayatollah*. London: I.B. Tauris, 1999.

Moslem, Mehdi. *Factional Politics in Post-Revolutionary Iran*. Syracuse, NY: Syracuse University Press, 2002.

Mottahedeh, Roy. *The Mantle of the Prophet: Religion and Politics in Iran*. 2nd ed. Oxford: Oneworld, 2000.

Paidar, Parvin. *Women and the Political Process in Twentieth-Century Iran*. Cambridge: Cambridge University Press, 1995.

Parsa, Misagh. *Social Origins of the Iranian Revolution*. New Brunswick, NJ: Rutgers University Press, 1989.

Sanasarian, Eliz. *Religious Minorities in Iran*. Cambridge: Cambridge University Press, 2000.

Schirazi, Asghar. *The Constitution of Iran: Politics and the State in the Islamic Republic*. London: I.B. Tauris, 1996.

Tajbakhsh, Kian. "Political Decentralization and the Creation of Local Government in Iran: Consolidation or Transformation of the Theocratic State?" *Social Research* 67, no. 2 (Summer 2000): 377–404.

Vahdat, Farzin. *God and Juggernaut: Iran's Intellectual Encounter with Modernity*. Syracuse, NY: Syracuse University Press, 2002.

Zahedi, Dariush. *The Iranian Revolution Then and Now: Indicators of Regime Instability*. Boulder, CO: Westview, 2000.

Zonis, Marvin. *The Political Elite of Iran*. Princeton, NJ: Princeton University Press, 1971.

## INTERNET RESOURCES

Iran Daily (English language daily newspaper): **www.iran-daily.com**

Ministry of Foreign Affairs, Islamic Republic of Iran: **www.mfa.gov.ir**

Payvand (news and information portal): **www.payvand.com**

*Encyclopaedia Iranica:* **www.iranica.com/newsite/**

Iranian Studies Group at MIT: **www.isg-mit.org**

The Middle East Network Information Center (MENIC), University of Texas, Austin: **menic.utexas.edu/Countries_and_Regions/Iran/**

## ENDNOTES

1. From Population Action International: (accessed at http://www.populationaction.org/news/press/news_042302_Youth.htm).

2. From the Washington Institute: (accessed at http://washingtoninstitute.org/templateC05.php?CID=1556).

3. All existing maps showing the linguistic and ethnic groups that make up Iran's population have to be used with caution. Census questions do not include ethnic or linguistic affiliation, and few areas have an ethnically or linguistically homogeneous population. Internal migrations and urbanization have uprooted many people from their original home area. Besides, ethnic self-identification is not equally important to all people. Among the Kurds, for instance, those who are Sunni are much more likely to identify subjectively as Kurds than those who are Shiites. We therefore dispense with a map here.

4. Abdul-Hadi Hairi, *Shiism and Constitutionalism in Iran* (Leiden: Brill, 1977).

5. Nikki R. Keddie, *Modern Iran: Roots and Results of Revolution* (New Haven, CT: Yale University Press, 2003), 123.

6. Mark Gasiorowski, "The 1953 *Coup d'Etat* in Iran," *International Journal of Middle East Studies* 19, no. 3 (1987): 261–86.

7. See James A. Bill, *The Eagle and the Lion: The Tragedy of American-Iranian Relations* (New Haven, CT: Yale University Press, 1988), 319–78.

8. Richard W. Cottam, *Iran and the United States: A Cold War Case Study* (Pittsburgh, PA: University of Pittsburgh Press, 1988), 156–69.

9. Ahmad Ashraf and Ali Banuazizi, "The State, Classes, and Modes of Mobilization in the Iranian Revolution," *State, Culture, and Society* 1 (Spring 1985): 3–39.

10. Misagh Parsa, *Social Origins of the Iranian Revolution* (New Brunswick, NJ: Rutgers University Press, 1989).

11. Ironically, even the shah himself believed in the omnipotence of the United States and Britain: after his ouster, he blamed these countries for having engineered his demise.

12. Ruhollah Khomeini, "Islamic Government," in *Islam and Revolution: Writings and Declarations of Imam Khomeini*, trans. and annotated by Hamid Algar (Berkeley, CA: Mizan, 1981).

13. See H. E. Chehabi, "The Political Regime of the Islamic Republic of Iran in Comparative Perspective," *Government and Opposition* 36 (Winter 2001): 48–70.

14. Kaveh Ehsani, "Islam, Modernity, and National Identity," *Middle East Insight* 11, no. 5 (July–August 1995): 48–53.

15. For the prerevolutionary period, see Hossein Mahdavy, "Patterns and Problems of Economic Development in Rentier States: The Case of Iran," in M. A. Cook, ed., *Studies in the Economic History of the Middle East: From the Rise of Islam to the Present Day* (London: Oxford University Press, 1970), 428–67. For the Islamic Republic, see Hootan Shambayati, "The Rentier State, Interest Groups, and the Paradox of Autonomy: State and Business in Turkey and Iran," *Comparative Politics* 26 (April 1994): 307–31.

16. Homa Katouzian, *The Political Economy of Modern Iran* (New York: New York University Press, 1981).

17. On these parastatal foundations, see Suzanne Maloney, "Agents or Obstacles? Parastatal Foundations and Challenges for Iranian Development," in Parvin Alizadeh, ed., *The Economy of Iran: Dilemmas of an Islamic State* (London: I.B. Tauris, 2000), 145–76.

18. Bahman Baktiari, *Parliamentary Politics in Revolutionary Iran: The Institutionalization of Factional Politics* (Gainesville: Florida University Press, 1996).

19. Abdol-Karim Lahiji, "Moruri bar vaz'-e hoquqi-ye Iranian-e gheyr-e mosalman," *Iran Nameh* 19 (1379–80/2001): 19. On the legal discrimination of women, see section discussing gender relations later in this chapter.

20. Mehran Kamrava and Houchang Hassan-Yari, "Suspended Equilibrium in Iran's Political System," *Muslim World* 94 (October 2004): 495–524.

21. Asghar Schirazi, *The Constitution of Iran: Politics and the State in the Islamic Republic* (London: I.B. Tauris, 1998), 134.

22. Mehdi Moslem, *Factional Politics in Post-Revolutionary Iran* (Syracuse, NY: Syracuse University Press, 2002).

23. Kian Tajbakhsh, "Political Decentralization and the Creation of Local Government in Iran: Consolidation or Transformation of the Theocratic State?" *Social Research* 67, no. 2 (Summer 2000): 377–404.

24. Before World War I, Westerners considered Iran and other non-Western but nominally sovereign countries, such as China and Thailand, to be "semi-civilized" nations, which had some but not all of the attributes of a full-fledged member of the international community. See Gerrit Gong, *The Standard of "Civilization" in International Society* (Cambridge: Cambridge University Press, 1984).

25. Ahmad Ashraf, "The Appeal of Conspiracy Theories to Persians," *Princeton Papers* 5 (Winter 1997): 57–88.

26. See L. Carl Brown, *International Politics and the Middle East* (Princeton, NJ: Princeton University Press, 1984), 233–52.

27. Mansoor Moaddel and Taghi Azadarmaki, "The Worldviews of Islamic Publics: The Case of Egypt, Iran, and Jordan," in Ronald Ingelhart, ed., *Human Values and Social Change: Findings From the Values Survey* (Leiden: Brill 2003), 81.

28. This line of reasoning is based on Azadeh Kian-Thiébaut, "Entrepreneurs privés: entre développement statocentique et démocratisation politique," in *Les Cahiers de l'Orient* 60 (2000): 65–92.

29. Peter J. Chelkowski and Hamid Dabashi, *Staging a Revolution: The Art of Persuasion in the Islamic Republic of Iran* (New York: New York University Press, 1999), 130–31.

30. Ehsani, "Islam, Modernity, and National Identity," 51.

31. Farideh Farahi, "The Antinomies of Iran's War Generation," in Lawrence C. Potter and Gary G. Sick, eds., *Iran, Iraq and the Legacies of War* (New York: PalgraveMacmillan, 2004), 101–20.

32. Moaddel and Azadarmaki, "The Worldviews of Islamic Publics."

33. Ahmad Sadri, "The Varieties of Religious Reform: Public Intelligentsia in Iran," in Ramin Jahanbegloo, ed., *Iran: Between Tradition and Modernity* (Lanham, MD: Lexington Books, 2004), 117–28.

34. Marvin Zonis, *The Political Elite of Iran* (Princeton, NJ: Princeton University Press, 1971).

35. Frances Bostock and Geoffrey Jones, *Planning and Power in Iran: Ebtehaj and Economic Development Under the Shahs* (London: Frank Cass, 1989).

36. Khosrow Fatemi, "Leadership by Distrust: The Shah's *Modus Operandi*," *Middle East Journal* 36 (Winter 1982): 48–61.

37. Mehran Kamrava, *The Modern Middle East: A Political History Since the First World War* (Berkeley: University of California Press, 2005), 261.

38. Figures are from Wilfried Buchta, *Who Rules Iran? The Structure of Power in the Islamic Republic* (Washington, DC: The Washington Institute for Near East Policy and the Konrad Adenauer Stiftung, 2000), 68.

39. Assef Bayat, *Street Politics: Poor People's Movements in Iran* (New York: Columbia University Press, 1997).

40. In his discussion of charismatic authority, Max Weber points out that charismatic leaders oppose tradition, and he summarizes this attitude in the famous statement ascribed to Jesus: "It has been written . . . , but *I* say unto you." *Economy and Society* (Berkeley: University of California Press, 1976), 1115.

41. Schirazi, *The Constitution of Iran*, 67–68.

42. Quoted in Said Amir Arjomand, *The Turban for the Crown: The Islamic Revolution in Iran* (New York: Oxford University Press, 1988), 182.

43. In fact, Ahmadinejad belongs to a current of thought that considers the return of the Twelfth Imam imminent. This messianic expectation sets him apart from most other leaders of the Islamic Republic and may yet be the source of friction.

44. For details, see H. E. Chehabi, "Ardabil Becomes a Province: Center-Periphery Relations in the Islamic Republic of Iran," *International Journal of Middle East Studies* 29 (Spring 1997): 235–53.

45. For an inside account, see Elaine Sciolino, *Persian Mirrors: The Elusive Face of Iran* (New York: Free Press, 2000), 248–60.

46. For details see Buchta, *Who Rules Iran?* 156–70.

47. How this multiplicity of power centers affects individuals is seen in the story of Dariush Zahedi, an Iranian-American political scientist who had met with dissidents while visiting Iran one recent summer for his research. He was arrested by the ministry of information and held prisoner for two months, before being told that, as far as the ministry was concerned, he was innocent. Except that upon leaving the prison he was immediately rearrested by the intelligence agency of the Revolutionary Guards, who held him for another two months in solitary confinement and subjected him to similar interrogations as his preceding jailers, only in a less respectful tone. He was finally released and returned to the United States through the intervention of a number of Iranian diplomats after academics in the United States had publicized his plight.

48. Maloney, "Agents or Obstacles?" 149.

49. This is based on H. E. Chehabi's conversations with music officials and musicians in Iran.

50. From Earth Policy Institute: (accessed at http://www.earth-policy.org/Updates/Update4ss.htm).

51. The data are from the 2006 edition of *Der Fischer Weltalmanach* (Frankfurt/Main: Fischer, 2005), 500–15. The source of most figures is the World Bank.

52. Massoud Karshenas and Hassan Hakimian, "Oil, Economic Diversification and the Democratic Process in Iran," *Iranian Studies* 38, no. 1 (March 2005): 67–90.

53. "Youth Employment in Islamic Republic of Iran" (report prepared by the Department of International Affairs of the National Youth Organization, October 2004).

54. Mehrangis Kar, "*Shari'a* Law in Iran," in Paul Marshall, ed., *Radical Islam's Rules: The Worldwide Spread of Extreme Sharia Law* (Freedom House, Center for Religious Freedom, 2005), 41–64.

55. The numbers are from Amnesty International.

56. Abdolmohammad Kazemipur and Ali Rezaei, "Religious Life Under Theocracy: The Case of Iran," *Journal for the Scientific Study of Religion* 42, no. 3 (2003): 347–61.

57. See Mahmoud Sadri, "Sacral Defense of Secularism: Dissident Political Theology in Iran," in Negin Nabavi, ed., *Intellectual Trends in Twentieth-Century Iran* (Gainesville: University Press of Florida, 2003), 180–92.

58. Mahmud Abbasi, *Qanun-e Mojazat-e Eslami* (Islamic Penal Code) (Tehran: Hoquqi, 2002), 108.

59. Following the victory of the Mujahidin in Afghanistan, as the Iranian government became keen on repatriating Afghan refugees to Afghanistan, tens of thousands of Iranian women who had married Afghan refugee men in Iran were told by the authorities that they faced the choice of either seeking a divorce from their husbands or following him to his country.

60. Mehrangiz Kar, "Women's Political Rights After the Islamic Revolution," in Lloyd Ridgeon, ed., *Religion and Politics in Modern Iran: A Reader* (London: I.B. Tauris, 2005), 253–78.

61. Mansoor Moaddel and Taghi Azadarmaki, "The Worldviews of Islamic Publics: The Case of Egypt, Iran, and Jordan," in Ingelhart, ed., *Human Values and Social Change*, 77.

62. Moaddel and Azadarmaki, "The Worldviews of Islamic Publics," 78. Forty-five percent of Iranians agree with this statement, while 88 and 89 percent of Egyptians and Jordanians agree, respectively.

63. Moaddel and Azadarmaki, "The Worldviews of Islamic Publics," 79.

64. For details, see *The International Encyclopedia of Women and Sport* (New York: Macmillan, 2001), s.v. "Iran," 586–87. For an eyewitness account by a Western journalist, see Geraldine Brooks, *Nine Parts of Desire: The Hidden World of Islamic Women* (New York: Anchor Books, 1995), 201–11, "Muslim Women's Games."

65. Asked whether she would ever "want to throw off the head scarf in public," she answered: "Do you want to issue me my death sentence?" *International Herald Tribune*, 3 April 2003, 2.

66. On this point, see Vali Nasr, "Regional Implications of Shi'a Revival in Iraq," *Washington Quarterly* 27 (Summer 2004): 7–24.

67. Najmedin Meshkati, "Iran's Nuclear Brinkmanship, the U.S. Unilateralism, and a Mounting International Crisis: Can Civil Aviation Industry Provide a Breakthrough?" *Iran News*, 26 July 2004, 14. (available at http://www.irannewsdaily.com/asp/iran_news.asp).

68. Arang Keshavarzian, "Contestation Without Democracy: Elite Fragmentation in Iran," in Marsha Pripstein Posusney and Michelle Penner Angrist, eds., *Authoritarianism in the Middle East: Regimes and Resistance* (Boulder, CO: Lynne Rienner, 2005), 63–88.

JAMMU AND
KASHMIR
Srinagar

HIMACHAL
PRADESH
Shimla

PUNJAB
Chandigarh

HARYANA

DELHI

UTTARANCHAL

Dehradun

SIKKIM

ARUNACHAL
PRADESH

Itanagar

MEGHALAYA

Gangto

RAJASTHAN

UTTAR
PRADESH

ASSAM
Dispur

Kohima

NAGALAND

Jaipur

Lucknow

Patna
BIHAR

Shillong

Imphal

MANIPUR

Ganges R.

GUJARAT
Gandhinaga

Bhopal

JHARKHAND

Agartala

Aizawl

Narmada River

MADHYA PRADESH

Ranchi

WEST
BENGAL
Calcutta

TRIPURA

MIZORAM

DIU

DAMAN

DADAR & NAGAR
HAVELI

MAHARASHTRA

CHHATTISGARH

INDIA

Godavari R.

Mumbai
(Bombay)

Raipur

ORISSA
Bhubaneshwar

Bay of

Bengal

0    100   200   300   400   500 Miles

0  100 200 300 400  500 Kilometers

Arabian

Sea

Hyderabad

Krishna River

YANAM
(Pondicherry)

Panaji
GOA

ANDHRA
PRADESH

ANDAMAN
ISLANDS

KARNATAKA
Bangalore

MAHE
(Pondicherry)

Chennai
(Madras)

Port Blair

TAMILNADU

PONDICHERRY
(Puducherry)

Cauvery R.

KERALA

KARAIKAL
(Pondicherry)

ANDAMAN & NICOBAR ISLANDS

Thiruvananthapuram

INDIAN OCEAN

# POLITICS IN INDIA

*Subrata K. Mitra*

## Country Bio

**Population**
1.103,37 billion (2005)

**Territory**
1,269,338 square miles

**Year of Independence**
1947

**Year of Current Constitution**
1950

**Number of Constitutional Amendments**
93 (as of April 2006)

**Head of State**
President Pratibha Patil

**Head of Government**
Prime Minister Manmohan Singh

INDIA

**Official Languages**
English, Hindi (primary tongue of 30% of the people), Bengali, Telugu, Marathi, Tamil, Urdu, Gujarati, Malayalam, Kannada, Oriya, Punjabi, Assamese, Kashmiri, Sindhi, Sanskrit. ***Note:*** There are 24 languages, each of which is spoken by a million or more people.

**Religion**
Hindu 80.5%, Muslim 13.4%, Christian 2.3%, Sikh 1.9%, Buddhist 0.8%, Jain 0.4%, other 0.6% (Census 2001)

**Scheduled Castes**
16.2% of population

**Scheduled Tribes**
8.2% of population

There was a time, not so long ago, when India was seen as a poor democracy, set in a political culture of placid but functional anarchy. With its holy cows, *sadhus*, mendicants, mutilated beggars, ramshackle cities, and poor infrastructure, India was the epitome of backwardness. Most visitors to India today will readily testify that many of these external symbols of poverty and underdevelopment still persist. However, the past decade has added a new sense of optimism, both within India as well as to its image abroad. The ubiquitous mobile phones and highway flyovers in cities, where foreign firms and brand names jostle for space with traditional merchandise, speak for India's rapid integration into the global market economy. In contrast to the recent past, today Indian tourists and business travelers are frequently seen in major international cities. Leaders of business, industry, and powerful states are frequent visitors to the new centers of power and high finance—such as Bangalore, Hyderabad, and Mumbai—in addition to the obligatory visits to New Delhi, the national capital.

Are these symbols of high-tech affluence merely the latest addition to the multilayered diversity of India, or are they the much awaited take off to sustainable growth? This chapter answers this question by analyzing the interaction of the modern state and traditional society in contemporary India, beginning with a discussion of the policy challenges facing the country. The subsequent analysis looks at the present dilemmas and institutional solutions in the context of India's complex and diverse political process, the political tradition steeped in a culture of hierarchy, and its steady transformation under the impact of the democratic process. As in the case of all changing societies, the institutionalization of these achievements is one of the key problems in India. The interplay of federalism, elections, and party competition, India's impartial judiciary, and the watchful eye of Indian and international human right movements have combined to produce a political environment that has helped the sustainability of democracy and development.

In addition to being an interesting story in its own right, the Indian case holds great interest for cross-cultural comparisons of the transition to democracy and development. India—with its democratic political system, secular constitution, liberalized but still *mixed economy,* mass poverty, and complex ethnic composition—is a favorite example for general theories of development and modernization of both capitalist and socialist persuasions. Both of these perspectives saw some limitation on political participation as a necessary price to pay for the transformation of underdeveloped societies into liberal democracies. India, with its dual commitment to democratic rights and development, constitutes a test case. As things stand now, India has not radically changed its Constitution, institutional arrangements or democratic practice. Yet fast economic growth is being achieved. The chapter looks at the apparent contradiction between conventional theories of political transition and the Indian case by analyzing India's history, society, economy, institutions, and policy process.

## CURRENT POLICY CHALLENGES

Rapid economic growth and nuclearization have caused the politics of South Asia to emerge as a new worldwide focus of interest. The emerging markets, joint ventures, and the availability of skilled, low-cost professionals adept at new information technologies (IT) present challenges as well as opportunities for Western business and industry. The new international environment has posed a sharp challenge to India's traditional policy of nonalignment—known in India as *panchasheela*—which was typical of post-war Indian foreign policy.

Indo-Pakistani rivalry, with its potential for nuclear war, remains a source of great anxiety. The international community geared up for an arms race and the intensification of conflict in South Asia following the nuclear tests of 1998. But contrary to such apprehensions, soon after the tests, India and Pakistan started a series of negotiations and **confidence-building measures (CBMs).** The hope that the introduction of nuclear deterrence would lower tensions along the

Kashmir border was short-lived. The outbreak of armed conflict in the Kargil district of Kashmir in 1999, and the buildup of more than a million Indian and Pakistani troops along the line of control (LoC) in Kashmir following the terrorist attack on the Indian Parliament on December 13, 2001, again heightened international fears of yet another Indo-Pakistani confrontation, this time, with the possible use of nuclear weapons. However, the subsequent events belied this pessimistic outcome.

In the aftermath of the attacks in the United States on September 11, 2001, Pakistan reemerged as the key strategic partner of the U.S. government in South Asia. This development temporarily reversed the middle-term goal of U.S. policy to improve Indo-U.S. relations and made the United States a key player in South Asia's regional politics. Subsequently, the attraction of India as an emerging market and a possible balancing factor against China, as well as the efforts of the Indian government to gain recognition of its nuclear status, have introduced a sense of moderation and pragmatism into Indo-U.S. relations. On the Indian side, in place of the shrill ideological rhetoric of the past, one now finds a more moderate, pragmatic, and nuanced approach to the United States, as well as to Pakistan.

India's style of politics—which draws on symbols from culture and religion on the one hand and modern political institutions and the market on the other—is both complex and sophisticated, despite its outwardly naive appearance. After nearly six decades of **postindependence** politics based on democratic participation, protest movements, and accommodation within the limits of modern institutions, this mode of politics has come to characterize virtually all the arenas of the state. There are numerous examples of this. Most **ethno-nationalist** movements attract media attention when they first appear with their customary fury, mass insurgency, and military action, but eventually they find an institutional solution within the Indian political system. And though continued political unrest in Kashmir challenges this thesis, the case of Punjab in the 1990s and Tamil Nadu earlier in the 1960s illustrate this mode of successful conflict resolution in India.

India's Kashmir policy has a complex history and is the subject of endless debate in the press and in scholarly accounts.[1] India's reluctance to honor Jawaharlal Nehru's pledge to the United Nations to hold a plebiscite in Kashmir appears contradictory to the Indian government's support of international organizations. The conflict over Kashmir led to war between India and Pakistan in 1947–1948, 1965, 1971, and 1999. In addition, there is an ongoing "proxy war," fought between the Indian army and Kashmiri militants and cross-border terrorists, called *Mujahiddin*, supported by Pakistan. Contrary to Indian arguments, Pakistan claims that the terrorists are freedom fighters, seeking to liberate Kashmir from Indian rule. Kashmir, deeply evocative of the memory of India's partition and the contradictory ideologies about the role of religion espoused by India and Pakistan, is thus a complex issue that needs to be understood in its historical context.[2]

In retrospect, the politics of Kashmir appears as a mute testimony to the ideological battle between two different concepts of the state, namely, the secular and the confessional. The controversy was started by Jinnah, the founder of Pakistan, and Gandhi before India's Independence by Jinnah advocating the "two-nation" theory and Gandhi opposing it. After the Partition of British India into Pakistan, carved out as a homeland for Muslims, and secular India, Kashmir became the new symbol of this old struggle. Kashmir with its Muslim majority is claimed by Pakistan on the basis of the **two-nation theory.** Challenging the Pakistani claim to Kashmir on account of its Muslim majority, India justifies its claim to Kashmir as essential to the credibility and sustainability of its status as a secular state. In 1948, in the face of an invasion of Kashmir by armed tribals from the Northwest (with the backing of regular Pakistani troops), Nehru did not let the much better equipped Indian army push the Pakistani invaders all the way back to the northwestern frontier of Kashmir. The United Nations, instead of ordering the invaders to go back where they had come from, as Nehru had demanded, sent monitors to supervise the actual Line of Control (LoC) that separated the troops. From then on, the Kashmir issue was embroiled with the Cold War. Kashmir became a pawn in the rivalry between India and Pakistan, supported, respectively, by the Soviet Union and the United States.

Current developments point toward cautious optimism that a solution to the Kashmir problem might be acceptable to India, Pakistan, and the majority of the people of Kashmir. Indian public opinion continues to favor a negotiated solution to the problem (see Table 17.1). Quite noticeably, Indian opinion in favor of a negotiated outcome to the Kashmir conflict has gone up from 33.5 percent to 59.3 percent and support for a military solution has come down from 11.1 percent to 8.8 percent. The most remarkable fact in this context is that support for negotiation is higher than the average among the educated who are also the wielders of opinion in their localities. The initiative taken by the Bharatiya Janata Party (BJP) at the head of the **National Democratic Alliance (NDA)** coalition to negotiate with Pakistan has been followed by the current Congress Party-led United Progressive Alliance government (UPA). A negotiated outcome to the Kashmir problem emerged as the second best option for the Pakistani government of President Pervez Musharraf, continuously in search of domestic legitimacy and international acceptability. The acquisition of nuclear weapons and missiles has helped Pakistan overcome the handicap of its relatively smaller arsenal of conventional weapons against India. Finally, Pakistan's nuclear threat has given further salience to the Kashmir problem by drawing the attention of a world keen to avoid regional nuclear conflict.

The international visibility of India's successful IT sector; the outsourcing of routine, clerical functions by many of the world's major companies to India to take advantage of lower wages; and the rate of economic growth at about 8 percent have shifted attention from India's mass poverty. The fact remains, however, that even by India's modestly defined poverty rate, about 29 percent of the population continues to be classified as poor.[3] The reduction in numbers, which were as high as 50 percent in 1995, gives some scope for optimism. But the gains of economic growth have not trickled down to the hard-core poor, trapped in inaccessible parts of the country which are beyond the reach of the market and the competitive political process. To the list of the deprived one has to add the "new poor"—deeply indebted farmers, whose sad fate has come to the attention of the world through tragic cases of suicides.

In terms of mass literacy, India still lags behind the industrial nations, as well as China and most of the "tiger" economies of East Asia. The intellectual backup for India's prowess in IT, biotechnology, and medical research is provided by a few elite institutions—such as the world-famous IIT (Indian Institution of Technology), IIM (Indian Institute of Management), and the major metropolitan universities. Beyond these

| | | | TABLE 17.1 |
|---|---|---|---|
| Changing Opinion with Regard to India's Kashmir Strategy: Comparing 1996 and 2004 | | | |

**Question: Opinions are divided on the issue of the Kashmir problem.**
**Should the agitation be suppressed or resolved by negotiation?**

| | *1996* | | *2004* | |
|---|---|---|---|---|
| | **Negotiation** | **Suppression** | **Negotiation** | **Suppression** |
| **Religion** | | | | |
| Hindu | 31.3 | 11.9 | 57.4 | 9.0 |
| Muslim | 48.5 | 6.3 | 71.0 | 6.6 |
| Christian | 42.0 | 7.1 | 61.8 | 10.1 |
| Sikh | 46.8 | 12.7 | 67.9 | 9.4 |
| Other | 42.9 | 7.1 | 52.3 | 9.7 |
| **Education** | | | | |
| Nonliterate | 15.3 | 4.8 | 39.8 | 6.4 |
| Up to Primary | 32.0 | 10.5 | 59.8 | 7.8 |
| Up to Matric | 50.9 | 14.8 | 72.9 | 10.6 |
| College and Above | 60.8 | 26.5 | 79.5 | 12.7 |
| **Total** | 33.5 | 11.1 | 59.3 | 8.8 |

Source: National Election Study (NES) 1996, 2004. Conducted by the Center for the Study of Developing Societies, New Delhi.

institutions, which cater to the educational needs of a small portion of the population, the infrastructure for mass literacy and for the kind of technical training that a growing economy demands is sorely lacking. Under the federal division of powers, education is the responsibility of India's regional governments, which makes coordination for mass education difficult to achieve at the national level.

India's infrastructure, particularly road transport and shipping facilities, are inadequate to meet the needs of a fast-growing economy. The current project to build a system of expressways that would link India's major cities indicates the importance the government attaches to this issue. The problem has a historical background to it. India's transport network, particularly the railway, was originally put in place by the British colonial rulers. The main objective was to safeguard the need to move troops rapidly from one corner of the vast subcontinent to the other. As such, the rail network that independent India inherited was vast in terms of mileage, but the connectivity of ports with hinterlands and mines was lacking. The acceleration of the pace of economic growth and the challenge of global competition have added saliency to the issue of infrastructure.

## THE TWIN LEGACIES OF COLONIAL RULE AND THE ANTICOLONIAL MOVEMENT

Numerous ancient monuments, land grants, stone inscriptions, and sophisticated waterworks provide ample historical evidence of the existence of the premodern state in India. Sacred texts, like *Ramayana* and *Mahabharata*, and those specifically addressed to the needs of administration, such as the *Arthasastra*—the "science of government"—reputed to have been written in the fourth century B.C., also support this fact. To sustain such activities, taxes had to be collected, law and order needed to be maintained, and conflicts had to be settled between the king and his subjects as well as between different groups of individuals.

While there is general agreement that these functions were discharged properly and that the state existed well before the coming of European traders and then the colonial rulers, the institutional form and social basis of the early state is the subject of considerable historical controversy. Burton Stein, in his seminal work, questions the conventional notion of the highly organized feudal state with one paramount ruler and an omnipotent bureaucracy.[4] Instead, he suggests that the early state was "segmentary," where political authority and control were localized, and was part of loosely organized empires, drawing on many different factors, such as agrarian systems, kinship, and religious networks.[5] Once the British established their rule, they succeeded in bringing various local and regional units under a central government, which nevertheless drew heavily on indirect rule through quasi-autonomous intermediaries, such as native princes, tribal leaders, and ***zamindars*** (Hindi for landlords).[6]

The continuity between India's premodern history and its modern institutions helps to explain the resilience of India's political system. The complex legacies of colonial rule and the resistance to it have deeply affected modern India. In contrast to China and the former Soviet Union—which made self-conscious attempts to cut themselves off from their prerevolutionary history—no general anti-British campaign with racial overtones occurred in India either before or after its independence. The anticolonial movement based its struggle on a platform that combined agitation for self-rule with institutional participation. The movement as a whole was constitutionalist and liberal in nature. Although it had elements of nativism, religious intolerance, and a lot of radical, socialist rhetoric, the movement remained under the control of leaders who had been educated in the West and believed in accommodation and consensus and stood generally against the use of race or religion as the basis of politics. Thus, independence meant a transfer of power to the elite who were at the forefront of the national struggle during the last phase of British rule. Muslim leaders who had fought for the creation of Pakistan as the homeland for South Asia's Muslims migrated to the new country. The Indian National Congress was the main political party in the Constituent Assembly that produced the Indian Constitution and subsequently formed the government, having won the first general election.

**Mahatma Gandhi,** the most outstanding leader of India's struggle for independence and a continued source of moral inspiration, was trained as a barrister in England. He developed the method of ***satyagraha***—nonviolent resistance—while he was in South Africa working for an Indian law firm. The South African experience also taught Gandhi the importance of cross-community coalitions, a strategy that he subsequently transformed into Hindu-Muslim unity. This factor became a salient feature of Gandhi's politics upon his return to India in 1915. Under his leadership, the Indian National Congress became increasingly sensitive to the gap between the predominantly urban

Gandhi had a keen understanding of the nature of Indian politics and of the difficulties inherent in uniting a population easily divided by race, religion, and caste. His resistance to the Salt Tax provided a "common denominator" for mobilizing the Indian population to "nonviolent resistance."

Margaret Bourke-White/Time Life Pictures/Getty Images

## Gandhi: The Story of Independence

Mohandas Karamchand Gandhi, popularly known as Mahatma—The Great Soul—was born in 1869 in Porbandar, a small seaport in the western state of Gujarat. He was trained as a barrister in England. After his return to India, he went to South Africa to take a position as a lawyer. There, he initiated a protest movement against the discrimination experienced by the Indian community and became well known for his method of nonviolent resistance. Back in India in 1915, he immediately joined the Freedom movement led by the Congress Party. Drawing on his South African experience, he developed the concept of *satyagraha* as a principle and technique of nonvio-

lence and civil disobedience to fight injustice and to revolt against British colonial rule. In 1920 he became the undisputed leader of the Congress Party and turned it into a mass movement, uniting all the different and sometimes even mutually hostile strands of Indian society. Gandhi was against the partition of British India on the basis of religion and tried to reconcile the growing antagonism between Hindus and Muslims. In 1948, only one year after his vision of an independent India had been reached, he was assassinated by Nathuram Godse, a young Hindu fanatic, who accused him of appeasement of Pakistan and the Muslim community.

middle-class Congress Party and the Indian masses, and it shifted its attention to the Indian peasantry (see Box 17.1).

Under Gandhi's leadership, the Indian National Congress steadily broadened its reach, both in terms of social class and geography. In 1918, while introducing *satyagraha* in India, Gandhi courted arrest in support of the indigo plantation workers of Bihar. There were similar movements in Punjab, Gujarat, and other parts of India. To mobilize mass support, Gandhi also introduced other indigenous political practices, such as fasting and general strikes or *hartal* (a form of boycott accompanied by a work stoppage). In choosing civil disobedience to resist the Salt Tax imposed by the British, Gandhi showed his brilliance as a strategist. When the British rulers responded with repressive measures, their actions only intensified the struggle.

Gandhi's tactics became a model for subsequent civil disobedience movements through which he mobilized peasants and workers as well as the urban middle classes. He combined the techniques of political negotiation with more coercive direct action (such as *hartal* and *satyagraha*) and derived both the political resources and the methods from within Indian culture and tradition.

The British responded to increasingly vocal demands for political participation with the Government of India Act of 1935. This act is a landmark in India's constitutional development and, subsequently, an important blueprint for the independent India.

Even though the voting franchise continued to carry a property qualification, the electorate still expanded from 6 million to 30 million. Provincial elections held under this act gave the Congress Party a valuable experience in electoral campaigns and governance. Both became crucial assets for the establishment of an orderly political process after India's independence.

While the political and constitutional developments that took place under British rule are important legacies on their own, the effect of British rule itself on Indian society was also very important in terms of the psychological impact on Indian identity and selfhood.[7] The first social reformers, whose agenda included some of the programs advocated by British Utilitarians, looked up to the British colonial government as allies in a joint struggle. The Congress Party, which brought the reformist and political strands of Indian nationalism together, acquired a new social base as the movement, under Gandhi's leadership, mobilized the peasantry, labor, and other occupational groups in rural and urban areas. The Congress Party, as an office-seeking and anticolonial movement, therefore, became the instigator and beneficiary of reform. The 1909 constitutional reforms had conceded limited Indian representation, but the extension of the franchise and the responsibility of elected members were severely circumscribed. The reforms of 1919 then provided for a relatively large measure of responsibility at the local and provincial levels in areas such as education, health, and public works that were not "reserved" or deemed crucial for colonial control. The Congress Party took advantage of these reforms to participate in the local and municipal elections, which greatly enhanced the potential for democratic government after India's independence. By making common cause with middle-class aspirations, it earned the trust and loyalty of the middle class while challenging the authority and legitimacy of British rule. These same social groups were among its more important social bases of support. In addition, the Congress Party developed an ability for the aggregation of interests, a talent for sustained and coordinated political action, and skills of administration through vigorous participation in elections, particularly those to the provincial legislature under the 1935 Government of India Act. The leaders of the Congress Party also gained what few anticolonial movements had—namely, a taste of genuine political competition and the experience of patronage as a tool of political transactions and means to power.

For over half a century, following its formation in 1885 and the final coming of independence in 1947, the Congress Party remained the focus of the national struggle against British rule. It followed a strategy that combined political objectives with those of social reform and nation-building. This complex repertoire of competition and collaboration with the foreign rulers became the hallmark of the Congress Party. It steadily expanded the political agenda to include virtually all aspects of national life, exerting pressure on the British to concede more power to Indian hands. It used the power and resources thus gained to strengthen the organization and political network. When the British thought that they had conceded enough and the negotiations came to a standstill, the Congress Party took to direct action and mobilization, imposing pressure until the British returned to the negotiations. This legacy of direct action, mass movement, and transactional politics based on patronage became an important ingredient of the political culture that sustained democratic rule in India after independence. The Gandhian blend of British parliamentary methods and indigenous techniques made direct political action, such as *satyagraha*, an integral part of political culture and tradition in postindependence India.[8]

After 150 years of British colonial rule, often referred to as the British *raj*, India became independent on August 15, 1947. **Jawaharlal Nehru,** India's first prime minister, was a leading figure in the anticolonial campaign and a proponent of nonalignment for India. He soon became a leader of the whole Third World (see Box 17.2). Unlike the postrevolutionary elite of China and the Soviet Union, Nehru and his associates formed a national leadership through consensus building, by including rather than eliminating challengers, and accommodating a broad political spectrum. The character of the new political system was shaped by the legacies of Indian history and social

## Jawaharlal Nehru to Sonia Gandhi: Democracy and Dynastic Rule

BOX 17.2

Born in 1889 in Allahabad as the eldest son of Motilal Nehru, a prominent nationalist leader and close friend of Mohandas K. Gandhi, Jawaharlal Nehru—like Gandhi—was educated in England before he returned to his hometown as a barrister. He entered national politics in the 1920s and joined a long and close association with Gandhi. Inclined to socialist ideas and to the vision of a rapid process of modernization, it is Nehru who in many ways was the architect of independent India. He announced the birth of the Indian state in his famous "Freedom at Midnight" speech, where he caught the spirit of the historical moment. Soon afterwards Nehru became the first prime minister of India, a position he occupied until his death in 1964. But the Nehru "dynasty" continued to dominate Indian politics in the person of his daughter Indira Gandhi, who became prime minister in 1966, and subsequently his grandson Rajiv Gandhi, who was prime minister from 1984 until 1989. Following Rajiv's death in an explosion carried out by a Tamil suicide bomber from Sri Lanka, his Italian born widow, Sonia Gandhi, was gradually inducted into national politics. Following the victory of the UPA-coalition under her leadership in 2004, Sonia was invited to become the prime minister. She declined, preferring instead to provide leadership from outside the government, as the president of the Congress Party.

diversity, but most of all by the nature of the local and regional resistance to colonial rule. The middle class, which included many of these leaders, had an ambiguous relationship to the British presence in India. Some of this class fought for the *raj* and some against it, but the class as a whole was the product of British rule.

## THE "GIVENS" OF INDIAN SOCIETY: FROM HIERARCHY TO PLURALITY

The key to many of the issues arising out of India's politics is found in the interaction of India's traditional institutions and social diversity on the one hand, and the modern democratic political process on the other. This interaction explains why, despite a culture traditionally based on social hierarchy and authoritarianism, steeped in mass poverty and high illiteracy, India has established a resilient democratic political order.

### Religious Diversity and Political Conflict

India is a multicultural, a multidenominational, and, according to the Indian Constitution, a secular state. According to data generated by India's decennial census, India is a Hindu "majority" country, as the latest measurement classifies 80.5 percent of the population as Hindus. But Hindus themselves are divided into many sects and denominations as well, to the point where some scholars question the status of Hinduism as a religion altogether.[9] Additionally, all other major religions of the world are present in India. The state of Jammu and Kashmir has a Muslim majority. Three smaller Indian states each have a Christian majority, and Punjab has a Sikh majority.

The rapid rise of the Hindu-nationalist Bharatiya Janata Party, however, is a reminder of the political appeal of pan-Indian Hinduism as an ideology. The idea of a politically mobilized Hindu majority, threatening the plural and democratic character of the political process, is a source of some anxiety among the minorities (see Figure 17.1). Recent survey findings reinforce the impression that opinions on the issue of **Ayodhya** (Box 17.3) are polarized. Asked, if "only the Ram temple should be built on the spot where the mosque stood," 68 percent of Muslims disagree compared with only 20 percent of Hindus. However, support among Hindus for the proposition that "India

should make greater efforts for friendly relations with Pakistan" remains around 40 percent, although support among Muslims has slightly decreased from the earlier 72 percent to 65 percent.[10] Judging from the findings of opinion polls, while India's political process continues to reinforce group consciousness—and thus a political distance among different communities—it also generates a sense of personal efficacy that leads to the emergence of new, short-term alliances among opposing groups.

India's political process, therefore, appears to be robust enough to inject a degree of moderation to extreme sectional demands. The logic of electoral politics, as we shall see later in this chapter, accounts both for the origin of such movements and, once in power, for the moderation of their more extreme demands.[11] Cultural plurality is an integral part of Hinduism. Its many sects and their separate traditions influence one another, leading to the growth of new forms.[12] Many Hindus believe in the concept of "unity in diversity." While from the outside Hinduism appears as a vast phalanx that is internally undifferentiated and externally bounded, in reality it is far from being so. It has a rich diversity in spite of attempts to simplify and standardize ritual and social practice.[13] Each cultural-linguistic area has its own "little" tradition and local gods, and it is within the local sects that most Hindus live their religious life. The classical ideals of Hinduism and local traditions have freely interacted with each other in the past, leading to the growth of regional traditions and cross-regional movements.[14]

An earlier generation of Indian political specialists thought that religious beliefs impeded the functioning of the modern state and economy and were a major obstacle to social transformation. By an extension of the same argument, they believed that with modernization, religion would decline in importance.[15] In contrast, recent political developments have shown that religion, as one can notice from the political mobilization of minorities, can also become a political vehicle for social movements. It can impart a sense of identity to social groups feeling discriminated against or threatened by other groups. This confluence between the search for identity and political competition appears in a number of ways.[16] When adherents of a religion are regionally concentrated, such as Sikhs in Punjab and Muslims in Kashmir, there is a convergence between religion and regional identity. This convergence generates a corresponding demand that the regional government

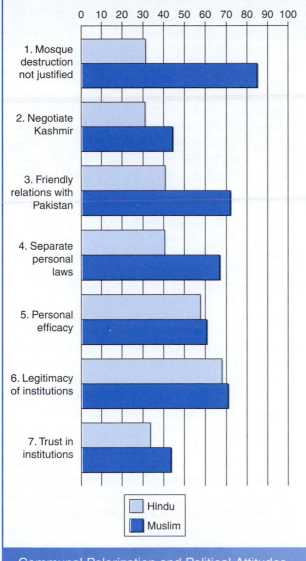

Key:

The numbers 1–7 show for the percentage (%) of the respective responses to the following questions:

1. "Some people say that the demolition [of Babri Mosque in 1992 by a mob of Hindu fanatics in the northern city of Ayodhya] was justified while others say it was not justified. What would you say—was it justified or not justified?" (not justified)

2. "People's opinions are divided on the issue of the Kashmir problem. Some people say that government should suppress the agitation by any means while others say that this problem should be resolved by negotiations. What would you say, should the agitation be suppressed or resolved by negotiations?" (solved by negotiations)

3. "India should make more efforts to develop friendly relations with Pakistan. Do you agree?" (agree)

4. "Every community should be allowed to have its own laws to govern marriage and property rights. Do you agree or disagree?" (agree)

5. "Do you think your vote has an effect on how things are run in this country, or do you think your vote makes no difference?" (vote makes a difference)

6. "Suppose there were no parties or assemblies and elections were not held—do you think that the government in this country can be run better?" (no)

7. "How much trust do you have in political institutions?" (somewhat + great deal)

**Communal Polarization and Political Attitudes**                    **FIGURE 17.1**

Source: The data in this table were collected from a national sample of 10,000 men and women representing the Indian electorate. The survey was conducted by the Centre for the Study of Developing Societies, Delhi, in May–June 1996.

incorporate the sacred beliefs of the religion. This demand severely stretches the limit of the secular state in India.[17]

Hindu nationalist movements extend this logic by demanding the embodiment of Hindu cultural ideals within the structure of the modern state at the national level. Political parties and movements that draw their strength from religious beliefs and aspirations are also quite strong in political and cultural self-assertion. Following their impressive gains in the parliamentary elections of 1996 and 1998 at the expense of the centrist forces (the communist vote has remained low but stable), Hindu nationalist parties have formed the government at the center and in several states. The 2004 parliamentary elections, which voted the Hindu nationalist NDA coalition out of power, appears to have arrested the growth curve of cultural nationalism. Still, religion—particularly the exclusive right to places of worship and the right to make religious processions in a religiously mixed

**BOX 17.3**

## Ayodhya (1992) and Its Aftermath, Godhra (2002)

The city of Ayodhya in the northern State of Uttar Pradesh came to international prominence on December 6, 1992. A long-standing point of contention between Hindus and Muslims was a mosque, built in 1528 by the first Moghul emperor Babur, that Hindus claim, stood where a temple once marked the birthplace of Rama. The Hindu nationalist Bharatiya Janata Party (BJP)—then head of the state government—launched a *rathyatra* (pilgrimage) to Ayodhya in order to destroy the mosque and to rebuild in its place a Hindu temple, but it could not discipline the frenzied crowd. The mosque was demolished by the *karsevaks* (activists) of two front organizations of Hindu-nationalism, followed by communal riots in many parts of India. The BJP's dilemma became apparent again during the communal clashes on the eve of the tenth anniversary of the Babri mosque's destruction in February 2002, when an attack by a Muslim mob on a train with Hindu activists returning from a demonstration in Ayodhya resulted in more than fifty dead, mostly women and children. This incident triggered a pogrom against the Muslim minority in Gujarat, causing several hundred victims. The opposition accused the BJP-led state government of complicity with anti-Muslim mobs; the government defended itself with statistics showing that about a third of the casualties were caused by police shooting under orders, mostly against Hindu mobs.

neighborhood—is one of the main causes of conflict in India today. North India is dotted with mosques that stand next to Hindu temples or are built on spots where Hindu temples are believed to have stood. This is an integral part of the popular memory of the Islamic conquest of India from the eighth century onward. Many of these Islamic structures are now at the center of the religious storm that, judging from the Gujarat riots of 2002, continues to incite religious fervor and political passion (see again Box 17.3).

Muslims constitute 13.4 percent of the population, and they are a vocal, assertive, and politically organized minority. The demand for a separate homeland for Muslims by the Muslim League during the British colonial rule led to the **partition** of British India and the creation of Pakistan in 1947, a new state with the explicit purpose of becoming the homeland of South Asia's Muslims. About two-thirds of Indian Muslims and the bulk of the leaders of the Muslim League subsequently left India for Pakistan following the partition. Over the past decades, the Muslim community in India has, however, developed a new leadership, identity, and political assertiveness. Muslim representation in legislative bodies and in public life has grown since India's independence and political competition has enhanced the sense of group assertion and a substantial increase in the number, intensity, and geographic spread of communal conflict.[18]

Sikhism—born about 400 years ago as a resistance movement against Islamic invaders—took on many of the theological and organizational features of both Hinduism and Islam. Some Sikhs feel that their identity is threatened by modernization and assimilation with Hinduism. They envision the creation of a sovereign Khalistan state as an exclusive homeland for Sikhs. Sikhs form a tenuous majority in the northern Indian state of Punjab, but this is constantly depleted through emigration to other parts of India and abroad. Punjab is home to the Akali Dal, a Sikh political party that was a partner in the NDA coalition.[19] Some Sikhs fear the further loss of the Sikh majority because of the influx of non-Sikhs from poorer parts of India, attracted to Punjab by better wages. Some perceive even further threats to Sikh identity and traditions from new habits being inculcated by the youth through modernization and from the growth of revisionist sects within Sikhism. These anxieties fueled a political movement that took an increasingly violent turn, leading to the army's siege of the Golden Temple in the holy city of Amritsar, and in revenge, the assassination of Prime Minister Indira Gandhi by two of her Sikh bodyguards on October 31, 1984.[20] However, a combination of repression of dissidents and accommodation of some of their leaders has seen peace return to Punjab.

The cultural diversity of India is also enriched by its modern associations, trade unions, and all manners of

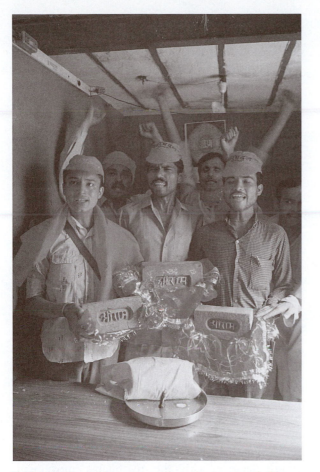

With the Ramshila movement emotively named after the consecrated bricks for the constructing of a Hindu temple to replace a mosque in the northern Indian city of Ayodhya, militant Hindus have launched an offensive to counter Muslim fundamentalism.

*India Today International,* 21 October 1989.

movements in which people come together to obtain material advantages. Group formation has frequently led to communal strife initiated or exacerbated by groups promoting their shared interest. Social solidarity becomes an important means of political mobilization. Political groups, which are created out of the fission and fusion of traditional social groups, define their newly found identity as a mechanism for gaining benefits. The absence of nationwide, cohesive, homogeneous primordial groups has impeded the growth of an equivalent kind of tribal politics that has stymied the growth of democracy and modern institutions in Africa. With the exception of Kashmir, the Indian state has kept separatist movements in check through a combination of

firmness and flexibility. The direction and pace of the process depend largely on the leadership that emerges, the nature of its demands, and how effective the central and regional governments are in dealing with them. India, with all its diversity, has been relatively successful in managing and containing these conflicts through a process of political bargaining, accommodation, repression, and institutional change.[21]

## Caste and Politics

Local **castes** (*jatis*) are the basic social units that still govern marriages, social networks, food taboos, and rituals in India. In the past, caste regulated the choice of occupation as well, which was typically caste-specific and hereditary at the same time. This has changed rapidly because of modernization, legislation, and urbanization. In addition, the government quota system has opened up top jobs that once were the prerogative of the upper castes.

There are more than 2,000 *jatis* in India, traditionally divided into four hierarchically ranked broad categories called *varnas:*

1. the Brahmins, who originally performed the traditional function of priests;
2. the Kshatriyas, who were the rulers and the warriors;
3. the Vaisyas, who were the mercantile classes; and
4. the Sudras, who were the service groups, agriculturists, and artisans.

Originally, the caste system presupposed the interdependent relationship of occupational groups, referred to as the *jajmani* system.[22] *Jatis* were linked to one another through ties of reciprocal economic, social, and political obligations. In the center of this scheme of reciprocity stood social groups with controlling interests in land, whom other castes provided with services, and from whom they received a share of the harvest. The relationship of the lower castes to the high-caste landowners was hereditary, but their dependent status also carried some traditional rights, such as distress relief at the time of natural calamities. All behavior within the system, however, emphasized social hierarchy and inequalities of power, wealth, and status. Control over land was the critical lever of social status and power. These institutions and traditions derived their legitimacy from the unifying concept of *dharma*, which signified the natural order of things. Though specific to Hinduism, dharma dominated local society, tradition, and belief systems. The oppressive aspects of the caste system have been increasingly contested by those at the bottom of the pyramid, particularly the former "untouchables" and the lower castes, mentioned in the Constitution, respectively, as Scheduled Castes (SC), Scheduled Tribes (ST), and Other Backward Classes (OBC).

The former untouchables are excluded from social interaction with the four *varnas*, because of the "polluting" nature of their traditional occupation as scavengers. They make up about a sixth of India's population. Attempts to elevate them into full membership in society through legislation, affirmative action, and competitive politics have accelerated since Independence. Politically conscious and increasingly assertive, former untouchables now refer to themselves as ***dalits,*** which in Hindi means "the suppressed groups." The Bahujan Samaj Party, currently the most important advocate of *dalit* self-assertion, is an important factor in the politics of northern India. It has placed many of its members in major ministerial positions.

Many Indians see the caste system as the cause of India's social fragmentation and economic backwardness. But castes are also the only basis of identity and social interaction for vast numbers of people. Democracy and economic change have thus sometimes worked at cross-purposes, creating conflict, fragmenting large castes into new social groups, and fusing several existing groups into caste associations. As new opportunities for enterprise and political linkage open up, castes are increasingly the basis of community formation. The new "political caste" is an instrument for the promotion of collective interest by social groups that come together for that purpose. The instrumental role that caste plays in raising consciousness and electoral mobilization actually undermines the ideological basis of social hierarchy and helps question the more odious aspects of caste domination.[23] The politics of northern India has been recently dominated by coalitions of former untouchables and the "Backward Classes," who usually belong to the lowest *varna*.

The situation of India's aborigines, known as **tribals** who represent 8.2 percent of the population, parallels that of the former untouchables. The colonial practice declared the areas largely inhabited by them as reserved or "scheduled areas," where tribal lands could not be easily acquired by nontribals. This policy has continued after India's independence. Although tribals exist all over India, and some tribal groups living in nontribal areas have caste-like status, the majority are concentrated in three main regions: the Northeast (in Nagaland, Meghalaya, and Arunachal Pradesh), the hill areas of central India, and western India. Overall, these regions are socially and economically backward, but the spirit of political competition pervades them as well. Movements for the creation of autonomous regions are indicative of this tribal self-assertion.

## Language

Along with caste and religion, language is one of the key components of identity. Language is also one of the main social cleavages in other South Asian nations, such as Pakistan or Sri Lanka. India's major languages, each having evolved over many centuries, are concentrated in different regions. As such, the mother tongue has become the focus of regional identity. Although Hindi is common in northern India, the different regions (and subregions) have their distinct dialects. Many are very highly developed, and they have their own distinguished literary traditions. In the 1920s, subnational loyalties based on language had developed simultaneously with the nationalist movement. The Indian National Congress demanded that Britain redraw the map of India along linguistic lines. Congress itself was organized on the basis of regional languages as early as 1920. Later, in 1956, the government redrew the administrative map of India and since then the Indian states have been reorganized on the basis of the mother tongue. The elevation of the main vernacular to the status of official language of a region has reinforced the multinational character of the Indian political system.

Indian languages can be divided into two main groups: the Indo-Aryan languages of the North (such as Punjabi, Hindi, Kashmiri, and Bengali) and the Dravidian languages of the South (such as Telugu, Tamil, Kannada, and Malayalam). The largest single language in India is Hindi, which, along with English, is recognized as an official language of India. The languages of North India all have a common Sanskritic base. A complex three-language formula gives Hindi the status of the national language while equalizing the chances of non-Hindi speakers of India for public services by conceding to English the status of a link language. Regional languages are the main medium for official purposes within regions. Linguistic movements in India have thus contributed to the greater differentiation of the political system as well as to the overall legitimacy of the state, without, at the same time, damaging the basis of national integration.

## Social Class

Unlike in China and Vietnam, despite the presence of both mass poverty and radical politics, India did not develop a revolutionary peasant movement. When peasant uprisings inspired by Marxism appeared in southern India shortly after India's independence and in West Bengal in the 1960s, they did not spread to other parts of India. The nature of colonial rule and Indian resistance to it—particularly the role of Gandhi, the Indian class structure, and the country's social fragmentation—are responsible for the muted nature of class conflict in India. The slow pace of industrialization and urbanization and castes, tribes, and ethnic groups that cut across class lines led to a highly uneven pattern of class formation. This pattern has severely inhibited the development of class identities and political mobilization based on class appeals.

As a group, India's industrial working class is quite small and only a minority is unionized. Protected by strong labor legislation and surrounded by workers in insecure jobs, unionized labor constitutes something of a labor aristocracy. The rural class system is even more complex. The land reforms of the 1950s eliminated some landlords (*zamindars*). In their place, there emerged a powerful new rural force composed of a mixed-status group of middle-peasant cultivators. These middle peasants, called "bullock capitalists," control 51 percent of the agricultural land and constitute 35 percent of the rural households and 25 percent of the total population of India.[24] They are a powerful political force in rural India. Championed by peasant parties like the Bharatiya Kranti Dal and the Lok Dal, they have challenged urban interests, upper-caste-dominated parties, and the formally dominant position of the older social notables. However, with the independent mobilization of the former untouchables, who constitute the social layer just below, their position is also gradually being challenged.

The landless and small landowners (those holding fewer than 2.5 acres of land), divided by caste as well as by class lines, in states like Uttar Pradesh and Bihar, do not share a common interest. The small landowners also do not identify with the needs and aspirations of the rural landless population. Under the pressure of mechanization, which requires a larger unit of production, the pressure on land has increased, leading to enhanced landlessness. The dominant social groups are being pressed in some parts of India through the independent political organization of the former untouchables, who are frequently landless agricultural workers. Such movements—as for example, the *dalit* movements in western India and the Bahujan Samaj Party in northern India—constitute an important challenge to the dominance of the upper social strata.

In summary, from a comparative perspective, India is a highly pluralistic and segmented society where the twin process of modernization and democratization has transformed a hierarchical society into groups that see themselves as legitimate political actors. But the cultural basis lacks uniformity at the national level because social networks are often confined to region and locality. Regions have increasingly acquired their own distinct identity in terms of economic and political status, and cross-regional coalitions deeply influence the course of national politics.

## POLITICAL INSTITUTIONS AND THE POLICY PROCESS

At independence in 1947, India, like many former British colonies, adopted the model of British parliamentary democracy. This model includes the accountability of the executive to the legislature, a professional and politically neutral military and career civil service, and the rule of law—all operating within the framework of a parliamentary system. Some salient features of the political system of the United States—such as federalism, the separation of powers, and fundamental rights of individuals protected by a Supreme Court—were also introduced. The leaders of the underprivileged—most notably Bhim Rao Ambedkar, the chief architect of the Constitution, and Jawaharlal Nehru—wanted to give shape to a broad vision of a modern, secular, democratic India, mobilizing its resources toward the twin objectives of growth and redistribution.

Compared to many other postcolonial states, India in 1947 started with several advantages that eventually facilitated the growth of a parliamentary democracy. The transition from colonial rule provided

| The Separation and Division of Powers in India | | | TABLE 17.2 |

| Levels of Government | Powers | | |
|---|---|---|---|
| | Executive | Legislative | Judicial |
| National | President-in-Council | Parliament | Supreme Court |
| Regional | Governor-in-Council | Assembly | High Court |
| Local | District Magistrate | Zilla Parishad | District Court |

a continuity of both the leadership and the institutional structure. A professional bureaucracy and security apparatus, already manned mostly by Indians, was immediately available. Above all, the development of the Congress Party into a nationwide electoral organization made for a unified exercise of power. The partition of India, by removing the Muslim League, which had been the main political challenger to the Congress Party, produced a smaller but more cohesive political system. The leaders of the successor state quickly adapted themselves to the new, competitive political environment, based not so much on nationalist ideals as on the pragmatic politics of patronage and public policy. This led to the creation of a political system that institutionalized representation, competition, and accountability. Finally, Nehru's adoption of nonalignment as the cornerstone of India's foreign policy created a generation of political leaders focused on domestic politics who saw elections and the growth of a self-reliant economy as the main basis of legitimacy.

This basic institutional structure has survived the challenges of the past six decades, a period that includes the demise of the generation of leaders who were in charge at the time of India's independence, the mobilization of new social groups, left- and right-wing radicalism, famine, mass poverty and large-scale changes in the economy, a major border war against China in 1962, and three wars against Pakistan.

One legacy of the Indian resistance to British rule was a deep distrust of power and a determination to secure the maximum possible freedom for citizens. The members of the Constituent Assembly, which met from 1947 to 1950, gave shape to these aspirations in the institutions they devised. In some cases, they drew on India's cultural and political legacies, but in others they borrowed widely from the major constitutions of the western world. The result was the separation of power among the executive, the legislature, and the judiciary at the national level. This separation is represented by the

president and the Council of Ministers, the Parliament, and the Supreme Court, respectively. An equally robust division of power between the federal government and the regions was also established (see Table 17.2).

In its solicitude for the decentralization of power, the Constituent Assembly did not stop there. There were strong hopes for the devolution of power below the level of the regional governments, to be exercised directly by the representatives of the people. This hope took a concrete shape in 1957 when the Balwantrai Mehta Committee recommended the creation of a *panchayati raj* (literally, the rule of the five), to set up representative bodies at the district, subdistrict, and village levels. They were endowed with a measure of administrative autonomy, charged with developmental functions, and for that purpose given financial means. The implementation of *panchayati raj* has been far from uniform, but thanks to the Seventy-third Amendment to the Constitution in 1993, all of India's half-million villages are covered by some form of direct exercise of power by the residents.

The resultant structure had tremendous potential for political fragmentation and social conflict. But India's "state-dominated pluralism" provided the right balance between central direction and respect for regional and local autonomy.[25] To cope with extraordinary situations where rapid action was imperative, the Constitution gave a series of emergency powers to the national executive to meet the challenge of grave political crises. Although the Constitution formally vested authority in the president, everyday exercise of executive power and legislative initiative were intended to be in the hands of the prime minister.

## The President

The role of the president as the head of the state was designed with the British monarch in mind. In practice, however, the office combines the ceremonial roles of head of the state with some substantive powers. Under the Indian Constitution, executive power is formally vested in the president, and he is expected to exercise these powers on the advice of the Council of Ministers, with the prime minister at its head. The real lines of control, as shown in Figure 17.2, nevertheless indicate otherwise.

The president appoints the prime minister and has the authority to dismiss him. But, by convention, these powers are severely limited. The president invites the leader of the majority party or coalition in the Lok Sabha to form the government, and so far, unlike in Pakistan, no president has dismissed a prime minister. The Indian president exercises his authority as advised by the prime minister. But that does not mean that the president is merely a rubber stamp. The president might identify a potential leader when there is no clear parliamentary majority. This was the case in 1989 with V. P. Singh, who was invited to form the government when the leader of the Congress Party stated that he did not intend to form the cabinet. More recently, after the 2004 parliamentary elections, the president invited

Manmohan Singh to form the government again after the leader of the Congress Party decided not to become the prime minister. Since 1989, the president has been extraordinarily watchful in upholding of constitutional norms and in preventing the use of governmental powers for partisan purposes. This attentiveness has greatly contributed to the growth in the stature of the presidency.

Unlike the British head of state, the Indian president is elected. The election procedure involves the political representation and active participation of all regions of the country as well as the national and regional political parties (see Figure 17.2). Early presidents, like Rajendra Prasad and S. Radhakrishnan, were eminent statesmen who were not seen as politicians even though they were elected. That is not the case anymore. The president's five-year term can be renewed. Although no president has experienced it, the president can be removed through impeachment by the Parliament. The president is elected through proportional representation by a single transferable vote, a complicated voting procedure that has been

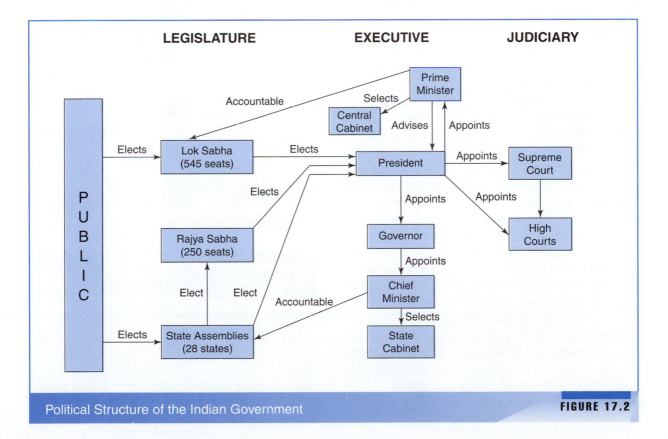

Political Structure of the Indian Government **FIGURE 17.2**

explicitly designed to ensure uniformity among the states as well as parity between the regions as a whole and the nation.

Rajendra Prasad, the first Indian president, closely cooperated with Nehru as prime minister, which set the precedent for subsequent occupants of the office (see Figure 17.3). The fact that both offices were held by leaders linked to the Congress Party facilitated cooperation during the early years of the Republic. This informal practice has become increasingly difficult to sustain as the hegemony of the Congress Party has given way to coalition governments. But politicians have used other ways of achieving coordination, such as extensive multiparty negotiation before presidential elections. This is important for the smooth functioning of India's political institutions, because the Constitution confers an impressive range of powers on the president. It provides the president with the authority to suspend fundamental rights and to declare a state of national **emergency** under Article 352, to impose the "President's rule" in a region, under which the state is ruled directly by the union executive (Article 356), and with a provision for financial emergency under Article 360. But, in true republican fashion, even while leaving the decision to the president and the prime minister, the Constitution requires the presidential proclamations to be laid before Parliament for approval within two months, failing which they will lapse.

The appointment of the highest elected executive of India appears democratic in contrast with many developing countries where replacement of the chief executive often occurs by nondemocratic means (see Chapter 6). However, some analysts point out that for thirty-eight out of sixty years since its independence, India was ruled by members of the Nehru family.[26] A more serious criticism is the failure of democratic government, leading to authoritarian rule that compromised India's democratic status through the imposition of a national emergency in 1975 (see Box 17.4).[27] Dismissing elected governments at the regional level and applying direct rule from Delhi had become more frequent during the prime ministership of Indira Gandhi. However, K. R. Narayanan set an important precedent in 1998 by turning down a cabinet recommendation to impose the president's rule on the state of Bihar.[28] One can still point to the robustness of Indian democracy by showing that authoritarian rule, rather than

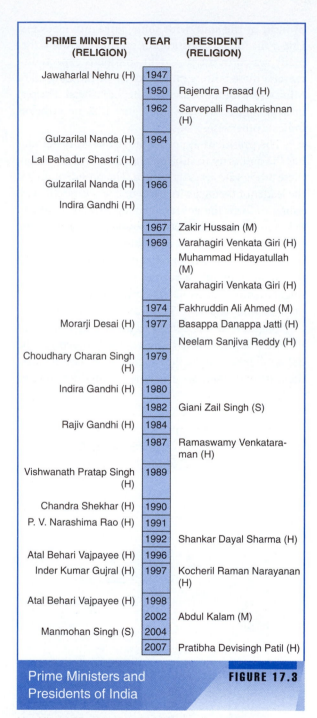

| PRIME MINISTER (RELIGION) | YEAR | PRESIDENT (RELIGION) |
|---|---|---|
| Jawaharlal Nehru (H) | 1947 | |
| | 1950 | Rajendra Prasad (H) |
| | 1962 | Sarvepalli Radhakrishnan (H) |
| Gulzarilal Nanda (H) | 1964 | |
| Lal Bahadur Shastri (H) | | |
| Gulzarilal Nanda (H) | 1966 | |
| Indira Gandhi (H) | | |
| | 1967 | Zakir Hussain (M) |
| | 1969 | Varahagiri Venkata Giri (H) |
| | | Muhammad Hidayatullah (M) |
| | | Varahagiri Venkata Giri (H) |
| | 1974 | Fakhruddin Ali Ahmed (M) |
| Morarji Desai (H) | 1977 | Basappa Danappa Jatti (H) |
| | | Neelam Sanjiva Reddy (H) |
| Choudhary Charan Singh (H) | 1979 | |
| Indira Gandhi (H) | 1980 | |
| | 1982 | Giani Zail Singh (S) |
| Rajiv Gandhi (H) | 1984 | |
| | 1987 | Ramaswamy Venkataraman (H) |
| Vishwanath Pratap Singh (H) | 1989 | |
| Chandra Shekhar (H) | 1990 | |
| P. V. Narashima Rao (H) | 1991 | |
| | 1992 | Shankar Dayal Sharma (H) |
| Atal Behari Vajpayee (H) | 1996 | |
| Inder Kumar Gujral (H) | 1997 | Kocheril Raman Narayanan (H) |
| Atal Behari Vajpayee (H) | 1998 | |
| | 2002 | Abdul Kalam (M) |
| Manmohan Singh (S) | 2004 | |
| | 2007 | Pratibha Devisingh Patil (H) |

**Prime Ministers and Presidents of India**     **FIGURE 17.3**

H = Hindu, M = Muslim, S = Sikh

becoming terminal as in many developing countries, is often used as a temporary measure. It is seen more as a self-corrective procedure written into India's Constitution.[29]

The National Emergency of 1975–1977 and the
Challenge of "Popular" Authoritarianism

**BOX 17.4**

The national emergency from 1975 to 1977 that saw the suspension of fundamental rights, postponement of the general election by one year, arbitrary exercise of power, and incarceration of over 150,000 people, including several members of Parliament who stood up against it, was the first major trial of the strength and resilience of India's democracy. Both the motivation behind its declaration and the relative ease with which it could be imposed exposed the vulnerability of the Indian political system to authoritarian rule. But the electoral defeat of **Indira Gandhi** at the polls following the withdrawal of the state of emergency and the manner in which this defeat came about have produced an important political precedent against possible temptations of the authoritarian "alternative" on the part of political adventurers.

## The Prime Minister

The connecting link between the cabinet and the president as well as between executive and Parliament, the prime minister continues to be as Nehru used to describe it, "the linchpin of Government" (see again Figure 17.2). Nevertheless, the fact that power is exercised mostly by coalitions in contemporary Indian politics requires much more consultation with other parties. This sometimes leads to the open articulation of defiance against the authority of the prime minister, a situation that would have been unthinkable during the days of Nehru. Together with the ministers, the prime minister controls and coordinates the departments of government and determines policy through the submission of a program for parliamentary action. When the prime minister commands the majority in the Lok Sabha, his government is secure. But if he is defeated on any major issue, or if a no-confidence motion is passed, he must, by the conventions of cabinet government, resign. This has happened several times.

Other practices of cabinet government have become institutionalized in India as well. The cabinet provides the necessary backing to the prime minister. It provides a balance to his authority through its collective weight. This model was sorely tested during the tenure of Indira Gandhi, whose authoritarian tendencies and distrust of colleagues reduced the cabinet's role as a source of policy and administrative leadership, in sharp contrast to previous practice. The phenomenon was described as "deinstitutionalization."[30] Subsequent governments have restored the conventions of parliamentary government and the principle of collective responsibility.

The steady rise in the stature of Prime Minister Narasimha Rao in the 1990s was a testimony to the institutionalization of the office. Starting as a temporary replacement for Rajiv Gandhi and then as a compromise leader, Rao brought about radical changes in the management of the economy even without a solid legislative majority. His leadership skills were immensely valuable in ensuring a smooth transition after the assassination of Rajiv Gandhi and during the post-Ayodhya period. He maintained a delicate balance between the opposing factions of the Congress Party. So deeply entrenched are the principles of consensus and accommodation as core values of the political system that even after the end of Congress Party dominance and the coming of non-Congress Party governments, there has been no radical discontinuity in civil servants, policy mechanisms, or even policy orientations.

As prime ministers, Rao's successors, first Deve Gowda and then Inder Kumar Gujral, followed very much in the mold of consensus and accommodation. The real test came only in 1998 with the Vajpayee-government inducting into the central government leadership many individuals who lacked previous ministerial experience. However, the Bharatiya Janata Party (BJP) government continued to rule through consensus within the coalition, thus maintaining continuity in the areas of reform and security policy. The dexterity—with which Manmohan Singh has continued the tradition of prime ministerial leadership despite the presence of a large contingent of communists in the United Progressive Alliance (UPA) coalition and the long shadow of Sonia Gandhi on his government—is further testimony to the resilience of the practice of consultation and cohesion at the highest echelon of government in India.

## The Parliament

Even while they campaigned against British rule in India, the leaders of India's Freedom Movement aspired to a parliamentary democracy modeled on British institutions. For many of them, schooled in the British tradition, independence brought the opportunity to design India's Constitution. The main inspiration came from Britain, but with important differences. The principle of hereditary membership of landed aristocrats in the House of Lords has no equivalence in India. Besides, unlike Britain, India is a federation. As such, the upper house—the **Rajya Sabha** (the Council of States)—has some features of the U.S. Senate. In the same vein, reflecting the philosophy of social justice that underpinned the Freedom Movement, the system provides for some special features, such as the guaranteed representation of the former untouchables and tribals in the Lok Sabha through a quota system of "reserved seats."

The Parliament of India consists of two houses, the Lok Sabha, the lower house, and the Rajya Sabha, the upper house (see again Figure 17.2). The **Lok Sabha** (House of the People) consists of 545 members: 543 are directly elected and two are nominated by the president of India as representatives of the Anglo-Indian community. Elections of the members of the Lok Sabha take place on the basis of a simple majority, from single-member constituencies. The term of the Lok Sabha is five years, unless it is extended because of emergency conditions. The Lok Sabha can be dissolved before the end of its five-year mandate, or extended beyond five years, by the president on the advice of the prime minister (the latter has happened only once, during the emergency of 1975–1977).

The Parliament is designed to be an instrument of democratic accountability. The Constitution specifies that the Lok Sabha must meet at least twice a year, with no more than six months between sessions. The business of Parliament, avidly reported in the press, is transacted primarily in English or Hindi, but provision is made for the use of other Indian languages. Keeping to the British practice, a number of parliamentary committees impart a sense of continuity and specialization to the functioning of the Parliament. Some are primarily concerned with organization and parliamentary procedure. Others, notably the three

finance committees, act as watchdogs over the executive. Specific committees scrutinize the budget and governmental economy, appropriations and expenditures, the exercise of delegated power, and the implementation of ministerial assurances and promises.

The first hour of the parliamentary day (known as the zero hour) is devoted to questions that bring the ministers to public scrutiny. Written questions are submitted in advance—a process that extends the principle of parliamentary and public accountability to the bureaucracy—as well as through supplementary questions, which test the minister's ability to master the technical details of governance.

The Lok Sabha's ultimate control over the executive lies in the motion of no-confidence that can bring down the government. After the long years of hibernation during the era of uninterrupted Congress Party rule, the Parliament now exercises its right to hold the government responsible during the recent phase of coalition politics and unstable majorities. However, this has not created the kind of paralysis that occurred in the Fourth Republic of postwar France (see Chapter 8). The current number of leaders with ministerial experience both in the government and in the opposition ensures that the Parliament is both the scene of continuous challenges to the government as well as an opportunity to collaborate in the interest of governance.

The Rajya Sabha (Council of States) was seen merely as a "talking shop" during the earlier periods of Congress Party hegemony when the party dominated both houses of Parliament. Because most of the real power of accountability and finance inhere in the lower house, the center of political gravity naturally lies beyond the reach of the smaller, and constitutionally less powerful, upper house. Still, the increasingly competitive character of the Indian political process has increased the importance of the Rajya Sabha, too.

The Rajya Sabha consists of a maximum of 250 members, of which twelve are nominated by the president for their "special knowledge or practical experience" in literature, science, art, or social service. Reflecting the federal principle, the allocation of the remaining seats corresponds with the size of the respective population of the regions, except that small states have a larger share than their actual population proportion would imply. The members of the state legislative assembly elect members of the Rajya Sabha for a term of six years. The terms are staggered, so that elections are held for one-third of the seats every two years.

The role of the Parliament is normally confined to the scrutiny of legislation for its technical aspects because, reflecting the conventions of parliamentary democracy, most of the initiative for legislation lies with the cabinet. The legislators do not have the finances or the personnel that the political system of the United States bestows on the members of Congress. Indian committee hearings are not public occasions and therefore do not have the power of U.S. House or Senate committee hearings. As such, they provide only a forum for wide political consultation.[31]

The legislative process generally follows the British practice. Laws are initiated in the form of government bills or private members' bills. The latter are more an opportunity to air grievances and to draw attention because few if any ever become laws. The initiation of most legislation clearly lies with the government. All bills except money bills—with implications for spending, revenue, borrowing, or India's financial reserves—can be introduced in either house. The Ministry of Law and the Attorney General of India are consulted on legal and constitutional aspects. Ordinary bills go through three readings in each house. The second reading is the most vital because at this stage the bill receives the most detailed and minute examination and may be referred to a Select Committee or a Joint Committee of both houses of the Parliament. These committees do not have the same standing or resources as the committees in the U.S. House or Senate. They are neither called on to investigate the affairs of the government in public hearings nor asked to approve executive appointments. Their strength within the Indian system derives from the tradition of bipartisanship which, as in the United Kingdom, creates great confidence and respect for them within the government as well as the opposition parties.

Once both houses pass a bill, it requires the president's assent to become a law. This assent is not a mere formality. The president sometimes asks for technical details and expert advice in order to examine the constitutional implications of a bill before giving his assent. Potentially, this is a formidable threat in view of the fragility of coalitional politics where a united stand by the cabinet against an adversary is relatively difficult to sustain. A president determined to delay or obstruct legislation can do so through the simple expedient of not returning a bill, with or without assent, before the end of the current parliamentary session. In effect, this means that the government will repeat the entire legislative process for the bill in the next session. If the president withholds his assent and the Parliament passes the bill again, he would be obliged to give it the presidential assent. But these are exceptional situations. Unlike in the United States, the president is not expected to take legislative initiative, and there is no concept of the presidential veto as a source of influence on the policy process or an exercise of checks and balances.[32]

As a bill must be passed by both houses, joint sessions are used to resolve conflicts. Because of its larger size, the Lok Sabha plays a dominant role in such meetings. In matters relating to initiating money bills, the Lok Sabha has exclusive authority. The Rajya Sabha may only recommend changes; it cannot initiate, delay, or reject. When the majority of the ruling party or coalition in the Lok Sabha is narrow and the opposition has a majority in the Rajya Sabha, the potential peril of defeat in a joint session encourages the government to think in terms of cooperation rather than confrontation. This happened after 1977 when the Congress Party lost to the Janata Party in the parliamentary election and thus lost its majority in the Lok Sabha. Because only one-third of the seats of the Rajya Sabha are up for election every two years, the Congress Party continued to hold a majority in that house. When the Janata Party tried to amend the Constitution to remove the authoritarian measures that the Congress Party had introduced during the preceding emergency, it realized that it lacked the necessary majority in both houses. A compromise was struck and the Janata Party achieved only part of its legislative objectives. The parliamentary elections of 1996, 1998, and 2004 have produced situations where the two houses of the Parliament did not have the same majority coalitions. As such, the Rajya Sabha has gained in power and has begun to play an independent role in the matters of scrutiny and accountability.[33]

The lack of party discipline is the nemesis of parliamentary democracy, especially in countries like India, where modern institutions lack deep historical roots. Cross-party voting and defections can drive a government to paralysis and reduce parliamentary democracy to personal sovereignty or anarchy. The rapid governmental instability in the 1960s that resulted from the end of the Congress Party's hegemony gave India a warning of this potential danger.[34] Since then, government control over legislation was considerably strengthened by the passage of the anti-defection law. Under this act, voting against the party line is considered to be a defection, which leads to the loss of the seat by the member. This law and the electorate's disapproval of political opportunism have induced some stability at the level of the central and state governments.

## The Judiciary

The Constitution of India committed itself to individual rights of equality and liberty. However, it did not incorporate the American concept of natural justice where the U.S. Supreme Court is the ultimate defender of the "natural" rights of the individual. India's leaders had learned of parliamentary politics under British rule, and these principles led to a judicial system that is both independent from external control and free to interpret the law. It was originally intended to be supreme only within the "procedure established by law," and law itself is the domain of the legislature. On numerous occasions, however, the Court has vehemently defended its exclusive right to exercise control over legislation.

The Supreme Court has original and exclusive jurisdiction in disputes between the Union government and one or more states, or disputes between two or more states. It has appellate jurisdiction in any case, civil or criminal, that is certified as involving a substantial question of law in the meaning and intent of the Constitution. The Supreme Court is the interpreter and guardian of the Constitution, the supreme law of the land. Unlike the British system, where no national court exists to hold an act of Parliament invalid, all legislation passed in India's national or state governments must conform with the Constitution. The Supreme Court determines the constitutionality of any enactment. A remarkable feature of judicial review is the power of the Supreme Court to rule a constitutional amendment invalid if it violates the "basic structure" of the Constitution, but the scope of judicial review in India is not as wide as in the United States.

Although the modern legal system has largely displaced traditional customary law, traditional groups use the modern system for their own ends. The Supreme Court has dealt with such contentious issues as the Ayodhya case, which brought the dispute into the political system rather than let it slip out of the process of adjudication altogether (see again Box 17.3). The Court's landmark decisions—for example,

its ruling that *hindutva,* the core of the ideology of the BJP, was part of Indian culture and not necessarily of a religion—have deeply influenced the nature of political discourse in India. Recent survey findings rate the Indian Supreme Court along with the Election Commission as the most trustworthy of institutions.[35]

Since the core judicial doctrine of the Constitution of India puts the "procedure established by law" as superior to the American doctrine of "natural justice," the Supreme Court was initially accorded a status below the Parliament but above the national executive in terms of authoritative interpretation of the law. But gradually the Supreme Court has asserted its supremacy in such matters as well. This evolution was facilitated by the steady erosion of the massive legislative majorities since the early decades after India's independence, the rise of media influence, and the mobilization of interest groups at the national level. The emergency rule of Indira Gandhi (1975–1977) dented its authority and autonomy. But since then, the Court has bounced back.[36] The Court has reached a high level of esteem and trust in the eyes of the Indian public by drawing on the initiatives taken and innovations made in judicial practice and procedure. The Court exercises wide judicial review, on subjects ranging from the highly abstract and technical, such as personal law and industrial jurisprudence, to topical and controversial issues. The Court has also appointed itself as the guardian of vulnerable social groups and neglected areas of public life, such as the environment. Known as Public Interest Litigation (PIL), this is one of the most celebrated and contentious innovations of India's Supreme Court.

Today, the Supreme Court of India is seen as an important symbol of liberty, secularism, and social justice. It could all have turned out completely differently as in many changing societies where the pace of political mobilization overtakes that of the rule of law. That India did not follow this tragic course only goes to show the long evolution of the judicial culture under colonial rule and the important role played by lawyers in India's freedom struggle.

## The Bureaucracy

One of the main achievements of the Indian political system is a bureaucratic apparatus that is both professionally organized and politically accountable. The Indian bureaucracy is an enormously complex system that combines national or all-India services with regional and local services, as well as technical and managerial staff running public-sector undertakings. Public recruitment by merit with stiff competitive examinations is the general rule, with political appointments such as those in the United States being the rare exception.

The main services—like the Indian Administrative Service (IAS) and the Indian Police Service (IPS)—retain some of the features of their preindependence structures. But like the rest of the top services of India, they have been reorganized to create a federal balance in recruitment. The representation of the former untouchables, tribals, and women receive special attention. Recruitment is supervised by the Union Public Service Commission—an independent advisory body appointed by the president—and extensive new facilities exist for training new recruits. Although candidates are recruited centrally, the IAS is composed of separate cadres for each region. This composition strengthens federal links, because regional loyalties are balanced by the provision that at least half of the members of the IAS cadre come from outside the region. This practice creates language problems for officers who originate from outside, but it also encourages India's top administrators to learn the local language, contributing to the process of nation-building and cross-regional linkages. Members of district administration seek to combine rule of law, efficient management and coordination, and, increasingly, local democracy. These values are often hard to reconcile in practice: the extent to which a regional government succeeds in achieving this ideal acts as a crucial parameter of how successful it is in achieving the goal of democratic governance.

## THE FEDERAL STRUCTURE

Political unrest in Kashmir, separatist movements in Punjab and in the North East in the 1980s, and the occasional outbreak of intercommunity violence have generated considerable anxiety about India's national unity. The fear of "balkanization" greatly concerned India's leaders who lived through the bloody partition of the country. They saw demands for states' rights as the thin end of the wedge that could eventually dismember India. The successful accommodation of separatist demands increased the number of federal states to twenty-eight, and those movements are now seen as a democratic articulation of legitimate interests. The call for a federal division of powers, advocated by the

Indian National Congress in the 1920s when it organized its provincial committees on the basis of linguistically contiguous areas, originated from the need to safeguard regional and sectional identities. But economic policy, especially in a country with formidable problems of development, required central coordination. Out of these contradictory needs emerged what is known as the "cooperative" federalism of India.

Numerous special features of the Indian Constitution give it its highly centralized form. Of these, the two most important are the division of powers between the central government and the states with a bias in favor of the center, and the financial provisions affecting the distribution of revenues. In India, unlike in the United States, the federal states do not have their own separate constitutions. The state of Jammu and Kashmir is an exception, because the princely ruler acceded to the Indian Union on the condition that the central government would not interfere with the internal affairs of the state. Article 370, therefore, provides for separate constitutions for Jammu and Kashmir.

Kashmir has emerged as a test case of the integrative ability of the Indian political system. During British colonial rule, Kashmir was one of about six hundred princely states, ruled by Indian princes under British suzerainty. As a part of the general arrangements for the transfer of power, Britain agreed to partition the territories under direct rule into the sovereign states of India and Pakistan, and to transfer the right to decide for themselves—"paramountcy"—to the Indian princes who could join either of the two successor states or remain independent. Unlike most princely rulers who chose to join India or Pakistan, the king of Kashmir hesitated, because the king was Hindu while most of his subjects were Muslims. Within about a year of independence, however, when Pathan tribesmen, aided by Pakistan, invaded Kashmir, the king signed the Instrument of Accession to join India. India promptly airlifted troops to halt the invasion at the **line of control (LoC),** which became, thereafter, the unofficial frontier between Pakistan-Occupied Kashmir (PoK) and the area under Indian control. Since the state of Jammu and Kashmir has a special status under Article 370 of the Indian Constitution, it possesses more autonomy than other states. However, in practice, many of these special rights have been whittled down, bringing the states almost to the same level of control from the center as the federal states of the Indian Union.[37]

The Constitution of India, in the tradition of written agreements between the central government and the states, defines the division of powers between both sides in its seventh schedule. The Union List gives the center exclusive authority to act in matters of national importance; this list includes ninety-seven items, such as defense, foreign affairs, currency, banking, and income tax. The State List, which allocates exclusive rights of legislation to the states, includes sixty-six items of local and regional importance, such as public order and police, welfare, health, education, local government, industry, agriculture, and land revenue. The Concurrent List contains forty-seven items in which the center and the states share legislative authority. In case of a conflict, the central law prevails. Civil and criminal law, and social and economic planning are the important items in this list, as these subjects are crucial to issues of identity and economic development. The residual power lies with the Union. Unlike the classic model of federalism, in India the central government, acting through the Parliament, can create new states, alter the boundaries of existing ones, and even abolish a state by ordinary legislative procedure without recourse to constitutional amendment.

Not only does the central government have a wide range of powers under the Union List, but these powers are enhanced because the central government has a variety of powers that enable it, under certain circumstances, to extend its authority to the domain of the states. These special powers take three forms: (1) the emergency powers under Articles 352, 356, and 360; (2) the use of Union executive powers under Articles 256, 257, and 360; and (3) special legislative powers granted under Article 249.

The emergency powers in the Indian Constitution can enable the Union executive to transform the federation into a unitary state when the president makes a declaration to that effect. Under these emergency provisions, the central executive and legislature can simply substitute the corresponding organs of the regional governments. Even under nonemergency conditions, the central government may assume executive powers over regional governments in "national" interest. These powers, used by the president at the advice of the prime minister, are closely monitored by the Parliament, the media, and the judiciary. In this context, the Rajya Sabha acts as the custodian of the states' interests.

The center's right to influence the federal division of powers is reinforced by the Constitution's financial provisions. The central government has vast powers over the collection and distribution of revenue, which make the states depend heavily on the central government for financial support. Financial assistance flows from the central government to the states in several ways. Most of the lucrative taxes, like income tax, corporate tax, and import and export duties, are collected by the central government. The center and the states share these funds under a formula devised by the Finance Commission, which is appointed by the president but is guaranteed independence from interference by the center and states governments. The center alone has the power over currency, banking, and international borrowings. The states also have their own sources of income. But these taxes, like land revenue or irrigation taxes, for example, have not been particularly lucrative. Agricultural income is notoriously difficult to ascertain, and taxes on such income are difficult to collect.

As a result of the financial provisions envisaged in the Constitution and their evolution over time, the states are routinely short of funds. These shortfalls are met through central assistance in the form of loans, grants-in-aid, and overdraft facilities—provisions that compromise the autonomy of the states. This situation has been further reinforced by the centralizing tendencies of the national five-year plans and the powers exercised by the Congress Party on state governments, ruling both at the center and in the states virtually uninterrupted for two decades following India's independence.

Despite these centralizing tendencies, however, the Indian political system has a distinct pattern of cooperation between the center and the states. This cooperation was helped by rapid economic growth in some cases and the assertion of cultural identity and autonomy in others. Freed from the tutelage of central dominance because of the decline of the "one-dominant-party system" of the Congress Party, and liberalization of the economy since 1991, Indian federalism has become more robust in recent years. Additionally, the adoption of regional languages as administrative languages brings government closer to the people. The regional languages have experienced a renaissance, spurred on by the textbook market; public funds for regional culture; cinema and television; the National Sahitya Academy (the National Academy of Literature, which promotes the national language Hindi as well as the regional languages); and the national film festivals, which offer special prizes for the best regional films. The regional elite, confident in their language and identity, have rediscovered the virtues of learning English and Hindi, which give access to competitive jobs under the central government, to prestigious national universities, and to business and industry in other regions of India and abroad. Thus the language conflict, which split East Pakistan from West Pakistan and continues to threaten the integrity of Sri Lanka, has been relatively muted in India.

These institutions show how the Indian political system has combined elements of a modern state with the historical legacies of the premodern past. The Constitution includes countervailing forces—a wide spectrum of institutions with a sense of corporate identity, political power, agenda, and political base—that would make it difficult, though not impossible, for a potential dictator to transform the political system into an authoritarian regime. In the process, the state has become the initiator of change, the author of a nation in the making.

Next, we will see how the political process produces a continuous interaction between the values of individualism, liberty, egalitarianism, and secularism on which the system is based, and the hierarchical and organic norms of the society within which it is ensconced. In the process, the system has sometimes been stretched to the limit but without breaking down altogether, and it has managed to bounce back in a transformed shape and with renewed vigor.

## THE ARTICULATION OF INTERESTS

The aggressive pursuit of interests by a politically mobilized citizenry can strain the limited capacity of political institutions in rapidly changing societies. This section examines how interest and pressure groups, and an assortment of protest movements, engage in political transaction at the national, regional, and local levels. Despite the pressure on the institutions and the occasional political crisis, the system has so far maintained its resilience.

The formal representation of interest in India reflects three key features. First is the vast range of modes of representation, stretching from efficiently organized, modern organizations of employers, businessmen, industrialists and labor on the one extreme to traditional forms, involving caste, tribe, and ethnic groups, on the other extreme. In addition, there are unconventional political forms like *satyagraha, dharna, boycott,* or *rasta roko*, inspired by Gandhi. Then, there are also radical organizations that resort to collective violence and suicide. The second feature is that there is no practice of "closed shop," where specific organizations have monopoly control over the representation of particular interests. Instead, considerable competition among organizations fragments interests. This situation has stymied the growth of interest articulation as an independent and powerful phenomenon in its own right, which is usually the case in industrial liberal democracies. Third, people with a cause or a grievance combine effectively in various forms of action and organizations, such as parties, interest and pressure groups, movements, and spectacular forms of political protest. Consequently, India's level of interest articulation and aggregation is comparable to the one found in long-established and more prosperous western democratic states even in the absence of formal organizations of interest representation at the same scale.

## Trade Unions and Employers' Associations

Under India's labor law, any seven workers can formally set up a trade union. State-appointed labor inspectors provide counsel and inquire into the conditions of work. Trade unionism in India today is built on the historical legacy of some leading trade unions and employers' organizations which date back to British colonel rule. For example, the All India Trade Union Congress (AITUC), one of the largest central trade union organizations in the country, it was established in 1920 and is the oldest Indian trade union. The AITUC was founded by the Indian National Congress as a mainstream labor organization during India's independence movement, in which it played a significant role. Since independence, the AITUC has been affiliated with the Communist Party of India. A second example is the All India Railwaymen's Federation (AIRF), founded in 1925, which today has a membership of more than a million railway workers.

Similar to that of workers, several well-organized interest representations of employers can be found in India. One famous example is the Confederation of Indian Industries (CII), founded in 1895 as the Engineering and Iron Trades Association. CII is now the most visible business association in India with over 4,700 member companies, eleven overseas offices, and institutional partnerships with 216 organizations in ninety-four countries. Similarly, the Federation of Indian Chambers of Commerce and Industry (FICCI) together with the Associated Chambers of Commerce and Industry (ASSOCHAM) function as the apex for trade associations and industry in India. Both groups are key actors in policy formulation and the socioeconomic transformation of the country. They also have a significant role in the making of government economic policy.

Unlike in liberal democracies where interest groups concentrate on the conditions of work that they seek to improve through collective bargaining, India's unions are closely affiliated to political parties and thus become specially active at election time. The culture of effective collective bargaining is not deeply entrenched. Rather than organized strikes as the ultimate weapon, India's unions often resort to illegal stoppage of work (referred to as "wildcat strikes") and rely on state intervention on their behalf to win better conditions. Additionally, they are highly fragmented, with an increasing number of unions competing for a stagnant pool of workers. Also, intraunion feuds reduce the effectiveness of the union movement as a whole.[38]

Trade unionism has gone through four broad phases after India's independence, corresponding to structural changes in the economy. The first phase, 1950 to the mid-1960s, saw the government pursuing a planned economy and an import substitution strategy, which corresponded to the rise of public-sector unionism. The second phase lasted up to the late 1970s and was a period of relative economic stagnation and political instability. It witnessed rising labor discontent, interunion rivalries, and industrial conflict. Organizations like the Hind Mazdoor Sabha emerged as leading voices in the labor movement. The third phase, 1980 to 1991, was characterized by uneven economic development so that decentralized bargaining and independent trade unionism gained ground. Interstate and interregional variations in the labor-management regimes grew wider with unions strengthened in the more prosperous economic sectors. The fourth phase started with the economic reforms of the early 1990s. It is characterized by demands for greater labor market flexibility, especially in employment and industrial dispute management. Reforms are considered vital to stimulate India's manufacturing sector, but they are resisted particularly by the left parties which, since 2004, lent outside support to the ruling UPA coalition.

## Indigenous Interests

There are also indigenous variations of interest articulation. Some, like *satyagraha* ("holding on to truth"), were originally inspired by Gandhi as a form of passive resistance to British rule. The tradition of unconventional direct action has spawned many variants.[39] These are supplemented by social movements. For example, the *Chipko* movement in northern India fought for the protection of the Himalayan forests. Based on Gandhian principles, it used nonviolent protest and attracted attention with its tactic of village women hugging trees to prevent the trees from being chopped down. Their first protest action took place in April 1973, and the movement had its major success in 1980 when it secured a fifteen-year ban on "green felling" in the Himalayan forests of Uttar Pradesh.

There are also more specialized pressure groups, such as the Bharatiya Kisan Union (BKU), also known as the Indian Peasant Union, which has organized *kisans* (working peasants). The *kisans* are divided between two broad sections; namely, the small self-sufficient landowners who cultivate land with family labor and do not employ outside labor, and more affluent peasant proprietors whose holdings are usually well above the subsistence level.

## Local Politics: Democracy at the Grassroots Level

The emergency of 1975–1977 brought together a wide range of political forces for the defense of civil liberties (see again Box 17.4). These groups—consisting of lawyers, journalists, academics, social workers, and political activists—became an important pressure group starting in the 1980s. Their presence and intervention have publicized the struggles of vulnerable social groups and exposed acts of administrative injustice and, in more extreme cases, state repression. Thus, the greatly restricted scope for interest articulation and aggregation caused by the 1975–1977 events produced nonparty political movements, local protest movements, and civil rights activists.

This development has led to the emergence of a new social class of mediators in the political process, generally called the "social activists." These are often upper and middle-class citizens, who identify themselves with the lower orders of society, a whole variety of social strata ranging from the untouchable castes to the destitute among the tribes and ethnic minorities. One speaks today of political movements as a generic form of political action. There is a new genre of "movements" that have an economic content, but are multidimensional and cover a large terrain in practice. This new genre includes the high-profile environmental movements, the women's movement, the civil liberties movement, movements for regional self-determination and autonomy, and the peasants' movement. Other groups focus on peace, disarmament, and denuclearization. Democracy has appeared as the power of the powerless. The powerful, in their turn, have learned some lessons about the hidden costs of authoritarian solutions to political problems from the emergency of 1975–1977. The coalition that brought the Janata Party to power in 1977 in many ways benefited from the widespread desire for democratic participation and access to the center of decision making. The trend continues.

At a larger, systemic level, the rise of this new consciousness of civil rights provides a balancing factor to the growth of authoritarian tendencies and the advocacy of a muscular, developmental state, committed to rational management and modern technology. These grassroots movements also signify a new understanding of the democratic process, which has moved from an almost exclusive preoccupation with parties and elections to new issues that the political system has not addressed. The period of erosion of parliamentary, party, and federal institutions and of the decline of the authority of the state has been accompanied by the rise of new actors on the scene, new forms of political expression, and new definitions of the content of politics.[40] The growth of local protest movements as a method for articulating interests and demanding administrative redress was facilitated by the wide acceptance of lobbying and contacting decisionmakers, and other techniques of direct action, such as forcing public officials to negotiate by *dharna*—a form of sit-in strike—or to bear on them by physically surrounding them *(gherao)*.[41]

A survey of over 200 local elites in two Indian states revealed wide acceptance of collective protest as a means to get state officials to listen to local demands and meet local needs. The perception of this "room for maneuver in the middle" gives a new focus and depth to democratic institutions because it acts as a sanction against official complacency and inadequacy in implementation while undercutting the appeal of violent revolution as a more effective solution to problems.[42] The growth of political consciousness and the mobilization of interests have created a situation in India where the level of legitimacy and the sense of individual efficacy exceed the trust people have in politicians or in their ability to deliver the goods. This situation creates the potential for instability, because landslide victories can fizzle out at the first sign of failure by a leader. This was the case for **Rajiv Gandhi,** who won the biggest victory the Congress Party ever had at the polls in 1984 and then rapidly lost popular support when rumors about bribery by the Swedish company Bofors began to circulate. In a situation like this, politicians may attempt to escape popular wrath by taking recourse to abstract rhetoric and populist promises rather than concrete policy that might involve some sacrifice. The obverse side of chaotic populism is a dose of authoritarianism, which offers to set things right and carries a disgruntled citizenry away with it. India has already had a taste of such methods during Indira Gandhi's Emergency rule.

## Democracy and the Challenge of Governance

When political demands overtake the capacity of the system to satisfy them, as American political scientist Samuel Huntington had warned in the 1960s, the gap can enhance political disorder.[43] But when political participation occurs in the context of a state that combines accommodation with the repression of antisystem forces, the combined effort can lead to the resilience of a democratic political process. In this context, India's record on the management of law and order, which has successfully brought down the number of riots per million inhabitants from its peak in the mid-1980s (see Figure 17.4), deserves special attention, particularly because of the critical focus that

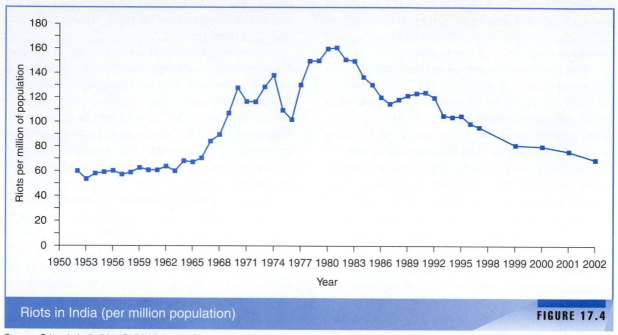

**Riots in India (per million population)**

**FIGURE 17.4**

Source: *Crime in India* (New Delhi: Ministry of Home Affairs; various years).

India has recently received about human rights violations from human rights groups within the country and abroad.

The Indian case demonstrates how transactional politics within firm boundaries laid down and defended with overwhelming force by the state have helped in the functioning of representative political institutions. They provided the channels of political recruitment to aspiring social elites as well as the means for upward mobility to the lower social strata. One consequence is the absence of significant social groups that feel sufficiently discriminated against to undertake collective rebellion. However, the recent spate of suicides by indebted and impecunious farmers shows the limitation of this strategy of accommodation.

## The Military

The military and paramilitary forces of India deserve special attention. Although the number of armed military has increased significantly, the civilian government of India remains firmly in control. In contrast to many developing countries, especially in Africa, the Indian middle classes had opted for civil service and professional jobs under colonial rule, and have continued to prefer political careers after independence. In

India, this situation contributed to the professional and apolitical character of the army. Consequently, the officer corps of India, traditionally accustomed to civilian control and indoctrinated with the appropriate disposition in the course of their training, has remained nonpartisan even during political turmoil.

The absence of a leadership vacuum at the upper and middle levels of the system and the fragmented character of the command structure of the military in India are other contributory factors to the relative immunity of the Indian political system from a military takeover. The second source of danger for the political system from the breakdown of law and order is contained through a large police force of about a million men and women.

Under India's federal division of powers, law and order is a state subject. As such, the basic components of the Indian police are recruited, trained, and deployed by the regional governments. However, the central government also exercises considerable power over law and order management through different methods. In the first place, some special police forces are recruited and trained by the central government. In principle, central forces can be sent to trouble spots in the regions at the request of the state governments, and once deployed they are placed under the orders of state officials. The district magistrate and the superintendent of police normally belong to the Indian Administrative Service and the Indian Police Service, both of which are central services. As such, these officials typically have some accountability to the central government in their professional judgments.

As the situation in Ayodhya in 1992 and Gujarat in 2002 revealed, however, even the presence of a large paramilitary force is no guarantee of the effective management of law and order when the central and state governments do not agree on the policy to be followed. In extreme cases, therefore, the Constitution provides for a direct rule by the center under Article 356 (the president's rule, which we discussed earlier). Central intervention in Punjab and Kashmir occurred under similar conditions where the regional government proved either unwilling or unable to take effective measures. Effective law and order management certainly contributed to the restoration of the political process in Punjab. The regions of India and the state itself continuously share with each other knowledge of law and order management, which results in the creation of new forces or major changes in equipment, training, and service conditions.

## THE PARTY SYSTEM

The party system of contemporary India is the result of the six decades of growth under British rule prior to India's independence. It is a complex system, characterized by the continuous presence of the Congress Party in the national political arena, the emergence of a powerful Hindu nationalist movement, the world's longest elected communist government at the regional level, and the occasional lapse into authoritarian rule (which, nonetheless, did not become terminal as in the case of the majority of postcolonial societies). The picture becomes much clearer if we divide the postindependence period into the "one-dominant-party system" period (1952–1977) and its subsequent transformation into a multiparty system.[44] The relative ease with which India developed electoral democracy and a competitive party system might appear puzzling.

Universal adult franchise was introduced in 1952. All political parties, including communists and the extreme right-wing Jan Sangh, were authorized to participate in the election. Thanks to the extension of suffrage, the electorate expanded and brought into the political arena a large number of voters with no previous electoral experience. Such a sudden influx of new voters could have been a recipe for disaster for democracy and political order, particularly in conjunction with the violence that accompanied the partition of India. But the subsequent course of parliamentary democracy—thanks to the continuity of the institutions of state and the structures of leader-constituent relations—saw parties and elections becoming an essential part of the political culture of postindependence India. Voter turnout, spread over all social classes, went up steadily, from 45.7 percent in the first general election to the Lok Sabha held in 1952 to 58 percent in the third general election held in 1962. It has remained stable at almost 60 percent between 1962 and the fourteenth elections in 2004 (see Figure 17.5).

How do India's political parties combine, on the one hand, elections based on single-member constituencies and franchise based on the idea of individual choice, with, on the other hand, the existence of castes, tribes, and other groups based on collective identities? Factions—short-term alliances of individuals and groups that come together opportunistically to cash in their numerical strength in the ballot box—is a possible answer to this puzzle. Elections and party competition have thus played a double role by empowering both individuals and groups, leading to the continuous creation of new groups and coalitions. Rather than inhibiting the growth of party competition, social conflict, interwoven with political conflict, deepens political partisanship. Elections with limited franchise under British rule facilitated political transition by acting as the institutional context in which power was transferred to elected Indian leaders.

After India's independence, the same process accelerated the pace of social change, leading to a second phase of political change when the generation from the freedom movement was replaced by younger leaders. Many of these new leaders came from upwardly mobile, newly enfranchised, lower social classes. The entry of the Bharatiya Janata Party, widely seen as the party of business and industry, into government brought these groups closer to power. All sections of Indian society thus have had links to the structure of power at one time or another, if not in the national arena, then at least in one or more regional governments.

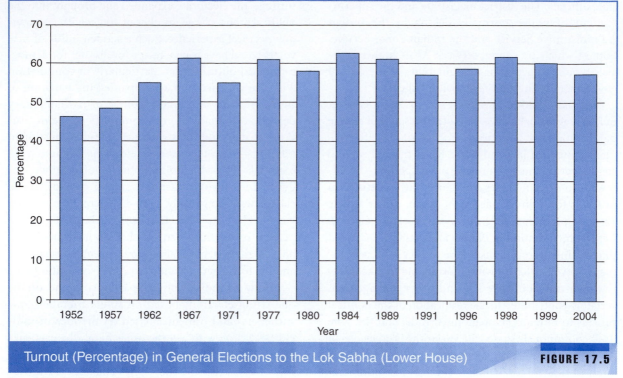

Turnout (Percentage) in General Elections to the Lok Sabha (Lower House)    **FIGURE 17.5**

Source: Election Commission of India.

## The Congress System

The first two decades following independence in 1947, roughly corresponding to Nehru's stewardship of Indian politics, were crucial to the transition from a colonial state to a democratic government. The years between 1950 and 1967 were the period of solid dominance of the Congress Party. Although the opposition parties did not alternate with the dominant party in controlling the government, their exclusion from the formation of public policy was more formal than real. In fact, they were vital for the functioning of the **Congress system.** Their importance is amply demonstrated by the extent to which government policy was influenced (even though this influence was exercised indirectly) by opposition parties. This was the basic characteristic of the one-dominant-party system that distinguished it from a one-party system as well as from a multiparty system (see Figure 17.6).

During the first two decades after Independence, the Congress Party ruled at the center as well as in the states. It achieved this remarkable feat by drawing on its legacy as the party of Gandhi, Nehru, and the Freedom Movement. It also succeeded through engaging

in patronage, accommodating often conflicting interests, and developing an internal pattern of factions that made the party open to new interests. This unique achievement caused the specialists of Indian politics to call this period the Congress "system"; that is, "a system of patronage [within which] traditional institutions of kin and caste were . . . accommodated and a structure of pressures and compromises was developed."[45]

Ironically and fortuitously, the authoritarian ways of the Congress Party facilitated the growth of a bargaining political culture and the recruitment of new elites—both of which are indispensable for the transition to democracy in developing societies. Thus, the system achieved competition despite the fact that the Congress Party was the ruling party virtually everywhere in India. Individuals who had risen to power in the Congress Party organization sometimes constituted the chief opposition to the government and provided an alternative route to influence over policy. In this process, elections at various levels of the party organization played an important role, as did the selection of party candidates for the general elections.

The relative strength of political parties in the Parliament meant that during the two decades

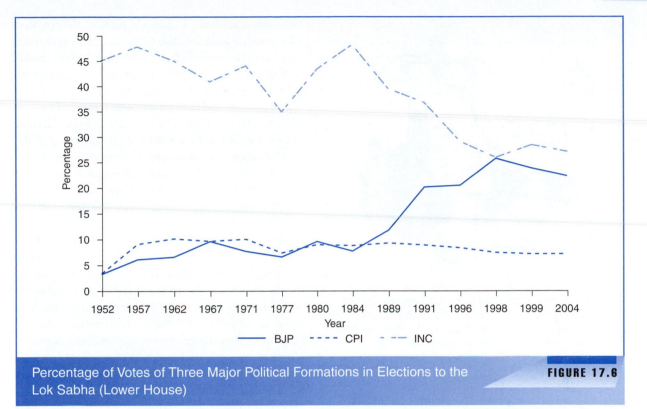

**Percentage of Votes of Three Major Political Formations in Elections to the Lok Sabha (Lower House)**    **FIGURE 17.6**

Note: The label INC includes: Indian National Congress (1967), Congress (Requisionist) (1971), Congress (Indira) (1980). BJP (Bharatiya Janata Party) was, until 1976, named BJS (Bharatiya Jana Sangh). The BJS did not participate in the elections of 1977 and 1980 under its own name because it formed part of the Janata party coalition. The label CPI includes the CPI (Communist Party of India) and the CPI (M) (Communist Party of India [Marxist]).

following independence, non-Congress parties had no possibility of exercising political power directly. Nevertheless, they had influence over policy as well as civil servants. The opposition parties in this system were "parties of pressure," operating outside the Congress Party but constantly criticizing, pressuring, censoring, and influencing opinion and interests both inside and outside the Parliament. This restrained the Congress Party from taking too intransigent a position on policy.

The Congress Party itself contained factions ranging from the ideological left to the right, and encompassing various regional and parochial interests as well as more secular and modern pressure groups. Furthermore, the opposition parties constantly exerted a latent threat to the Congress Party that, if the latter strayed too far from the centrist position, it would be displaced from power by a coalition of the aggrieved factions. This element of internal competition facilitated the mobilization of new interests and the recruitment of new social groups into power.

The Congress Party established its dominance essentially by a process of progressive expansion of its social base, so that ever new layers of recruitment and support were available to it, making it able to tilt a majority in its favor in most regions and to continue in its position of dominance.[46] This expansion occurred in several ways. Soon after India's independence, the Congress Party co-opted landed gentry, businessmen, peasant proprietors, new industrialists, and the rural middle class—socially and economically entrenched groups in society—into its organization. This action provided the party with a strong and ready structure of support, with electoral "link men" that controlled various "vote banks," serviced through patronage. The process of co-optation replaced higher castes that dominated the party machine in the regions and districts. Wherever the process was successful, it expanded the social base of the Congress Party and continued its ascendancy. In addition, the Congress Party developed an elaborate network of patronage, which made it possible to bargain with a wide spectrum of social groups for

A cartoon of Sonia Gandhi, the Italian-born widow of former Prime Minister Rajiv Gandhi, as the new imperatrice of India. Her decisive role in the election of Mr. Manmohan Singh as the leader of the PDA coalition and Prime Minister in 2004 shows her continuing influence in Indian politics.

*India Today International*, September 21, 1998, p 9.

political support in return for economic and social benefits with various social strata in rural and urban areas.

All this enabled the Congress Party to be a catch-all party and further consolidated its electoral organization on the basis of the traditional social structure as well as the emerging structure of economic opportunities.[47] Both the traditionally entrenched social groups and the new aspirants developed a stake in the Congress Party, internalized the symbolism and procedures of the electoral and parliamentary systems, and got actively involved in the overall framework of authority and decisionmaking represented by the Congress Party. The resulting distribution of consensus proved highly functional to the development of democratic values and procedure among the large masses of the Indian electorate.

Such a process necessarily confronted the Congress Party with new issues and new pressures. These have been addressed by neutralizing the more glaring sources of conflict in Indian society by timely and often anticipatory legislation—the abolition of *zamindars,* far-reaching protective labor legislation, the removal of gross social inequalities by granting special rights and advantages to backward groups, and linguistic reorganization of the states. These progressive legislative measures were often supplemented with firm suppression of secessionist

and violent activities in various parts of the country. Along with legislation, the Congress Party attempted both "penetration" of labor unions and "accommodation" of minority communities, and at the same time an informal but elaborate system of conciliation and resolution of conflicts and factional disputes through the mediation of prominent individuals at various levels. All these steps jointly led to a considerable strengthening of the party of consensus and a corresponding weakening of the potential sources of cleavage that might have gravely affected the stability of the political system.

It is important to remember that many of the advantages attributed to independent India were also available to other successor states that grew out of the British Empire. Whereas in Pakistan postindependence politics eventually led to the growth of antidemocratic social forces, in India it led to a fusion of cultural pluralism and political transaction, thus creating an authentically Indian political process. By making politics the great engine of mobilization and identity, the postindependence political process brought wide sections of society to the fold of the new political order, dispersed the symbolism of parliamentary government and economic development, and socialized traditional and emerging elites into the norms of democratic politics.

The method of interest articulation and aggregation that took place within the framework of the one-dominant-party system made the state the inevitable intermediary between competing interests in disputes involving labor and management as conceptualized in the Industrial Disputes Act of 1947. The same applied to landowner and peasant, student and university, and virtually every conceivable social conflict. This development led to the multiplication of the number of unions, all competing for basically the same pool of workers. It contributed to "involuted pluralism"— growth in the number of unions and labor militancy accompanied by the diminution of average membership and financial viability.[48] This system of interest articulation, aggregation, and conflict management was seriously challenged for the first time during the emergency of 1975–1977 (see again Box 17.4).

## The Bharatiya Janata Party

In the early 1990s, the **Bharatiya Janata Party (BJP)** confirmed its position as the main challenger to the Indian National Congress in northern India. Its presence outside the Hindi-heartland of North

India—where neither Hindi nor the religious dispute, centered on a temple for **Rama** in Ayodhya, predominate—is a phenomenon of great significance. The steady evolution of the party in the national Parliament is equally impressive. From the low point of two seats in the Lok Sabha in 1984, the party went up to eighty-five in 1989 and 182 seats in the parliamentary elections held in 1999. However, in the parlimentary election of 2004 the number of seats has dropped to 138.

In the course of its rapid rise to power, the party had drawn on the desire of many Hindus to see a more prominent role for Hindu culture within the institutions of the secular state and to deny special treatments to minorities, such as a special status for the Muslim majority state of Jammu and Kashmir. The BJP came to power riding the crest of Hindu nationalism and promising to build a temple for Rama in the city of Ayodhya where the Babri mosque stood. It failed to find a solution to the conflict between Hindus and Muslims, each of whom demand exclusive ownership of the site. When the mosque was demolished by a mob of Hindu zealots, the state government, led by the BJP, accepted responsibility for its failure to uphold law and order and resigned. Subsequently, the imperatives of India's coalitional politics have caused the party to moderate its stand on cultural and religious issues.

During the short-lived tenure of Vajpayee as prime minister (1998–1999), the party spoke more of good governance and less of Hindu nationalism. Back in office in 1999 and with a clear majority for the National Democratic Alliance, of which the BJP was the largest partner in the Lok Sabha, Prime Minister Vajpayee announced the commitment of his government to follow the same moderate policies that he had launched during his previous tenure.

The general election of 2004 to the Lok Sabha took place about six months before the end of the five-year term of the National Democratic Alliance government, led by the BJP. When the government called for early elections, nearly all opinion polls predicted a comfortable victory on the strength of its record in office as well as the personal popularity of Prime Minister Vajpayee. Thus, the upset victory by the Congress Party-led **United Progressive Alliance (UPA)** took everyone by surprise. In retrospect, the NDA's campaign slogan "India Shining," which celebrated its achievements on the unprecedented rate of growth of the economy, seems to have backfired. Those who had not gained from the liberalization of the economy, those who

stood to lose from the removal of subsidies, the population in rural areas of India, and some religious minorities appear to have voted against the coalition. For the first time, the Congress Party made preelection alliances with regional parties opposed to the Hindu nationalist BJP on a "secular" platform. The Congress Party used the votes cast in favor of the UPA efficiently, greatly enhancing the number of its own seats in the Lok Sabha.

## Communist Party

Founded in 1927, the Communist Party of India is one of the oldest in the world. It was proscribed for most of the time under British rule except toward the end when the party came out openly in support of the war effort once the Soviet Union came under attack from Nazi Germany. The party went through factional struggle and several splits on ideological grounds following India's independence. The Telengana uprising of 1946–1947, modeled after the Chinese revolution, was rapidly put down by the Indian army. This discredited the leftist faction. Under the leadership of the right faction, the party came to terms with Indian democracy and took part in the first general election, emerging as the second largest party after the Congress Party, though it was far behind it in terms of actual number of seats. More success was to follow.

The Communist Party won the regional election in the southern state of Kerala in 1957, a first victory for communism in a democratic election. Coinciding with the resolution of the Soviet Communist Party to support "peaceful transition to democracy," the party looked poised for a bigger role in Indian politics. However, that was not to be. The dismissal of the communist government of Kerala after two years in office by the Congress Party in the Center under Article 356 of the Constitution showed the limits of "bourgeois democracy," exactly as the left faction of the party had argued. More bad news was to follow. Differences with China on the boundary led to a border conflict in 1962, which caused members of the left faction to come out in favor of China, leading to their incarceration. The split was formalized in 1964 with the founding of the Communist Party of India (Marxist) (CPM), which followed a radical, pro-Chinese line compared with the Communist Party of India (CPI) which stuck with a more moderate, pro-Congress and pro-Soviet line. The CPM itself split five years later when its own left wing emerged as a new party—the Communist Party of India (Marxist-Leninist)—and initiated a peasant uprising in the Naxalbari district in the foothills of the Himalayas. The peasant uprising was put down by the security forces amid much bloodshed.

Two main trends have emerged since these turbulent times. The CPM, which came to power in West Bengal in the late 1970s, has become one of the longest serving, democratically elected communist governments anywhere in the world. At the center, the sixty communist members of the Parliament, whose support from the "outside" is crucial to the continuation of the UPA government, constitute an important source of influence on public policy. However, the urge for revolution, powerfully articulated by the "Naxalites"—this is how the Indian Maoists named themselves—lives on, under different names in different parts of India, whose violent activities continue to be a source of anxiety for the Indian government, particularly in view of the success of Maoists in neighboring Nepal.

## The Social Bases of the Parties

Drawing on survey data provides the basic information about the distribution of support to the main political parties across social formations (see Table 17.3).

| Social Profile for Major Political Formations, 2004 (in percentages) | | UPA Congress+ | NDA BJP+ | Left | BSP | SP | Share in Survey Sample | TABLE 17.3 |
|---|---|---|---|---|---|---|---|---|
| **Area** | Rural | 37 | 37 | 8 | 6 | 5 | 79.5 | |
| | Urban | 38 | 38 | 9 | 3 | 4 | 20.5 | |
| **Gender** | Male | 36 | 37 | 7 | 5 | 5 | 55.2 | |
| | Female | 37 | 35 | 9 | 5 | 5 | 44.8 | |
| **Caste/Community** | Upper Caste | 24 | 56 | 9 | 1 | 3 | 15.7 | |
| | Peasant proprietors | 37 | 47 | 4 | 1 | 3 | 8.4 | |
| | Upper OBC | 36 | 39 | 4 | 3 | 8 | 20.0 | |
| | Lower OBC | 36 | 39 | 10 | 3 | 4 | 16.0 | |
| | Dalit | 37 | 23 | 10 | 21 | 3 | 16.1 | |
| | Adivasi | 42 | 33 | 8 | <1 | <1 | 7.5 | |
| | Muslim | 53 | 11 | 7 | 3 | 16 | 9.9 | |
| | Sikh | 26 | 47 | 8 | 5 | 3 | 2.4 | |
| | Christian | 54 | 21 | 11 | 1 | — | 3.4 | |
| | Others | 27 | 30 | 23 | 3 | 1 | 0.5 | |
| **Caste/Community/Group** | Hindu upper caste | 9.8 | 25.6 | 17.8 | 1.9 | 8.6 | 15.7 | |
| | Hindu peasant proprietor | 6.8 | 11.8 | 3.3 | 1.0 | 2.8 | 8.6 | |
| | Subtotal (upper): | 16.6 | 37.4 | 21.1 | 2.9 | 11.4 | 24.3 | |
| | Hindu upper OBC | 21.2 | 21.9 | 9.4 | 7.3 | 34.1 | 19.8 | |
| | Hindu lower OBC | 15.4 | 17.5 | 19.7 | 6.2 | 9.8 | 16.1 | |
| | Subtotal (middle): | 36.6 | 39.4 | 29.1 | 13.5 | 43.9 | 35.9 | |
| | Dalit | 16.6 | 9.6 | 19.2 | 76.7 | 6.2 | 16.0 | |
| | Adivasi | 8.5 | 5.4 | 7.1 | 0.6 | 0.0 | 7.2 | |
| | Muslim | 15.0 | 2.5 | 9.3 | 3.8 | 37.5 | 9.8 | |
| | Subtotal (lower): | 40.0 | 17.5 | 35.6 | 81.1 | 43.7 | 33.0 | |
| | Others | 6.9 | 5.7 | 14.0 | 2.5 | 1.0 | 6.8 | |
| **Percent of Respondents** | | 27.6 | 29.5 | 7.6 | 3.7 | 2.7 | 100 | |

Source: *Economic and Political Weekly*, 18 December 2004, 5392–5393.

The social base of the Congress Party cuts across all social groups and cleavages of India, making it India's quintessential catch-all party. Nevertheless, the Congress Party has relatively greater support in the lower social order and among religious minorities.

The social profile of the Hindu nationalist BJP presents a sharp contrast. It is very much a party of the "Hindu-Hindi-belt," which normally indicates the northern Indian Gangetic plains. The table shows that the BJP continues to be very much a party of the upper social order and Hindu upper caste, but has nevertheless already succeeded in extending its reach to the former untouchables and tribals and even to a small section of Muslim voters and politicians.

By the standards of its national support base, the left, consisting of both Communist parties (CPM and CPI), attracts proportionally more support from the lower social classes as well as support from the more educated voters. The rise of India's regional parties is comparatively a recent phenomenon. Like the Congress Party, in the regional context these parties cut across all social groups and compete with the Congress Party, for the same social base, except for the Other Backward Classes (OBC), a social group sandwiched between the Hindu upper classes and the former untouchables. The leaders of many of India's regional parties are drawn from the OBC, which in consequence tend to exert proportionally more support to the regional parties.

At India's independence, the introduction of universal adult franchise empowered underprivileged social groups with a new political resource. The right to vote by secret ballot—exercised at a polling booth conveniently located at a public place where one could vote freely—created an environment that was helpful for political participation. The right to vote in secrecy and without coercion acted as a direct challenge to social dominance posed by newly mobilized lower castes and religious minorities who felt empowered thanks to the value of the vote.

Social mobilization and its political containment appear to have taken place in India as two independent but ultimately convergent processes. The pace of social change has accelerated through social reform legislation, recruitment of new social elites into the political arena, and political mobilization through electoral participation. Their overall impact on the stability of the political system has been moderated by intermediary functions and parties at the regional and local levels.

Lloyd and Susanne Rudolph have described the process as *vertical, horizontal* and *differential* mobilization.[49] Typically, as the marginal social groups discovered the negotiable value of the vote during the early years after independence, they became avid players in the political arena at the local and regional levels. Established *jajmani* systems—reciprocal social bonds based on the exchange of service and occupational specialization—broke down to create new groupings. Finally, caste associations, based on shared social and economic interests, emerged as links between parties and the society.[50] These developments created useful room to maneuver for the national, regional, and local elites.[51]

## POLITICAL SOCIALIZATION AND POLITICAL CULTURE

India's per capita gross national product in terms of purchasing power parity is about 6 percent of U.S. GNP and its literacy rate is low (about 65 percent according to the 2001 Census). But despite mass poverty and low literacy India has sustained the democratic form of government it adopted at independence. The contradiction between these two important "preconditions" of democracy and Indian reality is puzzling. To explain this phenomenon, it is necessary to analyze the political attitudes that underpin political behavior in Indian society and how people came to acquire them (see Box 17.5).

### The Interaction of Tradition and Modernity

Those unfamiliar with Indian politics might be amazed at the mingling of modern institutions and premodern practices and symbols within the framework of the modern state. In his introduction to India's political culture, W. H. Morris-Jones explains this phenomenon in terms of three idioms: the modern, the traditional, and the saintly.[52] The modern idiom understands politics as a competitive process of articulation and aggregation of interests. This modern idiom of Indian politics consists of the Constitution and the courts, parliamentary debate, the higher administration, the upper levels of all the main political parties, and the entire English press and much of the Indian language press. The main debates of Indian politics—on issues of federalism, economic development, planning or defense expenditure, for example—take place in the modern language of politics, and as such are accessible to Western students of Indian politics.[53]

## The Right to Vote: Power of the Powerless

BOX 17.5

A report in *India Today*, India's most widely circulated newsmagazine, gives an interesting insight into the strong support given by the backward classes to the government of the Janata Dal in the 1995 elections. A 55-year-old Dalit woman, "pointing to the stain of indelible ink on her finger," says, "I voted for Laloo." The reporters "point to the gaping cracks in her roof, her grandchildren who have nothing to wear, the medicine she does not have, the two meals she cannot afford, and ask, "Why?" She replies, "All that has been there for thousands of years." Saying this, she remembers the day the chief minister's helicopter landed on the nearby paddy field. "Laloo came to visit us," she announces. "Since I was born, not even a crow has flown over our village." The second report is equally revealing. A 45-year-old landless laborer, when asked about Laloo, breaks into what looks like a strange dance. He falls on his knees, and with hands stretched in front, presses his forehead flat against the ground and begins to crawl backwards. "Now I don't do this when my landlord walks by," he shouts, "because Laloo said so."

Source: Raj Kamal Jha and Farzand Ahmed, "Laloo's Magic," *India Today,* 30 April 1995.

However, there is rarely an occasion when Indian politicians do not take recourse to some traditional concepts, like *jati* or *dalits,* or some that are deeply embedded in Indian religions and values, like *shaheed* (martyrs) or *ahimsa* (nonviolence).

The saintly idiom mobilized with insuperable skill by Gandhi's *satyagraha* reflects on the core values of society that cut across both modern and traditional cleavages and does not necessarily refer to the spiritual or the otherworldly. Messages from leaders like Gandhi expressed in this mode can reach the whole society and "stir the imagination of the advanced radical and the conservative traditionalist alike."[54]

Although these three political idioms are conceptually distinct, they are not necessarily separate in reality. In fact, the same individual may combine all three: a University of California–trained computer engineer based in Bangalore might have daily transactions with his business partner in California's Silicon Valley. He might have an arranged marriage within his *jati* and linguistic region, and punctiliously follow the food taboos and social rituals of his caste. He might also belong to an Internet network, avidly exchanging messages with the worldwide network of the VHP, the World Council of Hindus.

Depending on the region, locality, length and depth of colonial rule, and the individual's class, gender, and age, one idiom may be more clearly pronounced than another. Political actors manipulate all those idioms in terms of their perception of particular cases and contexts. Consequently, the three appear functionally related to one another in the competitive political marketplace of India. The tribe, or *jati* network—operating as a caste association—can very well carry the modern message of individual rights, entitlement, and electoral preferences to people who are first-generation voters. Simultaneously, modern satellite television, broadcasting the *Ramayana* and *Mahabharata* (Hindu religious classics), can spread the message of an indigenous Indian identity that claims to be unique, authentic, and exclusive. Since India's independence, such interactions have created new political forms and processes as well as the emergence of two new themes of Indian political culture: the instrumentality of politics and the politics of identity.

Indians use many forms of political participation, such as voting, lobbying, and contacting, and failing these (or sometimes in addition to these), the coercive methods of direct action. These forms are found all over the country, in areas where European powers first settled 400 years ago as well as in those that have never had any direct experience of European rule—among affluent elites well versed in the form of modern politics as well as among the poorest, illiterate peasants who have been mobilized into electoral politics only recently. Reports in the Indian media bear witness to such widespread attitudes of empowerment by village women and poor peasants.

The simultaneous use of participation and protest drawing on modern institutions and traditional symbols and networks has caused the three idioms of politics to conflate. Consequently, the political process in

India acts as a channel for the expression of a collective identity. Also contested are the power and position of the English-speaking elite that had hitherto seen itself as urban, urbane, and secular. This search for identity expresses itself not only in terms of national movements like those associated with Hindu nationalism, but also in the assertion of Sikh identity in Punjab and the tribal Jharkhand identity in southern Bihar. Similar aspirations for welfare and identity also underpin politics in Kashmir and India's Northeast, violently clashing with one another and the Indian state in their determination to assert their own vision of the state and nation.

Open articulation of such discord and violent clashes over interest and identity might give the impression that there is no central or unifying theme behind political attitudes in India, no "Indian way" of doing things. In the heyday of India's freedom movement, Gandhi and the Congress Party defined this central thrust of India's political culture. After independence, Nehru and the Congress Party government articulated the core values of India's political culture in terms of secularism, socialism, and democracy. Six decades later, the Congress Party and its program no longer occupy that central place it once held. Instead, the political system is uneasily groping toward a redefinition of India's core values in terms of communal accommodation, capitalism, and democracy. Once in power, cultural-nationalist parties have downplayed separatist themes, like a Tamil homeland or an exclusive homeland for the sons of the soil, and they have gradually accommodated themselves within the Indian Union. The Communist Party of India (Marxist), in power in West Bengal, is also trying to accommodate itself within the new political culture of enterprise. The press reports that the Left Front government is busy, simultaneously, sending "high-profile delegations to woo foreign investment and attract European investment in agriculture," while the draft resolution for the next party conference "deprecates the trend towards liberalization which has resulted in a bonanza for foreign capital and Indian big business."[55]

## Political Learning

The complex interaction between tradition and modernity can be further investigated through specific questions: How do Indians acquire their political attitudes? How do the contenders for power communicate their positions on issues facing Indian society? How do the perception of authority and the evaluation of political leaders vary across regions and sections of the population? Why has the electronic media achieved such prominence in India's electoral politics over the past years? We will now analyze how the process of political socialization in the context of a traditional society is undergoing rapid change.

Conventionally, in stable democracies the individual is politically socialized through family, school, secondary association, and workplace. Totalitarian political systems usually inculcate the "right" political attitudes by guiding the individual through school, youth groups, front organizations, and party membership for the privileged few. Neither model is completely available to India. Modernization has greatly diluted the effective role that family, caste, and kin once played in molding attitudes. The totalitarian path is forbidden by the Constitution that guarantees the fundamental freedom of thought, belief, faith, association, and movement and, in action, by a functioning and occasionally fractious political process.

Indian analysts started using the public opinion surveys quite early, which has made it possible to track changing opinions and attitudes that show a steady rise in political consciousness, a sense of empowerment, and political information. Television, which is no longer a state monopoly, has accelerated the spread of political information in recent years.

Social change has influenced political socialization through means other than family, caste, or tribe. But as far as the conventional instruments of political socialization are concerned, the state in India has two main institutional constraints. Schooling is a limited instrument because it is still not accessible to a large section of the population. In addition, primary schooling is not a federal subject, which makes it difficult to have a national policy. Even regional governments have prudently avoided the temptation of interfering with the contents and administration of schooling, though recent attempts by some regional governments to introduce a new ideological bias into school books created a nationwide protest from educators. A similar attempt by the communist government of Kerala in 1959 led the president of India to dismiss the Kerala government on the grounds that lawful government of the state was not possible. This precedent restrained the enthusiasm of newly elected governments to spread their ideas by incorporating them into textbooks and school administration. As we learn from Lloyd and Susanne Rudolph, such attempts are ultimately self-defeating.[56]

The foregoing suggests that educational institutions, for constitutional and political reasons, are not an effective institutional medium for the Indian state to promote a cohesive national political culture. But that is not the same as saying that schooling has no impact on promoting legitimacy and personal efficacy. Formal education is associated with the legitimacy of the electoral process; the individual's sense of efficacy increases with education, as does confidence in politicians. However, many illiterates evaluate the personal accountability of individual politicians at a level below the average, and some of that group do not believe that elections are the only way to conduct politics. These are the parts of the population in which leaders of mass movements are likely to find potential support.

In the past, mass illiteracy was the other main obstacle to state-sponsored political socialization through the print media. This factor has been overcome by the electronic media, which are neither restrained by the inability to read and write nor by the remoteness of villages from the capital, thanks to televisions, mobile phones, and cheap Internet access. Additionally, the introduction of competition into broadcasting has brought in diversity and sensitivity to consumer demands, and thereby vastly enhanced the appeal of the electronic media. An innovation in this respect is to set up Internet sites that expose corruption in high quarters.[57]

Until the liberalization and penetration by the electronic media, the process of political participation and electoral campaigns were the most effective tools of political socialization. New political attitudes and skills have evolved through participation. The preindependence legacies have also been enriched and sometimes replaced by developments since independence. As a result, Indian society today is as affected by recent changes in its political and economic form as by its historical inheritance.

In the early years after 1947, the modernizing leaders around Nehru and the Congress Party leadership paid routine homage to a vaguely defined Indian nationalism, social democracy, economic self-reliance through import substitution, and secularism, understood as both the separation of state and religion and

equal respect for all religions. But, in sharp contrast to other new states, these broad and abstract ideas were not made into a dogma. The Congress Party itself harbored many factions that differed widely from one another in personal loyalties as well as ideological leanings. As a result, in each of these major initiatives undertaken by the state, a significant variation of normative theory was used. The socialist aspirations of Nehru and the myth of the independent peasant producer were intertwined in the policies of land reforms. The neo-Gandhian approach—embodied in *panchayati raj* and community development—were juxtaposed with an equally powerful belief in the rational individual as the basis of voting decisions. These programs relied on the ability of such individuals to identify parties as well as candidates as a result of their knowledge about the relationship of issues to voting choices. The market as the driving force behind production, consumption, credit, and communication was promoted with equal vigor as central planning and bureaucratic implementation, and therefore aimed at achieving the same objective. These ideas, whether indigenous to India or gleaned from elsewhere, were formulated at the apex of the system and were expected to trickle down to the regional and local arenas.

## Elections

Part of the answer to the puzzling growth of a democratic political culture in the context of a traditional society is the historical continuity between the political process, elite-mass linkage, and top leadership before and after independence. Following partition, parts of India that had a long experience of British rule and Indian resistance to it remained within India. The Congress Party's top leaders, known as the High Command, flew into the task of getting the vote out in the first general election of 1952 by spreading the message of nationalism, democracy, development, and secularism. The Congress Party organization, fortified with the tremendous resources at its command, became the fountainhead of patronage.

After independence, political transaction and election campaigns thus became the chief instrument of political socialization in India. In a daring move, India's leaders put everything on the auction block of electoral politics right at the outset, in the first general election of 1951–1952. Even the very definition of the nation, its physical boundaries, and the basic principles of its economic organization were not considered over and above politics. Since then, every election (and there have been a great many—parliament, state assembly, district and local councils and municipalities, and a myriad of school committees and other groups) became an occasion for individuals to recognize the value of their votes. The result was that the great school of democracy quickly multiplied the numbers of its enthusiastic pupils and continued to produce both knowledge and skill even when the first teachers left the scene.

Since regular and frequent political consultation was the most effective instrument of political socialization, we need to examine indicators of political participation. Revealing statistics can be found from participation in the general elections to the Lok Sabha, the lower house of the federal legislature and the highest repository of legislative authority and governmental accountability in the country. These are illustrative of India's success at organizing an electoral process at a continental scale. Large-scale poverty and illiteracy notwithstanding, India, under the supervision of the independent Election Commission, has organized elections involving very large electorates who, by law, have to be provided with polling booths within easy walking distance. The campaigns themselves are strictly monitored. It is not unusual for polling to be stopped and repolling ordered in the event of electoral fraud or violence.[58]

The level of participation, shown earlier in Figure 17.5, has stabilized around 60 percent, a little lower than the longer established and more affluent democracies of Europe. General elections to the federal Parliament and its regional equivalent, the State Assemblies, and elections to popular bodies at the local level are very much a part of normal political life in India. The general election of 1951–1952 was the first time that a national electorate, the bulk of which had never voted before, took part in an election under universal adult franchise. The right to vote and a secure environment within which citizens can participate in polling freely have now been generally established. Men tend to turn out in greater numbers than women, but the participation of women has grown over the years. An equally interesting phenomenon is the participation of the former untouchable castes, which, both for men and women, keeps pace with the population as a whole, a significant achievement considering their oppressive exclusion by the upper social strata in the past.

## POLITICAL RECRUITMENT

If political participation is a minimum criterion of democratic rule, then a persuasive case can be made that India has caught up with the West. To facilitate the growth of political socialization, high levels of participation are necessary but not sufficient. We therefore call on two further sources of evidence: political recruitment to the highest legislature of the country and the social composition of the local elite. Political recruitment is important because once people have the knowledge of the normative structure of the system and the skill with which to engage in political transactions, they tend to elect representatives who reflect the main cleavages of society. Of course, the representative character of the elected elite is unlikely to become mathematically accurate, because very small groups, thanks partly to the "first-past-the-post" system of voting, tend to get penalized. However, by looking at the data over time and across different regions, one can draw some general conclusions.

The percentage of politicians of rural origin has grown in the Lok Sabha over the years and correspondingly the weight of "agriculturists" as well. The percentage of women has doubled but is still far below their share of the population.[59] The percentage of Brahmins has dropped significantly. The former untouchables and tribals, who continue to occupy a little over a fifth of the membership, reflect their weight in the population of the country. This results from a system of "reservation," which sets a quota for these underprivileged groups. Quite interestingly, though there is no quota system for the election of Muslims to the Parliament (and the electoral rules do not provide for proportional representation), their total number is not far below their proportion in the Indian population.

The picture of the social base of the national elite from the Lok Sabha is reinforced by the data on local elites. Many regional governments—following the seventy-third Amendment to the Constitution, which requires one-third of the seats in *panchayats* to be filled by women—have become an important recruiting ground for new leaders and a school for training these potential leaders in the art of governance.

Political participation and the recruitment of new elites act as powerful agents of political socialization. The data on efficacy and legitimacy present two interesting facets of political socialization in India (see Figure 17.7). Efficacy, which measures individuals'

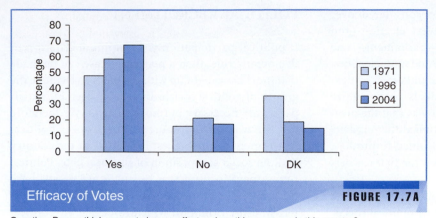

Efficacy of Votes

**FIGURE 17.7A**

Question: Do you think your vote has an effect on how things are run in this country?

Source: National Election Study (NES), Center for the Study of Developing Socities, Delhi.

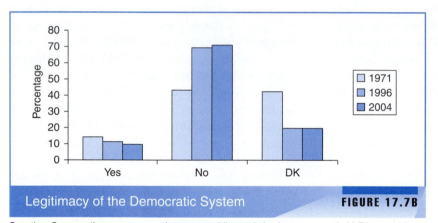

Legitimacy of the Democratic System

**FIGURE 17.7B**

Question: Suppose there were no parties or assemblies and elections were not held. Do you think the government in this country can be run better?

Source: National Election Study (NES), Center for the Study of Developing Societies, Delhi.

A majority of people believe that their vote has an effect on the political state of affairs in the country. The percentage of such people has gone up from 48.5 percent in 1971 to 67.5 percent in 2004. A second important fact is the decline, over the past 25 years, of those who could not answer this question has gone down from 35.5 percent in 1971 to 15 percent in 2004.

As individual perceptions go, efficacy and legitimacy are the two faces of democracy. A question designed to measure legitimacy, asked *Suppose there were no parties or assemblies and elections were not held—do you think that the government in this country can be run better?* The question was deliberately phrased in the negative, requiring the interviewees to show their commitment to democracy by formulating the answer in the negative—not a simple thing to do, considering the radical difference in the status of the interviewer and interviewee in the backdrop of a traditional society where social deference and a tendency to agree with those who represent superior power point in the same direction. Those who consider India's current institutional arrangement to be consistent with their own value preferences have steadily gone up from 43.4 to 70.5 (Figures 17.7A and 17.7B).[60]

self-perception with regard to the powers-to-be, shows a steady rise over the recent past. Legitimacy of the political system has also climbed, from 68 percent in 1996 to 72 percent in 2004.

In view of the right to universal adult franchise and the political culture that has grown around it, the normative perception of the vote gives us the most general measure of individual efficacy. The question *"Do you think your vote has effect on how things are run in this country, or, do you think your vote makes no difference?"* was asked in all three surveys, to measure the sense of efficacy that actors attach to their vote. The results are quite revealing of the strength and reach of India's democracy at the level of individual perception.

These data show a paradoxical situation exists, where ordinary people feel empowered enough to "kick the rascals out." But in the end, when the vital foundations of democracy are threatened by political adventurers, support for it ebbs and democratic institutions reemerge. Once again, as we can see from the example of the national emergency of 1975–1977 (see again Box 17.4), the Indian political system has experienced situations where this potential is transformed into the breakdown of democracy and the rise of popular authoritarianism, with democracy eventually bouncing back.

## POLICIES TO ADDRESS THE ECONOMY, WELFARE, AND POVERTY

According to recent statistics, India's economy grew at an annual rate of 6.9 percent in 2004–2005 (see Figure 17.8).[61] Measured in terms of purchasing power parity (PPP), India has reached $2,196 per capita. In terms of PPP, India surpassed Pakistan in 2000 for the first time. Within the region, only the Chinese economy shows higher growth rates than the Indian.

In terms of absolute poverty, denoted by the number of people who live on less than $1 a day, India's estimated 390 million (as of 2005, approximately 38 percent of the population) is a dire indication of mass poverty.[62] Although the picture is slightly better in terms of relative poverty, measured by the percentage share of the income of the lowest 20 percent as compared with the United States, China, or Brazil (see Table 1.4 in chapter 1), the poor performance on the indicators of welfare (such as access to sanitation, safe water, or infant mortality) reinforces the picture of mass poverty in India.

In spite of slow and incremental growth and industrialization, India is still a predominantly agricultural country with about two-thirds of its population dependent on agriculture. Most are marginal peasants with small holdings or no land at all. The majority of India's peasants draw their livelihood from rain-fed, subsistence agriculture. The economic legacy at the time of independence included a small industrial base that with the business sector contributed only 5 percent of the GNP. India also inherited one of the largest rail systems in the world, which did not link the ports with the economic hinterland, but rather with the capital cities, reflecting the security needs of a colonial power.

### Politics of Incremental Growth and Redistribution

Though nationalism and communal harmony were the main organizing principles of India's Freedom Movement, mass poverty was always high on the nation's political agenda. If the symbolic articulation of this commitment to the welfare of the poor came from the austere lifestyle of the top leadership, the antipoverty programs came from the Congress Socialists, whose main leader was Jawaharlal Nehru. After independence, the Congress Party government

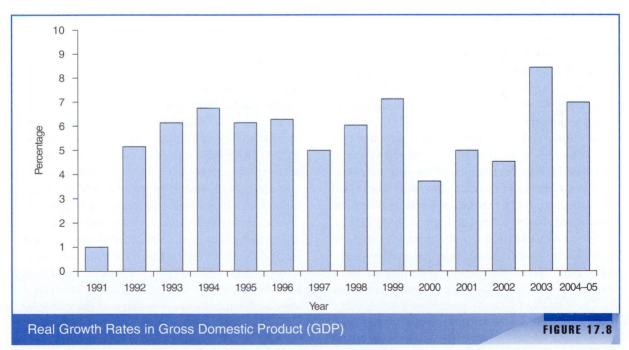

Real Growth Rates in Gross Domestic Product (GDP)

**FIGURE 17.8**

The survey question asked to measure legitimacy of democratic institutions in 2004 gave two choices to those who did not explicitly say that "democracy was better". The 9.7 percent who say 'yes' in 2004 thus comprise two groups—of 3.7 percent who say dictatorship is better, and 6 percent who are indifferent between democracy and dictatorship. Data from World Research Institute (accessed at www.earthtrends.wrl.org on 8 June 2006).

created a mixed economy in which the state built the infrastructure and key industries. The private sector focused on manufacturing and distribution. National planning, conceived by technocrats but under the guidance of key members of the central cabinet and the National Development Council, was charged with balancing the needs of growth with the imperative of social justice and redistribution. Besides introducing new notions of entitlement, the Constitution promised a life of dignity and economic opportunity to the underprivileged, particularly to the former untouchables and tribal population. While development remained high on the agenda, it was not placed outside the political arena, as occurred in "developmental" states like Japan or South Korea, where development policy became the preserve of a technocratic and financial elite. In India, economic policy involved national and regional politics, and institutions like the Planning Commission. The adoption of a mixed economy as the framework of development guaranteed that economic policy was not shifted outside public scrutiny and accountability. This model of a democratic planning was further reinforced by a number of reforms that protected the rights of workers, extended electoral democracy to the village councils (*panchayats*), removed intermediary rights of large landlords (*zamindars*) and princely rulers, and attempted to introduce land ceilings and cooperative farming.[63]

As a consequence of these policies, Indian development during the early decades after independence, while unspectacular in any specific area, nevertheless strengthened India's political institutions. It also eliminated famine and a reliance on imported food within the lifetime of one generation. The first gains came in the 1950s through an expansion of the area under cultivation and irrigation works. The 1960s accelerated agrarian production through a series of technical innovations, like seeds of the high-yielding variety, new pesticides, chemical fertilizer, and the supply of precise information on weather and market conditions. This "Green Revolution" transformed India from a net importer of food to a self-sufficient country. Through the 1970s the government developed a complex system of storage and market interventions called "Food Procurement" that guaranteed prices to maintain a steady flow of food production and supply to consumers. India's food policy had evolved in reaction to chronic food shortage that necessitated food imports at huge financial and political costs,

particularly during the Vietnam War when India opposed U.S. policy. The food program finally started yielding rich dividends in the 1980s. India's system of food security became so resilient that even the severe droughts of 1987 did not lead to significant fluctuations in the prices of agricultural commodities.[64]

The modernizing leadership around Nehru intended to raise the general standard of living and protect the country's newly won freedom through a mixed economy. This model of import substitution, planned economic growth, and a policy of self-reliance did not leave much room for integration into the international market. In part this situation reflected a certain Gandhian nostalgia for *swadeshi*—the consumption of only homemade goods—but also a basic distrust of the West. During the first half of the twentieth century, from 1900 to 1946, Indian national income under colonial rule had risen by 0.7 percent annually, while its population grew at the rate of 0.8 percent. The lesson was not lost on the generation of Nehru. Thanks to the developmental initiatives from 1950–1951 to 1990–1991, India more than doubled the size of its economy. While its growth rate was well above preindependence levels, it fell far below expectations. India was considerably below the 8 to 10 percent of the fastest-growing countries in Asia—Japan, South Korea, Taiwan, Hong Kong, and Singapore—and lagged substantially behind China.

In spite of its poor performance relative to worldwide economic growth, India did achieve some spectacular results. By the late 1980s, industry contributed 29 percent of the Indian GNP. Despite the low level of industrialization, by the mid-1980s India was one of the twenty most industrialized nations in terms of total industrial production. India was self-sufficient in consumer goods and in basic commodities, like steel and cement. It also produced a range of intermediate-level manufactured goods, ships, locomotives, trucks, machine tools, and sophisticated electronic equipment. In a departure from its classic patterns of international trade based on primary exports, India started a modest export of manufactured goods. However, the slowing down of India's economy and the visible inefficiency of the basic model of import substitution became compelling factors for a radical change.

The model of planned development based on a mixed economy—where the "*commanding heights*" of the economy were dominated by the public sector—achieved a certain amount of welfare, but it also produced some less desirable side effects. While state control over the market managed to simultaneously keep inflation and budget deficits low by the standards of developing countries, the system created what is known as a *quota-permit-raj*.[65] It also bred rampant corruption and inefficiency, all but snuffing out the spirit of enterprise. The result was a general slowing down of growth, which the government tried to stimulate in the early 1980s by borrowing from the international market. However, this was done without any radical changes in the structure of the management of the economy. The result was a serious financial crisis by the end of the 1980s. Most alarmingly for India's policymakers and the international financial establishment, India's debt-to-GDP ratio went up by 100 percent in the span of a decade. In 1991, Manmohan Singh, then finance minister, and Prime Minister Narasimha Rao introduced the first structural reform of the economy, which came to be known as "liberalization" (see Box 17.6).

The first policies introduced by Manmohan Singh sought a drastic reduction of state control over the market, whether open or disguised. The government reduced subsidies on several items and relaxed strict import and export controls. The system of licensing new industries and closing those that were no longer profitable but could not be closed off because of labor protection legislation was amended to bring a new flexibility to the market. Areas of production that the government had brought under its control during the heyday of nationalization in the 1970s under the

concept of "essential commodities" were gradually returned to the market. Important areas of production—such as electricity generation, parts of the oil industry, domestic air transport, roads, and some telecommunications—were opened up for private initiative and enterprise. The government welcomed foreign investment and participation in the process of production through "joint ventures." India attempted to make itself attractive for foreign investors by lowering tariffs in a significant departure from the previous policy of import substitution and autarchy. There was an easing up of imports, and Singh encouraged export through the devaluation of the rupee by 24 percent in 1991. The rupee was also made partly convertible. The heavy taxes on entrepreneurs were gradually reduced, as was the direct tax on income. The top rate of income tax came down from 56 percent to 40 percent and of corporate tax from 57.5 percent to 46 percent.[66]

These measures were reinforced with a communication revolution that saw a deregulation of broadcasting. This development gave Indian consumers easy access to foreign-made televisions and radios, and to the hitherto unavailable choice of programs through satellite and cable channels. The state broadcasting took on the challenge and introduced a modest degree of variety through internal competition.

In some ways, the fiscal policies of 1991 to liberalize the economy and implement a policy of privatization of public-sector undertakings went against the grain of Indian politics. As far as ancient Indian tradition goes, the *Arthasastra* had allocated a number of

---

## Manmohan Singh

**BOX 17.6**

The current Indian prime minister, Manmohan Singh, is the first Sikh to occupy the most important political office of the country. He is an economist by training with a distinguished academic record in Oxford, Cambridge, and Delhi, and prestigious appointments with the Reserve Bank of India and the World Bank. When India faced a severe fiscal crisis in 1991, as India's finance minister he initiated the structural reform of India's economy, which subsequently came to be known as the process of liberalization. Following the victory of the UPA-coalition in the 2004 parliamentary elections, Manmohan Singh was drafted

in as the leader of the UPA parliamentary coalition. Consequently, the president of India invited him to form the central cabinet. Sonia Gandhi, leader of the Congress Party, has institutionalized the process of regular consultation between her and the prime minister, creating in the process the scope for two centers of power within the coalition. However, the coordination between Sonia Gandhi and Manmohan Singh appears to have worked out quite effectively, facilitating better coordination among the constituent parties of the ruling coalition and also a sense of cohesion about the government.

Dr. Manmohan Singh (right), a career economist and India's first Sikh Prime Minister, shaking hands with President Hu Jin-Tao of China, indicating the growing relations between the two neighbors.

Gurinder Osan/AP Images

key sectors of the economy to the exclusive authority of the king. This tradition of state monopoly was continued by practically all the rulers of India, coming to a peak under British colonial rule. Indian commercial and industrial entrepreneurs had chafed against the British monopoly and colonial obstacles to the expansion of their activities, and they had enthusiastically supported the *swadeshi* program of Mahatma Gandhi. They were content after independence to find a secure niche for themselves within the structure of the mixed economy. Each obstacle to free enterprise was also the visible tip of a powerful vested interest. As such, it comes as no surprise that attempts to roll the state back have produced a powerful backlash from a formidable coalition: socialists who want to protect the poor and underprivileged from the ravages of capitalism, rich farmers who fear the loss of government subsidies, the *swadeshi* lobby that is apprehensive about the loss of Indian political autonomy and cultural identity, and regional leaders who fear the growing gap between rich and poor parts of India without the presence of a powerful, redistributive center.

Liberalization has thus sparked a heated debate among India's political parties. India's communist parties predictably came out with a staunch opposition to the liberalization of trade regulations. They saw these reforms as an attempt by the international financial establishments like the International Monetary Fund and the World Bank to dictate terms to India. They demanded that the entry of foreign capital be governed by the technological "needs" of India, which are presumably to be determined by India's planners. For the left, the public sector as a whole, and especially public-sector employment, needed to be defended against attempts at privatization that could lead to job losses. The Congress Party, which had introduced the liberalization measures in the first place, was muted in the defense of liberalization, having sensed its lack of electoral appeal. The Bharatiya Janata Party, which had traditionally drawn support from the trading communities and the better educated and urban populations, took a complex position on this whole issue. The party manifesto called for "full liberalization and calibrated globalization"; it argued in favor of initiative and enterprise but wanted to retain the role of the state in protecting national industry and trade against "unfair" international competition. The BJP also intended to exclude foreign intrusion from areas crucial to India's security interests, and foreign competition from consumer goods industries with catchy slogans like "computer chips yes, potato chips no."

In a context where coalitional politics is inordinately sensitive to popular mood swings, the uncertain feelings of the electorate are also reflected in the radical fluctuations of public policy. It was therefore remarkable that the BJP-led NDA government continued the policy of liberalization started by its predecessor in spite of the opposition among its ranks. In the wake of the nuclear tests of 1998, when sanctions against India threatened to stymie its economic growth, the BJP government sent its top troubleshooters to the finance capitals of the world to salvage the situation by clearing the applications for joint ventures. These efforts were partly neutralized by the nationalist euphoria created by the spectacle of India "standing up" to the West, which some elements of the cultural-nationalist parties interpreted as the right moment to throw foreign products out of India. Still, the NDA government kept the momentum of liberalization intact. However, the electoral dividends it had expected from its "India shining" campaign achievements did not materialize. Following the electoral defeat of the NDA in 2004, however, the UPA coalition has kept the course of liberalization, thus reinforcing India's policy stability despite governmental change.

Going by the record of the past few years, Prime Minister Manmohan Singh, the architect of the first major reform, has become quite adept at balancing the pressure of a significant contingent of communists in the ruling coalition with the steady stream of incremental reform.

There are still problems aplenty: poor infrastructure, political wrangling over educational quotas, deep pockets of poverty and illiteracy, and tragic farmers' suicides as a form of protest against the side effects of globalization. But over and above it all there is also a sense of euphoria about close to double-digit growth and low inflation, and a widespread sense of opportunity knocking at the door. This sense of buoyancy is borne out by recent public opinion data.[67]

## CONCLUSION: DEMOCRACY AND DEVELOPMENT

Barely a decade after India began its journey as a multiparty democracy, Selig Harrison, voicing the pessimism of many Western observers, warned: "Odds are almost wholly against the survival of freedom . . . the issue is, in fact, whether any Indian state can survive at all."[68] These opinions echoed misgivings expressed about self-rule leading to chaos.[69] After six decades of democratic rule and fourteen national elections, the issue of India's survival as a democracy could probably be taken off the agenda.

Back Roll: Just when diplomatic initiative was helping restore the shaken confidence of investors in a postatomic test India, the Sangh Parivar, a collective reference to extreme right Hindu nationalist groups, started needling the BJP-led government. With the Swadeshi jagran Manch, a Hindu nationalist-front organization, trying to impose its agenda, it's a case of one step forward, two steps back.

*India Today International,*
21 September 1998, 7.

**BOX 17.7**

## A Nuclear Surprise

The 1998 nuclear test by India, followed within weeks by Pakistan, set alarm bells ringing in the major capitals of the world. India and Pakistan are not signatories of the Nuclear Nonproliferation Treaty (NPT). Therefore, although the tests were not violating a treaty agreement as such, it was feared that they would jeopardize the cause of nonproliferation, and thus increase the likelihood of nuclear conflict. Thanks to the confidence-building measures (CBMs) that India and Pakistan have since put in place, South Asia appears to have entered a period of moderate stability.

India's nuclear program actually started in 1946. Subsequently, the Atomic Energy Commission (AEC) was established in 1948, and the first two civilian nuclear reactors opened in 1956 and 1960. Simultaneously with the developing of nuclear energy for peaceful purposes, India advocated general global disarmament, including nuclear weapons in particular. However, with the Chinese testing of the nuclear bomb (1964)

and the feeling among India's leaders that the world powers were unlikely to jettison their nuclear stockpiles, India attempted to enter the nuclear club with a "peaceful nuclear device" in 1974. However, this was to no avail. For the next three decades, other nations placed heavy sanctions on India, cutting off the supply of nuclear know-how, technology and sufficient fuel supply. Following the 1998 test, India's leaders have strongly justified their claim to membership of the exclusive nuclear club. Besides the military and political reputation and respect it creates, nuclear power is also crucially important for India's continued economic growth in view of its chronic dependence on imported petroleum. With the tests of 1998, India finally entered the exclusive nuclear league. The Indo-U.S. agreement of February 27, 2006, once it is ratified by the U.S. Congress, would help integrate India's nuclear program with the international market and control regimes in fissile material.

---

The key question that now confronts us is what kind of Indian democracy will emerge over the next decades. Will it be an elitist, affluent, and secure India, able to sustain the pace of reform and the current rate of growth? Or, will India remain a majoritarian democracy, reforming but still poor, armed with nuclear teeth (see Box 17.7), threatening its neighbors and scuttling the chances of nuclear nonproliferation, wishing, nevertheless, to enjoy the benefits of trade and scientific exchange with the rest of the world?

Drawing on the development of institutions and the policy process in India during the past six decades, this chapter has argued that the likelihood of the collapse of the Indian state and its democratic political system is slim.[70] The sense of optimism is reflected in public opinion. The national elite, evolved over the years, has understood the benefits of cooperation and compromise with all sections of the population. India's leaders of all political shades increasingly voice their concerns about national security and prosperity.

India's experience contrasts with the political experience of other countries of the subcontinent, which share some of India's cultural, political, and historical legacies. The difficulties faced by the democratic process

in these countries confirm the postulates of conventional social theory: that successful political democracy requires the preconditions of literacy and economic development,[71] institutionalization of political power prior to the introduction of popular participation,[72] or a victorious bourgeoisie acting as the social base for democratic institutions.[73] The Indian "counter example" thus raises a main question: Why has India—despite a culture based on social hierarchy and authoritarianism, mass poverty, and high illiteracy—been able to establish a successful democratic political order?[74]

With over one billion inhabitants living in twenty-eight federal states and six union territories, and eighteen major languages with different scripts, India is a country of continental proportions and dramatic extremes, where spirituality is juxtaposed with religious hatred, mass poverty with affluence, philosophies espousing multiculturalism and universality with those committed to sectarianism and bigotry. From scholar to philanthropist, India in its many parts evokes weary admiration, tinged with disbelief and despair. Our analysis here has pointed away from Indian "exceptionalism," and the explanation that the hidden genius of Indian culture accounts for the resilience of democracy, its success at state formation and, more recently, state contraction without the ensuing chaos that has blighted the end of Soviet rule. This chapter has provided some insights into understanding India's apparently exceptional features, which conventional theory has drawn on to make pessimistic predictions about the future of modern political institutions in India.

Unlike the majority of postcolonial countries, India retains the territory, constitution, and political system that marked its emergence as an independent country in 1947. In spite of external conflicts and internal insurgencies, elections have been held regularly and with rates of participation between almost 50 percent in the early elections and about 60 percent since the 1960s. India has achieved a minimum of welfare and food security, and inflation and explosive population growth have been tamed; and now, with the liberalization of India's economy, international business confidence in India remains high. Despite these achievements, some dark spots continue to blight the democratic credentials of India—mass poverty and illiteracy persist.

Just as the imperative of governance had forced Hindu nationalists in power to moderate their stance, so has the political temptation to garner the advocates of *hindutva*—believers in the rightful claim that Hindu values are central to the Indian state—led to the outbreak of pogroms between Hindus and Muslims.[75] The puzzles of India's democracy are rooted in these contradictions.[76]

This chapter has formulated answers to some of these questions by drawing on India's political resources—its social and cultural diversity, its experience of colonial rule and the resistance to it, the efforts of a modernizing and visionary leadership at nation- and state-building, and its major institutions and policy process since India's independence. These were the main components that facilitated democratic rule, and in the present context, orderly state contraction. With its political parties, movements, elections, multiple conflicts, and conflict-solving mechanisms, India is a rich source of data for students of comparative politics, especially with regard to an illustration of the main theoretical concepts of the discipline—from interest articulation, aggregation, and adjudication, to the interaction of politics, policy, and economic development. For those interested in the resilience of democratic political systems, India offers an interesting contrast to Western liberal democracies.

This resilience of India's democratic political system appears even more astounding because India's main political institutions—the legislature, executive, judiciary, and individual rights—have not evolved entirely from within its society and culture. On the contrary, many of these are colonial transplants. Yet, their legitimacy is not questioned by India's main political parties, including those that draw their strength from mobilization along the lines of religious cleavages or class conflict.

In attempting to answer these questions, this chapter has pointed not in the direction of India's political institutions, process, and the political culture that has evolved from the conflict and conflation of tradition and modernity. It has pointed toward cross-culturally comparable factors that account for the Indian success at sustaining a stable political system that combines both democracy and development. In India, norms of democracy are widely shared by all major political parties—including the Communist Party, and right-wing Hindu nationalist parties like the Shiv Sena and the Bharatiya Janata Party—although they differ radically in their ideological positions. Even in the lowest political arenas, the right to democratic participation is no longer considered an exotic idea. This Indian achievement—puzzling in view of the negative implications of conventional social theory about the survival of democracy in poor, postcolonial, preindustrial societies—needs to be understood in the larger comparative context.

One sometimes comes across the criticism that the political process of India accepts democracy only at the level of interest aggregation and accommodation and not at the level of liberal values, such as respect for the freedom and dignity of individuals. A further extension of this argument is that vote counting is neither necessary nor sufficient as a guarantee for the long-term survival of a democracy. Scholarly concerns about the rise of popular authoritarianism in the wake of competitive and aggressive populism are based on such misgivings. These criticisms reinforce the apprehensions of a possible collapse or a surreptitious gnawing away at democratic institutions until the system is reduced to an empty shell.[77]

The findings presented here suggest that challenges to Indian democracy—emanating from such problems as political insurgency, denial of equal rights to minorities, communal riots, political violence, "criminalization of politics,"[78] and the rise of "popular authoritarianism"—are not accidental or incidental features of India's political system. Ironically, they sometimes originate from the same process that gives rise to, and sustains, representative political institutions in the first place. India's democratic process continues to be open and inclusive, so much so that sometimes locally influential politicians with criminal records manage to get elected to legislatures and political activists resort to forceful methods of protest leading to the disturbance of public order. As one learns from the reelection of Indira Gandhi, the unrepentant author of the emergency of 1975–1977, authoritarian political leaders managed to get a popular mandate in 1980. These practices are tolerated if not condoned by the democratic political process. But the countervailing forces of India's democracy, federalism, and regulatory agencies like the Supreme Court and the Election Commission ensure that they do not spread beyond a point that would choke the vitality of the democratic process and the rule of law altogether.

The existence of the danger of a collapse of democracy cannot be ruled out altogether, but survey data regarding legitimacy; efficacy; the empowerment of former untouchables, religious minorities, and women; and the recruitment of new local elites show the strength and the potential for a further unfolding of "prodemocracy" forces in India. This is further supported by statistical data on governance, political order, participation, and legitimacy. The results of national surveys are supplemented with evidence of the upward social mobility of underprivileged social groups and the complementarities of institutional as well as radical modes of participation at the local level. The marketplace of politics continues to operate as an arbiter of the contradictory values of the dignity of the individual and the identity of the group, and more recently, of the imperative of integration with the international political economy. At the same time, the need to maintain India's cultural distinctiveness as well as the interests of the least privileged remains.

In the final analysis, the universal significance of the Indian experiment lies in showing the democratic potential of politics from below. When it is combined with representative political institutions and tied to political competition and social reform, it can produce unexpected results that support and promote democratic transition and consolidation. This process occurs notwithstanding the absence of material affluence or religiocultural roots of individual rights. At the same time, it must also be remembered that the process is unlikely to be fully consensual. Empowerment of the marginal social groups, while crucial to the functioning of the Indian system, is, in India as everywhere in the world, contested by entrenched and privileged social groups. But the commitment of India's key institutions—such as the judiciary, the Parliament, the media, the army, and the national and regional leaders—to democracy and secularism remain steadfast. The Indian case shows how its "million mutinies," ensconced in the context of a responsive state and elites well versed in the art and science of governance, can pave the way of transition to liberal democracy despite predictions to the contrary.[79]

## KEY TERMS

Ayodhya
Bharatiya Janata Party (BJP)
castes
confidence-building measures (CBMs)
Congress system
dalits
dharma
dharna
emergency

ethno-nationalist
Gandhi, Indira
Gandhi, Mahatma
Gandhi, Rajiv
gherao
hindutva
jajmani
jatis
liberalization
line of control (LOC)

Lok Sabha (House of the People)
mixed economy
National Democratic Alliance (NDA)
Nehru, Jawaharlal
Panchasheela
panchayati raj
postindependence partition
raj

Rajya Sabha (Council of States)
Rama
satyagraha
swadeshi
tribals
United Progressive Alliance (UPA)
varnas
zamindars

## SUGGESTED READINGS

Ahluwalia, Isher Judge. *Industrial Growth in India: Stagnation Since the Mid-sixties.* Delhi: Oxford University Press, 1985.

Austin, Granville. *The Indian Constitution: Cornerstone of a Nation.* Oxford: Clarendon Press, 1966.

Bardhan, Pranab. *The Political Economy of Development in India.* Delhi: Oxford University Press, 1984.

Brass, Paul R. *Language, Religion, and Politics in North India.* London: Cambridge University Press, 1974.

———. *The Politics of India Since Independence.* Cambridge: Cambridge University Press, 1990.

Brown, Judith. *India: The Origin of an Asian Democracy.* Delhi: Oxford University Press, 1985.

Cohen, Stephen. "The Military and Indian Democracy." In Atul Kohli, ed., *India's Democracy: An Analysis of State-Society Relations.* Princeton, NJ: Princeton University Press, 1988.

Das Gupta, Jyotirindra. "Democracy, Development, and Federalism: Some Implications of Constructive Constitutionalism in India." In Subrata Mitra and Dietmar Rothermund, eds., *Legitimacy and Conflict in South Asia.* Delhi: Manohar, 1997.

Embree, Ainslie, ed. *Sources of Indian Tradition.* Vol. 1, *From the Beginning to 1800.* New Delhi: Penguin, 1991.

Forster, E. M. *A Passage to India.* Harmondsworth, England: Penguin, 1985; first published in 1924.

Frankel, Francine. *India's Political Economy, 1947–77: The Gradual Revolution.* Princeton, NJ: Princeton University Press, 1978.

Fuller, C. J. *The Camphor Flame: Popular Hinduism and Society in India.* Princeton, NJ: Princeton University Press, 1992.

Haq, Mahbub ul. *Human Development in South Asia, 1997.* Karachi: Oxford University Press, 1997.

Haq, Mahbub ul, and Khadija Haq. *Human Development in South Asia, 1998.* Karachi: Oxford University Press, 1998.

Hardgrave, Robert, and Stanley Kochanek. *India: Government and Politics in a Developing Nation.* Fort Worth, TX: Harcourt Brace Jovanovich, 1993.

Harrison, Selig. *India: The Most Dangerous Decades.* Princeton, NJ: Princeton University Press, 1960.

Hay, Stephen, ed. *Sources of Indian Tradition.* Vol. 2, *Modern India and Pakistan.* New Delhi: Penguin, 1991.

Inden, Ronald. *Imagining India.* Oxford: Blackwell, 1990.

Indira Gandhi Institute of Development Research, *India Development Report, 2004/05.* Delhi: Oxford University Press, 2005.

Jeffrey, Robin. *What's Happening to India? Punjab, Ethnic Conflict, and the Test for Federalism,* 2nd ed. London: MacMillan, 1994.

Jenkins, R. *Democratic Politics and Economic Reform in India.* Cambridge: Cambridge University Press, 2000.

Joshi, Vijay, and I. M. D., Little, *India: Macroeconomics and Political Economy, 1964–1991.* Delhi: Oxford University Press, 1994.

Kashyap, Subhas. *Our Parliament.* Delhi: National Book Trust of India, 1989.

Kohli, Atul. *The State and Poverty in India: The Politics of Reform.* Cambridge: Cambridge University Press, 1987.

———. *The Success of India's Democracy.* Cambridge: Cambridge University Press, 2001.

Kothari, Rajni. *Politics in India.* Boston: Little Brown, 1970.

Manor, James. *From Nehru to Nineties: The Changing Office of the Prime Minister in India.* London: Hurst, 1994.

Mitra, Subrata K., ed. *The Post-colonial State in Asia: The Dialectics of Politics and Culture.* Hemel Hempstead, England: Wheatsheaf, 1990.

———. *Power, Protest, and Paticipation: Local Elites and the Politics of Development in India.* London: Routledge, 1992.

———. *Culture and Rationality.* Delhi: Sage, 1999.

———. *The Puzzle of India's Governance,* London: Routledge, 2005.

Mitra, Subrata K., and V. B. Singh, *Democracy and Social Change in India: A Cross-sectional Analysis of the Indian Electorate.* Delhi: Sage, 1999.

Mitra, Subrata K., Mike Enskat, and Clemens Spiess, eds. *Political Parties in South Asia.* Westport, CT/London: Praeger, 2004.

Mitra, Subrata K., Siegfried Wolf, and Jivanta Schoettli. *A Political and Economic Dictionary of India.* London: Europa, 2006.

Mitra, Subrata K. and V. B. Singh, *When Rebels become Stakeholders: Democracy, Agency and Social Change in India. Delhi: Sage;* 2009.

Moore, Barrington. *Social Origins of Dictatorship and Democracy: Lord and Peasant in the Making of the Modern World.* Boston: Beacon Press, 1966.

Morris-Jones, W. H. *The Government and Politics of India.* Wistow, England: Eothen Press, 1987.

Naipaul, V. S. *India: A Million Mutinies Now.* London: Heinemann, 1990.

Nandy, Ashis. *The Intimate Enemy: Loss and Recovery of Self Under Colonialism.* Delhi: Oxford University Press, 1983.

Omvedt, Gail. *Reinventing Revolution: New Social Movements and the Socialist Tradition in India.* London: East Gate, 1993.

Potter, David C. *India's Political Administrators: 1919–1983.* Oxford: Clarendon, 1986.

Rudolph, Lloyd, and Susanne Rudolph. *The Modernity of Tradition: Political Development in India.* Chicago: University of Chicago Press, 1967.

———. In *Pursuit of Lakshmi: The Political Economy of the Indian State.* Chicago: University of Chicago Press, 1987.

Sheth, D. L., ed. *Citizens and Parties: Aspects of Competitive Politics in India.* Delhi: Allied, 1975.

Smith, D. E. *India as a Secular State.* Princeton, NJ: Princeton University Press, 1963.

Sontheimer, Guenter D., and Hermann Kulke, eds. *Hinduism Reconsidered.* Delhi: Manohar, 1989.

Weiner, Myron. *Party Building in a New Nation: The Indian National Congress.* Chicago: University of Chicago Press, 1968.

World Bank, *World Development Report, 2006. Equity and Development.* New York: Oxford University Press, 2005.

## INTERNET RESOURCES

Government of India: Directory of official websites: **www.goidirectory.nic.in**

Indian Parliament: **www.parliamentofindia.nic.in**

Prime Minister's Office: **www.pmindia.nic.in**

Combined access to Indian newspapers: **www.samarchar.com**

Bharatiya Janata Party: **www.bjp.org**

Indian National Congress: **www.indiannationalcongress.com**

Constitution of India: **www.indiacode.nic.org**

World Resources Institute: **www.earthtrends.wri.org**

## ENDNOTES

1. For a detailed analysis of the background to the separatist movement in Kashmir, see Subrata Mitra, "Nehru's Policy Towards Kashmir: Bringing the State Back in Again," *Commonwealth and Comparative Politics* 35 (1997): 55–74.

2. Subrata Mitra, "War and Peace in South Asia: A Revisionist View of India-Pakistan Relations," *Contemporary South Asia* 10 (2001): 361–79.

3. According to World Bank data derived on the basis of the Indian national poverty line (http://devdata.worldbank.org/AAG/ ind_aag.pdf; accessed on 25 July 2006).

4. Burton Stein, *Peasant, State, and Society in Medieval South India* (Delhi: Oxford University Press, 1980).

5. See Hermann Kulke, ed., *The State in India, 1000–1700* (Delhi: Oxford University Press, 1985), for an excellent introduction to the diversity of historical scholarship on the political form and social base of the early state in India.

6. Judith Brown, *Modern India: The Origins of an Asian Democracy* (Delhi: Oxford University Press, 1985).

7. Ashis Nandy, *The Intimate Enemy: Loss and Recovery of Self Under Colonialism* (Delhi: Oxford University Press, 1983).

8. Subrata Mitra, "Room to Maneuver in the Middle: Local Elites, Political Action, and the State in India," *World Politics* 43 (April 1961): 390–413.

9. Guenter Sontheimer and Hermann Kulke, eds. *Hinduism Reconsidered* (Delhi: Mahohar, 1989).

10. National Election Study (Delhi: CSDS, 1999).

11. Yogendra Malik and V. B. Singh, "Bharatiya Janata Party: An Alternative to Congress (I)?" *Asian Survey* 32 (April 1992): 318–36.

12. For excellent sources on the origin of political institutions and attitudes in India, see *Sources of Indian Tradition*, Vol. 1, *From the Beginning to 1800*, Ainslie Embree, ed. (London: Penguin, 1991); and Vol. 2, *Modern India and Pakistan*, Stephen Hay, ed. (London: Penguin, 1991).

13. See *Sources of Indian Tradition* op.cit. for references to the attempts and movements to develop a standard form of worship, to simplify ritual, and to spread egalitarian norms within the Hindu community.

14. The Jagannath cult of Orissa is an example of this form of syncretism. See Subrata K. Mitra, "Religion, Region, and Identity: Sacred Beliefs and Secular Power in a Regional State Tradition of India," in Noel O. Sullivan, ed., *Aspects of India: Essays on Indian Politics and Culture* (Hull, England: University of Hull, 1994), 46–68.

15. "There is a good chance that 20 years from now, many of India's constitutional anomalies regarding the secular state will have disappeared. It is reasonable to expect that by that time there will be a uniform civil code and that Hindu and Muslim law, as such, will have ceased to exist. Legislation having already dealt with the most serious abuses in Hindu religion there will be little need for further interference by the state." D. E. Smith, *India as a Secular State* (Princeton, NJ: Princeton University Press, 1963), 134.

16. Subrata Mitra, "The NDA and the Politics of 'Minorities' in India," in *Coalition Politics and Hindu Nationalism*, Katherine Adeney and Lawrence Sáez, eds. (London: Routledge, 2005), 77–96.

17. Subrata Mitra, "Desecularizing the State: Religion and Politics in India After Independence," *Comparative Studies in Society and History* 33 (October 1991): 755–77.

18. For a comprehensive dimension, see Robert Hardgrave and Stanley Kochanek, eds., *India: Government and Politics in a Developing Nation,* (Fort Worth, TX: Harcourt Brace Jovanovich, 1993).

19. See Robin Jeffrey, *What's Happening to India: Punjab, Ethnic Conflict, and the Test for Federalism*, 2nd ed. (London: MacMillan, 1994).

20. Gurharpal Singh, "Ethnic Conflict in India: A Case-study of Punjab," in John McGarry and Brendan O'Leary, eds., *The Politics of Ethnic Conflict Regulation* (London: Routledge, 1993), 84–105.

21. Subrata Mitra, "The Rational Politics of Cultural Nationalism: Subnational Movements of South Asia in Comparative Perspective," *British Journal of Political Science* 25 (1995): 57–78.

22. Alan Beals, *Gopalpur: A South Indian Village* (New York: Holt, Rinehart & Winston, 1963), 41.

23. Caste consciousness transforms caste from an ascriptive status to a politically convenient self-classification. For a discussion of the efforts to improve the material conditions of the former untouchables through the policy of reservation and the upper-caste backlash against it, see Subrata Mitra, "The Perils of Promoting Equality," *Journal of Commonwealth and Comparative Politics* 25 (1987): 292–312.

24. Lloyd Rudolph and Susanne Rudolph, *In Pursuit of Lakshmi: The Political Economy of the Indian State* (Chicago: University of Chicago Press, 1987), 49.

25. Lloyd Rudolph and Susanne Rudolph, *In Pursuit of Lakshmi*, 247, 255–58.

26. The dynastic "theory" of succession in India—popularized in the West by Tariq Ali, *The Nehrus and the Gandhis: An Indian Dynasty* (London: Pan Books, 1985)—has been questioned in Subrata Mitra, "Succession in India: Dynastic Rule or Democratization of Power?" *Third World Quarterly* 10 (1988): 129–59.

27. The legal basis of the emergency rule of 1975–1977 has been the subject of an intense controversy. Most observers see this period as a breakdown in the democratic political system in India. See W. H. Morris-Jones, "Creeping but Uneasy Authoritarianism in India," *Government and Opposition* 12 (1977): 39–47.

28. The President's rule, under which a region is ruled directly by the center for a specific period, is indicative of a failure of representative government. It happened relatively infrequently during the first two decades of Independence; the most celebrated case was the dismissal of the elected Communist government of Kerala in 1959. It became more common during the governmental instability of the mid-1960s, with the imposition of the president's rule eight times during the prime ministerial tenures of Nehru and Shastri (1950 to 1966). However, during the two periods of tenure of Mrs. Gandhi, the president's rule was imposed 42 times.

29. If the president of India is satisfied that a grave emergency exists whereby the security of the nation or of any part of the territory thereof is threatened, whether by war, external aggression or internal disturbance, he may make a declaration to that effect (Article 352). While a proclamation of emergency is in operation, nothing in Article 19 "shall restrict the power of the state to make any law or to take any executive action" (Article 358). Article 356 makes similar provisions for the suspension of democratic government in a region. It should be pointed out that emergencies are conceived of as temporary and the scope for legislative accountability is not altogether absent.

30. James Manor, who had earlier talked about the "deinstitutionalization" of India, has more recently talked about the "regeneration" of institutions. See James Manor, *From Nehru to Nineties: The Changing Office of the Prime Minister in India* (London: Hurst, 1994).

31. For a more detailed discussion, see "The Legislative Process: How Laws Are Made," in Subhas Kashyap, *Our Parliament* (Delhi: National Book Trust of India, 1989), 121–56.

32. For a brief period during the last years of the presidency of Zail Singh, presidential assent became an effective instrument to delay legislation. But commentators on Indian politics have attributed this more to the personal pique of Singh against Prime Minister Rajiv Gandhi than to any explicit policy difference between them.

33. Such situations are not unknown in parliamentary democracies. But the French solution of "cohabitation" of a president and a legislative majority belonging to different parties or the German "grand coalition" are not yet available, though they cannot be excluded in the future.

34. See Subrata Mitra, *Governmental Instability in Indian States* (Delhi: Ajanta, 1978), for an analysis of the rapid rise and fall of governments in Indian states during the 1960s.

35. The survey was conducted through face-to-face interviews during May–June 1996, in the aftermath of the eleventh parliamentary elections. A representative sample of about 10,000 adults was interviewed under the guidance of the Center for the Study of Developing Societies (CSDS), Delhi.

36. S. K. Verma and Kusum, eds., *Fifty Years of the Supreme Court of India: Its Grasp and Reach* (Delhi: Oxford University Press, 2000), narrates this success story.

37. The central government is referred to as the Union government and the Indian federation is referred to as a Union of States in Article 1 of the Indian Constitution.

38. Rudolph and Rudolph (1987) refer to the two phenomena respectively as "state dominated pluralism" and "involuted pluralism." See Lloyd Rudolph and Susanne Rudolph, 259–89.

39. Subrata Mitra, Siegfried Wolf, and Jivanta Schoettli, *A Political and Economic Dictionary of South Asia* (London: Europa, 2006), 96.

40. For a discussion on new social movements in India, see Gail Omvedt, *Reinventing Revolution: New Social Movements and the Socialist Tradition in India* (London: East Gate, 1993).

41. Subrata Mitra, *Power, Protest, and Participation: Local Elites and the Politics of Development in India* (London: Routledge, 1992).

42. See Subrata Mitra, "Room to Maneuver."

43. Samuel Huntington, *Political Order in Changing Societies* (New Haven, CT: Yale University Press, 1968).

44. See Subrata K., Mitra, Mike Enskat, and Clemens Spiess, eds., *Political Parties in South Asia* (Westport, CT/London: Praeger, 2004).

45. Rajni Kothari, *The State Against Democracy: In Search of Humane Governance* (Delhi: Ajanta, 1988), 164–65.

46. See Myron Weiner, *Party Building in a New Nation: The Indian National Congress* (Chicago: University of Chicago Press, 1968).

47. See Subrata Mitra, "Party Organization and Policy Making in a Changing Environment: The Indian National Congress," in Kay Lawson, ed., *How Political Parties Work Perspectives from Within* (Westport, CT: Praeger, 1994), 153–77.

48. Lloyd Rudolph and Susanne Rudolph, *In Pursuit of Lakshmi*, 255.

49. Vertical mobilization refers to political linkages that draw on and reinforce social and economic dominance. Horizontal mobilization takes place when people situated at the same social and economic levels get together to use their combined political strength to improve their situation. Differential mobilization refers to coalitions that cut across social strata. Lloyd Rudolph and Susanne Rudolph, *The Modernity of Tradition: Political Development in India* (Chicago: University of Chicago Press, 1967).

50. For the formulation of these ideas in terms of an analytical framework on elections and social change in India based on a model of electoral norms and organizational structures corresponding to them, see Subrata Mitra, "Caste, Democracy and the Politics of Community Formation in India," in Mary Searle-Chatterjee and Ursula Sharma, eds., *Contextualising Caste* (London: Blackwell/The Sociological Review, 1994), 49–72.

51. For an application of this concept as a framework for the discussion of political participation in India, see Subrata Mitra, "Room to Maneuver."

52. W. H. Morris-Jones, *The Government and Politics of India* (Wistow, England: Eothen Press, 1987), 58.

53. This theme has been developed further in Jyotirindra Dasgupta, "India: Democratic Becoming and Combined Development," in Larry Diamond, Juan Linz, and Seymour Martin Lipset, eds., *Democracy in Developing Countries* (Boulder, CO: Lynne Rienner, 1989), 62.

54. W. H. Morris-Jones, *Government and Politics,* 61. The statement, first made in 1962, turned out to be prophetic, because J. P. Narayan became a rallying point for opposition to the Emergency in 1975.

55. Manas Ghosh, "Lack of Identity: Options Before the CPI(M)," *Statesman Weekly,* 22 April 1995.

56. Lloyd Rudolph and Susanne Rudolph, "Cultural Policy, the Text Book Controversy, and Indian Identity," in A. Jeyaratnam Wilson and Dennis Dalton, eds., *The States of South Asia* (London: Hurst, 1982), 131–54.

57. In March 2001, Tehelka, the Internet News Agency, uncovered a bribery scandal among leading government officials, which caused the resignation of Defense Minister George Fernandes, BJP Party President Bangaru Laxman, as well as the president of the Samata Party, Jaya Jaitly.

58. Following allegations of irregularity in the northern Indian constituency of Amethi where Prime Minister Rajiv Gandhi was a candidate, the Election Commission, an independent body that supervises the conduct of polling, ordered new voting to take place. Thus, one can notice both the political will and institutional capacity at the systemic level to minimize the cases of electoral tampering.

59. The percentage of women representatives in India's highest legislature is low in terms of absolute numbers but does not compare too unfavorably to those in developed European democracies. Only 6 percent of the members of the then House of Commons of Britain were women. "United Nations Economic Commission for Europe," *Economist,* 18–24 March 1995, 33.

60. The survey question asked to measure legitimacy of democratic institutions in 2004 gave two choices to those who did not explicitly say that "democracy was better." The 9.7 percent who say "yes" in 2004 thus comprise two groups—of 3.7 percent who say dictatorship is better, and 6 percent who are indifferent between democracy and dictatorship.

61. Data from World Research Institute (accessed at www.earthtrends.wri.org on 8 June 2006).

62. World Bank India Country Brief 2005 (accessed at www.worldbank.org/in on 8 June 2006).

63. The Indian model of development has had sharp critics like Barrington Moore (Moore 1996), who saw India's efforts at combining growth with democracy as "tall in talk but short in action." One defender, Jyotirindra Das Gupta (1997), described the Indian model as a method of "combined development," based on a "creative exercise in the autonomy of political initiative."

64. See John Wall, "Foodgrain Management: Pricing, Procurement, Distribution, Import, and Storage Policy in India," *Occasional Papers,* World Bank Staff Working Paper No. 279 (Washington, DC: World Bank, 1978), 88–89.

65. A pejorative epithet, usually implying the proclivity of the Congress Party regime to practice patronage politics; literally, a regime based on disbursing largesse, such as quotas for commodities whose supply is controlled by the government, and giving permits to set up industries or run specific businesses for which government permission is needed. Liberalization has attempted to put an end to these practices by removing these areas of enterprise from the government control.

66. *Economist,* 21–26 January 1995, 7.

67. When asked in a national opinion survey in 2004 about the financial prospects they expected, 49.2 percent of the national sample thought their financial conditions would improve, 6.2 percent thought they would worsen, 19.4 percent thought they would remain the same, and about 25 percent were not sure. In the same survey, 67.5 percent thought their vote had an effect on how things are run in the country, compared with 17.5 percent who thought the opposite. Delhi: National Election Survey, Center for the Study of Developing Societies, 2004.

68. Selig Harrison, *India: The Most Dangerous Decades* (Delhi: Oxford University Press, 1960), 338.

69. Conservative opinion in Britain was generally opposed to Indian independence before an acceptable solution to the communal problem between Hindus and Muslims was found. This cautious approach was criticized by some who cited the successful functioning of elected governments in eight out of eleven provinces after the 1937 elections held under the Government of India Act of 1935; see Henry Noel Brailsford, *Democracy for India* (London: Fabian Society, 1942).

70. These arguments are stated in detail in Subrata Mitra, *Culture and Rationality* (Delhi: Sage, 1999); and Subrata Mitra and V. B. Singh, *When Rebels become Stakeholders: Democracy, Agency and Social Change in India* (Delhi: Sage; 2009).

71. Seymour M. Lipset, "Some Social Requisites of Democracy: Economic Development and Political Legitimacy," *American Political Science Review* 53 (1959): 69–105. Lipset suggests that in order to succeed as a democracy, a society has to attain certain levels of social and economic development.

72. Samuel P. Huntington, *Political Order in Changing Societies* (New Haven, CT: Yale University Press, 1968), 55.

73. The puzzle has a direct bearing on the pessimistic prognosis of Barrington Moore (1966).

74. Indian experience stands in sharp contrast to its South Asian neighbors. Universal adult franchise was introduced in Ceylon in the early 1930s, even before limited franchise was available in some Indian provinces. The Muslim League—which under the leadership of Jinnah, championed the cause of Pakistan—became the ruling party in the new state after Independence. Neither of the two states has been as successful as India in sustaining democracy. See Mick Moore, "Sri Lanka: The Contradictions of the Social Democratic State," and Hamza Alavi, "Authoritarianism and the Legitimation of State Power in Pakistan," in Subrata Mitra, ed., *The Postcolonial State in Asia: The Dialectics of Politics and Culture* (Hemel Hempstead, England: Wheatsheaf, 1990).

75. There is considerable controversy among scholars regarding the causes and probability of Hindu-Muslim conflict. See Ashutosh Varshney, *Ethnic Conflict and Civic Life: Hindus and Muslims in India* (New Haven: Yale University Press, 2002) and Paul Brass, The *Production of Hindu-Muslim Violence in Contemporary India* (Seattle: University of Washington Press, 2003) for contrary views. Christophe Jaffrelot gives a graphic account of Hindu-Muslim riots in Gujarat in "Communal Riots in Gujarat: The State at Risk?" *Heidleberg Papers in South Asian and Comparative Politics,* No. 17 (2003) http://www.sai.uniheidelberg.de/SAPOL/HPSACP.htm. Steven Wilkinson suggests a link between electoral competition and ethnic riots in India in *Votes and Violence: Electoral Competition and Ethnic Riots in India* (Cambridge: Cambridge University Press, 2004).

76. "Nothing in India is identifiable, the mere asking of a question causes it to disappear or to merge into something else." E. M. Forster, *A Passage to India* (Harmondsworth, England: Penguin, 1985; first published in 1924), 92.

77. The Emergency of 1975–1977, which is seen as an aberration of the political process in India, is a major landmark in the country's political development. For further information, see "Images of the Emergency," the theme of a symposium on the subject in *Seminar* (Delhi, March 1977), and P. B. Mayer, "Congress (I), Emergency (I): Interpreting Indira Gandhi's India," *Journal of Commonwealth and Comparative Politics* 22 (1984): 128–50.

78. The rise of lawlessness and the criminalization of politics have been observed by several scholars. See the epilogue in W. H. Morris-Jones, *The Government and Politics of India,* (259–72). The mass-circulation *India Today* talks about "the elevation of violence, defiant indiscipline, and lawlessness to a cult" everywhere in the country, "not just [among] the armed militants of the Jammu and Kashmir Liberation Front or the Khalistan Commando Force, but ordinary people, lawyers, policemen, shopkeepers, civil servants, students, trade unionists" as well. "Cult of Anarchy," *India Today,* 31 August 1990.

79. V. S. Naipaul, *India: A Million Mutinies Now* (London: Heinemann, 1990), 517.

# NIGERIA

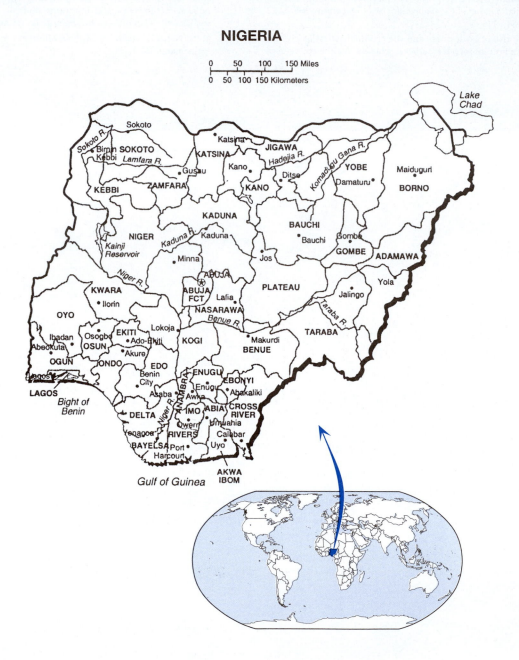

# POLITICS IN NIGERIA

*Robert J. Mundt, Oladimeji Aborisade, and A. Carl LeVan*

## Country Bio

**Population**
149 million

**Territory**
356,668 square miles

**Year of Independence**
1960

**Year of Current Constitution**
1979 Constitution still partially in force; draft
1995 Constitution published and revised in 1999,
(the 1999 Constitution)

**Head of State**
President Umar Musa Yar'Adua

**Head of Government**
President Umar Musa Yar'Adua

**Languages**
English (official), Hausa, Yoruba, Igbo, and 250
other ethnic groups

**Religions**
Muslim 50%, Christian 40%, indigenous
beliefs 10%

NIGERIA

In the African context Nigeria is a megastate. Even on a world scale, Nigeria is a major country. Larger than France or Britain, it claims over one-fifth of the people in Africa and has the world's largest black population. Its petroleum and its substantial standing military force guarantee its prominence in international relations; and with seventy-six universities, Nigeria contains a large proportion of Africa's centers of learning and research.

For these reasons alone, one should know about Nigeria. But learning about Nigeria is also an efficient approach to learning about Africa, because Nigeria embodies much of the variety of African political experience within its borders. Its traditions include the large-scale emirates of the north and the small kingdoms and village-level republics of the south. Although both were administered by Britain, the north and south of Nigeria experienced different versions of colonial rule. Its culture is divided by ethnicity and by religion, especially between Christians and Muslims. Its history since independence includes coups, countercoups, and civil war; recently, along with many other Africans, Nigerians have been groping toward a renewal of democracy. The problems and prospects of many African ministates are found in Nigeria, but at a more daunting scale and level of complexity. To know Nigeria is not necessarily to know Africa, but to one who is well acquainted with the Nigerian experience there will be little that is surprising in politics elsewhere on the continent.

Nigeria's prominent place in the world is more potential than real, however, because in recent years Nigeria has been a *sick* giant. Its economy is in shambles and the provision of public services has broken down. This chapter examines the causes of this illness and assesses the democratic government's remedies to it.

## CURRENT POLICY CHALLENGES

Of all the countries considered in this book, Nigeria might be the only one whose continued existence is currently in doubt. The country's ethnic, regional, and religious divisions have intensified in recent years, and important political actors have recently suggested breaking up the country into a weak federation or even completely independent states if political power cannot be distributed in a manner all can accept. This situation is not all that unusual: Nigeria has existed for only forty-nine years. After roughly seventy years of existence, the Soviet Union split apart over regional and policy issues, and the cohesiveness of Canada and of the United Kingdom remain open to question in some quarters today. It may be easier to explain why Nigeria is likely to fall apart in the short term than it is to specify conditions for its long-term stability.

It is against this stark reality that politics and policy must be viewed in Nigeria today. In 1999 Nigeria returned to formal civilian rule, when Olusegun Obasanjo was elected president. A few weeks later a new democratic legislature was also elected. In 2003, President Obasanjo was reelected in a landslide, and his party also captured most other important political offices. Even though Nigeria has returned to constitutional rule, that constitution will continue to be tested by Nigerians' frustration over the failure of their potentially wealthy country to provide basic human needs, education, potable water, reliable transportation and communications, and politics free of rampant corruption. Income levels per capita are barely a tenth of income in the United States or Western Europe, and among the 177 nations ranked in the United Nations' Human Development Index, Nigeria ranked number 159—among the poorest quarter of nations. Similarly, in the 2005 Corruption Perceptions Index developed by Transparency International, only five ranked worse out of the 159 countries studied.

From the outset, the government has struggled to move Nigeria in a new direction. If a democratic regime cannot address these demands in reasonably short order, that regime will suffer the fate of those before it and chaos or renewed authoritarian rule will be the likely outcome. Yet, Nigerians always seem to draw on a wellspring of optimism, even as they maintain an attitude of skepticism. The following analysis will help the reader determine the degree to which that optimism is warranted.

## THE EFFECTS OF HISTORY

More than forty years ago, anthropologist Clifford Geertz titled an essay on the developing nations "Old Societies and New States."[1] This title is an apt characterization of Nigeria, for although the concept of Nigeria dates only to 1914, and the independent state only to 1960, the cultures that compose it have ancient roots.

In one sense, then, there are "many" Nigerias. That is, there are distinct political cultures with precolonial origins, and there are the varied colonial experiences of north, east, and west. We will consider these causes of variety separately.

### The Enduring Effects of Precolonial Events

Our images of precolonial Africa have been plagued by misunderstandings, sometimes in the form of simple ignorance, but often the result of prejudice. Many in the industrial world still view traditional Africa as "primitive," composed of a series of "tribes."[2]

A common response is that "Africa had its empires also." As we shall see, this is quite true. However, to insist that empires are a sign of advanced culture is to accept that the successful implementation of authoritarian rule over large numbers of people is "civilized." It can be argued that those peoples who at the village level developed complex systems of limitations on their rulers were at least as politically sophisticated as those who built empires. All these peoples interacted in trade, cultural diffusion, and war for many centuries before the creation of today's nation-states, and their belief systems were as complex and nuanced as any in the world.

To reiterate, there was no single Nigeria a century ago. Some of the peoples inhabiting the land that now constitutes Nigeria were organized only at the village or extended family level (for example, the **Igbo** in the southeast), while in other areas there were kingdoms and states. Where one group had subjugated the peoples around them, we can identify empires, such as that of Kanem-Bornu around Lake Chad between the eleventh and fourteenth centuries, the Oyo Empire in the western region of present-day Nigeria from the thirteenth to the eighteenth centuries, and the Fulani Empire of the nineteenth century.[3]

The **Hausa** people began forming city-states in northern Nigeria between 1000 and 1200 A.D., and came under the influence of Islam no later than the fifteenth century. By the next century, mosques and Koranic schools were flourishing, and Hausa princes were international rivals of Morocco and the

Ottoman Empire. The fortunes of these systems waxed and waned through the centuries, but they were decisively changed when non-Hausa court officials rose against them early in the nineteenth century. These officials were **Fulani,** a people with their origins in western Sudan who had entered into the Hausa lands as herders and, more importantly, as teachers, traders, and eventually court advisers. By their own accounts they were ardent Muslims who found the Hausa leaders lax in their faith and decadent. A Fulani scholar and preacher, Usman dan Fodio, inspired a religious and political revolt against the Hausa kings (he found responsive audiences to his denunciation of taxes, even among Hausa commoners). A Fulani-dominated caliphate was established in Sokoto, now northern Nigeria. This Fulani Empire controlled most of the north until the British defeated it in 1903. Sokoto retains its role as the Muslim religious capital of Nigeria to this day. The Hausa and Fulani cultures have become so intertwined, with extensive intermarriage and with Hausa the primary language of both, that the dominant culture of the north is usually referred to as **Hausa-Fulani.** The descendants of the rulers of the Hausa-Fulani kingdoms, identified by the Islamic title *emir*, continue to hold court in the major cities of northern Nigeria.

In the forest region the **Yoruba** and Bini peoples of the southwest began forming kingdoms between the twelfth and fifteenth centuries at Oyo, Ife, and Benin. In the seventeenth and eighteenth centuries the kingdom of Oyo subdued its rivals and extended its control over the entire southwestern part of Nigeria. These political systems developed intricate methods of limiting the powers of their rulers. For example, the ruler of Oyo, the Alafin, was chosen by a council of chiefs, the Oyo Mesi. The historian Michael Crowder recounts that "if they felt the Alafin had exceeded his powers [the Oyo Mesi] could divine that all was not well between the Alafin and his spiritual double and force him to commit suicide. . . . However, the Oyo Mesi were restrained from abuse of this power by the fact that one of their number had to die with the Alafin."[4] Clearly, limited government has other sources than the Magna Carta and comes in a variety of forms. The successors to the Yoruba kings, or *obas*, continue to act out symbolic leadership roles in many cities in southwestern Nigeria.

Because Nigeria was defined through the colonial experience, we must ask how and why the eventual British domination occurred. The immediate cause for British interest in West Africa was trade, and the first such international trade of any importance was in slaves. Coastal groups began exchanging captives for goods with European trading ships as early as the sixteenth century. Wars among the various kingdoms ensured a plentiful supply of captives, particularly in southwestern Nigeria. For the next 300 years this trade was sustained: Benin, Lagos, Bonny, and Calabar thrived as slave trade centers, exporting upward of 20,000 persons per year to the Americas. Nigeria lost some of its most able-bodied inhabitants during those "barren three centuries" of relations between Europe and Africa.

In 1807 the British Parliament outlawed the slave trade. In a remarkable turnabout, the British navy replaced British slave ships and began patrolling the West African coast to cut off the trade, which was not completely eliminated until about 1850. The established slave-trading patterns were gradually converted to other goods. British consuls established themselves on the coast and began to intervene in local politics, favoring those candidates for ruling positions who would give them commercial advantages over other European traders. The British succeeded in obtaining treaties of British protection and trade along the coast. These were treaties between unequals, increasingly favorable to the British as they first established commercial and then political control.

## The Colonial Interlude (1900–1960)

With tongue in cheek, Nigerian journalist Peter Enahoro once described his nationality in this fashion: "Today, the conglomeration of tribes assembled compulsorily at the 1884 Berlin conference are assigned as Nigerians—for want of a substitute collective noun."[5] Indeed, the name "Nigeria" itself was coined by Flora Shaw, an Englishwoman who later married Sir Frederick Lugard, the architect of colonial Nigeria. Enahoro's characterization refers to the origins of Nigeria's boundaries and those of most countries of contemporary Africa. In order to avoid war resulting from the competition for colonies, the great European powers met as the Conference of Berlin in 1884–1885 and divided Africa into spheres of influence. In effect, the European powers decided to seize control of the continent rather than merely trade with its rulers and merchants. In a wave of negotiations, imperialist wars, and conquests, their efforts were successful, and by the beginning of World War I in 1914 maps of Africa showed clearly drawn lines with areas color-coded according to the European power claiming control. Thus, in 1886 the Royal Niger Company was granted a royal charter to control Nigerian trade. That charter was replaced in 1900 by the creation of the Colony of Lagos and the Protectorates of Northern and Southern Nigeria.

There was an unfortunate interaction between the colonial penetration and West Africa's natural environment: cultures tend to be affected by climate and ecology, as people adapt differently to life in the rainforest, grasslands, or desert. In West Africa, the prevailing climate and ecological zones run east and west (see Figure 18.1). However, the colonial thrust was from the coast of the Gulf of Guinea inland, and colonial boundaries were established on the coast and then extended northward, intersecting the climate zones. This virtually guaranteed that the colonies thus established would be composed of peoples coming from vastly different cultures.

Nigeria first became an entity in 1914, when the Northern and Southern Protectorates and Lagos were brought under a single colonial administration. This unifying action was largely symbolic, however, as its two parts continued to be governed separately. The Northern and Southern Provinces replaced the Protectorates, each under a lieutenant governor. Northern Nigeria remained apart as such political structures as a legislative council evolved in the south. Northerners did not sit on the Nigerian Legislative Council until 1947. Indeed, the north proved to be the perfect setting for the "indirect rule" elaborated by the governor, Lord Lugard: the British administration would not intervene directly into everyday life in its colonies, but would support the rule of traditional leaders, such as the Fulani emirs. This, Lugard argued, was the most efficient means of controlling the colonies. In southern Nigeria, however, Western-educated elites challenged the authority of the traditional rulers where they existed (as among the Yoruba); in southeastern Nigeria, among the Igbo and other peoples, there really were no traditional kings or chiefs. Attempts to create village chiefs where the concept was unknown produced results that were sometimes comical and often tragic. Novelist Chinua Achebe has an English colonial officer describe such a situation:

> Chief Ikedi was still corrupt and high-handed but he had become even more clever than before. The latest thing he did was to get his people to make him an *obi* or king, so that he was now called his Highness Ikedi the First, Obi of Okperi.

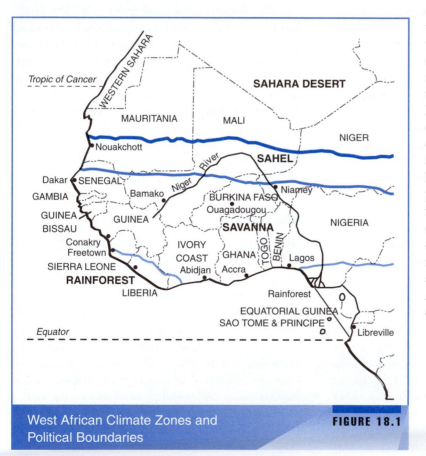

**West African Climate Zones and Political Boundaries**

**FIGURE 18.1**

This among a people who never had kings before! This was what British administration was doing among the Ibos, making a dozen mushroom kings grow where there was none before.[6]

Thus the different applicability of indirect rule served to further distinguish the political experiences of the regions.

The British colonial administration also faced the problem of incompatible objectives. In order to make the colony self-sustaining, Britain needed an export economy. However, the conversion of peasant societies from subsistence to a market orientation eroded the foundations of traditional rule. Except in the north, chiefs and kings had no traditional right to collect taxes, yet this became a central duty in the colonial system. Also, the development of a modern system of transportation and communication, necessary to stimulate commerce, encouraged the movement of people from the countryside to cities and from one part of the country to another, all under the protection of the colonial authorities. Urbanized populations and immigrants from other cultures could scarcely be expected to show deference to traditional rulers, nor did they see any good reason for paying taxes.

Along with commerce and administration, the British brought missionaries and education. Missionaries of many denominations—Anglicans, Presbyterians, Catholics, Baptists, Adventists, and others—brought the Gospels to Nigeria, although only to the south; the northern emirates had an understanding with the British that Christian proselytizing would not be permitted in their domains. Christianity spread especially rapidly in the southeast, and somewhat less so in the southwest; with it went formal schooling. As Nigerian children learned the English language and customs, they acquired the tools with which to challenge colonial rule on the rulers' own terms. However, the Western-educated elite that emerged came largely from the south. Thus, the culture is divided north and south along religious lines, but the difference has to do with much more than religion.

Modern constitutional development began within a few years of the creation of Nigeria as a single colony, with elective office first provided in 1922. An early nationalist leader, Herbert Macaulay, established a political party soon thereafter. As a Nigerian-centered political life grew up among the formally educated, other organizations arose, and the British colonial administration was pressed with demands for participation. The spirit of the times was captured by Nigerian writer Wole Soyinka as he recalled that

> Suddenly there was Oge-e-e-ed Ogendengbe (Herbert) Macaulay and there was Ze-e-e-ek (Nnamdi Azikiwe, nationalist leader). His oratory, we learnt, could move mountains. Some young, radical nationalists were being jailed for sedition, and sedition had become equivalent to demanding that the white man leave us to rule ourselves.[7]

From then on, constitutions promulgated by various governors (and named after them) were always somewhat behind the expectations of Nigerian political activists. What southern politicians judged conservative, however, was usually seen as radical by the conservative elites in the north. These differences of opinion among Nigerians resulted in 1954 in the creation of a federal system of three regions, Northern, Eastern, and Western. A single ethnic group dominated each region: The Hausa-Fulani in the north, the Igbo in the east, and the Yoruba in the west. Under pressure from their leaders, the Eastern and Western regions received self-government in 1957; the north became self-governing in 1959, a few months before national independence.

## Nigerian Independence

As Nigeria approached independence, there was a general consensus that the nation should come to independence as a single country. Independent Nigeria was born on October 1, 1960.

Nigeria's independent governments at the federal and state levels experienced a very short "honeymoon." Within two years, conflict had torn apart the ruling coalition in the Western Region. The next year suspicions about the national census (as we will see later) destroyed what little trust there was among the regions. Finally, in 1965 law and order broke down in the Western Region over election-related fraud and violence, and the military ended the First Republic in a January 1966 coup.

An awareness of these experiences is critical to an understanding of political conflict in independent Nigeria. Although the colonial experience was comparatively brief, it left a legacy of political ideas that were difficult to reconcile with precolonial values and structures. Many modern Nigerians remain profoundly Yoruba or Hausa; but is there a role for obas and emirs in modern Nigeria? This is not just a clash between the "traditional" and the "modern," because there are many, perhaps hundreds of "traditions." The blending of these various influences was all the less likely given the short time allowed for political evolution prior to independence. Nigerians and other Africans are today grappling with the resultant confusion, which has produced political instability, economic woes, and constant military interventions. And the difficulties on Nigeria's road to independence are obviously related to the absence of any start in that direction prior to independence.

## ENVIRONMENTAL POTENTIAL AND LIMITATIONS

Why has Nigeria's economic development been so dismal? Why are most of its people so poor? Are these conditions the result of physical environment, history, and socioeconomic context, or do they result from the Nigerian political process and the policy decisions that Nigerian governments have made?

Nigeria is counted among the world's less developed, or Third World, countries. Its gross domestic product (GDP) in 2004 was $72.1 billion or $560 per capita (we will discuss Nigeria's GDP later in this chapter; see Table 18.4 and accompanying text). This figure put it well below the United Nations criterion for "low-income countries." Previously, from 1980 to 1991, GNP per capita actually declined by 1.7 percent annually. Controlling for purchasing power parity (PPP), per capita GDP was $1,154 in 2004.

### Conditions Affecting Agricultural Production and the Sale of Primary Commodities

Colonial policies not only retarded Nigeria's political development but also had profound, if mixed, effects on its economy. Since early in the colonial period, southern Nigerians have been producing cocoa, palm oil, timber, and rubber. The timber, sold mostly as tropical hardwoods for use in furniture and construction, came from the now-dwindling rainforests in the south. In the north the principal market products were cattle, hides and skins, cotton, and peanuts.

The growth of trade in these commodities was not entirely spontaneous. The British interest in Nigeria was primarily commercial, with its origins in the United Africa Company (UAC). When the UAC was granted a charter as the Royal Niger Company in 1886, it was given police and judicial power, and it was authorized to collect taxes and to oversee commerce. Not surprisingly, its policies aimed at developing the Nigerian economy to be compatible with British needs. Also, public sentiment in Britain never solidly favored creating a colonial empire, and powerful voices in Parliament favored keeping the costs of the empire to a minimum. Colonial administrations were under heavy pressure to be self-sufficient—to develop local sources of revenue to cover their costs of administration. As a result, colonial administrators pressured peasant farmers away from subsistence agriculture and into commercial farming, particularly of export crops. Furthermore, cost-efficient marketing meant emphasis on just a few of the most needed products; in Nigeria (and elsewhere in West Africa), these turned out to be palm oil, cocoa, peanuts, and cotton. Thus British raw material priorities and the need to provide a self-sufficient colonial administration distorted African economies toward dependence on the sale of a small number of primarily agricultural commodities.

The combination of population growth and the commercialization of agriculture strained relationships between agricultural techniques and the ecology that had been in place for centuries. Colonial officials sometimes assumed that productivity could be greatly increased in tropical regions with the introduction of "modern" methods without recognizing the different ecological conditions of production in a tropical setting. Lush tropical rainforest could not simply be replaced by plantations. Rainfall, temperature, and soil conditions meant that farming techniques effective in England or North America would be unsuccessful or even disastrous. Only gradually, and much later, were the efforts of agronomists applied to maximizing agricultural production in the tropics, especially to food production for local consumption. There is still a large "research deficit" between the resources expended for agricultural research in temperate zones, as opposed to that in tropical zones.

Thus, Nigeria came to independence with an economy typical of Africa and other Third World areas. It was based on the production and export of

A street market bustles at an exit to the raised superhighway connecting Lagos Island to the mainland.

A. Hermann/UPI Bettmann/Corbis

agricultural commodities, principally palm oil (of which Nigeria was the world's leading exporter) and cocoa. Because Nigeria was larger and more ecologically diverse than most African colonies, its exports showed greater diversity than in the typical case. Still, production in each of its regions was focused on one or a few commodities, and the country as a whole depended on commodity markets in the industrial countries for its foreign exchange.

Like other newly independent countries, Nigeria broke with some colonial economic development policies, especially as concerned the need to diversify production. But the need for foreign exchange meant that agriculture continued to emphasize exportable commodities, even as investment capital was largely directed toward industrialization. Economists in both the industrial and Third World countries associated industry with prosperity, and agriculture was seen as the "cash cow" from which to extract savings for investment in other areas. Also, Nigerian government officials, trained in the need to balance budgets, balanced appropriations bills with overly optimistic estimations of "expected revenue." When these fell short, the difference was made up from cash reserves accumulated by the Central Produce Marketing Board. However, "since those reserves were derived from the price differential between what was paid to the farmer and what the Board earned in export earnings . . . for close on a decade, Nigeria existed only through the exploitation of her farmers."[8]

In addition to keeping agricultural prices low to provide such reserves, Nigerian governments also tried to satisfy urban demands for cheap food by holding down the price paid to farmers in the domestic market. This action contributed to the unattractiveness of agricultural work and enhanced the lure of the cities.

## Disease

Physical illness is a part of the human condition, and the higher disease rates of poorer nations are largely explained by the lack of resources to acquire medicines, medical facilities, and personnel. But environment contributes as well: some of the most common human diseases, including malaria, can survive only in tropical climates. In tropical Africa, virtually every long-term resident carries the malaria virus, and large proportions of the population are affected by it. It is usually not fatal, but it is extremely debilitating, and it has a documented effect on labor productivity. Various river-borne diseases also account for long-term illness and fatalities, contributing especially to the high mortality rate among children. As with agricultural problems, research can attack these diseases; yet a vastly disproportionate share of the world's resources applied to health problems is focused on ailments more common to the industrialized world. In recent times, AIDS has topped the list of the most dreadful diseases in Africa. The Joint United Nations Program on HIV/AIDS reported in 2006 that 3.9 percent of all Nigerians were infected; given the country's huge population, this amounts to over 5 million people between the ages of 15 and 49. In many African countries, the AIDS epidemic is slowing down the agricultural economy in particular and national productivity in general.

## Population Growth

Nothing is more striking to a visitor to Nigeria than the youth of the population; everywhere there are multitudes of children. About 45 percent of the Nigerian population is less than 15 years of age.[9] Children are considered a valuable resource in labor-intensive agricultural societies, and in a country with high infant mortality rates and no social security system, parents would be imprudent not to have enough children so that some would grow up to provide for them in their old age. This behavior becomes dysfunctional at the societal level, of course, as increasing populations struggle to survive on a limited physical environment. Figure 18.2 illustrates the projected population growth through 2020. Between 1975 and 2000, the population of Nigeria grew an average of 2.9 percent annually. With slow economic growth (only about 2.4 percent annually in the 1990s), this means when measured in per capita terms, GDP growth was actually negative. During this same period, the urban population grew from approximately 23 percent to 44 percent, a major leap. In this environment of rapid population growth and urbanization, children become economic liabilities. Thus, the "dependency ratio" (the proportion of the nonworking population to the working population) has steadily risen since the early 1960s, placing a great strain on the country's underdeveloped facilities for social welfare and education.[10]

Counting the population in Nigeria has always been controversial because of its implications for the distribution of resources and political districting. There has not been a widely accepted census since 1963 (see pp. 699–700). When the government conducted its most recent census in March 2006, it eliminated questions about religion and ethnicity from the questionnaire in order to ease popular concerns and encourage participation. Instead, it asked questions about education levels, income, water supply, occupation, and access to telephones and televisions.

Nevertheless, the census encountered significant resistance, particularly from separatists in the East; about fifteen people were killed during various protests and violence. The logistical issues of surveying over one hundred million people also hampered the effort. Workers claimed they had not been paid and that not enough forms were provided, and some claimed that no one counted them. Additionally, the government asked all citizens to stay home for the weeklong duration of the census until they were counted, which many small business owners saw as a hardship. The National Population Commission released the results in 2007 and they were forwarded to the president in November 2008. However they remain controversial and still have not been formally approved.

## Urbanization

Nigeria shares a pattern of urbanization common in Africa: although the country is still primarily rural, it is urbanizing rapidly. Nigeria's population is projected to be over 50 percent urban by the year 2010. In the

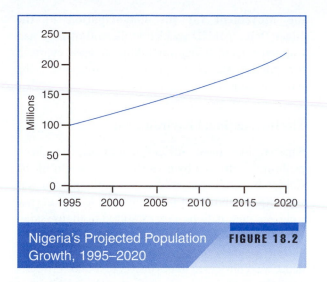

**FIGURE 18.2**

Nigeria's Projected Population Growth, 1995–2020

process, the development of urban infrastructure is added to the long list of demands on government. For example, the government ministry in charge of Abuja, the federal capital, announced in 2002 that the population of the city had exceeded 4 million, whereas city planners had estimated that the population would only be about 1.5 million at this stage of development.[11]

The population shift means that a smaller proportion of the labor force is available for agricultural work. That is a normal pattern of modernization, of course, but unless the productivity of agricultural workers increases, it means a drop in food production per capita. That has been the Nigerian experience: self-sufficient in food at independence, Nigeria is now heavily dependent on imports, paid for from oil revenues.

## Petroleum

The magnitude of Nigeria's petroleum reserves became apparent in the 1950s with the first shipload of crude exported in 1958. Nigeria was engulfed in a bloody civil war from 1967 to 1970, which brought a halt to oil exports. At war's end, however, Nigerian petroleum production began to boom, and it grew at a dramatic rate through the 1970s. Although such a valuable mineral resource is an asset to any country, its effects on Nigeria were not all beneficial. The country's economy became distorted by the great disparity of value between petroleum and the traditional agricultural products: soon young workers were abandoning

their farms and villages and flocking to the cities and the oil fields.

Oil revenues peaked in 1979. World demand for oil decreased each year from 1979 to 1983. At the same time, oil production in countries that were not part of the Organization of Petroleum Exporting Countries (OPEC), especially Mexico, Norway, and the United Kingdom, grew substantially. Nigeria's planners were slow to realize the implications of rising supply and stagnant demand. The glory days of seemingly limitless oil revenues ended abruptly in April 1982, when production of crude oil in Nigeria dropped from 2.1 million to 0.9 million barrels per day; oil export revenues fell correspondingly, from $1.35 billion to $0.7 billion per month. In the preceding decade, Nigeria had become dependent on oil revenues for imports and large-scale development projects. As was commonly the case in the Third World, Nigeria fell behind in its debt payments, which forced the government to impose unpleasant austerity measures. A further fall in oil prices in 1986 pushed the country into a severe recession from which it has never recovered. Moreover, Nigerian fortunes became even more closely tied to oil revenues: Figure 18.3 shows that the source of Nigeria's hard currency shifted dramatically

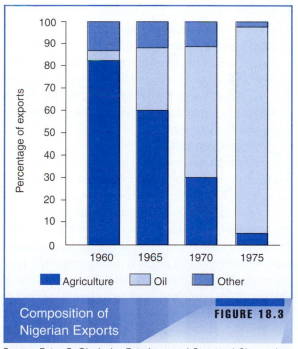

**FIGURE 18.3**

Composition of Nigerian Exports

Source: Peter O. Olayivola, *Petroleum and Structural Change in a Developing Country* (New York: Praeger, 1987).

from agricultural products to petroleum in the early 1970s. Since then petroleum has accounted for over 90 percent of export earnings. After world oil prices increased due to the Iraq War that began in 2003, Nigeria again began earning huge revenues, which it has applied toward its foreign debt.

### The Geographic Distribution of Natural Resources: Political Effects

Nigeria's oil fields are found in the Niger delta basin, an area of 43,500 square miles, or 8 percent of the country. As a natural resource that is both geographically concentrated and far more valuable than any other, Nigerian petroleum presents a classic problem for distributive justice. To Nigerian federal governments, it is a "national patrimony." Its potential value was an important motivation behind the Eastern Region's declaration of independence as **Biafra** in 1967, and oil certainly helps explain why the rest of the country was so obstinately determined to keep the region within Nigeria. But had Biafra maintained its independence, the question of oil field ownership would not have gone away, for the people who traditionally inhabited that area were minorities in the Igbo-dominated Biafra. And even though the federal government won the civil war, local peoples continue to protest the spread of oil wealth over the whole country while their land pays the price of environmental degradation from the oil operations. Southern Nigerians in general wonder why the riches should be shared with the distant north. The oil-producing region is the least developed in Nigeria, and unrest will continue there until the Delta peoples believe they have been fairly treated.

In recent years bitter and violent combat has broken out among the youth of the various Delta peoples. Massive protests have been organized by organizations, such as the Movement for the Actualization of the Sovereign State of Biafra (MOSSOB). Hundreds of its members have been arrested for participating in peaceful rallies, prayer sessions, and even soccer matches organized to promote Igbo causes. The government's harsh response to a "stay at home" protest in August 2004 prompted criticism by human rights groups.[12] Such organizations are testing Nigeria's commitment to democratic freedoms. If these groups feel impeded from expressing themselves, they may become more militant. This seems to be the case with the **Movement for the Emancipation of the Niger Delta (MEND),** which at the end of 2006 had claimed responsibility for taking at least eighteen foreigners hostages as a protest of conditions in the oil-producing areas.

### The International Environment

Nigeria, like most African countries, has been profoundly affected by its birth at the height of the Cold War, and by the sudden end of the bipolar war with the dissolution of the Soviet Union. During the Cold War, new nations were pressured to choose sides. The West and East granted foreign aid to developing nations as a reward for loyalty. Nigeria at independence was considered to be conservative and "prowestern," especially in contrast to such radical regimes as that of Kwame Nkrumah in Ghana. The prime minister at independence, Tafawa Balewa, announced the country's gratitude "to the British whom we have known first as masters, then as leaders, and finally as partners, but always as friends."[13]

Many Nigerian intellectuals equated the West's capitalism with colonialism, however, which they contended continued after independence through **neocolonial** economic ties. Political discourse through the first thirty years of Nigerian independence was often based on the ideological poles of capitalism and socialism, and relationships with the major powers involved staking a position between the two camps. In the civil war that resulted from the Eastern Region's declaration of independence as Biafra in 1967, the Soviet Union sided with the Nigerian federal government, while the U.S. government attempted to maintain a neutral position, even though the Biafran cause was widely supported by Americans. Economics finally dictated Nigeria's international position: the West was best equipped to prospect for Nigeria's oil fields, and only the West had the technology to extract and market this natural resource. Thus developed a close relationship between the Nigerian federal government and some of the world's major oil companies.

The end of the Cold War brought a new era to the relations of Nigeria and other poorer nations with the industrial world. The West's fear of the spread of communism had caused them to pay some attention to even the smallest and least-endowed countries. In the colonial period, Britain had provided virtually all foreign aid to Nigeria. In the Cold War environment at independence, Nigeria adopted a deliberate policy of diversification that diluted British influence and brought aid from the United States, Canada, the European Common Market (now the European Union), Japan, and Sweden. By the 1990s, however, those Third World countries without significant resources or with serious developmental problems were simply less interesting to the developed world; it is commonly perceived that Africa particularly has been "marginalized." In the Nigerian case, official loans and grants have not loomed large in recent years in any event, given access to oil revenues; foreign aid represented only about $2 per person in 1990.

Nigeria shared in a common Third World experience following the oil crisis of 1973 as it accumulated massive international debts. A sudden boom in oil prices resulted in huge new deposits in the world's banks. This surge in deposits without an increase in the demand for credit posed a serious problem to the lending agencies: they had to find borrowers. The increasing value of Nigeria's commodities made the nation appear extremely creditworthy. Although Nigeria's military government at the time was already busy spending the booming oil profits, there was a great demand for new infrastructure and for an expansion of public services. Banks had little difficulty convincing the Nigerian government to borrow additional sums. This borrowing seemed to make sense to all sides, given high inflation, rising prices for commodities, and the "excess liquidity" of bank deposits. Late in the 1970s commodity prices fell, however, and petroleum prices also did not remain as high as predicted. Third World debt mushroomed in the 1980s, and several governments defaulted. Nigeria's indebtedness grew from $8.9 billion in 1980 to $34.5 billion in 1991; by 1995 it represented 274.5 percent of the annual value of the country's exports, and 140.5 percent of GNP. After the transition to democracy, President Obasanjo made debt reduction a high priority for his administration and in 2000 Nigeria rescheduled $20 billion of its debt. In 2006, thanks in large part to earning from the high price of oil, Nigeria became the first African country to pay off its Paris Club debt, reducing its total debt by $30 billion. It still owes money to the World Bank and to some private lenders.

A final aspect of Nigeria's international environment is its regional context, West Africa. As an accident of colonial rule, Nigeria is entirely surrounded by former French colonies—Benin (formerly Dahomey), Niger, and Cameroon. Because France and the French-speaking West African countries have been suspicious of Nigeria's intentions and have developed close economic ties among themselves, Nigeria has had difficulty in developing the leadership role in the region that its size and strength would suggest.

As the oil boom drained the rural workforce, signs urged Nigerians to return to agriculture.

Bruno Barbey/Magnum Photos, Inc.

# POLITICAL CULTURE AND SUBCULTURES

The political culture of Nigeria is extremely heterogeneous and complex. Analysis of it must take into account a Western value system overlaid on those of its various precolonial traditions; it must assess the impact of a variety of religious beliefs and of the continuing effects of Christian and Muslim proselytizing efforts. Since the colonial experience have come new divisions based on social class and on the different experiences of urban and rural dwellers. The whole range of modern political ideologies is found among the belief systems of the politically active population. Here we will give greatest attention to the political implications of ethnic identity, religious beliefs, social and economic status, contact with urban life, and civil society.

## Ethnic Identity

Because of the geographic separation of ethnic groups, Nigerians can be easily identified based on language and cultural traits. These groups vary tremendously in size, and only three of them—the Hausa, Igbos, and Yoruba—are particularly numerous and influential in the country's politics. The influence of these three major groups is a cause of great concern to the remaining minority groups. Because there has been a high degree of geographical separation of ethnic groups in Nigeria (a result of the country's policies during and since the colonial period), Nigerians can easily identify the origins of their fellow citizens by observing their dialect (or accent in English), their manner of dress (if it is traditional), and in some cases by "tribal marks," patterned facial scars that formerly were created as part of rites of passage to indicate ethnic identity. There are also differences in wealth and political awareness.

In the absence of a widely accepted census, the size of Nigerian ethnic groups can only be approximated. Approximately one-half of the country's population is in the north, and about one-fourth each in the southeast and southwest. The Hausa represent about two-thirds of the north's total population, the Igbo about two-thirds in the east, and the Yoruba about two-thirds in the west. Thus, other groups represent about one-third in each region, and one-third overall. Here we will briefly consider the three largest groups.

*Hausa-Fulani* The Hausa-Fulani people mostly live in the northern half of the country. As noted earlier, this hyphenated identity came from the imposition of Fulani rule over the Hausa population in the nineteenth century. The two cultures became intricately intertwined, although they have never become completely homogenized. Thus, the term "Hausa" is often used as a short form of "Hausa-Fulani." "Hausaland" actually straddles the border between Nigeria and Niger to the north, a former French colony, and the people in these two countries maintain many cultural and commercial ties. A greater proportion of Hausas engage in subsistence agriculture and live in rural villages than is true of southern Nigerians. There are sizable Hausa communities in cities all over Nigeria, where they carry on trade and commercial activities while maintaining kin and client relationships with their home region. The vast majority of Hausas (but not all) are Muslim. The Hausa heartland is itself still organized as a series of emirates: each of the major cities in northern Nigeria is the seat of an emir, one of the kings through whom the British applied their indirect rule. There is no official role for the emirs in modern Nigeria, and their unofficial role is hotly disputed, even in the north. Yet they retain great influence in their localities and, through Hausa prominence in national politics, in the rest of the country as well.

*Igbo* The Igbo (also spelled Ibo) occupy the southeastern part of the country, from the banks of the Niger River east. Most of the region is developed for market agriculture, with Igbo farmers growing palm products, rice, and yams. The Igbo people lived in politically independent, socially endogamous villages, usually no larger than 8,000 people, and did not have a sense of common Igbo identity until the colonial period.

The Igbo are known for the enthusiasm with which they adopted Western culture. Although the encounter with British colonialism was a wrenching shock forcefully described in Chinua Achebe's novel *Things Fall Apart*, the Igbo responded enthusiastically to Western education and the missionaries who brought it, and aggressively sought advancement in modern commerce and civil service. Igbo people also emigrated widely throughout the country and seem less concerned than other groups with maintaining separate communities where they are "strangers." (In Nigeria, the term "stranger" refers specifically to a person living outside his or her "home" community.)

They are employed on the basis of their education and modern skills in all parts of the country, including the north.

Igbo officers led the first military coup in 1966, and thousands of Igbos living in northern cities were attacked and killed in reaction to that coup. The Igbos retreated to their home region. The next year they followed the call of one of their own, Lieutenant Colonel Ojukwu, in the secession from Nigeria of Igbo-dominated Biafra. The three-year civil war that ended in the defeat of Biafra in 1970 caused great hardship, but within a few years Igbos were again active in commerce (they were by then generally barred from government work in other localities) across the land. Nevertheless, the Biafran experience and the civil war left long-term mistrust between the Igbos and other Nigerians.

*Yoruba* The Yoruba mostly live in the southwestern part of Nigeria, including the metropolitan area of **Lagos,** the former federal capital and major urban center. Traditionally subsistence farmers, rural Yoruba people began growing cocoa and palm products for export in the colonial period. Although they share a common language, traditional religion, and myths of origin, the precolonial Yoruba were divided into a number of independent and warring kingdoms that give them separate identities today as Ijebu, Egba, Awori, Oyo, Ekiti, Igbomina, and others. The Yoruba have a long tradition of commerce, and both men and women are prominent in trade networks and markets throughout West Africa.

The Yoruba kingdoms were marked by complicated institutions that balanced power between an *oba* (king) and lineage chiefs, as in the relationship between the Alafin of Oyo and the Oyo Mesi described earlier. In their effort to impose indirect rule, the British upset these structures by supporting the obas against all challengers. In the process, the obas frequently became autocratic and lost much of their legitimacy with their own people; their influence in contemporary politics varies greatly, but is generally much less than that of the northern emirs.

Because the Yoruba had, on the one hand, a highly stratified society complete with kings and, on the other hand, were quite receptive to missionaries and their schools, they are often seen as in an intermediate position between the stratified and change-resistant Hausa and the egalitarian and innovative Igbo. In their sometimes strident assertion of their identity and interests, they also have provoked their share of mistrust among other Nigerians, as their candidates have generally been shut out of national leadership positions.

Given the ethnic-based strife so common in the world today, it should not come as a surprise that group identities are deeply rooted and emotionally charged in Nigeria as well. Ethnic rivalries often have their roots in precolonial warfare and are frequently refreshed by economic rivalries. While nationalism may serve as a cement where the feeling is shared by a country's entire population, the same feeling at a subnational level can destroy a political system. In Nigeria, these attachments are multilayered, and different levels of association can become charged at different times, as demonstrated in the Ibadan-Ijebu rivalry (see Box 18.1). Strong ethnic ties often are felt and expressed in kinship terms, and thus are often central to the definition of self. However, the Nigerian case demonstrates that ethnicity is often wrongly understood as primordial. While ethnic identity indeed has ancient roots, this does not mean that one's ethnic identity is identical with that of one's distant ancestors. In Africa, and in Nigeria in particular, we

---

## The Ibadan-Ijebu Controversy

**BOX 18.1**

Ibadan is one of the two largest cities in Nigeria. An old Yoruba city, it is plagued by a historic rivalry between its two major groups, the Ibadan and the Ijebu—both claiming descent from Oduduwa (whose descendants seem as quarrelsome as Abraham's!). The Ijebu lived closest to the coast and thus were the first to enter into commerce with European traders. Their attempt to control trade with the interior—that is, with Ibadan—is said to have produced their long-standing animosity. At the same time, the animosity is not always felt at the individual level, for intermarriage between the two groups is common.

see extraordinary change, as in the bonding of two separate groups to form the Hausa-Fulani culture, in the emergence of a "Yoruba" identity over what were previously separate societies in conflict, and in the formation of an Igbo identity among villagers who previously were largely unaware of one another. Both in the colonial period and since, ethnic identities have been manipulated for political purposes.

In Nigeria some of the first associational groups were based on the perception of common ethnic bonds in "nontraditional" settings. As a student in London, the early nationalist leader Obafemi Awolowo formed the Egbe Omo Oduduwa as a cultural organization grouping expatriate Yorubas. This group was to become the basis for the Action Group, the political party Awolowo later formed.

Because the major ethnic groups are regionally based, political issues affecting such groups are often defined geographically, and Nigeria has preserved a sense of permanent attachment between a people and its "traditional" homeland to the degree that it is more difficult to become a "citizen" of another state in Nigeria than it would be for a Nigerian to acquire citizenship in many foreign countries. The ethnic exclusiveness found in each state and local authority is euphemistically referred to as Nigeria's "federal character," and it has strong effects on the nature of national policy. Thus, as Nigerians respond to educational or economic opportunities in other parts of the country, they find it necessary to organize into ethnic associations to protect and promote their interests. Hausas in the south usually live in a ghetto called the *sabo*, where they speak their language and practice their Muslim faith. Nigerians at the lowest socioeconomic level often belong to a single association, that of their ethnic group; the more educated members of these "stranger" communities will often overlay the purely ethnic associations with others in which they interact across ethnic lines.

Multiple ethnic identities even at the local level have had a fragmenting effect on political structure. Particularly since 1976, there have been numerous disputes over the site of local government headquarters, with the "loser" often petitioning to the state and federal governments for a division of the local government area. The conflict between the Ife and Modakeke in Oranmiyan local government (see Box 18.2) is but one of many examples that could be cited. Local ethnic conflict affects policy outputs as well, where local

---

## The Conflict Between Modakeke and Ile-Ife

**BOX 18.2**

Early in the nineteenth century, Yorubas from Old Oyo were driven south by a Fulani invasion, and some settled in and around Ile-Ife. They were at first well received by Ile-Ife's traditional ruler, the Ooni, but soon got into a violent quarrel with the local population. The Oyo refugees were then reduced to servitude, and some were sold into slavery. Later, however, in an internal dispute, they sided with the ruler, who rewarded them with a settlement of their own, Modakeke. Strife continued between the two groups, and in an 1882 battle the Modakeke burned down the sacred city of Ife. Throughout the colonial period, the Ooni often used their conflict to play one group against the other. As independence neared, the Modakeke sought a local government independent of Ife. Also, the Ife leaders supported the Action Group (party), while Modakeke supported the National Council of Nigeria and the Cameroons (NCNC).

After independence, Ife and Modakeke were in the same local government (Oranmiyan), but they fought constantly until Oranmiyan was split in 1989. There was peace until August 1997, when the government moved one local government from an Ife to a Modakeke location and then to supposedly neutral ground. Violent conflict broke out among young men of each side. Whole villages were burned and hundreds of lives were lost. In January 1999, the Osun state administrator invited the two communities to an open meeting, at which both groups agreed to a ceasefire. The Ooni stated that he had in fact requested General Abacha to create a new state, and that Abacha had declined but had given him the new local government as a consolation prize. The traditional leader's request and the government's response inadvertently rekindled historic animosities, with tragic results. In April 2002, the federal government mandated Osun State to create an Area Office for Modakeke as part of a peace process. The Area Office was created without delay, and it is yielding some positive results within the Modakeke community.

governments build health centers or markets that are not used by some ethnic groups, thus throwing off planners' projections.

## Religion

Each of the groups identified in the previous section had traditional religious institutions and beliefs in place long before the arrival of Christianity and Islam. In some cases these earlier beliefs have maintained their vigor, especially among many Yoruba. However, the missionaries brought their religion with formal education in the southern regions; most major Christian churches are well established in the south, and indigenous Christian sects have split off from them in a myriad of denominations. Not surprisingly, the Christian denominations themselves tend to be geographically and ethnically concentrated, with a higher proportion of Roman Catholics among the Igbo, a Baptist concentration among the Yoruba of Ogbomoso, the Evangelical Church of West Africa predominant in Igbomina and Kwara State, and so on. A significant proportion of Yoruba—perhaps half—are Muslim. Under the agreement between the colonial administration and the northern emirates, Christian proselytizing was barred from the north, and, except for the "strangers" living there, almost the entire population is at least nominally Muslim, and the Hausa bring their religion with them when they move south. This movement is offset by the establishment of churches in northern cities by immigrants mostly from the south.

Missionaries built and staffed the great majority of schools during the colonial period. Thus the north-south education gap, with its effect on political awareness, attitudes toward civil rights, and the like itself derives from the prohibition of missionaries in the north.

There is, then, an overlay of religion on ethnicity that intensifies the north-south cultural split, and the case can be made that the most sensitive issues now involve religion rather than ethnicity. These overlapping cleavages are more dangerous because they accentuate regional differences. Nigeria has a special problem in this regard in that the Christian–Muslim split is near fifty-fifty, whereas in almost all other African states Muslims are either the large majority of the population or compose a clear minority.

The brother of Usman dan Fodio, the leader of the nineteenth-century *jihad* (holy war) in northern Nigeria, wrote a four-volume work on the nature of legitimate Islamic government. It does not allow for the possibility of a conflict between secular concepts of justice and welfare and those in the *sharia* (Muslim religious law). These values are well-rooted in the region: a survey of 686 students at Bayero University in Kano in 1983 found that 92 percent of them "believed an Islamic state was inherently superior to a secular state."[14] In the 1980s the Maitatsine Islamic movement, composed largely of young men marginalized by the socioeconomic changes of the period, rioted against the Christian presence in northern Nigeria (as well as against police repression), with loss of life estimated in the thousands. On the other side, a failed coup against the Babangida regime in 1990 is widely thought to have been a "Christian coup against the northern Muslim leadership."[15] Because fundamentalist elements in both Christianity and Islam have frequently found it unacceptable to live in a pluralist society, those seeking a basis for political stability in Nigeria must be sensitive to finding a balance between the two major faith groups. For that reason there was great distress in the south when, in 1986, President **Ibrahim Babangida** proposed that Nigeria join the Organization of the Islamic Conference (OIC), a group of more than fifty predominantly Muslim countries formed in 1970. In 1991, Babangida asserted that the membership was "in abeyance," which is perhaps the only resolution of the issue that will not exacerbate religious tensions.

## The Evolution of Nigerian Nationalism

All of our preoccupation with Nigerian subcultures should not obscure the fact that the British colonial administration was responding to Nigerian nationalist forces when it granted independence in 1960. There were three major sources of nationalist sentiment. The first was a small number of freed slaves from North America and others of African descent from the Caribbean who settled on the West African coast and developed a culture unrelated to any of those indigenous to the country. Second, nationalist fervor grew out of the experience of Nigerians who fought for the British in World War II and felt frustration at the lack of recognition of their service. A third category of nationalists consisted of those Nigerians who studied in England and especially in the United States, including one of the most prominent among them, **Nnamdi**

## The Story of Nnamdi Azikiwe

Although an Igbo, Nnamdi Azikiwe was born in Zungeru in northern Nigeria in 1904. He received his basic education in Nigeria, then went to the United States, where he studied at Lincoln University in Pennsylvania, Stores College in West Virginia, and the University of Pennsylvania. He also worked in the United States as a coal miner, laborer, and dishwasher. Upon his return home, he joined the Nigerian Youth Movement. His interest in self-rule led to his presence at the founding of the National Council of Nigeria and the Cameroons (NCNC) and to his founding of a pro-self-rule newspaper, the *West African Pilot*. He then moved to the Gold Coast (now Ghana), where he published an article, "Has the African a God," that resulted in a sedition charge. He won his case on appeal and went on to serve as the premier of the Eastern Region, and from 1963 to 1966 as president of Nigeria. He died in 1996 at the age of 92.

Azikiwe (see Box 18.3). Although they came from a variety of ethnic backgrounds, in their quest for independence, these activists developed a sense of Nigerian nationalism and succeeded in forming cross-ethnic alliances.

Civil war also stimulated Nigerian nationalism. The two military coups before the Biafran war were clearly ethnic in their origins. However, the Biafran conflict brought together a military force that was cross-ethnic (excluding, of course, Igbos, who were at the heart of the Biafran succession). Although the officer corps is increasingly dominated by Muslims, it has continued to recruit nationally.

A study of Nigerian political culture must focus on orientations toward national (federal) political institutions. Nigerians oriented toward public political activities can be identified by (1) exposure to formal education and (2) involvement in the modern economy. As concerns interest in public policy, many Nigerians, particularly in rural areas and in the north, are *subjects*, not *participants*. Although such people may be unaware of, and uninterested in, issues of general political concern, they still have to deal with local government officials on issues affecting themselves and their families. In Nigeria, as elsewhere in Africa and the Third World, such concerns are likely to be handled through personal interest contacting. In general, Nigerians are more likely than most to feel that the government should provide for individual needs (see Figure 3.3 in Chapter 3). A 2002 survey reported that 93 percent of Nigerians believe that it is "important or very important" for the government to provide basic necessities.[16] In most cases, such contacting is part of a *clientelist* arrangement: citizens go to an individual who is politically influential for help and expect to "pay" for help through a long-term arrangement that may include payment in kind (as in bribes), or by turning out to vote when asked to do so, even while remaining uninterested in politics. Political activity is widespread and virtually all-embracing; interest in public affairs is strongly conditioned by education and employment.

## Democratic Norms and Values

In order to assess Nigeria's chances for achieving political democracy, we must first consider the distribution of norms that might support democratic institutions. The legitimacy of opposition, manifested as tolerance for criticism, opposition, and competition for control, is an obvious prerequisite for stable democracy.[17] The performance of political activists in Nigeria from 1960 on suggests problems, even under democratic civilian regimes. As single parties gained control in each region, opponents were treated very roughly, often in the physical sense, with armed thugs hired to disrupt their meetings and attack their leaders.

Nevertheless, strong support has emerged for democratic norms since the military's exit in 1999. Today 81 percent of Nigerians say "democracy is preferable to any other form of government." In addition, 83 percent say that the freedom to criticize the government is "very important or important."[18]

## The Political Role of Women

In Nigeria's ethnic diversity, the position of women varies considerably. In Igbo, Yoruba, and other southern Nigerian traditions, women had considerable control over their own affairs in what anthropologists label "dual-sex" systems. That is, there were parallel systems of political and social organization for men and women. P. C. Lloyd concluded that "the Yoruba wife's status is characterized by great overt submission to her husband together with considerable economic independence."[19] Scholars of colonial history contend that women lost most of their autonomy under colonialism, because British custom at the time gave women less control of their own affairs than did the African societies they controlled. A famous case in point is the Igbo "Women's War" (referred to by the colonial government as the "Aba riots"), in which Igbo women used traditional means of protest against taxation and were harshly repressed by the colonial government (see Box 18.4).

In the north, Islamic custom greatly restricts women's roles in society. Although Hausa women have considerably more freedom than their counterparts in the Middle East, including significant roles in local production and trade, they generally were not allowed an active political role at the time of independence. Northern women voted for the first time in 1979.

The contemporary involvement of women in political leadership is similar to that of many countries: in most parts of the country, Nigerian women vote in equal numbers with men but are generally underrepresented in politics. Since the 1998–1999 elections, women have made modest gains in politics, moving from three to nine senatorial seats (out of 109), and from twelve to thirty house seats (out of 360). Yet men still hold more than 90 percent of the elected and appointed positions, including only six out of 42 federal ministerial positions.

## Political Corruption

A traveler on Nigerian roads meets frequent police checkpoints and barricades. Ostensibly in place to check for arms and smuggled goods, their actual function is to extort payments from travelers by uncovering various minor violations. Many Nigerians do not take offense at this behavior, noting that police officers' pay is low and often comes late.

Pervasive corruption has been a problem ever since the late colonial era; it was the central theme of Chinua Achebe's novel *No Longer at Ease*, in which an idealistic young administrator is gradually pressured by personal problems and the prevalence of corruption into accepting bribes. Achebe is only one of many Nigerians to condemn corruption; each political regime comes to power promising to eliminate the practice and punish offenders, only to fall into the same pattern. The huge sums of money that passed through officials' hands as a result of the oil boom greatly aggravated the problem: unprecedented forms of flagrant corruption appeared when oil revenues began to fill the federal treasury of General Yakubu Gowon in the early 1970s. His military governors spent large sums on openly lavish lifestyles, thus tarnishing the image of the military, which had supposedly come to power in reaction to the corruption of the First Republic. The coup against Gowon in 1975 was a direct result, as was the assassination of his successor General Murtala in 1976.[20] Achebe asserts that corruption has grown more "bold and ravenous" under each new regime.[21] It is widely believed that the deceased leader **Sani Abacha** and his family channeled enormous sums of money from petroleum revenue

---

### The Igbo Women's War

BOX 18.4

"In November of 1929, thousands of Igbo women ... converged on the native Administration centers.... The women chanted, danced, sang songs of ridicule, and demanded the caps of office (the official insignia) of the Warrant Chiefs.... At a few locations the women broke into prisons and released prisoners. Sixteen Native Courts were attacked, and most of these were broken up or burned.... On two occasions, British District Officers called in police and troops, who fired on the women and left a total of more than 50 dead and 50 wounded. No one on the other side was seriously injured." The women's actions were "an extension of their traditional method for settling grievances with men who had acted badly toward them."

Source: Judith Van Allen, "'Aba Riots' on 'Ibo Women's War'? Ideology, Stratification and the Invisibility of Women," in Nancy J. Hafkin and Edna G. Bay, eds. *Women in Africa: Studies in Social and Economic Change* (Stanford, CA: Stanford University Press, 1976), 59–85.

accounts into their private coffers at home and abroad. As part of its campaign to promote transparency in government and fight corruption, the Obasanjo administration successfully recovered $2 billion from the Sani Abacha family.

In 2002, the National Assembly passed the **Economic and Financial Crimes Commission (EFCC)** Establishment Act. Its purpose is to "prevent, investigate, prosecute and penalize economic and financial crimes." Crimes within its jurisdiction include money laundering, Internet fraud, bank fraud, bribery, and misuse of public funds. To run the EFCC, President Obasanjo appointed Mallam Nuhu Ribadu, who claims credit for recovering over $5 billion and successfully prosecuting eighty-two people.

Yet the EFCC has also been widely accused of selective prosecution of the president's political enemies. For example, it launched an investigation of Vice President Atiku Abubakar in 2006, when he was running for president. The Commission's critics suspected that the charges were brought because Abubakar had opposed President Obasanjo's efforts to amend the Constitution so as to make him eligible for a third term in office.[22] The EFCC's report accused Abubakar of misappropriating $100 million in public funds. In light of the charges the People's Democratic Party (PDP) suspended him from the party for three months to prevent him from contesting the December 2006 presidential primaries. The Senate also launched an investigation into whether he should be impeached.

## POLITICAL SOCIALIZATION

Nigerians develop their political beliefs and attitudes through the influence of socialization "agents," such as the family, primary and secondary groups, formal education, the media, and government-sponsored activities.[23] A caveat is necessary, however, when comparing the political socialization process in Nigeria to the established liberal democracies. Political socialization in the developed world occurs through fairly stable institutions. We treat the fluidity of party alignments in France or events such as the Vietnam War in the United States as exceptional, whereas in Nigeria people have grown up under political arrangements that shift constantly, even to their very core. Add to this the upheaval of urbanization and of the sudden and dramatic impact of petroleum on the culture and

the economy, and the need for a different perspective on socialization is apparent. Nevertheless, there is a universal quality to the importance of the agents of socialization we have identified, even as the nature of those institutions and the objects of political attitudes and values they shape may differ greatly from those in Europe or North America.

### The Family

The family, whether nuclear or extended, remains the core unit of political activity in Nigeria. In many Nigerian traditions, families are identified with a particular trade or role in society. Thus, among the Yoruba a family of warriors is called *Jagunjagun*, farmers are *Agbe*, and traders are *Onisowo*. To traditionally minded Nigerians, such identification remains important to the determination of one's appropriate role in modern politics.

Many Nigerians have grown up in polygamous families.[24] There is no law preventing a man from taking more than one wife, although Muslims are theoretically limited to a maximum of four and Christians of mainstream denominations to one. All indigenous traditions in Nigeria accept polygamy, and little stigma is attached to the practice. Some Christian denominations in Nigeria enforce monogamy only on those men who hold office in the church.

The large family units that result from polygamous households and the broader definition of family give kinship special political importance. A politician may be able to count on the support of literally hundreds of actual kin, and even larger numbers if one considers clan affiliations based on a sense of kinship even where exact genealogical ties cannot be demonstrated. Kinship provides the most powerful sense of identity and loyalty to many in Nigeria and elsewhere in Africa, and it is the model (and often the real-world basis) for clientelist relationships.

### Schools

In most contemporary nations, the schools play a central role in developing a sense of community. This is clearly an important mission in Nigerian schools, and balancing various loyalties is a delicate task for Nigerian educators. Also, formal education is one of the principal benefits Nigerians expect from government. The school certificate is highly regarded throughout the developing world as a means to economic and social advancement, and this is especially true in Nigeria: "It seems safe to say that by the 1930s and 1940s no people in the world placed a higher value on education or regarded its consequences more optimistically than did the inhabitants of this area."[25]

As Nigeria approached independence in the 1950s, the two southern regions invested massively in expansion of their educational systems, especially at the primary level. There is a broad consensus that primary education should be free and universal. Beyond that basic agreement, however, Nigeria has struggled with how to shape the curriculum and how to make it available.

The oil boom of the 1970s stimulated a massive wave of secondary school expansion and the university system, which grew from one in 1948 to five in 1962 to forty-five by 2002. Just between 1999 and 2002, sixteen state universities and six private ones were created. In addition to universities, the higher education system includes seventy-five polytechnics and colleges of technology and of education.

Even in the prosperous 1970s, a lack of resources threatened this educational boom, and there was a lack of properly trained instructors at all levels. With the economic collapse of the 1980s, funds for education dried up, and education suffered at all levels. Equal access has remained illusory for years, and the problem becomes more acute as one moves from the primary to the secondary and to the postsecondary level. The bias is on the one hand socioeconomic—children of the elite occupy a disproportionate share of the enrollments—and it also reflects gender. In 2002, girls constituted only about 44 percent of the students in primary schools, and this figure showed no improvement over the preceding ten years. Enrollment rates did increase dramatically after the transition to democracy, surging from 76 percent in 1998 to 95 percent in 2000. The African Development Bank reported a decline in adult illiteracy over the same years from 39 percent to 36 percent, and it has continued to drop. As a result, the level of political awareness has arguably risen too. Unfortunately other important disparities, notably those between north and south, persist.[26]

There have been indirect political effects of the education gap across regions. As the number of secondary graduates increased in the south, many of them sought jobs in the north and were embittered at northern rejection. At the same time, northerners grew alarmed at the prospect of being inundated by educated southerners. Differences in educational achievement thus contributed to the resentments that exploded in violence in 1966. Today northern political dominance in the face of higher educational achievement in the south continues to aggravate interregional political conflict.

The conference center in Abuja, the new capital.

Betty Press/Woodfin Camp & Associates

Language is an aspect of community-building that is often taken for granted, but language usage in school can have a major impact on political attitudes. As noted previously, English is the official language of Nigeria and remains the vehicle of instruction in Nigeria from primary school through the university. Furthermore, English is the language of government and, for the most part, of the mass media. Because English is a second language in most Nigerian homes, school plays an especially critical role in enabling access to the political system.

As a nation-building effort the three major indigenous languages—Hausa, Igbo, and Yoruba—are also taught through secondary school and are topics in the Senior School Certificate Examinations. Proficiency in English is required for admission to a university, where the local languages are used only in programs where they might specifically be required. The connection between English usage and government activities gives added weight to the usual relationship between education and political efficacy.

Whatever the effect of intentional socialization in the schools, studies of political culture invariably affirm the effect of education on political participation. This is especially true in less developed countries, where the cultural gap between those with and without formal education is especially great. Data from the 1999 World Values Survey in Nigeria find that only 25 percent of illiterate Nigerians are very interested in politics, compared with 46 percent among the most educated.

## The Mass Media

The presence of a lively and politically independent press goes back at least to Azikiwe's *West African Pilot.* By the time of independence a considerable number of competing newspapers existed in Nigeria (virtually all published in Lagos, then distributed nationwide). Yet the current combined circulation of daily newspapers is only about 2.7 million, or about twenty-four per 1,000 people.

The political effect of the press is naturally limited in a country where one third of the adults are illiterate. A 2000 survey found that approximately 30 percent of Nigerians get their news from newspapers at least once a week. That same survey reported that 64 percent of Nigerians are somewhat or very interested in politics, and 65 percent say they discuss politics and the

government with people "sometimes" or "often."[27] Today, newspaper readership includes all politically active Nigerians, and the perspectives in the press undoubtedly have a wide word-of-mouth circulation.

Most Nigerians get their news from radio and 60 percent of Nigerians list television as a source of news at least once a week. Radio and television have always been state-controlled and thus are faithful purveyors of the government's "spin" on political events. Shortwave broadcasts from the BBC, Voice of America, and other outside sources have been available as independent sources for decades, however. In recent years, indigenous television competes with satellite news services and since 1999 new independent media outlets have opened. In the year 2000 alone, Nigerians saw several new newspapers launched and six new privately operated radio stations. Although only a tiny proportion of the country's population have access to satellite telecasts or the Internet, such advanced communications technology permits outside views of Nigerian events to be introduced into the country, then spread by word of mouth or reflected in the print media.

The authoritarian regimes imposed a substantial number of restrictions on the media. According to the Center for Free Speech, a Nigerian watchdog organization, the military issued twenty-one decrees between 1966 and 1995 limiting press freedoms or even proscribing particular publications outright. There was a high level of tension between military governments and the press, and the life of a journalist was not easy. Many journalists were arrested, and in 1986 a prominent critic of the government was killed by a letter bomb.

The Constitution promulgated in 1999 reversed many restrictions instituted under General Sani Abacha and previous military rulers. Article 39 states: "Every person shall be entitled to freedom of expression, including freedom to hold opinions and to receive and impart ideas and information without interference." Although this article guarantees broad freedom for the media, journalists can still face criminal punishment for defamation of public officials, and a 1999 decree requires them to be accredited by a government-run media council. In other ways journalists are still subject to harassment. Reporters without Borders lists Nigeria as one of the countries in Africa where violence against journalists is "routine" and goes unpunished; twenty journalists suffered physical attacks in 2005 and "scores" of others were imprisoned for what they wrote. One newspaper publisher was detained without charge after running a negative story on the First Lady.[28]

## The State

The Nigerian government has at its disposal the modern means of mass communication that oil revenues have allowed it to develop. Periodically it launches propaganda campaigns on one issue or another, as in Operation Feed the Nation and Free Primary Education (in the 1970s), the War Against Indiscipline (in the 1980s), or the more recent Road Safety Operation, for which the government recruited author Wole Soyinka as director.

As part of its "transition program" to democracy (between 1986 and 1993), the regime of General Ibrahim Babangida inaugurated the Directorate for Social Mobilization, also known as MAMSER (Mass Mobilization for Self-Reliance, Economic Recovery and Social Justice). MAMSER's ostensible purpose was to shape a mass political culture that would be congenial to democracy. The government devoted considerable resources to this effort, although many questioned its effectiveness and some its sincerity. In 1995, the Abacha regime replaced it with a smaller organization intended to work through local governments. In 1990, the Babangida regime also established the Center for Democratic Studies (CDS) in Abuja, to conduct research on democratization and present seminars on that topic for government officials. In 1996, it too was closed by Abacha.

Nigerian political attitudes are far more likely to be affected by everyday contact with the state than by the state's direct, intentional efforts to shape attitudes. In Nigeria's federal system, direct contact comes largely through local officials. Rural residents without English-language proficiency find that, even at the local level, officials are much more educated than they and generally expect and get deference. Government is remote and must be approached through some form of informal mediation. For those with formal education, contact with local government is relatively simple; furthermore, because Nigerian policy is to hire civil servants from their home areas, there is neither a social nor a cultural difference between the educated citizen and the public servant. Nigerians expect to pay for expeditious service, and while they are aware of norms of honesty and ethics that are higher than the behavior they perceive, they are not scandalized by the

difference. Perceptions of policymakers are not usually the result of direct contact.

Nigerians generally express great cynicism about the motivations of policymakers at all levels, civilian or military, but for the most part this results from media accounts of venality and corruption. Whether through direct contact or media portrayal, they most often get what they expect from governmental officials, which of course becomes a self-fulfilling prophecy:

> The Complete Nigerian civil servant unlike his predecessor is not self-effacing behind an array of coded titles. You meet him here, you see him there, and you talk to him yonder. He is eager to make your acquaintance. He takes you into little corners to confide in you. For instance, he tells you how much it would cost you to have your file speeded up, which I think is very nice.[29]

One would expect that the unhappy experience with military rulers would leave Nigerians cynical and disillusioned. There certainly have been such effects, but there is a remarkably abiding faith in the importance of politics, especially among the educated. There is an impact here of the oil economy. Profits from the sale of petroleum have flowed through the central government, so that the stake in access to those in government, especially at the top, is high. For many intellectuals, however, the knowledge that important resources will be distributed through the government is offset by the uncertainty of the outcome of any attempt to become involved. They tend, thus, to leave the political field to a collection of seasoned politicians, those who have assembled a voter base every time a regime has offered the prospect of new elections.

## Contact with Urban Life

Massive population movement from the countryside to the cities is a nearly universal characteristic of less developed countries. Today over 46 percent of Nigeria's population lives in urban areas, reflecting an urbanization trend that began in the 1970s with the oil boom, when the massive infusion of wealth stimulated employment opportunities in construction and other areas. From 1970 to 1995, Nigeria's urban population increased from 20 to 39 percent of the total. The subsequent economic downturn left many of the new urban residents in an economically marginal position that was all the more precarious because they were removed from the possibility of subsistence production, the usual option of peasants when profits from marketed goods are low. In such an environment, urban residents are "available" for political mobilization; they are physically close to political institutions that might be held responsible for their problems, and communication about political events can spread quickly. Political unrest in Nigeria's most populous city, Lagos, was an important consideration in the military regime's decision in the 1970s to move the federal capital to Abuja, a city much farther to the north.

### Religion

Given the importance of religion in many Nigerians' lives, it is not surprising that religious institutions and religious leaders affect political orientations. According to the 2000 survey mentioned earlier, nearly 80 percent of all Nigerians say they belong to religious associations, and half of those say they are active members. A dramatic example is the activity against political authorities in northern Nigeria inspired by religious leader Alhaji Mohammed Marwa Maitatsine. In the 1970s, the rapid urbanization of the country produced a marginalized stratum of youth in the towns and cities of northern Nigeria. Fundamentalist Muslim reformers were active at the time, with financial support from Saudi Arabia and other Arab countries. The fundamentalist message, especially as preached in the Izala movement—an acronym for the Society for the Removal of Heresy and Reinstatement of Tradition— proved appealing to the young urban migrants and directed them religiously and politically against the dominant leadership in the north. They were thus mobilized into the region's political factionalism:

> Religion is a powerful instrument of mobilization in Northern Nigeria . . . ambitious politicians and local notables supported the creation of the Izala movement . . . support for a religious movement by a politician offers political rewards. This is all the more so given the fact that religious leaders mediate between the politicians and the civil society. Moreover, with the pledge by the military to hand over power in 1979, and with the heightened inter- and intra-party competition, one observed an intensification of contacts between politicians, local notables and religious leaders.[30]

With the return of democracy in 1999, Nigeria has experienced a new wave of religious tension, especially in the north where several states have declared their intention to implement Sharia, or Islamic law. Christian associations have opposed these changes and the conflicts have sometimes been dramatic: more than 10,000 people have been killed in religious conflicts between 1999 and 2003. The ongoing sensitivity over Islam in Nigeria was brought to the world's attention in one unfortunate incident in 2002. When the Miss World Beauty Pageant took place in Abuja, a newspaper suggested that the contestants were so beautiful that the religion's founding prophet would have chosen one of them. Over 200 people died when tensions between Christians and Muslims flared up.[31] At the same time, scholars such as John Paden maintain that Islam also provides cultural frameworks that northern Nigerians draw upon in order to resolve potential conflicts.

## POLITICAL RECRUITMENT

All the chief executives of Nigeria since independence are identified in Table 18.1. Several conclusions are apparent. First, northerners have dominated the leadership of the country under both civilian and military rule, in the first case because the population of the north is about the same as in the east and west combined, and in the case of the military regimes, because of increasing dominance of the officer corps by northerners.

In the early years of independence, a military career lacked prestige, especially among educated southerners. In an effort to speed the replacement of remaining British officers, the Balewa government actively recruited university graduates into the officer ranks. One result was the introduction of large numbers of educated Igbos into officer ranks; another was the politicization of the army. Three of the first six university graduates to enter the army led the first coup.

Because the military controlled the country between 1983 and 1999, an officer's commission has come to be seen as the most regular path to political power. It seems that the ethos of the military has changed in this regard. The first coup leaders in 1966 professed great regret at the necessity to intervene and promised that their stay would be temporary. They were removed and killed in the second 1966 coup before their sincerity could be tested. The longevity of General Gowon's regime was made necessary by the need to prosecute the civil war, and then to lay a constitutional framework for civilian rule. When

## Nigerian Chief Executives, 1960–2007

**TABLE 18.1**

| Dates | Name | Title | Ethnicity | Cause of Departure |
|---|---|---|---|---|
| 1960–Jan. 1966 | Tafawa Balewa | Prime Minister | Hausa-Fulani (North) | Coup (killed) |
| 1963–Jan. 1966 | Nnamdi Azikiwe | President [appointed] | Igbo (East) | Coup (removed) |
| Jan.–July 1966 | Agusi Ironsi | Military Head of State | Igbo (East) | Coup (killed) |
| July 1966–1975 | Yakubu Gowon | Military Head of State | Tiv ("Middle Belt") | Coup (removed) |
| 1975–1976 | Murtala Muhammed | Military Head of State | Hausa-Fulani (North) | Coup (killed) |
| 1976–1979 | Olusegun Obasanjo | Military Head of State | Yoruba (Southwest) | Handed power to civilian government |
| 1979–1983 | Shehu Shagari | President | Hausa-Fulani (North) | Coup (removed) |
| 1983–1985 | Muhammed Buhari | Military Head of State | Hausa-Fulani (North) | Coup (removed) |
| 1985–1993 | Ibrahim Babangida | Military Head of State | Gwari (North) | Forced out of office |
| Aug.–Nov. 1993 | Ernest Shonekan | Interim Head of State [appointed] | Yoruba (Southwest) | Forced out of office |
| Nov. 1993–June 1998 | Sani Abacha | Head, Provisional Ruling Council | Kanuri (North) | Died in office |
| May 1998–May 1999 | Abdulsalami Abubakar | Head, Provisional Ruling Council | Gwari (North) | Handed power to civilian government |
| May 1999–May 2007 | Olusegun Obasanjo | President | Yoruba (Southwest) | Civilian-to-civilian transfer |
| May 2007–present | Umar Musa Yar'Adua | President | Hausa-Fulani(North) | |

Gowon seemed inclined to settle in for the long term, he was removed, and General Obasanjo set and abided by his 1979 deadline. Thus, through the first period of military rule, although there was serious profit-taking on the part of many military leaders, none of them expected to have long-term political careers.

The second round of military power (1983 to 1999) produced a gradual change in the perspectives of at least some military officers. Many observers have wondered about the military leadership's annulment of the 1993 presidential election results and the abolition of state and local elective offices already filled. Most feel that if the presumed winner, Moshood Abiola, had been allowed to assume power, he would have been unable to deal effectively with the country's problems, would quickly have lost an already dubious legitimacy, and would thus have prepared the way for a return of the military with acceptance by the population. As it was, the Abacha regime faced massive resistance and was able to rule only on the basis of force, at least in much of the south. Many assume that Abacha's actions, while certainly supported by elements in the north that could not stomach a Yoruba president, also reflected the strong desire of a new generation of military officers to enjoy the fruits of power that come from oil revenues and from the potential profits that flow from the corruption of public office. The country witnessed open jockeying for positions as state governors or "chairmen" of local governments, which were allocated according to military rank. National-level offices were usually filled by generals, brigadiers, or colonels; state governors were mostly colonels; and local chairmen were lieutenant colonels and majors, often retired from active service. Politics in Nigeria is still largely a game of money; therefore, the retired military, the business group, and some retired civil servants dominate the elective positions while a few academics have political appointments, like minister, commissioner, and the foreign service.

Nigerian universities produce large numbers of trained public administrators, and they follow long-term careers in federal, state, or local administration that usually are not affected by changes at the top. An analysis of the educational backgrounds of the "administrative class" (assistant secretaries to permanent secretaries) just before the restoration of civilian rule in 1979 showed that all but 11 percent of them held university degrees.[32] An appropriate educational level had come to be expected in the civil service.

There has been some upheaval in the civil service following regime changes: an estimated 11,000 administrators were removed when Murtala Muhammed came to power in 1975 and took vigorous action against corruption. But to the degree that the administrative system continues to function through the many regime changes, it does so because of the permanence of the civil service.

Recruitment into political positions at the local and state levels generally exclude "strangers," even though they may be long-time residents of a community and, of course, Nigerian citizens. There are some exceptions: where "strangers" are sufficiently numerous, they can run and win. In most places, however, regulations have expressly limited candidacy to indigenous candidates. In addition to simple democratic fairness, the advantage of creating a multiethnic council is that it stimulates identity and participation in the community on the part of populations that are otherwise excluded. The overriding characteristic of recruitment into political or administrative office, however, is the effort faithfully to "reflect the federal character of Nigeria"—that is, to fill positions to have a government that is an ethnic microcosm of the locality or state it controls.

In the past, appointments of military personnel to government posts also reflected the country's "federal character": northern officers were appointed in the northern states, Yorubas and others from the southwest to states in that region, and so on, although Abacha introduced a pattern of more random assignments, placing southern officers in the north and vice versa. However, the highest military positions have come from the combat arms, which recently have been dominated by northerners; without the northern preponderance in these positions, Abacha's control of the country could not have been maintained.

Even northerners have not always been reliable: press reports claimed that a majority of junior officers had voted in 1993 for the southern civilian, **Moshood Abiola.** Abacha's support base was narrowed even further when, in March 1995, he arrested former head of state **Olusegun Obasanjo** and one of the most prominent senior northern military leaders, Shehu Musa Yar'Adua. Obasanjo was released by Abubakar after Abacha's death in 1998; Yar'Adua died in prison in December 1997. The same month, Abacha arrested the chief of the general staff, General Oladipo Diya, on the charge of plotting a military coup, and thus removed

the most senior Yoruba officer. Ethnic politics are still very much dominating the politics of Nigeria. However, President Olusegun Obasanjo has made use of the zoning structure, which breaks Nigeria into six divisions for the purpose of appointments and the distribution of infrastructures, but the minority—especially in the Delta areas of the oil-producing region—would want more functional roles in government. On many occasions, the oil-producing regions have usurped the laws and frictions developed between them. The federal government had to break it up. It is to be noted that the oil-producing regions have been neglected even by other administrations.

## POLITICAL STRUCTURE

It is open to question whether we can realistically describe the "structure" of the decisionmaking process in a country that has experienced five successful coups, three civilian constitutions, and a particularly amorphous arrangement from President Babangida's annulment of the 1993 elections to the election of Obasanjo in February 1999. It is, however, useful to be familiar with the range of constitutional arrangements the country has known and the patterns in their evolution.

The first political institution in which Nigerians participated as Nigerians was the legislative council mandated by the Clifford Constitution of 1922, which provided for elected representatives from Lagos. Elections were introduced in this way and stimulated political activity. Through successive constitutional changes in the 1940s and 1950s, elective office was extended to local and regional governments and the first provisions for a federal structure were introduced.

### The Development of the Constitution of 1999

As Babangida postponed the return to civilian rule in 1993, his standing with the population, and even within the military, moved ever lower. When he delayed announcing the outcome of the June 12, 1993, presidential election, apprehensions grew, for it was popularly believed that Moshood Abiola had won. Two days after the election, initial results released by the National Election Commission (NEC) showed that Abiola had won in eleven of fourteen states. Later, a private human rights coalition, the Campaign for

Democracy, published election results indicating that Abiola had won in nineteen of the thirty states. A few days later, the military government declared the election invalid. At the same time, Babangida promised new elections, and once again promised a return to civilian rule. He appointed a transition committee chaired by a Yoruba, Ernest Shonekan, and Babangida vacated the capital without fanfare—in a technical sense meeting his deadline for the restoration of civilian rule. However, Shonekan had virtually no support and was pushed aside by General Sani Abacha three months later in November 1993. General Abacha maintained the myth of a return to civilian government and created the Constitutional Conference to draft yet another governing document. The Constitutional Conference was inaugurated on June 27, 1994, but two weeks earlier, on the anniversary of the annulled election, Moshood Abiola had declared himself president. Abiola was arrested on June 23, 1994, and charged with three counts of treason. One count stated that he "solicited, incited, addressed, and endeavored to persuade people to take part in unconstitutionally overthrowing the head of state," an ironic indictment from a government whose leader seized control by force. Abacha seemed to manipulate the system to remain president, but his strategy was aborted by his death of a reported heart attack in May 1998. Meanwhile, Abiola had maintained his claim from prison, but he also died of a reported heart attack two months after Abacha, just as he was negotiating his release with Abacha's successor, Abdulsalami Abubakar. The succession of deaths, first of Shehu Yar'Adua in prison (November 1997), then Abacha (May 1998), and Abiola (July 1998), was seen by many Nigerians as an entirely improbable set of events. Even though the departed represented an extreme range of political positions, conspiracy theories have since then been widely floated.

From 1983 to 1999, politics in Nigeria took the form of a succession of military regimes that constantly planned a return to democracy. Administrative and judicial proceedings continued as though a constitutional structure were in place. The 1995 Constitution was widely discussed and even cited as the basis for election procedures in 1997 and 1998—yet the document was only officially promulgated by General Abubakar in May 1999 as he handed power over to a civilian regime. The overall structure of the current Constitution is outlined in Figure 18.4.

## Federalism

In a country as vast and complex as Nigeria, many political decisions are not made at the national level. A federal system was established as Nigeria moved to independence in 1954. In a uniquely Nigerian scenario, two of the regions, the Eastern and the Western, gained self-governing status in 1957; the north followed in 1959. Thus a very decentralized federal system was already in effect at independence. The Constitution of 1960 was explicitly federal, dividing responsibilities between the federal government and the three regions. Federalism has been a constant in the three constitutions (1963, 1979, and 1989) since that time, and in the constitution developed but never promulgated under Abacha in 1995, which Abubakar used as the basis for his return of the country to civilian rule in 1999. Indeed, it is difficult to imagine a stable political structure that would not allow a considerable devolution of power to leaders of the three major ethnic groups at least. There have been two attempts to impose a unitary system: in the first coup in 1966, General Ironsi attempted to end the autonomy of the regions, and there seemed to be a similar thrust in the aborted coup of 1990. In each case, reactions to the suggestion of a unitary system were decidedly cool.

In the face of formal federalism, however, stands a fiscal condition that calls the federal concept into question: all levels of government derive the largest portion of their revenues from the national oil monopoly, distributed through the national government. Beyond this fiscal fact of life, there has been the control of Nigeria by military governments for twenty-nine of forty-seven years of independence. It is difficult to define federalism under a military chain of command. Nonetheless, any permanent civilian constitution will undoubtedly be genuinely federal. As political activists in the south have become convinced that northerners are bent on dominating any central government in Nigeria, they have argued for greater state or regional autonomy. Moreover, with the emergence of militant groups, such as MOSSAB and MEND (see page 664), the federal government has had to confront an increasingly visible and viable secessionist movement in the south.

Some southerners even call for separate military forces for the major regions. We can be certain that defining state and local government boundaries will continue to be a central issue confronting any regime, civilian or military.

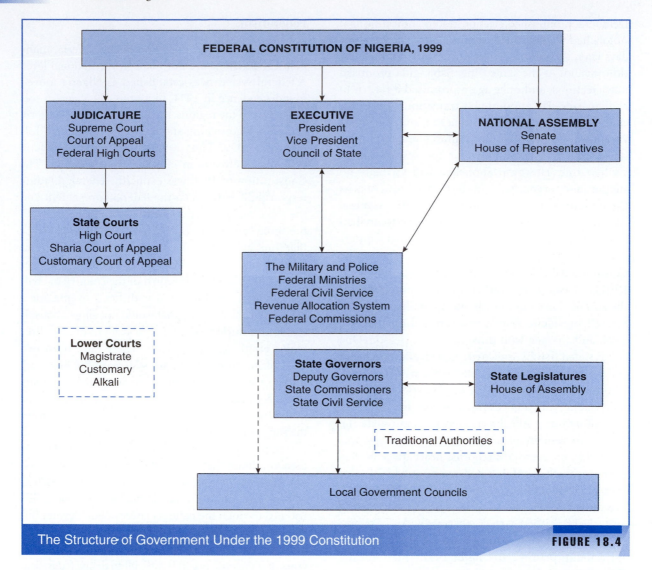

**FEDERAL CONSTITUTION OF NIGERIA, 1999**

**JUDICATURE**
Supreme Court
Court of Appeal
Federal High Courts

**EXECUTIVE**
President
Vice President
Council of State

**NATIONAL ASSEMBLY**
Senate
House of Representatives

**State Courts**
High Court
Sharia Court of Appeal
Customary Court of Appeal

The Military and Police
Federal Ministries
Federal Civil Service
Revenue Allocation System
Federal Commissions

**Lower Courts**
Magistrate
Customary
Alkali

**State Governors**
Deputy Governors
State Commissioners
State Civil Service

**State Legislatures**
House of Assembly

Traditional Authorities

Local Government Councils

The Structure of Government Under the 1999 Constitution

**FIGURE 18.4**

In our discussion of culture, we noted the effect of ethnic fragmentation on local government boundaries. When the federal military government created 301 local government administrations (LGAs) in 1976, boundary lines were drawn in Lagos with minimal consultation locally, and communities were not allowed to change them. When the country returned to civilian rule in 1979, however, elected officials were much more receptive to demands for subdividing local government areas. Within a year there were 716 local governments, an increase of 238 percent. Naturally, such a large number of local administrations placed a heavy burden on a country with limited financial and human resources. Since the local governments themselves had little potential for generating revenue,

they were unable to provide the services demanded by local populations. Interethnic competition to ensure responsive government produced units that were unable to respond to those who had "won" their own local governments.

The next military government addressed this situation. After seizing power on December 31, 1983, it returned the country to 301 local governments, plus three in the new Federal Capital Territory. Even the military was susceptible to local demands, however: the number again began to grow, and now at the "grassroots" there are 774 LGAs, a new high.

State-level politics has often been dominated by local ethnic rivalries, as states are called upon to settle local government boundary disputes and to decide on the competence of various traditional institutions. Pressures analogous to those at the local level have led to an expansion of the number of states. The three colonial regions, which became the states of federal Nigeria, quickly became four. With the outbreak of civil war in 1967, the country was divided into twelve states, a number that was increased to nineteen in 1976, to thirty in 1991, and to thirty-six in 1996 (plus the Federal Capital Territory; see Figure 18.5).

All these tensions finally converge at the national level, the source of most government resources. Recent federal governments have attempted to calm the ethnic struggle with a Nigerian version of affirmative action based on the country's "federal character." Various regions (and thus ethnic groups) are guaranteed a proportionate share of federal positions. This is an application of the consociational model, a common solution where countries are deeply divided by religion or ethnicity.[33] If appointments were made on competence alone, the educational advantage of the southernmost populations would result in their having a disproportionate share of civil service jobs. The major exception to apportioning positions according to federal character may be an indication of priorities. The Nigerian national football (soccer) team is not selected with attention to geographic representation!

Both the 1979 and 1989 Constitutions describe a three-level federalism. In such other large federations as the United States, Canada, and Australia, the constitution focuses on the federal-state relationship, with local government principally in the domain of the state or province. The fact that Nigerian constitutions have specified a uniform structure and common functions for local government is rather unusual. While there are no doubt advantages to this uniformity of structure and function, it does not allow for local governments to reflect the diversity of local cultures present in the country, nor is experimentation possible of the sort that has produced the manager and commission systems at the local level in the United States. Since colonial times, however, local government has really been little more than local administration of federal policy, a situation unlikely to change until local governments acquire independent sources of revenue. Clearly, in an oil-centralized system the demand for local governments cannot be explained by the control of decisionmaking. Rather, ever more local government is attractive because of the formula-driven allocation of funds that supports local activities. In 1981, the Second Republic's National

Assembly decided to allocate 10 percent of federal revenues and 10 percent of state revenues to the localities. However, not only were state governments unwilling to abide by this mandate, but they frequently tapped for their own purposes the federal allocation that was transmitted to them for distribution at the local level. To remedy this situation, the 1989 Constitution provided direct payment of the federal allocation to local governments; in 1990 that allocation was increased to 15 percent, and a few years later to 20 percent of federal revenues, where it stands as of 2007.

The process of subdividing administrative and political units has fueled a growth of the public sector. Employment in the public service is an indicator of the growth of government. At independence, there were 71,693 employees of federal and regional government; by 1974 there were about 630,000, not counting the 250,000 in military service. A study of local governments in 1978 and 1979 found another 386,600 positions at that level, not counting general laborers or district or village heads. The drop in oil revenues in the mid-1980s brought an end to government growth. However, the Buhari administration imposed a 15 percent across-the-board personnel reduction that started a long period of stability in government employment.[34] Since 1999 competition among states for the distribution of federal revenues is acute in two arenas: first in disagreements between the president and the National Assembly over the amount of money that should be returned to the oil-producing areas, or what Nigerians refer to as the "derivation formula." Second, the controversy has played out between the states and the federal government in a series of major Supreme Court decisions in 2002 concerning states' entitlement to off-shore oil revenues and the federal government's right to exempt certain expenses from funds distributed under the derivation formula.

Some suggest that a genuine federalism would help to cure Nigeria's political problems, which almost always involve the tremendously large stakes in the oil-rich nation's federal government. Perhaps a national government with limited resources would result in a federation that is not viewed as a high-stakes zero-sum game.

## Parliamentary vs. Presidential Government

Without exception, British colonies came to independence with a parliamentary system based on the mother country's Westminster model. Initially, Nigeria

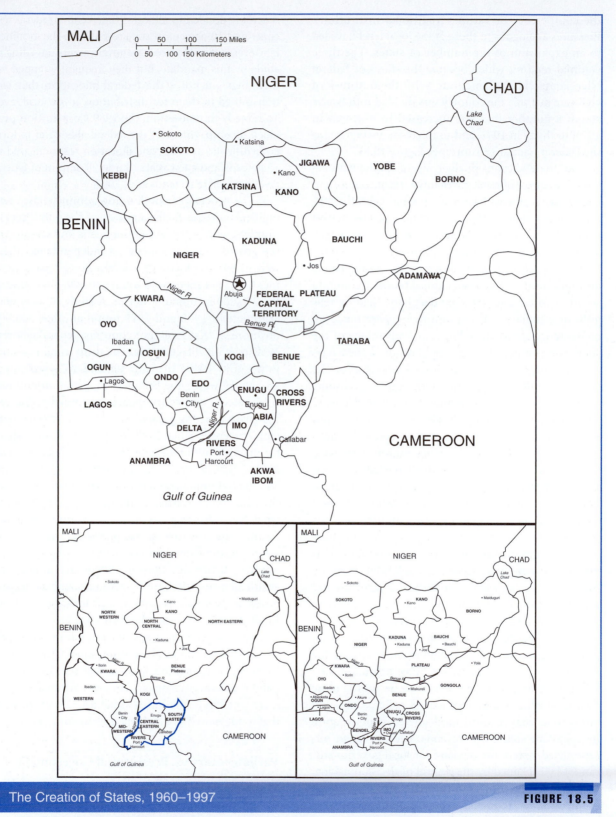

The Creation of States, 1960–1997

FIGURE 18.5

Note: Lower left: Dark color border (lower-left map) shows original three regions, increased to four by the creation of the Midwestern Region, and to twelve in 1967. Lower right: Nineteen states, 1976–1991. Above: 30 states, 1991–1997. (Current 36 states are shown at the beginning of the chapter.)

followed the Commonwealth pattern, with a ceremonial governor-general named by the British monarch. In 1963, the formal structure was redesignated a republic, with Nnamdi Azikiwe as president with mostly ceremonial powers; the parliamentary system was maintained, with a prime minister as head of government. Because Nigeria's first experience with civilian rule ended disastrously in 1966, it is not surprising that the previous system was called into question as a new constitution was being framed in the 1970s. The 1979 Constitution of the Second Republic was unabashedly modeled on the U.S. presidential model: an independently elected president was balanced against a two-house National Assembly at the federal level, with governors and legislatures following the same model at the state level. The disorder in the Second Republic might have brought presidentialism into disrepute as well, but the principal aspects of the presidential system were maintained in the 1989 and 1995 Constitutions.

The 1999 Constitution provides for an independently elected president and a dual chamber National Assembly at the federal level. Governors and single-house legislatures follow the same basic model at the state level. The speaker of the house presides over the House of Representatives, while the president of the Senate, who is in the line of presidential succession after the vice president of the republic, presides over the upper chamber. Each of Nigeria's thirty-six states has three senators (plus one for the Federal Capital Territory of Abuja), while population determines the number of constituencies in each state for a total of 360 representatives. Senators and representatives serve four-year terms and are elected at the same time, rather than in staggered elections. One legacy of the long years of military rule is that many of the legislators elected in 1999—nearly 80 percent in each chamber—had no previous legislative experience. There are about sixty standing committees in each chamber with jurisdiction over different issues. Committees are still getting accustomed to their role in the legislative process, and many bills are not amended or debated until they reach the floor for debate. As permitted by the Constitution, the Executive Branch introduced the federal budget and other major pieces of legislation, and how much the National Assembly can or should modify these bills has been a hotly contested issue since the transition to democracy. Differences of opinion between the two branches of government have been dramatic, even

though the president's party has consistently enjoyed a majority in both legislative chambers since 1999.

Nigeria's problems with achieving stable constitutional rule have made it an important case study in arguments over the relative advantages of the two systems in conditions of cultural pluralism. On the face of it, the fault may seem to lie with defects in the various constitutional frameworks, but the problem may actually be the intractable nature of Nigerian pluralism. A constitutional document cannot succeed at papering over a lack of trust among the country's subcultures. The lack of trust has led to suggestions of a "zoning" arrangement, which would require that the presidency and other top posts rotate automatically among the various geographical "zones" in the country, such that every major group could have a turn. The Constitutional Conference of 1995 gave a general endorsement to zoning at all levels of government— that is, for governorships of states and chairmanships of local governments as well as at the federal level. The National Assembly proposed similar constitutional reforms in 2001. But would such a plan really inspire trust, or would it inspire officeholders to even more rapacious rent seeking, knowing they would be in a given office only for one term?

## The Judiciary

Nigeria came to independence with a well-established legal system that included a court system and a thriving legal profession in the British tradition. The federal and state courts are integrated into a single system of trial and appeal courts. Thus the 1999 Constitution provides a Supreme Court, a Court of Appeal, and state and federal High Courts with original and appellate jurisdictions. Traditional authorities maintain their greatest influence in their judicial powers, for states are explicitly allowed to constitute customary and Sharia (Muslim Koranic law) courts, both original and appellate. Ten northern states maintain Sharia courts, a point of contention between Muslim authorities and those who see such official recognition as divisive.

It has been one of the greater anomalies of Nigeria's often chaotic politics that the independent judiciary has survived, even through military regimes that rule by decree. The final blow to judicial independence may have come, however, under the Abacha regime, which showed no inclination to respect any semblance of legal system autonomy. It reacted to court orders by changing the rules—even constitutional provisions—that might be used against it. It also established special military tribunals for robbery and firearms violations, for the trial of Ken Saro-Wiwa and others in Ogoniland, and for those accused of supporting coups against Abacha in 1995 and 1997.

## INTEREST ARTICULATION

There are at least two aspects of political influence in Nigeria. First is the effect of organized interest groups, such as unions and trade associations and religious bodies. The second involves the more informal channels of participation through individual relationships often described by the term "clientelism."

Nigerian author Wole Soyinka describes how some of the first formal interest groups formed during the colonial period out of previously nonpolitical associations:

> Much later, we heard of the formation of the Nigerian Women's Union. The movement of the *onikaba*, begun over cups of tea and sandwiches to resolve the problem of newly-weds who lacked the necessary social graces, was becoming popular and nation-wide. And it became all tangled up in the move to put an end to the rule of white men in the country.[35]

The activities of formal associations and institutions often offer the most vigorous expression of societal independence from a government. Characteristically, voluntary associations were either brought under control or abolished in the authoritarian regimes that took hold in Africa soon after independence. This was not, however, the case in Nigeria, where even during military regimes organizations such as the Nigerian Women's Union have maintained an independent existence, even as their political influence was reduced.

### Ethnic and Religious Associations

Many of the first formal associations in Nigeria had an ethnic base. The Igbo Federal Union (later the Igbo State Union) was "inaugurated by politically conscious representatives of the Igbo intelligentsia."[36] The Egbe Omo Oduduwa was organized among young, urban, Yoruba professionals. Minority groups especially found comfort in formal associations such as

the Ibibio State Union, the Edo National Union, the Urhobo Renascent Convention, and others. These associations often formed the organizational base for parties, and contributed to the latter associations' ethnic orientations. In the north, where individual clientelist ties are relatively stronger, associations even of the ethnic type have played less of a role. An ethnic association of contemporary significance is the Movement for the Survival of the Ogoni People (MOSOP), founded by **Ken Saro-Wiwa.** MOSOP claims to speak for the 500,000 Ogoni people whose land is now occupied by Shell Oil drilling rigs. The Ogoni complain that they have borne the brunt of the inconvenience of Nigeria's oil industry and have received little in return. By the early 1990s they had begun to disrupt production, and Saro-Wiwa was arrested. He won his freedom and continued to campaign overseas against Shell Oil and the Nigerian government. When four Ogoni chiefs were murdered by young militants, Saro-Wiwa was again placed under arrest (along with fourteen other Ogonis) and charged with murder for inciting the youths. In October 1995, he and eight codefendants were convicted by a military court. In November they were hanged, despite pleas of clemency from around the world. After five years in the grave, in July 2002, the federal government allowed their families to exhume bodies of Ken Saro-Wiwa and others for a proper burial.

As in many other countries, religious institutions and associations play an important part in Nigerian politics. These groups are especially durable and resilient, because when political activity is repressed they remain organized around denominational objectives, and where an ethnic association might have to play a less obvious role, neither Christian nor Muslim religious groups and leaders find it necessary to camouflage their identities. As in other countries, religious-based interest groups take several forms: the formal institutions (churches, Koranic schools); leadership roles such as bishops, pastors, and *mallams* (Muslim teachers and learned men); and voluntary denominational associations. The effectiveness of religious institutions in articulating concerns to government has been reduced by intergroup conflicts, most frequently between Christians and Muslims, that put the government in the role of mediator.

Not surprisingly, associational life is most active in the south; however, the north is home to an Islamic "mystic brotherhood," the Tijaniyya, which is particularly influential among lower-class Hausa Muslims and is looked on with suspicion by the representatives of orthodox Islam (another brotherhood, the Khadiriyya, is identified with the traditional elite of the north). The existence of such groups blurs the distinction between "modern" associations and "traditional" institutions. A new breed of ethnic organizations has emerged under democracy, with groups such as the Arewa People's Congress, which declares its mission as "defending northern interests," and the Odua People's Congress militating for its version of Yoruba interests in the southwest.

## Associational Groups

In the more urban and industrialized areas of the country, one encounters a range of associational interest groups common to the politics of any modern nation. Trade unions have played a role in Nigerian politics since the colonial period, sometimes collectively through the Nigerian Labor Congress (NLC) and its seventeen affiliated unions. However, labor action is organized more frequently by sector. Groups representing the petroleum workers can have an immediate impact on the national economy and consequently have the potential for great political influence, as was demonstrated in 1994 strike actions by the **National Union of Petroleum and Gas Workers (NUPENG)** and the Petroleum and Natural Gas Senior Staff Association (PENGASSAN). Groups such as the Nigerian Union of Local Government Employees (NULGE) are especially influential because of their immediate impact on government.

Professional organizations—such as the Nigerian Bar Association, the Nigerian Medical Association, and especially the Nigerian Union of Journalists—are politicized as issues concern them directly. Military governments periodically force the dissolution of such groups by arresting their leaders. After the NLC met in Kaduna in July 1994 and voted a general strike, the Abacha government arrested Frank Kokori, secretary of NUPENG, and most members of the petroleum industry unions eventually returned to work. (Kokori was one of the first political prisoners released by General Abubakar following the death of Abacha.)

The universities are another modern sector that has a tradition of political activism. Faculty (the term "staff" is used in Nigeria), as well as students, were some of the earliest critics of military rule, and military governments have tried to marginalize their

role in the country. Strikes by staff and students are common, and the campuses were the most vocal opponents of Abacha's continuation of military rule. However, because recent military regimes have been content to let the universities deteriorate, campus political activities have not had the impact on policy as have parallel actions of, say, petroleum workers.

The National Democratic Coalition (NADECO) and the Campaign for Democracy (CD) are groupings of civil rights and democracy activists that are particularly influential in intellectual circles and among students. In 1994 they were at the front of much anti-Abacha activity. These groups played leading roles criticizing General Abubakar's approach to a return to civilian rule.

During the long periods of military rule, politicians at all levels who were turned out by the military have constituted an interest group united around their desire to be allowed back into the circles of power. They were a force pushing for the return to civilian rule, even as many of them were content to be "co-opted" into administrative service under the military.

## Nonassociational Groups

A clear Nigerian example of the nonassociational interest group, but shadowy in its definition, is the famous **"Kaduna Mafia."** Hardly any informal conversation on Nigerian politics fails to mention this network of powerful northern leaders who are said to maintain strong influence over the military and Nigerian politics. Richard Joseph offers this description:

> In a general sense [Kaduna Mafia] refers to members of the northern intelligentsia who assumed positions of political and social influence during the decade of military rule after the civil war. These individuals are, on the whole, better educated than their predecessors in the emirate North who held similar positions in the first decade after independence. [They also] were less dependent on the patronage of the traditional rulers to advance in their careers.[37]

This group was highly influential in the Babangida years, but Sani Abacha distanced himself from it, and the arrest and death in prison in 1997 of General Yar'Adua, a leading figure in the Kaduna Mafia, suggests that the organization has lost its influence, at least temporarily.

Given that most of Nigeria's labor force is involved in agriculture, one expects to find strong associational activity among farmers. However, the ethnic divisions in the country have prevented the formation of any national-level farm organizations. Those groups that do exist are usually engaged in local cooperative activities and are not active beyond the regional level. More commonly, the interest articulation activities of farmers are of the anomic protest variety (that is, spontaneous and unorganized), or take the form of clientelism (as we will discuss later).

Finally, one institution is far more than an interest group: the military itself. We will address its political role later. The Nigerian military is not a cohesive interest, as was demonstrated in the transition from Abacha to Abubakar. The enlisted personnel and lower ranking officers have not seen any direct benefit from military rule, and many supported efforts to return to civilian rule. Also, the country's ethnic divisions are reflected in the military as well, although they compete there with a well-ingrained military professionalism. The military rank-and-file were originally drawn mostly from northern non-Hausa minorities. Later recruitment drew from all over the country, but the minorities, especially from the "Middle Belt," remain disproportionately numerous. The early preponderance of Igbo officers ended with the second coup and the Biafran civil war, which resulted in the northern dominance in the officer corps that is present today. However, there is wide ethnic diversity among the officers, and ethnicity is only one factor in the complex disputes within the military. There is a constant possibility that new factions will emerge to challenge the current leadership, to forestall or delay the return to civilian control. The Abacha regime cited a conspiracy to that end when, in March 1995, it ordered the arrest of "a group of over-ambitious and misguided officers and civilians." According to then second-in-command General Oladipo Diya, the coup plotters included "a cross-section of the country, officers from all parts of the country." Ironically, Diya himself was arrested as part of an alleged coup plot two years later.

The role of a vital civil society as a balance to political authority was played by a range of interest groups in the wake of General Sani Abacha's seizure of power in November 1993. Trade unions and unions of the academic staff at secondary schools and the universities engaged in a series of strikes against the Abacha regime. These activities were designed to force Abacha to release Moshood Abiola from prison, to agree to political activity on Abiola's part, and to turn over power to a civilian regime. Their strike stimulated an increase in world prices of raw crude oil and in pressing shortages in refined petroleum products in Nigeria. Abacha responded by arresting the union leaders and replacing them with his handpicked successors. Many Nigerians thought that strike and demonstration action would force Abacha out, but he stubbornly clung to power until his death.

Abacha's regime was not without substantial support. An organization called the Association for a Better Nigeria, formed under Babangida, went to court to seek an injunction against certification of the 1993 election. This and other associations represented those in the country who profited from the existing arrangement and were not eager for a new constitutional regime, and so continued their vocal support of the Babangida and Abacha regimes both in Nigeria and abroad. These elements were largely discredited after Abacha's death, and a number of their leaders made public pleas for forgiveness.

## Patron-Client Networks

An alternative structure for interest representation is found in the **patron-client network.** Powerful Nigerian political figures are able to mobilize support through personal "connections" with subordinates, who may themselves serve in a corresponding role of "patron" for a yet-lower set of "clients." **Clientelism** was an integral aspect of political life in the larger scale precolonial systems of the Hausa, the Yoruba, and others. Those who are not represented by formal associations may be able to take advantage of their connections to achieve political ends, particularly at the local level, and where traditional rulers and their political systems maintain some influence. Furthermore, the pattern of personal contacts is ingrained in the culture and thus remains important as an approach to powerful modern figures independent of any local traditional context.

Resting on these patron-client networks in Nigeria is a patronage system in which a ruler or an official gives a public office to an individual client in return for his loyalty in delivering political support at some lower level. The prevalence of such a system in Nigeria is not dependent on particular regimes, civilian or military.[38] Their durability makes the "restructuring" of Nigerian administration difficult when regimes are under pressure to develop an "austerity" budget.

## POLITICAL PARTICIPATION

The forms of action that Nigerians take in pursuit of political goals cover the whole spectrum of possibilities, from voting to participating in the terribly violent civil war of 1967–1970. Given the lack of either good census data or reliable voter registration figures, it is difficult to be precise about voter turnout figures, but estimates are in the range of 40 to 60 percent in some earlier elections, an impressive level for a majority poor and illiterate populace. Some of the explanation is found in the prevalence of patron-client systems, the "machine politics" that ties ordinary voters into the electoral process through personalistic ties with political activists.

Interest in elections, even in the mobilization of patron-client networks, declined during the long transition to civilian rule, but it rose again with the return to civilian rule. In the presidential election of February 1999, turnout was estimated at 52 percent. Voter turnout for the 2003 election was an estimated 69 percent.

Violence also is employed frequently, from the use of "thugs" by political parties in both republics to the confrontations with police in Lagos and the southwest during the last days of the Babangida regime and in the challenges to Abacha's seizure of power. Violence by the state, although less common than in many authoritarian regimes, has played a major role in Nigeria politics: upward of fifty people were executed for participating in the failed coups of 1986 and 1990; death sentences against those accused in 1995 were not carried out, only because members of the PRC could not agree among themselves on whether to do so. The greatest example of political violence was, of course, the Biafran civil war from 1967 to 1970. Nigeria has experienced over 2 million deaths in wars from 1960 to 1992, the vast majority of them during the civil war.

Nigeria has been a highly politicized country ever since independence, although alienation and frustration with the failure to develop stable, honest, and responsive institutions are increasingly evident.

## PARTIES AND ELECTIONS

After the Babangida government voided the national elections of 1993 and Abacha came to power, party activities were banned in Nigeria. The exception was the artificially created five-party system that contested local and state elections under Abacha; these parties were allowed to exist only if they refrained from any criticism of the regime, and they leaned so far in the other direction that all five named Abacha their presidential candidate! In 1998 the Abubakar regime allowed new parties to be formed and contested the 1998–1999 elections. The rebirth of party activity is evidence that the evolution of political parties and their effect on Nigerian politics are worthy of attention.[39]

The first modern party was formed by Herbert Macaulay in Lagos in 1923. Several such movements contended for power at the local level under the colonial regime, and a diverse nationalist movement emerged in 1944, under the leadership of Macaulay and Nnamdi Azikiwe, the National Council of Nigeria and the Cameroons (NCNC).[40] This organization advocated increased representation in the Nigerian colonial government. Chapters were established across Nigeria. However, when the British introduced a more democratic and decentralized constitution in 1951, the NCNC broke up along ethnic lines. The 1951 Constitution mandated indirect assembly elections in the three regions; Lagos was in the Western Region, where the Yoruba were in the majority. An opposition party, the Action Group (AG), emerged under the leadership of a young Yoruba lawyer, Obafemi Awolowo, with an initial organizational base in the Egbe Omo Oduduwa, a Yoruba cultural society. Although Azikiwe's NCNC won in multiethnic Lagos, the AG won the majority of seats in the Western Region. The NCNC won overall in the Eastern Region, where Azikiwe's own Igbo ethnic group was in the majority.

From the beginning there were forces within both the NCNC and the AG arguing for movement in a multicultural, issue-based, cross-regional direction. The AG was especially split along liberal (cross-regional, pushing for quick movement toward independence) and conservative (ethnic-based, evolutionary) lines. Elected offices were first established regionally, and only later (in 1957) at the national level. This favored the forces of regionalism. Azikiwe particularly was committed to action at the national level, but it became clear that a regional power base was essential, and Azikiwe also was constrained to center his party on its strength in the east. Thus the NCNC came to be identified with that region and the Igbo people (see Table 18.2).

In the north, Britain's successful application of indirect rule had resulted in an alliance between the

| Ethnic Distribution of Party Leaders, 1958 | | | **TABLE 18.2** |
| --- | --- | --- | --- |
| **Party*** | **Igbo** | **Yoruba** | **Hausa-Fulani** |
| NCNC | 49.3 | 26.7 | 2.8 |
| AG | 4.5 | 68.2 | 3.0 |
| NPC | — | 6.8 | 51.3 |

*NCNC: National Council of Nigeria and the Cameroons; AG: Action Group; NPC: Northern People's Congress.

Source: Richard Sklar and C. S. Whitaker, Jr., "Nigeria," in James S. Coleman and Carl Rosberg, eds., *Political Parties and National Integration in Tropical Africa* (Berkeley: University of California Press, 1964).

colonial administration and the traditional emirs that impeded the formation of modern political movements. Whereas in the south such movements had arisen among a Western-educated elite outside the control of any traditional authority, in the north the only youth to receive a modern education came from the families of the traditional elites. Although reformist political organizations were formed—notably the Northern Elements' Progressive Union (NEPU) under Mallam Aminu Kano—they operated only at the margins and tension points of the emirates. A more conservative movement, the Northern Peoples' Congress (NPC), was taken over by the Sardauna (a traditional title) of Sokoto and a Hausa commoner, Abubakar Tafawa Balewa. The NPC, the traditional emirates, and the preindependence administrative structure were intertwined such that young administrators could run successfully for public office, but only if they had the support of their administrative superiors and of the local traditional elite. This political structure grew up among a population that was not as educated (less than 15 percent were literate) as in the south, and that was much more loyal to their traditional authorities. In the 1959 Northern House of Assembly, 24 percent of NPC delegates were sons of incumbent or former emirs, and over a third were blood relatives of emirs. The elite origins of the party's officers and candidates were deemphasized through both communal (ethnic) and religious (Islamic) appeals to the electorate. Not surprisingly, the NPC did not give high priority in its program to achieving national independence. The NPC was challenged in northern elections, but with only occasional success.

Unlike the NCNC and AG, neither the NPC nor its northern rivals even tried to obtain political support outside their own region.

When General Ironsi assumed power following the breakdown of political order in the Western Region and the first coup, one of his first moves was to abolish all parties and a large number of political associations. The country remained without formal parties from 1966 until the preparations for a return to civilian rule in 1979. General Yakubu Gowon (head of state from 1966 to 1975) had considered the creation of a one-party state in Nigeria, with himself as leader of a "national movement." Nigeria's diversity and the plurality of its power bases made that concept impossible to achieve: to northern leaders, it suggested southern domination, while to the politicians waiting for the return of civilian rule, it meant the end of their ambitions. Gowon was unable to decide on a course of action and was deposed before any plan had been adopted.

After taking power, Murtala Muhammed set in motion a process to return to civilian rule. The military regime established the Constitution Drafting Committee, and in his address to its opening session, Murtala Muhammed laid down several principles relating to parties. He encouraged them to "discover some means by which Government can be formed without the involvement of political parties," but otherwise that they should draft a plan to guarantee "genuine and truly national political parties," while striving to work out "specific criteria by which their number would be limited."[41] The drafters responded with a constitution that was carefully crafted to promote national parties. It specified that to be elected president, a candidate would have to poll at least 25 percent of the votes cast in each of at least two-thirds of the states. Elections were to be controlled by the Federal Election Commission (FEDECO), with which all parties must register. Parties were to offer membership to any Nigerian, and party governing boards were to reflect the country's "federal character"—specifically, coming from at least two-thirds of the states. The Electoral Decree was published in 1978; in that same year political parties were again made legal, and they came in a flood—some 150 were formed.

The elections of 1979 and 1983 are difficult to analyze because five parties competed for president, Senate and House seats, and state assemblies with varying degrees of success. Looking at the Senate, House, and state assemblies overall, most states were controlled by a single party. Awolowo's United Party dominated five of the nineteen states, all in the Yoruba west and the midwest (a "minority" area). Azikiwe's NPP carried three states, two of which were in the Igbo-dominated east. Aminu Kano's northern opposition party carried only its leader's own state, Kano, in the north. The GNPP won two states in the northeast, home region of its presidential candidate. However, the ethnic factor was complicated by the success of the NPN in building cross-regional alliances. The NPN controlled eight states; five of these were in the north, but three were in the southeast.

In order to participate in the elections of 1998 and 1999, parties were required to demonstrate a nation-wide organization. On the basis of the cases they submitted, nine parties were qualified to compete in the local elections of December 1998. The three parties that received the highest number of votes in the 774 local governments were then allowed to compete in the state and national elections of 1999. The People's Democratic Party (PDP) won in 389 local governments, the All People's Party (APP) in 182, and the Alliance for Democracy (AD) in 100, with other parties winning in the remaining 103. As the presidential elections of February 1999 approached, the APP and AD negotiated to present a single candidate—in other words, the normal effect of a winner-take-all situation pushed toward the creation of a two-party system. There were ultimately just two candidates, Olusegun Obasanjo representing the PDP and Olu Falae leading the APP. Obasanjo won with 62.8 percent compared with Falae's 37.2 percent. The **Independent National Election Commission (INEC)** created by the Abubakar regime for this election declared Obasanjo the winner.

In 2003, Obasanjo ran for reelection. The APP, which had in the meantime renamed itself the **All Nigeria People's Party (ANPP),** selected Muhammed Buhari, another former military ruler, as its presidential candidate. Despite the internal tensions in the PDP, the party increased its majority in both houses of Congress and won twenty-eight out of thirty-six governorships. Obasanjo was reelected by a landslide, winning almost twice as many votes as Buhari. He and the PDP particularly improved their position in the southwest, where they captured five governorships from the AD. Table 18.3 shows the results of the 2003 elections. At every level, the PDP consistently demonstrated its dominance. Because of the very public tensions between President Obasanjo and Vice President Atiku Abubakar, the future of the PDP is uncertain. The broader party system is also in flux, as INEC has registered a score of new parties. The PDP secured majorities in the House and Senate again in 2007, and won most of the governorships. But many results are being contested. By early 2009, the courts had thrown out 11 gubernatorial and nine senatorial elections. In fact, the 2007 election of President Yar'Adua was not upheld by the Supreme Court until December 2008.

## Ethnic Solidarity and Party Loyalty

Figure 18.6 shows the formation of Nigerian political parties, notably their reemergence with the same ethnic bases after suppression by military regimes. Governments, especially the military ones, have tried to force Nigerians to express their will through cross-ethnic parties. However, because ethnicity drives much of the political organizing in the country, political leaders have succeeded in subverting the goal of truly national parties through their calls to ethnic identity. A political career is started in a local community on an ethnic

| Results of 2003 National Elections | | | | **TABLE 18.3** |
|---|---|---|---|---|
| | PDP (%) | ANPP (%) | AD (%) | Others (%) |
| Presidential vote | 61.9 | 32.2 | Did not contest | 5.9 |
| National assembly vote (seats) | 54.5 (213) | 27.4 (95) | 9.3 (31) | 8.8 (7) |
| Senate vote (seats) | 53.7 (73) | 27.9 (28) | 9.7 (6) | 8.7 (0) |

Note: PDP: People's Democratic Party; ANPP: All Nigeria People's Party; AD: Alliance for Democracy.

Source: The Independent National Electoral Commission, preliminary results, http://www.inecnigeria.org.

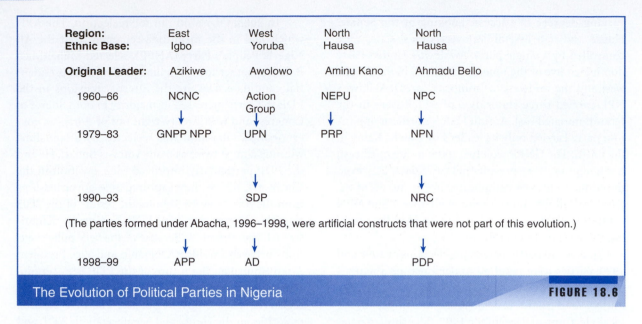

| Region: | East | West | North | North |
|---|---|---|---|---|
| Ethnic Base: | Igbo | Yoruba | Hausa | Hausa |
| Original Leader: | Azikiwe | Awolowo | Aminu Kano | Ahmadu Bello |
| 1960–66 | NCNC | Action Group | NEPU | NPC |
| 1979–83 | GNPP NPP | UPN | PRP | NPN |
| 1990–93 | | SDP | | NRC |

(The parties formed under Abacha, 1996–1998, were artificial constructs that were not part of this evolution.)

| 1998–99 | APP | AD | | PDP |
|---|---|---|---|---|

**The Evolution of Political Parties in Nigeria**                    **FIGURE 18.6**

basis, and a cross-ethnic party is, in that situation, nothing more than a coalition of ethnic interests. The Hausas have been most successful in this situation; they captured the presidency each time this national office was filled by election until Obasanjo's victory in 1999. With envy and bitterness, many political activists in the south were convinced that the Hausas knew they could assemble an electoral majority under their control and that they act accordingly. Many charged that Obasanjo, although not Hausa, could not have won without their support and was in effect the "northern" candidate.

The NPN won the ultimate prize, the presidency, in 1979, essentially on the basis of a combination of northern voters and minority voters in the southern regions. The most significant difference for parties between the First and Second Republics turned out to be the carving up of the original three regions into nineteen states. Ethnic groups other than the "big three" were dominant in a number of these states and had thus broken free of regional ethnic dominance. Party strategists henceforth combined a strong base in one of the main ethnic group areas with a successful appeal for support among minorities and potentially among dissident groups in the home bases of the other two major groups.

The same five parties remained in existence through the four years of the Second Republic, and contested again in 1983 for the presidency, seats in the Senate and House, and state-level positions. However, the smallest parties, the PRP and the GNPP, had been weakened by their lack of access to resources. And, as is normal in a presidential system where the ultimate prize, the presidency, is a winner-take-all election, there were pressures on the two major opposition parties to combine against the incumbent. Such cooperation proved impossible, however, when neither Azikiwe nor Awolowo would defer to the other as presidential candidate. In a campaign marked with violence and vote-rigging, the NPN won a solid victory, recording gains against the opposing parties in their home areas.

The NPN victory was short-lived. Three months into its second term it met an early demise at the hands of Nigeria's fourth military coup. Party financing in the 1983 elections was based on unprecedented political corruption, even as the country's financial situation had greatly deteriorated, and was among the reasons offered by the military for again abolishing the country's political parties. The public's acceptance of that action was rooted in the civilian government's failure to address in policy the issues raised during the campaign. For example, both the UPN and the NPP promised full employment and free education at all levels. These promises were beyond the regime's fiscal capacity and showed a serious lack of responsibility; it is not surprising that they contributed to voter cynicism.

The two-year reign of Muhammadu Buhari (1983–1985) presented no timetable for a return to electoral politics. However, Buhari's successor, Ibrahim Babangida, began outlining conditions for a return to civilian rule in 1986 that revealed his view of the country's problems. Babangida announced that forty-nine politicians convicted of corruption would be banned from politics for life. Between 1987 and 1989, a series of decrees created the National Election Commission (NEC) to replace the defunct FEDECO in managing the electoral process. The NEC provided for nonpartisan local council elections in 1987; set a timetable for the creation of political parties and the sequential election of legislators and executives at the local, state, and national levels; and promulgated a constitution to come into effect in 1992.

The NEC was entrusted with the task of establishing guidelines for party formation that would result in the emergence of a de facto two-party system. In 1989 the ban on party activities was lifted and associations were invited to form, with the proviso that they have a national following and an internally democratic structure. Some fifty parties sprang up overnight.

The effect of forcing a two-party system on this political chaos was not clear. Some feared it would lead to a polarization along north-south, Christian-Muslim lines. Such a polarization would imply the papering over of serious splits among northerners and between powerful interests in the southeast and southwest; in this context, the emergence of two monolithic political movements would not automatically occur. Thirteen groups eventually petitioned the NEC for recognition. After careful scrutiny, the NEC certified five parties to the Armed Forces Ruling Council (AFRC). The AFRC response was extremely innovative: all thirteen associations, including those certified by the NEC, were dissolved, and two parties were established by the military government, perhaps the only time in history that an authoritarian leadership had imposed a two-party system!

Babangida charged the NEC to examine the various documents of the dissolved parties and synthesize them into two discrete philosophies, one for a party "a little to the left," the other to fit a party "a little to the right" on the political spectrum. However, they were to have identical constitutions, providing for the choice of candidates by primary election. Even the parties' names were assigned by the government: the party on the left would be the Social Democratic Party, that on the right the National Republican Council. The impact of the American model on Nigerian constitution-making had never been more obvious.

The government built headquarters buildings for both parties at each local government and provided generous "take-off grants" to sustain their organizing efforts. In a first round of elections, party officials at all levels were elected. However, powerful politicians had naturally formed parallel organizations and set about using their clientelist networks to capture one or the other party at various levels.

Nigerians reacted to these developments with a mixture of cynicism and hope. It was difficult for intellectuals to accept a "democracy" based on parties and elections mandated by an authoritarian government; yet it was the "only game in town" and promised to bring the country back to civilian rule, however constraining the new rules might be. Many participated in the 1990 elections of local government secretaries and councils under the two party labels. The next year saw the election of state governors and legislators and a National Assembly. And the process was inevitably building to the election of a president, in 1992, at which time the military would hand over power.

The process was set back late in 1992, when the regime nullified the results of the parties' efforts to produce presidential candidates. The process had indeed been so poorly handled as to justify a postponement of the process. Yet Nigerians were ever more skeptical as to whether the military really intended to leave, or were just playing an elaborate game to buy time.

Babangida scheduled a new election for June 1993, ordered the parties to produce new candidates, and set August 27, 1993, as the date for turning over power to the civilian government. Under more careful control, the parties reconvened their national conventions and nominated new candidates. The National Republican Council selected a relatively unknown figure, Bashir Tofa (a Kanuri from the northeast), while the Social Democrats nominated a rich businessman from the southwest, Moshood Abiola. Abiola was inexperienced in politics but, like Tofa, had close ties to the military hierarchy. He seemed to have an ideal combination of identities for Nigeria's plural culture: although a Yoruba, he, like his opponent, was also a Muslim. Significantly, both had been active supporters of the NPN in the Second Republic.

The election finally took place on **June 12, 1993.** Nigerian and international observers reported that it was a generally fair election, certainly the cleanest Nigeria had ever seen; the NRC had not announced any plans to contest the outcome. Perhaps equally as important as its relative fairness, the election produced a unifying outcome that was everything advocates of a two-party system could have desired. Abiola, from the south, appeared to have won a majority of the votes in nine northern states, including his opponent's home state of Kano. The results seemed to suggest that, under a two-party system, factionalism in each region and state could be exploited to prevent a strictly regional outcome.

The 1993 results were never officially announced, however, and two weeks later Babangida annulled the election. "June 12" became a term forever etched into Nigerian memory, particularly for political activists in the southwest who claimed the Yoruba had been denied the presidency. Party politics, even the contrived variety invented by the Babangida regime, had once again proved to be an exercise unacceptable to the military leadership and their allies. The Abacha regime announced guidelines for the creation of new parties in June 1996, and political entrepreneurs immediately began forming alliances, even though NADECO and other opposition groups denounced the exercise as a sham. We have seen that the five parties certified for local elections in March 1997 all nominated Abacha for the presidency.

On July 20, 1998, Abubakar announced the dissolution of the five parties, the nullification of the local and state elections, and a new start toward democracy with freely formed parties and a promise to hand over power to an elected president on May 29, 1999. A new organ, the Independent National Electoral Commission, was created to supervise the electoral process. Of the nine parties originally certified in October 1998, the three that survived the local elections represented some degree of continuity with earlier party formations—each with a base among one of the three major ethnic groups. However, because of the requirement to have a national base and for other strategic considerations, the candidates of each party were not necessarily of the ethnic group presumably dominant in it. Most importantly, even though the PDP is said to have its base in the north, its leaders threw their support for the presidential nomination to General Obasanjo, who had only recently been released from Abacha's prison. As both a southerner (both he and his principal opponent Olu Falae were Yoruba) and a former military ruler, Obasanjo was seen by many both inside and outside the country as the individual most likely to provide effective leadership in the postmilitary state. However, some of those active in the various human rights and democracy movements were dubious that a former authoritarian leader was an appropriate president for a democratic state, and his northern backing raised doubts among many southerners. And the question still remained: Would the military be ready to return to the barracks? The answer came with the inauguration of Obasanjo as president on May 29, 1999.

For Nigeria's third attempt at democracy to succeed, the new Yar'adua administration will have to tackle significant problems, including corruption driven by substantial new oil revenues, a bureaucracy in need to retraining, ongoing ethnic and religious conflicts, and serious economic inequalities. Even though the president's party holds a majority in the National Assembly, there have been significant tensions between the Executive and legislative branches. Since 1999, corruption investigations have resulted in two changes of leadership in the Senate and two in the House. In 2002, PDP members in the Assembly responded with an impeachment campaign against President Obasanjo.

The elections of April 19, 2003, in Nigeria, were the first civilian-conducted elections in twenty years. This development represents a big step toward establishing an enduring democracy in Nigeria. It was the first election in Nigeria where three retired army generals contested for the presidency. President Olusegun Obasanjo won with 62 percent of the votes to Muhammed Buhari's 32 percent; other candidates had 6 percent, including Odumegu Ojukwu, the former seccessionist leader of Biafra (1967–1970). Olusegun Obasanjo's PDP captured most of the governorships, and supermajorities in the House and Senate. Election observers reported significant irregularities, concluding they "severely limited and even denied in some parties of the country, the ability of Nigerians to express their franchise" during both the legislative and presidential elections. The National Democratic Institute's observation report continued: "The cumulative effect of these problems seriously compromised the integrity of the elections where they occurred." Despite these flaws, Obasanjo was widely accepted as the winner and the international community interpreted the elections as a step toward democracy.

**Umar Musa Yar'adua,** the governor of Katsina State, emerged as the winner of the 2007 presidential contest. The election marked the first civilian-to-civilian transfer of power in the country's history, although power remained firmly entrenched in the ruling People's Democratic Party. It also marked the return of power to the north, since Yar'adua comes from a traditional Hausa-Fulani background.

International observers and domestic monitors criticized election preparations and the conduct of voting even more harshly than in 2003. The major national civil society coalition, the Transition Monitoring Group, called for the results to be cancelled outright. The European Union's Observation Mission said the "State and Federal elections have fallen far short of basic international and regional standards for democratic elections." A report issued immediately after the elections noted "significant evidence of fraud" and concluded that the elections "cannot be considered to have been credible." In some states where little or no voting took place, INEC pledged to hold special elections. In 2007 many candidates, including the defeated Vice President Atiku Abubakar, promised to challenge results using election tribunals and the courts. Other politicians, including the defeated ANPP candidate Muhammadu Buhari, expressed little confidence in these procedures given the sluggish dispute resolution process in 2003 and the numerous elections overturned by tribunals in 2007. In sum, the peaceful transfer of power is historic but the new government must also overcome lingering doubts about its legitimacy and its commitment to democratic procedures.

## POLICY FORMATION AND IMPLEMENTATION

Many people have stopped bothering themselves with classifying African regimes as democratic or otherwise. They instead keep asking: How much do the regimes address themselves to the needs and aspirations of the people? I am one, I tell you,

all these noises about democracy and democratic are mere luxuries to the sufferers.[42]

In comparing Nigeria's various civilian and military regimes, the ultimate question must always be their *performance.* This is certainly the "bottom line" for Nigerians, whose support of these various regimes is based on the quality of life they experience under them. This section thus focuses on the *decisions* governments have made, particularly in raising revenues, dispersing funds, and implementing programs; it will also discuss some background issues, such as planning and conducting the federal census, the results of which underlie all policy; and finally it presents the constraints imposed on Nigerian decisionmaking by the outside world, particularly in the World Bank-supported **Structural Adjustment Program (SAP).** Dealing with "SAP," as the economic restructuring program is commonly called, leads us back to the discussion of environment with which we began. Policy relating to Nigeria's international economic situation has responded to initiatives from other African countries, world powers, international organizations, and multinational firms. Here we consider the critical constraints that the world economy puts on the choices available to a Third World country, even one as large and resource-rich as Nigeria.

The third elected President of Nigeria, 2007: Umar Musa Yar'adua.

Don Emmert/AFP/Getty Images

## Extractive Performance

> The tax people brought this paper, they say that, because I have a large farm, I am to get a special assessment. They say that I am *Gbajumo* (well-to-do) because I have a large farm, but they say nothing about the thirteen children and four women who depend on the farm for gari [food], no. They say I am *gbajumo* with a large farm.[43]

Nigeria inherited a fiscal system in 1960 that depended mainly on taxes on international trade. Indirect taxes provided 64 percent of total revenues, direct taxes only 16.5 percent, and other revenues 19 percent. The colonial system had developed a revenue system that operated through agricultural marketing boards. Ostensibly created to provide price stability to farmers, marketing boards accumulated surplus funds in good years that tempted government officials with development projects in mind. Peasant farmers also paid direct taxes, of which they were much more aware: widespread tax riots broke out in the Western Region in 1968 and 1969, a period during which tax collection was halted, eventually to be replaced by a lower, much simpler flat tax.

In the First Republic and under the Gowon administration, the state governments collected the personal income, sales, and poll taxes. Tax collections generally declined as new states were created, without fiscal institutions in place and with smaller tax bases than the old regions. At the same time, rising oil revenues strengthened the fiscal position of the federal government (and those states with oil fields).

Oil production began in earnest in 1958. At independence, the federal government was collecting modest royalties from private Western oil companies. In 1971, within a few years of the Biafran civil war, Nigeria joined the **Organization of Petroleum Exporting Countries (OPEC)** and also formed the **Nigerian National Oil Corporation (NNOC)** to participate directly in oil production. NNOC acquired a one-third interest in the AGIP Company and Elf, both French-controlled firms. At the time, this was seen as retribution for French support of the Biafran separatist effort, but within a few years the government had acquired a majority interest in all oil-production activities. The NNOC was merged with the Ministry of Petroleum Resources to form the Nigerian National Petroleum Corporation. Over this same period (the mid-1970s), petroleum prices had risen dramatically,

from $3.30 per barrel in 1972 to $21.60 in 1979. Thus the sale of crude oil directly by the Nigerian federal government to multinational oil companies came to provide the greater part of federal government revenues and, through the federal system, of state and local revenues as well.

In a pattern typical of Third World oil-exporting countries, Nigeria today depends almost entirely on the revenues from this single industry. Since there is no indication that the world's appetite for oil will diminish in the near future, it is a reliable revenue source that substitutes for the various forms of taxes on private income. Nigerians are fortunate that they have not been directly burdened with the cost of supporting government programs; they are perhaps unfortunate that governments, especially authoritarian military regimes, can tap this vast wealth without risking the wrath of taxpayers. The exceptions to this general rule are enterprises and property owners in Lagos state, which has a large share of the country's modern enterprises and generates over half its revenues, and the Ogonis and other peoples who inhabit the oil-producing region, who do not feel they benefit from the natural resources of their home area.

Given their control of vast petroleum reserves, Nigerian regimes have not actively sought large amounts of direct foreign aid. Whereas low-income countries received an average of $10.20 per capita ($24.50 excluding China and India) in 1991, Nigeria's per capita aid totaled only $2.60 that year—a mere 0.8 percent of GNP. At the same time, Nigeria used its oil reserves as the collateral for massive borrowing from foreign and international banks in the 1970s and 1980s. The funds supported massive capital expenditures and gave Nigeria an enormous external debt, which rose from 10 percent of GNP to 140.5 percent between 1980 and 1995. Oil wealth did not bring the country financial independence; quite the contrary, the debt gave international lenders a predominant voice in Nigeria's allocation of public funding. With the debt payoffs in 2005 and 2006, Nigeria will now be substantially insulated from such outside influences.

## Distributive Performance

As a producer of high-grade petroleum, Nigeria has an unusually great potential to move out of the ranks of the less developed into the middle-income nations. In the 1970s, impressive projects, such as road development and irrigation projects as well as the launching of Abuja as the nation's capital, were signs that potential might become reality.

Unfortunately, political corruption grew apace, and probably began consuming a higher proportion of national wealth than in the pre-oil period. When oil revenues suddenly began their decline in 1980, "corruption and mismanagement prevented any kind of disciplined adjustment," and "the economy was plunged into depression and mounting international indebtedness. . . . Sucked dry of revenue by the corruption, mismanagement, and recession, state governments became unable to pay teachers and civil servants or to purchase drugs for hospitals, and many services (including schools) were shut down by strikes."[44]

In spite of the country's raw material advantage, Nigerians have not seen their lives improve in recent years. The United Nations Development Program publishes the Human Development Index based on three factors: life expectancy at birth, adult literacy, and per capita GDP. Table 18.4 shows some development rankings for Nigeria, its immediate neighbors (Benin, Niger, and Cameroon), and a sample of other countries. Nigeria has a rank of 159 out of 177 countries on the HDI, and a rank of 157 on per capita GDP alone. It is not surprising to find the less-developed countries low on these listings. However, GDP per

capita is a good measure of distributive potential; thus the comparison of per capita GDP and the HDI ratings can be an indicator of how well a country has done for its people compared with other countries with similar capacity. Although the Nigerian data are comparable to those of its neighbors and to Africa as a whole, these data suggest that the Nigerian advantage in oil revenue has had little noticeable impact on the overall quality of life.

Budgetary priorities are important in analyzing distributive performance. In the case of a country ruled by the military for most of the last decade, one might expect that military expenditures would loom especially large. This is not the case in Nigeria, where published sources put the 2000 military budget at $234 million. At the peak of General Abacha's rule, the per capita expenditure on the military was only $2 per annum, for a rank of 154 out of 160 countries. However, there are believed to be significant additional military expenditures that are not publicly reported. Extremely modest in size at independence, Nigeria's armed forces grew to 250,000 at the height of the Biafran civil war. Then the Gowon regime began a program of gradual attrition that reduced the force to about 100,000 in the mid-1980s. Further shrinkage since then has resulted in a total force of 77,000. This still leaves Nigeria a major military force, and despite

| | | | | | | | **TABLE 18.4** |
|---|---|---|---|---|---|---|---|

Nigeria's Ranking on GDP per Capita and Human Development Index (HDI)

| Country | Life Expectancy at Birth, 2004 | Adult Literacy Rate (%) 2004 | Real GDP per Capita 2004* | Human HDI 2004 | Rank in per Capita GDP, 2004 | Rank by HDI | Per Capita GDP-HDI |
|---|---|---|---|---|---|---|---|
| United States | 77.5 | 99.0 | 39,676 | .948 | 2 | 8 | −6 |
| Japan | 82.2 | 99.0 | 29,251 | .949 | 18 | 7 | 11 |
| Britain | 78.5 | 99.0 | 30,821 | .940 | 10 | 15 | −5 |
| Mexico | 75.3 | 91.0 | 9,803 | .821 | 60 | 53 | 7 |
| Botswana | 34.9 | 81.2 | 9,945 | .570 | 58 | 131 | −73 |
| Indonesia | 67.2 | 67.2 | 3,609 | .711 | 116 | 108 | 8 |
| China | 71.9 | 90.9 | 5,896 | .768 | 90 | 81 | 9 |
| Cameroon | 45.7 | 67.9 | 2,174 | .506 | 131 | 144 | −13 |
| Nigeria | 43.4 | 66.8 | 1,154 | .448 | 158 | 159 | −1 |
| Benin | 54.3 | 34.7 | 1,091 | .428 | 161 | 163 | −2 |
| Niger | 44.6 | 28.7 | 779 | .311 | 170 | 177 | −7 |

*Note: These figures are in U.S. dollars converted at purchasing power parity (PPP) rates.

Source: United Nations Development Program, *Human Development Report 2006*.

its use as a springboard to political power, Nigeria's army remains one of the more professional on the continent. As we will discuss later, Nigerian leaders have used this military strength to maintain a high profile in West Africa.

Nigerians have a great enthusiasm for education, and parties and regimes have promised universal access to it. Some progress can be noted. In 1964 Nigeria ranked twenty-ninth among African nations in enrollments, with 5 percent of the school-age population in primary school; it was nineteenth in secondary enrollments, with 5 percent of the appropriate age group in school. Ten years later, 24 percent of the school-age population was in school, and Nigeria was fifteenth in Africa on this measure. In 1990, 60 percent of the school-age population was in primary school, an impressive accomplishment given population growth in that period; but it had fallen back to nineteenth in rank on the continent. Current information about primary and secondary enrollment is scarce, but youth literacy was 87 percent in 2000, up from 65 percent in 1985.

The Nigerian government's performance in the area of health has been mediocre. The 1990 expenditure of $906 million was only $9 per capita, compared with a continentwide average of $24. Part of this poor performance is seen in the low foreign assistance component in Nigeria's effort. Only 6 percent of its health expenditure came from that source, the third lowest proportion in Africa. But here again there has been progress in outcomes: Nigeria's infant mortality rate has dropped from 185 in 1960, to 139 in 1970, 114 in 1980, and 98 in 2003. However, the under-age-5 mortality rate per 1,000 births is now 198, meaning nearly 20 percent of Nigerian children do not reach age 5. This trend reflects an unfortunate and perhaps surprising increase over the last several years.

With petroleum firmly established as the major source of foreign exchange in Nigeria, and with that industry under government control, the distribution of wealth is heavily influenced by policy decisions. Private consumption surged as oil revenues multiplied in the 1970s, about 8 percent per year. This average figure conceals tremendous increases in wealth at the top; the lower 40 percent of the population benefited very little. Government expenditure grew at an even greater rate than private consumption, both in absolute terms and as a proportion of GDP.[45] This aspect of expenditure, of course, includes sums lost in corrupt payments to individuals. Nigeria should have reaped another windfall during the Gulf War, as petroleum prices temporarily shot up, but increased revenues never showed up in national accounts. In 1994, economist Pius Okigbo examined the books of the Central Bank of Nigeria; he reported (as he left the country) that $12.6 billion were not accounted for. The skimming of oil profits had indeed reached astronomical proportions.

Income distribution is also affected by inflation, which followed from the rapid increase in the money supply during the 1970s oil boom and continued apace later on, as governments followed a time-honored approach to balancing budgets when revenues decline: they printed money. The result was continuous inflation, a problem that became especially serious in the 1990s, as shown in Figure 18.7. The case study (see Box 18.5) shows the effect of this inflation on individual income. Inflation has fluctuated since the return of democracy, ranging from about 4 percent in 2002 to nearly 27 percent in 2005.

Governments have attempted to deal with inflation by enforcing an official exchange rate for

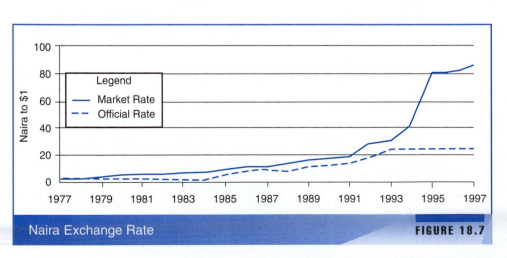

Naira to $1

Legend
— Market Rate
-- Official Rate

1977  1979  1981  1983  1985  1987  1989  1991  1993  1995  1997

**Naira Exchange Rate**                    **FIGURE 18.7**

## The Effects of Inflation: A Case Study

BOX 18.5

A young graduate with a new doctoral degree won a position as an instructor at a Nigerian university in 1977. His salary and benefits totaled 6,000 naira per year. At that time, one naira equaled $1.50, so his salary was the equivalent of $9,000—modest by industrial-world standards but very comfortable in Nigeria. Twenty years later, this same man achieved the rank of full professor, at a salary of 51,000 naira per year, with fringe benefits raising his total annual compensation to 90,000 naira. However, at the parallel market exchange rate of 80 naira to the dollar, his salary was the equivalent of $1,125 per year, a figure not taking into account

the effect of inflation on the purchasing power of the dollar since 1977. In 1998, a national review of faculty salaries increased the professor's salary to the equivalent of $5,000 per year. This discussion implies that salaries are regularly paid. However, in early 1999, the Abubakar government was in such financial straits that it failed to provide salary payments at all. In 2000, President Obasanjo improved the workers' pay generally and moved university teachers' pay to 130,000 naira per month, the equivalent of $1,000 per month. He did this to discourage brain drain in Nigeria and to promote high-level productivity in all sectors.

the **naira**—Nigeria's national currency. The result was a huge divergence in official and market exchange rates, causing chaos in the financial system. That chaos dried up investments and stimulated corruption, since anyone with access to foreign exchange at the official rate can then sell the foreign currency "on the street" for a large profit. Since 1999, the government has reduced its role in stabilizing the currency, allowing the value of the naira to be largely determined by forces of supply and demand.

As a policy issue, distribution in a large country such as Nigeria is also seen as a geographic question, not just one of policy priorities. Nigerians have a fondness for referring to the national budget as the "national cake," and they see state and local governments as the major recipients of slices. The federal government now spends between two-thirds and three-fourths of public monies, and also has great control over how the money distributed to state and local governments will be spent. On the contentious question of how to distribute resources as the number of states and local governments expanded, governments settled on relatively straightforward formulas, a combination of equality (across-the-board distributions to all states) and population. States other than Lagos now depend on the federal Revenue Allocation System (RAS) for 70 to 90 percent of their recurrent revenues. In order to fund local governments, the RAS was extended to cover them directly in 1981. Beginning in 1982, federal revenues were shared according to set

percentages among the three levels of government. Given the set formulas in the RAS, it is not surprising that regions and localities strive for statehood and local autonomy, and that population counts loom large as a political issue.

### Dealing with Debt and Structural Adjustment

Nigeria's recent debt repayments are historic—both for the country and for Africa. It solves a problem that began with fiscal indiscipline during the 1970s oil boom, when the government paid insufficient attention to the lack of productivity of public spending. Much of the money was applied to an increase in welfare expenditures, to developing an unprofitable steel industry, and to building the new capital at **Abuja.** Late in the 1970s, commodity prices fell, while oil prices remained high; African governments borrowed at an even faster pace, and the continent's total indebtedness increased between 1978 and 1982 from $27 billion to $72 billion. As African governments became unable to make debt payments, international financial institutions, principally the International Monetary Fund (IMF) and the World Bank, were called in to monitor a restructuring and rescheduling of the debt. Nigeria's total indebtedness continued to increase in the 1980s, from $8.9 billion in 1980 to $34.5 billion in 1991; by 1991 it represented 257 percent of the annual value of the country's exports and 109 percent of GNP. The annual cost of servicing the debt consumed

25 percent of the value of exports (up from 4 percent in 1980); the weight of this burden almost ensured that the debt would continue to grow. Throughout the past decade, the question of how to deal with the external debt was a principal focus of political discussion in Nigeria.

The debt problem that began under military rule became much more acute during the Second Republic (1979–1983). The Buhari regime approached the IMF for relief in the form of new loans and more favorable repayment terms but rejected the severe conditions the IMF attached to its help. The naira would have to be devalued, trade restrictions would have to be dropped, and subsidies for domestic gasoline consumption ended. These and similar measures have been the issues involved in Nigeria's Structural Adjustment Program (SAP). It was clear to the military leadership that such measures would be extremely unpopular with the Nigerian public and would lead to outbursts of political violence. When Ibrahim Babangida seized power in 1985, he opened a "national debate" on the issue. He claimed to fashion a Nigerian version of structural adjustment (while at the same time negotiating with the IMF). As the program's austerity measures began to be felt, the SAP became extremely unpopular. In his parallel program of moving back toward civilian rule, Babangida forbade candidates to criticize the program, but at the same time he eased off on the necessary austerity measures. The net result was that, although Nigerians were suffering from the country's poor position in international finance, the SAP did not reduce the debt or reform the financial system. Rather than allow the naira to float as urged by the IMF, the Abacha regime maintained the official exchange rate of 22 naira to the dollar, a decision certainly supported by those who were able to take advantage of it. In 1995 the exchange rate was partially opened to market forces, but the N22 to $1 exchange rate was maintained for government transactions. This neither stabilized the economy nor satisfied the international sector. The total external debt reached almost $8 billion, and the Nigerian National Petroleum Corporation owed over $1 billion to its foreign partners. In responding to gasoline shortages, however, the government lowered the subsidy on petroleum products. Nigeria once had the lowest fuel prices in the world, but in 1994 gasoline prices were raised 400 percent—still at the lower end of the range of prices in the world. Holding the price down had

deprived the country of gasoline, as stocks were spirited over the borders to fetch higher prices or sold along the roadside at "unofficial" prices. However, the sharp price rise seemed one more hardship to endure for those on low and fixed incomes, already suffering from rapid inflation. The discomfort increased when extreme fuel shortages reappeared in 1997. Long lines at official stations prompted a black market rate of up to 80 naira ($3.60) per liter (about one quarter gallon), or about seven times the normal price; the shortage was attributed to deteriorating conditions in Nigeria's four refineries as well as to mismanagement and diversion of maintenance funds and to massive smuggling of petroleum out of the country for personal profit by high-placed government officials.

There could hardly be a more dramatic demonstration of policy failure: a country rich in petroleum incapable of providing its citizens with fuel. In 1998 the Abubakar government imposed a variety of measures to remedy the situation, from severe penalties for fuel diversion to emergency funds to repair refineries and pay for increased imports of refined petroleum. The government also raised the price at the pump from 11 to 25 naira per liter. At the same time, the government and its partner oil companies were bedeviled by increasing unrest and violence in the oil-producing areas and against the pumping operations themselves. By late 1998 these disruptions were having a serious impact on Nigerian oil production, a situation that complicated the inauguration of a stable civilian government. After President Obasanjo was inaugurated in May 1999, he tried to bring calm to the situation by voiding all contracts awarded in the six months prior to his administration. Since then, each attempt by the government in 2000, 2001, and subsequent years to raise the price at the pump has been met with the return of lines at filling stations. Efforts to reduce government spending by eliminating the petroleum subsidy for domestic consumption remain highly controversial because those efforts impact not only the cost of public transportation but also food and other daily essentials.

## Regulative Performance

At independence in 1960, the Nigeria Police Force was essentially regionalized. Because the police were frequently mobilized for political purposes during the rough and tumble politics of the 1960s, the military regime decided to consolidate the police function at the national level. It is this national police force that now enforces traffic laws and other government legislation. However, it is often still the case that "law and order" is maintained in individual communities—especially in rural areas—through traditional institutions and norms. Traditional leaders not only prevent deviant behavior but also take responsibility for the welfare of the "strangers" who, in accord with accepted procedures, have taken up residence in their communities.

Although Nigeria was under military rule from 1983 to 1999, the average citizen has not felt oppressed by an authoritarian state. That citizen is aware of the police presence at checkpoints along the country's highways, but fear of authority does not restrict citizen's actions to a significant degree. As in most Third World countries, there simply are not the resources available to the Nigerian government to keep close tabs on its large population.

Nigeria's judicial system remains vigorous, and until the advent of Abacha's reign it had been surprisingly diligent at following a rule of law through the various informally constituted regimes. Still, military regimes intruded on that rule of law. The regime imposed the State Security (Detention of Persons) Decree in 1984, which allows detention without trial of those "suspected of posing a threat to national security." State officials seemed to intervene with increasing frequency into the judicial system where political questions are involved.

Freedom of expression was reduced even further as Sani Abacha held onto power. Repression touched members of the political and military elite and internationally famous figures who hitherto had appeared to be safe. In 1994, writer Wole Soyinka was prevented from leaving the country by air, and his passport was seized. (He later slipped across the border and criticized the regime from abroad until after Abacha's death.) Prominent political prisoners under Abacha included former head of state (and future president) Olusegun Obasanjo and Moshood Abiola and former presidential candidate Shehu Yar'Adua. Abacha showed himself to be unconcerned about international opinion in allowing the execution of Ken Saro-Wiwa in the face of an international outcry and in ignoring Pope John Paul II's plea for release of political prisoners during a 1998 visit.

**The Census Issue**  One policy issue has overshadowed all the others since independence, because the outcome often determines how political goods will be distributed. A minor policy issue in some countries, in Nigeria population counts have been fraught with conflict. In a country where federal subsidies make up the lion's share of budgetary allocations at all levels, the distribution of population directly affects the distribution of resources. (Americans will recognize a similar issue that arose concerning undercounting of some ethnic groups and the homeless after the 1990 census in the United States, and in the debate over whether to use representative samples rather than the whole population in some aspects of the 2000 census.)

After a false start in 1962, a national census was conducted in 1963. It reported a total population of 55.6 million, making Nigeria the tenth largest country in the world. However, it found a majority of that population (30 million) to be in the north, a finding that was then and is always questioned by southern Nigerians, who maintain that a flyover or drive through the north and south will easily demonstrate that population densities are higher in the latter (although it is also true that the area of the north is much larger). Nevertheless, the 1963 census, or straight-line projections from it, remained the official source of population statistics for almost twenty years. At the same time, voices are continually raised in favor of a new "fair" count in the regions that perceive themselves undercounted.

In 1973, General Gowon's Supreme Military Council attempted a census update, and ordered that enumerators be accompanied by unarmed soldiers. With the prestige and integrity of the armed forces behind the count, the resulting figures presumably could be trusted, and used for economic planning, electoral preparation, and military disengagement. Gowon's optimism was misplaced. The 1973 census figures, when finally released, appeared as politically manipulated and inflated as the discredited results of a decade earlier. . . . Apparent overcounting in certain areas, especially in the north, revived the latent fears of regional domination that periodically roil Nigerian politics.[46]

After almost two additional decades of continued reliance on the 1963 figures, the Babangida government commissioned a new census to be conducted by a

National Population Commission. Following methodical pretesting and sampling, a census in November 1991 put the country's total population at 88.5 million, a substantial downward revision from estimates that had exceeded 100 million. According to this census, the highest population concentrations were in the states of Bauchi, Kaduna, Kano, Katsina, and Sokoto in the north, and Lagos, Oyo, and Rivers in the south. The census caused new consternation in the south, where feelings ran high that the figures had again been "cooked" to favor the north. As mentioned earlier, the recent 2006 census effort fared only slightly better.

## Conclusions on Performance

While our judgments on performance should be nuanced given the complexity of Nigeria's political environment and the problems it faces, an overall conclusion emerges unfailingly. In comparison to other countries with equivalent natural resources, skilled human resources, and size, Nigeria has not done well.

That outcome caused Chinua Achebe to write *The Problem with Nigeria*, in which he concluded that the "problem" was leadership. Until Nigerians can settle on a constitutional arrangement that provides responsive leadership from the national to the local levels, the country will continue to fall far short of its potential. Although the Second Republic failed, it was a significant improvement over the first in reining in the politicization of ethnicity. There was reason to be optimistic that the Constitution developed in the later years of the Babangida regime would introduce another increment of correction. Although Abubakar was able to move the country to civilian rule, his decision to base the transition on the poorly articulated Constitution drafted under Abacha in 1995 did not inspire confidence in most Nigerians that the new regime would be based on the rule of law. Democracy cannot be "delivered" by a military regime; indeed, further progress in democratization will depend on the formation and maintenance of a coalition with the strength to force the country in that direction.

A fatal flaw in political culture may have developed in Nigeria since independence, and it is part of the "curse of oil": public policy is often seen in Nigeria as the "national cake," and the unfortunate analogy suggests that "they"—the government—bake a cake that is distributed in slices sized to match the political influence of various constituencies. At least at the mass level, constituencies are defined in ethnic terms, and politics becomes a competition among ethnic groups for larger slices of cake. The analogy could of course be used to describe the politics of many countries, but not to the extreme degree that it applies in Nigeria. There, communities look to the government to provide for them. A successful Nigerian constitution must not only provide responsive leaders; it must also shift responsibility so that extractive and distributive performance come from the same budget, and so that there is some relationship between the amounts one pays into and receives from the public sector. Public goals based on community effort were the norm in most Nigerian traditions; that norm must be rediscovered.

## NIGERIA IN AFRICA AND IN THE WORLD

Nigeria (now along with South Africa) has the population and resource base to be a regional power, and it has stimulated hopes and fears among its neighbors concerning that potential. Under the First Republic (1960–1966), Nigeria generally focused inward and played a rather minor role in the continent's turbulent politics. But then came the civil war over Biafra in 1966; Nigeria's army grew from 10,000 to 250,000, the country's oil potential became known, and, as we have seen earlier, world powers took an interest in the war's outcome.

Some West African governments offered clear support to Biafra, a support Nigerians suspected grew from a desire to see their country divided up and thus reduced in influence. This was thought especially to be the case with Cote d'Ivoire (the Ivory Coast) under President Houphouet-Boigny, who favored Biafra with French support. When the war ended, relations among these countries were, as might be expected, strained.

Subsequently, Nigeria under General Gowon took a leading role in establishing, in 1975, the **Economic Community of West African States (ECOWAS),** hoping both to bring Nigeria closer to other West African countries while at the same time countering French influence in the region. The Ivoirian government had taken the lead in forming the Economic Community of West Africa, an exclusively French-speaking organization, and was wary of the predominant position that Nigeria might play in a wider regional organization. But Nigeria was successful in first approaching Togo, Benin, and Niger, the French-speaking countries with which it already had close ties, offering attractive economic inducements that included special petroleum prices. With this group in hand, Nigerian diplomats cast their net wider, and the representatives of sixteen West African governments signed the Treaty of Lagos. The ECOWAS treaty specified a two-year phase during which intracommunity tariffs would be frozen, followed by an eight-year period that would end with the removal of duties on trade among members. Finally, a common external tariff wall would be created.

Thus, West Africa under Nigerian leadership is partaking in the worldwide movement toward free-trade zones. As elsewhere, however, progress has been difficult. Ten years after its creation, ECOWAS reported that it had not made "tangible progress in practical terms," and by 1989 the member governments were $80 million in arrears in their contributions to the organization. The proportion of intracommunity trade in the member countries' total international trade has not changed since 1980. At the same time, ECOWAS has had better success as a regional political organization, especially in mediating disputes among member states, and in 1990 a Nigerian proposal was approved that created a standing mediation committee.[47]

Nigeria has played a prominent role in the region through commitment of its substantial military capacity, notably in supplying the leadership and the majority of troops for ECOMOG, the ECOWAS-sponsored peacekeeping force in Liberia. That operation was viewed a success, with armed conflict halted and elections held. Nigerian troops have also been stationed in Sierra Leone to protect that country's borders from incursions of Liberian rebels, and have confronted a Sierra Leonean military junta that overthrew an elected civilian government, an action more than a bit ironic, given the origins of the Abacha regime. Nigeria has participated in wider ranging United Nations operations in Lebanon, Rwanda, the former Yugoslavia, and Somalia. However, as in other countries, these overseas deployments are seriously questioned at home, given the country's financial difficulties.

Because of its prominence on the continent, Nigeria's international financial problems have been especially embarrassing. Forced along with other African nations to accept stringent structural adjustment planning from the World Bank and International Monetary Fund, Nigeria has reacted with frustration and anger. It has led the region's governments in their critique of international lenders' policies, hosting the meeting that led to the Lagos Plan of Action as a response to international debt-structuring proposals.

Of all the world powers, France plays the most prominent role in West Africa. Although the French interest focuses on its own former colonies, in recent years the French have come to believe that Nigeria's size and potential wealth should not be overlooked, and France actively promotes closer economic ties with Nigeria, a move that upsets Nigeria's French-speaking neighbors. The Western powers, especially Britain and the United States, were openly critical of Nigeria's military rulers and supported the country's return to civilian rule, especially during the Babangida regime and once again with Abdulsalami Abubakar. The United States and Britain condemned Babangida's 1993 election annulment, and they suspended aid as a result. However, this relationship was not important enough to Nigeria's rulers to modify their behavior. Presumably an embargo on purchases of Nigerian oil would have had that effect, but the industrial nations' governments did not have the will to take such a drastic step. Most observers saw the Abacha regime's treatment of dissenters as a calculation of how far it could silence opposition without provoking more severe international sanctions. In contrast, many Nigerians were critical of what they saw as the West's premature enthusiasm over actions that until then were only *promised* by Abubakar in 1998. Western support returned with enthusiasm upon Obasanjo's inauguration.

## PROSPECTS FOR DEVELOPMENT

Nigeria's political and economic setbacks do not equal the tragedies of Rwanda, Sudan, or Somalia, but the frustrations are nonetheless deep and enduring. Billions of desperately needed naira have been wasted, a few have grown rich at the expense of the poor, and accountability in government has proved highly elusive. Poet Tanure Ojaide captured this frustration in "No Longer Our Own Country," written in 1986:

> We have lost it,
> the country we were born into.
> We can now sing dirges
> of that commonwealth of yesterday—
> we live in a country
> that is no longer our own.[48]

In much of the world, the attraction of democracy has been its association with prosperity. Like other people, Nigerians are more interested in the outcome of the political process than in the process itself. Calls for better leadership and the welcome initially extended to some military regimes suggest that Nigerians' highest priorities are economic security and the rule of law. If these could be provided by generals, the country would probably accept an authoritarian system. However, at least since Plato we have known that benevolent authoritarianism is an elusive concept. Western democracies have developed on the premise that democracy is a necessary, if not sufficient, condition for accountable leadership. And Nigerians have had enough opportunities to compare the results of military rule with their expectations so that a majority of them are ready for another try at elective civilian rule. Perhaps another constitutional correction will be enough to usher in the long-term political stability for which they have hoped.

We have focused this discussion on those aspects of the Nigerian situation most amenable to correction. There remain several rather intractable problems that will be overcome only with truly revolutionary change. Larry Diamond has identified as a central problem for Nigeria the relationship between the economy and the state. In his words, "Stable democracy is associated with an autonomous, indigenous bourgeoisie, and inversely associated with extensive state control over the economy. In Nigeria, and throughout much of Africa, the swollen state has turned politics into a zero-sum game in which everything of value is at stake in an election, and hence candidates, communities, and parties feel compelled to win at any cost."[49] The answer appears to be the emergence of a vigorous private sector less dependent on government subsidies and freed from the kinds of patronage costs that have drained the initiative and resources of the private sector. In West Africa and the world, Nigerians have a reputation for entrepreneurship. The challenge is to reduce the role of government to that of providing necessary infrastructure and public welfare safety nets so that Nigerian entrepreneurial initiative can thrive. Oil revenues remain critical. As the sense of public duty among some of the military elite declined from Gowon and Murtala to Babangida and Abacha, a subculture developed among officer ranks that can be identified as "when do I get my turn?" Such corruption of values is common, but the availability of oil revenues means that authoritarian leaders need not seek their rents directly from the populace. Rather, they have learned that all they must do is control the spigot and the narrow slice of the population that operates and protects it, and opponents will be helpless. The oil workers' unions and the people whose homelands are located where the drilling is done must be neutralized; the rest could safely be ignored.

Mancur Olson observed that "resolute autocrats can survive even when they impose heinous amounts of suffering upon their peoples. When they are replaced it is for other reasons (e.g., succession crises) and often by another stationary bandit." He then concluded that democracy appears under "historical conditions and dispersions of resources that make it impossible for any one leader or group to assume all power."[50] These conditions are not close at hand for Nigeria, with its economy overwhelmingly dependent on oil and the state's resources controlled directly by the regime. In this situation, interactions among the military become supremely important. Abubakar proved not to be "another stationary bandit," but instead represented a faction of military leaders with no taste for politics and a desire to reprofessionalize the military services. Had he and his supporters not taken a longer term view than Abacha, the continued existence of Nigeria as a single state would have been in doubt. After inheriting a fifteen-year legacy of continuous military rule and misgovernment, there is some indication that the Obasanjo administration was able to achieve some successes. For example, privatization achieved success in the areas of telephone and domestic transportation. Other areas in which progress has been made are water, housing, and electricity. Nigeria is gradually becoming a service-oriented country, but profound political and social challenges remain.

# KEY TERMS

Abacha, Sani

Abiola, Moshood

Abuja

All Nigeria People's Party (ANPP)

Azikiwe, Nnamdi

Babangida, Ibrahim

Biafra

clientelism

Economic and Financial Crimes Commission (EFCC)

Economic Community of West African States (ECOWAS)

Hausa, Hausa-Fulani

Igbo (Ibo)

Independent National Election Commission (INEC)

Kaduna Mafia

Lagos

Movement for the Emancipation of the Niger Delta (MEND)

naira

National Union of Petroleum and Gas Workers (NUPENG)

neocolonial

Nigerian National Oil Corporation (NNOC)

Obasanjo, Olusegun

Organization of Petroleum Exporting Countries (OPEC)

patron-client network

Saro-Wiwa, Ken

Structural Adjustment Program (SAP)

Yar'Adua, Umar Musa

Yoruba

# SUGGESTED READINGS

Abernethy, David B. *The Political Dilemma of Popular Education: An African Case.* Stanford, CA: Stanford University Press, 1969.

Achebe, Chinhua. *A Man of the People.* New York: Doubleday-Anchor, 1967.

———. *The Trouble With Nigeria.* Enugu: Fourth Dimension Press, 1983.

Beckett, Paul, and Crawford Young, eds. *Dilemmas of Democracy in Nigeria.* Rochester, NY: University of Rochester University Press, 1997.

Coleman, James S. *Nigeria: Background to Nationalism.* Berkeley: University of California Press, 1958.

Crowder, Michael. *The Story of Nigeria,* 4th ed. London: Faber & Faber, 1978.

Diamond, Larry. *Class, Ethnicity, and Democracy in Nigeria: The Failure of the First Republic.* Syracuse, NY: Syracuse University Press, 1988.

———. "Nigeria: Pluralism, Statism and the Struggle for Democracy." In Larry Diamond et al. eds., *Democracy: Africa.* Boulder, CO: Lynne Rienner, 1988, 33–91.

Diamond, Larry, Anthony Kirk-Greene, and O. Oyediran, eds. *Transition Without End: Nigerian Politics and Civil Society Under Babangida.* Boulder, CO: Lynne Rienner, 1997.

Dudley, Billy. *An Introduction to Nigerian Government and Politics.* Bloomington: University of Indiana Press, 1982.

Gordon, David F. "Debt, Conditionality, and Reform: The International Relations of Economic Restructuring in Sub-Saharan Africa." In Thomas M. Callaghy and John Ravenhill, eds., *Hemmed In: Responses to Africa's Economic Decline.* New York: Columbia University Press, 1993, 90–129.

Graf, William D. *The Nigerian State: Political Economy, State Class and Political System in the Post-Colonial Era.* Portsmouth, NH: Heinemann Educational Books, 1988.

Guyer, Jane I. "The Spatial Dimensions of Civil Society in Africa: An Anthropologist Looks at Nigeria." In John W. Harbeson, Donald Rothchild, and Naomi Chazan, eds., *Civil Society and the State in Africa.* Boulder, CO: Lynne Rienner, 1994, 215–29.

Joseph, Richard A. *Democracy and Prebendal Politics in Nigeria: The Rise and Fall of the Second Republic.* Cambridge, England: Cambridge: University Press, 1987.

Kane, Ousmane. "The Rise of Muslim Reformism in Northern Nigeria: IZALA (The Society for the Removal of Heresy and Reinstatement of Tradition)." In Martin Marty and Scott Appleby, eds., *Accounting for Fundamentalisms.* Chicago: University of Chicago Press, 1994.

Koehn, Peter H. *Public Policy and Administration in Africa: Lessons From Nigeria.* Boulder, CO: Westview, 1990.

Lewis, Peter M., Pearl T. Robinson, and Barnett R. Rubin. *Stabilizing Nigeria: Sanctions, Incentives, and Support for Civil Society.* Washington, DC: Brookings Institution Press, 1998.

Metz, Helen Chapin, ed. *Nigeria: A Country Study.* 5th ed. Washington, DC: U.S. Government Printing Office, 1992.

Nafziger, E. Wayne. *The Economics of Political Instability: The Nigeria-Biafran War.* Boulder, CO: Westview, 1983.

Normandy, Elizabeth. "Nigeria." In Mark W. Delancey, ed., *Handbook of Political Science Research on Sub-Saharan Africa.* Westport, CT: Greenwood Press, 1992.

Ogbondah, Chris W. *Military Regimes and the Press in Nigeria, 1966–1993.* Lanham, MD: University Press of America, 1994.

Ohiorhenuan, John F. E. *Capital and the State in Nigeria.* New York: Greenwood Press, 1989.

Olagunju, Tunji, Adele Jinadu, and Sam Oyovbaire. *Transition to Democracy in Nigeria (1985–1993).* Ibadan, Nigeria: Safari Books, 1993.

Olayiwola, Peter O. *Petroleum and Structural Change in a Developing Country: The Case of Nigeria.* New York: Praeger, 1987.

Oyediran, O., ed. *Nigerian Government and Politics Under Military Rule 1968–79*. London: Macmillan, 1979.

Oyewole, Anthony. *Historical Dictionary of Nigeria*. Metuchen, NJ: Scarecrow Press, 1987.

Paden, John. *Muslim Civic Cultures and Conflict Resolution*. Washington, DC: Brookings Institution Press, 2005.

*Publius: The Journal of Federalism* 21, no. 4 (Fall 1991) [special issue on Nigeria].

Soyinka, Wole. *AkÈ: The Years of Childhood*. Ibadan, Nigeria: Spectrum Books, 1968.

Suberu, Rotimi T. *Federalism and Ethnic Conflict in Nigeria*. Washington, DC: U.S. Institute of Peace, 2001.

## INTERNET RESOURCES

**http://www.AllAfrica.com**

Federal government of Nigeria: **www.nigeria.gov.ng**

Current information on Nigeria, including news from the major daily papers in Lagos, can be obtained through the Nigeria

page of *Africa South of the Sahara: Selected Internet Resources*: **www-sul.stanford.edu/depts/ssrg/africa/guide.html**

## ENDNOTES

1. Clifford Geertz, *Old Societies and New States: The Quest for Modernity in Asia and Africa* (New York: Free Press of Glencoe, 1963).

2. Because Africans have frequently referred to their ethnic groups as "tribes" and to the conflicts among those groups as "tribalism," these terms seem appropriate to our discussion of ethnicity in Nigeria. The problem from an outside perspective is that the term "tribe" has been applied indiscriminately to small groups of villages or whole empires, and often in conjunction with the adjective "primitive." Thus "tribe" has lost any specific meaning and imparts prejudicial notions. One may ask whether, if the Yoruba or Igbo of Nigeria are tribes (of 30 million or 40 million), are not the less numerous peoples known as Norwegians or Irish also tribes? What is the distinction? And if ethnic conflict in Africa is "tribalism," the same phenomenon in Yugoslavia, Britain, Germany, or the United States deserves the same label.

3. This discussion relies principally on A. Oyewole, *Historical Dictionary of Nigeria* (Metuchen, NJ: Scarecrow Press, 1987); Michael Crowder, *The Story of Nigeria*, 4th ed. (London: Faber & Faber, 1978); and James S. Coleman, *Nigeria: Background to Nationalism* (Berkeley: University of California Press, 1958).

4. Crowder, *The Story of Nigeria*.

5. Peter Enahoro, *How to Be a Nigerian* (Ibadan, Nigeria: Caxton, 1966), 2.

6. Chinua Achebe, *Arrow of God* (Garden City, NY: Anchor Books, 1967) 65.

7. Wole Soyinka, *AkÉ: The Years of Childhood* (Ibadan, Nigeria: Spectrum Books, 1981), 200.

8. Billy Dudley, *An Introduction to Nigerian Government and Politics* (Bloomington: University of Indiana Press, 1982), 230.

9. World Bank, "World Development Indicators," in *World Development Report 2006* (Washington, DC: World Bank, 2006).

10. Patrick Smith, "Economy," in *Africa South of the Sahara 1994* (London: Europa 1994), 660.

11. "Abuja Faces Population Explosion Crisis," *This Day*, 12 September 2002.

12. "Government Cracks Down on Biafra Secessionist Movement," IRIN, 19 April 2005; and "More Than 100 People Arrested at Separatist Biafra Rally," IRIN, 10 May 2005.

13. E. Wayne Nafziger, *The Economics of Political Instability: The Nigeria-Biafra War* (Boulder, CO: Westview, 1983), 73.

14. Barbara J. Callaway, *Muslim Hausa Women in Nigeria* (Syracuse, NY: Syracuse University Press, 1987), 93.

15. Naomi Chazan and Victor Lavine, "Africa and the Middle East," in John Harbeson and Donald Rothchild (eds.), *Africa in World Politics* (Boulder: Westview 1991), 202–27.

16. Afrobarometer Round 1: Compendium of Comparative Data From a Twelve Nation Survey (March 2002). For earlier evidence of this same pattern, see Sidney Verba, "The Parochial and the Polity," in Sidney Verba and Lucian Pye, eds., *The Citizen and Politics: A Comparative Perspective* (Stamford, CT: Greylock Publishers, 1978), 3–28.

17. Robert A. Dahl, *After the Revolution* (New Haven, CT: Yale University Press, 1971); see also the discussion in Billy Dudley, *An Introduction to Nigerian Government and Politics* (Bloomington: Indiana University Press, 1982), 80–83.

18. Afrobarometer Round 1.

19. P. C. Lloyd, "The Yoruba of Nigeria," in James L. Gibbs, Jr., ed., *Peoples of Africa* (New York: Holt, Rinehart & Winston, 1965), 565.

20. See the discussion in Dudley, *An Introduction to Nigerian Government*, 80–83.

21. Chinua Achebe, *The Trouble with Nigeria* (Enugu, Nigeria, Fourth Dimension Press, 1983), 42.

22. BBC News, "Nigerian Leaders 'Stole' $380 billion," 20 October 2006; BBC News, "Nigeria Governors in Graft Probe," 28 September 2006; and BBC News, "Obasanjo Accuses Deputy of Fraud," 7 September 2006.

23. The discussion that follows draws on Crawford Young's treatment of socialization in his chapter on "Politics in Africa" in earlier editions of this book.

24. In anthropological usage, polygamy is a general term for marriage to more than one spouse. Polygamy is preferred to describe the marriage of one man to more than one woman (and polyandry for the reverse). However, polygamy is the term in general use in Nigeria and elsewhere in English-speaking Africa.

25. David B. Abernethy, *The Political Dilemma of Popular Education* (Stanford, CA: Stanford University Press, 1969), 18.

The description of education development that follows draws on this same source.

26. *A Handbook of Information on Basic Education 2003* (Abuja: Federal Ministry of Education and UNESCO 2003).

27. Afrobarometer Survey, "Attitudes Toward Democracy and Markets in Nigeria," 2000; U.S. Department of State, "Country Reports on Human Rights Practices: Nigeria," 4 March 2002; and Committee to Protect Journalists, Attacks on the Press in 2001 (Washington, DC: Brooking Institution, 2002).

28. Reporters Without Borders, *Annual Report 2006;* and "Publisher Under Arrest After 'Greedy Stella' Obasanjo Story," IRIN, 9 May 2005.

29. Peter Enahoro, *The Complete Nigerian* (Lagos: Malthouse Press, 1992), 121.

30. Ousmane Kane, "The Rise of Muslim Reformism in Northern Nigeria," in Martin Marty and Scot Appleby, eds., *Accounting for Fundamentalism* (Chicago: University of Chicago Press, 1994).

31. Associated Press, "Hundreds Flee Nigerian City Swept By Riots," 25 November 2002.

32. Peter H. Koehn, *Public Policy and Administration in Africa* (Boulder, CO: Westview, 1990), 16.

33. As noted in Chapter 5, the concept of consociational arrangement comes from Arend Lijphart, *Democracy in Plural Societies* (New Haven, CT: Yale University Press, 1977).

34. Keohn, *Public Policy and Administration in Africa*, 17–18, cites various sources for these totals.

35. Soyinka, *AkÉ*, 199–200.

36. Richard Sklar and C. S. Whitaker, Jr., "Nigeria," in James S. Coleman and Carl G. Rosberg, Jr., eds. *Political Parties and National Integration in Tropical Africa* (Berkeley: University of California Press, 1964), 636.

37. Richard A. Joseph, *Democracy and Prebendal Politics in Nigeria* (Cambridge: Cambridge University Press, 1987), 133–34.

38. Joseph, *Democracy and Prebendal Policy in Nigeria*. Joseph calls the Nigerian version of patronage prebendalism, "patterns of political behavior which rest on the justifying principle that such offices should be competed for and then utilized for the personal benefit of officeholders as well as for their reference or support group. The official public purpose of the office often becomes a secondary concern, however much that purpose may have been originally cited in its creation or during the periodic competition to fill it" (8).

39. This account of party development through the first years of independence is taken from Sklar and Whitaker, "Nigeria."

40. "Cameroons" here refers to the English-speaking portion of the contemporary country of Cameroon (French Cameroun) on Nigeria's eastern border. The former German colony of that name was divided into League of Nations Trust Territories after World War I under British and French control. The NCNC was meant to include members from the British trust territory as well as from Nigeria, but in a pre-independence plebiscite, the English-speaking Cameroonians opted for incorporation into Cameroon. The NCNC then was renamed the National Convention of Nigerian Citizens.

41. Address of Brigadier Murtala Muhammed, reprinted as the preface to the *Report of the Constitution Drafting Committee* (Lagos: Ministry of Information, 1976), quoted in Dudley, *Introduction to Nigerian Government*, 127.

42. Letter to the editor, *Lagos,* 1983; quoted in Joseph, *Democracy and Prebendal Politics in Nigeria.*

43. Wole Soyinka, *AkÉ*, 201.

44. Diamond, "Nigeria," 53.

45. I. William Zartman, with Sayre Schatz, "Introduction," in I. William Zartman, ed., *The Political Economy of Nigeria* (New York: Praeger, 1983), 13. The military figures cited here come from Ruth Sivard, "World Military and Social Expenditures 1996" (Leesburg, VA: WMSE Publications, 1996), and "The Military Balance 2001–2002" (London: Oxford University Press, 2001).

46. Claude E. Welch, *No Farewell to Arms?* (Boulder, CO: Westview, 1987), 10.

47. The preceding treatment of the formation of ECOWAS is drawn from Carol Lancaster, "The Lagos Three: Economic Regionalism in Sub-Saharan Africa," in John W. Harbeson and Donald Rothchild, eds., *Africa in World Politics* (Boulder, CO, Westview Press, 1991), 249–67.

48. Tanure Ojaide, *The Blood of Peace and Other Poems* (London: Heinemann, 1991), 9.

49. Diamond, "Nigeria," 69.

50. Mancur Olson, "Dictatorship, Democracy, and Development," *American Political Science Review* 87 (September 3): 573.

# UNITED STATES

0  250  500  750  1000 Miles

0  250  500  750  1000 Kilometers

MAINE
Augusta
VERMONT
NEW HAMPSHIRE
Montpelier
Concord
MASSACHUSETTS
Boston
Albany
Providence
NEW YORK
Hartford
RHODE ISLAND
CONNECTICUT
PENNSYLVANIA
NEW JERSEY
Harrisburg
Trenton
Dover
Annapolis
DELAWARE
WEST
WASHINGTON, DC
VIRGINIA
MARYLAND
Richmond
Charleston
VIRGINIA
Frankfort

WASHINGTON
Olympia
Columbia R.
Salem
Helena
Missouri R.
NORTH DAKOTA
MINNESOTA
Lake Superior
MONTANA
Bismark
OREGON
IDAHO
Snake R.
SOUTH DAKOTA
WISCONSIN
St. Paul
MICHIGAN
Boise
Pierre
Madison
Lake Michigan
Lake Huron
Lansing
Lake Erie
Lake Ontario

WYOMING
IOWA
Cheyenne
Des Moines
OHIO
NEVADA
NEBRASKA
ILLINOIS
INDIANA
Columbus
Sacramento
Carson City
Lincoln
Salt Lake City
Springfield
Indianapolis
UTAH
Denver
KENTUCKY
CALIFORNIA
COLORADO
Topeka
Ohio R.
KANSAS
MISSOURI
Jefferson City
NORTH CAROLINA
Raleigh
OKLAHOMA
Nashville
ARKANSAS
TENNESSEE
SOUTH CAROLINA
Santa Fe
Colorado R.
Columbia
PACIFIC
ARIZONA
Oklahoma City
Atlanta
OCEAN
NEW MEXICO
Little Rock
ALABAMA
ATLANTIC
Phoenix
GEORGIA
OCEAN
TEXAS
MISSISSIPPI
Montgomery
Rio Grande
LOUISIANA
Jackson
Tallahassee
Austin
Baton Rouge
Mississippi R.
Missouri R.
Mississippi R.

FLORIDA

0  400 MI
0  400 KM
Arctic
Ocean
ALASKA
Juneau
Pacific Ocean

Honolulu
HAWAII
0  100 Miles
0  100 Kilometers
Pacific Ocean

Caribbean Sea
San Juan
PUERTO RICO
0  30 Miles
0  30 Kilometers

# POLITICS IN THE UNITED STATES

*Austin Ranney and Thad Kousser*

## Country Bio

### UNITED STATES

**Population**
300 million

**Territory**
3,475,031 square miles

**Year of Independence**
1776

**Year of Current Constitution**
September 17, 1787, effective March 4, 1789

**Head of State**
President Barack Obama

**Head of Government**
President Barack Obama

**Languages**
English, Spanish (spoken by a sizeable minority)

**Religions**
Protestant 52%, Roman Catholic 24%, Muslim 1%, Mormon 1%, Jewish 1%, none or not stated 21%

> And what should they know of England
> Who only England know?
>
> RUDYARD KIPLING[1]

Why a chapter on the United States in a book on comparative politics? One reason is that most of its readers are Americans,[2] and politics in the United States affects our lives far more than politics in any other country. Moreover, however feeble we may feel is our personal power to influence the actions of our government, it is certainly greater than our personal power to influence the actions of other nations' governments.

The question Rudyard Kipling asked about the English in the quotation above can be asked with equal relevance about Americans. There are, of course, many excellent textbooks on the American political system written by American authors and intended for American students. But most of them make few references to, let alone systematic comparisons with, other political systems. Thus, viewing American politics with a special focus on how it resembles and differs from politics in other nations will help us better meet our version of Kipling's challenge. It may even give us some

insight into how the distinctive ways of American politics are likely to affect our country's ability to meet the enormous challenges it will face in the years ahead.

## CURRENT POLICY CHALLENGES

The policy challenges facing the United States were radically altered by the events of September 11, 2001 (see Box 19.1). The day after the terrorist attacks President George W. Bush announced that they had been planned and executed by members of Al Qaeda, an international terrorist organization of radical Muslim fundamentalists led by Osama bin Laden (described further in Chapter 1). Bush declared that the attacks "were more than acts of terror, they were acts of war." He added that the "war against terror" would be resolutely fought by the United States and its friends not only against Al Qaeda but also against any nation-state that sheltered terrorists, financed them, or supported them in any way.

The new war was unlike any other in American history. The enemy was not another nation-state, such as Nazi Germany or Imperial Japan in World War II, or

**BOX 19.1**

## September 11, 2001

At 8:45 A.M. on that fateful Tuesday, a hijacked American Airlines Boeing 767 was flown into the north tower of the World Trade Center in New York City, setting it on fire. At 9:03 A.M. a hijacked United Airlines Boeing 767 was flown into the Center's south tower, setting it on fire. At 9:43 A.M. a hijacked American Airlines Boeing 757 was flown into the west side of the Pentagon outside Washington, D.C. And at 10:10 A.M. a hijacked United Airlines Boeing 757 crashed in a rural area near Pittsburgh (it is believed that the plane was targeted on the White House or the U.S. Capitol, but

that some passengers' efforts to recapture the plane deflected its course). At 10:05 A.M. the Trade Center's south tower, its structural steel fatally weakened by the fire's intense heat, collapsed from the top down, followed at 10:28 A.M. by the north tower.

The deaths totaled nearly 3,000, including the airplanes' hijackers, passengers, and crews, and the people caught in the burning buildings. This was the most killed in any peacetime disaster in the nation's history and far more than those slain in any other terrorist attack anywhere.

even a seceding section of the United States, like the Confederacy in the American Civil War. Consequently, there were no organized armies to be defeated in battle by the U.S. armed forces, no enemy governments to acknowledge defeat and sign peace treaties, indeed, no way to tell when the war was over and whether the United States had won. Instead, the enemy was an unknown number of shadowy, hard-to-find secret cells of terrorists dedicated to attacking American civilians, who had no way of knowing what "victory" would be and how we would recognize it. So the United States now faces a long and difficult twilight struggle in which most of its other policy challenges will take second place.

Nevertheless, many such challenges will remain. In domestic affairs, the problem of the economic and social status of African-Americans—some version of which has bedeviled the nation from its beginnings—remains high on the agenda. While African-Americans today are in many respects better off than they were a generation ago, they still lag behind whites in many areas, including family incomes, crime and imprisonment rates, formal education, housing quality, family stability, vulnerability to such diseases as AIDS and prostate cancer, and life expectancy. The nation's attention was focused on many of these inequalities after Hurricane Katrina flooded and destroyed many areas of New Orleans, a heavily African-American city, in August 2005. The lack of planning for this frequently-predicted emergency and the agonizingly slow response to it by all levels of government led many, both black and white, to question whether the

race and poverty of New Orleans' residents put them especially at risk.

In the new millennium, our nation of immigrants will once again debate immigration policy and the nature of U.S. citizenship. The acceleration in recent decades in the ethnic and linguistic diversity of nearly every state, along with a rise in the number of illegal immigrants, has led to demands for a more inclusive citizenship policy as well as calls for increased border security. During the spring of 2006, Latino activists led a series of demonstrations in favor of a more open immigration policy that echoed the civil rights marches of the 1960s in their scale, fervor, and level of controversy. Conflicts over immigration policy, affirmative action, and the use of languages other than English will surely continue well into the twenty-first century.

Other, equally familiar domestic policy challenges will continue, including such diverse matters as the "war on drugs," measuring national standards of educational achievement by uniform tests, reconciling environmental protection with economic growth, and addressing the bitter conflict over abortion between pro-choice and pro-life forces.

In the early years of the twenty-first century, the American economy, the largest in the world, was struggling with a brief recession, a weakening dollar, and a stock market that from 2000 to 2003 lost over 40 percent of its value. While the market and the economy overall recovered from that fall, stocks crashed even more rapidly in late 2008 as home foreclosures, rising gas prices, and a credit crunch sent America and then much of the world into a spiraling recession. As the nation struggles to recover from this immediate crisis, long-term challenges remain. Unfunded liabilities in Social Security and particularly in the Medicare system threaten to consume much of the federal government's budget and dampen economic growth in future decades. While the United States stands today as the world's economic leader, the expanding economies of China and India promise to threaten its position eventually.

In foreign policy, the unchallenged position of the United States as the world's most powerful nation and leader of the forces supporting democratic governments will certainly continue in the early twenty-first century. But national hubris is not warranted, for such a position carries perils in international affairs.

Perhaps the biggest issue is whether the United States should conduct its foreign policy mainly or solely through the structures and procedures of the United Nations (UN) or do what the U.S. president thinks is imperative even if the UN votes against it. This policy choice arose starkly in 2002–2003 in the debate over the Bush administration's intention to invade Iraq and remove its dictator, Saddam Hussein, without the clear authorization of a resolution by the United Nations, over the strong protests of public opinion in most nations, and over the determined opposition of such traditional allies as France and Germany.

The rationale underlying the Bush administration's choice is known as the "Bush doctrine." First enunciated by President George W. Bush after the Al Qaeda attacks of September 11, 2001, the doctrine declares that the United States should no longer wait to be attacked before it acts. It should, with the help of allies if possible but alone if necessary, take preemptive military action against any nation or terrorist group that possesses weapons of mass destruction that might be used against the United States. It was intended to replace such earlier policies as the Truman doctrine (containment of hostile regimes), the Reagan doctrine (support all Freedom Fighters), and the Clinton doctrine (always act multilaterally).

The doctrine guided the Bush administration's decision in March 2003 to invade Iraq despite the U.S. failure to win endorsement from the UN Security Council. The war was quick, and Baghdad fell within weeks. Yet winning the peace has proved much more difficult than winning the war, as it has become clear

that the United States committed too few troops and was too optimistic in its hopes to be welcomed as a liberator. The ongoing conflict with insurgents who oppose the American presence in Iraq has intensified, and more than 4,200 American soldiers had been killed in Iraq by December 2008. Even after the first democratic elections in January 2005 and the formation of a cabinet in May 2006, it appeared that continued U.S. presence in Iraq was required to maintain order. Perhaps most damaging to America's international prestige, President Bush's domestic approval, and the prospects for future use of the Bush doctrine, no weapons of mass destruction have been found in Iraq. American voters signaled their support for a new foreign policy direction in 2008 by electing Barack Obama, who pledged to adopt a multilateral approach and to remove combat troops from Iraq within 16 months of taking office.

This brief sketch of some of the high-priority domestic and foreign policy challenges facing the United States in the new century underlines the gravity, and in some cases the intractability, of its problems. Let us see how well or poorly its political system is equipped to deal with them.

## THE UNITED STATES AMONG THE WORLD'S NATIONS

### History

The world today is divided among more than 190 nations. The great majority of them are "new nations," that is, nations that have recently broken away from older countries and become independent sovereign nations. Indeed, 73 percent of all modern nations have achieved their independence since the end of World War II in 1945.

Some of these nations have established political systems capable of meeting enough of their citizens' needs that their polities have remained relatively stable and peaceful. Unhappily, however, many of them have changed their political systems with some frequency since independence and have yet to find one that works well enough to stay in business very long (Cambodia, Ethiopia, Rwanda, Somalia, and Yugoslavia are among the sadder examples).

Seymour Martin Lipset has argued that the United States was the world's "first new nation," in the sense that the problems it faced in its efforts to establish a stable and principled political system after winning its independence from Great Britain in 1783 were in many respects similar to those faced by the nations created after 1945.[3] Thus, the United States, which is so often described as a young nation, is actually an old one—not as old as, say, Great Britain, France, or Japan, but much older than most other modern nations. The United States has the world's oldest written constitution still in effect. It can fairly claim to have become a democracy well before any other large modern nation. In the 1790s, it developed the world's first modern political parties, and today's Democratic Party is generally recognized as the world's oldest active political party.

We will touch on several developments in American history throughout this chapter, but here we will emphasize only that the Civil War (1861–1865) is the United States' great historical watershed. Before 1861 it was a much-disputed question whether the United States was merely a convenient alliance among independent sovereign states, which had every right to secede whenever they wished, or an indissoluble sovereign nation whose people chose to divide power between the national government and the state governments. After 1865, in both law and fact, it was established that the United States was, as every American schoolchild is drilled to know, "one nation, indivisible," and not a federation of sovereign states.

Before 1861 many Americans, especially those in the eleven southern states that seceded to form the Confederacy, felt that they were first and foremost citizens of their states and derived their American citizenship from the membership of their states in the union. (The most famous example was Robert E. Lee: he strongly opposed both slavery and secession, and yet when Virginia seceded he refused command of the Union Army and cast his lot with Virginia because he felt he owed his primary loyalty to his state, not his nation.) The Fourteenth Amendment to the Constitution, ratified in 1868, removed all doubt by declaring: "All persons born or naturalized in the United States and subject to the jurisdiction thereof, are citizens of the United States and of the State wherein they reside." In short, all Americans are now primarily citizens of the United States, and derivatively become citizens of the state in which they reside. (Interested readers can see the broader discussion of federalism in Chapter 6.)

## Geography

The United States has jurisdiction over a territory totaling 3,475,031 square miles. This makes it geographically the fourth largest nation in the world, smaller only than Russia (6,592,800 square miles), Canada (3,849,674 square miles) and the People's Republic of China (3,696,100 square miles).[4] The United States is bounded by the Atlantic Ocean on the east, the Pacific Ocean on the west, Canada on the north, and Mexico on the south. This secure location—great oceans on two sides, militarily weak nations on the other two sides—made feasible the foreign policy of isolation from alliances and wars with foreign countries that the United States pursued until the end of the nineteenth century. In these days of intercontinental ballistic missiles, orbiting spy satellites, and international terrorism, however, no nation, including the United States, can count on its geographical location to keep it isolated from world politics.

## Population

The U.S. Bureau of the Census estimated that the total population in the United States surpassed 300 million in 2006. This makes it the third most populous nation in the world, behind China with 1.3 billion and India with 1.1 billion.[5] The U.S. rate of population increase has been impressive. The first census in 1790 reported a total population of 3.9 million, and so the 2004 figure represents a staggering increase of 7,413% percent in 214 years. Over 50 million people have moved from other parts of the world to the United States—a phenomenon characterized by the British analyst H. G. Nicholas as "the greatest movement of population in western history."[6] Accordingly, one of the most important facts to recognize about the United States is that, more than any other nation in history, it is a nation of immigrants. The census classifies only 1.8 percent of the population as being of Native American or Hawaiian ancestry;[7] the rest are immigrants or descendants of immigrants from all over the world.

Most immigrants came in one or the other of three historic waves: first, 1840–1860, mainly from Western Europe and Scandinavia; second, 1870–1920, mainly from Asia and Eastern Europe; and third, 1965 present, mainly from Latin America and Asia. In the 1920s, Congress imposed a ceiling on the number of immigrants allowed, and the immigration rate dropped sharply. It rebounded after the Immigration and Nationality Act was amended in 1965 to eliminate caps on the number of people who could migrate from each country. Today, about 700,000 to one million *legal* immigrants continue to arrive in America every year. In addition, an estimated seven million *illegal* immigrants—those who are foreign born and enter the country without inspection or violate the terms of a visa—reside in the United States[8] Figure 19.1 divides up America's foreign-born population (including both legal and illegal immigrants) according to places of birth.

Thus, from its beginnings the United States has received far more immigrants than any other nation in history, and it has the most ethnically and culturally diverse population the world has ever seen (only India comes close). Later, we will consider some of the consequences for American politics.

## Economy

At the end of the 1990s the United States had the world's largest economy. In 2003, its gross national product (GNP), or the total value of all the goods and services it produced, was calculated at $11.0 trillion, compared with Japan's $4.4 trillion and Germany's $2.1 trillion.[9] The American dollar continues to be the world's basic monetary unit; the value of most nations' currencies is customarily measured by how many euros, pounds, rubles, yen, and other units it takes to exchange for part or all of a dollar.

**Birthplaces of Foreign-Born Population, 2003**    **FIGURE 19.1**

Source: *Statistical Abstract of the United States: 2006* (Washington, DC: Bureau of the Census, 2006), Table 44, 45.

Some economists believe that American economic dominance has ended. The United States, which for many years was the world's greatest creditor nation, has become the world's greatest debtor nation, in part because Americans continue to buy billions of dollars more of foreign goods than foreigners buy of American goods, and in part because of the longstanding enormous deficits in the federal government's budget. From 1980 through 1997, the federal government spent a total of $3.1 trillion more than it took in, then ran modest surpluses from 1998 to 2001, but has returned to record-setting deficits since then. By 2005, the accumulated gross national debt was more than $8 trillion.[10]

America has long been regarded as the citadel of capitalist economic ideas and institutions, and the main antagonist of people and nations who believe in socialism. If we measure the degree of capitalism in an economy by the proportion of economic enterprise that is privately owned and operated for profit, that characterization is correct. Even so, American economic institutions and practices have never come close to meeting the standards for completely free enterprise laid down by such laissez-faire economists as Adam Smith in the eighteenth century and Milton Friedman in the twentieth. These economists advocated the barest minimum of government interference in economic affairs, including no government regulation of the operations, profits, and wages paid by successful businesses and no government subsidies or "bailouts" for unsuccessful businesses.

Yet even before Congress authorized a $700 billion bailout of financial institutions and other large corporations in the fall of 2008, American governments have subsidized American businesses in many ways. They conduct research that businesses can use to develop new products, and pay to market American products in other countries. State, local, and federal governments work together to provide public goods, such as education and a transportation infrastructure. Federal tax law subsidizes the pensions and health plans that businesses offer to their employees, creating a hybrid public/private safety net that works something like a European welfare state, though only for those who get a job with good benefits.[11] Congress imposes tariffs and import quotas on certain foreign manufactured goods so as to prevent them from undercutting American manufacturers. Federal laws guarantee that all workers will be paid a certain minimum wage regardless of what they would get in a truly free market—and so on. Most of these goodies have come from political pressure by business associations, labor unions, and other pressure groups. Thus, it seems fair to say that, while most Americans say they believe in free enterprise, they prefer to practice safe enterprise.

### America's Position in World Politics

Until the end of the nineteenth century the United States followed an isolationist foreign policy and was only a minor player in world politics. The changeover began with the Spanish-American War (1898), Theodore Roosevelt's mediation of the Russo-Japanese War (1905), and America's belated entry (1917) into World War I (1914–1918). Since 1918 America has been a leading player on the world stage.

From 1945 to 1989, world politics was dominated by the "Cold War" between the two great superpowers and their allies: the United States, leading an alliance of Western capitalist/democratic nations; and the Soviet Union, leading an alliance of Eastern communist/authoritarian nations. The Cold War came to an end in the early 1990s when the Soviet Union was formally dissolved (see Chapter 12) and Eastern European nations established their independence.

In the first years of the new millennium, the United States continues to be the world's most powerful nation, but a new international order is emerging. Whatever its final shape may be, the United States will continue to play a leading role, though that role is bound to be different from what it was during the Cold War.

### THE CONSTITUTIONAL SYSTEM

As in most modern nations (Great Britain and Israel are two notable exceptions), the basic structure of the American system of government is set forth in a written constitution—the Constitution of the United States, a document drawn up in 1787, ratified in 1788, and inaugurated in 1789. It is the world's oldest written constitution still in force.

Of course, the Constitution of the 2000s differs from that of 1789 in a number of important ways. It has been formally amended twenty-seven times, the most recent being the 1992 amendment that provided that no law changing the compensation for members of Congress shall take effect until an election of members of the House has been held.[12] Among the most important amendments are the following. The first ten, known collectively as the **Bill of Rights,** list the rights of individuals that the national government is forbidden to abridge (see Box 19.2).

The Fourteenth Amendment, ratified just after the Civil War, makes national citizenship legally superior to state citizenship, and prohibits the states from violating the "privileges and immunities" of U.S. citizens—which, by judicial interpretation, has come to mean nearly all the rights guaranteed against the national government by the first ten amendments. Other major amendments have outlawed slavery (the Thirteenth), guaranteed the right to vote to former slaves (the Fifteenth) and women (the Nineteenth),

---

### The U.S. Bill of Rights

**BOX 19.2**

1. Freedom of religion, speech, press.
2. Right to bear arms.
3. Freedom from quartering soldiers without owner's consent.
4. No unreasonable searches and seizures.
5. Trial of civilians only after indictment by a grand jury; no double jeopardy; prohibition against compelled self-incrimination; no deprivation of life, liberty, or property without due process of law; no taking of private property for public use without just compensation.
6. In criminal prosecutions, right to speedy and public trial by an impartial jury; defendant must be informed

of the nature and cause of accusations; defendant has power to compel testimony by witnesses in his or her favor; right to assistance of counsel.

7. Guarantee of trial by jury where the amount in controversy is over twenty dollars.
8. No excessive bail, no excessive fines, no cruel and unusual punishments.
9. Enumeration of certain rights in the Constitution shall not be construed to deny or diminish others retained by the people.
10. Powers not delegated to the national government nor prohibited to the states are reserved to the states or to the people.

limited presidents to two elective terms (the Twenty-Second), and spelled out the conditions under which an incapacitated president can be replaced (the Twenty-Fifth). Even with these amendments, most of the basic elements of the 1789 Constitution have remained in force, whereas the written constitutions in many other countries and in most of the American states have been replaced altogether several times. Thus, if durability is a mark of constitutional strength, the Constitution of the United States is one of the strongest in history.

Yet the words in the Constitution do not tell all there is to be told about the basic structure of the American constitutional system. A number of customs, usages, and judicial decisions have significantly altered our way of governing without changing a word in the Constitution. Examples are the addition of judicial review, the development of political parties, and the conversion of the presidential selection process from a closed process by small cliques of insiders to popular elections open to all citizens. We will say more about each of these changes below.

Taken together, the provisions of the written Constitution of the United States and their associated customs and usages add up to a constitutional system that has three distinctive features: federalism, separation of powers, and judicial review.

## Federalism

**Federalism** is a system in which governmental power is divided between a national government and several subnational governments, each of which is legally supreme in its assigned sphere. This system has some ancient precursors, notably the Achaean League of Greek city-states in the third century B.C. and the Swiss Confederation founded in the sixteenth century A.D. But the men who wrote the American Constitution established the first modern form of federalism. They did so because they had to. The 1787 convention in Philadelphia was called because its members felt that the new nation needed a much stronger national government than the Articles of Confederation provided, but the representatives from the small states refused to join any national government that did not preserve most of their established powers. The framers broke the resulting stalemate by dividing power between the national and the state governments, and gave each state equal representation in the national Senate. Only

thus could the large and small states agree on a new constitution.

Even so, some of the framers regarded federalism as more than a political expedient. James Madison, for example, believed that the greatest threat to human rights in a popular government is the tyranny of popular majorities that results when one faction seizes control of the entire power of government and uses it to advance its own special interests at the expense of all other interests. He saw a division of power between the national and state governments, combined with separation of powers, as the best way to prevent such a disaster.

Federalism has been widely praised as one of the greatest American contributions to the art of government. A number of nations have adopted it as a way of enabling different regions with sharply different cultures and interests to join together as one nation. The clearest examples of such nations today are Australia, Canada, Germany, and Switzerland, but significant elements of federalism are also found in systems as disparate as those of Brazil, India, and Mexico.

The American federal system divides government power in the following principal ways:

- Powers specifically assigned to the federal[13] government, such as the power to declare war, make treaties with foreign nations, coin money, and regulate commerce between the states.
- Powers reserved to the states by the Tenth Amendment. The main powers in this category are those over education, marriage and divorce, intrastate commerce, and regulation of motor vehicles. However, the federal government often grants money to the states to help them build and operate schools, construct and repair highways, make welfare payments to the poor and the sick, and so on. The states do not have to accept the money, but if they do they also have to accept federal standards governing how the money is to be spent and federal monitoring to make sure it is spent that way.
- Powers that can be exercised by both the federal government and the states, such as imposing taxes and defining and punishing crimes.
- Powers forbidden to the federal government, mainly those in the first eight amendments, such as abridging freedom of speech, press, and religion, and various guarantees of fair trials for persons accused of crimes.
- Powers forbidden to the state governments. Some of these are in the body of the Constitution, but

the main ones are the Fourteenth Amendment's requirements that no state shall "abridge the privileges or immunities of citizens of the United States; nor shall any State deprive any person of life, liberty, or property without due process of law; nor Deny to any person within its jurisdiction the equal protection of the laws." A series of U.S. Supreme Court decisions have interpreted these phrases to mean that almost all the specific liberties guaranteed against the federal government in the first eight amendments are also guaranteed against the state governments by the Fourteenth Amendment.

When all is said and done, however, perhaps the most important single point to note about the nature of American federalism is made in Article VI of the Constitution:

> This Constitution, and the laws of the United States which shall be made in Pursuance thereof; and all Treaties made, or which shall be made, under the Authority of the United States, shall be the supreme Law of the Land; and the Judges in every State shall be bound thereby, any Thing in the Constitution or Laws of any State to the Contrary notwithstanding.

In short, while the federal government cannot constitutionally interfere with the powers assigned exclusively to the states, whenever a state constitution or law is inconsistent with a law or treaty the federal government has adopted in accordance with its proper powers, the conflicting state constitution and law must yield. Moreover, it is the Supreme Court of the United States, an organ of the federal government and not of the state governments, that decides which acts of the federal government and the state governments are within their respective powers. Thus, to the extent that the American federal system is a competition between the national government and the states, the chief umpire is a member of one of the two competing teams.

## Separation of Powers

Since most analysts of the American system maintain that separation of powers is the most important single difference between the U.S. system (which is called a **presidential democracy**) and most other democratic systems (which are called *parliamentary democracies*), let us be clear on the institution's main features.

**Separation of powers** means the constitutional division of government power among separate legislative, executive, and judicial branches (see Figure 19.2). The Constitution of the United States specifically vests the legislative power in Congress (Article I), the executive power in the president (Article II), and the judicial power in the federal courts, headed by the Supreme Court (Article III).

The three branches are separated in several ways, the most important of which is the requirement in Article I, Section 6: "No Person holding any Office under the United States, shall be a Member of either House during his Continuance in Office." This provision means that each branch is operated by persons entirely distinct from those operating the other two branches. Thus, for example, when Representative Norman Mineta was appointed Secretary of Transportation in 2001, he had to resign his seat in the House before he could take up his new post. This, of course, is the direct opposite of the fusion-of-powers rule in parliamentary democracies, such as Great Britain and Germany, which require the head of the executive branch to be a member of Parliament.

The persons heading each branch of the U.S. government are selected by different procedures for different terms. Members of the House of Representatives are elected directly by the voters for two-year terms, with no limit on the number of terms they can serve. Members of the Senate are elected directly by the voters for six-year terms without term limits, and their terms are staggered so that one-third of the Senate comes up for election or reelection every two years.[14]

The president is elected indirectly by the **electoral college** (which is selected by direct popular election) for a four-year term, and is limited to two full elected terms. All federal judges, including the members of the Supreme Court, are appointed by the president with the approval of a majority of the Senate, and they hold office until death, resignation, or removal by Congress.

The other main devices ensuring the separation of powers are the **checks and balances** by which each branch can keep the other two branches from invading its constitutional powers. For example, the Senate can disapprove top-level presidential appointments and refuse to ratify treaties. The two chambers of Congress acting together can impeach, convict, and remove the president or federal judges from office. They can (and

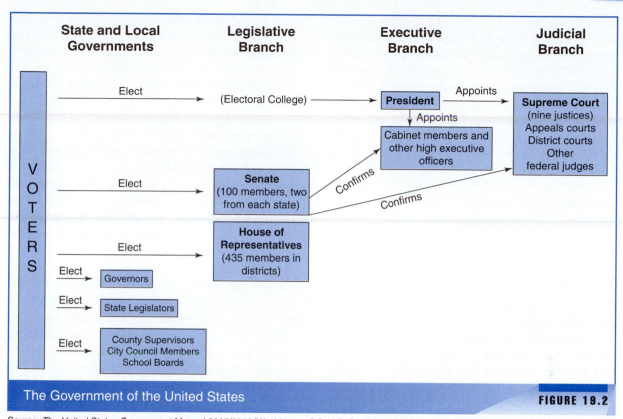

**State and Local Governments** | **Legislative Branch** | **Executive Branch** | **Judicial Branch**

VOTERS

Elect → (Electoral College) → **President** — Appoints → **Supreme Court** (nine justices) Appeals courts District courts Other federal judges

President → Appoints → Cabinet members and other high executive officers

Elect → **Senate** (100 members, two from each state) — Confirms → Cabinet members and other high executive officers

Senate — Confirms → Supreme Court (nine justices) Appeals courts District courts Other federal judges

Elect → **House of Representatives** (435 members in districts)

Elect → Governors

Elect → State Legislators

Elect → County Supervisors City Council Members School Boards

**The Government of the United States**

**FIGURE 19.2**

Source: *The United States Government Manual 2005/2006* (Washington, DC: U.S. Government Printing Office, 2005), 21.

often do) deny the president the legislation, appropriations, and taxes he requests. The president, in turn, can veto any act of Congress, and the Constitution requires a two-thirds vote of both chambers to override the veto. The president also makes the initial appointments of all federal judges. Presidents have normally nominated judges who are likely to agree with their political philosophies and policy preferences, but once appointed and confirmed judges rule without political supervision.

The Supreme Court, through its power of judicial review, can declare any act of the president or Congress null and void on the ground that it violates the Constitution. Such a decision can be overturned only by a constitutional amendment or by the Court, usually with new members, changing its mind.

Some scholars believe that the American system is more accurately described as a system of "separated branches exercising shared powers," since getting government action usually requires some kind of joint action by the Congress and the president, with the acquiescence of the Supreme Court. Separation

of powers is what most political scientists have called this feature of the system since the time of the *Federalist Papers*. Whatever it is called, this constitutional feature, more than any other, makes the American system different from most other democratic systems.[15]

## Judicial Review

**Judicial review** can be defined as the power of a court to render a legislative or executive act null and void on the ground of unconstitutionality. All American courts, including the lower federal courts and all levels of the state courts, exercise this power on occasion. But the final word on all issues involving an interpretation of the national Constitution (which, as we have seen, is "the supreme law of the land") belongs to the U.S. Supreme Court.

Although every democracy has to determine who has the final word on what its constitution allows and prohibits, the United States is one of the few democracies in which that power is given to the top appellate court of the regular court system. Some countries, such as Italy, give the final word to special tribunals rather than to bodies in their regular court systems, while in others (such as Mexico and Switzerland) the power includes only the "federal umpire" power, and not the power to override decisions of the national executive and legislature. Thus, judicial review is a prominent but not exclusive feature of the American constitutional system.

## POLITICAL CULTURE AND SOCIALIZATION

The American constitutional system, though important to how Americans make political decisions, is not the whole story. To a considerable degree, the American political system functions as it does because it is operated by Americans rather than by Britons, Italians, Mexicans, or Iraqis, and it does what it does because Americans have a distinctive political culture that underlies, animates, and shapes all of the formal institutions we have reviewed.

Two of this book's editors say that "a **political culture** is a particular distribution of political attitudes, values, feelings, information, and skills" that "affects the conduct of [a nation's] citizens and leaders throughout the political system."[16] Chapter 3 discusses political culture and socialization in a comparative perspective, and America's unique political culture deserves close attention.

### Melting Pot or Patchwork Quilt?

Most Americans are immigrants or descendants of immigrants who came from many different cultures in Africa, Asia, Western and Eastern Europe, and Latin America. Thus, throughout most of its history the United States has had to deal with how best to fit the immigrants and their different cultures into American economic, social, and political life.

Throughout our history, two visions of how immigrants should become incorporated into society have clashed in intellectual discourse, policy debates, and actual practice. One vision is of a **"melting pot"** that blends all the different cultures of immigrants into one uniquely American culture, which was to be expressed and passed on in one language, the American version of English. Some room was left for

such special ethnic folkways as Polish weddings, Irish wakes, and Mexican food, but the paramount task given to the educational system was to turn everyone into an English-speaking American imbued with the main values and attitudes of the nation's political culture.

A contrasting vision sees America as a true cultural **"patchwork quilt"** (the phrase is Jesse Jackson's)—an array of the languages, history, customs, and values of each of the nation's major ethnic groups, each receiving the same attention, respect, and importance as every other, with none dominant. This view rejects the melting pot idea that the ancient and distinct cultures of immigrant groups should be homogenized into one prevailing national culture—a culture which, they say, is not truly a blend of all cultures but rather the culture of Western Europe, especially Great Britain. While the patchwork quilt metaphor was recently coined and is today associated with some leaders among the African-American, Latino, and Asian communities, members of various immigrant groups have sought to cling to their cultural identities and native languages for over a century. Italian, Irish, and especially German immigrants often resisted melting into America's customs and language, and reshaped the mainstream culture and even the English language.

Among the policies advocated by adherents to the patchwork quilt vision are bilingual education (educating minority-group children in their native languages rather than forcing them to learn English as their primary language); printing ballots and other official documents in languages other than English; and broadening school curricula so as to give full and fair attention to the contributions of African, Asian, and Latin cultures as well as of British and Western European cultures.

Some opposition has set in against this movement. One manifestation is the laws adopted by several states and the May 2006 vote by the U.S. Senate declaring English to be the official language. Political scientist Sam Huntington's book, *Who are We? The Challenges to America's National Identity* offered a controversial defense of the Anglo-Protestant culture against a threatened erosion by today's wave of immigration from Latin America. The clash between the competing melting pot and patchwork quilt visions of immigrant assimilation will likely continue throughout the twenty-first century.

| | United States | Great Britain | France | Germany | Italy |
|---|---|---|---|---|---|
| **Trust in Government in Five Western Nations (in percentages)** TABLE 19.1 | | | | | |
| Most elected officials are trustworthy | 44 | 39 | 30 | 32 | 26 |
| Elected officials care what people like me think | 41 | 43 | 26 | 20 | 15 |
| Government is really run for the benefit of all the people | 48 | 57 | 52 | 30 | 16 |
| Trust the government | 40 | 57 | 33 | 41 | 35 |
| Average | 43 | 49 | 35 | 31 | 23 |

Source: *1997 Deconstructing Distrust Survey*, Pew Research Center for the People and the Press.

## Main Elements of the Traditional American Political Culture

The first dimensions of political culture that political scientists usually consider are called trust in institutions, and trust in government and/or trust in leaders. How do Americans compare with other peoples on these dimensions? Some of the answers are presented in Table 19.1, which compares the levels of popular trust in government in the United States and four Western European nations.

Table 19.1 shows that significantly greater proportions of Americans than of British, Germans, French, or Italians believe that most elected officials are trustworthy. On the other hand, fewer Americans than Britons or French believe that government is really run for the benefit of all the people. Averaging the answers on all four trust-in-government questions shows that Americans rank above the French, Germans, and Italians, but below the British. These findings do not support the charge made by some commentators that Americans are exceptionally "alienated" from their government. Moreover, other studies have shown that more Americans say they are very proud of their country (80 percent) and are willing to fight for it (71 percent) than the citizens of Great Britain, Spain, Italy, France, and Germany say about their countries (where the proportions range from 55 and 62 percent in Great Britain down to 21 percent and 35 percent in Germany).[17]

Thus, while Americans may trust their governments to do what is right less than some Western Europeans do, they are nevertheless more proud of being Americans and more willing to fight for America than the Western Europeans are for their countries. How can we explain this paradox?

The answer may lie in the fact that throughout history most Americans have strongly held two ideas that may be logically (but not emotionally) inconsistent. One is the idea that ordinary Americans are good, solid, reliable folks with plenty of common sense, and that America is a wonderful country. Conversely, they feel that the *government*, which is not the same thing as the country, is, as former President Ronald Reagan put it, "the problem, not the solution," and they feel that the professional politicians who fill its offices, lead its parties, and conduct its business are self-seeking lightweights more interested in winning votes and getting reelected than in making courageous and forward-looking policies to solve the nation's problems. Thus many Americans love their country but distrust the politicians who run its governments.

Another dimension of political culture is the degree to which ordinary people believe that their preferences significantly influence public officials. One of the findings of the first major comparative study of political cultures was that Americans score higher on this dimension than people in Great Britain, Germany, Italy, and Mexico, and that in all five countries better educated people score higher than less educated people.[18] Subsequent studies have confirmed that Americans generally feel more "politically efficacious" in this sense than do the citizens of most other nations.

Political scientists usually think of ideology as a comprehensive and strongly held set of convictions about how governments ought to make their decisions and/or what those decisions ought to be. The ideologies that receive the most attention in discussions of the political cultures of other nations are socialism and capitalism, with the Left leaning more toward socialism and the Right leaning more toward capitalism. Considerable attention is also paid to democracy and authoritarianism, and constitutionalism and totalitarianism. Almost every comparative study of political cultures concludes that ideology plays a smaller role in American political culture than in many others, with only handfuls of Americans supporting such classically European ideologies as socialism, communism, or fascism.[19]

Another exceptional feature of our nation is the depth of the conviction among most Americans—black and white, women and men, young and old—that they have certain basic rights and that often the best way to make sure they get their rights is not to wait for executives, legislatures, and bureaucrats to do the right thing but to file lawsuits to force public officials—and other private individuals—to honor their rights. The **litigiousness** of Americans—that is, their tendency to file lawsuits against government officials and other private citizens for violating their rights—gives the courts a central role in America. American legal scholar Robert Kagan argues that litigation in the United States accomplishes (at a much higher cost) the same things that European nations accomplish through regulation.[20] America has pursued this different path most likely because of the notion, espoused by populists like President Andrew Jackson, that the common man has enough wisdom to supervise everything, even his government.

## Political Socialization

Political socialization is the process by which children are introduced to the values and attitudes of their society, shaping their notions of what the political world is like and which people, policies, and institutions are good and bad. That process in America is much the same as in every other modern populous industrialized democracy. Political socialization begins in children as young as age 3 or 4 and continues until old age and death. Children typically begin by perceiving some political figures, notably the president and the local policeman, as important persons outside their own families. As they grow older their perceptions broaden and deepen, and they learn about political parties, legislators, judges, and public policies and issues.

The main agencies shaping Americans' political socialization are their families (especially their parents), schoolteachers, friends, schoolmates, work associates, and the mass communications media. Most recent studies agree that parents continue to have the most powerful impact on most people's political socialization. However, as the influence of the mass communications media has increased in recent years, parents' impact has lessened. This should not surprise us, for most analysts of political life in America and the other large-scale industrial democracies agree that the mass media, especially television, have become one of the most important forces—many would say *the* most important force—affecting people's political socialization, attitudes, and behavior.

The term **mass communications media** includes all the devices used to transmit information, thought, or feeling to a mass audience that does not see the communicator face-to-face. They fall into two categories: the print media (newspapers, magazines, books, and pamphlets) and the electronic media (radio, broadcast television, cable and satellite television, and the Internet).

The relative political importance of these media in America and three European democracies is shown in Table 19.2. It demonstrates that television is the most important source of information about politics for most Americans, as well as for most Britons, Germans, and French, with newspapers a distant second in all four nations. In all four nations the other media, such as direct communications among people, are less important. Note that the figures on Internet usage, taken from surveys conducted in 2000 and 2003, likely understate its growing importance.

The United States, like most other industrialized democracies, has a mixture of publicly owned and privately owned television and radio stations and networks. The privately owned media are much more important than the publicly owned in America: there are three times as many private as public broadcasting stations, and the public stations usually have only about 10 percent of the viewers. Additionally, nearly all high-circulation newspapers, magazines, and websites are privately owned and supported by advertising revenues and subscribers.

The political content produced by print media outlets is almost entirely unregulated by government because of the First Amendment's protection of freedom of the press (see again Box 19.2). About the only restrictions on what is printed are libel and slander laws, but in the landmark case of *New York Times v. Sullivan* (1964), the U.S. Supreme Court held that public officials and public figures cannot collect damages for remarks made about them in the print media unless those comments are (1) knowingly false

**TABLE 19.2**

Most Important Source of Political Information (in percentages)

|  | United States 2000 | Great Britain 2003 | Germany 2003 | France 2003 |
|---|---|---|---|---|
| Television | 70 | 54 | 75 | 66 |
| Newspapers | 39 | 44 | 59 | 40 |
| Radio | 15 | 28 | 38 | 36 |
| Internet | 11 | 18 | 14 | 15 |
| Magazines, other print media | 4 | 16 | 24 | 23 |
| Personal discussion | — | 18 | 20 | 25 |
| Other | 1 | 33 | 14 | 19 |

Source: Russell J. Dalton, *Citizen Politics: Public Opinion and Political Parties in Advanced Industrial Democracies*, 4th ed. (Washington, DC: C.Q. Press, 2006), Table 2.1, 23.

or made with a "reckless disregard" for their truth and (2) made with proved "malice" as a deliberate attempt to damage the victim's public reputation and standing—a charge that is very difficult to prove.[21]

By contrast, radio and television stations are much more closely regulated than the print media. They can broadcast only if they are granted a license by the Federal Communications Commission (FCC). That license requires that the political content of programs meet certain standards. For example, the stations must make available to all candidates for a particular political office an equal opportunity to make their appeals; they do not have to *give* any of them free time, but if they do give time to one candidate they must give it to all. If they sell time to one candidate, they must sell it to all at the same rates and offer comparably desirable times. They cannot charge political advertisers higher rates than they charge commercial advertisers.

The U.S. Supreme Court has consistently upheld the government's power to impose such restrictions on the electronic media while denying government any comparable power over the print media. The reasons have to do with what is generally called the **scarcity doctrine:** the Court has found that there is no limit, other than economic, on the number of newspapers, books, magazines, or pamphlets that can be printed and circulated. But there is a physical limit on the number of television or radio stations that can operate in a given portion of the broadcast spectrum. Accordingly, said the Court, broadcasting is a public resource, much like the national parks or navigable rivers; this gives the government the right not only to

allocate frequencies, but also to set standards to ensure that their use will promote "the public convenience, interest, or necessity."[22]

Perhaps the most liberated media outlets are independent Internet sites, which are not subject to licensing requirements, do not have to stay in the good graces of a large range of advertising clients, and have little reputation to lose if they publish news reports that become discredited. Web logs, or "blogs," authored by activists from every part of the ideological spectrum, play an increasingly important (and often-criticized) role in campaigns, with their ability to spread fact, rumor, and baseless accusation across cyberspace with unchecked speed. Because of the Internet's rising importance in politics, regulation of its political content is an evolving area of policy and jurisprudence.

## POLITICAL PARTICIPATION AND RECRUITMENT

### Participation by Voting

Since voting in elections is the main way in which ordinary citizens in all democracies actually participate in their nations' governing processes, most political scientists believe that **voting turnout**—the percentage of all the people eligible to vote who actually do so—is one of the most important indicators of any democratic system's health. Studies of voting turnout in the world's democracies, like that in Table 19.3, usually find that the turnout is lower in the United States than in any other democracy except Switzerland.

## TABLE 19.3

### Average Voting Turnout in Elections to Lower House, 1961–1999

| Nation | Average Turnout |
| --- | --- |
| Australia† | 95 |
| Belgium† | 92 |
| Italy† | 90 |
| Sweden | 88 |
| New Zealand | 87 |
| Germany | 86 |
| Canada | 75 |
| United Kingdom | 75 |
| France | 75 |
| Japan | 69 |
| India | 59 |
| United States | 52* |
| Switzerland | 52 |

†Compulsory voting law
*Presidential elections

Source: Adapted from Mark N. Franklin, "The Dynamics of Electoral Participation," in Lawrence LeDuc, Richard G. Niemi, and Pippa Norris, eds., *Comparing Democracies* 2 (Thousand Oaks, CA: Sage 2002), Table 7.1, 150.

Many commentators in America have also pointed to figures suggesting that voter turnout has declined dramatically here over the past few decades as signs of a deep sickness in U.S. politics. They have claimed, variously, that it is a symptom of too much negative campaigning, too few good candidates, the rising role of money in campaigns, the diminishing role of parties in grassroots politics, and many other ills. However, recent research shows that these are false diagnoses of what turns out to be a healthy patient: turnout has remained fairly stable in America over the past thirty years.

The conventional wisdom that turnout had dropped was wrong because it relied on a misleading approximation of turnout, which calculated the percentage of those old enough to vote who actually did so. The problem with this measure is that many people who are old enough to vote in the United States are not eligible to cast a ballot, some because they are not citizens and some because they are convicted felons living in states that bar them from voting. As the percentage of Americans who are noncitizens (including both legal and illegal immigrants) or felons has grown in recent decades, a smaller portion of the voting age population

has been eligible to vote. Scholars who counted up these groups and correctly calculated the percentage of eligible voters who participate found that turnout in presidential elections has remained steady at 55–60 percent since 1972 (after the Twenty-Sixth Amendment gave 18-year-olds the right to vote, and turnout in fact dropped).[23]

Further scrutinizing what goes into these turnout figures makes America look better compared to the rest of the world, and points out a key obstacle to voter participation here. When voting turnout is counted in exactly the same way in the United States as it is in other democracies—as a percentage of registered voters—the American record looks much better. In America, as in most of the world's other democracies, citizens' names must appear on voting registers before they can legally vote. But the United States differs from other nations in one important respect: in most other countries, getting on the register requires no effort by the voter. Public authorities take the initiative to get all eligible citizens enrolled, a job often made easier in countries that have a national list of residents. As a result, almost every citizen of voting age is registered to vote.

In the United States, by contrast, there is no list of residents, and each state regulates **voting registration.** In most states, would-be voters must make an effort to get on the register; no public official will do it for them. Moreover, in most democratic countries when voters move from one part of the country to another, they are automatically struck off the register in the place they leave and are added to the register in the place they move to, all with no effort on their part. In contrast, when people move from one U.S. state to another they are not automatically added to the register in their new state.[24] One study that compared turnout of registered voters in the United States, which averages 86.8 percent, with turnout of registered voters in twenty-four other democracies found that the United States ranks eleventh highest on this measure.[25]

This ranking is still lower than many might expect from the world's self-described citadel of democracy. Another explanation for America's low voting turnout arises from the fact that American voters are called on to cast far more votes than the citizens of any other country (only Switzerland comes close). In the parliamentary democracies, the only national elections are those for the national parliament, in which voters normally vote for one candidate or for one party. They also vote periodically for a candidate or a party in the elections for the city or rural district in which they live. In the federal systems, they also vote for a member of their state or provincial parliament. Hence, in most democracies other than the United States and Switzerland, the typical voter makes a total of only four or five voting decisions over a period of four or five years.[26]

In the United States, the combination of separation of powers, federalism, the direct primary, and, at the state and local levels, the initiative and referendum means that citizens may be faced with several *hundred* electoral decisions in a period of four years. At the national level, voters are called on to vote in the presidential primaries of their parties, and in the general election to decide (mostly) between the Democratic and Republican candidates. They are also expected to vote in primary elections and general elections every two years for members of the House of Representatives and twice in every six years for members of the Senate. At the state and local levels not only are the leading executive officials (governors and mayors) and members of the legislatures nominated in primary elections and elected in general elections, but in most states and localities a considerable number of other offices that are appointed positions in most other democracies—for example, state secretaries of state, attorneys general, treasurers, superintendents of education, judges, school superintendents, and members of local school boards, sanitary commissions, park commissions, and so on—are selected by much the same primary-plus-general election procedures.

Direct democracy processes, such as the **direct initiative** (a proposal for a new law that goes before voters if enough of them sign a petition), and the **popular referendum** (a vote on whether or not to keep an existing law), give many Americans even more choices to make at the ballot box. Although the U.S. federal government has never held a direct democracy election, twenty-four states and many local governments make the initiative process available, meaning that about 70 percent of Americans live in a city or state with the initiative.[27] This sometimes adds as many as thirty complex policy choices to a ballot.

Thus American citizens are called on to vote far more often and on more questions than those of any other country except Switzerland (where voters in many cantons also have direct democracy). Surely the opportunity to vote in free, fair, and competitive elections is a *sine qua non* of democratic government, and therefore a good thing. Yet a familiar saying is that there can be too much of a good thing, and many Americans leaving their polling places after casting their ninetieth (or more) vote

of the year are likely to conclude that the sheer number of voting decisions in America is a case in point.[28]

## Participation by Other Means

Voting, of course, is only one of several ways citizens can participate in politics. They can also serve in office; work in political parties; donate money to candidates, parties, and causes; attend rallies; take part in street demonstrations; send letters, telegrams, faxes, and e-mail messages to their elected representatives; write letters and op-ed pieces to newspapers; call radio and television talk shows; try to persuade families and friends; file lawsuits against public officials; and so on. These other forms of participation have not been studied as extensively as voting, but Russell Dalton has collected some interesting comparative data on conventional and unconventional forms of participation in the United States and some Western European countries (see Table 19.4).

The responses in Table 19.4 show that citizens of France are more likely than citizens of the United States, Great Britain, or Germany to participate in demonstrations and political strikes, whereas Americans are more likely than the others to persuade other people how to vote and to work with citizen groups.

Several other studies have found that the form of participation most frequently claimed by Americans is voting in elections (53 percent), followed by stating their political opinions to others (32 percent), contributing money to campaigns (12 percent), displaying political bumper-stickers and signs (9 percent), and attending political meetings or rallies (8 percent). Only 4 percent report belonging to a political club or working for a political party.[29]

In short, Americans participate in politics in ways other than voting in elections as much or more than the citizens of the other Western democracies for whom we have reliable information. These data certainly do not support the conclusion that Americans are in any way more alienated or lazier than the citizens of other democracies.

## RECRUITMENT OF LEADERS

Recruitment is the process whereby, out of the millions of a nation's citizens, emerge the few hundreds or thousands who hold elective and appointive public office, play leading roles in parties and pressure

| Nonvoting Forms of Political Participation in Four Democracies (in percentages) | | | | TABLE 19.4 |

| Activity | United States | Great Britain | Germany | France |
|---|---|---|---|---|
| **Voting** | | | | |
| Voted in national election | 53 | 72 | 74 | 61 |
| **Campaign Activity** | | | | |
| Attempt to convince others how to vote | 49 | — | 28 | 29 |
| Attend meeting/rally | 8 | 3 | 5 | 6 |
| Work for party/candidate | 3 | 3 | 7 | 7 |
| **Communal Activity** | | | | |
| Sign a petition | 81 | 81 | 47 | 68 |
| Membership in public interest group | 33 | 8 | 8 | 6 |
| **Protest Activity** | | | | |
| Participate in lawful demonstrations | 21 | 13 | 22 | 39 |
| Join in boycott | 25 | 17 | 10 | 13 |
| Participate in unofficial strike | 6 | 9 | 2 | 12 |

Source: All figures are from Russell J. Dalton, *Citizen Politics in Western Democracies*, 4th ed. (Washington, DC: C.Q. Press, 2006). Voting figures are taken from p. 40, campaign activity from pp. 44–46, communal activity from p. 49 and p. 68, and protest activity from p. 68.

groups, decide how the mass communications media will portray politics, and, within the limits permitted by the general public, make public policy.

Many scholars have studied leadership recruitment in many countries and have found certain general tendencies that are also evident in American politics. For instance, American leaders, like leaders in other countries, are drawn disproportionately from the middle and upper ranges of wealth and status. The reason lies not in the existence of any conspiracy to oppress the lower classes but in the kinds of knowledge and skills a person must have to win the support needed for selection as a leader. These skills are more likely to be acquired and developed by well-educated rather than poorly educated people. For example, people's chances to climb in a political party or a pressure group, to be selected for public office, or to be appointed to higher administrative offices are considerably enhanced if they have the ability to speak well in public, and, for elected officials increasingly, to look and sound good on television.

The federal and state governments choose most of their administrative employees by procedures and standards other than the unabashed political patronage that prevailed until the late nineteenth century. In today's system, initial selection is made according to the applicants' abilities to score well on standardized examinations or possession of other abilities and experience desired by their employers, and salary increases and promotions depend on job performance rather than on party connections. Since the merit system was established in 1883, more and more federal positions have been placed under it or under the "general schedule" category, and today only about 1 percent are available for purely political appointments.

Accordingly, in most respects elite recruitment in the United States differs very little from its counterparts in other advanced industrialized democracies. But in one aspect of that process—the nomination of candidates for elective office—the United States is unlike any other nation in the world.

## The Unique Direct Primary

We can divide the process of electing public officials into three parts: (1) *candidate selection*, the process by which political parties decide which people to name as their standard-bearers and campaign for; (2) *nomination*, the process by which public authorities decide which people's names will be printed on the official ballots; and (3) *election*, the process by which the voters register their choices among the nominees.

Many political scientists believe that candidate selection is the most important of the three processes. After all, the recruitment of public officials is essentially one of narrowing the choices from many to one. For example, in 2000 about 130 million Americans satisfied all the constitutional requirements for being elected president. Theoretically, all 130 million names could have been printed on the ballot and each voter could have had an absolutely free choice among them. But, of course, no voter can possibly make a meaningful choice among 130 million alternatives, and so a practical democratic election requires that the choices be narrowed down to a manageable number. The same is true for elections to office in all democratic countries.

In the United States, as in every other democracy, the narrowing process is accomplished mainly by the political parties. Each party chooses its candidates and gives their names to the election authorities, and those names appear on the ballot.[30] Accordingly, in 2004 the Democrats chose John Kerry to be their presidential candidate over Howard Dean, Wesley Clark, John Edwards, Al Sharpton, Carol Moseley Braun, Bob Graham, Dick Gephardt, Dennis Kucinich, and Joe Lieberman. President George W. Bush did not face any serious contenders for the Republican Party's nomination. These nominations made it relatively easy for the voters to make the final choice between Bush and Kerry.

Given the crucial role of candidate selection in democratic elections, it is important to recognize that the United States is the only nation in the world that makes most of its nominations by direct primaries. In nearly all the parliamentary democracies, the parties' candidates for parliament are chosen by the parties' leaders or by small groups of card-carrying, dues-paying party members. A few countries, such as Germany and Finland, require the parties to choose their candidates by secret votes of local party members in procedures that resemble but, strictly speaking, are not direct primaries. Consequently, in every nation except the United States the candidates are selected by only a few hundred, or at most a few thousand, party insiders.[31]

In the United States, nominations for almost all major elective public offices[32] are made by **direct primaries,** in which candidates are selected directly by the voters in government-conducted elections rather than indirectly by party leaders in caucuses and conventions. Moreover—and this is the key difference between America's direct primaries and the primary-like procedures in other countries mentioned earlier—public laws, not party rules, determine who is qualified to vote in a particular party's primary. In 2002, twenty-seven states held **closed primaries,** in which only persons pre-registered as members of a particular party could vote in that party's primary. Eleven states held **crossover primaries,** which are the same as closed primaries except that voters do not have to make a public choice of the party primary in which they will vote until election day. Nine states held **open primaries,** in which there is no party registration of any kind, and voters can vote in whichever party primary they choose (they can, however, vote in only one party's primary in any particular election) with no public disclosure of their choice.[33] In its 2000 *California Democratic Party v. Jones* decision, the U.S. Supreme Court prohibited California's **blanket primary** (which allowed voters to switch back and forth between the parties in voting for nominees for particular offices) on the grounds that it violated a party's First Amendment right to free association. This decision, which also caused Alaska and Washington to alter their primary systems, makes clear the extent to which nomination procedures are formal, regulated by the government, and structured by the Constitution.

Direct primaries make candidate selection in the United States by far the most open and participatory in the world. As noted earlier, in all other countries only a few thousand dues-paying party members at most participate in choosing candidates; in the United States they are chosen by any registered voter who wants to participate, and millions do in every election cycle. To give just one example: although American presidential candidates are formally selected by national nominating conventions, a great majority of the delegates to both conventions are chosen by direct primaries. In 2004, a grand total of 24,227,443 votes were cast in the Democratic and Republican presidential primaries.[34]

The American system for choosing its presidents may be wiser or more foolish than the ways other democracies select their top political leaders, but it is far more participatory.

## INTEREST ARTICULATION: PRESSURE GROUPS AND PACS

As we have seen throughout this book, every society has a number of different and conflicting political interests,[35] and the more advanced the economy and the more heterogeneous the society the more individuals and groups there are with interests that to some degree conflict with other interests. The inevitable clash of these interests generates the political process, which consists of two main parts: (1) interest articulation, by which the persons and groups make known their desires for government action or inaction; and (2) interest aggregation, by which various demands are mobilized and combined to press for favorable government policies. That is why many political scientists agree with Harold D. Lasswell that the essence of government is deciding "who gets what, when, and how."[36]

In most democracies interests are articulated mainly by pressure groups and political parties, and the governing parties also aggregate interests in formulating and implementing their programs. In the United States, however, the political parties are much weaker and less cohesive than those in most other democratic systems. Consequently, pressure groups play a major role in both interest articulation and aggregation in the United States.

Many foreign observers of America's peculiar politics have been especially struck by the great variety and power of our organized political groups.[37] Today they are even more numerous and important than in the past. They take two main forms, each of which specializes in a particular technique for influencing government: (1) political action committees and campaign contributions, and (2) pressure groups and lobbying.

## PACs and Campaign Contributions

Strictly speaking, a **political action committee (PAC)** is any organization that is not formally affiliated with a particular party or candidate and spends money to influence the outcome of elections. PACs differ from political parties in two main respects. First, unlike parties, they do not nominate candidates and put them on ballots with PAC labels; rather, they support or oppose candidates nominated by the parties. Second, PACs are interested mainly in the policies public officials make, not in the party labels those officials bear. Hence, they often support candidates of both major parties who are sympathetic to the PACs' particular policy preferences.

Such organizations have operated in American politics at least since the Civil War, and some of them have had considerable success. For example, the Anti-Saloon League was founded in 1893 to support both Democratic and Republican candidates for Congress pledged to support a constitutional amendment outlawing the manufacture and sale of alcoholic beverages. Most historians believe that it deserves much of the credit (blame?) for the adoption of the Eighteenth Amendment (prohibition) in 1919. One of the most powerful organizations in the second half of the twentieth century was the Committee on Political Education (COPE) of the AFL-CIO, which has supplied millions of dollars and thousands of election workers for candidates (mostly but not entirely Democrats) sympathetic to organized labor.

The greatest increase in the number and activity of PACs in American history has come since 1974 as an unanticipated (and, by many, unwanted) consequence of that year's amendments to the Federal Election Campaign Act. The amendments set low limits on the amount of money individuals could contribute to a candidate or a party, but considerably higher limits on what organizations could contribute. They also stipulated that although labor unions and business corporations could not directly contribute money to election campaigns, they could sponsor PACs and their PACs could make campaign contributions as long as the funds came from voluntary contributions by sympathetic individuals rather than by direct levies on union and corporate funds.

In ruling on the constitutionality of these rules, the Supreme Court upheld the limits on direct contributions, but said that limiting the amounts of money that an individual or an organization can spend on behalf of a candidate (that is, by broadcasting or publishing ads *not* controlled by candidates or parties) was a violation of the First Amendment's guarantee of free speech.[38]

These changes in the substance and interpretation of the campaign finance laws led most politically active interests to conclude that forming a PAC was the best way to influence election outcomes, and that is just what they have done. In 1974, only 608 PACs operated in national elections; by 2006 the number had exploded to 4,210 (see Box 19.3).

At present, each PAC must register with the Federal Election Commission and periodically report its receipts (who contributed and how much) and its expenditures (to what candidates it gave contributions and how much, and how much it spent on its own independent campaigning). A PAC can contribute $5,000 to a particular candidate in a primary election and another $5,000 in the general election. Yet there is

## Top Ten PACs in Overall Spending, 2003–2004

BOX 19.3

| Rank | PAC Name | Overall Spending |
|---|---|---|
| 1 | MoveOn PAC | $30,043,750 |
| 2 | Emily's List | 26,051,693 |
| 3 | America Coming Together | 15,154,735 |
| 4 | American Federation of State, County & Municipal Employees-PEOPLE, Qualified | 14,056,945 |
| 5 | United Auto Workers Voluntary Community Action Program | 13,336,541 |
| 6 | National Rifle Association Political Victory Fund | 12,772,488 |
| 7 | Service Employees International Union Committee on Political Education | 12,461,614 |
| 8 | Democratic Republican Independent Voter Education PAC for International Brotherhood of Teamsters | 10,468,934 |
| 9 | Republican Issues Campaign | 7,959,860 |
| 10 | Voice of Teachers for Education/Committee on Political Education of New York State United Teachers | 7,634,014 |

Source: Harold W. Stanley and Richard G. Niemi, *Vital Statistics on American Politics, 2005–2006* (Washington, DC: Congressional Quarterly, 2006), Table 215, 107–08.

no limit on the total amount it can contribute to all candidates and party committees. There is also no limit on the amount it can spend on behalf of a particular candidate or party as long as its beneficiaries have no say in how the money is spent. The enactment in 2002 of the McCain-Feingold bill prohibited all "soft money" contributions—formerly unlimited contributions that were made to federal, state, and local political parties. However, a perceived loophole in this law has allowed "527 Committees" (a name that comes from their categorization in the tax code) to play the role that parties formerly played by collecting the same sorts of unlimited contributions and spending them independently to influence campaigns.

Although many PACs take some part in presidential election campaigns, the federal government finances most of the costs of those campaigns. Thus, most PACs make most of their contributions to House and Senate campaigns. It is estimated that they now contribute about 28 percent of all the funds for those campaigns.[39]

The most important PACs can be classified in one of three main categories:

1. *Narrow material interest PACs.* These are PACs concerned mainly with backing candidates who will support legislation that favors a particular business or type of business (for example, Chrysler, Coca Cola, General Electric, General Motors, Texaco), and many other corporations have their own PACs, as do many labor unions, including the Air Line Pilots Association, the American Federation of State, County & Municipal Employees, and the American Federation of Teachers. In addition, a number of PACs represent the interests of whole industries, such as the Dallas Energy Political Action Committee (oil), Edison Electric Institute (electric power), and the National Association of Broadcasters (radio and television).

2. *Single, nonmaterial interest PACs.* These PACs promote candidates who favor their positions on a particular nonmaterial issue. For example, the National Abortion Rights Action League (prochoice) and the National Right to Life Committee (antiabortion) are concerned with the abortion issue and the National Rifle Association (anti-gun-control) and Handgun Control, Inc. (pro-control) focus on the gun control issue.

3. *Ideological PACs.* Finally, a number of PACs support candidates committed to strong liberal or conservative ideologies and issues. Liberal PACs include MoveOn, the National Committee for an Effective Congress, and the Hollywood Women's Political Committee. Conservative PACs include the Republican Issues Campaign and the Conservative Victory Committee.

## Pressure Groups and Lobbying

Another tactic that PACs use to advance their interests is **lobbying** through their Washington representatives. This stratagem concentrates on inducing public officials already in office to support government action (including administrative and judicial rulings as well as legislative acts) the groups favor and to block those the groups oppose.

In the bad old days, pressure groups often used straight bribes in the form of cash payments or guarantees of well-paid jobs after retirement. Sadly, bribes are still occasionally offered and accepted, but the laws against them are strict and the mass media's investigative reporters love to expose bribe-taking. In a recent example, the San Diego *Union-Tribune*'s 2005 investigation of Congressman Randall "Duke" Cunningham for accepting over $2 million in bribes in exchange for influencing defense contracts led to an eight-year prison term for Cunningham, as well as a Pulitzer prize for the newspaper. Congress reacted to the Cunningham scandal and the investigations that forced the resignation of House Majority Leader Tom DeLay and sent former lobbyist Jack Abramoff to jail by considering new ethics legislation. These scandals played a major role in the Democratic surge in the 2006 congressional elections (see Box 19.5). Calls for reform are likely to fade, though, as the scandals pass. Such was the case with the "Teapot Dome" influence-peddling scandal of the 1920s, which caused huge outrage at the time but is now a quaint historical footnote. Bribery is quite rare in everyday American politics, since most interest groups and public officials have decided that giving or taking bribes is either too immoral, too risky, or both.

The main tactic of lobbyists is now *persuasion*— convincing members of Congress (and their staffs, who play key roles in making most members' decisions) that the legislation the lobbyist seeks is in the best interests of the nation and of the member's particular district or state. After all, almost all members of Congress feel that their job is to do the best they can for the interests of their particular constituents. Since it is those constituents rather than the rest of the nation who determine whether or not the members will get reelected, their likely reactions must be the members' first concern.

Accordingly, lobbyists for all interests use the most persuasive evidence and arguments they can to convince a particular member that the actions their groups want will be in everyone's best interest—the voters in the particular district or state, the member's, and the nation's. Lobbyists who work for interest groups that also have PACs may sometimes hint that the PAC will be contributing to the campaigns of legislators who see the light on their issues. Surprisingly, however, most lobbyists and PACs work quite independently of one another, and a great volume of studies by political scientists have failed to provide any clear evidence that campaign contributions influence the votes cast by legislators. Contributions may ensure access to politicians, scholars have found, but it does not buy votes.

Although American interest groups most frequently employ electioneering and lobbying, they sometimes use tactics that are more widely used in other countries, such as mass political propaganda, demonstrations, strikes and boycotts, nonviolent civil disobedience, and sometimes even violence. There is one tactic, however, in which the United States leads the world: the use of **litigation** for political purposes. Tocqueville wrote in 1835, "Scarcely any political question arises in the United States that is not resolved, sooner or later, into a judicial question."[40] Political scientists Benjamin Ginsberg and Martin Shefter note that from 1955 to 1985 the number of civil cases brought in federal district courts increased from 50,000 a year to over 250,000 a year. One of several reasons for that enormous increase, they say, is the fact that a growing number of interest groups that have done poorly in both elections and lobbying have filed suits in the courts to reverse their losses in other arenas:

> Civil rights groups, through federal court suits, launched successful assaults on Southern school systems, state and local governments, and legislative districting schemes. . . . Environmental groups used the courts to block the construction of highways, dams, and other public projects that not only threatened to damage the environment but also provided money and other resources to their political rivals. Women's groups were able to overturn state laws restricting abortion as well as statutes discriminating against women in the labor market.[41]

Conservative groups have countered by trying to ensure that **conservatives** rather than liberals or feminists are appointed to the Supreme Court and other federal judgeships. Liberal groups have also organized campaigns to influence appointments and confirmation battles in order to populate the judicial branch with those who are sympathetic to their goals. Ever since Democrats in the Senate failed to confirm President Ronald Reagan's nomination of Robert Bork to the U.S. Supreme Court in 1987, nearly every appointment to the nation's highest court has been fought with intense lobbying, public pressure, and even with avalanches of television ads. The fact that interest groups are involved in judicial battles far more in America than in any other democracy should not surprise us, because the popularity of pursuing one's individual rights through litigation is one way in which the political culture of America differs significantly from the political cultures of most other countries.

The most important special trait of interest articulation and aggregation in the United States, however, is the very different party environment in which they take place. In most of the democracies discussed in this book most interests operate closely within political parties. (Indeed, in several instances particular interest groups are formally associated with particular parties, such as the trade unions with the British Labour Party.) Their main tactic is to persuade the parties with which they are associated to give their demands prominent places in the parties' programs and actions in government.

In contrast, American political parties are so much weaker and so much less important players in the policymaking process that the interest groups operate largely outside the parties and are little concerned about whether they are helping or hurting the parties. In 1980, for example, the National Organization for Women (NOW) fought for a rule in the Democratic Party to prevent the party from helping to elect any Democratic candidate who opposed the Equal Rights Amendment. In 1984 NOW said that it would refuse to support the party's national ticket unless a woman was nominated for the vice presidency (and, indeed, Geraldine Ferraro was nominated). In the 2004 election, Emily's List, a PAC supporting women candidates, spent a total of $26,051,693 to help women's campaigns, the second-largest amount spent by any PAC.[42]

The same observation applies to the Republican Party. For some time before 1994 many business PACs contributed much more campaign money to incumbent Democrats than to their Republican challengers even though the Republican political philosophy is much closer to that of business. The national leaders of the Republican Party complained bitterly about what they regarded as treason to the party and to conservatism, but Doug Thompson, the leader of the National Association of Realtors, rejected the Republicans' complaints and has spelled out his PAC's political priorities:

> We are a special interest group. Our interest is real estate and housing issues; it is not Contra aid, it is not abortion, it is not the minimum wage. . . . Our members are demanding a lot more accountability. Gone are our free-spending days when we poured money into a black hole called "challenger candidates." Our marching orders on PAC contributions are very clear: Stop wasting money on losers.[43]

Since the Republicans won control of Congress in the 1994 election there have been more Republican than Democratic incumbents, and Republicans have received more PAC contributions than Democrats. (This may change after the 2006 elections handed control of Congress back to Democrats.) In short, interest articulation and aggregation are in many respects different in the United States because its political parties are in most respects very different from those in any other democracy.

## THE SPECIAL CHARACTERISTICS OF AMERICAN POLITICAL PARTIES

### A Two-Party System

The American party system is usually a nearly pure two-party system; that is, one in which two major parties are highly competitive with one another and taken together win almost all the votes and offices in elections.[44] The most notable exception since the 1930s came in 1992, as Figure 19.3 shows, when independent H. Ross Perot won 19 percent of the popular votes for president (Democrat Bill Clinton won 43 percent and Republican incumbent George H. W. Bush won 38 percent). After the election Perot founded the Reform Party and ran as its presidential candidate in 1996, but, as the figure shows, his vote share fell to 8.6 percent. He did not run in 2000, but his party's presidential candidate, Pat Buchanan, got less than 1 percent of the votes.[45]

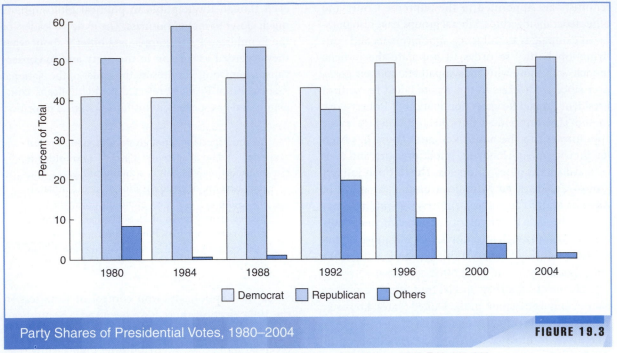

Party Shares of Presidential Votes, 1980–2004

**FIGURE 19.3**

Source: *Statistical Abstract of the United States: 2006* (Washington, DC: Bureau of the Census, 2006), Table 384, 247.

In 2004, in addition to Republican George W. Bush and Democrat John Kerry (see Box 19.4), there were presidential candidates from twenty-three other parties on the ballot in at least one state. However, all these other parties polled a combined 1.3 percent of the popular vote. In addition, nearly all the members of the House and Senate for the past several decades have been affiliated with one of the two major parties. The United States is one of the most distinctive two-party systems in the world.

### The "Americanization" of Electioneering

Electioneering—what parties and candidates do in campaigns to maximize their votes in elections—has changed considerably in most democratic nations since the 1950s, and the United States is generally credited with (or blamed for) leading the way. Before the 1950s electioneering in democracies was conducted mainly by party leaders and workers. The party workers made direct contacts with their candidates' known and potential supporters, and used the mass media mainly to publish newspaper advertisements and to print pamphlets and flyers for the party workers to distribute.

Since the 1950s, American parties and candidates have replaced the old techniques. They now depend mainly on paid television advertisements and broadcasters' interviews and talk shows to showcase their candidates and policies to the voters. They employ experts to conduct frequent polls of the voters to test how well their strategies are working. They canvass voters by telephone rather than by ringing doorbells. They store and analyze information about the demographics and past electoral behavior of election districts in computerized databases. They also have transferred control of electioneering from party politicians to paid professional campaign consultants trained in advertising agencies rather than party organizations. They have made televised debates among the candidates the most important events in campaigns.

Party leaders and candidates in other democracies have watched U.S. electioneering. Many have deplored it, and some have vowed never to "Americanize" (their term) their own campaigns. Nevertheless, campaigners in most democracies have adapted some or all of the high-tech American methods for their own uses. For example, the United States held its first nationally televised debates between presidential candidates in 1960.

Similar debates among leading parties and candidates are now regularly held also in Brazil, Chile, Denmark, France, Germany, Mexico, Norway, Sweden, and Venezuela. Most parties in most democracies now hire professional campaign consultants, some of them American or trained in America, to plan their campaigns. They use private polls to assess the effectiveness of their campaigns, and they use the mass media, especially television, as their main device for soliciting the voters' support. They have followed America's lead by increasingly using negative advertising to sharpen the contrasts between candidates or to ruin an opponent's reputation. In short, while the "Americanization" of electioneering may or may not be a healthy development, it has happened to some degree in all democracies and to a considerable degree in many.[46]

## Differences Between the Major Parties

Throughout the 1950s and 1960s, foreign observers (and many Americans) saw few differences between the Democratic and Republican parties. Their nominees were sometimes likened to "Tweedle Dee and Tweedle Dum" twins, and their members were internally divided on issues such as civil rights and the Vietnam War. Today, however, the split between the two major

---

## The Presidential Election of 2004                    **BOX 19.4**

| Candidate | Popular Votes | Electoral Votes |
|---|---|---|
| George W. Bush, Republican | 61,872,711 | 286 |
| John Kerry, Democrat | 58,894,584 | 251 |
| Others | 1,582,185 | 1 |

Like the presidential election of 2000, the race in 2004 was a close contest in which a razor-thin margin separated two candidates who espoused widely different governing philosophies, with neither winning a certain victory when most Americans went to bed on election night.

But unlike in 2000, they awoke the next day to a concession speech from Democratic nominee John Kerry when it became clear that Republican President George W. Bush had carried Ohio by a percentage margin of 51–49, giving him the electoral votes he needed to secure reelection. Bush won in both the Electoral College and in the popular vote, a feat he had not managed four years before, and the nation was spared another long, drawn out legal battle over the presidency. Yet despite the relative clarity of the final election result, Bush's prospects for reelection were in doubt throughout the campaign, and his narrow win left him far short of the mandate that he, like nearly all political victors, quickly claimed.

After receiving high approval ratings for his job performance in the wake of the terrorist attacks, on September 11, Bush began to lose popularity throughout 2002 as Democratic voters objected to his domestic policy stances and confrontational approach to Iraq. After the United States invaded Iraq in March 2002, voters rallied to their Commander in Chief. As the success of the initial strike into Baghdad gave way to the more difficult task of stabilizing and rebuilding an entire country, the war began to lose its popularity and opposition to it galvanized many Democratic activists. Yet the party's voters were divided on their support for the war, as was their party's nominee.

Senator John Kerry, a decorated Vietnam War veteran who had voted for a resolution supporting President Bush's tough stance toward Iraq, emerged as the party's mainstream choice to challenge Bush. Throughout the summer of 2004, though, Kerry's equivocal positions on the war stalled his campaign. At the Democratic convention, he had difficulty explaining why he had voted against a bill authorizing $87 billion to continue to fund the Iraq War, and his Vietnam War record came under fire from the dubious charges of a group (financed by conservative activists) calling itself "Swift Boat Veterans for Truth." President Bush remained consistent in his prowar position, even as "Texans for Truth" (started by a Democratic political consultant) criticized his stateside service in the National Guard during the Vietnam Era. With Iraq and terrorism remaining the top issues throughout the campaign, the candidates traded slight leads during the summer and fall of 2004. By November, 52 percent of registered voters remained in favor of the war, 48 percent approved of the president's performance overall, and he survived by winning 50.6 percent of the vote.

parties is sharp and meaningful. There is a vast gap between the views of Democratic and Republican voters on President Bush's job performance, on the Iraq War, and on many policy issues. In Congress, the Democratic caucus has moved further and further to the left since 1970, just as Republicans have become increasingly conservative.[47] Thus, the level of mass and elite **partisan polarization** in America is now quite high, as it is in most European nations.

This does not mean that there is no one left in the middle of the American political spectrum: indeed, most Americans see themselves as moderates who lean only slightly in the liberal or conservative direction. Instead, the increase in partisan polarization reflects the fact that Americans today have sorted themselves into the party that most accurately reflects their ideology.[48] No longer are there many conservative Democrats in the South or liberal Republicans in New England or the Midwest. This sorting has taken place among elected officials, party activists, and ordinary voters alike. Because of it, the parties now differ significantly in both the social composition of the voters who identify with them and the policy positions taken by their elected leaders.

As is shown in Figure 19.4, Americans are almost evenly divided among Democrats (35 percent), Republicans (36 percent), and independents (29 percent). (It should be noted, though, that most of these independents lean toward one party and vote for its nominees quite loyally.)[49] Democrats have greater support among women than men, among blacks than whites, and among people with lower incomes and educations than

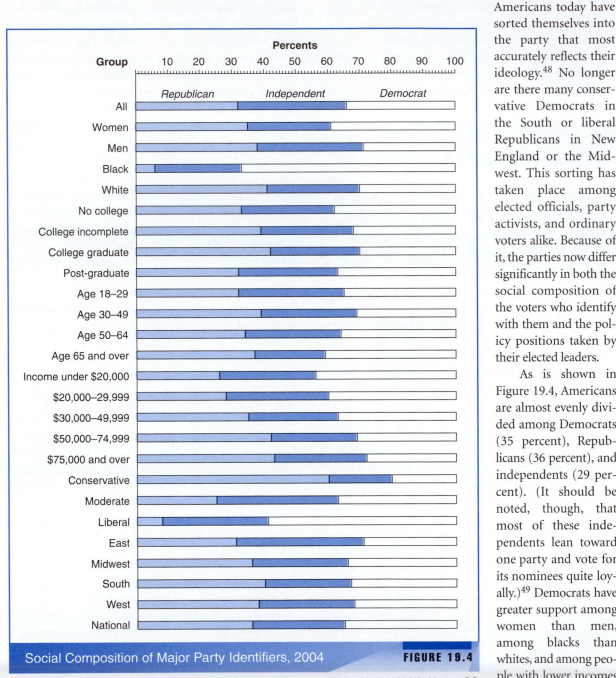

**Social Composition of Major Party Identifiers, 2004**    **FIGURE 19.4**

Source: Harold W. Stanley and Richard G. Niemi, *Vital Statistics on American Politics, 2005–2006* (Washington, DC: CQ Press, 2006), Table 3–2, 119.

upper-status people. Other research shows that the link between income and party affiliation has grown in recent decades: "The relatively poor are increasingly Democratic and the rich Republican."[50] Thus, as income inequality has increased in America, the gap between the two parties has widened. Finally, the parties now differ more than ever in how religious their members are, with Republican presidential candidates doing better among regular churchgoers than Democrats.[51]

These rising differences in each party's social base help to explain why Democratic and Republican members of Congress increasingly take different policy positions. Table 19.5 explores these divisions by looking at roll call votes on some significant issues before the House and Senate from 1993–2003. It shows that there are significantly more liberals than conservatives among the Democrats in both houses of Congress and significantly more conservatives than liberals among the Republicans—although on most issues some

Democrats vote for conservative positions and some Republicans vote for liberal positions.

Generally, Democrats tend to believe that government should take a major and active role in dealing with the nation's problems, while most Republicans tend to agree with Ronald Reagan that "big government *is* the problem." Thus, compared with Republicans most Democrats favor higher levels of government spending on aid for the poor and homeless, education, medical care, public housing, and the like. On the so-called social issues, Democrats tend to favor less government intervention in people's moral, religious, and intellectual lives, while Republicans favor policies that allow greater government involvement in such matters as limiting or outlawing abortions, prohibiting the exhibition of obscene films and art, and encouraging prayer in the public schools.

Democrats also tend to be more egalitarian than Republicans. That is, Republicans tend to support

## Selected Votes in Congress, 1993–2003　　　TABLE 19.5

| | Republicans | | | Democrats | | |
|---|---|---|---|---|---|---|
| | Liberal | Conservative | Cohesion Index* | Liberal | Conservative | Cohesion Index* |
| **House** | | | | | | |
| Lift ban, leave gays-in-military issue to Clinton | 101 | 157 | 22 | 163 | 11 | 88 |
| Welfare reform | 30 | 165 | 70 | 226 | 4 | 96 |
| Impeach Clinton for perjury | 5 | 223 | 98 | 200 | 5 | 98 |
| Bush-proposed tax cut, 2001 | 0 | 219 | 100 | 197 | 10 | 91 |
| Iraq War | 6 | 215 | 95 | 126 | 81 | 22 |
| Partial-birth abortion ban | 4 | 218 | 96 | 137 | 63 | 37 |
| Bush-proposed tax cut, 2003 | 1 | 224 | 99 | 198 | 7 | 93 |
| **Senate** | | | | | | |
| "Brady bill" for handgun control | 8 | 47 | 70 | 28 | 16 | 28 |
| Welfare reform | 1 | 51 | 96 | 23 | 23 | 0 |
| Bush-proposed tax cut, 2001 | 0 | 50 | 100 | 38 | 12 | 52 |
| McCain-Feingold campaign finance reform | 12 | 38 | 52 | 47 | 3 | 88 |
| Iraq War | 1 | 48 | 96 | 21 | 29 | 16 |
| Partial-birth abortion ban | 3 | 47 | 88 | 30 | 17 | 28 |
| Bush-proposed tax cut, 2003 | 3 | 48 | 88 | 46 | 2 | 92 |

*The cohesion index is a measure of the extent to which members of a particular party in a legislature vote alike on matter of public policy. The percentages of the members voting each way are calculated, and the smaller percentage is subtracted from the larger. If they all vote alike the index is 100. If they split evenly the index is 0. If they split 75–25 the index is 50.

Source: *Congressional Quarterly Reports, 1993–2003.*

measures for equal opportunity (giving every citizen an equal chance to engage in fair competition for material riches and the other good things in life), while Democrats tend to support measures for "equal conditions" (giving all citizens a guaranteed minimum of the good things in life even if they cannot earn them by their own efforts).

Although there are some issues on which legislators from both parties agree—in fact, many bills in Congress are passed by unanimous votes—a number of contentious issues reveal a split between the parties in America that is deep and growing.

## Decentralized Organization

Most political parties in most democracies are organized as **hierarchies,** with a national leader and national organization at the top holding the power to supervise the activities of local and regional party organizations. In sharp contrast, the American Democratic and Republican parties are organized, in Samuel Eldersveld's apt phrase, as "**stratarchies.**"[52] That is, their organizations at the national, state, and local levels have little power, legal or extralegal, over the organizations at the other levels. Moreover, within each level most parties have an executive organization and a legislative organization, and neither has any power over the other.

At the national level, for example, the Democrats and Republicans each have a **presidential party** and a **congressional party.** For the party that holds the presidency, the presidential party consists of the president, the national committee, the national chairman, and the national nominating conventions. The party that does not hold the presidency has no single person as its universally acknowledged leader.

Each party in each house of Congress has a caucus, consisting of all the party's members in the particular chamber (and thus equivalent to what in most democracies is called the parliamentary party). A floor leader is selected by the caucus to serve as the main coordinator of the party's legislative strategy and tactics. A policy committee, chosen by the caucus, advises the floor leader and the caucus on matters of substantive policy and legislative tactics. The whips are chosen by the caucus to serve as channels of communication between the leaders and the ordinary members. The campaign committees are chosen by the caucus to raise money and distribute it among the campaigns of selected candidates for the particular chamber.

We should emphasize, however, that the presidential party has little formal connection with the congressional party, and that any effort by the president (to say nothing of the national committee or the national chairman) to intervene in the congressional party's selection of its leaders or the determination of its policies or strategy is resented and rejected as "outside interference." On the other hand, in the 1998–1999 impeachment and trial of Democratic President Clinton, most Republican members sought his **impeachment,** conviction, and removal from office, while most Democrats supported him.

At the state level, both parties usually have a gubernatorial party and a legislative party. The gubernatorial party consists of the governor (the other party has no single, acknowledged leader), the state central committee, the state chair, and the state conventions. The legislative parties, like the congressional parties, usually have caucuses, elected floor leaders, policy committees, and whips. But each state's gubernatorial and legislative parties have no power over one another, and the national parties have no power over any part of the state parties. The national and state parties are simply different strata, not higher and lower levels in a chain of command headed by the national agencies.

At the various local levels there are congressional district committees, county committees, city committees, ward and precinct committees, and others too numerous to list here. In most states the local party committees and conventions are, both in law and in fact, independent of the state and the national party agencies. Hence, they constitute a third stratum, which is just as independent from the state agencies as the state agencies are from the national agencies.

Far more than almost any major party in any other modern democratic nation, then, American party organizations are agglomerations of hundreds of different leaders and committees distributed among various organizational strata, each of which has little or no power to command or obligation to obey any other agency in its own stratum, let alone any agency in any other stratum. Former Georgia governor and Senator Zell Miller's speaking career exemplifies this. A moderate Democrat from a state with many such voters, he delivered the keynote address to the Democratic National Convention in 1992. After growing disenchanted with national Democrats and supportive of President Bush, Miller gave the keynote at the Republican National Convention in 2004, but remains a Democrat.

## Low Cohesion

The parliamentary parties in most modern democratic nations have high **party cohesion,** a term that denotes the degree to which the members of a legislative party vote together on issues of public policy. Abstentions and even votes against the party leaders' wishes are not unknown in those parties, and in some countries their frequency has increased, though very slowly, in recent years. But these are, at most, minor deviations from the norm that all the members of parliamentary parties in other countries vote solidly together in most parliamentary votes.

By sharp contrast, the only matters in either chamber of Congress on which all Democrats regularly vote one way and all Republicans vote the other way relate to "organizing" the chamber—that is, selecting the speaker of the house, the president pro tem of the Senate, and the chairs of the leading standing committees. On all other issues they rarely vote unanimously, though most usually vote together.

On the issues shown in Table 19.5, party cohesion was generally higher among House Democrats than among Senate Democrats, and even higher among House and Senate Republicans. On some issues one party or the other approached the cohesion levels of most major parties in other democracies. For example, the House Democrats' opposition to President Clinton's impeachment was very high, while House Republicans had perfect cohesion for President George W. Bush's tax cut proposal in 2001. On the other hand, House Democrats split more evenly on gays in the military and Bush's tax cut.

Consequently, the congressional parties have some party cohesion. It is especially high on such issues as higher spending for social welfare measures and greater regulation of business—with the Democrats usually voting predominantly, but not unanimously, Yes; and the Republicans usually voting predominantly, but not unanimously, No. On the other hand, on issues that cut sharply across party lines—especially moral issues such as abortion, capital punishment, and the regulation of pornography—both parties regularly split relatively evenly. Thus, in comparison with the major parliamentary parties in most other democratic nations, the American congressional Democrats and Republicans have low cohesion on most issues.

This situation has important consequences for the role of American parties in the policymaking process, which we will consider later. It also has several causes, the most important of which is the fact that, compared with most other democratic parties, the leaders of the Democrats and the Republicans have very weak disciplinary powers.

## Weak Discipline

The leaders of most major parties in the world's democracies have a number of tools to ensure that the legislators bearing their parties' labels support the parties' policies in the national legislatures. For one, they can make sure that no unusually visible or persistent rebel against the party's positions is given a ministerial position or preferment of any kind. If that fails to bring the fractious member into line, they can expel him or her from the parliamentary party altogether. Many parties in many countries give their leaders the ultimate weapon: the power to deny the rebel reselection as an official party candidate at the next election.

In sharp contrast, in the United States any person who wins a party's primary for the House or Senate in any congressional district or state automatically becomes the party's legal candidate for that office, and no national party agency has the power to veto the nomination. On one notable occasion, called by historians "the purge of 1938," Franklin D. Roosevelt, an unusually popular and powerful national party leader, tried to intervene in the primary elections of several states to prevent the renomination of Democratic senators who had opposed his New Deal policies. He failed in twelve of thirteen attempts, and most people have since concluded that any effort by a national party leader to interfere in candidate selection at the state and local levels is bound to fail.

To be sure, presidents and their parties' leaders in Congress can and often do plead with their fellow partisans to support the president's policies for the sake of party loyalty and/or to increase the party's chances at the next election or to keep the party from looking foolish. If persuasion does not work, leaders can (but rarely do) promise to provide future campaign funding to a reluctant member or grant a hearing to a stalled bill authored by that member. Unless they have some strong reason to do otherwise, most members of Congress go along. However, unlike the leaders of most parties in most other countries, neither the president nor his party's congressional leaders have any effective disciplinary power to compel their members in Congress to vote in ways contrary to their consciences—or to what they perceive to be the interests and wishes of their constituents.

## A Special Consequence: Divided Party Control of Government

In a pure parliamentary democracy, one party cannot control the legislature while another party controls the executive. If the parliament refuses a cabinet request, the cabinet either resigns and a new cabinet acceptable to the parliament takes over, or the parliament is dissolved, new elections are held, and a new cabinet is formed that has the support of the new parliamentary majority. There can never be more than a short interim period in which the parliamentary majority and cabinet disagree on any major question of public policy.

In the United States, in contrast, separation of powers and the separate terms and constituencies for the president, the members of the House, and the members of the Senate make it possible for one party to win control of the presidency and the other party to win control of one or both houses of Congress. How often does it actually happen? From the election of 1832 (when most historians say the modern electoral and party systems began) through the election of 2000, there have been a total of eighty-seven presidential and midterm elections. Each of these elections could have resulted in either divided party control or unified party control. In fact, fifty-five (63 percent) produced unified control, and thirty-two (37 percent) produced divided control.

Even more noteworthy is the fact that since the death of Franklin D. Roosevelt in 1945, **divided party control** has occurred so frequently that many observers feel it has become normal, not exceptional. In the period from 1946 through 2008 there have been thirty-two elections. Only thirteen (40 percent) have produced unified control (ten with Democratic presidents and congresses, and three with a Republican president and congress), and nineteen (60 percent) have produced divided control (see Figure 19.5).

The election of 2000 initially produced unified Republican control, with President George W. Bush joining the Republican-controlled Congress. But it didn't last long: in 2001, Senator James Jeffords of Vermont announced that he was leaving the

| Year | Congress | President |
|------|----------|-----------|
| 1946 | Republicans | |
| 1948 | Democrats | Harry S Truman, Democrat |
| 1950 | Democrats | |
| 1952 | Republicans | Dwight D. Eisenhower, Republican |
| **1954** | Democrats | |
| **1956** | Democrats | |
| **1958** | Democrats | |
| 1960 | Democrats | John F. Kennedy, Democrat |
| 1962 | Democrats | |
| 1963 | Democrats | Lyndon B. Johnson, Democrat |
| 1964 | Democrats | |
| 1966 | Democrats | |
| **1968** | Democrats | Richard M. Nixon, Republican |
| **1970** | Democrats | |
| **1972** | Democrats | |
| **1973** | Democrats | Gerald R. Ford, Republican |
| **1974** | Democrats | |
| 1976 | Democrats | James E. Carter, Democrat |
| 1978 | Democrats | |
| **1980** | S–R, H–D | Ronald W. Reagan, Republican |
| **1982** | S–R, H–D | |
| **1984** | S–R, H–D | |
| **1986** | Democrats | |
| **1988** | Democrats | George H. W. Bush, Republican |
| **1990** | Democrats | |
| 1992 | Democrats | William J. Clinton, Democrat |
| **1994** | Republicans | |
| **1996** | Republicans | |
| **1998** | Republicans | |
| **2000** | S–D, H–R | George W. Bush, Republican |
| **2002** | Republicans | |
| **2004** | Republicans | |
| **2006** | Democrats | |
| **2008** | Democrats | Barack Obama, Democrat |

**FIGURE 19.5** United/Split Party Control of the Presidency and Congress, 1946–2008

Republican Party to become an Independent, and that he would vote with the Democrats. That gave the Democrats only a 50–49 margin, but with Jeffords' support they regained control of the Senate and once again became part of a divided government. In 2002, the voters restored control of both houses to the Republicans, but then delivered both the Senate and the House of Representatives to Democrats in 2006 and the presidency to Democrats in 2008 (see Figure 19.5).

The most obvious cause for this situation, which is both unknown and impossible in parliamentary democracies, is the fact that the chief executive and the members of both houses of Congress are, as we have seen, elected separately by overlapping constituencies

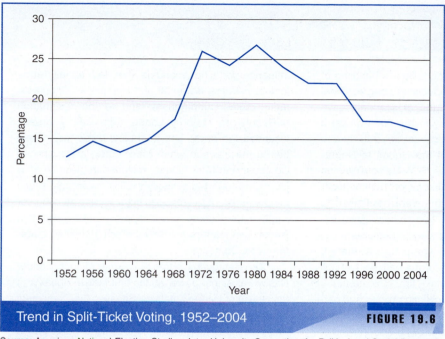

Trend in Split-Ticket Voting, 1952–2004

**FIGURE 19.6**

Source: American National Election Studies, Inter-University Consortium for Political and Social Research, University of Michigan, compiled by Gary Jacobson. Data points are the percentage reporting a different vote for the presidential and House of Representatives elections; third-party candidates are excluded from the calculations.

## THE POLICYMAKING PROCESS IN AMERICA

When we consider the policymaking process in the United States, we must first understand that the constitutional framework within which the process operates was carefully designed to keep government from doing bad things, not to make it easier for it to do good things. To be sure, in writing the Constitution the men of Philadelphia hoped to get a more effective national government than that provided by the Articles of Confederation. But making and implementing effective, coherent, and forceful national policies was not their prime goal.

and with different terms. The constitutional structure thus makes it possible for American voters to do something that voters in most parliamentary democracies cannot do, namely, "split their tickets"—that is, vote for a member of one party for president and for a member of the other party for Congress.

**Ticket-splitting** explains the increasing frequency of divided party control. Figure 19.6 shows the changing percentages of respondents in the National Election Studies of all presidential elections from 1952 through 2004 who reported voting for the presidential candidate of one party and a candidate of another party for the House of Representatives. This figure shows that split-ticket voting rose steadily from 1952 until 1980. It has fallen since then, as partisan polarization in the electorate has increased, but in 2004 it was still higher than it was in 1952.

However, divided government apparently does not significantly weaken (or strengthen) the federal government's ability to make public policies. David Mayhew's careful study of the most important pieces of legislation passed from 1946 to 1990 shows that the rate of production was about the same in periods of divided party control as in periods of unified control.[53]

They believed that government should never be regarded as some kind of benevolent mother, doing whatever is necessary to keep all her children well fed and feeling good. We should never forget, they warned, that government is a powerful and dangerous institution created by fallible human beings. Its prime objective—indeed, its only legitimate reason for existing and being obeyed—is to secure every person's God-given right to life, liberty, and property. Anything that government does beyond that, they believed, is not only less important but not even acceptable if it in any way abridges those basic rights.

The best way to make a government strong enough to secure the rights of its citizens without becoming so powerful that it overrides them, they believed, is to disperse its power among many different agencies—among the federal and state governments by federalism, and within the federal government by separation of powers. The power should be so divided, they held, that no single faction would likely ever get control of the whole power of government and promote its interests at the expense of all the others.[54]

Accordingly, they did not think that policy deadlocks, in which the government cannot act because one of its parts blocks action by other parts, are some

BOX 19.5

## The Congressional Elections of 2006

Voters dissatisfied with President Bush's handling of the Iraq War and with the Republican congressional leaders' handling of a multitude of scandals gave Democrats a landmark victory in the 2006 midterm elections. The Democratic Party captured thirty-one new seats, to take control of the House of Representatives for the first time since 1994. It also picked up six Senate seats, securing its first majority in the upper house since 2002. These gains were not limited to Washington, D.C.: Democrats won six new governorships and retook control of four state legislatures.

What brought about this sharp turn to the left across the nation? The results of the national exit poll conducted by the Edison/Mitofsky firm indicate that it represented a rejection of Republican policies and performance, more than an embrace of the Democratic platform. The 57 percent of voters who disapproved of George W. Bush's handling of his job voted overwhelmingly for congressional Democrats, as did the 61 percent of voters who thought Congress was performing poorly. A majority of voters disapproved of the war in Iraq, and 92 percent said that corruption and scandals in government were important in their decision about how to vote in their district's congressional race. The

influence-peddling scandals that led to jail terms for lobbyist Jack Abramoff and Republican Congressman "Duke" Cunningham, and to the resignation of Republican Majority Leader Tom DeLay, greatly wounded the party. The fatal blow came just weeks before the election when Mark Foley, a Republican Congressman from Florida, resigned in disgrace after journalists reported sexually explicit instant messages that he had sent to teenaged boys serving as congressional pages. Voters who disapproved of the way that Republican leaders handled the scandal voted three-to-one for Democrats.

The Democratic surge put former Minority Leader Nancy Pelosi into power as the first female Speaker of the House of Representatives. Because the Democrats did not set forth a clear and united policy on Iraq, Pelosi has faced the tough task of leading a party and a House that is divided over how to improve the situation there. Still, this is nothing new in American politics. The historical record of landmark congressional elections shows that the largest swings have come after wars, scandals, and economic downturns. Just as in 2006, they are more often a rejection of past performance than a clear prescription for future policies.

---

kind of terrible failure that should be avoided wherever possible and unblocked as soon as possible. Rather, they regarded such deadlocks as highly preferable to any government action that rides roughshod over the interests and objections of any significant part of the community. Consequently, whenever a deadlock blocks today's government from making effective policies to deal with budget deficits, mounting national debt, crime, health care, campaign finance, the war on terror, or any other public problem, the least we can say is that the policymaking process is operating as the framers intended.

### Traditional Ways of Avoiding Deadlocks

Alexis de Tocqueville wrote: "I have never been more struck by the good sense and the practical judgment of the Americans than in the manner in which they elude the numberless difficulties resulting from their Federal

Constitution."[55] He had a point. From the opening of the First Congress in 1789 to the twenty-first century, Americans have found that, however dangerous to human rights it may be, the government of the United States has to make and implement at least *some* policies. It has to regulate interstate and foreign commerce, increase or decrease the supply of money, conduct relations with foreign nations, levy taxes, make appropriations, and so on. As Tocqueville rightly observed, Americans have developed ways of getting policies made despite the constitutional system's many roadblocks and general tendency toward inertia. One set of ways has been traditionally used in ordinary times, and the other set has been called on in times of great crisis.

In ordinary times, public policies in America have been made mainly by putting together ad hoc, issue-specific coalitions of interests by bargaining and cutting deals among their representatives. The main

Democratic leader: Nancy Pelosi celebrates after the 2006 elections.

J. Scott Applewhite/AP Images

coalition builders have included public officials of all kinds, including presidents and their chief political aides in the Cabinet and the Executive Office of the President; members of Congress and their professional staffs; political heads and permanent civil servants in the executive departments and the independent agencies; and federal judges and their clerks. At least as active and often as powerful as these inside players are the outside players, especially the lobbyists representing the major organized interest groups that feel they have major stakes in the policy outcomes. The usual result is that, while each contest over each policy produces winners and losers, it never produces total victory or total defeat for any highly involved interest. Each contestant gets something of what it wants but never all; and each manages to stave off total disaster.

Many commentators, past and present, have been highly critical of this process. They claim that it usually takes far too long to get anything done, and that what is done is usually messy, full of inconsistencies, self-defeating, and in constant need of repair. They are also struck by how difficult it is to get closure on any major policy: typically, when a coalition loses in the

presidency, it tries in the Congress; when it loses in the Congress, it tries in the bureaucracy; when it fails to persuade incumbent elected and appointed officials, it tries to replace them; and when it loses everywhere else, it turns to the courts to upset or water down policies made by the other agencies.

In recent years, for example, environmentalists have increasingly focused their efforts on lobbying the federal agencies that implement natural resources legislation rather than only the members of Congress who pass it. As another example, when civil rights advocates in the 1950s failed to get Congress to abolish racial segregation in the schools, they turned to the U.S. Supreme Court and won their victory in the landmark decision of *Brown v. Board of Education* (1954). Those who today advocate same-sex marriage rights have found success in several court cases while they have generally lost in legislative fights and in initiative battles.

Without doubt the ordinary-times process falls far short of the neat, orderly, and swift policymaking process that parliamentary democracies usually enjoy because of their fusion of powers and the consequent impossibility of prolonged deadlock between the executive and the legislature. Yet the American process has undeniably produced a large number of major national policies, many of them quite successful: for example, the establishment of Alexander Hamilton's economic development program in the 1790s, the western expansion of the country in the nineteenth century, the absorption of millions of immigrants, the Progressive reforms of the early 1900s, the New Deal, the constant (though to some too slow) advance in the status of African-Americans since the end of slavery, the Great Society welfare and health care programs of the 1960s, the drastic overhaul of the tax system in 1986, and so on. Even at its best, however, the ordinary-times process has always taken a lot of time to produce results, and there have been occasions in American history when the danger that it would not work fast enough to meet the needs made the nation turn to a less rigid but more controversial type of policymaking process: unilateral action taken by presidents.

When the Southern states started seceding in 1861, Abraham Lincoln took a number of steps that were far outside the ordinary policymaking process. By executive proclamations he suspended the writ of *habeas corpus;* called for volunteers to join the Union

Army; spent government money to buy them food, uniforms, and weapons; and made the fateful decision to provision Fort Sumter even though he expected the action would start a civil war. Then, after having done all this, he summoned Congress into session, told them what he had done, and asked for retroactive authority—which they had no choice but to give him.

Since then, presidents have often taken the view that when the national interest requires prompt action, they either should do it on their own, as Lincoln did, or persuade Congress to rush through their radical reform measures, as Franklin D. Roosevelt did in the 1930s when it seemed clear that in the absence of extraordinary measures the economy would collapse under the stress of the Great Depression.

Presidents usually exert these extraordinary powers in foreign rather than domestic crises, as when Truman ordered American troops into Korea in 1950; Kennedy and Johnson followed suit in Vietnam in the 1960s; the first Bush ordered troops to Panama, the Persian Gulf, and Somalia in the 1980s and early 1990s; Clinton sent troops to Haiti in 1994 and to Bosnia in 1995; and the second Bush in 2001–2002 sent American soldiers and airmen to Afghanistan to overthrow the terrorist-sheltering Taliban government, and in 2003, sent the armed forces to invade Iraq and depose Saddam Hussein. The War Powers Act of 1974 was designed to limit the president's power to take this kind of action without congressional approval, but in fact it has restrained presidents very little. No one doubts that in any future crisis, especially in foreign affairs, presidents will again bypass the ordinary policymaking process and do what they feel needs to be done.

Recent experience, however, makes it clear that the **presidential-dictatorship** escape valve does not stay open indefinitely. When a military action drags on for months and years with huge expense, many casualties, and little hope of a clean-cut final victory—Korea and Vietnam are so far the leading examples, and Iraq seems to be taking its place on the list—the president eventually loses popular and then congressional support, and the nation returns to the ordinary process. In any case, a leader who is held to account for his actions in free elections every four years is no dictator.

He can also be checked by the courts and by the press, which happened to President George W. Bush with increasing frequency. The *New York Times* revealed in December 2005 that the National Security Agency, at the president's request, was conducting surveillance on domestic and international telephone calls without obtaining court warrants as proscribed by the Foreign Intelligence Surveillance Act (FISA). The Bush administration argued that the presidency's inherent powers justify going around this congressional act during a time of war, but the president faced tough questioning on this issue from reporters and from some members of Congress. In June 2006, the U.S. Supreme Court ruled that detainees held at Guantanamo Bay could not be put on trial before secretive military commissions, in part because the commissions were created without congressional authority. This landmark case points out the limits of executive power, even in wartime.

## POLICY PERFORMANCE

### Tax Policies

When considering policy performance in the United States, it is important to remember that we are dealing with the outputs of many governments, not just the one in Washington, D.C.[56] In 2002, there were over 87,000 governmental units in America, including the federal government, 50 states, 3,034 counties, 19,429 municipalities, 16,504 townships, 13,306 local school districts, and 35,052 special districts—each of which had some constitutional or statutory power to make policies.[57]

Of these 87,576 authorities, the federal government extracts the greatest share of revenues: it collects 62 percent of all taxes and 57 percent of revenues from all sources. Its share is, of course, smaller than the shares taken by the national governments of unitary nations—such as Great Britain, Japan, and Sweden—but it is larger than those taken by the national governments in any of the federal systems except Austria.[58]

Table 19.6 displays the main types of taxes as percentages of total revenue in the United States and eight other industrialized nations in 2000. This table shows that the United States relies more on personal income taxes than any other nation. Social Security taxes paid by employees in America are higher than average. The United States relies less on sales and other taxes on consumption than any other country. Part of the reason is that, unlike most European governments, the U.S. national government has never levied a sales tax or a value-added tax, although most American states

| | Personal Income | Corporate Income | Employees' Social Security | Employers' Social Security | Sales and Consumption | Specific Goods |
|---|---|---|---|---|---|---|
| Great Britain | 29.1 | 9.8 | 6.9 | 9.6 | 18.3 | 12.4 |
| Canada | 37.0 | 11.2 | 5.7 | 8.0 | 14.3 | 8.7 |
| France | 18.0 | 6.9 | 9.0 | 24.8 | 16.9 | 8.2 |
| Germany | 25.3 | 4.8 | 17.2 | 19.2 | 18.4 | 8.8 |
| Italy | 25.7 | 7.5 | 5.4 | 19.8 | 15.8 | 10.0 |
| Japan | 20.2 | 13.2 | 13.9 | 18.2 | 8.7 | 7.7 |
| United States | 42.4 | 8.5 | 10.2 | 11.8 | 7.5 | 6.3 |

**TABLE 19.6** Tax Sources as Percentages of Total Revenue, 2000

Source: *Statistical Abstract of the United States: 2006* (Washington, DC: Bureau of the Census, 2006), Table 1336, 878.

levy sales taxes as well as income taxes. Accordingly, the tax structure in the American federal system as a whole is more progressive (in the sense of placing the heaviest burden on people with the greatest ability to pay) than that in most but not all other nations.

Americans frequently complain about the heavy tax burden they bear, and Republican presidents Ronald Reagan, George H. W. Bush, and George W. Bush all made cutting taxes the cornerstones of their economic programs. Just how great is the tax burden of Americans compared with that borne by the residents of other industrialized democracies?

The answer depends on what measure is used. Expressed as a percentage of gross domestic product (GDP), American taxes take a total of 25.6 percent, the lowest figure among the major industrialized nations (Sweden, at 50.6 percent, is the highest). Moreover, its take from GDP has increased at a slower rate than in any other industrialized democracy since 1980. (Again, Sweden leads with the highest rate of increase.)[59] In summary, compared with the tax systems of most other industrialized countries, the American system is one of the more progressive in its structure but takes a smaller proportion of the GDP than any of the others.

### Distributive Performance

Figure 19.7 gives an overview of how the federal government spent its $2.5 trillion budget in 2005. This figure shows the federal government spent 64 percent of its budget on domestic welfare and education functions, 20 percent on defense-related functions, 7 percent for interest on the national debt, and 9 percent in other areas.

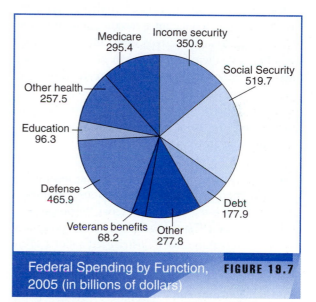

**FIGURE 19.7** Federal Spending by Function, 2005 (in billions of dollars)

Medicare 295.4
Income security 350.9
Social Security 519.7
Other health 257.5
Education 96.3
Defense 465.9
Veterans benefits 68.2
Other 277.8
Debt 177.9

Source: *Statistical Abstract of the United States 2006* (Washington, DC: Bureau of the Census, 2006), Table 463, 319.

Among the world's other democratic governments, only Israel spends as high a proportion of its budget on defense as the United States. (Some developing countries, such as North Korea, Oman, and Saudi Arabia, spend even higher proportions.) Some Americans argue that defense spending is far too high, especially now that the Cold War has ended. Others counter that the events of September 11, 2001, demonstrate that the world is still a dangerous place, and America needs to spend whatever it takes to win the **war on terror.** Whatever the merits of these positions, the trend up to 2001 was toward lower proportions of federal spending on defense, but defense spending then climbed from 2002 through 2005.

Other international comparisons show that U.S. per capita expenditures on health care are by far the highest in the world, followed at some distance by Switzerland and Germany.[60] And in proportion of the GDP spent on education, the United States (with 7.3 percent) ranks second behind South Korea (8.2 percent) and ahead of Denmark (7.1 percent), Iceland (6.7 percent), and Sweden (6.5 percent).[61]

## Regulatory Performance

Like all modern industrialized democracies, the United States is a welfare state in the sense that many of its policies proceed from the conviction that government has an obligation to guarantee certain minimum levels of life's basics to all its citizens, especially to those who cannot provide them for themselves. However, nations differ markedly both in the particular items of basic needs that government should provide and the levels at which they should be provided. In this section we briefly review the major policies adopted by American governments in three main problem areas.

*Social Insurance*   The United States was among the last of the modern industrialized nations to embrace the goals of the welfare state, and today the proportion of the nation's GDP spent on public welfare programs is lower than that in most industrialized nations. Even so, the federal, state, and local governments together have a wide range of policies intended to put a floor beneath the income and living conditions of the poor. For that purpose they use two main instruments: social insurance and public assistance.

*Social Insurance and Welfare*   This category includes programs to protect citizens against the risk of loss of income due to old age, retirement, sickness, industrial accidents, and unemployment. The basic federal legislation is the Social Security Act of 1935, which established a fund from mandatory contributions by employees and employers from which all wage earners are entitled to receive cash payments at retirement or on reaching a certain age. Since the benefits are available to all who contribute, most Americans regard its benefits as entitlements, not handouts. No stigma attaches to receiving Social Security checks, and most Americans of all income levels approve of the program.

*Public Assistance*   This category includes both direct cash and in-kind payments to poor people, such as cash aid to families with dependent children, food stamps, free milk for young children, and day care for children of working mothers with low incomes. Unlike Social Security, these programs are noncontributory and thus constitute obvious income transfers from upper income people to lower income people. As a result, some social stigma does attach to receiving public assistance benefits, and these welfare programs are much more controversial than the social insurance programs.

For years, there were many complaints that the welfare system, especially Aid for Families With Dependent Children (AFDC), was removing recipients' incentives to work and making them into lifelong dependents on government handouts. Then, in 1996, the Republican Congress passed and President Clinton signed a bill for **welfare reform.** The new law ended the federal guarantee of direct AFDC payments to all eligible families. Instead, the federal government gave $16.4 billion in block grants to the states to develop and fund their own new welfare programs, *provided* that the states impose work requirements for welfare recipients, develop job training programs for them, and put time limits on welfare benefits (thereby replacing welfare with "workfare," according to the new law's advocates).[62]

*Education*   In the United States as in other industrialized nations, education is provided mainly by schools financed and operated by the government, although there are more privately owned and operated schools, especially universities (including such famous institutions as Columbia, Harvard, Princeton, Stanford, and Yale), in America than in most other countries (they are also important in Japan and Great Britain).

What sets the American school system apart from systems in other countries is its high degree of decentralization. Most schools, from kindergartens through universities, are financed and regulated by state and local governments, although the federal government provides considerable subsidies for many special programs, each of which carries restrictions on how the money is to be spent. For example, in awarding federally funded scholarships and other forms of financial aid for students, schools may not discriminate against applicants because of their race or gender. The local financing and regulation of schools has many consequences, not the least of which is the fact that schools

| Educational Attainment, Ten Top Nations (11 with a tie), 2002 (percent of persons 25 to 64 years old) | | | **TABLE 19.7** |
|---|---|---|---|
| **Rank** | **Nation** | **Secondary Education (%)*** | **University Education (%)** |
| 1 | United States | 87 | 29 |
| 2 | Norway | 86 | 28 |
| 3 | Denmark | 80 | 23 |
| 4 | Netherlands | 66 | 22 |
| 5 | Canada | 83 | 21 |
| 6 | Japan | 84 | 20 |
| 7 | Australia | 61 | 20 |
| 8 | Iceland | 59 | 20 |
| 9 | Great Britain | 64 | 19 |
| 10 | Sweden | 82 | 18 |
| 10 | South Korea | 71 | 18 |

*Included in university education.

Source: *Statistical Abstract of the United States 2006* (Washington, DC: Bureau of the Census, 2006), Table 1326, 872.

in poor states and poor districts generally spend considerably less money per pupil than schools in richer states and districts.

Whatever the consequences of these differences, the United States, as Table 19.7 shows, still has a higher proportion of its population with secondary or university degrees than any other nation. It also has the second highest proportion (after Japan) of 17-year-olds in secondary schools, the highest proportion of 21-year-olds in colleges and universities, and the highest proportion of college graduates going on to graduate and professional schools.[63]

A number of industrialized nations operate on the theory that higher education should be reserved for only the most talented and accomplished students. They therefore require that only those students who do well in demanding nationally administered tests after finishing one level may advance to a school at the next higher level. The United States, in contrast, operates on the theory that as many people as possible should be given a chance at a college education. As educational sociologist Martin Trow sums it up, "If Europe's slogan for higher education has been 'nothing if not the best,' America's has been 'something is better than nothing.'"[64] Consequently, it is much easier for American 18-year-olds to enter some kind of postsecondary education—a four-year college or university, or a two-year community college—than for their peers in any other country, and many more do so.

In 2002, 29 percent of Americans between the ages of 25 and 64 had university educations—a higher proportion than in any other industrialized democracy.

What about the *quality* of American education? Many scholars, school administrators, and politicians in America have long and inconclusively debated that question, and the literature on the subject is far too vast and complicated to survey in detail here. We will note only that U.S. students score just above the mean for industrialized countries on a combined reading scale and just below the mean on math and science scales.[65]

**Environmental Protection** Of the policy areas considered here, environmental protection is the most recent to take center stage, not only in the United States but in most other industrialized nations as well. From the beginning of the Industrial Revolution in the late eighteenth century until well after World War II, one of the highest goals of every nation was economic growth—constantly increasing the nation's production of goods and services, both for home consumption and for sale abroad.

For many purposes that goal remains highly desirable today, since economic growth allows governments to reach a diverse set of policy goals, including boosting their military strength and diplomatic clout; providing more food, shelter, and medical care for the poor; or increasing the coverage and improving the quality of health and education. In recent years, however, policymakers in many nations, including the United States, have come to realize that economic growth, especially unrestrained and rapid growth, has great costs. Nowhere is this cost greater than in the area of toxic emissions and solid wastes that have been the by-products of large-scale industrialization.

As a result, policymakers in the United States and elsewhere have become increasingly aware that they must grapple with environmental problems. Some nations, especially Japan and Great Britain, have approached these problems less by relying on government regulations than on encouraging corporations and labor unions to work together to develop their own plans for dealing with pollution. Early in the era of environmental policy, the United States took a quite different approach. It enacted a series of stringent laws, beginning with the Clean Air Act of 1970. These laws require manufacturers to reduce sharply their emissions that pollute the air and water by installing expensive devices (such as smoke scrubbers and water purifiers) to recycle solid wastes, and to clean up, mostly at their own (and/or their insurance companies') expense, the toxic waste dumps they have previously created. The federal government established a special agency, the Environmental Protection Agency (EPA), to make sure that these laws are strictly enforced.

More recently, U.S. policymakers have moved away from stringent regulations and toward incentives, voluntary industry goals, and tradable permits that seek to reduce pollution in the most cost-effective way possible. Perhaps the clearest indication that the United States has moved away from the forefront of environmental regulation is the federal government's refusal to ratify the Kyoto Protocol, an international agreement designed to stave off global warming by reducing emissions of "greenhouse gases," such as carbon dioxide. Opponents have argued that abiding by the protocol's targets would slow down economic growth in the United States, and that it places too much of a burden on industrialized nations while putting much looser limits on developing countries. During his campaign, Barack Obama argued against this position, promising swift action to limit greenhouse gas emissions and more energetic American leadership in the fight against global warming.

# AMERICAN EXCEPTIONALISM: MYTH OR REALITY?

## The Idea in History

During much of its history, many of the United States' leaders and citizens—and some foreign commentators and many of the millions of immigrants who left their native countries to become Americans—have regarded the United States as not just another polity in a world of many polities, but as significantly different from other political systems. Some have viewed it as a great social experiment from which all political systems can and should learn lessons relevant to founding and reforming their own systems.

Thus in his first Inaugural Address, George Washington said, "The preservation of the sacred fire of liberty, and the destiny of the republican model of government, are justly considered as deeply, perhaps as finally staked, on the experiment intrusted to the hands of the American people."[66]

In December 1862, when the very existence of the American system was at stake in the Civil War, Abraham Lincoln said to the Congress, "We of this Congress and this administration, will be remembered in spite of ourselves.... The fiery trial through which we pass, will light us down, in honor or dishonor, to the latest generation.... We shall nobly save, or meanly lose, the last, best hope of earth."[67]

## How True Is It?

It seems altogether fitting and proper that we should end this chapter by asking not whether the idea of **American exceptionalism** is noble or vainglorious, but rather how true it is. That is, in what respect and to what degree does the American system resemble and differ from the world's other political systems? Our conclusions are summarized in Table 19.8.

*How the American System Closely Resembles Other Systems* It is a government that has jurisdiction over a certain territory and peoples. It makes laws governing their behavior and enforces them with means up to and including capital punishment.

American society is composed of many different groups with different interests, and its political process is essentially a contest among them to advance their interests. Few if any policies benefit all groups and interests equally, and most political decisions have, relatively speaking, some winners and some losers.

The new immigrants:
Mexicans crossing the Rio
Grande to enter the
United States.

J.P. Laffont/Sygma

In addition, this book's basic theoretical scheme for comparing governments is as applicable to the United States as to any other nation.

### How the American System Resembles a Few Nations but Differs from Most

As Table 19.8 notes, the United States is a democracy along with other democracies. It is based on the principle of constitutionalism. Its society is diverse in the ethnic and religious makeup of its residents.

The United States is a presidential democracy rather than a parliamentary democracy, based on the separation of powers rather than on their fusion. The head of government is elected rather than hereditary. Furthermore, the roles of chief of state and head of government are performed by the same official.

Democratic leaders: President
Barack Obama and Vice
President Joe Biden.

AP Images

The United States is also unusual because it is a federal system rather than a unitary system.

The legislative system also displays differences from other systems. The presiding officers of its legislative chambers are partisan rather than neutral. Its legislative committees play a critical role in the legislative process. And American legislators are largely free of party discipline and control their own votes.

The U.S. legal system is based on the English common law rather than on the continental European civil law. This means that our legal precedents are derived from the prior decisions of judges rather than from an extensive codification of principles constructed by legislative or executive branch officials. Also, its highest court has the power to declare acts of other government officials and agencies unconstitutional and thereby render them null and void.

U.S. elections use the single-member, plurality system rather than proportional representation. Because of this, they are almost always contested by only two major parties. Not only can different parties control different branches of government at the same

## The U.S. Compared with Other Nations: A Summary

**TABLE 19.8**

| Characteristic | How the U.S. Is Like Other Nations | How the U.S. Resembles a Few Nations but Differs from Many | How the U.S. Is Unique or Nearly So |
|---|---|---|---|
| Society | Consists of many different groups with different interests | Large population of immigrants and descendants of immigrants | |
| | | High religious diversity | |
| Political System | Has a government, which makes and enforces laws | Is a democracy | |
| Structure of Government | | Based on principles of constitutionalism | Extensiveness of system of checks and balances |
| | | Federal system | |
| Executive Branch | Has a chief executive | Presidential system rather than parliamentary system | |
| | | Chief of state and head of government roles performed by same person | |
| | | President is directly elected through an electoral college | |
| Legislative Branch | Has a national legislature | Both houses of the legislature are directly elected | Legislative committees play a critical role |
| Judicial Branch | Courts settle civil and criminal disputes | All national judges appointed; some state and local judges elected | Many political issues settled by courts rather than by parties or legislatures |
| | | Most courts have power of judicial review | |
| Parties and Elections | Has regular elections | Has a two-party system | Candidates selected by direct primaries |
| | | Elections use single-member districts and plurality decisions | Voter registration is decentralized and responsibility of voter |
| | | Elections held on fixed dates; no power of dissolution | Voters have many elections and many choices at each |
| | | Parties closely regulated by law | Party leaders have no power to admit or expel party members |
| | | Executive and legislative branches can be and often are controlled by different parties | Parties are decentralized and largely undisciplined and uncohesive |

time, but they often do. American elections are held on fixed dates, and there is no power of dissolution. The practice is well established by law and custom that members of the national legislature must live in the states and districts they represent. Particularly in some states and localities, though not at the national level, there is extensive use of popular initiatives and referendums.

### How the United States Is Unique or Nearly So

Finally, Table 19.8 highlights many of the unique aspects of the American political system. For instance, committees within Congress are more powerful and autonomous than committees in nearly every other national legislature.

American political parties choose most of their nominees for office by direct primaries conducted and regulated by public law, not by party rules. Many of its executive officers, particularly at the state and local levels, are directly elected and nominated by direct primaries; consequently, the U.S. voter faces more frequent elections and more decisions to make at each election than voters in any other democratic nation except Switzerland. In addition, America's systems for registering voters are largely decentralized and put most of the burden on the voters.

Political parties are closely regulated by law. But political parties do not control who can become and remain their members, and the parties are, compared with those in other democratic systems, uncohesive, undisciplined, and decentralized.

Because candidates run as individuals rather than as local representatives of national party teams, and because no publicly financed free media time is given to parties or candidates, the raising and spending of large amounts of money are more important in American elections than in most other democracies.

The court system is also unusual. A higher proportion of political issues are settled in the courts than in any other democracy. Consequently, lawyers play a more important role in the American political system than in any other.

## CONCLUSION

It seems fitting to end this chapter comparing the American political system to the world's other systems with a quotation from one of its greatest foreign observers, the English scholar and statesman, Lord Bryce:

> All governments are faulty; and an equally minute analysis of the constitutions of England, or France, or Germany would disclose mischiefs as serious . . . as those we have noted in the American system. To any one familiar with the practical working of free governments it is a standing wonder that they work at all. . . . What keeps a free government going is the good sense and patriotism of the people . . . and the United States, more than any other country, are governed by public opinion, that is to say, by the general sentiment of the mass of the nation, which all the organs of the national government and of the State governments look to and obey.[68]

## REVIEW QUESTIONS

- Why is voter turnout lower in the United States than it is in most democracies?

- How has immigration policy changed over the past century? What effect has this had on American political culture?

- What impact has the direct primary had on the power of political parties in the United States? Why?

- How has America's traditional approach to environmental issues differed from the strategies pursued in Europe? In what ways has our approach changed recently?

- On which areas of government does the United States spend more than the rest of the world does?

## KEY TERMS

| | | | |
|---|---|---|---|
| American exceptionalism | checks and balances | conservatives | direct primaries |
| Bill of Rights | closed primaries | crossover primaries | divided party control |
| blanket primary | congressional party | direct initiative | electoral college |

federalism
hierarchies
impeachment
judicial review
liberals
litigation
litigiousness
lobbying

mass communications
media
melting pot vs. patchwork quilt
open primaries
partisan polarization
party cohesion
political action committee (PAC)

political culture
popular referendum
presidential democracy
presidential dictatorship
presidential party
scarcity doctrine
separation of powers

stratarchies
ticket-splitting
voting registration
voting turnout
war on terror
welfare reform

## SUGGESTED READINGS

Abraham, Henry J. *The Judiciary: The Supreme Court in the Governmental Process*, 10th ed. New York: New York University Press, 1996.

Ansolabehere, Stephen, Roy Behr, and Shanto Iyengar. *The Media Game: American Politics in the Television Age*. New York: Macmillan, 1993.

Bryce, James. *The American Commonwealth*, 2nd ed. London: Macmillan, 1889.

Davidson, Roger H., and Walter J. Oleszek. *Congress and Its Members*, 7th ed. Washington, DC: Congressional Quarterly Press, 2000.

Delli Carpini, Michael S., and Scott Keeler, *What Americans Know About Politics and Why It Matters*. New Haven, CT: Yale University Press, 1996.

Epstein, Leon D. *Political Parties in the American Mold*. Madison: University of Wisconsin Press, 1986.

Fiorina, Morris P. *Culture War? The Myth of a Polarized America*. New York: Pearson-Longman, 2005.

Ginsberg, Benjamin, and Martin Shefter. *Politics by Other Means: The Declining Importance of Elections in America*, rev. ed. New York: Basic Books, 1999.

Hamilton, Alexander, James Madison, and John Jay. *The Federalist Papers*, ed. Clinton Rossiter. New York: New American Library, 1961.

Jacobson, Gary C. *A Divider, Not a Uniter: George W. Bush and the American People*. New York: Pearson-Longman, 2007.

Jones, Charles O. *Separate but Equal Branches: Congress and the Presidency*. Chatham, NJ: Chatham House Publishers, 1995.

King, Anthony S., ed. *The New American Political System*. Washington, DC: American Enterprise Institute, 1978.

————. *Running Scared: Why American Politicians Campaign Too Much and Govern Too Little*. New York: Martin Kessler Books, 1997.

Mayhew, David R. *Divided We Govern: Party Control, Lawmaking, and Investigations, 1946–1988*. New Haven, CT: Yale University Press, 1991.

McCarty, Nolan, Keith T. Poole, and Howard Rosenthal, *Polarized America: The Dance or Ideology and Unequal Riches*. Cambridge: MIT Press, 2006.

McClosky, Herbert, and John Zaller. *The American Ethos: Public Attitudes Toward Capitalism and Democracy*. Cambridge, MA: Harvard University Press, 1984.

Neustadt, Richard E. *Presidential Power and the Modern Presidents: The Politics of Leadership From Roosevelt to Reagan*. New York: Free Press, 1990.

Nicholas, Herbert G. *The Nature of American Politics*, 2nd ed. New York: Oxford University Press, 1986.

Peltason, Jack W. *Corwin & Peltason's Understanding the Constitution*, 14th ed. Fort Worth, TX: Harcourt Brace 1997.

Polsby, Nelson W. *Congress and the Presidency*, 4th ed. Englewood Cliffs, NJ: Prentice Hall, 1986.

Robinson, Donald L., ed. *Reforming American Government: The Bicentennial Papers of the Committee on the Constitutional System*. Boulder, CO: Westview Press, 1985.

Rourke, Francis E. *Bureaucracy, Politics, and Public Policy*. Boston: Little, Brown, 1984.

Schlozman, Kay Lehman, and John T. Tierney, *Organized Interests and American Democracy*. New York: Harper & Row, 1986.

Tocqueville, Alexis de. *Democracy in America*, 2 vols. Henry Reeve text, revised by Francis Bowen, edited by Phillips Bradley. New York: Alfred A. Knopf, 1945.

Wildavsky, Aaron. *The New Politics of the Budgetary Process*, 2nd ed. New York: HarperCollins, 1992.

## INTERNET RESOURCES

White House: **www.whitehouse.gov**

U.S. Senate: **www.senate.gov**

U.S. House of Representatives: **www.house.gov**

U.S. Courts: **www.uscourts.gov**

Library of Congress: **lcweb.loc.gov**

National Political Index: **politicalindex.com**

# ENDNOTES

1. "The English Flag," in *Barrack-room Ballads and Other Verses* (London: Methuen, 1892), stanza 1.

2. Strictly speaking, "America" means all the nations located in North and South America, including Canada and the countries in Central America, the Caribbean, and South America. Yet, for better or worse, most people around the world use "American" to label anything connected with just one of those nations, the United States of America. With apologies to the citizens of other Western Hemisphere nations, we will use this common, though technically incorrect, label in this chapter.

3. Seymour Martin Lipset, *The First New Nation: The United States in Historical and Comparative Perspective* (New York: Basic Books, 1963).

4. *The World Almanac and Book of Facts 2002* (New York: World Almanac Books, 2002), 782, 804.

5. *Statistical Abstract of the United States, 2006* (Washington, DC: U.S. Census Bureau, 2006), Table 1314, 836.

6. H. G. Nicholas, *The Nature of American Politics*, 2d ed. (New York: Oxford University Press, 1986), 4.

7. *Statistical Abstract of the United States, 2006*, Table 13, 15.

8. See *Statistical Abstract of the United States, 2006*, Table 5, 9, for figures on legal immigration, and Table 7, 10, for estimates and definition of illegal (or unauthorized) immigration.

9. *Statistical Abstract of the United States, 2006*, Table 1327, 873.

10. *Statistical Abstract of the United States, 2006*, Table 459, 317.

11. See Jacob Hacker, *The Divided Welfare State: The Battle Over Public and Private Benefits in the United States* (New York: Cambridge University Press, 2002).

12. The Twenty-First Amendment repeals the Eighteenth (prohibition) Amendment, so there are, in effect, only twenty-five amendments. The resistance to amending the Constitution even with quite popular provisions was demonstrated in June 2006, when an amendment that would have given Congress the power to ban flag burning fell one vote short of gaining the required two-thirds majority in the U.S. Senate. See Johanna Neuman and Faye Fiore, "Flag Measure Fails by 1 Vote," *Los Angeles Times*, 28 June 2006.

13. A word about this usage: strictly speaking, the government in Washington, DC, is the "national" government, and the whole divided-powers system of national and state government is the "federal" government. However, most Americans use the terms "national" and "federal" interchangeably to mean the government in Washington, DC. We will do the same, but the reader should be aware of the ambiguity of this usage.

14. Fifteen states have term limits for members of their legislatures. A number have also tried to impose similar limits on their members of Congress, but the U.S. Supreme Court ruled in 1995 (*U.S. Term Limits, Inc. v. Thornton*) that the states have no constitutional power to limit the terms of national legislators.

15. In recent years an old dispute has been revived by a number of political analysts who argue that presidential democracy is inherently inferior to parliamentary democracy, and the United States should convert to a system of parliamentary democracy similar to Great Britain's. Other analysts reply that, judging by the results—effective policies, loyal citizens, and stability—the American system has done at least as well as the parliamentary systems. See Chapter 2 for a discussion of the issues and arguments in the dispute's current version.

16. Gabriel A. Almond, G. Bingham Powell, Jr., and Robert J. Mundt, *Comparative Politics: A Theoretical Framework* (New York: HarperCollins, 1993), 55.

17. James Q. Wilson and John J. DiIulio, *American Government*, 6th ed. (Lexington, MA: D. C. Heath, 1995), Table 4.3, 81.

18. Gabriel A. Almond and Sidney Verba, *The Civic Culture: Political Attitudes and Democracy in Five Nations* (Princeton, NJ: Princeton University Press, 1962), 186.

19. See, for example, Seymour Martin Lipset, *Political Man: The Social Bases of Politics*, 2nd ed. (London: Heineman, 1983); and Angus Campbell et al., *The American Voter* (New York: John Wiley, 1960).

20. Robert A. Kagan, *Adversarial Legalism: The American Way of Law* (Cambridge: Harvard University Press, 2003).

21. *New York Times v. Sullivan*, 376 U.S. 254 (1964).

22. The two key cases are *National Broadcasting Co. v. United States*, 319 U.S. 190 (1943), and *Red Lion Broadcasting Co. v. Federal Communications Commission*, 395 U.S. 367 (1969).

23. See Michael P. McDonald and Samuel Popkin, "The Myth of the Vanishing Voter," *American Political Science Review* 95, no. 4 (December 2001), 963–74.

24. In 1993 Congress passed the "Motor Voter" act, which was intended to make registration much easier and thereby increase voting turnout. The legislation requires the states to allow citizens to register when applying for a driver's license, to permit registrations by mail, and to provide registration forms at public assistance agencies, such as those distributing unemployment compensation and welfare checks. While most political scientists applaud the new law, its effectiveness is not yet clear. Turnout of eligible voters, which stood at 61 percent in the 1992 presidential election, *dropped* to 53 percent in 1996. It rose to 56 percent in 2000, and then to 61 percent in 2004.

25. David Glass, Peverill Squire, and Raymond E. Wolfinger, "Voter Turnout: An International Comparison," *Public Opinion* (December 1983/January 1984), 49–55.

26. Russell J. Dalton, *Citizen Politics*, 2nd ed. (Chatham, NJ: Chatham House,1996), 45–47.

27. See John G. Matsusaka, *For the Many or the Few: The Initiative, Public Policy, and American Democracy* (Chicago: University of Chicago Press, 2004).

28. One distinguished foreign observer of American politics argues persuasively that American public officials, such as members of the House of Representatives, face elections far more frequently than do their counterparts in other democracies. Consequently, he says, they have to spend large parts of their time in office raising money, touring their districts, appearing on television, and otherwise preparing for the next election. These necessities leave them less time than is needed for the careful study of public issues and the formulation of good public policy. See Anthony S. King, *Running Scared: Why America's Politicians Campaign Too Much and Govern Too Little* (New York: Martin Kessler Books, 1997).

29. Robert S. Erikson, Norman R. Luttbeg, and Kent L. Tedin, *American Public Opinion*, 4th ed. (New York: Macmillan, 1991), Table 1.2, 5.

30. In the United States, as in many democratic countries, voters can write names other than the parties' nominees on their ballots, but few voters do so and write-in candidates almost never get more than a handful of votes. An exception came in the 2004 mayor's race in San Diego, when write-in candidate Donna Frye came within a few hundred votes (and a disputed vote tabulation procedure) of getting elected mayor of the nation's seventh largest city.

31. See Reuven Y. Hazan, "Candidate Selection," in *Comparing Democracies 2*, ch. 5.

32. The exception to this rule is the presidential "caucus-convention," to which all party registrants or loyalists are invited and which selects a nominee after debate, persuasion, and many rounds of voting by attendees. In the 2004 presidential contest, at least one of the major parties used a caucus to select its nominee in 20 states, according to Harold W. Stanley and Richard G. Niemi, *Vital Statistics on American Politics 2005–2006* (Washington, DC: CQ Press), 69–70.

33. William J. Keefe and Marc J. Hetherington, *Parties, Politics, and Public Policy in America*, 9th ed. (Washington, DC: CQ Press, 2003), 61–63.

34. Federal Election Commission, *Election Results for the U.S. President, the U.S. Senate and the U.S. House of Representatives* (Washington, DC: Federal Election Commission, 2005).

35. We take the term *political interest* to mean something of value to a person or group, to be gained or lost by what government does or does not do.

36. Harold D. Lasswell, *Politics: Who Gets What, When, How* (New York: Meridian Books, 1936).

37. See, for example, Alexis de Tocqueville, *Democracy in America*, Vol. 1, pp. 191–93; and Michel Crozier, *The Trouble With America*, translated by Peter Heinegg (Berkeley: University of California Press, 1984), 81.

38. *Buckley v. Valeo*, 424 U.S. 1 (1976).

39. Marjorie Randon Hersey, *Party Politics in America*, 11th ed. (New York: Pearson Longman, 2005), 222.

40. *Democracy in America*, Vol. 1, 280.

41. Benjamin Ginsberg and Martin Shefter, *Politics by Other Means: The Declining Importance of Elections in America* (New York: Basic Books, 1990), 151–52.

42. Harold W. Stanley and Richard G. Niemi, *Vital Statistics on American Politics 2005–2006* (Washington, DC: Congressional Quarterly, 2006), Table 2–15, 107–08.

43. *New York Times*, 21 November 1988.

44. Arend Lijphart puts the United States at the top of his list of democratic nations with the smallest number of effective legislative parties, closely followed by New Zealand, the United Kingdom, and Austria: *Democracies: Patterns of Majoritarian and Consensus Governments in Twenty-One Countries* (New Haven, CT: Yale University Press, 1984), Table 7.3, 122. Austin Ranney's ranking of "two-partyness," based on the somewhat different measure of "party fractionalization," which includes both the number of effective parties and the closeness of electoral competition between them, ranks the U.S. parties second behind New Zealand (although in 1995 New Zealand adopted proportional representation, and since then it has had a multiparty system): *Governing: An Introduction to Political Science*, 8th ed. (Englewood Cliffs, NJ: Prentice Hall, 2001), Table 8.6, 181.

45. Richard Scammon, Alice McGillivray, and Rhodes Cook, *America Votes*, 24 (Washington, DC: Congressional Quarterly Press, 2001), 8.

46. For a recent survey of changes in electioneering in the United States and other democratic nations, see David Butler and Austin Ranney, eds., *Electioneering: A Comparative Study of Continuity and Change* (New York: Oxford University Press, 1992).

47. Gary C. Jacobson, *A Divider, Not a Uniter: George W. Bush and the American People* (New York: Pearson-Longman, 2007), chs. 1–2.

48. Morris P. Fiorina, *Culture War? The Myth of a Polarized America* (New York: Pearson-Longman, 2005) 18, 5.

49. Bruce E. Keith et al., *The Myth of the Independent Voter* (Berkeley: University of California Press, 1992).

50. Nolan McCarty, Keith T. Poole, and Howard Rosenthal, *Polarized America: The Dance or Ideology and Unequal Riches* (Cambridge, MA: MIT Press, 2006), 12. But note that the very rich often vote for and contribute to Democrats, making the 90210 ZIP code in Beverly Hills a top fundraising area for the Democratic Party.

51. Morris P. Fiorina, *Culture War? The Myth of a Polarized America*, 70.

52. Samuel J. Eldersveld, *Political Parties in American Society* (New York: Basic Books, 1982), 133–36.

53. David Mayhew, *Divided We Govern* (New Haven, CT: Yale University Press, 1991).

54. The fullest exposition of this philosophy is, of course, *The Federalist Papers*, especially the tenth paper, by James Madison. See Clinton Rossiter, ed., *The Federalist Papers* (New York: New American Library, 1961).

55. *Democracy in America*, Vol. 1, 167.

56. Hundreds of books have been written comparing American public policies with their counterparts in other nations. We have drawn heavily on two: Arnold J. Heidenheimer, Hugh Heclo, and Carolyn Teich Adams, *Comparative Public Policy*, 3rd ed. (New York: St. Martin's Press, 1990); and Harold Wilensky and Lowell Turner, *Democratic Corporatism and Policy Linkages* (Berkeley: Institute of International Studies, University of California, 1987).

57. *Statistical Abstract of the United States, 2006*, Table 415, 272.

58. *Comparative Public Policy*, Table 6.5, 198.

59. OECD, *Revenue Statistics 1965–2004* (Washington, DC: OECD, 2005), Table 3, 68.

60. *Statistical Abstract of the United States, 2006*, Table 1323, 871.

61. OECD, *OECD in Figures, OECD Observer 2005/Supplement 1* (Washington, DC: OECD, 2005), 66–67.

62. For the law's details, see *Congressional Quarterly Almanac, 1996* (Washington, DC: Congressional Quarterly Press, 1997), 6–13 to 6–24.

63. *Comparative Public Policy*, Table 2.1, 30.

64. Quoted in *Comparative Public Policy*, 29.

65. OECD, *OECD in Figures, OECD Observer 2005/Supplement 1* (Washington, DC: OECD, 2005), 67–68.

66. *The Addresses and Messages of Presidents of the United States*, compiled by Edwin Williams (New York: Edward Walker, 1846), Vol. 1, 32.

67. Address to Congress, 1 December 1862, in Roy P. Basler, ed., *The Collected Works of Abraham Lincoln* (New Brunswick, NJ: Rutgers University Press, 1953), Vol. 5, 537.

68. *The American Commonwealth*, Vol. 1, 300–301.